FINANCIAL ACCOUNTING
In an Economic Context

Eighth Edition

JAMIE PRATT
Indiana University

WILEY

John Wiley & Sons, Inc.

VICE PRESIDENT & EXECUTIVE PUBLISHER: George Hoffman
PUBLISHER: Christopher DeJohn
PROJECT EDITOR: Ed Brislin
PRODUCTION MANAGER: Dorothy Sinclair
SENIOR PRODUCTION EDITOR: Valerie A. Vargas
MARKETING MANAGER: Ramona Sherman
CREATIVE DIRECTOR: Harry Nolan
DESIGNER: Wendy Lai
PRODUCTION MANAGEMENT SERVICES: Aptara Corporation
PHOTO MANAGER: Hilary Newman
EDITORIAL ASSISTANT: Jackie Kepping
MEDIA EDITOR: Greg Chaput
SENIOR MARKETING ASSISTANT: Laura Finley
COVER PHOTO: ©Ralph Mercer/Stone/Getty Images, Inc.
PART AND CHAPTER OPENER PHOTOS: ©iStockphoto

This book was set in Times by Aptara Corporation and printed and bound by RRD-JC. The cover was printed by RRD-JC.

This book is printed on acid free paper. ∞

Founded in 1807, John Wiley & Sons, Inc. has been a valued source of knowledge and understanding for more than 200 years, helping people around the world meet their needs and fulfill their aspirations. Our company is built on a foundation of principles that include responsibility to the communities we serve and where we live and work. In 2008, we launched a Corporate Citizenship Initiative, a global effort to address the environmental, social, economic, and ethical challenges we face in our business. Among the issues we are addressing are carbon impact, paper specifications and procurement, ethical conduct within our business and among our vendors, and community and charitable support. For more information, please visit our website: www.wiley.com/go/citizenship.

Evaluation copies are provided to qualified academics and professionals for review purposes only, for use in their courses during the next academic year. These copies are licensed and may not be sold or transferred to a third party. Upon completion of the review period, please return the evaluation copy to Wiley. Return instructions and a free of charge return shipping label are available at www.wiley.com/go/returnlabel. Outside of the United States, please contact your local representative.

To order books or for customer service, please call 1-800-CALL WILEY (255-5945).

Jamie Pratt
Financial Accounting in an Economic Context, 8th edition
ISBN-13 978-0470-63529-2

Printed in the United States of America

10 9 8 7 6 5 4 3 2

Brief Contents

Contents

PART 2: MEASUREMENT, MECHANICS, AND USE OF FINANCIAL STATEMENTS   77

3 THE MEASUREMENT FUNDAMENTALS OF FINANCIAL ACCOUNTING 77

4 THE MECHANICS OF FINANCIAL ACCOUNTING 112

5 USING FINANCIAL STATEMENT INFORMATION 176

PART 3: ASSETS: A CLOSER LOOK   241

6 THE CURRENT ASSET CLASSIFICATION, CASH, AND ACCOUNTS RECEIVABLE 242

7 MERCHANDISE INVENTORY 290

The Relative Size of Inventories   292

Accounting for Inventory: Four Important Issues   292

Acquiring Inventory: What Costs to Capitalize?   293
What Items or Units to Include? 293   What Costs to Attach? 295

Carrying Inventory: Perpetual Method   297

Selling Inventory: Which Cost Flow Assumption?   301
Specific Identification 301   Three Inventory Cost Flow Assumptions: Average, FIFO, and LIFO 302   Inventory Cost Flow Assumptions: Effects on the Financial Statements 304 Inventory Cost Flow Assumptions: Effects on Federal Income Taxes 305   Choosing an Inventory Cost Flow Assumption: Trade-Offs 306

Ending Inventory: Applying the Lower-of-Cost-or-Market Rule   310

The Lower-of-Cost-or-Market Rule and Hidden Reserves   311

International Perspective: Japanese Business and Inventory Accounting   312

ROE Exercise: Management of Inventory and Return on Equity   313

Inventory Turnover   313

ROE Analysis   314

8 INVESTMENTS IN EQUITY SECURITIES 332

Equity Securities Classified as Current   333
The Existence of a Ready Market 334
The Intention to Convert: Another Area of Subjectivity 335

Trading and Available-for-Sale Securities   335
Purchasing Trading and Available-for-Sale Securities 336   Declaration and Receipt of Cash Dividends 336   Sale of Securities 337   Price Changes of Securities at the End of the Accounting Period 337   Reclassifications and Permanent Market Value Declines 340   Mark-to-Market Accounting and Comprehensive Income 340

PART 4: LIABILITIES AND SHAREHOLDERS' EQUITY: A CLOSER LOOK   435

10 INTRODUCTION TO LIABILITIES: ECONOMIC CONSEQUENCES, CURRENT LIABILITIES, AND CONTINGENCIES 436

11 LONG-TERM LIABILITIES: NOTES, BONDS, AND LEASES 484

14 THE STATEMENT OF CASH FLOWS 639

Financial Accounting in an Economic Context is a trendsetting textbook in the area of introductory financial reporting and analysis. Since the publication of the first edition in 1989, this text has become an important part of the curriculum at a large and impressive group of forward-thinking schools. The eighth edition continues to build on the strengths of previous editions, while it introduces new ideas and refinements that better communicate the book's economic decision-making theme.

CONTINUING TO CHANGE THE WAY STUDENTS LEARN

The eighth edition contains new elements designed to improve and sharpen the text's economic decision-making theme, and the real-world references have been updated. For the most part, however, this eighth edition maintains the same style and content of the seventh edition, which was very well received by a wide variety of universities, colleges, and other institutions.

New to this Edition

In response to the changing financial reporting environment, thoughtful suggestions from reviewers, and the needs of today's students and tomorrow's business leaders, we have reengineered the text in the following ways.

 GLOBALIZATION OF BUSINESS AND FINANCIAL REPORTING STANDARDS. Business is becoming more global with each passing day, and International Financial Reporting Standards (IFRS) are used throughout the world, including in the United States. While the eighth edition still is based on U.S. GAAP, IFRS standards and concepts are woven throughout the entire text. Starting with Chapter 1, IFRS is included in our definition of generally accepted accounting principles, and the ongoing process of converging toward a single global system is described and discussed. Chapter 2 features a complete set of IFRS-based financial statements, published by Unilever, a Dutch-based consumer-goods company, and discusses the conceptual differences between U.S. GAAP and IFRS. Throughout the remainder of the text, conceptual and mechanical differences between U.S. GAAP and IFRS are highlighted via international boxed-in

items that do not interrupt the flow of the text, but allow interested readers to see where differences between the two systems reside. In addition, many end-of-chapter exercises, problems, and issues for discussion deal directly with IFRS-based financial statements, and in a number of places complete IFRS-based financial statements are illustrated and discussed. Note as well that IFRS is not the only evidence of globalization featured in this edition. Differences in business practices and cultures, differences in financial disclosure and format practices, and environmental differences across national borders are all highlighted. Indeed, we live in a global business world, and the eighth edition reflects what future business leaders need to know to operate effectively within it.

STATEMENT OF CASH FLOWS. Prior editions illustrated and discussed the statement of cash flows from the very first chapter, and demonstrated how to prepare the statement directly from the activity in the cash T-account in Chapter 4. Mechanical differences between accruals and cash flows were introduced and illustrated in Appendix 4A through the process of reverse T-account analysis, but the actual preparation of the statement of cash flows, using the indirect form of presentation, did not occur until Chapter 14.

In the eighth edition we have expanded Appendix 4A to include not only reverse T-account analysis but also the preparation of a relatively simple statement of cash flows under both the direct and indirect forms of presentation. Throughout the remaining chapters we have worked in special boxed-in items, where appropriate, that invite the reader to consider differences between accruals and cash flows, normally in terms of the adjustments to net income in the operating section of the statement of cash flows prepared under the indirect method. This feature constantly reminds the reader of the reconciliation between net income and net cash from operations, a very important part of understanding financial statements, and it better prepares the students for Chapter 14, which covers the statement as a whole. Readers who understand Appendix 4A and make note of the boxed-in items will find that Chapter 14 is no more than a helpful review.

FAIR MARKET VALUE ACCOUNTING. Students in today's business environment should understand the basics of fair market value accounting, and how it differs from the traditional matching model. U.S. GAAP is showing signs of moving toward a fair market value–based system (e.g., the fair value option for financial instruments), and IFRS relies more heavily on fair values than does U.S. GAAP. To address this development, fair market value accounting is weaved throughout the eighth edition. In addition to frequent references to market and firm valuation, the text also discusses recent difficulties in the financial markets and security valuation issues related to the collapse of major financial institutions. Appendix A covers valuation and the time value of money. Other prominent examples appear in:

Chapter 2—Differences between U.S. GAAP and IFRS in their reliance on fair market value accounting.

Chapter 3—Measurement fundamentals of financial reporting, including a discussion of asset valuation in terms of fair market value vs. historical cost.

Chapter 5—Discussion of financial statement analysis and firm valuation.

Chapter 8—Illustrations and discussions of fair market value applications to asset valuation and the fair value option for financial instruments under U.S. GAAP. This chapter also introduces acquisitions and the valuation of goodwill.

Chapter 9—Special section dealing with accounting for long-lived assets using the matching model vs. the fair market value option available under IFRS.

Chapter 11—Discussion of the fair market value of long-term debt vs. long-term debt accounting under the effective interest method.

Chapter 12—Discussion of market value vs. book value of common stock.

MORE COMPLETE FINANCIAL STATEMENT ANALYSIS PACKAGE. In earlier editions, Chapter 5 has been devoted to financial statement analysis, and Appendix 5A has covered shareholder value creation, how it relates to the return on equity model, and cash flow analysis. The eighth edition enhances this package in two important ways. First, the chapter now includes a section devoted to business segment analysis, which introduces real-world disclosures and links these disclosures to overall financial statement analysis. Second, Appendix 5A has been expanded to include a section on the mechanics of projecting financial statements. Both of these improvements help to complete the coverage of financial statement analysis in Chapter 5, and end-of-chapter items are devoted to both business segment analysis and projection of financial statements.

CONTINUING THE APPROACH

The eighth edition has retained and improved upon many of the popular features used in previous editions, such as ethics cases, Internet exercises, brief end-of-chapter real-world exercises and issues for discussion, and a set of interesting and challenging "quality of earnings" cases. This edition also includes an updated glossary considered by many to be the very best of its kind. But perhaps most important, this edition has maintained and improved upon its most distinctive feature—the economic decision-making approach and the balanced coverage of three important themes: economic factors. measurement issues, and mechanics.

Economic Factors

Financial accounting is meaningless without an understanding of the economic environment in which it exists. Each chapter in the eighth edition, therefore, includes frequent references to actual events and companies; quotes from well-known business publications and corporate annual reports—information about industry practices, debt covenants, compensation arrangements, and debt and equity markets; and in-depth discussions of legal liability, ethical issues, and management's incentives and influence on financial reports. The annual report of NIKE, which is the subject of short case questions at the end of each chapter, is also provided at the end of the text. Further-more, ratio analysis and international issues are introduced early and integrated throughout the text, and the coverage still reflects a strong user orientation with a distinct "quality and persistence of earnings" flavor. The important role of the economic environment in this text makes it more than simply a study of financial accounting. It is a study of modern business management as seen through the financial accounting process.

Measurement Issues

As future managers and users, students must understand the measurement issues underlying the financial statements before they can interpret and meaningfully use them. The eighth edition devotes considerable attention to the conceptual and theoretical foundation of financial accounting measurement, with special emphasis on how the financial statements provide useful measures of solvency and earning power. Cash and accrual statements are treated as equally important, with the statement of cash flows being covered from the very beginning. Chapter 3 provides a framework for accounting measurement that is used throughout the remainder of the text.

Mechanics

Using financial statements without understanding the underlying mechanics is like trying to interpret a foreign language without knowing the vocabulary. Consequently, the eighth edition provides a strong mechanical foundation and stresses mechanics early and throughout the text. Journal entries and T-accounts play an important role, but they are never treated as a goal. Rather, they are characterized as an efficient way to communicate how economic events are reflected on the financial statements. A special coding is used throughout the text to link the form of each entry to the basic accounting equation and financial statements. Thorough mechanical coverage is especially important in a text that takes a user orientation because effective users must be able to infer transactions from the financial statements. This mechanical skill, referred to as *reverse T-account analysis,* is covered several times in the text, and many exercises and problems are designed to test it.

Decision-Making Perspective

This text presents financial accounting in a way that helps managers make decisions—a decision-making perspective. At a fundamental level, managers make two kinds of decisions: attracting capital and investing capital. Simply put, managers must attract capital from debt and equity investors and then invest it in operations, producing assets, and investment securities. Successful management is defined by generating a return from these investments that exceeds the cost of capital. As depicted in Figure P-l, these two kinds of decisions can be matched with the three themes discussed above (mechanics, measurement issues, and economic factors) to produce six basic questions that must be answered by managers who use financial accounting information when making decisions.

FIGURE P–1

	Management Decisions	
	Attract Capital	**Invest Capital**
Mechanics	1 **How do the transactions affect the financial statements?**	4 **How are financial ratios computed, and how can transactions be inferred from the financial statements?**
Measurement Theory	2 **How do these financial statement effects influence outside perceptions of the company's earning power and solvency?**	5 **How do the financial statements and ratios indicate a firm's solvency and earning power?**
Economics	3 **How do these financial statement effects influence decisions of outsiders as well as debt and compensation contracts?**	6 **What action should be taken (e.g., invest, extend credit, adjust loan terms)?**

In their effort to attract capital, managers must address three questions when considering whether to enter into certain transactions: How do the transactions affect the financial statements? (cell 1); how do these financial statement effects influence outside perceptions of the company's earning power and solvency? (cell 2); and how do these financial statement effects influence the decisions of outsiders as well as debt and compensation contracts? (cell 3). These questions must be answered if management is to understand the economic consequences of the transactions under consideration.

In their effort to invest capital, managers must address three different questions: How are financial ratios computed, and how can transactions be inferred from the financial statements? (cell 4); how do the financial statements and ratios indicate a firm's solvency and earning power? (cell 5); and what action should be taken (e.g., invest, extend credit, adjust loan terms)? (cell 6). These questions must be answered if management is to understand how to use financial accounting information properly.

The decision-making perspective simply means that all six questions are addressed in this text. These are the areas where management decision making intersects with financial accounting information, or, in other words, this is what managers need to know about financial reporting and analysis. It is this perspective that makes *Financial Accounting in an Economic Context* different from all other texts.

SUCCESSFUL FEATURES RETAINED FROM PREVIOUS EDITIONS

With few exceptions, the text retains the main features of previous editions. Below is a brief description of the most important ones.

FLEXIBLE MODULES. Chapter 3 (The Measurement Fundamentals of Financial Accounting), Chapter 4 (The Mechanics of Financial Accounting), and Chapter 5 (Using Financial Statement Information) have been written so that they can be covered in any order. This modular structure adds an important dimension of flexibility to the text.

REAL WORLD REVIEW. Throught each chapter real world applications of chapter topics are highlighted and boxed. In the eighth edition, these boxed items also include real-world insights on general international issues, IFRS, and the reconciliation of net income with net cash from operations on the statement of cash flows.

REVERSE T-ACCOUNT ANALYSIS. An important user-oriented, analytical skill, called *reverse T-account analysis,* is covered in detail in Appendix 4A. This material shows students how to derive transactions from the financial statements, and many exercises and problems throughout the text require students to use it.

ETHICS VIGNETTES. Each chapter closes with a short business scenario that introduces an ethical issue related to the material covered in the chapter. Several questions that follow each scenario are designed to encourage meaningful class discussion.

INTERNATIONAL COVERAGE. At the end of each chapter, we discuss timely, relevant, and important international issues. These sections encourage students to think more broadly about global business issues and how they relate to accounting.

INDUSTRY DATA. Many of the chapters contain tables that compare accounting practices and show students the importance of accounting numbers and ratios across different industries and well-known companies. Updated in the eighth edition, these tables illustrate that the financial accounting issues faced by retailers, manufacturers, service enterprises, and financial institutions are quite different. A brief explanation of

the operations of companies in different industries and how these operations give rise to different financial accounting concerns follows each table.

EXCERPTS FROM BUSINESS PUBLICATIONS AND PROFESSIONAL JOURNALS. Over 10,000 references from various business publications (*Wall Street Journal, Forbes,* and other professional and academic journals) are integrated throughout the text. Updated to reflect the most recent developments, these references document and clarify important chapter concepts and introduce students to information sources that will be useful to them in their business careers.

NIKE CONSOLIDATED FINANCIAL STATEMENTS. The financial statements of NIKE appear in Appendix C at the end of the text. In addition to being referenced periodically throughout the text, each chapter contains an end-of-chapter case that requires students to relate the financial statements to accounting issues covered in the chapter.

STUDENT LEARNING AIDS

STUDY GUIDE. Designed to have a conceptual flavor that complements the textbook, this invaluable study aid includes for each chapter: (1) a review of key concepts and (2) a set of practice questions and exercises to enhance learning. This approach highlights important concepts and relations introduced in the textbook.

SUPPLEMENTS FOR THE INSTRUCTOR

INSTRUCTOR'S MANUAL. This instructor's resource includes a synopsis that highlights general chapter topics, a text/lecture outline that summarizes the chapter in detail, lecture tips for areas in which students commonly have difficulty, answers to chapter questions, and an assignment classification table.

TEST BANK. More than 1,700 questions are included in both the printed and microcomputer versions of the Test Bank. Learning outcomes are provided for each question.

SOLUTIONS MANUAL. This supplement provides complete solutions to all exercises and problems in the text.

POWERPOINT PRESENTATION SLIDES. Lecture slides highlight the major concepts of each chapter. The slides may be printed out for use on an overhead projector.

FINANCIAL ACCOUNTING WEB SITE (http://www.wiley.com/college/pratt). This password-protected instructor resource provides the Solutions Manual, Instructor's Manual, Test Bank, and PowerPoint Presentation Slides in an easily downloadable format.

For more information on these or other supplemental materials, please contact your local Wiley sales representative or visit us on the Web at www.wiley.com/college/pratt.

Acknowledgments

This text benefited significantly from the constructive and insightful comments provided by many individuals, including:

Ajay Adhikari, American University
Stephen Bier, Molloy College
Charles Caliendo, University of Minnesota
Linda Chase, Baldwin-Wallace College
Paquita Davis-Friday, Baruch College
Alan Glazer, Franklin and Marshall College
John Steven Grice, University of Alabama–Birmingham
Stephen Moehrle, University of Missouri–St. Louis
Beverly Rowe, Letourneau University
James Schweikart, Boston University
Douglas Stevens, Florida State University
Richard A. Turpen, University of Alabama–Birmingham
Xue (Sue) Wang, Emory University
Larry Weiss, Georgetown University
Ray Wilson, Boston University

Many other people deserve thanks and recognition for the contributions they have made to this text. I appreciate the efforts of all those who prepared ancillary material.

I am especially grateful to Tom Rearick, a colleague who helped with the initial revision and checked the exercises, problems, and discussion issues while preparing the solutions manual. Aleksandrina Pratt, my daughter-in-law, also painstakingly reviewed the entire text offering a number of insightful comments.

The John Wiley editorial, design, and marketing staff represent a first-rate group of professionals. Their high-quality work helped to ensure that the manuscript was comprehensive, coherent, and completed in a timely and orderly fashion.

Finally, heartfelt and sincere thanks go to my wife, Kathy, and children, Jason, Ryan, and Dylan. Their consistent support and understanding over the past 25 years has certainly enabled and motivated me to push forward toward the completion of now the eighth successful edition of this text.

Jamie Pratt

About the Author

Jamie Pratt holds the A. L. Prickett Chair of Accounting at Indiana University in Bloomington, Indiana. He received his undergraduate degree from Purdue University in 1973 and his doctoral degree from Indiana in 1977. Prior to joining the Indiana faculty in 1990, Jamie served on the faculties at the University of Washington in Seattle, Northwestern University, the University of Zurich (Switzerland), and INSEAD, an MBA program in Fontainebleau, France. Jamie teaches in executive programs throughout the world and has won numerous teaching awards and honors. He served as the Associate Editor of *The Accounting Review,* is very active in the American Accounting Association, and continues to publish in the top academic journals in accounting. In addition to this text, Jamie has authored a variety of educational products, including a case book, a spreadsheet-based financial analysis simulation, and state-of-the-art interactive financial reporting cases. His newest text, co-authored with Professor Eric Hirst, focuses on the link between share-holder value creation and financial reporting.

An Overview of Financial Accounting

In early 2010, after the Christmas season, stock market analysts following Apple, Inc.—manufacturer of the popular iPhone, iPod, and Macintosh computer—were very optimistic about the company's future revenues and earnings. Based largely on bullish expectations concerning the recently upgraded smart phones and a new tablet computer rumored to be released later in 2010, analysts elevated Apple's earnings forecast from $7.66 to $7.81 per share, boosting the share price to $213.35, a whopping 27 times earnings.

What are revenues and earnings? How do they relate to stock prices? What role do analysts and their expectations play? Would an investment in Apple be a wise move? Answering such questions begins with an understanding of the business environment, investment decisions and financial statements—topics addressed in Part 1 of this textbook.

CHAPTER 1
Financial Accounting and Its Economic Context

CHAPTER 2
The Financial Statements

CHAPTER 1

Financial Accounting and Its Economic Context

KEY POINTS

The following key points are emphasized in this chapter:

- The economic role of financial accounting statements.

- The four financial statements and the information each provides.

- The standard audit report, management letter, and footnotes to the financial statements.

- The two forms of investment—debt and equity—and how the information on the financial statements relates to them.

- The nature and importance of corporate governance and the role of financial statements.

- The current status of accounting standard setting—both in the U.S. and internationally.

Like schoolchildren who have practiced fire drills dozens of times, investors know exactly what to do when news leaks out that a company's financial records may not be in order. First, sell the stock; then, look around to see who else might get sucked up into the budding scandal, and drop them like a "hot potato." Investors followed their "fire drill" to the letter when they learned that the financial records of New Century, one of the nation's leading lenders of high-risk loans, were misstated. Its stock price plummeted; it was forced to declare bankrupty; and one of the worst credit crises in U.S. history was underway.

The situation described above is all too common. Billions of dollars are lost each year by investors who base their investment decisions on misleading reported numbers. This text, beginning with this first chapter, explains how that could happen. It also describes how you can avoid the fate of those investors who, believing the profits reported by New Century, chose to invest their hard-earned money and lost much of it. The first step involves understanding the **financial accounting** process.

FINANCIAL REPORTING AND INVESTMENT DECISIONS

Financial reporting plays an important role in investment decisions.

1. *Profit-seeking companies*—Managers of profit-seeking companies prepare reports containing financial information for the owners of these companies. In addition to other information, these reports contain four financial statements: the balance sheet, the income statement, the statement of shareholders' equity, and the statement of cash flows.

2. *Owners and other interested parties (users)*—Although prepared primarily for the owners, these financial reports are available to the public and are read by other interested parties who use them to assess the financial condition and performance of the company as well as the performance of its managers. Such interested parties, called users in this text, include potential investors, bankers, government agencies, and the company's customers and suppliers.

3. *User decisions*—Users obtain information from the financial reports that helps assess the company's past performance, predict its future performance, and control the activities of its managers. Financial reports, therefore, help users to make better decisions. Investors, for example, use financial reports to choose companies in which to invest their funds; bankers use them to decide where to loan their funds and what interest rates to charge.

4. *Effects of user decisions*—User decisions affect the financial condition and performance of the company and the economic well-being of its managers. For example, a banker may use the information contained in a financial report to decide not to loan a certain company much-needed funds. Such a decision may cause the company to struggle and may cost managers their jobs and owners their investments.

Figure 1–1 illustrates how financial reporting relates to investment decisions. Note its dynamic nature: The financial information provided by managers of a profit-seeking company is used by interested parties to make decisions that, in turn, affect a company's financial condition and the economic well-being of its managers. Managers need to understand the process depicted in Figure 1–1 from two perspectives:

1. Economic consequences
2. User orientation

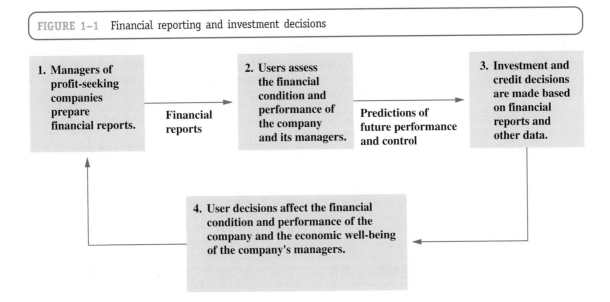

FIGURE 1-1   Financial reporting and investment decisions

Economic Consequences

To run a company effectively, management must be able to attract capital (funds) from outsiders who use financial statements to evaluate the company's performance and financial health. Managers apply for loans from bankers, for example, who use the financial statements to determine whether to grant the loan and, if so, what interest rate to charge. Since using financial statements by outsiders leads to economic consequences for managers and the companies they operate (e.g., higher interest rates), it is important that they know how economic events (e.g., business decisions) affect the financial statements. Consider a case where management is deciding to either purchase or rent equipment. When making such a decision, an astute manager would consider how the choice affects the financial statements because it could influence the way in which the company is viewed by outsiders. Considering and understanding how such events affect the financial statements are referred to in this text as an **economic consequence perspective.**

User Orientation

Managers are also users of financial statements, such as when they are called upon to assess the performance and financial health of other companies. Questions such as the following are often answered by analyzing financial statements provided by those companies.

- Should we purchase a company?
- Should we use a company as a supplier?
- Should we extend credit or loan funds to a company?

Accordingly, managers also need to know how to read, evaluate, and analyze financial statements. We call this perspective a **user orientation.**

The next section develops a scenario designed to highlight issues particularly important to users of financial statements. That same scenario serves as the basis for the next section, which covers the economic environment in which financial statements are prepared and used. Appendix 1A introduces managerial, tax, and not-for-profit accounting.

> **?** Some managers, particularly in certain high-tech companies, claim that required methods for computing manager pay overstate the company's costs and unfairly understate its performance. They argue that they are being penalized by these requirements. Others maintain that the financial performance of high-tech companies cannot be properly assessed unless manager pay is computed in line with the requirements. Which of the two arguments takes an economic consequence perspective, and which takes a user orientation? Discuss.

THE DEMAND FOR FINANCIAL INFORMATION: A USER'S ORIENTATION

Suppose that you recently learned that a long-lost relative died and left you a large sum of money. You know little about financial matters, so you consult Mary Jordan, a financial advisor, to help you decide what to do with the funds. She tells you that you have two choices: You can consume it or you can invest it.

Consumption and Investment

In consuming your new fortune, you would spend the money on goods and services, such as a trip around the world, expensive meals, a lavish wardrobe, or any other expenditures that bring about immediate gratification. Consumption expenditures, by definition, are enjoyed immediately and have no future value.

In investing the fortune, you would spend the money on items that provide little in the way of immediate gratification. Rather, they generate returns of additional money at later dates. In essence, investments trade current consumption for more consumption at a later date. Examples include investing in stocks and bonds, real estate, or rare art objects, or simply placing the money in the bank.

Where to Invest?

You decide to invest the money, and with a little direction from Mary, you begin to explore investment alternatives. You find that investments come in a number of different forms, however, and you quickly become overwhelmed, confused, and frustrated. Just as you are about to give up your search and put all your money in the bank, a man by the name of Martin Wagner knocks at your door. Through a mutual friend, Martin has heard of your recent windfall and states that he has an interesting offer for you.

Martin claims that he manages a very successful research company, called Microline, owned by a group of European investors. In its short history, the company has earned a reputation for innovation in software development. As Martin describes it, Microline's research staff is on the verge of designing a voice-activated word-processing system that will revolutionize word processing in the future.

Martin has come to you for capital—$1 million, to be exact. The company's research and development efforts have run short of funds, and money is still needed to complete the design. With your money, Martin asserts that the software system can be completed and sold, producing millions of dollars of income, some of which will provide you with a handsome return on your investment. Without your capital, Martin believes that the project may have to be abandoned.

The Demand for Documentation

You have listened to Martin's story and now must decide what to do. Your first thought is that you simply cannot accept his word without some documented evidence. How do you really know that he has successfully managed this business for the past two years and that $1 million will enable the company to turn this design into a fortune in the future?

After careful consideration, you decide that you need to see some proof before making a final decision. You ask for specific documents to show that Microline has been run successfully for the past two years, is currently in reasonably good financial condition, and has the potential to generate income of the magnitude Martin suggests. He agrees to provide you with such documentation because he knows that if he does not, you will invest your money elsewhere, and both he and Microline will suffer.

Several days later, Martin returns with a set of financial statements prepared by Microline's accountants. He explains the meanings of the numbers on the statements and further claims that the records at his office can be used to verify them. Taken at face value, the figures look promising, but somehow Martin's explanation is not convincing. It occurs to you that Martin might fabricate or at least influence the figures. After all, Microline needs money, and who would blame Martin for showing you only the figures that make Microline's situation look attractive to a potential investor?

The Demand for an Independent Audit

You require that Martin go one step further. He must return again with financial statements that have been checked and verified by an independent outsider who is an expert in such matters. You insist that the person not be employed by Microline or have any interest whatsoever in the company and have the appropriate credentials to perform such a task. In essence, you demand that Martin hire a **certified public accountant (CPA)** to verify Microline's financial statements. You require, in other words, that Microline subject itself to an **independent audit.** Martin agrees because, once again, if he does not, you will take your money and invest it elsewhere. At the same time, Martin is somewhat troubled. He knows that hiring and working with a CPA can be very costly and time-consuming.

Martin and the CPA: Different Incentives

Time passes and you become concerned that Martin has taken too long to return with the financial statements. You have thought of several questions since Martin's last visit and decide to call on him in person. You arrive at Microline's office and are seated by Martin's secretary. While you are waiting, you hear Martin's voice through the partly open door to his office. He seems to be discussing Microline's financial statements with the CPA. While you cannot understand exactly what is being said, it is clear that they are not in complete agreement and that they are both strong in their convictions.

You wonder why Martin and the CPA might view the financial statements from different perspectives and speculate that perhaps the CPA recommended presenting Microline's financial condition in a way that was unsatisfactory to Martin. You reason that Martin should probably follow the CPA's recommendation because, after all, the CPA is the expert in financial reporting. You realize, however, that Martin wants the statements to be as attractive as possible and that he may have some influence over the CPA. Indeed, Martin did hire the CPA and does pay the CPA's fee.

Before long, the CPA leaves and Martin invites you into his office. During your short discussion, you mention nothing of what you think you have heard. Martin answers your questions confidently and assures you that the statements will be ready within the week. Satisfied, you return home.

The Auditor's Report, the Management Letter, and the Financial Statements

Martin arrives at your home with seven official-looking documents: (1) an **auditor's report,** a short letter written by the auditor that describes the activities of the audit and comments on the financial position and operations of Microline; (2) a **management letter,** signed by Martin, which accepts responsibility for the figures on the statements; (3) a balance sheet; (4) an income statement; (5) a statement of shareholders' equity; (6) a statement of cash flows; and (7) a comprehensive set of footnotes, which more fully explains certain items on the four statements listed above. You briefly review the documents and tell Martin that you will have a decision for him soon.

THE AUDITOR'S REPORT

You begin your examination by reviewing the auditor's report, from which you hope to learn how credible the financial statements actually are (see Figure 1–2).

FIGURE 1–2
The standard
audit report

TO THE BOARD OF DIRECTORS AND SHAREHOLDERS OF MICROLINE:

We have audited the accompanying balance sheet of Microline as of December 31, 2010 and 2009, and the related statements of income, shareholders' equity, and cash flows for the years then ended. We have also audited management's assessment of the effectiveness of its internal control over financial reporting. These financial statements and the effectiveness of the internal controls are the responsibility of the Company's management. Our responsibility is to express an opinion on these financial statements and management's assessment of the internal controls based on our audit.

We conducted our audit in accordance with the standards of the Public Company Accounting Oversight Board. Those standards require that we plan and perform the audit to obtain reasonable assurance about whether the financial statements are free of material misstatement. An audit includes examining, on a test basis, evidence supporting the amounts and disclosures in the financial statements. An audit also includes assessing the accounting principles used and significant estimates made by management, as well as evaluating the overall financial statement presentation. Our audit of internal control over financial reporting included obtaining an understanding of internal control over financial reporting and testing and evaluating the design and operating effectiveness of the internal controls. We believe that our audit provides a reasonable basis for our opinion.

In our opinion, the financial statements referred to above present fairly, in all material respects, the financial position of Microline as of December 31, 2010 and 2009, and the results of its operations and its cash flows for the years then ended, in conformity with generally accepted accounting principles. Also, in our opinion management maintained effective internal control over financial reporting as of December 31, 2010.

Arthur Price

Arthur Price, Certified Public Accountant
March 12, 2011

Overall, you are reassured by the auditor's report. It indicates that the auditor reviewed Microline's records thoroughly and concluded that the statements (1) were prepared in conformity with generally accepted accounting, principles, (2) present fairly Microline's financial condition and operations, and (3) resulted from an effective internal control system. You suspect that the auditor could have rendered a much less favorable report, such as that the statements were not prepared in conformance with generally accepted accounting principles, or that no opinion could be reached because Microline's accounting system and internal controls were so poorly designed, or that Microline was in danger of failure. You also realize, however, that you know very little about internal control systems, auditing standards, and generally accepted accounting principles, and that Microline's management made a number of significant estimates when preparing the statements. This discovery is somewhat troubling because, even with the audit, it seems that Microline's management may have had some subjective influence on the financial statements.

THE MANAGEMENT LETTER

You next read the management letter, hoping to learn more about how the financial statements were prepared and audited (see Figure 1–3).

FIGURE 1–3
Management's letter

MANAGEMENT'S RESPONSIBILITIES:

Management is responsible for the preparation and integrity of the financial statements and the financial comments appearing in this financial report. The financial statements were prepared in accordance with generally accepted accounting principles and include certain amounts based on management's best estimates and judgments. Other financial information presented in this financial report is consistent with the financial statements.

The Company maintains a system of internal controls designed to provide reasonable assurance that the assets are safeguarded and that transactions are executed as authorized and are recorded and reported properly. The system of controls is based upon written policies and procedures, appropriate division of responsibility and authority, careful selection and training of personnel, and a comprehensive internal audit program. The Company's policies and procedures prescribe that the Company and all employees are to maintain the highest ethical standards and that its business practices are to be conducted in a manner which is above reproach.

Arthur Price, an independent certified public accountant, has examined the Company's financial statements, and the audit report is presented herein. The Board of Directors has an Audit Committee composed entirely of outside directors. Arthur Price has direct access to the Audit Committee and meets with the committee to discuss accounting, auditing, and financial reporting matters.

Martin Wagner

Martin Wagner, Chief Executive Officer
March 12, 2011

Once again, you are both reassured and troubled. It is comforting to know that Microline's management is accepting responsibility for the integrity of the statements, which have been prepared in conformance with generally accepted accounting principles, and that the company has an **internal control system** that safeguards the assets and reasonably ensures that transactions are properly recorded and reported. It is also nice to know that Microline's policies prescribe that its employees maintain high ethical standards. However, you still do not understand generally accepted accounting principles, are still

concerned that the statements reflect management's estimates and judgments, and have very little idea about the function of Microline's Board of Directors and Audit Committee.

THE FINANCIAL STATEMENTS

You briefly review the four financial statements (see Figure 1–4) and note first that dollar amounts are listed for both 2010 and 2009. This discovery is somewhat discouraging because only information about the past is included on the statements and is subject to the auditor's report and management letter. Nothing about Microline's future prospects is included in the financial statements—but the future is what interests you most. Whether Microline is able to provide an acceptable return on your $1 million

FIGURE 1–4

Financial statements for Microline

Microline
Financial Statements
As of December 31, 2010 and 2009

	2010	2009
BALANCE SHEET		
ASSETS		
Cash	$ 100,000	$ 60,000
Accounts receivable	80,000	90,000
Equipment	330,000	300,000
Land	500,000	500,000
Total assets	$1,010,000	$ 950,000
LIABILITIES AND SHAREHOLDERS' EQUITY		
Short-term payables	$ 50,000	$ 30,000
Long-term payables	420,000	450,000
Common stock	400,000	400,000
Retained earnings	140,000	70,000
Total liabilities and shareholders' equity	$1,010,000	$ 950,000
INCOME STATEMENT		
Revenues	$1,650,000	$1,500,000
Expenses	1,450,000	1,350,000
Net income	$ 200,000	$ 150,000
STATEMENT OF SHAREHOLDERS' EQUITY		
Beginning balance in common stock and retained earnings	$ 470,000	$ 400,000
Plus: Net income	200,000	150,000
Less: Dividends	130,000	80,000
Ending balance in common stock and retained earnings	$ 540,000	$ 470,000
STATEMENT OF CASH FLOWS		
Net cash flow from operating activities	$ 250,000	$ 120,000
Net cash flow from investing activities	(50,000)	(340,000)
Net cash flow from financing activities	(160,000)	280,000
Net increase (decrease) in cash	$ 40,000	$ 60,000
Beginning cash balance	60,000	0
Ending cash balance	$ 100,000	$ 60,000

investment depends primarily on what happens in the future. The past is often a poor indicator of the future.

You also observe that each statement emphasizes a different aspect of Microline's financial condition and performance. The balance sheet, for example, lists the company's assets, liabilities, and shareholders' equity. On the income statement, expenses are subtracted from revenues to produce a number called net income. The statement of shareholders' equity includes (1) the beginning and ending common stock and retained earnings balance, which can be found on the 2009 and 2010 balance sheets; (2) net income, which is the bottom line on the income statement; and (3) dividends. The statement of cash flows includes the beginning and ending balance of cash, which can be found on the 2009 and 2010 balance sheets, and net cash flows from operating, investing, and financing activities. It becomes clear quite quickly that you do not understand these terms and that you know very little about the information conveyed by these statements and, therefore, cannot begin to assess whether Microline would be a good company in which to invest.

THE FOOTNOTES

At this point you decide to examine the **footnotes,** hoping that they will clear up some of your uncertainty about the financial statements (Figure 1–5). They state that many of the numbers on the statements are the result of assumptions and estimates made by Microline's management, which does not surprise you because both the audit report and the management letter made similar statements. It is also clear from the footnotes that Microline was able to choose from a number of different acceptable accounting methods. While you know little about generally accepted accounting principles, you confidently conclude that they do not ensure exact and unbiased statements. Alternative accounting methods, as well as assumptions and estimates by Microline's management, are very evident.

FIGURE 1–5 Notes to the financial statements

Cash. **Cash consists of cash on hand and cash in a bank checking account.**

Accounts Receivable. **The balance in accounts receivable has been adjusted for an estimate of future uncollectibles.**

Equipment. **Equipment is carried at a cost and includes expenditures for new additions and those that substantially increase its useful life. The cost of the equipment is depreciated using the straight-line method over an estimated useful life of ten years.**

Land. **Land is carried at cost.**

Short-Term Payables. **Short-term payables consist of wages payable, short-term borrowings, interest payable, taxes payable, and an estimate of future warranty costs.**

Long-Term Payables. **Long-term payables consist primarily of notes that must be paid back after one year.**

Common Stock. **Common stock represents the contributions of the company's shareholders.**

Revenue Recognition. **Revenues from sales are reflected in the income statement when products are shipped. Revenues from services are estimated in proportion to the completion of the service.**

Expenses. **Expenses include selling and administrative expenses and estimates of uncollectible receivables and depreciation on the equipment.**

Descriptions of Financial Statements

After your initial examination, you decide that Microline may be a reasonable investment, but your lack of knowledge renders you incapable of making a confident choice. You decide to return to Mary Jordan, your financial advisor, for help. Perhaps she can explain the nature of the financial statements and improve your understanding of the decision that faces you. Mary begins by defining some of the fundamental terms used on the financial statements.[1]

The **balance sheet,** which lists Microline's assets, liabilities, and shareholders' equity, is a statement of the company's financial position as of a certain date. **Assets,** representing items that will bring future economic benefit to Microline, include the cash balance, the dollar amounts due from Microline's customers (accounts receivable), and the original cost of the equipment and land purchased by the company. **Liabilities,** which represent current obligations, consist of the amounts currently owed by Microline to its **creditors.** Satisfying these liabilities will generally require cash payments in the future. Common stock and retained earnings comprise the **shareholders' equity** section. **Common stock** represents the initial investments by Microline's owners, and **retained earnings** is a measure of Microline's past profits that have been retained (reinvested) in the business. Without the balance sheet, investors would have difficulty assessing the current financial condition of the company.

The **income statement** is divided into two parts: **revenues,** a measure of the assets generated from the products and services sold, and **expenses,** a measure of the asset outflows (costs) associated with selling these products and services. The difference between these two amounts is a number called **net income (profit or earnings),** which measures the success of Microline's operations over a particular period of time. Without the income statement, investors would be unable to determine the company's performance during the period.

The **statement of shareholders' equity** describes the changes in the shareholders' equity items (common stock and retained earnings) from one year to the next: There was no change in common stock for Microline, so in this case the statement only includes the increases and decreases to retained earnings, which is a measure of Microline's past profits. The net income, profit, or earnings amount from the income statement is first added to the beginning balance of retained earnings. **Dividends,** the assets paid to Microline's owners as a return for their initial investment, are then subtracted from this amount to compute ending retained earnings. The ending retained earnings amount appears on the balance sheet and becomes the beginning balance of the following period. The change in retained earnings indicates in any given year how dividends compare to profit.

The **statement of cash flows** summarizes the increases and decreases in cash over a period of time. The beginning cash balance is adjusted for the *net cash flows* (cash inflows less cash outflows) associated with Microline's operating, investing, and financing activities. **Operating activities** are associated with the actual products and services provided by Microline for its customers. **Investing activities** include the purchase and sale of assets, such as equipment and land. **Financing activities** refers to the cash collections and payments related to Microline's capital sources. Examples include cash borrowings and loan payments as well as collections from owners' contributions and the payment of dividends. Without the statement of cash flows, investors would have difficulty assessing the company's cash management strategies.

---

1. This section of the text provides basic definitions for important terms. These definitions are expanded upon in later chapters, and a complete glossary is provided at the end of the text.

Analysis of Financial Statements

After defining the terms on the financial statements, Mary notes that Microline appears to be in reasonably strong financial shape. She focuses first on the statement of cash flows, pointing out that the company's cash position has been increasing and that operating activities have contributed $120,000 and $250,000 in cash in the last two years. She also notes that Microline has invested heavily in new assets since its inception and that $160,000 was paid during 2010 for dividends and to reduce outstanding debts. In short, Microline has demonstrated the ability to generate cash. Mary believes this is very important, because in order to remain solvent, the company must be able to generate enough cash to meet its debts as they come due. She comments that **solvency** is a requirement for financial health.

Mary then moves to the income statement and statement of shareholders' equity, noting that Microline has shown profits of $150,000 and $200,000 over the past two years and, at the same time, has paid significant dividends to its owners, specifically $80,000 in 2009 and $130,000 in 2010. These numbers show that Microline has demonstrated **earning power,** the ability to grow and provide a substantial return to its owners. Mary also notes that the balance sheets indicate Microline's assets have increased during the past year from $950,000 to $1,010,000, while its liabilities (payables) have decreased from $480,000 to $470,000. She indicates that such a trend is promising.

To further support Microline's financial strength, Mary computes a few ratios by using the dollar values on the income statement and balance sheet. She points out that net income as a percentage of revenues increased from 10 percent ($150,000/ $1,500,000) in 2009 to over 12 percent ($200,000/$1,650,000) in 2010. Total payables as a percent of total assets decreased from over 50 percent ($480,000/$950,000) in 2009 to less than 47 percent ($470,000/$1,010,000) in 2010. Dividends as a percent of net income increased substantially over the two-year period—to 65 percent. After consulting some statistics covering the industry in which Microline is a member, Mary reports that Microline's financial ratios, in general, are stronger than those of many other similar firms.

> In its 2008 annual report, Bed Bath & Beyond, a leading housewares retailer, reported sales of $7.2 billion; net income of $425 million; total assets and total liabilities of $4.3 billion and 1.1 billion, respectively; and net cash flows from operating activities of $584 million. On which of the financial statements were each of these values reported, and what values were reported for each of the following items: total expenses, shareholders' equity, and the net income to sales ratio?

What Form of Investment: Debt or Equity?

The definitions and analysis provided by Mary are encouraging, and you decide that Microline is a good investment. However, Mary states that now you must decide what form your investment should take. Should it be in the form of a loan, or should you purchase ownership (equity) in Microline? She explains that the risks you face and the potential returns associated with these two forms of investment are really quite different. Moreover, the relative importance to you of the different kinds of information disclosed on the financial statements depends on the kind of investment you make.

A DEBT INVESTMENT

You would make a **debt investment** if you loaned the $1 million to Microline. You would then become one of the company's creditors and would require that Microline's management sign a **loan contract,** specifying (1) the *maturity date,* the date when the loan is to be paid back; (2) the **annual interest** payment, the amount of interest to be paid each year; (3) *collateral,* assets to be passed to you in case the principal or the interest on the loan is in *default* (not paid back); and (4) any other **debt restrictions** you feel you should impose on Microline to protect your investment. The contract might specify, for example, that Microline maintain a certain cash balance throughout the period of the loan or that dividends during that period be limited.

As one of Microline's creditors, your first concern would be Microline's ability to meet the loan's interest and principal payments as they come due. Since such payments are made in cash, you would be especially interested in Microline's cash management record and its ability to generate cash over the period of the loan. Thus, the information in the statement of cash flows would be very relevant. You would also be interested in the selling prices of assets that could be used as collateral and in the amounts of the loans and other liabilities owed by Microline to other creditors. The balance sheet, therefore, which lists Microline's assets and liabilities, would also contain some useful information.

Mary reminds you that many of Microline's assets are valued on the balance sheet at **historical cost,** the dollar amount paid when the assets were acquired, which, in many cases, was several years ago. This discovery is worrisome because the historical cost of an asset is rarely the same as its current selling price, the relevant amount if an asset is to be considered as collateral for the loan.

AN EQUITY INVESTMENT

Rather than loaning Microline the $1 million, you may wish to purchase **equity** in the company. As an equity investor, you would become one of the owners, or **shareholders,** of Microline.

Equity investments give rise to considerations that are somewhat different from those of debt investments. As a shareholder, for example, your return would be primarily in the form of stock appreciation and dividends, which would tend to be large if Microline performed well and small, or nonexistent, if the company performed poorly. Unlike a loan investment, for which interest and principal payments are specified by contract, dividend payments are at the discretion of Microline's **board of directors,** which is elected annually by the shareholders to represent their interests. Such representation involves (at least) quarterly meetings where company policies are set, dividends are declared, and the performance and compensation of the company's upper management are reviewed. The board of directors has the power to hire and fire upper management as well as determine the form and amount of their compensation.

As a shareholder who could vote in the election of the board of directors, your primary concern would be the performance of Microline's management—specifically, its ability to generate and maintain earnings in the future. To achieve such an objective, management must both ensure that cash is available to meet debts as they come due and invest in assets that produce a satisfactory return in the long run. Consequently, shareholders are interested in the information contained in all four of the financial statements: the balance sheet because it indicates Microline's assets and liabilities, the income statement and statement of shareholders' equity because they indicate Microline's earning power and dividend payments, and the statement of cash flows because it provides a report of Microline's past cash management policies. As a shareholder, however, you

would be especially interested in the income statement, since the board of directors often sets dividends as a percentage of income, which is generally considered to be the overall measure of management's performance and the company's earning power.

You would also be interested in the methods used to compensate Microline's upper management. You may wish, for example, to encourage the board of directors to institute a system of compensation that paid upper management on the basis of its performance. One way to implement such a system would be to set compensation levels at amounts expressed as percentages of net income. This would motivate Microline's management to increase net income and, accordingly, their compensation. Such a result should also mean increased earning power and greater dividend payments in the future. At the same time, however, you realize that management can influence the manner in which net income is measured.

A Decision Is Made, but Important Questions Still Remain

After a lengthy discussion with Mary, you decide to invest in the equity of Microline. From the information contained in the audit report, the management letter, the financial statements, and the footnotes, you have concluded that Microline is a legitimate operation that is solvent, has shown significant earning power, and has provided a reasonable return to its shareholders. You reason further that if Martin is correct in his prediction that their new voice-activated word-processing system will revolutionize the industry, there is a distinct possibility of large returns in the future. Shareholders would receive such returns in the form of an increase in the value of their investment and/or larger dividends, while payments to creditors would be limited to the contractual interest and principal payments.

You thank Mary for her advice and feel satisfied with your decision. You realize, however, that the future is uncertain and that your investment involves risks.

> **?** The asset side of the balance sheet for the Bank of New York Mellon, as well as many other financial institutions, is composed primarily of loans, while the Coca-Cola Company's assets include a large percentage of equity investments in other companies. What is the difference between these two kinds of assets, and why would these two companies rely more heavily on one than the other?

THE ECONOMIC ENVIRONMENT IN WHICH FINANCIAL REPORTS ARE PREPARED AND USED

Recent and significant financial disasters perpetrated by poor risk assessment and sometimes even fraudulent financial statements underscore the importance of accurate and credible financial reporting for the United States and the world economy. Financial statements provide measures of firm performance that support decisions by a wide variety of individuals and entities leading to billions of dollars in resource transfers each year. Indeed, the world economy depends to an important extent on the reliability and validity of financial statements.

Figure 1–6 illustrates the key elements of the financial accounting environment introduced earlier in the Microline scenario. In that scenario, as a potential investor

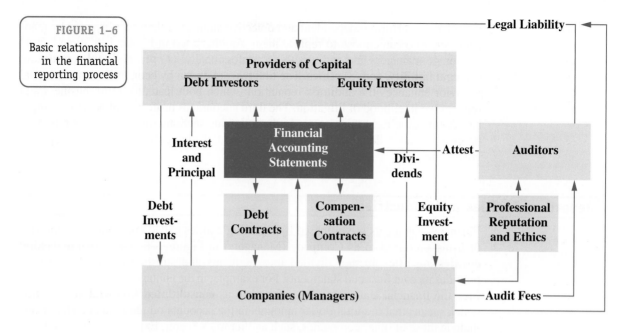

FIGURE 1–6
Basic relationships in the financial reporting process

you acted as a provider of capital, Martin Wagner and Microline represented the company (manager), and Arthur Price was the auditor. The figure shows that providers of capital (debt investors and equity investors) invest in (send funds to) companies operated by managers. In return, creditors (debt investors) expect to receive interest and principal payments, and equity investors expect to receive returns in the form of dividends and/or stock price appreciation. Company managers (1) hire auditors to attest to the financial information and (2) enter into debt and/or **compensation contracts.** Auditors add credibility to the financial statements by attesting to whether they were prepared in conformance with financial reporting standards and fairly present the company's financial performance and position, and contracts either protect the interests of creditors or are structured to encourage management to act in the interest of the company's owners—the shareholders.

In this environment, financial reporting information plays two fundamental roles. First, it helps debt and equity investors evaluate management's past business decisions and predict future performance. Second, it contains numbers (e.g., net income) used in debt and compensation contracts that influence management behavior.

> On its 2008 income statement General Electric reported over $17 billion of net income. Explain how this number could be used to evaluate GE management's past business decisions, predict GE's future performance, and influence GE management to make decisions in the interests of GE's shareholders.

An important feature of this environment is the level of **corporate governance,** which refers to mechanisms encouraging management to act in the interest of—and report in good faith to—the shareholders. Strong corporate governance is necessary because management has incentives to act and report in its own interest at the expense of the shareholders, and auditors face conflicting goals—they are responsible to capital

providers to perform independent and objective audits, but their fees are paid by management, who can choose to replace them. As illustrated in Figure 1–6, three factors encourage managers and auditors to act professionally: (1) **professional reputation,** (2) **legal liability,** and (3) **ethics.** The first two are driven by economics—professional behavior enhances the auditor's reputation, which both leads to future business and reduces the likelihood of litigation. The third encourages professional behavior simply because it is the right thing to do. In the following sections we describe the reporting process in more detail and discuss the essential elements of effective corporate governance.

Reporting Entities and Industries

Financial statements are prepared by reporting entities called companies, businesses, or firms—referred to as Company (Managers) in Figure 1–6. These **profit-seeking entities** are often further divided into segments and subsidiaries, each of which provides its own financial statements. For example, in the annual report of The Limited, Inc., the financial statements are referred to as **consolidated financial statements,** which means that the total dollar amounts in the accounts on the financial statements include those of other companies, such as Victoria's Secret, Express, and Bed & Body Works, which The Limited owns. These companies, called **subsidiaries,** prepare their own separate financial statements. Furthermore, The Limited is divided into retail divisions, and financial reports on each of these are compiled.

Financial statements are also prepared by entities not established to make profits, including counties, cities, school districts, other municipalities, charitable organizations, and foundations. In this text we limit our coverage to financial reports prepared by profit-seeking entities.

Companies are often grouped into **industries** based on the nature of their operations. While there are many industry classifications, they can be summarized into three basic categories: manufacturing, retailing, and services (general and financial). Manufacturing firms like General Motors, IBM, and PepsiCo acquire raw materials and convert them into goods sold either to consumers, usually through retailers, or to other manufacturers who use them as raw materials. Retail firms like Wal-Mart, Home Depot, Lowe's Home Improvement, Kohl's, Toys "Я" Us, and JCPenney purchase goods from manufacturers and sell them to consumers. The service industry includes firms like AT&T, Federal Express, and H&R Block, which provide general services, as well as firms like Citicorp, American Express, and Prudential Insurance, which provide financial services. Internet firms, such as Google, Yahoo!, and Amazon.com, are also part of the service industry. Specific industry classifications are provided by the well-known Standard Industrial Classification (SIC) Index, which assigns a 1- to 4-digit code to industries—the more digits in the code, the more specific the industry classification.

Knowledge of industries is important when analyzing financial statements because the relative importance of different aspects of financial performance and condition varies across firms in different industries. Managing outstanding loans, for example, is very important for lending institutions (banks) but less important for retailers like Wal-Mart that extend limited credit to customers. Furthermore, it is difficult to assess management's performance without knowledge of the overall performance of the company's industry, and without benchmarking management's performance against the performance of companies facing similar economic environments normally in the same industry.

Into what industry category (manufacturing, retail, service) would each of the following firms be placed? Boeing, Tommy Hilfiger, DuPont, American Express, General Electric, Microsoft, eBay, Southwest Airlines, and Sprint Nextel.

CORPORATE GOVERNANCE

As indicated earlier, corporate governance refers to mechanisms that encourage management to act in the interest of—and report in good faith to—the shareholders. Components of corporate governance include financial information users and capital markets, contracts between management and debt and equity investors, financial reporting regulations and standards, independent auditors, boards of directors and audit committees, internal controls ensuring that the company is in compliance with financial reporting regulations, legal liability, professional reputation, and ethics. As discussed below, each of these components somehow involves the financial statements, and an effective financial reporting system is critical for effective corporate governance.

Financial Information Users and Capital Markets

Financial statements are used by a variety of groups and can be divided into three categories: equity investors, debt investors, and others (including management).

EQUITY INVESTORS

Equity investors (often referred to simply as investors) purchase shares of stock, which represent ownership interests in a company. Ownership of an equity security entitles the holder to two basic rights: (1) to vote for company directors at the annual shareholders' meeting and (2) to receive dividends if paid. Equity investors can be classified into two groups. The first owns a substantial amount of the company's stock and uses the voting rights associated with that ownership to exert influence on, or control over, the activities of the company. The majority of equity investors, however, fall into a second group, where the ownership interest is too small to exert significant influence on the company through voting power. These investors have little direct influence over management, so their main concern is the returns (dividends and price appreciation) associated with holding the equity security.

Equity investors, and their representatives, such as financial and security analysts and stockbrokers, are interested in financial information because it helps them ascertain whether management is making wise business decisions. If the financial statements indicate that management has failed, investors holding large equity interests often use voting power to replace management while investors with relatively small equity interests normally sell their ownership interests. Indeed, management's performance as depicted by the financial statements plays an important role in monitoring and enforcing management's accountability to the shareholders. Simply stated, the financial statements tell shareholders how well their capital is being managed.

DEBT INVESTORS (CREDITORS)

Creditors provide capital (funds) to companies through loans. These investments involve loan contracts that normally specify: (1) a maturity date, the date when the loan is to be repaid; (2) an annual interest payment, the amount of interest to be paid each year;

(3) collateral, assets to be transferred to the creditor in case the loan payments are not met (default); and (4) additional debt restrictions generally designed to reduce default risk.

Creditors have limited influence over the company other than through the terms of the debt contract. They use financial information because it helps them assess the likelihood of default (the company is unable to make the loan payments), which in turn helps to establish terms of the debt contract. Normally, if the financial statements indicate that the risk of default is increasing, the terms of the debt contract become harsher—the interest rate and need for collateral increase, and the creditor may impose additional restrictions to further limit management's behavior. Consequently, a company's financial condition and performance, as indicated by the financial statements, are directly linked to how much it costs to borrow funds from creditors.

MANAGEMENT AND OTHER FINANCIAL STATEMENT USERS

Management often uses the financial statements of other firms to assess the financial strength and strategies of competitors, and to decide whether to enter into business relationships with other firms (e.g., suppliers, customers). It also uses its own financial statements to determine dividend payments, set company policies, and, in general, to help guide business decisions.

Other users include government bodies, such as the Federal Trade Commission, which often base regulatory decisions on information disclosed in the financial statements, and public utilities, which normally base their rates (the prices they charge their customers) on financial accounting numbers such as net income. Labor unions have also been known to use accounting numbers to argue for more wages or other benefits.

CAPITAL MARKETS

Equity and debt securities (investments) are held by both individuals and entities. Billions of shares of stock are held in large U.S. corporations, which, in turn, hold shares in each other. Debt securities in the form of loans are held primarily by banks, while debt securities in the form of bonds issued by large corporations are held by individuals and institutions.

Equity and debt securities are traded on public exchanges in the United States and in other countries. The *New York Stock Exchange (NYSE)* is by far the largest, but active exchanges exist in most of the major cities throughout the world. Large U.S. companies normally have their stocks listed on several exchanges, and many non-U.S. firms are listed in New York. More information about the NYSE, and the firms listed on it, can be found on the Internet at www.NYSE.com.

Publicly traded firms are so named because their shares of stock are owned by the public and traded on the public stock exchanges. As of December 18, 2009, for example, one share of Microsoft, a publicly traded firm, could be purchased by anyone for $30.36. So that investors can be adequately informed, the U.S. government requires publicly traded firms to meet extensive reporting requirements, and the financial statements of these companies can easily be accessed by anyone at any time. Recently, large investing firms, such as KKR and Blackstone, have purchased via the public exchanges all the outstanding shares of many publicly traded firms, "taking them private." Briefly discuss why Blackstone might want to take such an action, and describe some of the implications to the managers of the purchased firm and the investing public.

The prices at which equity and debt securities trade on the financial markets vary from day to day based largely on changes in investor expectations about the issuing company's future performance. Good news about the company tends to lead to increases in the *market prices* of its outstanding equity and debt securities, whereas bad news normally is associated with price declines. Price changes are widely considered to be a measure of management's performance, although they are determined by a variety of factors, only some of which are under management's control. Financial statements are an important source of the information used by those who invest in capital markets in setting expectations about a company's future prospects and in determining whether the company met those expectations. Consequently, financial statements are directly linked to the market prices of the company's equity and debt securities.

> In the introduction to Part 1 of this text we noted that stock market analysts were optimistic about Apple's future revenues and earnings. In response, the market price of Apple stock rose. Explain why the price increased, and how capital markets through the financial statements can incent or discipline management behavior.

Contracts: Debt Covenants and Management Compensation

Capital providers (debt and equity investors) normally require management to enter contracts designed to reduce risk and encourage business decision making consistent with capital-provider interests. Such contracts take two general forms: debt covenants and management compensation.

Debt covenants are included in debt contracts, often requiring management to maintain certain levels of financial performance or position to help ensure that management will be able to make the debt payments when they come due. Violating these requirements (technical default) normally gives the debtholder the right to demand that the entire debt be paid immediately, often leading to more costly debt terms. *Management compensation contracts* typically base management pay on certain net income or stock price goals, which can encourage desirable management decision making. Debt covenants and management compensation contracts provide examples where numbers taken from the financial statements are used in contracts written by capital providers to shape management behavior.

> Motorola has an employee incentive plan that makes annual payments to eligible employees based on whether they achieve specified business goals, many of which are expressed in terms of financial statement numbers. Recently the company paid over $250 million for these awards. Explain why Motorola has such a plan and how it works.

Financial Reporting Regulations and Standards

In 1934 the U.S. Congress created the **Securities and Exchange Commission (SEC)** to implement and enforce the Securities Act of 1933 and the Securities Exchange Act of 1934. The Securities Act of 1933 requires companies that raise capital (collect

funds) through public equity and debt exchanges (e.g, the New York Stock Exchange) to file a registration statement (Form S-1) with the SEC. The Securities Exchange Act of 1934 states that, among other requirements, companies with equity and/or debt securities listed on the public security markets (called *listed companies*) must (1) annually file a **Form 10-K** (audited financial reports), (2) quarterly file a **Form 10-Q** (unaudited quarterly financial statements), and (3) annually provide audited financial reports to the shareholders. Non-U.S. listed companies are required to file the SEC **Form 20-F.** The Forms 10-K, 10-Q, and 20-F contain a wealth of publicly available information and can be obtained by accessing the Electronic Data Gathering, Analysis, and Retrieval (EDGAR) system at the Web site www.sec.gov. Annual reports for individual companies are sent directly to shareholders, but can be obtained by anyone through the company's Web site (e.g., homedepot.com).

Annual reports published by major U.S. and non-U.S. companies typically include audited balance sheets for the two most recent years and audited statements of income, shareholders' equity, and cash flows for the three most recent years. They also include:

- A letter to the shareholders from a high-ranking officer
- A description of the business
- Management's discussion and analysis of the company's financial condition and performance
- Footnotes that describe the estimates, assumptions, and methods used to produce the numbers on the financial statements
- Selected quarterly data
- Summaries of selected financial information for at least the last five years
- Information about each of the company's major segments
- A letter from management stating its reporting responsibilities
- A letter from the company's outside (external) auditors stating whether the financial statements were prepared according to acceptable standards
- A listing of the members of the board of directors and executive officers

A large portion of the Form 10-K (including financial statements and footnotes) of NIKE, Inc. is provided in Appendix C at the end of this text. Take a few minutes to review it because we refer to this report frequently throughout the remainder of the text.

Generally Accepted Accounting Principles

Under current SEC regulations, U.S. companies whose securities are publicly traded on the U.S. exchanges must prepare their financial statements in accordance with **U.S. Generally Accepted Accounting Principles (U.S. GAAP),** and non-U.S. companies can use either U.S. GAAP or **International Financial Reporting Standards (IFRS).** External auditors must attest that these standards have been followed in the preparation of the financial statements. U.S. GAAP is established by a privately financed body called the **Financial Accounting Standards Board (FASB),** and IFRS is established by the **International Accounting Standards Board (IASB).** In the remainder of this text we use the phrase **Generally Accepted Accounting Principles (GAAP)** to describe either U.S. GAAP or IFRS.

These standards are useful because they lend credibility to the financial statements and help facilitate meaningful comparisons across different companies. However, the standards are often controversial because reporting requirements impose costs on companies required to follow them, many of which argue enthusiastically that these costs exceed the benefits created by the standards. Consequently, the accounting standard-setting process can be very political, involving controversial input from companies,

government regulators (e.g., SEC), Congress, financial statement users (financial and security analysts), and sometimes even the general public.

Figure 1–7 illustrates the political nature of the accounting standard-setting process. Policymakers, represented by the SEC, FASB, and IASB, are influenced in their deliberations by public input from Congress, the White House, government agencies, public hearings, and letters from interested parties. The result is GAAP, which sets the standard for actual accounting practices. These practices, in turn, create costs and benefits to investors, creditors, managers, auditors, and others (economic consequences) that underlie the public input targeted at the policymakers.

FIGURE 1–7

The accounting policymaking process

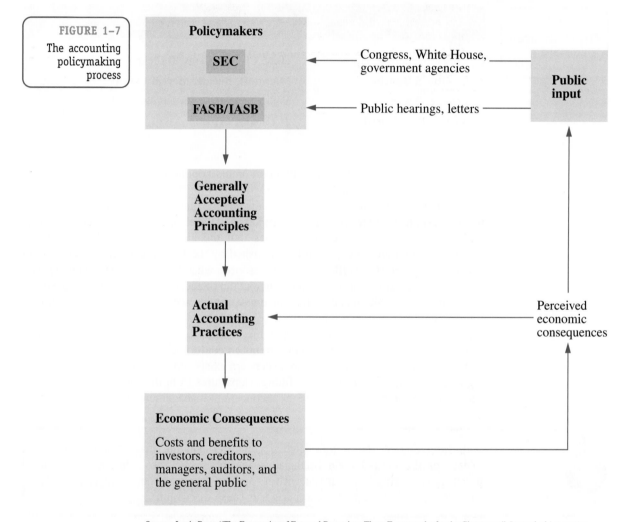

Source: Jamie Pratt, "The Economics of External Reporting: Three Frameworks for the Classroom," *Journal of Accounting Education* (1987), p. 182.

Many executives contend that financial accounting standards requiring that management compensation be measured in a way that reduces net income will negatively affect their firms. Accounting standard setters claim that the only objective is to improve financial reporting without regard for the consequences of its decisions. What do you think?

Independent Auditors

Major U.S. companies incur considerable costs to have their financial statements audited by independent public accounting firms. Four public accounting firms, known as the **"Big 4,"** audit most of the large companies. These firms and a selection of their major clients are listed in Figure 1–8. Many regional and local public accounting firms are located throughout the United States. Their audit clients comprise the thousands of mid-sized and small companies that, for various reasons, have their financial statements audited.

FIGURE 1–8
"Big 4" accounting firms and major clients

Accounting Firm	Major Clients
PricewaterhouseCoopers	eBay, Cisco Systems, DuPont
Deloitte & Touche	Microsoft, Boeing, Merrill Lynch
Ernst & Young	Wal-Mart, Intel, Hewlett Packard
KPMG Peat Marwick	JCPenney, PepsiCo, Xerox

The result of the audit is the audit report or audit opinion. The standard audit report, which is normally divided into three paragraphs, is illustrated in Figure 1–2. The first paragraph states that the financial statements and the internal controls were audited but that the responsibility for preparing the reports and the effectiveness of the controls rests with management; the second describes that the auditor conducted the audit in accordance with auditing standards established by the **Public Company Accounting Oversight Board (PCAOB)** and briefly describes what that means; the final paragraph states the conclusion, normally indicating that the financial statements present the company's financial position and performance fairly and in accordance with GAAP, and the internal controls are reasonably effective. However, a standard audit opinion is not always rendered to all companies. Sometimes auditors find that they are unable to reach a conclusion, the financial statements are not in conformance with GAAP, the internal control system is not effective, or some concern exists about the company's viability as a going concern in the foreseeable future. Departures from the standard audit opinion can signal problems that can cause great concern to management and capital providers.

Dell, Inc., one of the world's leading computer manufacturers, postponed the release of its audited 2006 financial statements while the company discussed possible accounting irregularities with its auditor, PricewaterhouseCoopers. Briefly comment on what might have occurred in these discussions.

Board of Directors and Audit Committee

The *board of directors,* elected annually by the shareholders, oversees management to ensure that it acts in the interest of the shareholders. Such oversight involves periodic (at least quarterly) meetings where company policies are set, dividends are declared, and the performance and compensation of the company's officers are reviewed. The board, normally composed of both company officers and nonmanagement representatives, has the power to hire and fire the officers as well as determine the form and amount of their compensation.

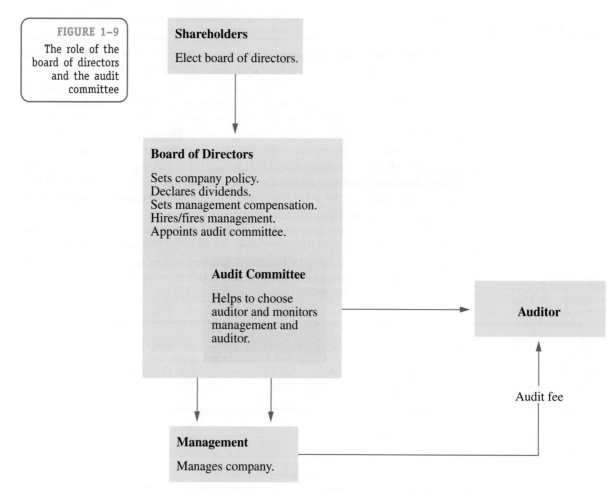

FIGURE 1–9

The role of the board of directors and the audit committee

Shareholders

Elect board of directors.

Board of Directors

Sets company policy.
Declares dividends.
Sets management compensation.
Hires/fires management.
Appoints audit committee.

Audit Committee

Helps to choose auditor and monitors management and auditor.

Auditor

Audit fee

Management

Manages company.

Figure 1–9 illustrates that the shareholders elect the board of directors, which appoints a subcommittee of outside (non-management) directors called the **audit committee.** This committee works with management to choose an auditor, and it monitors the audit to ensure that it is thorough, objective, and independent. Despite these controls, management still pays the audit fee and has considerable influence over whether the auditing firm is hired again. Such influence can threaten the auditor's independence. *Accountancy* magazine reports that "auditors may be loath to report faults in their clients' operations for fear of losing their audit contract." Some managers have been known to shop around for favorable audit opinions. For example, when Broadview Financial Corporation, a large Ohio company, switched auditors, it was revealed later that the switch was due to disagreements about proper methods of accounting. "Opinion shopping" is expressly prohibited by the SEC, and significant disagreements with the auditor are supposed to be reported and described by publicly traded companies in the Form 8K, which is filed with the SEC.

? Much criticism has been directed at audit committees for their lack of financial expertise, and the SEC recently enacted rules to help ensure that audit committee members are financially literate. Explain why it is important that audit committee members understand financial statements.

Sarbanes–Oxley Act

The **Sarbanes–Oxley Act,** passed by Congress in 2002 in response to a series of corporate financial statement frauds leading to billions of dollars in investor losses, is an attempt to bolster corporate governance and restore confidence in the U.S. financial reporting system. It enacted sweeping changes in the responsibilities of management, financial disclosures, independence and effectiveness of auditors and audit committees, and oversight of public companies and auditors. The Act requires the principal executive and financial officers to certify that the financial reports have been reviewed, do not contain untrue statements or omit important information, and fairly present the company's financial condition and performance. It also places additional responsibilities on management and the auditor to ensure that adequate *internal controls* are in place to provide reasonable assurance that the financial records are complete and accurate. Management must also file an annual report on internal controls over financial reporting, and the external auditor must attest to and report on management's assessment of internal controls. In summary, this Act places heavy emphasis on the quality of a company's internal control system and significantly increases the auditor's role in ensuring that the control system meets high standards.

When a company discovers an accounting error, the company must restate all previous financial statements affected by the error. Such restatements have risen consistently and dramatically in recent years. Some believe that the Sarbanes–Oxley Act accounts for this shift. Explain why.

Legal Liability

Management is legally responsible to the shareholders to act in their interests and to report in good faith. Auditors are legally responsible to the shareholders to conduct a thorough and independent audit. These responsibilities create a legal liability to those who rely on the financial statements. If management or auditors fail in these responsibilities and as a result investors and others suffer financial losses, management and the auditors can be sued to recover those losses. Litigation brought against management and auditors by shareholders is common and very costly and seems to increase each year in the United States. Some of the greatest financial frauds in the history of the United States recently have led to billions of dollars in losses borne by innocent investors, creditors, employees, and others. Enron, WorldCom (now MCI), HealthSouth, Xerox Corp., Rite Aid, and Qwest Communications International provide vivid examples of how internal control breakdowns and flawed and dishonest management and auditing can result in misstated financial statements that ultimately cost the U.S. economy billions of dollars; in each case huge litigation settlements were brought against corporate management and the auditor. Indeed, in the last 20 years, two huge auditing firms—Laventhol & Horwath and Arthur Andersen—have met their demise, in large part due to the costs of litigation. Legal liability definitely plays a critical role in corporate governance, creating a powerful economic incentive for managers and auditors to act professionally and ethically.

Professional Reputation and Ethics

The many aspects of corporate governance (e.g., capital markets, contracts, reporting regulations, independent auditors, boards of directors and audit committees, and legal liability) suggest that a large amount of mistrust exists among shareholders, managers,

and auditors. This observation is difficult to question given that cases of management fraud and embezzlement have risen significantly in recent years, and that audit firms have increasingly been found guilty of misconduct. Some even suggest that U.S. business is suffering from an ethics crisis. Indeed, businesspeople in general are often viewed as greedy, driven, and unscrupulous.

Notwithstanding these developments, little doubt exists that ethics is a major business asset and that ethical behavior is in the long-run best interest of managers, shareholders, and auditors. Clifford Smith, a professor of finance at the University of Rochester, stated in the *Journal of Applied Corporate Finance* that "ethical behavior is profitable." In recognition of the value of ethics, major U.S. companies, such as Boeing, General Mills, and Johnson & Johnson, have instituted special programs designed specifically to instill ethical behavior in their employees. Most of the top business schools offer courses in ethics. The **American Institute of Certified Public Accountants (AICPA),** the professional organization of CPAs, has a strong professional code of ethics designed to instill higher ethical standards in the members of the accounting profession.

Such efforts are not only moral, but they are driven by sound economic logic. Companies with reputations for quality, service, and ethical business practices are highly valued by investors and creditors partially because their financial statements can be trusted. Such companies and their managers are sued less frequently. As the employee manual of Wetherill Associates states, "We do not try to make profits or avoid losses. Instead, we try to take the 'right action' in the best way we know; the profits are a natural by-product."

Auditors also benefit from ethical behavior and strong reputations. Independent and respectable auditors face fewer liability suits and can generally charge client companies higher fees, primarily because their audit reports are trusted by the public. Consequently, it is important to realize that while the financial accounting process is a system of control, and manager and auditor fraud will continue to occur, it is best to be ethical, from both a moral and an economic standpoint. Not surprisingly, the most successful companies and audit firms enjoy the best reputations for high ethical standards.

> In its annual report General Electric devotes an entire section to governance, stating that "GE's directors have adopted corporate governance principles aimed at ensuring that the Board is independent, and fully informed of the key risks and strategic issues facing GE." The section includes a Web site containing these principles (www.ge.com/governance). Explain why GE has established such principles.

INTERNATIONAL PERSPECTIVE: MOVEMENT TOWARD A SINGLE GLOBAL FINANCIAL REPORTING SYSTEM

For many years the different histories, economies, political systems, and cultures of countries throughout the world gave rise to vastly different financial reporting systems. In North America, the United Kingdom, and Australia, for example, the financial reporting systems were oriented toward the decision needs of equity investors and designed to measure management performance in a true and fair manner. In European countries and Japan, the financial reports were heavily influenced by government requirements (e.g., tax law), and the statements were targeted more toward the needs of creditors, giving management much more discretion in the preparation of the

reports. In these settings financial reporting also tended to be intentionally conservative instead of designed to report management's true performance. In today's fast-moving, global marketplace this situation is quickly changing.

As described earlier, two sets of financial reporting standards are currently accepted by the SEC: U.S. GAAP and IFRS. Non-U.S. companies that follow IFRS are accepted by the SEC, and while U.S. companies still must follow U.S. GAAP, it is likely that soon they will be allowed (perhaps required) to report under IFRS. The advent of international accounting standards dates back to 1973, but recently their acceptance has grown remarkably fast. Since 2005, for example, all public companies in the European Union have been required to report under IFRS, and virtually all of the major non-U.S. stock exchanges (e.g., London, Tokyo, Frankfurt, Paris) now accept IFRS. Indeed, in 2007 for the first time the SEC accepted IFRS-based financial statements from non-U.S. companies filing the SEC Form 20-F.

While the fundamental principles underlying U.S. GAAP and IFRS are the same and there is huge overlap in the content, significant differences do exist. In 2002 the FASB and IASB addressed these differences by entering into the Norwalk Agreement, reaffirmed in 2006, agreeing that the two boards will work to converge existing financial reporting standards and coordinate future efforts in an attempt to create a single set of global standards. Further, in 2008 the SEC established a roadmap that anticipates mandatory reporting for U.S. publicly traded companies under IFRS beginning in 2014, 2015, or 2016, depending on their size.

The future remains uncertain, but momentum continues to build for a single set of high-quality global standards. In this text most of the discussion is based on U.S. GAAP, but throughout we describe and illustrate important differences between the two systems as they arise. In the future you are very likely to be exposed to IFRS-based financial reporting in one form or another.

> Discuss some of the problems associated with two different sets of financial reporting standards, and why a single set of global standards might be desirable. Would there be any drawbacks to a single set of standards?

APPENDIX 1A

THREE OTHER KINDS OF ACCOUNTING

This text is devoted almost exclusively to financial accounting. However, you should be aware of the three other kinds of accounting usually covered in other accounting courses: not-for-profit accounting, managerial accounting, and tax accounting.

Many economic entities do not have profit as an objective. Municipalities, such as cities, simply receive money from taxes, service fees, and debt investors and allocate it to address public needs. For example, a city allocates funds to a police department to ensure public safety. The process of recording these fund inflows and outflows and reporting them to the public is quite logically called **not-for-profit accounting.**

Managers need *internal information systems* to generate timely and accurate information that helps them plan and operate efficiently on a day-to-day basis. To guide their decisions, managers rely to some extent on the information produced by the financial accounting system. However, more important to such decisions is information that is not available to the public and is produced strictly for management's own use. Such information is referred to as **managerial accounting** information, and managerial accounting is usually covered in a separate course.

The area of accounting devoted to understanding and applying the tax law is known as **tax accounting**. Our complicated and constantly changing tax structure requires that thousands of accountants specialize in this area. Furthermore, tax law is extremely detailed and complicated; even a moderate coverage of tax accounting requires a number of separate accounting or law courses.

An important distinction should be made between the income number resulting from applying income tax laws (called *taxable income*) and the income number that results from financial accounting (called *net income*). The *Internal Revenue Code* specifies the rules to be followed to calculate taxable income. An entity's tax obligation is then computed as a percentage of this taxable income. Financial accounting income, or net income, is determined by applying financial accounting principles and procedures, which differ in many ways from the tax laws stated in the Internal Revenue Code. As a result, net income is not necessarily equal to taxable income. Tax laws are enacted for purposes quite different from those that drive the development of financial accounting principles. Accounting students often confuse these two sets of rules.

Figure 1A–1 compares not-for-profit, managerial, and tax accounting to financial accounting. The top of the chart depicts a sequential process in which the managers of an economic entity follow certain accounting processes that convert financial facts

FIGURE 1A–1   Four kinds of accounting

Economic Entity	Managers	System	Financial Information	Recipients	Decisions
FINANCIAL ACCOUNTING					
Profit-making companies	Finance or accounting department	U.S. Generally Accepted Accounting Principles or IFRS	Income statement Balance sheet Statement of shareholder's equity Statement of cash flows Other disclosures Auditor report	*External* Investors Creditors Suppliers Employees Managers Government General public	Equity and debt investments Contract negotiations Regulation Dividend payments
NOT-FOR-PROFIT ACCOUNTING					
Nonprofit entities	Finance or accounting department	Fund accounting principles	Balance sheet Funds flow statements	*External* Creditors Government General public	Debt investments Budget allocations
MANAGERIAL ACCOUNTING					
All entities	Internal accounting department	Company information system	Manager reports Production costs Performance evaluation, etc.	*Internal* Managers	Operating decisions
TAX ACCOUNTING					
All entities	Finance or accounting department	Internal Revenue Code	Official tax forms: 1040 for individuals 1120 for corporations	*External* Internal Revenue Service	Collection of government revenues

about the entity into a set of financial statements. Interested parties then use this information for a variety of business decisions.

SUMMARY OF KEY POINTS

The key points of this chapter are summarized as follows.

⬤ *The economic role of financial accounting statements.*

Investors and creditors demand that management provide financial accounting information for two fundamental economic reasons. First, they need financial numbers to monitor and enforce the debt and compensation contracts written with management. Second, they need financial information to decide where to invest their funds. Companies incur the costs of providing the statements and having them audited because they need to attract capital from investors and creditors, and managers want to maintain their levels of compensation. Management hires auditors who must act independently because they face high levels of legal liability and must follow professional ethical standards.

⬤ *The four financial statements and the information each provides.*

The four financial statements are (1) the balance sheet, (2) the income statement, (3) the statement of shareholders' equity, and (4) the statement of cash flows. The balance sheet lists the assets, liabilities, and shareholders' equity of a company at a given point in time. The income statement contains the revenues earned and expenses incurred by a company over a period of time. Revenues less expenses equals net income. The statement of shareholders' equity describes the changes in the shareholders' equity accounts from one period to the next. The statement of cash flows reconciles the cash amount from one period to the next. It lists net cash flows from operating activities, investing activities, and financing activities.

⬤ *The standard audit report, management letter, and footnotes to the financial statements.*

The auditor's report is divided into three paragraphs. The first states that the financial statements and internal controls are the responsibility of management, they have been audited, and the auditor's responsibility is to express an opinion on them. The second indicates that the examination of the company's records and internal controls was made in accordance with standards established by the PCAOB and that the auditor has obtained reasonable assurance that the financial statements are free of material misstatement. The final paragraph states that the financial statements present fairly the financial position of the company, the results of operations, and its cash flows in conformity with generally accepted accounting principles, and that the internal controls are reasonably effective.

The management letter normally states that the company's management is responsible for the preparation and integrity of the statements, that the statements were prepared in accordance with generally accepted accounting principles, and that certain amounts were based on management's best estimates and judgments. It further indicates that the company maintains a system of internal controls designed to safeguard its assets and ensure that all transactions are recorded and reported properly. The footnotes provide additional information about the dollar amounts on the financial statements. They indicate which accounting methods were used and where the numbers on the statements are the result of assumptions and estimates made by management.

⬤ *The two forms of investment—debt and equity—and how the information on the financial statements relates to them.*

There are two forms of investment: debt and equity. A debt investment is a loan, and debt investors are called *creditors*. When debt investments are made, management is normally required to sign a loan contract. Creditors are primarily concerned that the interest and principal payments are met on a timely basis. Since such payments are made in cash, creditors are interested in financial information that helps them predict future cash flows over the period of the loan.

Equity investments involve purchasing ownership interests in a company. Equity owners of corporations are called shareholders. Their returns come in the form of dividends (or *stock price appreciation*), which tend to be large if the company performs well and small, or nonexistent, if it performs poorly. The primary concern of shareholders is the performance of the company's management—specifically, its ability to generate and maintain earning power in the future. To achieve this objective, management must ensure that cash is available to meet debts as they come due and also invest in assets that produce satisfactory returns in the long run. Consequently, shareholders are interested in the information contained in all four of the financial statements.

● *The nature and importance of corporate governance and the role of financial statements.*

Corporate governance refers to mechanisms that encourage management to act in the interest of, and report in good faith to, the shareholders. Components of corporate governance include financial information users and capital markets, contracts between management and debt and equity investors, financial reporting regulations and standards, independent auditors, boards of directors and audit committees, internal controls ensuring that the company is in compliance with financial reporting regulations, legal liability, professional reputation, and ethics. The credibility of the financial reporting process depends on the effectiveness of these components, and recent financial frauds, imposing huge costs on the global economy, highlight what can happen when corporate governance fails.

● *The current status of accounting standard setting, both in the U.S. and internationally.*

For many years financial accounting practices and standards used in countries throughout the world were quite diverse due to different histories, cultures, economies, and political systems. Efforts by the International Accounting Standards Board (IASB) have attempted to bring greater uniformity to worldwide accounting practice by creating International Financial Reporting Standards (IFRS), and virtually all non-U.S. stock exchanges have accepted these standards. The SEC currently allows non-U.S. companies to file their financial statements using IFRS. The FASB and IASB have pledged to work together to create a single set of global accounting standards, and the SEC has established a road map leading to U.S. firms adopting IFRS in 2014, 2015, or 2016, depending on their size.

KEY TERMS

Note: Definitions for these terms are provided in the glossary at the end of the text.

American Institute of Certified Public
  Accountants (AICPA) (p. 25)
Annual interest (p. 13)
Annual reports (p. 20)
Assets (p. 11)
Audit committee (p. 23)
Auditor's report (p. 7)
Balance sheet (p. 11)
"Big 4" (p. 22)
Board of directors (p. 13)
Certified public accountant (CPA) (p. 6)
Common stock (p. 11)
Compensation contracts (p. 15)
Consolidated financial statements (p. 16)
Corporate governance (p. 15)
Creditors (p. 11)
Debt covenants (p. 19)
Debt investment (p. 13)

Debt restrictions (p. 13)
Dividends (p. 11)
Earning power (p. 12)
Economic consequence perspective (p. 4)
Equity (p. 13)
Ethics (p. 16)
Expenses (p. 11)
Financial accounting (p. 3)
Financial Accounting Standards Board
  (FASB) (p. 20)
Financing activities (p. 11)
Footnotes (p. 10)
Form 10-K (p. 20)
Form 10-Q (p. 20)
Form 20-F (p. 20)
Generally Accepted Accounting Principles
  (GAAP) (p. 20)
Historical cost (p. 13)

ETHICS in the Real World

the independence required of audit firms, which highlights a federal requirement that auditors severely limit additional services provided for audit clients and under no circumstances own stock in their clients.

While granting clean audit opinions on the financial statements by Vienna software maker MicroStrategy, Inc., auditor PricewaterhouseCoopers was also serving as middleman in the sale of MicroStrategy products. Wearing those two hats can compromise

ETHICAL ISSUE Is it ethical for the same firm to provide an independent audit service for a client while also providing business advisory services, and can an auditor maintain an independent perspective while owning equity securities in an audit client?

INTERNET RESEARCH EXERCISE

Recall the reference to Apple, Inc., at the beginning of the chapter. Start with the Apple Web site (www.apple.com/investor/) and find the most recent SEC Form 10-K. Find the income statement and the revenues and net income numbers for the last three years.

ISSUES FOR DISCUSSION

ID1–1

Financial statement users

Financial accounting statements are used by many parties. Describe how each of the following parties might use them: security analysts and shareholders, bank loan officers, a company's customers and suppliers, public utilities, labor unions, and a company's managers.

ID1–2

Auditors and management fraud

The AICPA's list of red flags, alerting auditors to the possibility of management fraud, includes a "domineering management with a weak board of directors." Briefly explain the role of the board of directors and how such a situation could indicate management fraud. Why are auditors concerned with management fraud?

ID1–3

Audit committees

Explain the function of the audit committee, and describe why it is important that it consist of outside (nonmanagement) directors.

ID1–4

Banks, the credit crunch, and the financial statements

One of the factors contributing to the 2008–2009 recession was the unwillingness of commercial banks to extend loans to customers, some of whom were quite creditworthy. This unwillingness led to what was called a "credit crunch." Discuss reasons why banks would become reluctant to extend credit to customers, and how the financial reporting system represents these loans on the banks' financial statements.

REAL DATA

ID1–5

Financial statement relationships

In its 2008 annual report, Home Depot reported that fiscal 2008 sales decreased to $71.3 billion (from $77.3 billion the previous fiscal year), while profits decreased to $2.26 billion (from $4.395 billion). Total assets decreased from $44.3 billion to $41.2 billion, while shareholders' equity during the same time period remained flat at $17.7 billion. The company's cash balance increased $74 million with cash flows from operating activities (+$5.5 billion), investing activities (−$1.7 billion), and financing activities (−$3.7 billion). Discuss possible explanations for these financial results.

REAL DATA

ID1–6

Debt covenants

Continental Airlines signed contracts with its major creditors (mostly banks) that require the company to maintain a minimum cash balance of $600 million, a minimum shareholders' equity balance of $972 million, and dividend payments restricted to no more than $576 million. Discuss why the creditors impose such restrictions on Continental.

REAL DATA

ID1–7

Managing reported profits

Fortune magazine ran an article titled "New Ethics or No Ethics? Questionable Behavior Is Silicon Valley's Next Big Thing," which recounts stories of Internet companies that aggressively inflate their revenues, delay the recognition of expenses, and report sales that are not exactly sales. In many cases the actions of these companies, while aggressive, are not in direct violation of generally accepted accounting principles. Discuss why companies might engage in such behavior, and comment on the ethical implications.

REAL DATA

ID1–8

Audit report

The following quote was taken directly from the audit report written by Pricewaterhouse Coopers on the 2009 financial statements of Kroger.

In our opinion, the accompanying consolidated balance sheets and related consolidated statements of operations, cash flows and changes in shareholders' equity present fairly, in all material respects, the financial position of Kroger Co. and its subsidiaries at January 31, 2009 and February 2, 2008, and the results of their operations and their cash flows for each of the three years in the period ended January 31, 2009 in conformity with accounting principles generally accepted in the United States of America.

Explain the meaning of the quote and the terms used in it.

REAL DATA

ID1–9

Corporate governance

In a report to its clients on the implications of the Sarbanes–Oxley Act of 2002, KPMG states that the Act is intended to expand corporate governance, increase public confidence in financial reporting information, and strengthen our capital market systems.

Describe the meaning of corporate governance and how it relates to financial accounting statements. Also, comment on how Sarbanes–Oxley can achieve the intentions stated in the KPMG report.

REAL DATA

ID1–10

Ethics and accounting

In a survey conducted by two accounting professors, the *Wall Street Journal* reported that a number of high-level corporate managers indicated that they would choose investments that would boost current net income to meet the expectations of analysts following their companies in favor of better investments that produced much larger returns in the future. "To the professors' surprise, the financial officers were eager to talk about how companies would forgo projects that would give them economic gain in order to put a finer gloss on earnings."

Comment on the ethical implications of management's behavior.

ID1–11

Global reporting standards

The FASB and IASB are working on converging U.S. GAAP and IFRS into a single reporting system. Currently, the SEC accepts IFRS financial statements from non-U.S. companies, while requiring U.S. GAAP from U.S. companies. Comment on the difficulties faced by

financial analysts who analyze financial statements to assess the financial condition and performance of companies. Consider, for example, the plight of an analyst in the pharmaceutical industry who must assess and compare the financial performance of giants Novartis (a Swiss firm using IFRS) and Johnson & Johnson (a U.S. firm using U.S. GAAP).

ID–12

International accounting standards

The Securities and Exchange Commission has established a road map that will ultimately require U.S. companies to use International Financial Reporting Standards (IFRS). Already, the SEC allows foreign companies to list their securities in the United States and file IFRS financial statements. In general, IFRS policies are considered to be based on general accounting *principles*, while the U.S. Generally Accepted Accounting Principles are very detailed and are based on numerous *rules*. Accounting experts are debating the effectiveness of the two standards: the international guidelines that employ general concepts and priniciples versus the U.S. approach of anticipating all situations with a detailed set of rules. Discuss the advantages and disadvantages of a system based on concepts versus a system based on rules.

ID1–13

Appendix 1A

Distinguish managerial accounting from financial accounting, and describe how the information provided by the two systems is used differently.

Excerpts taken from the SEC Form 10-K of NIKE, Inc. are reproduced in Appendix C.

REAL DATA

ID1–14

The SEC Form 10-K of NIKE

REQUIRED:

Review the 10-K of NIKE, and answer the following questions.

a. Briefly describe the operations of NIKE, and indicate whether it is a manufacturing, retail, or service company.
b. Which accounting firm audits NIKE? Briefly explain the contents of the audit report.
c. What dollar amounts for net income were reported in 2009, 2008, and 2007?
d. Compute NIKE's liabilities as a percent of total assets in 2009 and 2008. Did the percentage increase or decrease?
e. How much cash was provided by operating activities during 2009, 2008, and 2007?
f. Comment on NIKE's financial performance and condition.

The Financial Statements

KEY POINTS

The following key points are emphasized in this chapter:

- The three basic activities of a business and how they are reflected in the financial statements.

- The balance sheet, income statement, statement of shareholders' equity, and statement of cash flows and how these financial statements are used.

- Similarities and differences between non-U.S. and U.S. financial statement format and terminology.

In 2008, Borders Group, Inc., one of the nation's largest book retailers, reported a loss from operations of $185 million, a significant change from a $20 million operating loss in the prior year. This deterioration occurred partly as a result of a decrease in revenue of $313 million. From early February 2008 to January 2009, Borders' liabilities decreased by nearly $500 million. Over the same period the company's cash position decreased by $5 million, even though the company used over $260 million in cash to repay debt and over $6 million to pay dividends to shareholders. These kinds of activities, so vital to Borders or any other company, are reflected in different ways on the financial statements—the balance sheet, income statement, statement of shareholders' equity, and statement of cash flows. In this chapter we discuss the financial statements in more detail.

As you read this chapter, consider the following questions. How do operating, investing, and financing decisions affect the dollar amounts reported on the financial statements? What information on the financial statements can be used to assess solvency and earning power? How might investors and creditors use the dollar values shown on the financial statements to control and monitor the business decisions of managers? Why and how do firm stock prices react to reported financial information? Is management able to influence the preparation of these statements so that solvency and earning power are depicted attractively? Such questions give economic meaning to financial statements and cannot be ignored by savvy managers and investors.

CAPITAL FLOWS AND OPERATING, INVESTING, AND FINANCIAL ACTIVITIES

Figure 2–1 illustrates the flow of capital through the firm, highlighting a number of concepts that we rely on heavily throughout the text. Management must (1) attract money, often called capital, from two sources: shareholders by selling the ownership (equity) of the firms and debtholders (creditors) through borrowings. Management

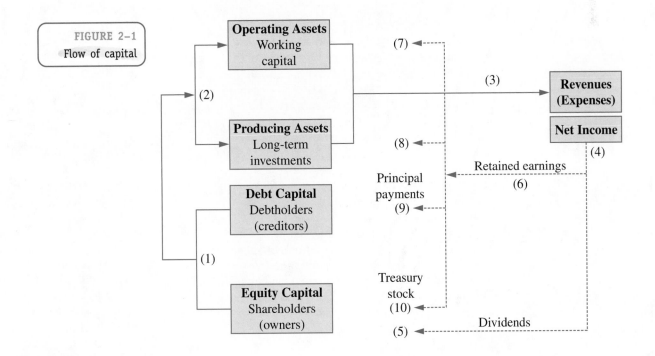

FIGURE 2–1
Flow of capital

normally attracts this capital by presenting historical and prospective information to these potential investors, explaining how it expects to use the capital to create returns for the investors. Shareholders (equity investors) expect returns in the form of price appreciation of their investments and/or dividends. Debtholders (debt investors) expect returns in the form of interest.

Management invests the capital (2) in both producing assets (e.g., property, plant, equipment; other companies; intangible assets; ideas) and operating assets (e.g., inventory), often referred to as working capital. Producing assets typically provides benefits for the firm over many periods by supporting the operating activities, the management of the assets used in day-to-day operations. Managing the producing and operating assets generates revenues (e.g., sales of inventories or services), which are matched against the expenses incurred to generate them (e.g., wages and salaries), including interest on the outstanding debt (3). The difference between revenues and expenses (4) is called net income, profit, or earnings and represents a measure of the wealth created by management for the shareholders during a given time period. The shareholders, normally through the board of directors, decide whether to take the created wealth out of the firm in the form of dividends (5) or to reinvest it in the firm (6). The reinvestment is called retained earnings, a measure of resources management can use to (7) purchase working capital and (8) purchase assets, (9) pay off loans, and/or (10) buy back ownership interests (shares of stock) from the shareholders in the form of treasury stock.

This process highlights three fundamental activities involved in managing a business: (1) operating activities, (2) investing activities, and (3) financing activities. **Operating activities** involve managing the operating assets, which includes activities related to the production and sale of goods and services (e.g., sales, receivables, inventory, and payables management). **Investing activities** involve acquiring and disposing of producing assets, the assets used to produce and support the goods and services provided (e.g., buildings, equipment, know-how). **Financing activities** involve raising capital through equity or debt issuances and the related payments to capital providers such as debt payments, dividends, and share repurchases.

> In its 2008 annual report, Zimmer Holdings, Inc., a well-known medical parts manufacturer, reported cash provided by operating activities of over $1 billion, cash used by investing activities of $924 million, and cash used for financing activities of $344 million. Describe some of the transactions that led to each of these three cash flow numbers.

The remainder of the chapter is devoted to describing and interpreting the financial statements. As you study them, keep in mind that they are designed to measure different aspects of businesses as depicted in Figure 2–1. The balance sheet includes assets (working capital and producing assets) and financing sources (equity, debt, and reinvestments from net earnings) as of a point in time. The income statement is a measure of operations, the activities involved in selling the goods and services. The statement of shareholders' equity keeps track of the investments made by the shareholders— either through equity investments or reinvested earnings—reduced by dividends paid to the shareholders. The statement of cash flows reports the cash inflows and outflows associated with the operating, investing, and financing activities of the business. Managers must understand the link between the financial statements and the company's financial condition and performance, as well as how their operating, investing, and financing decisions are reflected on the statements.

THE CLASSIFIED BALANCE SHEET

We now turn to more in-depth discussions of the four financial statements. Figure 2–2 shows the balance sheet for Harbour Island Company as of December 31, 2011. It is entitled a **classified balance sheet** because the asset and liability accounts are grouped into classifications: current assets; long-term investments; property, plant, and equipment; intangible assets; current liabilities; and long-term liabilities.

A Photograph of Financial Condition

Think of the balance sheet as a photograph of the business at a specific point in time. The title includes a specific date (December 31, 2011). As of this date, the balance sheet measures the financial condition of Harbour Island Company. In fact, some companies refer to the balance sheet as the *statement of financial condition.* This "photograph" of financial condition shows that as of December 31, 2011, Harbour Island has $220 in cash, total assets of $18,615, contributed capital of $9,550, retained earnings of $1,385, and total liabilities plus shareholders' equity of $18,615.

The balance sheet lists Harbour Island's assets and their sources as of December 31, 2011. The company's total assets (valued at $18,615) came from three separate sources: (1) $7,680 (41 percent) came from various forms of borrowing (total liabilities) and must be repaid in the future; (2) $9,550 (51 percent) was received when the company sold (issued) stock to the shareholders (contributed capital); and (3) $1,385 (8 percent), the dollar amount in the retained earnings account, was generated through the company's operating activities and not returned to the shareholders in the form of dividends. The addition of (2) and (3) represents the entire investment made by the shareholders in the business, and on this investment they expect some form of return in the future.

Balance Sheet Classifications

Assets are divided into current assets ($1,415); long-term investments ($4,000); property, plant, and equipment ($11,500); and intangible assets ($1,700). These categories and the order of the accounts within them are listed in order of **liquidity.** The assets listed near the top of the balance sheet (e.g., current assets) are expected to be converted into cash within a shorter time period than those listed at or near the bottom. They are, therefore, considered to be more liquid. The assets in the current asset category are also listed in order of liquidity. Cash, the most liquid of all assets, is understandably listed at the top.

Explain why total assets on the balance sheet of McDonald's Corporation consists of over 70 percent property, plant, and equipment, while property, plant, and equipment comprises only about 20 percent of Google's total assets.

Liabilities are divided into current liabilities ($740) and long-term liabilities ($6,940). These two categories, and the accounts within them, are also listed in order of liquidity. Those near the top (e.g., current liabilities) are expected to require the payment of cash within a shorter time period than those at or near the bottom. Study these categories and the order of the accounts contained within them. This is the general format required under U.S. generally accepted accounting principles, and it is important that you be familiar with it.

FIGURE 2–2

Classified balance
sheet for Harbour
Island Company

Harbour Island Company
Classified Balance Sheet
December 31, 2011

ASSETS

Current assets:			
Cash		$ 220	
Short-term investments		150	
Accounts receivable	$ 350		
Less: Uncollectibles	5	345	
Inventory		600	
Prepaid expenses		100	
Total current assets			$ 1,415
Long-term investments:			
Long-term notes receivable		$1,000	
Land		500	
Securities		2,500	
Total long-term investments			4,000
Property, plant, and equipment:			
Property		$6,000	
Plant	$4,000		
Less: Accumulated depreciation	1,100	2,900	
Equipment	$3,500		
Less: Accumulated depreciation	900	2,600	
Total property, plant, & equip.			11,500
Intangible assets:			
Goodwill		$ 800	
Patent		200	
Trademark		700	
Total intangible assets			1,700
Total assets			$18,615

LIABILITIES AND SHAREHOLDERS' EQUITY

Current liabilities:			
Accounts payable		$ 250	
Wages payable		25	
Interest payable		155	
Short-term notes payable		75	
Current maturities of long-term debts		60	
Deferred revenues		75	
Other payables		100	
Total current liabilities			$ 740
Long-term liabilities:			
Long-term notes payable		$1,500	
Bonds payable		3,500	
Mortgage payable		1,940	
Total long-term liabilities			6,940
Shareholders' equity:			
Contributed capital		$9,550	
Earned capital (primarily retained earnings)		1,385	
Total shareholders' equity			10,935
Total liabilities and shareholders' equity			$18,615

Many non-U.S. firms that publish IFRS-based balance sheets list their assets in the opposite order, starting with non-current assets, followed by current assets.

Assets

We now discuss the individual balance sheet accounts. This section reviews current assets; long-term investments; property, plant, and equipment; and intangible assets.

CURRENT ASSETS

Assets categorized as current are expected to be realized or, in most cases, converted into cash in the near future, usually within one year.[1] They are grouped into a separate category because they are considered to be highly liquid. The amount of highly liquid assets held by a company can be an indication of its ability to meet debt payments as they come due. Consequently, the current asset category is often reviewed by financial statement users who are interested in assessing a company's solvency position. **Current assets** include cash, short-term investments, accounts receivable, inventory, and prepaid expenses, and they often represent a significant portion of a company's total assets.

Explain why the current assets of Sears Holdings Corporation, a major retailer, typically comprise nearly 50 percent of total assets, while current assets for AT&T comprise only 8 percent of total assets.

CASH. Cash represents the currency a company has access to as of the balance sheet date. It may be in a bank savings account, a checking account, or perhaps on the company premises in the form of petty cash. Cash amounts that a company can use immediately should be separated on the balance sheet from cash that is restricted. As a condition of granting a loan, for example, banks often require that the borrowing company maintain a certain cash balance with the bank while the loan is outstanding. Cash amounts of this nature, called *compensating balances,* are normally described in the footnotes to the financial statements so that readers can draw a distinction between available cash and restricted cash. Such a distinction can be useful when assessing how much cash is available to meet an outstanding debt. For example, ARCO, a subsidiary of BP Amoco, notes in its financial reports that "the company maintains compensating balances for some of its various banking services and products."

SHORT-TERM INVESTMENTS. **Short-term investments** include stocks (equity investments in other companies), bonds (debt investments in the government or other companies), and similar investments. These securities are both *readily marketable* (i.e., able to be sold immediately) and intended by management to be sold within a short period of time, usually less than one year. A company often purchases these kinds of securities to earn income with cash that would otherwise be idle for a short time. The dollar value of this account is the total selling price (market value) of securities held by a company as of the balance sheet date. For purposes of solvency assessment, this dollar amount is normally viewed to be the same as available cash.

---

1. The actual definition of "current asset" is an asset expected to be converted into cash or used within one year or the operating cycle, whichever is longer. Operating cycles are discussed in Chapter 6.

Why do you think that WellPoint, an insurance company with assets of over $48 billion, carries cash and short-term investments of over $4.8 billion?

ACCOUNTS RECEIVABLE. The **accounts receivable** account represents the amount of money a company expects to collect from its customers. Such receivables arise from sales of products or services for which customers have not yet paid. These sales are often referred to as *credit sales* or *sales on account.* The dollar amount appearing on the balance sheet for this account is computed by taking the total dollar amount of the receivables owed and subtracting an estimate for *uncollectibles,* those accounts not expected to be received. The uncollectibles estimate is highly subjective, and users must be careful not to conclude that all reported receivables will necessarily lead to cash receipts.

Briefly explain why the giant bank JPMorgan Chase carries receivables in excess of $720 billion, which is approximately 35 percent of the company's total assets, while an even larger company, Wal-Mart, carries receivables of only about $4 billion.

INVENTORY. Inventory represents items or products on hand that a company intends to sell to its customers. It is often called **merchandise inventory.** The dollar value in this account is very important because a company's success often depends on its ability to sell these items. Users are very interested in the sales value of a company's inventory, but unfortunately, the balance sheet value of inventory is the cost of acquiring (purchasing or producing) it or the cost of replacing it as of the balance sheet date, whichever is lower.

Why do companies like Home Depot and Goodyear Tire & Rubber Company carry inventories that comprise most of their current assets and a large portion of total assets, while companies like Yahoo! and Bank of America carry no inventories at all?

A second kind of inventory account is called *supplies inventory*. It represents items used to support a company's operations; office supplies and spare parts are two common examples. The dollar amount of this account on the balance sheet is usually the cost of acquiring the items. Major manufacturers often carry a substantial inventory of spare parts. Normally about 10 percent of The Boeing Company's total inventory is composed of spare parts.

PREPAID EXPENSES. Prepaid expenses are exactly what the name suggests: expenses that have been paid by a company before the corresponding service or right is actually used. Insurance premiums, for example, are normally paid prior to the period of coverage. Similarly, rent is usually paid before the rental period. A prepaid expense, therefore, is considered an asset because it represents a benefit to be enjoyed by the company in the future; it is not considered an expense, appearing on the income statement, until it is used. Prepaid expenses are originally recorded on the balance sheet at the cost of acquiring them. For most companies, prepaid expenses are a very small, often insignificant, part of total assets. Also, prepaid expenses do not create future cash inflows, a fact that users must recognize when assessing a company's solvency position.

On its 2009 balance sheet, Walt Disney Company lists a current asset in the amount of $631 million called television costs. Explain what kind of prepaid expense this might be.

LONG-TERM INVESTMENTS

Long-term investments are acquired by companies to provide benefits for periods of time usually extending beyond one year. Examples include long-term notes receivable and investments in land and debt and equity securities.

The notes receivable account includes company receivables that are evidenced by promissory notes. *Promissory notes* are contracts (formal, legally enforceable documents) that state the face value of the receivable, the date when the face value is due, and the periodic interest payments to be made while the note is outstanding. The date when the receivable is due, called the *maturity date,* is often beyond one year, so this account is often listed in the long-term investment section of the balance sheet. However, if the maturity date of a note receivable is within one year, it should be disclosed as a current asset.

Notes receivable often arise because companies receive notes in exchange for the sale of expensive items. For example, The Boeing Company often receives notes in payment for sold aircraft and currently carries over $5.8 billion in long-term notes receivable. Alternatively, such notes can result from direct company loans to employees and others. It also happens that customers with large, overdue accounts are asked to sign promissory notes. Like accounts receivable, an estimate—often subjective—for uncollectibles must be provided for notes receivable.

The long-term investment section of the balance sheet can also include a number of other investments. Land, for example, may be purchased and held as a long-term investment. Investments in debt and equity securities that are not intended to be sold in the near future represent other common examples. Most major U.S. companies have made significant investments in the equity securities of other, usually smaller, companies, intending to exert long-term influence over their management. Owens Corning, for example, has major investments in the equity securities of over twenty different companies. Users should learn as much as possible about such investments, usually by reading the footnotes, because they signal areas where management has chosen to devote considerable attention.

PROPERTY, PLANT, AND EQUIPMENT

The property, plant, and equipment section of the balance sheet includes assets acquired for use in the day-to-day operations of the business. For many companies, especially manufacturers, this is the largest asset category on the balance sheet. For example, the property, plant, and equipment account for oil giant ConocoPhillips is valued at nearly $84 billion, which represents approximately 59 percent of its total assets. This account often contains the results of management's major investing activities, an important concern of financial statement users.

The **property** account represents the land on which the company conducts its operations. It is carried on the balance sheet at the original price for the land, which is not adjusted as the value of the property appreciates (i.e., increases). Be sure not to confuse this account with land in the long-term investment section. That land is held for investment purposes only and is not used in the operations of the business.

Plant and equipment represent the physical structures that a company owns and uses in its operations. The plant account, for example, includes the value of factory and office buildings and warehouses, while the equipment account includes machinery, vehicles, furniture, and similar items. The dollar amount in these accounts on the balance sheet is the original cost at the time the assets were purchased, reduced by an amount that loosely approximates the asset's lost usefulness or deterioration over time. This amount is called *accumulated depreciation.* Subtracting accumulated depreciation from the acquisition cost results in the *net value* or **net book value** of the assets. The excerpt below, which illustrates the methods used to disclose property, plant, and equipment, was taken from the 2008 annual report of Johnson & Johnson (dollars in millions).

IN MILLIONS	2008	2007
Land, buildings, and equipment:		
Land and land improvements	$ 886	$ 756
Buildings and building equipment	7,720	7,913
Machinery and equipment	15,234	14,554
Construction in progress	3,552	3,243
Total land, buildings, and equipment	$27,392	$26,466
Less accumulated depreciation	13,027	12,281
Net land, buildings, and equipment	$14,365	$14,185

INTANGIBLE ASSETS

Intangible assets are so named because they have no physical substance. In most cases they represent legal rights to the use or sale of valuable names, items, processes, or information. Many companies, such as Coca-Cola, have patents on certain formulas that grant them the sole legal right to produce and sell certain products. When NBC paid over $1 billion to acquire exclusive rights to broadcast the Olympics, it recognized an intangible asset on its balance sheet. In a similar way, the cost a company incurs to create a trademark (e.g., the golden arches of McDonald's) or its name (e.g., Goodyear Tire & Rubber) can also be accounted for as an intangible asset. Perhaps the most common intangible asset, called *goodwill,* represents the cost of purchasing another company over and above the total market price of that company's individual assets and liabilities. The goodwill account is prominent on the balance sheets of many major U.S. companies because they often purchase other companies, called *subsidiaries.* For example, when Google purchased Double Click in 2008, it recognized approximately $2.3 billion in goodwill on the transaction. Similar to property, plant, and equipment, intangibles are of interest to users because they often represent the results of a company's major investing activities.

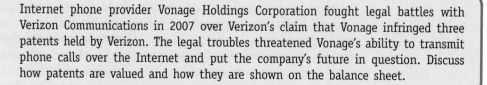

Internet phone provider Vonage Holdings Corporation fought legal battles with Verizon Communications in 2007 over Verizon's claim that Vonage infringed three patents held by Verizon. The legal troubles threatened Vonage's ability to transmit phone calls over the Internet and put the company's future in question. Discuss how patents are valued and how they are shown on the balance sheet.

Intangible assets are carried on the balance sheet at net book value, which is equal to the cost of acquiring an intangible asset, reduced by a dollar amount, called *accumulated amortization,* which loosely approximates the asset's reduction in usefulness over time.[2]

2. Certain intangible assets, including goodwill, are not subject to amortization.

The following excerpt was taken from the 2008 annual report of Merck, a leading pharmaceutical (dollars in millions):

	2008	2007
Goodwill	$1,438.7	1,454.8
Intangible subject to amortization:		
Patents and product rights	1,656.4	$1,656.3
Other	779.2	781.0
Total acquired cost	2,435.6	2,437.3
Patents and product rights	1,528.5	1,494.4
Other	1,528.5	1,494.4
Total accumulated amortization	381.7	274.7
	$1,910.2	$1,724.1

Almost 20 percent of the total assets of Cisco Systems, a worldwide leader in networking for the Internet, is composed of goodwill. What does this fact tell you about the growth strategy used by the company?

Liabilities

This section covers current and long-term liabilities. The dollar amounts disclosed in these sections of the balance sheet are very important to users who are interested in the timing of a company's future cash obligations, which is important when assessing whether a company can meet its debts when they come due. Total liabilities, as a percentage of total assets, vary significantly across companies in different industries. For example, ConocoPhillips carries liabilities of about 61 percent of total assets, while the liabilities of Citigroup represent approximately 93 percent of total assets.

CURRENT LIABILITIES

Current liabilities are obligations expected to be paid (or services expected to be performed) with the use of assets listed in the current asset section of the balance sheet. Examples include *accounts payable, wages payable, interest payable, short-term notes payable, income taxes payable, current maturities on long-term debts,* and *deferred revenues.*

Accounts payable are usually obligations to a company's suppliers for merchandise purchases made on account. Wages payable are obligations to a company's employees for earned but unpaid wages as of the balance sheet date. Interest payable and short-term notes payable are dollar amounts owed to creditors, often banks and other financial institutions. Income taxes payable are amounts owed to the government for taxes assessed on a company's income. **Current maturities of long-term debts** are portions of long-term liabilities that are due in the current period. They often arise when the principal amounts of long-term liabilities are due in installments over time. Deferred revenues represent services yet to be performed by a company for which cash payments have already been collected.

Financial statement users often closely examine a company's current liabilities as they assess a company's solvency position because most current liabilities require cash payments in the short-term future. Retailers rely heavily on suppliers as a source of financing. For example, on the balance sheet of The Gap, Inc., one of the largest liabilities is accounts payable—$975 million and approximately 13 percent of total assets.

Many non-U.S. firms that publish IFRS-based balance sheets list current liabilities directly below current assets, leading to the computation of net current assets (current assets − current liabilities). This format emphasizes the important relationship between current assets and current liabilities when assessing the firm's solvency position.

LONG-TERM LIABILITIES

Long-term liabilities are obligations expected to require payment over a period of time beyond the current year. These obligations are usually evidenced by formal contracts that state their principal amounts, the periodic interest payments, and maturity dates. The form of these debt contracts, however, can vary widely. Common examples include accounts like *long-term notes payable, bonds payable,* and *mortgage payables.*

Long-term **notes payable** refer to obligations on loans that are normally due more than one year beyond the balance sheet date. They usually involve either direct borrowings from financial institutions or arrangements to finance the purchase of assets. **Bonds payable** represent notes that have been issued for cash to a large number of debt investors (called *bondholders*). Issuing bonds is a common form of financing for many major U.S. companies, which often use the funds to expand operations. During 2006, Lowe's, a home improvement retailer, issued approximately $990 million in bonds. The proceeds were used to finance capital expenditures and reduce other debt. **Mortgage payables** are obligations that are secured by real estate and are usually owed to financial institutions. The contractual terms (e.g., interest notes and covenant restrictions) associated with long-term debts are particularly important to financial statement users because they identify short-term cash outflows and constraints that may inhibit management's future activities.

Provide a reasonable explanation for why the current liabilities of Bank of America are much larger than long-term liabilities and represent well over 50 percent of the total assets.

Shareholders' Equity

The **shareholders' equity** section of the balance sheet is basically divided into two parts: contributed capital and earned capital (primarily retained earnings). Note in Figure 2–2 that the total amount of shareholders' equity ($10,935) is equal to total assets ($18,615) less total liabilities ($7,680). This dollar amount is called the *net book value* of the company, and it also represents the total investment made by the shareholders in the company.

CONTRIBUTED CAPITAL

Contributed capital is a measure of the assets that have been contributed directly to a company by its owners.[3] Such contributions are made by purchasing the equity securities issued by the company, contributing cash or other noncash assets, or providing services.

---

3. Contributed capital is not used as a title of a balance sheet section. It encompasses a group of accounts that reflect owner contributions.

Whatever the form, the investor's contribution is exchanged for ownership interests (e.g., shares of stock) in the company. Such interests usually carry with them the right to have a voice in the management of the company (e.g., vote for the board of directors) as well as the right to receive assets (e.g., dividends), if they are distributed. In many cases, these ownership interests can be purchased and sold freely (e.g., through public stock markets), but such transactions have no effects on the company's balance sheet.

During the late 1990s, as with many high-tech companies, issuing stock was the principal form of financing used by Amazon.com—with three major common stock issuances, raising over $1 billion.

EARNED CAPITAL

Earned capital is composed of two components: retained earnings and other accumulated comprehensive income.[4] **Retained earnings** is a measure of the assets that have been generated through a company's operating activities but not paid out to shareholders in the form of dividends. This account is particularly troublesome to accounting students who tend to visualize it as a tangible pool of cash. Nothing could be further from the truth. The $1,385 in Harbour Island's retained earnings account in Figure 2–2 is not in the form of cash in the company treasurer's office or in the bank. In fact, it is not associated with any specific asset or group of assets. It is simply a measure of the amount of the assets appearing on the balance sheet that have been provided by profitable operations. All we know from the balance sheet in Figure 2–2 is that $1,385 of the $18,615 total in the asset account has been provided by the company's profitable operations.

The relative size of retained earnings on the balance sheets of major U.S. companies varies significantly across industries. Bank of America, for example, normally reports retained earnings of only 4 percent of total assets, while Boeing is currently reporting retained earnings of about 42 percent of total assets. Users normally consider a large balance in retained earnings to be a positive sign because it indicates that the company has been profitable in the past and has chosen to reinvest those profits. However, young companies often report negative retained earnings because it takes several years to become profitable. Also, some very successful companies report relatively low levels of retained earnings because they pay large dividends.

After three years as a well-known, publicly traded company, Amazon.com reported a deficit in retained earnings of over $800 million. Explain how this could have occurred.

ORGANIZATIONAL FORM AND THE EQUITY SECTION

A business entity in the United States can be legally organized in either of two basic ways: as a corporation or as a partnership (called a *proprietorship* if there is only one owner).[5] A *corporation* is a legal entity that is separate and distinct from its owners. It can be taxed or sued, and the owners, called *shareholders* or *stockholders,* are legally liable only for the amount of their original contributions to the corporation. Shareholders acquire ownership interests by purchasing shares of stock in the corporation.

---

4. Other accumulated comprehensive income tends to be relatively small and is discussed later in the text.
5. Other business forms exist that have characteristics of both partnerships and corporations. Examples include subchapter S corporations and limited liability corporations.

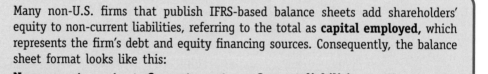

Corporation		Partnership	
Shareholders' equity:		**Owners' equity:**	
Contributed capital	$20,000	Capital account, Ms. A	$12,000
Retained earnings	14,000	Capital account, Mr. B	15,000
Total shareholders' equity	$34,000	Total owners' equity	$27,000

Their interests give them the right to vote for its board of directors at annual share-holders' meetings as well as the right to receive dividends, which are distributed on a per-share basis, if declared by the board.

A *partnership,* or *proprietorship,* on the other hand, is not a legal entity. It can neither be taxed nor sued, and the legal liability of the owners, called *partners* or *proprietors,* is not limited to their original contributions. Asset distributions to partners are called *withdrawals.*

The differences between corporations and partnerships are reflected in differences in the equity sections of their balance sheets. The shareholders' equity section of a corporate balance sheet, as illustrated in Figure 2–2, draws a distinction between contributed capital, the measure of the assets directly contributed by the shareholders, and retained earnings, the assets generated through the company's operating activities and not returned to shareholders in the form of dividends.

On the other hand, the equity section on a partnership's balance sheet, called **owners' equity,** makes no distinction between contributed capital and retained earnings. Instead, it consists of separate accounts for each partner, which show the status of each partner's personal capital balance, reflecting all contributions and withdrawals. Figure 2–3 illustrates the differences between the shareholders' equity section of a corporation and the owners' equity section of a partnership with two partners. Throughout most of the text, the discussions and illustrations assume the corporate form of organization.

Many non-U.S. firms that publish IFRS-based balance sheets add shareholders' equity to non-current liabilities, referring to the total as **capital employed,** which represents the firm's debt and equity financing sources. Consequently, the balance sheet format looks like this:

Non-current assets + Current assets – Current liabilities = Non-current liabilities + Shareholders' equity

Explain how this format differs from the U.S. format.

THE INCOME STATEMENT

The income statement, sometimes called the statement of operations, measures operating performance over a particular period—the activities associated with the acquisition and sale of the company's inventories or services. An example, for the Harbour Island Company covering the year ended December 31, 2011, is illustrated in Figure 2–4. Note that it consists of three categories: operating revenues ($5,000), operating expenses ($3,895), and other revenues and expenses (−$20). The net amount of these three numbers yields a number called *net income* or *loss, net earnings,* or *profits* ($1,085). Net income is a very common and useful measure of operating performance.

FIGURE 2–4

Income statement for Harbour Island Company

Harbour Island Company
Income Statement
for the Year Ended December 31, 2011

Operating revenues:		
Sales	$4,000	
Fees earned	1,000	
Total operating revenues		$5,000
Operating expenses:		
Cost of goods sold	$1,500	
Wage expense	1,000	
Rent expense	295	
Selling expense	300	
Depreciation expense	500	
Amortization expense	300	
Total operating expenses		3,895
Operating income		$1,105
Other revenues and expenses:		
Other revenues	$ 880	
Other expenses	900	
Net other revenues and expenses		(20)
Net income		$1,085

Most analysts, investors, creditors, and managers agree that net income is the most important number disclosed on the financial statements.

Operating Revenues

Operating revenues represent the inflow of assets (or decrease in liabilities) due to a company's operating activities over a period of time. Examples include sales and fees earned. The ability to generate operating revenues is often viewed as one of the important keys to success for a company.

Sales is perhaps the most common revenue account. It represents a measure of asset increases (usually in the form of cash or accounts receivable) due to selling a company's products or inventories. Operating revenues for Google increased by over 350 percent from 2006 to 2009.

If a company provides a service (e.g., a law firm or accounting firm) instead of selling a product, the revenue account reflecting such activity is called **fees earned** or **service revenue.** Walt Disney's income statement routinely includes both sales and service revenues. Sales are recognized when Disney products are sold, and service revenues come from its theme parks and films.

Many non-U.S. companies, especially in Europe, use the term "turnover" instead of revenue.

Operating Expenses

Operating expenses represent the periodic and usual outflow of assets (or creation of liabilities) required to generate operating revenues. Examples include cost of goods

sold and expenses related to wages, rent, selling, depreciation, and amortization. As important as generating revenues, controlling expenses is also a barometer of a company's success. Many consider Dell Computer to be a leading computer-systems company because it does an excellent job of using the Internet to reduce operating costs.

The **cost of goods sold** account represents the original cost of the inventory items (purchase price or cost of manufacturing) that are sold to generate sales revenue. For retail and manufacturing companies, this *inventory expense* is normally separated from other operating expenses because it is comparatively large, and it is often compared to sales revenue to indicate the relationship between the selling price of the inventory and its cost. Users pay close attention to this percentage because it indicates by how much the sales price exceeds the cost of a good. Cost of goods sold as a percentage of sales for The Gap, a large retailer, exceeds 60 percent, while Monsanto, a large manufacturer, typically reports cost of goods sold in the 45 percent range.

> Why do you think that H&R Block, a firm that offers tax services, reports no cost of goods sold?

The remaining operating expenses differ based on the nature of a company's operations. For retailing companies, which simply purchase finished goods and then sell them (e.g., Wal-Mart), this expense category contains accounts reflecting the decrease in assets (or creation of liabilities) due to such items as commissions to salespersons, salaries, wages, insurance, advertising, rentals, utilities, property taxes, equipment maintenance, depreciation of plant and equipment, and amortization of intangible assets. Manufacturing companies, on the other hand (e.g., General Motors), typically include only selling and administrative expenses in this category. Note from the expenses listed on the income statement in Figure 2–4 that Harbour Island is a retailer.

> As investors cheered company profit reports in spring and summer of 2009, the stock market rallied. With the chill of fall and winter, however, came skepticism about the sustainability of future earnings. Many analysts feared that corporate expenses had been cut as low as possible by reducing workforces, and revenue growth would be difficult to achieve due to the continuing economic recession. Explain why analysts were skeptical about future profits.

Other Revenues and Expenses

The category *Other revenues and expenses* (sometimes called Other gains and losses) can include a number of items. It usually contains revenues and expenses from activities not central to a company's operations; therefore, the dollar amount of this category is also usually small. Other revenues include interest on bank accounts, rent collected on the rental of excess warehouse space, and book gains recognized when assets are sold for amounts that exceed those costs. Other expenses include interest on outstanding loans and book losses recognized when assets other than inventory are sold for amounts that are less than their original costs. It is very important that users appreciate the difference between revenues and expenses generated by core business activities and those generated by "one-shot" transactions. Presumably, core activities can be expected to recur, whereas "one-shot" transactions cannot.

The large electric utility TXU Corporation reported a quarterly loss of $497 million. However, TXU reported that its operating income for the quarter was $444 million. At the time of the announcement, TXU was in the process of being purchased by a private equity investment group for $32 billion; the stock market reacted to the loss by pushing up TXU shares by 46 cents to $66.62 per share. Discuss how net income from operating activities can be positive, while net income is negative. Also discuss the stock market's reaction to the company's news.

THE STATEMENT OF SHAREHOLDERS' EQUITY

The statement of shareholders' equity, which is illustrated for Harbour Island in Figure 2–5, explains the changes in the shareholders' equity accounts (contributed capital and retained earnings) over a period. It represents a summary of the activity in the accounts that keep track of the shareholders' investment in the company. The shareholders' investment increases when capital is collected from the sale (issuance) of equity securities (contributed capital) and when profits, which belong to the shareholders, are reinvested in the business (earned capital). Dividends paid to the shareholders reduce their investment in the company. Note that the beginning dollar balances, which come from the December 31, 2010 balance sheet, are adjusted for the activity during 2011 leading to the ending dollar balances, which appear on the December 31, 2011 balance sheet. During 2011 Harbour Island collected $3,100 from common stock issuances, recorded net income of $1,085, and paid dividends of $200.

FIGURE 2–5
Statement of shareholders' equity for Harbour Island Company

	Contributed capital	Retained earnings	Total
December 31, 2010	$6,450	$ 500	$ 6,950
Net income		1,085	1,085
Less: dividends		(200)	(200)
Common stock issuance	3,100		3,100
December 31, 2011	$9,550	$1,385	$10,935

Retained earnings represents past profits that have not been returned to the shareholders in the form of dividends. By comparing dividends to profits across time, a user can ascertain a company's dividend policy.

Johnson & Johnson consistently pays significant dividends to its shareholders—normally on the order of 30 to 40 percent of net income. How would this be reported on the financial statements, and what portion of earnings is normally reinvested in the business?

It is important to realize that retained earnings is nothing in and of itself, but rather a measure of something else. It is not cash, nor is it an asset that can be touched or used. Instead, it is similar to an inch, a gallon, or a pound, all of which are measures of something tangible. An inch reflects a length of rope, the width of a table, or the height of a person, while retained earnings represents a measure of the assets, all of which are

listed on the asset side of the balance sheet, that have been generated through profitable operations and retained in the business. Recall that assets can come from three sources: borrowings, contributions from owners, and profitable operations. Retained earnings is a measure of the third source.

Under IFRS, the requirements for a complete set of financial statements (balance sheet, income statement, statement of shareholders' equity, and statement of cash flows) are very similar to those under U.S. GAAP.

THE STATEMENT OF CASH FLOWS

The statement of cash flows is a summary of the activity in a company's cash account over a period of time. Understanding the statement of cash flows is simply a matter of recognizing that certain transactions entered into by a company during a given period increase the cash account, while others decrease it. The statement summarizes these transactions and, in the process, explains how the cash balance at the beginning of the period came to be the cash balance at the end of the period. The statement of cash flows for Harbour Island Company for the year ended December 31, 2011, appears in Figure 2–6.[6]

The statement of cash flows is divided into three basic categories: (1) operating activities, (2) investing activities, and (3) financing activities. The transactions summarized within each of these three categories either increased or decreased cash during the period, and the net result of the three totals explains the change in a company's overall cash balance. For example, on Harbour Island's cash flow statement, operating activities increased cash by $1,470, investment activities decreased cash by $4,100, and financing activities increased cash by $2,750. The net result is $120 ($1,470 − $4,100 + $2,750), the increase in the cash balance during 2011.

The statement of cash flows provides important information to investors and creditors, especially those who are interested in assessing a company's solvency position. In a recent survey of over 60,000 companies that failed, over 60 percent blamed their failure on factors linked to cash flows.

A recent report from the Georgia Institute of Technology indicates that companies are inconsistent in how they define operating, investing, and financing activities when they prepare the statement of cash flows. Several years ago, for example, Avis Budget Group announced that it was reclassifying a $45 million cash outflow from its Operating section to its Investing section for the quarter. The "Net Increase in Cash" reported on the statement did not change, but the categorizations were altered. Why would investors care if cash flow was considered Investing instead of Operating? Why do you think the company made the change and publicized it in a press release?

6. The operating section of this statement of cash flows can be presented under either the direct or indirect method. The statement in Figure 2–6 uses the direct form of presentation. Most major U.S. companies use the indirect form of presentation, which we cover later and throughout the text.

FIGURE 2-6

Statement of cash
flows for Harbour
Island Company

Harbour Island Company
Statement of Cash Flows
for the Year Ended December 31, 2011

Operating activities:		
Cash collections from sales	$ 4,800	
Cash collections from rent	800	
Cash collections from interest	10	
Cash provided by operating activities		$ 5,610
Cash paid to suppliers	$(1,800)	
Cash paid to employees	(1,050)	
Cash paid for rent	(290)	
Cash paid for selling activities	(300)	
Cash paid for interest and taxes	(700)	
Cash disbursed for operating activities		(4,140)
Net cash increase (decrease) from operating activities		$ 1,470
Investing activities:		
Purchase of investment securities	$ (100)	
Purchase of property	(4,500)	
Proceeds from sale of investment securities	500	
Net cash increase (decrease) from investing activities		(4,100)
Financing activities:		
Proceeds from issuing equity	$ 3,100	
Principal payments on short-term notes	(100)	
Principal payments on long-term debt	(50)	
Cash dividends to shareholders	(200)	
Net cash increase (decrease) from financing activities		2,750
Increase (decrease) in cash balance		$ 120
Beginning cash balance (December 31, 2010)		100
Ending cash balance (December 31, 2011)		$ 220

Cash Flows from Operating Activities

Cash flows from operating activities include those cash inflows and outflows associated with the acquisition and sale of a company's products and services. The items
found in this section are closely related to those found on the income statement because both measure operating inflows and outflows. However, the dollar amounts of
these items on the statement of cash flows do not necessarily agree with the dollar
amounts appearing for these items on the income statement. The statement of cash
flows records only cash inflows and outflows; the income statement consists of revenues and expenses, which reflect more general asset and liability inflows and outflows. Cash is just one of a company's many assets.

Consider, for example, the sale of a service in exchange for a receivable. This transaction produces no cash; therefore, it has no effect on the statement of cash flows. It does,
however, appear as a revenue on the income statement because an asset in the form of a
receivable has been created. Consequently, net cash flow from operating activities on the
statement of cash flows is rarely equal to net income on the income statement. In the case

of Harbour Island, for example, net cash flow from operating activities in Figure 2–6 is equal to $1,470, while net income for the same period (see Figures 2–4 and 2–5) is equal to $1,085.

Two well-known companies that emerged in the 1990s are Yahoo! and Amazon.com. Yahoo! showed negative cash flows from operations in its first few years but began showing positive numbers in 1998. Amazon reported negative cash flows from operations until 2002. Where would these numbers be reported, and how might an analyst react to them?

Cash Flows from Investing Activities

Cash flows from investing activities include the cash inflows and outflows associated with the purchase and sale of a company's investments. Cash effects from the purchase or sale of a company's marketable securities or property, plant, and equipment are common examples. Note in Figure 2–6 that Harbour Island used $100 and $4,500 to purchase long-term investment securities and property, respectively. It also generated $500 in cash by selling long-term investments. These transactions in total reduced Harbour Island's cash balance by $4,100.

In the same year that Yahoo! reported net cash used by investing activities of $346 million, Amazon reported cash inflows from investing activities of $813 million. What kinds of transactions might have led to these two amounts?

Cash Flows from Financing Activities

Cash flows from financing activities include the cash inflows and outflows associated with a company's two sources of outside capital: liabilities and contributed capital. Cash proceeds from and cash principal payments on short- and long-term liabilities are reflected in this section of the statement of cash flows. As indicated in Figure 2–6, while Harbour Island borrowed no additional funds during 2011, it made cash principal payments on both short-term notes ($100) and long-term debt ($50). Cash proceeds from shareholder contributions, or equity issuances, and cash dividends to shareholders are also included in this section. Note that Harbour Island collected $3,100 in cash from issuing equity and paid cash dividends of $200.

In their early years, Yahoo! and Amazon both experienced fast growth and relied heavily on common stock issuances to raise capital. Do you expect that they showed positive or negative net cash flows from financing activities during this time period? Explain.

RELATIONSHIPS AMONG THE FINANCIAL STATEMENTS

Figure 2–7 presents a general overview of the four basic financial accounting statements for Harbour Island Company and shows how they relate to one another. Take some time to study it.

Note the four statements indicated by the numbers: (1) balance sheet, (2) income statement, (3) statement of shareholders' equity, and (4) statement of cash flows. Note also that an additional balance sheet, prepared at the end of the period, is included on the right side of the figure. The account balances on this balance sheet are different from those on the balance sheet on the left. To explain how the balance sheet accounts changed during the year, examine the other three financial statements: the statement of cash flows, the statement of shareholders' equity, and the income statement.

The statement of cash flows explains the activity during the year in the company's cash account. At the beginning of 2011 the balance in the cash account was $100. During the year, operating, investing, and financing transactions affected the cash balance, and the end result was $220. The statement of cash flows ties into the cash accounts listed on the balance sheet at the beginning and end of 2011.

The statement of shareholders' equity, like the statement of cash flows, also explains the activity in balance sheet accounts during 2011—contributed capital and retained earnings, which appear in the shareholders' equity section of each balance sheet. The beginning and ending balances tie directly to the balance sheets for the beginning and end of 2011.

The income statement contains revenues and expenses, which are reflected in the statement of shareholders' equity through the net income number. The income statement connects directly to the retained earnings account, which in turn connects directly to the two balance sheets.

As a result of these interrelationships, every transaction affecting the income statement affects the balance sheet in at least two places. Revenues and expenses are components of retained earnings and increase or decrease the retained earnings balance accordingly. In addition, each account on the income statement has a related account in either the asset or liability section of the balance sheet. Recognizing a sale, for example, can affect *cash and accounts receivable*. Recognizing an expense, such as wage expense, can affect *cash and wages payable*. Thus, the balance sheet and the income statement are closely related. As you work through this text, it is important that you clearly understand these relationships.

INTERNATIONAL PERSPECTIVE: AN EXAMPLE OF INTERNATIONAL FINANCIAL REPORTING STANDARDS

International Financial Reporting Standards (IFRS) are becoming increasingly important and, as we discussed in Chapter 1, are already accepted by the SEC. The consolidated balance sheet, income statement, and cash flow statement of Unilever, one of the world's leading suppliers of consumer brands (e.g., Knorr, Lipton, Dove, Hellman's), are provided below. These statements have been prepared according to IFRS, and the Unilever Group is registered in the Netherlands. Its shares are listed on the London and New York stock exchanges.

Note first that the financial statements cover up to December 31, 2008, and are expressed in euros, not U.S. dollars. While not a requirement under IFRS, Unilever's balance sheet, like many non-U.S. companies, is organized by listing non-current assets first, followed by current assets, current liabilities, non-current liabilities and, finally, shareholders' equity.

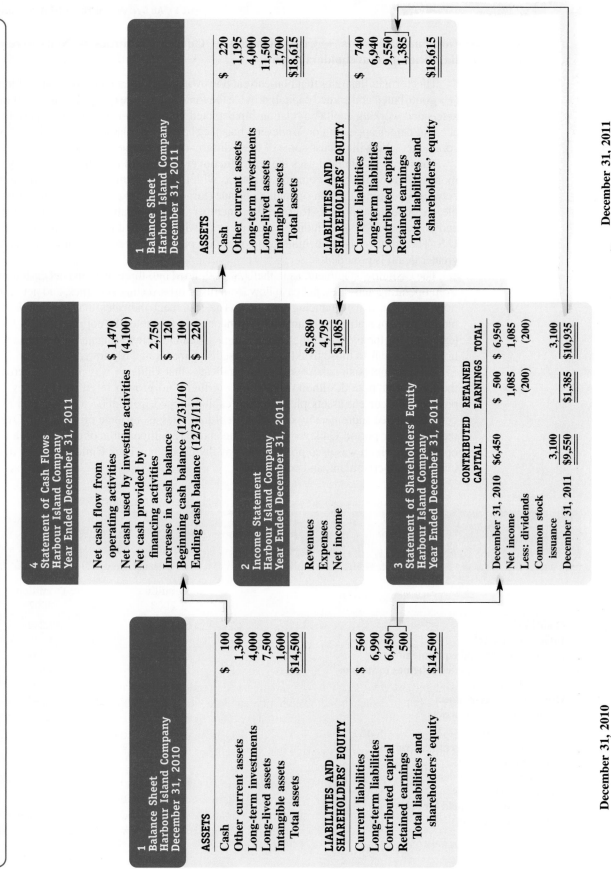

FIGURE 2-7 Relationships among the financial statements

1
Balance Sheet
Harbour Island Company
December 31, 2011

ASSETS

Cash	$ 220
Other current assets	1,195
Long-term investments	4,000
Long-lived assets	11,500
Intangible assets	1,700
Total assets	$18,615

LIABILITIES AND SHAREHOLDERS' EQUITY

Current liabilities	$ 740
Long-term liabilities	6,940
Contributed capital	9,550
Retained earnings	1,385
Total liabilities and shareholders' equity	$18,615

4
Statement of Cash Flows
Harbour Island Company
Year Ended December 31, 2011

Net cash flow from operating activities	$ 1,470
Net cash used by investing activities	(4,100)
Net cash provided by financing activities	2,750
Increase in cash balance	$ 120
Beginning cash balance (12/31/10)	100
Ending cash balance (12/31/11)	$ 220

2
Income Statement
Harbour Island Company
Year Ended December 31, 2011

Revenues	$5,880
Expenses	4,795
Net income	$1,085

3
Statement of Shareholders' Equity
Harbour Island Company
Year Ended December 31, 2011

	CONTRIBUTED CAPITAL	RETAINED EARNINGS	TOTAL
December 31, 2010	$6,450	$ 500	$ 6,950
Net income		1,085	1,085
Less: dividends		(200)	(200)
Common stock issuance	3,100		3,100
December 31, 2011	$9,550	$1,385	$10,935

1
Balance Sheet
Harbour Island Company
December 31, 2010

ASSETS

Cash	$ 100
Other current assets	1,300
Long-term investments	4,000
Long-lived assets	7,500
Intangible assets	1,600
Total assets	$14,500

LIABILITIES AND SHAREHOLDERS' EQUITY

Current liabilities	$ 560
Long-term liabilities	6,990
Contributed capital	6,450
Retained earnings	500
Total liabilities and shareholders' equity	$14,500

December 31, 2010

December 31, 2011

Non-current assets + Current assets − Current liabilities = Non-current liabilities + Shareholders' equity

This format illustrates that non-current borrowings and investments by shareholders (via contributed and earned capital) provide the financing for the company's non-current assets and working capital, a relationship depicted in Figure 2-1. For the most part, the account names appearing on Unilever's balance sheet are similar to those used by U.S. companies. We will discuss some of these differences as we move through the text.

The income statement uses the term "**turnover**" instead of revenue, which is common for many European companies, and, as with the U.S. format, makes a distinction between operating and non-operating revenue (turnover) and expenses. Note, for example, that operating profit is followed by a number of non-operating increases (income) and decreases (costs), including "finance costs," which is called interest expense in the U.S. The numbers listed behind many of the account names refer to footnotes, where greater detail is provided.

The cash flow statement, as in the U.S., is divided into three sections: net cash flow from operating activities, net cash flow from (used in) investing activities, and net cash flow from (used in) financing activities. The statement indicates that the detail explaining the operating cash amount is contained in footnote 28 (not provided in this text), and for the most part the account items listed in the investing and financing sections are similar to those listed in U.S.-based statements of cash flow.

A brief analysis of these statements indicates that Unilever was profitable across the three-year period, although there was virtually no growth in either revenues or profits. Non-current assets plus working capital dipped from 2007 to 2008, and the company relied more heavily on non-current liabilities as a source of financing. Over the three-year period Unilever did generate about 12 billion euros of cash through its operations, which was used primarily to pay dividends, buy back Unilever shares, and invest in property, plant, and equipment.

Unilever
Consolidated Balance Sheet
as at 31 December

	€ million 2008	€ million 2007
Goodwill[9]	11,665	12,244
Intangible assets[9]	4,426	4,511
Property, plant, and equipment[10]	5,957	6,284
Pension asset for funded schemes in surplus[20]	425	2,008
Deferred tax assets[12]	1,068	1,003
Other non-current assets[11]	1,426	1,324
Total non-current assets	24,967	27,374
Inventories[13]	3,889	3,894
Trade and other current receivables[14]	3,823	4,194
Current tax assets	234	367
Cash and cash equivalents[15]	2,561	1,098
Other financial assets[15]	632	216
Non-current assets held for sale[27]	36	159
Total current assets	11,175	9,928

	€ million 2008	€ million 2007
Financial liabilities[16]	(4,842)	(4,166)
Trade payables and other current liabilities[18]	(7,824)	(8,017)
Current tax liabilities	(377)	(395)
Provisions[19]	(757)	(968)
Liabilities associated with non-current assets held for sale[27]	—	(13)
Total current liabilities	(13,800)	(13,559)
Net current assets/(liabilities)	(2,625)	(3,631)
Total assets less current liabilities	22,342	23,743
Financial liabilities due after one year[16]	6,363	5,483
Non-current tax liabilities	189	233
Pensions and post-retirement healthcare liabilities:		
Funded schemes in deficit[20]	1,820	827
Unfunded schemes[20]	1,987	2,270
Provisions[19]	646	694
Deferred tax liabilities[12]	790	1,213
Other non-current liabilities	175	204
Total non-current liabilities	11,970	10,924
Share capital[21]	484	484
Share premium[21]	121	153
Other reserves[21]	(6,469)	(3,412)
Retained profit[21]	15,812	15,162
Shareholders's equity	9,948	12,387
Minority interests[21]	424	432
Total equity	10,372	12,819
Total capital employed	22,342	23,743

Unilever
Consolidated Balance Sheet
for the Year Ended 31 December

	€ million 2008	€ million 2007	€ million 2006
Continuing operations			
Turnover[2]	40,523	40,187	39,642
Operating profit[2]	7,167	5,245	5,408
After (charging)/crediting:			
Restructuring[3]	(868)	(875)	(704)
Business disposals, impairments and other[3]	2,137	306	196
Gain on US healthcare and UK pensions[3]	—	—	266
Net finance costs[5]	(257)	(252)	(721)
Finance income	106	147	128
Finance costs	(506)	(550)	(590)
Preference shares provision	—	(7)	(300)
Pensions and similar obligations	143	158	41

(Continued)

Unilever
Consolidated Balance Sheet
for the Year Ended 31 December (Continued)

	€ million 2008	€ million 2007	€ million 2006
Share of net profit/(loss) of joint ventures[11]	125	102	78
Share of net profit/(loss) of associates[11]	6	50	36
Other income from non-current investments[11]	88	39	30
Profit before taxation	7,129	5,184	4,831
Taxation[6]	(1,844)	(1,128)	(1,146)
Net profit from continuing operations	5,285	4,056	3,685
Profit for the year from discontinued operations[27]	—	80	1,330
Net profit	5,285	4,136	5,015
Cash flow from operating activities[28]	5,326	5,188	5,574
Income tax paid	(1,455)	(1,312)	(1,063)
Net cash flow from operating activities	3,871	3,876	4,511
Interest received	105	146	125
Purchase of intangible assets	(147)	(136)	(113)
Purchase of property, plant and equipment	(1,142)	(1,046)	(1,013)
Disposal of property, plant, and equipment	190	163	192
Sales and leaseback transactions resulting in operating leases	—	36	—
Acquisition of group companies, joint ventures and associates	(211)	(214)	(96)
Disposal of group companies, joint ventures and associates	2,476	164	1,873
Acquisition of other non-current investments	(126)	(50)	(90)
Disposal of other non-current investments	47	33	61
Dividends from joint ventures, associates and other non-current investments	132	188	120
(Purchase)/sale of financial assets	91	93	96
Net cash flow from/(used in) investing activities	1,415	(623)	1,155
Dividends paid on ordinary share capital	(2,086)	(2,182)	(2,602)
Interest and preference dividends paid	(487)	(552)	(605)
Additional financial liabilities	4,544	4,283	2,154
Repayment of financial liabilities	(3,427)	(2,896)	(5,364)
Sale and leaseback transactions resulting in finance leases	(1)	25	2
Capital element of finance lease rental payments	(66)	(74)	(73)
Share buy-back programme	(1,503)	(1,500)	—
Other movements on treasury stock	103	442	98
Other financing activities	(207)	(555)	(182)
Net cash flow from/(used in) financing activities	(3,130)	(3,009)	(6,572)
Net increase/(decrease) in cash and cash equivalents	2,156	244	(906)
Cash and cash equivalents at the beginning of the year	901	710	1,265
Effect of foreign exchange rate changes	(697)	(53)	351
Cash and cash equivalents at the end of the year[15]	2,360	901	710

REVIEW PROBLEM

The following information was taken from the 2008 annual report of Bed Bath & Beyond. All dollar values are in thousands.

Net sales for Bed Bath & Beyond increased 2.3 percent from fiscal 2007 to fiscal 2008, and 6.5 percent from 2006 to 2007. Gross profit (net sales less cost of sales) decreased over the three years, dropping from 43 percent (2006) to 40 percent (2008). Operating profit saw a similar decline, as selling, general and administrative expenses ate up a large share of sales. Analysts would view these earning power trends negatively, and might be concerned about sales growth and increased expense control in the future.

The balance sheet shows growth in total assets, with the largest change coming from short-term liquid assets. Inventories as a percentage of total assets are down, suggesting that even though profits are down, inventories are not building up. Current liabilities decreased, while current assets increased, implying greater solvency. The company has no interest-bearing debt, and retained earnings has increased.

The statement of cash flows shows that the company, even in a recession, has the ability to generate cash from its operating activities, which is being used to purchase investments, acquire long-term assets (capital expenditures), and repurchase outstanding shares of its own stock. Both the statement of cash flow and the statement of shareholders' equity show that in each of the three years (2006, 2007, and 2008) the company paid no dividends, and both issued and bought back its own stock.

In summary, from 2007 to 2009, Bed Bath & Beyond's earning power experienced some challenges from a recessionary environment, which affected all retailers. Sales growth was down from previous years, while profits were hurt by expense growth. Cash flow remained strong, and although the company paid no dividends, cash was distributed to shareholders through stock buybacks. Bed Bath & Beyond's solvency position remained excellent with increased liquid assets, very little debt, and the ability to generate cash from operations. Further, the company continued to invest in its future through capital expenditures.

Bed Bath & Beyond Inc. and Subsidiaries
Consolidated Statements of Earnings

	FISCAL YEAR ENDED		
(*In thousands, except per share data*)	February 28, 2009	March 1, 2008	March 3, 2007
Net sales	$7,208,340	$7,048,942	$6,617,429
Cost of sales	4,335,104	4,123,711	3,782,027
Gross profit	2,873,236	2,925,231	2,835,402
Selling, general and administrative expenses	2,199,340	2,087,209	1,946,001
Operating profit	673,896	838,022	889,401
Interest income	9,412	27,210	43,478
Earnings before provision for income taxes	683,308	865,232	932,879
Provision for income taxes	258,185	302,424	338,635
Net earnings	$ 425,123	$ 562,808	$ 594,244
Net earnings per share—Basic	$ 1.66	$ 2.13	$ 2.12
Net earnings per share—Diluted	$ 1.64	$ 2.10	$ 2.09
Weighted average shares outstanding—Basic	256,410	264,824	280,199
Weighted average shares outstanding—Diluted	258,619	268,409	284,956

See accompanying Notes to Consolidated Financial Statements.

Bed Bath & Beyond Inc. and Subsidiaries
Consolidated Balance Sheets

(In thousands, except per share data)	February 28, 2009	March 1, 2008
ASSETS		
Current assets:		
Cash and cash equivalents	$ 668,209	$ 224,084
Short term investment securities	2,000	—
Merchandise inventories	1,642,339	1,616,981
Other current assets	250,251	238,646
Total current assets	2,562,799	2,079,711
Long term investment securities	221,134	326,004
Property and equipment, net	1,148,435	1,121,906
Other assets	336,475	316,472
Total assets	$ 4,268,843	$ 3,844,093
LIABILITIES AND SHAREHOLDERS' EQUITY		
Current liabilities:		
Accounts payable	$ 514,734	$ 570,605
Accrued expenses and other current liabilities	247,508	258,989
Merchandise credit and gift card liabilities	165,621	171,252
Current income taxes payable	25,105	13,266
Total current liabilities	952,968	1,014,112
Deferred rent and other liabilities	227,209	192,778
Income taxes payable	88,212	75,375
Total liabilities	1,268,389	1,282,265
Commitments and contingencies		
Shareholders' equity:		
Preferred stock—$0.01 par value; authorized—1,000 shares; no shares issued or outstanding	—	—
Common stock—$0.01 par value; authorized—900,000 shares; issued 314,678 and 312,229 shares, respectively; outstanding 259,701 and 258,920 shares, respectively	3,147	3,122
Additional paid-in capital	878,568	813,568
Retained earnings	4,154,921	3,729,766
Treasury stock, at cost	(2,031,642)	(1,983,590)
Accumulated other comprehensive loss	(4,540)	(1,038)
Total shareholders' equity	3,000,454	2,561,828
Total liabilities and shareholders' equity	$ 4,268,843	$ 3,844,093

See accompanying Notes to Consolidated Financial Statements.

Bed Bath & Beyond Inc. and Subsidiaries
Consolidated Statements of Cash Flows

	FISCAL YEAR ENDED		
(In thousands)	February 28, 2009	March 1, 2008	March 3, 2007
Cash Flows from Operating Activities:			
Net earnings	$ 425,123	$ 562,808	$ 594,244
Adjustments to reconcile net earnings to net cash provided by operating activities:			
Depreciation	175,601	157,770	132,955
Amortization of bond premium	—	1,538	3,532
Stock-based compensation	43,708	43,755	52,596
Tax benefit from stock-based compensation	(1,183)	2,719	6,691
Deferred income taxes	(22,325)	2,315	(87,225)
Other	476	—	—
(Increase) decrease in assets, net of effect of acquisition:			
Merchandise inventories	(25,358)	(96,673)	(204,080)
Trading investment securities	(17)	(3,020)	(2,958)
Other current assets	(3,065)	(16,217)	(38,241)
Other assets	(954)	529	(695)
(Decrease) increase in liabilities, net of effect of acquisition:			
Accounts payable	(40,863)	(31,764)	75,883
Accrued expenses and other current liabilities	(13,301)	15,774	9,784
Merchandise credit and gift card liabilities	(5,631)	24,430	30,223
Income taxes payable	24,676	(74,530)	21,575
Deferred rent and other liabilities	27,083	25,102	19,348
Net cash provided by operating activities	583,970	614,536	613,632
Cash Flows from Investing Activities:			
Purchase of held-to-maturity investment securities	—	—	(124,125)
Redemption of held-to-maturity investment securities	—	494,526	309,818
Purchase of available-for-sale investment securities	—	(1,495,155)	(1,443,115)
Redemption of available-for-sale investment securities	107,550	1,546,430	1,177,250
Capital expenditures	(215,859)	(358,210)	(317,501)
Investment in unconsolidated joint venture, including fees	(4,786)	—	—
Payment for acquisition, net of cash acquired	—	(85,893)	—
Net cash (used in) provided by investing activities	(113,095)	101,698	(397,673)
Cash Flows from Financing Activities:			
Proceeds from exercise to stock options	17,650	22,672	43,393
Excess tax benefit from stock-based compensation	3,652	5,990	14,001
Repurchase of common stock, including fees	(48,052)	(734,193)	(301,002)
Payment of deferred purchase price for acquisition	—	—	(6,667)
Net cash used in financing activities	(26,750)	(705,531)	(250,275)
Net increase (decrease) in cash and cash equivalents	444,125	10,703	(34,316)
Cash and cash equivalents:			
Beginning of period	224,084	213,381	247,697
End of period	$ 668,209	$ 224,084	$ 213,381

See accompanying Notes to Consolidated Financial Statements.

Bed Bath & Beyond Inc. and Subsidiaries
Consolidated Statements of Shareholders' Equity

(In thousands)	COMMON STOCK SHARES	COMMON STOCK AMOUNT	ADDITIONAL PAID-IN CAPITAL	RETAINED EARNINGS	TREASURY STOCK SHARES	TREASURY STOCK AMOUNT	ACCUMULATED OTHER COMPREHENSIVE INCOME (LOSS)	TOTAL
Balance at February 25, 2006	306,156	$3,062	$575,559	$2,632,224	(25,166)	$ (948,395)	$ —	$2,262,450
Net earnings				594,244				594,244
Shares sold under employee stock option plans, including tax benefit	2,603	26	61,628					61,654
Issuance of restricted shares, net	991	10	(10)					—
Stock-based compensation expense, net			61,744					61,744
Repurchase of common stock, including fees					(7,5100)	(301,002)		(301,002)
Adoption of SAB 108			38,288	(72,612)				(34,324)
Adoption of SFAS No. 158							4,385	4,385
Balance at March 3, 2007	309,750	3,098	737,209	3,153,856	(32,676)	(1,249,397)	4,385	2,649,151
Adoption of FIN 48				13,102				13,102
Comprehensive Income (Loss):								
Net earnings				562,808				562,808
Temporary Impairment of auction rate securities, net of taxes							(4,516)	(4,516)
Pension adjustment, net of taxes							(736)	(736)
Currency translation adjustment							(171)	(171)
Comprehensive Income								557,385
Shares sold under employee stock option plans, including tax benefit	1,463	14	31,367					31,381
Issuance of restricted shares, net	1,016	10	(10)					—
Stock-based compensation expense, net			45,002					45,002
Repurchase of common stock, including fees					(20,633)	(734,193)		(734,193)
Balance at March 1, 2008	312,229	3,122	813,568	3,729,766	(53,309)	(1,983,590)	(1,038)	2,561,828
Comprehensive Income (Loss):								
Net earnings				425,123				425,123
Change in temporary impairment of auction rate securities, net of taxes							(615)	(615)

Unrealized loss included in net earnings, net of taxes							3,528	3,528
Pension adjustment, net of taxes							(4,593)	(4,593)
Currency translation adjustment							(1,822)	(1,822)
Comprehensive Income								421,621
Shares sold under employee stock option plans, including tax benefit	1,218	12	19,910					19,922
Issuance of restricted shares, net	1,224	13	(13)					—
Stock-based compensation expense, net			44,906					44,906
Director fees paid in stock	7		197					197
Repurchase of common stock, including fees					(1,668)	(48,052)		(48,502)
SFAS No. 158 change in measurement date effect				32				32
Balance at February 28, 2009	314,678	$3,147	$878,568	$4,154,921	(54,977)	$(2,031,642)	$(4,540)	$3,000,454

See accompanying Notes to Consolidated Financial Statements.

SUMMARY OF KEY POINTS

● *The three basic activities of a business and how they are reflected in the financial statements.*

Businesses must first attract capital and then invest it in productive assets that can be used to produce saleable goods and/or services. The three basic activities involved in conducting a business are (1) financing activities, (2) investing activities, and (3) operating activities. Financing activities involve the collection of capital through equity or debt issuances and any associated payments, such as dividends and debt payments. Investing activities involve the acquisition and sale of producing assets, the assets used to produce and support the goods and services provided. Operating activities involve the sale of the goods and services. Operating activities produce additional capital that can be reinvested in the producing assets, used to service debt payments, and distributed to the owners in the form of dividends.

The balance sheet lists assets (goods and producing assets) and financing sources (equity, debt, and reinvestments from net earnings) at a particular point in time. The income statement is a measure of operations, the activities (revenues and expenses) involved in selling the goods and services. The statement of shareholders' equity measures changes in contributed capital and the extent to which the business reinvests its net earnings and pays dividends. The statement of cash flows contains the cash inflows and outflows associated with the operating, investing, and financing activities of the business.

● *The balance sheet, income statement, statement of shareholders' equity, and statement of cash flows and how these financial statements are used.*

The asset accounts reported on the balance sheet are listed in order of liquidity and are divided into four categories: (1) current assets, which include cash, short-term investments, accounts receivable, inventory, and prepaid expenses; (2) long-term investments, which include long-term notes receivable, land, securities, the cash value of life insurance, and special investment funds; (3) property, plant, and equipment; and (4) intangible assets, which include patents, trademarks, and other intangibles, such as goodwill.

Liabilities are divided into two categories: (1) current liabilities, which primarily include short-term payables; and (2) long-term liabilities, which include items such as long-term notes, bonds, and mortgages payable. The shareholders' equity section for a corporation contains contributed capital and retained earnings; the owners' equity section for a partnership contains an account for each partner that records the cumulative balance of the partner's contributions less withdrawals.

The income statement consists of two basic categories: revenues and expenses. Revenues, which represent asset inflows (or liability decreases) associated with operating transactions during a given period, include sales, fees earned, service revenues, and other revenues (e.g., interest, book gains). Expenses, which represent the asset outflows (or liability increases) required to generate the revenues, include cost of goods sold, operating expenses (e.g., wages, rent), and other expenses (e.g., interest, book losses). Revenues less expenses equal net income.

The statement of shareholders' equity consists of the changes in two basic accounts: (1) contributed capital (e.g., the funds collected from shareholders through stock issuances) and (2) earned capital, primarily retained earnings, which represents past reinvested (not paid to the shareholders in the form of dividends) profits. The statement of cash flows contains three categories: (1) cash flows from operating activities; (2) cash flows from investing activities; and (3) cash flows from financing activities.

This information enables external users to assess the earning power and solvency position of the company. Assets generate cash through their use and sale, and liabilities represent cash requirements. The income statement indicates how profitable the company's operations have been, and the statement of cash flows shows how the company's cash is managed. The statement of shareholders' equity provides information about the investment in the company made by the shareholders.

(?)

Similarities and differences between non-U.S. financial statement format and terminology

The financial statement format used by non-U.S. companies is very similar to that of the U.S. for the income statement, statement of cash flows, and statement of shareholders' equity. For the balance sheet, many non-U.S. companies begin with non-current assets, add current assets, and then subtract current liabilities. This computation reflects the resources (non-current assets and working capital) management has at its disposal to generate revenues and profits. The balance sheet then lists non-current liabilities and then shareholders' equity, which represents the financing source of those resources, and is often referred to as "capital employed." Other terminology differences exist, and we noted, for example, that "turnover" is often used to describe revenue, and "financing cost" is used to describe interest expense. Additional terminology differences will be discussed in the text as they arise.

KEY TERMS

Note: Definitions for these terms are provided in the glossary at the end of the text.

Accounts payable (p. 42)
Accounts receivable (p. 39)
Bonds payable (p. 43)
Capital employed (p. 45)
Classified balance sheet (p. 36)
Contributed capital (p. 43)
Cost of goods sold (p. 47)
Current assets (p. 38)
Current liabilities (p. 42)
Current maturities of long-term
    debts (p. 42)
Earned capital (p. 44)
Fees earned (p. 46)
Financing activities (p. 35)
Financing cost (p. 63)
Intangible assets (p. 41)
Investing activities (p. 35)

Liquidity (p. 36)
Long-term investments (p. 40)
Merchandise inventory (p. 39)
Mortgage payables (p. 43)
Net book value (p. 41)
Notes payable (p. 43)
Operating activities (p. 35)
Owners' equity (p. 45)
Plant and equipment (p. 41)
Prepaid expenses (p. 39)
Property (p. 40)
Retained earnings (p. 44)
Sales (p. 46)
Service revenue (p. 46)
Shareholders' equity (p. 43)
Short-term investments (p. 38)
Turnover (p. 54)

ETHICS in the Real World

For years German and Swiss accounting rules allowed management to "manage" earnings through discretionary adjustments. For the most part, the adjustments "smooth out" earnings variability across time, and many were used to German and Swiss managers argued that such adjustments were in the best interest of the firm, its shareholders, and the overall economy.

Many of these companies have since adopted International Financial Reporting Standards (IFRS), which makes it more difficult to "manage" earnings. Many believe that these reporting standards encourage more transparency between corporate management and the investing community. Nonetheless, some Swiss companies were not quick to adopt IFRS, arguing that the standards imposed significant additional costs and simply made it more difficult for management to run their companies.

ETHICAL ISSUE Discuss the ethical issues facing a Swiss manager who is hesitant to adopt IFRS.

INTERNET RESEARCH EXERCISE

Review the discussion about Borders in the introduction to this chapter and provide a brief description and discussion of Borders' recent financial performance and core business. Begin your search at www.borders.com.

BRIEF EXERCISES

REAL DATA

BE2–1

Dividends as a percentage of net income

Revenues and expenses for PepsiCo during 2008 were $43.3 billion and $38.2 billion, respectively. The December 31, 2007 and 2008 balances in retained earnings were $28.2 billion and $30.6 billion, respectively. Compute dividends paid by PepsiCo during 2008. What percentage of net income did PepsiCo pay out in dividends during 2008?

REAL DATA

BE2–2

Financing assets

A summary of a recent balance sheet for Boeing Co. is as follows (dollars in billions):

Assets		Liabilities and Shareholders' Equity	
Current assets	$27	Current liabilities	$32
Property, plant, and equipment	8	Long-term debt	18
Other assets	24	Shareholders' equity	9
Total	$59	Total	$59

What amount and what percentage of Boeing's assets were financed by (1) current liabilities, (2) long-term debt, and (3) shareholders' equity?

REAL DATA

BE2–3

Assessing solvency

In BE2–2, Boeing's current assets consisted primarily of cash and short-term investments of $9.3 billion, accounts receivable of $5.7 billion, inventory of $9.6 billion, and miscellaneous current assets of $2.4 billion. Does the company appear solvent? Why or why not? Can Boeing pay off its current liabilities with liquid assets? Would it be more or less solvent if the dollar amounts in accounts receivable and inventory were reversed?

REAL DATA

BE2–4

The statement of cash flows across time

Excerpts from the annual report of AT&T, Inc., are as follows.

Statement of Cash Flows (Dollars in Millions)

	2008	2007	2006
Net cash from operating activities	$?	$34,242	$15,688
Net cash from investing activities	(29,143)	(18,616)	(8,366)
Net cash from financing activities	(4,691)	?	(6,128)
Net change in cash	?	(448)	?
Cash balance at beginning of year	1,970	?	?
Cash balance at end of year	1,792	?	2,418

Compute the missing values and briefly discuss AT&T's sources and uses of cash during the three-year period.

REAL DATA
BE2-5

Balance sheet
format differences

A recent balance sheet of Royal Dutch Shell, a huge oil and gas company that prepares financial statements using IFRS, reported the following dollar amounts (in millions).

Non-current assets	$154,073
Current assets	115,397
Current liabilities	94,384
Non-current liabilities	49,118
Equity	125,968

First, format these balance sheet sections in a manner that is used by many non-U.S. companies (see the Unilever analysis in this chapter), and then format the sections in the manner most common in the U.S. Comment on the differences, and how they highlight different concepts.

EXERCISES

E2-1

Identifying
financing, investing,
and operating
transactions

Listed below are eight transactions. In each case, identify whether the transaction is an example of financing, investing, or operating activities and which of the financial statements it would affect.

1. Common stock is issued for $500,000 in cash.
2. Twenty units of inventory are sold for $50 each.
3. Employee wages are paid.
4. A new warehouse facility is purchased.
5. Principal payments on outstanding debt are paid.
6. Dividends are paid to the shareholders.
7. A 4-year-old vehicle, used as a delivery truck, is sold for $9,000, its book value.
8. A utility bill for March is paid in April.

E2-2

Identifying
financing, investing,
and operating
transactions

Listed below are eight transactions. In each case, identify whether the transaction is an example of financing, investing, or operating activities and which of the financial statements it would affect.

1. Company borrows $50,000 in cash, signing a 10-year note payable.
2. Twenty units of inventory are purchased from suppliers on account for $12,000.
3. The utility bill is paid at the end of the month, $5,200.
4. Services are performed, and customers are billed for $13,000.
5. Five parcels of real estate are purchased for a total of $55,000 in cash.
6. A long-term investment in an equity security is sold for $4,500 cash.
7. Principal payments are made on outstanding debts.
8. Cash is received from customers for services completed in a previous period.

E2-3

Balance sheet or
income statement
account?

Listed below are accounts that may appear on either the balance sheet or the income statement.

a. Equipment
b. Fees Earned
c. Retained Earnings
d. Wage Expense
e. Patent
f. Cost of Goods Sold
g. Common Stock
h. Dividend Payable
i. Accumulated Depreciation

j. Prepaid Expense
k. Gain on Sale of Short-Term Investments
l. Rent Revenue
m. Supplies Inventory
n. Accounts Receivable
o. Land
p. Insurance Expense
q. Interest Payable
r. Deferred Revenue

For each account, indicate whether a company would ordinarily disclose the account on the balance sheet or the income statement.

E2-4

Financial statement and the lending decision

Assume a banker is interested in finding answers to the following questions about a company applying for a loan. In each case, indicate which of the four financial statements the banker should examine first to answer the question. If appropriate, also indicate which other financial statement(s) would provide further support for the answer.

1. What percent of earnings was retained in the business during each of the last three years?
2. What percent of sales revenue is spent on employee compensation?
3. How has the mix of assets and liabilities, both short-term and long, changed over the last two years?
4. How much cash has the company spent on new long-term assets?
5. What sources of capital does the company use to finance its operations?
6. Is the company growing?
7. How much above the cost of its products does the company charge its customers?
8. How quickly does the company pay its debts?

REAL DATA

E2-5

Relationships between retained earnings and revenues and expenses across time

Duke Energy Corporation is one of America's leading diversified energy companies. At the end of 2008 the company had a balance in its retained earnings account of $1.6 billion. Compute the missing amounts in the following table, and comment on the company's performance. Specifically, analyze the company's sales growth, profits, profits as a percentage of sales, and dividends declared as a percentage of net income (dollar amounts in billions).

	2008	2007	2006
Beginning retained earnings	$?	$ 5.7	$ 5.3
Revenues for the period	13.2	12.7	10.6
Expenses for the period	11.8	?	8.7
Dividends declared	1.2	5.8	?

E2-6

Relationships between retained earnings and revenues and expenses across time

At the end of 2009 a fast-growing advertising agency had a negative balance of $596 million in its retained earnings account. Compute the missing amounts in the following table, and comment on the company's performance. Specifically, analyze the company's sales growth, profits, profits as a percentage of sales, and dividends declared as a percentage of net income (dollars in millions).

	2009	2008	2007
Beginning retained earnings	$ (758)	$ (523)	$ (499)
Revenues for the period	?	1,522	1,383
Expenses for the period	1,550	1,608	?
Dividends declared	5	?	0

REAL DATA

E2-7

Using working capital to assess solvency

La-Z-Boy Incorporated included the following information in its 2009 annual report (dollars in millions).

	2009	2008
Cash	$ 17	$ 14
Accounts receivable	148	200
Inventory	140	178
Other current assets	43	35
Total current assets	$348	$427
Current liabilities	126	164
Current assets minus current liabilities	$222	$263

Define solvency and discuss how this information might be useful in assessing the company's solvency position. What drawbacks are associated with using this information in such a way?

Suppose that La-Z-Boy in E2–7 signed a debt covenant specifying that current assets must exceed current liabilities by $200 million. Assume further that in early January 2010, the company planned to purchase a $200-million piece of machinery and had two possible methods of paying for it: (1) short-term note payable or (2) long-term note payable. Compute the effect of each alternative on the difference between current assets and current liabilities, and discuss which method seems to be the most feasible.

The information below was taken from the 2009 annual report of Cisco Systems, a worldwide leader in networking for the Internet. As of the end of 2009, Cisco had a cash balance of $5.7 billion. Compute the missing amounts in the following table. Describe and evaluate the company's cash management activities in each of the three years (dollars in millions).

	2009	2008	2007
Beginning cash balance	$5,191	$?	$ 3,297
Net cash flow from operating activities	9,897	?	10,104
Net cash flow from investing activities	(9,959)	(4,193)	?
Net cash flow from financing activities	?	(6,433)	(1,331)
Ending cash balance	$5,718	$?	$ 3,728

Southwest Airlines is a major airline. The following information was taken from its 2008 annual report. As of the end of 2008, Southwest had a cash balance of $1.4 billion. Compute the missing amounts in the following table. Describe and evaluate the company's cash management activities in each of the three years (dollars in millions).

	2008	2007	2006
Beginning cash balance	$?	$1,390	$?
Net cash flow from operating activities	(1,521)	2,845	1,406
Net cash flow from investing activities	?	(1,529)	(1,495)
Net cash flow from financing activities	1,654	?	(801)
Ending cash balance	$1,368	$2,213	$?

From the following transactions, prepare a statement of cash flows for Lana and Sons in the proper form. The company began the year with a cash balance of $13,000. Describe and evaluate the company's cash management activities during the year.

1.   The shareholders contributed $7,000 in cash.
2.   Performed services for $5,000, receiving $4,000 in cash and a $1,000 receivable.
3.   Incurred expenses of $4,000; paid $3,000 in cash and $1,000 is still payable.
4.   Purchased machinery for $10,000; paid $3,000 in cash and signed a long-term note payable for the remainder.
5.   Paid the shareholders a $1,500 dividend.

From the following transactions, prepare a statement of cash flows for Emory Inc. in the proper form. The company began the year with a cash balance of $25,000. Describe and evaluate the company's cash management activities during the year.

1.   Borrowed $30,000 from a bank, signing a long-term note.
2.   Performed services for $45,000, receiving $40,000 in cash and a $5,000 receivable.
3.   Incurred expenses of $34,000; paid $23,000 in cash and $11,000 is still payable.
4.   Purchased equipment for $28,000; paid $23,000 in cash and signed a long-term note payable for the remainder.
5.   Paid the shareholders a dividend in an amount that ensured an ending cash balance of $25,000.

E2–13

Preparing financial
statements from
simple transactions

George began a business, and after collecting $6,000 from an equity investor and borrowing $5,000 from a bank, he purchased a piece of land for $8,000. During the year, he leased the land to Sheila and received $3,000 in cash. He paid $2,500 cash for expenses during the year and paid an $800 dividend to the equity investor.

   Prepare an income statement, a statement of shareholders' equity, a balance sheet, and statement of cash flows for the period. What did George do that may have concerned the bank? Explain.

E2–14

Preparing financial
statements from
simple transactions

Mary began a business, and after collecting $30,000 from an equity investor and borrowing $15,000 from a bank, she purchased a piece of land for $40,000. During the year, she leased the land to Karl and received $12,000 in cash, paying $14,000 cash for expenses. She paid a $1,000 dividend to the equity investor at year-end.

   Prepare an income statement, a statement of shareholders' equity, a balance sheet, and a statement of cash flows for the period. Evaluate Mary's decision to pay the $1,000 dividend.

PROBLEMS

P2–1

Classifying balance
sheet accounts

Presented below are the main section headings of the balance sheet:

a.   Current assets
b.   Long-term investments
c.   Property, plant, and equipment
d.   Intangible assets

e.   Current liabilities
f.   Long-term liabilities
g.   Contributed capital
h.   Retained earnings

REQUIRED:
Classify the following accounts under the appropriate headings, and prepare a balance sheet in proper form without account balances.

1. Dividends payable
2. Payments received in advance
3. Allowance for uncollectible accounts
4. Inventories
5. Capital stock
6. Accumulated depreciation—building
7. Bonds payable
8. Machinery and equipment
9. Accounts receivable
10. Short-term investments
11. Buildings
12. Patents

13. Property
14. Investment fund for plant expansion
15. Wages payable
16. Cash
17. Accumulated depreciation—equipment
18. Prepaid rent
19. Trademarks
20. Land held for investment
21. Current portion due of long-term debt
22. Accounts payable
23. Short-term notes payable

P2–2

Classifying income
statement accounts

The main section headings of the income statement are:

a.   Sales
b.   Fees earned
c.   Other revenues

d.   Cost of goods sold
e.   Operating expenses
f.   Other expenses

REQUIRED:
Classify the following descriptions under the appropriate headings and prepare an income statement in proper form without account balances.

1. Office salary expense
2. Sales of services provided
3. Insurance expense
4. Sales of inventories
5. Salespeople commission expense

6. Depreciation expense
7. Office supplies expense
8. Loss on sale of equipment
9. Income from interest on savings account
10. Income from dividends on investments

11. Advertising expense
12. Loss on sale of building
13. Interest expense on outstanding loans

14. Cost of sold inventories
15. Gain on sale of short-term investments

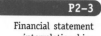

P2-3

Financial statement
interrelationships

Review Figure 2–7, and complete the blanks below to show the relationships among the four financial statements for Nimmo Brothers Corporation:

Balance Sheet (12/31/2010)	
Cash	$ 420
Other current assets	1,300
Long-term assets	1,400
Total assets	$3,120

Statement of Cash Flows (year ending 12/31/2011)	
Cash—Operating	$ 275
Cash—Investing	(200)
Cash—Financing	330
Δ in cash	?
Cash—12/31/10	?
Cash—12/31/11	?

Balance Sheet (12/31/2011)	
Cash	$?
Other current assets	1,550
Long-term assets	1,600
Total assets	?

Current liabilities	$ 620
Long-term liabilities	1,000
Contributed capital	1,000
Retained earnings	500
Total	$3,120

Income Statement (year ending 12/31/2011)	
Revenue	$4,200
Expenses	4,050
Net income	?

Current liabilities	$ 995
Long-term liabilities	1,200
Contributed capital	1,200
Retained earnings	?
Total	?

Statement of Shareholders' Equity
(year ending 12/31/2011)

	Contributed Capital	Retained Earnings
12/31/10	$1,000	$500
Net income		?
Dividends		(70)
Stock issuance	200	?
12/31/11	?	?

P2-4

Preparing a balance
sheet in proper form
and comparing U.S. and
non-U.S. practices

The following information is available relating to the activities of Johnson Co. as of December 31, 2011.

- Cash balance on 12/31/11 is $8,000.
- Short-term investments have a fair market value of $40,000 on 12/31/11.
- Accounts receivable balance of $125,000 on 12/31/11 includes $2,400 that is not likely to be collected.
- Inventory costing $165,000 has a replacement cost (market value) of $161,000 on 12/31/11.
- Buildings having a fair market value of $68,500 were purchased for $35,000 and have accumulated depreciation of $8,000.
- Accounts payable at year-end total $110,000.
- Taxes payable at year-end total $29,400.
- Balance in the long-term notes payable account at the end of the period is $79,100.
- Fair market value of the Johnson Co. stock is $10 per share on 12/31/11. When originally issued, 12,500 shares were sold for $8 per share.
- The total amount of net income earned by Johnson Co. since its inception several years ago is $65,000. Over that same period, Johnson Co. has paid $24,900 in dividends.

REQUIRED:
Prepare a balance sheet as of 12/31/11 in proper form for Johnson Co. Would you invest in this company? Why or why not? Reformat the balance using the balance sheet format used by Unilever, illustrated on pp. 54. Does this format highlight anything differently?

P2–5

Balance sheet and income statement relationships across five years

Compute the missing values for the following chart and analyze the financial performance and position of this company. The first year of operations is 2005.

	2011	2010	2009	2008
Assets:				
Cash	$500	$200	$ 300	$ 300
Accounts receivable	700	?	300	200
Inventory	400	400	?	500
Land	400	400	200	100
Property, plant, and equipment (net)	800	700	600	700
Liabilities and shareholders' equity:				
Accounts payable	?	500	300	200
Bonds payable	700	800	600	500
Contributed capital	600	600	400	?
Retained earnings	600	300	800	400
Sales	?	700	1,100	1,000
Expenses	(600)	?	?	(400)
Net income	?	(100)	400	?
Dividends	200	?	?	?

REAL DATA

P2–6

Using financial statements to assess solvency and earning power

Excerpts from the financial statements for Kroger, a major supermarket retailer, are as follows (dollars in millions).

	2009	2008
Cash	$ 263	$ 242
Accounts receivable	944	786
Inventory	4,859	4,849
Property, plant, and equipment	13,161	12,498
Other assets	3,984	3,918
Accounts payable	3,822	3,867
Other short-term debts	3,807	4,816
Long-term debt	10,406	8,696
Shareholders' equity	5,176	4,914
Sales	76,000	70,235
Expenses	74,751	69,054

REQUIRED:

Organize these numbers into income statement and balance sheets, and comment on Kroger's solvency and earning power positions.

P2–7

Balance sheet value and the fair market value of the assets

Because of consistent losses in the past several years, Eat and Run, a fast-food franchise, is in danger of bankruptcy. Its most current balance sheet follows.

Assets		Liabilities and Shareholders' Equity	
Cash	$ 25,000	Accounts payable	$ 42,000
Short-term investments	15,000	Wages payable	20,000
Accounts receivable	35,000	Other short-term payables	34,000
Inventory	42,000	Long-term notes	75,000
Prepaid insurance	10,000	Mortgage payable	25,000
Property, plant, and equipment	82,000	Contributed capital	50,000
Other assets	50,000	Retained earnings	13,000
		Total liabilities and	
Total assets	$259,000	shareholders' equity	$259,000

Additional information:

- The fair market value of the marketable securities is $19,000.
- The sale of the accounts receivable to a local bank would produce about $25,000 cash.
- A portion of the inventory originally costing $21,000 is now obsolete and can be sold for $3,000 scrap value. The remaining inventory is worth approximately $30,000.
- Prepaid insurance is nonrefundable.
- In the event of bankruptcy, the property, plant, and equipment owned by Eat and Run would be divided up and sold separately. It has been estimated that these sales would bring approximately $100,000 cash.
- Other assets (primarily organizational costs) cannot be recovered.

REQUIRED:

a. The book value (balance sheet assets less liabilities) of Eat and Run is $63,000. Comment on why this balance sheet value may not be a good indication of the value of the company in the case of bankruptcy.

b. If Eat and Run goes bankrupt, what would you consider to be the value of the company?

c. When a company goes bankrupt, the creditors are usually paid off first with the existing assets, and then, if assets remain, the shareholders are paid. If Eat and Run goes bankrupt, would the shareholders receive anything? If so, how much?

P2–8

Analyzing financial statements

The chief executive officer of Romney Heights has included the following information from the financial statements in a loan application submitted to Acme Bank. The company intends to acquire additional equipment and wishes to finance the purchase with a long-term note.

	2011	2010
Balance Sheet		
Current assets	$ 14,000	$ 12,000
Long-term assets	50,000	43,000
Current liabilities	7,000	6,000
Long-term liabilities	26,000	21,000
Contributed capital	25,000	25,000
Retained earnings	6,000	3,000
Income Statement		
Revenues	$ 35,000	$ 32,000
Expenses	23,000	26,000
Statement of Cash Flows		
Net cash flow from operating activities	$ 15,000	$ 9,000
Net cash flow from investing activities	(14,000)	(12,000)
Net cash flow from financing activities	7,000	5,000
Change in cash balance	$ 8,000	$ 2,000
Beginning cash balance	3,000	1,000
Ending cash balance	$ 11,000	$ 3,000

REQUIRED:

Assume that you, a bank loan officer, review the financial statements and recommend whether Romney Heights should be considered for a loan. Support your recommendation with calculations.

P2–9

Analyzing financial statements

Ted Tooney has operated a small service company for several years. The following information is from the financial statements prepared by Ted's accountant.

	2011	2010
Balance Sheet		
Current assets	$ 9,000	$ 8,000
Long-term assets	18,000	15,000
Current liabilities	7,000	4,000
Long-term liabilities	9,000	7,000
Contributed capital	9,000	9,000
Retained earnings	2,000	3,000
Income Statement		
Revenues	$92,000	$89,000
Expenses	78,000	72,000
Statement of Cash Flows		
Net cash flow from operating activities	$12,000	$15,000
Net cash flow from investing activities	(8,000)	(5,000)
Net cash flow from financing activities	(5,000)	(8,000)
Change in cash balance	$(1,000)	$ 2,000
Beginning cash balance	5,000	3,000
Ending cash balance	$ 4,000	$ 5,000

REQUIRED:

Assume that you have some capital to invest and that Ted asked you to consider making an equity investment in his company. Review the financial statements and describe how you would respond to Ted's request. Support your recommendation with calculations.

P2–10

Debt covenants can limit investments and dividends

A summary of the December 31, 2011 balance sheet of Ellington Industries follows:

	2011
Assets	
Current assets	$12,000
Land investments	55,000
Total assets	$67,000
Liabilities and Shareholders' Equity	
Accounts payable	$ 9,000
Long-term liabilities	30,000
Shareholders' equity	28,000
Total liabilities and shareholders' equity	$67,000

On January 1, 2012, the company borrowed $40,000 (long-term debt) to purchase additional land. The debt covenant states that Ellington must maintain a current asset balance at least twice as large as its current liability balance over the period of the loan.

REQUIRED:

a. As of January 1, 2012, how much of the $40,000 can Ellington invest in land without violating the debt covenant?

b. Assume that Ellington invested the maximum allowable in land. Prepare Ellington's balance sheet as of January 1, 2012. Compute the following ratios: current assets/current liabilities and total liabilities/total assets.

c. Assume that Ellington invested the maximum allowable in land and that during 2012 it generated $150,000 in revenues (all cash), paid off the accounts payable outstanding as of December 31, 2011, and incurred $130,000 in expenses, of which $123,000 was paid

in cash. The company neither purchased nor sold any of its long-term land investments, made no principal payments on the long-term debt, and issued no equity during 2012. Prepare a balance sheet as of the end of 2012, and compute how large a dividend the company can pay without violating the debt covenant. Compute total liabilities/total assets assuming that the company declares the maximum allowable dividend.

ISSUES FOR DISCUSSION

REAL DATA

ID2–1

Relationships among cash flows, income, and dividends

For over a year, Center Energy Corporation, a utility company in Ohio, had negative cash flow from operating activities, caused primarily by the escalating costs of one of its nuclear plants outside Cleveland. Yet the company reported positive earnings and paid a dividend to its shareholders of $2.56 per share.

REQUIRED:
a. Briefly explain how a company could have negative cash flow from operating activities, have a positive net income, and still pay dividends.
b. Could a company continue such a strategy over an extended period? Why or why not?

REAL DATA

ID2–2

Income statement classifications

In early May 2007, Walt Disney Company released its earnings for its fiscal second quarter. In the release, the company discussed its various operations, including

* Revenue from a surprising movie hit, *Wild Hogs*
* Upcoming revenue from two summer blockbuster movies, *Pirates of the Caribbean* and *Ratatouille*
* Sports programming costs at the television network ESPN
* A new licensing business model for ESPN mobile phone service
* Broadcasting revenue at its various television networks
* Merchandise sales related to its *Cars* movie release
* Softer theme park revenue

REQUIRED:
Discuss how the areas outlined above would be presented and classified on the income statement of Disney.

REAL DATA

ID2–3

Debt covenants

The following excerpt was taken from a financial report of Cummins Engine Company, a manufacturer of heavy-duty truck engines.

Loan agreements contain covenants that impose restrictions on the payment of dividends and distributions of stock, require maintenance of a 1.25:1 current ratio, and limit the amount of future borrowings. Under the most restrictive covenants, retained earnings of approximately $351 million were available for payment of dividends.

REQUIRED:
a. Briefly explain the meaning of this excerpt.
b. Why would a bank or other creditor impose such restrictions on a borrowing company?
c. Explain the role of financial accounting numbers in the restrictions described above.

REAL DATA

ID2–4

Statement of cash flow patterns across companies

The following information was taken from the 2008 annual reports—statements of cash flows—of Hewlett-Packard, Southwest Airlines, and The Boeing Co., Inc. (dollars in millions).

Company	Cash from Operations	Cash from Investing	Cash from Financing
HP	$14,591	$(13,711)	$(2,020)
Southwest	(1.521)	(978)	1,654
Boeing	(401)	1,888	(5,202)

REQUIRED:

Each of these companies shows a different cash flow pattern. Explain what these patterns might indicate about each company.

REAL DATA

ID2-5

Statement of cash flow patterns across time

The following information was taken from the 2008 annual report—statements of cash flows—of Goodrich Corporation, a major company in the aerospace and defense industry (dollars in millions).

Year	Cash from Operations	Cash from Investing	Cash from Financing
2006	265.5	(250.6)	(90.4)
2007	593.7	(279.3)	(202.5)
2008	786.6	(410.0)	(414.4)

REQUIRED:

What does this pattern of cash flows indicate about Goodrich's business strategy, performance, and cash balances from 2006 to 2008?

REAL DATA

ID2-6

Balance sheet—non-U.S. format

The following balance sheet (prepared according to IFRS) was taken from the 2008 annual report of GlaxoSmithKline, a British pharmaceutical company (British pounds in millions).

GlaxoSmithKline
Consolidated Balance Sheet at 31st December 2008

	Notes	2008 £m	2007 £m
NON-CURRENT ASSETS			
Property, plant and equipment	17	9,678	7,821
Goodwill	18	2,101	1,370
Other intangible assets	19	5,869	4,456
Investments in associates and joint ventures	20	552	329
Other investments	21	478	517
Deferred tax assets	14	2,760	2,196
Derivative financial instruments	41	107	1
Other non-current assets	22	579	687
Total non-current assets		22,124	17,377

(Continued)

GlaxoSmithKline
Consolidated Balance Sheet at 31st December 2008 (*Continued*)

	Notes	2008 £m	2007 £m
CURRENT ASSETS			
Inventories	23	4,056	3,062
Current tax recoverable	14	76	58
Trade and other receivables	24	6,265	5,495
Derivative financial instruments	41	856	475
Liquid investments	32	391	1,153
Cash and cash equivalents	25	5,623	3,379
Assets held for sale	26	2	4
Total current assets		17,269	13,626
Total assets		39,393	31,003
CURRENT LIABILITIES			
Short-term borrowings	32	(956)	(3,504)
Trade and other payables	27	(6,075)	(4,861)
Derivative financial instruments	41	(752)	(262)
Current tax payable	14	(780)	(826)
Short-term provisions	29	(1,454)	(892)
Total current liabilities		(10,017)	(10,345)
NON-CURRENT LIABILITIES			
Long-term borrowings	32	(15,231)	(7,067)
Deferred tax liabilities	14	(714)	(887)
Pensions and other post-employment benefits	28	(3,039)	(1,383)
Other provisions	29	(1,645)	(1,035)
Derivative financial instruments	41	(2)	(8)
Other non-current liabilities	30	(427)	(368)
Total non-current liabilities		(21,058)	(10,748)
Total liabilities		(31,075)	(21,093)
Net assets		8,318	9,910
EQUITY			
Share capital	33	1,415	1,503
Share premium account	33	1,326	1,266
Retained earnings	34	4,622	6,475
Other reserves	34	568	359
Shareholders' equity		7,931	9,603
Minority interests	34	387	307
Total equity		8,318	9,910

Approved by the Board on 3rd March 2009

Sir Christopher Gent
Chairman

REQUIRED:

Identify where the format of this balance sheet differs from that required under U.S. GAAP, and prepare a balance sheet as close as possible in accordance with U.S. GAAP.

REAL DATA

ID2–7

Net income vs. cash flow from operations

The *Wall Street Journal* (April 16, 2004) reports, "For as long as companies have published cash-flow statements, investors have used them to gauge the credibility of earnings. The most closely watched portion of these reports is the part called cash flow from operating activities. If a company shows strong earnings but generates little cash flow from its core operations, it could be a warning sign that the earnings are illusory. Conversely, many investors take comfort in the quality of a company's earnings if they also see robust operating cash flow."

REQUIRED:

Comment on this quote.

REAL DATA

ID2–8

How transactions affect the balance sheet and statement of cash flows

In late 2009 General Electric, Vivendi SA, and the cable television company Comcast entered into a complicated transaction to change the ownership of the television and production company NBC Universal. Prior to the transaction, GE owned 80 percent of NBC, and Vivendi owned a minority share of 20 percent. GE bought the 20 percent of NBC owned by Vivendi (giving GE the entire company), and then sold 51 percent of NBC to Comcast. Both purchases were paid for with cash.

REQUIRED:

Explain why GE and Comcast would enter into such a transaction, and describe how these exchanges would affect the balance sheet and statement of cash flows of GE.

REAL DATA

ID2–9

Should the SEC have dropped the requirement to reconcile IFRS with U.S. GAAP?

Up until 2007 non-U.S. firms that published IFRS-based financial statements and wished to raise capital on the U.S. stock markets (e.g., New York Stock Exchange) were required to file with the SEC a Form 20-F that included reconciliations of both net income and shareholder's equity as measured under U.S. GAAP and IFRS. The reconciliations provided detailed explanation of the different ways in which net income and shareholders' equity were measured under the two systems.

REQUIRED:

Assume that you are an analyst attempting to compare the financial condition and performance of NIKE, which publishes U.S. GAAP–based financial statements, and adidas, which publishes IFRS-based financial statements. Would you be pleased with the SEC's decision to drop the reconciliation requirement? Explain.

REAL DATA

ID2–10

The SEC Form 10-K of NIKE

Excerpts taken from the SEC Form 10-K of NIKE are reproduced in Appendix C.

REQUIRED:

Review the NIKE Form 10-K, and answer the following questions.

a. Compute cost of sales, selling, general & administrative expenses, interest costs, and taxes as a percent of revenues for 2009, 2008, and 2007, and explain how NIKE's net income has changed over the three-year period.

b. Compute current and noncurrent assets as a percent of total assets, and explain how NIKE's asset structure changed from 2008 to 2009.

c. Compute current and long-term liabilities as a percent of total assets, and explain how NIKE's reliance on liabilities as a source of financing changed from 2008 to 2009.

d. Review the statement of cash flows, and comment on whether NIKE is growing and which financing sources have financed this growth.

e. Approximately what portion of NIKE's net income is paid to the shareholders in the form of dividends each year? Are there other methods that NIKE uses to return cash to shareholders?

Measurement, Mechanics, and Use of Financial Statements

General Motors was the dominant automobile manufacturer throughout the world for decades. The company's car line spanned several brand names and its dealer network was ubiquitous in the United States. Annually, the company's market share for new car sales in the U.S. was well ahead of rival firms, both domestic and international. However, in the latter part of the first decade of this century, sales dropped while expenses, often locked in at contractual rates, grew substantially. Competition from the likes of Toyota and Honda eroded market share and profitability, while GM and its dealers became dependent on offering steep rebates to move cars. Eventually, the company's losses grew so much that the U.S. government, in an unprecedented move, took over ownership of the firm and negotiated GM into and then out of bankruptcy court. Only recently is GM beginning to rebound and reduce the government's ownership stake.

How do you measure profit margins? How can profits turn quickly into losses? How does management affect the financial statements? And how do investors respond to the present success but the future uncertainty of changing markets and competition? These kinds of questions are addressed in Part 2 of this textbook.

CHAPTER 3
The Measurement Fundamentals of Financial Accounting

CHAPTER 4
The Mechanics of Financial Accounting

CHAPTER 5
Using Financial Statement Information

The Measurement Fundamentals of Financial Accounting

KEY POINTS

The following key points are emphasized in this chapter:

- Four basic assumptions of financial accounting.

- The markets in which business entities operate and the valuation bases used on the balance sheet.

- The principle of objectivity and how it determines the dollar values that appear on the financial statements.

- The principles of matching, revenue recognition, and consistency.

- Two exceptions to the principles of financial accounting measurement: materiality and conservatism.

- Fundamental differences between U.S. GAAP and IFRS.

Apple, Inc. has led the market for so-called smart phones with its iPhone, while competitors crowd the market daily with products such as the Pre from Palm and the Droid from Motorola. Manufacturers that sell these products are producing both hardware and software for their customers, selling the phone but also providing services to make the phone as functional as possible. Historically, the companies would record the revenue from the sale over the assumed life of the product, typically two years. Recently, however, the FASB approved changes that allow these companies to record more of the revenue in earlier periods of the phone's use. How do companies recognize revenue, and how are the financial statements affected? What might motivate management to recognize revenue early, and how might a company's stock price react to such behavior? This chapter covers the measurement fundamentals of financial accounting, which consists of the basic assumptions, principles, and exceptions underlying the financial statements. The principles of revenue recognition are an important part of these fundamentals.

ASSUMPTIONS OF FINANCIAL ACCOUNTING

There are four basic assumptions of financial accounting: (1) economic entity, (2) fiscal period, (3) going concern, and (4) stable dollar. These assumptions are important because they form the building blocks on which financial accounting measurement is based. Some are reasonable representations of the real world, and others are not. As each assumption is discussed, try to understand why it has evolved, and be especially aware of those that fail to capture the world as it really is.

Economic Entity Assumption

The most fundamental assumption of financial accounting involves the object of the performance measure. Should the accounting system provide performance information about countries, states, cities, industries, individual companies, or segments of individual companies? While it is important that each of these entities operate efficiently, financial accounting has evolved in response to a demand for company-specific measures of performance and financial position. Consequently, financial accounting reports provide information about individual, profit-seeking companies.

The process of providing information about profit-seeking entities implicitly assumes that they can be identified and measured. Individual companies must be entities in and of themselves, separate and distinct from both their owners and all other entities. This statement represents the **economic entity assumption,** the first basic assumption of financial accounting. This assumption provides an important foundation on which the financial accounting system is built, and in certain situations it plays a critical role in determining the scope of financial statements.

For example, after Walt Disney acquired the common stock of Capital Cities/ABC, Inc., a major broadcasting company, it included all of ABC's assets and liabilities on its consolidated balance sheet. For financial reporting purposes, therefore, ABC, which publishes its own separate financial statements, is included within the economic entity referred to as The Walt Disney Company. In fact, the consolidated balance sheet of Disney includes the assets and liabilities of many other companies, called *subsidiaries,* each of which prepares its own financial statements. NBC, another major broadcasting company, is owned by General Electric and the cable giant Comcast.

Fortune Brands, Inc. is an entity called a holding company, consisting of many businesses, including Titleist, Master Brand Cabinets, Moen Faucets, and Clos du Bois Wines. The company reports separate financial statements for each business as well as a set of consolidated financial statements. Why might it be useful to maintain separate accounting records for each company? Might there be some difficulties maintaining separate records?

Fiscal Period Assumption

Once the object of measurement has been identified (i.e., the economic entity), we must recognize that to be useful, measures of performance and financial position must be available on a timely basis. Investors, creditors, and other users of financial information need periodic feedback if they are to monitor the performance of management as well as control and direct its decisions.

The need for timely performance measures underlies the **fiscal period assumption,** which states that the operating life of an economic entity can be divided into time periods over which such measures can be developed and applied. Most corporations, for example, prepare annual financial statements, providing yearly feedback and performance measures to their shareholders. The Securities and Exchange Commission requires that publicly traded companies provide financial statements (called *Form 10-Q*) to their shareholders on a quarterly basis.

TIMELY VS. OBJECTIVE FINANCIAL INFORMATION

The fiscal period assumption introduces a trade-off between the timeliness of accounting information and its objectivity. Users need timely information, and thus, they generally prefer fiscal periods that are relatively short. However, as the fiscal period becomes shorter, the applications of certain accounting methods become more arbitrary and subjective. The quarterly accounting reports published by major U.S. corporations, for example, are not audited and are generally more subjective than the audited annual reports. To illustrate, the Form 10-Q report published by Amazon.com, Inc., for the third quarter of 2009, contained the following statement:

We have prepared the accompanying consolidated financial statements pursuant to the rules and regulations of the Securities and Exchange Commission for interim financial reporting. These consolidated financial statements are unaudited.

Cisco Systems and Alcoa have real-time financial information used exclusively for internal decision making. Cisco, for example, has hourly information on revenues, bookings, discounts, and product margins. While certainly there are advantages associated with real-time information systems, can you think of a possible disadvantage?

A CALENDAR YEAR OR FISCAL YEAR?

Another consequence of the fiscal period assumption is that companies must choose the dates of their reporting cycles. Most major U.S. corporations report on the calendar year. That is, they publish an annual report each year as of December 31, and their quarterly statements cover periods ending March 31, June 30, September 30, and

December 31. However, a number of companies report on twelve-month periods, called **fiscal years,** that end on dates other than December 31.[1] In most cases a company chooses a fiscal reporting cycle because its operations are seasonal, and the financial statements are more meaningful if the reporting period includes the entire season.

Large retailers, like Target, Wal-Mart, and Kohl's, for example, often end their fiscal years on January 31, after the completion of the Christmas season. Many companies in the food industry, such as General Mills, prepare annual financial statements in May or June, just after the winter grain crops are harvested. Companies in the farm machinery industries, such as Deere & Co., close their books in September or October, following the summer season when sales are heaviest. Universal Leaf Tobacco, a major processor in the tobacco industry, ends its fiscal year on June 30, immediately after the previous year's tobacco crop has been cured.

Going Concern Assumption

The **going concern assumption** follows logically from the fiscal period assumption. If we assume that an entity's life can be divided into fiscal periods, we must further assume that its life extends beyond the current period. In other words, we assume that the entity will not discontinue operations at the end of the current period over which its performance is being measured. Taken to the extreme, this assumption states that the life of the entity will continue indefinitely.

The role of the going concern assumption in financial accounting is as fundamental as the definition of an asset. Recall that assets are defined to have *future* economic benefit, that is, benefits that extend beyond the current period. The cost of equipment, for example, is placed on the balance sheet because the equipment is expected to provide benefits in the future. The Financial Accounting Standards Board invoked the going concern assumption when, in Statement of Financial Concepts No. 3, it defined assets as "probable *future* economic benefits obtained or controlled by a particular entity as a result of past transactions or events."[2]

> *MarketWatch* reported in April 2007 that Carrington Labs, Inc. had received a "going concern" opinion from its auditors. The opinion was rendered because the company had recorded substantial losses and was in need of additional financing. Why would auditors be concerned about a company's losses and its future prospects? What does financing have to do with a company's ability to operate as a going concern? Why do investors need to know an auditor's opinion about the future viability of a company?

Stable Dollar Assumption

To measure the dimensions, quantity, or capacity of anything requires a unit of measurement. Height and distance, for example, can be measured in terms of inches, feet, centimeters, or meters; volume can be measured in gallons or liters; and weight can be

---

1. According to a survey conducted by the American Institute of Certified Public Accountants, 37 percent of the merchandising and industrial companies in the United States close their books on dates other than December 31.
2. Financial Accounting Standards Board, "Elements of Financial Statements of Business Enterprises," *Statement of Financial Concepts No. 3* (Stamford, Conn.: FASB, December 1980), xi and xii.

measured in pounds or kilograms. Mathematical operations, such as addition or sub-traction, on any such measure require that the unit of measurement maintain a constant definition.

To illustrate, suppose that you weighed yourself at the beginning of the year and found that your weight was 120 pounds. At the end of the year, you weighed yourself again and noted that your weight was 128 pounds. You conclude that you gained 8 pounds during the year, but implicit in this conclusion is the assumption that the def-inition of a pound was the same at the beginning and the end of the year. Had a pound at the beginning of the year equaled 16 ounces, but at the end of the year 15 ounces, for example, you would actually have gained no weight at all. You would have weighed 1,920 ounces at both points in time.

The logical unit of measurement for the financial performance and condition of a company is the monetary unit used in the economic transactions entered into by that company. In the United States, for example, the monetary unit is the dollar. Conse-quently, the financial statements of U.S. companies are expressed in terms of dollars.

The measures of financial performance and position on the financial statements all involve the addition, subtraction, or division of dollar amounts. Total assets on the bal-ance sheet, for example, represent the addition of the dollar values of all the individual assets held by a company at a particular point in time. The ratio of current to total as-sets and the debt/equity ratio involve dividing certain balance sheet dollar amounts by other balance sheet dollar amounts. As with the measures discussed previously, valid use of these mathematical operations requires that the definition of the dollar be con-stant. Thus, a **stable dollar assumption** is implicit in the measures of performance and financial condition used to evaluate and control management's decisions.

INFLATION: THE DOLLAR'S CHANGING PURCHASING POWER

A dollar's value is defined in terms of its **purchasing power,** the amount of goods and services it can buy at a given point in time. During inflation, which has come to be a fact of life, the purchasing power of the dollar decreases steadily. Therefore, financial statements, which are based on the assumption that the purchasing power of the dollar is constant (i.e., no inflation), can be seriously misstated.

Suppose, for example, that on January 1 you have $1,000, and at that time the cost of rice is $1 per bag. You could purchase 1,000 bags of rice, but you decide instead to use the money to purchase (invest in) a small tract of land. During the year, the infla-tion rate is 10 percent. At year-end, the price of the rice is $1.10 per bag, and the value of the land is $1,100. You decide to sell the land, and on your income statement you recognize a gain on the sale of $100 ($1,100 − $1,000). You read your income state-ment and count the cash in your hand and conclude that your economic wealth has in-creased by $100. However, you use the $1,100 to buy rice and you are surprised to learn that it buys only 1,000 bags, the exact amount you could have purchased at the beginning of the year. Consequently, your wealth has not increased at all, even though your income statement indicates otherwise.

Johnson & Johnson reported that sales increased from $61 billion in 2007 to $64 billion in 2008, claiming roughly a 5 percent jump. Yet, during 2008 the con-sumer price index rose by 4 percent, meaning that on average the prices of goods and services increased in 2008 by 4 percent. Comment on Johnson & Johnson's claim.

A LIMITATION IN THE FINANCIAL STATEMENTS

The stable dollar assumption is one instance in which the financial statements are based on an unrealistic assumption. Financial accounting standard–setting bodies have recognized this problem for many years and have attempted to solve it many times. The most recent effort occurred in 1979, when the FASB required certain large U.S. companies to provide information about the effects of inflation in their annual reports. However, this requirement was subsequently rescinded. Companies complained that the disclosures were costly, and financial statement users showed little interest in them, probably because they believed them to be unreliable. It is important that financial statement users at least recognize that this limitation exists and, in some cases, learn how to adjust financial statements for the effects of inflation. Indeed, in some countries inflation continues to be a problem, and under international financial reporting standards (IFRS) financial statements should be restated for the effects of inflation.

> JCPenney's 2008 annual report lists as assets merchandise inventory that was purchased in 2008 and property, plant, and equipment, much of which was acquired many years before 2008 when the dollar's purchasing power was significantly different. Discuss the implications to the users of JCPenney's financial statements.

Summary of Basic Assumptions

Our discussion of the basic assumptions of financial accounting is now complete. In summary, we have assumed the existence of a separate, measurable business entity (economic entity), whose infinite life (going concern) can be broken down into fiscal periods (fiscal period) and whose transactions can be measured in stable dollars (stable dollar). Each of these assumptions is briefly defined in Figure 3–1.

FIGURE 3–1
The basic assumptions of financial accounting

Assumption	Definition
Economic entity	**Profit-seeking entities, which are separate and distinct from their owners and other entities, can be identified and measured.**
Fiscal period	**The life of the economic entity can be divided into fiscal periods, and the performance and financial position of the entity can be measured during each of those periods.**
Going concern	**The life of the economic entity will extend beyond the current fiscal period.**
Stable dollar	**The performance and financial position of the entity can be measured in terms of a monetary unit that maintains constant purchasing power across fiscal periods.**

Now that the basic assumptions of financial accounting have been established, we can explain how dollar amounts are attached to the assets, liabilities, equities, revenues, expenses, and dividends of economic entities. In the course of this explanation, we consider (1) valuations on the balance sheet and (2) the principles of financial accounting measurement.

> **?** While we refer to the fourth assumption as the stable dollar assumption, keep in mind that non-U.S. companies normally prepare their financial statements using a currency other than the dollar. Daimler, a German auto maker, prepares its statements in euros, while Mitsubishi Motors publishes statements expressed in Japanese yen. Comment on how this difference might affect how an analyst would conduct a comparison between the two companies.

VALUATIONS ON THE BALANCE SHEET

The dollar values attached to the accounts on a company's balance sheet are largely determined by the markets in which the company operates. To understand these markets, it is helpful to view a business entity in the following way.

Inputs ⟶ **Entity Operations** ⟶ **Outputs**
(purchase prices)   (sales prices)

A business entity operates in two general markets: an **input market,** where it purchases inputs (e.g., materials, labor) for its operations, and an **output market,** where it sells its outputs (services or inventories). Input market values (prices) are normally less than output market values (prices). For example, local automobile dealers purchase automobiles from manufacturers, such as Toyota, Daimler, and Ford Motor Company, and sell them to consumers. The prices paid for automobiles by dealers in their input market are generally less than the prices paid by consumers in the output market. A new Honda, for example, may cost a dealer $19,000 in the input market and may be sold to you, a customer, for $23,000 in the output market.

Moreover, input and output markets are defined in terms of specific entities: one entity's output market may be another entity's input market. DuPont, for example, supplies complete front and back assemblies for the General Motors cars produced at a GM plant near Kansas City, Missouri. When GM purchases these assemblies, the transaction takes place in the output market of DuPont and the input market of GM.

Viewing a business entity in terms of both its input and output markets introduces a number of different ways to value the accounts on the balance sheet. Should assets, for example, be valued in terms of prices from the input market or prices from the output market—or is there a way to reflect both input and output prices in their valuations? For example, should the value of the Honda on the dealer's balance sheet be expressed in terms of the dealer's input cost ($19,000) or the selling price in the output market ($23,000)?

Four Valuation Bases

Four different **valuation bases** are used to determine the dollar amounts attached to the accounts on the balance sheet. They are (1) present value, (2) fair market value, (3) replacement cost, and (4) original cost. **Present value,** the computation of which is discussed and illustrated in Appendix A at the end of the text, represents the discounted future cash flows associated with a particular financial statement item. The present value of a note receivable, for example, is calculated by determining the amount and timing of its future cash inflows and then adjusting the dollar amounts for the time value of money. **Fair market value (FMV),** or sales price, represents the value of the item in the output market. **Replacement cost,** or current cost, is the current price paid for an item in the input market. **Original cost** represents the input price paid when the item was originally purchased. Figure 3–2 provides definitions of the four valuation bases in terms of an entity's input and output markets.

FIGURE 3–2

Markets and valuation bases

Valuation Bases

1. **Present value—discounted future cash flows from input and output markets**
2. **Fair market value—current sales price in output market**
3. **Replacement cost—current cost to replace in input market**
4. **Original cost—historical cost in input market**

To illustrate, assume that on January 1, Watson Land Developers purchased an apartment building for $100,000, which an outsider recently offered to buy for $140,000. Watson estimates that if it continues to manage the apartment, it would produce net cash flows for the next ten years at a rate of $25,000 per year. The company also recently investigated replacing the apartment building with a comparable structure and learned that it would cost $175,000. The present value, fair market value, replacement cost, and original cost of the apartment building are provided in the following list. In other words, Watson purchased an apartment building for $100,000 that could now be sold for $140,000 and/or replaced for $175,000. Continuing to manage the apartment would produce cash flows of $25,000 per year, which is equivalent to a present value of $153,614.

Present value = **$153,614 ($25,000 × 6.14457*)**
Fair market value = **$140,000**
Replacement cost = **$175,000**
Original cost = **$100,000**

*Present value factor (ten-year ordinary annuity, 10 percent discount rate)

Avis Budget Group, Inc., the parent company of Avis Rental Cars, reports over $7.1 billion worth of vehicles on its balance sheet. Which of the four valuation bases does the $7.1 billion represent? Discuss how Avis could compute the present value, the fair market value, and the replacement cost of its fleet of vehicles, and describe how these different valuations might be considered useful information.

Valuation Bases Used on the Balance Sheet

All four of the valuation bases described in the previous section are contained in balance sheets prepared under generally accepted accounting principles. This point is illustrated in Figure 3–3, which provides a balance sheet with the valuation base for each account indicated in parentheses. The code for each valuation base is located below the balance sheet.

During the financial crisis of 2008–2009, banks and other investment firms had a difficult time establishing the balance sheet value of investment securities made up of subprime home mortgage loans. Regulators and investors wanted the securities shown at "market value," though many of the securities could not be sold for any price due to the underlying uncertainty of the subprime mortgages that comprised the investments. These "toxic assets," as they became known, were difficult to value in the market because, in effect, no market existed for their sale. In this situation, should the bank's balance indicate a value of zero for these investments, or would it be better to value them on the balance sheet at what the bank paid for the investments?

FIGURE 3-3

Valuation bases
on the
balance sheet

Harbour Island Company
Balance Sheet
December 31, 2011

ASSETS

Current assets:		
Cash	$ 220 (FMV)	
Short-term investments	150 (FMV)	
Accounts receivable	345 (FMV)	
Inventory	600 (LCM)	
Prepaid expenses	100 (OC)	
Total current assets		$ 1,415
Long-term investments:		
Long-term notes receivable	$1,000 (PV)	
Land	500 (OC)	
Securities	2,500 (OC)	
Total long-term investments		4,000
Property, plant, and equipment:		
Property	$6,000 (OC)	
Plant	2,900 (OC)	
Equipment	2,600 (OC)	
Total property, plant, and equipment		11,500
Intangible assets:		
Patent	$1,000 (OC)	
Trademark	700 (OC)	
Total intangible assets		1,700
Total assets		**$18,615**

LIABILITIES AND SHAREHOLDERS' EQUITY

Current liabilities:		
Accounts payable	$ 200 (FMV)	
Wages payable	150 (FMV)	
Interest payable	30 (FMV)	
Short-term notes payable	200 (FMV)	
Other payables	60 (FMV)	
Unearned revenues	30 (FMV)	
Dividends payable	70 (FMV)	
Total current liabilities		$ 740
Long-term liabilities:		
Long-term notes payable	$1,500 (PV)	
Bonds payable	3,500 (PV)	
Mortgage payable	1,940 (PV)	
Total long-term liabilities		6,940
Shareholders' equity		10,935
Total liabilities and shareholders' equity		**$18,615**

Valuation base code: FMV = fair market value; LCM = lower of cost or market; OC = original cost; PV = present value.

Cash and all current liabilities are valued using a specific form of fair market value called **face value.** This valuation reflects the cash expected to be received or paid in the near future. The statement of cash flows, which explains changes in the cash account, is completely expressed in terms of face value. Short-term investments are valued at fair market value. Accounts receivable are valued at **net realizable value,** another form of fair market value reflecting the amount of cash expected to be collected from the outstanding accounts. Inventories are valued at original cost or replacement cost, whichever is lower. This example of the conservative **lower-of-cost-or-market rule,** which ensures that the dollar value of this account is not overstated, illustrates that under certain circumstances replacement costs are found on the balance sheet.

Land, securities held as long-term investments,[3] and property used in a company's operations are all valued at original cost unadjusted for amortization or depreciation. Prepaid expenses, plant and equipment, and all intangible assets are carried on the balance sheet at their original costs **(historical costs),** reduced by accumulated amortization or depreciation. This adjusted cost dollar value is often referred to as *net book value.*[4]

Long-term notes receivable and long-term liabilities are valued at present value. The dollar amount attached to each of these accounts is calculated by determining the amount and timing of the future cash flows associated with the account and adjusting the dollar amounts for the time value of money (see Appendix A).

Technically, the shareholders' equity section of the balance sheet is not valued in terms of any valuation base. It represents the residual interests of the shareholders or the book value of the company, or the total investment made by the shareholders in the business. The shareholders' equity section can be viewed as the difference between the total balance sheet value of the company's assets and the total balance sheet value of the company's liabilities.

So far we have assumed that economic entities can be identified and measured, their infinite lives can be divided into fiscal periods, and their performance and financial position can be measured in terms of stable dollars. We have also observed that a number of different valuation bases (present value, fair market value, replacement cost, and original cost) are used to determine the dollar amounts of the accounts on the balance sheet. The next section presents the principles of financial accounting measurement, which explain why particular valuation bases are used for some accounts and not for others and how the valuation bases are used to measure net income.

> **?** Take a quick look at the 2009 balance sheet published by NIKE in Appendix C. Note the asset items and consider the valuation base used in each case.

THE PRINCIPLES OF FINANCIAL ACCOUNTING MEASUREMENT

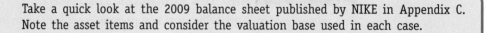

There are four basic principles of financial accounting measurement: (1) objectivity, (2) matching, (3) revenue recognition, and (4) consistency.

3. A special method, called the equity method, is used to value certain long-term equity investments on the balance sheet. This method is based on the original cost of the investment, but certain additional adjustments to original cost are made periodically. This method is discussed and illustrated in Chapter 8, which covers long-term investments.
4. Net book value can be applied to an individual balance sheet item, or to the company as a whole, where it is equal to total assets less total liabilities.

The Principle of Objectivity

Financial accounting information provides useful measures of performance and financial position. In doing so, financial accounting statements must provide information about value: the value of entire companies, the value of company assets and liabilities, and the value of the specific transactions entered into by companies.

The economic value of an entity, an asset, or a liability is its present value, which reflects both the future cash flows associated with the entity, asset, or liability and the time value of money.[5] There is, however, one critical problem with the present value calculation: It assumes that future interest rates and future cash flows are perfectly predictable. This assumption presents no problems in theory, but users of accounting measures of performance and financial position need reliable measures that can be audited at reasonable costs.

For example, Union Carbide Corporation, a subsidiary of the Dow Chemical Company, annually invests millions in new plant assets. Reporting this investment on the company's balance sheet at present value would require an estimate of the net future cash flows generated by the new facilities, as well as an estimate of future interest rates. Such estimates, which would be the responsibility of the company's management, are simply too subjective for the financial statements. Auditors would be unwilling and unable to verify these subjective judgments, and the legal liability faced by both managers and auditors would make such verification potentially very costly.

The principle of **objectivity,** which is perhaps the most important and pervasive principle of accounting measurement, states that financial accounting information must be verifiable and reliable. It requires that the values of transactions and of the assets and liabilities created by them be objectively determined and backed by documented evidence. Although it ensures that the dollar amounts disclosed on the financial statements are reasonably reliable, the principle of objectivity also precludes much relevant and useful information from ever appearing on the financial statements.

> **?** Many companies are valuable because they have knowledge not possessed by other companies, often referred to as intellectual property rights. While most believe that these assets have value, they do not appear on the companies' balance sheets. Why not?

PRESENT VALUE AND THE FINANCIAL STATEMENTS

The principle of objectivity ensures that present value cannot be used as the valuation base for all assets and liabilities. In some cases, however, the future cash flows associated with certain assets and liabilities are predictable enough to allow for sufficiently objective present value calculations. Suppose, for example, that on December 31, The Boeing Company received payment from United Airlines for an order of jumbo jets in the form of a note receivable. The note states that United will pay Boeing $1 million at the end of each year for the next two years. Certainly, this note should appear as an asset (receivable) on Boeing's December 31 balance sheet and as a payable on the balance sheet of United, but at what dollar amount should it be reported?

If we assume a discount rate of 10 percent and realize that the note is actually a two-period $1 million cash flow, we can use the present value calculation to

5. The following discussion assumes that you understand the present value calculation. If not, refer to Appendix A at the end of the text.

P. 719

place a value on the note ($1.735 million = $1 million × 1.735 [Table 5: $n = 2$, $i = 10\%$]).[6] Furthermore, the auditors of Boeing and United would be willing to attest to this valuation because the future cash flows are objectively determined in a legal contract, entered into and signed by both Boeing and United in an *arm's-length transaction*. The auditors for the most part are protected from legal liability because the responsibility to provide the contractual payments rests with United. The result is that a $1.735 million note receivable would appear on Boeing's balance sheet and a $1.735 million note payable would appear on United's balance sheet. In this case, present value would be used to provide a balance sheet value for both an asset and a liability.

In general, present value is used on the financial statements only in those cases where future cash flows can be objectively determined. As illustrated, contractual agreements like notes receivable and payable represent cases that meet this criterion. Mortgages, bonds, leases, and pensions are other examples of contracts that underlie cash flows and remove much of the subjectivity associated with cash flow prediction.

Refer again to the balance sheet in Figure 3–3, and note that present value is used as the valuation base for long-term notes receivable, long-term notes payable, bonds payable, and mortgages payable.

> **?** The FASB has issued a standard that sets the parameters for deciding when and how to use present value to determine the fair market value of an asset or a liability when the amount or timing of future cash flows is uncertain. Comment on trade-offs that might be introduced by such a standard.

MARKET VALUE AND THE FINANCIAL STATEMENTS

Using market value (i.e., fair market value or replacement cost) as a valuation base for the accounts on the financial statements can be attractive because, in many cases, market value represents the best estimate of present value. If, for example, buyers and sellers in a given market use their individual estimates of present value when bidding on an asset, the resulting market price of the asset should approximate its actual present value. In addition, fair market value is often more objective than present value. Market prices for the equity securities of major U.S. companies, for example, are listed on public stock exchanges and can therefore be objectively verified. To illustrate, the market price of a share of DuPont common stock as of the end of trading on January 10, 2010, was $34.01.

Unfortunately, while market values are sometimes objectively determinable, in most situations they are not objective enough for use in the financial statements. The market values of securities that are not traded on the major stock exchanges, most inventories, long-term investments, property, plant, and equipment, and intangible assets are not easily determined. The market values of such items may be very informative, but they fail to meet the principle of objectivity.

Refer again to the balance sheet in Figure 3–3, and note that market values are used in the valuation of relatively few accounts. Short-term investments are valued at fair market value, accounts receivable are valued at net realizable value, which approximates fair market value, and inventories are valued at original cost or market value, whichever is lower.

6. Table 5 appears at the end of Appendix A, located at the end of the text.

ORIGINAL COST AND THE FINANCIAL STATEMENTS

Note also in Figure 3–3 that the remaining accounts on the balance sheet (prepaid expenses, land, securities, property, plant, and equipment, and intangible assets) are valued at original cost, the price paid when the asset was originally acquired, or net book value, which is original cost adjusted for depreciation or amortization. Original costs can be objectively verified and supported by documented evidence. They are reliable, can be audited at reasonable cost, and do not violate the principle of objectivity.

Under IFRS, unlike U.S. GAAP, companies are allowed in certain situations to value property, plant, and equipment and intangible assets at fair market value. What does this difference imply about the role of the principle of objectivity under the two systems?

The Principles of Matching and Revenue Recognition

Objectivity is the most pervasive principle of financial accounting. It affects all areas of measurement, including operating performance, which is the focus of the matching and revenue recognition principles.

The **matching** principle, which states that the efforts of a given period should be matched against the benefits that result from them, underlies the measures of operating performance. It is initiated when a company incurs a cost (e.g., pays wages, purchases equipment, invests in a security) to generate benefits, normally in the form of revenues.[7] If the revenues are generated immediately, the cost is treated as an expense, appearing on the income statement of the current period. If the revenues are expected to be realized in future periods, the cost is considered an asset, or capitalized, and appears on the balance sheet. In future periods, as the revenues are realized, the assets are converted to expenses appearing on the income statements of the future periods. Thus, costs incurred to generate revenues are matched against those revenues in the time periods in which the revenues are realized. This process produces a periodic measure of net income, or company performance.

The most critical question in the matching process, as described in Figure 3–4, occurs at Step 2: In what time period will the revenue be realized? The cost incurred in Step 1 cannot be treated as an expense, and the matching principle cannot be applied until this question is answered. The answer, unfortunately, is not always obvious because there are many possibilities. The principle of **revenue recognition** provides the guidelines for answering this question.

To understand the principle of revenue recognition, it is helpful to view the selling of a good or a service as involving the four steps illustrated in Figure 3–5. A good or service is (1) ordered, (2) produced, (3) transferred to the buyer, and then (4) paid for by the buyer. These four steps make a complete production/sales cycle.

The principle of revenue recognition helps to determine at which of these four points the revenue from the sale of a good or service should be recognized on the income statement. The most common point of revenue recognition is Step 3, when the good or service is transferred to the buyer. At this point, a company has normally completed the earning process and is entitled to recognize the revenue. Yet, there are times when each of the other steps may be the point at which revenue should be

7. Benefits can also be in the form of cost savings.

FIGURE 3–4   Income measurement via revenue recognition and matching

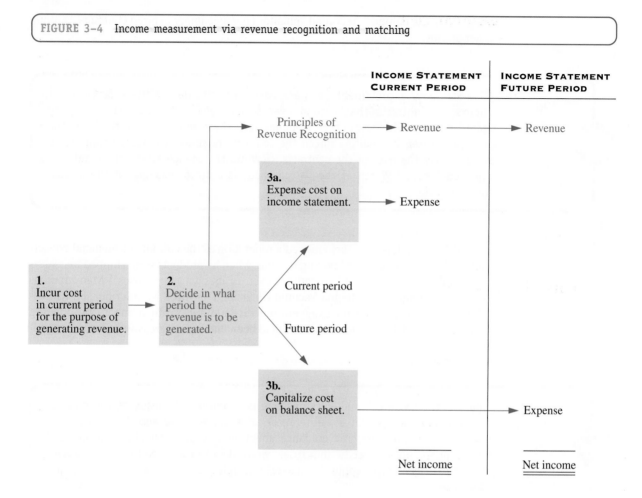

recognized. The principle of revenue recognition states that four criteria must be met before revenue can be included in the income statement:

1. The company has completed a significant portion of the production and sales effort.
2. The amount of revenue can be objectively measured.
3. In the case of physical goods, if the title has transferred; and in the case of a service, if the service has been performed.
4. The eventual collection of the cash is reasonably assured.

While these guidelines are helpful, defining the point in time when all four criteria are met still requires much judgment and can be very important because it often dramatically affects the dollar amounts on the financial statements.

In a story reported in the *Wall Street Journal*, for example, the SEC investigated Gemstar-TV Guide International, Inc. for improperly booking revenue. The investigation

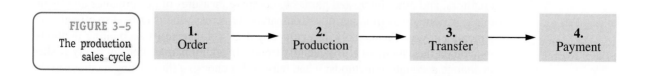

FIGURE 3–5
The production
sales cycle

| 1. Order | 2. Production | 3. Transfer | 4. Payment |

alleges that the company recorded "phantom revenue under expired contracts," among other abuses.

MicroStrategy, a prominent software company, provides software services for clients on contracts that extend over several years. At first, the company recorded the entire amount of revenue from these multiyear contracts in the first year. Later, its auditors forced the company to spread the recognition of the revenue over the lives of the contracts. How did the change affect MicroStrategy's reported income? Which of the two methods is a better example of the matching process?

IBM, which has for years enjoyed a reputation as the epitome of financial conservatism, has been cited "for booking revenue when its products were shipped to dealers who could return them and sometimes even to its own warehouses." Many famous accounting frauds (e.g., Regina Vacuum Cleaners, Phar-Mor, MiniScribe, and Knowledge Ware) were based on exaggerating revenue and profit numbers by creating fictitious sales. Blockbuster Video has also been cited for aggressive revenue recognition practices.

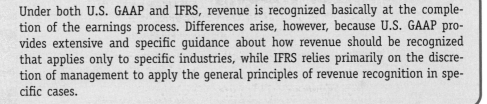

Under both U.S. GAAP and IFRS, revenue is recognized basically at the completion of the earnings process. Differences arise, however, because U.S. GAAP provides extensive and specific guidance about how revenue should be recognized that applies only to specific industries, while IFRS relies primarily on the discretion of management to apply the general principles of revenue recognition in specific cases.

The Principle of Consistency

Generally accepted accounting principles allow a number of different, acceptable methods to be used to account for the assets, liabilities, revenues, expenses, and dividends on the financial statements. For example, several acceptable methods may be used to account for each of the following assets: accounts receivable, inventories, long-term investments, and fixed assets. Such variety exists for two reasons: (1) No method is general enough to apply to all companies in all situations and (2) generally accepted accounting principles are the result of a political process in which interested parties who face widely different situations are allowed and encouraged to provide input.

The principle of **consistency** states that, although there is considerable choice among methods, companies should choose a set of methods and use them from one period to the next. Its primary economic rationale is that consistency helps investors, creditors, and other interested parties to compare measures of performance and financial position across time periods. Comparability across time is critical to effective financial analysis. Presumably, if a company does not change its accounting methods, outside parties can more easily identify trends. In addition, management rarely wishes to change accounting methods; it had reasons for choosing the existing methods in the

first place, and changing from one method to another could be viewed by outsiders as an attempt to manipulate the financial statements, reducing credibility.

Although consistency is important, it does not mean that companies never change accounting methods. If management can convince the independent auditor that the environment facing the company has changed to the point that an alternative accounting method is appropriate, the company is allowed to switch. However, such changes are not easily granted, and when approved, the effects of the change on the financial statements are clearly disclosed. The change is described in the footnotes and mentioned in the auditor's report, and prior years' financial standards are restated to maintain comparability. It also happens that the FASB mandates certain accounting method changes. In such cases the FASB provides guidelines regarding how the change should be implemented.

In 2005 Boeing, Duke Energy, and Amazon.com made accounting changes for a variety of items. In each case, (1) the financial effect of the change was reported on the income statement; (2) the change was described in the footnotes; and (3) an entire paragraph in the audit report was devoted to describing the changes.

> **?** During America Online's period of tremendous growth, the company, previously part of Time Warner, capitalized (treated as assets) all costs associated with acquiring new customers. The company subsequently changed its treatment to expense all such costs. This accounting change had a dramatic effect on the financial statements. Where in the annual report could an investor find information about this accounting change?

TWO EXCEPTIONS TO THE BASIC PRINCIPLES: MATERIALITY AND CONSERVATISM

Under certain circumstances, the costs of applying the principles of accounting exceed the benefits. In these situations, management is allowed (and, in some cases, required) to depart from the principles. All rules have exceptions, even the measurement principles of financial accounting. Two important exceptions are materiality and conservatism.

Materiality

Materiality states that only those transactions dealing with dollar amounts large enough to make a difference to financial statement users need be accounted for in a manner consistent with the principles of financial accounting. The dollar amounts of some transactions are so small that the method of accounting has virtually no impact on the financial statements and, thus, no effect on the related evaluations and control decisions. In such cases, the least costly method of reporting is chosen, regardless of the method suggested by the principles of accounting measurement. The dollar amounts of these transactions are referred to as immaterial, and management is allowed to account for them as expediently as possible.

For example, the matching principle indicates that the cost of a wastebasket should be included on the balance sheet and converted to expense over future periods because its usefulness is expected to extend beyond the current period. However, the cost of an individual wastebasket is probably immaterial, and it is costly in terms of management's

time and effort to carry such items on the books. For practical reasons, therefore, the purchase price is immediately treated as an expense. Granted, such treatment misstates income for both the current period and the future periods of the wastebasket's useful life. This misstatement, however, is extremely small (i.e., immaterial) and would have no bearing on the decisions of those who use the financial statements. In this case, the costs of capitalizing and depreciating the purchase price of the wastebasket simply exceed the benefits it would provide.

While materiality is practical, it represents a major problem area in accounting because it requires judgments that can differ considerably among investors, creditors, managers, auditors, and others. The U.S. Supreme Court has provided one of the few guidelines, defining a material item as one to which "there is substantial likelihood that a reasonable investor would attach importance in determining whether to purchase a security."

For many years, companies used *quantitative* (objective) methods to determine the materiality of a financial statement item (e.g., 5 percent of net income). The SEC has issued a statement eliminating that practice, requiring instead the use of *qualitative* analysis when determining whether a reported item is material. In this context, what is the difference between quantitative and qualitative analysis?

In determining materiality, the size of an item is always considered, but whether it would affect the decisions of an investor or creditor is often unclear. A dollar amount that is too small to make a difference in a large company may be very significant in a small company, and not only must the size of an item be considered, but its nature can also be important. A small adjustment to the inventory account, for example, may be far more significant to financial statement users than a large adjustment to an account in the shareholders' equity section of the balance sheet. What about a very small accounting adjustment that allows a company to just achieve its earnings forecast? Would that be considered immaterial? Finally, the user must be considered. A creditor's definition of materiality, for example, may be very different from that of an investor.

In summary, materiality is an important and practical exception to the principles of financial accounting measurement. The standard unqualified auditor's report states that "the financial statements are free of material misstatement." Materiality is, nonetheless, very ambiguous. As stated in *Forbes*, "Too often, investors miss important information because companies deem it 'immaterial.' What does this mean? Nobody knows—and that's a big problem." The article goes on to report that Rockwell International, a multibillion-dollar conglomerate, chose not to disclose a loss that could have been as large as $220 million because it was considered "immaterial."

The principle of consistency and the concept of materiality are treated very similarly under U.S. GAAP and IFRS.

Conservatism

Another important exception to the principles of financial accounting measurement is conservatism. Like materiality, conservatism is practical and has evolved over time in response to cost/benefit considerations. In its simplest form, **conservatism** states that, *when in doubt,* financial statements should understate assets, overstate liabilities, accelerate the recognition of losses, and delay the recognition of gains.

Conservatism does not suggest, however, that the financial statements should be intentionally understated. When objective and verifiable evidence about a material transaction is given, the principles of accounting measurement should be followed, and no attempt should be made to intentionally understate assets or overstate liabilities. Only when there is significant uncertainty about the value of a transaction should the most conservative alternative be chosen.

The economic rationale for conservatism is partially driven by the liability associated with overstating incorrectly the financial condition and performance of a company. Jeffrey Block, a well-known attorney, has observed many lawsuits against firms that have overstated earnings. As he stated for the *Boston Globe,* "The lesson from all these cases is for executives to be more upfront and disclose negative news to shareholders a lot earlier."

There are many examples of conservatism in the financial statements. The lower-of-cost-or-market rule, which is used to value inventories, has already been mentioned in this chapter and is perhaps the most evident example. Others are discussed as they arise later in the text.

There is evidence that extreme forms of conservatism were practiced for many years by non-U.S. companies, and that specific-country reporting rules in some cases actually encouraged intentional understatements of earnings and assets as well as overstatements of obligations. While such practices are more difficult now that IFRS is being used, many believe that the additional discretion available to management under IFRS, relative to U.S. GAAP, is still used to reduce reported earnings, especially in high-performing years. Consider, for example, Unilever (see financial statements at the end of Chapter 2), which booked a special expense in each of fiscal 2007, 2008, and 2009 (called restructuring), totaling over 2.5 billion euros. In the footnotes, Unilever explains that these charges relate in many cases to plant closings and employee layoffs that will be implemented in the future. Comment.

INTERNATIONAL PERSPECTIVE: FUNDAMENTAL DIFFERENCES BETWEEN U.S. GAAP AND IFRS

The assumptions, principles, and exceptions discussed in this chapter that form the basis for U.S. GAAP also underlie IFRS. Economic entity, objectivity, matching, revenue recognition, consistency, and conservatism, as well as the others, are all important in the preparation of IFRS-based financial reports, and the overlap between the two systems is much greater than the departures. However, some important differences do exist, and they tend to result from differences in how these concepts are applied to individual situations.

U.S. GAAP and IFRS differ in two fundamental ways. First, IFRS is more "principles-based" while U.S. GAAP tends to be more "rules-based." U.S. GAAP is

characterized by more "bright line" rules. Under U.S. GAAP, for example, there are different rules for revenue recognition for different industries, while IFRS tends to rely on a single basic revenue recognition standard. Similarly, accounting for leases under U.S. GAAP contains specific criteria for the recognition of assets and liabilities; under IFRS, the lease standard is much more general and open-ended. This basic difference leads to greater levels of required disclosure under U.S. GAAP, and most managers would agree that it is more difficult and costly to comply with the reporting requirements under U.S. GAAP. IFRS, on the other hand, generally leaves more discretion to management when choosing how to account for transactions, and relies on management's judgment to find the method resulting in financial statements that depict the company's financial performance and condition in a "true and fair" manner.

A second fundamental way in which the two systems differ is related to the manner in which asset values are carried on the balance sheet. Under U.S. GAAP, the principle of objectivity ensures that fair market values are not used unless they can be objectively determined. Thus, assets such as inventory, long-term investments, property, plant, and equipment, and intangibles tend to be carried on the balance sheet at historical cost. When the values of these assets change, the concept of conservatism dictates that fair market value is used only if it is below historical cost, which means that the balance sheet values of these assets can be reduced when their fair market values drop, but they are never increased—even when their fair market values rise.

IFRS seems less dependent on the principle of objectivity and the concept of conservatism. In many more situations, IFRS allows adjustments to the balance sheet values of assets like long-term investments, property, plant, and equipment, inventories, and certain intangible assets. In addition, under IFRS these assets can be adjusted to reflect changes in market value both downward and upward. Combined with the additional discretion available under IFRS, being able to adjust assets to their market values gives management more power to subjectively influence the financial statements, power that can be used to either enlighten or confuse investors. This fact helps to explain why the SEC has been relatively slow to accept IFRS-based financial statements.

The differences described above reflect general tendencies, and there are some instances where they may not be completely descriptive. We will address those cases as they arise in the text.

SUMMARY OF KEY POINTS

 Four basic assumptions of financial accounting.

The four basic assumptions of financial accounting are (1) the economic entity assumption, (2) the fiscal period assumption, (3) the going concern assumption, and (4) the stable dollar assumption. The economic entity assumption states that a company is a separate economic entity that can be identified and measured. The fiscal period assumption states that the life of an economic entity can be broken down into fiscal periods. The going concern assumption states that the life of an economic entity is indefinite. The stable dollar assumption states that the value of the monetary unit used to measure an economic entity's financial performance and position is stable across time.

 The markets in which business entities operate and the valuation bases used on the balance sheet.

A business entity operates in two general markets: an input market, where it purchases inputs for its operations; and an output market, where it sells the outputs that result from its operations. The four valuation bases (present value, fair market value, replacement cost, and original cost) can be defined in terms of these two markets.

The present value of an asset or liability represents the discounted future cash flows associated with the asset or liability. Fair market value represents the sales price in the output market. Replacement costs (or current costs) are the current prices paid in the input market. Original costs are the input prices paid when the input was originally purchased.

The financial statements contain a wide variety of valuation bases. Face value is used to value cash and short-term liabilities. Short-term investments are carried at fair market value, and inventories are valued at the lower of cost or market. Accounts receivable are valued at net realizable value, a form of market value. Notes receivable, notes payable, and most long-term liabilities are valued at present value. Prepaid expenses, fixed assets, and intangible assets are valued at original cost less an adjustment for depreciation or amortization.

⬤ *The principle of objectivity and how it determines the dollar values that appear on the financial statements.*

The principle of objectivity requires that the values of transactions and the assets and liabilities created by them be verifiable and backed by documentation. It ensures that present value is reported on the financial statements only in cases, such as contracts, where future cash flows can be objectively determined. It also ensures that market values such as fair market value and replacement costs, which are often difficult to objectively determine, are rarely reported on the financial statements (e.g., marketable securities and the lower-of-cost-or-market rule applied to inventories). Objectivity also ensures that many accounts on the financial statements are valued at original costs.

⬤ *The principles of matching, revenue recognition, and consistency.*

The matching principle states that the efforts of a given period should be matched against the benefits they generate. In determining net income, benefits are usually represented as revenues, and efforts are represented by expenses, which cannot be matched against revenues until the revenues have been recognized. The principle of revenue recognition determines when revenues can be recognized. In short, the principle of revenue recognition triggers the matching principle, which in turn is necessary for determining the measure of performance. The principle of consistency states that accounting methods should be consistent across time.

⬤ *Two exceptions to the principles of financial accounting measurement: materiality and conservatism.*

Two important exceptions to the principles of financial accounting measurement are materiality and conservatism. Materiality suggests that the principles of financial accounting measurement can be violated if the dollar amount involved in a particular transaction is so small that it would not affect the decisions of financial statement users. Conservatism guides accountants, when in doubt, to understate assets, overstate liabilities, accelerate the recognition of losses, and delay the recognition of gains. These two exceptions guide departures from the principles of financial accounting measurement when the costs of following them exceed the benefits. Conservatism, in particular, makes economic sense because the legal liability facing auditors and managers imposes a high potential cost on errors due to overstating assets or understating liabilities.

⬤ *Fundamental differences between U.S. GAAP and IFRS.*

U.S. GAAP and IFRS differ in two fundamental ways. IFRS is more "principles-based" while U.S. GAAP tends to be more "rules-based." This basic difference leads to greater levels of required disclosure under U.S. GAAP, and it is more difficult and costly to comply with the reporting requirements under U.S. GAAP. IFRS generally leaves more discretion to management when choosing how to account for transactions. In addition, under U.S. GAAP, the principle of objectivity ensures that fair market values are not used unless they can be objectively determined, and the concept of conservatism dictates that fair market value is used only if it is below historical cost. IFRS allows adjustments to the balance sheet values of assets for changes in market value, and these adjustments can be upward or downward.

KEY TERMS

Note: Definitions for these terms are provided in the glossary at the end of the text.

Conservatism (p. 95)
Consistency (p. 92)
Economic entity assumption (p. 79)
Face value (p. 87)
Fair market value (FMV) (p. 84)
Fiscal period assumption (p. 80)
Fiscal years (p. 81)
Going concern assumption (p. 81)
Historical costs (p. 87)
Input market (p. 84)
Lower-of-cost-or-market rule (p. 87)
Matching (p. 90)

Materiality (p. 93)
Net realizable value (p. 87)
Objectivity (p. 88)
Original cost (p. 84)
Output market (p. 84)
Present value (p. 84)
Purchasing power (p. 82)
Replacement cost (p. 84)
Revenue recognition (p. 90)
Stable dollar assumption (p. 82)
Valuation bases (p. 84)

ETHICS in the Real World

Microsoft Corporation changed its accounting for the sale of operating systems when it released Vista in 2007. The company now recognizes all revenue when a copy of Vista is sold; in previous years the company withheld a portion of revenue to be recognized in future periods when software updates were made available to customers. Historically, Microsoft lobbied the FASB and SEC to support strict guidelines for revenue recognition for software companies, but the company now has adopted some of the aggressive policies it had previously decried.

ETHICAL ISSUE Is Microsoft acting ethically when it changes its position on an important financial accounting principle? Discuss the implication of market forces on Microsoft's decisions.

INTERNET RESEARCH EXERCISE

Find the most recent Form 10-K filed by Microsoft with the Securities and Exchange Commission. Briefly describe the contents of the form, and identify the net income, total assets, and net cash from operations reported by the company. Begin your search at www.sec.gov and use the EDGAR Database provided by the SEC. The database offers a complete listing of the filings required by the SEC for publicly traded companies.

BRIEF EXERCISES

REAL DATA

BE3–1

Accounting assumptions, principles, and exceptions

The following excerpts were taken from the annual reports of a variety of companies:

1. The company's reporting period ends on the Saturday closest to January 31 (The Limited).
2. The consolidated financial statements include the accounts of Federal Express and its wholly owned subsidiaries (Federal Express).

3. Inventories are valued primarily at the lower of cost or market value (JCPenney).
4. Certain reclassifications have been made for prior years to conform with this year's presentation (Wendy's International).
5. Revenues from the distribution of motion pictures are recognized when motion pictures are exhibited (Walt Disney).
6. In an ongoing investigation, the Antitrust Division of the U.S. Department of Justice requested information from Microsoft concerning various issues. Management currently believes that resolving these matters will not have a material adverse impact on the company's financial position or operations (Microsoft).
7. Flight equipment is depreciated on a straight-line basis over a 20-year useful life (Delta Air Lines).
8. Intangible assets are carried on the balance sheet at cost (Merck).
9. Property and equipment are recorded at cost (Apple, Inc.).
10. Inflation rates, even though moderate in many parts of the world, continue to have an effect on worldwide economies but have had no effect on the company's reported financial position and performance (Johnson & Johnson).

Match each of the ten assumptions, principles, and exceptions below with one of the ten excerpts.

Assumptions	Principles	Exceptions
Economic entity	Objectivity	Materiality
Stable dollar	Matching	Conservatism
Fiscal period	Revenue recognition	
Going concern	Consistency	

EXERCISES

REAL DATA

E3–1

The effects of inflation on holding cash

Recently Boeing has maintained a cash balance of over $6 billion. At an annual inflation rate of about 2 percent, does cash have more or less purchasing power at the end of a given year than at the beginning? By how much? Is such a gain or loss reflected on the company's financial statements? Why or why not? Why would Boeing want to keep its cash balance as low as possible? Why doesn't the company reduce its cash balance to zero?

E3–2

The effects of inflation on holding land

Palomar Paper Products purchased land in 1993 for $15,000 cash. The company has held the land since that time. In 2011 Palomar purchased another tract of land for $15,000 cash. Assume that prices in general increased by 60 percent from 1993 to 2011.

a. Assuming that Palomar made only these two land purchases, what dollar amount would appear in the land account on Palomar's balance sheet as of December 31, 2011?
b. Palomar used $15,000 cash to make each land purchase. Would $15,000 in 1993 buy the same amount of goods and services as $15,000 in 2011? If not, how much more or less, and why?
c. Explain how one could adjust the dollar amount reported in the land account as of December 31, 2011, if the stable dollar assumption were dropped.

E3–3

Valuation bases on the balance sheet

Name the valuation base(s) that are used for each of the asset and liability accounts shown here. Some assets and liabilities can use more than one valuation base.

	Original Cost	Fair Market Value (FMV)	Present Value	Replacement Cost
Cash				
Short-term investments				
Inventories				
Prepaid expenses				
Long-term investments				
Notes receivable				
Machinery				
Equipment				
Land				
Intangible assets				
Short-term payables				
Long-term payables				

REAL DATA

E3–4

Fundamentals of inventory valuation

The 2009 annual report for Cisco Systems contains the following information (dollars in millions):

	7/25/2009	7/26/2008
Inventory	**$1,074**	**$1,235**

On the income statement Cisco reported that the cost of sales related to the inventory was $10.5 billion ($11.7 billion for the year ending 7/26/2008). Based on these dollar amounts, inventory is an important investment for Cisco's business cycle. In the notes to the financial statements the company reports, "Inventories are stated at the lower of cost or market. . . . The Company provides inventory write-downs based on excess and obsolete inventories determined primarily by future demand forecast. The write-down is measured as the difference between the cost of the inventory and market based upon assumptions about future demand and charged to . . . cost of sales."

a. Explain what would happen to the balance sheet value of inventory ($1.074 billion in the year ending 7/25/2009) if the company determined that a portion of its inventory was "obsolete."

b. Who is ultimately responsible for determining the forecast for future demand for the company's inventories?

c. Discuss how the concepts of objectivity, conservatism, and market value enter into how Cisco values its inventory on the balance sheet.

E3–5

Revenue recognition

Cascades Enterprises ordered 4,000 brackets from McKey and Company on December 1, 2011, for a contracted price of $40,000. McKey completed manufacturing the brackets on January 17 of the next year and delivered them to Cascades on February 9. McKey received a check for $40,000 from Cascades on March 14.

a. Assume that McKey and Company prepares monthly income statements. In which month should McKey recognize the $40,000 revenue from the sale?

b. Justify your answer in (a) in terms of the four criteria of revenue recognition.

c. Are there conditions under which the revenue could be recognized in a different month than the month you chose in (a)?

d. Provide several reasons why McKey's management might be interested in the timing of the recognition of revenue.

E3–6

The effects on income of different methods of revenue recognition

Lahmont Bridge Builders built a bridge for the state of Maryland over a two-year period. The contracted price for the bridge was $600,000. The costs incurred by Lahmont and the payments from the state of Maryland over the two-year period follow.

	Period 1	Period 2	Total
Costs incurred by Lahmont	**$300,000**	**$100,000**	**$400,000**
Payments from Maryland	400,000	200,000	600,000

a.   Prepare income statements for Lahmont for the two periods under the following
     assumptions:
     (1) Revenue is recognized at the end of the project.
     (2) Revenue is recognized in proportion to the costs incurred by Lahmont.
     (3) Revenue is recognized when the payments are received.
b.   Calculate the total net income over the two-year period under each assumption.

E3–7

Assets and
depreciation—
which assumption
sand principle?

RDP and Brothers purchased a panel truck for $25,000 on January 1, 2011. It estimated the
life of the truck to be five years, and it planned to depreciate an equal amount in each of the
five years.

a.   In line with generally accepted accounting principles, determine the amounts required here.

	2011	**2012**	**2013**	**2014**	**2015**
Original cost					
Depreciation expense					
Accumulated depreciation					
Net book value					

b.   Why did you decide to initially recognize the cost as an asset rather than treat it as an
     expense? What basic assumption of financial accounting are you relying upon in this
     decision?
c.   Why did you allocate a portion of the cost to each of the five years? What basic princi-
     ple of financial accounting measurement are you relying upon in this decision?

E3–8

The concept of
materiality

All large U.S. companies have policies in which all expenditures under a certain dollar amount
are expensed. Many of these expenditures are for assets, items that are useful to the company
beyond the period in which they were purchased.

a.   Explain the proper accounting treatment for expenditures for items that are expected to
     generate benefits in the future.
b.   Explain why it might make economic sense to expense some of these items. Upon what
     exception to the principles of financial accounting would such a decision be based?

E3–9

Changing
accounting methods
and net income

The net income amounts for Hauser and Bradley over the four-year period beginning in 2009
follow.

2009	**2010**	**2011**	**2012**
$21,000	**$24,000**	**$23,000**	**$29,000**

After further examination of the financial report, you note that Hauser and Bradley made
accounting method changes in 2010 and 2012, which affected net income in those periods.
In 2010, the company changed depreciation methods. This change increased the book value
of its fixed assets in each subsequent year by $5,000. In 2012, the company adopted a new
inventory method that increased the book value of the inventory by $9,000.

a.   Calculate the effect of each of these changes on net income in the year of the change.
b.   Prepare a chart that compares net income across the four-year period, assuming that
     Hauser and Bradley made no accounting changes. How would your assessment of the
     company's performance change after you learned of the accounting method changes?
c.   What principle of financial accounting makes it difficult to make such changes? Describe
     the conditions under which Hauser and Bradley would be allowed to make changes in
     their accounting methods.

E3–10

Adjusting for market
value—U.S. GAAP
vs. IFRS

At the end of every year NIKE and adidas record inventory write-downs for items (footwear
and apparel) that have lost value due to a variety of reasons, such as changing styles, defective merchandise, and lost items. Occasionally, the values of some of these inventories

recover in subsequent periods. NIKE reports under U.S. GAAP, and adidas reports under IFRS.

a. Explain in general how the changes in inventory values are reflected on U.S. GAAP–based vs. IFRS–based balance sheets.
b. How might NIKE's accounting for these events differ from that of adidas?

PROBLEMS

P3–1

The effects of inflation on reported profits

On January 1, 2011, you purchased a piece of property for $10,000. On December 31 of that year, you sold the property for $20,000. Assume that the general rate of inflation for 2011 was 10 percent.

REQUIRED:
a. According to generally accepted accounting principles, how much gain would be recorded in the income statement due to the sale of the property?
b. The $10,000 you used to purchase the property on January 1 could have been used to purchase any number of goods and services on January 1. Would the $20,000 you received at the end of the period enable you to purchase twice as many goods and services? Why or why not?
c. How much of the accounting gain computed in (a) could be attributed to inflation, and how much could be attributed to the fact that the property rose in value? Do generally accepted accounting principles make such a distinction? Why or why not?

P3–2

Inflation and bank loans

Assume that on January 1, Bush Enterprises borrowed $4,760 from Banking Corporation, promising to pay $5,000 at the end of one year. The effective rate of interest on the loan is approximately 5 percent ([$5,000 − $4,760]/$4,760). Suppose that the general rate of inflation for that year was 10 percent.

REQUIRED:
a. How much interest revenue did Banking Corporation recognize for the year? (*Hint:* The difference between the cash payment and the face value of the note receivable is interest revenue that Banking Corporation will earn over the life of the note.)
b. Do you think that Banking Corporation is better off at the end of the year by the amount of the interest revenue? Did Banking Corporation have more or less purchasing power at the end of the year? How much?
c. Which of the two parties, Bush Enterprises or Banking Corporation, seems to have ended up with the better deal? Could one determine this from a careful examination of the financial statements prepared on the basis of GAAP? Why or why not?

P3–3

The irrelevance of original cost

Three years ago Yeagley and Sons purchased the three assets listed in the following table. The chief financial officer, Kathy Dillon, is presently trying to decide what to do with each asset. She has three choices for each asset: (1) sell it, (2) sell it and replace it with an equivalent asset, or (3) keep it. The following information is provided to aid her decision.

Asset	Original Cost	Replacement Cost	Fair Market Value	Present Value of Future Cash Flows Produced by Old Asset	Present Value of Future Cash Flows of Equivalent Asset
A	$4,000	$1,000	$1,500	$2,500	$5,000
B	1,500	2,000	500	2,500	3,500
C	2,000	3,500	3,000	2,500	5,000

REQUIRED:

a. Assuming that Kathy chooses to keep Asset A and Asset B and sell and replace Asset C, evaluate her decisions. What decisions should she have made? Support your choices.
b. How useful was the original cost of each asset in the evaluation of Kathy's decisions?
c. Assume that Kathy proceeds with her decisions. According to generally accepted accounting principles, at what dollar amount would each asset be carried on Yeagley's balance sheet? What principles of financial accounting would be involved?

P3–4

Are dollars really stable?

Sales data for the fiscal years 2006, 2007, and 2008 for Bed Bath & Beyond follows (dollars in billions):

	2006	2007	2008
Sales	**$6.6**	**$7.0**	**$7.2**

According to the financial statements, sales increased by 9 percent from 2006 to 2008. Assume that the general rate of inflation as well as the price increase for Bed Bath & Beyond's products for the period 2006 to 2008 was 6 percent.

REQUIRED:

a. Considering price increases, did sales actually increase by 9 percent from 2006 to 2008? By how much did the company's sales actually grow from 2006 to 2008? By what percent did sales increase?
b. If prices had increased 10 percent from 2006 to 2008, what would have been the effect on the growth of sales?
c. Describe how the stable dollar assumption could have misled the users of Bed Bath & Beyond's financial statements.

REAL DATA

P3–5

Comparing across currencies and accounting systems

Selected financial information is provided below for three major pharmaceuticals: Glaxo-SmithKline (Britain), Sanofi-Aventis (France), and Pfizer (U.S.). GlaxoSmithKline's numbers were taken from the 2008 SEC Form 20-F, it uses IFRS, and the numbers are expressed in British pounds; the numbers for Sanofi-Aventis were also taken from the 2008 SEC Form 20-F and it too uses IFRS, but the numbers are expressed in euros; Pfizer is a U.S. company that uses U.S. GAAP, and the numbers are expressed in dollars and were taken from the 2008 SEC Form 10-K. As of the end of 2008, 1 U.S. dollar was equivalent to .69 British pounds and .71 euros. All numbers are in billions.

	GlaxoSmithKline	Sanofi-Aventis	Pfizer
Sales	24.3	27.5	48.2
Total assets	39.3	71.9	111.1
Shareholders' equity	7.9	45.1	57.5

a. Which company is the largest, and by how much?
b. Explain why it may be difficult to clearly state which is the largest.

REAL DATA

P3–6

The economic value of a company vs. its book value

The December 31, 2008, balance sheet and the income statement for the period ending December 31 for Manpower, Inc., a world leader in staffing and workforce management solutions, follow (dollars in millions). (This problem requires knowledge of present value. Refer to Appendix A.)

Balance Sheet

					Income Statement	
Current assets	**$4,690**	**Liabilities**	**$4,134**		**Sales**	**$21,553**
Long-lived assets	**1,928**	**Common stock**	**1,283**		**Expenses**	**21,334**
		Retained earnings	**1,201**		**Net income**	**$ 219**
		Total liabilities and				
Total assets	**$6,618**	**shareholders' equity**	**$6,618**			

You are interested in purchasing Manpower and have analyzed the future prospects of the company, estimating that it should be able to maintain at least its current earnings amount for the next ten years, at which time the assets would be worthless. You also estimate that the discount rate over that time period will be 12 percent.

REQUIRED:

a. Assuming that net income is equal to cash inflows, how much should you be willing to pay for Manpower?
b. What is the book value of Manpower?
c. Explain why there is a difference between the book value of Manpower and the amount you are willing to pay for it. What assumptions and/or principles of financial accounting are important here?

P3-7

Economic value and income vs. book value and income

On January 1, 2011, Barry Smith established a company by contributing $90,000 and using all of the cash to purchase an apartment house. At the time, he estimated that cash inflows due to rentals would be $65,000 per year, while annual cash outflows to manage and maintain it would be $45,000. He felt that the apartment house had a ten-year life and could be sold at the end of that time for $40,000. He also estimated that the effective interest rate during the ten-year period would be 10 percent. (This problem requires knowledge of present value. Refer to Appendix A.)

REQUIRED:

a. What is the book value of the building as of January 1, 2011? Assuming that Barry's estimates are correct, what is the economic value of the building? In your opinion, did Barry make a wise investment?
b. On December 31, 2011, Barry prepares financial statements and observes that his estimates were exactly correct. Assuming that cash inflows equal revenues, cash outflows equal expenses, and the net cost of the apartment, $50,000 ($90,000 − $40,000), is depreciated evenly over the ten-year period, prepare the income statement and balance sheet for Barry's apartment house.
c. Calculate the economic income of the apartment building for 2011. Economic income equals the difference between the present value at the beginning of the year and the present value at the end of the year plus any cash received during the year. Why is there a difference between accounting income and economic income?
d. What is the value on Barry's books of the apartment building at the end of 2011? What is the present value of the apartment building at that time?

P3-8

The differences between present value, book value, and liquidation value

The December 31, 2011, balance sheet of Myers and Myers, prepared under generally accepted accounting principles, follows. (This problem requires knowledge of present value calculations. Refer to Appendix A.)

Assets		Liabilities and Shareholders' Equity	
Cash	$ 10,000	Current liabilities	$ 8,000
Short-term investments	14,000	Long-term liabilities	20,000
Land	20,000	Common stock	80,000
Buildings and machinery	80,000	Retained earnings	16,000
		Total liabilities and	
Total assets	$124,000	shareholders' equity	$124,000

An investor believes that Myers and Myers can generate $20,000 cash per year for ten years, at which time it could be sold for $80,000. The FMVs of each asset as of December 31, 2011, follow:

Cash	$ 10,000
Short-term investments	14,000
Land	60,000
Buildings and machinery	40,000
Total FMV	$124,000

REQUIRED:

a. What is the book value of Myers and Myers as of December 31, 2011?
b. What is the value of Myers and Myers as a going concern (i.e., present value of the net future cash inflows) as of December 31, 2011? Assume a discount rate of 10 percent.
c. What is the liquidation value of Myers and Myers (i.e., how much cash would Myers and Myers be able to generate if each asset were sold separately and each liability were paid off on December 31, 2011)?
d. Discuss the differences among the book value of the company, the present value, and the liquidation value. Calculate goodwill, and explain it in terms of these three valuation bases.

P3–9

Three different measures of incomes

Suppose that Myers and Myers in P3–8 paid no dividends during 2012 and that the December 31, 2012, balance sheet looks like the one below. (This problem requires knowledge of present value calculations. Refer to Appendix A.)

Assets		Liabilities and Shareholders' Equity	
Cash	$ 30,000	Current liabilities	$ 6,000
Short-term investments	20,000	Long-term liabilities	20,000
Land	20,000	Common stock	80,000
Buildings and machinery	76,000	Retained earnings	40,000
		Total liabilities and	
Total assets	$146,000	shareholders' equity	$146,000

Assume that the investor in P3–8 was correct (i.e., the company produced $20,000 cash during 2012) and that the investor's expectations at the end of 2012 are unchanged. Assume further that an objective appraisal of the company's assets revealed the following FMVs as of December 31, 2012:

Cash	$ 10,000
Short-term investments	20,000
Land	66,000
Buildings and machinery	32,000
Total FMVs	$148,000

REQUIRED:

a. What dollar amount did Myers and Myers report in 2012 for net income under generally accepted accounting principles?
b. Calculate net income during 2012, using fair market values as the asset and liability valuation bases (i.e., $FMV_{2012} - FMV_{2011}$).
c. Calculate economic income for 2012 (i.e., cash received during 2012 plus the change in present value). The discount rate is still 10 percent.
d. Discuss the differences among these three measures of income. Discuss some of the strengths and weaknesses of each measure.

P3–10

Comparing companies using different accounting methods

The net income and working capital accounts for two companies in the same industry, ABC Company and XYZ Company, follow:

	ABC	XYZ
1/1–12/31 Net income	$10,000	$24,000
12/31 Working capital	16,000	30,000

After reviewing the complete financial statements of the two companies, you note that ABC and XYZ use different inventory valuation and depreciation methods. ABC uses method A to value its inventory, while XYZ uses method B. Had ABC used B and XYZ used A, their inventory accounts would have been $10,000 greater and $10,000 smaller, respectively. Similarly, ABC uses method X depreciation, while XYZ uses method Y. Had XYZ used X

and ABC used Y, their depreciation expenses for the year would have been $8,000 higher and $8,000 lower, respectively.

REQUIRED:

a. Calculate net income and working capital for the two companies under the following assumptions. (*Hint:* Working capital equals current assets less current liabilities).

Inventory Method	Depreciation Method	ABC Income/ Working Capital	XYZ Income/ Working Capital
B	Y		
B	X		
A	Y		
A	X		

b. Given this information, which combination of inventory and depreciation methods gives rise to the highest income and working capital numbers? Can you think of reasons why a manager would choose one method over another? Would managers always choose the method that results in the highest income? Why or why not?

c. If you were an investor attempting to decide in which company to invest, how would you treat the fact that the two companies used different methods to account for inventory and fixed assets? Is there a principle of accounting that covers this situation? Why or why not?

P3–11

Different methods of recognizing revenue

The Maple Construction Company agreed to construct twelve monuments for the city of Elderton. The total contract price was $2.4 million, and total estimated costs were $1,140,000. The construction took place over a four-year period, and the following schedule indicates the monuments completed, costs incurred, and cash collected for each period:

Year	1	2	3	4	Total
Monuments completed	2	6	3	1	12
Costs incurred	$380,000	$380,000	$285,000	$ 95,000	$1,140,000
Cash collected	$600,000	$900,000	$300,000	$600,000	$2,400,000

REQUIRED:

a. How much revenue should Maple recognize in each of the four periods under the following three assumptions?
   (1) Revenues are recognized each year in proportion to the monuments completed.
   (2) Revenues are recognized each year in proportion to the percentage of costs incurred.
   (3) Revenues are recognized each year in proportion to the cash collected each year.

b. For each of the three assumptions, match the appropriate amount of cost against the recognized revenue. Determine net income for each period under the three assumptions.

c. Compare the total revenue, total cost, and total net income that result from each of the three assumptions. Note that although the timing of the recognition differs across the three assumptions, the total amount of income recognized is the same.

P3–12

Revenue recognition and net income

Hydra Aire, Inc., sells appliances to Seasons Department Store. A recent order requires Hydra Aire to manufacture and deliver 500 toasters at a price of $100 per unit. Hydra Aire's manufacturing costs are approximately $40 per unit. The following schedule summarizes the production and delivery record of Hydra:

Year	1	2	3	Total
Toasters produced	200	200	100	500
Costs incurred	$ 8,000	$ 8,000	$ 4,000	$20,000
Toasters delivered	150	200	150	500
Cash received	$10,000	$15,000	$20,000	$45,000

REQUIRED:

a. Assuming that Hydra Aire recognizes revenue when the toasters are produced, how much revenue should be recognized in each of the three years?

b. Assuming that Hydra Aire recognizes revenue at delivery, how much revenue should be recognized in each of the three years?

c. Calculate net income for the three periods under each of the two assumptions above.

d. If Hydra Aire's management is paid an income-based bonus, which of the two assumptions would be preferred?

P3–13

The economics of
conservatism

Joe McGuire is a CPA who has recently completed the audit of Nelson Repairs, Inc. The audited balance sheet and income statement follow:

Balance Sheet

Current assets	$ 60,000	Liabilities	$ 80,000
Long-term assets	140,000	Shareholders' equity	120,000
		Total liabilities and	
Total assets	$200,000	shareholders' equity	$200,000

Income Statement

Sales	$160,000
Expenses	130,000
Net income	$ 30,000

During his examination, Joe learned that a lawsuit is soon to be filed against Nelson. The lawsuit accuses Nelson of negligence and asks for damages of $60,000 over and above the insurance. If Nelson were to lose the lawsuit, the future of the business would be in jeopardy. However, as the lawyers described it to Joe, the probability that Nelson will lose the lawsuit is very low, approximately 20 percent.

Joe is unsure about whether he should require Nelson to disclose the lawsuit on the financial statements. The president of Nelson does not want it disclosed because he believes that the disclosure would cause undue concern among the company's shareholders. Joe does not want to ignore the president's request because Nelson is his most important client. On the other hand, Joe knows that if he does not require disclosure, and Nelson loses the lawsuit, he may be legally liable for the losses of the shareholders. Joe constructed the following framework to help him make his decision.

	Lawsuit Outcome	
Decision	Win (80%)	Lose (20%)
Require disclosure	Error 1	Correct decision
Do not require disclosure	Correct decision	Error 2

REQUIRED:

a. Study Joe's framework, and note that he can choose to require or not to require disclosure. Requiring disclosure and winning the lawsuit gives rise to Error 1. Not requiring disclosure and losing the lawsuit gives rise to Error 2. Comment on the costs that Joe would incur from each of these two errors. Which of the two errors would be more costly? Which of the two outcomes (winning or losing the suit) is more likely to occur?

b. Suppose that Joe estimates that the cost of Error 1 is $10,000 and the cost of Error 2 is $50,000. Ignoring the costs and benefits of correct decisions, should Joe choose to require disclosure?

c. Explain the concept of conservatism in terms of Joe's framework.

ISSUES FOR DISCUSSION

ID3-1

Revenue recognition
and matching

Most airlines offer promotional programs in which passengers accumulate miles over time; when they have earned enough miles, they receive free tickets. In the past, airlines did not make any accounting entries for these free tickets. The free rider merely uses available seats or, on occasion, displaces a ticketed passenger.

The FASB adopted a method of accounting for tickets issued under these programs. They require that a portion of the fare paid when a passenger in such a program pays for a ticket be deferred until the free ride is used. For example, if a passenger purchases a $200 ticket, a portion, say $20, would not appear as revenue to the airline until the free trip is taken. It would be considered unearned revenue until then.

REQUIRED:
a. Evaluate the accounting standard in terms of the principle of revenue recognition and matching. List the criteria of revenue recognition, and suggest when it would be appropriate to recognize the revenue from a ticket sale. Given your suggestion, how should the related costs be accounted for?
b. Continental Airlines changed the way it accounts for "frequent flyer" credits, deferring more of the revenue it recognizes from this program until the service is actually provided. How would this change affect income in the year of the change, and does it appear to be a better application of matching? Why or why not?

ID3-2

Aggressive revenue
recognition in the
Internet industry

Many Internet firms "gross up" their revenues by reporting the entire sales price a customer pays at their site, when in fact the company keeps only a small percentage of that amount. Take Priceline.com, for example, the company made famous by those William Shatner ads about "naming your own price" for airline tickets and hotel rooms. In SEC filings for the year ended 2006, Priceline reported that it earned over $1.1 billion in revenues, but that included the full amount customers paid for tickets, hotel rooms, and rental cars. Traditional travel agencies call that amount "gross bookings," not revenues. And much like traditional travel agencies, Priceline keeps only a small portion of the "gross bookings," namely, the difference between the customers' accepted bids and the price it pays for the merchandise or service. The rest, which Priceline calls "cost of revenues," are paid to the airlines and hotels that supply the tickets and rooms. In 2006, those costs came to $722 million, leaving Priceline just $401 million. After subtracting other costs—like advertising and salaries—Priceline netted a profit of $74 million.

REQUIRED:
a. Comment on Priceline's method of booking "revenue."
b. Like Priceline, many Internet companies reported losses in the early years, forcing analysts to focus on other reported numbers. For example, at one time Priceline's stock price per share was 23 times its revenue per share, and 214 times its gross profit (revenue − product costs) per share. Can you think of a reason why Priceline might want to include "gross bookings" as revenue?
c. Why do you think that the SEC is clamping down on unethical accounting practices of Internet companies—most importantly, including as revenue "gross" versus "net" bookings?

ID3-3

Revenue recognition

A report on Blockbuster Video commented that Blockbuster seems to have unusual success in opening new franchises during the Christmas season. It appears that during each of the past few years, product sales to new franchises have increased significantly in the fourth quarter. The report also noted, however, that Blockbuster recognizes revenue when products are shipped, and there is no indication that the new franchises receiving the merchandise were actually open for business. Blockbuster is not alone. U.S. Robotics, which reports revenues when it ships items to dealers and wholesalers, has been criticized for puffing up reported sales by stuffing inventory into dealers.

REQUIRED:

a. How could the policy of recognizing revenue when products are shipped enable a company like Blockbuster or U.S. Robotics to "manage" earnings?

b. Is recognizing revenue when products are shipped necessarily a violation of GAAP? Explain.

ID3-4

Consistency and accounting changes

In 2003, Campbell Soup Company booked a special charge (reduction) to earnings totaling $31 million; the expense was a change in the way the company capitalized certain acquisition costs. These earnings numbers reported by the company for 2001, 2002, and 2003 (dollars in millions) are as follows.

2001	**$649**
2002	**525**
2003	**595**

REQUIRED:

a. Recalculate net income for 2003, assuming that the accounting change had not been made. Which is the more appropriate comparison—the reported amounts or the recalculated amounts? Why?

b. In what three places in Campbell Soup's annual report would an investor be able to find a reference to this accounting change?

c. Does it appear that Campbell Soup is practicing any of the reporting strategies discussed earlier in the text? Which one and why?

ID3-5

Comparability across time

MarketWatch and the news organization Reuters posted the following announcement on January 23, 2007:

Excluding One-Time Expenses, Johnson & Johnson Beats Estimates

Johnson & Johnson released its fourth quarter 2006 earnings . . . announcing that net income rose to $2.17 billion (Earnings Per Share of $0.74), from $2.1 billion (EPS of $0.70) during the prior year quarter. Excluding a one-time charge surrounding the acquisition of Pfizer Inc.'s consumer healthcare unit, Johnson & Johonson earned $0.81 EPS.

The report goes on to say that financial analysts were expecting earnings per share of 79 cents.

REQUIRED:

a. Which earnings per share figure (the 74 cents actually earned or the 81 cents earned if the special charge is ignored) is more important to investors interested in Johnson & Johnson?

b. Were the financial analysts who follow Johnson & Johnson pleased with the company's results?

c. What challenges will investors face when reviewing future financial statements of Johnson & Johnson?

ID3-6

Comparability

General Electric (GE) depreciates its fixed assets using a method that recognizes a relatively large portion of depreciation in the early years of an asset's useful life. IBM, on the other hand, uses the straight-line method.

REQUIRED:

Briefly describe the adjustments an investor would have to make when comparing GE's performance and financial position to that of IBM.

REAL DATA

ID3–7

Matching and
mismatching

Much has been written about the accounting fraud and subsequent bankruptcy of WorldCom. The *Baltimore Sun* reported that the "fraud was brazen (and) easy to spot. . . . The scheme was not complicated: the company's financial officers recorded routine maintenance expenses totaling $3.9 billion as capital expenditures, which can be written off over decades rather than booked as immediate expenses."

REQUIRED:
a.   Explain how capitalizing an item, instead of expensing it, affects the financial statements.
b.   Which principle of accounting is being violated? Are other principles involved? Discuss.

REAL DATA

ID3–8

Earnings restatements
and fiscal period,
matching, and
consistency

The *Wall Street Journal* reported in early 2010 that CitiBank acknowledged a series of errors in accounting for the investment in the firm by the U.S. government. These errors overstated the company's quarterly earnings in 2008 and 2009, and were corrected with an adjusting entry in the fourth quarter of 2009 that contributed to a large reported loss for the company. A stock analyst following Citi lamented that he was very concerned about these errors.

REQUIRED:
Discuss how CitiBank's accounting errors relate to the concepts of the fiscal period assumption, the consistency principle, and the matching principle. Further, discuss why the analyst is so concerned.

REAL DATA

ID3–9

Inventory recoveries
under IFRS

The 2008 Form 20-F published by Unilever, which uses IFRS, notes that during 2008 assets were written down by 246 million euros to market value for damaged, obsolete, and lost inventories. It also noted that the market value of certain inventories written down in prior periods was recovered, leading to an increase in the 2008 inventory value of 23 million euros.

REQUIRED:
a.   Compute the net adjustment recorded by Unilever for inventory market value changes during 2008.
b.   If Unilever followed U.S. GAAP instead of IFRS, what would have been the net adjustment?
c.   Briefly discuss fundamental differences between U.S. GAAP and IFRS.

REAL DATA

ID3–10

Income management
and conservatism

Whitney Tilson, a noted analyst, warns investors in an article in *The Motley Fool* that more than any other type of company, financial companies have immense discretion regarding what earnings to report. The key is the rate of loan losses that they expect to experience, which must be estimated at the end of every period. By changing this estimate, which in turn changes one of the largest expenses on their income statement, financial companies can manage net income. Tilson specifically cites Farmer Mac, the agency created by the federal government to provide funds in the agricultural lending market, which many analysts believe smooths its earnings across time by simply changing its estimate on loss rates.

REQUIRED:
a.   What does it mean to "smooth earnings across time"? How might a financial company practice this strategy, and why might it engage in this activity?
b.   Earnings smoothing has also been associated with conservatism. Why?

ID3–11

Economic entity

Enron was one of the world's largest power companies before it went bankrupt in one of the most spectacular financial frauds in history. One aspect of the fraud involved the creation of a separate entity that borrowed a large amount of money and then used the money to acquire facilities, which were then leased and used by Enron. Because Enron owned less than 50 percent of the stock of the separate entity, Enron was not required to include the entity in its consolidated financial statements. This arrangement was attractive to Enron management because the company did not have to report the huge debt held by the entity on its consolidated balance sheet.

The arrangement was deceptive to shareholders and potential investors because they were unaware of this debt, which turned out to be the responsibility of Enron. Recently, the FASB issued a standard requiring companies to include such separate entities in their consolidated financial statements.

REQUIRED:

Describe the economic entity assumption, and provide reasons why the FASB is requiring the consolidation of such entities. Do you think that the separate entity should have been considered part of the economic entity called Enron? Why?

ID3–12

Valuation bases

The 2006 annual report of KeyCorp, a regional bank holding company headquartered in Cleveland, indicates that marketable securities are listed on the balance sheet at fair value. In addition to its marketable securities, Key notes that it also has "Other Investments" that include principal investments made predominantly in privately held companies that are also listed at "fair value." Finally, Key documents that it also has investments, including equity and real estate instruments, that "do not have readily determinable fair value." This last category of investments is carried at estimated fair value.

REQUIRED:

a. Using terminology from the chapter, what are the valuation bases used by KeyCorp for its investments?
b. What are some of the challenges facing KeyCorp in valuing its "principal investments"?
c. What are some issues that investors should understand about "estimated fair value" of certain investments?

REAL DATA

ID3–13

Fair value accounting

The FASB requires that companies report the fair value of their equity and debt securities on the balance sheets. The FASB described fair value as a market exit price—an estimate of the price an entity would have realized if it had sold the asset or paid if it had been relieved of the liability on the reporting data in an arm's-length exchange motivated by normal business conditions.

REQUIRED:

a. Which of the four valuation bases discussed in the chapter is the FASB suggesting that companies use for their equity and debt securities?
b. Prior to the requirement, most of these securities were reported at cost. How did reporting them at fair value affect the income reported by companies?
c. Do you agree with the FASB? Why or why not?
d. Explain the basic differences between U.S. GAAP and IFRS regarding the use of fair market values on the balance sheet.

REAL DATA

ID3–14

The SEC Form 10-K of NIKE

Excerpts taken from the SEC Form 10-K of NIKE are reproduced in Appendix C. This chapter listed and defined four basic assumptions, four principles of measurement, and two exceptions.

REQUIRED:

Review the NIKE Form 10-K, and find at least one example of each of the ten concepts. Indicate the accounts on NIKE's balance sheet that use present value as a valuation base. Also indicate the accounts on NIKE's balance sheet that use fair market value as a valuation base.

The Mechanics of Financial Accounting

KEY POINTS

The following key points are emphasized in this chapter:

- Two criteria necessary for economic events to be reflected in the financial statements.

- The accounting equation and how it relates to the balance sheet, income statement, statement of shareholders' equity, and statement of cash flows.

- Journal entries (and T-accounts) and how they express the effect of economic events on the basic accounting equation and the financial statements.

- Why managers need to understand how economic events affect the financial statements.

- Why the financial statements are adjusted periodically to reflect certain economic events.

The U.S. General Accounting Office (GAO) periodically reports to Congress on the performance and accountability of various U.S. government agencies. In its report on the Small Business Administration (SBA), established to help small U.S. businesses, the GAO concluded:

The SBA continues to have difficulties producing complete, accurate, and timely financial statements. It incorrectly calculated the accounting losses on loan sales and did not perform key analyses to determine the overall financial impact of the sales. These errors and lack of key analyses also mean that congressional decision-makers are not receiving accurate financial data to make informed decisions about the SBA's budget and appropriations.

This quote reflects a problem confronting many large and well-known U.S. companies, not just governmental agencies—a lack of high-quality internal control designed to ensure that all transactions are recorded in a timely and accurate manner. As discussed in Chapter 1, the Sarbanes–Oxley Act recently placed greater emphasis on the need for internal control, as many believe that costly corporate financial frauds are in part due to internal control breakdowns.

This chapter covers the mechanics underlying the preparation of financial statements and how they help to ensure that a company's transactions are accurately and completely accounted for. After completing it, you should be able to construct financial statements from economic events.

Understanding the mechanics underlying the preparation of financial statements is crucial for effective management. Timely and accurate reporting is critical. Also, managers often choose among transactions, and such choices should not be made without considering the financial statement effects and the associated economic consequences. Consequently, managers must understand the mechanics that link transactions to the financial statements.

Managers must also understand how to read, interpret, and analyze financial statements. To do so effectively, it is useful to be able to infer from the financial statements events and transactions that occurred during the accounting period. A mechanical process, called T-account analysis, can enable users to make such inferences. This process is also helpful when preparing and understanding the statement of cash flows, and it is covered in Appendix 4A.

ECONOMIC EVENTS

Economic events reflected in the financial statements must be both relevant to the financial condition of a company and objectively measurable in monetary terms.

Relevant Events

Relevant events have economic significance to a particular company and include any occurrence that affects its financial condition. Events of general economic significance, like the election of a new U.S. president, the passage of federal legislation, or the outbreak of war, could be considered relevant. Events that are more company-specific, like the signing of a new labor agreement, the hiring of a new chief executive officer, the sale of an item of inventory, or simply the payment of monthly wages, are also relevant. Each of these events could have a significant impact on the financial resources of a particular company. Anyone interested in the company's financial status (shareholders, investors, creditors, managers, auditors, and other interested parties) wants to be able to assess the financial impact of all such events.

Objectivity

Unfortunately, only a small percentage of all relevant events are reflected on the financial statements. The dollar values assigned to the accounts on the financial statements must be determined in an objective manner.

In general, a dollar value is considered objective if it results from an exchange in which two parties with differing incentives reach agreement. To illustrate, in 2008 when Nokia offered to purchase NAVTEQ, a U.S.-based digital mapping company, from NAVTEQ's shareholders, Nokia's and NAVTEQ's shareholders had differing incentives. Nokia wanted to pay as little as possible, while the shareholders wanted to receive as much as possible. When they reached agreement on the value of NAVTEQ, a transaction took place. NAVTEQ passed to Nokia for a price of 5.3 billion euros. The price represented an objective valuation of NAVTEQ because two parties with differing incentives reached agreement on it. The transaction was accompanied by documented evidence (e.g., receipts, canceled checks, vouchers, a bill of sale) that could be used to verify its entry into Nokia's financial records, and after the purchase, an investment of 5.3 billion euros was reflected on Nokia's balance sheet.

Unfortunately, the most relevant information is not always the most objective. CBS Television Distribution, for example, is a television syndicator with the rights to *Jeopardy, Wheel of Fortune,* and *Oprah,* which generate millions of dollars in licensing fees. Yet, these rights are valued on the balance sheet at their purchase costs, less accumulated amortization, which are much less. Similarly, a partner at a major accounting firm once noted: "Coca-Cola is one of the best-recognized trademarks in the world, but it is not on their books. It got that recognition through advertising, but you don't book advertising as an asset, because you don't know if it will have future value."

> **?**
>
> In the pharmaceutical industry, when a drug passes its clinical tests, huge value is created. In the software industry, when software passes a beta test, it suddenly becomes valuable. In these two examples, do the pharmaceuticals and the software companies become more valuable when these events occur? Are the events recorded in the financial statements? Explain.

THE FUNDAMENTAL ACCOUNTING EQUATION

The four financial statements are all based on a mathematical equation, which states that the dollar value of a company's assets equals the dollar value of its liabilities plus the dollar value of its shareholders' equity. In fact, the balance sheet is a statement of this equation.

Assets = Liabilities + Shareholders' Equity

The mechanics of accounting are structured so that this equality is always maintained. If the two sides of this equation are unequal, the books do not balance, and an error has been made. However, maintaining this equality does not ensure that the financial statements are correct; errors can exist even if the **accounting equation** balances.

Assets

Assets are items and rights that a company acquires through objectively measurable transactions that can be used in the future to generate economic benefits (i.e., more

assets). Such acquisitions are usually made by purchase: An asset is received in exchange for another asset (often cash) or a payable. Assets include cash, securities, receivables from customers, land, buildings, machinery, equipment, and rights such as patents, copyrights, and trademarks. Simply, the left side of the accounting equation represents the dollar values of the items and rights that have been acquired by a company and are expected to benefit the company in the future.

Assets come from three sources: (1) They are borrowed; (2) they are contributed by shareholders (owners); and (3) they are generated by a company's operating activities. The right side of the equation, liabilities and shareholders' equity, represents the dollar values attached to these three sources. For each dollar amount on the asset side of the equation, a corresponding dollar amount is reflected on the liability and shareholders' equity side.

Liabilities

Liabilities consist primarily of a company's debts or payables. They are existing obligations for which assets must be used in the future. The dollar amount of the total liabilities on the balance sheet represents the portion of the assets that a company has borrowed and must repay.

> The Associated Press reported in November, just as the 2009 holiday shopping season was beginning, that retail industry analysts were expecting shoppers to have a more difficult time finding the popular toys for Christmas presents, as stores were intentionally keeping their inventory levels to a minimum. Items such as robotic hamsters and the latest Barbie dolls were purchased by retailers in lower quantities in 2009, as stores had been hurt with excessive and slow-moving inventory during Christmas 2008. When a retailer purchases inventories from a supplier, how are the financial statements affected?

Shareholders' Equity

Shareholders' equity consists of two components: (1) **contributed capital,** the dollar value of the assets contributed by shareholders; and (2) **retained earnings,** the dollar value of the assets generated by operating activities and retained in the business (i.e., not paid to the shareholders in the form of dividends).[1] Operating activities are those transactions directly associated with the acquisition and sale of a company's products or services. Dividing shareholders' equity into its components, the fundamental accounting equation appears as follows:

Assets = Liabilities + Contributed Capital + Retained Earnings

That is, the dollar value of the assets is equal to the sum of the dollar amounts owed, the dollar amount of shareholders' contributions, and the dollar amount retained from profitable operations.

---

1. The second component of shareholders' equity is actually earned capital; the primary part of it is retained earnings. Later in the text we introduce another part of earned capital, called accumulated comprehensive income.

?

A summary of the 2008 balance sheet for Zimmer Holdings, a manufacturer of healthcare products, is provided below (dollars in millions). Describe it in terms of the basic accounting equation.

Current assets	$2,179	Liabilities	$1,585	
Noncurrent assets	5,060	Contributed capital	1,268	
		Retained earnings	4,386	
Total	$7,239	Total	$7,239	

BUSINESS TRANSACTIONS, THE ACCOUNTING EQUATION, AND THE FINANCIAL STATEMENTS

Companies conduct operations by exchanging assets and liabilities with other entities (e.g., individuals and businesses). These economic events are referred to as **business transactions.** Exchanging cash for a piece of equipment, for example, is a transaction that represents the purchase of equipment. Borrowing money is a transaction in which a promise to pay in the future (i.e., note payable) is exchanged for cash. The sale of a service on account is a transaction in which the service is exchanged for a receivable. In each of these exchanges, and in all business transactions, something is received and something is given up. *These receipts and disbursements affect the financial condition of a company in a way that always maintains the equality of the fundamental accounting equation. That is, each business transaction is recorded in the books so that the dollar values of a company's assets always equal the dollar values of its liabilities and shareholders' equity.*

Transactions and the Accounting Equation

The six transactions described here were entered into by Joe's Landscaping Service during 2011, its first year of operations. Figure 4–1 shows how each transaction affects the accounting equation. Study it carefully and read the following discussion of each transaction.

FIGURE 4–1   Business transactions and the accounting equation

Transaction	Assets	=	Liabilities	+	Contributed Capital	+	Retained Earnings
(1)	$+10,000	=			$+10,000		
(2)	+ 3,000	=	$+3,000				
(3)	+ 5,000	=					
	− 5,000						
(4)	+ 8,000						
	+ 4,000	=					$+12,000
(5)	− 9,000	=					− 9,000
(6)	− 1,000	=					− 1,000
End-of-year balance	$ 15,000	=	$ 3,000	+	$ 10,000	+	$ 2,000

TRANSACTION (1). Joe, the owner of the company, contributes $10,000. This dollar amount increases the company's cash balance, an asset, by $10,000 and is also recorded on the right side of the accounting equation under contributed capital. Note that both sides of the accounting equation are increased by $10,000, so its equality is maintained.

TRANSACTION (2). $3,000 is borrowed from a bank. The dollar amount of this exchange also increases the company's cash balance, but in this case liabilities are also increased; the company now owes $3,000 to the bank.

TRANSACTION (3). The company purchases equipment for $5,000 cash. This exchange both increases and decreases the company's assets. It now has an asset called *equipment,* and its cash balance is reduced by $5,000. Still, the equality of the accounting equation is maintained because the asset side was both increased and decreased by $5,000.

TRANSACTION (4). The company performs a service for $12,000. This transaction increases the company's cash balance by $8,000 and creates a receivable of $4,000. Thus, total assets increase by $12,000. The corresponding $12,000 adjustment on the right side of the equation, which maintains its equality, is reflected in retained earnings because the company generated this $12,000 through its own operations.

TRANSACTION (5). The company pays $9,000 for expenses—wages, interest, and maintenance. This transaction decreases the company's cash balance by $9,000 and maintains the equality of the equation by decreasing retained earnings in the amount of $9,000. Retained earnings is decreased because, as in Transaction (4), these expenses are associated with the company's operating activities.

TRANSACTION (6). Joe pays himself a $1,000 dividend as a return on his original investment. The dollar amount of the dividend reduces the company's cash balance by $1,000 and is also reflected on the right side of the equation by a $1,000 reduction in retained earnings. Retained earnings is reduced because the fundamental objective of the company's operating activities is to provide a return for the owner, and retained earnings is the measure of the assets that have been accumulated through operations.

During 2008, the Coca-Cola Company purchased property, plant, and equipment in the amount of $2.0 billion. The company also borrowed over $4.3 billion. How were these transactions reflected in the basic accounting equation?

The Accounting Equation and the Financial Statements

This section introduces and defines the concept of an account and describes the preparation of simplified versions of the balance sheet, statement of cash flows, income statement, and statement of shareholders' equity for Joe's Landscaping Service.

ACCOUNTS AND THE ACCOUNTING EQUATION

For purposes of recording transactions and preparing financial statements, the main components of the accounting equation (assets, liabilities, and shareholders' equity) can be further subdivided into separate categories called accounts. The general category of assets is normally divided into a number of accounts including, for example, a cash account, a receivables account, and an equipment account. Liabilities normally consist of various payable accounts, and as mentioned earlier, shareholders' equity can be divided into a contributed capital account and a retained earnings account.

Accounts serve as "storage units," where the dollar values of business transactions are initially recorded and later compiled into the financial statements. The accounts that appear on the financial statements represent a balance between enough detail to provide meaningful breakdowns of assets, liabilities, and shareholders' equity but not so much as to overwhelm the user.

In Figure 4–2, the main components of the accounting equation are divided into separate accounts for the purpose of recording the six transactions entered into by Joe's Landscaping Service. Note that Figure 4–2 is very similar to Figure 4–1. It differs only in that it records the transactions in more specific categories, which represent the accounts that eventually appear on the financial statements.

FIGURE 4–2   Accounts and the accounting equation

	Assets			=	Liabilities	+	Shareholders' Equity		
Transaction	Cash	+ Receivables	+ Equipment	=	Loan Payable	+	Contributed Capital	+	Retained Earnings
(1)	$+10,000			=			$+10,000		
(2)	+ 3,000			=	$+3,000				
(3)	− 5,000		$+5,000	=					
(4)	+ 8,000	$+4,000		=					$+12,000
(5)	− 9,000			=					− 9,000
(6)	− 1,000			=					− 1,000
Total	$ 6,000	+ $ 4,000	+ $ 5,000	=	$ 3,000	+	$ 10,000	+	$ 2,000

Note that total assets in Figure 4–2 ($15,000 = $6,000 + $4,000 + $5,000) equal total assets in Figure 4–1 as well as total liabilities plus shareholders' equity ($15,000 = $3,000 + $10,000 + $2,000). The components of the accounting equation have simply been divided into more specific "storage units." In the next sections, the information contained in Figure 4–2 is used to prepare the financial statements.

The basic accounting equation and its relationship to the individual accounts are exactly the same under IFRS as they are under U.S. GAAP.

THE BALANCE SHEET

The balance sheet is the statement of the basic accounting equation as of a particular date: in this case, the end of 2011. It is called a balance sheet because assets are always in balance with liabilities plus shareholders' equity. That is, there is a source for each asset the company has acquired. Figure 4–3 shows the balance sheet for Joe's Landscaping Service at the end of its first year of operations. This balance sheet was prepared by simply listing and grouping the totals of the individual asset, liability, and shareholders' equity accounts, which appear at the bottom of Figure 4–2.

FIGURE 4–3

Balance sheet for Joe's Landscaping

Joe's Landscaping Service
Balance Sheet
December 31, 2011

ASSETS		LIABILITIES AND SHAREHOLDERS' EQUITY	
Cash	$ 6,000	Loan payable	$ 3,000
Receivables	4,000	Contributed capital	10,000
Equipment	5,000	Retained earnings	2,000
		Total liabilities and	
Total assets	$15,000	shareholders' equity	$15,000

STATEMENT OF CASH FLOWS

The statement of cash flows in Figure 4–4 was prepared directly from the activity recorded in the cash account in Figure 4–2. Each dollar value on the statement of cash flows corresponds to an increase or decrease in the cash account indicated in Figure 4–2. Note also that the ending cash balance of $6,000 on the statement of cash flows equals the balance in the cash account on the balance sheet. The statement of cash flows is nothing more than a summary of the activity in the company's cash account, divided into three sections—operating, investing, and financing activities.

FIGURE 4–4

Statement of cash flows for Joe's Landscaping

Joe's Landscaping Service
Statement of Cash Flows
for the Year Ended December 31, 2011

Operating activities:		
Sale of a service (4)	$ 8,000	
Payments for expenses (5)	(9,000)	
Net cash from operating activities		$ (1,000)
Investing activities:		
Purchase of equipment (3)	$ (5,000)	
Net cash from investing activities		(5,000)
Financing activities:		
Borrowings (2)	$ 3,000	
Owner contributions (1)	10,000	
Payment of dividends (6)	(1,000)	
Net cash from financing activities		12,000
Increase in cash balance		$ 6,000
Cash balance at beginning of year		0
Cash balance at end of year		$ 6,000

INCOME STATEMENT

The income statement is a measure of the assets generated from the company's operating activities during a period of time. It compares *revenues* (the asset inflows due to operating activities) to *expenses* (the asset outflows required to generate the revenues). The difference between revenues and expenses is called *net income* or *net loss*. If revenues exceed expenses, there is net income or profit; if expenses exceed revenues, there is a net loss.

In terms of the accounting equation, revenues, expenses, and dividends are reflected in the retained earnings account. Like the general categories of assets, liabilities, and shareholders' equity, retained earnings can be further subdivided into revenue accounts, expense accounts, and dividend accounts. Recording a transaction in a revenue account increases retained earnings; recording a transaction in an expense or dividend account decreases retained earnings.

In the example of Joe's Landscaping Service, revenues in the form of cash and a receivable were generated in Transaction (4), the sale of landscaping services for $12,000. Expenses were recognized in Transaction (5), which reflects payments made for wages, interest, and equipment maintenance. The dollar amounts of these two transactions are recorded in the retained earnings account in Figure 4–2, but in practice they would be recorded in separate revenue and expense accounts, which are components of retained earnings. An income statement can be prepared by disclosing revenues and expenses in the manner shown in Figure 4–5.

<table>
<tr><td>

FIGURE 4–5

Income statement for Joe's Landscaping

</td><td>

Joe's Landscaping Service
Income Statement
for the Year Ended December 31, 2011

Revenues: Fees earned for service	$12,000
Expenses: Wages, interest, maintenance	9,000
Net income	$ 3,000

</td></tr>
</table>

STATEMENT OF SHAREHOLDERS' EQUITY

The statement of shareholders' equity describes the changes during 2011 in the shareholders' equity accounts—in this case, contributed capital and retained earnings. The statement appears in Figure 4–6, and note that it simply summarizes the activities in the contributed capital and retained earnings accounts indicated on Figure 4–2, except that the net income number appears on the statement instead of the individual revenues and expenses.

<table>
<tr><td>

FIGURE 4–6

Statement of shareholders' equity

</td><td>

Joe's Landscaping Service
Statement of Shareholders' Equity
for the Year Ended December 31, 2011

	Contributed Capital	Retained Earnings	Total
Beginning balance (1/1/2011)	$ 0	$ 0	$ 0
Contribution by owner	10,000		10,000
Net income		3,000	3,000
Less: Dividends		(1,000)	(1,000)
Ending balance (12/31/11)	$10,000	$2,000	$12,000

</td></tr>
</table>

A summary of the 2009 financial statements of Target follows (dollars in millions). Discuss each statement in terms of the basic accounting equation.

Income statement:

Revenues	$62,884
Expenses	(60,670)
Net income	$2,214

Balance sheet:

Current assets	$17,488	Liabilities	$30,393
Non-current assets	26,618	Contributed capital	2,826
		Earned capital	10,887*
Total	$44,106	Total	$44,106

Statement of cash flows:

Cash from operations	$ 4,430
Cash used for investing	(4,373)
Cash used for financing	(1,643)
Decrease in cash	(1,586)
Beginning cash	2,450
Ending cash	$ 864

Statement of shareholders' equity:

	Contributed Capital	Earned Capital	Total
Beginning balance	$ 2,724	$12,583	$15,307
Share issuances	106		106
Net income		2,214	2,214
Less: Dividends		(471)	(471)
Other	(4)	(3,439)	(3,443)
Ending balance	$ 2,826	$10,887	$13,713

*Recall that earned capital is primarily comprised of retained earnings.

THE JOURNAL ENTRY

In the previous section, we demonstrated how economic events affect the accounting equation and, ultimately, the financial statements. **Journal entries** provide a more efficient way to represent such effects. They are used to represent relevant and measurable economic events, and their content and structure indicate how such events affect the accounting equation. The form of a typical journal entry follows:

	Debit	Credit
Equipment	5,000	
Cash		5,000

Purchased equipment for cash

The affected accounts in this entry are equipment and cash, and the dollar amount of the transaction is $5,000. Placing the $5,000 assigned to equipment on the left side of the entry indicates that the equipment account has been increased by $5,000. That account is said to have been *debited*. In the terminology of financial accounting, to

debit an account simply means to place the dollar amount assigned to it on the left side of the journal entry.

Placing the $5,000 assigned to the cash account on the right side of the entry, or crediting it, indicates that the cash account has been decreased by $5,000. To **credit** an account means to place it on the right side of the journal entry. The sample entry indicates that equipment was purchased for $5,000 cash.

Compound journal entries are treated in exactly the same way, but they involve more than two accounts. For example, if equipment is purchased for $5,000 cash and a $10,000 note payable, we would record the following compound journal entry:

	Debit	Credit
Equipment	15,000	
Cash		5,000
Notes payable		10,000

*Purchased equipment for cash and a
note payable*

THE DOUBLE ENTRY SYSTEM

Note in the preceding journal entries that the total dollar value on the left side is always equal to the total dollar value on the right side and that at least two different accounts were affected. Both characteristics are true of all journal entries and illustrate the **double entry system,** which is the cornerstone of financial accounting. The equality of the debit and credit sides maintains the equality of the accounting equation, and the fact that at least two different accounts are affected indicates that in all exchange transactions, something is received and something is given up.

THE JOURNAL ENTRY BOX

A useful way to learn journal entries is to view them as shown in Figure 4–7, which provides a systematic way of converting exchange transactions to journal entries. The top of the box is an expression of the accounting equation. Answers to the three questions identify the three components of each transaction: (1) the accounts affected, (2) the direction of the effect, and (3) the dollar value of the transaction.

Increases in asset accounts (Cell A) and decreases in liability and shareholders' equity accounts (Cell D) are always represented on the debit (left) side of the journal entry. Decreases in asset accounts (Cell C) and increases in liability and shareholders' equity accounts (Cell B) are always recorded on the credit (right) side of the journal entry. It is important to recall that revenue, expense, and dividend accounts are all part of the shareholders' equity account, retained earnings. Thus, revenues, which increase retained earnings, are recorded on the credit side of the journal entry. Expenses and dividends, which decrease retained earnings, are recorded on the debit side of the journal entry.

Figure 4–7 shows that journal entries have been devised so that transactions are recorded in a way that always maintains the equality of the accounting equation. Debits always equal credits, and accordingly, assets always equal liabilities plus shareholders' equity.

JOURNAL ENTRIES AND THE ACCOUNTING EQUATION: EXAMPLES

In Figure 4–8, seven different transactions give rise to seven different journal entries, affecting the accounting equation in seven different ways. The equality of the accounting equation is always maintained, and the debit side of each journal entry is exactly

FIGURE 4–7   The journal entry box

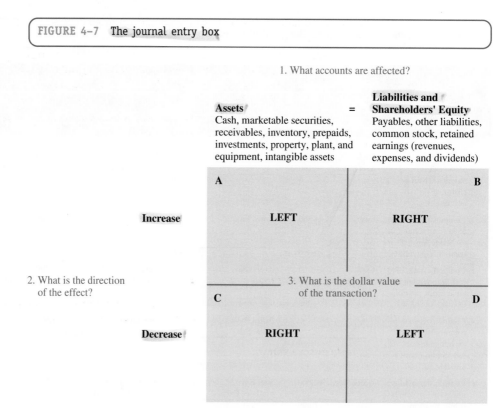

equal to the credit side. Note especially Transactions 5, 6, and 7, where the equality of the accounting equation is maintained through the effect of a revenue, an expense, and a dividend on retained earnings. The explanations on the right side of the chart indicate how the journal entry box was used to construct each journal entry.

The account names in each journal entry contained in Figure 4–8 are followed by parenthetical notations designed to indicate how the entry affects the fundamental accounting equation. We use this notation throughout the remainder of the text because it emphasizes the important relationship between the economic event represented by the journal entry and the accounting equation and, ultimately, the financial statements.

During 2006, Cisco Systems recorded revenues of $36.1 billion, most of which were recorded on account. Describe how these transactions would be represented in Figure 4–8.

T-ACCOUNTS

When analyzing the effects of many economic events on the financial statements, it is useful to keep running tallies of the balances for each asset, liability, shareholders' equity, revenue, expense, and dividend account. This can be achieved by creating a T-account for each of the financial statement accounts. **T-accounts** are so named because they are in the form of a T—the left side of the T represents the debit side of

FIGURE 4-8   Journal entries and the accounting equation

Transaction	Accounting Equation			Journal Entry			
	Assets		= Liabilities and Shareholders' Equity		Debit	Credit	Explanation*
1. Company receives $100 cash in payment from a customer on account.	Cash Accts. Rec.	+100 −100 0 =	0	Cash (+A)** Accts. Rec. (−A)	100	100	Cash, an asset, is increased. Accts. Rec., an asset, is decreased.
2. Company borrows $500 from a bank in exchange for a short-term note payable.	Cash	+500 +500 =	Notes Pay. +500 +500	Cash (+A) Notes. Pay. (+L)	500	500	Cash, an asset, is increased. Notes Pay., a liability, is increased.
3. Company pays $300 cash in payment of an account payable.	Cash	−300 −300 =	Accts. Pay. −300 −300	Accts. Pay. (−L) Cash (−A)	300	300	Cash, an asset, is decreased. Accts. Pay., a liability, is decreased.
4. Company issues common share in exchange for an outstanding note payable.		0 =	Notes Pay. −1,000 Com. Stk. +1,000 0	Notes. Pay. (−L) Com. Stk. (+CC)	1,000	1,000	Notes Pay., a liability, is decreased. Com. Stk., an equity, is increased.
5. Company provides a service for which it bills its clients $2,000.	Accts. Rec.	+2,000 +2,000 =	Ret. Earn. +2,000 via Fees Earned +2,000	Accts. Rec. (+A) Fees Earned (R, +RE)	2,000	2,000	Accts. Rec., an asset, is increased. Fees Earned, a revenue, increases Retained Earnings.
6. Company pays $500 in salaries to its employees.	Cash	−500 −500 =	Ret. Earn. −500 via Salary Expense −500	Salary Exp. (E, −RE) Cash (−A)	500	500	Cash, an asset, is decreased. Salary Exp. decreases Retained Earnings.
7. Company declares an $800 dividend to be paid later to its owners.		0 =	Dividends Pay. +800 Ret. Earn. −800 via Dividends 0	Dividends (−RE) Dividends Pay. (+L)	800	800	Dividends Pay., a liability, is increased. Dividends decreases Retained Earnings.

Note: Accts. Rec. = Accounts Receivable; Accts. Pay. = Accounts Payable; Com. Stk. = Common Stock; Dividends Pay. = Dividends Payable; Notes Pay. = Notes Payable; Ret. Earn. = Retained Earnings; Salary Exp. = Salary Expense.
*See journal entry box in Figure 4–7.
**Typically, journal entries would not include the information in parentheses:
+ = increase and − = decrease; A = Asset; L = Liability; SE = Shareholders' Equity; R = Revenue; E = Expense; Ga = Gain; Lo = Loss; CC = Contributed Capital; RE = Retained Earnings
Balance Sheet (A = L + SE)
Income Statement (R + Ga − E − Lo = NI). Note: No gains or losses are illustrated in this example.
SE = CC + RE

the entry, and the right side corresponds to the credit side. Since journal entries also have a debit and credit side, the debited and credited dollar amounts are easily transferred (posted) to their respective T-accounts.

Figure 4–9 illustrates the relationships among the basic accounting equation, T-accounts, and journal entries. The following example demonstrates how financial

statements can be prepared from a group of economic events (transactions), each of which is represented by a journal entry. The balances are maintained in T-accounts.

FIGURE 4–9   Relationships among basic accounting equation, T-accounts, and journal entries

Basic accounting equation:

Assets   =   Liabilities   +   Shareholders' Equity

Contributed Capital   Retained Earnings

Revenues − Expenses − Dividends

Corresponding T-accounts:

Assets	Liabilities	Contributed capital	Revenues	Expenses	Dividends
+ | −	− | +	− | +	− | +	+ | −	+ | −

Sample journal entries:

Issue stock:	*Cash (+A)*	X	Sell service:	*Asset (+A)*	X
	Contr. Cap. (+CC)	X		*Revenue (+RE)*	X
Borrow:	*Cash (+A)*	X	Pay salaries:	*Expense (−RE)*	X
	Liability (+L)	X		*Asset (−A)*	X
Buy Asset:	*Asset (+A)*	X	Pay dividend:	*Dividend (−RE)*	X
	Cash (−A)	X		*Cash (−A)*	X

AN EXAMPLE. The December 31, 2011, balance sheet of Maple Services Company appears in Figure 4–10. The journal entries and associated T-accounts for ten transactions, entered into during 2012, are provided in Figure 4–11. Note first that the account balances from the balance sheet are the beginning balances in the T-accounts. Note also that the journal entries, numbered 1–10, are posted in the T-accounts. Review each journal entry and trace the dollar amounts of the debits and credits to the T-accounts. The financial statements, which appear in Figure 4–12, can be prepared directly from the T-accounts.[2]

FIGURE 4–10

Maple Services balance sheet

Maple Services Company
Balance Sheet
December 31, 2011

ASSETS		LIABILITIES AND SHAREHOLDERS' EQUITY	
Cash	$12,000	Salaries payable	$ 4,000
Accounts receivable	9,000	Notes payable	6,000
Land	15,000	Contributed capital	21,000
		Retained earnings	5,000
		Total liabilities and	
Total assets	$36,000	shareholders' equity	$36,000

---

2. The closing process is not illustrated in this example. It is illustrated, however, in the review problem at the end of the chapter (p. 163).

FIGURE 4-11   Maple Services Company

JOURNAL ENTRIES

(1) Cash (+A)	5,000			(6) Rent Expense (E, −RE)	500		
Common Stock (+CC)		5,000		Cash (−A)		500	
Issued common share				*Paid rent*			
(2) Land (+A)	7,000			(7) Insurance Expense (E, −RE)	100		
Cash (−A)		7,000		Cash (−A)		100	
Purchased land				*Paid for insurance coverage*			
(3) Salaries Payable (−L)	4,000			(8) Salary Expense (E, −RE)	3,000		
Cash (−A)		4,000		Cash (−A)		3,000	
Paid salaries owed at the end				*Paid salaries*			
of 2008				(9) Interest Expense (E, −RE)	500		
(4) Cash (+A)	6,000			Notes Payable (−L)	2,000		
Accounts Receivable (−A)		6,000		Cash (−A)		2,500	
Received cash on outstanding				*Paid interest and principal on an*			
accounts receivable				*outstanding loan*			
(5) Cash (+A)	7,000			(10) Dividends (−RE)	1,000		
Service Revenue (R, +RE)		7,000		Cash (−A)		1,000	
Received cash for services provided				*Paid cash dividend*			

T-ACCOUNTS

Cash				Accounts Receivable		Land		Salaries Payable		
	12,000			9,000		15,000				4,000
(1)	5,000	(2)	7,000		(4) 6,000	(2) 7,000		(3)	4,000	
(4)	6,000	(3)	4,000	3,000		22,000				0
(5)	7,000	(6)	500							
		(7)	100							
		(8)	3,000							
		(9)	2,500							
		(10)	1,000							
	11,900									

Notes Payable			Contributed Capital		Retained Earnings		Service Revenue	
		6,000		21,000		5,000		(5) 7,000
(9)	2,000			(1) 5,000				
		4,000		26,000				

Salary Expense		Rent Expense		Insurance Expense		Interest Expense	
(8)	3,000	(6)	500	(7)	100	(9)	500

Dividends	
(10)	1,000

FIGURE 4-12

Financial
statements for
Maple Services
Company

Income Statement
for the Year Ended December 31, 2012

Service revenue		$7,000
Expenses:		
Salaries	$3,000	
Rent	500	
Insurance	100	
Interest	500	
Total expenses		4,100
Net income		$2,900

Statement of Shareholders' Equity
for the Year Ended December 31, 2012

	Common Share	Retained Earnings	Total
Beginning balance	$21,000	$ 5,000	$26,000
Common share issuances	5,000		5,000
Net income		2,900	2,900
Less: Dividends		(1,000)	(1,000)
Ending balance	$26,000	$ 6,900	$32,900

Balance Sheet
December 31, 2012

ASSETS		LIABILITIES AND SHAREHOLDERS' EQUITY	
Cash	$11,900	Notes payable	$ 4,000
Accounts receivable	3,000	Contributed capital	26,000
Land	22,000	Retained earnings	6,900
		Total liabilities and	
Total assets	$36,900	shareholders' equity	$36,900

Statement of Cash Flows
December 31, 2012

Operating activities:		
Cash receipts for services	$ 7,000	
Cash receipts from accounts receivable	6,000	
Cash payments for salaries	(7,000)	
Cash payments for rent	(500)	
Cash payments for insurance	(100)	
Cash payments for interest	(500)	
Cash increase (decrease) due to operating activities		$ 4,900
Investing activities:		
Cash payment for purchase of land	$(7,000)	
Cash increase (decrease) due to investing activities		(7,000)
Financing activities:		
Cash receipt from issuing share	$ 5,000	
Cash payment for loan principal	(2,000)	
Cash payment for dividends	(1,000)	
Cash increase (decrease) due to financing activities		2,000
Increase (decrease) in cash balance		$ (100)
Beginning cash balance		12,000
Ending cash balance		$11,900

INCOME STATEMENT. The income statement for the period ending December 31, 2012, is prepared by subtracting the balances in the expense T-accounts (salary expense, rent expense, insurance expense, and interest expense) from the balances in the revenue T-accounts (service revenue), resulting in net income.

The statement of shareholders' equity for that same period consists of adding the $5,000 common share issuance to the beginning balance in common share, coming to the ending (2012) balance of $26,000. Common stock is a form of contributed capital. The reconciliation of the retained earnings account consists of the addition of net income less the amount of dividends declared during the period. The result ($6,900) is the ending (December 31, 2012) balance in retained earnings.

BALANCE SHEET. The December 31, 2012, balance sheet consists of the balances in the asset (cash, accounts receivable, land), liability (notes payable), and shareholders' equity (contributed capital and retained earnings) T-accounts. Note that the ending balance in retained earnings ($6,900), which was computed on the statement of share-holders' equity, appears on the balance sheet.

The dollar amounts on the balance sheet represent the beginning balances for asset, liability, and shareholders' equity T-accounts for the next period (2013). Since the dollar amounts in the revenue, expense, and dividend accounts are reflected in the ending balance of retained earnings, the revenue, expense, and dividend T-accounts begin the next period (2013) with zero balances. The balance sheet accounts are described as **permanent** because their balances accumulate from one period to the next. The income statement and dividend accounts are described as **temporary** because their balances begin each new period at zero.[3]

STATEMENT OF CASH FLOWS. The statement of cash flows is prepared from the cash T-account. Each cash inflow and outflow is classified as operating, investing, or financing and then placed on the statement. This statement reconciles the change in the cash balance during the period, expressing it in terms of cash increases (decreases) due to operating, investing, and financing activities.

RECOGNIZING GAINS AND LOSSES

Companies often sell investments and noncurrent assets, receiving dollar amounts that do not match the amounts at which the investments are carried on the balance sheet. In such cases, a gain or loss must be recognized in the amount of the difference between the proceeds and the carrying amount.

> **?** When JCPenney sold the Eckerd drugstore chain to CVS Corporation for $4.53 billion, it recorded a $77 million loss on the transaction. How can a company sell a subsidiary for over $4 billion and record a loss on the transaction?

When McDonnell Douglas sold its North American Field Service business for $100 million, it recognized a $29 million gain because the investment was carried on the company's balance sheet at $71 million. Assuming that the business was acquired

---

3. In actual accounting systems, the year-end balances in the revenue, expense, and dividend accounts are formally transferred to retained earnings through a series of journal entries. This closing process zeroes out the balances in the temporary accounts so that they begin at zero the next period. This process is illustrated in the review problem at the end of this chapter.

for $71 million, the following journal entries were used to record these events. (Dollar amounts are in millions.)

Investment (+A)	71	
Cash (−A)		71

Acquired North American Field Service for cash

Cash (+A)	100	
Investment (−A)		71
Gain on Sale (Ga, +RE)		29

Sold North American Field Service for gain

If McDonnell Douglas had sold the business for an amount less than the $71 million carrying amount, $55 million for example, a loss would have been recognized in the following manner.

Cash (+A)	55	
Loss on Sale (Lo, −RE)	16	
Investment (−A)		71

Sold North American Field Service for loss

The gain or loss in the entry represents the profit or loss on the transaction in the amount of the difference between the proceeds and the balance sheet value of the investment. Note also that the gain or loss appears on the income statement, and the cash proceeds from the sale would appear on the statement of cash flows under cash flows from investing activities.

Goodyear Tire & Rubber sold assets in its Latin American and European segments for $53.3 million. The value of the assets on the balance sheet prior to the sale was $27.6 million. How did Goodyear record this transaction?

PERIODIC ADJUSTMENTS

Up to now the discussion has focused on the financial statement effects of exchange transactions—transactions backed by documented evidence, in which assets and/or liabilities are transferred between parties. Assets and liabilities, however, are often created or discharged without the occurrence of a visible, document-driven exchange transaction. They sometimes build up or expire as time passes. Interest, for example, is earned continually on bank savings accounts, and machinery depreciates as it is used in a company's operations. Such phenomena are not evidenced by exchange transactions, but they can be very important to a company's performance and financial condition.

Net income for a particular period is measured by (1) recognizing revenues when the earning process is complete and (2) matching against those revenues the expenses incurred to generate them. Under this view of performance, called the **accrual system of accounting,** revenues are booked when assets are created (or liabilities are discharged) and expenses are recorded when liabilities arise (or assets are reduced). In other words, revenues and expenses can be recognized either before or after the related cash is received or paid. The accrual system requires that periodic adjustments be made to the financial statements so that net income for a given period of time will be the result of a proper matching of the revenues and expenses within that period.

Periodic adjustments take one of three forms: (1) accruals, (2) deferrals, and (3) revaluations. The first two are covered in this chapter; revaluation adjustments are covered in subsequent chapters as they arise.

Accruals

Accruals refer to amounts in asset and liability accounts that build up over time. The term *accrue* simply means to build up gradually.[4] Two very common examples are accrued wages and accrued interest.

ACCRUED WAGES

Suppose that employees of Taylor Motor are paid at the end of each week. The total weekly payroll is $10,000, which is earned at a rate of $2,000 per day for each of the five working days. Assume that December 31 falls on a Tuesday, and the financial statements are prepared as of that day. Figure 4–13 illustrates these facts and the journal entries that would be recorded under accrual accounting.

FIGURE 4–13   Accrued wages

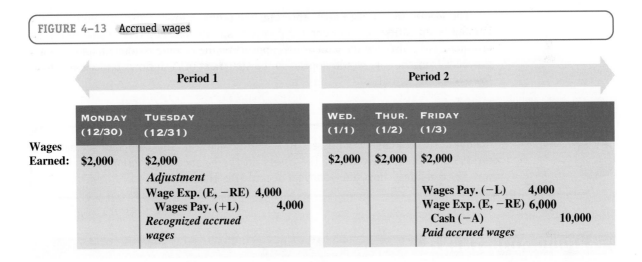

In applying the accrual system, it must be recognized that although no cash has been paid as of December 31, a liability has been created. The company owes its employees two days' worth of wages, or $4,000. This liability is recognized with an adjusting journal entry of the form indicated in Figure 4–13. Wage expense of $4,000 is reflected on the income statement of the period ending on December 31 (Period 1). Wages payable of $4,000 appears in the liability section of the December 31 balance sheet, and the amount is carried into Period 2. Note that on Friday, when the $10,000 cash payment for wages is made, $4,000 serves to remove the wages payable (the liability is discharged), and $6,000 is charged to wage expense of Period 2 and thus will appear on the income statement of Period 2.

The adjustment in this example achieves matching, in that it matches the cost of the effort expended by the employees in Period 1 with the revenues generated in Period 1. Wage expense of $4,000 is subtracted from Period 1 revenues in the computation of

---

4. Note that the term *accrual* refers to a system of accounting that recognizes revenues and expenses as assets and liabilities are created or discharged, as well as one of two kinds of adjusting entries. The double meaning of this term can be a source of confusion, and it is important that you be aware of the context in which it is used.

Period 1 net income. Similarly, the cost of the effort expended by the employees in Period 2 ($6,000) is matched against Period 2 revenues on the Period 2 income statement.

It is also important to realize that Taylor would prepare statements of cash flows for Periods 1 and 2 and the entire $10,000 cash payment would be reflected in the operating section of that statement in the second period only. None of it would appear on the statement of cash flows of Period 1. As Figure 4–14 indicates, the total resource expenditure recognized under the accrual system is the same as that recognized under the cash system. The difference lies in the timing of the recognition. Due to the adjustment, the accrual system recognizes $4,000 in Period 1 and $6,000 in Period 2.

FIGURE 4–14 Expenditure recognition	**Accounting System/Financial Statement**	**Period 1**	**Period 2**	**Period 3**

Accounting System/Financial Statement	Period 1	Period 2	Period 3
Accrual/Income statement	$4,000	$ 6,000	$10,000
Cash/Statement of cash flows	0	10,000	10,000

ACCRUED INTEREST

Suppose that on December 1, Bank of America Corporation loans $12,000 to Exxon Mobil Oil Company at an annual interest rate of 10 percent. Assume that the accounting period ends on December 31 and that Exxon pays Bank of America in full (principal and interest) on January 31 of the next year. Figure 4–15 illustrates these facts and the journal entries that would be recorded under accrual accounting.

FIGURE 4–15 Accrued interest revenue

Period 1		Period 2

DECEMBER 1	**DECEMBER 31**	**JANUARY 31**

Note Rec. (+A) 12,000
   Cash (−A)   12,000
Received note for cash
	Adjustment
	Interest Rec. (+A) 100
	   Interest Rev. (R, +RE) 100
	*Recognized accrued
	interest received*
		Cash (+A) 12,200
		   Interest Rec. (−A) 100
		   Interest Rev. (R, +RE) 100
		   Note Rec. (−A) 12,000
		*Received cash on
		outstanding note*

Bank of America records an adjustment on December 31 to reflect the fact that an asset, *interest receivable,* has been created. The company has earned $100 ([$12,000 × 10%]/12 months) in interest during the month of December. Interest receivable of $100 is recognized (debited), and *interest revenue* is credited. When the $12,200 cash payment is received on January 31, $12,000 serves to reduce the outstanding note receivable, $100 is charged against the interest receivable account, and the remaining $100 is recognized as interest revenue.

As in the example of accrued wages, the adjustment here helps to achieve a matching of revenues and expenses in the appropriate time period. It does so by dividing the

total interest earned on the loan ($200) into two components, based on the periods in which it was earned and the time when the asset, interest receivable, was created. Half of the $200 interest payment was earned in Period 1 and therefore should appear as a revenue on the income statement of Period 1. The remaining $100 should appear as a revenue on the income statement of Period 2 because the loan was outstanding during one month of Period 2.

Consider again the effect of these transactions on the statements of cash flows for Periods 1 and 2. No cash inflow related to interest is recorded in Period 1, and therefore nothing would be reflected on the statement of cash flows for that period. Instead, all $200 would appear on the statement of cash flows in Period 2, when the cash is actually received. Once again, the total interest recognized across the two periods under the cash system ($200) is the same as that recognized under the accrual system, but the timing of the recognition is different. The adjusting journal entry prepared under the accrual system ensures that $100 is recognized on the income statement of Period 1, with the remaining $100 appearing on the income statement of Period 2.

Figure 4–16, using the same facts as Figure 4–15, considers the borrower's (Exxon Mobil's) point of view. Examine the journal entries, and note especially how the adjusting journal entry matches revenues and expenses in the appropriate time period and gives rise to expense recognition in a time period when no cash payment is made.

FIGURE 4–16   Accrued interest expense

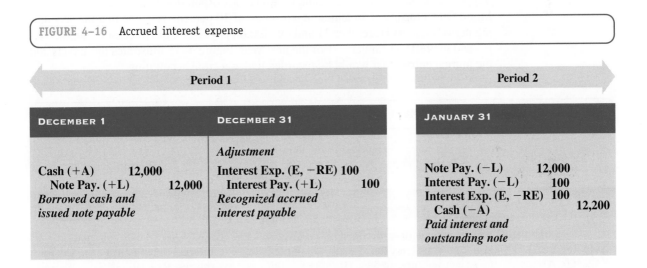

> Honeywell International, an advanced technology and manufacturing company, reported accrued liabilities of $6.0 billion on its 2008 balance sheet. Explain the meaning of that number.

Deferrals

The second type of adjustment is called a **deferral** (or **cost expiration**). Like accruals, these adjusting entries (1) are recorded in the books at the end of an accounting period to achieve an appropriate matching of revenues and expenses and (2) do not reflect cash exchanges. They are called deferrals because they are entries that serve to defer the recognition of an expense or revenue until the proper time.

ASSET CAPITALIZATION AND THE MATCHING PRINCIPLE

Before studying deferrals, you should understand one very important concept in financial accounting measurement—*asset capitalization* and how it relates to the matching principle. The **matching principle** involves a four-step process: (1) a cost is incurred in the current period for the purpose of generating revenue; (2) the revenue recognition principle determines the period in which the revenue is recognized; (3) if the revenue is recognized in the current period, the cost is **expensed** (appearing on the income statement as an expense); if the revenue is expected to be recognized in a future period, the cost is **capitalized** (appearing on the balance sheet as an asset); and (4) capitalized costs are converted to expenses (by recording cost expiration adjusting journal entries) in those future periods when revenue is recognized. Assets, by definition, are expected to generate economic benefits in the form of future revenues, and, according to the matching principle, the costs of acquiring assets should be matched against those benefits when they are recognized. The accrual system of accounting accomplishes this matching by initially capitalizing the costs of assets and then converting them to expenses (through periodic adjustments) as their usefulness expires and their benefits are realized.

To illustrate the important difference between expensing and capitalizing a cost, consider a company with the following simplified balance sheet as of December 31, 2011:

Assets	$1,000	Liabilities	$ 600
		Shareholders' equity	400
Total	$1,000	Total	$1,000

During 2012, the company recognizes $2,500 in revenues and $1,500 in expenses. In a separate transaction the company also spends $500 on its facilities. Should the $500 be considered an expense for 2012 or an asset? Figure 4–17 provides the resulting financial statements if the company expenses or capitalizes the $500 expenditure, assuming that all transactions were in cash.

FIGURE 4–17
Expensing vs. capitalizing

	Expenses $500	Capitalizes $500
Balance sheet:		
Assets	$ 1,500	$2,000
Liabilities	600	600
Shareholders' equity	900	1,400
Income statement:		
Revenues	$ 2,500	$2,500
Expenses	2,000	1,500
Net income	$ 500	$1,000

Note the differences in total assets, shareholders' equity, expenses, and net income. Assets and net income are clearly much higher if the company chooses to capitalize the $500 cost. As illustrated in the next section, however, if the cost is capitalized it will have to be amortized against revenues in future periods, reducing reported net income in those periods.

?

The *Baltimore Sun* reported that the WorldCom fraud, which cost investors billions of dollars, "was not complicated: the company's financial officers recorded routine maintenance expenses totaling $3.9 billion as capital expenditures. . . ." Explain how this scheme violated the matching principle and affected the financial statements.

EXPENSE OR CAPITALIZE EXAMPLES

Figure 4–18 illustrates the basic procedures used to account for expenses and capitalized costs. It is divided into two sections. The upper section depicts the matching process. The lower section consists of nine different transactions, each carried through the four steps involved in applying the matching principle.

FIGURE 4–18   Expense or capitalize?

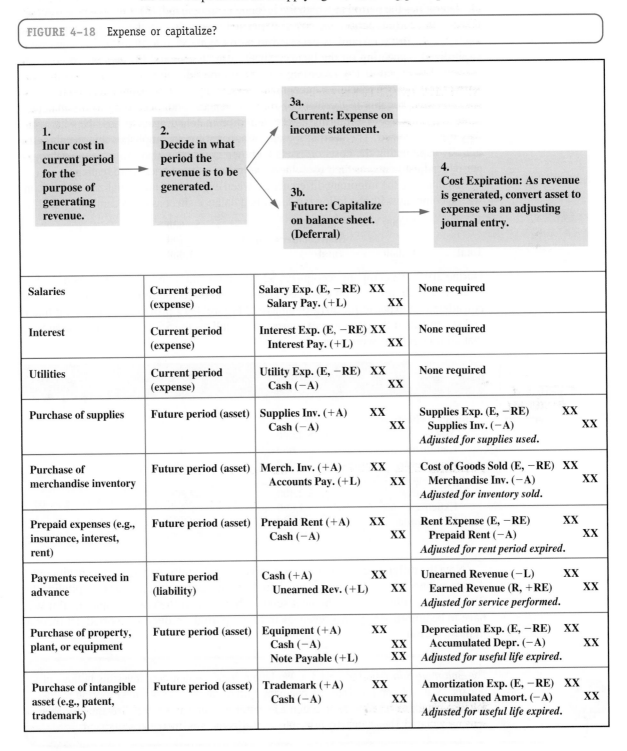

Salaries	**Current period (expense)**	Salary Exp. (E, −RE) XX Salary Pay. (+L) XX	None required
Interest	**Current period (expense)**	Interest Exp. (E, −RE) XX Interest Pay. (+L) XX	None required
Utilities	**Current period (expense)**	Utility Exp. (E, −RE) XX Cash (−A) XX	None required

Purchase of supplies	**Future period (asset)**	Supplies Inv. (+A) XX
		    Cash (−A) XX
			Supplies Exp. (E, −RE) XX
			    Supplies Inv. (−A) XX
			Adjusted for supplies used.

Purchase of merchandise inventory	**Future period (asset)**	Merch. Inv. (+A) XX
		    Accounts Pay. (+L) XX
			Cost of Goods Sold (E, −RE) XX
			    Merchandise Inv. (−A) XX
			Adjusted for inventory sold.

Prepaid expenses (e.g., insurance, interest, rent)	**Future period (asset)**	Prepaid Rent (+A) XX
		    Cash (−A) XX
			Rent Expense (E, −RE) XX
			    Prepaid Rent (−A) XX
			Adjusted for rent period expired.

Payments received in advance	**Future period (liability)**	Cash (+A) XX
		    Unearned Rev. (+L) XX
			Unearned Revenue (−L) XX
			    Earned Revenue (R, +RE) XX
			Adjusted for service performed.

Purchase of property, plant, or equipment	**Future period (asset)**	Equipment (+A) XX
		    Cash (−A) XX
		    Note Payable (+L) XX
			Depreciation Exp. (E, −RE) XX
			    Accumulated Depr. (−A) XX
			Adjusted for useful life expired.

Purchase of intangible asset (e.g., patent, trademark)	**Future period (asset)**	Trademark (+A) XX
		    Cash (−A) XX
			Amortization Exp. (E, −RE) XX
			    Accumulated Amort. (−A) XX
			Adjusted for useful life expired.

CURRENT EXPENSES. The first three transactions (salaries, interest, and utilities) represent resource expenditures, either through the creation of a liability or the payment of cash, for which the benefit is assumed to be realized in the current period. Salaries and interest in this case are accrued at the end of the current period with an accrual adjusting journal entry, and the associated cash payments are expected to follow in a future period. The utility expense is both recognized and paid in the current period. Since the benefit from each of these three expenditures is assumed to be realized in the current period, all are expensed, regardless of the timing of the cash payment. These expenditures have not been capitalized and, therefore, Step 4 in the matching process, an adjusting journal entry, is not necessary.

SUPPLIES INVENTORY. The fourth transaction in Figure 4–18, the purchase of supplies, is capitalized because supplies are normally expected to be useful beyond the current period. Typically, at the end of each period, an inventory of the remaining supplies is taken, and a cost expiration adjusting journal entry is entered in the books to reflect the cost of the supplies that were used (expired) during the period. This entry also restates the supplies inventory account on the balance sheet to reflect the supplies actually on hand at the end of the period.

   To illustrate, assume that during 2011 Weyerhaeuser Company purchased materials and supplies to support the manufacture of forest products at a total cost of $700. On December 31, a count revealed that supplies in the amount of $300 remained on hand. If the company began the year with $500 in the supplies account, the cost of the supplies used during 2011 would be computed as shown below, and the following journal entries would have been recorded to reflect these facts.

Supplies Used	=	Beginning Inventory	+	Purchases	−	Ending Inventory
$900	=	$500	+	$700	−	$300

2011: Purchase of Supplies			Dec. 31: Cost Expiration Adjusting Entry		
Supplies Inventory (+A)	700		Supplies Expense (E, −RE)	900	
Cash (−A)		700	Supplies Inventory (−A)		900
Purchased supplies			*Recognized use of supplies*		

   In this situation, supplies in the amount of $300 would be reported on the company's December 31 balance sheet.

MERCHANDISE INVENTORY. The purchase of merchandise inventory is capitalized because inventories are expected to generate revenues in the future when they are sold. According to the matching principle, the cost of the merchandise should be converted to an expense, cost of goods sold, in the period when the inventories are sold. According to the matching principle, the cost of the merchandise inventory should be converted to an expense (called cost of goods sold) when the revenue associated with the sale of the inventory is recognized. Assuming that Macy's sold merchandise inventory with a cost of $5,000, the journal entries following demonstrate how the capitalized cost would become cost of goods sold.

2011: Purchase of Merchandise			At Time of Sale		
Merchandise Inv. (+A)	5,000		Cost of Goods Sold (E, −RE)	5,000	
Cash (−A)		5,000	Merchandise Inv. (−A)		5,000
Purchased merchandise			*Adjusted for inventory sold*		

PREPAID EXPENSES. Prepaid expenses represent costs such as insurance, interest, and rent that are paid in advance, before the associated benefit is realized. Insurance

premiums, for example, are paid in advance and usually cover an entire year or more. Similarly, interest on loans is sometimes paid before the borrowed funds are used. In applying the matching principle, such prepayments are capitalized and then converted to expenses as the time period expires and benefits are realized. This periodic conversion is achieved through cost expiration adjusting journal entries.

To illustrate, assume that on January 1, 2011, Merck purchased a $1,000 insurance premium for a two-year period. The following journal entries would be made on the books of Merck over the life of the insurance coverage.

Jan. 1, 2011: Purchase of Insurance			Dec. 31, 2011 and 2012: Cost Expiration Adjusting Entry		
Prepaid Insurance (+A)	1,000		Insurance Expense (E, −RE)	500	
Cash (−A)		1,000	Prepaid Insurance (−A)		500
Paid insurance in advance			*Adjusted for expiration of insurance*		

In this example, Merck would report in the current asset section of its 2011 balance sheet $500 of prepaid (unexpired) insurance, which would be converted to an expense at the end of 2012.

UNEARNED (DEFERRED) REVENUES. Unearned revenues are the reverse of prepaid expenses. For every entity that prepays an expense before the associated benefit is realized, another entity receives a payment before it performs the required service. When applying the revenue recognition principle to the entity that receives payment and has yet to provide the service, a liability account, called **unearned revenues,** is credited when the cash is initially collected. This account is then converted to a revenue as the service is performed with an end-of-period adjusting journal entry.[5]

To illustrate, suppose that Delta Air Lines received $5,000 during 2011 for tickets not yet used. Delta's cash account would immediately increase by $5,000, but the company would not recognize revenue at that time because it had not yet performed the contracted service. Instead, Delta would recognize a $5,000 liability, indicating that it owed services in the form of airplane travel. Assume that as of the end of 2011, Delta had fulfilled 60 percent of the services. At that time, therefore, an adjusting journal entry would be recorded to remove 60 percent of the liability from the company's balance sheet and, at the same time, recognize 60 percent of the revenue. The following journal entries reflect these facts.

Receipt of Advance Payment			Cost Expiration Adjusting Entry		
Cash (+A)	5,000		Unearned Revenue (−L)	3,000	
Unearned Revenue (+L)		5,000	Fees Earned (R, +RE)		3,000
Received cash prior to providing *service*			*Recognized revenue from providing* *service*		

This sequence of journal entries would leave a liability for unearned revenues on Delta's 2011 balance sheet of $2,000, representing airline travel that Delta still had to fulfill.

PROPERTY, PLANT, AND EQUIPMENT. Transaction 8 in Figure 4–18 considers the costs of purchasing property, plant, and equipment. Since these assets are expected to

---

5. Technically, an unearned revenue does not represent a capitalized cost because it is not an asset, and therefore, the adjusting journal entry to convert it to a revenue is not a cost expiration adjusting journal entry. However, we have chosen to categorize it as such because the concept of deferring the recognition of a revenue until the service is performed is the same as deferring the recognition of an expense until the associated benefit is realized. Both are essential to implementing the matching principle.

help generate revenues beyond the current time period, the matching principle specifies that the acquisition costs be capitalized and systematically converted to an expense (**amortized**) over the estimated useful lives of the assets. At the end of each period of the estimated useful life, a cost expiration adjusting journal entry is recorded to amortize a portion of the capitalized cost. The process of amortizing the cost of property, plant, and equipment is called **depreciation.**

To illustrate, assume that Federal Express invested $10,000 in flight equipment on January 1, 2011. At the time of the purchase, FedEx management subjectively estimated that the equipment would have a useful life of ten years and chose to depreciate an equal amount of the capitalized cost ($1,000 = $10,000/10 years) at the end of each of the ten one-year periods. The following journal entries would have been recorded in FedEx's books.

Jan. 1, 2011: Purchase of Equipment			Dec. 31, 2011, 2012 . . . , 2020: Cost Expiration Adjusting Entry		
Equipment (+A)	10,000		Depr. Exp. (E, −RE)	1,000	
Cash (−A)		10,000	Accumulated Depr. (−A)		1,000
Purchased equipment			*Adjusted for depreciation on equipment*		

Note that the cost expiration adjusting journal entry involves a debit to depreciation expense that appears on the income statement for each of the ten years. It also involves a credit to an account called *accumulated depreciation,* instead of a credit to the equipment account itself. Accumulated depreciation is a special account that appears on the asset side of the balance sheet. It offsets the asset account to which it applies (i.e., *equipment*), maintaining an accumulated balance of the amount of depreciation taken on the asset up to the date of the balance sheet. Balance sheet accounts like accumulated depreciation, which are used to offset other balance sheet accounts, are called **contra accounts.** Subtracting the balance in the accumulated depreciation account from the original cost of the equipment on the balance sheet gives rise to a number referred to as **book value.**

Using the same information as in the preceding example, at the end of the second year (December 31, 2012) the equipment account would appear on FedEx's balance sheet as follows. The original cost of the equipment is $10,000, the accumulated depreciation is $2,000, and the net book value is $8,000.

Equipment	$10,000	
Less: Accumulated depreciation	2,000	$8,000

Estimating the useful life of property, plant, and equipment and choosing a method of allocating the capitalized cost to future periods is a subjective and difficult task for management. These choices can also have a significant effect on the amount of net income recognized each year because they have a direct bearing on the amount of depreciation expense that appears on the income statement. To illustrate the importance of such estimates, when Delta Air Lines decided to change the useful life estimate of its flight equipment from ten years to fifteen years, it disclosed in its financial report that the change decreased depreciation expense of that year by $130 million.

INTANGIBLE ASSETS. The final transaction in Figure 4–18 is the purchase of an intangible asset, such as a patent or trademark. The cost of this purchase is, once again, capitalized because the benefit of the purchase is expected to extend beyond the current period. Many intangibles have definable lives (often determined by law) over

which the capitalized cost is typically amortized. The cost expiration adjusting journal entry consists of a debit to *amortization expense* and a credit to the contra account, *accumulated amortization*.

To illustrate, assume that Johnson & Johnson, a leading manufacturer of consumer health care products, purchased a patent for $20,000, which was determined by law to have a twenty-year life. The following journal entries would be recorded by Johnson & Johnson over the patent's legal life.

Purchase of Patent			End of Each of 20 Subsequent Years: Cost Expiration Adjusting Entry		
Patent (+A)	**20,000**		**Amortization Exp. (E, −RE)**	**1,000**	
Cash (−A)		**20,000**	**Patent (−A)**		**1,000**
Acquired patent.			*Adjusted for amortization of patent.*		

Note that the *patent* account is credited directly in the entry to amortize the cost of the patent. This practice is common, although GAAP recommends the use of a separate accumulated amortization account.

Research and development (R&D) is a very important activity for pharmaceutical companies like Johnson & Johnson. In 2009 the company invested over $2.5 billion in these activities. Under U.S. GAAP Johnson & Johnson is required to treat these costs as expenses. However, under IFRS companies are allowed to capitalize the portion of R&D devoted to development. Comment on how this difference would affect the way in which an analyst compared the financial performance of Johnson & Johnson to Novartis, a Swiss pharmaceutical that uses IFRS.

CAPITALIZING AND MATCHING: EXAMPLES

Figure 4–19 contains several examples in which cost expiration adjusting journal entries are used to apply the matching principle. Such entries are designed to convert capitalized costs to expenses in future time periods as the benefits (revenues) from the initial expenditures are recognized. The transactions illustrated in Figure 4–19 consider supplies, merchandise inventory, prepaid insurance, unearned revenue, equipment, and a patent.

Note in Figure 4–19 that equal amounts of the cost of the equipment and the patent are depreciated, or amortized, in each of the three time periods. For example, the $9,000 equipment cost is depreciated at a rate of $3,000 per period. This method is referred to as **straight-line depreciation.** It is almost always used to amortize intangible assets, but it is only one of several methods that can be used to depreciate the capitalized costs of property, plant, and equipment.

During 2008, Eastman Kodak Company booked revenues of $9.4 billion; paid interest costs on outstanding debt of $108 million; purchased inventory of $7.3 billion; purchased property, plant, and equipment of $254 million; and recognized depreciation and amortization of $500 million. Explain each of these transactions in terms of Figures 4–18 and 4–19.

FIGURE 4-19   Capitalize and match

| CAPITALIZE → | ADJUSTING ENTRIES DURING COST EXPIRATION PERIOD → | | | EXPLANATION |
	1	2	3	

Supplies (+A)   100
  Cash (−A)   100
Purchased supplies.
	Sup. Exp. (E, −RE) 30
	  Supplies (−A) 30
	Supplies costing $70 on hand.
		Sup. Exp. (E, −RE) 50
		  Supplies (−A) 50
		Supplies costing $20 on hand.
			Sup. Exp. (E, −RE) 20
			  Supplies (−A) 20
			No supplies on hand.
				The cost of supplies is converted to expense as the supplies are used up.

Inventory (+A) 600
  Accts. Pay. (+L) 600
Purchased 6 items at $100 per item.
	COGS (E, −RE) 100
	  Inventory (−A) 100
	One item sold.
		COGS (E, −RE) 200
		  Inventory (−A) 200
		Two items sold.
			COGS (E, −RE) 300
			  Inventory (−A) 300
			Three items sold.
				The cost of inventory is converted to expense (Cost of Goods Sold) as the inventory is sold.

Pre. Ins. (+A)   300
  Cash (−A)   300
Paid 3 years of insurance coverage in advance.
	Ins. Exp. (E, −RE) 100
	  Prepaid Ins. (−A) 100
	The first year of insurance coverage expires.
		Ins. Exp. (E, −RE) 100
		  Prepaid ins. (−A) 100
		The second year of insurance coverage expires.
			Ins. Exp. (E, −RE) 100
			  Prepaid Ins. (−A) 100
			The third year of insurance coverage expires.
				The cost of prepaid insurance is converted to expense as the insurance coverage expires.

Cash (+A)   240
  Un. Rev. (+L)   240
Received $240 for services to be performed later.
	Un. Rev. (−L) 120
	  Fees Earned (R, +RE) 120
	Half of the service is performed.
		Un. Rev. (−L) 60
		  Fees Earned (R, +RE) 60
		One quarter of the service is performed.
			Un. Rev. (−L) 60
			  Fees Earned (R, +RE) 60
			One quarter of the service is performed.
				Revenue is recognized as the service is completed.

Equip. (+A)   9,000
  Notes Pay. (+L) 9,000
Purchased machinery with an estimated 3-year life and no salvage value.
	Dep. Exp. (E, −RE) 3,000
	  Accum. Dep. (−A) 3,000
	First year passes, assuming straight-line depreciation rate.
		Dep. Exp. (E, −RE) 3,000
		  Accum. Dep. (−A) 3,000
		Second year passes.
			Dep. Exp. (E, −RE) 3,000
			  Accum. Dep. (−A) 3,000
			Third year passes.
				The cost of machinery is converted to expense (Depreciation Expense) as the estimated useful life passes.

Patent (+A)   900
  Cash (−A)   900
Acquired patent with 3-year legal life.
	Amort. Exp. (E, −RE) 300
	  Accum. Amort. (−A) 300
	First year passes, assuming straight-line amortization rate.
		Amort. Exp. (E, −RE) 300
		  Accum. Amort. (−A) 300
		Second year passes.
			Amort. Exp. (E, −RE) 300
			  Accum. Amort. (−A) 300
			Third year passes.
				The cost of obtaining the patent is converted to an expense (Amortization Expense) as the legal life passes.

Revaluation Adjustments

At various points in the remainder of this text, we cover adjustments that do not fall into the categories of accruals or cost expirations. Such adjustments serve to restate certain accounts to keep their reported values in line with existing facts. For example, the balance sheet dollar amounts of short-term investments, accounts receivable, and inventories are sometimes adjusted when the market values of these assets change. The entries required in such situations are called **revaluation adjustments.**

REPORTING DIFFICULTIES FACED BY MULTINATIONAL COMPANIES

In this chapter we have covered the mechanics of preparing financial statements measured in U.S. dollars, written in the English language, and using U.S. GAAP. In this section we briefly discuss some of the reporting difficulties faced by **multinationals,** companies that have their home in one country but operate, own other companies (subsidiaries), and raise capital in other countries.

DuPont, for example, is a Delaware-based company that operates in approximately 90 different countries; has significant ownership interests in entities in the United States, Asia, Europe, and Latin America; and lists its common shares not only on the New York Stock Exchange, but also on a variety of non-U.S. exchanges. DuPont publishes U.S. GAAP-based financial reports expressed in U.S. dollars. Unilever, another world leader in consumer goods, is jointly based in the Netherlands and Britain and has significant ownership interests in entities operating in 23 different countries. Its common shares are listed on the New York, London, and Amsterdam stock exchanges, and it publishes IFRS-based financial statements expressed in euros.

We have already mentioned the difficulties faced by analysts who attempt to compare the financial performance of companies like DuPont and Unilever that publish financial statements based on different accounting standards expressed in different currencies. These same problems plague multinationals that must publish financial statements reflecting the financial performance of all the entities that make up the overall company.

All multinationals, U.S.-based and non-U.S.-based, report consolidated financial statements, meaning that the financial statements of all entities controlled by the parent company must be combined (consolidated) into a single set of financial reports. DuPont and Unilever, for example, both refer to their income statement as a "consolidated" income statement.

The process of consolidating all the different entities that comprise a company like DuPont or Unilever can be very difficult and costly. The separate entities that must be consolidated each prepare individual financial statements that often are expressed in different languages, using different currencies and different accounting standards. A subsidiary owned by DuPont and located in France, for example, may publish financial statements in French, expressed in euros, and using IFRS. In its effort to include this subsidiary's financial statements within the company's overall consolidated statements, DuPont must translate the French into English, convert the euro values into U.S. dollars, and adjust the IFRS-based financial statements to U.S. GAAP—and this process must be done for every one of DuPont's subsidiaries every time consolidated statements are prepared. Unilever has the same problem, but in its case the financial statements of the subsidiaries must be converted to euros and adjusted to IFRS standards.

These difficulties and the costs they impose on multinationals underscore the value of moving to a single global language, set of accounting standards, and currency. Right now almost all major multinationals publish financial statements in English, although a large percentage of non-U.S. companies publish financial statements in more than one language. U.S. GAAP and IFRS are the two predominant sets of financial reporting standards, and efforts are in place to eventually converge them. Differences in currencies across countries, on the other hand, are likely to persist well into the future, and as we discuss later, these differences introduce special risks, as well as reporting problems, faced by multinationals.

APPENDIX 4A

T-ACCOUNT ANALYSIS AND PREPARING THE STATEMENT OF CASH FLOWS

In this appendix we describe how the statement of cash flows can be prepared from two balance sheets and an income statement. The approach involves **T-account analysis,** a mechanical process by which by reconstructing activity in a T-account one can infer information not directly reported on the financial statements. T-account analysis is a valuable tool because it is used by companies to prepare the statement of cash flows, and it can be used by analysts to create useful information about a company not reported in the financial statements. We will also illustrate and differentiate the two methods used to present the statement of cash flows—the **direct method** and the more difficult but far more common **indirect method.**

Figure 4A–1 includes two balance sheets (2011 and 2010), an income statement (2011), and some additional information for Wildcat Industries. Figure 4A–2 includes the T-accounts corresponding to each of the accounts listed on the financial statements as well as the activity that took place in those accounts during 2011. The balance sheet accounts contain beginning balances (BB), which reflect the balances on the 2010 balance sheet as well as ending balances (EB), which reflect the balances on the 2011 balance sheet. Entries within the T-accounts correspond to the numbered journal entries listed in Figure 4A–3. Figure 4A–4 includes the statement of cash flows, derived using T-account analysis, using the direct form of presentation, and Figure 4A–5 includes the operating section of the statement of cash flows using the more common indirect form of presentation.

The statement of cash flows (direct form of presentation) in Figure 4A–4 was constructed from the activity in the cash T-account. Note that each of the amounts on the statement also appears in the cash T-account—cash increases on the left and cash decreases on the right. These cash amounts were derived as described below, divided into two categories: operating items and non-operating items.

OPERATING ITEMS

CASH FROM SALES (+$37,000). The income statement includes sales revenue of $40,000. Sales were made on account (see Additional Information on Figure 4A–1), which increased the accounts receivable T-account by 40,000 (1). Because the ending balance in accounts receivable was $15,000, accounts receivable must have been reduced during 2011 by $37,000, producing a cash increase of $37,000 (2). Customers must have made $37,000 in payments on account. The adjustment to convert the accrual-based sales revenue to cash inflow is illustrated below.

Income Statement Amount		Adjustment			Cash Flow
Sales revenue	$40,000	Less: Increase in accounts receivable	($3,000)	=	+$37,000

CASH FROM SERVICES (+$9,000). Service revenue of $12,000 on the income statement means that unearned revenue was reduced by $12,000 during 2011 (3). Cash is received in advance for services to be performed and the revenue is only recognized after the service is performed. Because the ending balance in unearned revenue is $5,000, cash received in advance for services to be performed during 2011 must have

FIGURE 4A-1   Two balance sheets and an income statement for Wildcat Industries

The following information was taken from the records of Wildcat Industries.

	2011	2010
BALANCE SHEET		
Cash	$ 8,000	$ 7,000
Accounts receivable	15,000	12,000
Inventory	18,000	15,000
Prepaid rent	5,000	3,000
Property, plant, and equipment	50,000	40,000
Less: Accumulated depreciation	(10,000)	(5,000)
Total assets	$86,000	$72,000
Accounts payable	8,000	4,000
Salaries payable	9,000	7,000
Dividend payable	2,000	3,000
Unearned revenue	5,000	8,000
Long-term debt	35,000	30,000
Contributed capital	19,000	15,000
Retained earnings	8,000	5,000
Total liabilities and stockholders' equity	$86,000	$72,000
INCOME STATEMENT		
Sales revenues	$40,000	
Service revenues	12,000	
Less:		
Cost of goods sold	30,000	
Salary expense	4,000	
Rent expense	6,000	
Depreciation expense	6,000	
Loss on sale of equipment	1,000	
Net income	$ 5,000	

Additional Information: Wildcat purchased property, plant, and equipment during the year in the amount of $15,000, paying cash, and borrowed $5,000 on a long-term note. All sales of goods and inventory purchases were made on account; cash received in advance for services to be performed is reflected in the unearned revenue account; and salaries are accrued and rent is paid in advance.

been $9,000 (4). During 2011, $9,000 was received from customers in advance, and services valued at $12,000 were performed. The adjustment to convert the accrual-based service revenue to cash inflow is illustrated below.

Income Statement Amount		Adjustment		Cash Flow
Service revenue	$12,000	Less: Decrease in unearned revenue	($3,000) =	+$9,000

CASH PAID TO INVENTORY SUPPLIERS (−$29,000). Cost of goods sold of $30,000 on the income statement means that the inventory T-account was reduced by $30,000 to reflect the outflow of sold inventory (5). Because the ending balance of inventory was $18,000, merchandise inventory in the amount of $33,000 must have been purchased from suppliers (6). Inventory purchases were made on account (see Additional Information on Figure 4A-1), meaning that the accounts payable T-account must have been increased by $33,000 (6). Because the ending balance in this account was

FIGURE 4A-2 Reconstructed Wildcat ledger

Cash			
BB 7,000			
(2) 37,000			
(4) 9,000			
	29,000	(7)	
(14) 3,000			
	2,000	(9)	
(15) 5,000	8,000	(11)	
(16) 4,000	15,000	(13)	
	3,000	(18)	
EB 8,000			

Accounts Receivable	
BB 12,000	
(1) 40,000	
	37,000 (2)
EB 15,000	

Property, Plant, and Equipment

BB 40,000	
(13) 15,000	
	5,000 (14)
EB 50,000	

Inventory	
BB 15,000	
	30,000 (5)
(6) 33,000	
EB 18,000	

Accumulated Depreciation

	5,000 (BB)
	6,000 (12)
(14) 1,000	
	10,000 EB

Prepaid Rent	
BB 3,000	
(11) 8,000	6,000 (10)
EB 5,000	

Accounts Payable	
	4,000 (BB)
	33,000 (6)
(7) 29,000	
	8,000 EB

Salaries Payable	
	7,000 BB
	4,000 (8)
(9) 2,000	
	9,000 EB

Dividend Payable	
	3,000 BB
	2,000 (17)
(18) 3,000	
	2,000 EB

Unearned Revenue	
	8,000 BB
(3) 12,000	
	9,000 (4)
	5,000 EB

Long-Term Debt	
	30,000 BB
	5,000 (15)
	35,000 EB

Contributed Capital	
	15,000 BB
	4,000 (16)
	19,000 EB

Retained Earnings	
	5,000 BB
	5,000 NI*
(17) 2,000	
	8,000 EB

Sales Revenue	
	40,000 (1)

Service Revenue	
	12,000 (3)

Cost of Goods Sold	
(5) 30,000	

Salary Expense	
(8) 4,000	

Rent Expense	
(10) 6,000	

Depreciation Expense	
(12) 6,000	

Loss on Sale of Equipment	
(14) 1,000	

* NI net income.

$8,000, $29,000 in cash must have been paid to inventory suppliers (7). The adjustment to convert the accrual-based cost of goods sold to cash payments to suppliers is illustrated below.

Income Statement Amount	Adjustment	Cash Flow
Cost of goods sold $30,000	Plus: Increase in inventory ($3,000)	=
	Less: Increase in accounts payable ($4,000)	= −$29,000

CASH PAID FOR SALARIES (−$2,000). Salary expense of $4,000 on the income statement means that salaries payable was increased by $4,000 during 2011 (see Additional Information on Figure 4A–1 stating that salaries are accrued, and entry (8) on Figure 4A–3). Because the ending balance in the salaries payable T-account was $9,000, $2,000 in cash must have been paid for salaries (9). The adjustment to convert the accrual-based salary expense to cash payments to employees is illustrated on next page.

FIGURE 4A-3   Reconstructed Wildcat journal entries

(1) Accounts Receivable (+A)	40,000	
Sales Revenue (R, +R/E)		40,000
(2) Cash (+A)	37,000	
Accounts Receivable (−A)		37,000
(3) Unearned Revenue (−L)	12,000	
Service Revenue (R, +R/E)		12,000
(4) Cash (+A)	9,000	
Unearned Revenue (+L)		9,000
(5) Cost of Goods Sold (E, −R/E)	30,000	
Inventory (−A)		30,000
(6) Inventory (+A)	33,000	
Accounts Payable (+L)		33,000
(7) Accounts Payable (−L)	29,000	
Cash (−A)		29,000
(8) Salary Expense (E, −R/E)	4,000	
Salary Payable (+L)		4,000
(9) Salary Payable (−L)	2,000	
Cash (−A)		2,000
(10) Rent Expense (E, −R/E)	6,000	
Prepaid Rent (−A)		6,000
(11) Prepaid Rent (+A)	8,000	
Cash (−A)		8,000
(12) Depreciation Expense (E, −R/E)	6,000	
Accumulated Depreciation (−A)		6,000
(13) Property, Plant, and Equipment (+A)	15,000	
Cash (−A)		15,000
(14) Cash (+A)	3,000	
Accumulated Depreciation (+A)	1,000	
Loss on Sale of Equipment (E, −R/E)	1,000	
Property, Plant, and Equipment (−A)		5,000
(15) Cash (+A)	5,000	
Long-Term Debt (+L)		5,000
(16) Cash (+A)	4,000	
Contributed Capital (+SE)		4,000
(17) Retained Earnings (−SE)	2,000	
Dividend Payable (+L)		2,000
(18) Dividend Payable (−L)	3,000	
Cash (−A)		3,000

Income Statement Amount		Adjustment		Cash Flow
Salary expense	$4,000	Less: Increase in salary payable	($2,000) =	−$2,000

CASH PAID FOR RENT (−$8,000). Rent expense of $6,000 on the income statement means that prepaid rent in the amount of $6,000 must have been expired, reducing the prepaid rent T-account (10). Because the ending balance in the account was

FIGURE 4A–4
Statement of cash
flows—direct
method of
presentation

**Statement of Cash Flows
for the Year Ended December 31, 2011**

Cash from sales (2)*	$37,000
Cash from services (4)	9,000
Cash paid to inventory suppliers (7)	(29,000)
Cash paid for salaries (9)	(2,000)
Cash paid for rent (11)	(8,000)
Net cash from operations	7,000
Cash paid for PP&E (13)	(15,000)
Cash received from equipment sale (14)	3,000
Net cash used for investing	(12,000)
Cash received from borrowings (15)	5,000
Cash received from stock issuance (16)	4,000
Cash paid for dividends (18)	(3,000)
Net cash from financing	6,000
Change in cash balance	1,000
Beginning cash balance	7,000
Ending cash balance	$ 8,000

Number in parentheses refer to entries numbered in Figure 4A–3.

FIGURE 4A–4
Statement of cash flows—direct method of presentation

$5,000, $8,000 of prepaid rent must have been paid for during 2011, reducing cash by $8,000 (11). The adjustment to convert the accrual-based rent expense to cash payments for rent is illustrated below.

Income Statement Amount		Adjustment		Cash Flow
Rent expense	$8,000	Less: Increase in prepaid rent	($2,000)	= −$6,000

NON-OPERATING ITEMS

CASH PAID FOR PROPERTY, PLANT, AND EQUIPMENT (PP&E) (−$15,000).

See Additional Information on Figure 14A–1 and entry (13) on Figure 4A–3. The $15,000 PP&E purchase increased the PP&E T-account by $15,000. Because the ending balance in the PP&E T-account was $50,000, PP&E with an original cost of $5,000 must have been sold (or disposed of) during 2011 (14).

FIGURE 4A–5
Operating section
of statement of
cash flows—
indirect method
of presentation

Net income	$5,000
Non-current items:	
Depreciation	6,000
Loss on sale of equipment	1,000
Current items:	
Less: Increase in accounts receivable	(3,000)
Less: Increase in inventory	(3,000)
Less: Increase in prepaid rent	(2,000)
Plus: Increase in accounts payable	4,000
Plus: Increase in salaries payable	2,000
Less: Decrease in unearned revenue	(3,000)
Net cash from operations	$7,000

FIGURE 4A–5
Operating section of statement of cash flows—indirect method of presentation

CASH RECEIVED FROM EQUIPMENT SALE (+$3,000). Depreciation expense of $6,000 on the income statement means that the accumulated depreciation T-account was increased by $6,000 (12). Because the ending balance in the accumulated depreciation T-account was $10,000, this account must have been reduced by $1,000 during 2011 (14), which means the PP&E sold during 2011 (see above) must have had accumulated depreciation attached to it of $1,000—in other words, its book value at the time of sale was $4,000 ($5,000 original cost − $1,000 accumulated depreciation). The loss on sale of equipment of $1,000 on the income statement means that when this equipment was sold, the cash proceeds ($3,000) were $1,000 less than the book value of the sold equipment (14).

CASH RECEIVED FROM BORROWING (+$5,000). The long-term debt T-account increased from $30,000 to $35,000 during 2011, indicating that the cash increase from (net) additional borrowings during the year equaled $5,000 (15).

CASH RECEIVED FROM STOCK ISSUANCES (+$4,000). The contributed capital T-account increased from $15,000 to $19,000 during 2011, indicating that the cash increase from (net) additional stock issuances during the year equaled $4,000 (16).

CASH PAID FOR DIVIDENDS (−$3,000). Net income reported on the income statement was $5,000 for 2011, meaning that the retained earnings T-account was increased by $5,000. Because the ending balance in retained earnings was $8,000, dividends declared by the board of directors, which reduces retained earnings and increases dividend payable, must have been $2,000 (17). Because the ending balance in the dividend payable T-account was $2,000, the cash payment to shareholders for dividends during 2011 must have been $3,000 (18).

INDIRECT FORM OF PRESENTATION

The explanations above describe how each of the items on the statement of cash flows—direct method of presentation (Figure 4A–4) was derived. Each of these items is represented on the cash T-account, and reflects an actual cash flow. The phrase "direct method of presentation" is used because each item is *directly* related to the cash account.

The statement of cash flows—indirect method of presentation (Figure 4A–5) is exactly the same as the Direct Method of Presentation *except for the manner in which net cash from operations ($7,000) is computed*. Rather than taking the operating cash flows directly from the cash T-account, the indirect method computes net cash from operations by first taking net income ($5,000) from the income statement (Figure 4A–1), and then adjusting it for the differences between the accrual-based measures of revenues and expenses and actual cash flows.

Depreciation ($6,000) and loss on sale of equipment ($1,000), for example, are both added back to net income in the calculation of net cash from operations. Both represent expenses on the income statement, recorded under the accrual basis, that reduced net income, but did not reduce operating cash flows. Note that in entries (12) and (14) on Figure 4A–3, neither involves an operating cash outflow. Consequently, both amounts are added back to net income in the calculation of net cash from operations.

The remaining adjustments all deal with changes in the current balance sheet accounts from 2010 to 2011. Each of these adjustments to the operating balance sheet items was illustrated earlier when we used T-account analysis to derive the cash flows associated with sales and service revenues, cost of goods sold, salaries, and rent. In each case the change in the current balance sheet account balance was added to or subtracted from net income in the calculation of net cash from operations. Table 4A–1 summarizes the relationships between changes in current balance-sheet account balances and the direction of the adjustment to net income in the calculation of net cash from operations.

TABLE 4A–1   Adjustments for changes in current balance sheet accounts on the statement of cash flows—Indirect form of presentation

	Increase	Decrease
Current Assets	*Subtract from net income*	*Add to net income*
Current Liabilities	*Add to net income*	*Subtract from net income*

Students normally have difficulty understanding T-account analysis and the adjustments to net income on the statement of cash flows in the calculation of net cash from operations. However, understanding T-account analysis and these adjustments is important because the indirect method of presentation is used by almost all major U.S. and non-U.S. companies, and T-account analysis can be a valuable tool for an analyst. Throughout this text we review these adjustments as they arise, and we return to the statement of cash flows in Chapter 14.

REVIEW PROBLEM

Consider the balance sheet of a small retail company, Kelly Supply, as of December 31, 2011 (Figure 4–20). Exchange transactions that occurred during 2012 are recorded in Figure 4–21 and posted to T-accounts in Figure 4–22. The financial statements are contained in Figures 4–23 and 4–24.

The December 31, 2011, balance sheet accounts are reflected in the T-accounts as beginning balances. The exchange transactions are numbered (1)–(11), and each is described and has been posted in the T-accounts.

At year-end, the adjusting journal entries are recorded and posted to the T-accounts. Adjusting entries are numbered (12)–(18). Entries (13), (16), and (17) are accruals, and entries (12), (14), (15), and (18) are cost expirations. Entries (19) and (20) close revenues, expenses, and dividends to retained earnings.

FIGURE 4–20

Balance sheet for Kelly Supply

Kelly Supply
Balance Sheet
December 31, 2011

ASSETS			LIABILITIES AND SHAREHOLDERS' EQUITY	
Cash		$12,000	Accounts payable	$ 8,000
Accounts receivable		15,000	Wages payable	3,000
Merchandise inventory		12,000	Interest payable	1,000
Prepaid rent		3,000	Dividends payable	2,000
Machinery	$25,000		Unearned revenue	3,000
Less: Accum. depr.	5,000	20,000	Short-term notes pay.	5,000
Patent		5,000	Long-term notes pay.	10,000
			Contributed capital	30,000
			Retained earnings	5,000
			Total liabilities and	
Total assets		$67,000	shareholders' equity	$67,000

FIGURE 4-21 General journal for Kelly Supply

Daily Journal Entries

(1) Cash (+A)   10,000
    Accounts Receivable (+A)   15,000
        Sales (R, +RE)   25,000
    Cost of Goods Sold (E, −RE)   9,000
        Merchandise Inventory (−A)   9,000
    Sold merchandise with a cost of $9,000
    for cash and on account.

(2) Cash (+A)   8,000
        Accounts Receivable (−A)   8,000
    Received cash on account.

(3) Merchandise Inventory (+A)   10,000
        Cash (−A)   3,000
        Accounts Payable (+L)   7,000
    Purchased merchandise inventory
    for cash and on account.

(4) Accounts Payable (−L)   10,000
        Cash (−A)   10,000
    Paid cash on account.

(5) Wages Payable (−L)   3,000
    Wage Expense (E, −RE)   7,000
        Cash (−A)   10,000
    Paid accrued wages.

(6) Interest Payable (−L)   1,000
    Interest Expense (E, −RE)   1,000
        Cash (−A)   2,000
    Paid accrued interest.

(7) Short-Term Notes Pay. (−L)   2,500
        Cash (−A)   2,500
    Paid short-term note.

(8) Cash (+A)   10,000
        Contributed Capital (+CC)   10,000
    Issued common stock for cash.

(9) Dividends Payable (−L)   2,000
        Cash (−A)   2,000
    Paid cash dividend.

(10) Machinery (+A)   1,000
        Cash (−A)   1,000
    Acquired machinery for cash.

(11) Dividends (−RE)   1,000
        Dividends Payable (+L)   1,000
    Declared dividends.

Adjusting Journal Entries

(12) Unearned Revenue (−L)   2,000
        Sales (R, +RE)   2,000
    Recognized 2/3 of goods delivered.

(13) Interest Receivable (+A)   50
        Interest Revenue (R, +RE)   50
    Recognized accrued interest on
    savings account.

(14) Depreciation Expense (E, −RE)   3,000
        Accumulated Depr. (−A)   3,000
    Recognized depreciation on
    machinery.

(15) Amortization Expense (E, −RE)   500
        Patent (−A)   500
    Recognized amortization of patent.

(16) Wage Expense (E, −RE)   1,000
        Wages Payable (+L)   1,000
    Recognized accrued wages.

(17) Interest Expense (E, −RE)   2,000
        Interest Payable (+L)   2,000
    Recognized accrued interest on
    note payables.

(18) Rent Expense (E, −RE)   1,000
        Prepaid Rent (−A)   1,000
    Recognized 1/3 of rent
    period expired.

Closing entry

(19) Sales   27,000
     Interest Revenue   50
        Cost of Goods Sold   9,000
        Wage Expense   8,000
        Rent Expense   1,000
        Interest Expense   3,000
        Deprec. Expense   3,000
        Amortization Expense   500
        Retained Earnings   2,550
    To close revenue and expense accounts to
    Retained Earnings.

(20) Retained Earnings   1,000
        Dividends   1,000
    To close dividends to Retained Earnings.

FIGURE 4-22   T-accounts for Kelly Supply

Cash			
	12,000		
(1)	10,000		
(2)	8,000		
		(3)	3,000
		(4)	10,000
		(5)	10,000
		(6)	2,000
		(7)	2,500
(8)	10,000	(9)	2,000
		(10)	1,000
	9,500		

Accounts Receivable			
	15,000		
(1)	15,000		
		(2)	8,000
	22,000		

Interest Receivable			
(13)	50		
	50		

Merchandise Inventory			
	12,000		
(3)	10,000		
		(1)	9,000
	13,000		

Prepaid Rent			
	3,000	(18)	1,000
	2,000		

Machinery			
	25,000		
(10)	1,000		
	26,000		

Accumulated Depreciation			
			5,000
		(14)	3,000
			8,000

Patent			
	5,000	(15)	500
	4,500		

Accounts Payable			
			8,000
		(3)	7,000
(4)	10,000		
			5,000

Wages Payable			
			3,000
(5)	3,000	(16)	1,000
			1,000

Interest Payable			
			1,000
(6)	1,000	(17)	2,000
			2,000

Dividends Payable			
			2,000
(9)	2,000	(11)	1,000
			1,000

Unearned Revenue			
			3,000
(12)	2,000		
			1,000

Short-Term Notes Payable			
			5,000
(7)	2,500		
			2,500

Long-Term Notes Payable			
			10,000
			10,000

Contributed Capital			
			30,000
		(8)	10,000
			40,000

Retained Earnings			
			5,000
(20)	1,000	(19)	2,550
			6,550

Sales			
(19)	27,000	(1)	25,000
		(12)	2,000
			0

Interest Revenue			
(19)	50	(13)	50
			0

Cost of Goods Sold			
(1)	9,000	(19)	9,000
	0		

Wage Expense			
(5)	7,000		
(16)	1,000	(19)	8,000
	0		

Rent Expense			
(18)	1,000		
		(19)	1,000
	0		

Interest Expense			
(6)	1,000		
(17)	2,000	(19)	3,000
	0		

Depreciation Expense			
(14)	3,000	(19)	3,000
	0		

Amortization Expense			
(15)	500	(19)	500
	0		

Dividends			
(11)	1,000	(20)	1,000
	0		

FIGURE 4-23

Financial statements for Kelly Supply

Kelly Supply
Income Statement
for the Year Ended December 31, 2012

Revenues:		
Sales	$27,000	
Interest revenue	50	
Total revenues		$27,050
Expenses:		
Cost of goods sold	$ 9,000	
Wage expense	8,000	
Rent expense	1,000	
Interest expense	3,000	
Depreciation expense	3,000	
Amortization expense	500	
Total expenses		24,500
Net income		$ 2,550

Kelly Supply
Statement of Shareholders' Equity
for the Year Ended December 31, 2012

	Contributed Capital	Retained Earnings	Total
Beginning balance	$30,000	$ 5,000	$35,000
Common stock issuances	10,000		10,000
Net income		2,550	2,550
Less: Dividends		(1,000)	(1,000)
Ending balance	$40,000	$ 6,550	$46,550

Kelly Supply
Balance Sheet
December 31, 2012

ASSETS			LIABILITIES AND SHAREHOLDERS' EQUITY	
Cash		$ 9,500	Accounts payable	$ 5,000
Accounts receivable		22,000	Wages payable	1,000
Interest receivable		50	Interest payable	2,000
Merchandise inventory		13,000	Dividends payable	1,000
Prepaid rent		2,000	Unearned revenue	1,000
Machinery	$26,000		Short-term notes pay.	2,500
Less: Accumulated			Long-term notes pay.	10,000
depreciation	8,000	18,000	Contributed capital	40,000
Patent		4,500	Retained earnings	6,550
			Total liabilities and	
Total assets		$69,050	shareholders' equity	$69,050

Kelly Supply
Statement of Cash Flows
for the Year Ended December 31, 2012

Operating activities:		
Collections from sales	$10,000	
Collections of accounts receivable	8,000	
Payments for inventory purchases	(3,000)	
Payments on accounts payable	(10,000)	
Payments for wages	(10,000)	
Payments for interest	(2,000)	
Net cash increase (decrease) from		
operating activities		$(7,000)
Investing activities:		
Purchase of machinery	$ (1,000)	
Net cash increase (decrease) from		
investing activities		(1,000)
Financing activities:		
Issuance of common stock	$10,000	
Payment of dividend	(2,000)	
Principal payments on short-term		
notes payable	(2,500)	
Net cash increase (decrease) from		
financing activities		5,500
Net cash increase (decrease) during 2012		$(2,500)
Beginning cash balance (December 31, 2011)		12,000
Ending cash balance (December 31, 2012)		$ 9,500

The income statement contains revenues and expenses; the statement of shareholders' equity explains the change in the contributed capital and retained earnings balances; and the balance sheet consists of the ending balances in the asset, liability, and shareholders' equity accounts. The statement of cash flows was prepared directly from the entries in the cash T-account. The indirect method of presentation for the statement of cash flows is illustrated in Figure 4–25 (see Appendix 4A).

Net income	$ 2,550
Non-current items:	
Plus depreciation	3,000
Plus amortization	500
Current items:	
Less increase in accounts receivable	(7,000)
Less increase in interest receivable	(50)
Less increase in merchandise inventory	(1,000)
Plus decrease in prepaid rent	1,000
Less decrease in accounts payable	(3,000)
Less decrease in wages payable	(2,000)
Plus increase in interest payable	1,000
Less decrease in unearned revenue	(2,000)
Net cash increase (decrease) from	
operating activities	$(7,000)

SUMMARY OF KEY POINTS

 Two criteria necessary for economic events to be reflected in the financial statements.

Economic events must be both relevant and objectively measurable in monetary terms if they are to be reflected on the financial statements. Relevant events have economic significance to the company. Objectively measurable events must be backed by documented evidence. Economic events must be relevant so that they can be used to evaluate the financial condition of the company; they must be objectively measurable so that they can be audited and viewed as credible by users.

The accounting equation and how it relates to the balance sheet, income statement, statement of shareholders' equity, and statement of cash flows.

The accounting equation states that assets equal liabilities plus shareholders' equity. The main components of the accounting equation (assets, liabilities, and shareholders' equity) are divided into subcategories, called *accounts,* in which transactions are recorded and from which the financial statements are compiled. When a business transaction occurs, two or more accounts are increased or decreased in such a way as to maintain the equality of the equation.

The balance sheet contains the balances as of a given point in time of all the asset, liability, and shareholders' equity accounts. It is a statement of the accounting equation.

The income statement contains a summary of the operating transactions, measured on an accrual basis, entered into by a company during a period of time. Operating transactions affect asset or liability accounts and always either increase or decrease retained earnings in the shareholders' equity section of the accounting equation.

The statement of shareholders' equity and the statement of cash flows summarize the transactions that affect the shareholders' equity and cash accounts, respectively. The statement of shareholders' equity includes the net effect of the operating transactions as well as transactions with shareholders. The statement of cash flows is composed of cash inflows and outflows and explains the change in the cash account during the period.

Journal entries (and T-accounts) and how they express the effect of economic events on the basic accounting equation and the financial statements.

Journal entries (and T-accounts) are structured to indicate three aspects about economic events: (1) the accounts affected, (2) the direction of the effect, and (3) the dollar amount of the effect. Increases (decreases) in asset accounts and decreases (increases) in liability and equity accounts are placed on the left (right) side of the entry. Recognized revenues (expenses) are always placed on the right (left) side of the entry because they are always accompanied by increases (decreases) in assets or decreases (increases) in equities, which are indicated on the left (right) side. Following these rules ensures that economic events will be recorded in a way that maintains the equality of the accounting equation, and understanding these rules enables one to efficiently communicate the effects of any economic event on the financial statements.

Why managers need to understand how economic events affect the financial statements.

Managers often face situations in which they must choose whether to enter into certain transactions or how to structure transactions. Such choices should not be made without considering their economic consequences. The financial statement effects of transactions can lead to important economic consequences because outsiders use financial statement numbers to control and evaluate the firm and its management. Therefore, astute managers must understand in advance how transactions and other economic events affect the financial statements. In addition, adequate internal controls over the recording process are crucial to ensure that all transactions are recorded in a timely and accurate manner.

Why the financial statements are adjusted periodically to reflect certain economic events.

A large number of economic events are not represented by exchange transactions (e.g., depreciation of productive assets, and accruals of salaries, interest, and rent), yet they meet the criteria

(relevant and objective) for inclusion on the financial statements. These events require that adjustments be made to the financial statements periodically. Normally such adjustments are made to apply the principles of revenue recognition and matching. Revenue recognition states that revenues should be recognized when the earning process is substantially complete, not necessarily when cash is received. Matching states that expenses should be recognized in those periods when the associated benefit (revenue) is realized, not necessarily when cash is paid. These principles are fundamental to an accrual accounting system.

KEY TERMS

Note: Definitions for these terms are provided in the glossary at the end of the text.

Accounting equation (p. 114)
Accrual system of accounting (p. 129)
Accruals (p. 130)
Amortized (p. 137)
Assets (p. 114)
Book value (p. 137)
Business transactions (p. 116)
Capitalized (p. 133)
Compound journal entries (p. 122)
Contra accounts (p. 137)
Contributed capital (p. 115)
Credit (p. 122)
Debit (p. 122)
Deferral (cost expiration) (p. 132)
Depreciation (p. 137)
Double entry system (p. 122)
Economic events (p. 113)
Expensed (p. 133)

Journal entries (p. 121)
Liabilities (p. 115)
Matching principle (p. 133)
Multinationals (p. 140)
Permanent accounts (p. 128)
Relevant events (p. 113)
Retained earnings (p. 115)
Revaluation adjustments (p. 139)
Shareholders' equity (p. 115)
Statement of cash flows—direct method
  of presentation (p. 141)
Statement of cash flows—indirect method
  of presentation (p. 141)
Straight-line depreciation (p. 138)
T-accounts (p. 123)
T-account analysis (p. 141)
Temporary accounts (p. 128)
Unearned revenues (p. 136)

ETHICS in the Real World

In an article about the subjectivity involved when deciding to capitalize or expense a cost, *Forbes* reports:

A dollar spent on a toaster doesn't reduce wealth in the same way as one spent on a Twinkie. One lasts, the other doesn't. But where do toasters end and Twinkies begin in [today's] economy? . . . Accountants understand the general problem, but they do not know what to do about it. Capitalizing anything that you can't drop on your foot—software, worker training, marketing expense—can be hugely speculative. You never find out whether such things have real future value until the future arrives.

A case in point involves Fine Host Corp., which spent huge dollar amounts to obtain new food service contracts. The company listed these costs on the balance sheet and depreciated them over time. When the company was accused of aggressive accounting, the share price dropped from $12 to $3 per share. Many believed that the food service contract costs should have been accounted for "as current expenses against revenue." Fine Host ended up restating its net income number, reducing it from $13 million to a loss of almost $18 million.

ETHICAL ISSUE Fine Host management was not convicted, or even accused, of fraud. The company just subjectively called an asset what many in the financial community considered an expense. Was it ethical for Fine Host to do so? Was management acting in the interests of the shareholders?

INTERNET RESEARCH EXERCISE

The chapter opener points out that there are some accounting problems in U.S. federal agencies. The government organization assigned to oversee budgeting and accounting for the federal government is the General Accounting Office (GAO). What is the GAO, what kind of reports does it provide, and how is it organized? Begin your search at www.gao.gov.

BRIEF EXERCISES

REAL DATA

BE4–1

Effects of transactions on the accounting equation

During 2008, Intel entered into the transactions listed below.

a.   On a separate sheet of paper, complete the following chart to show the effect of these transactions on the accounting equation and compute the net effect (dollars in millions).

Transaction	Assets = Liabilities + Shareholders' Equity
1. Paid $5,197 to purchase property, plant, and equipment.	
2. Issued common stock for $1,105.	
3. Recorded depreciation of $4,360.	
Net effect	

b.   Which one of the transactions did not appear to affect the accounting equation? Why didn't it?

REAL DATA

BE4–2

Effects of transactions on the accounting equation

During 2008, The Limited entered into the transactions listed below.

a.   On a separate sheet of paper, complete the following chart to show the effect of these transactions on the accounting equation and compute the net effect (dollars in millions).

Transaction	Assets = Liabilities + Shareholders' Equity
1. Repaid $15 of long-term debt.	
2. Paid cash dividends of $201.	
3. Repurchased common stock for $379.	
Net effect	

b.   Compare and discuss how transactions 2 and 3 affected the basic accounting equation.

REAL DATA

BE4–3

Effects of transactions on the accounting equation

During 2008, Yahoo!, Inc. entered into the transactions listed below.

a.   On a separate sheet of paper, complete the following chart to show the effect of these transactions on the accounting equation and compute the net effect (dollars in millions).

Transaction	Assets = Liabilities + Shareholders' Equity
1. Recognized service revenues of $6,426 in exchange for accounts receivable.	
2. Paid $1,322 for sales and marketing.	
3. Issued common stock for $363.	
4. Purchased marketable securities for $2,317	
Net effect	

b.   Which of these transactions would be reflected on the income statement? Which of these transactions would be reflected on the statement of cash flows?

EXERCISES

E4-1

Effects of
transactions on the
accounting equation

On a separate piece of paper, complete the following chart to show the effect of each transaction on the accounting equation.

Transaction	Assets = Liabilities + Shareholders' Equity

1. **Owners contributed $30,000 cash.**
2. **Purchased land for $20,000 cash.**
3. **Borrowed $9,000 cash from bank.**
4. **Provided services for $8,000 on account.**
5. **Paid $5,500 cash for expenses.**
6. **Paid $500 cash dividend to owners.**

E4-2

Effects of
transactions on
accounts

Consider the same transactions as in E4–1, but this time complete the following chart, using a separate sheet of paper.

	Assets			=	Liabilities	+	Shareholders' Equity	
Trans.	Cash	Accounts Receivable	Land	=	Notes Payable	+	Contributed Capital	Retained Earnings
1.								
2.								
3.								
4.								
5.								
6.								

E4-3

Preparing the
financial statements
from the accounts

Total each asset, liability, and shareholders' equity account in E4–2, and prepare an income statement, a statement of shareholders' equity, a balance sheet, and a statement of cash flows. Assume that the current year is the company's first year of operations.

E4-4

Preparing the
financial statements

Assume that Cathedral Enterprises, which is in its first year of operations, entered into the following transactions. Show how the five transactions affect the accounting equation, and prepare an income statement, statement of shareholders' equity, balance sheet, and statement of cash flows.

1. Shareholders contributed $10,000 cash.
2. Performed services for $8,000, receiving $6,000 in cash and a $2,000 receivable.
3. Incurred expenses of $6,000. Paid $3,000 in cash, and $3,000 is still payable.
4. Purchased land for $12,000. Paid $2,000 in cash and signed a long-term note for the remainder.
5. Paid the shareholders $400 in the form of a dividend.
6. Sold one-half of the land purchased in (4) for $7,000 cash.

The Brown Corporation experienced the following financial events on October 10, 2012:

E4-5

Which economic events
are relevant and
objectively measurable?

1. The company entered into a new contract with the employees' union that calls for a $2.00 per hour increase in wages, a longer lunch break, and cost-of-living adjustments, effective January 1, 2013.
2. The company issued $200,000 in bonds that mature on October 10, 2022. The terms of the bond issuance stipulate that interest is to be paid semiannually at an annual rate of 10 percent.
3. The company president retired and was replaced by the vice president of finance.
4. The company received $10,000 from a customer in settlement of an open account receivable.
5. The company paid $1,000 interest on an outstanding loan. The interest is applicable to September 2012 and is included on the books as a liability, "Accrued Interest Payable."

(Continued)

6. The market value of all the company's long-lived assets is $275,000. They are currently reported on the balance sheet at $250,000.

7. The company purchased a fire insurance policy for $1,500 that will pay the Brown Corporation $1 million if its primary production plant is destroyed. The policy insures the company from November 1, 2012, through October 31, 2013.

8. The company placed an order to have $10,000 of inventory shipped on October 17, 2012.

Indicate whether each of these economic events has accounting significance (i.e., whether the company would prepare a journal entry for the event). In each case, explain why or why not.

REAL DATA

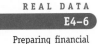

Preparing financial
statements

The following accounts and balances were taken from the records of US Airways (dollars in millions).

Flight equipment	$3,157	Accounts payable	$ 797
Passenger revenue	8,183	Common stock	1
Retained earnings	(2,307)	Fuel expense	3,618
Notes payable	3,634	Other revenues	912
Interest expense	253	Short-term investments	20
Accounts receivable	293	Depreciation expense	215
Prepaid expenses	684	Landing fees	562

Identify each account as an income statement or balance sheet account. Where is each account reflected in the basic accounting equation?

REAL DATA

E4-7

Preparing financial
statements

The following information was taken from the 2008 annual report of Bristol-Myers Squibb, a world-leading drug company (dollars in millions).

Cost of goods sold	$ 6,396	Cash and equivalents	$ 7,976
Net cash from operations	3,707	Short-term borrowings	154
Accounts receivable	3,710	Advertising and product expense	1,550
Restructuring expense	218	Accounts payable	1,535
Net cash from financing	(2,582)	Long-term liabilities	10,601
Shareholders' equity	12,241	Net sales	20,597
Net cash from investing	5,079	Property, plant, and equipment	5,405
Research and dev. expense	3,585	Other current assets	2,788
Other noncurrent assets	9,384	Other current liabilities	2,085
Other expenses	901	Selling and adm. expenses	4,792
Marketable securities	289	Accrued payables	2,936

Prepare an income statement, balance sheet, and statement of cash flows, and comment on the financial performance and condition of the company.

E4-8

Preparing a statement
of cash flows from
the cash ledger

The following cash T-account for Miller Manufacturing summarizes all the transactions affecting cash during 2012.

Cash

Beginning balance	9,000	Equipment purchases	24,000
Sales of services	45,000	Rent payable payments	7,000
Receivables collections	50,000	Bank loan principal	12,000
Sale of land	7,500	Loan interest	3,000
Issuance of common stock	15,000	Salaries	26,500
Long-term borrowings	16,000	Dividend payments	4,000
		Miscellaneous expenses	13,000
		Long-term investment purchase	10,000

a. Compute the ending cash balance.
b. Prepare a statement of cash flows.

E4-9

Preparing a statement
of cash flows from
journal entries

Small and Associates, a small manufacturing firm, entered into the following cash transactions
during January 2012:

1. Issued 600 shares of stock for $25 each.
2. Sold services for $4,000.
3. Paid wages of $1,600.
4. Purchased land as a long-term investment for $9,000 cash.
5. Paid a $2,000 dividend.
6. Sold land with a book value of $3,000 for $3,500 cash.
7. Paid $1,500 to the bank: $900 to reduce the principal on an outstanding loan and $600
    as an interest payment.
8. Paid miscellaneous expenses of $1,800.

a. Prepare journal entries for each transaction.
b. Prepare a cash T-account, and compute Small's cash balance as of the end of January.
    Assume a beginning balance of $5,000.
c. Prepare a statement of cash flows for the month of January.

E4-10

Preparing statements
from transactions

Ed's Lawn Service entered into the following transactions during 2012, its first year of
operations:

1. Collected $12,000 in cash from shareholders.
2. Borrowed $5,000 from a bank.
3. Purchased two parcels of land for a total of $10,000.
4. Paid $5,000 to rent lawn equipment for the remainder of the year.
5. Provided lawn services, receiving $10,000 in cash and $4,000 in receivables.
6. Paid miscellaneous expenses of $4,000.
7. Sold one parcel of land with a cost of $3,000 for $2,800.
8. Paid a $2,200 dividend to the shareholders.

a. In a manner similar to Figure 4–2, show how each transaction affected the fundamental
    accounting equation and prepare an income statement, a statement of shareholders' equity,
    a year-end balance sheet, and a statement of cash flows for 2012.
b. Journalize each transaction and post it in the appropriate T-accounts. From this informa-
    tion, prepare a year-end balance sheet, an income statement, a statement of shareholders'
    equity, and a statement of cash flows for 2012.

E4-11

Preparing the
statement of cash flows
from the cash
T-account

The following cash T-account for Holcomb Manufacturing summarizes all the transactions
affecting cash during 2012.

Cash			
Beginning balance	8,000	Inventory purchases	27,000
Sales of inventories	34,000	Accounts payable payments	7,000
Receivable collections	40,000	Bank loan principal payments	10,000
Sales of long-term investments	12,500	Loan interest	3,000
Issuance of common stock	14,000	Wages	16,000
Long-term borrowings	9,000	Dividend payments	4,000
		Administrative expenses	12,000
		Equipment purchases	11,000

a. Compute the ending cash balance.
b. Prepare a statement of cash flows (direct method).

E4-12

Classifying adjusting
journal entries

Eaton Enterprises made the following adjusting journal entries on December 31, 2011:

1. **Rent Expense**	1,200	
Rent Payable		1,200

(Continued)

2. Insurance Expense	5,000	
Prepaid Insurance		5,000
3. Depreciation Expense	20,000	
Accumulated Depreciation		20,000
4. Interest Receivable	1,500	
Interest Revenue		1,500
5. Unearned Revenue	200	
Fees Earned		200

a.   Give a brief explanation for each of the above entries.
b.   Classify each of the above entries as either a cost expiration adjusting entry or an accrual adjusting entry.

E4–13

Classifying transactions

Hog Heaven Rib Joint made the following journal entries on December 31, 2011:

1. Wage Expense	6,000	
Wages Payable		6,000
2. Interest Expense	1,000	
Cash		1,000
3. Cash	10,500	
Note Payable		10,500
4. Rent Expense	1,500	
Prepaid Rent		1,500
5. Insurance Expense	2,800	
Prepaid Insurance		2,800
6. Cash	2,000	
Unearned Revenues		2,000
7. Equipment	9,000	
Cash		9,000
8. Supplies Expense	12,000	
Supplies Inventory		12,000
9. Accounts Payable	8,000	
Cash		8,000
10. Depreciation Expense	13,000	
Accumulated Depreciation		13,000
11. Advertising Expense	8,000	
Cash		8,000
12. Advertising Expense	3,000	
Prepaid Advertising		3,000

Place each of the transactions above in one of the following five categories: (1) operating cash flow, (2) investing cash flow, (3) financing cash flow, (4) accrual adjusting journal entry, and (5) cost expiration adjusting journal entry.

E4–14

Recognizing accrued wages

The Hurst Corporation pays its employees every Friday for the five-day week just ended. On January 2, 2013, the company paid its employees $70,000 for the week beginning Monday, December 29.

a.   Assuming that the employees earned wages evenly throughout the week, prepare any adjusting journal entries that were necessary on December 31, 2012.
b.   Prepare the journal entry that would be recorded on Friday, January 2, when the wages are paid.
c.   Complete a chart like the following.

	2012	2013	Total
Wage expense			
Cash outflow associated with wages			

d.   What is the purpose of the adjusting journal entry on December 31?

REAL DATA

E4-15

Depreciating a
fixed asset

During 2009, Starbucks purchased fixed assets costing approximately $450 million. Assume that the company purchased the assets at the beginning of the year, uses straight-line depreciation, and normally depreciates its equipment over three years.

a. Compute the book value of the equipment at the end of each of the three years.
b. Complete a chart like the following.

	2009	2010	2011	Total
Depreciation expense				
Cash outflow associated with the purchase of the equipment				

c. What is the purpose of the adjustments at the end of each period?

E4-16

The difference
between accrual and
cash accounting

Washington Forest Products began operations on January 1, 2011. On December 31, 2011, the company's accountant ascertains that the following amounts should be reported as expenses on the income statement:

Insurance expense	$20,000
Supplies expense	11,000
Rent expense	14,000

A review of the company's cash disbursements indicates that the company made related cash payments during 2011 as follows:

Insurance	$29,000
Supplies	27,000
Rent	8,000

a. Explain why the amounts shown as expenses do not equal the cash paid.
b. For each expense account, compute the amount that should be in the related balance sheet account as of December 31, 2011. *Hint:* Note that Forest Products began operations on January 1, 2011.

E4-17

The difference
between net income
and net cash flow
from operations

The following journal entries were recorded by Lauren Retailing during the month of July:

1. Cash	5,000	
Accounts Receivable	3,000	
Sales		8,000
2. Cash	2,000	
Accounts Receivable		2,000
3. Inventory	5,800	
Accounts Payable		5,800
4. Accounts Payable	2,800	
Cash		2,800
5. Cost of Goods Sold	3,700	
Inventory		3,700
6. Accrued Expenses	2,500	
Accrued Payables		2,500

a. Prepare an income statement and the operating section of a statement of cash flows.
b. Explain why net income is not equal to net cash flow from operations, and reconcile the two numbers.

E4-18

Preparing a statement
of cash flows from
original transactions

Rahal and Watson, a small manufacturing company, entered into the following cash transactions during January of 2012:

1. Issued 800 shares of common stock for $30 each.
2. Collected $3,900 on outstanding accounts receivable.

(Continued)

3. Paid wages for the month of January of $1,530.
4. Purchased land as a long-term investment for $12,000 cash.
5. Paid a $6,000 dividend.
6. Sold a piece of equipment with a book value of $5,000 for $7,000 cash.
7. Paid $2,000 to the bank: $900 to reduce the principal on an outstanding loan and $1,100 as an interest payment.
8. Paid miscellaneous expenses of $5,000.

a. Prepare a journal entry for each transaction. Indicate the classification and the effect on the accounting equation.
b. Prepare a cash T-account, and compute the company's cash balance as of the end of January. Assume a beginning balance of $4,000.
c. Prepare a statement of cash flows (direct method) for the month of January.

E4–19

Cash and accrual accounting: comparison of performance measures

Peters Company was in business for two years, during which time it entered into the following transactions:

Year 1:
1. The owners contributed $24,000 cash.
2. At the beginning of the year, rented a warehouse for two years with a prepaid rent payment of $12,000.
3. Purchased $10,000 of inventory on account.
4. Sold half the inventory for $24,000, receiving $20,000 in cash and an account receivable of $4,000.
5. Paid wages of $6,000 and also accrued wages payable of $4,000.

Year 2:
1. Paid the outstanding balance for the inventory purchased in Year 1.
2. Paid the outstanding wages payable balance.
3. Sold the remaining inventory for $30,000 cash.
4. Received full payment on the outstanding accounts receivable.
5. Incurred and paid wages of $12,000.
6. Returned the cash balance to the owners and shut down operations.

a. Prepare an income statement and a statement of cash flows for both Year 1 and Year 2.
b. Complete a chart like the following.

Performance Measure	Year 1	Year 2	Total
Net income			
Net cash flow from operating activities			

REAL DATA

E4–20

Assessing economic consequences

Condensed balance sheets for 2007 and 2008 and the 2009 income statement for Goodyear, the world's largest tire company, are as follows (dollars in millions).

	2008	2007
Current assets	$ 8,340	$10,172
Long-term assets	6,886	7,019
Total assets	$15,226	$17,191
Current liabilities	$ 4,779	$ 4,664
Long-term liabilities	9,425	9,677
Shareholders' equity	1,022	2,850
Total liabilities and		
shareholders' equity	$15,226	$17,191
Revenues	$19,488	
Expenses	19,565	
Net loss	$ (77)	

   a. Early in 2009, assume that Goodyear is considering the following transactions. Treat each separately and compute how it would affect the company's ratios of current assets divided by current liabilities and total liabilities divided by total shareholders' equity.
      1. Purchase $1,000 in inventory on account.
      2. Issue common stock for $2,000 cash.
      3. Refinance a $500 short-term liability with a $500 long-term liability.
      4. Purchase equipment in exchange for a $400 long-term note payable.
      5. Pay a $1,000 short-term debt with cash.
   b. Assume that the terms of Goodyear's long-term debt require the company to maintain a ratio of current assets divided by current liabilities of 1.65. Is this covenant restriction relevant to whether the company should enter into any of the above transactions? Explain.
   c. How much cash could Goodyear pay for a long-term investment and still be in compliance with the covenant?

E4–21

Appendix 4A:
T-account analysis

Excerpts from the financial statements of Dunbar Manufacturing are provided below.

Wages

Cash payments for wages during 2012	$35,000
Wages payable as of December 31, 2012	17,000
Wage expense on the 2012 income statement	39,000

Rent

Prepaid rent as of December 31, 2011	$12,000
Prepaid rent as of December 31, 2012	15,000
Rent expense on the 2012 income statement	21,000

Accounts Receivable

Cash collected from customers during 2012	$38,000
Accounts receivable as of December 31, 2011	14,000
Sales revenue on the 2012 income statement	45,000

   a. Compute the wages payable as of December 31, 2011.
   b. Compute the cash payments for rent during 2012.
   c. Compute the accounts receivable as of December 31, 2012.

E4–22

Appendix 4A:
Depreciation and
cash flows

Your boss asks you to examine the following income statements of Hamilton Hardware and Watson Glass:

	Hamilton Hardware	Watson Glass
Sales	$900,000	$900,000
Cost of goods sold	(400,000)	(400,000)
Depreciation expense	(50,000)	(100,000)
Other expenses	(200,000)	(200,000)
Net income	$250,000	$200,000

In the notes to the financial statements, you notice that Hamilton Hardware uses the straight-line method of depreciation and that Watson Glass uses the double-declining-balance method.

   a. Assume that the dollar amounts for sales, cost of goods sold, and other expenses reflect total cash collections from customers, total cash paid for inventory, and total cash paid

for other expenses, respectively. Compute cash provided (used) by operating activities for each company, using each of the following:

1. The direct method format
2. The indirect method format

b. Why is the cash provided (used) by operations different from net income? Which of the two methods shows this more clearly?

c. Would you agree of disagree with the following statement? *Depreciation is an important source of cash for most companies.* Explain your answer.

E4–23

Appendix 4A:
Preparing a statement
of cash flows—direct
and indirect method of
presentation

Tony began a small retailing operation on January 1, 2012. During 2012, the following transactions occurred:

1. Tony contributed $20,000 of his own money to the business.
2. $60,000 was borrowed from the bank.
3. Long-lived assets were purchased for $25,000 cash.
4. Inventory was purchased: $25,000 cash and $15,000 on account.
5. Inventory with a cost of $25,000 was sold for $80,000: $20,000 cash and $60,000 on account.
6. Cash payments included $18,000 for operating expenses, $5,000 for loan principal, and a $2,000 dividend.
7. $15,000 in expenses were accrued at the end of the year, and depreciation expense of $1,000 was recorded.

a. Prepare journal entries for each economic event.
b. Prepare a balance sheet as of the end of 2012 and an income statement and statement of shareholders' equity for Tony's business.
c. Prepare a cash T-account and a statement of cash flows using the direct method.
d. Prepare a statement of cash flows using the indirect method, but this time prepare it from the company's two balance sheets, the income statement, and the statement of shareholders' equity earnings. Tony's first balance sheet contains all zero balances.

PROBLEMS

P4–1

Journal entries and
the accounting
equation

Below are several transactions entered into by Vulcan Metal Corporation during 2012. Unless otherwise noted, all transactions involve cash.

1. Purchased equipment for $150,000.
2. Paid employees $30,000 in wages.
3. Collected $15,000 from customers as payments on open accounts.
4. Provided services for $24,000: $16,000 received in cash and the remainder on open account.
5. Paid $50,000 on an outstanding note payable: $10,000 for interest and $40,000 to reduce the principal.
6. Purchased a one-month ad in the local newspaper for $5,000.
7. Purchased a building valued at $250,000 in exchange for $130,000 cash and a long-term note payable.
8. Sold investments with a cost of $20,000 for $35,000.

REQUIRED:

Prepare journal entries for each transaction and explain how each affects the accounting equation.

P4-2

T-accounts and the
accounting equation

The following T-accounts reflect seven different transactions that Rodman Container Company entered into during 2012:

Cash			
(a)	7,000	(c)	2,000
(f)	5,000	(d)	20,000
(g)	25,000	(e)	1,200

Accounts Receivable			
(a)	21,000	(f)	5,000

Equipment	
(d)	50,000

Inventory	
(b)	6,000

Accounts Payable			
(c)	2,000	(b)	6,000

Notes Payable		
	(d)	30,000

Common Stock	
(g)	25,000

Sales Revenue		
	(a)	28,000

Rent Expense	
(e)	1,200

REQUIRED:

For each transaction, describe what occurred and how it affected the accounting equation.

P4-3

Journal entries and
preparing the four
financial statements

No CFS

Ryan Hope, controller of Hope, Inc., provides you with the following information concerning Hope during 2012. (Hope, Inc. began operations on January 1, 2012.)

1. Issued 1,000 shares of common stock at $95 per share.
2. Paid $2,600 per month to rent office and warehouse space. The rent was paid on the last day of each month.
3. Made total sales for services of $190,000: $65,000 for cash and $125,000 on account.
4. Purchased land for $32,000.
5. Borrowed $75,000 on December 31. The note payable matures in two years.
6. Salaries totaling $80,000 were paid during the year.
7. Other expenses totaling $40,000 were paid during the year.
8. $56,000 was received from customers as payment on account.
9. Declared and paid a dividend of $26,000.

REQUIRED:

a. Prepare journal entries for these transactions.
b. Establish T-accounts for each account, and post the journal entries to these T-accounts.
c. Prepare an income statement, statement of shareholders' equity, a December 31, 2012, balance sheet, and statement of cash flows for 2012.

P4-4

Preparing the four
financial statements

The December 31, 2011, balance sheet for Morrison Home Services is summarized below.

Assets		Liabilities and Shareholders' Equity	
Cash	$10,000	Liabilities	$ 6,000
Receivables	4,000	Contributed capital	10,000
Long-term assets	10,000	Retained earnings	8,000
		Total liabilities and	
Total assets	$24,000	shareholders' equity	$24,000

During January of 2012, the following transactions were entered into:

1. Services were performed for $7,000 cash.
2. $3,000 cash was received from customers on outstanding accounts receivable.

(*Continued*)

3. $3,000 cash was paid for outstanding liabilities.
4. Long-term assets were purchased in exchange for a $6,000 note payable.
5. Expenses of $4,000 were paid in cash.
6. A dividend of $800 was issued to the owners.

REQUIRED:

a. Provide a journal entry for each transaction.
b. Treat each transaction independently and describe how each would affect the ratios of current assets divided by current liabilities, net income divided by shareholders' equity, and total liabilities divided by shareholders' equity; and Morrison's current ratio, return on equity, and debt/equity ratio, respectively.
c. Prepare the income statement, statement of shareholders' equity, the January 31 balance sheet, and the statement of cash flows (direct method) for January.
d. (Appendix 4A) Prepare the operating section of the statement of cash flows under the indirect method.

P4–5

Comprehensive
problem

The December 31, 2011, balance sheet of Tybee Corporation is provided below (in millions).

Assets		Liabilities and Shareholders' Equity	
Cash	$ 24	Accounts payable	$ 4
Accounts receivable	15	Interest payable	3
Supplies	6	Unearned revenue	12
Prepaid insurance	12	Other short-term payables	4
Equipment	50	Long-term note payable	50
Less: Acc. dep. (12)	38	Contributed capital	20
Land	10	Retained earnings	12
Total	$105	Total	$105

Transactions during January 2012:

- Paid $5 for employee wages.
- Collected $10 cash from customers for work previously performed and billed.
- Purchased equipment for $5 cash.
- Purchased $2 of supplies for cash.
- Paid $3 to a vendor for supplies previously purchased on credit in December 2011.
- Paid the interest owed as of December 31, 2011.
- Completed $18 in services for customers, receiving 50 percent payment in cash and billing the remainder.
- Paid $15 to reduce outstanding long-term note payable.
- Collected $5 for the issuance of common shares.

As of 1/31/12:

- Had performed 25 percent of the services for which it had been paid in advance.
- Owes $1 for interest that will be paid next month.
- Depreciated equipment in the amount of $4.
- Physical count of supplies reveals $3 on hand.
- Declared and paid a cash dividend in the amount of 50 percent of January's net income.

REQUIRED:

Prepare a complete set of financial statements as of January 31, 2012, and prepare the statement of cash flows under the direct and the indirect (Appendix 4A) method.

P4–6

Effects of transactions on the income statement and statement of cash flows

Ten transactions are listed below.

Transaction	Accounts	Direction	Net Income	Net Operating Cash Flow
1. Issued ownership securities for cash.	Cash	+		
	Contributed			
	Capital	+	NE	NE
2. Purchased inventory on account.				
3. Sold a service on account.				
4. Received cash payments from customers on previously recorded sales.				
5. Purchased equipment for cash.				
6. Paid cash to reduce the wages payable account.				
7. Sold a service for cash.				
8. Paid off a long-term loan.				
9. Made a cash interest payment.				
10. Sold land for an amount greater than its cost.				

REQUIRED:

For each one, indicate what specific accounts are affected as well as the direction (increase or decrease) of the effect. Also indicate whether the transaction would increase or decrease both net income (revenues minus expenses) on the income statement and net cash flow from operations (operating cash inflows minus operating cash outflows) on the statement of cash flows. Use the following key: increase (+), decrease (−), and no effect (NE). The first one has been completed for you.

P4–7

The effects of adjusting journal entries on the accounting equation

Beta Alloys made the following adjusting journal entries on December 31, 2011.

1. Wage Expense	10,000		
Wages Payable		10,000	
2. Insurance Expense	5,000		
Prepaid Insurance		5,000	
3. Interest Receivable	1,000		
Interest Revenue		1,000	
4. Unearned Rent Revenue	6,000		
Rent Revenue		6,000	
5. Depreciation Expense	20,000		
Accumulated Depreciation		20,000	
6. Supplies Expense	8,000		
Supplies Inventory		8,000	
7. Unearned Subscription Revenue	2,000		
Subscription Revenue		2,000	

REQUIRED:

Classify each adjusting entry as either an accrual adjustment (A) or a cost expiration adjustment (C), and indicate whether each entry increases (+), decreases (−), or has no effect (NE) on assets, liabilities, shareholders' equity, revenues, and expenses. Organize your answer in the following way. The first journal entry has been done for you.

Entry	Classification	Assets	Liabilities	Shareholders' Equity	Revenues	Expenses
(1)	A	NE	+	−	NE	+

P4-8

Preparing adjusting
journal entries

The following information is available for M&M Johnson, Inc.:

a. The December 31, 2011, supplies inventory balance is $85,000. A count of supplies reveals that the company actually has $30,000 of supplies on hand.

b. As of December 31, 2011, Johnson, Inc. had not paid the rent for December. The monthly rent is $2,400.

c. On December 20, 2011, Johnson collected $18,000 in customer advances for the subsequent performance of a service. Johnson recorded the $18,000 as unearned revenue, and as of December 31 two-thirds of the service had been performed.

d. The total cost of Johnson's fixed assets is $500,000. Johnson estimates that the assets have a useful life of ten years and uses the straight-line method of depreciation.

e. Johnson borrowed $10,000 at an annual rate of 12 percent on July 1, 2011. The first interest payment will be made on January 1, 2012.

f. Johnson placed several ads in local newspapers during December. On December 31, the company received a $28,000 bill for the ads, which was not recorded at that time.

g. On July 1, 2011, Johnson paid the premium for a one-year life insurance policy. The $350 cost of the premium was capitalized when paid.

REQUIRED:
Prepare the adjusting journal entries necessary on December 31, 2011.

P4-9

Inferring adjusting
journal entries
from changes in
T-account balances

The following information is available for Derrick Company:

Account	T-Account Balance before Adjustments	T-Account Balance after Adjustments
Prepaid Rent	14,500	11,800
Prepaid Insurance	8,500	7,800
Accumulated Depreciation	36,000	38,400
Salaries Payable	1,300	2,500
Unearned Revenues	800	600
Fees Earned	87,600	87,800
Rent Expense	6,500	9,200
Insurance Expense	5,500	6,200
Depreciation Expense	0	2,400
Salary Expense	3,500	4,700

REQUIRED:
Prepare the adjusting journal entries that gave rise to the changes indicated.

P4-10

Reconciling accrual
and cash flow
dollar amounts

Burkholder Corporation borrowed $28,000 from its bank on January 1, 2011, at an annual interest rate of 10 percent. The $28,000 principal is to be paid as a lump sum at the end of the period of the loan, which is after December 31, 2012. This is the only interest-bearing debt held by Burkholder.

REQUIRED:
The following chart below contains six independent cases, each related to the Burkholder Corporation. Compute the missing amount in each case, assuming that the loan described is Burkholder's only outstanding loan.

	Case 1	Case 2	Case 3	Case 4	Case 5	Case 6
12/31/11 interest payable balance	400	800	400	?	200	?
Cash interest payments—2012	3,000	?	2,300	2,600	?	2,500
12/31/12 interest payable balance	?	300	?	200	400	0

P4–11

Revenue recognition,
cost expiration, and
cash flows

Prustate Insurance Company collected $240,000 from Jacobs Printing Corporation for a two-year fire insurance policy on May 31, 2011. The policy is in effect from June 1, 2011, to May 31, 2012.

REQUIRED:

a. Assume that Prustate Insurance Company recorded the $240,000 cash collection as a liability on May 31, 2011.
  1. Prepare the entry to record the cash collection.
  2. Prepare the adjusting entry necessary on December 31, 2011.
  3. What was the purpose of the adjusting journal entry on December 31, 2011?
  4. Complete a chart like the following:

	2011	2012	Total
Insurance revenue			
Cash receipts associated with insurance			

b. Assume that Jacobs Printing Corporation recorded the $240,000 cash payment as an asset on May 31, 2011.
  1. Prepare the entry to record the cash payment.
  2. Prepare the adjusting entry necessary on December 31, 2011.
  3. What was the purpose of the adjusting journal entry on December 31, 2011?
  4. Complete a chart like the following:

	2011	2012	Total
Insurance expense			
Cash payments associated with insurance			

REAL DATA

P4–12

The effects of
transactions on
financial ratios

The balance sheet of Walgreens, a leading chain drugstore, as of August 31, 2009, appears as follows (dollars in millions):

Assets		Liabilities and Shareholders' Equity	
Cash	$ 2,587	Accounts payable	$ 4,308
Accounts receivable	2,496	Other short-term payables	2,461
Inventory	6,789	Long-term payable	3,997
Other noncurrent assets	13,270	Shareholders' equity	14,376
		Total liabilities and	
Total assets	$25,142	shareholders' equity	$25,142

REQUIRED:

Assume that the following eight transactions occurred the next year (dollars in millions). Indicate the effect of each transaction on net income (revenues minus expenses), the current ratio (current assets divided by current liabilities), working capital (current assets minus current liabilities), and the debt/equity ratio (total liabilities divided by total shareholders' equity) of Walgreens. Use the following key: increase (+), decrease (−), no effect (NE). Treat each transaction independently.

Transaction	Net Income	Current Ratio	Working Capital	Debt/Equity Ratio
1. Issued ownership shares for $100 cash.				
2. Purchased equipment costing $95 for cash.				
3. Paid off a $200 long-term liability				

(Continued)

Transaction	Net Income	Current Ratio	Working Capital	Debt/Equity Ratio
4. Sold inventory costing $500 for $685 cash.				
5. Declared a $152 dividend but have not paid.				
6. Paid $200 in wages payable.				
7. Received $75 from customers on account.				
8. Incurred and paid $30 in interest on short-term payables.				

P4–13

Effects of different forms of financing on financial ratios

The following condensed balance sheet for December 31, 2012, comes from the records of Buzz and Associates:

Assets		Liabilities and Shareholders' Equity	
Cash	$ 10,000	Current liabilities	$ 20,000
Other current assets	40,000	Long-term notes payable	20,000
Property, plant, and equipment	70,000	Contributed capital	30,000
		Retained earnings	50,000
		Total liabilities and	
Total assets	$120,000	shareholders' equity	$120,000

Buzz and Associates is considering the purchase of a new piece of equipment for $30,000. The company does not have enough cash to purchase it outright, so it is considering alternative ways of financing. As management sees it, there are three basic options: (1) issue 3,000 ownership shares for $10 per share, (2) take out a long-term loan (12 percent annual interest) for $30,000 from the bank, or (3) purchase the equipment on open account (must be paid in full in thirty days). Presently Buzz has 12,000 ownership shares outstanding.

REQUIRED:

a. Compute the present current ratio (current assets/current liabilities), the debt/equity ratio (total liabilities/shareholders' equity), and the book value of Buzz's outstanding ownership shares: (total assets minus total liabilities) divided by number of shares outstanding.

b. Compute the current ratio, debt/equity ratio, and book value per share under each of the three financing alternatives, and express your answers in the following format:

Financing Alternative	Current Ratio	Debt/Equity Ratio	Book Value per Share
1. Share issuance			
2. Long-term note			
3. Open account			

c. Discuss some of the pros and cons associated with each of the three financing options.

d. The chairman of the board of directors stated at a recent board meeting that with $50,000 in Retained Earnings, the company should be able to purchase the $30,000 piece of equipment. Comment on the chairman's statement.

REAL DATA

P4–14

Effects of events on financial ratios

The following balances were taken from the October 31, 2008, balance sheet of Hewlett-Packard (dollars in millions).

Current assets	$51,728
Long-term assets	61,603
Current liabilities	52,939
Long-term liabilities	21,450
Shareholders' equity	38,942

Early in fiscal 2009, Hewlett-Packard considered the financial effects of several events.

REQUIRED:

For each of the five events listed here, indicate how they would affect the financial ratios listed by completing the following chart. Assume that financial statements are prepared immediately after each event. Treat each event independently, and use the following key: Increase (+), Decrease (−), and No Effect (NE).

	Net Income / Shareholders' Equity	Current Assets / Current Liabilities	Total Liabilities / Shareholders' Equity
1. Purchase inventory on account.			
2. Sell assets for cash at a gain.			
3. Provide services to customers, receiving cash in return.			
4. Make a principal payment on an outstanding long-term liability.			
5. Issue common stock for cash.			

REAL DATA

P4–15

Effects of events on
financial ratios

The following balances were taken from the December 31, 2008, balance sheet of Manpower, Inc., a world-leading workforce provider (dollars in millions):

Current assets	**$4,690**
Long-term assets	1,928
Current liabilities	2,907
Long-term liabilities	1,228
Shareholders' equity	2,483

Early in 2009, Manpower considered the financial effects of several events.

REQUIRED:

For each of the five events listed here, indicate how each event would affect the financial ratios listed by completing the following chart. Assume that financial statements are prepared immediately after each event. Treat each event independently, and use the following key: Increase (+), Decrease (−), and No Effect (NE).

	Net Income / Sales	Current Assets / Current Liabilities	Total Liabilities / Shareholders' Equity
1. Purchase equipment for cash.			
2. Purchase machinery in exchange for a long-term note payable.			
3. Pay salaries, which have not been accrued, to employees.			
4. Declare a dividend.			
5. Issue common stock to satisfy a current obligation.			

The following balances were taken from the December 31, 2008, balance sheet of Time Warner (dollars in millions):

Current assets	**$16,602**
Long-term assets	**97,294**
Current liabilities	**13,976**
Long-term liabilities	**57,632**
Shareholders' equity	**42,288**

Early in 2009, Time Warner considered the financial effects of several events.

REQUIRED:

For each of the five events listed here, indicate how they would affect the financial ratios listed by completing the following chart. Assume that financial statements are prepared immediately after each event. Treat each event independently, and use the following key: Increase (+), Decrease (−), and No Effect (NE).

	Net Income / Total Assets	Current Assets / Current Liabilities
1. Purchase equipment in exchange for a note payable.		
2. Pay cash for marketing its services.		
3. Sell equipment for an amount less than its book value.		
4. Pay wages that were accrued in a previous period.		
5. Provide a service for which cash was collected in a previous period.		

P4–17

Comprehensive problem

The following balance sheet is presented for J.D.F. Company as of December 31, 2011.

J.D.F. Company
Balance Sheet
December 31, 2011

ASSETS

Cash		$ 170,000
Accounts receivable		188,000
Merchandise inventory		200,000
Prepaid insurance		74,000
Supplies inventory		40,000
Long-term investments		160,000
Equipment	$480,000	
Less: Accumulated depreciation	98,000	382,000
Machinery	$950,000	
Less: Accumulated depreciation	230,000	720,000
Patent		75,000
Total assets		$2,009,000

LIABILITIES AND SHAREHOLDERS' EQUITY

Accounts payable	$ 220,000
Wages payable	73,000
Mortgage payable	300,000
Bonds payable	500,000
Contributed capital	500,000
Retained earnings	416,000
Total liabilities and shareholders' equity	$2,009,000

During 2012, J.D.F. entered into the following transactions.

1. Made credit sales of $1,350,000 and cash sales of $350,000. The cost of the inventory sold was $700,000.
2. Purchased $820,000 of merchandise inventory on account.
3. Made cash payments of $400,000 to employees for salaries. This amount includes the wages due employees as of December 31, 2011.
4. Purchased $110,000 of supplies inventory by issuing a six-month note that matures on March 12, 2013.
5. Collected $850,000 from customers in payment of open accounts receivable.
6. Paid suppliers $870,000 for payment of open accounts payable.
7. Sold a long-term investment for $37,000. The investment had been purchased for $30,000.
8. Paid $148,000 in cash for miscellaneous operating expenses.
9. Issued additional common stock for $120,000 cash.
10. On September 30, 2012, a customer gave the company a note due on May 1, 2013, in payment of a $72,000 account receivable.
11. The company declared and paid a cash dividend of $50,000.
12. The company purchased stock in Microsoft as a long-term investment for $50,000.

J.D.F. used the following information to prepare adjusting journal entries on December 31, 2012.

(a) Forty percent of the prepaid insurance on January 1 was still in effect as of December 31, 2012.
(b) A physical count of the supplies inventory indicated that the company had $40,000 on hand as of December 31, 2012.
(c) A review of the company's advertising campaign indicates that of the expenditures made during 2012 for miscellaneous operating expenses, $25,000 applies to promotions to be undertaken during 2013.
(d) The company is charged at a rate of $3,500 per month for certain operating expenses. It paid $36,000 for these expenses during the year.
(e) The company owes employees $43,000 for wages as of December 31, 2012.
(f) The $72,000 note receivable accepted in payment of an account receivable (see [10] above) specifies an annual interest rate of 9 percent.
(g) Equipment has an estimated useful life of ten years, and machinery has an estimated useful life of twenty years. The patent originally cost $125,000 and had an estimated useful life of ten years. The company uses the straight-line method to depreciate and amortize all property, plant, equipment, and intangibles.
(h) The note issued by the company (see [4] above) has a stated rate of 10 percent and was issued on September 12, 2012.

REQUIRED:

a. Prepare an income statement, a statement of shareholders' equity, a balance sheet, and a statement of cash flows using the direct form of presentation.
b. (Appendix 4A) Prepare the operating section of the statement of cash flows under the indirect method.

P4-18

Appendix 4A:
T-account analysis

Excerpts from the financial statements of Tree Tops Services are as follows.

	2012	2011
Balance sheet:		
Accounts receivable	$ 2,500	$ 3,100
Unearned revenue	1,300	2,600
Income statement:		
Revenues from services	54,700	49,800
Statement of cash flows:		
Net cash from operations	62,400	58,700

Note: Net cash from operations consists of two components: (1) cash collections from services rendered and (2) cash payments due to operating activities.

REQUIRED:

For 2012, compute (1) cash collections from services rendered and (2) cash payments due to operating activities.

P4–19

Appendix 4A:
T-account analysis

Mayberry Enterprises has two sources of revenue. It sells advertising displays to retail firms and provides a consulting service on how to mount and use these displays. You represent a large manufacturing company that is considering purchasing Mayberry. You have reviewed Mayberry's most recent financial statements, excerpts of which are provided below and are concerned about which of the two revenue sources is growing in importance for Mayberry. Mayberry's customers always pay for the consulting services in advance, indicating that the accounts receivable balance is associated only with sales of advertising displays.

	2012	2011	2010
Income statement:			
Revenues	$89,500	$76,000	$67,000
Balance sheet:			
Accounts receivable	29,500	32,200	35,000
Statement of cash flows:			
Collections from display sales	43,500	41,500	39,500

REQUIRED:

Which of the two revenue sources is growing in importance for Mayberry? Support your conclusion with calculations.

P4–20

Appendix 4A:
T-account analysis

You are a credit analyst for First American Bank, and Badger Business has applied for a loan. The company claims to have more than tripled profits from 2011 to 2012 and believes that it should be given prime credit terms. In addition, you note that Badger has expanded its operations, recently paying $37,000 for new equipment that replaced older equipment, which was sold that same year. No other transactions affected the company's equipment account. Excerpts from the company's 2012 financial statements are provided below.

	2012	2011
Balance sheet:		
Equipment	$97,400	$84,800
Accumulated depreciation	(26,400)	(24,300)
Income statement:		
Net income	5,200	1,500
Depreciation expense	8,700	7,600
Statement of cash flows:		
Proceeds from equipment sale	23,400	0

REQUIRED:

Reconstruct the journal entry to record the sale of equipment, and comment on Badger's claim that profits more than tripled in 2012.

ISSUES FOR DISCUSSION

REAL DATA

ID4–1

A transaction and
its effect on the
accounting equation
and balance sheet

When MCI Communications Corporation (now part of Verizon Communications) purchased Satellite Business Systems (SBS) from International Business Machines Corporation (IBM), it issued common stock to IBM, valued at $376 million, and signed a note payable for $104 million. MCI received miscellaneous assets valued at $52 million and the SBS system.

REQUIRED:

Respond to the following:

a. At what dollar amount was the SBS system recorded on MCI's balance sheet?
b. Describe how this transaction affected the accounting equation from MCI's point of view.
c. Describe how this transaction affected MCI's balance sheet.
d. Identify the financial statement accounts affected, the direction of the effect, and the dollar amount of the effect on each account.
e. Prepare the journal entry MCI recorded when the transaction took place.

REAL DATA

ID4–2

The effect of a transaction on the basic accounting equation

When Campbell Soup purchased the European culinary business from Unilever, the acquisition was funded with available cash and a short-term notes payable. The $920 million purchase price was allocated: $100 million to fixed assets and inventory; $490 million to identifiable intangible assets (e.g., trademarks), and $330 representing the excess of the purchase price over the fair value of the individual assets acquired (goodwill).

REQUIRED:

a. How did the transaction affect the accounting equation from Campbell Soup's perspective?
b. How did the transaction affect the accounting equation from Unilever's perspective?
c. Describe how the transaction affected Campbell Soup's balance sheet.
d. Prepare the journal entry made by Campbell Soup to record the transaction.

REAL DATA

ID4–3

The effects of transactions on the accounting equation

In the late 1990s the Internet explosion sent the share values of well-known Internet companies soaring. Many of these companies took advantage of the high prices by making major share issuances and using the funds as their major source of financing. Lycos collected $111 million from a 1998 issuance; Yahoo! collected over $800 million over a three-year period; and America Online topped them all, collecting over $1 billion. While each company used the proceeds a little differently, they all used some of it to reduce debt, update equipment, and increase current assets.

REQUIRED:

a. Describe how the issuance of stock to reduce debt, update equipment, and increase current assets affects the fundamental accounting equation.
b. Explain how the issuance of stock could increase a company's credit rating.

REAL DATA

ID4–4

Cash flows and business failures

The W.T. Grant Company was the nation's largest retailer until it filed for bankruptcy only one year after it had reported profits of over $20 million for more than ten consecutive years. Yet cash flow provided by operations started dipping several years earlier and remained negative until the company's collapse.

REQUIRED:

a. What kind of items might account for such a divergence between net income and cash flow provided by operations?
b. What information on the financial statements could have provided some warning of the company's failure?

REAL DATA

ID4–5

Corporate frauds and the auditor

In "Behind the Wave of Corporate Fraud: A Change in How Auditors Work," the *Wall Street Journal* detailed several of the recent accounting scandals and the techniques management used to deceive both the auditors and the investing public. The article focused on audit techniques that contributed to the ability of management to undertake deceptive practices. For example, WorldCom reclassified ordinary expenses as assets, which the auditors missed because there was "no supporting documentation"; Tyco International, charged with inflating profits by over $1 billion, left "warning signs" that were not followed up on by auditors; and HealthSouth Corporation pulled it off by inflating the dollar amounts of a large number of small revenue recognition transactions because they "knew the auditors did not look at increases of less than $5,000."

REQUIRED:

a. Explain how WorldCom showed higher profits in the current period by inaccurately classifying expenses as assets. How would this technique affect the profits of future periods?

b. Explain why management may be tempted to inflate profits in the current period.

c. Explain why auditors might not check transactions below a certain dollar amount.

d. How could high-quality internal controls have helped in avoiding these frauds?

REAL DATA

ID4–6

Watch cash flow

Herbert S. Bailey, Jr., published the following poem in *Publishers Weekly* (Jan. 13, 1975), which was written in the meter of Edgar Allan Poe's famous poem, *The Raven*.

Though my bottom line is black, I am flat upon my back.
My cash flows out and customers pay slow.
The growth of my receivables is almost unbelievable;
The result is certain—unremitting woe!
And I hear the banker utter an ominous low mutter,
"Watch cash flow."

REQUIRED:

Explain Mr. Bailey's message.

REAL DATA

ID4–7

Income statement classification and International Financial Reporting Standards

In January 2004, Munich-based automaker BMW switched how it classified certain expenses to match what it anticipates to be the format approved by International Financial Reporting Standards (IFRS). Previously, BMW classified these expenses as part of operating profit, and now it has decided to move them to the nonoperating section of the income statement in line with IFRS. As reported in the *Wall Street Journal,* a Goldman Sachs analyst commented that BMW's action would significantly boost its operating income, and "if GM took BMW's approach, it would boost operating income by over $7 billion."

REQUIRED:

a. How would the change made by BMW affect net income, that is, its "bottom line"?

b. Provide several reasons why BMW might be interested in making this change.

c. Why would an analyst from Goldman Sachs be concerned about how operating profits are measured by BMW and GM?

d. Would BMW be allowed to make this change if it wished to issue stock on the New York Stock Exchange? Discuss.

The Associated Press reported:

REAL DATA

ID4–8

Problems with the federal government's accounting systems

The military's money managers last year made almost $7 trillion in adjustments to their financial ledgers in an attempt to make them add up, the Pentagon's inspector general said in a report released yesterday. The Pentagon could not show receipts of $2.3 trillion of those changes, and half a trillion dollars of it was just corrections of mistakes made in earlier adjustments. . . . The magnitude of accounting entries required to compile the financial statements highlights the significant problems [the Pentagon] has producing accurate and reliable financial statements with existing systems and processes . . . the military can't measure the results of closing a base; can't rationally decide whether to contract out a service or keep it in government hands; and may inaccurately peg the cost of programs under debate, from national missile defense to retirees' health care.

REQUIRED:

Discuss problems that might arise due to the significant weaknesses of the Pentagon's accounting systems.

REAL DATA

ID4–9

Debt transactions and the basic accounting equation

The *Wall Street Journal* (October 5, 2009) reported that analysts are worried about companies borrowing money to pay dividends and to repurchase outstanding shares of stock. Aircraft parts manufacturer TransDigm Group borrowed $360 million to pay dividends, while Intel Corporation borrowed $1.5 billion to buy back shares of stock. These concerns of

analysts are not new; in March 2007 the *Wall Street Journal* reported two instances of borrowings-for-dividends (Rexnord Corporation and Scotts Miracle-Gro) that sparked concerns. Companies have defended the actions, often citing historically low borrowing costs.

REQUIRED:

Discuss how the above transactions affect the basic accounting equation for the companies involved. What risks are posed when a company pursues such a strategy? What are the benefits of such a decision?

REAL DATA

ID4–10

Consolidated financial statements and multinationals

In October 2008 NIKE completed the acquisition of 100% of the common shares of Umbro, a leading United Kingdom–based global soccer brand. The acquisition price was approximately $576 million, and since the acquisition Umbro has operated as a wholly owned NIKE subsidiary. Umbro prepares its financial statements under IFRS and the amounts are denominated in British pounds.

REQUIRED:

Describe some of the difficulties faced by NIKE each year when it consolidates the financial statements prepared by Umbro into its overall consolidated financial statements.

REAL DATA

ID4–11

Real-time accounting

According to *The Internal Auditor* (April 2000):

In the past, credible financial reports could be produced, audited, and published only on a periodic basis, because the information needed to generate such reports was either impossible or too costly to obtain on a real-time basis. However, a growing number of important items on financial statements have come under real-time management, as information technology has made such practices both economically feasible and competitively necessary for survival.

REQUIRED:

What does it mean that information can be obtained on a real-time basis? What items on the financial statements do you think have come under real-time management, and what advantages might real-time accounting create?

REAL DATA

ID4–12

The SEC Form 10-K of NIKE

The SEC Form 10-K of NIKE is reproduced in Appendix C.

REQUIRED:

Review the NIKE Form 10-K, and answer the following questions.

a. In terms of the basic accounting equation, explain how NIKE accounts for prepaid expenses. What is the dollar value of prepaid expenses on the 2009 and 2008 balance sheets?

b. In terms of the basic accounting equation, explain how NIKE accounts for accrued liabilities.

c. How much cash did NIKE spend for capital expenditures and dividends during the year ended May 31, 2009? How did these transactions affect the basic accounting equation? How much cash was collected from share issuances through stock options, and how did these transactions affect the basic accounting equation?

d. What is the balance of accounts payable on NIKE's May 31, 2009, balance sheet, and how did it get there?

e. What does NIKE's management say in its management letter about its system of internal controls?

f. (Appendix 4A) Why is depreciation added to net income in the operating section of the statement of cash flows, and why is the increase in accounts receivable subtracted from net income?

Using Financial Statement Information

KEY POINTS

The following key points are emphasized in this chapter:

- Using financial accounting numbers to influence management decisions and predict future events.

- Five steps of financial statement analysis.

- Assessing the business environment.

- Assessing earnings quality and persistence.

- Analyzing financial statements.

- Difficulties involved in using annual report information to identify mispriced securities.

- Difficulties involved in using financial statements to compare the performance of companies operating in different countries.

When a company reports its results, it had better beat the expectations of the analysts who follow that company, or look out, stock price! Network equipment maker Juniper Networks, Inc. (JNPR) represents a prime example. You would think that when JNPR reported an 8 percent jump in 2009 quarterly revenue and a 14 percent increase in profits, the stock price would soar. Not true. JNPR stock was actually off 13 percent, down to $14.77 per share. Why? It seems that reported earnings per share and revenue, even though lofty, didn't quite make the consensus analyst earnings prediction as compiled by Thomson First Call.

Earnings predictions are prepared regularly by analysts who closely follow companies, and they are compiled by groups like Thomson First Call and Nelsons. Stock prices react to those predictions, and when they are not met, stock prices drop. To achieve or beat these expectations, companies often tell analysts that earnings will be lower than they really believe, or sometimes they use accounting discretion to boost reported earnings. How do analysts make earnings predictions, and what role do financial statements play?

The information that appears in the financial statements is used in many ways by a variety of individuals and entities. Investors and creditors use it to evaluate company performance and to predict the amount and timing of earnings and the future cash flows (e.g., dividends and interest) associated with their investments. They also use financial information to influence and monitor the activities of management. As representatives of the shareholders, the boards of directors of many companies base executive compensation on various measures of income, while creditors protect their loan investments by writing debt covenants in terms of financial statement numbers. Public utilities use financial accounting numbers to set customer rates, and labor unions use such information to negotiate with management for higher wages and better working conditions. Credit-rating agencies, such as Standard & Poor's, Moody's, and Dun & Bradstreet, use financial statement information to determine credit ratings. Indeed, financial accounting information plays an important role in a number of different kinds of business decisions.

CONTROL AND PREDICTION

Financial accounting numbers are useful in two fundamental ways: (1) they help investors and creditors influence and monitor the business decisions of a company's managers, and (2) they help to predict a company's future earnings and cash flows.

Financial Accounting Numbers and Management Control

Investors and creditors, who provide a company with its capital, can direct and monitor the actions of its managers by requiring that their contracts be written in terms of financial accounting numbers. Shareholders have incentives to encourage management to act in ways that maximize future dividend payments and stock price appreciation. Since such returns depend on a company's earning power and long-term profitability, shareholders want management to make business decisions that maintain high levels of earning power. A common method used to attain such a goal is to base management's compensation on reported profits. Such compensation schemes, which are set by a company's board of directors, can lead to payments in the form of either cash or shares of stock. Exxon Mobil Corporation, for example, has implemented a management incentive program that pays eligible employees a percentage of the company's earnings

if net income in a given year exceeds 6 percent of invested capital (as defined in the bonus plan). These bonuses have been paid in both cash and shares of Exxon Mobil common stock.[1]

Creditors are also interested in protecting their investments by influencing the business decisions of management. They are concerned that companies may not be able to meet their loan obligations because company assets may have been (1) paid to the shareholders in the form of dividends or purchases of outstanding stock, (2) pledged to other creditors, or (3) mismanaged. To reduce the probability of such events, a creditor may restrict certain business decisions of managers as a condition of the loan. Such restrictions are written into the loan contract and expressed in terms of financial accounting numbers.

For example, when Alcoa entered into an eight-year, $600 million revolving credit agreement with a group of banks, it required that during the period of the loan (1) the current ratio (current assets divided by current liabilities) not be less than 1:1 and (2) a minimum working capital (current assets—current liabilities) of $500 million be maintained. In other debt covenants, The Pillsbury Company, part of General Mills, is restricted with respect to paying dividends and purchasing its own common stock, and Delta Air Lines' covenants restrict its ability to grant liens, incur or guarantee debt, and enter into flight equipment leases.

Financial Accounting Numbers as Prediction Aids

Financial accounting numbers report on past events. In and of themselves, they are neither predictions nor forecasts. However, to the extent that past events are indicative of the future, financial accounting numbers can be used to make predictions about a company's future earnings and cash flows. Financial statement numbers, for example, have been used in statistical models to predict bankruptcy with reasonable accuracy, and auditors often use such models to predict whether potential clients will remain in business. Indeed, the main objective of financial reporting, as stated by the Financial Accounting Standards Board, is "to help present and potential investors and creditors and other users in assessing the amount, timing, and uncertainty of *future* cash flows."[2]

> Vonage provides communication services over the Internet. In February 2002 the company planned to raise funds by offering its stock for sale to the public for the first time. As reported in TheStreet.com, Vonage planned the public offering despite the fact that the company "has been losing money and plans to continue to do so." In the company's prospectus to potential investors, revenue growth is highlighted while the losses are explained by increases in marketing expenses.
>
> Discuss why investors would be interested in buying a company that is growing but continues to lose money. What do financial accounting concepts such as profit and operating cash flow tell investors about a company's *future* prospects? Discuss what information in addition to the financial reports is needed for investment decisions.

1. It is unclear whether basing management compensation on accounting measures of profit serves to maximize the long-term earning power of major companies in the United States. Some contend that such compensation schemes encourage management to manipulate reported profits and to make operating, investing, and financing decisions that increase profits in the short run, at the expense of long-term profitability.

2. Financial Accounting Standards Board, "Objectives of Financial Reporting by Business Enterprises," *Statement of Financial Accounting Concepts No. 1* (Stamford, Conn., 1979).

FRAMEWORK FOR USING FINANCIAL STATEMENTS TO PREDICT FUTURE EARNINGS AND CASH FLOWS

Equity investors use financial information to predict future earnings and cash flows in their efforts to identify securities that will provide high returns. Creditors use financial information to predict whether companies can generate enough cash in the future to cover debt payments. Future cash flows are at the heart of a company's true value, which is of interest to both investors and creditors. The balance sheet provides a measure of a company's value at a given point in time—its book value (assets − liabilities). Unfortunately, book value is a far cry from true value or even the stock market's estimate of true value. As of December 31, 2008, for example, the book value of Yahoo! was $11.25 billion, while the total market price of its outstanding shares of stock was just under $17 billion!

As illustrated in Figure 5–1, reported book value and true value differ for three reasons: (1) the financial statements do not reflect the company's prospects within its business environment, (2) the financial statements do not reflect important unrecorded events, and (3) management prepares the reports in a biased manner.

FIGURE 5–1   Framework for financial statement analysis

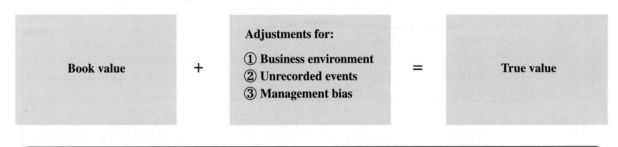

Business Environment

Book value fails to reflect "true value" primarily because the financial statements are backward looking, and what really matters in the valuation of a company is its future prospects. What is the prognosis for the economy—good or bad—and how closely are the company's fortunes tied to swings in the overall economy? What is the future for the industry in which the company operates—is it growing or dying? What is the company's strategy for generating profits within the industry? Does it compete by providing innovative products and/or services or by controlling its costs? The answers to these questions are critical in assessing a company's true value, and backward-looking financial statements are of limited use in answering them. It is often stated that trying to manage a company using the financial statements is like trying to drive a car by looking in the rearview mirror. It works if the future is just like the past, but watch out if a big truck is stopped in front of you and there is no truck behind you!

?   It is not unusual for companies with little or no profit to have reasonably high stock prices. Amazon.com, for example, reported no profits in its early years of operation, yet supported an impressive stock price. Similarly, as noted in the beginning of the chapter with Juniper Networks, companies reporting increasing profits are sometimes punished by the stock market. Explain why stock prices do not necessarily follow profit reports.

Unrecorded Events

The financial statements also leave out important current and historical information, which is relevant to assessing true value. For example, estimates of the value of a company's human resources are not included in the balance sheet. For many companies, especially those in the fast-growing service sector, human capital is the most important asset—yet, the balance sheet contains no asset called human capital. How can one assess the value of a basketball team without assessing the value of its players? How does one value a law firm or public accounting firm without considering the value of its professional staff?

Similarly, most of the assets on the balance sheet are carried at historical cost, not current market prices, and there is much doubt about the usefulness of historical costs for decision-making purposes. Consider, for example, land purchased ten years ago for $1,000 that now can be sold for $10,000. Under U.S. GAAP the land is carried on the balance sheet at $1,000, even though $10,000 is likely the more useful number.

Under IFRS, in certain situations the land can be carried on the balance sheet at $10,000, its current market value.

It is also true that financial statements prepared according to U.S. GAAP ignore the effects of inflation and that they are not published in a timely manner. Normally, the annual reports of most U.S. companies are published several months after the balance sheet date, allowing many important—but unreported—transactions to occur in the meantime.

In May 2007, Rupert Murdoch's News Corporation made an unsolicited offer of $60 per share to purchase Dow Jones & Company, the publisher of the *Wall Street Journal*. At the time of the offer, shares of Dow Jones were trading on the New York Stock Exchange for a little over $36 per share. A review of the December 31, 2006, balance sheet of Dow Jones showed that the book value per share (shareholders' equity according to GAAP divided by the number of shares outstanding) was approximately $6 per share. Which valuation is correct—the market value as determined on the NYSE, the market valued as determined by an experienced investor, or the book value as determined by GAAP? Discuss why an investor would be willing to pay such a premium over the book value and the existing market value.

Management Bias

Finally, the financial statements are limited by management's bias. Managers are not inherently unethical, and they do not attempt at every opportunity to exploit the investors and creditors who provide the company's capital. It is in the manager's long-term best interest to report truthfully. However, it is well known that managers choose accounting methods and estimates that report the results of operations in ways that protect and further their interests. They are fully aware that the financial statements are used by outsiders to evaluate and influence their actions and that their future levels of wealth are often directly tied to financial accounting numbers. Such influence may come in the form of choosing a particular accounting method or estimate and/or any number of other subjective operating, investing, financing, and reporting decisions.

> **?** In a growing practice, many companies are including in their annual reports what they refer to as "pro forma" financial information. Such information is used to describe what the financial statements or key financial numbers would look like, for example, after a proposed merger or acquisition. While the Securities and Exchange Commission (SEC) recognizes that pro forma numbers can be useful, in an official 2004 SEC release, it cautioned investors because pro forma numbers are normally not prepared in conformance with generally accepted accounting principles (GAAP), and "under certain circumstances can mislead investors if it obscures GAAP results." Explain how pro forma numbers could be useful and why the SEC is cautioning investors.

ELEMENTS OF FINANCIAL STATEMENT ANALYSIS

Given that the use of financial statements for predicting future earnings and cash flows is limited due to the lack of forward-looking information, unrecorded events, and management bias, it is important that financial statement analysis address the following issues:

- Assessing the business environment.
- Reading and studying the financial statements and footnotes.
- Assessing earnings quality.
- Analyzing the financial statements.
- Predicting future earnings and/or cash flows.

In this chapter these issues are discussed in a given order, but keep in mind that different analysts use different methods. Indeed, financial statement analysis is an art, not a science, where judgment plays an extremely important role.

ASSESSING THE BUSINESS ENVIRONMENT

The analyst must first learn about the company, its industry, and how the company and industry relate to the overall economy. What is the nature of the company's operations, and what strategy is the company using to generate profits within its industry? What is the company's industry, who are the major players and the company's competitors, and is it easy or difficult for outside firms to enter the industry? What are the relationships between the company and its suppliers and customers, and who holds the bargaining power? Finally, when the overall economy booms or goes into recession, how are the company's sales and profits affected? How quickly do the company's sales and profits change when the indices of overall economic activity change? An astute analyst addresses these questions before reviewing the financial statements. The answers provide a forward-looking perspective on the company and create a useful context in which to interpret the financial statements. They also help the analyst to target key items in the financial statements for especially close examination.

One way to quickly gain a sense of a company's operations and how other experts view its future prospects is to access investment services, such as Moody's (moodys.com), Value Line (valueline.com), Dun & Bradstreet (smallbusiness.dnb.com), and Standard & Poor's (spglobal.com). These information sources provide extensive analyses of the operations and financial position of many companies, as well as ratings of the riskiness

of their outstanding debts. These ratings reflect a company's future prospects within its business environment and have a direct bearing on its ability to issue debt with reasonable terms.

> Apple Computer, with both its iPhone and tablet computer iPad, charges customers a product price and a "data fee" (in conjunction with communications firm AT&T) to allow the device to connect to the Internet. Before the introduction of its latest products (dating back to the iPod), Apple had been more of a traditional hardware manufacturer, selling customers its Macintosh line of computers. With the newer personal electronic products, Apple provides a service in addition to the hardware product. What effect over time has this strategic shift had on the financial statements of Apple? Which arenas of the balance sheet, income statement, and statement of cash flows would be affected?

The *Wall Street Journal* reports almost daily the changes in a company's financial prospects and its credit ratings, which in turn affect the price of a company's stocks and bonds as well as its ability to raise additional funds. For example, a recent annual report of Hewlett-Packard states:

Standard & Poor's Ratings Services, Moody's Investors Service, and Fitch Ratings currently rate our senior unsecured long term debt A-, A3, and A and our short-term debt A-1, Prime-1, and F1, respectively. We do not have any rating downgrade triggers that would accelerate the maturity of a material amount of our debt. However, a downgrade in our credit rating would increase the cost of borrowings under our credit facilities. Also, a downgrade in our credit rating could limit, or, in the case of a significant downgrade, preclude our ability to issue commercial paper under our current programs.

READING AND STUDYING THE FINANCIAL STATEMENTS AND FOOTNOTES

After the analyst understands the company's business environment, financial statement information can be studied. This analysis consists of three steps: (1) read the audit report, (2) identify significant transactions and the company's important segments, and (3) read the income statement, balance sheet, statement of cash flows, statement of shareholders' equity, and footnotes.

The Audit Report

The audit report serves as the accounting profession's "seal of approval," stating whether, and to what extent, the information in the financial statements fairly reflects the financial position and operations of the company.

After reviewing the financial records of a company, the auditor usually renders a **standard audit report** stating that the financial statements fairly reflect the financial position and operations of the company and the internal control system is reasonably effective. Such a report also states that all necessary tests were conducted in concluding that a company's financial statements conform to generally accepted accounting principles.[3] In

---

3. Examples of the standard audit report can be found in Chapter 1 of this text and in Appendix C, where excerpts from NIKE's SEC Report 10-K is located.

such cases, the reader can be reasonably assured that the information in the statements is credible and that the company in question is in reasonable financial health.

Accounting Trends and Techniques (New York: AICPA, 2009) reported that, of the 600 major U.S. companies surveyed, the overwhelming majority received a standard audit report in 2009. The remainder of these companies received something other than a standard report. Auditors depart from the standard report for many different reasons, some of which can be quite serious. For example, in a recent study by John Grice, an accounting professor at Troy State University, over 50 percent of the publicly traded companies that go bankrupt receive an audit opinion in the year prior to bankruptcy indicating "substantial doubt" about the company's ability to continue as a going concern.

Not all companies are audited by certified public accountants. Only those companies whose equity securities are traded on public stock exchanges are legally required to do so. Such publicly traded companies tend to be the largest in the United States (in terms of annual sales or total assets), yet they represent only a small portion of the total number of U.S. companies. These other companies may or may not choose to have their statements audited. Many are required to do so as a condition for private equity issuances or bank loans, but most are not audited at all. A comprehensive audit by a public accounting firm can be very time-consuming and costly, and for many small companies, especially those that do not rely on outside sources of capital, the benefit from the audit simply does not justify the costs. In such cases, the financial statement user must proceed with extreme caution.

A controversy called "Big GAAP vs. Little GAAP" is brewing currently among accounting policymakers. It involves whether a separate set of less rigorous generally accepted accounting principles should be established for small and/or non-publicly traded companies. This same issue will arise if and when the United States moves to IFRS—that is, will a standard audit report require that non-public companies use IFRS instead of U.S. GAAP?

Significant Transactions and Important Segments

Predicting earnings and cash flows also involves reviewing significant transactions entered into by a company or significant recent events that might affect a company's performance. Such items can have an important effect on the future direction of a company and may distort the financial statements, making it more difficult to assess a company's financial position and operations. Examples include major acquisitions, the discontinuance or disposal of a business segment, unresolved litigation, major write-downs of receivables or inventories, offers to purchase outstanding shares (tender offers), extraordinary gains or losses, and changes of accounting methods. Usually, such transactions or events are discussed in the footnotes of the annual report, and the financial effects are prominently disclosed on the income statement and/or statement of cash flows.

Analysts must pay careful attention to how these items affect the income statement. They can dramatically impact reported income, yet reflect little about the company's future. An important concept in financial statement analysis is called **earnings persistence,** which refers to the extent to which an income statement item reported in the current period can be expected to reflect future income levels. An item with high

persistence would be expected to relate closely to future income amounts and be useful in predicting them, while low persistence earnings are normally associated with "one-time," nonrecurring events.

When Motorola sold its automotive electronics business, it booked a gain on the sale of $399 million. Including the gain, the company reported net income for the year of $3.6 billion. Comment on whether an analyst should include the gain in the assessment of management's past performance. Also comment on whether an analyst should consider the gain in the assessment of the company's future performance.

Like many large companies, Walt Disney is composed of several **business segments:** media networks, parks and resorts, studio entertainment, consumer products, and interactive media. Each is briefly described below.

Segment	Description	Percent of Company 2009 Revenues/Profits
Media networks	Television production	45/71
Parks and resorts	Theme parks	29/21
Studio entertainment	Motion pictures	17/3
Consumer products	Disney toys, apparel, etc.	7/9
Interactive media	Video games, online Web sites	2/loss

During 2009 media networks was by far the largest source of revenues and profits, parks and resorts and motion pictures were less profitable, and the relatively small interactive media segment actually posted a loss.

Disney's operations can also be broken down based on geographic segments. In 2009, 76 percent and 74 percent of Disney's revenues and profits, respectively, were generated in the United States and Canada, where 88 percent of Disney's fixed assets are invested; the remainder are in Europe, Asia, and Latin America.

Segment information can be very useful because it provides insight into how and where large companies invest their resources and generate their revenues and profits. Under both U.S. GAAP and IFRS, companies are required to disclose revenues, profits, and assets of their primary operating and geographic segments. Reviewing this information is essential for effective financial analysis.

Financial Statements and Footnotes

Financial statements were discussed in Chapter 2, and the information provided in the footnotes will be discussed and illustrated throughout the remainder of the text. There is, however, one important point worth mentioning here.

One goal of assessing a company's business environment is to identify key items on the financial statements. For example, success for companies in the retail industry, like Wal-Mart and Home Depot, depends on the quality of inventory management. Consequently, inventory, accounts payable, and cost of goods sold—and the related footnotes—are particularly important financial statement accounts for these companies. In financial services, companies like Bank of America loan billions of dollars each year to customers, which makes the collectibility of receivables especially important. Software manufacturers, such as Microsoft, invest heavily in research and development, an income statement expense account that consistently generates considerable attention from

analysts. Therefore, when reading the financial statements, it is important to recognize that the nature of the company's operations normally determines where the analysis should be focused. This is particularly true for Internet companies like Google, which invest heavily each year in the acquisition of new companies.

ASSESSING EARNINGS QUALITY

Earnings quality refers to the extent to which the reported financial statements deviate from the true financial condition and performance of the company. One aspect of assessing earnings quality involves determining the extent to which management's biases have influenced the financial statements. Four strategies used by managers to "manage" reported accounting numbers are well known. Each is discussed below.

Overstating Operating Performance

In certain situations, managers simply attempt to devise a more favorable picture by **overstating the performance** of the company. This is often achieved by accelerating the recognition of revenues or deferring the recognition of expenses. Young, fast-growing, aggressive companies sometimes use this reporting strategy to help them attract much-needed capital, and it is also common in situations where companies face financial difficulties.

In a well-known article entitled "Earnings Hocus-Pocus," *Business Week* reported that when the economy slows and Wall Street gets jittery, concerns grow that companies desperate to keep up earnings and stock prices practice even more aggressive accounting. Explain what this means and provide several examples of "aggressive accounting."

Taking a Bath

When a company experiences an extremely poor year, it sometimes chooses very conservative accounting methods, estimates, or judgments (e.g., recognize an accounting loss) that, in turn, further reduce the company's reported financial condition and operating performance in that year. This strategy, called **taking a bath,** enables companies to recognize losses in years that are already very poor, in hopes that these losses may be less obvious. Furthermore, by recognizing losses in the current year, management will not have to recognize them in future years, which in turn may improve future financial statements.

That same *Business Week* article (see above) noted, "The aim of many of today's giant write-offs is to front-load expenses. Charge off three years of expenses all at once, and by definition future earnings will be better. It's akin to making three years of mortgage payments all at once, and claiming that your income has grown [across the three-year period]." Explain the meaning of this quote and provide several examples of "front-loading expenses."

Creating Hidden Reserves

Very conservative accounting methods, estimates, and judgments may also be used by management in years of extremely good performance. This strategy, called **creating hidden reserves,** can help management to "smooth" reported earnings over time. Recognizing accounting losses in the current period ensures that reported earnings in that period are not too high and, in addition, guarantees that the loss will not have to be recognized in future periods when reported earnings may be less impressive.

Fannie Mae and Freddy Mac are companies that buy home mortgage receivables from banks, providing the banks with more money to make new loans. Consequently, the main assets held by Fannie and Freddy are receivables, which are of little value if the home mortgages are not paid on a timely basis. In 2003 and 2004 both companies were cited for using accounting discretion to make reported earnings look less volatile, and more recently, both were taken over by the federal government due to the falling value of the mortgage loans. Why would a company want to make its reported earnings look less volatile, and how might Fannie and Freddy have used accounting discretion to "smooth earnings"?

Employing Off-Balance-Sheet Financing

Managers have been known to structure financing transactions and choose certain accounting methods so that debt need not be reported on the balance sheet. By avoiding the recognition of debt, such activities, called **off-balance-sheet financing,** may make the reporting company appear less risky. As noted in *Forbes,* "The basic drives of man are few: to get enough food, to find shelter, and to keep debt off the balance sheet." In a very famous and costly financial fraud, Enron Corporation was charged with failing to report billions of dollars of liabilities on its balance sheet.

RadioShack Corporation leases rather than owns most of its facilities. These leases involve significant contractual commitments to make payments far into the company's future—sometimes as long as ten or twenty years. Such commitments in the year 2008 totaled $640 million. For the most part, these payments are accounted for on the income statement as rent expense as they are paid. Is there another way one might view these commitments, perhaps as a liability? Discuss.

Given such strategies, financial statement users must not only analyze the statements, but must also attempt to assess the extent to which management has had discretionary influence over the statements. To do so, users must examine the footnotes closely to identify the accounting methods that have been chosen, while being particularly aware of those areas in the statements that are most sensitive to the subjective estimates and judgmental reporting decisions of management. Users should also learn as much as possible about the situation faced by management or, in other words, "put

themselves in management's shoes" by investigating incentive compensation contracts, debt covenants, and the general economic environment in which the company itself and its industry exist. With such information, users can better understand the economic incentives that may have determined the reporting strategies chosen by management.

Assessing the quality of a company's reported numbers is useful because it enables users to adjust the statements and thereby make more accurate assessments of a company's true value. Indeed, in a recent study a well-known earnings quality analyst found that from 1998 to 2004, the fifty companies with the best-quality earnings had returns about four times the average for the stock market in total. The bottom fifty had zero returns.

IFRS relies more heavily than U.S. GAAP on management's discretion to choose the method of accounting that fairly reflects the company's financial condition and performance, and at the same time requires fewer disclosures. IFRS also more frequently allows the use of fair market values as the basis for asset measurement. Given these differences, comment on the amount and nature of earnings management practiced under the two systems.

Earnings Quality and Unrecorded Events

Assessing earnings quality also includes considering the unrecorded events not reflected on the financial statements. Once again, these limitations depend on the nature of the company under analysis. The financial statements of professional service companies, where the value lies in the professional staff, may be quite limited because the balance sheet does not contain a value for human capital. In such cases, the analyst can improve the quality of the statements by estimating the value of human capital. Companies in the high-tech industry may have patents and formulas and other intangible assets that are not valued accurately on the balance sheet. Here again, analysts may wish to adjust the reported values of these assets. Such adjustments are highly subjective and often must be based on information available outside the financial statements (e.g., industry trade journals, asset appraisals). Nonetheless, the goal of earnings quality assessment is to improve the quality of the reported numbers, and the analyst should make some attempt to achieve it.

During the financial crisis of 2008–2009, many bankers were laid off, as business prospects were bleak. Finally, in the second half of 2009, banks reported a return to profits, and the news service Reuters reported that investment banks, including J.P. Morgan and Goldman Sachs, were returning to the labor market, hiring investment bankers and traders. Reuters cited the increased activity of recruiting professionals, known as "headhunters," as a sign that the banks were seeing a brighter future. How do you think the stock market reacted to this news, and how was it reflected in the financial statements of the banks?

ANALYZING THE FINANCIAL STATEMENTS

Now that the analyst has examined the business environment, read the financial statements, and assessed the quality of the reported numbers, the statements can be analyzed. Financial statement analysis is a broad and complex topic. In this chapter, we discuss comparison analysis, which includes common-size analysis and ratio analysis. Appendix 5A introduces the concept of shareholder value creation and contains a framework designed to help identify it and analyze its determinants via the analysis of ratios as a package (called the ROE model).[4] It also describes the basics of cash flow analysis.

Accounting numbers are not very meaningful in and of themselves. They become useful only when they are compared to other numbers. For example, suppose that you read in the *Wall Street Journal* that PepsiCo reported net income of $1 billion for 2010. Would you interpret that announcement as favorable or unfavorable news? This question is difficult to answer in the absence of a basis for comparison. Income of $1 billion is neither large nor small in an absolute sense. It depends on such factors as the amount of net income reported by PepsiCo in previous years, the amount of net income reported by other companies similar to PepsiCo, normally in the same industry, the size of PepsiCo's operations and capital base, or even the profit expected by analysts. Thus, financial accounting numbers are only meaningful when compared to other relevant numbers. Such comparisons can be made in three ways: (1) across time, (2) across different companies within the same industry, and (3) within the financial statements of the company at a given point in time against a benchmark or target.

Comparisons across Time

Financial accounting numbers can be made more meaningful if they are compared across time. At a minimum, generally accepted accounting principles require that the financial statements of the current and the preceding years be disclosed side by side in published financial reports. Income statements, statements of cash flow, and statements of shareholders' equity are required for three years, while balance sheets are required for two. While this is helpful for identifying changes from one year to the next, many companies provide comparisons of selected items, accounting and nonaccounting, across five- or ten-year periods. Such disclosures can help a user to develop a "feel" for a company's activities and its general financial condition and, at the same time, can identify certain trends and turning points.

JCPenney Company, for example, provides a five-year comparison of most income statement items, selected per-share and balance sheet items, and the number of its employees. Delta Air Lines provides a ten-year comparison of most income statement items, selected per-share and balance sheet items, and such nonaccounting information as available seat miles, revenue passenger miles, and passenger load factor. Wendy's International provides a ten-year comparison of selected information about operations, financial position, per-share data, financial ratios (e.g., gross margin, current ratio, and debt/equity ratio), restaurant data (e.g., number of U.S. and international restaurants), and other data, including the numbers of shareholders and employees.

Comparison within the Industry

A second type of comparison that can enhance the meaningfulness of financial accounting numbers is to compare them to those of similar companies. Similar companies are

4. The ROE model is used as a framework for financial analysis periodically throughout the remainder of the text.

usually found in the same industry; thus, industry-wide statistics are often a useful basis for comparison. Information concerning industry averages is reported by such sources as (1) *Dun & Bradstreet's Key Business Ratios,* (2) *Robert Morris Associates' Annual Statement Studies,* (3) *Moody's Investors Service,* and (4) *Standard & Poor's Industry Surveys.*

Differences in what are considered normal accounting numbers across industries can be very significant. For example, in the hobby, toy, and games industry, on average, current assets account for 80 percent of total assets, while in the telecommunications industry, the average percentage is only 31. Consequently, it is very important that the accounting numbers of a given company in a given industry be evaluated in terms of the norms established in that industry.

Comparisons within the Financial Statements: Common-Size Statements and Ratio Analysis

A third way to analyze financial statement numbers is to compare them to other numbers on the financial statements of the company at a particular point in time. Such comparisons can take two forms: (1) common-size financial statements and (2) ratio analysis.

COMMON-SIZE FINANCIAL STATEMENTS

Financial statement numbers can be expressed as percentages of other numbers on the same statements. On the income statement, expense items and net income are often expressed as percentages of net sales. On the balance sheet, assets and liabilities can be expressed as percentages of total assets (or liabilities plus shareholders' equity). Presenting such information gives rise to **common-size financial statements.** Common-size income statements and balance sheets for La-Z-Boy Incorporated are contained in Figure 5–2.

Common-size financial statements can help to indicate why changes occur in a company's financial performance and financial condition. La-Z-Boy's sales decreased from 2007 to 2008, and its net loss worsened. Expenses as a percent of sales increased— leading to a greater loss as sales declined faster than expenses. On the balance sheet,

FIGURE 5–2
Common-size financial statements— La-Z-Boy, Inc. (dollar amounts in millions)

	2008	%	2007	%
INCOME STATEMENT				
Net sales	$1,227	100	$1,451	100
Cost of sales	(888)	72	(1,057)	73
Expenses and charges	(460)	37	(408)	28
Net income	$ (121)	(9)	$ (14)	(1)
BALANCE SHEET				
Current assets	$ 348	63	$ 427	56
Long-term assets	205	37	342	44
Total	$ 553	100	$ 769	100
Current liabilities	$ 126	23	$ 164	21
Long-term liabilities	121	22	154	20
Shareholders' equity	306	55	451	59
Total	$ 553	100	$ 769	100

total assets declined, and liabilities as a percent of total assets slightly increased. Also, the mix of the company's assets shifted in favor of short-term assets.

FINANCIAL RATIOS

Preparing common-size financial statements is simply a matter of computing ratios in which income statement or balance sheet items act as numerators and sales or total assets serve as denominators. Computing additional ratios using two or more financial statement numbers is also a common and useful practice, generally known as **ratio analysis.**

Two general points are particularly important when computing ratios. First, with only a few exceptions, there are no hard-and-fast rules for the computation of ratios. The ratios discussed here are merely representative of ratios that are widely used. Analysts can, and do, adjust them to fit different situations, and certainly other ratios might be equally or more relevant to a given decision.

Second, in the computation of many ratios, income statement numbers are compared to balance sheet numbers. Since the income statement refers to a period of time and the balance sheet refers to a specific point in time, in calculating these ratios it is usually best to compute an average for the balance sheet number. One way to compute such an average is to add the account balance at the beginning of the period to the account balance at the end of the period, and divide the result by 2. This method provides a simple average for the balance sheet dollar amount.[5] The following discussion divides the ratios into five categories: (1) profitability, (2) leverage, (3) solvency, (4) asset turnover, and (5) other ratios.

PROFITABILITY RATIOS. Net income, or profit, is the primary measure of the overall success of a company. This number is often compared to other measures of financial activity or condition (e.g., sales, assets, shareholders' equity) to assess performance as a percent of some level of activity or investment. These comparisons are referred to as **profitability ratios** and are designed to measure earning power.

Return on Equity. Return on equity compares the profits generated by a company to the investment made by the company's shareholders.

Net Income[6]/Average Shareholders' Equity

Net income, which appears in the numerator, is viewed as the return to the company's owners, while the balance sheet value of shareholders' equity, which appears in the denominator, represents the amount of resources invested by the shareholders (contributed capital + retained earnings).

This ratio is considered a measure of the efficiency with which the shareholders' investment is being managed. As the ratio increases, management tends to be viewed as more efficient from the owner's perspective. Shareholders often compare this ratio against the returns of other potential investments available to them to determine whether their investment in a company is performing satisfactorily.

Return on Assets. Another measure of return on investment is return on assets. This measure is broader than return on equity because it compares the returns to both shareholders and creditors to total assets, the total resources provided by shareholders and creditors.

{Net Income + [Interest Expense (1 − Tax Rate)][7]}/Average Total Assets

---

5. A weighted average, which is covered in advanced texts, may be more appropriate in certain cases.

6. Dividends paid on preferred stock are normally subtracted from net income in the numerator. However, because such dividends are normally small, we will assume that they are zero.

7. Since interest is deductible for tax purposes, the actual cost of the interest is reduced by the tax savings.

Accordingly, the numerator includes both the return to the shareholders (net income) and the return to the creditors (interest expense), while the denominator consists of the balance sheet value of total assets, which is equivalent to the investments of both the shareholders (shareholders' equity) and the creditors (total liabilities).

Return on Sales, or Profit Margin. Return on sales, or profit margin, is computed by dividing the return to the shareholders and creditors by net sales.

{Net Income + [Interest Expense (1 − Tax Rate)]}/Net Sales

This ratio provides an indication of a company's ability to generate and market profitable products and control its costs. It reflects the number of cents in profit for every dollar of sales.

Discuss the following information, reported by Eli Lilly, a major pharmaceutical company.

	2008	2007	2006
Return on equity	(20.5%)	24.1%	24.5%
Return on assets	(6.8%)	12.8%	12.2%
Return on sales	(9.3%)	16.8%	18.8%

LEVERAGE RATIOS. **Leverage** refers to using borrowed funds to generate returns for the shareholders. A company that borrows $10,000 at an 8 percent interest rate and invests the funds to generate a 12 percent return is using leverage effectively. Leverage is desirable because it creates returns for the company's shareholders without using any of their money, but it increases risk by committing the company to future cash obligations. Three well-known leverage ratios are common equity leverage, capital structure leverage, and the long-term debt ratio.

Common Equity Leverage. Common equity leverage compares the return available to the shareholders to the returns available to all capital providers.

Net Income[8]/{Net Income + [Interest Expense (1 − Tax Rate)]}

High levels of this ratio indicate that the shareholders are receiving a large portion of the total return generated by the company. These high levels are the result of the company either not using leverage (e.g., low levels of borrowing, and interest expense is very low) or using leverage very effectively (e.g., high levels of borrowing, but net income is still large relative to interest expense).

Capital Structure Leverage. Recall that a company can meet its financing needs in any of three ways: (1) borrowings, (2) shareholder contributions, or (3) undistributed profits (retained earnings). Capital structure leverage measures the extent to which a company relies on borrowings (liabilities).

Average Total Assets/Average Shareholders' Equity

This ratio increases above 1 as liabilities in the capital structure increase. It decreases toward 1 as liabilities decrease. High levels indicate that a company is using leverage—large potential earning power and high levels of risk.

8. Dividends on preferred stock are normally subtracted from net income in the numerator. In this chapter, however, we assume that such dividends are zero.

Another equivalent and common way to measure capital structure leverage is called the **debt/equity ratio,** which compares liabilities to shareholders' equity, and is computed in the following way.

Average Total Liabilities/Average Shareholders' Equity

Long-Term Debt Ratio. The long-term debt ratio measures the importance of long-term liabilities as a source of asset financing.

Long-Term Liabilities/Total Assets

Companies that have large investments in long-term assets tend to finance those investments with long-term liabilities.

Discuss the following information, reported by Eli Lilly, a major pharmaceutical.

	2008	2007	2006
Capital structure leverage	2.7	2.0	2.1
Long-term debt ratio	0.32	0.30	0.27

SOLVENCY RATIOS. There is additional pressure on companies with high levels of leverage to manage their solvency, which refers to a company's ability to meet its debts as they come due. Four ratios are often used to measure this ability: (1) the current ratio, (2) the quick ratio, (3) interest coverage, and (4) accounts payable turnover.

Current Ratio. The current ratio compares current assets to current liabilities as of the balance sheet date.

Current Assets/Current Liabilities

It measures solvency in the sense that current assets, for the most part, can be used to meet current liabilities.

Quick Ratio. The quick ratio is similar to the current ratio, except that it provides a more stringent test of a company's solvency position. Current assets like inventories and prepaid expenses, which are not immediately convertible to cash, are excluded from the numerator.[9]

(Cash + Marketable Securities + Net Accounts Receivable)/Current Liabilities

Interest Coverage. The interest coverage ratio compares the annual funds available to meet interest to the annual interest expense.

(Net Income + Tax Expense + Interest Expense)/Interest Expense

Income before taxes and interest is used in the numerator because these funds can be used to pay interest. Increasing levels of this ratio signal that a company is becoming more solvent.

Accounts Payable Turnover. Many companies, especially in the retail industry, use their suppliers as an important source of financing. By delaying payments on inventory purchases to suppliers, companies can free up large amounts of cash. Accounts

---

9. The quick ratio is sometimes computed by excluding accounts receivable from the numerator.

payable turnover measures how quickly, on average, suppliers are paid off or, in other words, the extent to which accounts payable is used as a form of financing.

Cost of Goods Sold/Average Accounts Payable

When computed in this way, the ratio indicates the number of times during the year that the accounts payable balance is paid off. Dividing this ratio into 365 days indicates the number of days, on average, that accounts payable balances remain outstanding. Wal-Mart, for example, turns over its accounts payable approximately 8 times per year, or every 45.6 days (365 days/8).

Interpreting this ratio can be difficult. Slow turnover (i.e., few times per year or many days) can signify solvency problems in that the company may be having difficulty generating the cash to pay its suppliers. On the other hand, it may signify a financially strong company that has the negotiating power with its suppliers to use them as an inexpensive form of financing. Similarly, fast turnover can indicate financial strength or low negotiating power with suppliers. As is true for many ratios, the appropriate interpretation will depend on an understanding of the company's business environment.

> **?**
>
> Discuss the following information, reported by Eli Lilly, a major pharmaceutical company.
>
> | | 2008 | 2007 | 2006 |
> | ------------------------ | ----- | ---- | ---- |
> | Current ratio | 0.95 | 2.27 | 1.91 |
> | Interest coverage | (4.7) | 18 | 15 |
> | Accounts payable turnover (days) | 75 | 74 | 81 |

ASSET TURNOVER RATIOS. Asset turnover ratios—typically computed for total assets, accounts receivable, inventory, and fixed assets—measure the speed with which assets move through operations, or the number of times during a given period that assets are acquired, used, and replaced. As with accounts payable turnover, these ratios can be divided into 365 days to determine the number of days, on average, that it takes for given assets to be turned over. In general, high levels of asset turnover indicate efficient asset management—that is, a company is using a relatively low level of assets to generate returns for the shareholders. In some situations, however, low asset investments can constrain profitability.

Receivables Turnover. Receivables turnover reflects the number of times the trade receivables were recorded, collected, and recorded again during the period.

Net Credit Sales/Average Accounts Receivable[10]

It measures the effectiveness of the credit-granting and collection activities of a company. High receivables turnover often suggests effective credit-granting and collection activities, while low turnover can indicate late payments and bad debts, probably due to credit being granted to poor-risk customers and/or to ineffective collection efforts. A very high turnover, however, is not always desirable; it may indicate overly stringent credit terms, leading to missed sales and lost profits.

---

10. Because credit sales are rarely disclosed by companies, analysts normally use total sales as a proxy for credit sales.

Inventory Turnover. Inventory turnover measures the speed with which inventories move through operations.

Cost of Goods Sold/Average Inventory

It compares the amount of inventory carried by a company to the volume of goods sold during the period, reflecting how quickly, in general, inventories are sold. Because profit (and often cash) is usually realized each time inventory is sold and substantial costs are often associated with carrying inventories, an increase in the inventory turnover is normally desirable. However, high inventory turnovers can indicate that inventory levels are too low, giving rise to lost sales and profits due to items being out of stock.

Fixed Assets Turnover. Fixed assets turnover measures the speed with which fixed assets are used up.

Sales/Average Fixed Assets

It compares the average level of fixed assets to the sales for the year, that is, the level of fixed asset investment necessary to generate the annual sales volume.

Total Asset Turnover. Total asset turnover measures the speed with which all assets are used up in operations, aggregating the turnover measures of the component assets (e.g., accounts receivable, inventory, and fixed assets).

Sales/Average Total Assets

It provides an overall measure of asset management efficiency.

Discuss the following information, reported by Eli Lilly, a major pharmaceutical company.

	2008	2007	2006
A/R turnover (days)	49	47	54
Inventory turnover (days)	209	206	213
Fixed asset turnover (days)	154	164	187
Asset turnover (days)	502	478	542

OTHER RATIOS. The financial community uses several other ratios to assess company performance: earnings per share, price/earnings ratio, dividend yield ratio, and stock price return.

Earnings per Share. Earnings per share is perhaps the best known of all the ratios, largely because the financial press often treat it as the primary measure of a company's performance. It measures profitability strictly from the standpoint of the common shareholders. Unlike return on equity or return on assets, which assess profitability relative to a measure of capital investment, this ratio assesses profitability relative to the number of common shares outstanding. According to generally accepted accounting principles, earnings per share must appear on the face of the income statement and be calculated in accordance with an elaborate set of complex rules that are beyond the scope of this book. The basic formula is provided below.

Net Income/Average Number of Common Shares Outstanding

Price/Earnings (P/E) Ratio. The price/earnings ratio is used by many financial state-ment analysts to assess the investment potential of common stocks.

Market Price per Share/Earnings per Share

Specifically, by relating the price of a company's common stock to its earnings, this ratio reflects the stock market's confidence that current earnings will lead to cash inflows in the future.

Dividend Yield Ratio. The dividend yield ratio relates the dividends paid on a share of common stock to its market price. It indicates the cash return on the shareholder's investment.

Dividends per Share/Market Price per Share

Stock Price Return. The annual return on investment provided by a share of common stock is computed by subtracting the market price at the beginning of the year (Market Price$_0$) from the market price at the end of the year (Market Price$_1$), adding the divi-dends per share paid during the year, and dividing the result by the market price at the beginning of the year:

$$\text{(Market Price}_1 - \text{Market Price}_0 + \text{Dividends)/Market Price}_0$$

This ratio provides a measure of the pre-tax performance of an investment in a share of common stock.

In its 2008 annual report Eli Lilly provides a graph that tracks the value of $100 if it had been invested at the beginning of 2004 in (1) Eli Lilly stock, (2) the Standard & Poor's Index (a measure of the overall return of the stock market), and (3) Eli Lilly's peer group (other major pharmaceuticals—for example, Abbott, Johnson & Johnson, Merck, Pfizer, Bristol-Myers Squibb). How has Lilly stock per-formed relative to the overall market and relative to its peer group?

	2008	2007	2006	2005	2004
Lilly	$67	$ 85	$ 80	$ 87	$ 83
S&P Index	90	142	135	116	111
Peer Group	94	112	110	97	97

SUMMARY OF FINANCIAL RATIOS AND COMPANY RATIO PROFILES

Figure 5–3 contains a summary of the ratios discussed in this chapter, and Figure 5–4 contains selected ratios from seven well-known companies from various industries, computed from their 2008 financial statements. Consider the nature of each company's operations and think about why the ratio profiles differ across the companies.

Several concluding points about ratio analysis are important. First, ratios should never be interpreted in isolation; each ratio should be considered in the context of the company's other ratios. Wendy's International, for example, maintains a current ratio well below 1.00, which if viewed by itself could signify a solvency problem. However, the company's strong earning power and cash flows provide adequate cash to meet the company's needs. Appendix 5A introduces a method (ROE model) for analyzing ratios as a package.

FIGURE 5–3   Summary of important financial ratios

Ratio	Formula
PROFITABILITY RATIOS	
Return on equity	Net Income/Average Shareholders' Equity
Return on assets	{Net Income + [Interest Expense (1 − Tax Rate)]}/ Average Total Assets
Return on sales (profit margin)	{Net Income + [Interest Expense (1 − Tax Rate)]}/Net Sales
LEVERAGE RATIOS	
Common equity leverage	Net Income/{Net Income + [Interest Expense (1 − Tax Rate)]}
Capital structure leverage	Average Total Assets/Average Shareholders' Equity
Debt/equity ratio	Average Total Liabilities/Average Shareholders' Equity
Long-term debt ratio	Long-Term Liabilities/Total Assets
SOLVENCY RATIOS	
Current ratio	Current Assets/Current Liabilities
Quick ratio	(Cash + Marketable Securities + Net Accounts Receivable)/ Current Liabilities
Interest coverage	(Net Income + Tax Expense + Interest Expense)/ Interest Expense
Accounts payable turnover*	Cost of Goods Sold /Average Accounts Payable
ASSET TURNOVER RATIOS*	
Receivables turnover	Net Credit Sales/Average Accounts Receivable
Inventory turnover	Cost of Goods Sold/Average Inventory
Fixed assets turnover	Sales/Average Fixed Assets
Total asset turnover	Sales/Average Total Assets
OTHER RATIOS	
Earnings per share	Net Income/Average Number of Common Shares Outstanding
Price/earnings ratio	Market Price per Share/Earnings per Share
Dividend yield ratio	Dividends per Share/Market Price per Share
Stock price return	(Market Price$_1$ − Market Price$_0$ + Dividends)/Market Price$_0$

*Each turnover ratio can be converted to "days" by dividing by 365 days.

?

Based on your knowledge of the companies in Figure 5–4, provide reasons why the value of some of the ratios varies so much across companies. For example, why is Bank of America's capital structure leverage ratio so large, and why do Kroger's receivables turn over so quickly while Bank of America's turn over so slowly? Why are some of the ratios NA (not available)?

FIGURE 5-4   Selected ratios for well-known companies

	Kimberly-Clark	Microsoft	Hewlett-Packard	Amazon	Kroger	Bank of America	AT&T
ROE	0.37	0.38	0.22	0.33	0.25	0.03	0.12
ROA	0.11	0.19	0.09	0.09	0.07	0.02	0.06
ROS	0.10	0.25	0.07	0.04	0.02	0.36	0.12
CEL	0.88	1.00	0.97	0.93	0.80	0.10	0.85
CSL	4.01	1.99	2.61	3.83	4.51	10.91	2.55
CR	1.22	1.82	0.98	1.30	0.95	1.12	0.53
IC	8.59	NA	32.83	13.56	5.05	1.11	6.87
ART (times)	7.69	4.72	7.80	25.02	87.86	0.13	7.70
IT (times)	5.49	14.28	11.26	11.46	17.07	NA	NA
AT (times)	1.06	0.78	1.17	2.59	3.34	0.06	0.46
EPS	4.06	1.63	3.25	1.52	1.92	0.56	2.17
P/E ratio*	14.81	18.10	15.30	78.61	11.25	26.38	11.67

*Yahoo! Finance (January 26, 2010).

Ratio analysis is also limited in a number of significant ways. Financial ratios draw from financial statement information, which has important limitations. Limited inputs are rarely improved, and are sometimes made worse, when combined into ratios. Ratio comparisons within a firm across time, across firms at a given point in time, and across firms from different countries are fraught with difficulties and must be done with extreme caution. Thus, while ratio analysis is a valuable tool for the analyst, it must be conducted thoughtfully and carefully.

PREDICT FUTURE EARNINGS AND/OR CASH FLOW

After the analyst completes the first four steps (assessing business environment, reading and studying the financial statements, assessing earnings quality, and analyzing the financial statements), a prediction is normally prepared. Analysts who follow equity securities predict future earnings or cash flow, using these predictions in mathematical models (e.g., present value)[11] that provide estimates of the value of a company's shares of stock. These estimates are compared to current market prices to determine whether a particular security is over- or underpriced. Credit analysts prepare cash flow predictions to see whether loan customers will be able to make their loan payments when they come due.

Predicting future levels of earnings or cash flow is a difficult and subjective process. Nonetheless, it is very important for success, and astute financial statement analysis can improve these predictions significantly.

---

11. See Appendix A in the back of the text for a discussion of present value. Appendix 5A at the end of this chapter provides a brief discussion of projecting future financial statements.

ANNUAL REPORT INFORMATION AND PREDICTING STOCK PRICES

It is well known that stock prices react to the disclosure of accounting information. Indeed, *USA Today* reported that "profits of public companies have the greatest and most immediate effect on the company's stock price," and in a number of accounting and finance research studies, stock prices of companies traded on the U.S. stock markets have been shown to react almost instantaneously to the disclosure of accounting information. It is important to understand, at the same time, that published annual reports are not available to the public until several months after the balance sheet date, and important numbers, such as net income, are announced quarterly and are available to the public almost as soon as they are determined. Thus, it is difficult, if not impossible, for investors to use the information contained in an annual report to identify undervalued stocks traded on the public securities markets. Such information is not timely enough because the market price has already reacted to important accounting numbers that were released at an earlier date.

While annual report information in and of itself may not be particularly helpful in identifying undervalued publicly traded securities, this certainly does not mean that it is useless. There is evidence, for example, that annual report information, if analyzed in a superior fashion, can lead to better-than-average returns in the stock market. Such analysis may also help an investor to better understand the expected risk and return levels associated with certain investments, to ascertain whether those levels are consistent with the investor's preferences. In addition, banks use financial statement analysis to guide loan decisions and to determine the terms of the loans they grant, and financial ratios have been used successfully by bankers and auditors to predict business failures. Financial ratios that deviate from normal expectations can be used to identify management report fraud, and financial statement analysis can also be useful when deciding whether to purchase equity or debt securities in companies that are not publicly traded. Finally, recall that financial ratios are used in contracts to influence the actions of managers.

INTERNATIONAL PERSPECTIVE: FINANCIAL STATEMENT ANALYSIS IN AN INTERNATIONAL SETTING

U.S. investors are showing increasing interest in foreign securities traded on foreign markets, and the securities of more and more non-U.S. firms using International Financial Reporting Standards (IFRS) are being listed on the U.S. exchanges. Such securities often provide returns that exceed those available from U.S. firms, and holding foreign stocks can help reduce an investor's risk by diversifying the investment portfolio to include securities of companies from more than one country. In most cases, the choice to buy or sell a foreign security is based on financial information provided by the investee company, which, in turn, presents the investor with the difficult challenge of analyzing and interpreting financial statements prepared according to foreign accounting (often IFRS) and business norms.[12]

Investors interested in comparing the financial performance and condition of companies from different countries often must contend with two difficult issues. First, if

---

12. Some non-U.S. companies, especially small ones, publish financial statements based on standards established by the government of their country.

the companies use different accounting standards (e.g., U.S. GAAP vs. IFRS), the reported values must be adjusted to a common basis so that reasonable comparisons can be made.

Consider, for example, an investor analyzing the cell phone industry and involved in comparing Finland-based Nokia, with IFRS-based financial statements, to U.S.-based AT&T, which publishes financial statements under U.S. GAAP. Until 2007, the SEC required non-U.S. companies traded on U.S. exchanges (like Nokia) to include, in their publicly available SEC Form 20-F, a reconciliation between IFRS-based and U.S. GAAP-based net income and shareholders' equity. This form explained the amount and nature of the differences between the IFRS- and U.S.-based dollar amounts. In 2006, for example, had Nokia used U.S. GAAP, its reported net income would have been about $30 million lower. The main reason for the difference is that Nokia capitalized development costs that under U.S. GAAP would have been expensed. Shareholders' equity under IFRS, on the other hand, was about $50 million lower than it would have been under U.S. GAAP. Together, these differences indicate that Nokia's ROE (net income/shareholders' equity) was substantially higher than it would have been had it used U.S. GAAP.

Knowledge that Nokia's reported ROE was higher than what it would have been under U.S. GAAP helps the investor make a more valid comparison to AT&T's reported ROE, which was based on U.S. GAAP. A review of the 20-F forms submitted to the SEC since 1994 shows that until 2006 annual IFRS-based income amounts exceeded U.S. GAAP-based amounts by an average of between 2 percent and 10 percent, and IFRS-based shareholders' equity was less than that under U.S. GAAP by an average of between 11 percent and 16 percent. Consequently, IFRS-based ROE amounts have, on average, exceeded U.S. GAAP-based ROE amounts by around 20 percent.

Unfortunately, in 2007 the SEC eliminated the requirement to reconcile IFRS-based income and shareholders' equity with income and shareholders' equity as measured under U.S. GAAP in the SEC Form 20-F. This move made it more difficult for investors to make valid comparisons between companies that use different accounting systems, further highlighting the benefits of a single global reporting system.

It is also unfortunate that adjusting financial statements to a common basis by itself may not be sufficient to achieve meaningful comparisons. Since the accounting statements are a product of the social, economic, legal, and cultural environment, it follows that differences across environments would further complicate the interpretation of the adjusted financial statements. In other words, not only must the financial statements of a foreign-based company be adjusted, but the resulting numbers can only be interpreted through an understanding of the foreign environment.

In an interesting study, Professor Frederick Choi and a number of colleagues from Japan, Korea, and the United States showed that understanding the institutional, legal, and cultural aspects of an environment is as important as adjusting the foreign financial statements for differences in accounting principles. The authors found that the Japanese and Korean firms, in general, were much more highly leveraged (higher debt/equity ratios) and less profitable (lower net income/sales) than their U.S. counterparts, but they noted further that important environmental and cultural characteristics explained these differences. For example, raising capital through equity issuances in Japan and Korea is relatively unusual for a number of reasons, one of which is that the local banks and government play a particularly important role in providing debt capital. The authors also reported that Japanese managers are much less concerned with short-term profits than U.S. managers and are more likely to make investments

that maximize long-term profitability, often at the expense of profits in the current period. As a result, Japanese and Korean firms may appear on the surface to be more highly leveraged and less profitable than U.S. firms, but in substance they may not be. They are simply products of a different business environment.

APPENDIX 5A

SHAREHOLDER VALUE, ROE, AND CASH FLOW ANALYSES

Management's goal is to create value for the shareholders, the owners of the firm, by generating a return on the shareholders' investment that exceeds the **cost of equity**—the return the shareholders could have earned if they invested their funds in an equally risky alternative investment. **Return on equity** (net income/average shareholders' equity) (**ROE**) defines the return on the shareholders' investment for a given period; therefore, **shareholder value creation** occurs in a given period if ROE is greater than the cost of equity. If ROE is less than the cost of equity, value has been lost. Management's success is defined by whether it creates shareholder value in the long run.

The cost of equity is very elusive, and even the best economists have been unable to agree on how it should be computed. It is not disclosed on the financial statements or related footnotes because it is simply too subjective. It must be estimated. Some companies discuss their cost of capital estimates in their annual reports, but it remains relatively rare. Most economists agree, however, that the cost of equity contains two components: a risk-free rate of return, which is shared by the entire economy, and a risk premium, which is unique to the particular investment.

Cost of equity = Risk-free rate of return + Risk premium

The rate of return on ten-year government treasury bills as of a particular date is often used to estimate the risk-free rate. Historically, it has ranged from around 3 to 8 percent, averaging about 6 percent. The more difficult part of estimating the cost of equity is the risk premium, which varies significantly across firms and industries. Following, we list estimates of the cost of equity for selected firms as of the end of 2008. The ten-year government treasury bill rate was approximately 4 percent.

Firm	Industry	Risk-free rate	Risk premium	Cost of Equity
Cisco Systems	Internet hardware and software systems	4%	12%	16%
DuPont	Science	4%	6%	10%
General Motors	Auto manufacturing and financial services	4%	13%	17%
Lowe's Corporation	Retail home improvement	4%	5%	9%
McDonald's	Fast food	4%	8%	12%
Nordstrom	Retail clothing	4%	8%	12%
Walt Disney	Entertainment and media	4%	7%	11%

DETERMINANTS OF VALUE CREATION: ANALYZING RETURN ON EQUITY

Because the comparison between ROE and the cost of equity is the indicator of shareholder value creation, analysts are very interested in changes in ROE across time for a given firm, as well as ROE comparisons across similar firms (e.g., in the same industry) as of a point in time. Changes in ROE across time for a firm indicate whether a company's value creation is improving or deteriorating; ROE comparisons across similar firms indicate which companies are creating the most value. Analysis can also include both simultaneously—that is, how does a company's value creation across time compare to that of other companies?

Analysts not only use ROE to track and compare value creation, but they are also interested in *why* value creation changes across time and *why* one company's value creation exceeds another's. What features about a company's operating, investing, and financing decisions drive changes in value creation or explain why one company creates more value than another? These features are called value drivers, and the identification and analysis of key value drivers is an important objective of financial statement analysis. Managers can use the same tools to predict and explain how their actions will lead to future value creation.

A well-known framework designed to identify value drivers, by analyzing changes in ROE across time and differences in ROE across companies, is called the DuPont (ROE) model, which is described by the following algebraic expression.[13]

Return on equity = Return on assets × Capital structure leverage × Common equity leverage

This expression defines three financial statement ratios (return on assets, capital structure leverage, and common equity leverage) that when multiplied together equal ROE. This equality means that changes in these ratios lead to changes in ROE. For example, if common equity leverage and capital structure leverage are unchanged, an increase in return on assets leads to an increase in ROE. An important goal for managers, therefore, is to increase ROE by taking actions that increase its determinants. Although increasing leverage can increase ROE, the additional reliance on debt associated with increasing leverage also elevates the firm's risk and cost of capital. Consequently, attempts to increase ROE should first be directed at improving operating and investing decisions, which should lead to increases in return on assets (ROA).

ROA can be decomposed further into the product of two key financial ratios—profit margin (or operating return on sales) and asset turnover. Changes in profit margin and asset turnover lead to changes in ROE through their effects on ROA. Consider a company, for example, that makes a decision that increases profit margin without decreasing asset turnover. This decision would lead to higher ROA, and if the leverage ratios were unchanged, higher ROE and the creation of shareholder value.

Return on assets = Profit margin (Return on sales) × Asset turnover

Figure 5A–1 illustrates the ROE framework and relates it to three important value drivers: (1) effective sales and expense management, (2) effective working capital and long-term asset management, and (3) effective capital structure management. **Effective sales and expense management** creates value by increasing profit margin, which increases ROA, which, in turn, increases ROE. **Effective working capital and long-term asset management** creates value by increasing asset turnover, which, in turn, increases ROA and ROE. **Effective capital structure management** can increase ROE by increasing the leverage ratios, but more leverage leads to more interest expense and may lead to lower common equity leverage. A close relationship also exists between these three value drivers and operating, investing, and financing activities. Operating activities involve both sales and expense and working capital management; investing activities involve long-term asset management; and financing activities involve capital structure management. In the next section we discuss financial statement ratios that measure these value drivers.

---

13. This version of the DuPont model was introduced in Selling, T. I., and C. P. Stickney, "Disaggregating the Rate of Return on Common Shareholders' Equity: A New Approach," *Accounting Horizons* 4, no. 4 (December 1990).

FIGURE 5A–1   Value drivers and financial statement ratios

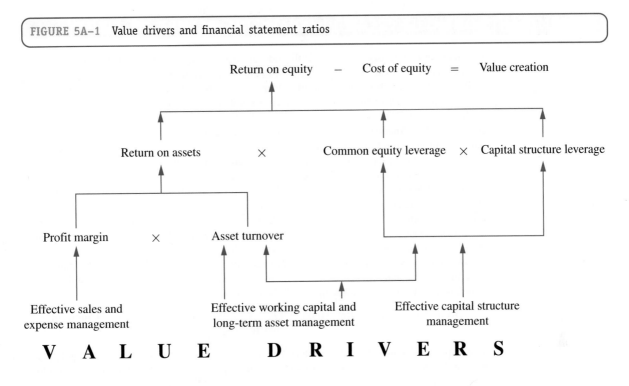

Figure 5A–2 expands Figure 5A–1 to include the financial ratios we have discussed in Chapter 5. In summary, management's goal is to create value by maximizing the extent to which ROE exceeds the cost of equity. To do so, it must effectively manage three key value drivers: (1) sales and expenses, (2) long-term assets and working capital, and (3) capital structure. Ratios constructed from numbers on the financial statements provide useful measures of these value drivers, and the decomposition of the ROE model shows how managing these measures links to value creation.

Several points should be emphasized. First, the three value drivers and the associated financial ratios can be expressed in terms of the three fundamental management activities: operating, investing, and financing. Operating activities are reflected primarily in the profit margin components (revenues and expenses) and working capital ratios (turnover and solvency ratios); investing activities are reflected primarily in the noncurrent asset turnover ratios; and financing activities are reflected primarily in the leverage and solvency ratios.

Second, any attempt to create value by managing a given ratio must consider effects on other parts of the model. For example, additional borrowing will no doubt increase capital structure leverage, but the ultimate effect on ROE cannot be determined without considering how the use of the borrowed funds affects common equity leverage and ROA.

SHAREHOLDER VALUE CREATION AND THE ROE MODEL: JCPENNEY VS. KOHL'S

Figures 5A–3 and 5A–4 summarize the financial ratios for two mid-market department stores, JCPenney and Kohl's, respectively, for 2008 and 2007, in a format consistent with the ROE framework. Figure 5A–5 compares selected ratios from Kohl's and Penney to those

FIGURE 5A-2   Complete ROE model

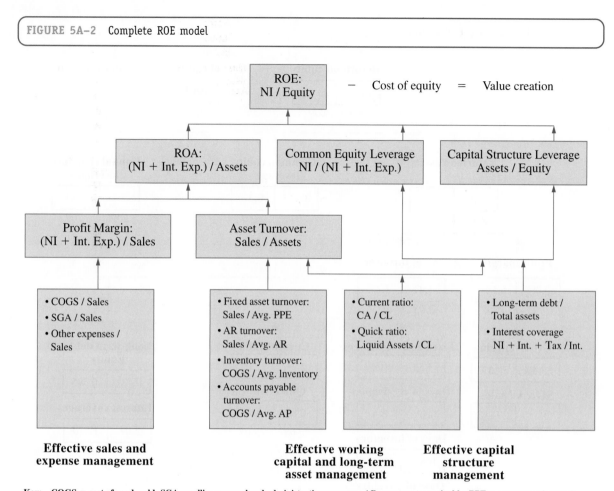

Key: COGS = cost of goods sold; SGA = selling; general and administrative expenses; AR = accounts receivable; PPE = property, plant and equipment; AP = account payable; CA = current assets; CL = current liabilities; Int. = interest expense

ratios computed across the members of their primary industry group, retail apparel and accessories.

Both companies performed profitably in 2008, a difficult and somewhat unique feat in the retail industry given the economic recession experienced during this time. Assuming an estimate of the cost of equity for each firm of 12 percent, both created wealth by generating returns in excess of this market standard. Both companies, however, generated lower returns in 2008 than in the previous year. As described below, the ROE model indicates that these companies generated their returns in different ways, and in a manner different from much of the industry.

JCPenney employs more leverage than Kohl's, using it to boost ROE; the company, in both 2007 and 2008, had lower profitability ratios but used higher capital structure leverage (CSL) to compensate for the lower returns. The 2.78 CSL ratio for Penney appears to be more aggressive than the 1.71 employed by Kohl's.

The more conservative approach to its capital structure taken by Kohl's was more than off-set by its superior ability to generate sales from its asset base, and then more efficiently convert those sales into profits. For every dollar in asset investment, Kohl's generated $1.50 in sales, compared to only $1.41 for JCPenney. Kohl's also outperformed Penney in controlling expenses, generating 5.9 cents in profit for every dollar of sales, compared to only 3.9 cents for Penney. The companies achieved similar gross margins (37 percent), but Kohl's managed its

FIGURE 5A–3   JCPenney ROE Analysis

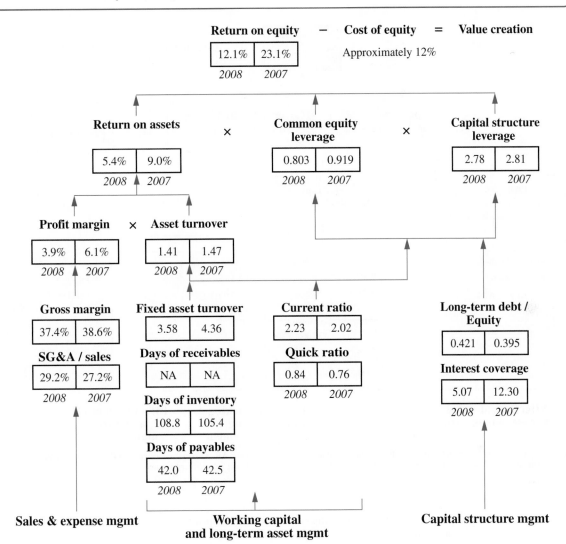

overhead (SG&A) expenses more efficiently. These two factors, which produced a higher ROA for Kohl's, allowed it to achieve a slightly higher ROE than JCPenney without having to bear the risk of the additional leverage.

With respect to industry comparison, both companies outperform the industry on ROE, ROA, and profit margin, but turn over their assets, especially inventory, more slowly. Some might interpret this to mean that the rest of the industry, relative to Kohl's and JCPenney, is chasing sales (volume and market share) at the expense of profits. Inventory turnover is very important in the retail industry, but it leads to sales—not necessarily profit—creation. Expense control is necessary to create profits.

This example shows how financial statement analysis can be useful in evaluating not only a company's overall performance but also the underlying reasons. Managers at JCPenney can use this analysis to pinpoint the need for a better control of overhead and corporate expenses, for example. Managers at Kohl's can use this analysis to consider what benefits would come from a more aggressive approach to its capital structure, and at what costs.

FIGURE 5A–4   Kohl's ROE Analysis

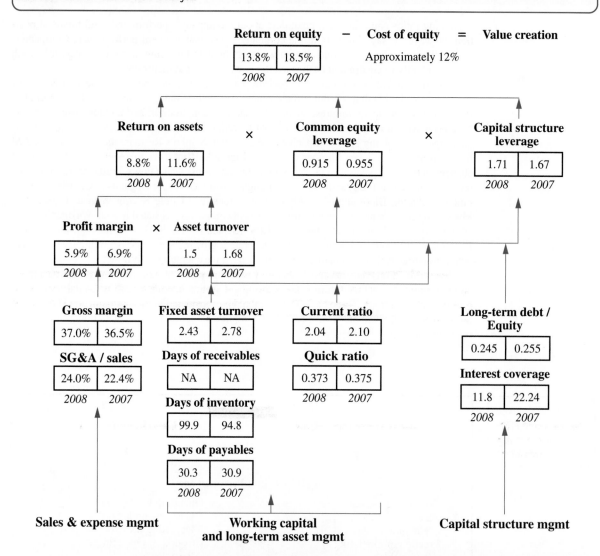

FIGURE 5A–5
JCPenney and
Kohl's—industry
comparison

	JCPenney	Kohl's	Industry Median*
Return on equity	0.121	0.138	0.112
Return on assets	0.054	0.088	0.047
Profit margin	0.039	0.059	0.021
Gross profit margin	0.374	0.370	0.342
Asset turnover	1.41	1.50	2.2
Days inventory	109	100	88
Long-term debt/equity	0.421	0.245	0.280
Current ratio	2.23	2.04	1.77
Quick ratio	0.840	0.373	0.500
Interest coverage	5.07	11.8	11.48

*Financial ratios provided by Hoover's, Inc.

CASH FLOW ANALYSIS

Analyzing ratios can indicate a great deal about a company's performance and financial position. However, it says little about the company's cash management performance. Companies, especially highly leveraged ones that rely heavily on debt financing, need to manage their cash flows prudently to ensure that cash is available when debt payments come due.

The investment community has become increasingly concerned with the assessment of solvency, concluding that it is not sufficient simply to analyze ratios. In large part this concern has stemmed from company failures, leading to huge investor, creditor, and auditor losses that may have been averted if better information about solvency had been available. For example, famous bankruptcies involving such companies as W.T. Grant, Sambo's Restaurants, Penn Central, AM International, and Wickes Lumber encouraged the FASB in 1981 to require the statement of changes in financial position, a predecessor to the statement of cash flows. Furthermore, economic recession in the late 1980s and late 1990s brought down such corporate giants as Campeau Corporation (including Bloomingdales, Abraham & Straus, and Circle K convenience stores), R.H. Macy, several major airlines, and a host of dot-com companies. As stated in Rick Wayman's article entitled "How to Evaluate the 'Quality' of EPS" (September 19, 2003), "Without question, cash is King on Wall Street, and companies that generate a growing stream of operating cash flow are better investments than companies that post . . . negative operating cash flow."

Cash flow analysis, also called **solvency assessment,** involves estimating future cash flows and determining whether future inflows are timed so that adequate cash is available to cover future cash obligations. Three basic factors should be considered in this assessment: (1) operating performance, (2) financial flexibility, and (3) liquidity. Figure 5A–6 depicts how these factors relate to solvency.

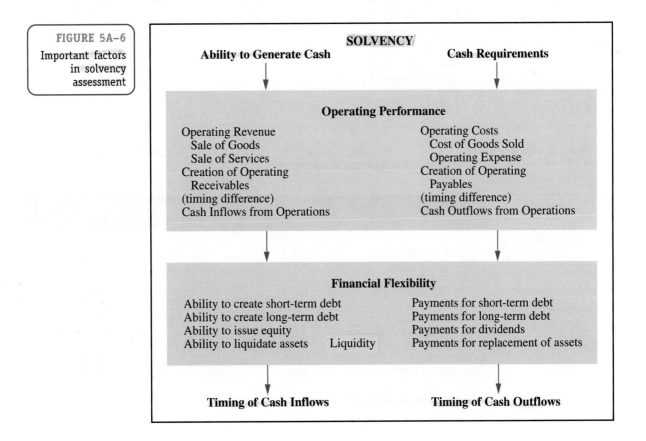

FIGURE 5A–6
Important factors in solvency assessment

Operating performance represents a company's ability to grow (increase its net assets) through operations. Since operations is perhaps the most important source of cash to a firm, this concept is very important for solvency assessment. The operating section of the statement of cash flows is especially useful here, as are the profitability and activity ratios discussed earlier.

Financial flexibility refers to a company's ability to produce cash through means other than operations: issuing debt, issuing equity, and selling assets. Companies capable of generating cash through a number of these options are considered financially flexible. Referring to the financial statement footnotes can be useful here because a company's ability to borrow and the condition of outstanding equity issuances are normally described in some detail. The balance sheet lists the assets of the company, but users must be cautious here because the assets are not carried at market value. The statement of cash flows may be helpful in assessing financial flexibility because it describes recent debt and equity issues and payments and recent asset acquisitions and sales.

Liquidity is part of financial flexibility. It represents the ability of a company to convert its existing assets to cash. Highly liquid assets increase a company's solvency position because they represent quick access to cash and can be used to secure outstanding loans. Liquidity can be assessed by reviewing the order of the assets listed on the balance sheet. A large percentage of current assets relative to total assets can indicate high liquidity. Also, the receivables and inventory turnover ratios reflect liquidity—high turnover normally indicates high liquidity.

CASH FLOW PROFILES

The statement of cash flows can also be used to identify the cash flow profile of a company. These profiles can indicate a company's strategy, position in its life cycle, or key characteristics of its current situation. Such profiles are defined simply by whether net cash from operating, investing, and financing activities are positive or negative. Note the eight combinations listed below. They are followed by a brief description of the company's activities, based on each profile.

	1	2	3	4	5	6	7	8
Net cash from operating activities	+	+	+	+	−	−	−	−
Net cash from investing activities	+	−	+	−	+	−	+	−
Net cash from financing activities	+	+	−	−	+	+	−	−

- *Profile 1.* This company is generating large amounts of cash, perhaps in anticipation of a large investment.
- *Profile 2.* This company is financing its growth through operations and by issuing debt and/or equity. *growing, buying new investments, financing w/ debt*
- *Profile 3.* This company is using operating cash and selling off long-term assets to reduce debt or pay shareholders.
- *Profile 4.* This company is financing both its growth and payments to capital providers with cash from operations. *good company that is doing well and making money "cash cow"*
- *Profile 5.* This company is selling off long-term assets and collecting cash from capital providers to finance operating cash flow losses. *going out of business (liquidating)*
- *Profile 6.* This company is collecting cash from capital providers to finance growth and operating cash flow losses. *start up company*
- *Profile 7.* This company is selling off long-term assets to finance operating cash flow losses and payments to capital providers.
- *Profile 8.* This company is using its cash reserves to finance operating cash flow losses, payments to capital providers, and growth.

PROJECTING FUTURE FINANCIAL STATEMENTS

A complete financial analysis includes an attempt to project future financial statements. These projections can be used in present value-based formulas that help to assess a company's market value, and they are often used internally by companies to establish budgets, standards that can be compared to actual results in the evaluation of management's performance. Used in this way, financial statement projections can motivate management to achieve higher levels of performance.

The process of projecting a future income statement and balance sheet involves the following steps.

1. Predict future sales.
2. Predict future profit margin.
3. Based on the sales prediction, estimate the level of assets necessary to support that level of sales.
4. Choose a target financing mix (liabilities vs. equity).

To illustrate how the process works, consider Kohl's Department Store, which reported the following dollar amounts (in millions) in 2008, 2007, and 2006.

	2008	2007	2006
Sales	$16,389	$16,474	$15,597
Net income	885	1,084	1,109
Total assets	11,334	10,560	9,034
Shareholders' equity	6,739	6,102	5,956

PREDICT FUTURE SALES. Although in the time period 2006–2008 Kohl's grew only about 5 percent, over the past five years sales have grown at an average rate of about 10 percent. We assume 10 percent growth, leading to expected sales for 2009 of $18,028 ($16,389 × 1.1).

PREDICT FUTURE PROFIT MARGIN. Over the past three years net income/sales has been around 6 percent. We assume a 6 percent profit margin, leading to expected 2009 profits of $1,082 ($18,028 × 6%).

ESTIMATED LEVEL OF ASSETS NECESSARY TO SUPPORT SALES. Over the past three years total assets/sales has varied from 58 percent to, most recently, 69 percent. We believe that Kohl's will work to drive this number down (i.e., increase asset turnover), so we assume a 64 percent asset/sales ratio, leading to an expected 2009 total asset investment of $11,538 ($18,028 × 64%).

TARGET FINANCING MIX. Over the last three years shareholders' equity/total assets has varied from 65 percent to around 60 percent, meaning that liabilities have financed from 35 percent to 40 percent of Kohl's assets. We assume that Kohl's will keep the level of liabilities at about 40 percent, leading to total liabilities and shareholders' equity for 2009 of $4,615 ($11,538 × 40%) and $6,923 ($11,538 × 60%), respectively.

This analysis results in the following projected income statement and balance sheet for 2009.

Income Statement

Sales	$18,028
Expenses	(16,946)
Net income	1,082

Balance Sheet

Assets	$11,538
Liabilities	4,615
Shareholders' equity	6,923

This simplified example illustrates the basic mechanical process involved in projecting financial statements. Clearly, much more analysis is involved in developing the predictions and estimates of the individual items, and often these predictions include the company's goals and objectives over a much longer time period. In addition, by making more detailed predictions about the timing of cash receipts and payments and about the various financing choices (e.g., dividends, equity issuances, treasury stock purchases), projected statements of cash flow and shareholders' equity can also be prepared.

REVIEW PROBLEM

The information below was taken from the 2009 annual report of Lowe's, a leading retailer in hardware and home improvement products (dollars in millions). From the information, compute the ratios discussed in the chapter (excluding the market ratios) and comment on the change in Lowe's earning power and solvency positions from 2008 to 2009. The company's tax rate during 2008 was approximately 37 percent.

Lowe's Companies, Inc.
Consolidated Statements of Earnings
(In millions, except per share and percentage data)

	January 30, 2009	February 1, 2008	February 2, 2007
Net sales	$48,230	$48,283	$46,927
Cost of sales	31,729	31,556	30,729
Gross margin	16,501	16,727	16,198
Expenses:			
Selling, general and administrative	11,074	10,515	9,738
Store opening costs	102	141	146
Depreciation	1,539	1,366	1,162
Interest	280	194	154
Total expenses	12,995	12,216	11,200
Pre-tax earnings	3,506	4,511	4,998
Income tax provision	1,311	1,702	1,893
Net earnings	$ 2,195	$ 2,809	$ 3,105

See accompanying notes to consolidated financial statements.

Lowe's Companies, Inc.
Consolidated Balance Sheets
(In millions, except par value and percentage data)

	January 30, 2009	February 1, 2008	February 2, 2007
Assets			
Current assets:			
Cash and cash equivalents	$ 245	$ 281	$ 364
Short-term investments	416	249	432
Merchandise inventory—net	8,209	7,611	7,144

(Continued)

Lowe's Companies, Inc.
Consolidated Balance Sheets
(In millions, except par value and percentage data)

	January 30, 2009	February 1, 2008	February 2, 2007
Deferred income taxes—net	166	247	161
Other current assets	215	298	213
Total current assets	9,251	8,686	8,314
Property, less accumulated depreciation	22,722	21,361	18,971
Long-term investments	253	509	165
Other assets	460	313	317
Total assets	$32,686	$30,869	$27,767
Liabilities and Shareholders' Equity			
Current liabilities:			
Short-term borrowings	$ 987	$ 1,064	$ 23
Current maturities of long-term debt	34	40	88
Accounts payable	4,109	3,713	3,524
Accrued compensation and employee benefits	434	467	425
Self-insurance liabilities	751	671	650
Deferred revenue	674	717	731
Other current liabilities	1,033	1,079	1,098
Total current liabilities	8,022	7,751	6,539
Long-term debt, excluding current maturities	5,039	5,576	4,325
Deferred income taxes—net	660	670	735
Other liabilities	910	774	443
Total liabilities	14,631	14,771	12,042
Shareholders' equity			
Preferred stock—$5 par value, none issued	—	—	—
Common stock—$.50 par value; Shares issued and outstanding January 30, 2009 1,470 February 1, 2008 1,458	735	729	762
Capital in excess of par value	277	16	102
Retained earnings	17,049	15,345	14,860
Accumulated other comprehensive (loss) income	(6)	8	1
Total shareholders' equity	18,055	16,098	15,725
Total liabilities and shareholders' equity	$32,686	$30,869	$27,767

See accompanying notes to consolidated financial statements.

Refer to the following table, which contains the 2009 and 2008 financial ratios for Lowe's. The definitions for the ratios can be found in Figure 5–3. These ratios can also be analyzed using the format described in Appendix 5A (see Figure 5–5).

	2009	2008
Return on Equity	0.129	0.177
Return on Assets	0.075	0.100
Return on Sales (Profit margin)	0.050	0.061
Common Equity Leverage	0.919	0.958
Capital Structure Leverage	1.86	1.84
Long-Term Debt Ratio	0.202	0.227
Current Ratio	1.153	1.121
Quick Ratio	0.082	0.068
Interest Coverage	12.35	23.78
Accounts Payable Turnover (days)	45.0	41.9
Receivables Turnover	NA	NA
Inventory Turnover (days)	91.0	85.3
Fixed Assets Turnover (days)	167	152
Asset Turnover (times)	1.52	1.65

FIGURE 5–5   Lowe's Companies ROE framework

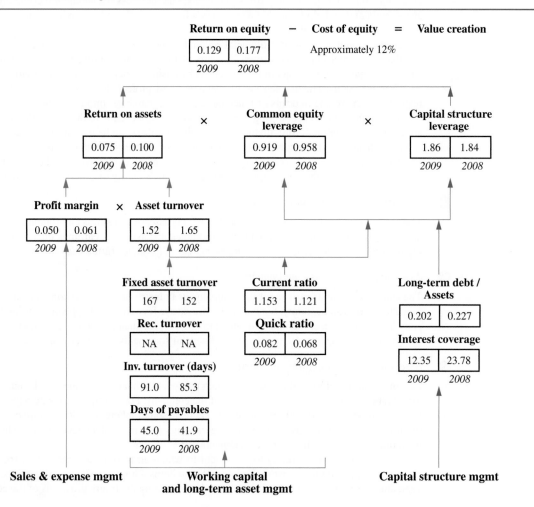

The profitability ratios (ROE, ROA, PM) as well as the effectiveness of its leverage (CEL) all dipped during 2009, while Lowe's slightly increased the amount of its leverage (CSL). Overall, asset turnover (AT) slowed, as did both fixed assets and inventory, while Lowe's took more time to pay its suppliers. With respect to solvency, the current ratio increased (mostly due to the increase in inventory levels), and the quick ratio shows that Lowe's became a bit more liquid during the year. Long-term debt remained roughly the same, but the ability of its operations to cover its debt service costs (IC) decreased significantly. In general, Lowe's did not have a very good year. Its ability to create sales from its investment in assets dropped off, as did its ability to control operating costs. Both its earning power and its ability to meet its debts suffered during 2009. On a positive note, however, 2009 was a very difficult year for retailers and Lowe's fared better than most in the industry.

SUMMARY OF KEY POINTS

The key points of the chapter are summarized below.

● *Using financial accounting numbers to influence management decisions and predict future events.*

Financial accounting numbers can be used in two fundamental ways: (1) they help investors, creditors, and other interested parties to influence the business decisions of a company's managers, and (2) they help to predict a company's future cash flows by providing an indication of earning power and solvency.

Investors and creditors use financial accounting numbers to influence managers by requiring that they enter contracts written in terms of financial accounting numbers. Shareholders encourage management to act in their interests by basing management's compensation on profits. Creditors constrain the actions of managers and protect their own interests by writing restrictions, expressed in terms of financial accounting numbers, into loan contracts.

Although financial accounting numbers report on past events, to the extent that past events are an indication of the future, financial accounting numbers can be used to predict a company's future cash flows. The income statement is designed to measure earning power, the balance sheet measures financial condition, and the statement of cash flows can be used to assess solvency—and all of these concepts relate to a company's ability to generate assets in the future.

● *Five steps of financial statement analysis.*

The five steps of financial statement analysis are: (1) assessing business environment, (2) reading and studying the financial statements and footnotes, (3) assessing earnings quality, (4) analyzing the financial statements, and (5) predicting earnings and/or future cash flows.

● *Assessing the business environment.*

The analyst must first learn about the company, its industry, and how the company and industry relate to the overall economy. Such analysis provides a forward-looking perspective on the company and creates a useful context in which to interpret the financial statements. It also helps the analyst to target the important parts of the financial statements for closer examination.

● *Assessing earnings quality and persistence.*

Earnings quality refers to the extent to which the reported financial statements deviate from the true financial condition and performance of the company. For example, since management prepares the reports, a certain bias may exist. There are other inherent limitations associated with the financial statements as well. Assessing earnings quality involves recognizing where these deviations occur and adjusting the statements accordingly.

Earnings persistence refers to the extent to which an income statement item (revenue or expense) is expected to persist in the future. Some items—low persistence—do not occur every year, and these items should be discounted when assessing the future prospects of the company.

Analyzing financial statements.

Comparison analysis consists of two components: (1) common-size analysis and (2) ratio analysis. Both involve comparisons across time, between companies, and within the financial statements. Ratio analysis consists of computing profitability, leverage, solvency, asset turnover, and other (e.g., market) ratios.

Difficulties involved in using annual report information to identify mispriced securities.

It is difficult to use annual report information to identify mispriced (under- or overvalued) securities because annual reports are typically not available until several months after the balance sheet date. Important financial information, such as net income, is normally released to the public long before the annual report is published, and market prices react almost instantaneously to such news releases. Consequently, stock prices already reflect much of the annual report information by the time it is available. Notwithstanding the untimely release of the annual report, it is possible—with superior financial statement analysis—to improve a variety of equity and debt investment decisions.

Difficulties involved in using financial statements to compare the performance of companies operating in different countries.

It is difficult to make meaningful comparisons across companies operating in different countries because of the varying formats of the financial accounting statements, the different accounting methods, and the political, economic, and cultural environment. Analysts must understand these differences and restate the financial statements to comparable bases before analysis can be meaningfully conducted.

KEY TERMS

Note: Definitions for these terms are provided in the glossary at the end of the text.

Business segments (p. 184)	Financial flexibility (p. 207)
Cash flow analysis (p. 206)	Leverage (p. 191)
Common-size financial statements (p. 189)	Liquidity (p. 207)
Cost of equity (p. 200)	Off-balance-sheet financing (p. 186)
Creating hidden reserves (p. 189)	Operating performance (p. 207)
Debt/equity ratio (p. 192)	Overstating the performance (p. 185)
Earnings persistence (p. 183)	Profitability ratios (p. 190)
Earnings quality (p. 185)	Ratio analysis (p. 190)
Effective sales and expense management (p. 201)	Return on equity (p. 200)
	Solvency assessment (p. 206)
Effective working capital and long-term asset management (p. 201)	Shareholder value creation (p. 200)
	Standard audit report (p. 182)
Effective capital structure management (p. 201)	Taking a bath (p. 185)

ETHICS in the Real World

Fortune magazine examined a series of published articles that explored increasingly common, and somewhat shady, business practices in the Internet world. These practices included: (1) how dot-coms intentionally inflate revenues, (2) how CEOs buy and sell large amounts of their own company's stock, (3) how boards of directors are often overly influenced by company management, and (4) how analysts who follow Internet companies are sometimes influenced by a company to make overly optimistic assessments of its future prospects.

ETHICAL ISSUE Why are these four business practices a possible violation of ethical business behavior?

INTERNET RESEARCH EXERCISE

Provide a brief description of Thomson Financial Network and explain what kind of information it provides for analysts. How might analysts use this information, and why are company managers interested in the information provided by Thomson about their companies? Begin your search at www.thomsonreuters.com.

BRIEF EXERCISES

REAL DATA

BE5–1

Analyzing financial statements

The following information was taken from the financial statements of Coca-Cola and PepsiCo (dollar amounts in millions). Tax rates for Coca-Cola and Pepsi were 22 percent and 27 percent, respectively.

Coca-Cola	2008	2007
Income Statement		
Sales	$31,944	$28,857
Interest expense	438	456
Net income	5,807	5,981
Balance Sheet		
Assets	$40,519	$43,269
Shareholders' equity	20,472	21,744

PepsiCo	2008	2007
Income Statement		
Sales	$43,251	$39,474
Interest expense	329	224
Net income	5,142	5,658
Balance Sheet		
Assets	$35,994	$34,628
Shareholders' equity	12,203	17,325

a. Compute return on equity, return on assets, common equity leverage, capital structure leverage, profit margin, and asset turnover for each company for 2008. Discuss the comparison.

b. (Appendix 5A) For each company, what number results from the following: return on assets × common equity leverage × capital structure leverage?

c. (Appendix 5A) For each company, what number results from the following: profit margin × asset turnover?

d. (Appendix 5A) Compare Coca-Cola to PepsiCo. Which company has the higher return on equity and why? Which company has the higher return on assets and why? Discuss whether the two companies are creating shareholder value.

REAL DATA

BE5–2

Segment analysis

The following sales information concerning Johnson & Johnson's primary business segments appeared in the company's 2008 SEC Form 10-K (dollars in millions).

	2008	2007	2006
Consumer			
U.S.	$ 6,937	$ 6,408	$ 4,573
International	9,117	8,085	5,201
Pharmaceutical			
U.S.	14,831	15,603	15,092
International	9,736	9,263	8,175
Medical Devices			
U.S.	10,541	10,433	10,110
International	12,585	11,303	10,173

a.   Which of the three primary business segments is the largest, and which of the three grew the most from 2006 to 2008?

b.   What percentage of Johnson & Johnson's total sales was generated in each of the three years outside the United States?

c.   Which of the three primary business segments generates the greatest percentage of sales outside the United States?

EXERCISES

REAL DATA

E5–1

Analyzing financial statements

Excerpts from the 2008 financial report of Cisco Systems, a leading Internet networker, are provided below (dollars in millions).

Review the information, calculate relevant ratios from Figure 5–3, and explain why Cisco appears to be a good or poor investment. The tax rate was 20 percent.

	2008	2007	2006
Balance Sheet			
Current assets	$44,177	$35,699	$31,574
Long-term assets	23,951	23,035	21,766
Current liabilities	13,655	13,858	13,358
Long-term debt	15,826	10,523	8,502
Shareholders' equity	38,647	34,353	31,480
Income Statement			
Sales	$29,131	$33,099	$29,462
Net income	6,134	8,052	7,333
Interest expense	346	319	377

REAL DATA

E5–2

Analyzing financial statements

Excerpts from the 2008 financial report of Intel, a computer-processor manufacturer, are as follows (dollars in millions).

	2008	2007	2006
Balance Sheet			
Current assets	$19,871	$23,885	$18,280
Long-term assets	30,844	31,766	30,088
Current liabilities	7,818	8,571	8,514
Long-term debt	3,809	4,318	3,102
Shareholders' equity	39,088	42,762	36,752

(*Continued*)

	2008	2007	2006
Income Statement			
Sales	$37,586	$38,334	$35,382
Net income	5,292	6,976	5,044
Interest expense	8	15	24

Review this information, calculate relevant ratios from Figure 5–3, and explain why Intel appears to be a good or poor investment. The tax rate was 31 percent.

E5–3

Analyzing financial statements

The chief executive officer of Ginny's Fashions has included the following financial statements in a loan application submitted to Priority Bank. The company intends to acquire additional equipment and wishes to finance the purchase with a long-term note.

	2012	2011
Balance Sheet		
Current assets	$ 21,000	$ 14,000
Long-term assets	52,000	50,000
Current liabilities	9,000	7,000
Long-term liabilities	24,000	26,000
Contributed capital	25,000	25,000
Retained earnings	15,000	6,000
Income Statement		
Revenues	$ 74,000	$ 70,000
Expenses	56,000	53,000
Statement of Cash Flows		
Net cash from operating activities	$ 9,000	$ 15,000
Net cash from investing activities	(12,000)	(14,000)
Net cash from financing activities	5,000	7,000
Change in cash balance	$ 2,000	$ 8,000
Beginning cash balance	9,000	1,000
Ending cash balance	$ 11,000	$ 9,000

Assume that you, a bank loan officer, review the financial statements, and recommend whether Ginny's Fashions should be considered for a loan. Support your recommendation with financial ratios. Assume a tax rate of 30 percent. Interest expense is $2,000 in 2012 and $2,000 in 2011.

E5–4

Computing ratios and preparing common-size financial statements

The 2011 and 2012 financial statements of Ken's Sportswear follow:

Balance Sheet	2012	2011
Assets		
Cash	$ 9,000	$ 7,000
Accounts receivable	12,000	9,000
Inventory	18,000	15,000
Long-lived assets (net)	60,000	50,000
Total assets	$99,000	$81,000

(Continued)

Balance Sheet	2012	2011
Liabilities and Shareholders' Equity		
Accounts payable	$16,500	$12,000
Long-term liabilities	46,000	40,000
Common stock	20,000	20,000
Additional paid-in capital	5,000	5,000
Retained earnings	11,500	4,000
Total liabilities and equity	$99,000	$81,000

Income Statement	2012	2011
Sales (all on credit)	$72,000	
Less: Cost of goods sold	30,000	
Gross profit	$42,000	
Operating expenses	12,000	
Net income from operations	$30,000	
Interest expense	5,000	
Net income before taxes	$25,000	
Income taxes	8,500	
Net income	$16,500	
Dividends	$ 9,000	
Per-share market price	$ 36	$ 30
Outstanding common shares	2,000	2,000

a. Compute all relevant ratios for 2012.
b. Prepare common-size financial statements.
c. Evaluate the company's financial performance and condition.

REAL DATA

E5–5

Solvency and
the role of
activity ratios

Excerpted financial information from the records of The Gap, Inc., a major clothing retailer, follows (dollars in millions):

	2008	2007	2006
Inventory	$ 1,506	$ 1,575	$ 1,796
Current assets	4,005	4,086	5,029
Accounts payable	975	1,006	772
Current liabilities	2,158	2,433	2,272
Sales	$14,526	$15,763	$15,923
Cost of goods sold	9,079	10,071	10,266

a. Compute the current ratio for each year.
b. Compute the gross margin for each year.
c. Compute inventory turnover and inventory days for 2007 and 2008; compute accounts payable turnover and accounts payable days for 2007 and 2008.
d. Comment on the company's solvency trend.

E5–6

Solvency and
the statemnet of
cash flow

Beecham Limited began operations in early 2010. Summaries of the statements of cash flows for 2012, 2011, and 2010 follow:

	2012	2011	2010
Net cash provided (used) by operating activities	$?	$(252)	$?
Net cash provided (used) by investing activities	150	?	$(400)
Net cash provided (used) by financing activities	(200)	400	800
Net increase (decrease) in cash balance	$?	$ (2)	$ 78
Beginning cash balance	76	?	0
Ending cash balance	$ 156	$ 76	$?

a. Compute the missing dollar amounts, and briefly comment on the company's cash man-
    agement policies during the three-year period.
b. Does the company appear to have faced any solvency problems during the period?
    Explain your answer.

E5-7

Using solvency and activity ratios together

The following data are from the 2012 financial report of Generic Clothing Company:

	2012	2011
Current assets:		
Cash	$ 15,000	$ 30,000
Short-term marketable securities	225,000	10,000
Accounts receivable (net)	90,000	95,000
Inventory	50,000	225,000
Prepaid insurance	20,000	25,000
Total current assets	$400,000	$385,000
Current liabilities:		
Accounts payable	$ 75,000	$ 60,000
Wages payable	10,000	10,000
Current portion of long-term debt	375,000	100,000
Total current liabilities	$460,000	$170,000

a. Based upon the above data, compute the following for Generic Clothing Company for
    both 2011 and 2012:
    (1) The current ratio
    (2) The quick ratio
b. Assume that net credit sales for the years ended December 31, 2011, and 2012, were
    $780,000 and $800,000, respectively, and that the balance of accounts receivable as of
    January 1, 2012, was $100,000. Compute the receivables turnover and days outstanding
    for both years.
c. Does it appear that the solvency position of the company improved or worsened from
    2010 to 2012? Explain.

E5-8

Explaining return on equity with inventory turnover

PLP Corporation began operations on January 1, 2009. The initial investment by the owners
was $100,000. The following information was extracted from the company's records.

	Net Income	December 31 Shareholders' Equity	December 31 Inventory	Cost of Goods Sold
2009	$510,000	$100,000	$200,000	$1,200,000
2010	490,000	290,000	255,000	1,350,000
2011	515,000	315,000	320,000	1,395,000
2012	505,000	510,000	365,000	1,400,000

a. Compute the return on equity for each year. Has the company been effective at manag-
    ing the capital provided by the equity owners?
b. Does the information about inventory and the cost of goods sold indicate any reason for
    the trend in return on equity? Support your answer with any relevant ratios.

E5-9

Using ratios and the statement of cash flows to assess solvency and earning power

The financial information below was taken from the records of Lotechnic Enterprises. The
company pays no dividends.

	2012	2011	2010	2009
Current assets	$ 35,000	$ 31,000	$24,000	$20,000
Non-current assets	93,000	86,000	64,000	33,000
Total assets	$128,000	$117,000	$88,000	$53,000

(*Continued*)

	2012	2011	2010	2009
Current liabilities	$ 30,000	$ 25,000	$ 13,000	$ 8,000
Long-term liabilities	40,000	40,000	35,000	15,000
Capital stock	20,000	20,000	20,000	20,000
Retained earnings	38,000	32,000	20,000	10,000
Total liabilities and shareholders' equity	$128,000	$117,000	$ 88,000	$53,000
Net cash provided (used) by operating activities	$ (2,000)	$ 3,000	$ 6,000	$ 7,000
Net cash provided (used) by investing activities	(10,000)	(20,000)	(31,000)	(12,000)
Net cash provided (used) by financing activities	15,000	15,000	25,000	8,000
Net increase (decrease) in cash	$ 3,000	$ (2,000)	$ 0	$ 3,000
Interest expense	$ 5,000	$ 5,000	$ 4,000	$ 2,000
Net income	24,000	21,000	14,000	13,000

a.   Compute the current ratio, the debt/equity ratio, and return on assets for each of the four years. Assume that the year-end balances in 2009 reflect the average balances during the year. Assume a tax rate of 30 percent.
b.   Prepare a common-size balance sheet for each of the four years.
c.   Use the statement of cash flows, and analyze the earning power and solvency positions of Lotechnic.

REAL DATA

E5–10

The effects of transactions on financial ratios

Monsanto Company, a leading global chemical manufacturer, entered into the following transactions during 2009.

1.   Purchased inventory on account.
2.   Purchased plant machinery by issuing long-term debt.
3.   Made a principal payment on long-term debt.
4.   Paid wages.
5.   Sold inventory on account for 20 percent over cost.
6.   Issued stock for cash.

The 2008 balance sheet of Monsanto is as follows (dollars in millions).

Assets		Liabilities and Shareholders' Equity	
Cash and marketable securities	$ 1,956	Current liabilities	$ 3,756
Other current assets	5,927	Long-term liabilities	4,065
Long-lived assets	9,994	Shareholders' equity	10,056
Total assets	$17,877	Total liabilities and shareholders' equity	$17,877

Fill in a chart like the following one by indicating whether each transaction would increase (+), decrease (−), or have no effect (NE) on the quick ratio, current ratio, and debt/equity ratio. Treat each transaction independently.

Transaction	Quick Ratio	Current Ratio	Debt/Equity Ratio
1.			

E5–11

Debt covenants limiting additional debt and dividend payments

At the end of 2011, Montvale Associates borrowed $120,000 from the Bayliner Bank. The debt covenant specified that Montvale's debt/equity ratio could not exceed 1.5:1 during the period of the loan. A summary of Montvale's balance sheet after the loan follows.

	2011
Assets	
Current assets	$130,000
Noncurrent assets	350,000
Total assets	$480,000
Liabilities and Shareholders' Equity	
Current liabilities	$130,000
Long-term liabilities	150,000
Shareholders' equity	200,000
Total liabilities and shareholders' equity	$480,000

a. Compute Montvale's debt/equity ratio immediately after the loan.
b. How much additional debt can the company incur without violating the debt covenant?
c. How large a dividend can the company declare and pay at the end of 2011 without violating the debt covenant?

d. If Montvale had declared, but not yet paid, a $20,000 dividend before it took out the loan, could the company pay the dividend afterward without violating the debt covenant? Why or why not?

REAL DATA

E5–12

Examining market ratios over time

The following information refers to the financial records of McDonald's Corporation over a three-year period (dollar amounts in millions except share price).

	2008	2007	2006
Net income	$4,313	$2,395	$3,544
Dividends declared	1,823	1,766	1,217
Closing per-share price	62.19	58.91	44.33
Number of shares outstanding	1,127	1,188	1,234

a. Compute dividends declared as a percentage of net income during each of the three years.
b. Compute the price-earnings ratio, dividend yield, and stock price return for 2006, 2007, and 2008.
c. Comment on the performance of an investment in McDonald's stock from 2006 to 2008.

REAL DATA

E5–13

Computing ratios and the effect of transactions on return on equity

Merck, a major pharmaceutical, generated $7,808 million in net income for the year ended December 31, 2008.

1. The company declared and paid $3,278.5 million in dividends during 2008.
2. Merck stock was selling for $57.37 per share on January 1, 2008, and for $30.40 per share on December 31, 2008.
3. As of January 1, 2008, the company had 2,169 million shares of common stock outstanding. During 2008, the company repurchased 35.7 million shares. Assume that the purchases were made evenly throughout the year.

a. Compute the following ratios:
   (1) Earnings per share
   (2) Price/earnings
   (3) Dividend yield
   (4) Stock price return
b. What effect (increase, decrease, or no effect) did each of the three events above have on Merck's return on equity ratio?

REAL DATA

E5–14

Segment analysis

The operating profits from 2006 to 2008 reported by each of Johnson & Johnson's primary business segments are provided below. Sales numbers for each of the segments are provided in BE5–2 of the Brief Exercises section of this chapter (dollars in millions).

	2008	2007	2006
Consumer	$2,674	$2,277	$1,374
Pharmaceutical	7,605	6,540	6,894
Medical devices	7,223	4,846	6,126

REQUIRED:
a. Which of the segments is the most profitable as a percentage of sales?
b. Which of the segments reports the fastest growth in profitability?

E5–15

Appendix 5A:
Interpreting
financial ratios

The following ratios were computed from the financial statements of INSEAD Incorporated:

	2012	2011	2010
Return on equity	0.28	0.25	0.22
Return on assets	0.15	0.18	0.20
Common equity leverage	0.85	0.88	0.90
Capital structure leverage	2.20	1.58	1.22
Profit margin	0.09	0.08	0.07
Asset turnover	1.67	2.25	2.85

Use the ROE model to analyze these ratios, and comment on the company's performance from 2010 to 2012 and why.

E5–16

Appendix 5A:
Interpreting
financial ratios

The following ratios were computed from the financial statements of LBS Products:

	2012	2011	2010
Return on equity	0.11	0.18	0.20
Return on assets	0.09	0.18	0.20
Common equity leverage	0.80	0.78	0.78
Capital structure leverage	1.50	1.30	1.30
Profit margin	0.06	0.13	0.13
Asset turnover	1.50	1.40	1.50

Use the ROE model to analyze these ratios, and comment on the company's performance from 2010 to 2012 and why.

E5–17

Appendix 5A

Assume that the following financial ratios are calculated for Royals Corporation in 2012:

Asset turnover	0.625
Common equity leverage	0.685
Capital structure leverage	2.50
Return on assets	9.50%
Return on sales (profit margin)	15.20%

a. What was the return on equity for Royals Corporation in 2012?
b. If Royals Corporation keeps all of its other ratios constant in 2013 but increases its capital structure leverage ratio to 2.75, what will be the 2013 return on equity?
c. If Royals Corporation keeps all of its other ratios constant in 2013 but increases its profit margin to 16%, what will be the 2013 return on equity?

REAL DATA

E5–18

Appendix 5A: Projected
financial statements

Selected financial information appearing in the SEC Form 10-K for Johnson & Johnson is reported below (dollars in millions).

	2008
Sales	$63,747
Net income	12,949
Total assets	84,912
Total shareholders' equity	42,511

REQUIRED:

Assume that company management expects sales growth of 8 percent during 2009, and during 2009 expects stable relationships between net income and sales, sales and total assets, and debt/equity. Prepare a projected income statement and balance sheet for 2009.

PROBLEMS

REAL DATA

Computing and
interpreting ratios

Imation, a global technology company, reported the following selected items as part of its 2008 annual report (dollars in millions):

	2008	2007
Cash	$ 97	$ 140
Accounts receivable	378	507
Inventory	363	366
Current assets	976	1,119
Current liabilities	504	631
Shareholders' equity	945	1,054
Sales	$2,155	
Cost of goods sold	1,805	
Interest expense	2	
Net loss before taxes	(35)	
Net loss	(33)	

REQUIRED:

Compute the following ratios:

1. Current ratio
2. Quick ratio
3. Receivable turnover (time and days)
4. Interest coverage
5. Return on assets
6. Inventory turnover (times and days)
7. Return on equity

P5–2

Borrow or issue
equity: effects on
financial ratios

Edgemont Repairs began operations on January 1, 2010. The 2010, 2011, and 2012 financial statements follow:

	2012	2011	2010
Assets			
Current assets	$ 30,000	$10,000	$ 8,000
Noncurrent assets	83,000	45,000	41,000
Total assets	$113,000	$55,000	$49,000
Liabilities and Shareholders' Equity			
Current liabilities	$ 12,000	$ 7,000	$ 5,000
Long-term liabilities	50,000	10,000	10,000
Shareholders' equity	51,000	38,000	34,000
Total liabilities and			
shareholders' equity	$113,000	$55,000	$49,000
Revenues	$ 70,000	$45,000	$37,000
Operating expenses	27,000	24,000	24,000

(*Continued*)

	2012	2011	2010
Interest expense	5,000	1,000	1,000
Income taxes	13,000	6,000	6,000
Net income	$ 25,000	$14,000	$ 6,000
Dividends	$ 12,000	$10,000	$ 2,000
Number of shares outstanding	10,000	10,000	10,000

On January 1, 2012, the company expanded operations by taking out a $40,000 long-term loan at a 10 percent annual interest rate.

REQUIRED:

a. Compute return on equity, return on assets, common equity leverage, capital structure leverage, profit margin, and asset turnover.

b. On January 1, 2012, the company's common stock was selling for $20 per share. Assume that Edgemont issued 2,000 shares of stock, instead of borrowing the $40,000, to raise the cash needed to pay for the January 1 expansion. Recompute the ratios in (a) for 2012. Ignore any tax effects.

c. Should the company have issued the equity instead of borrowing the funds? Explain.

REAL DATA

P5–3

Percentage changes and common-size financial statements

You are considering investing in Eli Lilly, a major pharmaceutical company. As part of your investigation of Lilly, you obtained the following balance sheets for the years ended December 31, 2008 and 2007 (dollars in millions):

	2008	2007
Assets		
Current assets:		
Cash	$ 5,497	$ 3,221
Short-term marketable securities	429	1,611
Accounts receivable	2,779	2,674
Inventory	2,493	2,524
Other current assets	1,255	2,286
Total current assets	$12,453	$12,316
Property, plant, and equipment	8,626	8,575
Other assets	8,134	5,984
Total assets	$29,213	$26,875
Liabilities and Shareholders' Equity		
Current liabilities:		
Short-term borrowings	$ 5,846	$ 414
Accounts payable	886	924
Wages payable	771	824
Dividends payable	537	514
Income taxes payable	229	238
Other current liabilities	4,841	2,523
Total current liabilities	$13,110	$ 5,437
Long-term debt	9,368	7,934
Contributed capital*	(902)	1,697
Retained earnings	7,655	11,807
Total liabilities and		
shareholders' equity	$29,213	$26,875

*Net, including treasury stock and other adjustments.

REQUIRED:

a. Compute the dollar change in each account from 2007 to 2008. Also compute the percentage change in each account from 2007 to 2008.

b. Convert the balance sheets to common-size balance sheets. Also compute the percentage change in the common-size numbers of each account from 2007 to 2008.
c. Does the information in (b) provide any additional data to that in (a)? Explain.

P5–4

Comprehensive
ratio analysis

You have just been hired as a stock analyst for a large stock brokerage company. Your first assignment is to analyze the performance of Gidley Electronics. The company's balance sheet for 2011 and 2012 is presented below and on the next page.

	2012	2011
Assets		
Current assets:		
Cash	$ 110,000	$ 115,000
Short-term marketable securities	175,000	220,000
Accounts receivable	350,000	400,000
Inventory	290,000	240,000
Prepaid expenses	55,000	35,000
Total current assets	$ 980,000	$1,010,000
Property, plant, and equipment	650,000	590,000
Less: Accumulated depreciation	(165,000)	(130,000)
Total assets	$1,465,000	$1,470,000
Liabilities and Shareholders' Equity		
Current liabilities:		
Accounts payable	$ 60,000	$ 50,000
Wages payable	15,000	20,000
Unearned revenue	50,000	35,000
Income taxes payable	55,000	35,000
Current portion of long-term debt	110,000	135,000
Total current liabilities	$ 290,000	$ 275,000
Bonds payable	380,000	440,000
Common stock ($10 par value)	220,000	170,000
Additional paid-in capital	145,000	115,000
Retained earnings	430,000	470,000
Total liabilities and shareholders' equity	$1,465,000	$1,470,000

The company's income statement and reconciliation of retained earnings for the years ended December 31, 2011 and 2012, are presented below.

	2012	2011
Income Statement		
Revenue:		
Net cash sales	$1,405,000	$1,255,000
Net credit sales	2,450,000	3,010,000
Total revenue	$3,855,000	$4,265,000
Cost of goods sold:		
Beginning inventory	$ 240,000	$ 300,000
Net purchases	1,755,000	2,005,000
Cost of goods available for sale	$1,995,000	$2,305,000
Less: Ending inventory	290,000	240,000
Cost of goods sold	$1,705,000	$2,065,000
Gross profit	$2,150,000	$2,200,000

(Continued)

	2012	2011
Selling and administrative expenses:		
Depreciation expense	(95,000)	(100,000)
General selling expenses	(470,000)	(450,000)
General administrative expenses	(580,000)	(620,000)
Net operating income	$1,005,000	$1,030,000
Interest expense	150,000	165,000
Net income from continuing		
operations before taxes	$ 855,000	$ 865,000
Income taxes	345,000	350,000
Net income	$ 510,000	$ 515,000
Reconciliation of Retained Earnings		
Beginning retained earnings balance	$ 470,000	$ 165,000
Plus: Net income	510,000	515,000
Less: Dividends	(550,000)	(210,000)
Ending retained earnings balance	$ 430,000	$ 470,000

The market prices of the company's stock as of January 1, 2011, December 31, 2011, and December 31, 2012, were $65, $69, and $54 per share, respectively. The January 1, 2011, balance in shareholders' equity was $450,000, there were no changes in the number of common shares outstanding or in accounts receivable during 2011, and the income tax rate was 40 percent for 2011 and 2012. Total assets as of January 1, 2011, were $1,450,000.

REQUIRED:

Answer the following questions (including any relevant ratios in your answers) for both 2011 and 2012. Unless the December 31, 2010, balance is provided, assume that the December 31, 2011, balance reflects the average balance during 2011.

1. How effective is the company at managing investments made by the equity owners?
2. Is the company using debt in the best interests of the equity owners?
3. Can the company meet its current obligations using current assets? Using cash-like assets?
4. How sensitive are stock prices to changes in earnings?
5. How many days is the average account receivable outstanding? Are the days outstanding increasing or decreasing?

P5-5

Comparing companies on earning power

The following information was obtained from the 2012 financial reports of Hathaway Toy Company and Yakima Manufacturing:

	Hathaway Toy	Yakima Mfg.
Interest expense	—	$ 195,000
Net income	$ 875,000	755,000
Current liabilities	240,000	25,000
Mortgage payable	—	1,850,000
Common stock ($10 par value)	800,000	350,000
Additional paid-in capital	915,000	150,000
Retained earnings	745,000	325,000
Total liabilities and shareholders' equity	$2,700,000	$2,700,000

Assume that the only change to shareholders' equity during 2012 is due to net income earned in 2012.

REQUIRED:

a. Which company is more effective at managing the capital provided by the owners?
b. Which company is more effective at managing capital provided by all investors?
c. Compute the earnings per share for each company.
d. Is Yakima Manufacturing using its debt effectively for the equity owners?

Excerpts from the 2008 financial statements for Goodyear are as follows (dollars in millions):

	2008	2007	2006
Balance Sheet			
Current assets	$ 8,340	$10,172	$10,179
Long-term assets	6,886	7,019	6,850
Current liabilities	4,779	4,664	4,666
Long-term liabilities	9,425	9,677	13,121
Contributed capital	(503)	1,248	(1,726)
Retained earnings	1,525	1,602	968
Income Statement			
Revenues	$19,488	$19,644	$18,751
Expenses	19,505	19,042	19,081
Statement of Cash Flows			
Net cash from operating activities	$ (745)	$ 105	$ 560
Net cash from investing activities	(1,136)	(829)	(532)
Net cash from financing activities	312	(1,333)	1,696
Change in cash balance	$(1,569)	$ (399)	$ 1,724
Beginning cash balance	3,463	3,862	2,138
Ending cash balance	$ 1,894	$ 3,463	$ 3,862

REQUIRED:

Assume that you have some capital to invest and that you are considering an equity investment in Goodyear. Review the financial statements and comment on Goodyear as an investment. Support your recommendation with financial ratios. Assume a tax rate of 30 percent. Interest expense is $320 in 2008, $450 in 2007, and $447 in 2006.

The following selected financial information was obtained from the 2012 financial reports of Robotronics, Inc. and Technology, Limited:

	Robotronics, Inc.	Technology, Ltd.
Interest expense	$ 100,000	$ 175,000
Unusual gain (net of taxes of $320,000)	—	1,300,000
Net income (including unusual items)	610,000	1,675,000
Current liabilities	140,000	25,000
Bonds payable	725,000	0
Mortgage payable	1,490,000	405,000
Common stock	500,000	600,000
Additional paid-in capital	215,000	325,000
Retained earnings	290,000	515,000
Total liabilities and shareholders' equity	$3,360,000	$1,870,000

Assume that total assets, total liabilities, and total shareholders' equity were constant throughout 2012.

REQUIRED:

a. Assume that you are considering purchasing the common stock of one of these companies. Which company has a higher return on equity? Would your conclusion be different if the impact of the unusual item had not been included in net income? Should unusual items be considered? Why or why not?

b. Which company uses leverage more effectively? Does your answer change if you do not consider the impact of the unusual item on net income?

P5–8

Preparing the
financial statements
from financial ratios

Tumwater Canyon Campsites began operations on January 1, 2012. The following information is available at year-end. Assume that all sales were on credit.

Net income	$ 25,000	Return on sales	8%
Receivables turnover	8	Gross margin	40%
Inventory turnover	5	Quick ratio	50%
Accounts payable	$200,000		

REQUIRED:

Prepare an income statement and the current asset and current liability portions of the
balance sheet for 2012. Current assets consist of cash, accounts receivable, and inventory.
Accounts payable is Tumwater's only current liability. (*Hint:* Begin by using return on sales
to compute net sales.)

P5–9

Common-size
financial statements

Bob Cleary, the controller of Mountain-Pacific Railroad, has prepared the financial statements
for 2011 and 2012, shown below and on the next page. The market prices of the company's
stock as of January 1, 2011, December 31, 2011, and December 31, 2012, were $50, $45, and
$70 per share, respectively. Assume an income tax rate of 34 percent and assume that interest
expense was incurred only on long-term debt (including the current maturities of long-term debt).

REQUIRED:

a.   Prepare common-size balance sheets and income statements for 2011 and 2012 and
analyze the results.

b.   Which income statement account experienced the largest shift from 2011 to 2012? Did
this shift appear to have any impact on the balance sheet? Explain.

c.   What benefits do common-size financial statements provide over standard financial
statements?

Balance Sheet	2012	2011
Assets		
Current assets:		
Cash	$ 10,000	$ 312,000
Short-term marketable securities	125,000	120,000
Accounts receivable	500,000	150,000
Inventory	200,000	210,000
Prepaid expenses	50,000	75,000
Total current assets	$ 885,000	$ 867,000
Long-term investments	225,000	225,000
Property, plant, and equipment	430,000	540,000
Less: Accumulated depreciation	(65,000)	(100,000)
Total assets	$1,475,000	$1,532,000
Liabilities and Shareholders' Equity		
Current liabilities:		
Accounts payable	$ 10,000	$ 50,000
Wages payable	5,000	2,000
Dividends payable	125,000	5,000
Income taxes payable	50,000	35,000
Current portion of long-term debt	100,000	175,000
Total current liabilities	$ 290,000	$ 267,000
Mortgage payable	350,000	450,000
Common stock ($10 par value)	200,000	110,000
Additional paid-in capital	135,000	95,000
Retained earnings	500,000	610,000
Total liabilities and shareholders' equity	$1,475,000	$1,532,000

Income Statement	2012		2011	
Revenue:				
Net cash sales	$1,955,000		$2,775,000	
Net credit sales	4,150,000		1,410,000	
Total revenue		$6,105,000		$4,185,000
Cost of goods sold:				
Beginning inventory	$ 210,000		$ 300,000	
Net purchases	4,005,000		2,475,000	
Cost of goods available				
for sale	$4,215,000		$2,775,000	
Less: Ending inventory	200,000		210,000	
Cost of goods sold		4,015,000		2,565,000
Gross profit		$2,090,000		$1,620,000
Selling and administrative				
expenses:				
Depreciation expense	$ 75,000		$ 90,000	
General selling expenses	575,000		600,000	
General administrative				
expenses	480,000	1,130,000	420,000	1,110,000
Net operating income		$ 960,000		$ 510,000
Interest expense		50,000		65,000
Net income from continuing				
operations before taxes		$ 910,000		$ 445,000
Income taxes		310,000		151,000
Net income before				
unusual items		$ 600,000		$ 294,000
Unusual loss—net of				
tax benefit of $60,000		115,000		—
Net income		$ 485,000		$ 294,000

Statement of Retained Earnings	2012	2011
Beginning retained earnings balance	$ 610,000	$ 326,000
Plus: Net income	485,000	294,000
Less: Dividends	(595,000)	(10,000)
Ending retained earnings balance	$ 500,000	$ 610,000

P5–10

Comparing ratios to
industry averages

Mountain-Pacific Railroad, whose financial statements are presented in P5–9, is interested in comparing itself to the rest of the industry. Bob Cleary, the controller, has obtained the following industry averages from a trade journal. (The industry averages were the same for 2011 and 2012.)

Return on equity	0.500
Current ratio	3.100
Quick ratio	1.850
Return on assets	0.300
Receivables turnover	8.150
Earnings per share ($)	41.150
Price/earnings ratio	0.451
Capital structure leverage	1.770
Profit margin	0.072
Dividend yield	0.375
Return on investment	0.102
Interest coverage	9.890
Inventory turnover	21.700

REQUIRED:

a. Compute these ratios for Mountain-Pacific Railroad for both 2011 (using year-end balances) and 2012 (using average balances where appropriate). Identify significant trends. Could the company experience solvency problems? Explain.

b. Compare the ratios of Mountain-Pacific Railroad to the industry averages. Do you think that Mountain-Pacific Railroad is doing better, worse, or the same as the industry? Explain your answer, being as specific as possible.

P5–11

Assessing the loan
risk of a potential
bank customer

You have just been hired as a loan officer for Washington Mutual Savings. Selig Equipment and Mountain Bike, Inc. have both applied for $125,000 nine-month loans to acquire additional plant equipment. Neither company offered any security for the loans. It is the strict policy of the bank to have only $1,350,000 outstanding in unsecured loans at any point in time. Since the bank currently has $1,210,000 in unsecured loans outstanding, it will be unable to grant loans to both companies. The bank president has given you the following selected information from the companies' loan applications.

	Selig Equipment	Mountain Bike, Inc.
Cash	$ 15,000	$ 160,000
Accounts receivable	215,000	470,000
Inventory	305,000	195,000
Prepaid expenses	180,000	10,000
Total current assets	$ 715,000	$ 835,000
Noncurrent assets	1,455,000	1,875,000
Total assets	$2,170,000	$2,710,000
Current liabilities	$ 285,000	$ 325,000
Long-term liabilities	950,000	875,000
Contributed capital	790,000	910,000
Retained earnings	145,000	600,000
Total liabilities and shareholders' equity	$2,170,000	$2,710,000
Net credit sales	$1,005,000	$1,625,000
Cost of goods sold	755,000	960,000

REQUIRED:

Assume that all account balances on the balance sheet are representative of the entire year. Based on this limited information, which company would you recommend to the bank president as the better risk for an unsecured loan? Support your answer with any relevant analysis.

P5–12

Issuing debt or
equity: effects on
ratios and owners

Watson Metal Products is planning to expand its operations to France in response to increased demand from the French for quality metal products to use in production processes. Ben Watson, president of Watson Metal Products, and his consultants have estimated that the expansion will require an investment of $5 million. They have also estimated that this expansion will cause net income before interest expense to increase by $1,500,000. The company is considering financing the expansion through one of the following alternatives.

Alternative 1: Issue 200,000 shares of common stock for $25 per share.

Alternative 2: Issue long-term debt at an annual interest cost of 15 percent. The principal would be payable in ten years.

Alternative 3: Issue 100,000 shares of common stock for $25 per share and finance the remainder by issuing long-term debt at an annual interest rate of 15 percent. The principal would be payable in ten years.

The income statement for the year ended December 31, 2012, of Watson Metal Products was as follows:

Sales	$150,000,000
Cost of goods sold	(90,000,000)
Other expenses	(45,000,000)
Income from operations	$ 15,000,000
Interest expense	4,000,000
Net income before taxes	$ 11,000,000
Income taxes	4,400,000
Net income	$ 6,600,000
Earnings per share	$ 3.30

Prior to the expansion, the total debt of Watson Metal Products was $35 million, and total shareholders' equity was $45 million. There were no changes in total debt and total shareholders' equity other than those due to net income and the expansion project. Federal and state income tax rates total 40 percent.

REQUIRED:

a. Assume that the company's net income from non-French operations in 2013 equals the income earned in 2012 and that the estimated income from operations on the expansion is realized in 2013. Compute earnings per share, return on equity, return on assets, common equity leverage, and the capital structure leverage as of December 31, 2013, if the company finances the expansion through the following:
   (1) Alternative 1
   (2) Alternative 2
   (3) Alternative 3
   Assume that the December 31, 2013, balances equal average balances during 2013.

b. Assume that you are currently a shareholder in Watson Metal Products. Which expansion alternative would you prefer? Explain your answer.

c. What amount of net income would Watson Metal Products have to generate from the expansion project so that earnings per share would be the same before and after the expansion under each alternative?

P5-13

Preparing financial statement data from financial ratios

The following relationships were obtained for Boulder Mineral Company for 2012:

Current ratio	3:1
Inventory turnover (average days supply)	12.167
Quick ratio	2:1
Debt/equity	0.4:1
Return on equity	0.75:1
Return on assets	0.65:1
Return on sales (profit margin)	0.2:1
Receivables turnover	25
Earnings per share	$16.00

Additional information:
1. Boulder Mineral Company generated $450,000 in net income during 2012.
2. Credit sales comprise 80 percent of net sales.
3. Cost of goods sold is 55 percent of net sales.
4. Current liabilities are 35 percent of total liabilities.
5. The balance in the cash account is $68,000.
6. The income tax rate was 34 percent.

REQUIRED:

Using the above information (and year-end balances), compute the following items.

a. Shareholders' equity
b. Total liabilities
c. Total assets
d. Interest expense
e. Net income before taxes
f. Net sales
g. Credit sales
h. Accounts receivable
i. Cost of goods sold
j. Inventory turnover
k. Inventory
l. Current liabilities
m. Current assets
n. Marketable securities
o. Noncurrent assets
p. The number of shares of common stock outstanding

REAL DATA

P5–14

Segment analysis

Information about Pepsico's five primary segments is provided below (dollars in millions). The information was taken from the company's 2008 SEC Form 10-K.

	Revenues	Profits	Assets
Frito-Lay North America	$12,507	$2,959	$6,284
Quaker Foods North America	1,902	582	1,035
Latin America Foods	5,895	897	3,023
Americas Beverages	10,937	2,026	7,673
U.K. & Europe	6,453	811	8,635
Middle East, Africa, Asia	5,575	667	3,961

REQUIRED:

a. Compute the percent each segment contributes to the total revenues reported for 2008.
b. Rank the segments in terms of profit margin.
c. Rank the segments in terms of return on assets.
d. Discuss.

REAL DATA

P5–15

Analyzing an
IFRS-based set of
financial statements

Review the 2008 consolidated income statement and balance sheet published by Unilever, which is located at the end of Chapter 2 in this text.

REQUIRED:

a. Compute the profitability, solvency, leverage, and turnover ratios listed in Figure 5–3. Comment on Unilever's earning power and solvency.
b. (Appendix 5A) Use the ROE analysis described in Appendix 5A and discuss the reasons for the change in ROE from 2007 to 2008.

ISSUES FOR DISCUSSION

REAL DATA

ID5–1

Linking company
characteristics to
the financial
statements

Financial profiles, expressing the dollar value of financial statement accounts as a percentage of total assets (for balance sheet accounts) and sales (for income statement accounts), are listed for four well-known companies.

1. Bed Bath & Beyond—housewares retailer
2. Kelly Services—provider of part-time employees

3. Bank of America—commercial bank
4. Hewlett-Packard—technology and consulting company

	1	2	3	4
Balance Sheet				
Cash	34	16	9	8
Accounts receivable	50	0	15	56
Inventories	0	39	7	0
Long-term assets	1	32	19	10
Other assets	15	13	50	26
Current liabilities	76	22	47	41
Long-term liabilities	15	7	19	14
Shareholders' equity	9	71	34	45
Income Statement				
Sales of goods	0	100	77	0
Sales of services	100	0	23	100
Cost of goods sold	0	60	59	0
Operating expenses	96	34	31	101
Net income	4	6	7	(1)

REQUIRED:

Link each profile with a company, and explain your choice.

REAL DATA

ID5-2

Linking company
characteristics to
the financial
statements

Financial profiles, expressing the dollar value of financial statement accounts as a percentage of total assets (for balance sheet accounts) and sales (for income statement accounts), are listed for four well-known companies.

1. Walgreen's—retailer of pharmacy and consumer goods
2. EchoStar Communications—provider of satellite television dishes and services
3. General Electric—diversified manufacturer and financial services firm
4. Campbell Soup—manufacturer of food products, growing by acquisitions

	1	2	3	4
Balance Sheet				
Cash	11	29	10	1
Accounts receivable	48	11	10	9
Inventories	2	2	27	14
Long-term assets	10	41	43	33
Other assets	29	17	10	43
Current liabilities	31	13	27	27
Long-term liabilities	56	10	16	61
Shareholders' equity	13	77	57	12
Income Statement				
Sales of goods	38	81	100	100
Sales of services	62	19	0	0
Cost of goods sold	30	69	72	60
Operating expenses	60	75	25	30
Net income	10	(44)	3	10

REQUIRED:

Link each profile with a company, and explain your choice.

Morningstar, a firm that evaluates and rates mutual fund performance, published an article on its Web site discussing a company's book value per share (shareholder's equity/number of shares outstanding) versus its market price per share. Morningstar claims that the price-to-book ratio (market price per share/book value per share) is a measure of the difference between the value the stock market attaches to a firm and the value GAAP attaches to the firm.

Business Week, in its 2003 Global 1000 Scoreboard, tracked the price-to-book ratio for the top companies in the world. Selected ratios are as follows.

Company	Country	Reporting System	Price-to-book
Exxon Mobil	U.S.	U.S. GAAP	3.3
BP Amoco	Britain	U.S. GAAP	2.2
Pfizer	U.S.	U.S. GAAP	9.9
Johnson & Johnson	U.S.	U.S. GAAP	6.7
Vodafone	Britain	IFRS	0.7
Novartis	Switzerland	IFRS	3.1
NTT DOCOMO	Japan	U.S. GAAP	3.6

REQUIRED:

Discuss why book value and market value are not the same. What factors would increase or decrease the price-to-book ratio? How could the nature of the business or the health of the economy affect the ratio?

Movie rental company Netflix announced first quarter 2009 earnings of $32 million, on revenue growth of 21 percent. Earnings per share ($0.54) beat the consensus analyst forecast of $0.50. In reaction to the news, Netflix's stock price rose nearly 5 percent to $47.70 per share.

REQUIRED:

a. What is a consensus forecast?
b. Why are companies concerned about meeting or beating the consensus forecast?
c. What strategies can companies use to help meet or beat the forecasts, and why might those who analyze financial statements be concerned?

Eastman Kodak Company announced plans to cut its workforce by 21 percent over a three-year period and booked an expense of approximately $1.5 billion, citing its planned transition from its traditional film business to new digital imaging technology. The expense, referred to as a "restructuring charge," covers employee severance payments and disposals of buildings and equipment planned to occur over the next couple of years. Most of the costs are in the areas of the company tied to manufacturing and distributing film and paper for traditional cameras, the focal point of the business for its entire history.

REQUIRED:

a. Is it likely that analysts anticipated that Eastman Kodak would be making such a move? Could they have anticipated the exact amount of the costs to Eastman Kodak of the transition? How do you think the stock market reacted to the news of the $1.5 billion charge? Discuss.
b. Explain why Eastman Kodak might have booked the entire charge well in advance of incurring the actual costs. Could the company be practicing earnings management? If so, how might that work?
c. If you were analyzing Eastman Kodak by computing financial ratios, how would you treat the restructuring charge?
d. Name several other companies whose fortunes are tied to a technology that is vulnerable to obsolescence.

A retailer is posting strong earnings growth in its bricks-and-mortar business, but its fledgling Internet operation is posting losses. In making their earnings estimates, should Wall Street analysts ignore those losses and focus only on the profitable business, or should they look at

the company's retailing operations as a whole, which means lowering their profit forecasts to reflect the dot-com losses? That is the crux of the battle among a growing number of companies, and recently a behind-the-scenes conflict heated up because Staples, Inc. was able to persuade many analysts to submit estimates for the office supplier's first quarter, omitting losses from its Staples.com division. Most retailers, including Wal-Mart, lump their Internet results in with everything else. Staples's competitor, Office Depot, which is making money on its Internet business, rolls the Internet side into its overall results. Toys "R" Us and Blockbuster also include losses from their Internet operations in their overall results.

REQUIRED:

Explain why Staples might want to separate the losses from its new start-up operation, and provide some reasons that company management may offer to justify the action. Do you think the losses should be reported, separated, included with the overall results, or ignored?

REAL DATA

ID5–7

Characteristics of a good investmen

Fortune ran an article on Bob Olstein, an investment analyst who was particularly bullish at the time on several well-known stocks. He said the following indicators were the keys to his success: (1) a recent dramatic drop in the stock price, (2) company reports of positive free cash flow (net cash from operations minus capital expenditures), (3) conservative accounting methods, (4) a buildup in raw materials and partially completed inventory compared to finished inventory, (5) an increase in discretionary expenditures such as research and development, (6) undervalued assets on the balance sheet, (7) little or no debt combined with a high return on assets, and (8) consistency between what the president's letter said and what had actually happened over the past few years.

REQUIRED:

Explain how each of the eight items could provide a positive sign about a company.

REAL DATA

ID5–8

Financial accounting information in an efficient market

In an article published in the *Journal of Accountancy,* James Deitrick and Walter Harrison noted that the major markets for common stocks (e.g., the New York Stock Exchange, the American Stock Exchange) have been found to be efficient. That is, "common stock prices behave as if they fully incorporate all existing information quickly and without bias. This implies that information, old and new, has been impounded into security prices as a result of the analysis and collective wisdom of investors and their advisors." This finding has encouraged many accountants to contend that the information contained in financial reports cannot be used to identify undervalued common stocks in an efficient market.

REQUIRED:

a. Provide the rationale for why the information contained in financial reports cannot be used to identify undervalued securities.

b. Explain how financial accounting information can be useful even though it may not be helpful in identifying undervalued securities that are traded in efficient markets.

REAL DATA

ID5–9

Company value, intangibles, and the new economy

Baruch Lev, a well-respected accounting professor at New York University's Stern School of Business, has commented about the lack of relevance in today's financial statements. He notes that the 500 largest companies in the United States have market-to-book ratios (the ratio between the market value of the company and its balance sheet value [total assets − total liabilities]) that, on average, are greater than six. What this means is that the balance sheet reflects only 10 to 15 percent of the value of these companies. He claims that intangibles are fast becoming substitutes for physical assets. *PR Newswire* reported: "The traditional standards of financial accounting—measuring a company's book value based solely on physical assets that appear on the balance sheet—is becoming obsolete."

REQUIRED:

What is Professor Lev referring to when he mentions intangibles? Explain the reasoning underlying his claim. Do you agree with him? Why or why not?

REAL DATA
ID5-10
Weak accounting

Billionaire investor Warren Buffett was once quoted in the *Financial Post* saying: "The reaction of weak management to weak operations is often weak accounting."

REQUIRED:

What does he mean? Provide some examples. What are the implications for financial statement users?

REAL DATA
ID5-11
Financial ratios,
earning power,
solvency, and
stock prices

An accounting professor at the University of California at Berkeley was once quoted in the *Wall Street Journal* as saying,

The most important items on the financial statements are trends in inventory, accounts receivable, and order backlogs. These are the strongest indicators and are more closely related to stock returns than reported earnings. In particular, investors should look at how companies' inventories of finished goods track their sales. If inventories are rising faster than sales, it's a bad signal. . . . For similar reasons, it pays to watch accounts receivable. . . . If these are rising faster than sales, not only can this signal trouble with sales but may show vulnerability to customer defaults.

REQUIRED:

a. Which of the financial ratios best captures the indicators suggested by the Berkeley professor?
b. Explain how these ratios provide information about solvency and earning power and why they might be more closely related to stock prices than earnings.

REAL DATA
ID5-12
Stock price
reactions to
earnings
announcements

The business press follows the movement of stock prices very closely, especially when companies post their earnings announcements. Interestingly, there is no set pattern for how stock prices react to earnings announcements. Sometimes companies report earnings increases and stock prices decrease, while sometimes companies report earnings decreases and stock prices increase.

REQUIRED:

Explain how this can occur.

REAL DATA
ID5-13
Initial public
offerings (IPOs)
yet to show profits

The June 4, 2007, edition of the *Wall Street Journal* reported that in 2007 many companies selling stock to the public for the first time—initial public offerings (IPOs)—are not yet profitable. According to a report issued by the research firm Sageworks, 46 percent of the companies that listed IPOs in early 2007 had shown nothing but losses, the highest percentage since the dot-com bubble in 1999 and 2000. The CEO of Sageworks was quoted as saying, "Traditionally, there have been some rules of thumb about when to go public, and one of them was that you should have profits." The research report was issued at the same time that the Dow Jones Industrial Average and the S&P 500 stock index hit their record highs.

REQUIRED:

a. Why did the research report compare the IPOs in 2007 to the era of Internet companies going public?
b. What are the risks to investors if a company has never shown profits?
c. What is the connection between the number of IPOs from unprofitable companies and the record levels of the stock market?
d. The article stated, "Investors now want more than pie-in-the-sky promises of future profits. They are looking at revenue and cash flow and want specific timetables for profitability before buying shares." Discuss this quote and its connections to the financial statements.

REAL DATA
ID5-14
Appendix 5A:
Analyzing the
financial statements
of Eli Lilly

The following pages contain the consolidated balance sheets and statements of income and cash flows taken from the 2008 annual report of Eli Lilly, a major pharmaceutical.

REQUIRED:

Analyze the statements by using the ROE model. Estimate whether Lilly created value for its shareholders and identify the company's primary value drivers.

CONSOLIDATED STATEMENTS OF OPERATIONS

Eli Lilly and Company and Subsidiaries
(Dollars in millions, except per-share data)

Year Ended December 31	2008	2007	2006
Net sales	$20,378.0	$18,633.5	$15,691.0
Cost of sales	4,382.8	4,248.8	3,546.5
Research and development	3,840.9	3,486.7	3,129.3
Marketing, selling, and administrative	6,626.4	6,095.1	4,889.8
Acquired in-process research and development (Note 3)	4,835.4	745.6	—
Asset impairments, restructuring, and other special charges (Note 5)	1,974.0	302.5	945.2
Other—net, expense (income)	26.1	(122.0)	(237.8)
	21,685.6	14,756.7	12,273.0
Income (loss) before income taxes	(1,307.6)	3,876.8	3,418.0
Income taxes (Note 12)	764.3	923.8	755.3
Net income (loss)	$(2,071.9)	$ 2,953.0	$ 2,662.7
Earnings (loss) per share—basic and diluted (Note 11)	$ (1.89)	$ 2.71	$ 2.45

See notes to consolidated financial statements.

Eli Lilly and Company and Subsidiaries
Consolidated Balance Sheets

December 31 (Dollars in millions)	2008	2007	2006
ASSETS			
Current Assets			
Cash and cash equivalents	$ 5,496.7	$ 3,220.5	$ 3,109.3
Short-term investments	429.4	1,610.7	781.7
Accounts receivable, net of allowances of $97.4 (2008) and $103.1 (2007)	2,778.8	2,673.9	2,298.6
Other receivables (Note 9)	498.5	1,030.9	395.8
Inventories	2,493.2	2,523.7	2,270.3
Deferred income taxes (Note 12)	382.1	642.8	519.5
Prepaid expenses	374.6	613.6	319.5
Total current assets	12,453.3	12,316.1	9,694.4
Other Assets			
Prepaid pension (Note 13)	—	1,670.5	1,091.5
Investments (Note 6)	1,544.6	577.1	1,001.9
Goodwill and other intangibles—net (Note 3)	4,054.1	2,455.4	130.0
Sundry (Note 9)	2,534.3	1,280.6	1,885.3
	8,133.0	5,983.6	4,108.7
Property and Equipment, net	8,626.3	8,575.1	8,152.3
	$29,212.6	$26,874.8	$21,955.4
LIABILITIES AND SHAREHOLDERS' EQUITY			
Current Liabilities			
Short-term borrowings and current maturities of long-term debt (Note 7)	$ 5,846.3	$ 413.7	$ 219.4
Accounts payable	885.8	924.4	789.4
Employee compensation	771.0	823.8	641.6

Sales rebates and discounts	873.4	706.8	508.3
Dividends payable	536.8	513.6	463.3
Income taxes payable (Note 12)	229.2	238.4	640.6
Other current liabilities (Note 9)	3,967.2	1,816.1	1,822.9
Total current liabilities	13,109.7	5,436.8	5,085.5
Other Liabilities			
Long-term debt (Note 7)	4,615.7	4,593.5	3,494.4
Accrued retirement benefit (Note 13)	2,387.6	1,145.1	1,586.9
Long-term income taxes payable (Note 12)	906.2	1,196.7	—
Deferred income taxes (Note 12)	74.7	287.5	62.2
Other noncurrent liabilities (Note 9)	1,383.4	711.3	745.7
	9,367.6	7,934.1	5,89.2
Commitments and contingencies (Note 14)			
Shareholders' Equity (Notes 8 and 10)			
Common stock—no par value			
Authorized shares: 3,200,000,000			
Issued shares: 1,136,948,610 (2008)			
and 1,135,212,894 (2007)	711.1	709.5	707.9
Additional paid-in capital	3,976.6	3,805.2	3,571.9
Retained earnings	7,654.9	11,806.7	10,926.7
Employee benefit trust	(2,635.0)	(2,635.0)	(2,635.0)
Deferred costs—ESOP	(86.3)	(95.2)	(100.7)
Accumulated other comprehensive income (loss) (Note 15)	(2,786.8)	13.2	(1,388.7)
	6,834.5	13,604.4	11,082.1
Less cost of common stock in treasury			
2008—888,998 shares	99.2	100.5	101.4
2007—899,445 shares	6,735.3	13,503.9	10,980.7
	$29,212.6	$26,874.8	$21,955.4

See notes to consolidated financial statements.

Eli Lilly and Company and Subsidiaries
Consolidated Statements of Cash Flows

Year Ended December 31 (Dollars in millions)	2008	2007	2006
Cash Flows from Operating Activities			
Net income (loss)	$(2,071.9)	$ 2,953.0	$2,662.7
Adjustments to Reconcile Net Income to Cash Flows from Operating Activities			
Depreciation and amortization	1,122.6	1,047.9	801.8
Change in deferred taxes	442.6	60.7	346.8
Stock-based compensation expense	255.3	282.0	359.3
Acquired in-process research and development, net of tax	4,792.7	692.6	—
Other, net	406.5	172.1	600.6
	4,947.8	5,208.3	4,771.2
Changes in operating assets and liabilities, net of acquisitions			
Receivables—(increase) decrease	799.1	(842.7)	243.9
Inventories—(increase) decrease	84.8	154.3	(60.2)
Other assets—(increase) decrease	1,648.6	(355.8)	(43.0)

Accounts payable and other liabilities—increase (decrease)	(184.7)	990.4	(936.0)
	2,347.8	(53.8)	(795.3)
Net Cash Provided by Operating Activities	7,295.6	5,154.5	3,975.9
Cash Flows from Investing Activities			
Purchases of property and equipment	(947.2)	(1,082.4)	(1,077.8)
Disposals of property and equipment	25.7	32.3	65.2
Net change in short-term investments	957.6	(376.9)	1,247.5
Proceeds from sales and maturities of noncurrent investments	1,597.3	800.1	1,507.7
Purchases of noncurrent investments	(2,412.4)	(750.7)	(1,313.2)
Purchases of in-process research and development	(122.0)	(111.0)	—
Cash paid for acquisitions, net of cash acquired	(6,083.0)	(2,673.2)	—
Other, net	(284.8)	(166.3)	179.0
Net Cash Provided by (Used for) Investing Activities	(7,268.8)	(4,328.1)	(608.4)
Cash Flows from Financing Activities			
Dividends paid	(2,056.7)	(1,853.6)	(1,736.3)
Net change in short-term borrowings	5,060.5	(468.5)	(8.4)
Proceeds from issuance of long-term debt	0.1	2,512.6	—
Repayments of long-term debt	(649.8)	(1,059.5)	(2,781.5)
Purchases of common stock	—	—	(122.1)
Issuances of common stock under stock plans	—	24.7	59.6
Other, net	(8.1)	(0.6)	9.9
Net Cash Provided by (Used for) Financing Activities	2,346.0	(844.9)	(4,578.8)
Effect of exchange rate changes on cash and cash equivalents	(96.6)	129.7	97.1
Net increase in cash and cash equivalents	2,276.2	111.2	102.6
Cash and cash equivalents at beginning of year	3,220.5	3,109.3	3,006.7
Cash and Cash Equivalents at End of Year	$ 5,496.7	$ 3,220.5	$3,109.3

See notes to consolidated financial statements.

Eli Lilly and Company and Subsidiaries
Consolidated Statements of Comprehensive Income (Loss)

Year Ended December 31 (Dollars in millions)	2008	2007	2006
Net income (loss)	$(2,071.9)	$2,953.0	$2,662.7
Other comprehensive income (loss)			
Foreign currency translation gains (losses)	(766.1)	756.6	542.4
Net unrealized losses on securities	(190.6)	(11.4)	(3.2)
Minimum pension liability adjustment (Note 13)	—	—	(18.8)
Defined benefit pension and retiree health benefit plans (Note 13)	(2,941.2)	943.8	—
Effective portion of cash flow hedges	23.2	(0.1)	143.3
Other comprehensive income (loss) before income taxes	(3,874.7)	1,688.9	663.7
Provision for income taxes related to other comprehensive income (loss) items	1,074.7	(287.0)	(43.1)
Other comprehensive income (loss) (Note 15)	(2,800.0)	1,401.9	620.6
Comprehensive income (loss)	$(4,871.9)	$4,354.9	$3,283.3

See notes to consolidated financial statements.

REAL DATA

ID5-15

Appendix 5A:
Projecting financial
statements

Review the Eli Lilly financial statements contained in ID5-14 and, based on the following assumptions, prepare a simplified 2009 income statement and balance sheet.

- Sales growth in 2009 is at the same rate as in 2008.
- Expense to sales ratio is 85 percent.
- Total assets to sales ratio remains at the same level as at the end of 2008.
- Total liabilities to total assets ratio remains at the same level as at the end of 2008.

REAL DATA

ID5-16

Appendix 5A:
Cash flow profiles and
company life cycles

Cash flow profiles over a three-year period are provided here for three well-known companies: Echostar Communications, Wal-Mart, and US Airways. Link each profile to one of the firms, explain what it means in terms of the company's cash management strategy, and describe how this analysis might reveal the company's age, maturity, and success.

	1	2	3
PROFILE 1			
Net cash flow from operations	+	+	+
Net cash flow from investing activities	−	−	−
Net cash flow from financing activities	+	+	+
PROFILE 2			
Net cash flow from operations	−	−	−
Net cash flow from investing activities	−	+	−
Net cash flow from financing activities	+	+	+
PROFILE 3			
Net cash flow from operations	+	+	+
Net cash flow from investing activities	−	−	−
Net cash flow from financing activities	−	−	−

REAL DATA

ID5-17

The SEC Form
10-K of NIKE

The NIKE 10-K Form is reproduced in Appendix C.

REQUIRED:
a. Review the NIKE SEC Form 10-K and analyze the financial statements by assessing NIKE's earning power and solvency, and provide support for your assessments. Start by using the ratio framework illustrated in Figure 5–3.
b. Find the operating segment information disclosed by NIKE. Which of NIKE's segments generates the most revenues, and what percent is it of the total? Which of the segments has the highest profit margin, and which segment has the fastest long-lived asset turnover?
c. (Appendix 5A) Use the ROE model to analyze the financial statements. Comment on whether NIKE created shareholder value and identify the primary value drivers.
d. (Appendix 5A) Based on the financial statements, make reasonable assumptions about NIKE's sales growth, expense/sales ratio, sales/total assets ratio, and liabilities to total asset ratio for 2010, and prepare a simplified income statement and balance sheet for NIKE for 2010.

Assets: A Closer Look

In a conference call with analysts, executives of Xerox Corporation discussed fourth quarter 2009 results, noting that earnings beat earlier estimates despite concerns about revenue levels. The company's CFO proudly reported, "Given the 2009 environment, we challenged our management teams around the world to manage cash as the number one priority. They did, and delivered cash from operations of almost $1 billion in the fourth quarter and $2.2 billion for the year versus a forecast of $1.7 billion. Achievements were where we wanted them to be, profit and working capital. Fourth quarter working capital improvements were $489 million and $758 million for the year. In addition, we managed CapEx [capital expenditures] to only $193 million for the year."

The key to success for Xerox and many other companies is their ability to efficiently manage assets—that is, have relatively low investments in receivables, inventories, and long-lived assets that produce large returns for the shareholders. Well-run companies get a lot of "bang for their buck." Part 3 of this textbook is devoted to managing and accounting for these assets.

The Current Asset Classification, Cash, and Accounts Receivable

KEY POINTS

The following key points are emphasized in this chapter:

- Current assets, working capital, current ratio, and quick ratio, and how these measures are used to assess the solvency position of a company.

- "Window dressing" and the reporting of current assets, working capital, and the current ratio.

- Techniques used to account for and control cash.

- Accounts receivable and how they are valued on the balance sheet.

- The allowance method for uncollectible receivables.

- Major concerns of financial statement users in the area of receivables reporting.

The world revolves around credit. Companies sell goods and services on account, while banks allow homeowners to borrow a substantial portion of the purchase price of a house. These loans, or "receivables," appear on the balance sheet as assets, but nobody knows for sure when or if they will become cash. In 2008 and 2009, the excesses of home loans extended to "subprime" borrowers caused the downfall of many household names in the world of finance. Merrill Lynch and Countrywide Mortgage were purchased at distressed prices by Bank of America with the help of the U.S. government. Investment bank Bear Sterns was purchased "on the cheap" (according to *Business-Week*) by JPMorgan Chase; and the 158-year-old investment bank Lehman Brothers went out of business. These well-known and previously dominant firms all invested in securities backed by mortgage loan receivables from borrowers with poor credit histories. When housing prices dropped and economic forces pushed borrowers beyond their ability to make their monthly payments, the mortgage receivables became worthless, causing massive losses for investors. Investment firms that were not able to cover their dwindling assets ceased to exist and, for a time, threatened the viability of the financial markets and those who depend on available credit to run their businesses. Deciding when and to whom to extend credit, and then managing those receivables, are indeed important considerations for managers in today's business world.

This chapter is divided into four sections. Section 1 covers the current asset classification and the measures of solvency and liquidity that use current assets. The dollar amounts in the cash and accounts receivable accounts make up an important part of current assets and are therefore important components of these measures. Sections 2 and 3 consider the definitions, disclosure rules, and methods of accounting for cash and accounts receivable. The chapter concludes with managing receivables expressed in foreign currencies, and a discussion of the link between receivables management and return on equity.

THE CURRENT ASSET CLASSIFICATION

Current assets are so named because they are intended to be converted to cash (or consumed) in the near future. The exact definition of the near future is subjective, so the accounting profession has provided guidelines. According to professional standards, a **current asset** is defined as any asset that is intended to be converted into cash within one year or the company's **operating cycle,** whichever is longer.[1] As illustrated in Figure 6–1, a company's operating cycle is the time it takes the company to convert its cash to inventory (to purchase or manufacture inventory), sell the inventory, and collect cash from the sale. In other words, the operating cycle is the time required for a company to go through all the required phases of the production and sales process.

FIGURE 6–1
The operating cycle

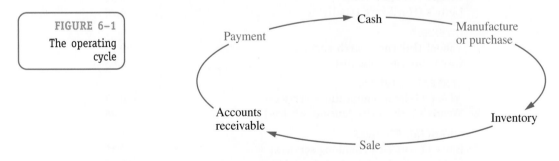

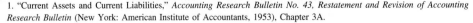

1. "Current Assets and Current Liabilities," *Accounting Research Bulletin No. 43, Restatement and Revision of Accounting Research Bulletin* (New York: American Institute of Accountants, 1953), Chapter 3A.

As the definition of current assets states, if the operating cycle is longer than one year, it serves as the time period for current assets. Companies with different operating cycles therefore use different time periods to define current assets. Compare, for example, the relatively short operating cycles of grocery chains like Safeway, Kroger, and Lucky Stores to the operating cycles of companies in the aerospace industry like The Boeing Company and Airbus, which require several years to manufacture aircraft. Indeed, the time periods for the current asset classification differ widely from company to company. However, the accounts included in the current asset section on the balance sheets of all companies are virtually the same. They are *cash, short-term investments, short-term accounts and notes receivable, inventories,* and *prepaid expenses.* The individual accounts that comprise the current asset classification were briefly discussed and illustrated in Chapter 2.

> **?** Discuss the differences in the operations and the operating cycles of Tommy Hilfiger, a clothing manufacturer; Toyota, an automobile manufacturer; Young & Rubicam, an advertising agency; and Yahoo!, an Internet portal.

The Relative Size of Current Assets across Industries

The relative size of current assets differs significantly across companies in different industries. Figure 6–2, which includes current assets as a percentage of total assets for selected well-known companies from various industries, shows that investment bank Goldman Sachs has a ratio of over 90 percent. In contrast, general services (AT&T and Wendy's) and manufacturing (GE and Chevron) are in the 10–30 percent range. The primary assets of financial services are short-term notes receivable and investments; the primary assets in the manufacturing and general services sectors tend to be property, plant, and equipment. Retailers, such as Kroger and Lowe's, carry relatively large

FIGURE 6–2 Current assets as a percentage of total assets	Current Assets/Total Assets
MANUFACTURING:	
General Electric (Manufacturer)	0.16
Chevron Texaco (Oil drilling and refining)	0.23
RETAIL:	
Kroger (Grocery retail)	0.31
Lowe's (Hardware retail)	0.28
INTERNET:	
Yahoo! (Internet search engine)	0.26
Cisco (Internet systems)	0.65
GENERAL SERVICES:	
AT&T (Telecommunications services)	0.09
Wendy's/Arby's (Restaurant services)	0.08
FINANCIAL SERVICES:	
Bank of America (Banking services)	0.31
Goldman Sachs (Investment services)	0.97

amounts of inventory, and many of the Internet firms (Yahoo! and Cisco) have large cash and short-term investment balances.

Measures Using Current Assets: Working Capital, Current Ratio, and Quick Ratio

The distinction between current and noncurrent assets is useful because it provides an easy-to-determine, low-cost measure of a company's ability to produce cash in the short run. Current assets are often compared to current liabilities (the liabilities expected to require cash payments within the same time period as current assets) as an indicator of a company's solvency position.[2] Reasoning that current liabilities are a measure of short-run cash outflows, we find that these comparisons appear to be logical. Three such comparisons, which were discussed in Chapter 5, are working capital and two solvency ratios, the current ratio and the quick ratio. **Working capital** is defined as current assets less current liabilities; the **current ratio** is equal to current assets divided by current liabilities; and the **quick ratio** divides the sum of cash plus short-term investments plus short-term receivables by current liabilities.

> Under IFRS the definition of current and the definition and use of working capital is the same as under U.S. GAAP. Many non-U.S. firms, however, include current assets at the bottom of assets on the balance sheet, and match them there against current liabilities.

Selected current ratio balances are presented in Figure 6–3. The variances are quite large—some well above 1.0 and others below 1.0. Internet companies, like Yahoo! and

FIGURE 6–3
Current assets as a percentage of current liabilities

	Current Assets/Current Liabilities
MANUFACTURING:	
General Electric (Manufacturer)	0.50
Chevron (Oil drilling and refining)	1.14
RETAIL:	
Kroger (Grocery retail)	0.94
Lowe's (Hardware retail)	1.15
INTERNET:	
Yahoo! (Internet search engine)	1.41
Cisco (Internet systems)	3.24
GENERAL SERVICES:	
AT&T (Telecommunications services)	0.53
Wendy's/Arby's (Restaurant services)	0.76
FINANCIAL SERVICES:	
Bank of America (Banking services)	0.42
Goldman Sachs (Investment services)	1.31

2. Current liabilities were introduced and listed in Chapter 2 and are discussed extensively in Chapter 10.

Cisco, tend to carry large amounts of cash and short-term investments and rely very little on short-term debt financing. Lowe's current ratio is driven by hefty cash and short-term investment balances, a large inventory of hardware goods, and a low level of accounts payable. Large companies in the high-tech telecommunications industry (AT&T) invest heavily in property, plant, and equipment, financing these investments with both short- and long-term debt. Such companies can afford to carry low current ratios because their operations can generate cash flows sufficient to meet their short-term debt payments. Also, they carry little in the way of inventories or receivables.

Approximately three-quarters of RadioShack's total assets are considered current, while the same ratio for shopping mall owner Simon Property Group is only about 5 percent. Why?

The Economic Consequences of Working Capital, the Current Ratio, and the Quick Ratio

Managers must understand how transactions affect working capital, the current ratio, and the quick ratio because investors, bankers, and other lenders (e.g., bondholders) often use these measures to help assess a company's ability to meet current obligations as they come due. For example, Dun & Bradstreet, a widely used service that rates the creditworthiness of a large number of U.S. businesses, includes both the current ratio and the quick ratio as solvency measures in its list of fourteen key business ratios. Another of these key ratios, sales/working capital, is described as indicating whether a company has enough (or too many) current assets to support its sales volume. The formula used by Dun & Bradstreet to determine a company's credit rating, which in turn relates to the company's ability to borrow funds and the terms of its outstanding loans, includes these fourteen ratios.[3]

The measures of working capital and the current ratio also appear in loan contracts and debt covenants, where they specify certain minimum dollar amounts or ratios that a debtor company must maintain. For example, a recent financial report of Cummins Engine Company, a manufacturer of heavy-duty truck engines, indicated that loan agreements entered into by the company require maintenance of a 1.25 current ratio. This means that Cummins must maintain a current ratio of 1.25, or the creditor has the right to call for the immediate payment of the entire loan principal. Similarly, The Limited, which specializes in high-end clothing, has revolving credit agreements with a number of banks specifying that the company must maintain a certain level of working capital.

Working capital, the current ratio, and the quick ratio are also used by auditors. For example, an AICPA list of "red flags" alerting auditors to possible management fraud includes "inadequate working capital." The AICPA reasons that low amounts of working capital may put pressure on management to fraudulently manipulate the financial records in an effort to deceive shareholders, creditors, investors, and others. In addition, examining a company's working capital and current ratio can help an auditor assess whether there is substantial doubt about a company's ability to continue operations in the future. Information that helps to predict business failures is valuable to auditors because such failures lead to investor and creditor losses, which in turn can lead to costly lawsuits against auditors.

3. Many of the fourteen ratios were discussed in Chapter 5, but Dun & Bradstreet uses others as well.

Limitations of the Current Asset Classification

While working capital, the current ratio, and the quick ratio are used extensively in business to assess solvency, they have a number of inherent and significant weaknesses. These limitations are related to the fundamental fact that current assets and current liabilities fail to accurately reflect future cash inflows and outflows, the essence of a company's ability to meet its debts as they come due. As noted by Leopold A. Bernstein,

The current ratio is not fully up to the task [of assessing short-term liquidity] because it is a static or "stock" concept of what resources are available at a given moment to meet the obligations at that moment. Moreover, working capital . . . does not have a logical or causative relationship to the future funds which flow through it. The future flows are, of course, the focus of our greatest interest in the assessment of short-term liquidity. And yet, these flows depend importantly on elements not included in the current ratio, such as sales, profits, and changes in business conditions.[4]

In addition, management has incentives to choose accounting methods and make operating decisions for no reason other than to "cosmetically" inflate the balances in the current asset accounts. For example, Datapoint, a computer manufacturer, once was charged by the SEC with materially overstating its receivables and revenues. The company was apparently shipping computers without customer authorization and thereby recording sales and receivables prematurely. In three successive years General Electric made accounting changes, all of which affected working capital and reduced earnings in total by approximately $2 billion. Such actions can have a significant impact on solvency ratios, which in turn may affect the company's credit rating as well as determine whether a company is in violation of a loan contract or debt covenant.

From these examples, it is clear that managers have discretion over the accounts in the current asset section of the balance sheet and thus have some control over measures like working capital, the current ratio, and the quick ratio. Exercising such discretion to inflate these measures is often called **window dressing** and includes choosing accounting methods or making operating decisions designed solely to make the financial statements appear more attractive. Keep in mind, however, that while the practice of window dressing is widespread, it may not serve management's long-term interest. Managers who attempt to deceive by manipulating the dollar amounts on the financial statements risk reducing the credibility of the statements, which may actually hinder their ability to raise debt and equity capital.

In a speech to the New York Center for Law and Business, Arthur Levitt, past chair of the SEC, commented that "earnings were like a bottle of fine wine; you wouldn't pop the cork before it was ready . . . but some companies are doing this with their revenue . . . recognizing it before a sale is complete." Explain how recognizing revenue before a sale is complete could be considered window dressing working capital.

A MOVEMENT TOWARD CASH FLOW ACCOUNTING

In view of these limitations, measures like working capital, the current ratio, and the quick ratio are rarely viewed as the only ways to assess solvency. Cash flow numbers have gained popularity as indicators of a company's ability to meet its debts as they come

4. Leopold A. Bernstein, "Working Capital as a Tool," *Journal of Accountancy* (December 1981), pp. 82, 84, 86.

due. The statement of cash flows, for example, which discloses the net cash flows from operating, investing, and financing activities, is also being used by investors and creditors to assess solvency. For example, Loyd C. Heath, an emeritus accounting professor at the University of Washington, states that "the emphasis in credit analysis has shifted from analysis of working capital position to dynamic analysis of future cash receipts and payments." A survey of investors published in *Management Accounting* notes that "investors use the statement of cash flows more, and the income statement less, than previously."

Nonetheless, solvency and liquidity measures based on the current asset classification are still important and widely used. Working capital, the current ratio, and the quick ratio are low-cost surrogates for cash flow measures and are still used extensively by investors and creditors and in loan contracts and debt covenants. It is important, therefore, that you as a manager understand how transactions affect these measures and how these measures can be used to assess solvency and earning power. As we move now into discussions of each individual current asset, keep in mind that the accounting methods and operating decisions that affect these assets also affect working capital, the current ratio, and the quick ratio.

> **?** The Wendy's/Arby's Group carries a current ratio that is approximately 75 percent, with relatively little investments in cash, receivables, inventories, and prepaid expenses. Explain why Wendy's/Arby's is not in danger of going bankrupt even though its current liabilities far exceed its current assets.

CASH

The cash account is the first asset listed in the current asset section of the balance sheet. It consists of coin, currency, and checking accounts, as well as money orders, certified checks, cashier's checks, personal checks, and bank drafts received by a company. Remember also that cash is the standard medium of exchange and thus provides the basis for measuring all financial statement accounts.

Companies use a number of different titles to describe the cash account on their balance sheets. *Accounting Trends and Techniques* (2009) provided the summary contained in Figure 6–4 of the balance sheet captions of 600 of the largest companies in the United States. Note that the title *Cash* is decreasing in popularity, while *Cash and Equivalents* is becoming much more common.

FIGURE 6–4
Cash: Balance sheet captions

	2009	2008	2007	2006
Cash	22	29	36	35
Cash and cash equivalents	528	515	505	501
Cash and equivalents	34	37	34	32
Cash, including certificates of deposit or time deposits	2	2	1	2
Cash and marketable securities	13	14	21	25
No amount for cash	1	3	3	5
Total companies	600	600	600	600

Source: *Accounting Trends and Techniques* (2009).

The relative size of the cash account on the balance sheet varies across companies in different industries. Figure 6–5 reports that Yahoo!, Wendy's/Arby's, and Cisco carry relatively large amounts of cash. Yahoo! may be holding cash intended for acquisitions, while Cisco built up a cash reserve as protection during the recession Wendy's/Arby's has to keep its cash registers full.

FIGURE 6–5 Cash as a percentage of total assets and current assets	Cash/Total Assets	Cash/Current Assets
MANUFACTURING:		
General Electric (Manufacturer)	**0.06**	**0.39**
Chevron (Oil drilling and refining)	**0.06**	**0.26**
RETAIL:		
Kroger (Grocery retail)	**0.04**	**0.12**
Lowe's (Hardware retail)	**0.01**	**0.03**
INTERNET:		
Yahoo! (Internet search engine)	**0.12**	**0.47**
Cisco (Internet systems)	**0.08**	**0.13**
GENERAL SERVICES:		
AT&T (Telecommunications services)	**0.01**	**0.08**
Wendy's/Arby's (Restaurant services)	**0.02**	**0.24**
FINANCIAL SERVICES:		
Bank of America (Banking services)	**0.02**	**0.06**
Goldman Sachs (Investment services)	**0.02**	**0.02**

Three issues concerning cash are particularly important to managers: (1) restrictions on the use of cash, (2) proper management of cash, and (3) control of cash.

Restrictions on the Use of Cash

In general, cash presents few problems from a reporting standpoint. There are no valuation problems because cash always appears on the balance sheet at face value. The only reporting issue is whether there are restrictions on its use.

Restrictions placed on a company's access to its cash are typically imposed by creditors to help ensure future interest and principal payments. As part of a loan agreement, for example, a creditor may require that a certain amount of cash be held in **escrow,** that is, controlled by a trustee until the debtor's existing liability is discharged. In addition, banks sometimes require that minimum cash balances be maintained on deposit in the accounts of customers to whom they lend money or extend credit. These amounts are called **compensating balances.**

Cash held in escrow and compensating balances are examples of cash amounts that a company may own but cannot immediately use. Such restricted cash should be separated from the general cash account on the balance sheet, and the restrictions should be clearly described either on the balance sheet itself or in the footnotes to the financial statements. If the restricted cash is to be used for payment of obligations maturing within the time period of current assets, the separate "restricted cash" account is appropriately classified as a current asset. If it is to be held for a longer period of time, it should be classified as noncurrent.

Owens Corning, for example, once noted in its financial report that $85 million, almost 96 percent of its $89 million cash balance, was restricted. Approximately $70 million was held in escrow, to be used in the following year for the payment of a long-term debt, and $15 million was temporarily "locked" in a Brazilian bank. That same year, Atlantic Richfield Company's financial report noted that "the company maintains compensating balances for some of its various banking services and products." Both Owens Corning and Atlantic Richfield included the restricted funds among their current assets. Manville Corporation, in its financial report, indicated that $278 million was placed in escrow in connection with bankruptcy proceedings. These funds were not included as current assets.

> **?** On its 2009 balance sheet, La-Z-Boy reported $17.3 million in "cash and equivalents" and $18.7 million in "restricted cash." Would you include both amounts in the calculation of working capital? Why or why not?

Proper Management of Cash

Proper cash management requires that enough cash be available to meet the needs of a company's operations, yet too much is undesirable because idle cash provides no return and loses purchasing power during periods of inflation. Maintaining a proper balance is one of management's greatest challenges. Enough cash must be available so that a company can meet its cash obligations as they come due. Purchases are often made in cash, and payments on accounts payable require cash. Wages, salaries, and currently maturing long-term debts must be honored in cash. Normally the cash needed for such operating activities is kept on the premises in the form of **petty cash** (small amounts of cash to cover day-to-day needs) or deposited in an interest-bearing checking account, where it earns a moderate rate of interest and can be withdrawn immediately as cash needs arise.

Cash in and of itself, however, is not a productive asset. Consider, for example, a popular TV game show that left $1 million under a plastic dome sitting out on the stage. The amount of annual interest income that was forgone by leaving that amount of cash idle, assuming a 10 percent interest rate, was $100,000 ($1,000,000 × 10%). Furthermore, during inflationary times, cash continually loses purchasing power. Assuming a 5 percent annual rate of inflation, it would require $1.05 million at the end of a year to buy the same goods and services that could have been purchased with $1 million at the beginning of the year. Consequently, cash over and above the amount needed for operations should be returned to shareholders as dividends or invested in income-producing assets such as short-term investments, inventories, long-term investments, property, plant, and equipment, and intangible assets.

A company that maintains a cash balance of more than is necessary for its day-to-day needs is not operating at its full potential. It is, of course, a desirable practice to keep a little extra in the checking account to meet unforeseen cash requirements, but in general, cash in excess of the amount necessary to cover day-to-day cash obligations should be invested in assets that produce a higher return. Determining this amount and where to invest the excess is a very important concern of a company's managers. Andrew Long, head of global payments and cash management for Asia Pacific, once noted, "If you are a treasurer of a company, one of the key concerns is managing cash."

In the same article in *Business Times*, Andrew Long notes that "cash management can cover a whole range of things." What does he mean?

Control of Cash

The control of cash is an important responsibility of a company's accounting system. It is a special concern for businesses such as grocery stores, movie theaters, restaurants, financial institutions, retail stores, department stores, and bars, which process frequent cash transactions. Two aspects of the control of cash are record control and physical control.

RECORD CONTROL OF CASH

Record control refers to the procedures designed to ensure that the cash account on the balance sheet reflects the actual amount of cash in the company's possession. Problems of record control arise when many different kinds of transactions involve cash, and it is difficult to record them all accurately. Proper control of cash records requires that all cash receipts and disbursements be faithfully recorded and posted. Periodically, the dollar amount of cash indicated in the cash account in the ledger should be checked against and reconciled with the cash balance indicated on the statement provided by a company's bank.

PHYSICAL CONTROL OF CASH

Physical control of cash refers to the procedures designed to safeguard cash from loss or theft. Problems of physical control arise because cash is the standard medium of exchange; it is universally desired and easily concealed and transported. Cash embezzlement by a company's employees is always a threat. Separation of duties is an important part of a well-controlled system. It requires that employees responsible for recording cash transactions should not also be responsible for the physical control of the cash.

Proper physical control of cash may require that a minimum amount of cash be kept on a company's premises at any one time. Petty cash amounts used to cover day-to-day office expenses and cash receipts from sales or receivable payments should be handled by as few employees as possible and stored in a safe or locked cash drawer. Cash amounts in excess of petty cash requirements should be taken to the bank at frequent intervals.

Sarah Hogg, chairperson of Frontier Economics, a leading European consulting firm, commented that "ignoring cash control is accountants' Achilles' heel." Explain what she means.

ACCOUNTS RECEIVABLE

Accounts receivable arise from selling goods or services to customers who do not immediately pay cash. Often backed by oral rather than written commitments, accounts receivable represent short-term extensions of credit that are normally collectible within thirty to sixty days. These credit trade agreements are often referred to as **open accounts.** Often many such transactions are enacted between a company and its

customers, and it is impractical to create a formal contract for each one. Open accounts typically reflect running balances, because at the same time customers are paying off previous purchases, new purchases are being made. If an account receivable is paid in full within the specified thirty- or sixty-day period, no interest is charged. Payment after this period, however, is usually subject to a significant financial charge. Credit card arrangements with department stores, like Macy's and JCPenney, and oil companies, like Exxon Mobil and Chevron, are common examples of open accounts.

The following journal entries illustrate the recognition of accounts receivable from (1) the sale of merchandise[5] and (2) the sale of a service.

Accounts Receivable (+A)	**500**	
Sales (R, +RE)		**500**

Sold two items of inventory for $250 each on account

Accounts Receivable (+A)	**150**	
Fees Earned (or Service Revenue) (R, +RE)		**150**

Provided consulting services for $150 on account

Note that the recognition of the account receivable in each case is accompanied by the recognition of a revenue: sales or fees earned (service revenue). Both the balance sheet and the income statement are therefore affected when accounts receivable are established. Note also that the recognition of an account receivable is an application of the accrual system of accounting. Recall from Chapter 3 that revenues are recognized when the four criteria of revenue recognition are met.[6] Accounts receivable, therefore, are established in those cases where these four criteria are met prior to cash collection.

Under IFRS, revenue recognition is based mainly on a single standard that contains general principles applied to different types of transactions. Under U.S. GAAP, the general principles are similar, but there is also extensive guidance for individual industries and different types of contracts.

As the following journal entry illustrates, when cash is ultimately received, the accounts receivable balance is removed from the balance sheet and no revenue is recognized.

Cash (+A)	**500**	
Accounts Receivable (−A)		**500**

Collected cash on account

The accounts receivable account therefore appears on the balance sheet during the time period between the recognition of a revenue and the receipt of the related cash payment.

In a well-known financial fraud, Cendant Corp. was found to have booked fictitious revenues. The fraud was discovered when an analyst noted that the accounts receivable balance was growing much faster than sales from one year to the next. Explain how one could be alerted to a possible fraud by comparing the growth of accounts receivable to the growth of sales.

---

5. The sale of merchandise also involves the outflow of inventory which must be recognized before financial statements are prepared.

6. The four criteria of revenue recognition are: (1) The earning process is substantially complete, (2) revenue is objectively measurable, (3) post-sale costs can be estimated, and (4) cash collection is reasonably assured.

Importance of Accounts Receivable

In our heavily credit-oriented economy, transactions that give rise to accounts receivable make up a significant portion of total business transactions. Figure 6–6 discloses the importance of accounts receivable to our selected group of well-known companies. Note first the sizable investment in receivables made by the financial institutions. Most of these receivables are loans made to customers and clients. Similarly, General Electric owns a financial subsidiary that is used to provide financing to customers who purchase big-ticket items, such as home appliances. The subsidiary also extends loans to large borrowers, much the same as Bank of America. These receivables make up half of the company's total assets. Many companies are moving away from extending credit to their customers. Lowe's, for example, does not issue its own credit cards, relying instead on cash sales, personal checks, and major credit cards such as VISA and MasterCard.[7] Some major retailers, like Nordstrom, issue their own credit cards and consequently carry large balances of accounts receivable.

In August 2009 the *Wall Street Journal* reported the results of a survey that considered the cash flow timing of large and small companies. The report found that, as the 2008–2009 recession wreaked its havoc, large companies with revenues of $5 billion or more sped up the collection of accounts receivable and slowed payment of accounts payable. On the other hand, smaller companies, with revenues of less than $500 million, took an extra 4.5 days to collect receivables and actually paid trade obligations two days faster during the recession. Discuss the advantages to companies of accelerating collections from customers and delaying payments to suppliers, and explain why larger companies may have an upper hand in this form of working capital management.

FIGURE 6–6 Receivables as a percentage of total assets and current assets		Receivables/ Total Assets	Receivables/ Current Assets
MANUFACTURING:			
General Electric (Manufacturer)		0.50*	3.21*
Chevron (Oil drilling and refining)		0.10	0.43
RETAIL:			
Kroger (Grocery retail)		0.04	0.13
Lowe's (Hardware retail)		NA	NA
INTERNET:			
Yahoo! (Internet search engine)		0.09	0.33
Cisco (Internet systems)		0.05	0.07
GENERAL SERVICES:			
AT&T (Telecommunications services)		0.06	0.71
Wendy's/Arby's (Restaurant services)		0.02	0.24
FINANCIAL SERVICES:			
Bank of America (Banking services)		0.50*	0.61*
Goldman Sachs (Investment services)		0.10	0.11*

Includes notes receivable.

7. When a customer uses a bank card to pay for an item or service (e.g., VISA or MasterCard), the selling company does not carry the receivable on its balance sheet. The receivable is "sold" to the finance company that issued the card. Such an arrangement is called *factoring*.

In which of these three companies do you think accounts receivable management and control are most important and why—General Electric (major manufacturing), Wal-Mart (discount retail), or Walgreens (pharmacies)?

Net Realizable Value: The Valuation Base for Accounts Receivable

The key factor in valuing accounts receivable on the financial statements is the amount of cash that the receivables are expected to generate. The cash is expected to be received in the future; in theory, therefore, present value should be used as the valuation base. The expected future cash receipt should theoretically be discounted. However, as indicated earlier, the period of time from the initial recognition of an account receivable to cash collection is normally quite short (thirty to sixty days). Consequently, the difference between the amount of cash to be received and the present value of the expected cash flows from the receivable is considered immaterial. For example, the difference between $100 and the present value of $100 to be received in one month, given a 10 percent annual interest rate, is approximately $0.76. Therefore, the face value of the receivable, the amount of cash to be collected, is judged to be a reasonable approximation of present value and, accordingly, provides the starting point for balance sheet valuation.

While the face value of the receivable represents a starting point, there are a number of reasons why it may not represent the actual amount of cash ultimately collected. Many companies, for example, offer cash discounts, allowing customers to pay lesser amounts if they pay within specified time periods. Other accounts receivable may produce no cash at all because customers simply refuse to, or cannot, pay (bad debts) or choose to return previously sold merchandise (sales returns). Each of these issues must be considered when placing a value on the accounts receivable account on the balance sheet.

Accordingly, the valuation base for the accounts receivable account is not the face amount of the receivables but rather the **net realizable value,** an estimate of the cash that is expected to be produced by the receivables.

Net Realizable Value of Accounts Receivable = Face Value − Adjustments for (1) Cash Discounts, (2) Bad Debts, and (3) Sales Returns

As of the end of fiscal 2009, Apple, Inc. had outstanding accounts receivables in the amount of $3.41 billion but only reported $3.36 billion on its balance sheet. Why?

Cash Discounts

When a good or service is sold on credit, creating a receivable, the company making the sale naturally wants to collect the cash as soon as possible. To encourage prompt payment, many companies offer discounts (called **cash [sales] discounts**) on the gross sales price. There are benefits associated with offering these discounts because collected cash can be used to earn a return, and eliminating receivables quickly reduces the costs of maintaining records for and collecting outstanding receivables. Presumably,

companies that offer cash discounts believe that these benefits exceed the reduction in future cash proceeds that results from the discount.

Cash discounts simply specify that an amount of cash less than the gross sales price is sufficient to satisfy an outstanding receivable if the cash is received within a certain time period. Certain sales on account, for example, may be subject to a 2 percent (of the gross sales price) cash discount if paid within ten days. Such terms are expressed in the following way: 2/10, *n*/30, which reads "two-ten, net thirty." This expression means "a discount in the amount of 2 percent of the gross sales price is available if payment is received within ten days. To avoid finance charges over and above the gross price, payment must be received within thirty days." Other terms on cash discounts are also common: 3/20, *n*/30, for example, means that a discount in the amount of 3 percent of the gross sales price is available if payment is received within twenty days, and finance charges over and above the gross price can be avoided if payment is received within thirty days; *n*/10, EOM means that the net amount of the sale (gross price less cash discount) is due no later than ten days after the end of the month.

CASH (SALES) DISCOUNTS VS. QUANTITY AND TRADE DISCOUNTS

Cash (sales) discounts, which can be viewed as incentives for prompt payment of open accounts, should be distinguished from quantity and trade discounts, which are simply reductions in sales prices. A **quantity discount** is a reduction in the per-unit price of an item if a certain quantity is purchased. "Cheaper by the dozen" is an example. Trade discounts are simply reductions in the sales price. A common form of trade discount, called a **markdown,** is quite common in retailing and normally is a sales price reduction due to decreased demand.

This distinction is important because cash (sales) discounts are reflected in the financial statements but quantity and trade discounts are not. To illustrate, in conjunction with an end-of-season sale, suppose that The Gap reduces the price of a certain line of shirts from $40 to $25. This $15 markdown is simply a reduction in the sales price of the shirts and would not be reflected in The Gap's books when the shirts are sold. The journal entry to record the sale would simply be:

Cash (or Accounts Receivable) (+A)	**25**	
Sales (R, +RE)		**25**

Sold merchandise for cash (or on account).

Note that the books give no recognition to the fact that the original sales price was $40. The asset (cash or accounts receivable) and the revenue (sales) are valued at the exchange price at the time of the transaction. The fact that the shirts were originally priced at $40 is ignored.

ACCOUNTING FOR CASH (SALES) DISCOUNTS

There are two ways to account for cash discounts: the **gross method** and the net method. We cover just the gross method because it is more straightforward and much more common in practice than the net method. Figure 6–7 illustrates the entries involved in the gross method.

The gross method initially recognizes the transaction at $1,000, the gross sales price, and thereby is based on the assumption that Buyer Company, the customer, will not receive the cash discount. If Buyer Company pays within the ten-day discount period (Case 1), a cash discount account is used to balance the difference between the gross receivable ($1,000) and the cash proceeds ($980). Cash discount is a temporary account that appears on the income statement of Seller Company. Its debit balance serves as a contra account to the credit balance in the sales account, giving rise to an

FIGURE 6–7   Accounting for cash discounts

GIVEN INFORMATION:
Assume that Seller Company sells goods on account with a gross sales price of $1,000 to Buyer Company on December 15, 2011 (terms 2/10, *n*/30). The following journal entries would be recorded on the books of Seller Company using the gross method for two different cases.

Initial sale on December 15.	Accounts Receivable (+A)	1,000	
	Sales (R, +RE)		1,000
	Sold goods on account.		
CASE 1:			
Assume that Seller Company receives full payment on	Cash (+A)	980	
December 20 (within the ten-day discount period).	Cash Discount (−R, −RE)	20	
	Accounts Receivable (−A)		1,000
	Paid on account.		
CASE 2:			
Assume full payment is received by Seller Company on	Cash (+A)	1,000	
January 3 (beyond the ten-day discount period).	Accounts Receivable (−A)		1,000
	Paid on account.		

income statement number called *net sales*. An example of the form of this disclosure follows.

Sales	$1,000
Less: Cash discounts	20
Net sales	$ 980

If Buyer Company misses the ten-day discount (Case 2), the $1,000 cash receipt after the expiration of the discount period exactly matches the gross amount in Seller Company's accounts receivable account.

An important caveat about cash discounts: In reality, many companies pay little attention to their terms. Consider, for example, a major retailer like Wal-Mart which is an extremely important customer to a large number of its suppliers. While the suppliers may offer cash discounts, encouraging Wal-Mart to pay its bills quickly, there is little they can do if Wal-Mart chooses to pay the discounted amount after the expiration of the discount period. The suppliers are very dependent on Wal-Mart's business, and that dependence gives Wal-Mart an advantage that many businesses in similar situations tend to exploit.

The Allowance Method of Accounting for Bad Debts (Uncollectibles)

In an ideal world, all receivables would be satisfied, and there would be no need to consider bad debts. However, accounts that are ultimately uncollectible are an unfortunate fact of life, and companies must act both to control them and to estimate their effects on the financial statements. To give you some idea of the magnitude of bad debts, Figure 6–8 shows 2008 uncollectibles as a percentage of outstanding receivables for several major U.S. corporations.

FIGURE 6–8
Bad debts as a percentage of outstanding receivables

Company	Bad Debts/ Outstanding Receivables
Verizon	7.4%
SUPERVALU	1.5%
General Electric	1.4%
Pier 1 Imports	8.3%

Source: *2008 annual reports.*

Controlling bad debts is a costly undertaking for many companies. The creditworthiness of potential customers can be checked by subscribing to credit-rating services such as Dun & Bradstreet, Moody's, or Standard & Poor's. Companies can create and maintain collection departments, hire collection agencies, and pursue legal proceedings. Certainly, each of these alternatives can improve cash collections, but each does so at a significant cost. In the extreme, management can institute a policy requiring that all sales be paid in cash. Such a policy would eliminate collection costs and drive bad debts to zero, but it could also be extremely costly because it could dramatically reduce sales revenue. Many companies sell their receivables to financial institutions by accepting credit cards, like VISA and MasterCard, but they are charged substantial fees for this service. Thus, a number of companies choose to extend credit to their customers, and for those companies bad debts are an inevitable cost of everyday operations that must be considered in the management of accounts receivable.

From an accounting standpoint, the inevitability of bad debts reduces the cash expected to be collected from accounts receivable. It thereby reduces the value of accounts receivable on the balance sheet. Bad debt losses also represent after-the-fact evidence that certain sales should not have been recorded, since the fourth criterion of revenue recognition (i.e., cash collection is assured) was not met for those sales. As a result, both accounts receivable and net income are overstated if bad debts are ignored. Proper accounting for bad debts, therefore, involves two basic adjustments: (1) an adjustment to reduce the value of accounts receivable on the balance sheet and (2) an adjustment to reduce net income.

?

"With China poised to enter the World Trade Organization, a fresh wave of foreign investors is preparing to take the plunge into its huge market. But as they do, these newcomers should learn a hard truth from their more seasoned, battle-worn predecessors: just because you make a sale doesn't mean you will get paid for it." Explain the meaning of this quote and how it might affect how U.S. companies do business in China.

The **allowance method** is used to account for bad debts. This method involves three basic steps: (1) the dollar amount of bad debts is estimated at the end of the accounting period; (2) an adjusting journal entry, which recognizes a bad debt expense on the income statement and reduces the net balance in accounts receivable, is recorded in the books; and (3) a write-off journal entry is recorded when a bad debt actually occurs. The following example illustrates the basic steps of the allowance method.

Suppose that during 2011, its first year of operations, Q-Mart had credit sales of $20,000 and a balance in accounts receivable of $6,000 as of December 31.

1. *Estimating bad debts*. After reviewing the relevant information, Q-Mart's account-ants estimate that 2.5 percent ($500) of its credit sales will not be collected.

2. *Adjusting journal entry*. The following journal entry would be recorded on December 31.

Bad Debt Expense (E or, −RE)	**500**	
Allowance for Doubtful Accounts (−A)		**500**
Recognized provision for doubtful accounts.		

On its 2006, 2007, and 2008 statement of cash flows in the operating section, Target adds back bad debt provisions of $380 million, $481 million, and $1,251 million, respectively, in the calculation of cash flow provided by operations. Why?

3. *Write-off journal entry*. On January 18, 2012, Q-Mart is notified that ABM Enter-prises has declared bankruptcy and will not be able to pay the $200 it owes to Q-Mart. The following journal entry would then be recorded in the books of Q-Mart.

Allowance for Doubtful Accounts (+A)	**200**	
Accounts Receivable/ABM (−A)		**200**
Wrote off uncollectible account/ABM.		

STEP 1: ESTIMATING BAD DEBTS

The allowance method requires that the dollar value of bad debts be estimated at the end of each accounting period. The most common method of estimating bad debts for finan-cial reporting purposes is the **percentage-of-credit-sales approach.**[8] This approach simply multiplies a percentage by the credit sales of the period. In the example given, $500 (2.5% × $20,000) of the credit sales during 2011 was estimated to be uncollectible.

The percentage of credit sales used in the calculation of bad debt expense is based primarily on a company's past experience. For a company such as Q-Mart, which is in its first year of operations, the typical bad debt rate of the other companies in its indus-try may provide a useful benchmark. Nonetheless, the percentage is an estimate, which by definition is inexact and uncertain. These estimates represent an area of potential disagreement between managers, who often want the financial statements to be as attractive as possible, and auditors, whose professional ethics and exposure to legal liability encourage them to prefer conservative reporting.

The problem of estimating bad debts is significant for financial institutions, which have a large portion of their assets in outstanding loans. However, most service, retail, and manufacturing companies, especially those that have been in business for many years, can estimate bad debts with reasonable accuracy. The major retail com-panies, in particular, experience bad debts at a fairly constant percentage of credit sales across time. Bad debt expenses for JCPenney, for example, have been less than 1 percent of sales for a number of consecutive years. Thus, while it may be difficult to predict whether an individual account will be uncollectible, many companies find it relatively easy to predict the percentage of bad debt losses from a large group of credit sales.

---

8. Later in the chapter we discuss another method of estimating bad debts, called the *aging method*.

STEP 2: ADJUSTING JOURNAL ENTRY

The proper method of accounting for bad debts requires an end-of-period adjusting journal entry that reduces both net income and the balance sheet carrying value of accounts receivable.

The credit side of the adjusting journal entry recorded by Q-Mart in the previous example, *allowance for doubtful accounts,* reduces the balance sheet value of accounts receivable by $500, the expected dollar amount of bad debts.[9] Allowance for doubtful accounts is a permanent contra asset account with a credit balance. It immediately follows and is subtracted from accounts receivable on the balance sheet. The form of this disclosure in the current asset section of the balance sheet follows:

Accounts receivable	**$6,000**
Less: Allowance for doubtful accounts	**500**
	$5,500

Disclosing the allowance for doubtful accounts account in this way reflects the fact that less cash than is indicated by the face value of the receivables is expected to be collected. In the case above, $5,500 of the outstanding receivables is expected to be received. Such disclosure helps to report accounts receivable at net realizable value.[10]

The debit side of the adjusting journal entry records a contra revenue on the income statement (bad debt expense). Recognizing the $500 contra revenue in 2011 indicates that certain (unidentifiable as of December 31) credit sales should not have been recorded in 2011. It thereby serves to reduce revenues for sales that actually were never made.[11]

For many years Sears offered financing to its customers through a separate credit card business. The company suffered from management problems in that business, recording increasingly large reserves (allowances) to cover growing bad debts. Several years ago Sears sold its credit card business to Citigroup, a large financial institution. What does it mean that Sears recorded "increasingly large reserves (allowances) to cover growing bad debts"? Why might Citigroup be better suited to manage receivables?

STEP 3: THE WRITE-OFF JOURNAL ENTRY

The write-off journal entry recorded by Q-Mart reduces both the allowance account and the accounts receivable balance. It is particularly important to note that this entry has no effect on the income statement and only serves to remove from the books the specific account receivable of ABM.

The write-off entry has virtually no effect on the financial statements because it simply identifies a specific bad debt that (on average) was known to be uncollectible and was recognized as such at the end of the previous accounting period. Indeed, the

---

9. The account title "Allowance for Doubtful Accounts" is used in this text. However, in a survey of 600 major U.S. companies, *Accounting Trends and Techniques* (2009) reports that slightly less than half of these companies use this title. The remaining companies use any of eight different descriptions, including Allowance, Allowance for Losses, and Reserve for Doubtful Accounts.

10. Many major U.S. companies do not disclose the dollar amount in the allowance account explicitly on the balance sheet. Instead, they simply report the net amount of receivables, after the dollar amount in the allowance account has been subtracted.

11. The bad debt estimate represents revenues that should never have been recorded because the fourth criterion of revenue recognition (cash collection is reasonably assured) was not met, giving rise to a contra revenue account, which is subtracted from sales on the income statement. However, generally accepted accounting principles do not specifically address how this charge should be disclosed, and some companies record the adjustment as an expense.

entry does not affect the net accounts receivable balance, current assets, working capital, the current ratio, quick assets, or net income.

To illustrate, the February 28, 2009, net accounts receivable of SUPERVALU, one of the nation's largest grocery retailers, appeared as follows (dollars in millions):

Accounts receivable	**$887**
Less: Allowance for doubtful accounts	**13**
	$874

The following year, assume that SUPERVALU receives notice that Catering Corporation will not be able to pay the $5 million it owes to SUPERVALU, and the following journal entry is recorded in SUPERVALU's books:

Allowance for Doubtful Accounts (+A)	**5**	
Accounts Receivable/Catering (−A)		**5**

Wrote off uncollectible account/catering.

This write-off entry reduces the balance of both accounts receivable and allowance for doubtful accounts by $5 million. Consequently, after the write-off entry, the net accounts receivable balance appears as follows:

Accounts receivable	**$882**
Less: Allowance for doubtful accounts	**8**
	$874

Note that the write-off entry had no effect on the net realizable value of accounts receivable. The net balance of $874 is unchanged because both accounts receivable and allowance for doubtful accounts were reduced by the same dollar amount. As a result, current assets, the current ratio, working capital, the quick ratio, and net income are all unaffected. The financial statement effect occurred at the end of the previous period (Step 2) when the adjusting journal entry was recorded.

So far we have implied that bad debts are discovered when a specific event occurs. For example, in the preceding illustrations the bad debt write-offs were recorded when a company received notice that a given customer was bankrupt or could not pay for some other reason. While bad debt write-offs can be recorded in this manner, it is probably more common for companies to write off bad debts when they decide that given receivables have been outstanding too long and are too costly to pursue. The following excerpt, which summarizes a typical write-off policy, was taken from a financial report of JCPenney Company, Inc.:

The Company's policy is to write off accounts when the scheduled minimum payment has not been received for six consecutive months, or if any portion of the balance is more than twelve months past due, or if it is otherwise determined that the customer is unable to pay.

The accounts receivable footnote in RadioShack's 2008 annual report provided the following information (dollars in millions).

The change in the allowance for doubtful accounts is as follows:

Balance at the beginning of the year	$2.5
Provision for bad debts	0.6
Uncollected receivables written off	(1.6)
Balance at the end of the year	$1.5

Explain the meaning of this information in terms of the three steps described above.

BAD DEBT RECOVERIES

Specific accounts that have been written off the books are occasionally recovered later. When such a receivable is reinstated, the write-off entry is simply reversed. This procedure corrects what was (in retrospect) recorded in error at a previous time. For example, the recovery of a previously written-off $5 million account receivable would be recorded as follows:

Accounts Receivable/Catering (+A)   5
   Allowance for Doubtful Accounts (−A)   5
Recovered $5 accounts receivable/catering.

Cash (+A)   5
   Accounts Receivable/Catering (−A)   5
Received $5 cash on account.

Inaccurate Bad Debt Estimates

Inaccurate bad debt estimates give rise to preadjustment balances in allowance for doubtful accounts. For example, if a company estimates $4,000 of bad debts on December 31, 2011, and actually incurs only $3,400 during 2012, as shown in Figure 6–9, allowance for doubtful accounts contains a $600 credit balance *before adjusting entries are recorded* at the end of 2012. If, instead of $3,400, bad debts of $4,400 actually occur during 2012, as shown in Figure 6–10, the *preadjustment December 31, 2012, balance* in allowance for doubtful accounts is a $400 debit.

FIGURE 6–9   Overestimated bad debts

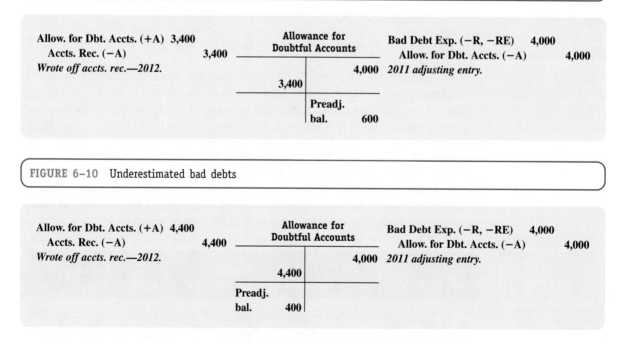

FIGURE 6–10   Underestimated bad debts

Because estimates are rarely correct, preadjustment balances in allowance for doubtful accounts are common. They are usually ignored because across time under- and overestimates in individual years tend to neutralize each other. However, a significant

debit or credit accumulation in the preadjustment balance over several periods may indicate that the estimates are not only inaccurate but also biased. Consistent overestimates give rise to preadjustment credit accumulations (Figure 6–9), while consistent underestimates create preadjustment accumulations on the debit side of allowance for doubtful accounts (Figure 6–10). Such accumulations, which often indicate that a company's estimating formula should be revised, can lead to balance sheet misstatements in the allowance account because they are reflected in the year-end, post-adjustment balance. Users can detect these misstatements by comparing the amount in the allowance account to such numbers as sales and accounts receivable across time. Unusual deviations or well-defined trends may reveal a problem in estimating bad debts, which may raise questions about management's competence and/or incentives.

In early 2004 Quovadx Inc., a business software company, was being investigated by the SEC. Apparently, in 2002 the company booked millions of dollars in revenue on sales made to a group of Indian information-technology companies, and as of early 2004 had not received any payments from them. How do you think Quovadx should account for these facts? Explain how a reader of the financial statements might have been able to detect such a problem.

AN AGING SCHEDULE: ANOTHER METHOD OF ESTIMATING BAD DEBTS

Another common method of estimating bad debt losses is to establish an **aging schedule** of outstanding accounts receivable. This method categorizes individual accounts in terms of the length of time each has been outstanding and applies a different bad debt rate to each category. The bad debt rate applied to categories comprising older accounts is greater than that applied to categories comprising younger accounts, on the assumption that the longer an account has been outstanding, the more likely it is to be uncollectible.

To illustrate how an aging schedule can be used to estimate bad debts, assume that each of the accounts that make up a $4,000 end-of-year balance in accounts receivable is placed into one of three categories that represent the lengths of time the accounts have been outstanding: (1) six to twelve months, (2) three to six months, and (3) less than three months. It is the company's policy to write off accounts when they become one year old. Assume also that the percentage of uncollectibles expected for each of the three categories is 30 percent for Category 1, 10 percent for Category 2, and 2 percent for Category 3. The bad debt estimate for the entire accounts receivable balance is computed in Figure 6–11. The $324 estimate is computed by totaling the dollar amount of the bad debts expected from each of the three categories.

FIGURE 6–11 An aging schedule	Age of Accounts	Amount	Percent Uncollectible	Estimate	
	6–12 months	$ 500	30%	$150	(500 × 30%)
	3–6 months	1,300	10%	130	(1,300 × 10%)
	Less than 3 months	2,200	2%	44	(2,200 × 2%)
	Total	$4,000		$324	

AGING AS A MANAGEMENT TOOL

Maintaining control over outstanding accounts receivable is an important part of effective management for many companies. Because of the time value of money, receivables should be collected as quickly as possible. Bad debts should also be held to a minimum. Aging schedules help companies control bad debts in a number of significant ways.

An aging schedule, for example, can identify slow-moving accounts, thus directing collection efforts and defining the maximum costs that should be incurred by those efforts. Collection efforts should be directed toward the accounts in the older categories, but the costs associated with these efforts should not exceed the expected loss from the accounts. For example, a company may have $10,000 of accounts receivable that have been outstanding for over six months. Past experience indicates that 20 percent of such accounts are uncollectible. The $2,000 ($10,000 × 20%) expected loss from these accounts determines a maximum dollar amount for the costs incurred to collect them.

An aging schedule can also be helpful in estimating how much money a company is losing in potential interest charges. Such information can be useful in deciding whether to offer cash discounts and in determining the appropriate terms for such discounts.

Although aging schedules can provide useful information, keep in mind that they can be costly to establish and maintain. For companies that rely on credit sales to a wide variety of customers, maintaining the age and balance of each account can be quite time-consuming. Computerized accounting systems are almost a necessity for efficient aging analyses and receivables control. Most large companies, of course, have computerized their receivables accounting, and when small companies change from manual to computerized accounting systems, receivables applications are often used first to improve control over accounts receivable.

There is a growing trend among companies seeking greater efficiencies to sell their outstanding receivables to financial institutions, which are well equipped to deal with potential bad debts. As reported in *Crain's Chicago Business Journal,* "The trend has been fueled by downsizing companies that no longer want to employ mid-level managers to oversee collection efforts, and the spread of sophisticated financial management techniques is leading more firms to conclude that a smaller amount of money now is worth more than the possibility of a larger amount later." These developments underscore the significant costs associated with managing your own receivables.

> **?** As president and CEO of newly formed Hilco Receivables LLC, Bruce Passen plans to tap into a growing trend among businesses to sell delinquent accounts receivable rather than hire collection agencies to try to recover the money owed. Collection firms with a stomach for a little risk now have an opportunity for higher returns. What does Mr. Passen plan to do?

Accounting for Sales Returns

For many companies, it is common that merchandise sold on account is returned by customers at a later date. These returns are important in the retail industry, and textbook publishers are especially affected because customers can often return large amounts of product sixty days or more after the initial sale. When returned items were initially sold, the sale and the associated account receivable were recognized on

the books. Because sales returns are usually accompanied by either the removal of the receivable or the granting of future credit, companies with significant returns must adjust both the income statement and accounts receivable on the balance sheet. The methods used to account for sales returns are similar to those used to account for bad debts; that is, at the end of each period an estimate of expected sales returns is made which, in turn, determines the dollar value of an adjusting journal entry that reduces income and establishes an allowance account. This account is disclosed on the balance sheet as a contra to accounts receivable. Actual returns are then debited against the allowance and credited against accounts receivable.

Under IFRS, the methods used to estimate and account for uncollectibles are very similiar to those under U.S. GAAP.

ACCOUNTS RECEIVABLE FROM A USER'S PERSPECTIVE

When accounting for short-term receivables, two general questions are of significant economic importance: (1) When should a receivable be recorded in the books? (2) At what dollar amount should a receivable be valued on the balance sheet?

When Should a Receivable Be Recorded?

Revenues and related receivables are recognized when the four criteria of revenue recognition have been met. Establishing exactly when this occurs, however, is difficult and subjective because managers have freedom to determine when and how a sale and the associated receivable are recorded. This freedom gives rise to widely different practices. For example, General Electric recognizes revenues when goods are shipped, while HarperCollins, a large book publisher, recognizes revenues when it invoices customers, sometimes a month before orders are shipped. Revenue recognition practices even differ among companies in the same industry. A survey of 200 software companies, for example, revealed that twenty-six (13 percent) companies waited until cash was received before recognizing a sale, while thirty (15 percent) companies recognized a sale as soon as an order was received.

Users of financial statements must realize that, even within the guidelines of generally accepted accounting principles, managers can use discretion to speed up or slow down the recognition of revenue. This concern is particularly important for transactions that occur near the end of an accounting period. Recognizing a receivable and a revenue on December 30 instead of January 2, for example, can significantly affect current assets, working capital, and net income on the December 31 financial statements.

A former executive of Computer Associates International pleaded guilty in U.S. District Court, noting that the company "kept quarters open," a practice of not closing the books until several days after the end of an accounting period. He noted that this practice allowed Computer Associates International to prematurely record more than $1 billion of revenue from 95 contracts. Explain what "keeping quarters open" means, and how it affects the financial statements.

To illustrate, suppose that current assets, current liabilities, and net income for Johnson and Sons as of December 29 are $45,000, $34,000, and $14,000, respectively. Johnson and Sons provides a service to Ace Manufacturing that is billed at $20,000. The service is ordered by Ace on December 30 and completed by Johnson and Sons on January 5. Payment is made by Ace after January 5. The current ratio, working capital position, and net income as of December 31 for Johnson and Sons are computed in Figure 6–12, assuming that (1) the revenue is recognized when the service is completed on January 5 and (2) the revenue is recognized when the service is ordered on December 30.

FIGURE 6–12 The timing of revenue and receivable recognition		(1) Revenue Is Recognized on January 5.	(2) Revenue Is Recognized on December 30.
December 31 current ratio			
(current assets ÷ current liabilities)		1.32	1.91
December 31 working capital			
(current assets − current liabilities)		$11,000	$31,000
Net income, year ended December 31		$14,000	$34,000

Note that the timing of revenue recognition can have a significant effect on important financial statement numbers. Recognizing the sale in the earlier period increased the current ratio by 45 percent and working capital and net income each by $20,000. Such effects have economic significance because they may influence a company's credit rating or determine whether it violates the terms of debt agreements. Since the timing of revenue and receivable recognition has a direct effect on net income and current assets, financial statement users should pay special attention to it.

Extreme cases of premature revenue and receivable recognition, or the complete fabrication of sales, is often interpreted as management fraud. Bear Stearns cited a 1999 study of over 200 corporate accounting fraud cases that occurred between 1987 and 1997, and concluded that the majority of these cases involved premature recognition of revenues (and receivables). In September of 2000 the SEC reported that it filed 30 enforcement actions for accounting abuses at a number of public companies, and many of these cases involved revenue recognition problems, such as booking revenue on shipments that never occurred. Two companies cited by the SEC were Raytheon, a defense contractor, and The Limited, a well-known clothing retailer, both of which have changed their revenue recognition practices. In each case the change led to the recognition of a major income write-down.

Other famous cases of inappropriate revenue recognition have involved such companies as MiniScribe, a software manufacturer, Regina Corporation, a well-known home appliance maker, and Orion Pictures, a motion picture studio that produced a number of box office hits. In all three cases, aggressive management, under intense pressure to perform, either fabricated sales or used questionable accounting practices to accelerate the recognition of revenues in an effort to increase reported profits and improve solvency measures. While these unethical behaviors may have delayed and obscured the companies' financial problems, they did little to solve them and in most cases made matters much worse.

A special problem has arisen in the world of the Internet. Given that Internet startup companies are now routinely valued on their revenues—since most generate

losses—the SEC has grown worried that some companies are overstating their revenues. When dot-com companies, for example, swap advertising with other Web sites, the swapping companies often book offsetting revenue and expense amounts. While the practice does not affect earnings, it does tend to overstate revenues.

When California Micro Devices Corp. wrote off over half of its accounts receivable, its stock price dropped by 40 percent. A court hearing later revealed that in the face of aggressive revenue goals, the company booked revenues on products that had been sold but were not shipped until after the end of the year. In terms of the principles of revenue recognition, explain why this practice is inappropriate. How could it lead to a receivables write-off?

Balance Sheet Valuation of Receivables

The appropriate dollar amount at which to value receivables on the balance sheet is primarily a question of whether the outstanding receivables will, in fact, be paid. Companies like Bank of America and General Electric have billions of dollars in outstanding receivables, many of which may never produce any cash. Estimating such uncollectibles, which can significantly affect both the income statement and the balance sheet, can be very subjective and can lead to substantial disagreements between management and its auditors. Several years ago, for example, a major auditing firm postponed rendering an opinion on Federal Home Loan Bank of Dallas because the bank carried $500 million of questionable receivables on its balance sheet. Bad debt write-offs can also be enormous. In 2008 alone, Bank of America wrote off $13 billion in bad debts. In addition, estimating bad debts involves judgment, and there is a real temptation for managers to use the estimate to report favorable earnings.

In 2008 Federated Department Stores was purchased by Macy's, Inc. Federated carried customer credit, but Macy's did not, selling Federated receivables to a financial institution. Explain Macy's decision.

These examples suggest that (1) bad debts can be significant, (2) estimating bad debts is subjective, and (3) management is often unwilling to establish large bad debt provisions. Users must be aware of these concerns and pay close attention to the size and activity in the allowance account as well as the annual bad debt expense. For example, consider a case where the following information is taken from the financial statements of a company you are currently reviewing as a possible investment:

	2012	2011
Balance Sheet		
Accounts Receivable	$12,500	$13,200
Allowance for Doubtful Accounts	(1,300)	(1,500)
Income Statement		
Sales	$99,000	$82,500
Bad Debt Expense	(1,700)	(1,650)
Net Income	5,000	4,200

At first glance, the company's financial performance appears to be strong and improving. Both sales and net income increased by 20 percent during 2012, and accounts receivable decreased, which suggests that receivables collections may have improved. However, a closer look at the activity in the allowance account and bad debt expense raises a concern. Using T-account analysis, as illustrated in Figure 6–13, you can see that the bad debt expense was insufficient, $200 less than the write-offs during 2012. Further review shows that the expense, as a percent of sales, decreased from 2 percent in 2011 to 1.7 percent in 2012. Had 2 percent been used in 2012, the expense would have been $1,980, and net income would have been lower by $280. Also, the allowance amount, as a percent of accounts receivable, decreased from 11.4 to 10.4 percent. It seems that management reduced the bad debt expense, which increased reported net income, even though bad debt write-offs did not decrease during 2012. Users must be cautious in these situations because bad debt estimates are based on information about the creditworthiness of their customers, which is available only to management. It is virtually impossible for outsiders to assess these estimates.

FIGURE 6–13

Analyzing the allowance for doubtful accounts T-account

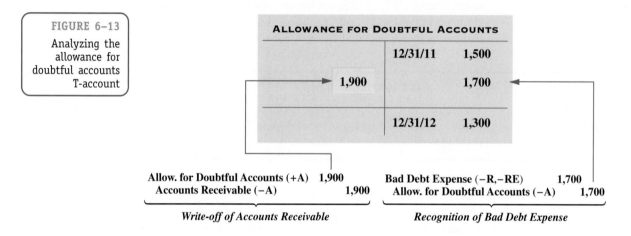

In one of its annual reports Sears, the well-known retailer, reported a profit of $1.4 billion, while reporting net cash from operations of negative $500 millions. One of the main reasons for the difference was a $4.86 billion increase in accounts receivable during the year. Sears subsequently sold off its credit-card receivables portfolio to concentrate its efforts on retail sales. What events may have accounted for the huge increase, and how might they influence an investor's interpretation of the company's current ratio and cash flow statement?

In summary, the methods used to account for accounts receivable can lead to significant economic consequences, affecting a company's credit rating, determining whether debt covenants are violated, accelerating bankruptcy proceedings, and introducing the potential for sizable lawsuits against managers and auditors. Recall from Chapter 5 that the combination of such economic effects and reporting subjectivity can encourage managers to use reporting strategies. Examples are overstating income and financial condition, "taking a bath," and building "hidden reserves," which can serve managers' interests at the expense of the shareholders. Recall also that practicing such strategies need not be fraudulent, because generally accepted accounting principles are sufficiently flexible to allow a large amount of management discretion.

FINANCIAL INSTITUTIONS AND UNCOLLECTIBLE LOANS

The collectibility of outstanding loans is a key concern for bank management and is at the heart of successful banking. In its 2008 financial statement, for example, JPMorgan Chase reported approximately $745 billion in outstanding loans, which was about 34 percent of total assets. The company estimated that $23.2 billion of these loans would be written off, and in 2008 the company recognized bad debt expense of $21 billion. Other financial institutions, such as savings and loans, insurance companies, and manufacturers that offer financing to their customers (Big 3 automakers, General Electric, Deere & Company), also carry significant receivables and face special collectibility problems. Such problems can involve much more than simply assessing the creditworthiness of customers. Major swings in the overall U.S. economy, certain sectors within the economy, or even entire countries and continents can have huge impacts on the financial health of these kinds of companies. Several years ago, for example, Westinghouse sold off its financial subsidiary due to nonperforming loans caused by a drop-off in the U.S. economy; banks with outstanding loans to companies in the southwest United States experienced severe financial hardship when oil prices slumped in the 1980s; and Citibank and other major U.S. banks recently booked huge losses due to the financial crisis in Asia.

> **?** On its 2006, 2007, and 2008 statement of cash flows in the operating section, General Electric subtracts increases in current receivables of $2,194 million, $868 million, and $24 million, respectively, in the calculation of cash from operating activities. Why?

The difficulties in America's financial institutions have brought about several significant changes relevant to accountants. First, the FASB has ruled that banks both disclose the market values of their outstanding loans and create larger reserves for bad debts. This rule, which generated much opposition from the banking industry, has reduced the balance sheet value of most U.S. banks. Difficulties in the financial institutions have also imposed additional legal liability on the audit profession. Leading accounting firms have been sued for billions of dollars for their alleged roles in the failures of hundreds of savings and loan companies. Such suits were initiated by both savings and loan shareholders and government regulators. Indeed, the accounting issues surrounding receivables can lead to significant economic consequences.

> **?** We mentioned in the introduction to this chapter that many financial institutions suffered large losses on investments composed primarily of mortgage receivables during the 2008–2009 recession. The losses were so large and so prevalent throughout the financial services industry that the U.S. government stepped in with an unprecedented infusion of capital into the banking system. Banks large and small, from Goldman Sachs in New York to Old National Bank in Evansville, Indiana, received capital infusions from the government's Troubled Asset Relief Program (TARP). How do losses on receivables affect a bank's capital position? Why was the government so concerned about losses on the banks' balance sheets?

INTERNATIONAL PERSPECTIVE: RECEIVABLES, FOREIGN CURRENCIES, AND HEDGING

As companies expand, they often search for new markets in other countries. Most major U.S. companies operate in more than one country, and many have operations in countries throughout the world. Of the $64 billion in worldwide revenues generated by Johnson & Johnson in 2008, for example, $31 billion (48 percent) came from outside U.S. borders. The internationalization of business introduces an issue of major concern to accountants—that is, many transactions with foreign entities involve currencies other than the U.S. dollar. When General Electric, a **multinational corporation,** sells products on account to Japanese customers, the contract often requires payment to be made in Japanese yen. An accounting problem arises because the accounts receivable must be expressed on GE's balance sheet in U.S. dollars, and the **exchange rate** between the U.S. dollar and the Japanese yen is constantly fluctuating.

Suppose, for example, that on December 1, 2010, Motorola delivered a shipment of wireless communicators to a German customer for a price of 1.5 million euros. Assume that on that date 1.4 U.S. dollar could be exchanged for 1 euro. Because Motorola prepares financial statements expressed in U.S. dollars, it would convert the receivable to an equivalent U.S. dollar amount and record the following entry:

Accounts receivable (+A)	2.10*	
Sales (R, +RE)		2.10

*(1.4 U.S. dollar/1 euro) × 1.5 million euros

Assume further that the U.S. dollar advances against the euro and that by December 31 the two currencies are trading 1:1—that is, 1 U.S. dollar can be exchanged for 1 euro. Consequently, as of December 31, the 1.5 million euros receivable is worth only $1.5 million dollars, and Motorola has experienced an **exchange rate loss** of $0.60 million. Accordingly, Motorola would record the following year-end adjusting entry:

Exchange rate loss (E, −RE)	0.60*	
Accounts receivable (−A)		0.60

*$2.10 million − $1.50 million

The loss occurred because Motorola held a contract promising the receipt of 1.5 million euros over a time period when the euro dropped in value relative to the U.S. dollar; simply, the value of the receivable went down. Of course, had the value of the euro advanced instead of declined against the U.S. dollar, Motorola would have recorded a gain, reflecting an increase in the value of the receivable.

Exchange rates among currencies can vary significantly across time, and these gains and losses can cause reported earnings to jump up and down erratically from one period to the next. U.S. firms with outstanding receivables expressed in non-U.S. currencies normally attempt to avoid bearing the risks associated with these kinds of gains and losses because they can lead to negative effects on stock prices, credit ratings, management compensation, and debt covenants.

Management has very little control over exchange rates, but it can reduce some of the risks associated with holding receivables denominated in foreign currencies through a strategy called **hedging.** There are many ways to practice hedging, some of which are discussed in Appendix 11B, but a simple way involves holding payables

expressed in foreign currencies that exactly counteract the effects of exchange rate fluctuations on outstanding receivables held in those same currencies.

Suppose in the preceding illustration that at the same time Motorola made the sale to the German customer, it simultaneously borrowed 1.5 million euros from a German bank. As of December 1, that payable would be expressed on Motorola's balance sheet at \$2.10 million [(2.10 U.S. dollars/1 euro) × 1.5 million euros]. As of December 31, after the U.S. dollar advanced against the euro, the payable would decrease in value and Motorola would recognize an exchange rate gain of \$0.60 million, which would exactly counteract the effect on reported net income of the exchange rate loss associated with the outstanding receivable.

Effective hedges can significantly reduce the variation in earnings across time associated with holding receivables denominated in foreign currencies. The following excerpt from the 2008 annual report of 3M, a multinational manufacturer, describes how the company deals with fluctuating exchange rates:

The company enters into foreign exchange forward contracts, options, and swaps to hedge against the effect of exchange rate fluctuations on cash flows denominated in foreign currencies and certain intercompany financing transactions.

ROE EXERCISE: MANAGEMENT OF WORKING CAPITAL AND RECEIVABLES AND RETURN ON EQUITY

Management's goal is to maximize shareholder wealth by choosing investments (e.g., people, inventories, plant and equipment, other companies) that generate an overall return exceeding the cost of the debt and equity capital used to finance the investments. Stated another way, management must manage its operating, investing, and financing decisions in a manner that maximizes the return on the shareholders' investment in the company. The ROE model, introduced and illustrated in Appendix 5A, provides a framework linking the management of a company's operating, investing, and financing activities to its return on the shareholders' investment (return on equity). The management of a company's working capital and receivables plays an important role in the ROE model via three financial statement ratios: current ratio (current assets/current liabilities), quick ratio ([cash + short-term investments + accounts receivable]/current liabilities), and receivables turnover (sales/average accounts receivable).

Current and Quick Ratios

The current and quick ratios provide measures of solvency—the ability to meet debt obligations as they come due. Companies that finance their operating and investing activities through borrowing (leverage) often maintain liquid-asset (e.g., cash, marketable securities, accounts receivable, inventories) balances because it lowers the risk borne by the lender by helping to ensure that the company will be able to meet the debt payments. The lower risk reduces the costs of borrowing (e.g., lower interest cost), and in some cases the debt contract requires liquid-asset balances. At the same time, liquid assets tend to provide minimal returns, indicating that holding overly large balances may not be in the shareholders' best interest. In terms of the ROE

model, the current and quick ratios indicate the extent to which the company is maintaining liquid assets that can be used to meet short-term obligations. It is important that adequate liquid assets be maintained, but the requirement to hold liquid assets imposes a cost on companies that practice leverage.

Accounts Receivable Turnover

Accounts receivable turnover provides a measure of a company's investment in its receivables. As indicated earlier, offering customer credit can increase sales, but outstanding receivable balances need to be financed at a cost, and managing receivables can be costly and risky. In terms of the ROE model, receivables turnover is a component of total asset turnover, meaning that changes in receivables turnover are reflected in changes in asset turnover, which in turn are reflected in return on assets (ROA), which in turn are reflected in return on equity (ROE). Thus, increasing the speed of receivables turnover (increasing sales relative to the investment in accounts receivable) puts upward pressure on both ROA and ROE.

ROE Analysis

Access the Web site http://wiley.com/college/pratt, and conduct ROE analyses on Caterpillar versus Deere & Company and/or IBM versus Hewlett-Packard, paying special attention to how the companies' solvency positions and receivables turnover impact ROE.

REVIEW PROBLEM

This section provides a review problem that covers the methods used to account for bad debts. The facts given are accounted for using the allowance method with a percentage-of-credit-sales estimate.

Assume that Credit Inc. began operations on January 1, 2011. The relevant transactions for 2011 and 2012 are summarized in the accounts receivable T-account provided in Figure 6–14. Sales on account during 2011 totaled $10,000, and cash receipts for those sales equaled $6,000. The accounts receivable balance at the end of 2011 was $4,000 ($10,000 − $6,000). Sales on account during 2012 totaled $12,000, and cash receipts during the same period, from sales made in both 2011 and 2012, were $11,000. On June 5, 2012, Credit Inc. received notice that a $500 account established in 2011 would not be collectible. This account was written off, and the December 31, 2012 balance in accounts receivable is $4,500 ($4,000 + $12,000 − $11,000 − $500). Assume that companies in Credit's industry typically experience bad debt losses of approximately 7 percent of credit sales.

The allowance method gives rise to end-of-period adjusting journal entries that decrease revenues in the appropriate period and reduce the value of accounts receivable on the balance sheet to net realizable value, the amount of cash expected to be collected from the receivables. The write-off entry on June 5, 2012, has virtually no effect on the financial statements of Credit Inc.

Note that the preadjustment balance in allowance for doubtful accounts as of December 31, 2011, is a $200 credit ($700 estimate − $500 write-off). Either Credit overestimated its bad debt losses for 2011 or certain outstanding accounts created from 2011's credit sales may still be written off. If this preadjustment balance accumulates over a period of several years, Credit should review and possibly revise its estimating formula. Otherwise, it is ignored.

FIGURE 6-14
Bad debt
review problem

General Ledger

Accounts Receivable

Beginning balance	0		
2011 credit sales	10,000		
		2011 cash receipts	6,000
12/31/11 balance	4,000		
2012 credit sales	12,000		
		2012 cash receipts	11,000
		2012 bad debt	500
12/31/12 balance	4,500		

**Allowance Method
(percentage-of-credit-sales estimate)**

<u>December 31, 2011</u>
$700 (7% × $10,000)

Estimate entry	Bad Debt Expense (E or −R, −RE)	700	
	Allow. for Doubt. Accts. (−A)		700

<u>June 5, 2012</u>

Write-off entry	Allow. for Doubt. Accts. (+A)	500	
	Accts. Rec. (−A)		500

<u>December 31, 2012</u>
$840 (7% × $12,000)

Estimate entry	Bad Debt Expense (E or −R, −RE)	840	
	Allow. for Doubt. Accts. (−A)		840

Allowance for Doubtful Accounts

		Beginning balance	0
		12/31/11	700
		12/31/11 balance	700
6/5/12	500		
		Preadj. balance	200
		12/31/12	840
		12/31/12 balance	1,040

SUMMARY OF KEY POINTS

● *Current assets, working capital, current ratio, and quick ratio, and how these measures are used to assess the solvency position of a company.*

Current assets are assets that can be converted into cash within one year or the company's operating cycle, whichever is longer. Working capital is equal to current assets less current liabilities, which are the liabilities expected to be required for payment with the assets listed as current. The current ratio is equal to current assets divided by current liabilities. The quick ratio is equal to cash plus marketable securities plus accounts receivable, divided by current liabilities.

These low-cost measures are useful in assessing a company's solvency position because they compare a measure of short-term cash inflows to a measure of short-term cash outflows. They are often used by banks and other lenders, and they appear in many loan agreements and debt covenants, enabling lenders to protect their investments by requiring that management maintain certain levels of liquidity.

● *"Window dressing" and the reporting of current assets, working capital, and the current ratio.*

Window dressing refers to management's use of discretion in reporting accounting numbers to make the financial statements appear more attractive. Such discretion is used, for example, to make it easier to attract capital, to increase bonus compensation, or to avoid violating the terms of debt contracts. Management can window dress in three basic ways: (1) management can choose to use accounting methods that improve the reported numbers, (2) it can bias the estimates required to apply a given accounting method, and (3) it can make operating, investing, and financing decisions that directly affect the reported numbers.

● *Techniques used to account for and control cash.*

Cash held in escrow or compensating balances are examples of restrictions on a company's use of its cash. Such restrictions should be clearly disclosed on the balance sheet or in the footnotes, and restricted cash should be included in separate accounts.

Two aspects to the control of cash that are largely the responsibility of the company's accountants are record control and physical control. Problems of record control arise because many transactions involve the cash account, and it is often difficult to ensure that the cash account on the balance sheet reflects the actual amount of cash in a company's possession. Problems of physical control arise because cash is universally desired and easily concealed and transported.

● *Accounts receivable and how they are valued on the balance sheet.*

Accounts receivable arise from transactions with customers who have purchased goods or services but have not yet paid for them. They are amounts owed by customers for goods and services sold as part of the normal operations of the business. Often backed up by oral rather than written commitments, accounts receivable represent short-term extensions of credit that are normally collectible within 30 to 60 days. Accounts receivable are valued at net realizable value, the gross amount of the receivables less adjustments for cash discounts, uncollectibles, and sales returns.

● *The allowance method for uncollectible receivables.*

Under the allowance method, the amount of uncollectibles is estimated at the end of each accounting period. Then an adjusting journal entry is made to reduce revenue via a contra revenue account, and a contra account to accounts receivable, allowance for doubtful accounts, is credited. Later, when the uncollectible is actually realized, both the value of accounts receivable and the allowance account are reduced.

● *Major concerns of financial statement users in the area of receivables reporting.*

For many companies, accounts receivable are a significant percentage of total and current assets. Accordingly, the methods used to account for them can have direct and often significant effects on such measures as current assets, working capital, the current ratio, the quick ratio, the collection period, and net income. Financial statement users must realize that managers can influence these measures by speeding up or slowing down the recognition of revenue and related receivables and that the estimate of uncollectibles is very subjective. Such practices can affect a company's credit rating, determine whether debt terms are violated, accelerate bankruptcy proceedings, and bring about sizable lawsuits against managers and auditors. In this area, users must pay close attention to the activity in sales, accounts receivable, bad debt expense, and allowance for doubtful accounts.

KEY TERMS

Note: Definitions for these terms are provided in the glossary at the end of the text.

Accounts receivable (p. 251)
Aging schedule (p. 262)
Allowance method (p. 257)
Cash (sales) discounts (p. 255)
Compensating balances (p. 249)
Current asset (p. 243)
Current ratio (p. 245)
Escrow (p. 249)
Exchange rate (p. 269)
Exchange rate loss (p. 269)
Gross method (p. 255)
Hedging (p. 269)
Markdown (p. 255)

Multinational corporations (p. 269)
Net realizable value (p. 254)
Open accounts (p. 0251)
Operating cycle (p. 243)
Percentage-of-credit-sales approach
   (p. 258)
Petty cash (p. 250)
Physical control (p. 251)
Quantity discount (p. 255)
Quick ratio (p. 245)
Record control (p. 251)
Window dressing (p. 247)
Working capital (p. 245)

ETHICS in the Real World

Allied Bancshares, a Houston-based group of banks, reported a string of 31 quarterly earnings increases. In an interview with three Goldman Sachs security analysts, one of the bank's senior officers explained that the bank intentionally overstates its bad debt expense in good quarters and understates it in poor quarters. In this manner, the fluctuations in earnings from one quarter to the next can be smoothed out. The bank's auditors have written clean opinions on the bank's financial statements over this time period, and this strategy maximizes the bonuses paid to the bank's executives. In addition, presumably it is in the best interest of the bank's shareholders, partly because it helps the bank maintain its legal reserve requirements.

ETHICAL ISSUE Is it ethical for companies like Allied Bancshares to intentionally overstate expenses in some periods and understate them in others to achieve consistent increases in reported net income across time?

INTERNET RESEARCH EXERCISE

For the most recent year, complete the chart below for JPMorgan Chase. Begin your search at www.jpmorganchase.com.

Activity in the *Allowance for Loan Losses* account:

Allowance for loan losses at January 1	?
Total provision for loan losses	?
Net charge-offs	?
Allowance for loan losses at December 31	?

BRIEF EXERCISES

REAL DATA

BE6–1

Analysis of accounts receivable

The following information was taken from the 2009 annual report of Emerson Electric Co., a leader in the network power sector (dollars in millions):

	2009	2008
Balance Sheet:		
Receivables, less allowance for uncollectibles of $93 and $90, respectively	**$3,623**	**$4,618**

a. Compute total accounts receivable as of the end of 2009 and 2008, and compute the bad debt allowance as a percentage of total accounts receivable. Did the percentage increase or decrease?

b. The bad debt expense reported on Emerson's 2009 income statement did not equal $93. Explain why.

REAL DATA

BE6–2

Uncollectible accounts expense

The following information was taken from the publicly available records of General Electric concerning the allowance for uncollectible account for its financing subsidiary, GE Capital Services (dollars in millions):

	2008	2007
Balance at Jan. 1	**$ 4,238**	**$ 3,945**
Increases	**7,518**	**4,431**
Decreases	**(8,162)**	**(5,966)**
Recoveries	**1,731**	**1,828**
Balance at Dec. 31	**$ 5,325**	**$ 4,238**

a. What dollar amounts of bad debt expense were recognized on the 2008 and 2007 income statements? Why do you think the figure changed so dramatically?

b. What dollar values of customer accounts were written off the books in 2008 and 2007?

c. By what percentage did the allowance account change from 2007 to 2008, and what are several reasons why this may have occurred?

REAL DATA

BE6–3

Uncollectible accounts expense

General Electric's financing subsidiary (GE Capital Services—GECS) provides financing services for GE's customers. If you purchase a GE appliance, for example, you could finance it through GECS. In 2008, GECS generated over $71 billion in revenue and reported profits of over $7 billion. These numbers represented approximately 40 percent of the company's total revenues ($182 billion) and 40 percent of the company's profits ($17.4 billion). In 2008, the bad debt provision reported on GE's income statement was $7.5 billion.

a. Compute bad debts as a percentage of revenues. Should you use GE overall revenues or revenues generated by GECS? Why?

b. If GECS prepared its own balance sheet, what would you expect to be the largest accounts?

c. Would you consider GE to be a manufacturing, retail, or service company? Discuss.

EXERCISES

E6–1

Classifying cash on the balance sheet

Boyer International is currently preparing its financial statements for 2011. The company has several different sources of cash and is trying to decide how to classify them. The sources of cash follow:

a. $30,000 in a checking account with The First National Bank.

b. $3,000 in checks dated December 4, 2011, received from customers.

c. $250,000 in certificates of deposit through The First National Bank, which are to mature on November 15, 2014.
d. $40,000 in a savings account with The First National Bank.
e. $1,000 in the petty cash fund. As of December 31, 2011, there are receipts totaling $600 in the petty cash drawer.
f. $50,000 held as a compensating balance for a loan with The First National Bank. The loan agreement requires Boyer International to maintain a compensating balance equal to 10 percent of the loan balance. During 2012, the outstanding principal balance will be reduced to $350,000.
g. $8,000 in a checking account with Interstate Federal Savings.

Indicate how each source listed should be classified on the December 31, 2011, balance sheet. Explain each answer.

E6–2

Classifying cash on the balance sheet

The following items were taken from the financial records of Melvin Construction Company.

a. $2,000 in a checking account.
b. $8,000 invested in a treasury note due to mature in 90 days.
c. $3,000 in a savings account that cannot be withdrawn until a $10,000 outstanding debt is paid off.
d. $18,000 invested in securities that will be sold in two years to finance an expansion of the plant.
e. $2,500 invested in IBM common shares. Management intends to liquidate this investment in less than six months.
f. $15,000 held in escrow by a bank, serving as earnest money that binds management to a real estate contract.
g. A $3,000 money order received in payment from a customer.

Classify each item as either (a) unrestricted cash, (b) restricted cash, or (c) investment.

E6–3

Accounting for cash discounts

On December 12, Woodington sold goods on account for a gross price of $40,000. The terms of the sale were 2/10, n/30. As of December 31, when financial statements were prepared, no payment had been received by Woodington. Full payment was received on January 5 of the following year.

a. Prepare journal entries for these transactions.
b. Assume that full payment was received on December 20. Prepare journal entries and discuss how the timing of the cash receipt affected the income statement and statement of cash flows.

E6–4

Accounting for cash discounts

On May 1, 2012, Crab Cove Fishing Company sold Maine lobster on account for a gross price of $30,000. On May 5, the company also sold cod on account for a gross price of $20,000. The terms of both sales were 3/10, n/30. Crab Cove received payment for the first sale on May 6, 2012, and payment for the second sale on May 31, 2012.

Provide all necessary journal entries.

E6–5

Bad debts under the allowance method

Arlington Cycle Company began operations on January 1, 2011. The company reported the following selected items in its 2012 financial report:

	2012	2011
Gross sales	$1,400,000	$1,500,000
Accounts receivable	600,000	650,000
Actual bad debt write-offs	22,000	10,000

Arlington estimates bad debts at 2 percent of gross sales.

Analyze the activity in the allowance for doubtful accounts T-account, and comment on whether the bad debt estimate has been sufficient to cover the write-offs.

E6–6

Accounting for
uncollectibles

In its 2011 financial report, Sound Unlimited reported the following items:

1. A credit balance of $200,000 in allowance for doubtful accounts.
2. A debit balance of $7,500,000 in accounts receivable.
3. Sales of $3,250,000.

During 2011, the company was involved in the following transactions that affected allowance for doubtful accounts.

1. Wrote off accounts considered uncollectible totaling $195,000.
2. Recovered $45,000 that had previously been written off.

Assume that historically 5 percent of sales has proven to be uncollectible.

a. Compute the December 31, 2010, balance in allowance for doubtful accounts.
b. Assume that all sales were on credit and cash collections from customers during 2011 totaled $4,200,000. Compute the 12/31/10 balance in accounts receivable.

REAL DATA

E6–7

Accounting for
doubtful accounts:
The allowance
method

The following items were extracted from the 2008 financial records of Cummins, Inc. (dollars in millions):

Allowance for doubtful accounts   12 (cr.)

During the following year, the company wrote off $11 of accounts receivable as uncollectible and then estimated $9 of the year's receivables to be uncollectible. The company did not recover any previously written-off accounts.

a. Prepare the entry to record the bad debt expense.
b. Compute the final balance in allowance for doubtful accounts.

E6–8

Inferring bad debt
write-offs and
reconstructing
related journal
entries

The 2012 annual report of Johnson Services reveals the following information. The dollar amounts are end-of-year balances.

	2012	2011
Credit sales	$75,300	$61,500
Accounts receivable	9,400	9,200
Allowance for doubtful accounts	1,300	1,000
Bad debt recoveries	55	70

Johnson estimates bad debts each year at 2 percent of credit sales.

a. Compute the actual amount of write-offs during 2012.
b. Infer the journal entries that explain the activity in accounts receivable and the related allowance account during 2012.

REAL DATA

E6–9

IFRS, bad debts,
and the statement
of cash flows

Kyocera is a Japanese telecommunications company that publishes IFRS-based financial statements. On its March 31, 2009, statement of cash flows in the operating section it reported a "provisions for doubtful accounts" of 671 million yen, and a "decrease in receivables" of 75,866 million yen.

a. Why were these two amounts reported in the operating section of the statement of cash flows?
b. How were these two amounts treated in the reconciliation of net income with net cash provided by operating activities?
c. During 2009 net cash from operating activities was more than 68,288 million yen higher than net income. Explain why.

E6–10

Preparing an
aging schedule

Potter Stables uses the aging method to estimate its bad debts. Sherman Potter, the company president, has given you the following aging of accounts receivable as of December 31, 2009, along with the historical probabilities that the account balances will not be collected.

Account Age	Balance	Noncollection Probability
Current	$290,000	2%
1–45 days past due	110,000	5%
46–90 days past due	68,000	8%
Over 90 days past due	40,000	15%

Compute total receivables and expected bad debts as of December 31, 2012.

E6–11

Exchange gains/losses on outstanding receivables

On January 1, 2012, Outreach Incorporated sold services to a Canadian supply company and accepted a three-year note in the amount of 11,000 Canadian dollars. Assume that exchange rates between the U.S. dollar and the Canadian dollar are as follows:

Date	U.S. Dollars Per Canadian Dollars
January 1, 2012	**$0.95**
December 31, 2012	**0.99**
December 31, 2013	**0.90**

Provide the journal entries (in U.S. dollars) prepared by Outreach to record the receipt of the note and the exchange gains/losses recognized on December 31, 2012, and December 31, 2013. Ignore any interest on the note.

E6–12

Hedging to reduce the risk of currency fluctuations

Assume that Outreach (in E6–10) hedged the 11,000 (Canadian dollar) receivable by borrowing 11,000 Canadian dollars from a Canadian bank on January 1, 2012. Use journal entries to demonstrate how this transaction removes Outreach's exposure to the risk of fluctuating exchange rates. Explain.

PROBLEMS

P6–1

Classifying cash on the balance sheet

On September 30, 2011, Print-O-Matic Inc. entered into an arrangement with its bank to borrow $250,000. The principal is due on October 1, 2016, and the note has a stated annual interest rate of 10 percent. Under the borrowing agreement, Print-O-Matic agreed to maintain a compensating balance of $60,000 in a non-interest-bearing account. As of December 31, 2011, Print-O-Matic has an additional $225,000 in various savings and checking accounts that earn an annual rate of 6 percent. The controller intends to classify the entire $285,000 in cash as a current asset.

REQUIRED:
a. Do you agree with the classification of the $285,000 of cash as a current asset? Explain your answer.
b. Print-O-Matic reported interest expense associated with this note for the year ended December 31, 2011, in the amount of $6,250 [($250,000 × 10%) × 1/4]. Do you agree with this classification? Should any other factors be considered in the interest cost? Explain.

P6–2

Cash discounts

During the month of March, QNI Corporation made the following credit sales and had the following related collections. QNI prepares financial statements for the first quarter of operations at the end of March.

March 3   **Sold goods to AAA company for a gross price of $1,400. The terms of the sale were 2/10, n/30.**

March 8   **Sold goods to BBB company for a gross price of $800. The terms of the sale were 2/10, n/30.**

March 11   Received full payment from AAA.

March 28   Received full payment from BBB.

March 29   Sold goods to CCC company for a gross price of $1,800.
The terms of the sale were 2/10, n/30.

REQUIRED:
a. Prepare the journal entries to record these transactions.
b. Note that BBB missed the discount period by ten days. Compute the annual interest rate BBB paid for the use of the $800 for that ten-day period. Assuming that BBB can borrow money from the bank at 9 percent, what should BBB have done differently?

P6–3

Bad debts over time

Financial information for CNG Inc. follows:

	2012	2011	2010
Credit sales	$205,000	$200,000	$180,000
Actual bad debt write-offs	11,000	10,000	6,000

The company estimates bad debts for financial reporting purposes at 3 percent of credit sales. The balance in allowance for doubtful accounts as of January 1, 2010, was $10,000.

REQUIRED:
a. Provide the journal entries related to allowance for doubtful accounts for 2010, 2011, and 2012.
b. Compute the balance in allowance for doubtful accounts as of December 31, 2012.
c. Comment on the sufficiency of the bad debt expense and allowance over the three-year period. How did you come to your conclusion?

P6–4

Accounting for uncollectibles over two periods

Glacier Ice Company uses a percentage-of-net-sales method to account for estimated bad debts. Historically, 3 percent of net sales have proven to be uncollectible. During 2011 and 2012, the company reported the following:

	2012	2011
Gross sales	$1,500,000	$1,800,000
Sales discounts	100,000	130,000
Sales returns	50,000	20,000

REQUIRED:
a. Prepare the necessary adjusting entry on December 31, 2011, to record the estimated bad debt expense for 2011.
b. Assume that the January 1, 2011 balance in allowance for doubtful accounts was $65,000 (credit) and that $70,000 in bad debts were written off the books during 2011. What is the December 31, 2011, balance in this account *after adjustments*?
c. Prepare the necessary adjusting entry on December 31, 2012, to record the estimated bad debt expense for 2012.
d. What is the December 31, 2012, balance in allowance for doubtful accounts? Assume that $85,000 in bad debts was written off the books during 2012.

P6–5

Accounting for uncollectibles over three periods

Albertson's Locksmith Corporation started operations on January 1, 2010. Albertson's estimates uncollectibles using the percentage-of-credit-sales method. The following information

pertains to the company's sales, receivables, and collections for the first three years of operation:

	2012	2011	2010
Credit sales	$240,000	$190,000	$105,000
Cash sales	8,000	4,000	1,000
Total sales	$248,000	$194,000	$106,000
Write-offs	8,400	6,000	3,000
Cash collections of A/R	214,000	161,000	92,000

Albertson's estimates uncollectible accounts at 4 percent of credit sales.

REQUIRED:
a. What is the balance of the allowance for uncollectibles account as of the end of 2010, 2011, and 2012?
b. What is the (net) balance of the accounts receivable account as of the end of 2010, 2011, and 2012?
c. Comment on Albertson's annual estimates.

REAL DATA
P6–6
Analyzing the activity in the allowance account

The information below was taken from the footnotes of JPMorgan Chase's 2008 annual report. The December 31, 2008, balance in the allowance account was $23,164 (dollars in millions).

	2008	2007	2006
Allowance at Jan. 1	$ 9,234	$ 7,279	$7,090
Provision for losses	23,765	6,549	3,231
Recoveries	929	829	842

REQUIRED:
Compute the actual write-offs recognized by JPMorgan Chase in 2006, 2007, and 2008. Comment on JPMorgan Chase's annual estimates. Discuss the reasons underlying the 2008 amounts.

P6–7
Ignoring potential bad debts can lead to serious overstatements

The following financial information represents Hadley Company's first year of operations, 2011:

Income Statement		Balance Sheet	
Sales	$200,000	Cash	$ 5,000
Cost of goods sold	102,000	Accounts receivable	85,000
Gross profit	$ 98,000	Other assets	40,000
Expenses	65,000	Total assets	$130,000
Net income	$ 33,000	Current liabilities	$ 13,000
		Long-term notes payable	80,000
		Shareholders' equity	37,000
		Total liabilities and	
		shareholders' equity	$130,000

After reading Hadley's financial statements, you conclude that the company had a very successful first year of operations. However, after further examination, you note that the sales figure on the income statement was not adjusted for a bad debt expense. You also realize that a large percentage of Hadley's sales were to three customers, one of which, Litzenberger Supply, is in very questionable financial health, although still in business. Litzenberger owes Hadley $50,000 as of the end of 2011.

REQUIRED:
a. Adjust the financial statements of Hadley Company to reflect a more conservative reporting with respect to bad debts. That is, establish a provision for the uncollectibility of

Litzenberger's account. Recompute net income. How does this adjustment affect your assessment of Hadley's first year of operations?

b.   Why would auditors probably require that Hadley choose the more conservative reporting?

c.   Hadley's chief financial officer claims that no bad debt expense should be recorded, because Litzenberger is still conducting operations as of the end of 2011. How would you respond to this claim?

P6–8

Estimating uncollectibles, financial ratios, and loan agreements

Excerpts from the 2011 financial statements of Finley, Ltd., a service company, follow:

Fees earned	**$240,000**
Accounts receivable	**68,000**
Allowance for doubtful accounts	**3,400**
Total current assets	**105,000**
Total current liabilities	**65,000**
Net income	**15,000**
Dividends declared	**5,000**
Bad debt expense	**3,400**

Auditors from Price and Company reviewed the financial records of Finley and found that a credit sale of $10,000 (for services rendered), which was included in the fees earned amount above, should not have been recognized until January 20, 2012. The auditors also noted that a more reasonable estimate of future bad debts would be 10 percent of the accounts receivable balance. The auditors have informed Finley's management that the audit opinion will be qualified if Finley does not adjust the financial statements accordingly.

REQUIRED:

a.   Compute the effect of the auditors' recommended adjustment on the 2011 fees earned, accounts receivable, allowance for doubtful accounts, current ratio, working capital, and net income reported by Finley.

b.   Assume that Finley has a loan agreement with a bank, requiring it to maintain a current ratio of 1.5 and limiting its annual dividend payment to 50 percent of net income. How might these restrictions have influenced the reporting decisions of Finley's managers?

P6–9

Uncollectibles: Ignoring an allowance

Fine Linen Service began operations on January 28, 2008. The company does not establish an allowance for doubtful accounts. It simply recognizes a bad debt expense when an account is deemed uncollectible. The company has written off the following items over the past five years:

July 6, 2008	**Wrote off $10,000 as uncollectible from a sale made on March 1, 2008.**
Feb. 3, 2009	**Wrote off $50,000 as uncollectible from a sale made on October 28, 2008.**
Mar. 11, 2010	**Wrote off $25,000 as uncollectible from a sale made on December 20, 2008 ($12,000) and a sale made on May 10, 2008 ($13,000).**
Mar. 24, 2010	**Recovered $5,000 that had been written off on February 3, 2009. It is company policy to credit bad debt expense when an account is recovered.**
Aug. 8, 2011	**Wrote off $75,000 as uncollectible from sales made in 2008 ($20,000), in 2009 ($25,000), and in 2010 ($30,000).**
Dec. 2, 2011	**Wrote off $5,000 as uncollectible from a sale made on April 26, 2011.**
Sept. 19, 2012	**Wrote off $90,000 as uncollectible from sales in 2008 ($5,000), in 2009 ($30,000), in 2010 ($25,000), in 2011 ($20,000), and in 2012 ($10,000).**

Over the period 2008 to 2012, Fine Linen Service realized the following sales and reported the following ending balances in accounts receivable.

	Sales	Accounts Receivable
2008	$1,000,000	$ 950,000
2009	975,000	900,000
2010	1,025,000	1,200,000
2011	1,032,000	1,175,000
2012	990,000	1,095,000

At the beginning of operations, a consultant had informed Fine Linen Service that the company should expect not to collect 8 percent of total sales.

REQUIRED:
a. List the bad debt expense and the balance sheet value of accounts receivable for each year over the five-year period under both Fine Linen's current method and the allowance method. Use the following format:

	2008	2009	2010	2011	2012
Current method:					
Bad debt expense					
Accounts receivable value					
Allowance method:					
Bad debt expense					
Accounts receivable value					

b. Compute the total bad debt expense over the five-year period under the two methods. Why is the allowance method preferred to Fine Linen's current method?

P6–10

Accounting for uncollectibles and the aging estimate

In an attempt to include all relevant information for decision-making purposes, Merimore Company estimates bad debts using the aging method. However, for external reporting purposes, the company estimates bad debts as a percentage of credit sales. Merimore prepares monthly adjusting journal entries. From trends over the past five years, the company controller has estimated that 2 percent of monthly credit sales will prove to be uncollectible. Following are the monthly credit sales and bad debt write-offs for Merimore Company for 2011.

Month	Cash Collections	Credit Sales	Write-Offs
January	$ 1,200,000	$ 1,000,000	
February	1,050,000	925,000	
March	910,000	1,010,000	
April	1,000,000	975,000	$ 87,000
May	875,000	950,000	
June	1,080,000	1,200,000	
July	950,000	1,150,000	52,000
August	1,011,000	1,075,000	
September	1,105,000	1,025,000	
October	980,000	980,000	
November	1,100,000	900,000	
December	865,000	750,000	100,000
Total	$12,126,000	$11,940,000	$239,000

On December 31, 2011, the controller prepared the following aging of accounts receivable:

Account Classification	Balance	Percent Uncollectible
Current	$ 700,000	2.0%
1–30 days past due	1,200,000	5.5%
31–75 days past due	550,000	10.0%
Over 75 days past due	800,000	25.0%

The allowance for doubtful accounts balance on January 1, 2011, was a credit of $70,000.

REQUIRED:
a. Prepare the adjusting journal entry necessary on December 31, 2011, so that the statements will be in accordance with the company's external reporting policies. Remember that the company prepares monthly adjusting journal entries.
b. Compute the balance in allowance for doubtful accounts after the entry in (a) has been recorded and posted.
c. Compute the balance in accounts receivable as of January 1, 2011.
d. Prepare the December 31 adjusting entry for bad debts, using the percentage-of-credit-sales method, and compute the estimated bad debts, using the aging method.
e. Why would a company want to estimate bad debts using two different methods? Which of the two methods is more costly and time-consuming to implement? Which provides more useful information?

P6–11

Inferring reporting strategies

Excerpts from the financial statements of Ticheley Enterprises are as follows.

	2012	2011	2010
Income Statement			
Bad debt expense	$ 1,700	$ 2,900	$ 2,100
Net income	15,800	15,300	14,400
Balance Sheet			
Accounts receivable	$27,400	$23,200	$23,100
Allowance for doubtful accounts (cr.)	2,100	3,000	2,300
Shareholders' equity	78,500	75,000	71,400

On December 27, 2011, Ticheley sent merchandise with a sales price of $8,500 to a major customer. The merchandise was in transit as of December 31. The cost of the inventory shipped was $2,900, and the company chose to record the sale and outflow of inventory on January 4, 2012, when the customer received the shipment. Ticheley's management is compensated partially on an annual bonus, where all managers share equally in a $10,000 bonus pool if reported net income exceeds 20 percent of shareholders' equity.

REQUIRED:
a. Ticheley's president recently stated in a letter to the shareholders that the company has reported profit increases consistently over the last three years. Comment on this statement.
b. Why would a company establish a management compensation system where a bonus is paid if reported income exceeds a certain percentage of shareholders' equity?
c. Identify any reporting strategy that Ticheley may be using, and support your position with calculations.
d. Explain why Ticheley may be using the strategy you mentioned above, and support your position with calculations.

P6–12

Exchange gains and losses

Hughes International is a U.S. company that conducts business throughout the world. Listed below are selected transactions entered into by the company during 2011.

1. Sold merchandise to Royal Equipment Company (a United Kingdom company) in exchange for an account receivable in the amount of 320,000 pounds. At the time, the exchange rate was 0.50 British pound per U.S. dollar.

2. Sold merchandise to Honda Automobile Company (a Japanese company) in exchange for a note receivable that calls for a payment of 350,000 yen. The exchange rate was 125 yen to the U.S. dollar.
3. Purchased inventory from Venice Leathers (an Italian company) in exchange for a note payable that calls for a payment of 500 euros. The exchange rate was 0.75 euro to the U.S. dollar.
4. Purchased inventory from B. C. Lumber (a Canadian company) in exchange for an account payable in the amount of 200,000 Canadian dollars. The exchange rate was 1.10 Canadian dollars per U.S. dollar.

On December 31, 2011, the exchange rates were as follows:

Foreign Currency	Currency Per U.S. Dollar
British pound	0.60
Japanese yen	115
Euro	0.85
Canadian dollar	1.05

REQUIRED:
a. Convert each transaction above to the equivalent amount in U.S. dollars.
b. Prepare journal entries to record each transaction.
c. Assume that the receivables and payables are still outstanding as of December 31, 2011. Compute the amount of exchange gain or loss for each transaction.
d. Why do fluctuating exchange rates give rise to exchange gains and losses?

P6–13

Fluctuating exchange rates, debt covenants, and hedging

International Services entered into a debt covenant requiring it to maintain a current ratio of at least 1.5:1. The company's condensed balance sheet as of December 31 follows:

Assets		Liabilities and Shareholders' Equity	
Current assets	$ 80,000	Current liabilities	$ 50,000
Noncurrent assets	200,000	Long-term liabilities	100,000
		Shareholders' equity	130,000
		Total liabilities and	
Total assets	$280,000	shareholders' equity	$280,000

International's primary customer is Buckingham, Ltd., a company located in Britain. As of December 31, Buckingham owed International 40,000 British pounds. The exchange rate as of December 31 between U.S. dollars and British pounds was $1.70 per pound.

REQUIRED:
a. What dollar amount of International's current assets on the balance sheet is associated with the receivable owed by Buckingham?
b. Assume that all account balances remain the same over the next year. Below what exchange rate (U.S. dollars per British pound) would International be in violation of the debt covenant?
c. Assume that $1,600 of accounts payable on the balance sheet represents a debt of 1,000 British pounds to a British bank. Below what exchange rate would International be in violation of the debt covenant now? Consider both the receivable and the payable.
d. Describe how International could hedge to reduce the risk of being in violation of the debt covenant.

ISSUES FOR DISCUSSION

REAL DATA

ID6-1

Restricted cash and
solvency ratios

Safeguard Scientifics, Inc. reported the following in its 2008 financial statements.

Note 7: Long-Term Debt.

The credit facility required the company to maintain cash collateral equal to the company's borrowings (amounts in thousands).

Cash held in escrow—current	**$ 6,433**
Cash held in escrow—long-term	**501**
Total Assets	**$232,402**

REQUIRED:
a. Why would a potential investor or creditor want to know about restrictions on cash?
b. Assume that the loans under the credit facility are expected to remain outstanding for two years. Should the restricted cash be disclosed as current or noncurrent? Discuss.
c. How might the disclosure of such a restriction affect the calculation of working capital, the current ratio, and the quick ratio?

REAL DATA

ID6-2

Revenue recognition,
ethics, and reputation

The *Wall Street Journal* reported, "For more than ten years, IBM has quietly turned to Merrill Lynch & Co. and others to execute a rare financial maneuver that propped up the results of IBM's big leasing business. The maneuver allowed IBM to book immediately all the revenue from a long-term computer lease—even though the actual dollars would flow in over the life of the lease. That didn't break any rules, but some accountants term it an end-run that many blue-chip companies would avoid. [IBM's external auditors] called the revenue booster troubling . . . and urged IBM to take immediate action to use the maneuver less." Later, the article states, "Questions about IBM's accounting could be awkward for the wounded computer giant [because] IBM long enjoyed a reputation as the epitome of financial conservatism, with triple-A-rated debt and the bluest of blue-chip stocks."

REQUIRED:
a. Discuss how using an aggressive method to recognize revenue, like the one just described, might affect IBM's reputation as "the epitome of financial conservatism."
b. Discuss some of the economic consequences associated with the use of such a method, mentioning some of the benefits and costs affecting IBM and its management.
c. The article mentions later that IBM requires all employees to swear that they have read the IBM "Business Conduct Guidelines" manual that warns them against not only reporting information inaccurately but also organizing it in a way that is intended to mislead or misinform. Comment on whether this policy is consistent with the use of the aggressive revenue recognition method mentioned above.

REAL DATA

ID6-3

Working capital,
debt covenants, and
restrictions on
management
decisions

Excerpts from the June 30, 1994, balance sheet of The Quaker Oats Company (now part of PepsiCo, Inc.) are provided below (dollars in millions).

	1994	*1993*	*1992*
Current assets:			
Cash and short-term investments	$ 140.4	$ 61.0	$ 95.2
Receivables	509.4	478.9	575.3
Inventories	385.5	354.0	435.3
Other current assets	218.3	173.7	150.4
Current liabilities	1,259.1	1,105.1	1,087.5

REQUIRED:

a. The notes to the company's 1992 financial statements state that "under the most restrictive terms of the various loan agreements . . . minimum working capital of $150 million must be maintained." Compute how close The Quaker Oats Company came to this restriction at the end of 1992, and discuss what has happened since that time.

b. In Quaker Oats' 1994 annual report, it states, "Under the most restrictive terms of the Revolving Credit Agreements, the company must maintain total shareholders' equity greater than $300 million." Comment on possible explanations for the changing restrictions.

REAL DATA

ID6–4

Analyzing the allowance account

The footnotes to the 2008 financial statements of Citigroup, the holding company for Citibank, contained the following information (dollars in millions):

	Allowance for Credit Losses		
	2008	2007	2006
Allowance for loan losses at beginning of year	$?	$?	$9,782
Provision for credit losses—consumer	28,282	15,599	6,224
Provision for credit losses—corporate	5,392	1,233	96
Consumer credit losses	20,002	10,645	8,629
Corporate credit losses	1,922	948	312
Consumer recoveries	1,600	1,661	1,547
Corporate recoveries	149	277	232
Allowance for loan losses at end of year	?	?	?

REQUIRED:

a. Fill in the missing values and comment on any trends across the three-year period.

b. As of the end of 2008, the company had outstanding loan receivables of $694,216: $519,673 in consumer loans and $174,543 in corporate loans. Which of the two categories appears to be the riskier? Why?

REAL DATA

ID6–5

Managing reserves for uncollectible receivables

The *Wall Street Journal* (March 12, 2007) reported that an analyst with the Center for Financial Research and Analysis found an interesting item in an earnings report from New Century Financial Corporation, a mortgage lending company specializing in "subprime" loans to borrowers with checkered credit histories. The analyst discovered that New Century had for the first time combined two categories of reserves for losses. New Century combined the reserve for losses on defaulted loans with a reserve for losses on real estate that had been acquired through foreclosure. By putting the two reserve accounts together, New Century could show that total reserves for losses had increased only slightly from the prior period. Hidden, though, was the fact that the reserve for losses on bad loans actually dropped by 8.7 percent. The Center for Financial Research and Analysis pointed out the discrepancy of a drop in reserves at a time when defaults on subprime mortgages were increasing across the country.

REQUIRED:

Discuss the effect of "reserves for loan losses" on the financial statements and why a company such as New Century might be reluctant to increase the reserve. Discuss what economic factors influence loan defaults (and especially loans in the subprime mortgage market).

REAL DATA

ID6–6

Provisions for loan losses and profits

Publicly traded companies release financial statements (unaudited) on a quarterly basis. For the quarter ended December 31, 2009, MarketWatch reported that Bank of America (B of A) and Wells Fargo had improved their results over the same period in 2008 but that "lingering signs of credit trouble" still existed for the banks. B of A reported a smaller loss than in 2008, but past-due loans in home mortgages, home equity loans, and commercial real estate loans all grew, as did past-due loans in its business loan portfolio. At Wells, the company showed a quarterly profit versus the prior year's loss, but its net write-offs as a percentage of loans rose to 2.71 percent from 2.11 percent for the same period a year earlier. MarketWatch

quoted an analyst who follows the banking industry as saying that he believes the problem loan situation is worse than what the banks have been disclosing.

REQUIRED:
Discuss the implications of a weakened real estate market on bank profitability. How would high unemployment, in addition to soft housing prices, affect banks' earnings? How does the provision for loan loss affect the balance sheet and the income statement of banks? Why do banks adjust the provision when market conditions change, and why do analysts sometimes question the amount of the reserve set aside by the banks?

REAL DATA

ID6–7

Bad debts, statement of cash flows, and U.S. GAAP vs. IFRS

Excerpts from the operating sections of the 2008 statement of cash flows for Target and Toyota are provided below. Target publishes U.S. GAAP-based financial statements and Toyota publishes IFRS-based financial statements (dollars in millions).

	Target	Toyota
Net earnings	**$2,214**	**$17,146**
. . .	. . .	. . .
Bad debt provision	**1,251**	**1,226**
. . .	. . .	. . .
Change in accounts receivable	**(458)**	**(2,064)**
. . .	. . .	. . .
Net cash from operations	**$4,430**	**$29,760**

REQUIRED:
a. What is the bad debt provision, and on which other financial statement would you find it?
b. Explain why the bad debt provision and the change in accounts receivable appear in the operating section of the statement of cash flows.
c. Provide several reasons why net cash from operations is so much larger than net earnings for both companies.
d. Does it look like U.S. GAAP and IFRS account for bad debts much differently? Explain.

REAL DATA

ID6–8

Earnings restatement due to misstated loan losses

In July 2006, Par Pharmaceuticals announced that it would restate financial results for fiscal years 2004 and 2005 and for the first quarter of fiscal 2006 due to an understatement of the allowance for uncollectibles for accounts receivable. The understatement resulted from delays in recognizing customer credits and uncollectible customer accounts. The company expects the restatement would total a deduction of $55 million of revenues for the time period.

The investing Web site seekingalpha.com (posted July 7, 2006) responded to Par's announcement with some calculations regarding receivables. Seekingalpha.com figured that receivables dropped 3.7 percent from 2004 to 2005 but that revenue dropped an even greater 37.2 percent over the same period. The relative growth in receivables (as compared to sales size) implies a slowing of the collection period. The Web site calculated that accounts receivables days grew from 79 days to 121 days; the site further states, "From this we see that on top of the decline in sales for 2005, the quality of the sales also declined—the company made sales on credit that it ultimately was unable to collect."

REQUIRED:
Discuss the implications of selling on credit to customers who ultimately do not pay. How is the basic accounting equation affected at the time of the sale and at the time of the realization that too many of the receivables will not be collected? What does it mean when receivables "days" increases? How can a reader of financial statements predict future restatements of revenue?

REAL DATA

ID6–9

Concentrations of credit risk

The following quote was taken from the 2009 annual report of Hewlett-Packard.

HP sells a significant portion of its products through third-party distributors and resellers and, as a result, maintains individually significant receivable balances with these parties.

If the financial condition or operations of these distributors and resellers deteriorates substantially, HP's operating results could be adversely affected. The ten largest distributor and reseller receivable balances collectively, which were concentrated primarily in North America, represented approximately 22% of gross accounts receivable at October 31, 2009 and 18% at October 31, 2008. No single customer accounts for more than 10% of accounts receivable.

REQUIRED:

a.   Why would an investor or other user of HP's financial statements be concerned that certain individual customers represent a large portion of the receivables balance?

b.   If problems arose with some of these customers, explain how it might affect HP's financial statements.

REAL DATA

ID6–10

Boosting earnings with bad debt estimates

Forbes noted that "Fairfield Company does set aside a reserve for bad debts, but last year it began tinkering with its provision for loan losses, reducing it from $6.5 million in one year to $5.39 million the next. It may not sound like much, but the reserve now covers only 4% of the company's time share sales, down from 6.5%—even though sales have increased by 30%. But, hey, that's tomorrow's problem. Today, Fairfield gets an extra $1 million in earnings."

REQUIRED:

a.   Provide several reasons why a company may reduce its bad debt reserve from $6.5 to $5.39 million. Would these reasons seem to be as reasonable when sales have increased by 30 percent?

b.   What does *Forbes* mean in the article by "that's tomorrow's problem"?

REAL DATA

ID6–11

Macroeconomic conditions and uncollectibles

In its November, 2009, press release discussing third quarter financial results, the construction management and consulting firm Hill International specifically cited an increase in bad debt expense as a drag on otherwise improved operating profits. Hill provides its services globally to companies involved in large construction projects.

REQUIRED:

Discuss the effects of an international real estate recession on construction projects and why this macroeconomic event would affect a company's bad debt expense. Who is on the other side of a company's bad debt expense? How does this expense affect the income statement and the balance sheet? How could an analyst following the global construction markets use a company's disclosure on bad debts to better understand the industry?

REAL DATA

ID6–12

Accounting for foreign currencies— An economic consequence

An article in *Forbes* noted that "accounting rules . . . can often change the way companies do business." Under the accounting rule covering receivables and payables denominated in foreign currencies, for example, "it is very important for companies to monitor their currency dealings." A case in point is R.J. Reynolds Industries, which "opened regional treasury offices in London and Hong Kong to keep tabs on worldwide cash flow and direct local borrowings." In that same article, a partner from a major accounting firm indicated that "more and more companies are centralizing their treasury-management function. Those that don't may be operating at a disadvantage."

REQUIRED:

a.   Explain why the methods of accounting for foreign currencies might cause a company to centralize its treasury-management function and why those that don't may be operating at a disadvantage.

b.   What is one of the main strategies used by U.S. companies to reduce the risks of holding receivables or payables denominated in non-U.S. currencies?

c.   Explain how the strategy in (b) works. Specifically, how might it be used to reduce the possibility of violating a covenant on an outstanding debt?

ID6–13

The SEC Form 10-K of NIKE is reproduced in Appendix C.

The SEC Form
10-K of NIKE

REQUIRED:

Review the SEC 10-K Form for NIKE, and answer the following questions.

a. Compute the change in NIKE's current ratio and working capital from 2008 to 2009. Which accounts are the most important in explaining that change?

b. What is included in NIKE's balance sheet cash account?

c. How large are NIKE's receivables relative to current assets and total assets? How important is receivables management to NIKE's operations? How large is the reserve (allowance) for bad debts? Explain.

d. What percent of revenue and accounts receivable results from international sales? What strategies does NIKE employ to mitigate risks related to foreign currency?

e. Why is the increase in accounts receivable listed in the operating section of the statement of cash flows?

CHAPTER 7

Merchandise Inventory

KEY POINTS

The following key points are emphasized in this chapter:

- Inventory and how it affects the financial statements.
- Four issues that must be addressed when accounting for inventory.
- General rules for including items in inventory and attaching costs to these items.
- The three cost flow assumptions—average, FIFO, and LIFO.
- The lower-of-cost-or-market rule.

When the shareholders of Ann Taylor Stores, a national retailer of upscale women's clothing, brought suit against company management, the company was accused of misleading investors by hiding the fact that it had accumulated huge amounts of excessive and overvalued inventory. Although the company reported disappointing results, surprising Wall Street, management denied any wrongdoing. The financial press often reports incidents where management uses inventory accounting to manipulate earnings. This chapter covers inventory accounting, providing analysts the knowledge necessary to recognize how decisions involving inventory accounting influence the financial statements.

Inventory refers to items held for sale in the ordinary course of business. It is very important to retail and manufacturing enterprises, whose performance depends significantly on their sales. The demand for a company's products and the effectiveness of its inventory management are often the most important determinants of a company's success. To illustrate, *BusinessWeek* once reported that the international grocery store, Aldi, stocked only 700 product lines, compared to 20,000 at competing grocers and up to 150,000 at Wal-Mart Supercenters. Analysts following the company have noted that handling fewer items allows the company better control over quality and price, and simplifies shipping and handling functions, yielding better-than-average operating profit margins.

> **?** The Small Business Adviser in *Business Today* once noted that "your inventory must be managed well to maximize profits. Uncontrolled inventories are inefficient and costly." What are "uncontrolled inventories," and how are they inefficient and costly?

Shareholders, creditors, managers, and auditors are all justifiably interested in the amount, condition, and marketability of a company's inventory. Shareholders are interested in future sales, profits, and dividends, all of which are related to the demand for inventory, and in the efficiency with which managers acquire, carry, and sell inventory. Creditors are interested in the ability of inventory sales to produce cash that can be used to meet interest and principal payments. Creditors may also view inventory as potential collateral or security for loans. Management must ensure that inventories are acquired (or manufactured) and carried at reasonable costs. Enough inventory must be carried and available to meet constantly changing consumer demands; yet carrying too much inventory can be very costly. Auditors must ensure that the inventory dollar amount disclosed in the financial statements is determined using generally accepted accounting principles and reflects the value of the inventories actually owned. The value and marketability of a company's inventory can also provide an indication of its ability to continue as a going concern.

Excerpts from the operating section of Target Corporation's statement of cash flows are provided below (dollars in millions).

	2008	2007	2006
Net earnings	$2,214	$2,849	$ 2,787
. . . .	. . . .	. . . .	. . . .
Change in inventory	77	(525)	(431)
. . . .	. . . .	. . . .	. . . .
Cash flow provided by operations	$4,430	$4,125	$ 4,862?

Did Target's inventory increase or decrease during 2006, 2007, and 2008, and why is the change added to or subtracted from net earnings in the calculation of cash flow provided by operations?

THE RELATIVE SIZE OF INVENTORIES

Note in Figure 7–1 that financial institutions and Internet firms carry little or no inventories, while inventory is very important to retailers and, to a lesser extent, to manufacturers. Inventory is by far the largest current asset for grocery store chains like Kroger; and for retailers like Lowe's, JCPenney, and Wal-Mart, efficient and effective inventory management is the key barometer for their success. Manufacturers, like GE, invest in inventories because raw materials are necessary for the manufacturing process, but because carrying inventory is costly, they strive to minimize inventory levels, hoping to send their finished products to distributors and retailers as soon as possible. Similarly, companies that extract natural resources, like Chevron, attempt to ship their product to refineries and processing stations, and then to market, as soon as it is taken from the ground.

FIGURE 7–1

Inventory as a percentage of total assets and current assets

	Inventory/ Total Assets	Inventory/ Current Assets
MANUFACTURING:		
General Electric (Manufacturer)	0.02	0.11
Chevron (Oil drilling and refining)	0.04	0.19
RETAIL:		
Kroger (Grocery retail)	0.21	0.67
Lowe's (Hardware retail)	0.25	0.89
INTERNET:		
Yahoo! (Internet search engine)	0.00	0.00
Cisco (Internet systems)	0.02	0.03
GENERAL SERVICES:		
AT&T (Telecommunications services)	0.00	0.00
Wendy's/Arby's (Restaurant services)	0.01	0.06
FINANCIAL SERVICES:		
Bank of America (Banking services)	0.00	0.00
Goldman Sachs (Investment services)	0.00	0.00

Both Hewlett-Packard, a world leader in technology development, and Yahoo!, a well-known Internet portal and search engine, play important roles in today's high-tech business economy. One carries virtually no inventories while the other carries a substantial amount. Which is which? Explain.

ACCOUNTING FOR INVENTORY: FOUR IMPORTANT ISSUES

Figure 7–2 summarizes four important issues that must be addressed when accounting for inventory. At the top of the figure, the life cycle of inventory is divided into four segments. Inventory is (1) acquired, through purchase or manufacture, and then (2) carried on the company's balance sheet. It then either (3) is sold or (4) remains on

FIGURE 7–2   Accounting for inventory: Four important issues

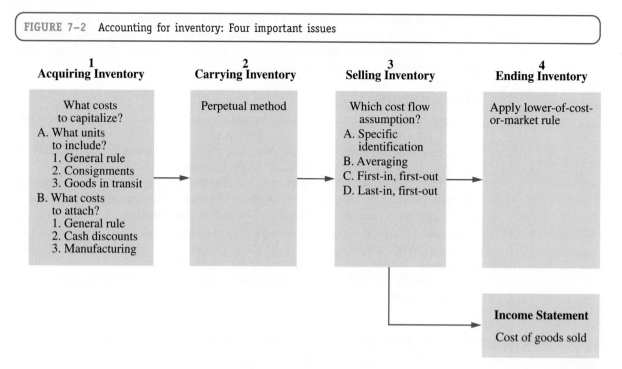

the balance sheet as ending inventory. At each of these four points, an important issue in financial accounting must be addressed. The remainder of the chapter covers these four points in order.

ACQUIRING INVENTORY: WHAT COSTS TO CAPITALIZE?

Inventory costs are capitalized because inventories are assets that provide future economic benefits. When inventories are sold, these benefits are realized. According to the matching principle, the capitalized cost should at this time be matched against the revenue recognized from the sale. Determining the amount of capitalized cost involves two steps: The number of items or units that belong in inventory must first be determined, and then costs must be attached to each item.

What Items or Units to Include?

Decisions as to what items or units to include in inventory are governed by a general rule. However, the general rule is not always simple to apply.

GENERAL RULE

Items should be included in a company's inventory if they are being held for sale and the company has complete and unrestricted ownership of them. Such ownership indicates that (1) the company bears the complete loss if the inventory is lost, stolen, or destroyed and (2) the company owns all rights to the benefits produced by the items.

In most cases, ownership is accompanied by possession: Companies that own inventory are usually in possession of it. Under these circumstances, determining the number of units that belong in inventory is straightforward: The number of inventory

units on the company's premises can simply be counted. In some cases, however, ownership is not accompanied by possession, and it becomes somewhat more difficult to find and determine the appropriate number of inventory units. Consignments and goods in transit are two common examples.

CONSIGNMENTS

In a **consignment,** a *consignor* (the owner) transfers inventory to a *consignee* (receiver), who takes physical possession and places the inventory up for sale. When it is sold, the consignee collects the sale proceeds, keeps a percentage of the proceeds for the service, and transfers the remainder to the consignor.

When accounting for consignments, it is important to realize that ownership, not physical possession, determines the balance sheet on which consigned inventory is disclosed. Since consigned inventory is owned by the consignor, it belongs on the consignor's balance sheet, even though it is physically located on the consignee's premises. When preparing or using financial statements, managers must be sure that consigned inventory has been treated in the appropriate manner. Misclassifying it would misstate the inventory balance, current assets, cost of goods sold, gross profit, and net income.

Saks, a fashion retail store, reported 2008 consignment inventories of $139 million not reflected on the company's balance sheet. Explain what consignment inventories are and why they would not be reflected on Saks's balance sheet.

GOODS IN TRANSIT

When inventory is sold, the seller records a sale and the buyer records a purchase. Theoretically, both parties should record the transaction at exactly the same moment: the point in time when the ownership of the inventory transfers from the seller to the buyer. For practical purposes, however, most sales are recorded when goods are shipped, and most purchases are recorded when goods are received. Since goods are often in transit between the seller and the buyer for as long as several days, sellers and buyers often record the same transaction at two different points in time. This practice is acceptable except in cases where there are **goods in transit** at the end of an accounting period. For example, suppose that Buyer & Co. (located in Seattle, Washington) purchased goods on account from Seller Inc. (located in New York) on December 29. Seller delivered the goods immediately to XYZ Trucking Co., and the goods are in transit on December 31, the balance sheet date for both Buyer and Seller.

Accounting for this transaction in an appropriate manner involves determining who owns the goods while they are in transit. The most common way of determining ownership is to examine the freight terms associated with the shipment. These terms normally indicate which party bears the responsibility for shipping the goods and thereby owns them while they are in transit. The freight term of FOB shipping point (destination) indicates that the purchaser (seller) owns the inventory during transit.

FOB (free on board) shipping point indicates that the seller is responsible for the goods only to the point from which they are shipped. In the example, if the goods were shipped FOB shipping point, Seller Inc. would be responsible to deliver the goods to XYZ Trucking. From that point to Seattle, Buyer would be considered the owner of the

goods, and their value would belong on Buyer's December 31 balance sheet. Both an inventory purchase on Buyer's books and a sale on Seller's books should be recorded.

FOB (free on board) destination indicates that the seller is responsible for the goods all the way to their destination. If the goods in the example were shipped FOB destination, Seller Inc. would be considered the owner of the goods until they reached Seattle. In this case, the goods would belong in Seller's inventory, and neither a purchase nor a sale would be recognized as of December 31.

Transactions near the end of an accounting period are often difficult to account for correctly. Managers must examine freight invoices and other related documents to ensure that sales and purchases are placed in the proper accounting periods and that, as of the balance sheet date, the number of inventory units on a company's balance sheet accurately reflects the inventory units actually owned. Similar to consignments, misclassifying goods in transit can misstate important financial statement numbers and ratios.

The 2008 annual report of Kellogg Company states, "The company recognizes sales upon delivery of its product to customers. . . ." What does this policy imply about goods in transit shipped by Kellogg? Explain how the revenue recognition policy influences the inventory amount carried on the balance sheet.

What Costs to Attach?

Once the number of items to be included in inventory has been determined, costs must be attached to these items to produce the total capitalized inventory cost. The general rule that guides this process and how it applies to inventory purchases and manufacturing operations is discussed in the following section.

GENERAL RULE

All costs associated with the manufacture, acquisition, storage, or preparation of inventory items should be capitalized and included in the inventory account. Included are the costs required to bring inventory items to saleable condition, such as the costs of purchasing, shipping in (called **freight-in** or **transportation-in**), manufacturing, and packaging. This rule is not difficult to apply in most cases, but two relatively common areas require further discussion. They are (1) accounting for cash (purchase) discounts on inventory purchases and (2) determining the costs of manufacturing inventories.

Lowe's Companies, Inc. reported in its 2008 annual report: "The cost of inventory also includes certain costs associated with the preparation of inventory for resale. . . ." Suppose that Lowe's paid $5 million in 2008 to assemble light fixtures before displaying them for sale. Explain how Lowe's would account for this cost.

ACCOUNTING FOR CASH (PURCHASE) DISCOUNTS

Chapter 6 discusses accounting for cash (purchase) discounts from the seller's point of view. There we commented that the gross method establishes a credit sale and the corresponding account receivable at the gross price and recognizes a discount if payment

is received within the discount period. Accounting for cash (purchase) discounts on inventory purchases is exactly the same, except now it is from the buyer's point of view. The inventory purchase is booked at the gross price, and if payment is made within the discount period, the carrying value of the inventory is reduced by the discount. If the discount is missed, the inventory is carried at the gross amount.

It is generally not advisable for companies to miss discounts. Under terms 2/10, n/30, for example, a purchasing company that makes a $1,000 payment 20 days after the expiration of the 10-day discount period would be paying a $20 financing charge. This situation is equivalent to borrowing cash at a 36.5 percent ([$20/$1,000] × [365 days/20 days]) annual rate of interest. Missing discounts, therefore, can be very expensive.

Companies that miss discounts because they are short of cash would be better off borrowing from a bank at a rate much lower than 36.5 percent and using the proceeds to pay those suppliers offering cash (purchase) discounts. Consequently, most purchasing companies attempt to make payment within the discount period. Inability to do so can be a sign of mismanagement and/or serious financial problems.

> **?** Dell is one of the leaders in the personal computer market, staking its claim with superior inventory management. Its 2008 annual report shows sales and cost of goods sold of $61 and $50 billion, respectively, and an investment in inventory of only $867 million. Almost incredibly, Dell turned its inventory over 49 times (every 7.4 days) during 2008. Discuss how effective inventory management can boost cash flow.

DETERMINING THE COSTS OF MANUFACTURING INVENTORIES

Retail companies, like Sears, Wal-Mart, Target, Macy's, and JCPenney, simply purchase inventories (usually from manufacturers) and sell them for prices that exceed their costs. Retailers primarily provide a distribution service, rarely changing or improving the inventories they sell. As a result, the capitalized inventory cost for a retail operation consists primarily of only two components: (1) the purchase cost and (2) freight-in, the cost of shipping the goods to the retailer. If Wal-Mart, for example, purchases merchandise for $5,000 cash and pays $500 to have the goods shipped to one of its stores, the following journal entry would be recorded:

Inventory (+A)	5,500	
Cash (−A)		5,500

Purchased inventory, including freight-in charges

The operations of **manufacturing companies,** like IBM, General Electric, General Motors, Procter & Gamble, RJR Nabisco, and Johnson & Johnson, are much more complex. These companies purchase raw materials and use processes involving labor and other costs to manufacture their inventories. The capitalized inventory cost therefore includes the cost of acquiring the raw materials, the cost of the labor used to convert the raw materials to finished goods, and other costs that support the production process. These other costs, called **overhead,** include such items as indirect materials (e.g., cleaning supplies), indirect labor (e.g., salaries of line managers), depreciation of fixed assets, and utility and insurance costs.

The capitalized inventory costs of manufacturing operations include all costs required to bring the inventory to saleable condition. In this general respect, accounting for manufacturing operations is no different from accounting for retail operations. However, in manufacturing, virtually any cost that can be linked to the production process

should be allocated to the inventory account. Therefore, costs like depreciation, wages and salaries, rent, and insurance are often capitalized as part of the inventory cost and, accordingly, are matched against revenues when the finished inventory is sold.

The footnotes to the 2008 financial statements of Intel Corporation contained the following information (dollars in millions):

	2008	2007
Raw materials	$ 608	$ 507
Work in process	1,577	1,460
Finished goods	1,559	1,403
	$3,744	$3,370

Is Intel a retailer or a manufacturer? What dollar amount appeared in the inventory account on the 2008 balance sheet? Provide several examples of the kinds of costs included in work in process and finished goods.

Financial statement users should be aware that allocating overhead costs to inventory is a very subjective process, requiring expertise, that can have significant effects on important financial numbers and ratios. These allocations give management substantial influence over the financial statements. General Electric, for example, once reported in the footnotes of its annual report that it "changed its accounting procedures to include certain inventory costs [including depreciation and other product costs] previously charged directly to expense." The change increased reported net income by $281 million.

CARRYING INVENTORY: PERPETUAL METHOD

Until relatively recently, many companies (especially large retail and manufacturing operations) had difficulty maintaining a continuous record of inventory balances due to the speed with which inventories flowed in and out of the business. The number and variety of transactions were just too great to perpetually maintain an accurate count at a reasonable cost. Consequently, to prepare financial statements (i.e., compute the cost of goods sold and ending inventory), companies were forced to periodically disrupt operations and count their inventories.

Electronic data processing has dramatically reduced the cost of record keeping, and now most companies have moved—or are moving—toward computerized systems that maintain perpetual inventory balances. The bar code systems you see in major grocery stores (e.g., Safeway) and retailers (e.g., Target) are common examples. While these systems do not eliminate the need to periodically count inventories, they offer a much greater level of control over inventories—a key element for the success of manufacturers and retailers. In this section, we describe the **perpetual inventory method.**

The perpetual inventory method is straightforward. When inventory is purchased, the inventory account is increased by the cost of the purchase; and when an inventory sale is made, the account is decreased by the amount of the cost of the sold inventory. Accordingly, perpetual balances are maintained in the inventory and cost of goods sold accounts. At the end of the accounting period, though not necessary for the preparation of the financial statements, an inventory count should be taken. The count provides an inventory amount that can be compared to the amount in the inventory account to

FIGURE 7–3

Perpetual inventory

Assume that inventory at the beginning of December is $2,500 (125 units at $20 per unit), and the following events occurred during December, and the inventory T-account follows.

<u>December 10:</u> Purchased 100 units of inventory on account for $20 per unit.

Inventory (+A)	$2,000^a$	
Accounts payable (+L)		2,000

<u>December 20:</u> Sold 50 units of inventory for cash at $30 per unit.

Cash (+A)	$1,500^b$	
Sales (R, +RE)		1,500
COGS (E, −RE)	$1,000^c$	
Inventory (−A)		1,000

<u>December 30:</u> An inventory count reveals that 170 units are on hand.

Loss (E, −RE)	100^d	
Inventory (−A)		100

Inventory				
Beginning balance	2,500			
12/10 purchase	2,000			
		12/20 sale	1,000	
Balance before count	3,500			
		Loss	100	
Balance after count	3,400			

^{a}(100 units × $20)
^{b}(50 units × $30)
^{c}(50 units × $20)
^{d}(175 units − 170 units) × $20

ascertain whether actual inventory matches the company's perpetual inventory record. Figure 7–3 provides an illustration.

Note that the perpetual method in combination with the end-of-period inventory count identifies a weakness in the company's inventory control procedures. One hundred and seventy-five units (125 + 100 − 50) were expected, but only 170 were found. Consequently, management is now alerted to an inventory control problem. The system does not offer an explanation for the five-unit shortage (e.g., theft, spoilage, inaccurate record keeping), but it does invite management to review the system.

Review Figure 7–3 again, and assume that the company lacked the technical ability (or chose not) to record the cost of the sold inventory ($1,000) for the December 20 sale. Instead, to compute cost of goods sold, the company relied upon the December 30 inventory count, and used the following formula.

Cost of goods sold	=	Beginning inventory	+	Purchases	−	Ending inventory
$1,100		$2,500	+	$2,000	−	$3,400 (170 units × $20 per unit)

This is an example of what is called the **periodic inventory method** because it computes cost of goods sold *periodically* (at the end of each reporting period) instead of *perpetually* (at the time of each sale). In this example it produces a cost of goods sold amount of $1,100, compared to the perpetual method, which produced a cost of goods sold amount of $1,000 and a loss due to the inventory shortage of $100. Under the

periodic method, management never learns that there is an inventory control problem; the cost of the problem is "buried" in the cost of goods sold number.

> CVS Corporation, a leading pharmacy retailer, takes independent physical counts on a regular basis at each location to ensure that the amounts reflected in the financial statements are accurate. Between physical counts, the company accrues for anticipated physical inventory losses on a location-by-location basis. Explain why CVS spends so much time and effort attempting to ensure accurate inventory counts.

ERRORS IN THE INVENTORY COUNT

Errors in the inventory count misstate both inventory on the balance sheet and net income on the income statement of that period. Such errors also misstate net income in the subsequent period by an equal dollar amount in the opposite direction. For example, an error in the inventory count taken at the end of 2011 that understates inventory by $2,000 will also understate 2011's net income by $2,000. In addition, this error if uncorrected will cause net income of 2012 to be overstated by $2,000.

To illustrate, assume that Rainier Corporation began operations on January 1, 2011. Figure 7–4 summarizes the transactions entered into by the company during 2011 and 2012 and contains accurate inventory balances and income statements for the two years. Assume that the only expenses incurred by the company were the costs of sold inventories.

FIGURE 7–4
Rainier
Corporation:
Transactions for
2011–2012

	Inventory	Sales
2011		
(1) Purchased 500 units of inventory for $1 per unit	$500	
(2) Sold 200 units of inventory for $3 per unit	(200)	$ 600
Ending inventory	$300	
Sales ($600) − Cost of Goods Sold ($200) = Net Income ($400)		
2012		
Beginning inventory	$300	
(1) Purchased 600 units of inventory for $1 per unit	600	
(2) Sold 700 units of inventory for $3 per unit	(700)	$2,100
Ending inventory	$200	
Sales ($2,100) − Cost of Goods Sold ($700) = Net Income ($1,400)		

Suppose that Rainier Corporation made no accounting errors during 2011 or 2012 except that it failed to include 20 items of inventory, each with a cost of $1, in its inventory count at the end of 2011. Inventory was thus determined incorrectly to be $280 instead of $300. Inventory was correctly counted at the end of 2012. The cost of goods sold and the inventory calculations for 2011 and 2012 appear in Figure 7–5. Income statements assuming accurate information and the miscounting error are shown in Figure 7–6.

In summary, a single error in the counting of inventory caused net income of 2011 and net income of 2012 to be misstated by equal dollar amounts ($20) in opposite directions. Although both income statements are incorrect, the balance sheet as of the end of 2012 is properly stated. The accurate inventory count at year-end corrected the

FIGURE 7–5
Inventory errors

Cost of Goods Sold Calculation:

	Cost of goods sold	=	Beginning inventory	+	Purchases	−	Ending inventory
2011:	$220	=	$0	+	$500	−	$280
2012:	$680	=	$280	+	$600	−	$200

FIGURE 7–6
Comparative income statements: Rainier Corporation

	Accurate	Error
2011		
Sales	$ 600	$ 600
Cost of goods sold	200	220
Net income	$ 400	$ 380
2012		
Sales	$2,100	$2,100
Cost of goods sold	700	680
Net income	$1,400	$1,420

inventory balance, and the $20 understatement of retained earnings due to understated net income in 2011 was counterbalanced by a $20 overstatement to net income in 2012.

Inventory errors are not unusual and at times can be quite significant. For example, the auditor for Comnet Corp., a computer software and health care products company, discovered that management had unintentionally overvalued inventories by $1.6 million on the company's financial statements. Consequently, Comnet's reported net income of $2.6 million was reduced to $1.0 million, and net income the following year was $1.6 million larger.

An article in the *Wall Street Journal* titled "Inventory Chicanery Tempts More Firms, Fools More Auditors" reported that "when companies are desperate to stay afloat, inventory fraud is the easiest way to produce instant profits and dress up the balance sheet . . . [and] the recent rise in inventory fraud is one of the biggest single reasons for the proliferation of accounting scandals." The article described how inventory frauds at Comptronix Corp., an Alabama electronics company, Laribee Wire Manufacturing, L.A. Gear, and the discount drugstore Phar-Mor were perpetrated simply by management creating fictitious inventories—undetected by the external auditor—that instantly increased profits. "Experts say that many companies overvalue obsolete goods and supplies. Others create phantom items in the warehouse to augment the assets needed for loan collateral. Still others count inventory that they pretend they have ordered but that will never arrive . . . [in these cases] the auditor was either taken or missed the obvious."

? In its 2008 annual report, The Gap reported ending inventory and net income of $1,506 million and $967 million, respectively. If The Gap had incorrectly counted its ending inventory at $1,700 million, what would have been its 2008 net income? (Do not account for income taxes.)

SELLING INVENTORY: WHICH COST FLOW ASSUMPTION?

Perhaps the most important and difficult question of inventory accounting involves how to allocate the capitalized inventory cost between the cost of goods sold and ending inventory. The examples so far have assumed that the cost of the sold inventory is known, but such situations are relatively unusual. In most cases, companies are unable to determine exactly which items are sold and which items remain in ending inventory. When this occurs, an assumption must be made about the cost flow of the inventory items. The assumption chosen can significantly affect net income, current assets, working capital, and the current ratio because it determines the relative costs allocated to the cost of goods sold and ending inventory.

This section first discusses the specific identification method, which is used when the cost of the sold inventory items can be determined. We then cover three cost flow assumptions that are used extensively in practice: averaging; first-in, first-out (FIFO); and last-in, first-out (LIFO).

Under IFRS, the last-in, first-out (LIFO) inventory cost flow assumption is prohibited. The cost of inventory generally is determined using the first-in, first-out (FIFO) or averaging assumption.

Specific Identification

In some cases, especially with relatively infrequent sales of large-ticket items (e.g., jewelry, furniture, automobiles, land), it is possible to specifically identify which inventory items have been sold and which remain. In such situations, the allocation of inventory cost between the cost of goods sold and ending inventory is relatively straightforward. Suppose, for example, that on March 1, Used Cars & Co. had three 2011 Honda Accords for sale. Cars 1 and 2 were purchased from the same dealer at a cost of $10,000 each. Car 3 was purchased recently at an auction for $12,000. The three cars are in comparable condition, and the selling price for each is $18,000. The March 1 inventory for Used Cars & Co. follows:

Car	Cost
1	$10,000
2	10,000
3	12,000
Total	$32,000

Assume that on March 15, Sammy Sportsman agrees to purchase any one of the three cars for $18,000. Used Cars gives Sammy Car 3 (cost = $12,000), and the following journal entries are recorded:

Cash (+A)	18,000	
Sales (R, +RE)		18,000
Sold Honda		
Cost of Goods Sold (E, −RE)	12,000	
Inventory (−A)		12,000
Recognized cost of goods sold for		
Honda with cost of $12,000		

It is fairly clear in this situation that $12,000 should have been allocated to cost of goods sold and $20,000 should remain in ending inventory. An inventory item (Car 3) with a cost of $12,000 was sold. Thus, the specific identification procedure is a relatively straightforward way to determine the cost of goods sold and ending inventory. Nonetheless, it does have limitations.

First, the **specific identification** procedure requires the tracking of specific inventory items, which can be difficult for some firms. A second limitation is that in many cases specific identification allows a manager to manipulate net income and the ending inventory value. Suppose in the example that the manager of Used Cars & Co. chose to give Sammy Sportsman either Car 1 or Car 2, instead of Car 3. Recall that Sammy was indifferent toward choosing among the three automobiles. In this situation, the following journal entries would have been recorded:

Cash (+A)	**18,000**	
Sales (R, +RE)		**18,000**
Sold Honda		
Cost of Goods Sold (E, −RE)	**10,000**	
Inventory (−A)		**10,000**
Recognized cost of goods sold for		
Honda with cost of $10,000		

The decision to give Sammy Car 1 or Car 2 would have produced net income and ending inventory values that were $2,000 ($12,000 − $10,000) greater than the decision to give Sammy Car 3. The specific identification procedure allowed the manager to manipulate income and inventory by choosing which inventory item to deliver to the customer. While manipulating the financial statement in this way is not a misrepresentation, it does allow management to influence the timing of income recognition.

Several years ago Amazon.com dropped the specific identification method in favor of the first-in, first-out (FIFO) inventory cost flow assumption. Explain why a growing company, like Amazon, might make such a change.

Three Inventory Cost Flow Assumptions: Average, FIFO, and LIFO

The inventories of many companies are acquired at so many different prices that it is often difficult to identify specifically the costs of the items sold and the costs of the items in ending inventory. In such cases, an assumption must be invoked.

To illustrate and compare the three different cost flow assumptions, consider the following example. The chart in Figure 7–7 provides information about the inventory purchases and sales for Discount Sales Company over a two-year period. Following this information are inventory T-accounts that track the information under three different cost-flow assumptions: average, first-in, first-out (FIFO), and last-in, first-out (LIFO).

Note in Figure 7–7 that inventory costs are increasing across time. The cost of the beginning inventory is $4 per unit; purchase costs in year 1 are $7 per unit; and purchase costs in year 2 are $8 per unit. Note also that the inventory purchases in years 1 and 2 are recorded in the same way across all three assumptions: $70 and $40 in years 1 and 2, respectively. The differences in the assumptions relate to the different dollar amounts attached to cost of goods sold (COGS) when the outflow of the sold inventory is recorded.

FIGURE 7-7

Inventory flow assumptions: Average, FIFO, and LIFO

Given Information:

Description	Units	Unit Cost	Total
Beginning inventory	3	$4	$12
Year 1			
Purchases	10	$7	$70
Sales	(8)		
Ending inventory	5		
Year 2			
Beginning inventory	5		
Purchases	5	$8	$40
Sales	(8)		
Ending inventory	2		

Inventory (Average Assumption)

Year 1:	Beginning inventory	12	
	Purchases	70	
			COGS (8u × $6.31[1]) 50
Year 2:	Ending inventory	32	
	Purchases	40	
			COGS (8u × $7.20[2]) 58
	Ending inventory	14	

Inventory (FIFO Assumption)

Year 1:	Beginning inventory	12	
	Purchases	70	
			COGS 47[3]
Year 2:	Ending inventory	35	
	Purchases	40	
			COGS 59[4]
	Ending inventory	16	

Inventory (LIFO Assumption)

Year 1:	Beginning inventory	12	
	Purchases	70	
			COGS 56[5]
Year 2:	Ending inventory	26	
	Purchases	40	
			COGS 58[6]
	Ending inventory	8	

[1] 3u × $4 = $12   [2] 5u × $6.31 = $32   [3](3u × $4) + (5u × $7)
    10u × $7 = $70   5u × $8.00 = $40   [4](5u × $7) + (3u × $8)
    13u $82   10u $72   [5]8u × $7
    $6.31 = $82/13u $7.20 = $72/10u   [6](5u × $8) + (2u × $7) + (1u × $4)

Under the **average assumption,** a weighted average cost of the units available for sale is computed at the time of the sale. For example, at the time of the sale in year 1, 13 units were available for sale—3 units @ $4 and 10 units @ $7, a weighted average (as illustrated in Figure 7–7, footnote 1) of $6.31. This amount is multiplied times the number of units sold (8) to compute both COGS and the reduction in the inventory account. The same procedure is followed in year 2, but note that the weighted average as of the date of the sale is different; it has risen to $7.20 per unit because the inventory purchase costs have risen.

Under the **first-in, first-out (FIFO) assumption,** the oldest available inventory costs are used to compute COGS. In year 1, it was assumed that 3 of the 8 units sold were from the beginning inventory ($4 per unit), while the remaining 5 units were from the purchase in year 1 ($7 per unit)—leaving an ending inventory ($35) composed of 5 units @ $7 per unit. In year 2, 5 of the 8 units were assumed to have come from the remaining 5 units purchased in year 1 ($7 per unit), while the remaining 3 units came from the year 2 purchase ($8 per unit). The $16 ending inventory is composed of 2 units @ $8 per unit, all from the year 2 purchase—the most current inventory costs.

Under the **last-in, first-out (LIFO) assumption,** the most current inventory costs are used to compute COGS. In year 1, it was assumed that all 8 units sold had a cost of $7, the most current purchase cost, leaving an ending inventory ($26) composed of 2 units @ $7 and 3 units @ $4 per unit. In year 2, the 8 units sold were assumed to have come from three groups: 5 units from the most current (year 2) purchase, 2 units from the remaining units purchased in year 1 ($7 per unit), and 1 unit from beginning inventory ($4 per unit). Year 2's ending inventory under LIFO ($8) is 2 units @ $4 per unit—inventory costs from before year 1.

Inventory Cost Flow Assumptions: Effects on the Financial Statements

Figure 7–8 compares the FIFO, average, and LIFO cost flow assumptions with respect to COGS, gross profit, and ending inventory for years 1 and 2. Assume that Discount Sales Company sold its inventory for $10 per unit in both years 1 and 2.

Refer first to year 1. FIFO gives rise to the largest gross profit ($33), and ending inventory ($35) while LIFO produces the lowest gross profit ($24) and ending inventory ($26). These differences arise because inventory costs are rising and LIFO uses the most current (highest) costs in computing COGS and allocates the oldest (lowest) costs to ending inventory. In general, in times of rising inventory costs, FIFO will give rise to higher net income and inventory numbers than LIFO. These differences reverse in periods when inventory costs decrease. The average assumption creates dollar values between FIFO and LIFO in either case. In times of increasing inventory costs,

FIGURE 7–8

Financial statement effects of the three inventory cost-flow assumptions

	FIFO	Average	LIFO
YEAR 1:			
Sales	$80	$80	$80
COGS	(47)	(50)	(56)
Gross profit	33	30	24
Ending inventory	35	32	26
YEAR 2:			
Sales	$80	$80	$80
COGS	(59)	(58)	(58)
Gross profit	21	22	22
Ending inventory	16	14	8

using the FIFO assumption can boost important financial ratios, such as return on equity, earnings per share, working capital, and the current ratio. Choosing LIFO, on the other hand, may value inventories at unrealistically low levels.

> Walgreen's uses the LIFO assumption for inventories. Inventory on the 2008 balance sheet was reported as $6.8 billion. Had the company used the FIFO assumption, ending inventory would have been $1.2 billion higher. Explain why ending inventory can be so different under two acceptable assumptions.

In year 2 the situation is different. LIFO's COGS ($58) is actually less than FIFO's ($59), which means that gross profit is higher for LIFO ($22) than FIFO ($21) even though inventory costs increased. While this result seems inconsistent with year 1, it occurs because during year 2 Discount Company sold more inventory items than it purchased, liquidating some of its inventory balance. The company began the year with 5 units and ended with only 2. This liquidation caused the LIFO assumption to "dip into old (low-cost) layers of inventory" in the calculation of COGS. Note in Figure 7–7, for example, that COGS under LIFO included 2 units from year 1 ($7 per unit) and 1 unit from inventory prior to year 1 ($4 per unit). The boost to profit associated with dipping into old inventory costs is called a **LIFO liquidation.**

Inventory Cost Flow Assumptions: Effects on Federal Income Taxes

As the previous example shows, if inventory costs and units are increasing, using the LIFO assumption gives rise to the lowest net income amount. During inflationary times, therefore, the LIFO assumption is an attractive alternative for determining a company's federal income tax liability, which is computed as a percentage of taxable income; less taxable income means less federal income tax liability.

Federal income tax law states that if a company uses the LIFO assumption for computing its tax liability, it must also use the LIFO assumption for preparing its financial statements. If a company uses a cost flow assumption other than LIFO for tax purposes, it can use the LIFO, averaging, or FIFO assumption for financial reporting. This regulation is called the **LIFO conformity rule,** and it causes most companies to use the same cost flow assumption for both income tax and financial reporting purposes. Companies that choose LIFO for tax purposes must use it for reporting purposes. Companies that want to use FIFO for reporting purposes may not use LIFO for tax purposes.

Figure 7–9 shows the effects of the different cost flow assumptions on federal income taxes. The comparison uses the numbers from Figure 7–8 (year 1), except that expenses of $10 are assumed for all cases and federal income taxes have been assessed

FIGURE 7–9

Income tax effects of the three inventory cost flow assumptions

	FIFO	Averaging	LIFO
Sales (35 units × $15)	$80	$80	$80
Cost of goods sold	47	50	56
Gross profit	$33	$30	$24
Expenses	10	10	10
Net income before taxes	$23	$20	$14
Federal income taxes (34%)	8	7	5
Net income after taxes	$17	$13	$ 9

as a percentage (34 percent) of net income before taxes and are listed as an expense on the income statement.

Note in Figure 7–9 that, in times of rising inventory costs, if a company chooses to minimize its federal income taxes by using the LIFO assumption, it must report lower net income and inventory on its financial statements. The effects on the financial statements of using LIFO can be significant. For example, as of December 31, 2008, the inventories of General Electric, a LIFO user, were valued at about $706 million less than they would be under FIFO. In another example, DuPont reduced its current assets and reported net income by $612 million when it changed from FIFO to LIFO. However, companies using the FIFO assumption to boost reported net income and ending inventory must pay additional federal income taxes. These additional tax payments can be very significant.

> **?** Earlier we mentioned that Walgreen's 2008 inventory balance under LIFO was $1.2 billion lower than it would have been under FIFO. Estimate how many dollars in taxes Walgreen's has saved by using LIFO instead of FIFO. Assume a 30 percent income tax rate.

Choosing an Inventory Cost Flow Assumption: Trade-Offs

Most companies find it impractical to specifically identify the inventory items sold during a given period. Management must therefore choose from among the three assumptions discussed above. *Accounting Trends and Techniques* (2009) reports that of the major U.S. companies surveyed, 36 percent used LIFO, 65 percent used FIFO, and 29 percent used averaging for at least some of their inventories. Most of these companies used different methods for different kinds of inventory. Of those using LIFO, only 4 percent use it for all inventories, but 52 percent used it for over half of their inventories. One of the primary reasons that large U.S. LIFO users use other assumptions as well is that they own non-U.S. subsidiaries that use IFRS, which does not allow LIFO. The choice of a cost flow assumption is a difficult problem that depends on the situation faced by a given company.

Before considering the trade-offs involved in choosing an inventory cost flow assumption, remember that the assumption does not necessarily reflect the actual movement of the inventory. In fact, there is often no relationship between the assumption used to value the inventory for reporting purposes and the actual cost of the inventory on hand. Choosing a cost flow assumption is largely independent of the nature of the inventory itself.

It is also difficult to change a cost flow assumption once it has been chosen. As discussed in Chapter 3, the principle of consistency requires that accounting methods be consistent from year to year, and such changes, even when approved by an auditor, must be fully described in the footnotes, and prior years' financial statements must be restated. Recently, only a few major U.S. companies have changed their inventory cost flow assumptions.

The trade-offs involved in choosing an inventory cost flow assumption are divided into two categories: (1) income and asset measurement and (2) economic consequences. *Income and asset measurement* refers to how well each assumption produces measures that reflect the actual performance and financial condition of a company. *Economic consequences* refer to the costs and benefits associated with using a particular assumption.

INCOME AND ASSET MEASUREMENT

In terms of income and asset measurement, most believe that FIFO is preferred. FIFO produces a more current measure of inventory on the balance sheet. Ending inventory

under FIFO reflects the costs of the most recent purchases; LIFO reports ending inventory in terms of older, less relevant costs. Using LIFO over a period of time, therefore, can give rise to ending inventory costs that are grossly outdated. Union Carbide's net worth (assets − liabilities), for example, was at one time understated by about 18 percent simply because it used LIFO, and the *inventory turnover* (cost of goods sold ÷ inventory) of Monsanto, another LIFO user, was overstated by approximately 50 percent.

The LIFO assumption is a better application of the matching principle because it allocates the most current purchase costs to cost of goods sold, where they are matched against current sales in the determination of net income. However, this LIFO advantage is normally relatively small because it is measured only over a single year. For example, DuPont's 2008 LIFO-based inventory was approximately $1 billion below its current cost. LIFO-based earnings, on the other hand, were only $200 million below FIFO-based earnings.

ECONOMIC CONSEQUENCES

The economic consequences of choosing an inventory flow assumption relate to such factors as income taxes and liquidity problems, bookkeeping costs, LIFO liquidations and purchasing practices, debt and compensation contracts, and the capital market.

INCOME TAXES AND LIQUIDITY. Often the most important economic consideration when choosing an inventory cost flow assumption is the tax consequence. When inventory costs are rising, LIFO yields a lower net income number than FIFO, resulting in a lower tax liability. Consequently, choosing LIFO can improve a company's cash flow by minimizing cash payments for income taxes. As mentioned earlier, the magnitude of such savings can be significant.

> The fact that LIFO is not allowed under IFRS raises an important potential impediment to the adoption of IFRS in the United States. Most LIFO users in the U.S. have chosen LIFO because it results in an income tax savings that has accumulated over many years. DuPont, for example, has saved over $150 million in income taxes because it uses LIFO. A shift to IFRS in the absence of any changes in the U.S. tax law could impose a huge and immediate tax burden on LIFO users in the U.S.

Using FIFO can create liquidity problems. In times of rising prices, FIFO produces higher income than LIFO because it matches relatively old costs against current revenues. Because old costs are lower than current costs, FIFO creates **paper profits,** profits that are due to rising inventory costs instead of efficient operations. Paper profits appear on the income statement, but they are not backed by cash inflows. Unfortunately, these inflated profits are also used to determine a company's tax liability, which must be paid in cash. As a result, operating cash inflows may not be sufficient to cover the required cash outflows, and the company's liquidity position suffers.

> In the early 1970s, the United States experienced a dramatic economic downturn and double-digit inflation. In one year alone, over 400 companies, most with cash flow problems, switched from FIFO to LIFO. Explain why so many companies would make such a shift.

BOOKKEEPING COSTS. While LIFO usually brings about a lower tax liability than FIFO, it requires more bookkeeping procedures and is generally more costly to implement. For example, one survey of FIFO users found that many companies did not adopt LIFO because the record-keeping requirements of LIFO were burdensome and costly. Indeed, short-cut methods for estimating LIFO have been devised to reduce the costs of maintaining LIFO records.

LIFO LIQUIDATION AND INVENTORY PURCHASING PRACTICES. As illustrated earlier, the use of LIFO can boost net income amounts when inventory levels are cut back. Consider, for example, Atlantic Richfield, a giant in the oil industry and a long-time LIFO user. In the early 1980s, the dollar amount in the company's inventory balance consisted of costs that were very old, extremely low, and outdated. Then an oil glut occurred, and the market price of oil decreased sharply. In response, Atlantic Richfield and a number of other oil companies cut inventory levels significantly. This action caused the low and outdated costs in inventory to be matched against Atlantic Richfield's current revenues. The result was a $105 million increase in the company's profits. That same year, the profits of Gulf Oil, Standard Oil of California, and Texaco, other LIFO users, were inflated for the same reasons, by $200 million, $165 million, and $315 million, respectively. Unfortunately, these high profits were due to the liquidation of LIFO inventories, not the effective and efficient operations of the oil companies or the condition of the oil industry, which at the time was suffering. Moreover, additional income taxes had to be paid on these profits.

Many LIFO users allow such inventory liquidations to occur, but other companies intentionally avoid them by maintaining their inventory purchases to prevent their inventory levels from diminishing. Such a practice avoids increased taxes, but at the same time, it can give rise to other problems. It may not be the appropriate time to purchase inventory. Inventory costs may be at a seasonal high, for example, or significant discounts may not be available. Furthermore, such action does nothing to solve the problem associated with LIFO's understated inventory valuation; it merely postpones a problem that grows worse with each passing year.

> **?** Ford Motor Company, a major automobile manufacturer, reported in its 2008 annual report that the reduction of its LIFO inventory quantities increased pre-tax net income by $209 million. Explain how reducing inventory could increase income. As an analyst, why would you be interested in such a disclosure?

DEBT AND COMPENSATION CONTRACTS. FIFO may be attractive to management because, when inventory costs are rising, FIFO produces higher reported net income and higher inventory values than LIFO. Compensation paid to management expressed as a percentage of FIFO income tends to be higher than compensation based on LIFO income. In addition, debt covenants using ratios based on FIFO will impose less restrictive constraints on managers than those based on LIFO.

The relative effects of LIFO and FIFO on the financial statements are reversed when prices are decreasing. For example, the annual report of May Department Stores once noted: "We value our department store inventories using the LIFO (last-in, first-out) method. Usually, this decreases earnings . . . [however, in the current year] we experienced deflation, which resulted in a pretax LIFO credit [earnings increase] of $46 million."

THE CAPITAL MARKET. Management may also choose FIFO over LIFO because it believes that FIFO's higher net income and inventory amounts are valued more highly

by investors and creditors in the capital market. They reason that using FIFO could improve the company's credit rating, which may lead to better terms on its borrowings and higher prices for its outstanding debt securities. Some believe that FIFO may also bring about higher prices for the company's outstanding equity securities. For example, in the survey mentioned earlier, when asked why the company did not use LIFO, one manager responded that using LIFO would depress the market price of its stock. If such assertions are correct, using FIFO would make it easier to raise capital as well as increase management's value in the managerial labor market.

The validity of this reasoning is open to question. A number of research studies in accounting suggest that the stock market "looks through" a company's accounting methods and values the company on the basis of the underlying cash flows. Since using LIFO usually saves taxes, these studies suggest that companies using LIFO are more highly valued by the stock market than companies using FIFO. However, the evidence is mixed, and all such conclusions are still tentative.

Under U.S. GAAP, companies using LIFO are required to report in the footnotes to the financial statements what the value of their inventories would be if they used FIFO. Also, they are required to report the income effects of any LIFO liquidations during the year.

General Motors reported the following information in Note 11 (Inventories) of its 2006 annual report (dollars in millions).

	2006	2005
Productive material, work in process, and supplies	$ 5,810	$ 5,512
Finished product, service parts, etc.	9,804	10,378
Total inventories at FIFO cost	15,614	15,890
Less LIFO allowance	(1,508)	(1,525)
Total	$14,106	$14,365

Inventories are stated at cost, which is not in excess of market. The cost of approximately 52 percent of U.S. inventories is determined by the last-in, first-out (LIFO) method. The cost of all other inventories is determined by either the first-in, first-out (FIFO) or average cost method.

During 2006 and 2005, U.S. LIFO inventory quantities were reduced. This reduction resulted in a liquidation of LIFO inventory quantities carried at lower costs prevailing in prior years as compared with the cost of 2006 and 2005 purchases, the effect of which decreased cost of goods sold by approximately $50 million in 2006 and $100 million in 2005, pre-tax.

What is the LIFO allowance, and why did the liquidation of LIFO inventory quantities reduce cost of goods sold?

THE LIFO RESERVE: A USER PERSPECTIVE. The footnotes to the 2008 financial statements of U.S. Steel Corporation (USS) stated, "Current acquisition costs were estimated to exceed (reported) inventory values at December 31 by approximately $1.1 billion in 2008 and $910 million in 2007." These dollar amounts are often referred to as **LIFO reserves,** and they provide useful information. For example, they enable users to compute the following for USS:

1. Inventory value under the FIFO assumption. USS reported LIFO inventory of $2,492 million as of December 31, 2008. Refer to the calculation below to see USS's

2008 inventory value if it used FIFO (dollars in millions). This calculation can help users compare the financial performance and condition of USS to that of other FIFO users.

2008 Inventory (LIFO) + 2008 LIFO Reserve = 2008 Inventory (FIFO)
$2,492   + $1,100   = $3,592

2. Net income and the additional tax liability if the company switched from LIFO to FIFO in 2008. Multiplying the reserve by the company's effective tax rate (which can be found in the footnotes) provides an estimate of the additional tax liability associated with changing from LIFO to FIFO in 2008 (dollars in millions):

2008 LIFO Reserve × Effective Tax Rate = Additional 2008 Tax
$1,100   ×   0.28   = $308

Such a change would result in recognizing the firm's oldest (and lowest) inventory cost in the 2008 cost of goods sold, thereby increasing taxable income and the associated tax liability. This calculation shows that USS would have paid additional taxes of $308 million if it had chosen to switch to FIFO in 2008. Another way to interpret this calculation is that it represents an estimate of the taxes saved by USS from the time it adopted LIFO to the present, assuming constant tax rates.

Assume that at the end of 2008 U.S. corporations were required to adopt IFRS, which does not allow LIFO, forcing U.S. Steel Corporation (USS) to immediately change from LIFO to FIFO. Do you think that USS would support such a requirement? Why?

3. FIFO net income in 2008 if the company had switched to FIFO in a prior year. An estimate of net income reported by USS if it had switched to FIFO in a prior year can be derived from multiplying the change in the LIFO reserve (from 2007 to 2008) by 1 minus the effective tax rate, and then adding that amount to net income reported under LIFO. Like the first calculation above, this calculation—provided below (dollars in millions)—can help users compare the financial performance and condition of USS to that of other FIFO users.

2008 Net Income (LIFO) +   Increase in LIFO Reserve   = 2008 Net Income (FIFO)
× Effective Tax Rate
$2,112   + [($1,100 − $910) × (1 − 0.28)] = $2,249

ENDING INVENTORY: APPLYING THE LOWER-OF-COST-OR-MARKET RULE

The inventory cost flow assumption determines the capitalized cost allocated to ending inventory. However, inventories on the balance sheet are not necessarily carried at this dollar amount. Based on conservatism, ending inventory is valued at cost or market value, whichever is lower.

Applying the lower-of-cost-or-market rule to ending inventory is accomplished by comparing the cost allocated to ending inventory with the market value of the inventory. If the market value exceeds the cost, no adjustment is made and the inventory remains at cost. If the market value is less than the cost, the inventories are written down to market value with an adjusting journal entry.

U.S. GAAP and IFRS use different market values when applying the lower-of-cost-or-market rule. Under U.S. GAAP, the market value is normally the replacement cost, the cost of replacing the inventory. Under IFRS, the market value is normally the realizable value, the amount at which the inventory could be sold.

Suppose, for example, that ABC Enterprises uses the FIFO assumption, which gives rise to an ending inventory of $100. If the market value of the inventory is $150, no adjusting journal entry need be recorded. The ending inventory remains at cost because cost ($100) is lower than market value ($150). If the market value of the inventories is $80, however, the inventory would have to be written down (reduced) from $100 to $80. The following journal entry represents one way of recording such a write-down:

Loss on Inventory Write-Down (Lo, −RE)	20	
Inventory (−A)		20

Wrote down inventory to market value ($100 − $80)

Inventory write-downs are fairly common and sometimes quite large. In a recent financial report, for example, Alcoa reported a write-down of approximately $213 million, while that same year Gerber Products Company recorded a $2.9 million charge to write down certain inventories to market value.

Under U.S. GAAP, inventory write-downs are considered permanent, meaning that they are not reversed even in cases when the market value of the written-down inventory rebounds. Under IFRS, on the other hand, if the market value of written-down inventory increases, an **inventory recovery** is recorded (i.e., the inventory is written up to the point of the original cost) and earnings are increased. This difference illustrates a case where IFRS treatment attempts to reflect the market values of assets more so than U.S. GAAP treatment.

THE LOWER-OF-COST-OR-MARKET RULE AND HIDDEN RESERVES

The lower-of-cost-or-market rule is often criticized because it treats inventory price changes inconsistently. Price decreases, based on difficult-to-determine market values, are recognized immediately, while price increases are not recognized until the inventory is sold in an objective and verifiable transaction. This conservative, but inconsistent, treatment can create "hidden reserves" that managers can use to manipulate income.

Consider a company that is just about to complete a very good year. Reported earnings are expected to be so high that management is seeking to reduce income and perhaps move some of the earnings to future periods that may be less successful. One way to execute this "income smoothing" strategy is to write down inventory in the current year and sell it in a future period. Suppose, for example, that management chooses to write down an inventory item with an original cost of $10 to its subjectively determined market value of $8. A $2 loss is immediately recognized, reducing the current year's net income. Assume further that during the following year, the inventory item is sold for $12, giving rise to a book gain that increases that year's net income by $4 ($12 − $8). Note that by writing down the inventory in the first year, management was able to transfer $2 of net income from the first to the second year. A "hidden reserve" was created by the write-down, which was realized in a subsequent period.

Certainly, the conservative and inconsistent nature of the lower-of-cost-or-market rule, combined with subjective inventory write-downs, can create "hidden reserves" that can be used to manage the reported values on the financial statements. However, it is important to keep in mind that conservative accounting is a response to the liability faced by those who must provide and audit financial statements. The potential costs to these parties associated with understating inventories and profits are typically less than those associated with overstating them. From an economic standpoint, therefore, the lower-of-cost-or-market rule may be justifiable, even though it produces questionable measures on the financial statements. In any event, investors, creditors, managers, auditors, and other interested parties must be aware of these weaknesses.

Olympic Steel, stock symbol ZEUS, announced early in April 2009 that it would record a $30 million charge to reduce the carrying cost of its inventory to market prices. The company had seen a 43 percent decline in its shipments during the 2008–2009 recession, and adjusted its inventory to reflect current market conditions. The $30 million expense represented approximately 12 percent of the value of the inventory on its March 31 balance sheet, and appeared in the operating section of the company's statement of cash flows as an add-back to net earnings in the calculation of net cash from operations. Why would a weak market for steel and related products affect the inventory on the balance sheet of a company like Olympic Steel, and why would the write-down appear as both an expense on the income statement and an add-back on the statement of cash flows?

INTERNATIONAL PERSPECTIVE: JAPANESE BUSINESS AND INVENTORY ACCOUNTING

We have commented several times in this text that knowledge of the business environment and practices in individual countries is important for understanding the financial statements used in those countries. The situation in Japan with respect to inventories provides an interesting example. Japan has a long history of what might loosely be described in the United States as "corporate groups." Typically, such groups are made up of a number of different entities, many of which perform different functions and hold equity interest in the others. The board of directors of each company is normally composed of representatives from each of the member entities. Mitsubishi, Sanwa, Nippon Steel, Hitachi, Nissan, and Toyota are all organized in such interlocking networks.

This group orientation, which is not evident in the United States, offers a number of significant advantages, most of which relate to planning and coordination among the group members. In most cases, for example, the presidents of the group companies hold meetings periodically to promote coordination and mutual understanding and to eliminate overlap in the activities conducted by the membership. These groups are then better able to share business risks, and when a company within a group faces difficulties, other group members pursue various means to assist it.

In many situations, such as in the Japanese auto and electronics industries, the group network contains both the manufacturer and its main suppliers. Proper coordination and planning among these parties can help to minimize material and product inventories as well as lead time and delivery items, giving rise to lower inventory carrying cost and better customer service. Just-in-time (JIT) inventory systems, which reduce the costs of carrying large amounts of inventory without jeopardizing customer service,

have long been a characteristic of this Japanese system and have given the Japanese a definite advantage when competing against U.S. industry.

The popularity and success of just-in-time inventory methods are often credited to Toyota, the Japanese car manufacturer. Companies following a JIT plan minimize their investment in idle inventory, purchasing inventory only as it is needed for production. Nick Koletic, an economics specialist at UCLA, published an article in *Inventory Management Review* (10/17/2005) that cited some risks associated with JIT inventory practices. In early 2010, Toyota suffered a quality control problem with accelerator pedals in many of its popular brands, leading to a massive recall; at the same time, Toyota's popular hybrid car, the Prius, faced problems with its brake system. Discuss what business risks a company, such as Toyota, takes when it minimizes the inventory it keeps on hand.

The implication for financial reporting is that Japanese manufacturers, in general, carry much lower levels of inventory that turn over at much higher rates than those in the United States. This difference decreases the importance of inventory accounting in Japan, making the effects on the financial statements of choosing among the various cost flow assumptions relatively insignificant. Consequently, unlike U.S. companies, which normally choose FIFO or LIFO for some significant economic reason, most companies in Japan use the averaging method. Furthermore, Japan has adopted international financial reporting standards (IFRS), which does not allow the use of LIFO.

ROE EXERCISE: MANAGEMENT OF INVENTORY AND RETURN ON EQUITY

The ROE model, introduced and illustrated in Appendix 5A, provides a framework linking the management of a company's operating, investing, and financing activities to its return on the shareholders' investment (return on equity). The management of inventory plays an important role in the ROE model primarily through the inventory turnover ratio. Recall as well that inventory is a current asset, so inventory management also influences working capital and the current ratio, discussed in Chapter 6.

Inventory Turnover

Inventory turnover (cost of goods sold ÷ average inventory) provides a measure of the level of a company's investment in its inventories. For retailers, adequate inventory levels must be maintained to properly service retail customers; for manufacturers, adequate levels of raw materials, work in process, and finished goods must be maintained to support the manufacturing process. Yet, inventories must be financed at a cost and they take up costly space, indicating that carrying overly high levels of inventories is not in the best interest of the shareholders. In terms of the ROE model, inventory turnover is a component of total asset turnover, meaning that changes in inventory turnover are reflected in changes in asset turnover, which in turn are reflected in return on assets (ROA), which in turn are reflected in return on equity (ROE). Thus, increasing inventory turnover (decreasing the investment in inventory relative to cost of goods sold) puts upward pressure on both ROA and ROE.

ROE Analysis

Access the Web site (http://www.wiley.com/college/pratt), and conduct ROE analyses on Barnes and Noble versus Amazon, or Nordstrom versus Saks, all of which carry substantial investments in inventory, paying special attention to how the companies' inventory turnover impacts ROE.

REVIEW PROBLEM

On December 1, Jane Lee contributed $1,000 of her own funds to begin an Oriental grocery store that sells white rice. The rice is kept in a large bin, and customers help themselves by filling plastic bags with a large scoop. The transactions described in Figure 7–10 took place during December. Assume that Jane incurred cash expenses (excluding the cost of goods sold and inventory shortages) of $400 during December, and she pays income taxes at a rate of 30 percent of net income before taxes on December 31.

Jane purchased rice on two occasions at two different prices. By multiplying the number of pounds purchased by the cost per pound, the total capitalized inventory cost for January can be computed ($510). Three hundred pounds of rice were sold for a price of $5/lb., creating total sales of $1,500 (300 lb. × $5).

FIGURE 7–10
December transactions for JL Oriental Foods

Date	Description	Total Inventory Cost
Dec. 1	Jane Lee, owner, contributed $1,000.	
7	Purchased 300 pounds of rice for $1.00 per pound.	$300
25	Sold 250 pounds of rice for $5.00 per pound.	
27	Purchased 150 pounds of rice for $1.40 per pound.	210
28	Sold 50 pounds of rice for $5.00 per pound.	
29	Paid cash expenses of $400.	
31	Paid income tax liability.	
Total capitalized inventory cost		**$510**

FIGURE 7–11
FIFO assumption

JL Oriental Foods
Income Statement
for the Month Ended December 31, 2011

Sales (300 lb × $5)	$1,500
Cost of goods sold	300[a]
Gross profit	$1,200
Expenses	400
Loss	14[b]
Net income before taxes	$ 786
Income tax expense ($790 × 0.30)	236
Net income after taxes	$ 550

[a](250 lb × $1) + (50 lbs × $1)
[b]10 lb × $1.40

FIGURE 7–11
(*Continued*)

JL Oriental Foods
Balance Sheet
December 31, 2011

Cash	$1,354[a]
Inventory	196[b]
Total assets	$1,550
Contributed capital	$1,000
Retained earnings	550
Total liabilities and shareholders' equity	$1,550

[a]Capital contribution − Purchases   + Sales   − Expenses − Taxes
   $1,000   − ($300 + $210) + $1,500 − $400   − $236
[b]140 lb × $1.40
   (150 lb × $1.40) − (10 lb × $1.40)

Assume that Jane took inventory (i.e., weighed the rice) on December 31 and noted that there were 140 pounds of rice on hand. Figures 7–11 and 7–12 contain the income statements and balance sheets prepared by JL Oriental Foods under the FIFO and LIFO cost flow assumptions. In Figure 7–13, the net income, ending inventory, and cash balance produced under the two cost flow assumptions are compared.

FIGURE 7–12
Periodic method:
LIFO assumption

JL Oriental Foods
Income Statement
for the Month Ended December 31, 2011

Sales (300 lb. × $5)	$1,500
Cost of goods sold	320[a]
Gross profit	$1,180
Expenses	400
Loss	14[b]
Net income before taxes	$ 766
Income tax expense ($766 × 0.30)	230
Net income after taxes	$ 536

[a](250 lb × $1) + (50 lb × $1.40)
[b](50 lb × 1.00) + (90 lb × $1.90)

JL Oriental Foods
Balance Sheet
December 31, 2011

Cash	$1,360[a]
Inventory	176[b]
Total assets	$1,536
Contributed capital	$1,000
Retained earnings	536
Total liabilities and shareholders' equity	$1,536

[a]Capital contribution − Purchases   + Sales   − Expenses − Taxes
   $1,000   − ($300 − $210) + $1,500 − $400   − $230
[b](50 lb × $1) + (100 lb × $1.40) − ($10 lb × $1.40)

FIGURE 7–13
Comparison of
FIFO to LIFO

	FIFO	LIFO
Net income	$ 550	$ 536
Ending inventory	196	176
Cash balance	1,354	1,360

Assume that on December 31 the market value of rice drops suddenly to $1.20 per pound. The total market value of Jane's 140 pounds of rice, therefore, is $168 (140 lb × $1.20). If Jane used the FIFO assumption, she would record the following journal entry to apply the lower-of-cost-or-market rule:

Loss on Inventory Write-Down (Lo, −RE)   28
    Inventory (−A)   28
Wrote down inventory to market value ($196 − $168).

If Jane prepared financial reports using IFRS and the market price of rice rebounded in the next period from $1.20 to $1.50 per pound, $0.10 above the original $1.40 cost, she would record a recovery of $28 ([$1.40 − $1.20] × 140 lbs.) with the following adjusting journal entry. This entry would increase net income, but only to the extent of the recovery ($0.20), not the entire market price increase ($0.30).

Inventory (+A)   28
    Inventory recovery (R, +RE)   28

Recovery of written-down inventory to original cost.

Under U.S. GAAP, no entry is recorded for the recovery because the write-down is considered permanent.

If Jane used the LIFO assumption, she would record the following journal entry:

Loss on Inventory Write-Down (Lo, −RE)   8
    Inventory (−A)   8
Wrote down inventory to market value ($176 − $168).

SUMMARY OF KEY POINTS

Inventory and how it affects the financial statements.

Inventory includes asset items held for sale in the ordinary course of business. The ending inventory balance appears on the balance sheet and, for manufacturing and retail companies, is often the largest current asset. The methods used to account for inventory affect the allocation of the capitalized inventory cost between ending inventory and cost of goods sold. This allocation, in turn, affects net income and the ending inventory amount reported on the balance sheet. The effects of inventory accounting methods in the current and subsequent periods can be assessed by examining the following formula:

Cost of Goods Sold = Beginning Inventory + Purchases − Ending Inventory

The ending inventory valuation of the current period decreases cost of goods sold, and thereby increases gross profit and net income. Ending inventory of the current period becomes

beginning inventory of the subsequent period. Beginning inventory increases cost of goods sold and decreases gross profit and net income.

Inventory write-downs reduce earnings, and are added back to earnings on the statement of cash flows because they require no cash outflow. Increases (decreases) in inventory balances are subtracted (added) to earnings on the statement of cash flows because they put downward (upward) pressure on the cash balance.

● *Four issues that must be addressed when accounting for inventory.*

Four issues that must be addressed when accounting for inventories are (1) what costs to include in the capitalized inventory cost (what items to include and what costs to attach to these items); (2) perpetual inventory method; (3) which cost flow assumption to use (specific identification, average, FIFO, or LIFO); and (4) how to apply the lower-of-cost-or-market rule.

● *General rules for including items in inventory and attaching costs to these items.*

Items held for sale should be included in a company's inventory if the company has complete and unrestricted ownership of them. Consigned inventory, though in the possession of the consignee, should be reported on the consignor's balance sheet. Shipping terms normally indicate how to account for goods in transit as of the balance sheet date.

Any cost required to bring an inventory item to saleable condition should be capitalized and treated as an inventory cost. This includes all costs that can reasonably be associated with the manufacture, acquisition, storage, or preparation of inventory items.

● *Three cost flow assumptions—average, FIFO, and LIFO.*

Under averaging, average costs are allocated to the goods sold and the goods that remain in ending inventory.

Under FIFO, the first items purchased are assumed to be the first items sold. This assumption matches old inventory costs with sales but places relatively up-to-date inventory costs on the balance sheet. In times of rising inventory costs, this assumption tends to inflate net income and increase a company's tax liability.

Under LIFO, the most recent items purchased are assumed to be the first items sold. This assumption matches current inventory costs with sales but tends to place old and outdated inventory costs on the balance sheet. LIFO can also be costly to implement and may encourage managers to purchase inventory items at inappropriate times. However, this assumption provides a reasonable measure of net income, and in times of rising inventory costs, it helps to minimize a company's tax liability. LIFO users also disclose the LIFO reserve, which allows the computation of FIFO inventory and net income as well as the accumulated tax savings associated with using LIFO. LIFO is allowed under U.S. GAAP but is not allowed under IFRS.

● *The lower-of-cost-or-market rule.*

Under the lower-of-cost-or-market rule, the cost of ending inventory is compared to its market value. If the cost is greater than the market value, the inventory is written down to market and a loss is recognized. If the cost is less than the market value, no write-down is necessary. The lower-of-cost-or-market rule is often criticized because it can be used to create hidden reserves, allowing managers to manipulate income, and it gives rise to reporting inconsistencies. Inventory recoveries are recorded under IFRS but not under U.S. GAAP.

KEY TERMS

Note: Definitions for these terms are provided in the glossary at the end of the text.

Average assumption (p. 304)
Consignment (p. 294)
First-in, first-out (FIFO) assumption
  (p. 304)
FOB (free on board) destination (p. 295)

FOB (free on board) shipping
  point (p. 294)
Freight-in (p. 295)
Goods in transit (p. 294)
Inventory recovery (p.311)

ETHICS in the Real World

It is well known that inventory fraud is an easy way for a company to produce instant profits and dress up the balance sheet. Many famous frauds have involved the creation of fictitious inventories.

   An article in the *Wall Street Journal* reported that "auditors at even the top accounting firms are often fooled [by such shenanigans] . . . outside auditors can fail to catch inventory scams because they either trust management too much or fear they will lose clients by being tougher . . . spotting inventory fraud requires bigger staffs than some accounting firms . . . are willing to send out to do the inventory audits. . . . If auditors were more skeptical of management claims, particularly in bad times, they would look at a far greater portion of the inventory in certain instances and do more surprise audits, which . . . nowadays are unusual."

   Auditors do face intense competition for clients, and audit fees have been reduced significantly in recent years. Accordingly, there is much pressure to control audit costs by reducing the number of audit hours in an effort to maintain profit levels, and inventory frauds are very difficult to uncover. Alan Winters, the AICPA's director of audit research, stated, "It is difficult if not impossible for the outside auditor to spot inventory fraud, [especially] if top management is directing it."

ETHICAL ISSUE Consider an auditor who has a large client in danger of being lost due to fee competition (i.e., a competitor has agreed to provide an audit for a lower fee). Is it ethical for this auditor to cut back on the number of hours devoted to auditing the inventory account so that the client can be charged a lower fee and a profit can still be made on this audit?

INTERNET RESEARCH EXERCISE

At the beginning of the chapter, we noted that the management of Ann Taylor Stores had come under fire for intentionally inflating its inventory values. Briefly describe the operations of Ann Taylor Stores and comment on how the company has performed over the past several years. Begin your search with the Hoover's Company Finder, which can be found at www.hoovers.com.

BRIEF EXERCISES

REAL DATA
BE7-1
Inventory

In its 2008 annual report, Hewlett-Packard reported beginning inventory of $8.0 billion, ending inventory of $7.9 billion on the balance sheet, and cost of goods sold of $69.3 billion on the income statement. Compute the inventory purchases made by Hewlett-Packard during 2008.

REAL DATA
BE7-2
Inventory

The following information was taken from the footnotes in the 2008 annual report of Johnson & Johnson.

	2008	2007
Raw materials and supplies	$ 839	$ 905
Goods in process	1,372	1,385
Finished goods	2,841	2,821
	$5,052	$5,110

a. From information in the footnote alone, indicate whether Johnson & Johnson is a retailer, manufacturer, or service firm. Explain.
b. From information in the footnote alone, indicate whether Johnson & Johnson uses the LIFO or FIFO inventory cost flow assumption. Explain. (*Hint:* What disclosures are required under LIFO? under FIFO?)

REAL DATA

BE7–3

FIFO vs. LIFO

General Electric uses the LIFO inventory cost flow assumption, reporting inventories on its 2008 balance sheet of $13.7 billion and a LIFO reserve of approximately $706 million. What would be GE's 2008 inventory balance if it used the FIFO assumption instead? Why is the disclosure of the LIFO reserve useful to financial statement users?

EXERCISES

E7–1

Goods in transit as of the end of the accounting period

Dallas Manufacturing engaged in five transactions involving inventory at the end of 2011:

1. Ordered $50,000 of inventory on December 29, 2011. The goods were shipped on December 30, 2011, with the terms FOB shipping point. Dallas received the inventory on January 4, 2012.
2. Received an order to sell inventory with a cost of $40,000. The goods were shipped to the customer on December 31, 2011, and received on January 3, 2012. The terms of the sale were FOB shipping point.
3. Received an order to sell inventory with a cost of $15,000. The goods were shipped to the customer on December 29, 2011, and received on January 2, 2012. The terms of the sale were FOB destination.
4. Ordered $10,000 of inventory on December 27, 2011. The inventory was shipped on December 27, 2011, with the terms FOB destination. Dallas received the inventory on December 31, 2011.
5. Ordered $75,000 of inventory on December 30, 2011. The inventory was shipped on December 31, 2011, with the terms FOB destination. Dallas received the inventory on January 3, 2012.

Assume that Dallas included in inventory (12/31/11) all items from the five cases above. Explain how the resulting financial statements would be misstated.

E7–2

Accounting for inventory purchases

Nick's Fish Market purchased Maine lobster on account on October 10, 2011, for a gross price of $76,000. Nick also purchased Alaskan king crab on account on October 11, 2011, for a gross price of $36,000. The terms of both sales were 2/15, n/30. Nick paid for the first purchase on October 20, 2011, and for the second purchase on October 30, 2011. He uses the perpetual inventory method.
Prepare journal entries for each transaction.

E7–3

Accounting for inventory purchases

Baymont Corporation purchased inventory on account on March 3, 2011, for a gross price of $50,000. The company purchased additional inventory on account on March 10, 2011, for a gross price of $140,000. The terms of both sales were 3/12, n/30. Baymont Corporation paid for the first purchase on April 25, 2011, and for the second purchase on March 20, 2011. The company prepares monthly adjusting journal entries and uses the perpetual inventory method.
Prepare journal entries for each transaction.

REAL DATA

E7-4

Compute the
missing values

The following information was extracted from annual reports of 3M (dollars in millions).

	2008	2007	2006
Beginning inventory	?	?	$ 2,162
Purchases	13,540	?	12,152
Goods available for sale	?	?	14,314
Ending inventory	?	2,852	?
Cost of goods sold	$13,379	$12,735	$11,713

Compute the missing information.

E7-5

Carrying
inventories:
Perpetual and
periodic methods

The following information comes from the records of Telly's Supply:

Beginning inventory	**$32,000**
Inventory purchases	**85,000**
Transportation-in	**4,300**

An inventory count taken at year-end indicates that inventory with a cost of $50,000 is on hand as of December 31, 2011.

Assume that inventory purchases and transportation-in are both reflected in the inventory account, which shows an ending balance of $52,000. Compute cost of goods sold along with any adjusting entries required at the end of the period.

REAL DATA

E7-6

The financial
statement effects of
inventory errors

The Finish Line, Inc. reported the following items in its fiscal 2008 financial report (dollars in millions).

	2008		2007	
Sales		$1,262		$1,277
Cost of goods sold:				
Beginning inventory	$ 268		$ 287	
Purchases	857		887	
Goods available for sale	$1,125		$1,174	
Less: Ending inventory	239		268	
Cost of goods sold		886		906
Gross profit		$ 376		$ 371

Assume that counting errors caused the ending inventory in 2007 to be understated by $50 and the ending inventory in 2008 to be overstated by $50.

a. Compute the impact of these errors on cost of goods sold for the year ended December 31, 2007, and on the inventory balance as of December 31, 2007.
b. Compute the impact of these errors on cost of goods sold for the year ended December 31, 2008, and on the inventory balance as of December 31, 2008.
c. What is the impact of these errors on cost of goods sold over the two-year period ended December 31, 2008?

REAL DATA

E7-7

Inventory and
the statement
of cash flows

The Japanese firm Sony prepares its financial statements using U.S. GAAP. Two items related to its inventory appeared in the operating section of the 2009 statement of cash flows, both in millions of yen: loss on impairment of assets (38,308) and change in inventories (160,432). On the statement of cash flows both items were being added to Sony's 2009 net loss of 98,938 in the calculation of a highly positive (407,153) net cash provided by operating activities number. Included in the loss on impairment of assets was a sizable inventory write-down.

a. Explain how net cash provided by operating activities can be such a large positive number while net income is negative.

b.   Provide the basic structure of the inventory write-down entry, and explain why this amount would appear in the operating section of the statement of cash flows and be added to the net loss in the calculation of net cash provided by operating activities.

c.   Did Sony's inventory increase or decrease during the year, and how do you know?

E7–8

Income manipulation under specific identification

Marian's Furs specializes in full-length mink coats. As of January 1, Marian had four top-of-the-line coats. Although the four coats are equivalent, they were purchased the previous year at different costs:

	Cost
Coat 1	$8,400
Coat 2	7,100
Coat 3	7,600
Coat 4	6,800

During January a customer decided to buy any one of the mink coats for $12,000. This was the only sale in January.

a.   If Marian wished to maximize January's profits and ending inventory, which of the minks would she have sold to the customer? Compute the gross profit on the sale and January's ending inventory. Discuss why Marian might wish to maximize profits and ending inventory.

b.   If Marian wished to minimize January's profits and ending inventory, which of the minks would she have sold to the customer? Compute the gross profit on the sale and January's ending inventory. Discuss why Marian might wish to minimize profits and ending inventory.

E7–9

Inventory assumptions and manipulating income under specific identification

Vinnie's House of Televisions has 75 identical 27-inch color monitors in stock on January 1, 2012. Vinnie maintains records of the serial number of each monitor to track its costs. Vinnie purchased the 75 monitors on December 5, 2011, for $450 each. He also purchased 50 on January 2, 2012, for $500 each and an additional 65 on January 15, 2012, for $600 each. Each monitor is priced to sell at $1,000. Vinnie sold 130 monitors during the month of January.

a.   Compute gross profit and ending inventory for the month if the company adheres to each of the following:
     (1) FIFO cost flow assumption
     (2) Averaging cost flow assumption
     (3) LIFO cost flow assumption

b.   Assume that Vinnie uses the specific identification method to compute the cost of goods sold. Explain how Vinnie could manipulate the gross profit number. What are the highest and the lowest gross profit amounts Vinnie could report? What are some possible factors that could motivate Vinnie to report either the highest or the lowest net income amount?

E7–10

Inventory cost flow assumptios

Watkins Corporation began operations on January 1, 2010. The 2010 and 2011 schedules of inventory purchases and sales are as follows:

2010:

Purchase 1	10 units @ $10 per unit	$100
Purchase 2	20 units @ $12 per unit	240
Total purchase costs		$340
Sales	15 units @ $30 per unit	$450

2011:

Purchase 1	10 units @ $13 per unit	$130
Purchase 2	15 units @ $15 per unit	225
Total purchase costs		$355
Sales	20 units @ $35 per unit	$700

Complete the following schedule, and briefly discuss the trade-offs associated with choosing an inventory cost flow assumption.

2010	FIFO	Weighted Average	LIFO
Cost of goods sold			
Gross profit (Sales − COGS)			
Ending inventory			

2011	FIFO	Weighted Average	LIFO
Cost of goods sold			
Gross profit (Sales − COGS)			
Ending inventory			

E7–11

Inventory flow assumptions over several periods and income taxes

Heller Bottling Company began business in 2008. Inventory units purchased and sold for the first year of operations and each of the following four years follow:

	Units Purchased	Cost per Unit	Units Sold
2008	10,000	$12	5,000
2009	12,000	16	16,000
2010	5,000	18	2,000
2011	10,000	21	10,000
2012	2,000	23	6,000

Inadequate cash flows forced Heller Bottling Company to cease operations at the end of 2012.

a. Compute cost of goods sold for each of the five years if the company uses the following:
    (1) LIFO cost flow assumption
    (2) FIFO cost flow assumption
    (3) Averaging cost flow assumption
b. Does the choice of a cost flow assumption affect total net income over the life of a business? Explain your answer.
c. If the choice of a cost flow assumption does not affect net income over the life of a business, how does the choice of LIFO give rise to a tax benefit?

REAL DATA

E7–12

Using the LIFO reserve

The following disclosure was included in the footnotes of Caterpillar's 2008 annual report. The company uses the LIFO cost flow assumption and reported net income of $3,557 for 2008. The company's effective tax rate is 21 percent (dollars in millions).

	2008	2007
Inventories at current cost	$11,964	$9,821
Less: Adjustment to LIFO basis	3,183	2,617
Inventories on LIFO basis	$ 8,781	$7,204

a. Compute 2008 ending inventory for Caterpillar assuming it changed from LIFO to FIFO at the end of 2008.
b. Compute the accumulated income tax savings enjoyed by Caterpillar due to the choice of LIFO as opposed to FIFO.
c. Compute 2008 reported net income for Caterpillar assuming it changed from LIFO to FIFO several years before.
d. Explain how the information generated in (a), (b), and (c) could be useful.
e. Explain why Caterpillar might oppose a requirement to adopt IFRS by U.S. companies.

E7-13

The lower-of-cost-
or-market rule and
hidden reserves

Central Incorporated has two items in inventory as of December 31, 2011. Each item was purchased for $40. Company management chose to write down Item #1 to $28, which at year-end was assessed to be its market value. Management did not write down Item #2 because its market value was estimated to be greater than $40. During 2012, each item was sold for $50 cash.

a. Prepare journal entries for each activity (i.e., the write-down, the sale of Item #1, and the sale of Item #2).
b. Compute the profit or loss associated with each item in 2011 and 2012.
c. Explain how management could manipulate reported earnings when applying the lower-of-cost-or-market rule.

REAL DATA

E7-14

Inventory accounting
under U.S. GAAP
and IFRS

In its 2008 annual report the Unilever Group, which published IFRS-based financial statements, reported the following in the inventory footnote (in million euros).

	2008	2007
Raw materials and consumables	1,437	1,406
Finished goods and goods for resale	2,452	2,488
Total inventories	3,889	3,894

"During 2008, 246 million euros (2007: 177 million euros) was charged to the income statement for damaged, obsolete, and lost inventories. In 2008, 23 million euros (2007: 25 million euros) was released to the income statement (recoveries) for inventory provisions taken in earlier years."

a. Is Unilever a manufacturer or a retailer, and how do you know?
b. Does Unilever use the FIFO or LIFO inventory assumption, and how do you know?
c. What is an inventory write-down and an inventory recovery? Record the entries made by Unilever at the end of 2008 for the write-down and recovery.
d. How would Unilever's accounting have been different if it used U.S. GAAP instead of IFRS?

PROBLEMS

P7-1

Purchases and cash
discounts

On November 15 and 26, Brown and Swazey purchased merchandise on account for gross prices of $8,000 and $12,000, respectively. Terms of both purchases were 2/10, n/30. None of these items has been sold, and both accounts are paid in full on December 2.

REQUIRED:
Provide all the journal entries that would be recorded for these events.

P7-2

The gross method
and partial
payments

Stober Corporation made two purchases of inventory on account during the month of March. The first purchase was made on March 5 for $30,000, and the second purchase was made on March 10 for $60,000. The terms of each purchase were 2/10, n/30. The first purchase was settled on March 13, and the second was settled on July 18.

REQUIRED:
a. Prepare all the necessary journal entries associated with these transactions.
b. Assume that with respect to the second purchase, the company settled two-thirds of the accounts payable balance on March 19 and settled the remaining balance on August 7. The first purchase was settled on March 13. Prepare all the necessary journal entries associated with the second purchase.

P7-3

The financial effects
of inventory errors

The following information was taken from the records of Eli Lilly, a major pharmaceutical (dollars in millions).

	2008	2007	2006
Sales	$20,378	$18,634	$15,691
Cost of goods sold	4,383	4,249	3,547
Gross profit	$15,995	$14,385	$12,144
Expenses	18,067	11,432	9,481
Net income (loss)	$(2,072)	$ 2,953	$ 2,663

Assume that ending inventory was overstated by $500 in 2006, understated by $150 in 2007, and overstated by $320 in 2008.

REQUIRED:

Compute the corrected cost of goods sold and net income for 2006, 2007, and 2008.

P7-4

The financial
statement and
income tax effects
of averaging, FIFO,
and LIFO

The purchase schedule for Lumbermans and Associates is as follows:

Date	Items Purchased	Cost per Item
March 15	6,000	$1.30
July 30	9,000	1.50
December 17	7,000	1.60
Total	22,000	

The inventory balance as of the beginning of the year was $15,000 (15,000 units @ $1), and an inventory count at year-end indicated that 11,000 items were on hand. Sales and expenses (excluding cost of goods sold) totaled $55,000 and $15,000, respectively. The federal income tax is 30 percent of taxable income.

REQUIRED:

a. Prepare three income statements, one under each of the assumptions: FIFO, average, and LIFO.

b. How many tax dollars would be saved by using LIFO instead of FIFO?

c. Assume that the market value of an inventory item dropped to $1.35 as of year-end. Apply the lower-of-cost-or-market rule, and provide the appropriate journal entry (if necessary) under the FIFO, averaging, and LIFO assumptions.

d. Repeat (a) above assuming that the costs per item were as follows:

Beginning inventory	$1.60
March 15	1.40
July 30	1.30
December 17	1.20

Which of the three assumptions gives rise to the highest net income and ending inventory amounts now? Why?

P7-5

Inventory accounting,
earnings, taxes, and
lower-of-cost-
or-market

The purchase schedule for Laundryman's Corporation is as follows:

Date	Items Purchased	Cost per Item
February 10	1,000	$75
May 15	3,000	$80
October 20	4,000	$82

The inventory balance as of the beginning of the year was $35,000 (500 units @ $70 each). During the year ended December 31, the company sold 6,000 units for $150 per unit. Expenses other than cost of goods sold totaled $125,000. The effective income tax rate is 30 percent.

REQUIRED:

a. Prepare three income statements, one under each assumption—FIFO, LIFO, average.
b. How many tax dollars would be saved by using LIFO instead of FIFO?
c. Assume the market value of an item of inventory dropped to $78 as of the end of the year. Apply the lower-of-cost-or-market rule, and provide the appropriate journal entry (if necessary) under the FIFO, LIFO, and average assumptions.
d. Repeat (a) above, assuming the costs per item were:

Beginning inventory	**$80**
February 10	**$78**
May 15	**$77**
October 20	**$75**

Which of the three assumptions now gives rise to the highest net income and ending inventory?

P7–6

The gross method, and the LIFO and FIFO cost flow assumptions

The Magic Teddy Bear Toy Company entered into the following transactions during January 2011:

January   3: Purchased 7,000 teddy bears at $20 each with the terms 2/10, n/30.
3: Sold 2,000 teddy bears at $50 each for cash.
9: Sold 4,000 teddy bears at $50 each on account.
10: Settled the purchase made on January 3.
15: Purchased 10,000 teddy bears. Three thousand of the bears were purchased for cash at $24.50 each, and the remaining bears were purchased on account for a gross price of $25.00 each (terms 2/10, n/30).
19: Purchased 7,000 teddy bears at $26 each with the terms 2/10, n/30.
23: Paid for one-half of the teddy bears purchased on account on January 15.
27: Purchased 4,000 teddy bears at $28 each for cash.
28: Settled the remaining open account from the purchase made on January 15.
28: Settled the open account from the purchase made on January 19.
29: Sold 6,000 teddy bears at $60 each for cash.
30: Sold 5,000 teddy bears at $60 each on account.
31: Purchased 2,000 teddy bears at $30 each for cash.
31: Received a freight bill in the amount of $30,000, covering all purchases made during January 2011.

The Magic Teddy Bear Toy Company has 5,000 teddy bears on hand at $19 each as of January 1, 2011.

REQUIRED:

Assume that The Magic Teddy Bear Toy Company accounts for purchase cash discounts under the gross method. Prepare all necessary entries, including adjusting journal entries, during January 2011, if the company uses the following:

a. LIFO cost flow assumption
b. FIFO cost flow assumption

(*Hint:* Compute the total cost per unit in order to calculate ending inventory and cost of goods sold.)

Financial statements as of December 31, 2008, for Johnson & Johnson are as follows. The company used the FIFO inventory cost flow assumption to prepare these statements (dollars in millions).

Income Statement

Sales		$63,747
Cost of goods sold:		
Beginning inventory	$ 5,110	
Purchases	18,453	
Goods available for sale	$23,563	
Less: Ending inventory	5,052	
Cost of goods sold		18,511
Gross profit		$45,236
Expenses		28,307
Net income before taxes		$16,929
Federal income tax (24%)		3,980
Net income		$12,949

Balance Sheet

Cash	$10,768	Current liabilities	$20,852
Inventory	5,052	Long-term liabilities	21,549
Other assets	69,092	Shareholders' equity	42,511
		Total liabilities and	
Total assets	$84,912	shareholders' equity	$84,912

Assume that on December 30, 2008, Johnson & Johnson decided to change from the FIFO to the LIFO inventory cost flow assumption. Assume that the ending inventory value under the LIFO assumption is $4,000.

REQUIRED:

a. Compute the change in Johnson & Johnson's current ratio associated with the change from FIFO to LIFO. Round to two decimal places.

b. Compute the change in Johnson & Johnson's gross profit and net income associated with the change from FIFO to LIFO. Assume that the dollar amount of the change is reflected in cost of goods sold.

c. How many tax dollars would be saved by the change from FIFO to LIFO?

d. Discuss some of the disadvantages associated with the change to LIFO.

Ruhe Auto Supplies began operations in 1998. The company's inventory purchases and sales in the first and subsequent years of operations are as follows:

Year	Units Purchased	Cost per Unit	Units Sold
1998	20,000	$ 5	4,000
1999	8,000	10	8,000
2000	7,000	15	9,000
2001	8,500	20	7,000
2002	6,000	25	7,500
2003	7,500	30	7,000
2004	9,000	50	8,000
2005	8,000	65	9,000
2006	9,500	70	9,000
2007	7,000	75	8,000
2008	8,500	80	8,500
2009	9,000	85	7,500
2010	8,500	90	9,500
2011	9,500	95	20,000

The company's federal income tax rate is 30 percent. For the year ended December 31, 2011, Ruhe Auto Supplies generated $3,000,000 in revenues and incurred $800,000 in expenses (exclusive of cost of goods sold). Ruhe Auto Supplies uses the LIFO cost flow assumption to account for inventory.

REQUIRED:

a. Compute ending inventory as of December 31, 2011. Identify the number of units in ending inventory and the costs attached to each unit.
b. Compute the company's 2011 income tax liability and net income after taxes for the year ended December 31, 2011.
c. Assume that Ruhe Auto Supplies was able to purchase an additional 10,500 units of inventory on December 31, 2011, for $95 per unit. Would you advise the company to purchase these additional units? Explain your answer.

P7–9

Using the LIFO reserve

You are a financial analyst currently reviewing the financial statements of Danner International and Brady Enterprises, two companies of similar size within the same industry. Net incomes of $39,300 and $42,700 were reported for 2011 by Danner and Brady, respectively. After a thorough comparison of the accounting methods used by the two companies, you find that they are similar except for the inventory cost flow assumption—Danner uses FIFO and Brady uses LIFO. You conduct a further review of Brady's footnotes and discover the following. Inventories declined during 2011, causing a LIFO liquidation, which accounted for $8,000 of the before-tax net income reported in 2011.

	2011	2010
Inventories at current cost	**$36,200**	**$42,400**
Less: Adjustment to LIFO	**3,500**	**4,800**
Inventories at LIFO	**$32,700**	**$37,600**

Brady's effective tax rate is 35 percent.

REQUIRED:

a. Restate Brady's net income assuming there was no LIFO liquidation in 2011. How does the restated amount compare to Danner's net income?
b. Restate Brady's 2011 reported net income as if the company had always been a FIFO user. Is Brady's restated reported income higher or lower than Danner's reported net income? Explain.
c. As of the end of 2011, how much accumulated income tax had Brady saved due to its choice of LIFO instead of FIFO? How much as of the end of 2010? Does LIFO save taxes in every year? Explain.
d. Would it be advisable for Brady to change its cost flow assumption from LIFO to FIFO? Discuss.

P7–10

Avoiding LIFO liquidations

IBT has used the LIFO inventory cost flow assumption for five years. As of December 31, 2010, IBT had 700 items in its inventory, and the $9,000 inventory dollar amount reported on the balance sheet consisted of the following costs:

When Purchased	Number of Items	Cost per Item	Total
2007	500	$12	$6,000
2009	200	15	3,000
Total	700		$9,000

During 2011, IBT sold 900 items for $75 each and purchased 350 items at $30 each. Expenses other than cost of goods sold totaled $20,000, and the federal income tax rate is 30 percent of taxable income.

REQUIRED:
a. Prepare IBT's income statement for the year ending December 31, 2011.
b. Assume that IBT purchased an additional 550 items on December 20, 2011, for $30 each. Prepare IBT's income statement for the year ending December 31, 2011.
c. Compare the two income statements, and discuss why it might have been wise for IBT to purchase the additional items on December 20. Discuss some of the disadvantages of such a strategy.

Inventory accounting under IFRS

The 2011 inventory activity for Helio Brothers, a discount retailer that prepares financial statements under IFRS using the FIFO cost flow assumption, is provided below.

Beginning inventory	**500 items @ $2.00/item**	**$ 1,000**
Purchases	**6,000 items @ $2.50/item**	**15,000**
Sales	**6,100 items @ $5.00/item**	**30,500**

Many of the items in the company's inventory at the end of 2011 were judged to be outdated, and on average the market value of the remaining inventory was estimated at $1.50 per item.

REQUIRED:
a. Compute Helio's ending inventory and net income for 2011.
b. Early in 2012 styles appeared to change, and the average market price of the inventory written down at the end of 2011 rebounded to $2.80 per item. Record the entry made by Helio to recognize the inventory recovery. What entry would Helio record if it used U.S. GAAP instead of IFRS?

ISSUES FOR DISCUSSION

REAL DATA

ID7-1

Choosing FIFO or LIFO

A partner from a major accounting firm made the following comment when asked about the accounting methods used by companies in the software industry: "Accounting policies that have adverse short-term effects on financial statements cannot help the industry raise capital."

After reading such a comment, one might conclude that managers who wish to raise capital by borrowing from banks or issuing equity or debt securities should choose the FIFO cost flow assumption instead of LIFO. Yet, others have written that they are "puzzled" about why thousands of U.S. companies use FIFO instead of LIFO.

REQUIRED:
Discuss the above comments.

REAL DATA

ID7-2

LIFO reporting

The following information was taken from the inventory footnote contained in the 2009 annual report of Deere & Company, the agricultural equipment manufacturer.

	2009	2008
Finished goods	**$2,437**	**$2,677**
Work in process	**387**	**519**
Raw materials	**940**	**1,170**
Inventories at FIFO	**3,764**	**4,366**
Excess of FIFO over LIFO	**(1,367)**	**(1,324)**
Inventories at LIFO	**$2,397**	**$3,042**

Most inventories owned by Deere & Company and its U.S. equipment subsidiaries are valued at cost, on the last-in, first-out (LIFO) basis. Remaining inventories are generally valued at the lower of cost, on the first-in, first-out (FIFO) basis, or market. The value of gross

inventories on the LIFO basis represented 59 percent and 64 percent of worldwide gross inventories at FIFO value on October 31, 2009 and 2008, respectively.

REQUIRED:

a. Why would a potential investor or creditor who is considering investing in Deere be interested in the difference between LIFO and FIFO inventory values?

b. Explain why reducing certain inventory quantities, valued under LIFO, would increase net income and why an investor would be interested in such a disclosure.

c. Deere's effective tax rate is 34 percent. Approximately how much more income tax would Deere have paid if at the end of 2009 it switched to FIFO for all of its inventory?

d. Explain why Deere & Company might resist adopting IFRS.

REAL DATA

ID7–3

LIFO liquidation and hidden reserves

In the early 1980s, an oil glut caused Texaco, a LIFO user, to delay drilling, which cut its oil inventory levels by 16 percent. The LIFO cushion (i.e., the difference between LIFO and FIFO inventory values) that was built into those barrels over the year amounted to $454 million and transformed what would have been a drop in net income to a modest gain.

REQUIRED:

Explain how using LIFO could be interpreted as building "hidden reserves."

REAL DATA

ID7–4

The lower-of-cost-or-market rule and the recognition of loss/income

TII Industries makes over-voltage protectors, power systems, and electronic products primarily for use in the communications industry. Several years ago, the company reported that it took "a substantial inventory write-down," resulting in a loss for its third quarter ending June 24. The write-down was estimated to be $12 million and stems from customers' changes in product specifications.

REQUIRED:

a. Provide the journal entry to record the write-down.

b. Assume that the original cost of the inventory was $52 million and that it was written down to its market value of $40 million. If TII Industries sells it for $48 million cash in the following period, what journal entries would be recorded? Assume that TII uses the perpetual inventory method.

c. Applying the lower-of-cost-or-market rule in this case would cause TII to recognize a loss in the period of the write-down and income in the subsequent period. Does such recognition seem appropriate? Why or why not?

REAL DATA

ID7–5

Inventory write-down

The *Wall Street Journal* (April 17, 1998) reported that "Valero Energy Corp. said it will take a first-quarter charge of $37.7 million, or 43 cents per share, related to lower prices for crude oil and refined products. The energy-refining and marketing company characterized the write-down as an accounting 'to reduce the carrying value of our crude oil and refined products inventories to their market value.'"

REQUIRED:

a. What exception to the principles of financial accounting is being followed by Valero when it writes down its inventories?

b. How would the write-down affect the financial statements?

c. How would the write-down affect the company's current ratio and its inventory turnover ratio (increase, decrease, or no effect)?

d. Explain how such a write-down could be used to manipulate earnings and what two reporting strategies Valero could be following.

e. If crude oil prices rebounded in 1999, explain how Valero, which uses U.S. GAAP, would account for the rebound. What if Valero used IFRS instead of U.S. GAAP?

REAL DATA

ID7–6

Interpreting the inventory footnote

The 2008 annual report of Sherwin Williams, a manufacturer of paint products, contained the following footnote (dollars in thousands).

Note 4-Inventories

Inventories were stated at the lower of cost or market with cost determined principally on the last-in, first-out (LIFO) method. The following presents the effect on inventories, net income, and net income per share had the Company used the first-in, first-out (FIFO) inventory valuation method adjusted for income taxes at the statutory rate and assuming no other adjustments. Management believes that the use of LIFO results in a better matching of costs and revenues. The information is presented to enable the reader to make comparisons with companies using the FIFO method of inventory valuation.

	2008	2007	2006
Percent of total inventory on LIFO	86%	83%	88%
Excess of FIFO over LIFO	$321,280	$241,579	$226,818
Decrease in net income due to LIFO	(49,184)	(7,844)	(24,033)
Decrease in net income per common share due to LIFO	(.41)	(.06)	(.17)

REQUIRED:

a. Sherwin Williams reported inventories on the balance sheet at $864,200 (2008), $887,465 (2007), and $825,179 (2006). Compute the company's ending inventory had it shifted to FIFO at the end of 2008 (dollars in thousands).

b. Estimate the taxes saved by Sherwin Williams because it uses LIFO instead of FIFO. Assume a tax rate of 33 percent.

c. Does LIFO provide a better matching of current costs to revenues in times of inflation? Why? Is the same true in times of deflation?

REAL DATA

ID7-7

"Thinning" inventories
during slow times

When it released its first quarter earnings for fiscal 2007, FedEx Corporation also projected that its shipping volume would be lighter and that its profit growth would be the lowest in years. As reported in the *Wall Street Journal* (March 22, 2007), FedEx cited the fact that many companies were "thinning inventories to ride out the economic slowdown."

REQUIRED:

a. What does it mean for a company to "thin" its inventories? How would such a business practice aid a company during an economic recession?

b. Where in the financial statements would a reader be able to discern that a company was thinning its inventories? What effect would this have on the reader's analysis of the company's financial performance?

c. Do the goods shipped by FedEx appear on FedEx's balance sheet? Discuss.

REAL DATA

ID7-8

Inventory and
the statement of
cash flows

The 2008 statement of cash flows for JCPenney reports (dollars in millions) net cash from operating activities of $1,155 (2008), $1,249 (2007), and $1,258 (2006). Included on the statement of cash flows (indirect method) in the computation of net cash from operating activities are adjustments for inventory of $382 (2008), −$241 (2007), and −$190 (2006).

REQUIRED:

Explain the nature of these adjustments and what they tell us about JCPenney's inventory balances in 2008, 2007, and 2006. Discuss the cash flow implications of these inventory adjustments.

REAL DATA

ID7-9

Different inventory
disclosures

JCPenney Company, Inc. discloses its inventory in the following manner on the balance sheet itself (dollars in millions).

	2008	2007
Merchandise inventory (net of LIFO reserves of $21 and $1)	$3,259	$3,641

SUPERVALU, Inc., on the other hand, disclosed information about its LIFO and FIFO values in a footnote to its 2009 financial statements. The balance sheet inventory values (in millions) were $2,709 and $2,776 for 2009 and 2008, respectively.

Approximately 81 percent and 82 percent of the company's inventories were valued using the last-in, first-out (LIFO) method inventories for fiscal 2009 and 2008, respectively. The first-in, first-out (FIFO) method is primarily used to determine cost for some of the remaining highly perishable inventories. If the FIFO method had been used to determine cost of inventories for which the LIFO method is used, the company's inventories would have been higher by approximately $258 million at February 28, 2009, and $180 million at February 23, 2008.

REQUIRED:

a. For which of the two companies is the difference between LIFO and FIFO larger as a percent of total inventories?
b. Compute ending inventory as of the end of 2008, assuming the FIFO method, for JCPenney and as of the end of 2009 for SUPERVALU.
c. Estimate the tax savings enjoyed by the two companies due to their use of LIFO instead of FIFO.
d. Why might SUPERVALU use FIFO for "highly perishable inventories"?

REAL DATA

ID7–10

Analyzing inventory management on the statement of cash flows

Target Corp. is a major U.S. retailer that historically has carried inventory balances in excess of 15% of its total assets, and in a typical year the cost of its sold inventory approximates 70% of total sales. In the operating section of its 2008 statement of cash flows, Target added the $77 million decrease in its inventory balance and subtracted the $389 million increase in its accounts payable balance to net earnings in the calculation of cash flow provided by operations.

REQUIRED:

a. Why were these adjustments reported on the statement of cash flows?
b. Assuming that most of the accounts payable are owed to its inventory suppliers, what does the difference between these two amounts indicate about how Target's operating cash flows were managed during 2008?

REAL DATA

ID7–11

Nike SEC Form 10-K

The Nike SEC Form 10-K is reproduced in Appendix C. Review it and answer the following questions.

REQUIRED:

a. How large is inventory compared to the other assets on NIKE's balance sheet? Did inventory increase, decrease, or remain the same as a percent of total assets from 2008 to 2009?
b. What is the primary cost associated with NIKE's cost of sales, and how did this account vary as a percent of sales from 2007 to 2009?
c. Did NIKE appear to pay off its suppliers faster or slower during 2009 compared to 2008?
d. Review the operating section of NIKE's statement of cash flows and comment on the cash flow implications associated with the changes in the primary working capital accounts during 2009.
e. See Note 1. Does NIKE use the LIFO, FIFO, or averaging assumption? See Note 2. Why are NIKE's inventories predominantly finished goods?

CHAPTER 8

Investments in Equity Securities

KEY POINTS

The following key points are emphasized in this chapter:

- Criteria that must be met before a security can be listed in the current assets section of the balance sheet.

- Trading and available-for-sale securities and how the mark-to-market rule is used to account for them.

- Why companies make long-term investments in equity securities.

- The mark-to-market method, the cost method, and the equity method of accounting for long-term equity investments, and the conditions under which each method is used.

- Consolidated financial statements, when they are prepared, and how they differ from financial statements that account for equity investments using the equity method.

In early 2000, Cisco Systems boasted the greatest market value in the history of Wall Street—nearly half a trillion dollars, with almost all of that wealth created since 1995. While its market value has since declined significantly, Cisco is still a great engineering company, well-managed and technically astute, and almost all of its growth has come from acquiring other companies. How it chose those companies has defined its corporate strategy; how it integrated them into its empire has defined its corporate politics; and how it retained the people acquired with the companies has defined its corporate culture. These acquisitions and others like it, where ownership is transferred, involve the purchase and sale of equity securities, the subject of this chapter.

An **equity investment** occurs when one company purchases another company's outstanding common stock. Recall from Chapter 1 that equity holders have the right to receive dividends, if declared, and to vote for the board of directors at the annual meeting of the shareholders. Companies make investments in equity securities for two basic reasons: (1) to earn investment income in the form of dividends and stock price appreciation and (2) to exert influence or control over the board of directors and management of the investee company. Relatively small equity investments are normally made to earn income over a short period of time, while larger, long-term equity investments often signal an attempt by the investing company to influence the operations of the target company.

To illustrate, as of its fiscal year-end 2009, Microsoft Corporation disclosed over $25.3 billion in marketable securities—debt and equity investments in a wide variety of companies. At the same time, the company held investments in companies in which between 20 and 50 percent of the equity securities had been purchased. These holdings were carried on the balance sheet at about $4.9 billion. During fiscal 2009, Microsoft purchased 100 percent of the outstanding stock of nine companies for a total price of $925 million.

The next section covers equity investments classified as current because they are readily marketable and intended to be sold within the time period of current assets. The chapter then discusses long-term equity investments and divides the coverage into three categories, based on the proportion of the common share holdings: (1) equity holdings of less than 20 percent, (2) equity holdings from 20 to 50 percent, and (3) equity holdings of greater than 50 percent. As we note later, these three situations are accounted for differently. Appendix 8A is devoted to consolidated financial statements, which are prepared when a company holds more than 50 percent of the outstanding common stock in another company.

EQUITY SECURITIES CLASSIFIED AS CURRENT

Idle cash held by a company earns no return and during inflation actually declines in purchasing power. Nevertheless, proper cash management must ensure that enough cash is available to meet a company's day-to-day cash needs. Such cash needs tend to fluctuate, sometimes unexpectedly, making it difficult for management to consistently strike an appropriate balance between available cash and return-producing investments. In an effort to both earn a return and be able to produce cash on short notice, companies often purchase readily marketable securities. Companies also use these investments to offset the risks of changing interest rates associated with certain liabilities. The annual report of Intel, for example, notes, "The company maintains its short-term investment portfolio to offset change in certain liabilities." Such investments, which include stocks and bonds traded on public security exchanges, provide income

through dividends, interest, or price appreciation and can be readily converted to cash when needed to meet current cash requirements.[1]

The relative size of short-term investments on the balance sheet varies significantly across companies in different industries. Retailers such as hardware, department, clothing, and sporting goods stores typically maintain dollar amounts of less than 3 percent of total assets. Financial institutions, insurance companies, and some services, on the other hand, which have greater needs for ready cash, often carry short-term investment portfolios that represent a larger percentage of total assets. Recent annual reports of Honeywell International and Goodrich Corporation show no holdings of short-term investments. JPMorgan Chase carries short-term investments of almost 34 percent of total assets. Starbucks holds short-term equity investments of over 3 percent of total assets.

Short-term investments are listed in the current assets section of the balance sheet. It is important to realize that they are distinct from long-term investments in equity and debt securities, which are included in the long-term investments section. Two criteria must be met for an investment in a security to be considered current and thus warrant inclusion as a current asset:

1.   The investment must be *readily marketable.*
2.   Management must *intend to convert* the investment into cash within the time period of current assets (one year or the operating cycle, whichever is longer).

If either criterion is not met, the investment must be included in the long-term investments section.

The 2008 annual report of Intel, a building block supplier to the world Internet economy, discloses short-term investments of $5.3 billion, representing about 10 percent of total assets. Describe the characteristics of these investments.

The Existence of a Ready Market

Readily marketable means that the security can be sold and converted into cash on demand. Stocks and bonds traded actively on the public stock exchanges (e.g., New York Stock Exchange, American Stock Exchange) usually meet this criterion. Objective market prices exist for such securities, which ensure that they can be sold on very short notice. In most cases, all a company must do is request that its stockbroker sell the security.

Some securities, on the other hand, are not publicly traded, often because there are restrictions on their sale. Common stocks of privately held corporations, for example, may have very limited markets because restrictions exist on who can own them (e.g., ownership is sometimes limited to family members). Objective market prices do not exist for such securities, and they cannot be readily converted into cash. Accordingly, they fail to meet the readily marketable criterion and should be listed in the long-term investments section of the balance sheet.

---

1. Short-term investments can also consist of certificates of deposit, money market accounts, and commercial paper. Certificates of deposit are usually purchased from banks in denominations of at least $5,000. They provide a fixed rate of return over a specified period of time. Money market accounts are similar to savings or checking accounts but provide a slightly higher rate of interest, and there are usually restrictions on the withdrawal of funds. Commercial paper is a short-term note issued by corporations with good credit ratings. They are usually issued in denominations of $5,000 and $10,000 and provide returns that exceed those of money market accounts.

The 2008 annual report of Intel discloses: "We account for non-marketable . . . investments . . . in other long-term assets." Why would Intel list its nonmarketable investments in the non-current section of its balance sheet?

The Intention to Convert: Another Area of Subjectivity

The second criterion, **intention to convert** the investment to cash, is much more difficult to determine objectively. Consequently, it can be a very difficult area for the auditor, who must determine whether a company's financial statements conform with generally accepted accounting principles. Simply asking managers whether they intend to sell securities within the time period of current assets does not provide sufficiently objective evidence. Recall that managers have incentives to window dress, which in this case might consist of including what would appropriately be a long-term investment in the current assets section. Such a decision might be made to increase a company's quick ratio, current ratio, or working capital number—an issue that users should consider when they analyze financial statements.

When PepsiCo acquired two Canadian soft-drink bottling operations for $246 million, the company listed these investments as current assets on its balance sheet because "it was management's intention to resell these operations." The following year PepsiCo sold only one of the investments and continued to include the remaining investment in the current assets section. In your opinion, did PepsiCo violate an accounting standard? Discuss.

TRADING AND AVAILABLE-FOR-SALE SECURITIES

Investments in readily marketable equity securities are classified into one of two categories: (1) trading securities or (2) available-for-sale securities. **Trading securities** are bought and held principally for the purpose of selling them in the near future with the objective of generating profit on short-term price changes. Investments not classified as trading securities are considered **available-for-sale securities.** Trading securities are always listed in the current section of the balance sheet, while available-for-sale securities are listed as current or long-term, depending on management's intention.[2]

Trading and available-for-sale are terms used under IFRS, and the accounting methods used for these securities are very similar to U.S. GAAP.

---

2. This chapter considers investments in equity securities, and this particular section is based on Statement of Financial Accounting Standards No. 115, "Accounting for Certain Investments in Debt and Equity Securities." Investments in debt securities are classified into one of three categories: (1) trading, (2) available-for-sale, or (3) held-to-maturity. The methods used to account for trading and available-for-sale debt securities are the same as those used for trading and available-for-sale equity securities. Accounting for debt securities held to maturity is covered in Appendix 11B of this text.

Both trading and available-for-sale securities are accounted for using the **mark-to-market rule,** which states that readily marketable securities be carried on the balance sheet at current market value. The following example considers four separate events: (1) the purchase of the securities, (2) the declaration and receipt of related cash dividends, (3) the sale of the securities (at either a gain or a loss), and (4) changes in the prices of the securities on hand at the end of the accounting period. The first three events use the same methods to account for trading and available-for-sale securities. The fourth event, however, applies the mark-to-market rule differently.

Purchasing Trading and Available-for-Sale Securities

When trading and available-for-sale securities are purchased, they are capitalized and recorded on the balance sheet at cost. As with other capitalized assets (inventory, long-term investments, fixed assets, and intangible assets), cost includes the purchase price as well as any *incidental acquisition costs,* such as brokerage commissions and taxes.[3] For example, assume that Goodyear Tire & Rubber Company purchased three different kinds of securities (Dow Chemical, Abbott Laboratories, and Eli Lilly) on December 1, 2011. Each security is readily marketable, and the company intends to sell the Dow and Abbott investments in the near future. Thus, the investments in Dow and Abbott are classified as trading securities, and the investment in Lilly is classified as available-for-sale. The following prices were paid:[4]

10 shares of Dow Chemical at $10/share	$100
20 shares of Abbott Laboratories at $12/share	240
15 shares of Eli Lilly at $20/share	300
Total cost	$640

Assuming that all prices *include* brokerage commissions, the following journal entry reflects the purchase of the three sets of securities:

Trading Securities (+A)	340*	
Available-for-Sale Securities (+A)	300	
Cash (−A)		640

Purchased trading and available-for-sale securities
*$100 (Dow) + $240 (Abbott)

Declaration and Receipt of Cash Dividends

Cash dividends declared on trading and available-for-sale securities, to which Goodyear has a legal right, are initially recognized as a receivable and a revenue. When the cash dividend is received, the receivable is exchanged for cash. Continuing the example, suppose that on December 15, 2011, the board of directors of Abbott declared dividends of $1 per share, to be paid to the holders of its common stock on January 15, 2012. The following journal entries would be recorded in Goodyear's books:

December 15—at declaration of dividend:

Dividend Receivable (+A)	20*	
Dividend Income (R, +RE)		20

Recognized declaration of dividend
*($1/share × 20 shares)

3. Actual brokerage commissions range from 1 to 5 percent.
4. For computational ease, the dollar amounts used in this example are unrealistically small. Multiplying the totals by 1,000 will produce numbers of a more realistic magnitude.

January 15—at receipt of dividend:

Cash (+A)	20	
Dividend Receivable (−A)		20

Received cash dividend

Sale of Securities

When trading and available-for-sale securities are sold, the balance sheet value is removed from the books, and the difference between the balance sheet value and the proceeds from the sale is recognized as a realized gain or loss. If the proceeds exceed the balance sheet value, a **realized gain** is recognized; if they are less than the balance sheet value, a **realized loss** is recognized.

Continuing the example, assume that on December 4, Goodyear sold all ten shares of Dow Chemical stock for $13/share and ten of the fifteen shares of Eli Lilly stock for $10/share. Assuming that brokerage commissions have already been deducted from the sales price, these sales would give rise to the following journal entries:

Cash (+A)	130	
Trading Securities (Dow) (−A)		100*
Realized Gain on Sale of Trading Securities (Ga, +RE)		30

Sold Dow Chemical stock
*($10/share × 10 shares)

Cash (+A)	100	
Realized Loss on Sale of Available-for-Sale Sec. (Lo, −RE)	100	
Available-for-Sale Securities (Lilly) (−A)		200*

Sold Lilly stock
*($20/share × 10 shares)

The realized gain and loss accounts represent the difference between the sale proceeds and the balance sheet value of the sold securities and, therefore, provide a measure of management's performance with respect to the buying and selling of these securities. These accounts appear on the income statement and thus figure in the determination of net income. Chapter 13 points out that these book gains and losses, and others like them, appear in a special section of the income statement, titled "Other Revenues and Expenses."

> Biomet, which designs, manufactures, and markets orthopedic products, reported dividend income and realized gains from short-term investments in the amounts of $0.3 million and $0.8 million, respectively, for 2009. Describe the transactions that gave rise to these two sources of income.

Price Changes of Securities on Hand at the End of the Accounting Period

At the end of each accounting period the current market values of all trading and available-for-sale securities held by the company are determined. Adjusting journal entries restate the balance sheet values of the securities to reflect their current market values. These adjustments give rise to **unrealized gains and losses,** often called **holding gains or losses.** In the case of trading securities, these gains or losses are considered temporary accounts, appear on the income statement, and are reflected in retained earnings. *In the case of available-for-sale securities, the **unrealized price changes***

are considered permanent accounts and are carried in the shareholders' equity section of the balance sheet.

END-OF-PERIOD ADJUSTMENTS: TRADING SECURITIES

Continuing the example, assume that Goodyear held all twenty shares of Abbott on December 31, 2011, the end of the accounting period. The shares were purchased for $12 each and are currently trading for $15 each. To mark the investment to market value, an adjusting journal entry of the following form would be recorded on December 31:

Trading Securities (Abbott) (+A)   60*
    Unrealized Gain on Trading Securities (Ga, +RE)   60
Revalued Abbott securities to market
*[($15 − $12) × 20 shares]

If instead of $15/share, the Abbott shares were trading for $10 each on December 31, the following adjusting journal entry would have been recorded:

Unrealized Loss on Trading Securities (Lo, −RE)   40*
    Trading Securities (Abbott) (−A)   40
Revalued Abbott securities to market
*[($12 − $10) × 20 shares]

The unrealized holding gain (loss) represents the extent to which Goodyear's wealth increased (decreased) due to holding Abbott securities from December 1 to December 31. Because the investment in these securities is classified as trading and therefore is expected to be sold in the near future, the unrealized holding gain (loss) is considered part of Goodyear's income for the accounting period. Note also that the balance sheet value of the investment in Abbott on December 31, 2011, reflects the current market price of the securities, which is carried into the next period and used in the determination of future realized and unrealized gains and losses.

END-OF-PERIOD ADJUSTMENTS: AVAILABLE-FOR-SALE SECURITIES

Assume that Goodyear held five shares of Eli Lilly stock on December 31, 2011, with a current market value of $22 each. (Recall that fifteen shares were originally purchased on December 1 at $20 each, and ten shares were sold on December 4 for $10 each.) To mark the investment to market value, the following adjusting journal entry would be recorded on December 31:

Available-for-Sale Securities (Lilly) (+A)   10*
    Unrealized Price Increase on Available-for-Sale Sec. (+SE)   10
Revalued Lilly securities to market
*[($22 − $20) × 5 shares]

If instead of $22/share, the Lilly shares were trading for $14 each on December 31, the following adjusting journal entry would have been recorded:

Unrealized Price Decrease on Available-for-Sale Sec. (−SE)   30*
    Available-for-Sale Securities (Lilly) (−A)   30
Revalued Lilly securities to market
*[($20 − $14) × 5 shares]

Again, the unrealized price increase (decrease) represents the extent to which Goodyear's wealth increased (decreased) due to holding Lilly securities from December 1 to December 31. However, because the investment in these securities is classified as

available-for-sale and therefore is not expected to be sold in the near future, the unrealized price change is not considered part of Goodyear's income for the accounting period. Therefore, it *affects only the shareholders' equity section of the balance sheet, and not the income statement.* Unrealized price increases (credits) increase shareholders' equity, while unrealized price decreases (debits) decrease shareholders' equity. Both the market value of the investment and the dollar amount of the unrealized price change in the shareholders' equity account are carried into the next accounting period and adjusted if the securities are sold or the market value of the securities changes. We illustrate below how the balance sheet values of the investment and unrealized price change accounts are adjusted under two separate conditions: (1) if the securities are sold in the next period and (2) if the market value of the securities changes in the next period.

> Apple, Inc.'s success with its Macintosh computer, iPod, and iPhone products can be seen in the growth of its short-term marketable securities. As of 9/26/2009, Apple owned $18.2 billion of these investments, up from $10.2 billion on 9/27/2008. This growth in marketable securities has come at a time of extreme stock market volatility. What effect would a strong bull or bear stock market have on Apple's financial statements? What management decision can radically affect how much an up or down market changes Apple's profitability?

(1) IF THE AVAILABLE-FOR-SALE SECURITIES ARE SOLD. Assume as in the most recent example above that Eli Lilly shares were trading at $14 each as of December 31, 2008, and a $30 unrealized price decrease (debit) was disclosed in the shareholders' equity section of the December 31 balance sheet. If Goodyear sold all five Lilly shares for $16 each on April 5, 2012, the following journal entry would be recorded:

Cash (+A)	80*	
Realized Loss on Available-for-Sale Sec. (Lo, −RE)	20	
Available-for-Sale Securities (Lilly) (−A)		70**
Unrealized Price Decrease on Available-for-Sale Sec. (+SE)		30
Sold Lilly securities		

*($16/share × 5 shares)
**($14/share × 5 shares)

Note first that cash is debited for the proceeds of the sale ($16/share × 5 shares). The $30 unrealized price decrease and the balance sheet value of the available-for-sale securities account, which reflects the market value of the securities as of December 31 ($14/share × 5 shares), are both written off the books because Goodyear no longer holds the securities. The realized loss of $20 is the "plug" that brings the entry into balance, but more importantly, it represents the difference between the original cost ($100 = $20/share × 5 shares) of the securities and the proceeds from the sale ($80).

> Most U.S. companies prefer to classify investments as available-for-sale instead of trading securities. This choice offers these firms a method of managing reported earnings by carefully choosing when to sell certain securities in their portfolio. Explain how this might work.

(2) IF THE MARKET VALUE OF THE AVAILABLE-FOR-SALE SECURITIES CHANGES. Assume once again that Eli Lilly shares were trading at $14 each as of December 31, 2011, and a $30 unrealized price decrease was disclosed in the shareholders' equity section of the December 31 balance sheet. If on December 31, 2012, the securities are still held by Goodyear and the price has changed to $16, the following journal entry would be recorded:

Available-for-Sale Securities (Lilly) (+A)	10*	
Unrealized Price Decrease on Available-for-Sale Sec. (+SE)		10

Revalued Lilly securities to market
*[($16 − $14) × 5 shares]

In this case, the available-for-sale account is adjusted to reflect its current market value and the unrealized price decrease account is reduced because the market price has increased since the previous balance sheet date. The December 31, 2012, balance in the unrealized price decrease account in the shareholders' equity section of Goodyear's balance sheet would be $20 ($30 − $10).

> In its 2009 annual report, Biomet reported net unrealized losses on available-for-sale equity securities of $0.6 million. Where on the financial statements would this amount be reflected? Had the equity investments been considered trading securities, where on the financial statements would the amount be reflected?

Reclassifications and Permanent Market Value Declines

Companies sometimes choose to change the classifications of security investments from trading to available-for-sale, or vice versa. In such cases, unrealized holding gains or losses should be recognized immediately as income. When transferring securities from the trading to the available-for-sale classification, unrealized holding gains and losses that accrued since the most recent financial statement date should be recognized as income on the date of the transfer. When transferring securities from the available-for-sale to the trading classification, unrealized holding gains and losses from two sources should be recognized as income on the date of the transfer: (1) those that accrued since the most recent financial statement date and (2) the unrealized price change disclosed in the shareholders' equity section of the most recent balance sheet.

Investments sometimes suffer a permanent market value decline; the price declines and is not expected to recover. In such cases, the security should be written down to its market value, and a *realized loss* that reduces net income should be recognized immediately whether the security is classified as trading or available-for-sale. Determining a permanent decline is very subjective, and GAAP provide very few guidelines. Perhaps the best way to assess such a decline is to consider the financial condition of the firm that issued the security. We return to this issue in Chapter 9, where we discuss permanent write-downs of fixed assets and how management can use its discretion in this area to manage reported financial numbers.

Mark-to-Market Accounting and Comprehensive Income

For years, accounting theorists have argued for a pure form of mark-to-market accounting, where assets are reported on the balance sheet at market value and changes

in asset prices are included on the income statement. The methods used to account for trading securities are completely consistent with this approach, while the methods used to account for available-for-sale securities report market values on the balance sheet but do not reflect changes in market prices on the income statement.

In a move toward pure mark-to-market accounting, the FASB now requires companies to provide a statement of comprehensive income. No specific format is required for this statement, but it must be displayed with the same prominence as the other financial statements.

> Under IFRS, a similar statement is required, most often referred to as the **Statement of Recognized Income and Expense (SORIE).**

The statement of comprehensive income must disclose total **comprehensive income,** which includes all nonowner-related changes in shareholders' equity that do not appear on the income statement and are not reflected in the balance of retained earnings. Several items fall into this category, including adjustments to shareholders' equity for the holding gains and losses associated with available-for-sale securities. Thus, while unrealized price increases and decreases of available-for-sale securities are not reflected on the income statement, they are reported on the statement of comprehensive income. When combined with net income, which is reported on the income statement, comprehensive income provides investors, analysts, and others with an estimate of the overall change in a company's wealth during the period.

> Major firms use a number of different methods to disclose comprehensive income on their annual reports. AT&T includes a statement of comprehensive income immediately after the statement of shareholders' equity; PepsiCo includes a line item called comprehensive income within the statement of shareholders' equity; Wendy's discloses a special financial statement devoted only to comprehensive income along with the other financial statements; and Johnson & Johnson includes a statement of comprehensive income in the footnotes to the financial statements. As an analyst, would you consider comprehensive income an important number, and how would you feel about the wide variety of disclosure options used by major companies?

LONG-TERM EQUITY INVESTMENTS

As indicated earlier in this chapter, companies make investments in the equity securities of other companies primarily for two reasons: (1) investment income in the form of dividends and stock price appreciation, and (2) management influence, where the voting power of the purchased shares allows the investor company to exert some control over the board of directors and management of the investee company. The primary motivation behind the long-term equity investments for most major U.S. companies is reason (2), influence over the investee company's operations and management.

Most large, well-known U.S. companies are constantly involved in acquisitions, whereby they purchase all, or a majority of, the outstanding common stock of another

company and then change the investee company's operations and/or management. Several years ago, for example, General Electric (GE) purchased for $6.4 billion all outstanding common stock of RCA Corporation, which at the time owned National Broadcasting Company (NBC). As reported in GE's financial report, "subsequent to the acquisition, GE sold . . . a number of RCA and NBC operations whose activities were not compatible with GE's long-range strategic plans."

In another example, Cisco Systems stated in its 2006 financial report that its February 24, 2006, acquisition of Scientific Atlanta Inc. cost $7.1 billion. Cisco made significant changes to the operations and management of the acquired company.

> **?** In 2004 FedEx Corporation acquired Kinko's copy center chain in a transaction valued at $2.4 billion. FedEx acquired Kinko's to better compete against UPS, which had previously acquired Mail Boxes Etc. Did FedEx and UPS make these investments to generate income in the form of dividends and stock appreciation or to exert influence over the investee company's operations and management? Discuss.

It is also common to exert influence over the operations and management of a company by purchasing a significant portion, but less than a majority (51%), of the company's outstanding common stock. *Accounting Trends and Techniques* (New York: AICPA, 2009) reports that, of the major U.S. companies surveyed, well over half reported such investments. For example, as of the end of 2006, Walt Disney held a 38 percent ownership in A & E Television Networks and a 40 percent ownership in E! Entertainment Television.

Accounting for Long-Term Equity Investments

Since long-term investments in equity securities are commonly made to exert influence over the operations and management of the investee company, financial accounting standards define the appropriate accounting method in terms of the potential for such influence—specifically, in terms of the percentage of outstanding voting stock owned by the investor company.

If the investor company owns less than 20 percent of the outstanding voting stock of the investee company, the potential for influence is relatively small, and the two entities can be viewed as independent. The equity investment, therefore, is accounted for using either the mark-to-market method or the cost method. When the percentage of ownership is between 20 and 50 percent, the investor company has the potential to exert "significant influence" over the investee company, and the two entities cannot be viewed as completely independent. The investor company uses the equity method to account for the equity investment. When the percentage of ownership is greater than 50 percent, the investor company has "control" over the investee company, and for accounting purposes, the two entities are viewed as one, and consolidated financial statements are prepared. Figure 8–1 summarizes the conditions that define the methods used to account for long-term equity investments.

The following discussion presents the mechanics involved in applying the cost and equity methods and the conditions under which each method is used.

FIGURE 8–1

Accounting for long-term investments in equity securities

Percentage of Stock Ownership	Potential to Influence	Accounting Method
Less than 20%	Small	Mark-to-market or cost method
20%–50%	Significant	Equity method
Greater than 50%	Control	Consolidated financial statements

The Cost Method

Some equity securities have no readily determinable market values. Equity securities in corporations whose securities are not publicly traded (i.e., closely held corporations or private companies), for example, may have restrictions on trading and therefore have no public market values. Relatively small investments (less than 20% of the outstanding voting stock) in such securities, which by definition cannot easily be liquidated, are accounted for using the **cost method.** It is impossible to apply the mark-to-market method to such securities because their market values cannot be determined.

Applying the cost method is very straightforward. Purchases of equity securities are recorded at cost, including incidental costs of acquisition; dividends are recorded as income when declared; and sales, when they eventually occur, give rise to realized gains or losses reflected on the income statement.

To illustrate, suppose that on January 15, 2011, Beldon Inc. purchased 100 equity securities in a closely held corporation for $10 per share. On December 15 Beldon received a $50 dividend that had been declared on November 29. No other activity occurred in the account until May 5, 2012, when Beldon sold the securities privately for $7 each. The journal entries contained in Figure 8–2 would reflect these transactions.

FIGURE 8–2

The cost method of accounting for long-term equity investments

2011:			
Jan. 15	Long-Term Investment in Equity Securities (+A)	1,000	
	Cash (−A)		1,000
	Purchased 100 equity shares at $10 per share		
Nov. 29	Dividend Receivable (+A)	50	
	Dividend Income (R +RE)		50
	Recognized a declared dividend to be received		
Dec. 15	Cash (+A)	50	
	Dividend Receivable (−A)		50
	Received previously declared $50 dividend		
2012:			
May 5	Cash (+A)	700	
	Loss on Sale of Long-Term Equity Securities (Lo, −RE)	300	
	Long-Term Investment in Equity Securities (−A)		1,000
	Sold 100 equity shares, originally purchased at $10 each, for $7 per share		

The Equity Method

Some companies have the ability to significantly influence the operating decisions and management policies of other companies. Such influence indicates a substantive economic relationship between the two companies and may be evidenced, for example, by

representation on the board of directors, the interchange of management personnel between companies, frequent or significant transactions between companies, or the technical dependency of one company on the other. Significant investments in the equity securities (voting stock) of another company may also indicate significant influence and a substantive economic relationship. To achieve a reasonable degree of uniformity, the accounting profession concluded that an investment of 20 percent or more in the voting stock of another company represents a "significant influence" and that equity investments from 20 to 50 percent of the voting stock should be accounted for using the **equity method.**

> As of 12/31/2008, Intel Corporation listed over $3 billion of long-term investments accounted for under the equity method. The company disclosed that its equity ownership of four of these companies consisted of the following percentages: 49 percent, 49 percent, 45 percent, and 8 percent. The first three ownership levels clearly fall into the category for equity method accounting. Under what conditions might a company use the equity for an investment that only constituted 8 percent of the affiliate company's outstanding common shares?

The accounting procedures used to apply the equity method reflect a substantive economic relationship between the investor and the investee companies. The equity investment is originally recorded on the investor's books at cost but is adjusted each subsequent period for changes in the net assets of the investee. As the balance sheet value of the investee increases or decreases, so does the long-term equity investment account of the investor.

Specifically, the carrying value of the long-term investment on the investor's balance sheet is (1) periodically increased (decreased) by the investor's proportionate share of the net income (loss) of the investee and (2) decreased by all dividends transferred to the investor from the investee. In other words, the equity method of accounting acknowledges a close economic link between the two companies. Investee earnings, which indicate net asset growth, and investee dividends, which represent net asset reductions, are reflected proportionately on the balance sheet of the investor.

To illustrate, assume that on January 1, 2011, American Electric Company purchased 40 percent of the outstanding voting stock of Masley Corporation for $40,000. During 2011, Masley recognized net income of $10,000 and declared (Dec. 1) and paid (Dec. 20) dividends of $1,500 to American Electric. During 2012, Masley recognized a net loss of $5,000 and declared (Dec. 1) and paid (Dec. 20) only a $500 dividend to American Electric. Under the equity method, the journal entries contained in Figure 8–3 would be recorded on the books of American Electric.

It is important to understand how the equity method reflects a significant economic relationship between the investor and investee companies. The net income (loss) of the investee serves to proportionately increase (decrease) the investment account of the investor. Thus, the investee's net asset growth or decline is reflected on the investor's balance sheet and income statement. Note also that dividends transferred from the investee to the investor are not treated as revenue on the investor's books.

2011:

Jan. 1   Long-Term Investment in Equity Securities (+A)   40,000
        Cash (−A)   40,000
        Purchased 40% of Masley's outstanding shares

Dec. 1   Dividend Receivable (+A)   1,500
        Long-Term Investment in Equity Securities (−A)   1,500
        Recognized $1,500 dividend declared by Masley

Dec. 20 Cash (+A)   1,500
        Dividend Receivable (−A)   1,500
        Received dividend declared on December 1

Dec. 31 Long-Term Investment in Equity Securities (+A)   4,000
        Income from Long-Term Equity Investments (R, +RE)   4,000
        Recognized 40% of Masley's 2008 net income
        ($10,000 × 40%)

2012:

Dec. 1   Dividend Receivable (+A)   500
        Long-Term Investment in Equity Securities (−A)   500
        Recognized dividend declared by Masley

Dec. 20 Cash (+A)   500
        Dividend Receivable (−A)   500
        Received dividend declared on December 1

Dec. 31 Loss on Long-Term Equity Investment (Lo, −RE)   2,000
        Long-Term Investment in Equity Securities (−A)   2,000
        Recognized 40% of Masley's 2009 net loss
        ($5,000 × 40%)

In December 2007 Boeing and Lockheed Martin Corp. entered into a 50/50 joint venture to create United Launch Alliance, which launches rockets for the U.S. government. Each company made an initial investment of about $500 million. What method of accounting did each company use, and how was the $500 million investment reflected in each company's financial statements?

Revenue is recognized when the investor's proportionate share of the investee's net income is recorded, not when the dividends are declared or transferred. Dividends are simply treated as an exchange of assets on the investor's books. The long-term investment account is decreased, dividends receivable is increased on the date of declaration, and the receivable is exchanged for cash on the date of payment.

Eli Lilly, the well-known pharmaceutical, carries long-term investments in equity securities using the equity method on its balance sheet. From the end of 2007 to the end of 2008, the investment account increased from $98.8 million to $127.8 million. Discuss the events that could have accounted for this change.

Figure 8–4 indicates the importance of investments accounted for under the equity method, relative to total assets, to several major U.S. corporations at fiscal year end, 2008. Investee companies that are 20 to 50 percent owned by investor companies are often referred to as **affiliate companies.**

FIGURE 8–4	Company	Amount of Investment (millions of dollars)	Percentage of Total Assets
The relative importance of investments in affiliate companies (selected U.S. companies)	Microsoft	$4,933	6%
	Coca-Cola	5,316	13
	DuPont	844	2
	Intel	3,032	6

Source: 2008 financial reports.

Under IFRS, affiliate companies are normally called associate companies.

Income from equity investments can also represent a material percentage of net income. In recent annual reports, for example, Starbucks, PepsiCo, and Bristol-Myers Squibb reported income from affiliate companies (as a percentage of total net income) of 31 percent, 7 percent, and 12 percent, respectively. The following excerpt, taken from the 2008, financial report of Goodyear Tire & Rubber Co., describes how the company accounts for equity investments in affiliate companies:

Investments in companies in which we do not own a majority and we have the ability to exercise significant influence over operating and financial policies are accounted for using the equity method.

At the end of 2008, Coca-Cola reported investments under the equity method totaling over $5.3 billion (13 percent of total assets) primarily in bottling companies, the largest of which was a 35 percent investment in Coca-Cola Enterprises, the largest soft-drink bottler in the world. During 2008 Coca-Cola Enterprises reported a net loss of $4.4 billion, while Coca-Cola reported an overall loss on its equity method investments of $874 million. How much loss did Coca-Cola report from its investment in Coca-Cola Enterprises? How well did all the other bottling operations perform during 2008?

Some Cautions to Financial Statement Users about the Equity Method

Several features about the equity method should cause financial report users to view it carefully. First, the equity method provides another reason why a company's net income (loss) differs from its cash flow from operations. The income recognized from the investee company rarely equals the cash dividends received by the investor. *Forbes* magazine once described the equity method as "misleading" because "the investor company never really sees any nondividend cash from the investee company" on which it often recognizes substantial income. For example, in 2008 Chevron recognized $5,366 million in income from affiliate companies, which represented 22 percent of its 2008 earnings. However, Chevron received only $4,926 million in cash dividends from the affiliates. An astute user can learn how much cash was received from affiliate investments by examining the operating section of the statement of cash flows. In

Chevron's case, the $440 million difference between reported equity income ($5,366 million) and cash received ($4,926 million) was subtracted from net income in the calculation of net cash from operations and described as "distributions less than income from equity affiliates."

In the operating section of its 2008 statement of cash flows, AT&T reported a line item entitled "undistributed earnings from investments in equity affiliates" in the amount of $654 million, which is subtracted from net income in the calculation of net cash provided by operating activities. Explain the meaning of this item.

In addition, the equity method ignores price (market value) changes in the affiliate's equity securities. For example, price decreases, even if substantial, are not recognized on the investor's books and, in fact, may even be accompanied by the recognition of income and the receipt of dividends if the affiliate reports positive income and declares dividends during the period of the price decline. Informed users should keep track of the price changes of the affiliate's equity shares, if they are publicly available.

Third, the percentage of ownership (20 percent to 50 percent) is not always a valid indication of "significant influence." Influence comes in many different forms. Time Warner, for example, was able to block a bid by Turner Broadcasting Systems (TBS) to acquire CBS even though Time Warner owned less than 20 percent of TBS stock. Time Warner did, however, have two members on the TBS board of directors. Similarly, it is possible to exert a controlling influence with less than 51 percent of the stock, especially when the remaining stock is owned by shareholders who represent a wide variety of interests.

Finally, as we discuss later in this chapter, using the equity method can be considered a method of off-balance-sheet financing because it fails to reflect the liabilities of the affiliate on the balance sheet of the investor company. Financial accounting standards require that a summary of the financial statements of all affiliate companies be included in the footnotes of the investor's financial statements. Users should review these summaries to see if including the affiliate's assets and liabilities on the investor's balance sheet would affect solvency and liquidity ratios.

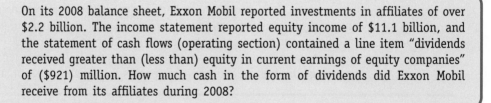

On its 2008 balance sheet, Exxon Mobil reported investments in affiliates of over $2.2 billion. The income statement reported equity income of $11.1 billion, and the statement of cash flows (operating section) contained a line item "dividends received greater than (less than) equity in current earnings of equity companies" of ($921) million. How much cash in the form of dividends did Exxon Mobil receive from its affiliates during 2008?

THE FAIR MARKET VALUE OPTION

In 2007 the FASB passed a financial reporting standard that allows companies to account for certain financial instruments (including investments in equity securities) at fair market value. This means that the equity investments we have covered thus far in this chapter (e.g., trading securities, available-for-sale securities, and equity method investments) can—*at the option of the company*—be accounted for using mark-to-market

accounting.[5] As we have already described, equity investments classified as trading securities must be accounted for in this manner, but this new standard allows companies, if they wish, to use mark-to-market for available-for-sale securities as well as equity investments designed to exert a "significant influence" over an affiliate company.

IFRS has a similar standard that gives companies the option to carry assets on the balance sheet at market value. As we discuss later, the IFRS standard applies to a much larger group of assets, including real estate and property, plant, and equipment.

Because fair market values can be very subjective, an important disclosure required when a company uses market values on its balance sheet relates to the basis for the market value estimate. Market values based on quoted prices in active markets for identical securities are called **Level 1 measurements;** market values based on less reliable, observable, indirect inputs are called **Level 2 measurements;** and market values based on much less reliable, unobservable inputs are called **Level 3 measurements.** These disclosures help the reader to better assess the uncertainties inherent in the market value estimates.

The **fair market value option** standard represents a major and important shift in U.S. GAAP toward the use of market values in the financial statements—a shift in the direction of IFRS, which already relies significantly on mark-to-market accounting. For the most part, mark-to-market accounting is still optional, but gradually more companies appear to be exercising the option. *Accounting Trends and Techniques* (2009) reported that over 20 percent of the major corporations surveyed in 2008 used fair market value as the basis for certain non-current balance sheet assets. By far the most common basis for the market value measurements was Level 1 (quoted prices for identical securities in active markets).

Business Acquisitions, Mergers, and Consolidated Financial Statements

A **business acquisition** occurs when an investor company acquires a **controlling interest** (more than 50 percent of the voting stock) in another company. If the two companies continue as separate legal entities, the investor company is referred to as the **parent company,** and the investee company is called the **subsidiary.** Several years ago, for example, Benetton Group paid $330 million to acquire Benetton Sportsystem, which carries Rollerblade, Prince tennis racquets, and Nordica ski boots. Sportsystem now operates as a Benetton subsidiary. In such cases, the parent prepares **consolidated financial statements** (including the income statement, balance sheet, statement of cash flows, and statement of shareholders' equity). Consolidated statements ignore the fact that the parent and the subsidiary are actually separate legal entities and, for reporting purposes, treat the two companies as a single operating unit.

Under IFRS, the definition of control for purposes of consolidation is often broader than the U.S. GAAP definition, including factors beyond ownership percent.

Consolidated statements are prepared for financial accounting purposes only. The parent and the subsidiary maintain separate legal status. In many respects they may

5. Recall that under mark-to-market accounting, the investment is carried on the balance sheet at its current market value, and changes in market value from one period to the next are reflected in earnings on the income statement.

continue to operate as relatively independent entities, and the subsidiary maintains a separate set of financial statements. Only because the parent has a controlling interest over the subsidiary do professional accounting standards require that the financial condition of the two companies be represented to the public as one.

A **merger,** or **business combination,** occurs when two or more companies combine to form a single legal entity. In most cases, the assets and liabilities of the smaller company are merged into those of the larger, surviving company. The stock of at least one company, usually the smaller one, is often retired, and it ceases to exist as a separate entity. When Chemical Bank was merged into Chase Manhattan, for example, the surviving entity was named Chase Manhattan. Chase Manhattan subsequently merged with J.P. Morgan, creating the new entity JPMorgan Chase. Technically speaking, consolidated financial statements are not prepared after a merger because no parent/subsidiary relationship exists. At least one of the companies involved in the combination no longer exists. However, the financial statements of the surviving company do reflect the assets and liabilities of the merged entities.

> **?** The financial statements of Target Corporation are all referred to as "consolidated." Explain what this means.

Most business acquisitions and combinations consummate when cash and/or other assets (often stock) of the parent are paid to the shareholders of the subsidiary in exchange for the assets and liabilities of the subsidiary.[6] Such transactions are commonly accounted for under the purchase method, when the assets and liabilities of the subsidiary are recorded on the balance sheet of the parent at fair market value (FMV), and the difference between the purchase price and the net FMV of the subsidiary's assets and liabilities is recorded as goodwill.

For example, when Delta Air Lines, Inc. purchased all the outstanding shares of Western Airlines, Inc. for $787 million, the purchase price consisted of $383 million in cash and Delta common stock valued at $404 million. Delta received the assets and liabilities of Western, which at the time of the transaction had fair market values as described in Figure 8–5.

FIGURE 8–5
Computation of goodwill

		Fair Market Value (in millions)
Current assets		$349
Property, plant, and equipment		748
Other assets		24
Less: Current liabilities	$310	
Long-term debt	431	(741)
Net FMV of Western's assets and liabilities		$380
Less: Purchase price		787
Goodwill (excess of purchase price over FMV of net assets)		$407

6. In the following discussion we use the terms *parent* and *subsidiary* to denote the investor and investee companies. In the case of business combinations, however, the term *parent* should be interpreted as the survivor company and the term *subsidiary* as the merged company.

In the preparation of its consolidated statements, Delta recorded the purchase by making an adjustment similar to the following entry. Western's assets and liabilities were then included on Delta's consolidated balance sheet.

Current assets (+A)	349	
Property, plant, and equipment (+A)	748	
Other assets (+A)	24	
Goodwill (+A)	407	
Current liabilities (+L)		310
Long-term liabilities (+L)		431
Cash (−A)		383
Common stock (+SE)		404
Purchased Western Airlines		

Goodwill

Goodwill is an asset listed in the noncurrent section of the balance sheet. As illustrated in the example above, it arises when a company (parent) pays an amount to acquire a controlling interest in a subsidiary that exceeds the fair market value of the subsidiary's net assets (total assets less liabilities). Acquiring companies are willing to pay this "premium" presumably because they believe that the value to them of owning the controlling interest exceeds the fair market value of the subsidiary's individual net assets. Companies that grow through acquisitions often carry huge goodwill balances on their balance sheets. Hewlett-Packard, for example, reported goodwill of over $32 billion on its 2008 balance sheet, an amount that increased by more than $10 billion over the previous year.

Up until 2002, each year a portion of the goodwill balance was amortized, reducing reported income in that year. However, a new accounting standard, effective January 1, 2002, ruled that goodwill should not be amortized. Rather, each year the balance in the goodwill account should be subjected to an impairment test to see if the balance sheet amount of the goodwill exceeds its estimated fair market value. If the balance sheet amount is judged to exceed the fair market value of the goodwill, the goodwill account should be written down to its fair market value.

To illustrate, if Company A's balance sheet amount of goodwill is $10,000 and the fair market value of the goodwill is estimated to be $8,000, Company A's goodwill would be considered impaired and the entry below would be recorded in Company A's books. If the fair market value of the goodwill was estimated to be $10,000 or more, no entry would be recorded in Company A's books.

Goodwill Impairment Charge (Lo, −RE)	2,000	
Goodwill (−A)		2,000

ConocoPhillips, a mega oil company, reported a goodwill impairment expense of $25.4 billion on its 2008 income statement. The company reported an overall net loss that year of $17 billion, compared to an $11.9 billion profit in 2007. What might have caused the impairment expense? The impairment expense also appeared in the operating section of the statement of cash flows as an add-back to net earnings in the calculation of net cash from operations. Why?

Estimating the fair market value of goodwill is highly subjective. It essentially involves attempting at the end of each year to place a value on the subsidiaries previously acquired by the company, most of which are no longer publicly traded and many of which do not operate as independent entities. This requirement imposes a large

burden on companies that carry large balances in the goodwill account, and the subjectivity involved offers yet another way for companies to manage reported earnings. In addition, goodwill impairment charges are difficult to audit because auditors normally have limited knowledge of the subsidiaries in question.

> General Electric included the following in the footnotes to a recent annual report: "We tested all our goodwill for impairment, and recorded a non-cash charge of $1.2 billion. Substantially all of the charge related to the GECS IT Solutions business and the GECS U.S. Auto and Home business. Factors contributing to the impairment charge were the difficult economic environment in the information technology sector and the heightened price competition in the auto insurance industry." Briefly explain the meaning of this quote.

Accounting for business acquisitions and mergers and preparing consolidated financial statements are actually more complex than we have indicated here. Further discussion can be found in Appendix 8A and in intermediate and advanced financial accounting texts.

The Equity Method or Consolidated Statements?

Accounting for an equity investment under the equity method can give rise to financial statements that are much different from those prepared as consolidated statements. The following example describes an equity investment, comparing the balance sheet produced under the equity method to a consolidated balance sheet.

Figure 8–6 shows the December 31, 2011, balance sheets of Megabucks, a large manufacturing company, and Tiny Inc., a smaller distribution outlet. Note initially that the debt/equity ratio of Megabucks is 67 percent ($20,000 ÷ $30,000). Assume that on December 31 Megabucks purchased the outstanding stock of Tiny Inc. for $10,000.

FIGURE 8–6

The balance sheets of Megabucks and Tiny Inc.

Megabucks
Balance Sheet
December 31, 2011

Assets	$50,000	Liabilities	$20,000
		Shareholders' equity	30,000
		Total liabilities and	
Total assets	$50,000	shareholders' equity	$50,000

Tiny Incorporated
Balance Sheet
December 31, 2011

Assets	$20,000	Liabilities	$15,000
		Shareholders' equity	5,000
		Total liabilities and	
Total assets	$20,000	shareholders' equity	$20,000

Under the equity method, Megabucks would record the following journal entry.

Long-term investment (+A)   10,000
    Cash (−A)   10,000
Purchased Tiny Inc. for $10,000

Note that the journal entry to record the investment has no effect on the total assets, total liabilities, total shareholders' equity, or the debt/equity ratio of Megabucks. The transaction is simply recorded as an exchange of two assets, a long-term investment and cash. In future periods under the equity method, Megabucks' total assets will reflect the net incomes (losses) reported by Tiny Inc., less any dividends.

If Megabucks accounts for this acquisition as a purchase and prepares consolidated financial statements, it would record the transaction with the following journal entry. Assume that Tiny's assets and liabilities are reported on its balance sheet at FMV.

Assets (+A)   20,000
Goodwill (+A)   5,000
    Liabilities (+L)   15,000
    Cash (−A)   10,000
Acquired Tiny Inc. for $10,000

In this case, both the assets and the liabilities of Megabucks would be increased by $15,000. The resulting consolidated balance sheet would appear as in Figure 8–7. Note that the debt/equity ratio is now 1.17 ($35,000 ÷ $30,000). Treating the transaction as a purchase and preparing a consolidated balance sheet, as opposed to using the equity method, increases the debt/equity ratio of Megabucks from 0.67 to 1.17.

FIGURE 8–7
Consolidated
balance sheet

Megabucks
Balance Sheet
December 31, 2011

Assets	$65,000	Liabilities	$35,000
		Shareholders' equity	30,000
		Total liabilities and	
Total assets	$65,000	shareholders' equity	$65,000

This difference between the equity method and preparing consolidated financial statements has encouraged many companies in the past to choose the equity method when possible, especially when the investee company carries considerable debt. Such a choice may come in the form of purchasing slightly less than 50 percent of the investee company's common stock, purchasing over 50 percent and claiming that "control is temporary or does not rest with the majority owner," or acquiring 100 percent and claiming that preparing consolidated statements would distort the financial statements because the subsidiary is so unlike the parent. The national director of a major accounting firm once noted that the equity method can be viewed as a method of off-balance-sheet financing. He pointed out that using the equity method can "present a more favorable impression of debt/equity ratios, working capital ratios, and returns on assets invested in the business." Consequently, financial statement users and auditors should pay special attention to cases where some question arises about whether the equity method should be used or consolidated financial statements should be prepared.

As of the end of 2008, Coca-Cola owned approximately a 30 percent interest in bottling companies that reported accumulated assets of $50.1 billion and accumulated liabilities of $35.3 billion. The balance sheet of Coca-Cola listed assets of $40.5 billion and liabilities of $20.1 billion. If Coca-Cola increased its ownership interest in these bottling companies so that it was required to include their assets and liabilities in a set of consolidated financial statements, what do you think would happen to Coca-Cola's liability-to-total-asset ratio?

Special Purpose Entities (SPEs)

Companies often create separate entities to carry out activities or transactions directly related to specific purposes. The entities (called **special purpose entities** or **special purpose vehicles**) take on various legal forms (e.g., corporations, partnerships) and create efficiencies for sponsoring companies by separating certain activities from their other activities. Primary motivations for the creation of SPEs include raising funds and transferring risks.

To illustrate, rather than directly purchasing property on which to conduct operations, suppose that Company A creates a separate entity (SPE), which raises capital by issuing debt or equity to investors. The SPE then uses these funds to purchase the property, which in turn is leased to Company A. Company A then uses the property, making periodic lease payments to SPE. Company A may prefer this arrangement to a direct purchase of the property because the responsibility for both raising the funds to finance the purchase and bearing the risks of owning the property has been transferred to SPE.

The key accounting question related to SPEs is whether the sponsoring company (e.g., Company A) should include (consolidate) the financial statements of the SPE with its own financial statements. According to professional standards, if the sponsoring company relinquishes control of the SPE, there is little reason to consolidate; if the sponsoring company retains control, the assets and liabilities should be consolidated. Unfortunately, determining who actually controls the SPE can be very subjective, and the transaction can be strategically structured by management to achieve the preferred accounting treatment, which sometimes fails to reflect the economic essence of the arrangement.

Accounting for SPEs is a difficult and controversial area, and in this section we only scratch the surface. It is important, however, because companies currently are using literally thousands of these vehicles. The vast majority of the SPEs are designed to achieve legitimate company goals, but occasionally they are used to mislead investors.

The recent interest in SPEs was in part motivated by the Enron fraud. It appears that Enron controlled a number of SPEs, many of which were financed by significant amounts of debt that were not consolidated on Enron's financial statements. Explain why Enron's management may not have wanted to consolidate the financial statements of the SPEs, and how not consolidating the SPEs may have misled investors.

Accounting for Equity Investments: A Summary

Figure 8–8 provides a framework that summarizes the methods used to account for investments in equity securities. It summarizes the appropriate accounting methods for all (short-term and long-term) investments in equity securities. In general, three questions must be answered before the appropriate accounting method and disclosure can be determined: (1) Is the security marketable? (2) Does management intend to liquidate the security within the time period of current assets? and (3) Is the proportion of ownership less than 20 percent, between 20 and 50 percent, or greater than 50 percent?

FIGURE 8–8   Accounting for equity securities

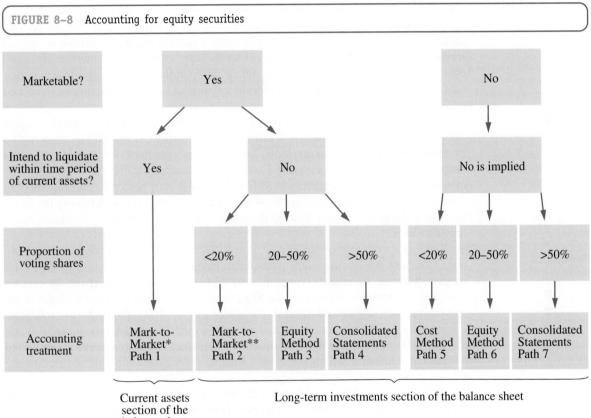

*Trading or available-for-sale securities, depending on expected liquidations.

**Available-for-sale securities.

If the purchased equity securities are marketable, and management intends to liquidate them within the time period of current assets, the investment is considered short-term. This is regardless of the proportion of ownership and whether it is considered trading or available-for-sale, and it is carried on the balance sheet at market value (Path 1). If the purchased securities are marketable, but management does not intend to liquidate them within the time period of current assets, the investment is considered long-term. Such long-term investments, where less than 20 percent of the voting shares are held, are considered available-for-sale and are carried on the balance sheet at

market value (Path 2). Long-term investments of between 20 and 50 percent of the voting shares are normally accounted for using the equity method (Path 3), but companies now have the option to use mark-to-market accounting. Long-term investments of 50 percent or more of the voting shares give rise to consolidated statements (Path 4).

Equity investments that are not marketable are accounted for using the cost method if they represent less than 20 percent of the voting shares (Path 5), or the equity method if they represent an investment of between 20 and 50 percent (Path 6). Consolidated statements should be prepared if such investments represent 50 percent or more of the voting stock (Path 7).

Preparing Consolidated Financial Statements for Multinationals

Multinational U.S. companies typically own a number of subsidiaries that have financial statements expressed in foreign currencies and prepared based on accounting standards other than U.S. GAAP (e.g., International Financial Reporting Standards). General Mills, for example, has major subsidiaries in several European countries, Canada, and Latin America, all of which publish their own financial statements denominated in local currencies. When General Mills prepares consolidated financial statements at year-end, the financial statements of these subsidiaries must first be converted to U.S. GAAP and then translated into U.S. dollars before they can be combined with the accounts of General Mills.

The process of translating the foreign currencies to U.S. dollars involves three steps: (1) classify the foreign subsidiaries, (2) translate the financial statements into U.S. dollars, and (3) consolidate the accounts. Foreign subsidiaries fall into two general categories: those (Type I) whose operations depend primarily on the parent (e.g., act as a supplier or channel of distribution); and those (Type II) that operate independently of the parent, transact primarily in the local currency, and are basically part of the countries in which they are operate.

When the financial statements of Type I foreign subsidiaries are translated into U.S. dollars, gains or losses resulting from the translation process are considered part of consolidated income because these subsidiaries transact with the parent in U.S. dollars, and gains and losses on changes in the exchange rates can affect the cash flows of the U.S. parent. Motorola, which has subsidiaries in China and a number of other non-U.S. companies, reported a loss on foreign currency exchange rates of $149 million on its 2008 income statement.

When the financial statements of Type II foreign subsidiaries are translated into U.S. dollars, the gains or losses resulting from the translation process are *not* considered part of consolidated income. Instead, these **foreign currency translation adjustments** are considered part of comprehensive income. As such, these adjustments appear on the statement of comprehensive income, and their cumulative balance appears in the shareholders' equity section of the balance sheet.

During 2008, on its statement of comprehensive income, General Electric reported a currency translation adjustment of approximately −$11.0 billion. The currency adjustment cumulative balance reported in the shareholders' equity section of GE's 2008 balance sheet was approximately −$299 million. Describe the nature of a currency translation adjustment, and estimate its balance on GE's 2007 balance sheet.

ROE EXERCISE: MANAGING INVESTMENTS IN EQUITY SECURITIES AND RETURN ON EQUITY

The ROE model, introduced and illustrated in Appendix 5A, provides a framework linking the management of a company's operating, investing, and financing activities to its return on the shareholders' investment (return on equity). In terms of this model, investments in equity securities can be viewed as either short-term or long-term.

Short-term investments in equity securities are part of working capital management, which is most directly concerned with maintaining liquid assets to meet debts as they come due. Management invests in short-term equity securities to achieve both liquidity and some level of return. The current and quick ratios reflect that level of investment, and the role of these two ratios in the ROE model is discussed in the ROE Exercise at the end of Chapter 6.

Long-term investments in equity securities are designed to generate returns for the shareholders. The success of such investments is measured by comparing the size of the return to the size of the investment. Accordingly, return on assets (ROA) is an important performance barometer for long-term investments in equity securities. As indicated in the ROE model, asset turnover is a key determinant of ROA, and ROA is a key determinant of ROE.

ROE ANALYSIS

Access the Web site (http://www.wiley.com/college/pratt), and conduct an ROE analysis on Kellogg vs. General Mills and/or AT&T vs. Verizon, paying special attention to how asset turnover impacts ROE.

APPENDIX 8A

CONSOLIDATED FINANCIAL STATEMENTS

Many companies expand by purchasing other companies and/or extending operations into other countries. For example, as of December 31, 2008, Johnson & Johnson, one of the world's largest consumer products companies, owned more than 200 companies that operated in almost every country of the world. In a typical year, Johnson & Johnson spends $1 billion acquiring other domestic and foreign operations. Each of these acquisitions involves acquiring large amounts of the outstanding equity securities of the investee companies. This appendix covers the methods used to account for investments in excess of 50 percent of the investee company's outstanding voting stock.

Such transactions give rise to consolidated financial statements, which reflect the combined accounts of both the investor and the investee companies. Virtually all major U.S. corporations prepare financial statements on a consolidated basis. The following excerpt is from the 2008 financial report of IBM and is typical of the disclosures made by other major U.S. companies.

The consolidated financial statements include the accounts of IBM and its controlled subsidiaries, which are generally majority owned. Investments in . . . business entities in which the company . . . has the ability to exercise significant influence . . . are accounted for using the equity method.

Accounting for Business Acquisitions and Mergers: The Purchase Method

Equity shares in other companies can be acquired by paying cash or other assets, issuing stock, or issuing bonds to the acquired company's shareholders. Often some combination of these forms of payment is used. When Delta Airlines acquired Western Airlines, for example, the $787 million payment to Western's shareholders consisted of $383 million in cash and 8.3 million shares of Delta stock, each with a value of $48.75.

For simplicity, in the following examples we assume that cash is paid for the acquired stock. To illustrate how the purchase method is used to account for business acquisitions and mergers, assume that on December 31, 2011, Multi Corporation acquired a controlling interest in the equity shares of Littleton Company. The December 31 balance sheets for both companies and some additional information for Littleton Company appear in Figure 8A–1.

FIGURE 8A–1   Balance sheets for Multi Corporation and Littleton Company (before acquisition)

Multi Corporation
Balance Sheet
December 31, 2011

ASSETS

Cash	$ 65,000
Accounts receivable	70,000
Notes receivable	35,000
Inventory	120,000
Long-lived assets (net)	230,000
Total assets	$520,000

LIABILITIES AND SHAREHOLDERS' EQUITY

Accounts payable	$ 90,000
Long-term notes payable	130,000
Common stock	200,000
Retained earnings	100,000
Total liabilities and shareholders' equity	$520,000

Littleton Company
Balance Sheet
December 31, 2011

ASSETS

Cash	$ 6,000
Accounts receivable	9,000
Inventory	10,000
Long-lived assets (net)	35,000
Total assets	$60,000

LIABILITIES AND SHAREHOLDERS' EQUITY

Accounts payable	$14,000
Long-term notes payable	16,000
Common stock	22,000
Retained earnings	8,000
Total liabilities and shareholders' equity	$60,000

Additional information:
Common shares outstanding	8,000

When a parent company (Multi Corporation) purchases a controlling interest in a subsidiary (Littleton), the parent is essentially purchasing the assets and liabilities of the subsidiary. It is important to realize that the historical costs of the subsidiary's assets, which are included on Littleton's balance sheet in Figure 8A–1, are of little consequence to the purchase decision. The parent is actually purchasing the fair market values (FMVs), not the historical costs, of the assets and liabilities of the subsidiary. An important rule, therefore, in understanding accounting for consolidated financial statements is: When a parent purchases a controlling interest in a subsidiary, the assets and liabilities of the subsidiary are recorded on the balance sheet of the parent at their FMVs.

Consequently, from Multi Corporation's standpoint, it is more appropriate to view the value of Littleton's net assets as shown in Figure 8A–2, where all assets and liabilities have been

valued at their individual FMVs. As of December 31, 2011, there were 8,000 shares of Littleton common stock outstanding. The per-share market value of the net assets, therefore, is $5 ($40,000 ÷ 8,000 shares).

FIGURE 8A–2

FMV of Littleton's net assets

Littleton Company Schedule of Fair Market Values of Assets and Liabilities December 31, 2011	
Cash	$ 6,000
Accounts receivable	9,000
Inventory	15,000
Long-lived assets	40,000
Accounts payable	(14,000)
Long-term notes payable	(16,000)
FMV of net assets	$40,000

The following sections account for Multi Corporation's purchase of Littleton shares under the two most common scenarios: (1) purchase 100 percent of the common stock for a price greater than the per-share market value of the net assets, and (2) purchase between 50 and 100 percent of the common stock for a price greater than the per-share market value of the net assets.[7]

CASE 1: PURCHASE 100 PERCENT OF STOCK AT A PRICE GREATER THAN THE PER-SHARE MARKET VALUE OF THE NET ASSETS

Assume that Multi Corporation purchased all 8,000 shares of the outstanding stock of Littleton for $8 per share, a total cost of $64,000. The purchase entry and illustrative adjusting entry appear in Figure 8A–3.[8]

FIGURE 8A–3

Consolidated journal entries for Multi Corporation: Case 1

Dec. 31	Investment in subsidiary (+A)	64,000	
	Cash (−A)		64,000
	Purchased 8,000 shares of Littleton common stock at $8		
	Cash (+A)	6,000	
	Accounts receivable (+A)	9,000	
	Inventory (+A)	15,000	
	Long-lived assets (+A)	40,000	
	Goodwill (+A)	24,000*	
	Accounts payable (+L)		14,000
	Long-term notes payable (+L)		16,000
	Investment in subsidiary (−A)		64,000
	Added assets and liabilities of Littleton at FMV and eliminated investment account		

*$3 ($8 price per share − $5 per-share market value of net assets) × 8,000 sh.

7. It is unusual for a company to be purchased for less than the FMV of its net assets, and we do not cover such cases in this text. These situations are covered in advanced financial accounting texts.

8. The purchase entry would be recorded on Multi Corporation's books. The adjusting entry, however, is only for illustrative purposes. It is not actually on Multi Corporation's books. It is reflected only in the consolidation process, as illustrated in Figure 8A–4.

The purchase price in this case ($64,000) exceeds the FMV of Littleton's net assets ($40,000) by $24,000; therefore, goodwill of $24,000 is recognized on the acquisition. Multi Corporation apparently believes that Littleton is worth more than the FMV of its net assets. It paid $3 per share over and above the $5 ($40,000 ÷ 8,000 shares) per-share market value of the net assets, resulting in a total payment of $24,000 ($3/sh. × 8,000 shares) for goodwill, which Littleton had accumulated up to the date of the purchase. Goodwill, an intangible asset, appears on the asset side of the consolidated balance sheet, usually below fixed assets. The consolidated balance sheet would be prepared using a work sheet, as illustrated in Figure 8A–4.

FIGURE 8A–4   Work sheet for Multi Corporation: Case 1

**Multi Corporation
Consolidated Work
Sheet December 31, 2011**

ACCOUNTS	MULTI CORP.	LITTLETON CO.	ADJUSTMENTS AND ELIMINATIONS DR.	CR.	CONSOLIDATED BALANCE SHEET
Cash	1,000	6,000			7,000
Accounts receivable	70,000	9,000			79,000
Notes receivable	35,000	—			35,000
Inventory	120,000	10,000	5,000		135,000
Investment in subsidiary	64,000	—		64,000	—
Long-lived assets	230,000	35,000	5,000		270,000
Goodwill	—	—	24,000		24,000
Total assets	520,000	60,000	34,000	64,000	550,000
Accounts payable	90,000	14,000			104,000
Long-term notes payable	130,000	16,000			146,000
Common stock	200,000	22,000	22,000		200,000
Retained earnings	100,000	8,000	8,000		100,000
Total liabilities and shareholders' equity	520,000	60,000	30,000		550,000

Transactions where 100 percent of a subsidiary's stock is purchased at a price that exceeds the per-share market value of the subsidiary's net assets are very common. In 2006 alone, Johnson & Johnson spent $18 billion in acquiring seven different businesses, including the consumer health care business of Pfizer.

CASE 2: PURCHASE BETWEEN 50 AND 100 PERCENT OF STOCK AT A PRICE GREATER THAN THE PER-SHARE MARKET VALUE OF THE NET ASSETS

Assume that Multi Corporation purchased 6,400 shares (80%) of Littleton's outstanding stock for $8 per share, a total cost of $51,200. The purchase entry and illustrative adjusting entry appear in Figure 8A–5.

In this case, both goodwill and **noncontrolling interest** are recognized. Goodwill is recognized because Multi Corporation paid $8 for each share, which is $3 more than the $5 per-share market value of the net assets. The total goodwill recognized by Multi Corporation on the transaction is still $24,000 because Multi Corporation still has control over Littleton. Noncontrolling interest is recognized, however, because Multi Corporation purchased only 80 percent

Dec. 31	Investment in subsidiary (+A)	51,200	
	Cash (−A)		51,200
	Purchased 6,400 shares (80%) of Littleton		
	common stock at $8		
	Cash (+A)	6,000	
	Accounts receivable (+A)	9,000	
	Inventory (+A)	15,000	
	Long-lived assets (+A)	40,000	
	Goodwill (+A)	24,000*	
	Accounts payable (+L)		14,000
	Long-term note payable (+L)		16,000
	Noncontrolling interest (+SE)		12,800
	Investment in subsidiary (−A)		51,200
	Added assets and liabilities of Littleton at FMV		
	and eliminated investment account		

*20% × $64,000 ($8/share × 8,000 shares)

of Littleton's stock. The amount of noncontrolling interest recognized on the transaction is computed by multiplying the number of Littleton's shares owned by the minority shareholders (1,600 = 8,000 × 20%) times the value of each share ($8), giving rise to $12,800.

Under IFRS, noncontrolling interest can be computed in the manner illustrated in Figures 8A–5 and 8A–6, or by multiplying the noncontrolling interest (20 percent) by the FMV of the net assets ($40,000), giving rise to $8,000. If this option is chosen, goodwill would be reduced to $19,200 ($24,000 − $4,800), reflecting the assumption that the minority shareholders have no equity interest in the goodwill.

The economic significance of noncontrolling interest is somewhat unclear. It can be interpreted as a liability in that it represents an interest held by outsiders in a portion of the net assets listed on the consolidated balance sheet. On the other hand, it resembles a shareholders' equity item because the interest held by outsiders is an equity interest held by outside shareholders. Very recently, U.S. GAAP was changed to require that noncontrolling interest be considered an item of shareholders' equity, a position consistent with International Financial Reporting Standards (IFRS).

The consolidated balance sheet would be prepared using a work sheet, as illustrated in Figure 8A–6.

Acquisitions where both goodwill and noncontrolling interest are recognized occur periodically in the United States but are much less common than those where 100 percent of the subsidiary's stock is purchased. Often such transactions are followed quite closely by the acquisition of the outstanding minority stock. For example, when Alcoa acquired approximately 91 percent of the outstanding stock of TRE Corporation for $326 million, the transaction recognized both goodwill and noncontrolling interest, which were included in Alcoa's balance sheet. Shortly after the acquisition, Alcoa acquired the remaining outstanding stock, and TRE became a wholly owned subsidiary of Alcoa.

FIGURE 8A–6   Work sheet for Multi Corporation: Case 2

Multi Corporation
Consolidated Work Sheet
December 31, 2011

ACCOUNTS	MULTI CORP.	LITTLETON CO.	ADJUSTMENTS AND ELIMINATIONS DR.	CR.	CONSOLIDATED BALANCE SHEET
Cash	13,800	6,000			19,800
Accounts receivable	70,000	9,000			79,000
Notes receivable	35,000	—			35,000
Inventory	120,000	10,000	5,000		135,000
Investment in subsidiary	51,200	—		51,200	—
Long-lived assets	230,000	35,000	5,000		270,000
Goodwill	—	—	24,000		24,000
Total assets	520,000	60,000	34,000	51,200	562,800
Accounts payable	90,000	14,000			104,000
Long-term notes payable	130,000	16,000			146,000
Noncontrolling interest	—	—		12,800	12,800
Common stock	200,000	22,000	22,000		200,000
Retained earnings	100,000	8,000	8,000		100,000
Total liabilities and shareholders' equity	520,000	60,000	30,000	12,800	562,800

Other Issues Concerning Consolidated Financial Statements

Accounting for acquisitions and mergers is a very complex and detailed topic. In this appendix we have only scratched the surface. For example, transactions between a parent and subsidiary (intercompany transactions) must be eliminated when the financial statements of the two companies are consolidated. In the examples above, we focused only on consolidating balance sheets for transactions that occurred at year-end. Many acquisitions and mergers occur during the year, and of course, the income statement, statement of cash flows, and statement of shareholders' equity must also be consolidated. Finally, consolidations between parents and subsidiaries that operate in different countries can be complex because, as discussed in the chapter, adjustments must be made for different currencies, and these adjustments sometimes are reflected on the income statement and sometimes only on the balance sheet.

REVIEW PROBLEM I

The following information relates to the marketable security investments of Macon Construction. Securities held on December 31, 2011, are described in the table on next page. AAA and BBB are classified as trading securities, and CCC is classified as an available-for-sale security.

Securities	No. of Shares	Cost/Share	Total Cost	Value/Share	Total Market Value
AAA	10	$14	$140	$17	$170
BBB	25	15	375	14	350
CCC	15	8	120	10	150
			$635		$670

Early in 2012, Macon sold all of its investment in AAA securities for $18 per share. The company also sold five shares of BBB for $13 per share. During 2012, Macon received dividends of $3 per share on the remaining twenty shares of BBB, and dividends of $2 per share were declared, but not yet received, on the 15 shares of CCC stock. The per-share market values of BBB and CCC on December 31, 2012, were $12 and $9, respectively. During 2013, Macon sold the remaining 20 shares of BBB stock for $13 per share and the 15 shares of CCC for $11 per share.

The journal entries that would be required for 2011 under the mark-to-market rule follow.

1. **Trading Securities (AAA) (+A)**   30*
       Unrealized Gain on Trading Securities (R, +RE)   30
   Revalued AAA securities to market
   *10 sh. × $3 per sh.

2. **Unrealized Loss on Trading Securities (Lo, −RE)**   25
       Trading Securities (BBB) (−A)   25*
   Revalued BBB securities to market
   *25 sh. × $1 per sh.

3. **Available-for-Sale Securities (CCC) (+A)**   30*
       Unrealized Price Increase on Available-for-Sale
       Securities (+SE)   30
   Revalued CCC securities to market
   *15 sh. × $2 per sh.

The journal entries that reflect 2012 activities involving short-term equity investments follow.

1. **Cash (+A)**   180*
       Trading Securities (−A)   170**
       Realized Gain on Sale of Trading Sec. (Ga, +RE)   10
   Sold ten shares of AAA stock at $18
   *10 sh. × $18 per sh.
   **10 sh. × $17 per sh.

2. **Cash (+A)**   65*
   Realized Loss on Sale of Trading Sec. (Lo, −RE)   5
       Trading Securities (−A)   70**
   Sold five shares of BBB stock at $13 per share
   *5 sh. × $13 per sh.
   **5 sh. × $14 per sh.

3. **Cash (+A)**   60*
   Dividend Receivable (+A)   30**
       Dividend Revenue (R, +RE)   90
   Received BBB dividends and recognized
   dividends declared on CCC stock
   *20 sh. × $3 per sh.
   **15 sh. × $2 per sh.

4. **Unrealized Loss on Trading Securities (Lo, −RE)**   40
    Trading Securities (BBB) (−A)   40*
    Revalued BBB shares to market
    *20 sh. × $2 per sh.

5. **Unrealized Price Increase on Available-for-Sale**
    Securities (−SE)   15
    Available-for-Sale Securities (CCC) (−A)   15*
    Revalued CCC shares to market
    *15 sh. × $1 per sh.

The journal entries that reflect the sales of short-term equity investments in 2013 follow.

1. **Cash (+A)**   260*
    Trading Securities (BBB) (−A)   240**
    Realized Gain on Trading Securities (R, +RE)   20
    Sold twenty shares of BBB stock at $13 per share
    *20 sh. × $13 per sh.
    **20 sh. × $12 per sh.

2. **Cash (+A)**   165*
    Unrealized Price Increase on Available-for-Sale
    Securities (−SE)   15
    Available-for-Sale Securities (CCC) (−A)   135**
    Realized Gain on Available-for-Sale
    Securities (Ga, +RE)   45
    Sold fifteen shares of CCC stock at $11 per share
    *15 sh. × $11 per sh.
    **15 sh. × $9 per sh.

REVIEW PROBLEM II

Trailor Corporation entered into the two transactions listed below on January 1, 2011.

a. On January 1, 2011, Trailor purchased 30 percent of the outstanding common stock of Rowers Company for $50,000. Income reported by Rowers during 2011 and 2012 was $15,000 and $8,000, respectively. Rowers declared and paid dividends to Trailor in the amount of $3,000 during each of the two years.

b. On January 1, 2011, Trailor purchased 100 percent of the outstanding common stock of Kleece Corporation for $20,000. The FMVs of the individual assets and liabilities of Kleece Corporation, as of the time of the acquisition, were $40,000 and $28,000, respectively.

The related journal entries that would be recorded for each transaction over the subsequent two-year period follow.

a. **2011:**
    Jan. 1   **Investment in Equity Securities (+A)**   50,000
              Cash (−A)   50,000
              Purchased Rowers common stock

    Dec. 31   **Investment in Equity Securities (+A)**   4,500*
              Income from Equity Investments (R, +SE)   4,500
              *$15,000 × 30%

(continued)

Cash (+A)	**3,000**	
Investment in Equity Securities (−A)		**3,000**

Recognized 30% of Rowers's income and
received dividends*

*Assume that dividends were declared and paid on the same day.

2012:

Investment in Equity Securities (+A)	**2,400***	
Income from Equity Invest. (R, +RE)		**2,400**

*\$8,000 × 30%.

Cash (+A)	**3,000**	
Investment in Equity Securities (−A)		**3,000**

Recognized 30% of Rowers's income and
received dividends*

*Assume that dividends were declared and paid on the same day.

b.   2011:

Jan. 1

Assets (+A)	**40,000**	
Goodwill (+A)	**8,000**	
Liabilities (+L)		**28,000**
Cash (−A)		**20,000**

Acquired Kleece Corporation

SUMMARY OF KEY POINTS

The key points of the chapter are summarized below.

 Criteria that must be met before a security can be listed in the current assets section of the balance sheet.

Two criteria must be met before an investment in a security can be listed in the current assets section of the balance sheet: (1) the security must be able to be converted into cash within the time period that defines current assets (i.e., the current operating cycle or one year, whichever is longer), and (2) management must intend to convert the security into cash within the time period that defines current assets.

 Trading and available-for-sale securities and how the mark-to-market rule is used to account for them.

Trading securities are bought and held principally for the purpose of selling them in the near future with the objective of generating profit on short-term price changes. Investments not classified as trading securities are considered available-for-sale securities. Trading securities are always listed in the current assets section of the balance sheet, while available-for-sale securities are listed as current or long-term, depending on management's intention. In applying the mark-to-market rule to trading and available-for-sale securities, four separate events must be considered.

1. *Purchase of securities.* When the securities are purchased, they are capitalized and recorded on the balance sheet at cost. The cost includes the purchase price as well as any incidental acquisition costs, such as brokerage commissions and taxes.
2. *Declaration and payment of dividends.* Cash dividends declared on these securities are initially recognized as receivables and revenues. When a cash dividend is received, the receivable is exchanged for cash.

3. *Sale of securities.* When these securities are sold, their balance sheet value is removed from the books and the difference between this amount and the proceeds of the sale is recognized on the books as either a realizable gain or a realized loss.

4. *End-of-accounting period adjustment.* Both trading and available-for-sale securities are adjusted to current market value at the end of the accounting period. In the case of trading securities, the related unrealized holding gain or loss is reflected directly in income; in the case of available-for-sale securities, the related unrealized price change is booked to shareholders' equity and included on the statement of comprehensive income.

● *Why companies make long-term investments in equity securities.*

Companies make long-term investments in the equity securities of other companies for two primary reasons: (1) investment income in the form of dividends and/or stock price appreciation and (2) management influence, where the voting power of the purchased shares allows the investor company to exert influence or control over the board of directors and management of the investee company. The primary motivation behind the long-term equity investments for most major U.S. companies is reason (2), influence over the investee company's operations and management.

● *The mark-to-market method, the cost method, and the equity method of accounting for long-term equity investments, and the conditions under which each method is used.*

The mark-to-market rule is used to account for trading securities, which are always considered current, and available-for-sale securities whether they are classified in the current or long-term assets section of the balance sheet.

Under the cost method, purchases of equity securities are recorded at cost, including incidental costs of acquisition, dividends are recorded as income when declared, and sales give rise to book gains or losses in the amount of the difference between the acquisition cost of the securities and the proceeds from the sale. The cost method is used for investments in nonmarketable securities that involve less than 20 percent of the investee company's voting stock.

Under the equity method, the purchase of equity securities is originally recorded at cost, and the carrying value of the long-term investment on the investor's balance sheet is (1) periodically increased (decreased) by the investor's proportionate share of the net income (loss) of the investee and (2) decreased by all dividends transferred to the investor from the investee. The equity method is used for investments in marketable or nonmarketable securities that involve from 20 to 50 percent of the investee company's voting stock.

Under both U.S. GAAP and IFRS, companies have the option of using mark-to-market accounting for investments in equity securities, and if they exercise that option, they must disclose the basis for the market value estimate.

● *Consolidated financial statements, when they are prepared, and how they differ from financial statements that account for equity investments using the equity method.*

Consolidated financial statements represent the combined financial statements of a parent company and any companies acquired by the parent. Such acquisitions occur when the parent purchases a controlling interest (51% of the outstanding voting stock) in another company, or as the result of a merger, where one or more of the merged companies ceases to exist. Consolidated statements should be prepared when a parent owns 51 percent or more of a subsidiary's outstanding common stock.

When the parent prepares consolidated financial statements, it includes the assets and liabilities of the subsidiary with its own. If the purchase price exceeds the FMV of the subsidiary's net assets, goodwill is also recognized on the balance sheet of the parent. Under the equity method, the assets and liabilities of the investee company are not included with those of the parent, and this, in turn, can represent a form of off-balance-sheet financing.

KEY TERMS

Note: Definitions for these terms are provided in the glossary at the end of the text.

Affiliate companies (p. 345)
Available-for-sale securities (p. 335)
Business acquisition (p. 348)
Business combination (p. 349)
Comprehensive income (p. 341)
Consolidated financial statements (p. 348)
Controlling interest (p. 348)
Cost method (p. 343)
Equity investment (p. 333)
Equity method (p. 344)
Fair market value option (p. 348)
Foreign currency translation
  adjustments (p. 355)
Holding gains or losses (p. 337)
Intention to convert (p. 335)
Level 1 measurements (p. 348)

Level 2 measurements (p. 348)
Level 3 measurements (p. 348)
Mark-to-market rule (p. 336)
Merger (p. 349)
Noncontrolling interest (p. 359)
Parent company (p. 348)
Readily marketable (p. 334)
Realized gains/losses (p. 337)
Special purpose entities (SPEs) (p. 353)
Special purpose vehicles (p. 353)
Statement of Recognized Income
  and Expense (SORIE) (p. 341)
Subsidiary (p. 348)
Trading securities (p. 335)
Unrealized gains/losses (p. 337)
Unrealized price changes (p. 339)

ETHICS in the Real World

The takeover battle for Gerber Products Co. included bids by a number of U.S. companies, including Quaker Oats (now part of PepsiCo), which entered a bid of $35 per share. Swiss drug giant Sandoz Ltd. won the battle quickly, however, by raising the ante to $53 per share. Some investment bankers claimed that the favorable accounting treatment for acquisitions practiced in Switzerland gave Sandoz the advantage it needed to outbid Quaker Oats.

ETHICAL ISSUE Is it ethical for the government or standard-setting body in a particular country to set accounting standards that are designed to provide international economic advantages enjoyed solely by the companies and capital markets in that country?

INTERNET RESEARCH EXERCISE

The chapter began by noting that the extraordinary growth experienced by Cisco Systems in the late 1990s was fueled by acquisitions of other companies. How much has Cisco grown since 1999? Has Cisco maintained high levels of performance? Begin your search at www.cisco.com.

BRIEF EXERCISES

REAL DATA

BE8–1

Short-term investments

The following table was taken from the 2008 annual report of Merck & Company, a major U.S. pharmaceutical company (dollars in millions).

	2008	2007	2006
Net income	$7,808	$3,275	$4,434
Other comprehensive income (loss)			
Net unrealized (loss)	(80.5)	58	26
Other	(1,647)	280	(10)
Comprehensive income	$6,080	$3,613	$4,450

REQUIRED:

a. What is comprehensive income and how does it differ from net income?

b. This table indicates that Merck carries certain kinds of investments on its balance sheet. What are they, and what happened to the values of those investments in 2008, 2007, and 2006?

REAL DATA

BE8–2

Available-for-sale securities

On the statement of comprehensive income within its 2008 annual report, Bristol-Myers Squibb included a ($37) million line item behind "available-for-sale securities." During 2008 the company maintained a portfolio of marketable securities in the current asset section of the balance sheet of nearly $289 million.

REQUIRED:

Explain the event that led to the ($37) million amount listed on the statement of comprehensive income, and where else on the financial statements this amount would be reflected.

REAL DATA

BE8–3

Equity method, the income statement, and statement of cash flows

PepsiCo, Inc. reported "bottling equity income" of $374, $560, and $553 on its income statements for 2008, 2007, and 2006, respectively (dollars in millions). The computation of net cash from operating activities on the company's statement of cash flows includes "bottling equity income, net of dividends" of ($202), ($441), and ($442) for the same three years.

REQUIRED:

a. Provide the entry made by PepsiCo to record affiliate net income in 2008.

b. Why is there a reference to bottling equity income on the statement of cash flows?

c. How many cash dividends did PepsiCo receive from its bottling affiliates during 2008, 2007, and 2006?

d. Discuss how PepsiCo management might evaluate the performance of these affiliates.

REAL DATA

BE8–4

Goodwill

Procter & Gamble's 2008 balance sheet reported a goodwill balance of $56.5 billion. Describe what goodwill is, how it was originally recorded, and what it indicates about Procter & Gamble.

REAL DATA

BE8–5

Goodwill accounting

Recently, Johnson & Johnson purchased the outstanding common stock of several businesses for $2.8 billion in cash. The purchase price exceeded the estimated fair market value of the acquired assets by $1.8 billion, and Johnson & Johnson assumed liabilities of $323 million.

REQUIRED:

Re-create the journal entry for the acquisitions, and describe how the transaction affected the basic accounting equation.

EXERCISES

E8–1

Accounting for
short-term equity
securities

Monroe Auto Supplies engaged in several transactions involving short-term equity securities during 2011, shown in the following list. The company had never invested in equity securities prior to 2011. All securities were classified as trading securities.

1. Purchased 1,000 shares of IBM for $50 per share.
2. Purchased 500 shares of General Motors for $80 per share.
3. Sold 750 shares of IBM for $60 per share.
4. Received a dividend of $1.50 per share from General Motors. Assume that the dividend was declared in a previous period.
5. Purchased 200 shares of Xerox for $40 per share.
6. Sold the remaining 250 shares of IBM for $30 per share.
7. Sold the 200 shares of Xerox for $58 per share.
8. Sold the 500 shares of General Motors for $60 per share.

a. Prepare journal entries for each transaction.
b. What effect did these transactions have on the company's 2011 net income?

E8–2

Mark-to-market
accounting

The following information was extracted from the December 31, 2011, current asset section of the balance sheets of four different companies:

	Wearever Fabrics	Frames Corp.	Pacific Transport	Video Magic
Trading securities	$800,000	$490,000	$645,000	$210,000
Available-for-sale securities	130,000	40,000	250,000	85,000
Short-term equity invest.	$930,000	$530,000	$895,000	$295,000

There were no transactions in short-term equity securities during 2012, and as of December 31, 2012, the controllers of each company collected the following information:

	Wearever Fabrics	Frames Corp.	Pacific Transport	Video Magic
Trading securities	$820,000	$480,000	$625,000	$220,000
Available-for-sale securities	122,000	52,000	246,000	88,000
Short-term equity invest.	$942,000	$532,000	$871,000	$308,000

a. Compute the change in the wealth levels of each of the four companies due to the market value changes in their equity investments.
b. Compute the effect on 2012 reported income for each of the four companies due to the market value changes in their equity investments.
c. Explain why the answers to (a) and (b) are not the same.
d. How would 2012 reported income change for each company if each chose to use the fair market value option for the available-for-sale securities?

E8–3

Mark-to-market
accounting

The following information relates to the activity in the short-term investment account of Lido International, which held no short-term investments as of January 1.

1. **January 28**   Purchased ten shares of Able Co. stock at $14 per share.
2. **February 18**   Purchased twenty shares of Baker Co. stock at $26 per share.
3. **March 15**   Received dividends from Able Co. of $1 per share.
4. **April 29**   Sold five shares of Able Co. for $15 per share.
5. **May 18**   Received dividends from Baker Co. of $2 per share.
6. **June 1**   Sold five shares of Baker Co. for $22 per share.
7. **June 30**   Market value of Able shares is $17 per share.
                      Market value of Baker shares is $20 per share.

a. Prepare journal entries for each transaction, excluding the June 30 adjusting entry. Use the asset account "Short-Term Investments," and assume that dividends were declared and paid on the same day.

b. Prepare the June 30 adjusting entry, and describe the effect on reported income, assuming that: (1) Able and Baker shares are both considered trading securities; (2) Able is considered a trading security, and Baker is considered an available-for-sale security; (3) Able is considered an available-for-sale security, and Baker is considered a trading security; and (4) both Able and Baker are considered available-for-sale securities.

c. Which combination in (b) depicts management as most successful in the current period? Explain.

E8–4

Activity in the short-term investment account across time periods

On November 11, 2011, Wadsworth Company purchased twenty shares of ZZZ for $8 per share. Wadsworth held the investment for the remainder of 2011, and as of December 31, the per-share market value of ZZZ had risen to $10. During 2012, Wadsworth sold ten shares of ZZZ for $9 each, and at the end of 2012, the per-share market price of the remaining ten shares was $12. During 2013, the remaining shares of ZZZ were sold for $14 each. Assume that Wadsworth held no other equity investments during this time period.

a. Complete the following chart. The first column assumes that the investment was classified as trading securities; the second column assumes that the investment was classified as available-for-sale securities.

	Trading	Available-for-Sale
2011 income		
12/31/11 balance sheet investment value		
2012 income		
12/31/12 balance sheet investment value		
2013 income		
Total income ('11 + '12 + '13)		

b. Comment on the differences.

REAL DATA

E8–5

Available-for-sale disclosures

Biomet, Inc. provided the following disclosures in Note 5 of its 2008 annual report. It describes the company's investments in available-for-sale equity securities (dollars in millions).

		Unrealized	
	Cost	**Gains**	**Losses**
2008	**$825.3**	**$0**	**$(0.6)**
2007	**42.9**	**0.1**	**(3.9)**

a. Compute the fair market value of Biomet's available-for-sale equity portfolio for both 2008 and 2007.

b. What was the effect on the company's comprehensive income amount associated with its available-for-sale securities?

c. Assume that Biomet sold its entire portfolio of available-for-sale securities at the end of 2008. How much income would be realized on the sale? Provide the journal entry.

E8–6

Reporting problems with mark-to-market accounting as applied to available-for-sale securities

Tom Miller and Larry Rogers each started separate businesses on December 1, 2011, by contributing $6,000 of their own funds. Early in December, both men purchased 120 shares of Diskette common stock, which was selling at the time for $26 per share, and classified the investment as available-for-sale securities. During December, they both also purchased $1,500 of inventory on account.

As of December 30, the market price of Diskette common stock had risen to $32 per share. Tom was delighted by the price increase but chose simply to hold the stock, expecting that the price would continue to appreciate for at least another month. Larry, on the other hand, sold his shares, but immediately repurchased them because he too believed that they would continue to appreciate.

a. Prepare separate year-end balance sheets for both Tom and Larry.
b. Compute net income, working capital, and the current ratio for both Tom and Larry.
c. From the financial statements alone, which of the two appears to be in the better financial position? Why?
d. Assume that there are brokerage commissions on all security purchases and sales. Which of the two is actually in the better financial position? Why?

E8–7

Classifying and accounting for equity investments

Hartney Consulting Services is involved in the following investments as of December 31, 2011:

1. Owns 40 percent of the common stock issued by Doyle Corporation. Doyle Corporation's stock is actively traded, and Hartney Consulting intends to hold this investment for at least five years.
2. Owns 55 percent of the common stock issued by Jacobs Automotive Parts Manufacturing. This stock is actively traded. Hartney Consulting intends to hold this investment indefinitely.
3. Owns 10 percent of the common stock issued by Markert Computers. Markert Computers is a closely held company with just two other shareholders.
4. Owns 45 percent of the common stock issued by Luther Brewery. Luther Brewery has just recently joined the New York Stock Exchange. Hartney intends to sell this investment to raise cash within the next five years.
5. Owns 15 percent of the common stock of Hartney Farms. The stock is publicly traded, but Hartney intends to hold the investment indefinitely.
6. On November 30, 2012, Hartney Consulting owned 18 percent of Whittenbach Industries. During December, Hartney Consulting purchased an additional 15 percent of the company. This company's stock is actively traded, and Hartney fully intends to hold this stock for four years.

a. Indicate whether each investment should be classified as short-term or long-term on the December 31, 2012, balance sheet. Also indicate the appropriate accounting treatment for each investment. Explain your answer.
b. Explain why the nonmarketable equity securities are disclosed in the long-term investment section of the balance sheet and are not carried at market value.

E8–8

The cost method

Mystic Lakes Food Company began investing in equity securities for the first time in 2011. During 2011, the company engaged in the following transactions involving equity securities. Assume that the stock of Thayers International and Bayhe Enterprises is not considered marketable and that ownership is less than 20 percent of the equity. Prepare journal entries to record these transactions.

1. Purchased 10,000 shares of Thayers International for $26 per share.
2. Purchased 25,000 shares of Bayhe Enterprises for $35 per share.
3. Thayers International declared a $2-per-share dividend to be paid at a later date.
4. Sold 4,500 shares of Bayhe Enterprises for $30 per share.
5. Sold 8,000 shares of Thayers International for $32 per share.

E8–9

Applying the mark-to-market rule

Refer to the data provided in E8–8.

a. Assume that the stock of Thayers International and Bayhe Enterprises is considered marketable, and Mystic Lakes Food Company wishes to hold all investments indefinitely. Prepare journal entries to record the transactions.
b. Assume that on December 31, 2011, the market values of Thayers International and Bayhe Enterprises are $25 and $32, respectively. Prepare the entry to adjust the company's long-term investments to market value.

E8–10

The equity method

On January 1, 2011, Nover Solar Systems purchased 10,000 shares of Reilly Manufacturing for $190,000. The investment represented 25 percent of Reilly's outstanding common stock. Nover intended to hold the investment indefinitely. During 2011, Reilly earned net income of $75,000, and during 2012, Reilly suffered a net loss of $6,000. Reilly paid dividends both years of $1.50 per share.

a. Prepare all relevant journal entries that would be recorded on Nover's books during 2011 and 2012.
b. Compute the book value of Nover's long-term equity investment account as of December 31, 2011, and December 31, 2012.

REAL DATA

E8-11

Inferring information from equity method disclosures

Duke Energy Corporation accounts for certain investments under the equity method, and as of December 31, 2008, Duke reported equity method investments of $473 million on its balance sheet and $696 million on its 2007 balance sheet. Equity income on the income statement totaled ($102) million for 2008.

a. Assume that Duke owns approximately 40 percent of the outstanding common stock of the affiliates and made no additional equity investment on sales during 2008. How much net loss did the affiliates report for 2008?
b. How much in dividends did Duke receive in 2008?

E8-12

Inferring information about the equity method from the financial statements

Mainmont Industries uses the equity method to account for its long-term equity investments from affiliates. The following information from the financial statements of Mainmont refers to an investment in the securities of Tumbleweed Construction, a company 30 percent owned by Mainmont:

	2011	2010
Long-term investment in equity securities	$29,000	$25,000
Income from equity securities	12,000	7,000

Mainmont neither purchased nor sold any equity securities during 2011.

a. How much net income did Tumbleweed Construction earn during 2011?
b. What was the dollar amount of the total dividend declared by Tumbleweed Construction during 2011?
c. Provide the journal entries recorded by Mainmont during 2011 with respect to its investment in Tumbleweed Construction.
d. Describe how this activity would be reported on Mainmont's statement of cash flows.

E8-13

Recording an acquisition under the purchase method

Multiplex purchased 100 percent of the outstanding common stock of Lipley Company for $900,000. At the time of the acquisition, the fair market values of Lipley's individual assets and liabilities follow:

Cash	$ 90,000
Accounts receivable	60,000
Inventory	160,000
Plant and equipment	560,000
Payables	300,000

a. Provide the journal entry recorded by Multiplex at the time of the acquisition.
b. Assume that the book values of the assets and liabilities on Lipley's balance sheet as of the date of the acquisition were $550,000 and $300,000, respectively. Explain how the book value of Lipley could be less than the net FMV of Lipley's assets and liabilities, which in turn is less than the price Multiplex paid for Lipley's common stock.

E8-14

Appendix 8A: 100 percent purchases in excess of the net market value of the assets and liabilities

The following chart describes six transactions where 100 percent of a subsidiary's voting stock was purchased for cash:

	Purchase Price	Book Value	Net FMV in Excess of Book Value	Goodwill
1.	?	$ 7,000	$1,000	$1,000
2.	$ 6,000	6,000	?	0
3.	12,000	?	4,000	3,000
4.	15,000	10,000	3,000	?
5.	?	2,000	1,000	3,000
6.	12,000	4,000	8,000	?

Provide the missing values.

E8–15

Appendix 8A:
Per-share book
and market value

The book value of a share of Camden common stock on December 31 is $12. The balance sheet value and the market value of the company's assets and liabilities as of that date follow:

	Balance Sheet Value	Market Value
Cash	$15,000	$15,000
Receivables	26,000	24,000
Inventories	15,000	25,000
Fixed assets	40,000	47,000
Liabilities	(60,000)	(60,000)
Net book value	$36,000	
Net market value		$51,000

On December 31, Conglomerate, Inc. purchased 100 percent of the outstanding stock of Camden for $22 per share.

a. How many shares of common stock did Camden have outstanding as of December 31?
b. Compute the per-share net market value of Camden's common stock.
c. Why would Conglomerate pay more than the per-share market value for a share of Camden common stock?
d. Prepare the entry that reflects the acquisition.

E8–16

Appendix 8A:
Computing goodwill
and noncontrolling
interest

Maxwell Industries paid $18 per share for 80 percent of the 10,000 outstanding shares of Kendall Hall. The balance sheet of Kendall Hall and additional market value information follow.

	Historical Cost	FMV
Current assets	$125,000	$150,000
Noncurrent assets	65,000	80,000
Liabilities	70,000	70,000
Shareholders' equity	120,000	—

a. Compute the amounts of goodwill and noncontrolling interest recognized by Maxwell.
b. Compute goodwill and noncontrolling interest assuming that Maxwell uses IFRS and chooses the accounting treatment that assumes that the minority shareholders have no equity interest in the goodwill.
c. Where on the balance sheet would noncontrolling interest be disclosed?

E8–17

Appendix 8A:
Completing
a consolidated
work sheet

Glover Chemical purchased 100 percent of the outstanding stock of Ward Supply on December 31 for $100,000 cash. As of that date, the FMVs of the inventory and fixed assets of Ward equaled $70,000 and $125,000, respectively. Assume that cash, accounts receivable, and the liabilities are on the books of Ward at FMV. Provide the information to complete the following consolidated work sheet, which already reflects the entry recorded at acquisition.

Accounts	Glover	Ward	Adjustments and Eliminations Dr.	Cr.	Consolidated Balance Sheet
Cash	73,000	10,000			
Accounts receivable	110,000	40,000			
Inventory	220,000	60,000			
Investment in subsidiary	100,000	—			
Fixed assets	615,000	120,000			
Goodwill	30,000	—			
Total assets	1,148,000	230,000			

(continued)

Accounts payable	80,000	70,000
Long-term notes	450,000	80,000
Common stock	500,000	70,000
Retained earnings	118,000	10,000
Total liabilities and shareholders' equity	1,148,000	230,000

PROBLEMS

P8–1

Applying the mark-to-market rule to investments in equity securities

O'Leary Enterprises began investing in short-term equity securities in 2011. The following information was extracted from its 2011 internal financial records. Houser and Miller were classified as trading securities, while Letter and Nordic were classified as available-for-sale securities.

Security	Purchases	Sales	Total Dividends Received	12/31/08 Market Value*
Houser Company	90 shares @ $22	60 shares @ $25	$40	$25
Miller, Inc.	180 shares @ $40	90 shares @ $30	85	35
Letter Books	75 shares @ $48	5 shares @ $55	30	46
Nordic Equipment	170 shares @ $70	145 shares @ $95	50	90

*Per share

REQUIRED:
a. Compute the effect on reported 2011 income from all investment transactions and price changes.
b. Compute the effect on reported 2011 income if O'Leary Enterprises exercised the fair market value option for all its investments.

P8–2

Trading securities: Purchases, sales, dividends, and end-of-period adjustments

Anderson Cabinets began operations during 2005. During the initial years of operations, the company invested primarily in fixed assets to promote growth. During 2011, H. Hurst, the company president, decided that the company was sufficiently stable that it could now invest in short-term marketable securities, classified as trading securities. During 2011, the company entered into the following transactions concerning marketable securities:

1.	March 10	Purchased 1,000 shares of Arctic Oil & Gas for $28 per share.
2.	March 31	Purchased 800 shares of Humphries Manufacturing for $10 per share.
3.	May 26	Received a cash dividend of $1.25 per share from Arctic Oil & Gas.
4.	July 10	Purchased 1,000 shares of Kingsman Game Co. for $18 per share.
5.	September 11	Sold 800 shares of Arctic Oil & Gas for $35 per share.
6.	September 27	Sold 500 shares of Humphries Manufacturing for $8 per share.
7.	October 19	Purchased 1,000 shares of Quimby, Inc. for $25 per share.
8.	November 6	Received a cash dividend of $1.25 per share from Arctic Oil & Gas.
9.	December 8	Sold the remaining shares of Arctic Oil & Gas and Humphries Manufacturing for $30 and $15, respectively.
10.	December 31	According to the *Wall Street Journal,* the market values of these securities at the close of business on December 31 follow:

Arctic Oil & Gas	$32
Humphries Manufacturing	14
Kingsman Game Company	15
Quimby, Inc.	26

REQUIRED:

a. Prepare the necessary journal entries for each of these transactions. Assume that any dividends were declared and paid on the same day.
b. Prepare the short-term equity securities section of the balance sheet as of December 31, 2011.
c. Compute the impact of these transactions on the income statement for the year ended December 31, 2011.

P8–3

Changing security investment classifications

On October 18, 2011, Daley Inc. purchased 100 shares of Orthon at $32 per share. The investment was classified as available-for-sale securities. The shares were held throughout the remainder of 2011 and 2012, and by December 31, 2011 and 2012, the per-share market price had risen to $40 and $50, respectively. On December 31, 2012, Daley decided to change the classification from available-for-sale to trading securities.

REQUIRED:

a. Provide the journal entries recorded at October 18, 2011; December 31, 2011; and December 31, 2012.
b. Assume that the investment was originally classified as trading securities and then changed to available-for-sale on December 31, 2012. Provide the journal entries recorded at October 18, 2011; December 31, 2011; and December 31, 2012.
c. Compute the 2011 and 2012 income effects under the two assumptions.

P8–4

Window dressing and the mark-to-market rule

Levy Company and Guyer Books made the same equity investment—200 shares of Watson Manufacturing at a cost of $12 per share—on November 18. On December 31, the market value of Watson had risen to $45 per share. Guyer Books held its investment in Watson, while Levy sold the shares and immediately repurchased them at the December 31 market value.

REQUIRED:

a. Compute the balance sheet value and income effect associated with these events recorded by the two companies, assuming that the investment was classified as trading and available-for-sale. That is, fill in the following chart with the appropriate dollar values.

	Guyer Books		Levy Co.	
	Balance Sheet Value	**Income Effect**	**Balance Sheet Value**	**Income Effect**
Investment classified as:				
Trading securities				
Available-for-sale securities				

b. Discuss the differences.

P8–5

Trading versus available-for-sale classifications

Rochester Enterprises purchased 500 shares of Newark Corporation for $15 per share on June 15, 2011, when Newark had approximately 10,000 equity shares outstanding. Rochester held the investment throughout 2011, and as of December 31, the per-share market price had risen to $18. On January 16, 2012, Rochester sold 300 shares for $19 per share, and on October 20 sold the remaining 200 shares for $13 each. The company held no other security investments during this time period.

REQUIRED:

a. Assume that Rochester classified the investment as trading securities, and provide the journal entries recorded on June 15, 2011; December 31, 2011; January 16, 2012; and October 20, 2012.

b. Assume that Rochester classified the investment as available-for-sale securities, and provide the journal entries recorded on June 15, 2011; December 31, 2011; January 16, 2012; and October 20, 2012.

c. Compute the net cash effect of these transactions across 2011 and 2012.

d. Compute the 2011, 2012, and total income effect, assuming that the investment was classified as trading securities.

e. Compute the 2011, 2012, and total income effect, assuming that the investment was classified as available-for-sale securities.

f. Comment on the difference between the two assumptions.

P8-6

Inferring from
balance sheet
disclosures

The following information was taken from the 2011 annual report of Orleans Enterprises:

	2011	2010
Trading securities	**$25,440**	**$27,000**

Related footnote: The 2011 and 2010 balances in the trading securities account consist of 1,600 and 1,800 equity shares of Atwater Company, respectively. During 2011, in the only transaction related to these securities, 200 shares were sold for $15.50 each.

REQUIRED:

a. Compute the 2011 income effect related to the company's investment in Atwater. Divide the effect into its realized and unrealized components.

b. Repeat (a), assuming that the securities were classified as available-for-sale and that Orleans's first investment in these securities occurred on December 31, 2010.

REAL DATA

P8-7

Inferring information
about trading and
available-for-sale
investments

JPMorgan Chase carries portfolios of both trading securities and available-for-sale securities. At the end of 2008 and 2007, the trading securities were valued at $347.4 billion and $414.3 billion, respectively; and the available-for-sale securities were valued at $205.9 billion and $85.4 billion, respectively. Together, the investments comprise about 25 percent of the company's total assets as of December 31, 2008. Unrealized gains reported on the 2008 income statement totaled $9.9 billion.

REQUIRED:

a. Trading securities are carried on the balance sheet at market value. Compute the net decrease in the investment in trading securities during 2008.

b. The net increase in the investment in available-for-sale securities reported on the statement of cash flows during 2008 was approximately $107.4 billion. Compute the unrealized net gains on the available-for-sale securities during 2008. On which financial statement would this dollar amount be found?

P8-8

Long-term equity
investments: The
mark-to-market
method versus the
equity method

A summary of the December 31, 2010, balance sheet of Masonite Tires follows:

Assets	$160,000	Liabilities	$ 70,000
		Shareholders' equity	90,000
Total	$160,000	Total	$160,000

On January 1, 2011, Masonite purchased 2,000 (20% of the outstanding common shares) shares of Bingo Boots for $40,000 and held the investment throughout 2011 and 2012. During 2011 and 2012, Bingo earned net income of $15,000 and $20,000, respectively. Bingo paid total dividends of $10,000 and $15,000 during 2011 and 2012. The per-share prices of Bingo common stock as of the end of 2011 and 2012 were $18 and $21, respectively. During 2011 and 2012, Masonite generated revenues (excluding revenues related to the investment in Bingo) of $85,000 and $75,000, respectively, and incurred expenses of $50,000 and $70,000, respectively. Assume that all these revenues and expenses involve cash. Masonite pays no dividends.

REQUIRED:

a. Assume that Masonite exercises its option to use the mark-to-market method.
   (1) Prepare a balance sheet as of January 1, 2011.
   (2) Prepare a balance sheet as of December 31, 2011, and an income statement for the year ended December 31, 2011.
   (3) Prepare a balance sheet as of December 31, 2012, and an income statement for the year ended December 31, 2012.

b. Assume that Masonite uses the equity method.
   (1) Prepare a balance sheet as of January 1, 2011.
   (2) Prepare a balance sheet as of December 31, 2011, and an income statement for the year ended December 31, 2011.
   (3) Prepare a balance sheet as of December 31, 2012, and an income statement for the year ended December 31, 2012.

c. Identify some reasons why the management of Masonite may wish to use the mark-to-market method instead of the equity method. Describe why the equity method might be preferred. Does holding 20 percent of a company's outstanding common stock necessarily mean that the investor company can exert substantial influence over the investee?

P8–9

The equity method versus consolidated financial statements

A summary of the 2011 balance sheet of Alsop, Ltd., follows:

Assets	$180,000	Liabilities	$ 90,000
		Shareholders' equity	90,000
Total	$180,000	Total	$180,000

On January 1, 2011, Alsop acquired 100 percent of the outstanding common stock of Martin Monthly for $62,000 cash. At the time of the acquisition, the fair market values of the assets and liabilities of Martin were $86,000 and $64,000, respectively. During 2011, Martin operated as a subsidiary of Alsop; it recognized $15,000 of net income and paid a $10,000 dividend.

REQUIRED:

a. Account for the acquisition as a purchase. Provide the journal entry to record the acquisition, and prepare Alsop's consolidated balance sheet as of January 1, 2011.
b. Account for the acquisition using the equity method. Provide the journal entry to record the acquisition, and prepare Alsop's balance sheet as of January 1, 2011.
c. Compute the debt/equity ratios produced by the two methods of accounting for this investment. Explain why Alsop's management might wish to use the equity method instead of preparing consolidated financial statements.

P8–10

Inferring information from the financial statements

Excerpts from the financial statements of Macy Limited are as follows. (Numbers are in thousands.)

	2011	2010
BALANCE SHEET		
Assets:		
Short-term investments	$290	$160
Investment in affiliate	530	0
Shareholders' equity:		
Unrealized price decrease on short-term investments	(20)	0
INCOME STATEMENT		
Realized gain on short-term investments	$ 80	
Unrealized gain on short-term investments	30	
Income on equity investment	40	

(continued)

STATEMENT OF CASH FLOWS

**Operating section (The following amounts were subtracted
    from net income in the calculation of net cash from
    operating activities.):**

Gains on short-term investments	$(110)
Equity income in excess of cash received	(30)
Investing section:	
Investment in affiliate	(500)
Investment in short-term investments	(280)
Sale of short-term investments	240

Footnotes:

Short-term investments. As of December 31, 2010, trading securities were valued at $130; during 2011, no available-for-sale securities were acquired or sold.

Investment in affiliate. On January 30, 2011, the company purchased 40 percent (50,000 shares) of the outstanding equity of Lehmon Financial Services at $10 per share.

REQUIRED:

Compute the following dollar amounts.

a.   The December 31, 2011, market value of the short-term equity investments classified as available-for-sale.

b.   The balance sheet carrying value of the trading securities sold during 2011.

c.   Compute the earnings-per-share dollar amount reported by the affiliate.

d.   Compute the per-share dividend declared by the affiliate.

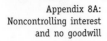

P8–11

Appendix 8A:
100 percent purchase
and the recognition
of goodwill

The condensed balance sheets as of December 31 for Rice and Associates and Rachel Excavation are as follows:

	Rice	Rachel
ASSETS		
Cash	$ 196,000	$ 10,000
Accounts receivable	150,000	40,000
Inventory	300,000	40,000
Fixed assets	400,000	130,000
Total assets	$1,046,000	$220,000
LIABILITIES AND SHAREHOLDERS' EQUITY		
Accounts payable	$ 80,000	$ 20,000
Long-term liabilities	300,000	50,000
Common stock	400,000	90,000
Additional paid-in capital	140,000	10,000
Retained earnings	126,000	50,000
Total liabilities and shareholders' equity	$1,046,000	$220,000

As of December 31, the market values of Rachel's inventories and fixed assets were $70,000 and $120,000, respectively. Liabilities are at FMV on the balance sheet.

On December 31, Rice and Associates purchased all of the outstanding common shares of Rachel Excavation for $180,000 cash. The preceding balance sheets were prepared immediately prior to the acquisition.

REQUIRED:

a.   Prepare the journal entry recorded by Rice to recognize the acquisition.

b.   Prepare a consolidated work sheet and a consolidated balance sheet.

P8–12

Appendix 8A:
Noncontrolling interest
and no goodwill

Assume that Rice and Associates in P8–11 purchased 80 percent of the outstanding shares of Rachel for $136,000 cash.

REQUIRED:
a.   Prepare the journal entry recorded by Rice to recognize the acquisition.
b.   Prepare a consolidated work sheet and a consolidated balance sheet.

P8–13

Appendix 8A:
Noncontrolling interest
and goodwill

Assume that Rice and Associates in P8–11 purchased 80 percent of the 10,000 shares of outstanding stock of Rachel for $140,000 cash.

REQUIRED:
a.   Prepare the journal entries recorded by Rice to recognize the acquisition.
b.   Prepare a consolidated work sheet and a consolidated balance sheet.
c.   Compute noncontrolling interest and goodwill assuming that Rice uses IFRS and exercises its option to compute noncontrolling interest assuming that the minority shareholders have no equity interest in the goodwill.

P8–14

Appendix 8A:
Allocating the excess
purchase price among
tangible assets and
goodwill

Assume the same facts as in P8–11, except that the FMVs for the inventory and fixed assets of Rachel are not as precisely specified. That is, appraisers have indicated that the FMV of the inventory is between $65,000 and $75,000 and that the FMV of the fixed assets is between $115,000 and $125,000. You, as the accountant for Rice and Associates, can use any value within these ranges to record the acquisition.

REQUIRED:
a.   Assume that you wish to maximize reported income in the next period. What dollar amounts would you allocate to Rachel's inventory, fixed assets, and goodwill when recording the acquisition? Explain.
b.   Assume that you wish to minimize reported income in the next period (e.g., when preparing the transaction for tax purposes). What dollar amounts would you allocate to Rachel's inventory, fixed assets, and goodwill when recording the acquisition? Explain.

P8–15

Appendix 8A:
Noncontrolling interest
and goodwill

Groomer purchased a controlling interest in three companies during 2011. Financial information concerning the three companies follows:

	Company X	Company Y	Company Z
Cash	$ 6,000	$ 4,000	$ 2,000
Accounts receivable	12,000	9,000	7,000
Inventory	30,000	12,000	18,000
Fixed assets	70,000	30,000	15,000
Total assets	$118,000	$55,000	$42,000
Current liabilities	$ 7,000	$12,000	$ 5,000
Long-term liabilities	25,000	20,000	18,000
Common stock	50,000	10,000	15,000
Retained earnings	36,000	13,000	4,000
Total liabilities and shareholders' equity	$118,000	$55,000	$42,000
FMV:			
Inventory	$ 45,000	$18,000	$18,000
Fixed assets	75,000	35,000	15,000
Shares of stock outstanding before acquisition	10,000	1,000	2,000

All other assets and liabilities on the balance sheet are at FMV.

Groomer purchased 8,000, 600, and 1,500 shares of Company X, Company Y, and Company Z, respectively. The share prices and cash payments follow.

Company X   8,000 × $10.60 = $84,800
Company Y   600 ×   40.00 =   24,000
Company Z   1,500 ×   11.00 =   16,500

REQUIRED:
For each company, prepare the journal entry to record the acquisition by Groomer. Then, for each company, prepare a journal entry that could have been recorded to include the individual assets and liabilities on the books of Groomer.

P8–16

Appendix 8A: Consolidated statements, the equity method, and debt covenants

Mammoth Enterprises purchased 50 percent of the outstanding stock of Atom, Inc. on December 31 for $60,000 cash. On that date, the book value of Atom's net assets was $70,000. The market value of Atom's assets was $180,000, $20,000 above book value. Mammoth's condensed balance sheet, immediately before the acquisition, follows:

Assets		Liabilities and Shareholders' Equity	
Current assets	$150,000	Current liabilities	$ 30,000
Noncurrent assets	350,000	Long-term liabilities	200,000
		Common stock	100,000
		Retained earnings	170,000
		Total liabilities and	
Total assets	$500,000	shareholders' equity	$500,000

Mammoth entered into a debt covenant earlier in the year that requires the company to maintain a debt/equity ratio of less than 1:1.

REQUIRED:
a. Compute Mammoth's debt/equity ratio both before and after the acquisition. Consider minority interest a liability.
b. Explain why in this situation Mammoth would probably prefer the equity method instead of treating this transaction as a purchase and preparing consolidated financial statements.

ISSUES FOR DISCUSSION

REAL DATA

ID8–1

Equity adjustments for marketable securities

H&R Block reported the following account on its statement of shareholders' equity (dollars in thousands):

	2007	2008	2009
Change in net unrealized gain on marketable securities	$(26,152)	$(4,197)	$(4,000)

REQUIRED:
a. Did the market value of H&R Block's marketable securities increase or decrease in 2007, 2008, and 2009?
b. How could H&R Block manage its earnings by choosing when to sell certain of its marketable securities?
c. Explain how the FASB requirement on comprehensive income will influence the reporting practices of H&R Block.

REAL DATA

ID8–2

Short-term equity investments classified as available-for-sale

The following was taken from the 2009 annual report of H&R Block:

Marketable securities—available for sale: *Proceeds from the sales of available-for-sale securities were $8.3 million, $13.9 million, and $3.5 million during fiscal years 2009, 2008, and 2007, respectively. Gross realized gains on those sales during 2009, 2008, and 2007 were $0.7 million, $0.4 million, and $0.3 million, respectively; gross realized losses were $1.3 million, $0.1 million, and $0.1 million, respectively.*

REQUIRED:

a. Describe the difference between trading securities and available-for-sale securities.
b. How is the company's total comprehensive income affected by the dollar values reported in the footnote?
c. Compute the cost of the securities sold during 2007, 2008, and 2009.

REAL DATA

ID8–3

Equity method

The following excerpts, all of which related to the equity investment account, were taken from the 2008 annual report of AT&T (dollars in millions):

	2008	2007
BALANCE SHEET		
Investment in affiliates	$2,332	$2,270
INCOME STATEMENT		
Equity in net income of affiliates	819	692
FOOTNOTES		
Dividends received from affiliates	165	

REQUIRED:

a. The statement of cash flows indicates that no equity investments in affiliates were sold in 2008. Estimate how much was invested in affiliates during 2008.
b. What would you expect to see on AT&T's 2008 statement of cash flows related to this investment activity?
c. Explain why equity income is or is not a good measure of the cash AT&T received from its equity investments.

REAL DATA

ID8–4

IFRS financial statements and the equity method

The 2008 IFRS-based financial statements of EADS N.V., the owner of Airbus, the French-based airline manufacturer, included the following account information (in million euros).

	2008	2007
INCOME STATEMENT:		
Share of profits from associates accounted for under equity method	188	210
BALANCE SHEET:		
Investments in associates accounted for under equity method	2,356	2,238
STATEMENT OF CASH FLOWS:		
Operating section—		
Results of companies accounted for by equity method	(188)	(210)
Investing section—		
Payments for investments in associates	(122)	(132)
Proceeds from disposals of associates	180	186

REQUIRED:

a. Explain the meaning of each of the 2008 disclosures.
b. Estimate the balance sheet carrying amount of the investments in associates disposed of during 2008. (*Hint:* Attempt to recreate the activity in the "investments in associates accounted for under the equity method" account.)
c. Was there a gain or loss on the disposal? How large?

REAL DATA

ID8–5

Equity method and the fair market value option

Sony Corporation, the Japanese electronics manufacturer, prepares U.S. GAAP-based financial statements (in million yen). On its 2008 balance sheet it reported investments in affiliate companies of 381,188 and 236,779 for 2008 and 2007, respectively. It also reported income

from equity investees of 31,509 on the 2008 income statement, and (31,509) appeared in the operating section of the 2008 statement of cash flows.

REQUIRED:

a. Describe the factors that may have explained the increase in the balance sheet value of investments in affiliate companies from 2007 to 2008.
b. Why does −31,509 appear in the operating section of the 2008 statement of cash flows?
c. How would income from these investments be computed if Sony chose to exercise the option to account for these equity investments using the fair market value option? What additional information would be needed, and what additional disclosures would be required?

In 2008, Chevron reported net income of $23.9 billion, $5.4 billion of which was income recognized on investments in affiliate companies accounted for under the equity method. In that same year, Chevron received much less than that amount in dividends from these affiliates. Some accountants have argued that the net income amount reported by Chevron from the equity method is distorted because the company received much less cash on its investment.

REQUIRED:

a. Comment on this criticism of the equity method. In your answer, explain the accounting procedures that characterize the equity method and why income is recognized that is not always backed up by cash receipts. Also explain why investors and creditors must be careful when analyzing financial statements that reflect the use of the equity method.
b. Chevron uses the indirect method of presenting the statement of cash flows. Indicate the direction of the adjustment to net income associated with earnings and dividends under the equity method that appears in the operating section of the statement.

Prior to Financial Accounting Standard 94 in 1988, wholly owned finance subsidiaries of major U.S. companies were accounted for by the parent using the equity method. These companies justified the procedure by claiming that the operations of the subsidiaries were so unlike those of the parents that consolidating the subsidiaries' financial statements would distort those of the parents. At the same time, by using the equity method, the parents were able to avoid including the subsidiaries' liabilities, which were often quite large, on their consolidated balance sheets. It was estimated, for example, that adding the liabilities of General Motors Acceptance Company, a finance subsidiary, to those of General Motors (GM), the parent, would have quadrupled GM's debt/equity ratio.

Forbes commented that if the FASB required such companies to consolidate their finance subsidiaries, it "could cause difficulties with bond indenture agreements and loan covenants requiring that certain ratios be maintained." Others have commented that such problems are of little concern because they can be avoided by writing debt covenants so that all financial ratios are defined in terms of generally accepted accounting principles. Moreover, most financial statement users are reasonably sophisticated and are already aware of the subsidiary's debt. Credit-rating agencies claim, for example, that as long as the debt of the subsidiary is disclosed, it matters little whether it is consolidated or not.

REQUIRED:

a. Briefly explain the difference between using the equity method and preparing consolidated financial statements, and describe how requiring the consolidation of subsidiary financial statements could "cause difficulties with bond indenture agreements."
b. How might the fact that most financial statement users are reasonably sophisticated affect the nature of the accounting standards developed by the FASB?

In its 2009 annual report, Starbucks shows that as of September 27, 2009, it owned $21.5 million in marketable securities designated as available-for-sale. On the same date, Starbucks owned $44.8 million in marketable securities designated as trading securities. Assume that Starbucks sold no marketable securities during the month of October, 2009.

REQUIRED:

a. What would have happened to Starbucks's net income for the month ended October 31, 2009, if the stock market crashed and share price valuations fell, on average, by 50 percent?

b. Under the same scenario as (a), what could management have done to lessen the impact of the crash on net income? What management decision would have increased the negative impact on net income?

c. Why might management want to classify marketable securities as available-for-sale instead of trading?

The *Wall Street Journal* recently reported quarterly earnings for the technology company Acer, Inc. and the oil company Royal Dutch Shell. In the opening paragraph of the Acer article, it stated that there was a "41 percent jump in first-quarter profits, thanks in part to the sale of shares held in other companies." Shell's strong profits were "boosted by gains from proceeds of sales in the company's portfolio of equity investments."

REQUIRED:

a. From the preceding quotes can you tell whether the securities were classified as available-for-sale or trading? Why?

b. Why would a financial statement reader want to separate profits from investment sales from other profits?

c. What earnings concept would an analyst be examining by separating different kinds of earnings?

Large U.S. corporations, especially banks, tend to hold larger portfolios of securities they classify as available-for-sale than of securities they classify as trading. On its 2008 balance sheet, for example, Bank of New York reported available-for-sale securities of $32.1 billion and trading securities of only $11.1 billion. Some have commented that classifying investments as available-for-sale gives management greater ability to manage reported earnings from one year to the next.

REQUIRED:

Explain how the methods used to account for investments classified as available-for-sale (compared to the methods used to account for trading securities) could give management greater ability to manage reported earnings.

A consolidated statement of comprehensive income for Eli Lilly, a major pharmaceutical, is provided below (dollars in millions).

	2008	2007	2006
Net income	$(2,072)	$2,953	$2,663
Other comprehensive income (loss):			
Foreign currency translation adjustments	(766)	757	542
Net unrealized gains (losses) on securities	(191)	(11)	(3)
Other items (inc. SFAS 158)	(1,843)	656	81
Comprehensive income	$(4,872)	$4,355	$3,283

REQUIRED:

Define comprehensive income and describe the events that led to the dollar values (positive and negative) associated with foreign currency translation adjustments and net unrealized gains (losses) on securities.

If a company owns over 50 percent of another company (subsidiary), the financial statements of the two entities are consolidated into one larger entity. For example, the 2008 financial statements of Verizon Communications, Inc. include the financial statements of Verizon Wireless, the cellular phone operator, owned 55 percent by Verizon Communications and 45 percent by Vodafone. Vodafone's interest in the assets and liabilities reported on Verizon's balance

sheet are represented in an account on the balance sheet called "minority interest" (noncontrolling interest) in the amount of approximately $37 billion, which is over 18 percent of Verizon's total assets.

REQUIRED:
a. Explain how noncontrolling interest ends up on the balance sheet.
b. Discuss whether it should be classified as an asset, a liability, or a shareholders' equity item.

REAL DATA

ID8–13

Nike SEC Form 10-K

The SEC Form 10-K of NIKE is reproduced in Appendix C.

REQUIRED:
Review Nike SEC From 10-K, and answer the following questions.

a. Does NIKE carry investment portfolios in trading and available-for-sale securities?
b. Has NIKE exercised the fair market value option for any of these investments? If so, which ones, and what level of measurement (1, 2, or 3) did NIKE rely upon to estimate the market values?
c. Did NIKE have any major acquisitions during 2008? Replicate the entry NIKE recorded to account for this acquisition.
d. How much goodwill did NIKE report on its 2009 and 2008 balance sheets? From 2008 to 2009, NIKE had a decrease in goodwill. What does this indicate about management's evaluation of the future of the companies it previously purchased? Is there any evidence on the 2009 income statement?
e. Why does a goodwill impairment appear in the operating section of the 2009 statement of cash flows?
f. Does NIKE have significant investments in companies in which it does not have control?

Long-Lived Assets

KEY POINTS

The following key points are emphasized in this chapter:

- How the matching principle underlies the methods used to account for long-lived assets.

- Major questions addressed when accounting for long-lived assets and how the financial statements are affected.

- Major economic consequences associated with the methods used to account for long-lived assets.

- Costs that should be included in the capitalized cost of a long-lived asset.

- Accounting treatment of postacquisition expenditures.

- How the cost of a long-lived asset is allocated over its useful life and the alternative allocation methods.

- Disposition of long-lived assets.

- The increasing importance of fair market value and issues that must be addressed when using fair market value as a basis for long-lived assets.

The Pepsi Bottling Group recently reported that its depreciation expense will be lower, boosting the bottom line, due to successful maintenance allowing changes in asset depreciation. Depreciation lives on manufacturing equipment, for example, are being changed to fifteen from ten years. The company said the change would reduce depreciation expense by about $58 million and increase earnings 22 cents a share. "The primary reason for this is that our extensive maintenance programs have enabled us to extend the operating lives of our assets well beyond their previous book lives," said company management.

The methods used to account for property, plant, and equipment vary greatly across companies and can have dramatic effects on reported income. These methods are covered in this chapter.

Long-lived assets are used in the operations of a business and provide benefits that extend beyond the current operating period. Included in this category of assets are land, buildings, machinery, equipment, natural resource costs, intangible assets, and deferred costs.

Land includes the cost of real estate used in the operations of the company. **Fixed assets,** such as buildings, machinery, and equipment, are often located on this real estate. **Natural resource costs** include the costs of acquiring the rights to extract natural resources. Such costs are very important in the operations of the extractive industries (e.g., mining, petroleum, and natural gas). **Intangible assets** are characterized by rights, privileges, and benefits of possession rather than physical existence. Examples include the costs of acquiring patents, copyrights, trademarks, and goodwill. **Deferred costs** represent a miscellaneous category of intangible assets, often including prepaid expenses that provide benefits for a length of time that extends beyond the current period, organization costs, and other startup costs associated with beginning operations (e.g., legal and licensing fees). These definitions are often firm-specific. Land, for example, represents the inventory of a real estate firm, but it is a long-lived asset for a retailer. Similarly, Boeing carries aircraft in its inventory that when sold becomes a fixed asset on the balance sheet of United Airlines, the purchaser. The methods used to account for land, fixed assets, natural resource costs (often using an account called property, plant, and equipment), and intangible assets and deferred costs are covered in this chapter.

Shareholders, investors, creditors, managers, and auditors are interested in the nature and condition of a company's long-lived assets because such assets represent the company's capacity to produce and sell goods and/or services in the future. Planning and executing major capital expenditures for such items as land, buildings, and machinery are some of management's most important concerns. Long-lived asset turnover (sales/average long-lived assets) is a financial ratio used to assess how efficiently a company uses its long-lived assets. In general, if the ratio is high, the company is generating large amounts of sales with a relatively small investment in long-lived assets. As discussed in the next section, this ratio may be particularly useful when comparing the relative performance of manufacturers and service enterprises.

THE RELATIVE SIZE OF LONG-LIVED ASSETS

As Figure 9–1 illustrates, investments in noncurrent assets tend to be large for services, manufacturers, and retailers, and relatively small for Internet firms and financial institutions. Services like AT&T must constantly invest in new technology, and restaurant services like Wendy's/Arby's continually add and update facilities. Retailers invest heavily in stores (Kroger and Lowe's), while natural resource production (Chevron)

FIGURE 9–1

Property, plant, and equipment plus intangibles as a percentage of total assets

	Property, Plant, and Equipment + Intangibles/Total Assets
Manufacturing:	
General Electric	**0.22**
Chevron (Oil drilling and refining)	**0.60**
Retail:	
Kroger (Grocery retail)	**0.66**
Lowe's (Hardware retail)	**0.70**
Internet:	
Yahoo! (Internet search engine)	**0.49**
Cisco (Internet systems)	**0.27**
General Services:	
AT&T (Telecommunications services)	**0.88**
Wendy's/Arby's (Restaurant services)	**0.87**
Financial Services:	
Bank of America (Banking services)	**0.06**
Goldman Sachs (Investment services)	**0.01**

relies heavily on property, plant, and equipment. The relative size of the facilities for financial institutions is swamped by investments in securities and loans, and the financial subsidiary of GE (GE Capital), with its large balance of receivables, dilutes the importance of property, plant, and equipment as a percentage of total assets. The main infrastructure for Internet firms (Yahoo and Cisco) is largely electronic, not "bricks and mortar."

? Chevron, Yahoo!, and Goldman Sachs are three well-known U.S. companies—one a major manufacturer, one an Internet company, and one a financial institution. Rank them in terms of how important fixed asset accounting is to their financial statements. Briefly explain.

LONG-LIVED ASSET ACCOUNTING: GENERAL ISSUES AND FINANCIAL STATEMENT EFFECTS

The matching principle states that efforts (expenses) should be matched against benefits (revenues) in the period when the benefits are recognized. The cost of acquiring a long-lived asset, which is expected to generate revenues in future periods, is, therefore, capitalized in the period of acquisition. As the revenues associated with the long-lived asset are recognized, these costs are **amortized** with a periodic adjusting journal entry. Stated another way, since expenses represent the costs of assets consumed in conducting business, at the end of each accounting period an entry is recorded to reflect the expense associated with the portion of the long-lived asset consumed during that period.

The form of journal entries to capitalize and amortize a piece of equipment follows. Assume that the equipment is purchased on January 1 for $10,000, and its cost is

amortized evenly over its four-year useful life. Recall that amortization of a fixed asset is called **depreciation** and that the dollar amount of the depreciation expense recognized each year is accumulated in an accumulated depreciation account.

Jan. 1	Equipment (+A)	10,000	
	Cash (−A)		10,000
	Acquired equipment		
Dec. 31	Depreciation Expense (E, −RE)	2,500	
	Accumulated Depreciation (−A)		2,500
	Recognized depreciation during first year		

Both Target Corporation and Carrefour, a giant French retailer that uses IFRS, report large depreciation add-backs in the operating section of the 2008 statement of cash flows. Why.

The preceding description and journal entries indicate implicitly that three basic questions must be answered when accounting for long-lived assets:

1. What dollar amount should be included in the capitalized cost of the long-lived asset?
2. Over what time period should this cost be amortized?
3. At what rate should this cost be amortized?

As the following illustration shows, the answers to these questions can have significant effects on the financial statements.

Assume that Rudman Manufacturing acquired equipment for a purchase price of $9,000 and paid an additional $3,000 to have it painted. Figure 9–2 compares the journal entries to record the acquisition and the depreciation charge and the resulting balance sheet value of the equipment in four different cases. In Case 1, Rudman capitalizes the entire $12,000 cost and depreciates it evenly ($4,000 per year) over a three-year period. In Case 2, Rudman capitalizes the $9,000 purchase cost, expenses the $3,000 painting charge, and depreciates the purchase cost evenly ($3,000 per year) over a three-year period. In Case 3, Rudman capitalizes the entire $12,000 cost and depreciates it evenly ($6,000 per year) over a two-year period. In Case 4, Rudman capitalizes the entire $12,000 cost and depreciates it over a three-year period using an accelerated rate; that is, greater depreciation charges are recognized in the early years of the asset's life.

Comparing Case 1 to Case 2 illustrates the financial statement effects of varying the amount of capitalized cost. Note that increasing the amount of capitalized cost (Case 1) reduces the total expense recognized in Year 1, but this increases the depreciation expense recognized during each year of the asset's useful life.

Comparing Case 1 to Case 3 illustrates the financial statement effects of varying the estimated useful life. As the life estimate gets shorter (Case 3), the amount of depreciation expense recognized in each year increases. In the extreme case, estimating the useful life of an asset at one year is equivalent to expensing its cost.

Delta Air Lines depreciates most of its airplanes over a 25-year life, while United normally uses a 30-year estimated useful life. Over the useful lives of these assets, how do these differences affect their balance sheet values and the income statement?

FIGURE 9-2   The effects of depreciation period on the financial statements: Rudman Manufacturing

CASE 1: $12,000 cost is capitalized and depreciated evenly over a three-year period.

YEAR 1		YEAR 2		YEAR 3	
Equipment (+A) 12,000					
Cash (−A)	12,000				
Depr. Exp. (E, −RE) 4,000		Depr. Exp. (E, −RE) 4,000		Depr. Exp. (E, −RE) 4,000	
Accum. Depr. (−A)	4,000	Accum. Depr. (−A)	4,000	Accum. Depr. (−A)	4,000
Balance sheet value:* $ 8,000		$4,000		$0	

CASE 2: $9,000 cost is capitalized and depreciated evenly over a three-year period.

YEAR 1		YEAR 2		YEAR 3	
Equipment (+A) 9,000					
Cash (−A)	9,000				
Maint. Exp. (E, −RE) 3,000					
Cash (−A)	3,000				
Depr. Exp. (E, −RE) 3,000		Depr. Exp. (E, −RE) 3,000		Depr. Exp. (E, −RE) 3,000	
Accum. Depr. (−A)	3,000	Accum. Depr. (−A)	3,000	Accum. Depr. (−A)	3,000
Balance sheet value:* $ 6,000		$3,000		$0	

CASE 3: $12,000 cost is capitalized and depreciated evenly over a two-year period.

YEAR 1		YEAR 2		YEAR 3	
Equipment (+A) 12,000					
Cash (−A)	12,000				
Depr. Exp. (E, −RE) 6,000		Depr. Exp. (E, −RE) 6,000			
Accum. Depr. (−A)	6,000	Accum. Depr. (−A)	6,000		
Balance sheet value:* $ 6,000		$0		$0	

CASE 4: $12,000 cost is capitalized and depreciated over a three-year period at an accelerated rate.

YEAR 1		YEAR 2		YEAR 3	
Equipment (+A) 12,000					
Cash (−A)	12,000				
Depr. Exp. (E, −RE) 6,000		Depr. Exp. (E, −RE) 4,000		Depr. Exp. (E, −RE) 2,000	
Accum. Depr. (−A)	6,000	Accum. Depr. (−A)	4,000	Accum. Depr. (−A)	2,000
Balance sheet value:* $ 6,000		$2,000		$0	

Balance sheet value, also known as book value, *equals capitalized cost less accumulated depreciation.*

Comparing Case 1 to Case 4 illustrates the financial statement effects of varying the depreciation rate. Using an accelerated rate (Case 4) increases the amount of depreciation expense recognized in the early years, but it gives rise to smaller amounts of depreciation expense in later years.

The differences among the four cases, with respect to the amount of expense recognized and the balance sheet value of the equipment, are summarized in Figure 9–3. Note that the total amount of expense recognized under the four cases is the same

FIGURE 9-3

Comparative expense amounts and balance sheet values

	Year 1	Year 2	Year 3	Total
CASE 1				
Expense	$4,000	$4,000	$4,000	$12,000
Balance sheet value	8,000	4,000	0	
CASE 2				
Expense	6,000	3,000	3,000	12,000
Balance sheet value	6,000	3,000	0	
CASE 3				
Expense	6,000	6,000	0	12,000
Balance sheet value	6,000	0	0	
CASE 4				
Expense	6,000	4,000	2,000	12,000
Balance sheet value	6,000	2,000	0	

($12,000). Varying the capitalized cost, estimated life, and depreciation rate affects only the timing of the expense recognition throughout the three-year period.

Choosing to capitalize and amortize or expense the costs associated with acquiring long-lived assets can have significant effects on the financial statements. When AOL chose to capitalize, instead of expense, its marketing cost, the company boosted earnings by $130 million. The major railroads, including Burlington Northern, CSX Santa Fe, Norfolk & Western, and Union Pacific, increased profits by an average of 25 percent when they chose to capitalize and amortize, instead of expense, the costs of laying track. The net income of Comserv, a Minneapolis-based maker of software systems, was boosted by $6.5 million because the company chose to capitalize and amortize, instead of expense, software development costs. Changing the useful-life estimate or adjusting the rate at which a long-lived asset is amortized can also significantly affect the financial statements and important financial ratios. The Pepsi Bottling Group decreased expenses by $58 million and increased earnings per share by 22 cents when it decided to depreciate the cost of its manufacturing equipment over a longer period of time. Blockbuster Video slowed the amortization period for its tapes from 9 to 36 months, a choice that added 20 percent to its reported income. Burlington Northern once disclosed that the company's net income was reduced by $336 million when it increased the rate at which it depreciated its railroad assets.

? American Airlines once chose to extend the depreciation lives of its aircraft to conform more closely with practices in the airline industry. How did this choice affect American's reported income that year? How would this change affect the statement of cash flows? Briefly explain.

AN OVERVIEW OF LONG-LIVED ASSET ACCOUNTING

Figure 9–4 summarizes and organizes the topics covered in the remainder of the chapter. As shown at the top of the figure, there are three points in time during the life of a long-lived asset when important accounting issues must be addressed: (1) when

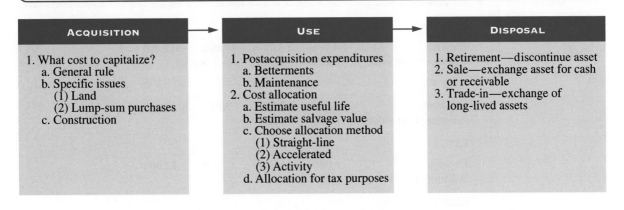

FIGURE 9–4   Accounting for long-lived assets

ACQUISITION	USE	DISPOSAL

1. What cost to capitalize?
  a. General rule
  b. Specific issues
    (1) Land
    (2) Lump-sum purchases
  c. Construction
	1. Postacquisition expenditures
	  a. Betterments
	  b. Maintenance
	2. Cost allocation
	  a. Estimate useful life
	  b. Estimate salvage value
	  c. Choose allocation method
	    (1) Straight-line
	    (2) Accelerated
	    (3) Activity
	  d. Allocation for tax purposes
		1. Retirement—discontinue asset
		2. Sale—exchange asset for cash
		  or receivable
		3. Trade-in—exchange of
		  long-lived assets

the long-lived asset is acquired (purchased or manufactured), (2) while the long-lived asset is in use, and (3) when the long-lived asset is disposed of.

ACQUISITION: WHAT COSTS TO CAPITALIZE?

The acquisition cost of a long-lived asset is determined by either (1) the fair market value (FMV) of the acquired asset or (2) the FMV of what was given up to acquire the asset, whichever is more readily determinable. In almost all cases, the FMV of what was given up is used because cash, which by definition is at FMV, is normally given up in such exchanges. Furthermore, the capitalized cost (i.e., the FMV of what was given up) should include all costs required to bring the asset into serviceable or usable condition and location.[1] Such costs include not only the actual purchase cost of the asset but also costs like freight, installation, taxes, and title fees. For example, suppose that the purchase cost of a piece of equipment is $25,000, and it costs $2,000 to have it delivered, $1,500 to have it installed, and taxes and title fees total $500 and $300, respectively. The total capitalized cost of the equipment would then be $29,300 ($25,000 + $2,000 + $1,500 + $500 + $300), and the following journal entry would be entered to record the acquisition, assuming that cash is paid for the equipment.

Equipment (+A)   **29,300**
  Cash (−A)   **29,300**
Acquired equipment

?   Zimmer, a major manufacturer of orthopedic equipment, increased its investment in property, plant, and equipment by almost $250 million during 2008. Briefly explain how these costs were accounted for. Where on the statement of cash flows would one find evidence of these additions?

---

1. Some costs (e.g., storage costs incurred while waiting to put an asset into service) are not required to bring the asset into usable condition and therefore should be expensed.

The Acquisition of Land

All costs incurred to acquire land and make it ready for use should be included in the land account. They include (1) the purchase price of the land; (2) closing costs, such as title, legal, and recording fees; (3) costs incurred to get the land in condition for its intended use, such as razing old buildings, grading, filling, draining, and clearing (less any proceeds from the sale of salvaged materials); (4) assumptions of any back taxes, liens, or mortgages; and (5) additional land improvements assumed to be permanent, such as landscaping, street lights, sewers, and drainage systems. While the costs incurred to acquire land and prepare it for use are capitalized, *they are not amortized* over future periods. The process of amortization requires the estimate of a useful life. Because land is considered to have an indefinite life, its cost cannot be amortized.

Under IFRS, a special land account called "investment property" is often found on the balance sheet. Such property is not used in the normal course of business, normally generating rental revenue and/or being held to take advantage of price appreciation. Under IFRS, investment property can be accounted for at cost or using mark-to-market accounting, which means that the balance sheet reflects its current market value, and changes in value from one period to the next are reflected in earnings. Under U.S. GAAP, investment property is included in the land account, and must be carried at cost.

Lump-Sum Purchases

A special problem arises when more than one asset is purchased at a single (lump-sum) price. In such situations, the total purchase cost must be allocated to the individual assets. If the FMVs of the purchased assets can be objectively determined, the total purchase cost can be allocated to each asset on the basis of its relative FMV. This cost allocation scheme is based on the assumption that costs vary in direct proportion to FMV.

To illustrate, assume that ABC Incorporated purchases three assets (inventory, land, and equipment) from Liquidated Limited, a company that is in the process of liquidation. The total price for the assets is $40,000. The individual FMVs of the three assets and the allocation of the $40,000 purchase cost to each asset appear in Figure 9–5.

FIGURE 9–5 Cost allocation on the basis of relative FMVs		FMVs	Allocation Formula	Allocated Cost
	Inventory	$20,000	[($20,000 ÷ $50,000) × $40,000]	$16,000
	Land	10,000	[($10,000 ÷ $50,000) × $40,000]	8,000
	Equipment	20,000	[($20,000 ÷ $50,000) × $40,000]	16,000
	Total	$50,000		$40,000

Note that the cost allocated to each asset is in direct proportion to the asset's portion of the total FMV. The inventory, for example, accounts for 40 percent ($20,000/$50,000) of the total FMV and thereby receives 40 percent ($16,000/$40,000) of the total costs. The equipment is treated similarly. Land accounts for 20 percent ($10,000/$50,000) of the total FMV and receives 20 percent ($8,000/$40,000) of the total cost.

Two features of this cost allocation approach are very important. First, it is based on FMVs, which by nature are very subjective and therefore are often expressed in terms of ranges rather than precise estimates. Second, while all three costs in this example are capitalized, each is treated differently in the future. The $16,000 inventory cost will be converted to cost of goods sold when the inventory is sold, the $8,000 land cost is not subject to amortization, and the $16,000 equipment cost will be depreciated over the equipment's useful life. Taken together, these two features indicate that the subjective choice of FMVs can have significant effects on future net income amounts, a fact that management may be able to exploit. For example, if management wishes to maximize income, it can choose from within the FMV ranges values that allocate as much cost as possible to land, which will not be amortized, and as little as possible to inventory, which will be converted to cost of goods sold relatively soon. On the other hand, management can minimize income (e.g., income tax reporting, building hidden reserves, or taking a bath) by allocating as much cost as possible to inventory and as little as possible to land.

To illustrate, assume in the previous example that the FMV of equipment was assessed at $20,000, but the FMVs of inventory and land were expressed as being somewhere within the following ranges: inventory ($15,000–$25,000), land ($5,000–$15,000). Figure 9–6 compares the resulting costs under two allocation schemes: (1) "Maximize future income" where the lowest value for inventory ($15,000) and the highest value for land ($15,000) are used, and (2) "Minimize future income" where the highest value for inventory ($25,000) and the lowest value for land ($5,000) are used.

FIGURE 9–6

Comparing cost allocation methods

(1) Maximize Future Income:

	FMVs	Allocation Formula	Allocated Cost
Inventory	$15,000	[($15,000 ÷ $50,000) × $40,000]	$12,000
Land	15,000	[($15,000 ÷ $50,000) × $40,000]	12,000
Equipment	20,000	[($20,000 ÷ $50,000) × $40,000]	16,000
Total	$50,000		$40,000

(2) Minimize Future Income:

	FMVs	Allocation Formula	Allocated Cost
Inventory	$25,000	[($25,000 ÷ $50,000) × $40,000]	$20,000
Land	5,000	[($ 5,000 ÷ $50,000) × $40,000]	4,000
Equipment	20,000	[($20,000 ÷ $50,000) × $40,000]	16,000
Total	$50,000		$40,000

The procedure of allocating costs on the basis of FMVs is also used when a company acquires the assets and liabilities of another company (i.e., through the purchase of outstanding stock) and must allocate the purchase price to those assets and liabilities (see Chapter 8 and Appendix 8A). As illustrated in Figure 9–6, such allocations can be very subjective, giving management much reporting discretion in this area.

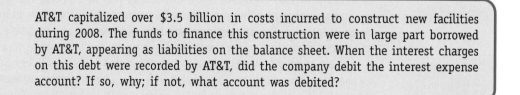

When Kellogg purchased the outstanding stock of Worthington Foods for $350 million, the purchase price was allocated to current and noncurrent assets ($218 million), liabilities ($62 million), and goodwill ($194 million). On what basis were these allocations made, and what kind of judgments were necessary to make them?

Construction of Long-Lived Assets

When companies construct their own long-lived assets, all costs required to get the assets into operating condition must be allocated to the long-lived asset account, including the costs of materials, labor, and overhead used in the construction process. The costs may also include interest on funds borrowed to finance the construction. Note the following excerpt from the 2008 annual report of Federal Express:

Interest on funds used to finance the acquisition and modification of aircraft . . . construction of certain facilities, and development of certain software up to the date the asset is ready for its intended use is capitalized and included in the cost of the asset if the asset is actively under construction.

Although determining the costs of materials and labor is relatively straightforward, allocating overhead and interest to the cost of long-lived assets can be difficult and is often arbitrary. Such issues are normally covered in management or intermediate financial accounting courses.

AT&T capitalized over $3.5 billion in costs incurred to construct new facilities during 2008. The funds to finance this construction were in large part borrowed by AT&T, appearing as liabilities on the balance sheet. When the interest charges on this debt were recorded by AT&T, did the company debit the interest expense account? If so, why; if not, what account was debited?

POSTACQUISITION EXPENDITURES: BETTERMENTS OR MAINTENANCE?

Costs are often incurred after an acquired or manufactured long-lived asset is placed into service. Such **postacquisition expenditures** serve either to improve the existing asset or merely to maintain it. Costs incurred to improve the asset are called

betterments, and costs incurred merely to repair it or maintain its current level of productivity are classified as **maintenance.**

The following guidelines are used to distinguish betterments from maintenance expenditures. In order to be considered a betterment, a postacquisition expenditure must improve the long-lived asset in at least one of four ways:

1. Increase the asset's useful life over that which was originally estimated.
2. Improve the quality of the asset's output.
3. Increase the quantity of the asset's output.
4. Reduce the costs associated with operating the asset.

Betterments are usually infrequent and tend to involve large dollar amounts. Maintenance expenditures, on the other hand, fail to meet any of the criteria mentioned above and tend to be periodic. Also, maintenance items are normally small, but certain expenditures (e.g., replacing a building roof every ten years) can be significant.

Postacquisition expenditures classified as betterments should be capitalized, added to the cost of the long-lived asset, and then amortized over its remaining life. Expenditures classified as maintenance should be treated as current expenses. For example, note the following excerpt from the 2008 annual report of Molson Coors Brewing Company:

Expenditures for new facilities and improvements that substantially extend the capacity or useful life of an asset are capitalized. . . . Ordinary repairs and maintenance are expensed as incurred.

The *Baltimore Sun* reported that the famous WorldCom fraud was easy to spot. "The scheme was not complicated: the company's financial officers recorded routine maintenance expenses totaling $3.9 billion as capital expenditures." Explain how this choice would affect the financial statements in the current and future periods.

Distinguishing between a betterment and a maintenance expenditure, even with the criteria mentioned above, is often difficult in practice, giving management reporting discretion in this area. In many cases, however, materiality plays an important role because postacquisition expenditures are frequently small, and in such situations they are expensed, regardless of their nature. To illustrate the accounting treatment for betterments and maintenance expenditures, assume that Jerry's Delivery Service purchased an automobile on January 1, 2011, for $10,000. The purchase cost was capitalized, and the useful life of the automobile was estimated to be four years from the date of purchase. Each year, Jerry had the car tuned up and serviced at a cost of $300. During the second year, the muffler was replaced for $80, and during the third year, the car was painted at a cost of $450. At the beginning of the fourth year, Jerry paid $1,000 to have the engine completely overhauled. The overhaul increased the automobile's expected life beyond the original estimate by an additional year. Figure 9–7 traces the book value, depreciation, and maintenance expenses associated with the automobile over its five-year life.

FIGURE 9–7		2011	2012	2013	2014	2015
Betterments and maintenance expenditures: Jerry's Delivery Service	Book value (1/1)	$10,000	$7,500	$5,000	$2,500	$1,750
	Overhaul				1,000	
	Less: Depreciation	2,500[b]	2,500	2,500	1,750[c]	1,750
	Book value[a] (12/31)	$ 7,500	$5,000	$2,500	$1,750	$ 0
	Maintenance expenses:					
	Tune-up	300	300	300	300	300
	Muffler replacement		80			
	Paint job			450		

[a]*Book value equals cost less accumulated depreciation.*
[b]2,500 = ($10,000 ÷ 4 years)
[c]1,750 = ($2,500 + $1,000) ÷ 2 years

Note that all postacquisition costs are treated as expenses except for the overhaul, which increased the automobile's life beyond the original four-year estimate. The $1,000 cost of the overhaul was capitalized at the beginning of the fourth year and, with the book value ($2,500) at that time, was depreciated evenly over the remaining two years of the car's useful life.

The 2008 annual report of Exxon Mobil states, "Maintenance and repairs, including planned major maintenance, are expensed as incurred. Major renewals and improvements are capitalized." Which of these costs are considered betterments? Which are considered maintenance? Explain.

COST ALLOCATION: AMORTIZING CAPITALIZED COSTS

Once the cost of a long-lived asset has been determined, it must be allocated over the asset's useful life. Such allocation is necessary if the costs are to be matched against the benefits produced by the asset. The allocation process requires three steps: (1) estimate a useful life, (2) estimate a salvage value, and (3) choose a cost allocation (depreciation) method.

Estimating the Useful Life and Salvage Value

Accurately estimating the useful life and salvage value of a long-lived asset is extremely difficult. An important consideration is the **physical obsolescence** of the asset. At what time in the future will the asset deteriorate to the point when repairs are not economically feasible, and what will be the asset's salvage value at that time? It is virtually impossible to predict accurately the condition of an asset very far into the future, let alone predict the **salvage value,** the dollar amount that can be recovered when the asset is sold, traded, or scrapped.

Robert Olstein, a veteran accounting expert, once noted, "Beware of companies that overestimate how much their fixed assets will be worth down the road. Optimistic assumptions allow a company to reduce the amount of depreciation it reports." Explain what he means. Who is he warning and why?

The problem of predicting useful lives and salvage values is complicated further by technological developments. The usefulness of a long-lived asset is largely determined by technological advancements, which could at any time render certain long-lived assets obsolete. **Technical obsolescence,** in turn, could force the early replacement of a long-lived asset that is still in reasonably good working order.

As a result, generally accepted accounting principles provide no clear guidelines for determining the useful lives and future salvage values of long-lived assets. In practice, many companies assume salvage value to be zero and estimate useful lives by referring to guidelines developed by the Internal Revenue Service. These guidelines, however, were established for use in determining taxable income and need not be followed in the preparation of the financial statements. Consequently, management can use its own discretion when estimating salvage values and useful lives. As long as the estimates seem reasonable and are applied in a systematic and consistent manner, auditors generally allow managers to do what they wish in this area. Sears, for example, depreciates its equipment generally over a five- to ten-year period and its real property over a forty- to fifty-year period. Figure 9–8 shows typical ranges of estimated useful lives for different kinds of fixed assets reported by major U.S. companies.

FIGURE 9–8
Estimated useful lives of fixed assets

Buildings and improvements	10–50 years
Machinery and equipment	3–20 years
Furniture and fixtures	5–12 years
Automotive equipment	3–6 years

These broad ranges can complicate the decisions of individuals who use financial statements to compare performance across companies. This problem is particularly evident in the airline industry, where the estimated lives used to depreciate aircraft often differ across companies. Delta Air Lines typically depreciates its planes over twenty-five years; other airlines, like United, estimate a life of thirty years for the same 727s that Delta writes off in twenty-five.

Emerson Electronics reports that estimated service lives for buildings range from 30 to 40 years, and for machinery and equipment range from 8 to 12 years. Explain why the ranges are so different for the two asset types, and how Emerson management could manage reported income with the choice of the estimated useful life of a new building.

Revising the Useful-Life Estimate

Estimating the useful life of a long-lived asset when it is acquired is a very subjective process. After using such assets for several years, companies often find that their

original estimates were inaccurate. For example, Delta Air Lines has increased the estimated useful life of its aircraft more than once. In these situations, the portion of the long-lived asset's depreciation base (cost − salvage value) that has not yet been depreciated is depreciated over the remainder of the revised useful life.

To illustrate, suppose that on January 1, 2006, ABC Airlines purchased aircraft for $110,000 and estimated the useful life of the aircraft and the salvage value to be ten years and $10,000, respectively. If the company depreciated equal portions ($10,000) of the amount subject to depreciation ($100,000) each year, it would have recognized $50,000 of accumulated depreciation by the end of 2010, and the aircraft would be reported on the 2010 balance sheet in the following manner:

Aircraft	**$110,000**	
Less: Accumulated depreciation	**50,000**	**60,000**

Assume that as of January 1, 2011, the company believes that the aircraft will actually be in service through 2021, ten years beyond the present time, and fifteen years from the date of acquisition (2006). In other words, the company changed its original useful-life estimate from ten to fifteen years. At that point, ABC would not make a correcting journal entry to restate the financial statements of the previous periods. Instead, it would simply depreciate the remaining depreciation base ($60,000 [book value] − $10,000 [salvage value]) over the remaining life of the aircraft (ten years). The following journal entry would be recorded in the company's books at the end of 2011 and at the end of each year until and including December 31, 2021.

Dec. 31	**Depreciation Expense (E, −SE)**	**5,000**	
	Accumulated Depreciation (−A)		**5,000**
	Recognized depreciation on aircraft ($50,000/10 yr)		

In late 2009 PepsiCo announced that its earnings should rise 11 percent to 13 percent for 2010, a growth rate considerably higher than in recent quarters. Analysts following the company and its rival Coca-Cola, however, stated that one of the reasons behind the higher projected earnings for PepsiCo was a change to its asset depreciation schedules. Why would the analysts mention the change to depreciation when discussing earnings growth, and how might PepsiCo respond? What steps should an analyst take when comparing the 2010 performance levels of PepsiCo and Coca Cola?

Depreciating the book value of the asset over the remaining useful life, as of the date of the estimate revision, is known as treating the revision *prospectively*. That is, no "catch-up" adjusting entry is recorded to restate the books. Estimate revisions are not considered errors, and therefore, the financial statements as of the time of the revision are not in need of correction. Instead, the new information that led to the revision affects only the manner in which the aircraft is accounted for in the future. However, if the revision gives rise to a reported net income amount that is materially different from what would have been reported without the revision, the company is required to describe the revision in the footnotes. The excerpt below was taken from an annual report of Delta Air Lines.

[T]he Company increased the estimated useful lives of substantially all of its flight equipment. . . . The effect of this change was a decrease of approximately $130 million in depreciation expense and a $69 million [after income taxes] increase in net income. . . .

Cost Allocation (Depreciation) Methods

The useful-life estimate determines the period of time over which a long-lived asset is to be amortized. The salvage value estimate in conjunction with the capitalized cost determines the **depreciation base**[2] (capitalized cost − salvage value): the dollar amount of cost that is amortized over the asset's useful life. The cost allocation methods discussed in this section determine the rate of amortization or, in other words, the amount of cost that is to be converted to an expense during each period of a long-lived asset's useful life. Three basic allocation (depreciation) methods are allowed under generally accepted accounting principles: (1) straight-line, (2) accelerated, and (3) activity.

THE STRAIGHT-LINE METHOD OF AMORTIZATION (DEPRECIATION)

The discussion and most of the examples so far have assumed that equal dollar amounts of a long-lived asset's cost are amortized during each period of its useful life. This assumption, which is referred to as the **straight-line method,** is used by most companies to depreciate their fixed assets and by almost all companies to amortize their intangible assets.[3] The straight-line method can be chosen for several reasons: (1) management believes that the asset provides equal benefits across each year of its estimated useful life, (2) in comparison with the other methods, it is simple to apply, and (3) it tends to produce higher net income numbers and higher long-lived asset book values in the early years of a long-lived asset's life. The following example illustrates the straight-line method.[4]

Assume that Midland Plastics purchased a van wagon for $15,000 on January 1, 2008. The life and salvage value of the wagon are estimated to be five years and $3,000, respectively. Under the straight-line method, the annual depreciation expense would be calculated as shown in Figure 9–9, which also includes the related adjusting journal entry.

FIGURE 9–9	
The straight-line method: Midland Plastics	**FORMULA**

FORMULA

Straight-line depreciation = (Cost	− Salvage value)* ÷ Estimated life
$2,400 per year = ($15,000 − $3,000)	÷ 5 years

JOURNAL ENTRY

Depreciation Expense (E, −RE)	2,400	
Accumulated Depreciation (−A)		2,400
Recognized annual depreciation		

*Depreciation base

Under the straight-line method, the same dollar amount of depreciation is recognized in each year of the asset's useful life. At $2,400 per year for five years, the total

---

2. *Depletion base* and *amortization base* are the terms used for natural resource costs and intangibles, respectively.

3. *Accounting Trends and Techniques* (New York: AICPA, 2009) reports that, of the U.S. companies surveyed, 99 percent used the straight-line method to depreciate at least some of their fixed assets. The straight-line method is used predominantly to depreciate buildings.

4. The information from this example is also used in the illustration of the accelerated method that follows.

amount of depreciation taken would be $12,000, the depreciation base. At the end of the wagon's estimated life, its book value ($15,000 − $12,000) is equal to its estimated salvage value ($3,000).

In the footnotes to its 2008 financial statements Target reported that depreciation was computed using the straight-line method over estimated useful lives. Fixtures and equipment were depreciated over useful lives ranging from 3 to 15 years, and the company reported $4.3 billion of fixtures and equipment on its 2008 balance sheet. Compute an estimate of the amount of depreciation Target recorded during 2008 on its fixtures and equipment.

DOUBLE-DECLINING-BALANCE METHOD

The next method discussed is the double-declining-balance method, an accelerated method of amortization. It is called an **accelerated method** because greater amounts of the capitalized cost are allocated to the earlier periods of the asset's life than to the later periods. Accelerated methods are used by some companies to depreciate fixed assets when preparing financial reports: Boeing, Inc., for example, uses double-declining-balance as one of its depreciation methods.[5]

To illustrate the **double-declining-balance method,** assume once again the facts of the preceding example. Figure 9–10 shows the general formula and calculations for each year.

Under the double-declining-balance method, each year's depreciation is computed by multiplying 2 by the book value of the asset (cost − accumulated depreciation) and dividing the result by N, the estimated useful life.[6] Note that salvage value is not part

FIGURE 9–10

The double-declining-balance method: Midland Plastics

FORMULA

Double-Declining-Balance Depreciation = (2 × Book Value) ÷ N
where   **Book value = cost − accumulated depreciation**
      N **= the estimated useful life**

CALCULATIONS

2008:	**(2 × $15,000) ÷ 5 =** **Accumulated depreciation = $6,000**	**$ 6,000**
2009:	**[2 × ($15,000 − $6,000)] ÷ 5 =** **Accumulated depreciation = $9,600 ($6,000 + $3,600)**	**3,600**
2010:	**[2 × ($15,000 − $9,600)] ÷ 5 =** **Accumulated depreciation = $11,760 ($9,600 + $2,160)**	**2,160**
2011:	**Reduce book value ($15,000 − $11,760) to salvage value ($3,000)** **Accumulated depreciation = $12,000 ($11,760 + $240)**	**240**
2012:	**No depreciation recognized because book value cannot be** **reduced below salvage value**	**0**
	Total depreciation expense recognized	**$12,000**

5. Another accelerated method used by a few companies (e.g., General Electric) is called sum-of-the-years'-digits. Compared to double-declining-balance, it is a less extreme form of accelerated depreciation.

6. The formula for the double-declining-balance method can also be expressed as ([cost − accumulated depreciation] × [2 × the straight-line rate]). The straight-line rate is equal to the percentage of the depreciation base charged each year under the straight-line method (1/N). Using the numbers in the example above, this formula appears as follows: ($15,000 − accumulated depreciation) × 40 percent.

of the general formula. However, the book value of the asset cannot be reduced below the asset's estimated salvage value. In 2011, for example, only the amount of depreciation ($240) necessary to bring the asset's book value ($15,000 − $11,760) to its estimated salvage value ($3,000) was recognized. For this same reason, no depreciation expense was recognized in 2012.

STRAIGHT-LINE AND DOUBLE-DECLINING-BALANCE: A COMPARISON

This section compares the financial statement effects of the two cost-allocation methods discussed above. The general formulas, the depreciation expenses, and the related book values for each year of the estimated useful life under each of the two methods appear in Figure 9–11. This comparison uses the same information given in the previous examples.

FIGURE 9–11

Depreciation methods compared

	Straight-Line			Double-Declining-Balance		
	$SL = (C - SV) \div N$			$\dfrac{2 \times BV}{N}$		
	EXPENSE	**BOOK VALUE**		**EXPENSE**	**BOOK VALUE**	
2008	2,400	15,000		6,000	15,000	
		− 2,400	12,600		− 6,000	9,000
2009	2,400	15,000		3,600	15,000	
		− 4,800	10,200		− 9,600	5,400
2010	2,400	15,000		2,160	15,000	
		− 7,200	7,800		−11,760	3,240
2011	2,400	15,000		240	15,000	
		− 9,600	5,400		−12,000	3,000
2012	2,400	15,000		0	15,000	
		−12,000	3,000		−12,000	3,000

The straight-line method results in the same amount of depreciation ($2,400) in each of the five years. The accelerated method shows greater amounts of depreciation in the early periods of the asset's life (2008 and 2009) and lesser amounts of depreciation in the later periods (2011 and 2012). Both methods recognize total depreciation of $12,000 over the five-year period and thus depreciate the long-lived asset only to its salvage value ($3,000).

Choosing between the two methods can have a significant effect on the timing of reported income. Assume that Midland Plastics, which purchased the wagon in the preceding examples, has revenues of $12,000 and expenses other than depreciation of $5,000 in each of the five years, 2008–2012. Figure 9–12 contains the income numbers for each of the two methods for each of the five years.

FIGURE 9–12

The comparative effects on net income of different depreciation methods

Methods	2008	2009	2010	2011	2012	Total
Straight-line	$4,600	$4,600	$4,600	$4,600	$4,600	$23,000
Double-declining-balance	1,000	3,400	4,840	6,760	7,000	23,000

Note: **The net income numbers were determined in the following manner:**

Net income = $12,000 (revenues) − $5,000 (other expenses) − depreciation expense

When Hewlett-Packard adopted the straight-line method of depreciation for all assets placed into service after a certain date, but continued with the use of accelerated methods for assets placed into service prior to that date, the company justified the change by claiming that straight-line is a better application of matching and that the new method more closely conforms to industry practices. How could straight-line be a better example of matching, and what advantage comes from conforming to industry practices?

Note first that the total income recognized across the five-year periods is the same ($23,000) under each method because each method recognizes $12,000 ($15,000 − $3,000) of depreciation expense over the life of the asset. However, the amount of depreciation recognized in each period differs, giving rise to different income patterns over the life of the asset. The graph in Figure 9–13 compares these income patterns.

FIGURE 9–13

Effects of depreciation methods on net income

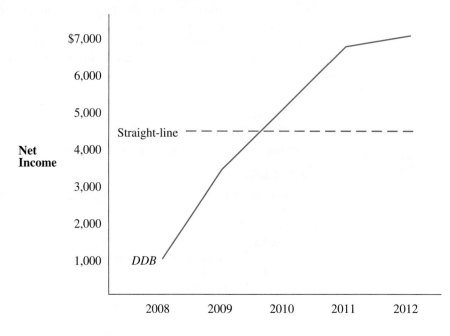

Note: DDB = Double-declining-balance.

Note that compared to double-declining-balance, net income under the straight-line method is higher in the early periods and lower in the later periods of the asset's estimated useful life. In the early periods, the double-declining-balance method produces low levels of net income that increase rapidly over the life of the asset.

Three major competitors in the aerospace industry include Boeing, Lockheed Martin, and Northrop Grumman use both accelerated and straight-line methods for different assets. To depreciate fixed assets, Boeing uses primarily accelerated methods, Lockheed Martin uses accelerated for the first half of the assets' lives followed by straight-line, and Tristar uses straight-line. Discuss difficulties that are encountered by analysts who attempt to assess the relative performance of these three companies.

THE ACTIVITY (UNITS-OF-PRODUCTION) METHOD AND NATURAL RESOURCE DEPLETION

The **activity method**[7] allocates the cost of a long-lived asset to future periods on the basis of its activity. This method is used primarily in the mining, oil, and gas industries to **deplete** the costs associated with acquiring the rights to and extracting natural resources. The following excerpt, for example, was taken from the annual report of Pennzoil, a large oil and gas mining company.

Provision for depreciation, depletion, and amortization is determined on a field-by-field basis using the units-of-production method.

The estimated life under the activity method is expressed in terms of units of activity (e.g., miles driven, units produced, barrels extracted) instead of years, as is done under the previous methods. In periods when an asset is very active (e.g., production is high), a relatively large amount of the cost is amortized. In periods when the asset is less active, relatively fewer costs are amortized.

To illustrate, assume that a company purchases mining properties for $1 million in cash. It estimates that the properties will yield 500,000 saleable tons of ore, and the company mines 10,000 tons during the first year of production. The computation of the depletion rate and the journal entries that would be made to record this series of events appear in Figure 9–14.

FIGURE 9–14
Depletion rate and related journal entries

DEPLETION RATE

$1,000,000 ÷ 500,000 estimated tons = $2 per ton

JOURNAL ENTRIES

Mineral Deposits (+A)	1,000,000	
Cash (−A)		1,000,000
Acquired right to extract ore		
Depletion Expense (E, −SE)	20,000	
Mineral Deposits (or Accumulated Depletion) (−A)		20,000
Recognized depletion for first year		
(10,000 tons × $2 per ton)		

?

ConocoPhillips, the large energy company, depreciates its fixed assets as follows: Property, plant, and equipment on the oil- and gas-producing properties are depreciated by the units-of-production method (activity method), while all other fixed assets are depreciated by the straight-line method. For those assets using straight-line, a 25-year useful life is used for refining assets, and 45-year useful life is used for pipeline assets. Why does ConocoPhillips use different methods of depreciation? What is unique about its business that might encourage management to adopt different methods of depreciation and different lines for different asset types? Which measurement principles of financial accounting are particularly applicable here?

---

7. Referred to as the *units-of-production method* in *Accounting Trends and Techniques* (New York: AICPA, 2006), p. 362.

Cost Allocation Methods and the Matching Principle

Recall that the matching principle states that efforts (expenses) should be matched against the benefits (revenues) they produce. In terms of this principle, the straight-line method assumes that the revenues generated by the depreciated asset are constant across the asset's life; the accelerated method assumes that such revenues are high in early periods and low in later periods; and the activity method assumes that revenues are generated in proportion to the asset's activity. While each of these methods may represent the best application of the matching principle for certain assets, the activity method is probably the most consistent overall. Presumably, the more active an asset is, the more benefits it should produce. The extent to which a given amortization method is consistent with the matching principle is an important factor that should be considered by management when choosing an allocation method. Such consistency helps to improve the quality and usefulness of the reported financial numbers. However, other economic factors, discussed in the next section, are also considered when making such decisions.

Under IFRS, depreciation accounting is very similar to U.S. GAAP. However, unlike U.S. GAAP, management has the option of periodically revaluing property, plant, and equipment to fair market value, if it can be reliably measured. Changes in fair market value are not reflected on the income statement, but rather affect a shareholder's equity account (the IFRS version of the statement of comprehensive income is called the statement of recognized income and expenses). Interestingly, very few companies exercise this option.

How Does Management Choose an Acceptable Cost Allocation Method?

Management may choose a given cost allocation method for a variety of economic reasons. Perhaps the most obvious is that the method has a significant and desired effect on important financial ratios, such as earnings per share, that are used by shareholders, investors, and creditors to evaluate management performance. When RTE Corporation, an electrical equipment manufacturer, more than doubled earnings per share by changing its depreciation method, its controller justified the action by stating: "We realize that compared to our competitors, our (past) conservative (accelerated) method of depreciation may have hurt us with investors because of its negative impact on net earnings." In a similar context, Inland Steel's controller once commented, "Why should we put ourselves at a disadvantage by depreciating more conservatively (i.e., accelerated methods) than other steel companies do?"

Note, however, that changing accounting methods, such as switching the depreciation method, to inflate net income in an effort to positively influence the assessments of investors and creditors may not be an effective strategy. When IBM shifted from the accelerated to the straight-line method, it increased reported earnings by $375 million. Did its share value increase? Some evidence suggests that stock market prices do not react positively to such changes, and many accountants question whether credit-rating services, like Dun & Bradstreet, adjust their ratings. In fact, knowledgeable shareholders, investors, and creditors may interpret a change to a less conservative depreciation method (e.g., from accelerated to straight-line) as a negative signal, indicating that management may be attempting to hide poor performance that it anticipates in the future. It is also true that the use of accelerated methods can lead to the creation of "hidden reserves," giving management greater ability to manage reported financial numbers in the future.

Management may also consider compensation contracts based on net income and debt covenants when choosing a depreciation method. Compared to accelerated methods, straight-line, for example, would tend to produce greater amounts of net-income-based compensation in the early periods of an asset's useful life. Similarly, the depreciation method chosen may affect whether a company violates a debt covenant.

Delta Air Lines operates under debt covenants where future borrowing may be restricted, subject to the performance of the company. Explain how the choice of a depreciation method could determine whether this covenant is violated.

Depreciation Methods for Income Tax Purposes

Management is not required to choose the same depreciation method for income tax purposes that it uses for financial reporting. Indeed, many companies cannot use for financial reporting purposes the depreciation methods that they are allowed to use for tax purposes. Most companies, such as Sundstrand Corporation (aerospace) and Merck & Company, Inc. (pharmaceuticals), use the straight-line method for financial reporting and an accelerated method for tax purposes. *Forbes* reports:

Like most businesses, Anheuser-Busch keeps two sets of books, one for tax purposes and one for its owners. [The company] uses accelerated depreciation for taxes but straight-line for reporting to investors.

Using accelerated depreciation for tax purposes gives rise to significant tax savings for these companies. In a single year, for example, Anheuser-Busch normally saves millions of dollars in taxes by using accelerated depreciation instead of straight-line for tax purposes.

We have shown that estimating useful lives and salvage values in addition to choosing among alternative depreciation methods gives management considerable flexibility in reporting the amount of depreciation on the financial statements. However, the current rules specified in the **Internal Revenue Code,** which cover depreciation for tax purposes, are much less flexible.

According to tax law, a fixed asset is placed into one of eight categories, and each category is assigned a minimum allowable useful life and a depreciation method, as indicated in Figure 9–15.

FIGURE 9–15

Depreciation rules for income tax purposes

Category	Estimated Life	Allowable Depreciation Method
1	3 years	Double-declining-balance
2	5 years	Double-declining-balance
3	7 years	Double-declining-balance
4	10 years	Double-declining-balance
5	15 years	150% declining-balance*
6	20 years	150% declining-balance*
7	27.5 years	Straight-line
8	31.5 years	Straight-line

*Formula − [1.5 × (cost − accumulated depreciation)] ÷ life

Automobiles, for example, are placed in Category 2, which allows them to be depreciated over a five-year life, using the double-declining-balance method. Equipment and machinery are normally included in Categories 1, 2, 3, or 4 and therefore are depreciated over lives ranging from 3 to 10 years, using the double-declining-balance method. Apartments, buildings, and warehouses are generally classified in Category 7 or 8; both categories are subject to the straight-line method over an estimated life of either 27.5 or 31.5 years.

For purposes of determining taxable income, management should use the depreciation strategy that provides the greatest economic benefit for the company, which normally means that management should choose the shortest allowable life and the most extreme form of accelerated depreciation. These choices are preferred for tax purposes because they save tax dollars in the early years of the asset's life and thereby minimize the present value of the stream of income tax payments.

> **?** During the fiscal year ending May 31, 2009, FedEx Corporation, which uses accelerated depreciation for tax purposes, recognized $3.9 billion of tax-deductible depreciation expense. Had the company used straight-line depreciation, it would have recognized only about $1.8 billion of depreciation. For that year the company's effective income tax rate was 37.6 percent. How much money did the company save in taxes by using accelerated, instead of straight-line, depreciation?

To illustrate, refer back to Figure 9–12, which compares net income numbers produced by the straight-line and double-declining-balance methods of depreciation. Note that the total income recognized under the two methods is the same ($23,000). Now assume a corporate income tax rate of 30 percent. The income tax payments reported in Figure 9–16 would then be due under each of the methods for each of the five years. The table also provides the present value of each stream of tax payments, assuming a 10 percent discount rate.[8]

FIGURE 9–16 Income tax payments (Tax rate equals 30 percent of income)

Method	2008	2009	2010	2011	2012	Total	Present Value
Straight-line	$1,380	$1,380	$1,380	$1,380	$1,380	$6,900	$5,231
Double-declining-balance	300	1,020	1,452	2,028	2,100	6,900	4,896

The tax payments included in Figure 9–16 are simply the income numbers in Figure 9–12 multiplied by the 30 percent tax rate. The total tax payments are equal for each method ($6,900), but the present values of the tax payments are not. The double-declining-balance method has a lower present value ($4,896), which means that the present value of the tax cost is less under double-declining-balance. Thus, the depreciation method chosen for tax purposes should be the one that recognizes the greatest amount of depreciation in the early years of an asset's life.

8. Appendix A, at the end of the text, covers the time value of money and the concept of present value.

The 2006 annual report of FedEx indicated that the company won a dispute with the Internal Revenue Service over the treatment of costs required to work on jet engines in the company's fleet of airplanes. FedEx had typically deducted the expenses immediately, characterizing them as routine jet engine maintenance costs. The IRS, on the other hand, argued that the expenditures should be capitalized and depreciated over a seven-year period. Explain the nature of this dispute, and why FedEx might want to deduct these costs.

DISPOSAL: RETIREMENTS, IMPAIRMENTS, SALES, AND TRADE-INS

Long-lived assets are acquired at cost, amortized as they are used in the operation of a business, and eventually disposed of. The disposal can take one of three forms: retirement, sale, or trade-in. The accounting procedures followed in all three cases have much in common. The depreciation is recorded to the date of the disposal, the cost and accumulated depreciation (or *net cost,* as in the case of intangibles and natural resources) of the long-lived asset are removed from the books, and any receipt or payment of cash or other assets is recorded when the asset is disposed of.[9] A gain or loss on the exchange is recognized in the amount of the difference between the book value of the asset and the net value of the receipt. Such gains and losses are usually found in the "other revenues and expenses" section of the income statement, but some manufacturers report them in cost of goods sold. Consider, for example, the following excerpt from the 2008 annual report of Kimberly-Clark Corporation:

When property is sold or retired, the cost of the property and related accumulated depreciation are removed from the consolidated balance sheet and any gain or loss on the transaction is included in income.

Retirement and Impairment of Long-Lived Assets

It is not unusual for companies to retire, close, or abandon their long-lived assets. **Retirement** of an asset can be due to obsolescence, the lack of a market for the asset in question, or closure by a regulatory body. On several occasions throughout their history, for example, the large U.S. automakers closed a number of plants in an effort to control costs. In such cases, the original cost and accumulated depreciation of the long-lived asset are simply written off the books. No gain or loss is recognized if the asset is fully depreciated at the time of the retirement. A loss is recognized if the asset is not yet fully depreciated.

Assume, for example, that Ajax and Brothers retired two pieces of equipment that were purchased ten years ago. Item 1 was purchased for $10,000 and was depreciated over eight years with no expected salvage value. At the time of its retirement, it was fully depreciated (i.e., accumulated depreciation was $10,000). Item 2 was purchased for $13,000 and was expected to have a $1,000 salvage value after its useful life of

9. Long-lived assets are rarely acquired or disposed of on the first or last day of the accounting period. In practice, therefore, companies must consider whether they wish to compute depreciation for partial periods. This text does not cover such computations for two reasons. First, many companies follow either of two policies: (1) recognize a full year of depreciation in the year of acquisition and zero depreciation in the year of disposition, or (2) recognize zero depreciation in the year of acquisition and a full year of depreciation in the year of disposition. Such policies eliminate the need to compute depreciation for partial periods. Second, computing depreciation for a partial period can get somewhat involved, especially under the accelerated methods, and we leave such discussion to intermediate accounting textbooks.

twelve years. At the time of its retirement, the accumulated depreciation account was equal to $10,000. The journal entries accompanying the retirement of the two pieces of equipment are as follows:

Accumulated Depreciation (+A) **10,000**
    Equipment (−A) **10,000**
Retired Item 1

Loss on Retirement (Lo, −RE) **3,000**
Accumulated Depreciation (+A) **10,000**
    Equipment (−A) **13,000**
Retired Item 2

No gain or loss is recognized on the retirement of Item 1 because an asset with a book value of zero was simply abandoned. The $3,000 loss on the retirement of Item 2 is recognized because the disposal of an asset with a book value of $3,000 generated no benefit.

Accounting for asset retirements is highly subjective and controversial. Generally accepted accounting principles require that when the value of an asset is "permanently impaired," it should be written down, but recent guidelines are subject to judgment, leaving management much discretion over the amount and timing of such write-downs. Simply, it is very difficult to determine exactly when an asset has been permanently impaired and by how much. In addition, these write-downs can be huge. General Motors, Chrysler, Ford, United, Sony, and Kyocera have each recorded multibillion-dollar asset write-downs in recent years. Almost no industry avoided huge impairment write-downs during the worldwide 2008–2009 recession. As part of an overall strategy to restructure company operations, management frequently chooses to record such write-downs in particularly poor years, enabling the company to "take the hit" when it does the least harm. This "taking a bath" strategy recognizes losses immediately that would normally be recorded as expenses (e.g., depreciation) in future years which, in turn, can improve future reported profits. The *Wall Street Journal* once reported that the FASB "cracked down on corporate America's habit of seizing upon restructurings as an occasion to take a bushel of write-offs all at once, making an earnings turnaround look speedier and more significant when it happens."[10]

Under IFRS, impairment charges on property, plant, and equipment are also recorded and reduce earnings. However, the criteria for when such charges should be recorded differ from U.S. GAAP, and the result is that under IFRS more frequent, but smaller, impairment charges are recognized. Also, under IFRS, recoveries from impairment charges recorded in prior periods serve to boost asset values and net income. These recoveries are not recognized under U.S. GAAP.

Management may also choose to record large "permanent impairment" write-downs in particularly good years. Polaroid, for example, recorded such a write-down in the same year it recognized a multibillion-dollar gain from a well-known legal settlement against Kodak for patent infringement. This reporting decision could be interpreted as "building a hidden reserve," which may enable Polaroid to "smooth" reported income over time. General Electric was once cited in the *Wall Street Journal* for using such write-offs frequently to "offset one-time gains."

10. Recently, the FASB passed a financial reporting standard that set criteria for asset write-downs. While these criteria may have reduced abuses, they are still very subjective.

When Eli Lilly, a major pharmaceutical, booked a $945 million restructuring and impairment charge on its income statement, it consisted primarily of two parts: asset impairments and employee termination severance costs, both of which resulted from shifting operations and closing plants in various parts of the world. The statement of cash flows included a $797 million add-back to net income for the restructuring charge. Discuss the general form of the journal entry made to record the restructuring charge, and why the statement cash flows included part of the charge as an add-back to net income.

Sale of Long-Lived Assets

Accounting for the sale of a long-lived asset is essentially the same as accounting for its retirement, except that cash is received in the exchange. For example, Computer Services purchased office furniture on March 1, 2008, for $24,000. At the time of the purchase, the company estimated the useful life of the furniture to be ten years and the salvage value to be $4,000, and it used the straight-line method of depreciation. On July 1, 2011 (three years and four months later), Computer Services remodeled its office and sold all the original furniture for $13,000. The company policy on recognizing depreciation for partial periods is to recognize no depreciation in the year of acquisition and a full year's depreciation in the year of disposition. The relevant calculations and the related journal entries appear in Figure 9–17.

FIGURE 9–17

The sale of a long-lived asset: Computer Services

Depreciation Computations		Depreciation Expense	Accumulated Depreciation
2008	(Year of acquisition)	$ 0	$ 0
2009	($24,000 − $4,000) ÷ 10 years	2,000	2,000
2010	($24,000 − $4,000) ÷ 10 years	2,000	4,000
2011	(Year of disposition)	2,000	6,000

JOURNAL ENTRIES

2011			
July 1	Depreciation Expense (E, −RE)	2,000	
	Accumulated Depreciation (−A)		2,000
	Recognized depreciation in year of disposition		
1	Cash (+A)	13,000	
	Accumulated Depreciation (+A)	6,000	
	Loss on Sale (Lo, −RE)	5,000	
	Furniture (−A)		24,000
	Sold long-lived asset		

In the operating section of its 2008 statement of cash flows, Target included a $33 million "loss on disposal of property and equipment" as an add-back to net earnings. Explain why and how a gain on disposal of property and equipment would be reported on the statement of cash flows.

On the date of sale, the depreciation is updated and the sale recorded. The loss on the sale ($5,000) represents the difference between the updated book value ($24,000 − $6,000) and the cash proceeds ($13,000).

> In May 2007 the *Wall Street Journal* reported that Japanese equipment manufacturer Konica Minolta returned to profitability in 2007 after it exited the camera and photo industries and concentrated on high-quality color printers. Current profitability was given a boost from the sale of fixed assets used in the exited business segments. How can the sale of a business segment give profits a boost? Would you expect this profitability boost to persist?

Trade-Ins of Long-Lived Assets

With a **trade-in,** two or more long-lived assets are exchanged, and cash is often received or paid. The methods used to account for such transactions depend on whether the exchanged assets are similar or dissimilar. This text limits its coverage to exchanges of **dissimilar assets,** those that are of a different general type, perform different functions, and are employed in different lines of business. The methods used to account for exchanges of similar assets are normally covered in intermediate accounting textbooks.

In general, the accounting procedures described in the section on retirements and the section on sales of long-lived assets also apply when dissimilar assets are exchanged.[11] That is, the depreciation of the asset given up is updated, its capitalized cost and accumulated depreciation are written off the books, and the receipt or payment of cash is recorded. However, a problem arises when accounting for exchanges because it is difficult to determine the dollar amount at which the asset received should be valued on the balance sheet. This problem, in turn, makes it equally difficult to measure the gain or loss that is recognized on the exchange.

The asset received in a trade-in should be valued on the balance sheet at either (1) the FMV of the assets given up or (2) the FMV of the assets received, whichever is clearly more evident and objectively determinable. Applying this rule is often difficult because the list price of an asset does not necessarily reflect its FMV, and determining the FMV of the asset given up is normally very subjective. Often the accountant must consult industry publications or obtain data on recent transactions involving similar assets to determine FMVs.

To illustrate, Mastoon Industries exchanged a delivery truck, which originally cost $17,000 (accumulated depreciation = $9,000) for a new printing press. The dealer agreed to accept the truck plus $12,000. Based on a list price of $18,000 for the printing press, the dealer claims to be granting a $6,000 ($18,000 − $12,000) trade-in allowance on the truck. However, the accountant for Mastoon finds that recent sales of comparable printing presses have realized, on average, $16,000, and a publication of used truck prices indicates that the value of the truck is approximately $4,000.

Given these facts, there are two acceptable ways to value the printing press on the balance sheet of Mastoon, each leading to the same result: (1) the FMV of the assets given up ($16,000 = $12,000 cash + $4,000 value of truck) or (2) the FMV of the

---

11. Keep in mind that a sale is simply the exchange of a long-lived asset for cash, a dissimilar asset.

asset received ($16,000, determined from recent sales). The resulting journal entry follows:

Printing Press (+A)	**16,000**	
Accumulated Depreciation (+A)	**9,000**	
Loss on Trade-In (Lo, −RE)	**4,000**	
Truck (−A)		**17,000**
Cash (−A)		**12,000**

Traded truck and cash for a press

Note also that the list price ($18,000) was not used as the FMV of the printing press. List prices are nothing more than invitations to negotiate, and astute buyers can often bargain for lower prices. Is it normally economically prudent, for example, to pay the list price for a new automobile? Moreover, since the actual FMV of the printing press seems to be $16,000 instead of $18,000, a better estimate of the trade-in allowance on the truck is $4,000 ($16,000 − $12,000), rather than $6,000 ($18,000 − $12,000). It is common for dealers, especially in the automobile industry, to lead customers to believe that they are receiving more for their trade-ins than they actually are.

?

Honeywell International reported the sale of four major business assets, recognizing losses on three of the sales ($131 million, $83 million, and $35 million) and a gain of $125 million on the fourth. Company footnotes disclose that Honeywell collected proceeds on these sales of $435 million in cash and investment securities. Discuss the general form of the entries made to record these sales, and how they affected the financial statements.

INTANGIBLE ASSETS

In Chapter 5 we noted that the value of a company as measured by the balance sheet (total assets − liabilities) rarely reflects its market capitalization value (value of a company as measured by the stock market). As of September 30, 2009, for example, the balance sheet value of Emerson Electric was $8.6 billion, while the stock market valued the company at $30.1 billion. The difference, $21.5 billion in this example, is often referred to as "intangibles," referring to those features about the company that are valued by the market but ignored by the balance sheet. These intangibles include the quality of a company's management, the value of its brands, good relationships with its customers and suppliers, and other factors that are important to the company's future but very difficult to measure. Certainly, the absence of these kinds of "assets" is a balance sheet weakness, and many argue that for a variety of companies, especially those in the Internet sector where "knowledge" is a company's most important asset, that weakness is quite significant. At present, neither U.S. GAAP nor IFRS allows the recognition of these kinds of assets. The principle of objectivity is just too strict. Consequently, analysts reviewing companies traded on U.S. markets must be content to rely on financial statements that do not capture some very important information.

In this section we discuss intangible assets, but only those that can be measured objectively. They are characterized by the rights, privileges, and benefits of possession rather than by physical existence. Some accountants also suggest that intangible

assets have a higher degree of uncertainty than tangible assets. Among other items, intangibles include the costs of acquiring copyrights, patents, trademarks, trade names, licenses, and goodwill. In general, the costs of acquiring intangible assets should be capitalized, and professional standards divide intangibles into two categories: those with definite lives (e.g., copyrights, patents, trademarks) and those with indefinite lives (e.g., goodwill). Those with definite lives should be amortized over their legal or useful lives, whichever is shorter. Most companies use the straight-line method for both reporting and tax purposes. Those with indefinite lives, similar to land, are not subject to amortization but must annually be considered for a possible impairment write-down.

> Under IFRS, intangible assets are also recorded on the balance sheet at cost. However, intangibles—except for goodwill—can be periodically revalued to fair market value if an active market for the intangible asset exists. The change in value, as for property, plant, and equipment, is not reflected on the income statement, but rather in shareholders' equity. Under IFRS, revaluing intangibles is an option, not a requirement. Under U.S. GAAP, revaluation is not an option.

COPYRIGHTS, PATENTS, AND TRADEMARKS

Copyrights are exclusive rights granted by law to control literary, musical, or artistic works. They are granted for seventy years beyond the life of the creator. Patents are granted by the U.S. Patent Office, and they give the holders exclusive rights to use, manufacture, or sell a product or process for a period of twenty years. A trademark or trade name is a word, phrase, or symbol that distinguishes or identifies a particular enterprise or product. The right to use a trademark is also granted by the U.S. Patent Office exclusively to the holder. The trademark lasts for a period of ten years but can be renewed indefinitely. Kleenex, Pepsi-Cola, Excedrin, and Wheaties are just a few examples of trade names that are so familiar that they are now a part of our culture.

THE COSTS OF DEVELOPING COMPUTER SOFTWARE

Statement of Financial Accounting Standards No. 86 specifies that the costs of developing and producing computer software products that will be available for sale or lease should be capitalized and amortized over their economic lives. Prior to this standard, all such costs incurred prior to the development of a prototype were expensed, and many small software development companies claimed that this practice understated net income, making it very difficult to attract outside capital. This standard had a significant impact on the financial statements of many companies involved in the development of computer software. For example, consider the excerpt below from a financial report of Wang Laboratories, Inc. Note that the net effect of the change increased net income by $19.3 million.

The Company adopted a change of accounting for costs of computer software. The change was made in accordance with provisions of Statement of Financial Accounting

Standards No. 86, which specifies that certain costs incurred in the development of computer software to be sold or leased to customers are to be capitalized and amortized over the economic life of the software product. Total costs capitalized during the year approximated $21.1 million, of which $1.8 million has been amortized and charged to expense.

GOODWILL

When one company purchases another for a dollar amount that is greater than the net FMV of the purchased company's assets and liabilities, goodwill is recognized on the purchasing company's balance sheet. Goodwill is a common asset on the balance sheets of major U.S. companies. *Accounting Trends and Techniques* (2009) reports that of the companies surveyed, 89 percent disclosed goodwill on their balance sheets. For many companies, such as Cisco Systems, Marriott Corporation, and General Electric, goodwill is quite significant. Importantly, goodwill is only recognized when it is acquired in an arm's-length transaction. It is never accrued on the balance sheet. The nature of goodwill and the methods used to account for it are discussed and illustrated in Chapter 8.

> **?**
>
> In 2008 Flowers Foods acquired the common stock of Holsum Holdings, which operates two bakeries in the Phoenix area. The purchase price was $144 million, and $65 million of that amount was allocated to intangible assets (other than goodwill), which appeared on the 2008 consolidated balance sheet of Flowers Foods. Of the $65 million in intangible assets, over $43 million was allocated to an account called "customer relationships." This intangible asset does not appear on the balance sheet of Holsum. What do you think this account refers to, and why does it appear on the balance sheet of Flowers Foods but not Holsum?

ORGANIZATIONAL COSTS

Organizational costs represent another subjective area in accounting for intangible assets. These costs are incurred prior to the start of a company's operations, typically including fees for underwriting, legal and accounting services, licenses, titles, and promotional expenditures. It is relatively clear that such costs are incurred to generate future revenues, and therefore, it seems that organizational costs should be capitalized. However, the service potential of such an asset cannot be associated with any future revenue in particular, and thus it is difficult to determine how it should be amortized. In a sense, organizational costs are of value to the company throughout its entire life. Does that mean that they should be left on the balance sheet indefinitely? Conceptually it may, but, similar to research and development costs discussed below, professional standards require that they be expensed.

RESEARCH AND DEVELOPMENT COSTS

Research and development (R&D) costs are incurred to generate revenue in future periods through the creation of new products or processes. Such costs are significant for many major U.S. manufacturers. In 2008, for example, Eli Lilly and

Company invested $3.8 billion in research and development, which amounted to about 19 percent of sales.

The matching principle suggests that R&D costs should be capitalized and amortized over future periods. However, it is difficult to match specific research and development expenditures with the creation of specific products or processes. Some R&D expenditures are for basic research, others lead to failures, and still others provide only indirect benefits or benefits that could not have been foreseen when the expenditure was incurred.

Concerned with the wide variety of practices used by companies to capitalize and amortize R&D expenditures, the FASB published *SFAS No. 2* in 1974. This pronouncement required that expenditures for most types of R&D costs be expensed in the year incurred, rather than capitalized and amortized as intangible assets. While this pronouncement promoted uniformity of accounting practices in the area of R&D, relieved pressures on auditors and managers to subjectively determine which R&D costs should be capitalized, and reduced some of management's ability to manipulate the financial statements, it is definitely inconsistent with the matching principle. In line with this standard, many R&D costs that will clearly benefit future periods are being immediately expensed. As with organizational costs, accounting for R&D costs represents an example of theoretical measurement principles being compromised in the interest of practical considerations.

The requirement to expense all R&D costs can have significant effects on the financial statements. Had Abbott Laboratories, for example, been allowed to capitalize half of its R&D expenditures in 2008, its net income would have increased by nearly $900 million. There is also some evidence suggesting that the negative effects on net income and other important financial ratios of *SFAS No. 2* serve to discourage companies from making R&D expenditures. In one particular case, for example, Boeing reduced its R&D expenditures in one year by $500 million. Some believe that the requirement to expense R&D may have been part of the cause.

> Under IFRS, under some circumstances internally generated development costs are capitalized and amortized. Such costs are expensed under U.S. GAAP.

IFRS VS. U.S. GAAP: REVALUATIONS TO FAIR MARKET VALUE

One very important way in which IFRS differs from U.S. GAAP involves the use of fair market value as a basis for valuation on the balance sheet and, as shown in this chapter, there is no better example of this difference than in the area of long-lived assets. Under U.S. GAAP, long-lived assets must be accounted for at original cost less accumulated depreciation (amortization), and if the market value of the asset permanently falls below the balance sheet carrying value, an impairment charge must be recorded, and cannot be reversed in later periods if the value of the asset recovers. Under IFRS, companies can either follow the U.S. GAAP method or they can periodically revalue their long-lived assets to fair market value—recognizing not only impairments, but also increases and recoveries of asset values. In essence, U.S. GAAP tends to follow a conservative "lower-of-cost-or-market" valuation principle, where market price reductions are recognized but market price increases are not. IFRS, by contrast, allows managers the option to more closely follow a pure market valuation principle, where both market value increases and decreases are recognized.

Interestingly, while IFRS companies have the option to follow a market value approach, most choose not to. Active markets often do not exist for long-lived assets because assets like property, plant, and equipment, as well as intangibles, are frequently customized for the specific needs of the company, resulting in limited markets for these kinds of assets. The lack of an active market discourages revaluations by making it difficult to find reliable market values. Further, asset write-ups increase the depreciation base, which in turn increases future depreciation expenses and lowers future reported profits—normally unattractive to management. With respect to market value accounting, the only area where most IFRS companies depart from the U.S. GAAP approach is that they tend to recognize recoveries of impairments recorded in prior periods.

As discussed in Chapter 8, U.S. GAAP now includes a provision—the fair value option—that allows companies to revalue financial instruments (not long-lived assets) to market value, with the change in market values being reflected in income (mark-to-market accounting). Recall as well that special disclosures (Levels 1, 2, and 3) are required to describe in more detail the basis for the market value estimates, and these disclosures signal the extent to which the estimates are reliable.

Both U.S. GAAP and IFRS appear to be moving toward more market-value-based accounting, and away from historical cost. This is a very important movement, but it may well be a long journey. There is no easy answer to which is better—a balance sheet consisting of assets reflecting useful, but relatively unreliable, market values or a balance sheet consisting of assets reflecting less useful, but very reliable, historical costs. Further, if market values are represented on the balance sheet, should the change in market value from one period to the next be reflected in earnings (and ultimately retained earnings), or should it skip the income statement and be reflected only in shareholders' equity (and comprehensive income)?

ROE EXERCISE: MANAGING LONG-LIVED ASSETS AND RETURN ON EQUITY

The ROE model, introduced and illustrated in Appendix 5A, provides a framework linking the management of a company's operating, investing, and financing activities to its return on the shareholders' investment (return on equity). For many companies (e.g., manufacturers, services, and companies that grow via acquisition) the management of long-lived assets is an important investment activity.

Long-lived asset turnover (sales ÷ average long-lived assets) is a measure of the extent to which the investment in long-lived assets generates sales volume. An increase in this ratio (i.e., increasing the level of sales per dollar invested in long-lived assets) puts upward pressure on total asset turnover, which puts upward pressure on return on assets (ROA), which in turn puts upward pressure on return on equity (ROE). Put simply, generating a large amount of sales with a small investment in long-lived assets is better for the shareholders than generating a small amount of sales with a large investment in long-lived assets. Consequently, an important role of management is to ensure that all long-lived assets (property, plant, and equipment and intangibles) are efficiently helping to generate the sales of goods and/or services. As indicated in the ROE model, effective management in this area can lead to higher shareholder returns.

ROE ANALYSIS

Access the Web site (http://www.wiley.com/college/pratt) and conduct an ROE analysis on Dow Chemical versus Dupont, and/or Kroger versus SuperValu, all of which carry significant investments in long-lived assets, paying special attention to how the management of the companies' various long-lived assets affects asset turnover, ROA, and ROE.

REVIEW PROBLEM

Norby Enterprises purchased equipment on January 1, 2009, for $8,000. It cost $1,500 to have the equipment shipped to the plant and $500 to have it installed. The equipment was estimated to have a five-year useful life and a salvage value of $1,000. On January 1, 2012, the equipment was overhauled at a cost of $1,000, and the overhaul extended its estimated useful life by an additional year (from five to six years). On January 1, 2013 the equipment and $13,000 cash were traded for a dissimilar piece of equipment with a FMV of $15,000. Norby uses the straight-line method of depreciation. The computations and journal entries related to the acquisition, depreciation, overhaul, and disposal of the equipment appear in Figure 9–18.

FIGURE 9-18   Solution to review problem: Norby Enterprises

Description/Date	Journal Entry			Accumulated Depreciation	Book Value[a]
Acquisition of equipment (1/1/09)	Equipment (+A) Cash (−A)	10,000[b] 	 10,000	0	10,000
Depreciation[c] (12/31/09)	Depreciation Expense (E, −RE) Accumulated Depreciation (−A)	1,800 	 1,800	1,800	8,200
Depreciation[c] (12/31/10)	Depreciation Expense (E, −RE) Accumulated Depreciation (−A)	1,800 	 1,800	3,600	6,400
Depreciation[c] (12/31/11)	Depreciation Expense (E, −RE) Accumulated Depreciation (−A)	1,800 	 1,800	5,400	4,600
Overhaul (1/1/12)	Equipment (+A) Cash (−A)	1,000 	 1,000	5,400	5,600
Depreciation[d] (12/31/12)	Depreciation Expense (E, −RE) Accumulated Depreciation (−A)	1,533 	 1,533	6,933	4,067

Trade-in (1/1/13)	Equipment (new) (+A)
	Accumulated Depreciation (+A)
	Loss on Trade-In (Lo, −RE)
	    Equipment (old) (−A)
	    Cash (−A)
		15,000
		6,933
		2,067
		
			11,000
			13,000		

[a]Book value = Equipment cost − accumulated depreciation
[b]Equipment cost: $8,000 purchase + $1,500 shipping + $500 installation = $10,000
[c]Depreciation expense before overhaul: ($10,000 cost − $1,000 salvage) ÷ 5-year life = $1,800
[d]Depreciation expense after overhaul: ($4,600 book value + $1,000 overhaul − $1,000 salvage) ÷ 3-year remaining life = $1,533

SUMMARY OF KEY POINTS

● *How the matching principle underlies the methods used to account for long-lived assets.*

Long-lived assets are used in the operations of the business, providing benefits that extend beyond the current accounting period. Included are land (not held for resale), buildings, machinery, equipment, costs incurred to acquire the right to extract natural resources, and intangible assets.

According to the matching principle, efforts (expenses) should be matched against benefits (revenues) in the period when the benefits are recognized. Since the benefits provided by long-lived assets extend beyond the current period, the costs of acquiring long-lived assets are capitalized in the period of acquisition and then amortized as their useful lives expire.

● *Major questions that are addressed when accounting for long-lived assets and how the financial statements are affected.*

Accounting for most long-lived assets consists primarily of answering three questions: (1) What dollar amount should be included in the capitalized cost of the long-lived asset? (2) Over what time period should this cost be amortized? (3) At what rate should this cost be amortized? These questions are addressed for all long-lived assets except land and goodwill, which is not subject to amortization.

Answering these questions in various ways can have significant effects on the timing of asset and income recognition. Capitalizing instead of expensing a cost defers expense recognition, giving rise to higher asset values and net income in the period of acquisition. Similarly, allocating the cost of a long-lived asset over a long period of time defers expense recognition and creates higher asset and income values in the early years of the asset's life. However, these financial statement effects are a matter of timing, not magnitude. That is, a method giving rise to higher asset and income values in the early years of an asset's life will create lower asset and income values in the later years.

● *Major economic consequences associated with the methods used to account for long-lived assets.*

The methods used to account for long-lived assets can have significant economic effects. The amount of cost to capitalize, the estimated useful life, the chosen amortization method, and the timing and amount of permanent write-downs can have significant effects on the timing of net income and important financial ratios. These numbers are used by interested parties to evaluate management and assess earning power and solvency, and to determine credit ratings. They are also used in compensation contracts and debt covenants to control and direct management behavior.

● *Costs that should be included in the capitalized cost of a long-lived asset.*

The acquisition cost of a long-lived asset is determined by either (1) the FMV of the acquired asset or (2) the FMV of what was given up to acquire the asset, whichever is more readily determinable. In almost all cases, the FMV of what was given up is used because cash, which by definition is at FMV, is normally given up in such exchanges. Furthermore, the capitalized cost (i.e., the FMV of what was given up) should include all costs required to bring the asset into serviceable or usable condition and location. This includes not only the cost of purchasing a long-lived asset, but also costs such as freight, installation, taxes, title fees, idle time while the asset is being installed, the costs of preparing land for use in the business, indirect overhead costs incurred while manufacturing a long-lived asset, and interest costs on borrowed funds used to construct long-lived assets. When long-lived assets are purchased as part of a group of assets for a single, lump-sum price, the overall price is allocated to each asset on the basis of its relative FMV.

● *Accounting treatment of postacquisition expenditures.*

Postacquisition expenditures are costs incurred subsequent to the acquisition or manufacture of a long-lived asset. Costs incurred to improve the asset (as defined by a set of criteria) are called

betterments and should be capitalized as part of the cost of the asset and amortized over its remaining life. Betterments are usually infrequent and tend to involve relatively large dollar amounts. Costs incurred to repair an asset or maintain its current level of productivity are classified as maintenance and are immediately expensed. Maintenance expenditures tend to be periodic and relatively small. It is often difficult to distinguish between a betterment and a maintenance expenditure, so management has much reporting discretion in this area.

● *How the cost of a long-lived asset is allocated over its useful life and the alternative allocation methods.*

To allocate the cost of a long-lived asset over its useful life, three issues must be addressed: (1) the useful life must be estimated, (2) the salvage value must be estimated, and (3) a cost allocation method must be chosen. The useful-life estimate defines the period of time over which the asset's cost is to be amortized. The capitalized cost less the salvage value defines the amortization base, the total amount of cost to be amortized. The cost allocation method determines the amount of cost to be amortized each period.

Three basic cost-allocation methods are considered systematic and reasonable: (1) straight-line, (2) accelerated, and (3) activity. The straight-line method recognizes equal amounts of depreciation each period throughout the life of the asset. Accelerated methods, including double-declining-balance, recognize larger amounts of depreciation in the early periods of an asset's life and smaller amounts in the later periods. The activity method bases the amount of amortization each period on the activity of the asset during that period. The life of the asset is expressed in terms of a unit of activity, and as each unit is produced, a portion of the asset's cost is amortized. This method is normally used to deplete the costs associated with mining natural resources.

● *Disposition and impairment of long-lived assets.*

Long-lived assets are disposed of through retirement, sale, or trade-in. When a long-lived asset is retired, depreciation is updated, the original cost and accumulated depreciation of the asset are written off the books, and a loss is recognized if the asset is not fully depreciated as of the time of the retirement. Determining when and how to write down such assets is very subjective, and long-lived assets should be periodically subjected to an impairment test to see if they need to be written down to market value.

When long-lived assets are sold for cash, depreciation is updated, cash is debited, the original cost and accumulated depreciation are written off the books, and a gain or loss, which represents the difference between the book value of the asset and the proceeds, is recognized on the transaction.

When two dissimilar assets and cash are exchanged, depreciation is updated, the cash receipt or payment is recorded, the original cost and accumulated depreciation of the asset given up are written off the books, the asset received is given a dollar value, and a gain or loss is recognized on the transaction. The general rule for valuing the asset received is to use the FMV of the assets given up (cash and the asset given up) or the FMV of the asset received, whichever is more objectively determinable.

● *The increasing importance of fair market value and issues that must be addressed when using fair market value as a basis for long-lived assets.*

IFRS relies more heavily on fair market value accounting than U.S. GAAP, while U.S. GAAP appears to be moving in this direction with the passage of the fair value option for financial instruments (see Chapter 8). This movement is motivated primarily by the belief that fair market values are more useful for decision making than historical costs. However, fair market values are less reliable, and when they are used to value balance sheet assets, it is important that they be accompanied by disclosures describing how they were determined. Also, when using fair market value for balance sheet assets, a major question arises concerning how to treat the changes in value from one period to the next: Should they be reflected on the income statement (and ultimately retained earnings), or should they not be reflected on the income statement and represented only in shareholders' equity (and comprehensive income)?

KEY TERMS

Note: Definitions for these terms are provided in the glossary at the end of the text.

Accelerated method (p. 399)
Activity method (p. 402)
Amortized (p. 386)
Betterments (p. 394)
Deferred costs (p. 385)
Deplete (p. 402)
Depreciation (p. 387)
Depreciation base (p. 398)
Dissimilar assets (p. 409)
Double-declining-balance method (p. 399)
Fixed assets (p. 385)
Intangible assets (p. 385)

Internal Revenue Code (p. 404)
Land (p. 385)
Maintenance (p. 394)
Natural resource costs (p. 385)
Physical obsolescence (p. 395)
Postacquisition expenditures (p. 393)
Retirement (p. 406)
Salvage value (p. 395)
Straight-line method (p. 398)
Technical obsolescence (p. 396)
Trade-in (p. 409)

ETHICS in the Real World

"With a simple bookkeeping change, companies can turn profits into losses—and vice versa. In many cases, the changes are perfectly justified, but the practice creates big opportunities for abuse."

So began a *Forbes* article that focused on the difficulty involved with determining the depreciation and/or amortization rates for long-lived assets and the level of discretionary judgment used by management in the area. Major U.S. companies, such as Cineplex Odeon, Blockbuster, General Motors, IBM, and Delta Air Lines, are cited in the article for the wide variety of methods they use. Blockbuster once changed the amortization period for its videotapes from nine to thirty-six months, adding nearly 20 percent to its reported income; GM added $2.55 to its earnings-per-share number by adjusting the way in which it amortizes its tools and dies; IBM increased its "bottom line" by $375 million by changing from accelerated to straight-line; and Delta depreciates its planes over fifteen years, while most of the rest of the airline industry uses a twenty- to twenty-five-year useful life. In each case, the policies were disclosed and within the guidelines of GAAP; the article notes further that "when it comes to amortization and depreciation, GAAP provides only the vaguest of guidelines."

However, the SEC chief accountant suggests that the disclosures are not adequate: "When a company says it's depreciating its plant over three to forty years, we don't know the intimate details and there is no practical way we could. I'd like accountants to take more responsibility for it."

ETHICAL ISSUE Is it ethical for management to use methods to account for long-lived assets that are within the guidelines of GAAP but fail to provide disclosure that is sufficient for shareholders to understand the financial condition and performance of the company?

INTERNET RESEARCH EXERCISE

The chapter points out that many companies are aggressively recognizing asset impairments, and some suspect that the companies are doing so as a way to manage earnings. The FASB recently established a standard to reduce these practices. Identify the number of this standard, when it was passed, and briefly describe its contents. Begin your search at www.fasb.org/st/.

BRIEF EXERCISES

BE9-1

Change in
depreciation method

A footnote to the financial statements of Allegheny Teledyne Incorporated stated the
following:

> *The straight-line method of depreciation was adopted for all property placed into service
> after July 1, 1996. Buildings and equipment acquired prior to that time are accounted for
> under accelerated methods. The company believes that the new method will more appropri-
> ately reflect its financial results by better allocating costs of new property over the useful
> lives of these assets. In addition, the new method conforms more closely to that prevalent in
> the industries in which Allegheny operates.*

a. What impact will the new method have on Allegheny's net income?
b. Briefly discuss some of the reasons that may have caused Allegheny to change the method
of depreciation.
c. Where else in the annual report could one find evidence that Allegheny changed its
method of depreciation?

BE9-2

Depreciation
and amortization

The Boeing Company reported in its 2008 annual report $1,325 million in depreciation
expense and $117 million in amortization expense for the year ending December 31, 2008.

a. Describe how the recognition of depreciation and amortization affects the basic accounting equation.
b. As reported in the footnotes, Boeing's accumulated depreciation balance grew during the
year from $12,280 million to $12,795 million. The historic cost of property, plant, and
equipment was $21,579 and $21,042 in 2008 and 2007, respectively. During 2008 the
company purchased property, plant, and equipment for a total of $1,674 million and col-
lected proceeds of $34 million on sales of property, plant, and equipment. Compute the
gain or loss on the sale of property, plant, and equipment in 2008. On which financial
statement would this appear, and how would these transactions affect the statement of
cash flows?

BE9-3

Acquisition of
fixed assets

The footnote below was taken from the 2008 annual report of Johnson & Johnson (dollars
in millions).

	2008	2007
Land and land improvements	$ 886	$ 756
Buildings and building equipment	7,720	7,913
Machinery and equipment	15,234	14,554
Construction in progress	3,552	3,243
	$27,392	$26,466
Less accumulated depreciation	13,027	12,281
	$14,365	$14,185

a. Approximately how much did Johnson & Johnson invest in land during 2008?
b. Why did accumulated depreciation increase during 2008?
c. Johnson & Johnson uses the straight-line method of depreciation. If the company used
an accelerated method, what effect would that decision have on the balance sheet?
d. What dollar amount appeared on Johnson & Johnson's 2008 balance sheet for property,
plant, and equipment?

BE9-4

IFRS, long-lived assets,
and the statement
of cash flows

In the operating section of its 2009 IFRS-based statement of cash flows, Kyocera, a Japanese
telecommunications firm, reported the following (in millions of yen):

	2009
Net income	298,040
. . .	. . .
Depreciation and amortization	985,626
. . .	. . .
Loss on impairment of PP&E and intangibles	27,576
. . .	. . .
Gain on sale of PP&E and intangibles	(83,980)
. . .	. . .
Net cash provided by operating activities	987,818

a. Describe the basic form of the entries recorded by Kyocera related to the three adjustments listed above to the operating section of the statement of cash flows.
b. Explain why these amounts appear on the statement of cash flows, and why depreciation and amortization and the loss on impairment of PP&E and intangibles are positive numbers, while the gain on the sale of PP&E and intangibles is a negative number.
c. Where on the statement of cash flows could you find the proceeds from the sales of PP&E and intangibles during 2009?
d. If Kyocera followed U.S. GAAP instead of IFRS, would you expect to see similar adjustments to the operating section of the statement of cash flows?

EXERCISES

E9–1

Determining the capitalized cost and depreciation base

Lowery, Inc. purchased new plant equipment on January 1, 2011. The company paid $920,000 for the equipment, $62,000 for transportation of the equipment, and $10,000 for insurance on the equipment while it was being transported. The company also estimates that over the equipment's useful life it will require additional power, which will cause utility costs to increase $90,000. The equipment has an estimated salvage value of $50,000.

a. What amount should the company capitalize for this equipment on January 1, 2011?
b. What is the depreciation base of this equipment?
c. What amount will be depreciated over the life of this equipment?

E9–2

Allocating cost on the basis of relative market value

AJB Real Estate purchased a ten-acre tract of land for $320,000. The company divided the land into four lots of two and one-half acres each. Lot 1 had a beautiful view of the mountains and was valued at $160,000. Lot 2 had a stream running through it and was valued at $120,000. Lots 3 and 4 were each valued at $60,000. Assume that each lot is sold for the values indicated. Compute the profit on each of the four sales.

E9–3

Which costs are subject to depreciation?

Firton Brothers purchased for $90,000 a tract of land that included an abandoned warehouse. The warehouse was razed, and the site was prepared for a new building at a cost of $10,000. Scrap materials from the warehouse were sold for $7,000. A building was then constructed for $140,000, a driveway and parking lot were laid for $32,000, and permanent landscaping was completed for $4,000. Firton Brothers depreciates fixed assets over a twenty-year period using the straight-line method.

a. Compute the amount of cost to be placed in the land, land improvements, and building accounts.
b. Assuming a salvage value of zero, compute the depreciation expense associated with the items above for the first year.

E9–4

Betterments or maintenance?

The following items represent common postacquisition expenditures incurred on machinery:

a. Lubrication service
b. Painting costs
c. Cleaning expenditures
d. Rewiring costs to increase operating speed
e. Repairs
f. Replacement of defective parts
g. An overhaul to increase useful life
h. Cost of a muffler to reduce machine noise
i. Costs of redesign to increase output

Identify each item as a betterment or a maintenance item.

E9–5

How the matching principle affects the timing of income recognition

The condensed balance sheet as of December 31, 2011, for Van Den Boom Enterprises follows:

Assets		Liabilities and Shareholders' Equity	
Current assets	$40,000	Liabilities	$35,000
Land	50,000	Shareholders' equity	55,000
		Total liabilities and	
Total assets	$90,000	shareholders' equity	$90,000

Revenues and expenses (other than amortization) are predicted to be $65,000 and $20,000, respectively, for 2012, 2013, and 2014. All revenues and expenses are received or paid in cash. On January 1, 2012, Van Den Boom pays $40,000 cash for an item.

a. Assume that Van Den Boom Enterprises engaged in operating activities only during 2012, 2013, and 2014. Prepare income statements for 2012, 2013, and 2014 and the balance sheet as of December 31 for 2012, 2013, and 2014, assuming the $40,000 cash payment is treated in each of the following ways:
   (1) Immediately expensed.
   (2) Capitalized and amortized evenly over two years.
   (3) Capitalized and amortized evenly over three years.
b. Compute the total income recognized over the three-year period under each assumption above.
c. What is interesting about the December 31, 2011, balance sheet prepared under all three assumptions?

E9–6

The effect of estimated useful life on income and dividends

Stork Freight Company owns and operates fifteen planes that deliver packages worldwide. The planes were purchased on January 1, 2008, for $1 million each. The company estimates that the planes will be scrapped after twelve years. Stork Freight uses straight-line depreciation.

a. Assume that in a typical year the company generates revenues of $50 million and operating expenses (excluding depreciation expense) of $25 million. Prepare an income statement for a typical year.
b. Assume that the company had originally estimated the useful life at six years instead of twelve. Prepare an income statement for a typical year. What is the percent change in net income?
c. Assume that the company policy is to pay dividends in the amount of 30 percent of net income. Compute the difference in the dividend payment between the two cases above.

E9–7

Revising the estimated life

Portland Products purchased a machine on January 1, 2008, for $60,000 and estimated its useful life and salvage value at five years and $12,000, respectively. On January 1, 2011, the company added three years to the original useful-life estimate.

a. Compute the book value of the machine as of January 1, 2011, assuming that Portland uses the straight-line method of depreciation.
b. Prepare the journal entry entered by the company to record depreciation on December 31, 2011.

E9-8

Different amortization methods achieve different objectives

The controller of Elton Furniture Store is currently trying to decide what depreciation method to use for a particular fixed asset. The controller has prepared the following list of possible objectives that might be accomplished through a depreciation method. Which method(s):

a. most closely matches the asset's cost with the benefits resulting from the asset's use?
b. allocates the cost of the asset over the asset's useful life?
c. generates the largest net income in the last year of the asset's useful life?
d. does not directly use the asset's salvage value in computing the depreciation expense?
e. is best for tax purposes (i.e., minimizes the present value of future tax payments)?
f. recognizes an equal charge to expense every period?
g. generates the largest depreciation expense in the asset's last year?
h. does not allow the asset's book value to drop below the asset's salvage value?

Consider each objective independently, and indicate the depreciation method(s) that achieve each objective.

E9-9

Computing depreciation and choosing a depreciation method

Benick Industries purchased a new lathe on January 1, 2011, for $300,000. Benick estimates that the lathe will have a useful life of four years and that the company will be able to sell it at the end of the fourth year for $60,000.

a. Compute the depreciation expense that Benick Industries would record for 2011, 2012, 2013, and 2014 under each of the following methods:
   (1) Straight-line depreciation
   (2) Double-declining-balance depreciation
b. If you were the president of Benick Industries, what might you consider when choosing a depreciation method for financial reporting purposes? Why?

E9-10

Depreciation calculations and journal entries

Stockton Corporation purchased a new computer system on January 1, 2011, for $300,000 cash. The company also incurred $25,000 in installation costs and $10,000 to train its employees on the new system. The computer system has an estimated useful life of five years and an estimated salvage value of $70,000.

a. Prepare the entry to record the acquisition of the computer system.
b. Calculate the depreciation expense recognized each year over the life of the system for each of the following assumptions:
   (1) Stockton uses straight-line depreciation.
   (2) Stockton uses double-declining-balance depreciation.
c. Provide the journal entry recorded by Stockton at the end of 2011 under the double-declining-balance method.

E9-11

The activity method of depreciation

Apex Trucking purchased a truck for $100,000 on January 1, 2011. The useful life of the truck was estimated to be either five years or 200,000 miles. Salvage value was estimated at $20,000. Over the actual life of the truck, it logged the following miles:

Year 1	48,000 miles
Year 2	35,000 miles
Year 3	40,000 miles
Year 4	25,000 miles
Year 5	35,000 miles
Year 6	10,000 miles

At the end of the sixth year, the truck was sold for $12,000.
   Prepare the journal entries to record depreciation over the life of the truck and its sale, assuming these methods:

1. Activity method
2. Straight-line method

E9-12

Depletion and matching

Natural Extraction Industries paid $4 million for the right to drill for oil on a tract of land in western Texas. Engineers estimated that this oil deposit would produce 100,000 barrels of crude oil.

a.   During the first year of operations, Natural Extraction extracted 30,000 barrels of oil. Prepare the entry to record depletion for the first year.

b.   During the second year, the company extracted 50,000 barrels. Prepare the entry to record depletion for the second year.

c.   What dollar amount would Natural Extraction report on its balance sheet at the end of the second year for oil deposits?

E9–13

An error in recording the acquisition of a fixed asset

Lewis Real Estate purchased a new photocopy machine on January 1, 2011, for $120,000. The company's bookkeeper made the following entry to record the acquisition:

Depreciation Expense (E, −RE)   120,000
   Cash (−A)   120,000

The photocopy machine has an estimated useful life of four years and an estimated salvage value of $20,000. Lewis Real Estate did not make any adjusting entry on December 31, 2011, or in any subsequent year associated with the photocopy machine. Furthermore, the company never discovered the error.

a.   Assume that Lewis Real Estate uses the straight-line method to depreciate its fixed assets. Compute the values for the following chart:

Year	Depreciation Expense per Company's Books	Correct Depreciation Expense	Annual Difference	Cumulative Difference
2011				
2012				
2013				
2014				

b.   In what direction and by how much will the accumulated depreciation account be misstated as of December 31, 2013?

c.   In what direction and by how much will the retained earnings account be misstated *prior* to closing entries on December 31, 2013?

d.   In what direction and by how much will the retained earnings account be misstated *after* closing entries on December 31, 2013?

E9–14

Fixed asset sales

Savory Enterprises reported the following information regarding the company's fixed assets in the footnotes to the company's 2011 financial statements:

Office furniture $500,000
Less: Accumulated depreciation   300,000   200,000

a.   Assume that Savory Enterprises sells all of its office furniture for $235,000 in cash on January 1, 2012. Prepare the entry to record the sale.

b.   Assume that Savory Enterprises sells all of its office furniture for $185,000 in cash on January 1, 2012. Prepare the entry to record the sale.

E9–15

Retiring, selling, and trading in a fixed asset

Paris Company purchased equipment on January 1, 2009, for $25,000. The estimated useful life of the equipment is five years, the salvage value is $5,000, and the company uses the double-declining-balance method to depreciate fixed assets.

a.   Provide the journal entry assuming the equipment is scrapped after three years.

b.   Provide the journal entry assuming the equipment is scrapped after five years.

c.   Provide the journal entry assuming the equipment is sold for $8,000 after three years.

d.   Provide the journal entry assuming, at the end of the fifth year, the equipment and $28,000 cash are traded in for a dissimilar asset with an objectively determined FMV of $30,000.

E9–16

Reverse T-account
analysis

The following financial information below was taken from the records of White Bones, Inc.

	2011	2010
BALANCE SHEET		
Equipment	$37,500	$32,700
Less: Accumulated depreciation	17,600	14,300
Net book value	$19,900	$18,400
INCOME STATEMENTS		
Depreciation expense	$ 7,200	$ 6,800
Gain on sale of equipment	2,100	0

Note: The company purchased equipment for $12,000 during 2011.

a.   How much cash was collected on the sale of equipment during 2011?
b.   Reconstruct the entry that recorded the sale of equipment during 2011.

REAL DATA

E9–17

Inferring
information from
the financial
statements

The information was taken from the 2008 annual report of Intel, a world-leading supplier to the Internet economy (dollars in millions).

	2008	2007
Property, plant, and equipment	$48,088	$46,052
Less: Accumulated depreciation	(30,544)	(29,134)
Depreciation expense	4,360	4,546
Investments in property, plant, and equipment	$ 5,197	$ 5,000

a.   From which of the financial statements was each figure taken?
b.   Estimate the cost of property, plant, and equipment sold during 2008.
c.   Estimate the accumulated depreciation associated with the property, plant, and equipment sold during 2008.
d.   Assume that the property, plant, and equipment was sold during 2008 for $100 million cash. Estimate the gain or loss recognized on the sale. On what financial statement(s) would this amount appear?

E9–18

Reverse T-account
analysis

The following financial information was taken from the records of Frederickson and Peffer.

	2011	2010
BALANCE SHEET		
Equipment	$26,900	$23,400
Less: Accumulated depreciation	10,500	9,800
Net book value	$16,400	$13,600
INCOME STATEMENT		
Depreciation expense	$ 3,800	$ 3,500
Loss on sale of equipment	900	0
STATEMENT OF CASH FLOWS		
Cash received on sale of equipment	$ 4,300	$ 0

a.   Reconstruct the entry that recorded the sale of equipment during 2011.
b.   How much equipment was purchased during 2011?

E9–19

Intangible assets:
Expense or capitalize
and amortize?

Swift Corporation incorporated on January 1, 2011, and incurred $45,000 in organization costs.

a.   Should Swift Corporation capitalize or expense these costs? Defend your answer.
b.   If these costs are capitalized, over what period of time should they be amortized? Provide the amortization journal entry for a single year if the maximum period of time is chosen.

    c. What arguments could be used to justify capitalizing organization costs but not allocating them to future periods?

    d. Assume that during 2011, Swift acquired a patent for $65,000. Should this cost be expensed or capitalized? Why one and not the other?

    e. Assume that during 2011, Swift invested $220,000 to research and develop new products. Should these costs be expensed or capitalized?

    f. What arguments could be used to justify capitalizing research and development costs, and if capitalized, how should these costs be amortized to future periods?

E9–20

The capitalized cost of a patent

The following information was taken from the internal financial records of Southern Robotics regarding a patent filed in 2011 for a new robotics arm used for manufacturing:

1. Legal and filing fees of $50,000 were paid during 2011 for filing the patent.
2. Legal fees of $200,000 were incurred and paid during 2012 to defend the patent against infringement by another company.

The patent was granted on December 31, 2011. The company estimated that the patent would provide an economic benefit to the company for five years. It is company policy not to amortize intangible assets in the year of acquisition.

    a. Assume that Southern Robotics successfully defended its patent against the infringement.
      (1) What amount should Southern Robotics report for this patent on the company's December 31, 2011, balance sheet?
      (2) What amount should Southern Robotics report for this patent on the company's December 31, 2012, balance sheet?
      (3) Prepare the entry to amortize the patent on December 31, 2012.
    b. Assume that Southern Robotics was unsuccessful in defending its patent against the infringement.
      (1) What amount should Southern Robotics report for this patent on the company's December 31, 2011, balance sheet?
      (2) What amount should Southern Robotics report for this patent on the company's December 31, 2012, balance sheet?
      (3) Prepare the entry to write off the patent.

REAL DATA

E9–21

Recognition of goodwill

When Bristol-Myers Squibb purchased DuPont Pharmaceuticals from E.I. DuPont de Nemours for $7.8 billion in cash, it acquired assets with a fair market value of $5.1 billion and assumed the liabilities of DuPont Pharmaceuticals valued at $1.1 billion.

REQUIRED:
    a. How much goodwill was recognized on the acquisition?
    b. Describe how this transaction affected the basic accounting equation.

REAL DATA

E9–22

U.S. GAAP/IFRS differences regarding fair market value

In the footnotes to its IFRS-based 2008 financial statements, European Aeronautical Defense and Space Company (EADS), parent company for Airbus, includes a description of a long-lived asset account called "investment property," which is leased to a third party. The historical cost of the property is 212 and accumulated depreciation is 125, leading to a balance sheet value of 87 (all in million euros). The footnote also reports that an estimate of the fair market value of the property is 88 million euros.

    a. Describe the differences between U.S. GAAP and IFRS regarding how this type of property is accounted for.
    b. How has EADS chosen to account for the investment property?
    c. What adjustment would EADS make to the 2008 financial statements if it chose to carry the investment property on its balance sheet at fair market value?

PROBLEMS

P9–1

How much
to capitalize?

Stonebrecker International recently purchased new manufacturing equipment. The equipment cost $1 million. The company also incurred additional costs related to the acquisition of the equipment. The total cost to transport the equipment to Stonebrecker's plant was $80,000, half of which was paid by Stonebrecker. The company also paid $8,000 to insure the equipment while it was being transported to its plant. The initial installation costs totaled $20,000. After installing the equipment, however, it was discovered that the floor under the equipment would have to be reinforced. Materials and direct labor to reinforce the floor totaled $15,000. While the equipment was being installed and the floor was being reinforced, the plant workers could not perform their normal functions. The cost to Stonebrecker of the employee downtime was $10,000. Stonebrecker estimates that the equipment will have a salvage value of $100,000 in ten years.

REQUIRED:
a.   What dollar amount should Stonebrecker capitalize on its books for this equipment?
b.   Prepare the journal entry to capitalize the equipment.
c.   What is the depreciation base of this equipment?
d.   Over the life of this equipment, what dollar amount will be depreciated under the straight-line method? Under the double-declining-balance method?

P9–2

Lump-sum purchases
and cost allocations

The JHP Company purchased a building, some office equipment, two cranes, and some land on January 1, 2011, for a total of $1 million cash. JHP has obtained the following appraisals of these assets:

Asset	FMV on 1/1/11	Estimated Life	Estimated Salvage Value
Building	$300,000	20 years	$75,000
Office equipment	150,000	3 years	35,000
Crane	75,000	5 years	15,000
Crane	75,000	5 years	15,000
Land	600,000	Indefinite	

JHP Company uses the straight-line method to depreciate fixed assets.

REQUIRED:
a.   Prepare the journal entry to record the purchase.
b.   Prepare the journal entry to record depreciation expense for each type of asset for the year ended December 31, 2011.
c.   Assuming that all of these assets are still held as of December 31, 2014, present these fixed assets as they would be shown on the December 31, 2014, balance sheet.

P9–3

Determining
capitalized cost
and depreciation

Gidley, Inc. purchased a piece of equipment on January 1, 2011. The following information is available for this purchase:

Purchase price	**$950,000**
Transportation	**$100,000[a]**
Installation	**$130,000[b]**
Salvage value	**$50,000**
Useful life	**4 years**

[a]Included in the transportation cost is $1,000 for insurance covering the shipment of the equipment to Gidley.
[b]Included in the cost of installation is $80,000 in wages paid to employees who helped install the equipment.

REQUIRED:

a. Compute the cost of the fixed asset that should be capitalized.
b. Prepare the entry to record depreciation expense for the year ended December 31, 2011, assuming the company uses each of the following:
   (1) Double-declining-balance depreciation method
   (2) Straight-line depreciation method
c. Assuming that the equipment was sold on January 1, 2012, for $250,000, prepare the entry to record the sale of the equipment using each of the following methods:
   (1) Double-declining-balance depreciation method
   (2) Straight-line depreciation method

P9–4

Expensing what should be capitalized can misstate net income

Westmiller Construction Company purchased a new truck on December 31, 2009, for $48,000. The truck has an estimated useful life of three years and an estimated salvage value of $12,000. When the truck was purchased, the company's accountant mistakenly made the following entry:

Depreciation Expense—Truck (E, −RE)   48,000
   Cash (−A)   48,000

Over the life of the truck, the company made no other entries associated with it.

REQUIRED:

a. What entry should Westmiller Construction Company have made on December 31, 2009?
b. Assuming that the straight-line method of depreciation should have been used and that the error was not discovered, in what direction and by how much was net income misstated in 2009 and 2010?
c. Assuming that the double-declining-balance method of depreciation should have been used and that the error was not discovered, in what direction and by how much was net income misstated in 2009 and 2010?

P9–5

Accounting for betterments and maintenance costs

McCartney Manufacturing purchased a dryer for $100,000 on January 1, 2008. The estimated life of the dryer is five years, and the salvage value is estimated to be $10,000. McCartney uses the straight-line method of depreciation.

On January 1, 2012, McCartney paid $160,000 to have the dryer overhauled, which increased the speed of the dryer and extended its estimated useful life to December 31, 2015. Each year, McCartney pays $1,000 to have the dryer serviced. On November 12, 2012, a major repair was required at a cost of $5,000. Salvage value is still estimated to be $10,000.

REQUIRED:

a. Provide the journal entry on January 1, 2008, to record the purchase of the dryer.
b. How should the service and repair costs be treated on McCartney's books?
c. Compute the depreciation expense that would be recognized during each year of the dryer's eight years of useful life.

P9–6

Accounting for betterments

Hulteen Hardware purchased a new building on January 1, 2007, for $1.5 million. The company expects the building to last twenty-five years and expects to be able to sell it then for $150,000. During 2012, the building was painted at a cost of $5,000. Almost ten years after acquiring the building, the roof was destroyed by a storm. The company had a new roof constructed at a cost of $200,000. The new roof was completed on January 1, 2017, and it extended the estimated life of the building by five years, to a total of thirty years. All other estimates are still accurate. Hulteen Hardware uses the straight-line method to depreciate the cost of all fixed assets.

REQUIRED:

a. Prepare the entry to record the purchase of the building, assuming that the company paid cash.
b. Prepare the entry to record the purchase of the new roof on January 1, 2017.
c. Prepare the entry to record depreciation expense for the year ended December 31, 2017.
d. Prepare the journal entry that would be recorded if the building was sold for $1.2 million on December 31, 2022.

P9–7

Revising the
estimated useful life

Burke Copy Center purchased a machine on January 1, 2006, for $180,000 and estimated its useful life and salvage value at ten years and $30,000, respectively. On January 1, 2011, the company added three years to the original useful-life estimate.

REQUIRED:
a. Compute the book value of the machine as of January 1, 2011, assuming that Burke recognizes the depreciation using straight-line.
b. Prepare the journal entry to record depreciation entered by the company on December 31, 2011, assuming that Burke uses straight-line.

REAL DATA

P9–8

Effects on an
accounting change

Effective January 1, 2003, Zimmer Holdings changed the method it used to account for hand-held instruments used by orthopedic surgeons. Prior to that date the cost of these instruments was carried as a prepaid expense, and when used, the cost was converted to an expense as part of selling, general, and administrative expenses. The new method recognizes these instruments as long-lived assets, and the costs are now included in property, plant, and equipment, and depreciated over a five-year period using the straight-line method. The effect of the change was to increase reported earnings $26.8 million.

REQUIRED:
Explain how this accounting change affected the basic accounting equation, and how it affects the computation of the current ratio and the fixed assets turnover ratio.

P9–9

Why is double-
declining-balance
preferred for tax
purposes?

Note: Knowledge of the time value of money is necessary for this problem (see Appendix A). Kimberly Sisters purchased equipment for $80,000 on January 1, 2011. Kimberly can use the double-declining-balance method for tax purposes but does not understand why it should be preferred over straight-line. The following information is available:

Estimated useful life	**4 years**
Estimated salvage value	**$20,000**
Expected revenues over each of the next four years	**$100,000**
Expected expenses (excluding depreciation) over each of the next four years	**$60,000**
Tax rate (percent of net income)	**35 percent**

REQUIRED:
a. Which of the two methods will give rise to the greater amount of depreciation over the life of the equipment? Support your answer with computations.
b. Which of the two methods will result in the payment of less taxes over the life of the equipment? Support your answer with computations.
c. Why is the double-declining-balance method preferred for tax purposes?
d. Assume a discount rate of 10 percent. How much money would be saved by using double-declining-balance instead of straight-line?

P9–10

The effect of
depreciation on
taxes, bonuses,
and dividends

Bently Poster Company pays income taxes on net income at the rate of 32 percent. The company pays a bonus to its officers of 8 percent of net income after taxes and pays dividends to its shareholders in the amount of 75 percent of net income after taxes. On January 1, 2011, the company purchased a fixed asset for $400,000. Such assets are usually depreciated over a ten-year period. Salvage value is expected to be zero. Assume that the bonus payment is not included as an expense in the calculation of taxable income and reported income.

REQUIRED:
Assume that revenues and expenses (excluding depreciation) for 2011 are $250,000 and $140,000, respectively. Compute the tax, bonus, and dividend payment for 2011 if the company uses the following:

a. The straight-line method of depreciation
b. The double-declining-balance method of depreciation
c. The straight-line method of depreciation, assuming a five-year useful life

P9–11

Natural resources:
Different methods
of cost allocation
depend on the
nature of the asset

Garmen Oil Company recently discovered an oil field on one of its properties in Texas. In order to extract the oil, the company purchased drilling equipment on January 1, 2011, for $800,000 cash and also purchased a mobile home on the same date for $54,000 cash to serve as on-site headquarters. The drilling equipment has an estimated useful life of twelve years but will be abandoned when the company shuts down this well. The mobile home has an estimated useful life of seven years and an estimated salvage value of $5,000. The company expects to use the mobile home on other drilling sites after work on this site is completed.

Company geologists estimated correctly that the well would produce two million barrels of oil. Actual production from the well for 2011, 2012, and 2013 was 600,000 barrels, 750,000 barrels, and 650,000 barrels, respectively. All extracted barrels were immediately sold. This well is now dry, and Garmen Oil has shut it down.

REQUIRED:
a. Prepare the entry to record the purchase of the drilling equipment and the mobile home.
b. Prepare the entries to record depletion expense for the drilling equipment using the activity method for 2011, 2012, and 2013.
c. Prepare the entries to record depreciation expenses for 2011, 2012, and 2013 for the mobile home using the straight-line method. Why are different methods used to allocate the costs of the drilling equipment and the mobile home?
d. Assume that Garmen Oil discovered that the well was dry at the end of 2012 (i.e., the well produced only 1,350,000 barrels of oil). Repeat parts (b) and (c).

P9–12

Selling and trading
in fixed assets

Webb Net Manufacturing purchased a new net weaving machine on January 1, 2009, for $500,000. The new machine has an estimated life of five years and an estimated salvage value of $100,000. It is company policy to use straight-line depreciation for all of its machines.

REQUIRED:
a. Assume that Webb Net Manufacturing sells this machine on January 1, 2012, for $325,000. Prepare the entry to record this transaction.
b. Assume that Webb Net Manufacturing sells this machine on June 30, 2012, for $320,000. Prepare the entry or entries to record this transaction.
c. Assume that Webb Net Manufacturing trades in this machine for a tract of land on January 1, 2012. The list price of the land is $250,000, and it has an appraised value of $210,000. The company is granted a trade-in allowance on the machine of $75,000 and pays an additional $175,000 in cash for the land. The net weaving machine is appraised at $75,000. Prepare the entry to record the trade-in, assuming that the land is valued as follows:
    (1) The FMV of the asset received.
    (2) The FMV of the assets given up.

P9–13

Recognizing
goodwill

On January 1, 2011, Diversified Industries purchased Specialists, Inc. for $1.8 million. The balance sheet of Specialists, Inc. at the time of purchase follows:

Assets		Liabilities and Shareholders' Equity	
Current assets	$650,000	Liabilities	$250,000
Long-lived assets	330,000	Shareholders' equity	730,000
		Total liabilities and	
Total assets	$980,000	shareholders' equity	$980,000

The total FMV of the individual assets of Specialists is $1.35 million, and the liabilities are valued on the balance sheet at FMV.

REQUIRED:
a. How can the FMV of Specialists' assets exceed the value of the assets on the balance sheet?
b. Why would Diversified pay more for Specialists than the FMV of the assets less the liabilities?

(continued)

c. Provide the journal entry to record the purchase.
d. In the recent past goodwill was amortized over a period of time not to exceed forty years. Provide an argument to challenge this position.

REAL DATA

P9–14

Goodwill accounting

When Zimmer Holdings purchased the common stock of Centerplus AG, a Swiss manufacturer of medical devices, for $3.4 billion, the fair market value of the assets acquired and liabilities assumed was estimated to be $2.3 billion and $1 billion, respectively.

a. Compute the goodwill acquired in the transaction.
b. Discuss why Zimmer paid significantly more for Centerplus than was indicated by the fair market value of Centerplus's net assets.

ISSUES FOR DISCUSSION

REAL DATA

ID9–1

Lump-sum sales and purchase

MGM Grand, Inc. purchased two Las Vegas casinos and the adjoining land for a total of $167 million. Soon afterwards, the company agreed to sell one of the casinos and 58.7 acres of adjacent land for $110 million.

REQUIRED:
a. What issues need to be addressed in order to determine the gain or loss resulting from the sale of one of the casinos? How should the cost of the sold casino be established?
b. Assume that each casino had a cost of $75 million and the adjacent land originally cost $17 million. Provide the journal entry prepared by MGM Grand to record the sale.
c. Explain how the casino and the land would each be valued on the balance sheet of the purchasing company.
d. Assume that an appraiser assesses the value of the land without the hotel to be $43 million. Compute the annual depreciation charge recognized by the purchasing company if it depreciates buildings using the straight-line rate over a period of twenty-five years. Assume no salvage value.

REAL DATA

ID9–2

Capitalizing marketing costs

Seattle FilmWorks capitalizes the costs of its direct mailings to prospective customers, expensing them over three years rather than in the year they're incurred. There's nothing wrong with this practice per se. If the customers netted by mailing come back with repeat business year after year, you really have booked an asset. But there is no guarantee that the first-time customer will become a regular. Consequently, large dollar amounts of marketing costs sit on the company's balance sheet as an asset.

This situation was familiar to America Online shareholders. By spreading its marketing expenses over several years, AOL was able to create artificially high earnings. The company finally changed its accounting policy. Result: A $385 million write-off.

REQUIRED:
Discuss the trade-offs involved with capitalizing marketing costs from a matching standpoint and from the perspectives of management, the shareholders, and the auditors.

REAL DATA

ID9–3

Capital acquisitions

Steel manufacturer V&M Star announced in early 2010 that it would spend $650 million to expand its Youngstown, Ohio, plant. The company indicated that funding from the federal government's stimulus bill, passed in response to the 2008–2009 recession, played an instrumental role in its decision to expand its existing facilities.

REQUIRED:
a. What issues must be considered when deciding whether to capitalize or expense the $650 million?
b. Under what conditions could the $650 million cost be expensed even if it improved instead of maintained the plant?

c. Assume that the $650 million cost is capitalized and that the expenditure extends the useful life of the existing facility. Explain how V&M will compute depreciation on its initial facility over its remaining useful life.

REAL DATA

ID9-4

U.S. GAAP/IFRS differences

In the footnotes to the IFRS-based 2008 financial statements of European Aeronautical Defense and Space Company (EADS), parent company for Airbus, research and development (R&D) expenses were reported at 2,699 million euros. Also included in the footnotes is a chart describing the activity during 2008 in an intangible asset account called "capitalized development costs," which shows the following (in million euros):

Beginning balance	957
Increases	31
Amortization	(107)
Ending balance	881

REQUIRED:
a. Explain the nature of the account called "capitalized development costs," and how EADS is accounting for R&D.
b. How would this account be treated if EADS followed U.S. GAAP?
c. Estimate the amount of R&D expense EADS would have recognized during 2008 if it had followed U.S. GAAP.
d Estimate the overall effect on 2008 net income of using IFRS vs. U.S. GAAP to account for R&D costs.

REAL DATA

ID9-5

Expense vs. capitalize

The 2008 annual report of Cisco Systems discloses that the company expenses all advertising and research and development costs, while capitalizing all software development costs.

REQUIRED:
Describe the effect of these two accounting treatments on the financial statements, discuss these treatments in terms of the nature of these particular costs and the matching principle, and comment on management incentives that might influence Cisco Systems to favor one or the other accounting treatment.

REAL DATA

ID9-6

Capital spending and profits

The *Wall Street Journal* once reported that hospitals plan to boost the amount of money spent on new property, plant, and equipment to meet increased demand from the aging demographics of the United States. The article stated that the increased capital spending "could squeeze already thin profits."

REQUIRED:
a. Discuss how hospital profits can be affected by increases in capital spending.
b. Discuss which financial statements would show the effects of increased capital spending.
c. How could you justify an increase in capital spending in terms of its potential effect on return on shareholders' equity?

REAL DATA

ID9-7

Asset impairments

The footnotes to the 2008 financial statements of McDonald's Corporation contain the following statement:

In accordance with SFAS No. 144, Accounting for the Impairment or Disposal of Long-lived Assets, long-lived assets are reviewed for impairment annually . . . and . . . if an individual restaurant is determined to be impaired, the loss is measured by the excess of the carrying amount of the restaurant over its fair value as determined by an estimate of discounted future cash flows.

REQUIRED:
a. Discuss the circumstances that could indicate that a McDonald's restaurant may be impaired.
b. Describe how McDonald's records an impairment charge.
c. How could management use the concept of an impairment charge to manage earnings?

After being asked how General Electric has maintained such consistent earnings growth over the past decade, Dennis Dammerman, the company's chief financial officer, said, "We're the best company in the world." However, the *Wall Street Journal* offered another explanation. It noted that over a ten-year period General Electric recorded six discretionary restructuring charges, ranging in magnitude from $147 million to over $1 billion—totaling $3.95 billion. Coincidentally, in each of the years when a restructuring charge was recognized, GE booked a sizable one-time gain. In one year, for example, the company recognized an $858 million one-time gain due to changes in accounting methods for taxes and inventory while taking a $1,027 million restructuring write-off. In another year, GE matched a $1 billion restructuring charge against the $1.4 billion one-time gain it recognized on the sale of an aerospace unit to Martin Marietta. "To smooth out fluctuations, GE frequently offsets one-time gains from big asset sales with restructuring charges; that keeps earnings from rising so high that they can't be topped the following year. GE also times sales of some equity stakes and even acquisitions to produce profit gains when needed."

REQUIRED:
a. Determine what reporting strategy GE seems to be using, and explain how it works.
b. Explain how discretionary restructuring charges help GE to implement that reporting strategy and why the company would want to pursue it.
c. The *Wall Street Journal* reported that "investors love restructurings" and that such charges seem to boost stock prices. Yet the FASB later cracked down on this popular corporate practice. Explain why investors might love restructurings, why stock prices seem to rise when they are announced, and why the FASB acted to limit such behavior.

U.S. accounting standards at one time contained a requirement that certain large companies disclose current values for inventories and fixed assets. Such disclosure included dollar amounts for cost of goods sold and depreciation that were based on current instead of historical cost. This requirement, however, was quickly abandoned in response to heated controversy.

REQUIRED:
a. Build an argument against requiring current values on the balance sheet.
b. Consider the usefulness of historical costs for decision-making purposes, and build a case for requiring current values on the balance sheet.
c. Which of the two arguments do you find most convincing?

A few years ago Kellogg, a maker of cereals and foods, hit its targeted earnings-per-share growth of 11 percent, and its stock price was up 25 percent. In the fourth quarter of that year, the company took a significant "one-time" charge against earnings when it wrote down assets—mostly property, plant, and equipment—from its overseas operations. Interestingly, this write-down was the ninth such charge in the past eleven quarters. Some analysts believe that Kellogg was using these charges to manage earnings and estimated that the company's earnings should actually have been 24 percent below the previous year.

REQUIRED:
a. Describe how Kellogg could use asset write-downs to manage earnings.
b. Explain why auditors may be less inclined to object to subjective asset write-downs compared to asset overstatements.
c. What is the FASB's position on asset impairments?

Burlington Northern released first quarter 2007 earnings below those of the same period for 2006. While revenues increased, mainly due to higher prices, earnings were down due to increased expenses, including a charge for the write-off of an outdated technology system.

REQUIRED:

a. Describe how the write-off of a technology system would affect the basic accounting equation and the financial statements.
b. What factors could lead to a company determining that its technology was overvalued?
c. Discuss how management might be able to manage earnings through such a write-off.

REAL DATA

ID9–12

U.S. GAAP/IFRS
differences

Until 2007 companies using IFRS with securities traded on the U.S. stock exchanges were required to include a statement that reconciled IFRS-based net income and shareholders' equity with U.S. GAAP-based net income and shareholders' equity in their Form 20-F filings with the SEC. These reconciliations provided useful information to analysts wanting to compare the financial performance of companies using IFRS to companies using U.S. GAAP. Nokia, the well-known communication company based in Finland, reported such reconciliations from 1994 to 2006. Some of the more significant items listed on the reconciliation included development costs and impairments. Over the 12-year period 1994–2006, for example, the accumulated adjustment (in millions of euros) from IFRS-based income to U.S. GAAP-based income was −102 and −47 for development costs and impairments of intangible assets (not including goodwill), respectively.

REQUIRED:

Discuss the differences between IFRS and U.S. GAAP with respect to long-lived asset accounting, and comment on how these differences could lead to the adjustments for development costs and impairments reported by Nokia.

REAL DATA

ID9–13

The SEC Form
10-K of NIKE

The SEC Form 10-K of NIKE is reproduced in Appendix C.

REQUIRED:

Review the NIKE SEC Form 10-K, and answer the following questions:

a. What percentage of total assets do property, plant, and equipment and long-lived assets in total make up?
b. What is the largest category of property, plant, and equipment?
c. How large is the depreciation and amortization expense relative to sales, and why is it listed on the statement of cash flows?
d. What method and estimated lives does NIKE use for its property, plant, and equipment?
e. What is the company's largest intangible asset?
f. What is NIKE's policy on asset impairments?
g. What event led to the large impairment change, and why are impairments listed on both the income statement and statement of cash flows?
h. How much did NIKE invest in property, plant, and equipment during 2008, and how much cash did it receive from disposals of property, plant, and equipment?

Liabilities and Shareholders' Equity: A Closer Look

In December 2009, The New York Times Company issued a very upbeat outlook for its business prospects, despite the lingering effects of the 2008–2009 recession and the tidal wave of change undermining the company's traditional print media business model. Print media advertising revenue for the *Times* was down 25 percent in the fourth quarter of 2009, and media industry experts talked of nothing except the Internet and technology's inevitable victory over newspapers and other traditional print media outlets. The New York Times Company, however, was optimistic in its outlook, citing digital and online advertising revenue growth, circulation revenue growth, and a more efficient cost structure. Playing a large role in the company's brightened, forward-looking statement was the change to its capital structure: The company had less debt and relatively more equity than in previous periods. Specifically, the company's CEO was quoted as saying, "We have made significant progress in reducing our debt level, with total debt expected to be approximately $800 million at year-end . . . down from $1.1 billion at the end of 2008." With such competitive forces aligned against the company, do you think its CEO is justified in her optimism with less debt and more equity? Why does the structure of a company's financing affect its future prospects? How do analysts incorporate debt and equity levels into their evaluation of a company's past and future performance? The next three chapters—10, 11, and 12—describe the components of a company's capital structure, helping to explain the logic behind the *New York Times'* positive outlook.

CHAPTER 10

Introduction to Liabilities:
Economic Consequences, Current Liabilities, and Contingencies

KEY POINTS

The following key points are emphasized in this chapter:

* Definition of a liability.

* Economic consequences associated with reporting liabilities on the financial statements.

* Determinable and contingent liabilities.

* Current liabilities.

* Bonus systems and profit-sharing arrangements and the reporting incentives they create.

* Methods used to account for contingencies.

Waste companies have great latitude in setting reserves (liabilities) for future environmental costs at their dumps. The process involves estimating how high the costs will be thirty years or more in the future and calculating how big a fund is needed in today's dollars to satisfy the future obligation. For example, Waste Management Inc., previously accused of using aggressive accounting methods, once recorded a $173.3 million cost that lowered its third-quarter profit by 63 percent. The cost included $45 million to boost cleanup reserves for some dumps, $26 million to increase reserves for litigation, and $72.3 million to boost reserves for future claims. Does anybody really know how large the liability should be? This example illustrates the difficulties involved in measuring liabilities, the topic of Chapters 10 and 11.

Liabilities, defined as obligations of a company to disburse assets or provide services in the future, are divided on the balance sheet into two categories: current liabilities and long-term liabilities. Current liabilities include primarily short-term payables to suppliers, employees, banks, and others. Long-term liabilities relate to long-term notes, bonds, leases, retirement costs, and deferred income taxes. This chapter introduces liabilities in general and covers the methods used to account for current liabilities and contingent liabilities, which can be either current or long-term. Accounting for retirement costs and deferred income taxes is briefly reviewed in Appendices 10A and 10B, respectively. Chapter 11 is devoted to long-term notes, bonds, and leases. These three liabilities are covered in a single chapter because the same basic method, called the *effective interest method,* is used to account for them.

 While a few relatively subtle differences exist between IFRS and U.S. GAAP accounting for liabilities, for the most part the two systems are quite similar.

WHAT IS A LIABILITY?

The FASB has defined liabilities as "probable future sacrifices of economic benefits arising from present obligations of a particular entity to transfer assets or provide services to other entities in the future as a result of past transactions or events." The board commented further that all liabilities appearing on the balance sheet should have three characteristics in common: (1) They should be present obligations that entail settlements by probable future transfers or uses of cash, goods, or services; (2) they should be unavoidable obligations; and (3) the transaction or event obligating the enterprise must have already happened.[1]

While the FASB's definition makes the measurement of most liabilities relatively straightforward, the liabilities listed on the balance sheet do encompass a wide variety of items, including credit balances with suppliers, debts from borrowings, services yet to be performed, withholdings from employees' wages and salaries, dividend declarations, product warranties, deferred income taxes, and a number of complex financing arrangements. As we will discuss later, there is some question whether all these items are liabilities in an economic sense as well as whether all the economic liabilities of a company are included on its balance sheet.

1. Financial Accounting Standards Board (FASB), "Elements of Financial Statements of Business Enterprises," *Statement of Financial Accounting Concepts No. 3* (Stamford, Conn.: FASB, 1980), pars. 28 and 29.

> **?** In its 2009 annual report, FedEx reported that it leased certain of its fixed assets. The contracts associated with those leases specified that $1.8 billion would have to be paid by the company in 2010. Yet this amount was not included in the liabilities listed on FedEx's balance sheet. Review the criteria for recognizing a liability and consider whether FedEx's accounting treatment was appropriate.

THE RELATIVE SIZE OF LIABILITIES ON THE BALANCE SHEET

Figure 10–1 contains liabilities as a percentage of total assets, often referred to as the **debt ratio,** for selected firms. The main financing source for financial institutions is clearly debt. Customer demand deposits and short-term debt are primarily responsible. General Electric's financial subsidiary, which is set up to provide financing to its customers on big-ticket sales, is basically a financial institution, accounting for GE's large debt ratio. Companies like AT&T and Kroger invest heavily in property, plant, and equipment that is financed through debt, while Internet firms have generated most of their financing by issuing equity.

FIGURE 10–1

Liabilities as a percentage of total assets

	Liabilities/ Total Assets
Manufacturing:	
General Electric (manufacturer)	0.87
Chevron (oil drilling and refining)	0.46
Retail:	
Kroger (grocery retail)	0.78
Lowe's (hardware retail)	0.45
Internet:	
Yahoo! (Internet search engine)	0.22
Cisco (Internet systems)	0.43
General services:	
AT&T (telecommunications services)	0.64
Wendy's/Arby's (restaurant services)	0.49
Financial services:	
Bank of America (banking services)	0.90
Goldman Sachs (investment services)	0.93

> **?** Internet companies like Yahoo! and Google carry very little debt on their balance sheets, while large manufacturers like Kimberly-Clark and General Electric have debt amounts that are well over 50 percent of total assets. Comment on why such differences might exist.

REPORTING LIABILITIES ON THE BALANCE SHEET: ECONOMIC CONSEQUENCES

The reported values of liabilities affect important financial ratios that shareholders, investors, creditors, and others use to assess management's performance and a company's financial condition. Seven of Dun & Bradstreet's fourteen key business ratios, for example, directly include a measure of liabilities: (1) quick ratio ([cash + marketable securities + receivables]/current liabilities), (2) current ratio (current assets/current liabilities), (3) current liabilities/net worth, (4) current liabilities/inventory, (5) total liabilities/net worth, (6) sales/net working capital, and (7) accounts payable/sales. These ratios and others that include liability measures are used by interested outside parties to determine credit ratings, assess solvency and future cash flows, predict bankruptcy, and, in general, assess the financial health of an enterprise. In addition to using liability measures to evaluate the future prospects of a firm, shareholders, investors, creditors, and managers are interested in the reported values of liabilities for other important reasons, several of which are discussed in the following paragraphs.

Shareholders and Investors

Debt financing can be very valuable to shareholders because funds generated by borrowing can be used to generate returns that exceed the cost of the debt. Since interest is tax deductible (reducing the cost of debt), this strategy (called leverage) is very common. However, shareholders and investors must pay close attention to the amount of liabilities and the contracts that underlie them because debt increases the riskiness of the company. Interest payments must be met before dividends can be distributed, and, in the event of liquidation, outstanding payables must be satisfied before shareholders are paid. Many loan contracts restrict the amount of dividends that can be paid in any one year to the common shareholders. For example, The Boeing Company, an aircraft manufacturer, operates under debt covenants that restrict the payment of dividends and other distributions on the company's stock. As of December 31, 2008, Boeing reported that it is in full compliance with these covenants.

Creditors

The creditors of a company have a special interest in the liabilities held by others. These liabilities compete for the resources that must be used to satisfy the obligations owed to them. Creditors often protect their interests by writing terms in loan contracts that require collateral in the case of default or that restrict a company's future borrowings. The 2008 annual report of engine manufacturer Cummins, Inc. contained the following excerpt, which describes the debt covenants imposed by its bank lenders:

Our debt agreements contain several restrictive covenants. The most restrictive of these covenants applies to our revolving credit facility which will, among other things, limit our ability to incur additional debt or issue preferred stock, enter into sale-leaseback transactions, pay dividends, sell or create liens on our assets, make investments and merge or consolidate with any other person. In addition, we are subject to various financial covenants including a maximum debt-to-EBITDA ratio and a minimum interest coverage ratio. As of December 31, 2008, we were in compliance with all of the covenants under our borrowing agreements.

Management

Management views short- and long-term borrowings and the related liabilities as important sources of cash for operating, investing, and financing activities. An article in *Forbes* stated: "Most companies spend lots of time figuring out when and how to borrow money. That makes sense. Proper timing of debt can save millions in interest payments." The bankruptcy of CIT Group was in large part due to its inability to borrow funds for its lending operations.

On its 2008 balance sheet, for example, General Electric disclosed about $693 billion of outstanding liabilities, representing almost 87 percent of its financing sources. That amount is a significant sum that requires astute and careful management to ensure that sufficient cash is on hand to meet the required payments as they come due. In 2008 alone, General Electric paid approximately $26 billion in interest to service its outstanding debt. Effective management of such debt is critical to a company's success and can be used to great advantage. As noted earlier, practicing leverage is a very popular strategy.

While management often chooses to rely on borrowings for its financial needs, it has incentives to understate liabilities on the balance sheet. Indeed, a well-known article in *Forbes* began: "The basic drives of man are few: to get enough food, to find shelter, and to keep debt off the balance sheet."

Additional debt on the balance sheet, for example, can reduce a company's credit rating, making it increasingly difficult to attract capital in the future. On June 25, 2009, Standard & Poor's Corp., an established credit-rating service, lowered the credit rating of aerospace company Moog, Inc. because the company had increased its debt levels due to a series of acquisitions. In reaction to Standard & Poor's announcement, the market price of the company's outstanding stock immediately dropped.

Additional debt on the balance sheet can also decrease the current ratio, increase the debt/asset ratio, and increase the debt/equity ratio. Such changes could cause a company to violate its debt covenants and, in general, cause it to be viewed as more risky by outside investors and creditors. The national director of accounting and auditing at Seidman & Seidman, for example, points out: "Removing large amounts of debt can present a more favorable impression of debt-to-equity ratios, working capital ratios, and the returns on assets invested in the business."

There are also situations, however, when management may wish to accelerate the recognition of liabilities, booking them in a current instead of a future period. For example, by reporting additional liabilities in the current period, management may be able to report higher net income amounts in future periods. Such a reporting strategy is not unusual for companies that are experiencing exceptionally poor years as well as for those experiencing exceptionally good years.

While in the midst of bankruptcy proceedings, for example, LTV Corporation "took a bath" by accruing a number of significant liabilities, none of which were required at the time by generally accepted accounting principles. A spokesman for LTV was quoted in the *Wall Street Journal* as saying:

[The company] took the special charges because it believes it should record all its liabilities while in [bankruptcy] proceedings. It's a unique opportunity for us to take it at a time when it does the least harm. . . . LTV likely wants a fresh start when it emerges from bankruptcy-law proceedings.

Companies experiencing exceptionally good years may also choose to accrue additional liabilities. The article just cited also pointed out that a number of companies "with strong equity positions" may wish to take early recognition of certain liabilities

and, in effect, "bite the bullet early." This reporting strategy, called "building hidden reserves," recognizes losses in a year when they will be overwhelmed by other items of income. It also avoids having to recognize the losses in later years that may not be so exceptional. Both General Electric and Microsoft have been cited for managing earnings through hidden reserves.

For years a tradition of conservative reporting has existed in Europe, and this conservatism often manifests itself through the subjective creation of liabilities, or "provisions" as they are often called.

Auditors

Auditors must attest that all liabilities are identified and properly reported on the balance sheet. Auditors are particularly careful in this area because significant unreported liabilities may lead to future investor and creditor losses for which auditors may be held liable. For example, the auditors for Bethlehem Steel cautiously noted in their report on the company's 2003 financial statements: "The continuation of the company as a going concern is contingent upon . . . the company's ability to comply with all debt covenants . . . and Bethlehem's ability to generate sufficient cash from operations and obtain financing sources to meet its future obligations." In the well-known Enron fraud, the demise of Arthur Andersen, Enron's auditor, was linked to billions of dollars of unreported Enron liabilities.

In two successive years, Motorola recorded charges against income for reorganization and other expenses of $4 billion and $2.6 billion, respectively. In those two years the company posted net losses of $3.9 billion and $2.5 billion. The following year the company bounced back, reporting a profit of $893 million, and noted in the annual report that a significant amount of the prior reorganization charges had not led to cash payments. What earnings management strategy might Motorola be practicing, and why should investors be concerned?

CURRENT LIABILITIES

Current liabilities are obligations expected to require the use of current assets or the creation of other current liabilities. They normally include obligations to suppliers (accounts payable), short-term debts, current maturities on long-term debts, dividends payable to shareholders, deferred revenues (services or goods yet to be performed or delivered that are expected to require the use of current assets), third-party collections (e.g., sales tax and payroll deductions), periodic accruals (e.g., wages and interest), and potential obligations related to pending or threatened litigation, product warranties, and guarantees.

Note that current liabilities are defined in terms of obligations "expected to require the use of current assets." Thus, reported obligations that are not expected to require the use of current assets are not disclosed as current. For example, an obligation due within a year may not be disclosed in the current liabilities section if it is either (1) expected to

be paid from assets that are presently listed as noncurrent or (2) expected to be replaced (refinanced) with a long-term liability or equity issuance. Such obligations would normally be disclosed as long-term.

An annual report for Manpower, Inc. stated, "Commercial paper borrowings . . . have been classified as long-term debt due to our intent and ability to refinance them on a long-term basis." An annual report of PepsiCo similarly states, "Short-term borrowings are reclassified to long-term when we have the intent and ability, through the existence of unused lines of credit, to refinance these borrowings on a long-term basis." How can these two companies classify debt with a short-term maturity as long-term?

The Relative Size of Current Liabilities on the Balance Sheet

Figure 10–2 shows that current liabilities are the main liabilities of financial institutions. As indicated earlier, customer demand deposits are the primary reason. Figure 10–1 indicated that Internet firms rely very little on debt, and in Figure 10–2 we see that the majority is current. In other words, Internet firms have relatively little long-term debt. AT&T, Chevron, and GE carry relatively small amounts of current liabilities, choosing to create their leverage with long-term debt. AT&T and Chevron also carry relatively large investments in property, plant, and equipment.

Current liabilities as a percentage of total liabilities for the Bank of New York and AT&T are approximately 92 percent and 25 percent, respectively. Explain why these two companies carry such different levels of current liabilities.

FIGURE 10–2

Current liabilities as a percentage of total liabilities

	Current Liabilities/ Total Liabilities
Manufacturing:	
General Electric (manufacturer)	0.36
Chevron (oil drilling and refining)	0.43
Retail:	
Kroger (grocery retail)	0.42
Lowe's (hardware retail)	0.55
Internet:	
Yahoo! (Internet search engine)	0.85
Cisco (Internet systems)	0.46
General services:	
AT&T (telecommunications services)	0.25
Wendy's/Arby's (restaurant services)	0.22
Financial services:	
Bank of America (banking services)	0.82
Goldman Sachs (investment services)	0.79

Valuing Current Liabilities on the Balance Sheet

Most liabilities involve future cash outflows that are specified by formal contract or informal agreement. They can therefore be predicted objectively, and present value methods can be used to value liabilities on the balance sheet. In the case of current liabilities, however, the time period until payment is relatively short and the difference between the **face value** (actual cash payment when the liability is due) of the liability and its present value (discounted future cash payment) is considered to be immaterial. Thus, in the interest of materiality, current liabilities are usually recorded on the balance sheet at face value.

Reporting Current Liabilities: An Economic Consequence

In most cases, the face value of a current liability is easy to determine, and balance sheet valuation is straightforward. The primary problem is one of discovery, ensuring that all existing current liabilities are reported on the balance sheet. Failure to discover and report an existing current liability misstates the financial statements and any of the financial measures that include current liabilities. Two particularly important financial measures are the current ratio and working capital, which help investors and creditors to assess a company's solvency position because they match current obligations against the assets on hand to satisfy them. These ratios are frequently found in loan contracts, such as those disclosed in the 2006 annual report of John B. Sanfilippo & Son Inc. The company was required to maintain a minimum amount of working capital; as of May 8, 2007, the company reported that it had violated the financial covenant and, if it failed to receive approval from its current lenders, would have to seek alternate financing.

Such debt restrictions can discourage management from reporting current liabilities on the balance sheet. Consider, for example, JFP Company, which borrows $1 million from Thrift Bank. The loan contract states that the loan is in default if JFP's current ratio, as reported on the balance sheet, dips below 2:1. Defaulting on this loan could mean that JFP must immediately pay the outstanding balance; in most cases, however, the company would be forced to renegotiate the terms of the loan with Thrift Bank. Such renegotiations would probably require that JFP make costly concessions, normally in the form of less desirable loan terms (e.g., higher interest rates, additional collateral).

At year-end, JFP's accountants determine that current assets equal $100,000. If current liabilities are determined to be $50,000 or less, the current ratio will be at least 2:1, and the loan will not be in default. On the other hand, if current liabilities are determined to be greater than $50,000, the current ratio would dip below 2:1, and JFP would be in violation of the loan contract, which could lead to serious financial problems.

If JFP's management fails, either intentionally or unintentionally, to report a given current liability on the balance sheet, it can avoid violating the terms of the loan contract and the related consequences. Management, therefore, has an incentive either to ignore existing current liabilities, postpone them, or structure transactions so that current liabilities do not have to be recorded. Auditors must make special efforts to ensure that all existing current liabilities are properly reported on the balance sheet, and financial statement users must be aware of these management incentives.

For many years the frequent-flyer programs offered by the major airlines have allowed customers to build up future flying credits—thus creating a liability for the airlines. That is, the airlines must provide free seats for its frequent flyers. Airlines now accrue current liabilities for these credits, but for many years they argued that it was unnecessary. Describe some of the economic consequences the airlines may have been trying to avoid by not accruing these liabilities.

DETERMINABLE CURRENT LIABILITIES

Determining the dollar amounts of all current liabilities, because they represent probable future outlays, involves an element of uncertainty. The relative degree of uncertainty gives rise to two current liability categories: (1) determinable and (2) contingent. Determining the dollar amount of a determinable current liability is relatively straightforward; determining the dollar amount of a contingent liability involves an estimate. Figure 10–3 provides an outline of the current liabilities covered in the next two sections.

FIGURE 10–3
Outline of
current liabilities

Determinable current liabilities	**Contingent liabilities**
A. Accounts payable	A. Lawsuits
B. Short-term debts	B. Warranties
1. Short-term notes	
2. Current maturities of long-term debts	
C. Dividends payable	
D. Unearned revenues	
E. Third-party collections	
F. Income taxes	
G. Incentive compensation	

In general, **determinable current liabilities** can be precisely measured, and the amount of cash needed to satisfy the obligation and the date of payment are reasonably certain. Determinable current liabilities include accounts payable, short-term debts, dividends payable, unearned revenues, third-party collections, and accrued liabilities.

Accounts Payable

Accounts payable are dollar amounts owed to others for goods, supplies, and services purchased on **open account.**[2] They arise from frequent transactions that are normally not subject to specific, formal contracts between a company and its suppliers. These extensions of credit are the practical result of a time lag between the receipt of a good, supply, or service and the corresponding payment. The time period is usually short (e.g., thirty to sixty days) and is indicated by the terms of the exchange (e.g., 2/10, n/30).

In the operating section of Target Corporation's 2008 statement of cash flows, a change in accounts payable of $389 million was subtracted from net earnings in the calculation of cash flow provided by operations. Did the accounts payable balance increase or decrease during 2008, and why is the change subtracted from net earnings?

Accounts payable are usually associated with inventory purchases, which were discussed in Chapter 7, and a Dun & Bradstreet survey found that accounts payable are the most popular source of financing for small business owners. The size of the balance in accounts payable can be an important indicator of a company's financial condition,

---

2. Accounts payable are sometimes referred to as *trade accounts payable. Accounting Trends and Techniques* (New York: AICPA, 2009) reports that 14 percent of the major U.S. companies surveyed used that phrase.

especially in the retail industry where suppliers are heavily relied upon to provide merchandise. The 1990 Christmas season for R.H. Macy, for example, did not produce sufficient revenues to cover the outstanding accounts owed to Macy's suppliers, which, in turn, delayed payments and caused the company's accounts payable balance to increase. Many financial analysts used this information to accurately predict that the company would soon declare bankruptcy. Robert Campeau, who built a retail empire in the 1980s, experienced similar problems prior to the empire's collapse in 1990. His companies paid suppliers so slowly that they ceased sending shipments.

Other companies use accounts payable as a source of financing, stretching the time to pay suppliers and using the cash for other purposes. Amazon.com's accounts payable turnover (in days), for example, rose from 49 in 2003 to almost 65 in 2009. Analysts following Amazon commented that this source of financing could not continue to grow very much before vendors would fight back and discontinue supplying the company.

JCPenney's accounts payable represent approximately 43 percent of its current liabilities, while the percentage for Biomet, a manufacturer in the medical industry, is only 16. Explain why accounts payable are so much more important for JCPenney.

Short-Term Debts

Short-term debts (or short-term borrowings) typically include short-term bank loans, commercial paper, lines of credit, and current maturities of long-term debt. **Commercial paper,** a popular means of providing short-term financing, represents short-term notes (30 to 270 days) issued for cash by companies with good credit ratings to other companies. A **line of credit** is usually granted to a company by a bank or group of banks, allowing it to borrow up to a certain maximum dollar amount, interest being charged only on the outstanding balance. Issued commercial paper and existing lines of credit are an indication of a company's ability to borrow funds on a short-term basis; thus, they are very important to investors and creditors who are interested in assessing solvency. Consequently, such financing arrangements are extensively described in the footnotes.

SHORT-TERM NOTES

Short-term notes usually arise from cash loans and are generally payable to banks or loan companies. In most cases, the life of a note is somewhere between thirty days and one year, and the bank or loan company lends the borrowing company less cash than is indicated on the face of the note. At the **maturity date** (when the loan is due), the borrowing company pays the lending institution the face amount of the note, and the difference between the face amount and the amount of the loan is treated as interest.

For example, suppose that on January 1, Freight Line Industries borrows $9,400 from Commercial Loan Company and signs a six-month note with a face amount of $10,000. The journal entry to record this transaction is provided below.

Cash (+A)	**9,400**	
Discount on Notes Payable (−L)	**600**	
Notes Payable (+L)		**10,000**
Issued short-term note payable		

The discount on notes payable account serves as a contra account to notes payable on the balance sheet and represents interest that is not yet owed but will be recognized in the future. Assuming that financial statements are prepared monthly, one-sixth of the discount would be converted to interest expense each month by an adjusting entry of the following form:

Interest Expense (E, −RE)	100	
Discount on Notes Payable (+L)		100
Recognized accrual of interest on a short-term note ($600/6)		

After this entry is recorded at the end of the first month, the balance of the discount would have been reduced to $500, and the balance sheet carrying amount of the note would be as follows:

Notes payable	$10,000	
Less: Discount on Notes Payable	500	$9,500

CURRENT MATURITIES OF LONG-TERM DEBTS

Long-term debts are often retired through a series of periodic installments. The installments that are to be paid within the time period that defines current assets (one year or the current operating cycle, whichever is longer) should be included on the balance sheet as current liabilities. The remaining installments should be disclosed as long-term liabilities.

For example, assume that on December 31, 2011, Wright and Sons borrows $50,000, which is to be paid back in annual installments of $7,000 each. The first payment, which is due on December 31, 2012, will consist of $5,000 in interest and $2,000 in principal. On the December 31, 2011, balance sheet, the associated payable would be disclosed in the following way. Note that the $50,000 principal amount is divided up into $2,000, which is due in the current period, and $48,000, which is long-term. The $5,000 in interest will be accrued at the end of 2012 after the company has had use of the funds.

Current Liabilities:	
Current Maturity of Long-term Debt	2,000
Long-term Liabilities:	
Long-term Notes Payable	48,000

> **?** Included as current liabilities in the 2008 annual report of Coca-Cola are accounts payable, accrued expenses, loans and notes payable, accrued income taxes, and current maturities of long-term debts. Define each of these items and explain why they are considered current liabilities.

Dividends Payable

A liability is created when the board of directors of a corporation declares a dividend to be paid to the shareholders. It is listed as current because dividends are usually paid within several weeks of declaration. The methods used to account for dividends are discussed in Chapter 12.

Unearned Revenues

Payments are often received before contracted services are performed. In such cases, an *unearned revenue, deferred revenue,* or *receipt in advance* liability is created because the companies receiving the payments are under obligations that must be

fulfilled. This liability is then converted to revenue as the related services are performed or the relevant goods are delivered. Recall that one of the primary criteria of revenue recognition is that the earning process must be complete before a revenue can be recognized. If providing the related services or relevant goods is expected to require the use of current assets, the unearned revenue liability should be classified as current.

> **?** Microsoft carries over $13 billion in unearned revenue in the current liability section of its 2009 balance sheet. What does this indicate about the nature of the contract between Microsoft and some of its customers? What responsibility does Microsoft have in the short-term future?

Unearned revenues arise from a number of different transactions: gift certificates sold by retail stores redeemable in merchandise, coupons sold by restaurants that can be exchanged for meals, tickets and tokens sold by transportation companies good for future fares, advance payments for magazine subscriptions, and returnable deposits. Two particularly interesting examples are common in the airline industry. Passenger tickets are frequently paid several months before they are used, often because special discount fares are available with prepayment. These receipts are not immediately treated as revenues by the airlines but are recorded as Air Traffic Liability and listed in the current liabilities section of the balance sheet. These liabilities are converted to revenue as the tickets are used. Similarly, the frequent-flyer programs offered by a number of the major airlines create obligations, as customers build up mileage credits that must be paid in the form of free airline tickets. While most airlines have neglected to do so, these liabilities should be recognized as the mileage credits are earned.

To illustrate the basic methods used to account for unearned revenues, assume that Seattle Metro Transit sells bus passes, good for one month, for $20 each. On December 15, the transit company sells 50 passes for a total of $1,000. The following journal entries would be recorded on December 15 and December 31, after one-half month had expired:

Dec. 15	Cash (+A)	1,000	
	Unearned Revenue (+L)		1,000
	Sold 50 bus passes for future service		
Dec. 31	Unearned Revenue (−L)	500	
	Fees Earned (R, +RE)		500
	Recognized completion of one-half future service		

> **?** On its 2008 balance sheet Continental Airlines reported a current liability titled "air traffic and frequent-flyer liability" that exceeded $1.8 billion. Explain the nature of this liability and distinguish it from accounts payable, another account that appears on the company's balance sheet.

Third-Party Collections

Companies often act as collecting agencies for government or other entities. The price paid for an item at Target, for example, includes sales tax, which Target must periodically remit to the proper government authority. Companies are also required by law to withhold from employee wages social security taxes as well as an amount approximating

the employee's income tax.[3] These withholdings are periodically sent to the federal government. In addition to payroll tax deductions, companies often withhold insurance premiums or union dues, which in turn must be passed on to the appropriate third party. In each of these cases, a liability is created; the company receives or holds cash that legally must be paid to a third party. The liability is discharged when the cash payment is made. These liabilities are usually considered current because payment is expected within the time period of current assets.

To illustrate, assume that Sears sells a small tractor for $1,000, which includes $50 in sales tax. The proper journal entry to record the sale follows:

Cash (or Accounts Receivable) (+A)	**1,000**	
Sales Tax Payable (+L)		**50**
Sales (R, +RE)		**950**

Sold merchandise and collected sales tax

When Sears pays the sales tax to the proper government authority, the following entry is recorded:

Sales Tax Payable (−L)	**50**	
Cash (−A)		**50**

Paid sales tax

Income Tax Liability

Income tax liability for a corporation is based on a percentage of taxable income in accordance with the rules stated in the Internal Revenue Code. The income tax rate currently paid by U.S. corporations is approximately 35 percent of taxable income. Most corporations are required by law at the beginning of each year to estimate their tax liabilities for the entire year and to make quarterly tax payments based on these estimates.

Incentive Compensation

Basing compensation on net income and/or stock prices is a very popular way to pay executives and managers. Such payments comprise a significant portion of the total compensation of virtually all upper-level executives in major U.S. corporations. Profit-sharing arrangements, which are also based on a measure of net income, are frequently used to compensate employees at lower levels of the corporate hierarchy. *Accounting Trends and Techniques* (AICPA, 2009) reported that virtually all major U.S. companies compensate their employees on some performance-based measure. "More and more, it's a system U.S. companies are using to recruit, keep, and motivate workers," says Whit Smith, owner of Whitney Smith Co. in Fort Worth.

Incentive compensation plans can take a number of different forms. AMP Incorporated, for example, has two incentive bonus plans: (1) a stock plus cash plan and (2) a cash plan. Executive compensation under the first plan is related to the market value of the company's stock; compensation under the second is a percentage of the company's net income. The formula for Chrysler's incentive compensation plan included a provision of 8 percent of consolidated net income. Exxon's incentive program indicates that the total amount distributed cannot exceed 3 percent of net income or 6 percent of capital invested (as defined by the plan). Figure 10–4 describes the incentive compensation formulas for selected large U.S. corporations.

---

3. Companies must not only withhold employee social security taxes; they must also match them. That is, employers must pay to the government a dollar amount equal to that withheld from the employee's wages. Such payments can be quite large. General Motors, for example, pays well over $100 million each year in matched social security taxes.

Aluminum Co. of America	15% of total cash dividends.
Ashland Oil	6% of after-tax net income.
The Boeing Co.	6% of before-tax net income.
Bristol-Myers Squibb	Lesser of 6% of before-tax net income or 8% of after-tax net income.
DuPont	20% of after-tax net income in excess of 6% of shareholders' equity.
Goodyear Tire & Rubber	10% of after-tax net income in excess of consolidated book value of outstanding capital stock.
ITT Corp.	12% of after-tax net income in excess of 6% of shareholders' equity.
International Paper	8% of after-tax net income in excess of 6% of shareholders' equity.
Rockwell International	2% of the first $100 million of before-tax net income plus 3% of the next $50 million of before-tax net income plus 4% of the next $25 million of before-tax net income plus 5% of the balance.
Unocal Corp.	3% of after-tax net income in excess of 6% of shareholders' equity.

From an accounting standpoint, liabilities associated with incentive compensation plans must be accrued at year-end because they are based on measures of performance (e.g., net income or stock prices) that cannot be determined until that time. They are listed as current on the balance sheet because they are typically distributed to employees early the following period, at which time the liability is discharged.

Suppose, for example, that Tom Turnstile, an executive for Maylein Stoneware, is paid a bonus each year in the amount of 3 percent of net income before income taxes. If net income before income taxes is determined at year-end to be $300,000, Turnstile's bonus is $9,000 ($300,000 × 0.03), and the following journal entry is recorded:

Bonus Expense (E, −RE)   9,000
  Bonus Liability (+L)   9,000
Accrued bonus liability

When the bonus is paid the following year, the following journal entry is recorded.

Bonus Liability (−L)   9,000
  Cash (−A)   9,000
Paid bonus liability

Incentive compensation plans are popular because they induce managers and employees to act in a manner consistent with the objectives of the shareholders. By basing compensation on net income or stock prices, such plans encourage management to maximize these measures of performance. Keep in mind, however, that managers have incentives to influence the measure of net income through operating decisions, the choice of accounting methods, estimates, assumptions, the timing of accruals, or even intentional misstatements.[4]

4. A number of research studies in accounting support the conclusion that management's choice of accounting methods (e.g., FIFO vs. LIFO; straight-line vs. accelerated depreciation) is influenced by the existence and nature of executive compensation plans.

To illustrate, suppose in the previous example that Tom Turnstile, who receives a bonus equal to 3 percent of net income each year, is the chief financial officer for Maylein Stoneware. At year-end, rather than reporting net income at $300,000 as stated in the example, he overlooks a $20,000 accrued expense, chooses an accounting method that recognizes $20,000 less of expenses (e.g., FIFO), or postpones $20,000 in research and development expenditures. Any of these acts would cause expenses to be $20,000 less than otherwise and net income to be $320,000 instead of $300,000. Tom's bonus would then be $9,600 ($320,000 × 0.03) instead of $9,000 ($300,000 × 0.03), an increase of $600.

Companies registered with the SEC are required to include in their proxy publications, which inform shareholders about the company and invite them to attend the annual shareholders' meeting, extensive disclosures about the nature and amount of the compensation paid to executives. For example, the 2008 proxy statement for Home Depot reported that Chairman and CEO Francis Blake was paid over $8 million in 2008, consisting of over $1 million in salary, approximately half a million in bonus, and over $6 million in stock-based awards. Discuss why shareholders should be interested in such information.

While executive compensation systems based on net income encourage management to act in the interests of the shareholders, they also encourage management to manipulate the measure of net income. In certain cases, such manipulations could be considered unethical, and furthermore, it may not even be in management's economic interest to do so. As illustrated throughout this text, accounting manipulations normally reverse themselves over time, and shareholders, investors, and creditors may discount the values of companies that provide financial statements of questionable credibility. Nonetheless, all interested parties should still be aware that management has incentives to manipulate income to increase compensation, and often controls the mechanism to do so.[5]

Executive compensation for banks and other financial services firms became a hotbed of discussion during the 2008–2009 recession and the federal government's unprecedented bailout of many firms. Banks such as Bank of America, Goldman Sachs, and JPMorgan Chase, insurance giant AIG, and industrial firms such as General Motors were all subject to public and congressional questioning for their large payments to executives at the same time that the taxpayers funded equity injections and/or takeovers of these firms. Discuss the pros and cons of high executive compensation and what disclosures in the financial statements can tell analysts and other readers about company pay practices.

CONTINGENCIES AND CONTINGENT LIABILITIES

As defined by the FASB, "a contingency is an existing condition, situation, or set of circumstances involving uncertainty as to possible gain or loss to an enterprise that will ultimately be resolved when one or more future events occurs or fails to occur."[6] A common example is an existing lawsuit that will be settled in the future by the decision of a court. If the possible future outcome represents an increase of assets

5. A popular method of compensating executives involves the use of stock options, which is covered in Chapter 12.
6. Financial Accounting Standards Board (FASB), "Accounting for Contingencies," *Statement of Financial Accounting Standards No. 5* (Stamford, Conn.: FASB, 1987), par. 1.

or a decrease of liabilities, the existing condition is considered a **gain contingency.** If the possible outcome represents a decrease in assets or an increase in liabilities, the condition is considered a **loss contingency.**

Before discussing the methods used to account for contingencies, study the following scenario carefully. It is designed to illustrate some of the economic issues involved in reporting contingencies.

Contingent Liabilities: A Scenario

Suppose that Harry Jones, the accountant for Chemical Enterprises, is preparing the financial statements as of December 31, 2011. Chemical Enterprises is in need of cash and plans to submit the financial statements to First National Bank with an application for a sizable loan. First National has required that the statements Harry prepares be audited by an independent CPA. To conduct the audit, Chemical has hired the firm of Arthur Mitchell & Co.

The preparation of the statements has gone smoothly for Harry, except for one rather significant problem. Several months ago, evidence of a small amount of toxic liquid, allegedly from one of Chemical's plants, was found in the water supply of a small midwestern town. The extent of Chemical's responsibility and the nature and extent of any physical harm to the town's residents are still uncertain, but the town has filed suit against Chemical for $1 million, a material amount, and a court case is currently in process. After reviewing the facts of the case, Chemical's lawyers estimate that there is a 70 percent chance that Chemical will successfully defend itself against the lawsuit.

Harry is uncertain how this lawsuit should affect the financial statements of Chemical as of December 31, 2011. As he sees it, the following alternatives represent the three possible ways to account for it.

1. Ignore the lawsuit on the financial statements.
2. Disclose and describe the lawsuit in the footnotes to the financial statements.
3. Recognize a loss on the income statement and a liability on the balance sheet in the amount of $1 million, and disclose and describe the lawsuit in the footnotes.

ALTERNATIVE 1: IGNORE

Under the first alternative, the lawsuit would not be mentioned anywhere in the financial statements. No loss has occurred as of December 31, 2011, and there is a 70 percent chance, according to the lawyers, that no loss will occur at all. Chemical's managers might be inclined to favor this alternative over the others because they suspect that disclosing the lawsuit (Alternative 2) or adjusting the financial statements to reflect it (Alternative 3) could endanger the bank loan or at least make the terms (e.g., interest rate) of the loan less favorable. Ignoring the lawsuit would avoid a negative effect on the financial ratios in general as well as on any contracts based on them.

However, the auditor, Arthur Mitchell & Co., is also aware of the lawsuit and is likely to render a qualified opinion on the financial statements unless some recognition is made of the potential loss. If it is not disclosed, and the auditor grants an unqualified (clean) opinion and the bank makes the loan, the auditor may be liable for any losses the bank incurs as a result of the litigation against Chemical. Ignoring the lawsuit would not be a conservative choice for either the auditor or management and may expose them both to significant legal liability.

ALTERNATIVE 2: DISCLOSE

The second alternative entails disclosing the nature and amount of the lawsuit as well as the opinions of Chemical's legal counsel. This alternative would describe the

situation to the bank as well as other financial report users, but it would have no effect on the dollar amounts in the financial statements. Consequently, financial ratios and contracts written in terms of financial statement numbers would remain unaffected. However, the bank could make any adjustments it saw fit and thereby assess for itself the magnitude of the potential problem.

ALTERNATIVE 3: ACCRUE

The final alternative is to accrue the loss and the related liability on the financial statements. If Harry chooses this action, he would make the following adjusting entry on December 31, 2011.

Contingent Loss (Lo, −RE)	1,000,000	
Contingent Liability (+L)		1,000,000

Accrued contingent liability

The contingent loss account is a temporary account that would appear on the income statement, reducing net income and, ultimately, shareholders' equity. The contingent liability account would appear on the liability side of the balance sheet and be classified as current if payment were expected to require the use of assets listed as current. If Chemical loses the suit and pays the residents of the town, the contingent liability will be written off in the following manner:

Contingent Liability (−L)	1,000,000	
Cash (−A)		1,000,000

Paid contingent liability

Alternative 3 would probably be very unattractive to the management of Chemical. Having to recognize the contingent loss and the associated liability on the financial statements would not only endanger the bank loan but could make important financial ratios appear much less favorable. It could, therefore, put the company in technical default on existing debt covenants as well as reduce compensation from bonus and profit-sharing plans. Furthermore, the court might interpret accrual of the loss as Chemical's own admission that the suit is lost, reducing Chemical's chances of successful defense.

On the other hand, accruing the contingent loss is the most conservative choice. It would therefore substantially reduce the potential legal liability faced by both the auditor and Chemical's management and possibly increase the credibility of both parties in the view of financial statement users. Furthermore, accruing the loss in this period would ensure that it would not have to be accrued in a future period.

In the pharmaceutical industry success involves the creation of effective drugs and the ability to patent them, restricting competitors from producing generic copies once the drug is released. Lawsuits charging patent infringement are common. In its 2008 annual report Eli Lilly, a major pharmaceutical, described four patent infringement lawsuits brought by the company against other pharmaceutical manufacturers attempting to market generic versions of four of Lilly's patented drugs. Lilly noted "it is not possible to predict the outcomes of this litigation and, accordingly, we can provide no assurance that we will prevail. An unfavorable outcome in any of these cases could have a material adverse impact on our consolidated results of operations, liquidity, and financial position." Discuss the related accounting issues.

Accounting for Contingencies

Choosing the appropriate accounting treatment for the situation depicted in the preceding scenario is not a simple matter. Each of the three alternatives is attractive in some respects and unattractive in others. The FASB addresses this problem in Standard No. 5, "Accounting for Contingencies," which provides guidelines that should be followed when accounting for contingencies. This standard first distinguishes between gain contingencies, which involve possible future gains, and loss contingencies, which involve possible future losses.

Figure 10–5 illustrates the methods used to account for both gain and loss contingencies. Note first that each is preceded by an initial event (e.g., the filing of a lawsuit). The probability of the related gain or loss is then assessed, usually by experts in the area, and classified as either "highly probable," "reasonably probable," or "remote." In all cases except highly probable contingent losses, this classification determines whether the gain or loss should be ignored or disclosed in the footnotes. In those cases where a contingent loss is considered highly probable, the question of whether it can be estimated is also addressed. If the loss can be estimated, it is accrued and disclosed. If it cannot, information about the loss is simply disclosed.

FIGURE 10–5
Accounting for contingencies

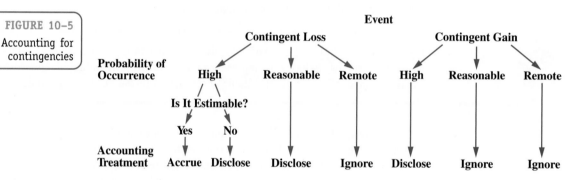

GAIN CONTINGENCIES

Gain contingencies are almost never accrued on the financial statements and are rarely disclosed in the footnotes. They are not recognized until they are actually realized, which is consistent with both the principle of objectivity and the concept of conservatism. It avoids any subjective estimates involved in predicting the outcomes of contingent events and ensures that the financial statements do not reflect gains that may not actually occur.

LOSS CONTINGENCIES

Loss contingencies, on the other hand, are often disclosed, and when highly probable and estimable, they are accrued. The resulting liability is considered current if it is expected to require the use of assets that are listed on the balance sheet as current.

Under IFRS the conditions under which contingent losses are accrued involve a lower threshold than under U.S. GAAP, resulting in more contingent losses being accrued under IFRS.

Classifying contingent losses as "remote," "reasonably probable," or "highly probable" and estimating the dollar amount of "highly probable" contingent losses is often quite subjective. Managers and auditors normally consult legal counsel or other experts, but in areas like lawsuits, it is difficult to predict outcomes accurately. Consequently, relatively few contingent losses stemming from lawsuits are actually accrued on the financial statements. The following quote, taken from an annual report of Johnson & Johnson, provides a typical example.

The Company is involved in numerous product liability cases in the United States, many of which concern adverse reactions to drugs and medical devices. The damages are substantial [and] it is not feasible to predict the ultimate outcome of litigation. However, the Company believes that if any liability results from such cases, it will be substantially covered by the Company's reserves.

When losses are accrued, loss ranges are usually specified in the footnotes, and a "reasonable estimate" within the range typically serves as the dollar amount for the accrual. Owens Corning, for example, accrued a huge liability for outstanding litigation related to asbestos claims dating as far back as 1960. The accompanying footnote described the range of possible settlements, and the amount of the accrual reflected "management's estimate." If no "reasonable estimate" can be agreed upon, the lowest amount in the range is normally used.

Under IFRS, the phrase "best estimate" is used instead of "reasonable estimate," the amount of the liability is represented by the present value of the future expected cash outflows, and the liability itself is referred to as a "provision."

Some accrued losses can be very significant. For example, Paragon Trade Brands, a maker of generic diapers, booked a contingent loss related to a patent infringement case with Procter & Gamble that wiped out its entire shareholders' equity. In another example, Rockwood Holding Co. was issued a qualified opinion by its independent auditors "in connection with litigation related to credit insurance." As reported in *Forbes,* such qualifications are issued by auditors to "protect themselves from future litigation" by alerting investors and "bank credit officers to important footnotes" and material uncertainties about the future of the company.

The 2008 annual report of Bristol-Myers Squibb, a major pharmaceutical, reported that as of December 31, 2008, $38 million was included in current liabilities for various product liability claims. What entry was made to record this liability, what conditions must have been met to justify this accrual, and what effect associated with this accrual would you expect to see on the statement of cash flows?

A major current issue in contingency reporting involves environmental cleanup costs, which some have estimated to be as much as $800 billion. Through "superfund legislation," the U.S. government has established both a fund to clean up pollution and a mandate for companies to clean up existing waste sites. This legislation also empowers the Environmental Protection Agency (EPA) to clean up existing waste sites and then be reimbursed by any party deemed responsible for contaminating the site. Being designated a "potentially responsible party" by the EPA can result in the imposition of

a huge liability. Some estimate that it will cost $65 billion to clean up existing waste sites, and each site is expected to cost an average of $25 million.

Environmental costs are a special concern for heavy manufacturing companies (e.g., petroleum products) and utilities (e.g., power plants) that have been in operation for many years. These companies are finding that they are increasingly being found responsible for environmental cleanup, often due to activities that occurred long before there was much public concern about the environment. While there is often great uncertainty about the actual dollar amount of these liabilities, more and more companies are incurring environmental cleanup costs and, at the same time, are disclosing and accruing contingent environmental liabilities in the annual report.

> **?** Insecticide manufacturer FMC Corporation reported in its 2008 annual report, "Environmental liabilities consist of obligations relating to waste handling and the remediation and/or study of sites at which we are alleged to have released or disposed of hazardous substances. . . . Accordingly, total reserves of $194.2 million and $188.6 million, respectively, before recoveries, were recorded at December 31, 2008 and 2007. . . . In addition, we have estimated that reasonably possible environmental loss contingencies may exceed amounts accrued by approximately $80 million at December 31, 2008." Discuss the company's treatment of environmental contingencies.

In addition to litigation and environmental costs, the contingency framework applies to many other important areas of accounting. The allowance method used to account for uncollectibles, for example, treats bad debts as highly probable and therefore accrues estimable loss contingencies. In the next section, we consider warranties, another important area of accounting that relies on the contingency framework.

WARRANTIES: ACCRUED LOSS CONTINGENCIES

In a **warranty,** a seller promises to remove deficiencies in the quantity, quality, or performance of a product sold to a buyer. Warranties are usually granted for a specific period, during which time the seller promises to bear all or part of the costs of replacing defective parts, performing necessary repairs, or providing additional services. From the seller's standpoint, warranties entail uncertain future costs. It is unlikely that all buyers will take advantage of the warranties granted to them, but enough of them do so to consider the future costs probable and reasonably estimable. Thus, warranties are normally accounted for as accrued contingent losses.

For example, suppose that Hauser and Sons sold ten word processors on July 1 for $1,000 each. Each word processor is under warranty for parts and labor for one year, and based on past experience, the company estimates that, on average, warranty costs will be $100 per unit. During the remainder of the year, several machines require servicing, and as of December 31, $350 of warranty costs had been paid. The following entries would be recorded to reflect these events:

Cash or Accounts Receivable (+A)	10,000	
Sales (R, +RE)		10,000
Sold ten word processors (10 × $1,000)		
Warranty Expense (E, −RE)	1,000	
Contingent Warranty Liability (+L)		1,000
Recognized contingent liability (10 × $100)		

Contingent Warranty Liability (−L)   350
   Cash (−A)   350
Paid warranty liability

    Several features of this accounting treatment are noteworthy. First, the contingent liability is created when the word processors are sold, because at that time Hauser and Sons are responsible for future services. Accordingly, the entire expected warranty expense related to the sale of the ten word processors is recognized in the period of sale, even though only a $350 cost is actually paid. The total warranty expense is thereby matched against sales revenue in the period of sale. Also, the balance in the contingent warranty liability account at the end of the period is $650 ($1,000 − $350), indicating that costs of $650 are still expected during the following six-month period due to warranties. This amount would be listed as a current liability on the December 31 balance sheet. As the following entry illustrates, the $650 contingent liability is removed from the books when costs are incurred to service the warranties as they are exercised in the second period.

Contingent Warranty Liability (−L)   650
   Cash (−A)   650
Paid warranty liability

> **?**
>
> Goodrich Corporation records an accrual for estimated future warranty claims at the time revenue is recognized. At the beginning of 2009, the company reported a warranty liability of $139.2 million; at year-end the amount also totaled $147.6 million. Warranty expense reported on the 2009 income statement totaled $52.3 million. Explain how Goodrich's accounting treatment for warranties is consistent with both contingency reporting and the matching principle. Estimate the cash payments made during 2009 to meet outstanding warranty claims.

PROVISIONS VS. CONTINGENT LIABILITIES: THE "DEVIL IS IN THE DETAILS"

Like most companies that publish IFRS-based financial statements, Unilever, a Dutch consumer-goods manufacturer, reports a balance sheet account called "**provisions**" with a sizable balance. Unilever's 2008 balance sheet, for example, includes a 377 million-euro provision classified as a current liability as well as a 646 million-euro provision classified as a long-term liability. The accounts consist of a collection of accrued liabilities where obligations exist related to past events, and reliable estimates can be made for the likely outcomes. Examples include estimates for unresolved legal and tax disputes, restructuring provisions involving estimated costs associated with projected factory closings and employee layoffs (e.g., severance pay), and other costs that are probable and can be reliably estimated. In these ways, provisions under IFRS are very similar to contingent liabilities under U.S. GAAP.

    However, there are important differences in how these concepts are applied. Provisions are more readily booked than contingent liabilities because under IFRS provisions are accrued when the obligation is "more likely than not," while under U.S. GAAP contingent liabilities are accrued when "highly probable," which is a much higher threshold. Further, under IFRS non-current provisions are valued at the present

value of the future expected cash flows; contingent liabilities under U.S. GAAP are valued at undiscounted cash flows. Finally, when there is a range of possible outcomes associated with the liability, under IFRS the "best estimate" is used, while under U.S. GAAP it is often the lowest value.

These differences illustrate that in many cases the differences between U.S. GAAP and IFRS are more at the application level than at the conceptual level. In concept, a provision and a contingent liability are very much the same, but large differences can arise because the guidelines for how to apply the concepts differ. Indeed, the "devil is in the details."

ROE EXERCISE: MANAGING CURRENT LIABILITIES

The ROE model, introduced and illustrated in Appendix 5A, provides a framework linking the management of a company's operating, investing, and financing activities to its return on the shareholders' investment (return on equity). The management of the nature and level of current liabilities represents important operating activities.

As illustrated by the ROE model, management can increase return on equity by practicing leverage—using borrowed funds to finance investments that provide returns that exceed the cost (e.g., interest) of borrowing. However, at the same time, this strategy imposes a responsibility on management to ensure that the company can remain solvent—generate enough cash to meet the obligations associated with the borrowings as they come due. Consequently, current liabilities play a particularly important role in the solvency ratios (see Chapter 5, Figure 5–3)—current ratio, quick ratio, interest coverage, and accounts payable turnover. Assessing how these ratios change relative to changes in a company's leverage position is an important part of financial statement analysis.

ROE ANALYSIS

Access the Web site (http://www.wiley.com/college/pratt), and conduct ROE analyses on Kohl's versus Dillards and/or Yahoo! versus Google, all four of which carry significant levels of current liabilities, paying special attention to the relationship between the companies' leverage and solvency positions.

APPENDIX 10A

RETIREMENT COSTS: PENSIONS AND POSTRETIREMENT HEALTHCARE AND INSURANCE

This appendix briefly defines and describes how to account for pension and postretirement healthcare and insurance liabilities.

PENSIONS

A **pension** is a sum of money paid to a retired or disabled employee, the amount of which is usually determined by the employees' years of service. For most large companies, pension plans are an important part of the employees' compensation packages, and they are part of almost all

negotiated wage settlements. Pension plans are backed by contractual agreements with the employees and are subject to federal regulation.

Most pension plans are structured so that an employer periodically makes cash payments to a pension fund, which is a legal entity distinct from the sponsoring company. The cash, securities, and other income-earning investments that make up the fund are usually managed by someone outside the company, and the assets in the pension fund do not appear on the company's balance sheet. The employer's cash contributions plus the income generated through the fund's management (i.e., dividends, interest, capital appreciation) provide the cash that is distributed to employees upon retirement. The terms of the pension plan determine the amounts to which individual employees are entitled (benefits).

There are two primary types of pension plans: a defined contribution plan and a defined benefit plan.

Defined Contribution Plan

Under a **defined contribution plan** an employer agrees only to make a series of contributions of a specified amount to the pension fund. These periodic cash payments are often based on employee wages or salaries, and each employee's percentage interest in the total fund is determined by the proportionate share contributed by the employer on the employee's behalf. Under this type of plan, the employer makes no promises regarding how much the employees will receive upon retirement. The actual benefits depend on the investment performance of the fund. The employer guarantees only the inputs (contributions), not the outputs (benefits). Most university business school professors are covered by such a plan.

Accounting for a defined contribution plan is relatively simple because once the employer makes the contribution, the sponsoring company faces no further liability. The cash payment is simply expensed, as in the following journal entry:

Pension Expense (E, −RE)	1,000	
Cash (−A)		1,000

Paid to a defined contribution plan

Defined contribution plans have gained in popularity over the last several years. Defined contribution plans, such as the very common 401(k)s, are considered much less expensive than defined benefit plans, which are covered in the next section. Home Depot, for example, contributed $159 million to its defined contribution pension plan during 2006.

Defined Benefit Plan

Under a **defined benefit plan** the employer promises to provide each employee with a specified amount of benefits upon retirement.[7] Such a guarantee is somewhat more difficult than promising to make specified contributions because the benefits are received by the employees in the future and therefore are uncertain. The benefits must be predicted, and the employer must contribute enough cash so that the contributions plus the earnings on the assets in the fund will be sufficient to provide the promised benefits as they come due. The employees of most major U.S. companies are covered by defined benefit plans.[8]

In the past, many employers under defined benefit plans either set aside no funds or failed to set aside enough to cover their future pension obligations. They simply paid the obligations as they came due, often out of the company's current operating capital. This practice not only represented poor financial management but, on occasion, left retired employees short of their rightful pension benefits. To help ensure that retired employees received what was promised

---

7. The social security system currently operating in the United States is a type of defined benefit pension plan; the federal government promises U.S. citizens a specified amount of benefits at age sixty-five. Presumably, these benefits are paid out of a fund that contains income-earning securities.

8. *Accounting Trends and Techniques* (New York; AICPA, 2009) reports that, of the major U.S. companies surveyed, almost 75 percent disclose the existence of a defined benefit pension plan.

them, Congress passed the **Employment Retirement Income Security Act (ERISA)** in 1974, which requires employers to fund their plans at specified minimum levels and provides other safeguards designed to protect employees.

The basic accounting procedures and the theories underlying accounting for defined benefit pension plans are really quite simple. In accordance with the matching principle, pension expense and the associated liability are accrued each period as employees earn their rights to future benefits (i.e., during the years when the employees provide services and help the company to generate revenues). The periodic adjusting entry to record this accrual takes the following form:

Pension Expense (E, −RE)	800	
Pension Liability (+L)		800

Recognized $800 pension liability

The periodic cash payments made by the employer to the pension fund simply reduce the pension liability as in the following journal entry, and the pension liability that appears on the balance sheet is simply the difference between the accrued liability and the cash payments. A large pension liability indicates that a significant amount of the expected pension costs has yet to be funded.

Pension Liability (−L)	500	
Cash (−A)		500

Paid $500 to pension fund

The primary difficulties in accounting for and managing a defined benefit plan are in (1) determining the appropriate dollar amount of the periodic accrual entry (i.e., Pension Expense debit and Pension Liability credit) and (2) deciding how much cash needs to be contributed to the pension fund to cover the eventual liability. The ultimate pension cost cannot be known for certain until the employees have received all the benefits to which they are entitled. This will not be known until the employees' deaths as well as the deaths of their survivors, who may also be entitled to certain benefits. Unpredictable factors such as employee life expectancies, employee turnover rates, future salary and wage rates, and pension fund growth rates all have a bearing on this determination.

Most companies hire actuaries (statisticians who specialize in such areas as assessing insurance risks and setting premiums) to establish estimates of the future pension costs and to provide methods for allocating those future costs to current periods (called *actuarial cost methods*). Generally accepted accounting principles require that an employer periodically recognize an expense and an associated liability in an amount that is established by one of many acceptable actuarial methods. The amount of this accrual is usually equal to an estimate of the present value of the pension benefits earned by employees during a given period. These amounts are very inexact, depending largely on subjective estimates and assumptions. As a matter of policy, contractual obligation, or law (ERISA), most companies make periodic cash payments to their pension plans in amounts that approximate the accruals they have chosen to record. Thus, the pension liability appearing on most balance sheets is either zero or relatively small.

Gains in the stock market in the late 1990s boosted the fair market values of company pension plans, creating gains that are reflected in reported net income. As *Newsweek* (April 24, 2000) suggested, "these gains are expected to pad the profits of some big companies for years to come," including General Electric, SBC Communications, IBM, Lucent Technologies, and BellSouth. Analysts warn that income from appreciated pension assets is not part of the company's core activities. While the news was good for these companies, it was not quite the same as rising earnings due to success in a company's core business. Indeed, stock market losses since that time have wiped out many of those gains.

As specified in *Financial Accounting Standards Nos. 87* and *88,* the accounting methods and disclosure requirements for pension plans are more comprehensive and complex than indicated in this appendix. The following excerpt from the 2008 annual report of Eli Lilly represents only a small portion of the required disclosures (dollars in millions).

As of the end of 2008, the pension benefit obligation was $6.35 billion and the market value of the assets designated to cover the obligation was $4.80 billion, indicating that the assets were not sufficient to cover the future obligation.

	Defined Benefit Pension Plans	
	2008	2007
Change in benefit obligation		
Benefit obligation at beginning of year	$ 6,561.0	$6,480.3
Service cost	260.1	287.1
Interest cost	409.8	362.4
Actuarial (gain) loss	(257.4)	(373.1)
Benefits paid	(338.4)	(311.0)
Plan amendments	(2.4)	32.7
Foreign currency exchange rate changes and other adjustments	(279.0)	82.6
Benefit obligation at end of year	6,353.7	6,561.0
Change in plan assets		
Fair value of plan assets at beginning of year	7,304.2	6,519.0
Actual return on plan assets	(2,187.8)	833.8
Employer contribution	223.7	202.9
Benefits paid	(326.1)	(301.4)
Foreign currency exchange rate changes and other adjustments	(217.9)	49.9
Fair value of plan assets at end of year	4,796.1	7,304.2
Funded status	(1,557.6)	743.2
Unrecognized net actuarial loss	3,474.8	1,143.3
Unrecognized prior service cost (benefit)	72.7	88.4
Net amount recognized	$ 1,989.9	$1,974.9

Accounting for pension plans is also quite subjective, relying heavily on estimates and assumptions. Furthermore, a small change in an important estimate can have a significant effect on both the amount funded by the company and the pension expense and liability reported on its financial statements. For example, to determine what a company must contribute to the pension plan each year, company accountants must estimate the fund's future annual return. The *Wall Street Journal* reported that over a three-year period, GM predicted an annual return on its pension fund of 11 percent but realized only an 8.7 percent return. Missing that target understated the company's pension expense by "a couple hundred million" and led to a funding shortfall of similar size.

POSTRETIREMENT HEALTHCARE AND INSURANCE COSTS

Most large companies cover a portion of the healthcare and insurance costs incurred by employees after retirement. Similar to pensions, such coverage is part of employee compensation and is earned over an employee's years of service. According to the matching principle, therefore, such costs should be accrued over the employee's tenure with the company, and then the associated liability should be written off as the benefits are paid after the employee's retirement. The issues of estimating this liability, providing adequate funds to meet required future payments, and accounting for such transactions are very similar to those involved with pensions, and accordingly, the appropriate accounting methods are basically the same.

The following excerpt comes from the 2008 annual report of Eli Lilly which, like many other companies, provides the same disclosures for postretirement healthcare costs as they do for pensions (dollars in millions).

| | Retiree Health Benefit Plans | |
	2008	2007
Change in benefit obligation		
Benefit obligation at beginning of year	$1,622.8	$1,740.7
Service cost	62.1	70.4
Interest cost	105.7	101.4
Actuarial (gain) loss	101.6	16.4
Benefits paid	(92.2)	(81.6)
Plan amendments	—	(227.7)
Foreign currency exchange rate changes and other adjustments	(3.7)	3.2
Benefit obligation at end of year	1,796.3	1,622.8
Change in plan assets		
Fair value of plan assets at beginning of year	1,348.5	1,157.3
Actual return on plan assets	(438.6)	147.4
Employer contribution	87.9	125.4
Benefits paid	(92.2)	(81.6)
Foreign currency exchange rate changes and other adjustments	—	—
Fair value of plan assets at end of year	905.6	1,348.5
Funded status	(890.7)	(274.3)
Unrecognized net actuarial loss	1,409.6	820.3
Unrecognized prior service cost (benefit)	(261.6)	(297.7)
Net amount recognized	$ 257.3	$ 248.3

APPENDIX 10B

DEFERRED INCOME TAXES

We have noted that the rules for computing income and expenses for purposes of taxation, as specified by the Internal Revenue Service, are different from generally accepted accounting principles, which specify how financial accounting net income is to be measured. These differences can be divided into two categories: permanent and timing differences. Permanent differences never reverse themselves, while timing differences do. Premiums paid on life insurance policies covering key employees, for example, are not deductible for tax purposes, but they are charged against income for financial reporting purposes. Interest received on municipal bonds is not included in taxable income but is recognized as revenue on a company's income statement. The different treatments for tax and financial accounting purposes in these two examples are considered permanent, because in neither case will the effect on income of the different treatments reverse itself over the life of the asset.

One of many common temporary differences arises when a company depreciates its fixed assets using an accelerated method when computing taxable income and the straight-line method when preparing the financial statements. This strategy causes taxable income to be less than accounting income in the early periods of the asset's life, but as illustrated in Chapter 9, this difference reverses itself in the asset's later years. Many accountants believe that timing differences of this kind create a liability, called deferred income taxes, in the asset's early years, which is discharged in the later years.

THE CONCEPT OF DEFERRED INCOME TAXES

Suppose that Midland Plastics purchased a piece of equipment on January 1, 2009, for $9,000. The equipment is expected to have a three-year useful life and no salvage value. Midland computes depreciation using the double-declining-balance (DDB) method for income tax purposes and straight-line for reporting purposes. In 2009, Midland's choice to use two different depreciation methods creates an income tax expense on the income statement, which is based on straight-line depreciation, that is greater than its income tax liability, which is based on double-declining-balance depreciation. In 2010 and 2011, the difference reverses itself, and the income tax expense is less than the income tax liability. Figure 10B–1 provides a schedule of these differences and, assuming an income tax rate of 30 percent, computes the tax effects associated with using DDB instead of straight-line for tax purposes.

FIGURE 10B–1

Income tax effects due to DDB depreciation

Year	DDB Depr.[a]		SL Depr.[b]		Excess (Under) Depr.		Tax Rate		Tax Benefit (Disbenefit)
2009	$6,000	–	$3,000	=	$3,000	×	30%	=	$ 900
2010	2,000	–	3,000	=	(1,000)	×	30%	=	(300)
2011	1,000	–	3,000	=	(2,000)	×	30%	=	(600)
Total	$9,000		$9,000		$ 0				$ 0

[a][$9,000 – accumulated depreciation] × 2[straight-line rate (33%)]
[b]$9,000/3 yr

Note that use of the DDB method, instead of straight-line, creates a tax savings of $900 in 2009, the first year of the equipment's useful life. In 2010 and 2011, however, this benefit reverses itself, giving rise to additional tax payments of $300 in 2010 and $600 in 2011. As of the end of 2009, Midland can view these additional tax payments as liabilities, because many consider them to be future obligations. Specifically, additional tax payments that total $900 ($300 + $600) are expected in 2010 and 2011. This liability is reported on the balance sheet and referred to as deferred income taxes. Midland Plastics, in other words, would report a deferred income tax liability of $900 in the liability section of its 2009 balance sheet.

During 2010 and 2011, as the tax benefit reverses itself and Midland pays the additional taxes, the deferred income tax liability is reduced by $300 in 2010 and by $600 in 2011. As of the end of 2011, therefore, after the useful life of the equipment has expired, the deferred income tax liability will have been reduced to zero.

ACCOUNTING ENTRIES FOR DEFERRED INCOME TAXES

Preparing the journal entry to record the recognition or discharge of deferred income taxes consists of three steps:

1. Compute the future income tax disbenefit ($900 = $300 + $600) as illustrated in Figure 10B–1. This dollar amount is entered as a credit to the deferred income tax account. The dollar amounts of the reversals (2010: $300, 2011: $600) are entered as debits to the deferred income tax account in future periods.

2. Compute the company's income tax liability (taxable income × corporate income tax rate). This dollar amount is entered as a credit to the income tax payable account.
3. Enter a debit to the income tax expense account in an amount that brings the journal entry into balance. Income tax expense is also equal to the net income before tax amount reported on the income statement multiplied times the company's effective income tax rate.

To illustrate, assume in the preceding example that Midland Plastics recognized taxable income in the amount of $4,000, $8,000, and $9,000 in 2009, 2010, and 2011, respectively.[9] At a 30 percent tax rate, the company's tax liability, therefore, is $1,200 (2009), $2,400 (2010), and $2,700 (2011). Given this information, Figure 10B–2 contains the journal entries, and the balance sheet carrying values of the deferred income tax account for the three-year period.

FIGURE 10B–2   Deferred income taxes

2009			2010			2011		
Inc. Tax Exp. (E, −RE)	2,100*		Inc. Tax Exp. (E, −RE)	2,100*		Inc. Tax Exp. (E, −RE)	2,100*	
Deferred Inc. Tax (+L)		900	Deferred Inc. Tax (−L)	300		Deferred Inc. Tax (−L)	600	
Inc. Tax Pay. (+L)		1,200	Inc. Tax Pay. (+L)		2,400	Inc. Tax Pay. (+L)		2,700
Balance sheet excerpt:								
Deferred income tax		900	(900 − 300)		600	(600 − 600)		0

*Plug or effective income tax rate times Net Income before Taxes.

In 2009, a deferred tax liability of $900 is recognized because Midland, which uses the DDB method for tax purposes, expects to pay additional income taxes of $300 and $600 over the next two years. An income tax liability of $1,200 is also recognized, and Income Tax Expense is debited for an amount ($2,100) that brings the journal entry into balance. In 2010 and 2011, as Midland pays the additional taxes, the deferred income tax account is reduced.

DEFERRED INCOME TAXES: ADDITIONAL ISSUES

The size of the deferred income tax liability account is usually related to the size of a company's investment in fixed assets. Note in Figure 10B–3 that large manufacturing companies, such as Merck, often carry huge balances in their deferred income tax accounts. Such companies normally depreciate their fixed assets using accelerated methods for tax purposes and straight-line for financial reporting purposes, and the resulting differences between their tax liability and income tax expense can be quite large. On the other hand, financial institutions, which carry limited investments in fixed assets, rarely show balances in the deferred income tax account. JPMorgan Chase, the American Express Company, and Safeco Insurance, for example, report no deferred income taxes on their balance sheets.

---

9. In this example, net income before taxes reported on Midland's income statement would be $7,000 (2009), $7,000 (2010), and $7,000 (2011), giving rise to an income tax expense of $2,100 ($7,000 × .30) for each year.

FIGURE 10B–3

Deferred income
tax liability
(selected U.S.
companies)

Company	Deferred Tax Liability (millions)	Percentage of Total Assets
Southwest Airlines	$1,904	13%
Merck	7,767	16%
Avis Budget	1,188	10%
Johnson & Johnson	1,432	2%

Source: 2008 annual reports.

As explained earlier, the deferred income tax account can be viewed as a liability, reflecting an obligation for additional income tax that must be paid in the future as certain tax benefits reverse. However, growing companies tend to purchase more fixed assets than they retire, which, in turn, causes fixed assets in the early (benefit) periods of their useful lives to exceed those in the later (disbenefit) periods. This phenomenon causes the credit balance in the deferred income tax account to accumulate, and many of the largest companies in the United States have amassed huge dollar amounts in deferred income taxes in this manner.

Another interesting aspect about deferred income taxes is that income statement gains and losses can be recognized when income tax rates change. Consider, for example, the General Electric (GE) Company, which at one time had accumulated excess depreciation (i.e., accelerated in excess of straight-line) of approximately $4 billion. At the then-current tax rate of 48 percent, these benefits translated to a deferred income tax liability of $1.92 billion ($4 billion × 48%), which GE reported on its balance sheet. However, when the corporate income tax rate was reduced to 34 percent, GE used the new tax rate and recalculated its deferred income tax liability to be $1.36 billion ($4 billion × 34%). Reducing the liability gave rise to an approximate gain of $560 million ($1.92 billion − $1.36 billion), which appeared on the income statement and was recorded with the following entry (dollars in millions):

Deferred Income Tax (−L)	560	
Gain on Change in Income Tax Rate (Ga, +RE)		560

Recognized gain due to reductions in future
income tax rates

Similarly, when corporate tax rates later went up from 34 to 35 percent, a number of companies were forced to recognize an additional liability and a charge to earnings. Coca-Cola Enterprises, for example, took a $40 million charge.

The methods used to account for deferred income taxes are controversial and much more complicated than indicated in this discussion. More in-depth coverage can be found in intermediate accounting texts. Nonetheless, this issue is important to all interested parties because calculating the amount of deferred income tax and reporting it as a liability or otherwise can have significant economic consequences. For example, should the computation of the debt/equity ratio include or exclude deferred income tax? Considering the size of the deferred income tax liability, how interested parties answer this question can affect their solvency assessments of certain companies.

THE CONSERVATISM RATIO

An important theme in this text is that meaningful financial statement analysis cannot be conducted without assessing the extent to which management has used its discretion when preparing the financial statements. We have often noted that such discretion can be used to understate (report conservatively) or overstate the financial condition and performance of a company.

A measure of the extent to which reported income is conservative, called the **conservatism ratio,** can be constructed from information disclosed in the annual report and is as follows.

Conservatism Ratio: Reported Income before Taxes/Taxable Income

The intuition underlying this ratio is based on the premise that for tax purposes companies accelerate tax-deductible expenses and defer taxable revenues as long as is allowable under income tax laws. Thus, taxable income (taxable revenues − tax-deductible expenses), the denominator of the ratio, reflects a very conservative measure of a company's income in a particular year. The extent to which reported income before taxes, the numerator of the ratio, exceeds (or is less than) taxable income indicates how conservative reported income is. Ratio amounts around 1.0 or less indicate relatively conservative levels, while reported income becomes increasingly less conservative as the ratio grows larger than 1.0.

Figure 10B–4 provides 2008 conservatism ratios for three major U.S. companies. Assuming that all three companies reported conservatively to the IRS, it appears that the 2008 financial reporting policies of GE were more conservative than those of FedEx, which were more conservative than those of Walgreens.

FIGURE 10B–4
Conservatism ratios

MANUFACTURING	
General Electric	**0.51**
SERVICE	
FedEx	**1.07**
RETAILER	
Walgreens	**1.29**

Source: 2008 annual reports.

The conservatism ratio cannot be computed entirely from the dollar amounts on the financial statements; additional information contained in the footnotes is also required. Reported income before taxes, the numerator, can be taken directly from the income statement. Taxable income, the denominator, must be computed indirectly, as follows:

Taxable Income = Current Year's Tax Liability/The Effective Income Tax Rate

Both the current year's tax liability and the effective income tax rate are required disclosures under GAAP and can be found in the footnotes.[10] The following excerpt is selected information taken from the footnotes of General Electric's 2008 annual report, followed by the calculation of GE's conservatism ratio in Figure 10B–5 (dollars in millions).

Footnote 7. Provision for Income Taxes

	2008	2007
Current tax expense	$2,336	$3,498
Deferred tax expense	(1,284)	657
Tax expense	1,052	4,155
Actual income tax rate	5.5%	15.6%

10. If the current year's tax liability is not immediately apparent in the footnotes, it can also be computed by subtracting the change in deferred income taxes on the balance sheet from the tax expense reported on the income statement. Increases (decreases) in net deferred income tax liabilities during the year should be subtracted from (added to) tax expense as reported on the income statement.

FIGURE 10B-5

The conservatism ratio of General Electric (dollars in millions)

Conservative ratio computation (2008):

Taxable income = Current year's tax liability/Effective tax rate
  $42,473   = $2,336   /   .055

Conservatism ratio = Reported income before taxes/Taxable income
   0.51   = $21,516*   / $42,473

*Reported on the 2008 income statement

The conservatism ratio provides a quick way to assess how conservative management's reporting choices have been in a particular year. Much more important, however, are the reasons and activities that explain the difference between reported income and taxable income, and these can be identified only through a close study of the footnotes.

The conservatism ratio for General Electric decreased from 1.13 in 2007 to 0.51 in 2008. Briefly explain what may have caused the change and how this information might be helpful to an analyst.

REVIEW PROBLEM

Before adjustments and closing on December 31, 2011, the financial records of Martin Brothers indicated the following balances:

Cash	$23,000	Accounts payable		$13,000
Accounts receivable	14,000	Short-term notes	$10,000	
Inventory	32,000	Less: Discount on notes	1,000	9,000
		Unearned revenue		3,000
		Other current liabilities		13,000
Total current assets	$69,000	Total current liabilities		$38,000

The terms of an outstanding long-term note payable state that Martin must maintain a current ratio of 1.5, or the note will be in default. The current ratio computed from the information above is 1.82 ($69,000 ÷ $38,000). However, the following transactions are not reflected in the above balances:

1. Merchandise purchased on account for $5,000 was in transit as of December 31, 2011. The terms of the purchase were FOB shipping point.
2. One-half of the interest on the $10,000 short-term note payable should be accrued as of December 31.
3. A $4,000 installment on a long-term debt will be due on March 31, 2012. Martin Brothers intends to withdraw $4,000 from a fund, listed on the balance sheet as a long-term investment, to meet the payment.
4. One-third of the unearned revenue has been earned as of December 31.
5. Wages in the amount of $4,000 are owed as of December 31. Federal income and social security taxes withheld on these wages equal $800 and $400, respectively.
6. The total income tax liability for 2011 was estimated at year-end to be $34,000. Income tax payments during the year totaled $32,000.
7. Albinus, Inc. brought suit against Martin Brothers early in 2011. As of December 31, Martin's legal counsel estimates that there is a 50 percent probability that Martin will lose the suit in the amount of $8,000. If Martin loses the suit, payment will be due within the next year.

The journal entry, if necessary, for each additional transaction and the current ratio after all adjustments have been recorded are as follows:

Trans-action	Current Assets	Journal Entry			Current Liabilities
	$69,000				$38,000
1.	+5,000	Inventory (+A)	5,000		
		Accounts Payable (+L)		5,000	+5,000
2.		Interest Expense (E, −RE)	500		
		Discount on Note (+L)		500	+500
3.		No entry—not payable from current assets.			
4.		Unearned Revenue (−L)	1,000		
		Earned Revenue (R, +RE)		1,000	(1,000)
5.		Wage Expense (E, −RE)	4,000		
		Federal Income Tax Payable (+L)		800 ⎤	
		Social Security Tax Payable (+L)		400 ⎬	+4,000
		Wages Payable (+L)		2,800 ⎦	
		Tax Expense (E, −RE)	400		
		Social Security Tax Payable (+L)		400	+400
6.		Income Tax Expense (E, −RE)	2,000		
		Income Tax Payable (+L)		2,000	+2,000
		Recorded income tax liability			
7.		Depends upon whether a 50 percent probability is considered "reasonably possible" or "probable."			
		If the loss is considered "reasonably possible," it is only disclosed and not included as a current liability.			
		If the loss is considered "probable," the contingent loss is accrued with the following journal entry:			
		Contingent Loss (E, −RE)	8,000		
		Contingent Liability (+L)		8,000	+8,000
	$74,000	Total current assets			
		Total current liabilities:			
		Not including contingent loss			$48,900
		Including contingent loss			$56,900

Current ratio not including contingent loss = 1.51 ($74,000/$48,900)
Current ratio including contingent loss = 1.30 ($74,000/$56,900)

Martin Brothers will be in default on the long-term liability if the contingent loss is accrued. The current ratio (1.30) will be below the ratio required in the debt covenant (1.5). If the contingent loss is only disclosed, the 1.51 current ratio will meet the requirements of the covenant.

SUMMARY OF KEY POINTS

● *Definition of a liability.*

The FASB has defined liabilities as "probable future sacrifices of economic benefits arising from present obligations of a particular entity to transfer assets or provide services to other entities in the future as a result of past transactions or events." All liabilities appearing on the balance sheet should have three characteristics in common: (1) They should be present obligations that entail settlements by probable future transfers or uses of cash, goods, or services; (2) they should be unavoidable obligations; and (3) the transaction or event obligating the enterprise must have already happened.

● *Economic consequences associated with reporting liabilities on the financial statements.*

Disclosing a liability on the balance sheet affects important financial ratios (e.g., current ratio, debt/equity, debt/assets) that are used by shareholders, investors, creditors, and others (1) to assess the financial performance and condition of a company and (2) to direct and control the actions of managers through contracts. Each of these parties has an economic interest in the amount of debt that a company must pay. Financial ratios, which use balance sheet liabilities, are also found in debt contracts to protect creditors by limiting future borrowings, dividend payments, and other management actions. Such economic consequences create incentives that encourage managers in certain situations to either understate or overstate liabilities.

● *Determinable and contingent liabilities.*

Determinable liabilities can be precisely measured, and the amounts of cash needed to satisfy the obligations and the dates of payment are reasonably certain. Examples include accounts and short-term notes payable, dividends payable, unearned revenues, third-party collections, and accrued liabilities. Determinable liabilities can also be conditional on certain events. Examples include liabilities associated with income tax and employee incentive compensation. Contingent liabilities result from existing conditions that can lead to negative outcomes in the future, depending on the occurrence of given events. Examples include lawsuits, uncollectibles, and warranties.

● *Current liabilities.*

Current liabilities are obligations that are expected to require the use of current assets or the creation of other current liabilities. They include obligations to suppliers, short-term notes payable, current maturities of long-term debts, dividends payable to shareholders, unearned revenues, third-party collections, periodic accruals, certain conditional liabilities, potential obligations related to pending or threatened litigation, and product warranties.

● *Bonus systems and profit-sharing arrangements and the reporting incentives they create.*

Bonus systems are popular because they provide a means for shareholders to induce management and other employees to act in a manner consistent with the objectives of the shareholders. Such incentives are created by basing compensation on profits. Managers have some control, however, over the measure of profits through operating, investing, and financing decisions, the choice of accounting methods, estimates, assumptions, and the timing of accruals. They can use this control to increase their bonus compensation.

● *Methods used to account for contingencies.*

Contingencies can be divided into two categories: gain contingencies and loss contingencies. Gain contingencies are rarely accrued and are only disclosed in the footnotes when they are highly probable. The probability of a loss contingency should be classified as either remote,

reasonably possible, or highly probable. If the probability is remote, the loss need not be disclosed. If the event is reasonably possible, the potential loss and all relevant information about it should be disclosed in the footnotes. If the event is viewed as highly probable and the amount of the loss can be estimated, the potential loss and associated liabilities should be accrued on the financial statements and described in the footnotes. When a sale is made that includes a warranty, the sale is recorded. Because the warranty liability is highly probable and can be estimated with reasonable accuracy, warranty expense and the contingent warranty liability should be recognized in the amount of the estimated future warranty costs at the same time. As the warranty costs are paid, the contingent liability is reduced.

KEY TERMS

Note: Definitions for these terms are provided in the glossary at the end of this text.

Commercial paper (p. 445)
Conservatism ratio (p. 465)
Debt ratio (p. 458)
Defined benefit plan (p. 458)
Defined contribution plan (p. 458)
Determinable current liabilities (p. 444)
Employment Retirement Income Security
   Act (ERISA) (p. 459)
Face value (p. 443)

Gain contingency (p. 451)
Line of credit (p. 445)
Loss contingency (p. 451)
Maturity date (p. 445)
Open account (p. 444)
Pension (p. 457)
Provisions (p. 456)
Warranty (p. 455)

ETHICS in the Real World

Earlier in the chapter we noted that FMC Corporation carries liabilities for environmental cleanup. The company estimates environmental expenses by choosing the lower end of the range of estimates in cases where no point within the range is more likely than any other. This policy ensures that the expense for environmental costs appearing on the income statement is as low as reasonably possible.

ETHICAL ISSUE Is it ethical for a company to choose the lower end of a range when estimating the level of expense to record for contingent losses such as environmental costs?

INTERNET RESEARCH EXERCISE

The costs associated with future environmental cleanup are significant, and companies like Waste Management, introduced at the beginning of the chapter, deal with estimating these costs continually. *SFAS No. 5* provides some guidance on accounting for these costs. When was the standard issued? Summarize its contents, and explain how it applies to the situation faced by Waste Management. You can begin your search at the FASB's home page (www.FASB.org).

BRIEF EXERCISES

REAL DATA

BE10–1

Cash flow
and accruals

Merck & Co. declared dividends (dollars in millions) of $3,250.4 (2008), $3,310.7 (2007), and $3,318.7 (2006). Cash payments for dividends reported on the statement of cash flows for the three years were $3,278.5 (2008), $3,307.3 (2007), and $3,322.6 (2006). Dividends payable at the end of 2007 totaled $831.1.

a. Briefly explain why dividends on the statement of shareholders' equity do not equal dividends on the statement of cash flows.
b. What kind of liability is dividends payable?
c. Calculate dividends payable at the end of 2008.

REAL DATA

BE10–2

Inferring financial
information

The following information was taken from the 2008 annual report of Target Corporation (dollars in millions):

	2008	2007
INCOME STATEMENT		
Cost of goods sold	$44,157	$42,929
BALANCE SHEET		
Inventory	6,705	6,780
Trade accounts payable	6,337	6,721

a. Compute the inventory purchases made by Target during 2008. Record a single entry that reflects these purchases.
b. How much cash did Target pay to its suppliers in 2008? Record a single entry that reflects these payments.

REAL DATA

BE10–3

Cash payments for
environmental cleanup

Monsanto's 2008 annual report stated that the company's liabilities for environmental remediation and litigation contingencies are $262 million as of 8/31/09 ($272 million as of 8/31/08).

a. Describe how the liabilities affected the basic accounting equation.
b. What accounting principle is being followed by Monsanto? Explain.
c. Assume $25 million was actually spent in 2009 to remediate environmental problems. Draw a T-account and reconstruct 2009 changes for contingencies.

REAL DATA

BE10–4

Cash flow implications

Target Corporation's 2008 financial statements included the following items (dollars in millions):

INCOME STATEMENT:	
Cost of sales	$44,157
STATEMENT OF CASH FLOWS (OPERATING SECTION):	
Increase in accounts receivable	458
Decrease in inventory	77
Decrease in accounts payable	389

a. Assuming that accounts payable refers only to inventory suppliers, compute the cash payments made by Target during 2008 to inventory suppliers.
b. Review the changes in the current accounts above and comment on the cash flow implications to Target (i.e., did they help to increase or decrease cash flows?).

EXERCISES

E10–1

Why are current liabilities carried at face value instead of present value?

Winslow Enterprises reports $40,000 in accounts payable on the balance sheet as of December 31, 2011. These payables, on average, will be paid in ten days.

a. Assuming a 12 percent annual discount rate, approximate the present value of the cash outflows associated with the accounts payable. (*Note:* Knowledge of present value [Appendix A] is required to do this exercise.)

b. Why are accounts payable carried on the balance sheet at face value instead of present value?

E10–2

Financing with long-term debt, contract terms, and the current ratio

Darrington and Darling borrowed $100,000 from Commercial Financing to finance the purchase of fixed assets. The loan contract provides for a 12 percent annual interest rate and states that the principal must be paid in full in ten years. The contract also requires that Darrington and Darling maintain a current ratio of 1.5:1. Before Darrington and Darling borrowed the $100,000, the company's current assets and current liabilities were $130,000 and $80,000, respectively.

a. Compute the company's current ratio if it invests $50,000 of the borrowed funds in fixed assets and keeps the rest as cash or short-term investments. To what dollar amount can current liabilities grow before the company violates the debt contract?

b. Compute the company's current ratio if it invests $80,000 of the borrowed funds in fixed assets and keeps the rest as cash or short-term investments. To what dollar amount can current liabilities grow before the company violates the debt contract?

c. Compute the company's current ratio if it invests the entire $100,000 of the borrowed funds in fixed assets. To what dollar amount can current liabilities grow before the company violates the debt contract?

E10–3

Accruals, the current ratio, and net income

Lily May Electronics recognizes expenses for wages, interest, and rent when cash payments are made. The following related cash payments were made during December 2011.

1. December 1   Paid $1,100 for rent to cover the subsequent twelve months.
2. December 5 and 20   Paid wages in the amount of $7,500. Wages in the amount of $7,500 are paid on the fifth and the twentieth of each month for the fifteen days just ended. The next payment will be on January 5, 2012.
3. December 15   Paid $600 interest on an outstanding note payable. The note has face value of $10,000 and a 12 percent annual interest rate. Interest payments in the amount of $600 are made every six months.

As of December 31, the current assets and current liabilities reported on Lily May's balance sheet were $24,000 and $15,000, respectively. Lily May's income statement reported net income of $7,500.

Compute Lily May's current ratio and net income if the company were to account for wages, interest, and rent on an accrual basis.

E10–4

Short-term notes payable and the actual rate of interest

On December 1, Spencer Department Store borrowed $19,250 from First Bank and Trust. Spencer signed a ninety-day note with a face amount of $20,000. The interest rate stated on the face of the note is 15 percent per year.

a. Provide the journal entry recorded by Spencer on December 1.

b. Provide the adjusting entry recorded by Spencer on December 31 before financial statements are prepared. Show how the note payable would be disclosed on the December 31 balance sheet.

c. Compute the actual annual interest rate on the note. (*Hint:* Note that Spencer had the use of $19,250 only over the period of the loan.)

d. Why is the actual interest rate different from the rate stated on the face of the note?

E10-5

Current maturities
and debt covenants

On January 1, 2007, Lacey Treetoppers borrowed $300,000, which is to be paid back in annual installments of $20,000 on December 30 of each year.

a. Assuming that Lacey has met all payments on a timely basis, how should this liability be reported on the December 31, 2011, balance sheet?

b. Assume that during December of 2011, the management of Lacey realizes that including the upcoming $20,000 installment as a current liability reduces the company's current ratio below 2:1, the ratio required in a long-term note payable signed by the company. Discuss how management might be able to avoid classifying the current maturity as a current liability.

E10-6

Gift certificates and
unearned revenue

Norsums Department Store sells gift certificates that are redeemable in merchandise. During 2011, Norsums sold gift certificates for $88,000. Merchandise with the total price of $52,000 was redeemed during the year. The cost of the sold merchandise to Norsums was $32,000. Norsums sold gift certificates for the first time in 2011.

a. Record the sale of the gift certificates.

b. Record the redemption during 2011. Assume that Norsums uses the perpetual inventory method.

c. Compute the balance in the unearned revenue account as of December 31, 2012, assuming that gift certificates were sold for $60,000 in 2012 and merchandise with a total price of $80,000 was redeemed.

REAL DATA

E10-7

Inferring a
cash payment

The following information was taken from the 2008 annual report of Bed Bath & Beyond, a leading household retailer (dollars in thousands).

	2008	2007
Cost of goods sold	$4,335,104	$4,123,711
Inventory	1,642,339	1,616,981
Accounts payable	514,734	570,605

a. Assume that accounts payable reflects only accounts with inventory suppliers, and compute the cash payments made to suppliers during 2008.

b. Would this dollar amount be disclosed on the statement of cash flows? Explain.

E10-8

Gain and loss
contingencies

Zeus Power has brought suit against Regional Supply in the amount of $825,000 for patent infringement. As of December 31, the suit is in process, and the attorneys have determined that there is a greater than 50 percent chance that Zeus Power will win the entire $825,000.

a. How should Zeus Power account for this situation?

b. How should Regional Supply account for the situation? Briefly describe some of the factors that might affect how Regional Supply chooses to account for this situation.

c. Why would the two companies account for the same facts in different ways?

E10-9

Bonus plans and
contingent losses

Jordan Brothers recently instituted a bonus plan to pay its executives. The plan specifies that net income must exceed $200,000 before any bonus payments are made. Cash in the amount of 10 percent of net income in excess of $200,000 is placed in a bonus pool, which is to be shared evenly by each of the executives. Ignore income taxes, and assume that the bonus payment is not included as an expense in the calculation of net income.

a. Briefly describe why a company would institute a bonus plan, and compute the amount in the bonus pool if Jordan Brothers shows net income of $300,000. Prepare the journal entry that would be recorded to reflect the bonus liability at the end of the year.

b. How much is in the bonus pool if Jordan Brothers shows net income of $180,000? Assume that Jordan Brothers is being sued for $60,000 as of the end of the year. The company's legal counsel believes that there is an 80 percent chance that Jordan will

lose the suit and that the entire $60,000 will have to be paid. Assume also that the suit was ignored when the $180,000 net income was computed. Why might Jordan's management wish to accrue the loss from the suit in the current year instead of simply disclosing it?

E10–10

Warranty costs:
Contingent losses
or expense as
incurred?

During 2011, Seagul Outboards sold 200 outboard engines for $250 each. The engines are under a one-year warranty for parts and labor, and from past experience, the company estimates that, on average, warranty costs will equal $20 per engine. As of December 31, 2011, 50 engines had been serviced at a total cost of $1,400. During 2012, engines were serviced at a total cost of $2,600. Assume that all repairs used cash.

a. Prepare the journal entries that would be recorded at the following times:
   (1) During 2011 to record the sale of the engines.
   (2) During 2011 to accrue the contingent loss on warranties.
   (3) During 2011 and 2012 to record the actual warranty cost incurred.
b. Assume that Seagul chose not to treat the warranty costs as contingent losses. Instead, it chose to expense warranty costs as they were paid. Compute the total net income for 2011 and 2012 for each of the two accounting treatments.

REAL DATA

E10–11

Deferred revenues
and cash receipts

Southwest Airlines is paid in advance for its ticket sales, recognizing a deferred revenue, called air traffic liability, when it receives the cash. The liability is then converted to revenue when the passenger takes the flight. During 2008 Southwest recognized passenger revenues in the amount of $10.5 billion. On the balance sheet Southwest reported air traffic liabilities of $963 million and $931 million as of the end of 2008 and 2007, respectively.

a. Explain why Southwest does not recognize revenue when it receives the payment from its customers.
b. What kind of a liability is air traffic liability? Discuss whether it should be considered current or long-term.
c. Compute the cash received by Southwest from passengers during 2008.

E10–12

Appendix 10A:
Pension
contributions and
unfunded pension
liability

Seasaw Seasons instituted a defined benefit pension plan for its employees three years ago. Each year since the adoption of the plan, Seasaw has contributed $16,000 to the pension fund, which is managed by Fiduciary Trust Associates. As of the end of the current year, it was estimated that contributions of $58,000 would have been necessary to maintain a fund large enough to provide the benefits promised to the employees when they retire.

a. Prepare the journal entries that were recorded by Seasaw as it contributed cash to the pension fund.
b. How much pension liability should be recorded on Seasaw's balance sheet as of the end of the current year?

E10–13

Appendix 10B:
Deferred taxes and
the tax rate

Swingley Company uses an accelerated method to depreciate its fixed assets for tax purposes and the straight-line method for financial reporting purposes. In 2011, the accelerated method recognized depreciation of $35,000, while the straight-line method recognized depreciation of $20,000. Taxable income and net income before taxes for that year were $65,000 and $80,000, respectively.

a. If the federal income tax rate is 35 percent, prepare the journal entry recorded by Swingley to accrue its 2011 tax liability.
b. If the federal income tax rate is 30 percent, prepare the journal entry recorded by Swingley to accrue its 2011 tax liability.
c. Briefly explain why the deferred income tax account is considered a liability on the balance sheet and why it is less when the tax rate is 30 percent rather than 35 percent.

E10–14

Appendix 10B:
Conservatism ratio

The following information was taken from the annual report of Busytown Industries.

	2011	2010
BALANCE SHEET		
Deferred income tax liability	$ 9,700	$8,300
INCOME STATEMENT		
Income before taxes	$68,000	
Income tax expense	(20,400)	
Net income	$47,600	
Effective income tax rate: 38%		

a. Compute Busytown's conservatism ratio, and comment on how conservative the company's reporting methods are.
b. Explain why the conservatism ratio provides a measure of the extent to which a company's financial accounting methods are conservative, and provide examples of accounting treatments that may increase or decrease the ratio.

E10–15

Appendix 10B:
Conservatism ratio

The following information was taken from the annual report of Sega-Venus Enterprises.

	2011	2010
BALANCE SHEET		
Deferred income tax liability	$ 18,300	$19,400
INCOME STATEMENT		
Income before taxes	$145,500	
Income tax expense	(54,000)	
Net income	$ 91,500	
Effective income tax rate: 34%		

a. Compute Sega-Venus's conservatism ratio, and comment on how conservative the company's reporting methods are.
b. Explain why the conservatism ratio provides a measure of the extent to which a company's financial accounting methods are conservative, and provide examples of accounting treatments that may increase or decrease the ratio.

PROBLEMS

P10–1

Distinguishing
current liabilities
from long-term
liabilities

Beth Morgan, controller of Boulder Corporation, is currently preparing the 2011 financial report. She is trying to decide how to classify the following items.

1. Account payable of $170,000 owed to suppliers for inventory.
2. A $60,000 note payable that matures in three months. The company is planning to acquire a five-year loan from its bank to pay off the note. The bank has agreed to finance the note.
3. A $500,000 mortgage: $75,000 payable within twelve months, and the remaining $425,000 to be paid over the next six years.
4. The sum of $8,000 owed to the phone company for service during December.
5. Advances of $25,000 received from a customer. The contract between the customer and Boulder Corporation states that if the company does not deliver the goods within six months, the $25,000 is to be returned to the customer.
6. The sum of $15,000 due the federal government for income tax withheld from employees during the last quarter of 2011. The government requires that withholdings be submitted by the end of the next quarter to the Internal Revenue Service.

7. A $125,000 note payable: $30,000 is payable within twelve months, and the remaining $95,000 is to be paid over the next two years. Boulder Corporation plans to issue common stock to the creditor for the portion due during the next twelve months.
8. The company declared a cash dividend of $50,000 on December 29, 2011. The dividend is to be paid on January 21, 2012.

REQUIRED:
a. Classify each of the items as a current liability or as a long-term liability. (*Note:* Some items may be classified partially as current and partially as long-term.)
b. Compute the total amount that should be classified as current liabilities.
c. Compute the total amount that should be classified as long-term liabilities.

P10–2

Recognizing current liabilities can restrict dividend payments

Linton Industries borrowed $500,000 from Security Bankers to finance the purchase of equipment costing $360,000 and to provide $140,000 in cash. The note states that the loan matures in twenty years, and the principal is to be paid in annual installments of $25,000. The terms of the loan also indicate that Linton must maintain a current ratio of 2:1 and cannot pay dividends that will reduce retained earnings below $200,000. The balance sheet of Linton, immediately prior to the bank loan and the purchase of equipment, follows:

Current assets	$ 120,000	Current liabilities	$ 100,000
Noncurrent assets	1,500,000	Long-term liabilities	300,000
		Capital stock	1,000,000
		Retained earnings	220,000
		Total liabilities and	
Total assets	$1,620,000	shareholders' equity	$1,620,000

REQUIRED:
The board of directors of Linton is about to declare a dividend to be paid to the shareholders early next year. After accepting the loan and purchasing the equipment, how large a dividend can the board pay and not violate the terms of the debt covenant?

P10–3

Recognizing current liabilities and violating debt covenants

Before adjustments and closing on December 31, 2011, the current accounts of Seymour and Associates indicated the following balances:

	Debit	Credit
Cash	$40,000	
Accounts receivable	50,000	
Allowance for doubtful accounts		2,000
Inventory	52,000	
Accounts payable		30,000
Unearned revenues		25,000
Warranty liabilities		5,000
Other current liabilities		10,000

The terms of an outstanding long-term note payable state that Seymour must maintain a current ratio of 2:1 or the note will become due immediately. The following items are not reflected in the balances above:

1. Bad debt losses in the amount of 6 percent of the outstanding accounts receivable balance are expected.
2. The warranty liability on outstanding warranties is estimated to be $12,000.
3. Forty percent of the unearned revenue had been earned as of December 31.
4. Five thousand dollars, listed above under "other current liabilities," is part of a line of credit and is expected to be immediately refinanced on a long-term basis when due.
5. The total income tax liability for 2011 was estimated at year-end to be $23,000. Estimated tax payments during the year totaled $20,000.

6. Trademans, Inc. brought suit against Seymour early in 2011. As of December 31, Seymour's legal counsel estimates that there is a 60 percent probability that the suit will be lost in the amount of $10,000. If the suit is lost, payment will most likely be due in the next year.

REQUIRED:

a. Prepare the journal entries that would be recorded (if necessary) for each of the six items listed.
b. After preparing the journal entries, compute the company's current ratio, assuming that the contingent liability described in (6) is not accrued.
c. After preparing the journal entries, compute the company's current ratio, assuming that the contingent liability described in (6) is accrued.
d. If you were Seymour's auditor, would you require that the contingent liability be accrued? Discuss.

P10–4

Issues surrounding the recognition of a contingent liability

While shopping on October 13, 2011, at the Floor Wax Shop, Tom Jacobs slipped and seriously injured his back. Mr. Jacobs believed that the Floor Wax Shop should have warned him that the floors were slick; hence, he sued the company for damages. As of December 31, 2011, the lawsuit was still in progress. According to the company's lawyers, it was probable that the company would lose the lawsuit. The lawyers also believed that the company could lose somewhere between $250,000 and $1.5 million, with a best guess of the loss at $742,000. The lawsuit was eventually settled in favor of Mr. Jacobs on August 12, 2012, for $690,000.

REQUIRED:

a. Discuss the issues that the Floor Wax Shop must address in deciding how to report this lawsuit in its 2011 financial report.
b. If you were auditing the Floor Wax Shop, how would you recommend that this lawsuit be reported in the 2011 financial report? Why?
c. Assume that a contingent liability of $742,000 is accrued on December 31, 2011. What journal entry would the company record on August 12, 2012, the date of the settlement?

P10–5

Accruing warranty costs before they are incurred

Arden's Used Cars offers a one-year warranty from the date of sale on all cars. From historical data, Mr. Arden estimates that, on average, each car will require the company to incur warranty costs of $760. The following activities occurred during 2011:

1. February 2   Sold five cars.
2. March 23   Sold ten cars.
3. May 30   Incurred warranty costs of $3,000 on four cars sold in 2010.
4. July 5   Sold eight cars.
5. September 2   Incurred warranty costs of $5,000 on five cars sold in 2011.
6. November 15   Incurred warranty costs of $6,000 on one car sold in 2011.
7. December 20   Sold twelve cars.

REQUIRED:

a. Assume that the cars were sold for cash for an average of $9,500. Prepare the entry to record the car sales during 2011 (combine all the sales and make one entry).
b. Prepare the individual entries to record the warranty costs incurred. Assume that the breakdown of warranty costs is 40 percent wages (paid in cash) and 60 percent parts.
c. Arden accrues its warranty liability with a single adjusting entry at year-end. Prepare that entry.
d. Compute the year-end warranty liability. The beginning balance in the warranty liability account was $3,500.
e. Explain why accountants estimate the warranty expense in the year of sale instead of recording the expenses as the costs are incurred.

P10-6

Advertising campaigns can give rise to contingent liabilities

To kick off its 2011 advertising campaign, Rachel's Breakfast Cereal is offering a $1 refund in exchange for five cereal box tops. The company estimates that the tops of 10 percent of the cereal boxes sold will be returned for the refund. The cereal boxes are sold for $2.00 each. During 2011 and 2012, 20,000 and 28,000 cereal boxes are sold, respectively, and 1,500 and 2,000 box tops are received for refunds during 2011 and 2012, respectively.

REQUIRED:

a. Prepare the journal entries to record the sale of the cereal boxes, the recognition of the contingent liability associated with the potential refunds, and the actual refund payments for 2011 and 2012.

b. Compute the liabilities associated with the potential refunds as of the end of 2011 and 2012.

REAL DATA

P10-7

Restructuring charges and the statement of cash flows

Pharmaceutical manufacturer Eli Lilly announced in the third quarter of 2009 that it was taking a $425 million restructuring charge due to the sale of its Tippecanoe Laboratories unit. Of the total expense, the company indicated that $364 million was related to "non-cash" asset impairment charges, with $61 million coming from severance packages for certain Tippecanoe employees. The third quarter 2009 statement of cash flows (operating section) contains a line item added back to net income for "other, net" in the amount of $364 million.

REQUIRED:

a. Provide the entry made by Lilly to record the charge.

b. Explain why the statement of cash flow contained the $364 million entry.

c. Assume Lilly's tax rate for 2009 was 26 percent. Compute the tax savings related to the charge.

P10-8

Appendix 10A: Accruing and funding pension liabilities

Shelby Company instituted a defined benefit pension plan for its employees at the beginning of 2007. An actuarial method that is acceptable under generally accepted accounting principles indicates that the company should contribute $40,000 each year to the pension fund to cover the benefits that will be paid to the employees. Shelby funded 80 percent of the liability in 2007 and 2008, 90 percent in 2009 and 2010, and 100 percent in 2011.

REQUIRED:

a. Prepare the journal entries to accrue the pension liability and fund it for 2007, 2008, 2009, 2010, and 2011.

b. Compute the balance in the pension liability account as of December 31, 2011.

P10-9

Appendix 10B: Deferred income taxes, changes in tax rates, and investment in long-lived assets

Acme, Inc. purchased machinery at the beginning of 2007 for $50,000. Management used the straight-line method to depreciate the cost for financial reporting purposes and the double-declining-balance method to depreciate the cost for tax purposes. The life of the machinery was estimated to be four years, and the salvage value was estimated as zero. Revenue less expenses other than depreciation (for financial reporting and tax purposes) equaled $100,000 in 2007, 2008, 2009, and 2010. Acme pays income taxes at the rate of 35 percent of taxable income.

REQUIRED:

a. Prepare the journal entries to accrue income tax expense and income tax liability for 2007, 2008, 2009, and 2010. Indicate the balance in the deferred income tax account as of the end of each of the four years.

b. Assume that the federal government changed the tax rate to 20 percent at the beginning of 2009. Repeat the exercise in (a). Would it be appropriate to recognize a gain at the end of 2009 to reflect the tax rate decrease? Why or why not? If so, how much of a gain?

c. Assume that Acme purchased additional machinery at the beginning of 2008 and 2010. Each purchase was for $50,000, and each machine had a four-year estimated life and no salvage value. Once again, the straight-line depreciation method was used for reporting purposes and double-declining-balance for tax purposes. Repeat the exercise in (a) assuming a tax rate of 35 percent. Why is the deferred income tax account one of the largest liabilities on the balance sheets of many major U.S. companies?

P10–10

Appendix 10B:
Conservatism ratio

You are a security analyst for Magneto Investments and have chosen to invest in one firm from the semiconductor manufacturing industry. You have narrowed your choice to either Owen-Foley Company or Amerton Industries, firms of similar size and direct competitors in the industry. The following information was taken from their 2011 annual reports.

OWEN-FOLEY COMPANY	2011	2010
BALANCE SHEET		
Deferred income tax liability	$ 18,400	$16,600
INCOME STATEMENT		
Income before taxes	$163,000	
Income tax expense	(52,000)	
Net income	$111,000	
Effective income tax rate: 36%		

AMERTON INDUSTRIES	2011	2010
BALANCE SHEET		
Deferred income tax liability	$ 18,800	$19,800
INCOME STATEMENT		
Income before taxes	$158,500	
Income tax expense	(53,500)	
Net income	$105,000	
Effective income tax rate: 36%		

REQUIRED:
On the basis of this information, explain which of the two firms seems to have the stronger earning power.

REAL DATA

P10–11

Appendix 10B:
Comparing
conservatism ratios

The following information was taken from the 2008 annual reports of Walgreens and The Limited (dollars in millions).

	Walgreens	The Limited
Net income before taxes	$3,164	$ 453
Income tax expense:		
Current	898	187
Deferred	260	46
Total	$1,158	$ 233
Effective tax rate	0.366	0.515

REQUIRED:
Compute the conservatism ratios for both companies and comment on the differences. Which company is more conservative, and why?

ISSUES FOR DISCUSSION

REAL DATA

ID10–1

Debt covenants and
reporting current
liabilities

FedEx Corporation, a world leader in express mail services, reported the following in its May 31, 2009, financial statements (dollars in millions):

	5/13/09
Current assets	$7,116
Current liabilities	4,524

The company's long-term debt contains restrictive covenants that require the maintenance of certain financial ratios. Assume that these covenants require that the company's current ratio be at least 1.0.

REQUIRED:

a. What additional dollar value of current liabilities could have been reported as of May 31, 2009, without violating the debt covenant?
b. List several current liabilities that management may have been able to control to ensure at year-end that the covenant was not violated, and explain how these liabilities could have been controlled.
c. Explain what could happen if the company violated the covenant.
d. Assume that at the end of 2009, FedEx considered a $3 billion fleet aircraft purchase. Assume also that the company has the necessary cash. Should the company pay cash or should it purchase the aircraft using long-term debt, and why? Support your answer with calculations.

REAL DATA

ID10-2

Receipts in advance:
Measurement theory
and financial
statement effects

Ingersoll-Rand manufactures specialized heavy-duty construction equipment. Included in a set of recent financial statements is the account "customers' advance payments," with a balance of over $15 million. The notes to the financial statements indicate that, although payments are collected in advance from customers, revenues are recognized when products are shipped. Products are normally shipped within six months of the advance payments.

REQUIRED:

a. On what financial statement and in which section of that statement would the account "customers' advance payments" be found?
b. Explain the accounting treatment associated with this account in terms of the principles of revenue recognition and matching.
c. Under this accounting treatment, how are important financial ratios, such as earnings per share, the current ratio, and the debt/equity ratio, affected (1) when the advance payments are received and (2) when the related goods are shipped?

REAL DATA

ID10-3

Contingency reporting

The 2008 annual report for HCA, Inc., a nationwide chain of hospitals, contains the following statement in the footnotes to the financial statements:

We operate in a highly regulated and litigious industry.

Furthermore, the company discloses,

Reserves for professional liability risks were $1.387 billion and $1.513 billion at December 31, 2008 and 2007, respectively. The current portion of this reserve, $279 million and $280 million at December 31, 2008 and 2007, respectively, is included in "other accrued [liabilities]" in the consolidated balance sheet. Provisions for losses related to professional liability risks were $175 million, $163 million and $217 million for 2008, 2007, and 2006, respectively (and) are included in "other operating expenses" in our consolidated income statement. Provisions for losses related to professional liability risks are based upon actuarially determined estimates. Loss and loss expense reserves represent the estimated ultimate net cost of all reported and unreported losses incurred through the respective consolidated balance sheet dates.

REQUIRED:

a. The term *reserve* refers to accrued liabilities. What portion of the reserves reported in 2008 and 2007 is listed in the current liability section of the balance sheet?
b. What entries were made in 2006, 2007, and 2008 to record additional reserves?
c. Estimate the cash payments made during 2008 to cover professional liability risks.
d. Discuss how management could manage earnings in this industry.

REAL DATA

ID10-4

Contingency
reporting in the
tobacco industry

Several years ago in its annual report, Philip Morris Companies, a major manufacturer of tobacco and food products, included footnote 16, which was almost five pages long. It consisted of a number of separate sections covering such topics as an overview of tobacco-related litigation, the type and number of cases, pending and upcoming trials, verdicts in individual cases, litigation settlements, smoking and health litigation, health care and cost-recovery litigation, and certain other tobacco-related litigation. During the year, over 500 smoking and health-related cases had been filed against the company, an increase of 30 percent over the previous year and 200 percent over the year before that. The company booked a pretax charge of over $3 billion, reducing reported net income to slightly over $5 billion.

REQUIRED:

Discuss Philip Morris's disclosure and accrual in terms of (1) the methods used to account for loss contingencies, and (2) the potential economic consequences associated with the disclosure and accounting treatment.

REAL DATA

ID10-5

Unreported assets

Lifschultz Industries, a small gas meter company, once reported a book value of less than zero (i.e., reported liabilities exceeded reported assets). Yet, in late March, the company's share price skyrocketed on news that it was pursuing a massive antitrust and racketeering lawsuit against three of the country's biggest trucking companies: Consolidated Freightways, Roadway Services, and Yellow Freight Systems. Lifschultz alleged that these trucking companies conspired to engage in anticompetitive activity, driving it out of the trucking business. The suit, filed in U.S. district court in South Carolina, sought $1.8 billion. The three trucking companies said nothing about the suit publicly other than to footnote it as a "contingency" in their annual reports.

REQUIRED:

a. Explain how Lifschultz can report negative book value and, at the same time, have its shares so highly valued in the stock market.
b. Explain the differences between how Lifschultz should account for the suit and how the three trucking companies should account for it.
c. Provide economic reasons why the plaintiff and defendants account for the same dispute differently.

REAL DATA

ID10-6

The economic
consequences of a
technical default

The following quote refers to the problems of Campeau Corporation, a Canadian-based retail empire that later declared bankruptcy. At the time, Campeau's department store chains included Bloomingdale's, Rich's, Burdines, Abraham & Strauss, and Lazarus.

Campeau Corp.'s announcement Friday that its bankers believe it has technically defaulted on $2.34 billion in debt probably will freeze new spring shipments, apparel makers say. Citibank, leader of the bank syndicate providing much of Campeau's debt financing, informed Campeau by letter last week that Campeau had violated certain covenants on debt and unless Campeau can remedy the default by December 31, Citibank stated it may demand full repayment of the loans.

REQUIRED:

a. What is a "technical default," and how did Citibank react to it?
b. Explain why apparel makers might "freeze new shipments" and why this presented great problems for the Campeau organization.

REAL DATA

ID10-7

Warranties and
contingencies

Agilent Technologies, Inc., a diversified technology company, sells extended warranties for the products and services provided to customers, deferring the revenue until future recognition. The following information about the extended warranty liability account was taken from Agilent's annual report (dollars in millions):

	2009	2008
Beginning balance	$29	$29
Deferral of revenue	50	51
Recognition of revenue	(51)	(51)
Ending balance	$28	$29

REQUIRED:

a. Draw a T-account for the extended warranty liability, record the activity disclosed above in that account, and explain how the entries represent an application of the matching principle.

b. Explain how the cash flow for warranties is different from the profitability of warranties.

REAL DATA

ID10–8

Deferred revenue

When Microsoft Corporation released earnings for its third quarter of fiscal 2007, profits hit a record $4.9 billion, driven in large part by revenue that was 32 percent higher than the previous year. However, the $14.4 billion in sales included $1.67 billion in deferred revenue from the redemption of upgrade coupons for the company's recently released operating system, Vista, that were never used. The coupons for Vista upgrades were given to customers prior to the release of the new program.

REQUIRED:

a. What is meant by "deferred revenue" and where does it fit in the financial statements?

b. Discuss the cash flow implications of the $1.67 billion in deferred revenue for Microsoft in the current and past fiscal quarters.

c. How do you think an analyst following the company would react to the above earnings announcement? How would the deferred revenues factor into the analysis?

REAL DATA

ID10–9

Current liabilities

Abbott Laboratories, a major pharmaceutical company, reported the following current liabilities in its 2009 annual report (dollars in millions).

	2009	2008	2007
Current liabilities:			
Short-term borrowings	$ 4,978	$ 1,691	$1,827
Trade accounts payable	1,281	1,352	1,219
Employee compensation	1,117	1,011	860
Other accrued liabilities	4,399	5,133	3,713
Dividend payable	621	559	505
Income tax payable	442	805	80
Current portion of long-term debt	211	1,041	899
Total current liabilities	$13,049	$11,592	$9,103

REQUIRED:

a. Briefly describe the transaction or event underlying each of the liabilities listed above.

b. What kinds of assets are expected to be used to meet these obligations?

c. Does Abbott plan in the foreseeable future to refinance any of these liabilities by issuing long-term debt? Explain.

d. Explain how proper management of these current liabilities can help Abbott improve its return on equity.

REAL DATA

ID10–10

Using executive compensation disclosures

The SEC requires additional information in the proxy statements that describe the compensation packages of a company's top executives. A *Wall Street Journal* article published soon after the requirement became effective offered a list of recommendations about how shareholders might use this additional information. Included in the list: Compare executive pay with shareholder returns, check to see if executive compensation is linked to stock market performance, find out how much company stock is owned by the executives, and beware of changes in the auditor.

REQUIRED:

Explain what a proxy statement is, and discuss how each of the recommendations listed above may provide useful information to the shareholders.

A major defense contractor, LTV, faced with huge liabilities, once declared Chapter 11 bankruptcy protection. Under Chapter 11, a company continues to operate but is protected from creditors while it tries to work out a reorganization plan. At that time, the company's management chose to accrue a $2.26 billion liability to reflect the potential cost of medical and life insurance benefits for its 118,000 current and retired employees, which was not required by generally accepted accounting principles. The *Wall Street Journal* reported that the company chose to recognize the charge because "if the company waited until after it negotiated new credit agreements and emerged from bankruptcy law proceedings before taking the $2 billion charge, the additional liability could trigger violations of its debt covenants."

REQUIRED:

a. Provide the journal entry to record the $2.26 billion charge recognized by LTV.
b. Explain how taking the charge before negotiating new credit agreements could avoid violating debt covenants.
c. It was also reported that LTV took several other significant charges while it was under bankruptcy proceedings. In addition to its concern about debt covenants, in general, why might management have chosen to take these charges at this time?

The following information was taken from the 2009 annual report of Emerson, a leader in process management, technology, network power, and industrial automation (dollars in millions).

	2009	2008	2007
Net income before taxes	$2,417	$3,591	$3,093
Income tax expense:			
Current	571	1,085	1,028
Deferred	122	52	(64)
Total	$ 693	$2,137	$ 964
Effective tax rate	28.7%	31.7%	31.2%

REQUIRED:

Comment on whether Emerson's financial accounting methods have been conservative or aggressive across the three-year period.

General Motors once posted net income of $552 million, compared with a loss of $112.9 million a year earlier. Over $200 million of the profit was due to an accounting adjustment in its North American operations because its expected taxes turned out to be lower than it had anticipated in earlier periods. David Healy, an analyst with S.G. Warburg & Co., noted that "Cynics would say that since they couldn't do it in the auto department, they did it in the accounting department."

REQUIRED:

a. Explain what Mr. Healy means.
b. Explain how a change in expected tax rates can lead to a positive effect on reported earnings.
c. Do you believe that the $200 million gain represents an increase in the overall wealth of GM?

The Internet phone company Vonage Holdings faced two separate patent infringement lawsuits initiated by Verizon and Sprint Nextel due to the technology used to provide Web-based communication services for its customers. The threat to Vonage's viability was severe, given

its narrow business focus and relatively short business life. Verizon and Sprint Nextel are much larger and better established companies.

REQUIRED:
a. What is a patent, and how is it accounted for on Verizon's and Sprint Nextel's financial statements?
b. Where might a financial statement user find evidence of the suit on Vonage's financial statements, how might it account for this suit, and how might Vonage's external auditors react to this situation?

REAL DATA
ID10–15
Provisions under IFRS

The 2008 IFRS-based balance sheet published by Volkswagen AG, a well-known German automaker, listed an account called "provisions" (divided into current and non-current categories) with a total balance (in million euros) of 17,546 (2008) and 17,558 (2007). The footnotes to the financial statements included the following statement and account information.

"In accordance with International Accounting Standard (IAS) 37, provisions are recognized when an obligation exists to a third party as a result of a past event; where a future outflow of resources is probable; and when a reliable estimate can be made. Provisions . . . are recognized at their (expected) settlement value discounted to the balance sheet date. Discounting is based on market rates."

December 31, 2007, balance:	**17,558**
Increases	**8,443**
Decreases	**(8,455)**
December 31, 2008, balance	**17,546**

REQUIRED:
a. Discuss differences between how provisions are accounted for under IFRS and how contingencies are accounted for under U.S. GAAP.
b. Explain how the increases listed above (8,443) affected the basic accounting equation, and list what kinds of items might be reflected in the 8,443 increase amount.
c. Explain how the decreases listed above (8,455) affected the basic accounting equation, and list what kinds of items might be reflected in the 8,455 decrease amount.

REAL DATA
ID10–16
The SEC Form
10-K of NIKE

The SEC Form 10-K of NIKE is reproduced in Appendix C.

REQUIRED:
Review the NIKE SEC Form 10-K, and answer the following questions.

a. What is working capital, and what is the trend in NIKE's working capital position in recent years?
b. How much did working capital change as a percentage of total assets over that time period?
c. What happened to NIKE's current ratio over the last year? What accounted for the change?
d. What are the most important current liabilities reported by NIKE?
e. Compute NIKE's accounts payable turnover (see Chapter 5) for the past two years. Comment on any change. (*Note:* The accounts payable at the end of 2007 totaled $1,040.3)
f. Is NIKE concerned with any major contingencies (see note 15)?
g. Briefly describe the five largest accrued liabilities, and the basic form of the entry lending to their recognition on the balance sheet.
h. (Appendix 10A). What kind of pension plan does NIKE provide for its employees? How much did the company contribute to the plan in the last three years?
i. (Appendix 10B). Compute NIKE's conservatism ratio over the last three years. Comment on whether the company's financial reporting was conservative or aggressive across the three-year period.

CHAPTER 11	Long-Term Liabilities: Notes, Bonds, and Leases

KEY POINTS

The following key points are emphasized in this chapter:

- Long-term notes payable, bonds payable, and leasehold obligations, and how companies use these instruments as important sources of financing.

- Economic consequences created by borrowing.

- Different forms of contractual obligations.

- The effective interest rate and how it is determined for contractual obligations.

- The effective interest method.

- How changes in market interest rates can lead to misstated balance sheet values for long-term liabilities.

- Operating leases, capital leases, and off-balance-sheet financing.

Ready Mix, Inc. is a publicly traded company that provides concrete mix to home-builders, subcontractors, pool builders, homeowners, and industrial property developers, primarily in the southwestern United States, a region stunned by the 2008–2009 housing crisis. Ready Mix finances its business and its fleet of concrete trucks with long-term debt, primarily from Wells Fargo and the National Bank of Arizona. In its 10-Q filing with the SEC for the third quarter of 2009, Ready Mix disclosed that it had violated financial covenants in the loan contracts with both banks. Wells Fargo waived the violations, but required additional fees and collateral; National Bank of Arizona had not yet waived the violations and could still demand immediate payment of the principal. The 10-Q also stated that Ready Mix expected, as of December 31, 2009, to be in violation of the Wells Fargo covenants, and "if [Wells Fargo] were to accelerate the payment requirements, the Company would not have sufficient liquidity to pay off the related debt and there would be a material adverse effect on the Company's financial condition and results of operations."

In addition to notes payable, many large companies finance their operations with bonds payable and leasehold obligations. **Notes payable** are obligations evidenced by formal notes that normally involve direct borrowings from financial institutions or arrangements to finance the purchase of assets. **Bonds payable** are obligations that arise from notes (bonds) that have been issued for cash to a large number of creditors, called *bondholders*. **Leasehold obligations** refer to future cash payments (e.g., rent) required for the use or occupation of property during a specified period of time. Each of these liabilities represents an obligation to disburse assets (usually cash) for a time that extends beyond the period that defines current assets. The formal contracts underlying such arrangements contain a number of terms including, for example, the principal amount of the debt, the periodic interest payments, the time period over which the interest and principal are to be paid, and security (e.g., collateral) and other provisions, many of which are designed to protect the interests of the lenders.

For the most part the methods used to account for long-term liabilities under U.S. GAAP and IFRS are very similar.

Long-term borrowing arrangements, such as notes, bonds, and leases, are a common and major source of capital and financing for companies throughout the world. Funds used to acquire other companies, purchase machinery and equipment, finance plant expansion, pay off debts, repurchase outstanding stock, and support operations are often generated by issuing long-term notes and bonds or entering into lease agreements. For example, when Walt Disney Company acquired ABC Family for $5.2 billion, it financed the purchase with long-term borrowings. In a typical year, U.S. companies will raise as much as $300 billion by issuing bonds.

Accounting Trends and Techniques (AICPA, 2009) reported that, of the major U.S. companies surveyed, 74 percent disclosed long-term notes payable, 24 percent disclosed bonds payable, and 41 percent disclosed leasehold liabilities. At the end of 2008 AT&T reported long-term liabilities of over $60 billion, consisting primarily of notes, bonds, and leasehold obligations.

> The 2008 statement of cash flows for Eli Lilly included the following disclosures (dollars in millions).
>
> | | 2008 | 2007 | 2006 |
> | --- | --- | --- | --- |
> | Proceeds from issuing long-term debt | $ 0.1 | $2,512.6 | $ 0 |
> | Repayments of long-term debt | (649.8) | (1,059.5) | (2,781.5) |
>
> Describe how this activity affected the company's 2008, 2007, and 2006 balance sheets.

THE RELATIVE SIZE OF LONG-TERM LIABILITIES

In Figure 11–1, we see that Internet firms carry a limited amount of long-term debt. It is also clear that while financial institutions rely very heavily on current liabilities (see Figure 10–2), their long-term debt is still greater than shareholders' equity. Recall from Figure 10–1 that the capital structure of financial institutions tends to be over 90 percent liabilities. GE has relied heavily on long-term debt primarily to finance its strategy to grow by acquiring other companies; note that its long-term debt is more than four times shareholders' equity. Over the years GE has reduced the size of its shareholders' equity by repurchasing its outstanding stock, which we discuss in Chapter 12. Lowe's, AT&T, and Chevron use long-term liabilities to finance large investments in property, plant, and equipment.

FIGURE 11–1

Long-term liabilities (LTL) as a percentage of total assets, total liabilities, and shareholders' equity[1]

	LTL/ Total Assets	LTL/ Total Liabilities	LTL/ Shareholders' Equity
MANUFACTURING:			
General Electric (Manufacturer)	**0.56**	**0.64**	**4.25**
Chevron (Oil drilling and refining)	**0.26**	**0.57**	**0.49**
RETAIL:			
Kroger (Grocery retail)	**0.45**	**0.58**	**2.01**
Lowe's (Hardware retail)	**0.20**	**0.45**	**0.37**
INTERNET:			
Yahoo! (Internet search engine)	**0.03**	**0.15**	**0.04**
Cisco (Internet systems)	**0.23**	**0.54**	**0.41**
GENERAL SERVICES:			
AT&T			
** (Telecommunications services)**	**0.48**	**0.75**	**1.31**
Wendy's/Arby's (Restaurant services)	**0.38**	**0.78**	**0.74**
FINANCIAL SERVICES:			
Bank of America (Banking services)	**0.16**	**0.18**	**1.69**
Goldman Sachs (Investment services)	**0.19**	**0.21**	**2.61**

1. Long-term liabilities in Figure 11–1 include deferred income taxes, but many accountants believe that deferred income taxes do not represent a liability in an economic sense. See Appendix 10B for further discussion on deferred income taxes.

Information from the 2008 balance sheets of the Bank of New York, Google, and 3M is provided below. Match each company with the proper profile and explain your reasoning.

	1	2	3
Fixed assets/total assets	1%	26%	16%
Current liabilities/total assets	82%	18%	7%
Long-term liabilities/total assets	7%	33%	4%

THE ECONOMIC CONSEQUENCES OF REPORTING LONG-TERM LIABILITIES

In recent years, the importance of long-term debt has grown to unprecedented levels in the United States, brought on primarily by numerous takeovers, mergers, and acquisitions involving billions of dollars. In the 1980s and 1990s individuals like Henry Kravis, Robert Campeau, Michael Milken, Rupert Murdoch, Merv Griffin, and Donald Trump as well as large companies like Walt Disney and WorldCom engineered mega-mergers financed by gigantic amounts of long-term debt. Following these mergers, companies were left with the challenge of generating enough cash to meet the staggering debt payment schedules created by such borrowings. In many cases, this situation has increased the pressure on companies to more carefully manage their debt payments and to pay special attention to how this debt is reported on the balance sheet.

Credit ratings have become increasingly important because companies realize that improved credit ratings lead to lower borrowing costs. For example, Emerson, which reports $3.8 billion in long-term debt and over $200 million in interest costs each year, notes in its 2009 annual report that "the company's strong financial position supports" ratings of A2 by Moody's Investor Service and A by Standard & Poor's as of September 30, 2009. Emerson has been approved to issue up to $2.25 billion in additional debt and equity securities.

Prior to Sun Microsystems' acquisition by Oracle Corporation, Standard & Poor's downgraded Sun's debt rating to BB+, a level considered "junk status" by the financial markets. S&P cited profitability concerns and lack of predictability in Sun's financial results as reasons for the downgrade. The rating covers approximately $1.3 billion of Sun's debt. Explain how S&P came to this conclusion, how the downgrade will affect Sun, and how these effects may be represented on the financial statements.

In such a debt-laden environment, measures of solvency, the debt/equity ratio, and debt covenant provisions take on a particularly important role. As such, management has strong incentives to manage financial statement numbers by employing reporting strategies like "off-balance-sheet financing."[2]

In response to this debt explosion and the threat of off-balance-sheet financing, the FASB passed a standard requiring companies to describe the risks associated with

---

2. Recall that "off-balance-sheet financing" involves the existence of debt obligations that are not listed in the liability section of the balance sheet.

financing arrangements not disclosed on the balance sheet. While this standard falls far short of providing all the information necessary to assess this risk, users can now better assess a company's potential obligations, whether or not they appear on the balance sheet.

Honeywell, an advanced technology manufacturer, includes in its annual reports a section titled "Financial Instruments" in which the company describes risks associated with fluctuating interest rates that could adversely affect the company, and how they are managed and controlled. Why is this disclosure necessary, and how is it useful to investors?

BASIC DEFINITIONS AND DIFFERENT CONTRACTUAL FORMS

Long-term obligations normally represent contractual agreements to make cash payments over a period of time. In addition to other terms, these contracts specify the period of time over which the payments are to be made as well as the dollar amount of each payment. Different contracts express these terms in different ways, giving rise to long-term obligations—and their associated cash flows—that take various forms.

Some contracts, called **interest-bearing obligations,** require periodic (annual or semiannual) cash payments (called **interest**) that are determined as a percentage of the **face, principal,** or **maturity value,** which must be paid at the end of the contract period. For example, a company may enter into an exchange in which it receives some benefit (e.g., cash, asset, or service) and, in return, promises to pay $1,000 per year for two years and $10,000 at the end of the second year. Such an obligation would have a life of two years, a **stated interest rate** of 10 percent ($1,000/$10,000), and a maturity, principal, or face value of $10,000. The cash flows associated with this contract are illustrated as follows:

Non-interest-bearing obligations, on the other hand, require no periodic payments, but only a single cash payment at the end of the contract period. For example, a company may enter into another exchange in which it receives a benefit and, in return, promises to pay $12,000 at the end of two years. This obligation, which is illustrated below, would have a life of two years, a stated interest rate of 0 percent, and a maturity, principal, or face value of $12,000. Although the stated rate is zero, as we discuss later these notes include an element of interest.

In an **installment obligation,** periodic payments covering both interest and principal are made throughout the life of the contract. For example, a company may enter into an exchange in which it receives a benefit and, in return, promises to pay $6,000 at the end of each of two years. The cash flows associated with this obligation are illustrated as follows:

Period:	0	1	2
Payment:	+Receipt	−$6,000	−$6,000

The contractual forms illustrated above represent three common ways to schedule the cash payments associated with long-term obligations. Furthermore, each of these contractual forms may contain additional terms that specify assets pledged as security or **collateral** in case the required cash payments are not met (**default**), as well as additional provisions (**restrictive covenants**) designed to protect the interests of the lenders.

> **?**
>
> Currently, NIKE has an outstanding bond liability with a stated interest rate of 5.375 percent and a principal of $25.1 million; Home Depot has capital lease obligations that require annual payments of $88 million; and Foothill/Eastern Transportation Corridor Agency has an outstanding zero coupon bond due January 15, 2032. Briefly describe the nature of the cash payments required for each of these three debts.

It is also useful to consider the nature of that which is received in exchange for the contractual obligation. In the examples above, we have simply referred to it as the "receipt." Often this "receipt" takes the form of cash, as in cases where companies borrow cash from financial institutions, promising to make payments in accordance with the terms of a loan contract. However, contractual obligations also can be exchanged for noncash items, such as long-lived assets, services, or other liabilities. Figure 11–2 illustrates the six possible kinds of notes that can be obtained by matching each of the three contractual forms with cash and noncash "receipts."

FIGURE 11–2

Six possible kinds of notes

1. **Installment**
   A. **Cash received (e.g., bank loan)**
   B. **Noncash received (e.g., lease or real estate purchase)**
2. **Non-interest-bearing**
   A. **Cash received (e.g., zero coupon bond)**
   B. **Noncash received (e.g., equipment purchase)**
3. **Interest-bearing notes**
   A. **Cash received (e.g., bond)**
   B. **Noncash received (e.g., equipment purchase)**

In the next section, we introduce the important concept of the effective interest rate in the context of each of the six combinations illustrated in Figure 11–2. We then discuss notes payable, which can be related to all six combinations; bonds payable, which typically relate to 3A; and capital leases, which relate to 1B.

> **?**
>
> In its 2008 annual report, AT&T reported long-term debt of $61 billion, composed of bonds, notes with varying stated interest rates (ranging from 2.95 to 9.10 percent), and leases. Briefly describe the basic contractual forms of each of these three forms of debt.

EFFECTIVE INTEREST RATE

The **effective interest rate** is the actual interest rate paid by the issuer of the obligation. It may or may not equal the interest rate stated on the contract (for interest-bearing notes). It is determined by finding the discount rate that sets the present value of the obligation's cash outflows equal to the fair market value (FMV) of that which is received in the exchange.[3] When contractual obligations are exchanged for cash (1A, 2A, and 3A in Figure 11–2), the cash amount received represents the FMV of the receipt. When contractual obligations are exchanged for noncash items (1B, 2B, and 3B), the FMV of the noncash items must be determined through appraisals or some other means.[4] The following examples show how the effective interest rate is determined for the three notes illustrated earlier: installment, non-interest-bearing, and interest-bearing.

In its 2008 annual report, Hewett-Packard listed nearly $14 billion in long-term debt, with annual interest rates ranging from 3.75 percent to 8.63 percent. The long-term debt includes notes, bonds, and leases. Consider these three types of long-term debts and discuss whether you think they are interest-bearing, non-interest-bearing, or installments. Are the interest rates indicated above stated rates or effective rates? Discuss.

Installment and Non-Interest-Bearing Obligations

Assume that Able Company entered into an installment obligation requiring the payment of $10,000 at the end of each of two years. In return, the company received a benefit (cash or noncash) with an FMV of $16,900. The cash flows associated with this exchange follow:

Period:	0	1	2
Payment:	+$16,900 ⟶	−$10,000 ⟶	−$10,000

In this case, the company has received a benefit of $16,900, promising to pay a $10,000, two-year, ordinary annuity. The effective (actual) interest rate on the obligation is calculated by finding that interest rate which, when used to discount the two $10,000 payments, results in a present value (PV) of $16,900. The calculation can be set up in the following way:

PV   = Annuity Cash Payment × (PV Table Factor Ordinary Annuity: n = 2, i = ?)
$16,900 = $10,000   ×   ?

Rearranging,

PV table factor = $16,900 ÷ $10,000 = 1.69
Since n = 2, i = 12% (effective interest rate)

The effective interest rate is equal to 12 percent because a $10,000, two-year, ordinary annuity discounted at 12 percent is equal to $16,900, the FMV of the benefit received by Able in the exchange.[5]

---

3. The material in this chapter requires an understanding of present value, which is covered in Appendix A.

4. If the FMV of the noncash item received in the exchange cannot be determined, the effective interest rate must be estimated by considering the effective interest rates of other similar contractual obligations.

5. This method of computing an effective interest rate is also described and illustrated in Appendix A at the end the text.

The method used to compute the effective interest rate for a non-interest-bearing obligation is the same as that used for an installment obligation, except that the table factor is taken from the Present Value of a Single Sum table instead of the Present Value of an Ordinary Annuity table. For example, if Baker Company entered into a non-interest-bearing obligation requiring a single $5,000 payment at the end of three years, receiving a benefit (cash or noncash) with an FMV of $3,969, the effective interest rate would be computed as follows:

PV   = Single Sum Cash Payment × (PV Table Factor Single Sum: n = 3, i = ?)
$3,969 = $5,000   ×   ?

Rearranging,

> **PV table factor = $3,969 ÷ $5,000 = 0.7938**
> **Since n = 3, i = 8% (effective interest rate)**

In both cases the effective interest rate of a given contractual obligation is determined by the FMV of the benefit received in the exchange. If, for example, the FMV of the benefit received in the non-interest-bearing case was $4,198 instead of $3,969, the effective rate would have been 6 percent instead of 8 percent. Similarly, in the installment case, if the FMV received was $17,355 instead of $16,900, the effective rate would have been 10 percent instead of 12 percent.

Interest-Bearing Obligations

Assume that Clyde Company entered into an interest-bearing obligation requiring interest payments of $1,000 at the end of each of two years and a principal payment of $10,000 at the end of the second year. In return, the company received a benefit (cash or noncash) with an FMV of $10,000. This obligation has a life of two years, a stated interest rate of 10 percent ($1,000/$10,000), and a maturity, face, or principal value of $10,000. The cash flows associated with this exchange follow:

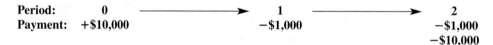

Period: **0** ————————————→ **1** ————————————→ **2**
Payment: **+$10,000**   **−$1,000**   **−$1,000**
                                                                                                              −$10,000

In this case, the company has received a benefit of $10,000, promising to pay a $1,000, two-year, ordinary annuity in addition to a $10,000 single sum payment at the end of two years. The effective (actual) interest rate on this obligation is calculated by finding that interest rate which, when used to discount all three payments, results in a present value of $10,000. The correct rate is 10 percent.[6]

Note in this case that the effective rate of interest (10 percent) equaled the interest rate stated on the obligation (10 percent). This equality occurred only because the FMV of the benefit received ($10,000) was equal to the maturity value of the obligation ($10,000). Had the FMV of the benefit received not equaled the maturity value, the effective rate of interest would not have equaled the stated rate. For example, had the FMV of the receipt equaled $9,662, the effective rate would have been 12 percent.

---

6. The correct rate can be found using a trial-and-error approach—that is, trying different interest rates until the present value of the cash payments is equal to the fair market value of the benefit. Most of you, however, have calculators that can compute the answer directly.

ACCOUNTING FOR LONG-TERM OBLIGATIONS: THE EFFECTIVE INTEREST METHOD

Understanding the effective rate of interest is important because it represents the actual rate of interest associated with an obligation. It is the foundation for the **effective interest method,** which is used to account for long-term contractual obligations—notes, bonds, and capital leases. This method consists of one basic rule:

The interest expense reported during each period of a long-term obligation's contractual life is computed by multiplying the effective interest rate by the balance sheet value of the obligation as of the beginning of the period.

The rationale underlying the effective interest method is that it leads to an interest expense amount each period that reflects the actual interest being paid on the obligation. In addition, it guarantees that the long-term liability on the balance sheet (note payable, bond payable, or lease liability) is reported throughout its life at the present value of its future cash flows, discounted at the effective interest rate. Recall from the discussion in Chapter 4 that present value is the theoretical goal of financial measurement.

At the end of 2008, Sherwin Williams reported long-term debt of $304 million on its balance sheet. At an average effective interest rate of 7.45 percent, estimate the interest expense associated with this debt reported by the company on its 2009 income statement.

ACCOUNTING FOR LONG-TERM NOTES PAYABLE

Issuing long-term notes is a popular way for major U.S. companies to raise cash. Both **secured** (backed by collateral) and **unsecured notes** are widely used. *Accounting Trends and Techniques* (AICPA, 2009) reported that, of the major U.S. companies surveyed, 74 percent disclosed unsecured notes and 13 percent disclosed notes backed by collateral.

The issuance of notes normally involves only one or a small group of lenders (usually financial institutions) and can take a number of different contractual forms. Interest-bearing, non-interest-bearing, and installment notes are all quite common, and they can be exchanged for cash and/or noncash items. A **mortgage,** for example, is a cash loan, exchanged for an installment note that is secured by real estate. Machinery and equipment purchases are often received in exchange for (financed with) installment notes. When a note payable is issued to satisfy another outstanding note payable, a **refinancing** has occurred.

The following example illustrates the methods used to account for a non-interest-bearing note exchanged for equipment (2B in Figure 11–2), which is almost identical to such a note being exchanged for cash (2A). Bonds are normally interest-bearing notes exchanged for cash, so the discussion of bonds later in the chapter will cover 3A in Figure 11–2. Capital leases are a form of financing the purchase of long-term assets with installment notes, so that discussion later in the chapter will cover 1B in Figure 11–2.

Assume that on January 1, 2011, Seabell Inc. acquired a piece of equipment with an FMV of $10,288 and, in return, signed a non-interest-bearing note payable with a maturity date of December 31, 2012, and a maturity value of $12,000. The transaction and the associated accounting entries are described in Figure 11–3.

FIGURE 11–3   Accounting for a non-interest-bearing note exchanged for equipment

Period:	1/1/11 ──────────▶	12/31/11 ──────────▶	12/31/12
Payment:	+Equipment	−$0	−$0
	(FMV = $10,288)		−$12,000

JOURNAL

Equipment (+A)	10,288	Interest Exp. (E, −RE)	823*	Interest Exp. (E, −RE)	889**	
Disc. on Notes Pay. (−L)	1,712	Disc. on Notes Pay. (+L)	823	Disc. on Notes Pay. (+L)		889
Notes Pay. (+L)	12,000			Notes Pay. (−L)	12,000	
				Cash (−A)		12,000

BALANCE SHEET VALUE

Notes payable	$12,000		Notes payable	$12,000		
Less: Discount	1,712	$10,288	Less: Discount	889	$11,111	

GENERAL LEDGER

Discount on Notes Payable

(1/1/11)	1,712			
		(12/31/11 adj.)	823	
(12/31/11)	889			
		(12/31/12 adj.)	889	
	0			

*$10,288 × 8%
**$11,111 × 8%

When Seabell acquires the equipment and issues the note, the equipment is recorded at its FMV, the notes payable account is recorded at its maturity value, and a discount on notes payable account is debited for the difference. The discount is listed on the balance sheet directly under notes payable and subtracted from it in determining the balance sheet value of the note payable, as illustrated in Figure 11–3. The discount can be viewed as a form of "unaccrued interest" because Seabell agreed to pay $12,000 for a piece of equipment that at present is worth only $10,288. Accordingly, the discount is amortized into interest expense over the two-year life of the note.

The effective interest method is then used to account for the note over its two-year life. First, the effective interest rate must be determined, which is equal to 8 percent, the interest rate that equates the present value of the note's future cash flows with the FMV of the equipment ($10,288). Then, the effective interest rate (8 percent) is multiplied by the book value of the note at the beginning of 2011 ($10,288) to determine the interest expense for 2011 ($823). The adjusting entry at the end of 2011 serves to recognize interest expense and amortize a portion of the discount. The remaining amount of the discount ($889) is then subtracted from the notes payable account to determine the book value of the liability as of the end of 2011 ($11,111). The same procedure is then followed at the end of 2012 to recognize interest expense and amortize the remainder of the discount ($889), and the maturity value ($12,000) is paid off at the end of the second year.

Several features of this example are important. First, the accounting treatment would have been virtually the same had a cash amount of $10,288 been received instead of equipment with an FMV of $10,288. Only the initial entry would have differed, reflecting a cash receipt instead of equipment.

Second, even though the note payable has no stated interest rate, it has an effective (actual) interest rate of 8 percent, which must be recognized over the life of the note. In line with the effective interest method, the interest expense in each period is simply the effective rate multiplied by the balance sheet value of the note at the beginning of that period. The interest expense recognized in the second period ($889) is greater than that in the first ($823) because the balance sheet value of the note increased from $10,288 to $11,111. The company was one year closer to the ultimate $12,000 payment. Finally, the effective interest method ensured that the balance sheet value of the note throughout its life was equal to the present value of the note's future cash flows, discounted at the effective interest rate. For example, the present value of $12,000 discounted back one year at 8 percent is equal to $11,111 ($12,000 × .92593) and discounted back two years is equal to $10,288 ($12,000 × .85734).[7] These fundamental features are very important because they apply to other forms of notes as well as bonds and capital leases.

> ?
>
> As of December 31, 2008, Verizon Communications reported notes and bond liabilities of $50.7 billion less an unamortized discount of $219 million. Compute the present value of the future cash payments associated with these debts, and explain what the unamortized discount is, how it was created, and how it will be accounted for in the future.

BONDS PAYABLE

Companies issue bonds to raise large amounts of capital, usually to finance expensive, long-term projects. For example, AT&T raised over $12.4 billion through bond issuances in 2008. Proceeds were used for working capital, capital expenditures, debt repayments, and acquisitions.

Bonds are normally sold to the public through a third party (called an underwriter), such as an investment banker or a financial institution.[8] They are usually interest-bearing notes that involve formal commitments requiring the issuing company to make cash interest payments to the bondholder and a principal payment (usually in the amount of $1,000 per bond) when the bond matures, normally between five and thirty years from the date of issuance. After bonds are initially issued, they are generally freely negotiable; that is, they can be purchased and sold in the open market. Both the New York and the American Security Exchanges maintain active bond markets.

---

7. Instead of the effective interest method, some companies amortize discounts on long-term obligations (e.g., notes and bonds) using the straight-line method. That is, they amortize equal amounts of the discount into interest expense during each period of the note's life. According to generally accepted accounting principles, the straight-line method is acceptable only if it results in numbers (i.e., interest expense and book value of the note payable) that are not materially different from those produced by the effective interest method. The straight-line method misstates periodic interest expense and the balance sheet value of the note because it fails to reflect the actual interest rate paid by the borrower.

8. Major underwriters include J.P.Morgan, Goldman Sachs, Credit Suisse First Boston, Salomon Smith Barney, Citigroup, Morgan Stanley, and Union Bank of Switzerland (UBS).

During 2008 Unilever issued bonds for approximately 801 million euros. How was this issuance reflected in the company's balance sheet and statement of cash flows?

Bond Terminology

Figure 11–4 summarizes the important components of a bond. The **life** of the bond is the time period extending from the date of its issuance to its maturity date. At the **maturity date,** the end of the bond's life, an amount of cash equal to the face value (*principal, par value,* or *maturity value*) is paid to the bondholder. The *face value,* the

FIGURE 11–4   Bond terminology

Issuance Date						Maturity Date
Time to Maturity						
0	6 months	1 year	6 months	2 years	(etc.) . . .	
Proceeds at Issuance	Interest Payment	Interest Payment	Interest Payment	Interest Payment	. . .	Interest Payment
						Face Value Payment

TERMS OF BOND CONTRACT

Life: Time period from date of issuance to the maturity date, usually from five to thirty years.

Maturity date: Date when the dollar amount written on the face of the bond (face value) and final interest payment are paid to the bondholder.

Face value: Dollar amount written on the bond certificate. Sometimes referred to as the *principal, par value,* or *maturity value,* the face value is usually $1,000.

Interest payment: The interest rate stated on the bond, multiplied by the face value. This rate is called the *stated rate,* or *coupon rate,* and it is usually fixed for the entire life of the bond.

Proceeds at issuance: Dollar amount collected when the bonds are issued, equal to the price the buyers paid for each bond multiplied by the number of bonds issued. This amount is usually net of issuance fees.

Effective interest rate: The actual interest rate paid on the bond. This rate, when used to discount the future interest and principal cash payments, results in a present value that is equal to the amount received by the issuer.

OTHER PROVISIONS OF THE BOND CONTRACT

Restrictions: The bond contract may restrict the issuing company in certain ways to ensure that the interest and principal payments will be made. For example, a certain current ratio or level of working capital may be required, dividends may be restricted, or additional debt may be limited.

Security: The bond contract may specify that collateral be paid in case of default (i.e., interest

or principal payments are not made). Unsecured bonds are called *debentures.*

Call provision: The bond contract may specify that the issuing company can buy back (retire) the bonds at a specified price after a certain date during the life of the bond. The specified price is usually greater than the face value.

amount written on the face of the bond, is usually $1,000. The **interest payment** (sometimes called coupon payment), which is paid to the bondholders on each semi-annual interest payment date, is computed by multiplying the annual interest rate stated on the bond (the stated or coupon rate) by the face value of the issuance. This amount is then divided by two because the stated rate is an annual rate, and the interest payments are made every six months. The **proceeds,** the amount collected by the issuing company when the bonds are issued, are equal to the price paid by the purchasers of the bonds multiplied by the number of bonds issued. This amount is usually net of the issuance costs incurred by the issuing company.[9]

To illustrate, assume that on January 1, 2009, Northern States Power Company issued 2,500 bonds, each with a face value of $1,000 and a stated interest rate of 5 percent, due to mature ten years later, on December 31, 2018. The company collected $990 on each bond, which totaled approximately $2.475 million for the entire bond issuance. In terms similar to those in Figure 11–4, the cash flows associated with this bond issuance and the calculations of the proceeds, the semiannual interest payment, and entire maturity value are shown in Figure 11–5.

FIGURE 11–5   Example of bond issuance: Northern States Power Company (dollars in thousands)

Issuance Date (1/1/09)	Time to Maturity: Thirty Years				Maturity Date (12/31/18)
0 ———→	6 months ———→	1 year ———→	6 months ———→	2 years ... ———→	10 years
Proceeds	Interest	Interest	Interest	Interest ...	Interest and face value
+$2,475,000[a]	−$62,500[b]	−$62,500	−$62,500	−$62,500	−$62,500 −$2,500,000

[a]2,500 bonds × $990 = $2,475,000
[b](2,500 bonds × $1,000 × .05%) ÷ 2 = $62,500

In addition to the face value, maturity date, and stated interest rate, the bond contract may include a number of other important provisions. Three such provisions are described in Figure 11–4: restrictive covenants, security, and call provisions.

Restrictive **covenants** are imposed by bondholders to protect their interests and may restrict management in a number of significant ways. Nordstrom, a large specialty store operating throughout the United States, stated in its annual report that the company has entered into long-term debt agreements that (1) limit additional long-term debt and lease obligations; (2) require that working capital must be at least $50 million or 25 percent of current liabilities, whichever is greater; (3) limit short-term borrowings; and (4) restrict dividends to shareholders.

Security provisions also protect the interests of bondholders by ensuring that assets are pledged in case of default. As of fiscal year-end 2008, for example, La-Z-Boy Inc. had outstanding bonds with a balance sheet value of $16.9 million, which were secured by land, buildings, and equipment. Bonds with no assets backing them are called

---

9. To simplify the discussion, these issuance costs are assumed to be zero in the remainder of the chapter.

unsecured bonds or debentures. At year-end, La-Z-Boy had outstanding debentures valued on the balance sheet at $35 million.[10]

A call provision grants to the issuing company the right to retire (repurchase) outstanding bonds after a designated date for a specified price. This provision serves to protect the interests of the issuing company, enabling it to remove the debt if economic conditions are appropriate. If interest rates fall, for example, a company may wish to repurchase outstanding bonds that require relatively high interest payments.

The following quote came from an annual report of CBS, a major television network:

The . . . debentures are due June 1, 2022 and may not be redeemed prior to June 1, 2002. On and after that date they may be redeemed, at the option of the company, as a whole at any time or in part from time to time, at specified redemption prices.

Interpret this quote and explain why CBS may want the option to redeem its outstanding long-term debt.

The Price of a Bond

Bond prices are basically determined by what potential bondholders are willing to pay for the right to receive the semiannual interest payments and cash in the amount of the face value at maturity.[11] The credit rating of the issuing company as well as the stated interest rate, covenants, security arrangements, call provisions, and many other terms of the bond contract directly influence the price at which bonds are issued. Bonds issued by companies with high credit ratings, offering high stated interest rates, and backed by collateral tend to sell for higher prices than unsecured bonds issued by companies with low credit ratings, offering low stated interest rates.

Bond prices are usually expressed as a percentage of the face value ($1,000) and may be less than, equal to, or greater than the face value. Bonds issued for less than $1,000 are issued at a *discount*. Bonds issued for $1,000 are issued at *face* (or *par*) *value*. Bonds issued for greater than $1,000 are issued at a *premium*.

As of the end of 2008, Exxon Mobil had long-term debt outstanding in the amount of $7.0 billion. Included in that amount were debentures due 2012 issued at a discount. What are debentures, and under what circumstances would they be issued at a discount?

The Effective Rate and the Stated Rate

As with other interest-bearing obligations, the effective (actual) rate of interest paid on a bond is not necessarily equal to the stated rate. Recall that the effective rate is that rate which, when used to discount the future contractual cash payments, results in a present value that is equal to the FMV of the receipt (i.e., issuance price). Depending

---

10. Debentures with a very low priority for the issuing company's assets in case of liquidation are referred to as *junk bonds:* bonds rated by credit-rating agencies at lower than investment grade.
11. A discussion of how bond prices are determined is contained in Appendix 11A.

on the relationship between the issuance price and the face value, the effective rate of interest on a bond may be lower than, equal to, or higher than the stated interest rate. Figure 11–6 illustrates these three relationships.

FIGURE 11–6 Bond prices and the relationship between the effective rate and the stated rate (bond terms: $1,000 face value, a 6 percent stated rate, and a five-year life)

Effective Rate		Stated Rate	Face Value	Price (Present Value)	Type of Issue
1. 8%	>	6%	$1,000	$ 919 = $30(8.1109) + $1,000(.6756)	Discount
2. 4%	<	6%	1,000	1,090 = $30(8.9826) + 1,000(.8203)	Premium
3. 6%	=	6%	1,000	1,000 = $30(8.5302) + 1,000(.7441)	Par

The effective interest rates of three different bonds are compared. Each bond has a $1,000 face value, a five-year life, and a 6 percent stated annual interest rate (paid semiannually). They differ in that #1 is issued at an $81 discount (91.9), #2 is issued at a $90 premium (109.0), and #3 is issued at par (100.0). In each case, the effective interest rate is determined by finding that rate which, when used to discount the interest and face value payments, results in a present value that equals the issue price.[12] The relationship among the price, the effective interest rate, and the stated interest rate is summarized as follows.

1. When the issuance price of a bond is greater than its face value (*premium*), the effective rate is less than the stated rate.
2. When the issuance price of a bond is less than its face value (*discount*), the effective rate is greater than the stated rate.
3. When the issuance price of a bond is equal to its face value (*par*), the effective rate is equal to the stated rate.

?

The effective interest rate on the debentures issued by Exxon Mobil, referred to on the previous page, was approximately 5 percent. Was the stated interest rate on the debentures above or below 5 percent? Explain.

Accounting for Bonds Payable

The effective interest method is used to account for bonds payable. The following examples use the effective interest method to account for two different bonds: one issued

---

12. When using present value tables to infer an effective interest rate or to compute the price of a bond, keep in mind that interest payments are made on a semiannual basis. Accordingly, when finding the table factors for the interest payment annuity and the lump-sum payment, the number of periods must be doubled and the discount rate must be halved. For example, the present value (PV) of a bond with a ten-year life, a $1,000 face value, and a 10 percent stated interest rate, discounted at 8 percent, would be computed as below. Note that the table factors are based on an *n* of 20 (10 × 2) and an *i* of 4 percent (8%/2).

PV = Semiannual interest (PV of annuity: n = 20, i = 4%) + Face value (PV lump sum: n = 20, i = 4%)

   = $50   (13.59)   + $1,000   (.456)
   = $679.50   + $456
   = $1,135.50

at face (par) value and one issued at a discount.[13] The following information is used in both cases.

Assume that Webster International issues ten bonds, each with a face value of $1,000, a stated interest rate of 10 percent, and time to maturity of two years. Interest payments of $500 [($10,000 × 10%)/2] are to be made semiannually. In Case 1, the bonds are issued at face (par), so that the effective rate (10 percent) equals the stated rate (10 percent). In Case 2, the bonds are issued at a discount, so that the effective rate (12 percent) is greater than the stated rate (10 percent). Figure 11–7 shows the cash flows associated with the two bond issuances. Note that the cash flows are identical for both, except for the issuance price.

FIGURE 11–7   Cash flows for bonds payable: Two cases compared

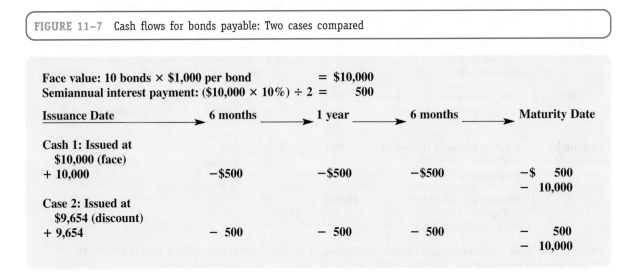

CASE 1: BONDS ISSUED AT PAR

In Case 1, the bonds are issued at par ($10,000) and the effective rate (10 percent) is equal to the stated rate (10 percent). The journal entries, balance sheet values of bonds payable, and present value of the future cash flows discounted at the effective interest rate are shown in Figure 11–8.

When bonds are issued at par, the journal entries are very straightforward because neither a discount nor a premium need be considered. The bonds payable account is simply carried on the balance sheet at $10,000 until maturity. Note that the present value of the remaining cash flows, discounted at 10 percent, is also equal to $10,000 throughout the life of the bond. The interest expense recognized in each six-month period ($500) appears on the income statement and is calculated by multiplying the effective interest rate (5% = 10%/2) by the balance sheet value of the bonds payable at the beginning of the period ($10,000). This calculation is the essence of the effective interest method and in this case gives rise to an amount equal to the $500 cash payment. These two dollar amounts are equal because the effective rate, which determines the interest expense, is equal to the stated rate, which determines the interest payment.

---

13. The methods used to account for bonds issued at a premium are very similar to those used to account for bonds issued at a discount. We do not illustrate them here because bonds issued at discounts are much more common.

FIGURE 11–8   Bonds issued at face value: Case 1

Date	Journal Entry			Balance Sheet Value	Present Value
Issue	Cash (+A)	10,000			
	Bonds Payable (+L)		10,000	$10,000	$10,000
	Issued bond				
6 months	Interest Expense (E, −RE)	500			
	Cash (−A)		500	10,000	10,000
	Paid interest				
1 year	Interest Expense (E, −RE)	500			
	Cash (−A)		500	10,000	10,000
	Paid interest				
6 months	Interest Expense (E, −RE)	500			
	Cash (−A)		500	10,000	10,000
	Paid interest				
Maturity	Interest Expense (E, −RE)	500			
	Cash (−A)		500	10,000	10,000
	Paid interest				
	Bonds Payable (−L)	10,000			
	Cash (−A)		10,000	0	0
	Paid principal				

Interest expense = Balance sheet value at beginning of period × [effective interest rate (10%) ÷ 2]
Cash interest payment = ($10,000 × 10%) ÷ 2
Balance sheet value = Face value ($10,000)
Present value = Remaining cash outflows discounted at effective interest rate (10%)

CASE 2: BONDS ISSUED AT A DISCOUNT

In Case 2, the bonds are issued at a $346 discount, and the effective rate of interest (12 percent) is greater than the stated rate (10 percent). Figure 11–9 shows the journal entries, balance sheet value of bonds payable, and present value of the future cash flows discounted at the effective interest rate.

The bond payable is initially recorded at $10,000, which is greater than the $9,654 cash proceeds; consequently, a $346 **discount on bonds payable** is recognized. This discount is disclosed on the balance sheet as a contra liability and is subtracted from the bonds payable account. It can be viewed as unaccrued interest waiting to be expensed over the life of the bond. The balance sheet disclosure of the bonds payable account and the discount at issuance appears as follows:

Bonds payable	$10,000	
Less: Discount on bonds payable	346	$9,654

In applying the effective interest method, interest expense is calculated each period by multiplying the effective interest rate (6% = 12%/2) by the balance sheet value of the bond liability at the beginning of the period. For example, at the end of the first six-month

FIGURE 11-9   Bonds issued at a discount: Case 2

Date	Journal Entry			Balance Sheet Value	Present Value
Issue	**Cash (+A)**	9,654			
	Discount on Bonds Payable (−L)	346			
	Bonds Payable (+L)		10,000	$ 9,654	$ 9,654
	Issued bond				
6 months	**Interest Expense (E, −RE)**	579			
	Discount on Bonds Payable (+L)		79	+ 79	
	Cash (−A)		500	9,733	9,733
	Paid interest and amortized discount				
1 Year	**Interest Expense (E, −RE)**	584			
	Discount on Bonds Payable (+L)		84	+ 84	
	Cash (−A)		500	9,817	9,817
	Paid interest and amortized discount				
6 months	**Interest Expense (E, −RE)**	589			
	Discount on Bonds Payable (+L)		89	+ 89	
	Cash (−A)		500	9,906	9,906
	Paid interest and amortized discount				
Maturity	**Interest Expense (E, −RE)**	594			
	Discount on Bonds Payable (+L)		94	+ 94	
	Cash (−A)		500	10,000	10,000
	Paid interest and amortized discount				
	Bonds Payable (−L)	10,000			
	Cash (−A)		10,000	0	0
	Paid principal				

Interest expense = Balance sheet value at beginning of period × [effective interest rate (12%) ÷ 2]
Cash interest payment = ($10,000 × 10%) ÷ 2
Balance sheet value = Face value ($10,000) less unamortized discount
                                            or
                    Balance sheet value at beginning of period + discount amortized during period
Present value = Remaining cash outflows discounted at effective interest rate (12%)

period, the $579 interest expense is computed thus: 6 percent × $9,654. The cash interest payment is only $500, so $79 is credited to the discount account. The $79 of amortized discount represents the interest cost, recognized in the first period, associated with receiving only $9,654 for a bond that requires a payment of $10,000 at maturity. The remaining (unamortized) portion of the discount ($267 = $346 − $79) is subtracted from bonds payable on the balance sheet to bring its balance sheet value to present value ($9,733).[14] This process is repeated every six months throughout the life of the bond, and eventually the entire discount is amortized into interest expense. Note also that the effective interest method ensures that the balance sheet value of the bond

14. Subtracting the unamortized portion of the discount from bonds payable is equivalent to adding the amortized amount of the discount to the balance sheet value, which is shown in Figure 11–9.

liability is equal to the present value of the remaining cash flows, discounted at 12 percent, throughout the life of the bond.

ISSUING BONDS AT PAR AND AT A DISCOUNT: A COMPARISON

Bond amortization tables for Case 1 (par) and Case 2 (discount) are contained in Figure 11–10. Recall that the effective (semiannual) interest rates for Cases 1 and 2 are 5 percent and 6 percent, respectively.

The effective interest method ensures that the actual interest rate on a bond issuance is constant throughout its life. Note, however, that interest expense is constant when bonds are issued at par and increasing when bonds are issued at a discount. This occurs because the effective rate is multiplied by the balance sheet value of the bonds payable, which is constant when bonds are issued at par and increasing when they are issued at a discount. In both cases, the balance sheet value is equal to the face value ($10,000) when the bonds are paid off at maturity.

La-Z-Boy issued $50 million in ten-year bonds to refinance other debt. The bonds had a stated rate of 5.25 percent. Assume that the bonds were issued on January 1 at an effective rate of 5.5 percent. Compute the proceeds from the bonds and the amount of interest expense recognized on the company's income statement.

FIGURE 11–10 Bonds amortization tables

Date	Interest Payment	Interest Expense	Amortization Discount/ Premium	Unamortized Discount/ Premium	Net Book Value
ISSUED AT PAR					
Issue					$10,000
6 months	$500	$500	0	0	10,000
1 year	500	500	0	0	10,000
6 months	500	500	0	0	10,000
Maturity	500	500	0	0	10,000
ISSUED AT DISCOUNT					
Issue				$346	$ 9,654
6 months	$500	$579	$79	267	9,733
1 year	500	584	84	183	9,817
6 months	500	589	89	94	9,906
Maturity	500	594	94	0	10,000

KEY:

Interest payment = Stated (semiannual) interest rate (5%) × maturity value ($10,000)
Interest expense = Effective interest rate × net book value at beginning of period
Amortized discount = Difference between interest payment and interest expense
Unamortized discount = Discount of prior period minus amortized discount
Net book value = Maturity value ($10,000) minus unamortized discount

The Effective Interest Method and Changing Interest Rates

We have stated on several occasions that the effective interest method ensures that long-term liabilities on the balance sheet are valued at the present value of the liability's future (remaining) cash flows, discounted at the effective interest rate *as of the date of issuance.* Under this method, the same effective interest rate is used throughout the life of the liability, even though interest rates in the financial markets may vary substantially. By ignoring changes in market interest rates, the effective interest method causes the balance sheet amount of the liability to equal something other than its actual present value. It fails to recognize economic gains and losses that affect the issuing company's financial condition.

To illustrate, assume that Olsen Foods issued ten bonds with a $1,000 face value for $1,000 each. The stated annual interest rate is 8 percent, and the bonds mature at the end of five years. Because the bonds were issued at face value, the effective interest rate is also 8 percent, and under the effective interest method, the following journal entry would be recorded at issuance:

Cash (+A)	**10,000**	
Bonds Payable (+L)		**10,000**
Issued bonds (10 × $1,000)		

Throughout their five-year life, the bonds payable would be carried on the balance sheet at $10,000, the present value (PV) of the remaining cash flows, discounted at 8 percent, the effective interest rate as of the issue date. If market interest rates fall by 2 percent during the first year of the bonds' life, however, the economic value of the bond liability becomes $10,702, the present value of the remaining cash flows discounted at 6 percent (8% − 2%).[15] As a result, Olsen would incur an economic loss of approximately $702 ($10,702 − $10,000). The intuition underlying such a loss is that Olsen is paying an effective rate of 8 percent on its outstanding bonds, while market rates are somewhat lower. In addition, the liability on Olsen's balance sheet is understated by $702.

If market interest rates rise by 2 percent during the first year, the economic value of the bond liability becomes $9,354, the present value of the remaining cash flows discounted at 10 percent (8% + 2%).[16] Olsen, therefore, would enjoy an economic gain of approximately $646 ($10,000 − $9,354). In this case, Olsen is paying only 8 percent on its outstanding bonds while market interest rates are somewhat higher, and the liability on Olsen's balance sheet is overstated by $646.

In its 2008 annual report, The Washington Post Company discloses long-term debt with a balance sheet value of $400 million and a fair market value of $398 million. Explain why the fair market value of the debt is less than its balance sheet value.

---

15. The economic value of the liability is equal to the liability's future cash flows discounted at the market rate.
   $10,702 = $400 (PV annual: n = 8, i = 3%) + $10,000 (PV single sum: n = 8, i = 3%)
          = $400   (7.01969)   + $10,000   (.78941)
16. The economic value of the liability is equal to the liability's future cash flows discounted at the market rate.
   $9,354 = $400   (PV annuity: n = 8, i = 5%) + $10,000 (PV single sum: n = 8, i = 5%)
         = $400   (6.46321)   + $10,000   (.67684)

FINANCIAL INSTRUMENTS, FAIR MARKET VALUES, AND OFF-BALANCE SHEET RISKS

Under the fair market value option, according to both U.S. GAAP and IFRS, companies can account for their long-term debts as described above (effective interest method, sometimes called amortized cost) or at fair market value. If the fair market value option is exercised, the amount of the debt is adjusted to fair market value, and the associated gain or loss appears on the income statement. In the illustration above with Olsen Foods, for example, when interest rates fell by 2 percent under the fair market value option, Olsen would book the following entry.

Loss on bonds payable	**702**	
Bonds payable		**702**

To record loss on decreasing market interest rates

If interest rates rose to 10 percent, the entry would have been:

Bonds payable	**646**	
Gain on bonds payable		**646**

To record gain on increasing market interest rates

While this option is available, most companies do not exercise it. Rather, they choose to disclose the fair market value of the debt in the footnotes. The following excerpt was taken from the 2008 annual report of Federal Express. The reader can ascertain from the footnote that market interest rates for Federal Express's long-term debt were below the debt's effective interest rates.

We had outstanding long-term debt with an estimated fair market value of $2.4 billion at May 31, 2009 and $1.9 billion at 2008 (balance sheet values were $2.6 billion and $2.0 billion, respectively). The underlying fair market values were estimated based on quoted market prices or the current rates offered for debt with similar terms and maturities.

Johnson & Johnson reported long-term debt of $8.3 billion and $7.1 billion as of the end of 2008 and 2007, respectively. The company reported that "the excess of the fair value over the carrying value of the debt was $1.4 billion in 2008 and $0.3 billion in 2007." Given that the effective interest rate of the long-term debt was similar in both years, what must have happened to make the difference between the balance sheet value and the market value so much greater in 2008?

Many companies also carry financial instruments that are not listed on the balance sheet, many of which involve significant risks. Examples include commitments to guarantee the credit of third parties (e.g., subsidiaries) and commitments to provide financing to customers who purchase certain inventory items. Another example is financing arrangements often designed to reduce the risks associated with fluctuations in interest rates and the value of foreign currencies relative to the U.S. dollar. While these arrangements are normally covered in advanced texts, users should know that the public disclosures of most major U.S. companies contain extensive descriptions of these instruments and that such instruments often reflect risks borne by the company that are captured nowhere on the balance sheet.

Bond Redemptions

Bonds can be **redeemed** (repurchased or retired) on or before the maturity date. When this occurs, amortization of any discount or premium is updated, the dollar amount in

the bonds payable account and any unamortized discount or premium are written off the books, a cash payment is recorded, and a gain or loss is recognized on the redemption if the cash payment differs from the net book value of the liability.

BOND REDEMPTIONS AT MATURITY

When bonds are redeemed at the maturity date, the issuing company simply pays cash to the bondholders in the amount of the face value and removes the bond payable from the balance sheet. At maturity, the bond payable is equal to the face value because, after the final entry to record interest expense, any discount or premium on the bonds will have been completely amortized. Journal entries to record bond redemptions at the maturity dates for bonds issued at face (Case 1) and at a discount (Case 2) appear in Figures 11–8 and 11–9, respectively. Note that in both cases, the journal entry to record the redemption takes the following form:

Bonds Payable (−L)   **10,000**
   Cash (−A)   **10,000**
Redeemed bonds with a $10,000 face value at maturity

BOND REDEMPTIONS BEFORE MATURITY

Many companies exercise call provisions or purchase their outstanding bonds on the open market before the maturity date. As indicated earlier, as economic conditions (especially interest rates) change, companies may wish to retire long-term debts.

To illustrate, consider companies that issued bonds in the mid-1980s when interest rates, compared to recent rates, were relatively high. As market interest rates dropped, many of these companies redeemed these bonds prior to maturity, recognizing losses because the market value of the debt exceeded its book value. Often new bonds were then issued at considerably lower rates. When Scott Paper Company, for example, retired $72.1 million of unsecured bonds (with an effective rate of 11.5 percent) prior to maturity, it recognized a $9.6 million loss on the transaction.

During the financial crisis of 2008–2009, the Federal Reserve Board pushed interest rates down and kept them at low levels to help boost economic activity. Explain what happened to bond prices while the Fed was pushing down interest rates, and how some companies with outstanding long-term debt before the crisis may have reacted to the lower rates, and why.

That same year, Scott issued additional debt with effective rates that averaged 8 percent to 9 percent.

To illustrate the redemption of a bond issuance prior to maturity at a loss, assume that bonds with a $100,000 face value and a $5,000 unamortized discount are redeemed for $102,000. The $7,000 loss on redemption would decrease net income and appear in a separate section of the income statement.

Bonds Payable (−L)   **100,000**
Loss on Redemption (Lo, −RE)   **7,000**
   Discount on Bonds Payable (+L)   **5,000**
   Cash (−A)   **102,000**
Redeemed bonds prior to maturity

If these same bonds are redeemed for $93,000, the following journal entry is recorded, and a gain on the redemption is recognized on the income statement as an extraordinary item:

Bonds Payable (−L)	**100,000**	
Discount on Bonds Payable (+L)		**5,000**
Cash (−A)		**93,000**
Gain on Redemption (Ga, +RE)		**2,000**
Redeemed bonds prior to maturity		

On a recent income statement, Cummins, Inc., a manufacturer of diesel engines, reported a loss from the early retirement of debt in the amount of $12 million. Explain what happened to result in the recognition of this loss and why the $12 million loss appeared in the operating section of the statement of cash flows as an add-back to net income.

LEASES

A **lease** is a contract granting use or occupation of property during a specified period of time in exchange for rent payments. Such contracts are a very popular way to finance business activities. Companies often lease rather than purchase land, buildings, machinery, equipment, and other holdings, primarily to avoid the risks and associated costs of ownership. *Accounting Trends and Techniques* (New York: AICPA, 2009) reports that, of the major U.S. companies surveyed, 99 percent disclosed some form of material lease arrangement. Many of the major retailers, for example, lease most of the facilities in which they conduct operations. The Limited stores are almost always leased for terms of ten years with multiple renewal options. The company's annual lease payments approximate $600 million. *Forbes* recently noted:

Today, about a third of all capital spending is financial via leases rather than through direct ownership. A quarter of a trillion dollars worth of capital investment is owned by the 100 top leasing companies, a 17% increase over last year.

Operating Leases

In a pure leasing (or rental) arrangement, an individual or entity (*lessor*) who owns land, buildings, equipment, or other property transfers the right to use this property to another individual or entity (*lessee*) in exchange for periodic cash payments over a specified period of time. Normally, the terms of the lease are defined by contract, and over the period of the lease, the owner is responsible for the property's normal maintenance and upkeep. The lessee assumes none of the risks of ownership, and at the end of the lease, the right to use the property reverts to the owner.

These types of agreements are called **operating leases,** and accounting for them is straightforward. The property is reported as an asset on the owner's balance sheet, and the periodic rental payments are recorded as rent revenue on the owner's income statement. If applicable, as in the case of a fixed asset, the capitalized cost of the property is depreciated by the owner. The lessee, on the other hand, recognizes no asset or liability but simply reports rent expense on the income statement as the periodic rent payments are accrued.

During 2008, JCPenney paid $302 million for its operating leases. How did the company account for these payments, and on which financial statements would activities associated with operating leases be reflected?

Capital Leases

Many contractual arrangements, which on the surface appear to be leases, are actually purchases financed with installment notes, where the risks and benefits of ownership have been transferred to the lessee. The present value of the periodic lease payments, for example, may approximate the FMV of the property. It is also possible that the property may revert, or be sold at a bargain price, to the lessee at the end of the lease period. Furthermore, the period of the lease may be equivalent to the asset's useful life. In such situations, the lessee has actually purchased the property from the lessor and is financing it with an installment note; that is, an asset has been received in exchange for an installment note payable. Such leases are referred to as **capital leases,** and they should be treated on the financial statements as purchases. That is, the leased property should be included as an asset on the balance sheet of the lessee, and the obligation associated with the future lease payments should be reported as a liability.

Suppose that on January 1, 2012, Hitzelberger Supply (lessee) signs an agreement to lease a bulldozer from Jones and Sons (lessor) for a period of two years. The contract specifies that Hitzelberger must pay $10,000 on December 31 of 2012 and 2013, and the bulldozer can be purchased by Hitzelberger at the end of the lease for a nominal sum. The market price of the bulldozer at the time of the agreement is $17,355, resulting in an effective interest rate of 10 percent, which is equivalent to the interest rate that would be charged if Hitzelberger borrowed funds to purchase the bulldozer.[17]

Hitzelberger should account for this arrangement as a capital lease because the present value of the lease payments discounted at the market rate of interest approximates the FMV of the bulldozer, and the company can purchase the bulldozer at the end of the lease period for a nominal sum. Although the transaction is described as a lease, in economic terms it is actually an installment purchase; stated another way, if Hitzelberger borrowed $17,355 from a bank to purchase the bulldozer and signed a two-year note with a 10 percent interest rate, the loan payment would be $10,000 per year for two years, the same payments required by the lease. Assuming that the bulldozer is depreciated on a straight-line basis over a five-year useful life, the entries shown in Figure 11–11 would be recorded by Hitzelberger over the life of the lease.

As with long-term notes payable and bonds payable, the effective interest method is used to compute the interest expense and amortize the lease liability. Specifically, the annual interest expense associated with the installment purchase is computed by multiplying the effective interest rate (10 percent) by the balance sheet value of the liability, and the dollar amount of the liability amortized each period is equal to the difference between the cash payment and the interest expense. This procedure ensures that the lease liability is carried on the balance sheet at present value throughout the life of the lease,

---

17. The effective rate of interest is determined by finding that rate which, when used to discount the future cash flows of the lease, results in a present value that is equal to the market price of the bulldozer. Refer to the discussion earlier in this chapter on the effective interest rate.

FIGURE 11–11

Accounting for a
capital lease:
Hitzelberger
Supply

GENERAL JOURNAL

2012	Jan. 1	Machinery (+A)	17,355	
		Lease Liability (+L)		17,355
		Recognized capital lease ($10,000 × 1.7355[a])		
	Dec. 31	Depr. Expense (E, −RE)	3,471	
		Accumulated Depr. (−A)		3,471
		Recognized depreciation ($17,355 ÷ 5)		
		Interest Expense (E, −RE)	1,736[b]	
		Lease Liability (−L) (plug)	8,264	
		Cash (−A)		10,000
		Made first lease payment		
2013	Dec. 31	Depr. Expense (E, −RE)	3,471	
		Accumulated Depr. (−A)		3,471
		Recognized depreciation ($17,355 ÷ 5)		
		Interest Expense (E, −RE)	909[c]	
		Lease Liability (−L) (plug)	9,091	
		Cash (−A)		10,000
		Made second lease payment		

[a]Present value of annuity table: n = 2, i = 10%
[b]10% × $17,355
[c]10% × $9,091 [Unamortized lease liability ($17,355 − $8,264)]

assuming that market interest rates remain constant over that time period. Note also that Hitzelberger depreciates the cost of the machinery, reflecting that, for purposes of financial accounting, Hitzelberger is considered the owner of the bulldozer.

SUPERVALU's fiscal 2009 balance sheet includes assets under capital leases and capital lease obligations of $1.03 billion and $1.3 billion, respectively. Where on the financial statements would these numbers be found, and how did SUPERVALU estimate them?

Operating Leases, Capital Leases, and Off-Balance-Sheet Financing

Both operating leases and capital leases are commonly reported on the financial statements of U.S. companies. *Accounting Trends and Techniques* (New York: AICPA, 2009) reports that, of the companies surveyed, 46 percent disclosed both operating and capital leases, 52 percent disclosed operating leases only, and 1 percent disclosed capital leases only.

Recall that from the lessee's standpoint, an operating lease simply gives rise to a periodic rent expense, while a capital lease involves the recognition of an asset, a leasehold liability, and an additional depreciation expense. Because accounting for capital leases increases liabilities and assets and recognizes depreciation expense, all of which can negatively affect important financial ratios (e.g., capital structure leverage and return on assets), companies have incentives to account for leases as operating. In 1977,

the Financial Accounting Standards Board issued an accounting standard that identified a set of criteria for distinguishing capital from operating leases. In general, these criteria attempt to identify when a leasing arrangement actually represents an installment purchase and therefore should be treated as such (i.e., a capital lease) on the financial statements. Specifically, if any of the four criteria listed in Figure 11–12 are met, the lease should be treated as a capital lease.

FIGURE 11–12 Capital lease criteria	1. **The lease transfers ownership of the property to the lessee.** 2. **The lease contains a bargain purchase option.** 3. **The lease term is 75 percent or more of the useful life of the property.** 4. **The present value of the lease payments equals or exceeds 90 percent of the FMV of the property.**

Although these criteria are useful, they have not removed the effects of management's discretion on classifying leases. A study sponsored by the Financial Accounting Standards Board, conducted four years after the FASB established the criteria, found that "a majority of the companies surveyed were structuring the terms of new lease contracts to avoid capitalization." Such attempts to finance asset acquisitions without having to report liabilities on the balance sheet may be economically sound in view of the importance of financial ratios in debt covenants and investor and creditor decisions. In one particular case, *Forbes* magazine reported that Dierckx Equipment Corporation, a small, privately owned company, could "endanger its credit rating" by capitalizing its leases. Consequently, financial statement users should closely review the lease terms disclosed in the footnotes to financial statements and ascertain for themselves whether a leasing arrangement is in fact a rental agreement or an installment purchase. Furthermore, generally accepted accounting principles require that companies disclose in the footnotes the future cash payments associated with both their operating and their capital leases. Financial statement readers can use this information to ascertain the extent to which the financial statements are affected by the lease accounting method. For example, one could reconstruct the financial statements as if all leases had been accounted for as capital leases by computing the present value of the cash flow payments associated with the company's operating leases and including that dollar amount as both a liability and an asset on the balance sheet.

Capital lease accounting is an area where IFRS differs from U.S. GAAP. Under IFRS, the four specific criteria listed above are not used. Instead, IFRS leaves more to the judgment of the manager, stating that capital lease accounting should be used if substantially all the risks and rewards incidental to ownership have been transferred from the lessor to the lessee. This difference is one of many where IFRS relies on judgment and U.S. GAAP relies on rules.

The following disclosure was taken from the 2008 annual report of Macy's Inc., which includes a wide variety of well-known retailers, including Bloomingdale's. It describes the company's leasing activities.

NOTES TO CONSOLIDATED FINANCIAL STATEMENTS

Minimum rental commitments (excluding executory costs) at January 31, 2009, for noncancellable leases are:

	Capitalized Leases	Operating Leases	Total
		(millions)	
Fiscal year:			
2009	$ 8	$ 235	$ 243
2010	7	236	233
2011	6	207	213
2012	5	191	196
2013	4	170	174
After 2013	32	1,709	1,741
Total minimum lease payments	$62	$2,738	$2,800
Less amount representing interest	27		
Present value of net minimum capitalized lease payments	$35		

Capitalized leases are included in the Consolidated Balance Sheets as property and equipment while the related obligation is included in short-term ($4 million) and long-term ($31 million) debt. Amortization of assets subject to capitalized leases is included in depreciation and amortization expense. Total minimum lease payments shown above have not been reduced by minimum sublease rentals of approximately $83 million on operating leases.

This computation is useful because it can help users make better comparisons across companies that capitalize different percentages of their leases. For example, Home Depot and Lowe's capitalize different percentages of their leases, which can complicate the interpretation of any financial ratio (e.g., return on assets or capital structure leverage) comparisons across the two companies. To address this problem, an analyst could assume that both companies capitalize all their leases, and financial ratios computed on the adjusted numbers would be more comparable.

?

The following information was taken from the fiscal 2009 annual reports of SUPERVALU and Wal-Mart (dollars in millions). Assuming that the terms of each company's lease contracts are approximately equivalent, which company seems to be practicing off-balance-sheet financing more aggressively, and why? Describe how you could make the financial ratios of the two companies more comparable.

Minimum lease payments under:

	Capital leases	Operating leases
SUPERVALU	$168	$ 426
Wal-Mart	569	1,161

INTERNATIONAL PERSPECTIVE: THE IMPORTANCE OF DEBT FINANCING IN OTHER COUNTRIES

The nature of capital markets plays an important role in determining the nature and use of an accounting system. U.S. companies, for example, rely heavily on both debt and equity capital, which, in turn, influences the accounting systems to provide information for both equity and debt investors. Accordingly, the importance of both earning power

and solvency in the assessment of a company's financial health has been emphasized throughout the text.

In certain other countries, however, the sources of capital are not as balanced between equity and debt. In Japan and much of Western Europe, for example, the environment is characterized by a few very large banks that satisfy the capital needs of most businesses. The local stock and bond markets, though increasingly becoming more active, are not as heavily relied upon as they are in the United States. The dependence on borrowing in Japan has caused the normal debt/equity ratio for a Japanese company to be well in excess of 75 percent, with most of the debt being in the form of long-term notes from one or more of the large banks.

This situation has had two significant effects on the different accounting systems. First, the accounting disclosure requirements in non-U.S. countries and IFRS are not as comprehensive as those in the United States, partially because the information needs of the major capital providers (i.e., banks) are satisfied in a relatively straightforward way—through personal contact and direct visits. In many non-U.S. countries, for example, it is not unusual for the banks to have members on the boards of directors of the companies for which they provide debt capital. Such direct access is an efficient and practical way to monitor a company's financial health, and it precludes the need for extensive accounting disclosures for external parties.

A second way in which the heavy reliance on debt affects non-U.S. accounting systems is that the required disclosures and regulations tend to be designed either to protect the creditor or to help in the assessment of solvency. For example, the Japanese Commercial Code, which until very recently determined Japanese accounting rules, also set a ceiling on the profits available for dividends to shareholders. Such a regulation helped creditors by ensuring that there was adequate cash to meet debt payments on the company's outstanding loans.

The *Wall Street Journal* reported that Prada, the well-known Italian fashion house, planned to cut its debt levels by 385 million euros by selling assets and reducing inventories, and with a large tax rebate from the Italian government. The company hoped to be able to raise funds by issuing equity, but the financial markets were worried that Prada's debt levels were much too high. Why would high levels of debt make it difficult to raise equity capital? Explain how Prada's financial statements would change if it was successful with its plans.

ROE EXERCISE: MANAGING LONG-TERM DEBT

The ROE model, introduced and illustrated in Appendix 5A, provides a framework linking the management of a company's operating, investing, and financing activities to its return on the shareholders' investment (return on equity). The management of the nature and level of long-term debt represents an important financing activity.

As illustrated by the ROE model, management can increase return on equity by practicing leverage—using borrowed funds to finance investments that provide returns that exceed the cost (e.g., interest) of borrowing. Issuing bonds and long-term notes and using capital leases can generate huge amounts of funds that can be invested in projects, creating shareholder returns without requiring any shareholder capital. The result is upward pressure on ROE. This strategy, however, does increase a company's risk because it creates obligations to make future cash payments regardless of whether the projects are successful.

Key ratios within the ROE model that address these issues include common equity leverage, capital structure leverage, long-term debt as a percent of total assets, interest coverage, and interest expense as a percent of sales (see Figure 5–3). Analyzing these ratios and how they relate to changes in ROE is useful in assessing how companies manage their financing activities and, accordingly, is an important part of financial statement analysis.

ROE ANALYSIS

Access the Web site http://www.wiley.com/college/pratt and conduct ROE analyses on New York Times versus Washington Post and/or Dow Chemical versus DuPont, all of which carry significant levels of long-term debt, paying special attention to the level of the companies' leverage and whether leverage is being used effectively.

APPENDIX 11A

THE DETERMINATION OF BOND PRICES

This chapter states that bond prices are determined by the dollar amount investors are willing to pay for them. That is, what will investors pay for the right to receive the semiannual interest payments and a cash payment in the amount of the face value at maturity? This appendix identifies and discusses factors considered by debt investors when deciding whether to purchase bonds. These factors have a direct bearing on bond prices.

Suppose, for example, that on June 9, 2011, you were reading the *Wall Street Journal,* looking to purchase a bond. You note that on that day Treetley Enterprises lists bonds with the following terms:

Face value	**$1,000**
Time to maturity	**18 years**
Stated annual interest rate (paid every 6 months)	**8%**
Current price	$85\frac{1}{4}$, **or $853**

The decision to buy the bond involves three steps: (1) determine the effective rate of return, (2) determine your required rate of return, and (3) compare the effective rate to the required rate.

Determine the Effective (Actual) Rate of Return

The procedure used to determine the effective rate of return is discussed in this chapter. Recall that the effective rate is that rate which, when used to discount the bond's future cash flows, results in a present value equal to the bond price. The effective rate of the Treetley bond is approximately 10 percent.

Determine the Required Rate of Return

Now that you have determined the effective rate, you must decide whether it is large enough to satisfy you. In other words, what rate of return do you require on a bond with these terms issued by Treetley Enterprises?

Your required rate of return is determined by adding the return you could receive from investing your money in a risk-free security (i.e., risk-free return) to the risk premium you would attach to the Treetley bonds:

Required Rate of Return = Risk-Free Return + Risk Premium

Determine the Risk-Free Return

The **risk-free** (or **riskless**) **return** is the annual return you could receive by investing in a riskless security, a security where there is virtually no doubt that the interest and principal payments will be honored. Such securities are often backed by the federal government. The annual returns on **treasury notes,** which can be purchased from the federal government and mature up to six months from the date of issue, provide an approximation of the risk-free rate. The bank interest rate on savings accounts probably represents the lowest estimate of the risk-free return. The annual return on **certificates of deposit,** where a given amount of money is lent to a financial institution for a specified period of time, represents another, perhaps more relevant, example.

Keep in mind that the actual risk-free return can only be approximated and that it fluctuates from day to day, based on such factors as changes in the **prime interest rate** (the interest rate charged by banks to their best customers), changes in the **discount rate** (the lending rate charged to banks by the Federal Reserve Board), and the inflation rate expected in the future. Assume that on June 9, 2011, when you considered purchasing Treetley bonds, a reasonable approximation of the risk-free return was 3 percent.

Determine the Risk Premium

The **risk premium** is expressed as a percentage and reflects the probability that Treetley will default on the periodic interest payments or face value payment at maturity. If this probability is high, these bonds would be considered "high risk" and the risk premium would be relatively large, say 5–10 percent. If the probability is low, the risk premium would be considerably less, say 1–3 percent.

The risk premium is associated specifically with the company issuing the bonds. It is determined by a number of factors, including the credit rating of the company and the bond issuance, the solvency and earning power of the company, future movements in the economy and how these movements may affect the operations of the company, and the terms of the bond issuance. For example, covenant restrictions on future debt and dividend payments as well as collateral and call provisions can affect the risk premium by changing the risk levels faced by the holder of the bonds. Analyzing financial statements is an important part of assessing the risk premium associated with investing in a particular company.

Assume that you have assessed the factors described above and have determined that the risk premium associated with the Treetley bonds is 6 percent.

Compare the Effective Rate to the Required Rate

The effective rate of return on the Treetley bond is 10 percent. You have determined that your required rate of return is 9 percent (3% risk-free rate + 6% risk premium). Since the effective rate exceeds the required rate, you will purchase the bond. The bond is selling for $853; in fact, you would be willing to pay $920 for it, the present value of the bond's future cash flows discounted at 9 percent, your required rate of return. Had your required return been greater than 10 percent, due to either a higher risk-free rate or a higher risk premium, you would not have purchased the bond and would not do so until the price decreased to the point where the effective rate exceeded your required rate.

Factors Determining Bond Prices

Bond prices, therefore, are determined by a market of investors, each assessing the economy-wide, risk-free rate as well as the risk premium associated specifically with the issuing company. Any factor affecting either of these two items affects bond prices. Factors that decrease either the risk-free rate or the risk premium tend to increase bond prices, while factors increasing either rate tend to decrease bond prices.

The *Wall Street Journal* often reports on how the actions of the Federal Reserve Board affect economy-wide interest rates. Almost without exception, when the Board acts to reduce interest rates, the bond market rallies, and when the Board acts to increase rates, bond prices fall. This relationship occurs because the Board's behavior has a direct effect on the risk-free rate of return. The *New York Times* once reported that Merrill Lynch & Company, which holds a huge portfolio of bond investments, "lost $250 million in a given month because its bond investments plummeted in value when interest rates surged."

The close relationship between the risk premium and bond prices illustrates why companies are so interested in their credit ratings. A decrease in a company's credit rating ordinarily leads to an increase in the market's assessment of the company's risk premium and, accordingly, a decrease in the value of the company's outstanding debt. For example, when Standard & Poor's noted that the credit quality of the U.S. chemical companies, in general, had demonstrated increasing signs of stability, most of the companies in the entire industry saw their bond prices rise.

APPENDIX 11B

INVESTING IN BONDS

Many companies include bonds in their investment portfolios. Compared to equity securities, bonds are relatively low risk, providing periodic interest income in addition to potential capital gains (and losses) as market values increase (decrease). To illustrate how large bond investments can be, as of December 31, 2008, General Electric Capital Service (GECS) included on its balance sheet bonds issued by U.S. companies valued at over $23 billion.

The method used to account for bond investments depends on management's intention, leading to three possible classifications: (1) held-to-maturity securities, (2) trading securities, and (3) available-for-sale securities. *Held-to-maturity securities* are, as the name suggests, bond investments that management does not intend to sell, intending instead to hold them until the maturity date, when the face value of the bond (usually $1,000) will be received. *Trading debt securities* are bought and held principally for the purpose of selling them in the near future with the objective of generating a profit on short-term price changes. *Available-for-sale debt securities* are neither intended to be sold in the near future nor intended to be held until maturity. The methods used to account for bond investments classified as trading or available-for-sale are very similar to those described in Chapter 8, which covered investments in equity securities. Both are carried on the balance sheet at market values; holding gains and losses for trading debt securities are reflected on the income statement; and holding gains and losses for available-for-sale debt securities are reflected in the shareholders' equity section of the balance sheet and are part of comprehensive income. Next we discuss the method used to account for held-to-maturity bond investments. Note that under the fair market value option, discussed in Chapter 8, management can choose to account for any of the three classifications of bond investments at fair market value.

Similar to bonds payable, the *effective interest method* is used to account for bond investments. Under the effective interest method:

When a bond is purchased, the bond investment is recorded at cost; interest revenue each period over the life of the bond is computed by multiplying the effective interest rate by the balance sheet value of the bond investment at the beginning of the period; and bond investment is carried on the balance sheet at the present value of the bond's future cash flows discounted at the effective interest rate.

To illustrate, assume that Clancy Company purchases a bond with a face value of $1,000, a maturity of two years, and a stated interest rate of 4 percent ($20 in interest to be received every six months). Clancy paid $929 for the bond, creating an effective interest rate of 8 percent, and intended to hold the bond until its maturity, two years in the future. Under the effective interest method, the bond investment would be accounted for over the two-year period as illustrated in Figure 11B–1.

FIGURE 11B–1   Accounting for held-to-maturity bond investments

Date	Journal Entry			Balance Sheet Value	Present Value
Purchase	Bond investment (+A)	929			
	Cash (−A)		929	$ 929	$ 929
6 months	Cash (+A)	20			
	Bond investment (+A)	17		+17	
	Interest revenue (R, +RE)		37	946	946
1 year	Cash (+A)	20			
	Bond investment (+A)	18		+18	
	Interest revenue (R, +RE)		38	964	964
6 months	Cash (+A)	20			
	Bond investment	18		+18	
	Interest revenue (R, +RE)		38	982	982
Maturity	Cash (+A)	20			
	Bond investment (+A)	18		+18	
	Interest revenue (R, +RE)		38	1,000	1,000
	Cash (+A)	1,000			
	Bond investment (−A)		1,000		

Interest revenue = Balance sheet value at beginning of period $\times \dfrac{\text{effective interest rate (8\%)}}{2}$

Cash interest receipt = $\dfrac{\$1{,}000 \times .04}{2}$

Balance sheet value = Balance sheet value + discount amortized during period
Present value = Remaining cash inflows discounted at effective interest rate (8%)

Note in the example that the discount on the bond, the difference between the face value ($1,000) and the purchase price ($929), is not separately disclosed. Rather, it is included in the bond investment account. Every six months the discount is amortized by increasing the bond investment account by the difference between the cash interest received and the interest revenue recognized. This method ensures that the bond investment on the balance sheet is equal to the present value of the remaining future cash inflows associated with the bond, discounted at the effective interest rate. In this way accounting for bond investments is very similar to accounting for bond liabilities, except asset and revenue accounts are involved instead of liability and expense accounts.

APPENDIX 11C

INTEREST RATE SWAPS AND HEDGING

Almost all major companies rely on long-term debt financing (e.g., bond issuances) where the issuing company makes fixed interest rate payments to debtholders over the life of the debt contract. As illustrated in this chapter, entering into fixed-interest-rate contracts exposes the issuing company to market rate risks—when market interest rates rise, the market value of the liability falls and the company experiences an economic gain; as market interest rates fall, the value of the liability rises and the company experiences an economic loss. Effective risk management attempts to reduce these risks as much as possible because investors avoid risky investments. Creditors impose stricter credit terms (e.g., higher interest rates, stricter debt covenants), and equity investors are willing to pay lower prices when they judge that a company's risk level rises.

A common method used by companies to reduce such risks is called **hedging,** where a company enters into a contract that creates risks that counteract or balance the risks attempted to be hedged (reduced). The most common method of hedging market interest rate risk is called an **interest rate swap.**

To illustrate how an interest rate swap can be used to hedge risks, assume that Peirson Company issues for face value ($1,000) a bond with a five-year maturity and a stated interest rate of 5 percent. This contract obligates Peirson to pay the bondholders $25 ([$1,000 × .05]/2) every six months for five years. Peirson realizes that the fixed 5 percent interest rate exposes the company to fluctuations in the market value of the debt as market rates change over the five-year period. To remove these risks, Peirson can approach a third party (normally a bank) and enter into an interest rate swap, a contract where Peirson receives fixed interest payments of $25 every six months, while agreeing to make periodic payments to the bank linked to the market rate of interest. If market rates increase above 5 percent, Peirson pays more than $25 for the six-month period; if market rates decrease below 5 percent, Peirson pays less than $25 for the six-month period. Note that the fixed payment made by Peirson to the bondholders ($25 every six months) exactly equals the fixed payment received by Peirson from the bank. Thus, by entering into the interest rate swap, Peirson is now paying an interest rate on the debt that is linked to the market rate. Consequently, when market rates change, the fair market value of the debt will not change, remaining at $5,000, the amount reported on the balance sheet.

The following excerpt was taken from a recent annual report of Emerson Electric, whose strategy ensures that the balance sheet value of the debt equals its market value over the life of the debt.

To efficiently manage interest costs, the company utilizes interest rate swaps as cash flow hedges of variable-rate debt or fair value hedges of fixed-rate debt.

REVIEW PROBLEM

Assume that Southern Carbide issues 500 bonds, each with a $1,000 face value on January 1, 2012. The five-year bonds have an annual stated interest rate of 6 percent, to be paid semi-annually on December 31 and June 30. The bonds are issued at 91.89, providing an effective annual interest rate of 8 percent. A call provision in the bond contract states that the bonds can be redeemed by Southern Carbide after December 31, 2012, for 96.0. Assume that Southern Carbide exercises this provision on July 1, 2013.

Figure 11–13 provides the cash flows, journal entries, discount balance, and net book value of the bonds from the time of the bond issuance to the redemption. An explanation of each calculation follows.

FIGURE 11–13 Review problem

Terms: Number of bonds issued: 500
Face value: $1,000
Stated interest rate: 6%
Time to maturity: 5 years
Call Provision: Redeemable after 12/31/12 for .9600

Interest payment dates: Dec. 31, June 30
Issue date: January 1, 2012
Price: .9189 ($459,450)
Effective interest rate: 8%

CASH FLOWS

12/31/11 ——→ 1/1/12 ——————→ 6/30/12 ——————————→ 12/31/12 ——————————→ 6/30/13
  +$459,450   −$15,000   −$15,000   7/1/13
  (proceeds)   (interest)   (interest)   −$15,000
                                                           (interest)
                                                           −$480,000
                                                           (redemption)

GENERAL JOURNAL

Cash	459,450
Discount	40,550
Bonds Pay.	500,000
Issued bond	

Int. Exp.	18,378	
Cash		15,000
Discount		3,378
Paid interest and		
amortized discount		

Int. Exp.	18,513	
Cash		15,000
Discount		3,513
Paid interest and		
amortized discount		

Int. Exp.	18,653	
Cash		15,000
Discount		3,653
Paid interest and		
amortized discount		

Bonds Pay.	500,000	
Loss on R.	10,006	
Discount		30,006
Cash		480,000
Redeemed bond		

DISCOUNT BALANCE

$40,550

$40,550 − $3,378
= $37,172

$37,172 − $3,513
= $33,659

$33,659 − $3,653
= $30,006 (before redemption)

NET BOOK VALUE

$500,000 − $40,550
= $459,450

$500,000 − $37,172
= $462,828

$500,000 − $33,659
= $466,341

$500,000 − $30,006
= $469,994 (before redemption)

Bonds Pay. = Bonds Payable
Int. Exp. = Interest Expense
Loss on R. = Loss on Redemption

Cash Flow Calculations

Proceeds. The proceeds of the bond issuance ($459,450) were calculated by multiplying the number of bonds issued (500) by the price per bond ($918.90).

Interest Payments. The semiannual interest payment ($15,000) was calculated by multiplying the number of bonds issued (500) by the face value of each bond ($1,000) by half the stated annual interest rate (3 percent).

Redemption Payment (7/1/13). The payment required to redeem the bonds on July 1, 2013 ($480,000), was calculated by multiplying the number of bonds issued (500) by the redemption price per bond ($960).

Journal Entry Calculations

At Issuance. Cash ($459,450) was equal to the cash proceeds. Bonds payable ($500,000) was calculated by multiplying the number of bonds issued (500) by the face value of each bond ($1,000). The discount ($40,550) represents an interest cost ("unaccrued interest") waiting to be recognized over the life of the bond. It arises because the bond issuance, which will require a $500,000 cash payment at maturity, generated only $459,450 at issuance.

Interest Payments and Discount Amortization. The calculation of the cash interest payments is described above. The effective interest rate (8 percent) was computed by finding the rate that produced a present value equal to the price ($459,450). The amount of interest expense recognized each period was calculated by multiplying half the effective interest rate (4 percent) by the net book value of the bond payable ($500,000 − unamortized discount) at the beginning of the period. The credit to the discount represents the additional interest expense recognized each period because the bonds were issued at a discount.

Redemption (7/1/13). The calculation of the cash payment at redemption ($480,000) was described earlier. The balance sheet value of the bonds at the time of the redemption (bonds payable: $500,000, discount: $30,006) is removed from the books. The loss on redemption ($10,006) represents the difference between the cash paid to redeem the bonds and the balance sheet value of the bonds as of July 1, 2013.

Discount Balance and Balance Sheet Value of Bonds Payable

The ending discount balance each period was calculated by subtracting the amount of the discount amortized during the period from the balance at the beginning of the period. The balance sheet value of the bonds payable at the end of each period was calculated by subtracting the unamortized discount from the face value of the bond issuance ($500,000).

SUMMARY OF KEY POINTS

 Long-term notes payable, bonds payable, and leasehold obligations, and how companies use these instruments as important sources of financing.

Long-term liabilities include notes payable, bonds payable, and leasehold obligations. They represent obligations that require the disbursement of assets (usually cash) at a future time beyond the period that defines current assets. Notes payable refer to obligations evidenced by formal notes. They normally involve direct borrowings from financial institutions or an arrangement to finance the purchase of assets. Bonds payable are notes issued for cash to a large number of creditors called *bondholders*. Leasehold obligations refer to future cash payments (i.e., rent) that are required for the use or occupation of property during a specified period of time.

Long-term notes, bonds, and leases are common and major sources of capital for companies throughout the world. Funds used to acquire other companies, purchase machinery and equipment, finance plant expansion, pay off debts, repurchase outstanding stock, and support operations are often generated by issuing long-term notes or bonds, or entering into lease agreements.

 Economic consequences created by borrowing.

Increased borrowing in the United States has forced managers to pay special attention to both their cash flow management policies and how the debt is reported in their financial statements. Credit ratings are assuming increasing importance because they link directly to the cost of borrowing and the firm's stock price. Management has entered into creative ways to generate sufficient cash to meet their debt obligations, and they manage the financial statement numbers by practicing strategies like "building hidden reserves," "taking a bath," and especially "off-balance-sheet financing."

 Different forms of contractual obligations.

There are three basic forms of contractual obligations: interest-bearing, non-interest-bearing, and installment. Interest-bearing obligations require periodic (annual or semiannual) cash payments (called interest) that are determined as a percentage of the face, principal, or maturity value, which must be paid at the end of the contract period. Non-interest-bearing obligations require no periodic payments but only a single cash payment at the end of the contract period. In an installment obligation, periodic payments covering both interest and principal are made throughout the life of the contract.

 The effective interest rate and how it is determined for contractual obligations.

The effective interest rate is the actual interest rate paid by the issuer of the obligation. It is determined by finding the discount rate that sets the present value of the obligation's cash outflows equal to the fair market value (FMV) of that which is received in the exchange. When contractual obligations are exchanged for cash, the cash amount received represents the FMV of the receipt. When contractual obligations are exchanged for noncash items, the FMV of the noncash items must be determined through appraisals or some other means.

 The effective interest method.

The effective interest method states that the interest expense reported during each period of a long-term obligation's contractual life is computed by multiplying the effective interest rate by the balance sheet value of the obligation as of the beginning of the period. It ensures that the long-term liability on the balance sheet is reported throughout its life at the present value of its future cash flows, discounted at the effective interest rate as of the issue date.

 How changes in market interest rates can lead to misstated balance sheet values for long-term liabilities.

The effective interest method ensures that over the life of an obligation its balance sheet value is equal to the present value of the obligation's future cash flows, discounted at the effective interest rate as of the date the obligation was issued. If the market rate of interest remains constant over the life of the obligation, then the obligation's balance sheet value will equal its present value. When market interest rates fluctuate, however, the actual present value of the obligation, discounted at the market rate, differs from the balance sheet value of the obligation, which is discounted at the original effective interest rate. In such cases, the balance sheet value of the liability is no longer an accurate measure of its present value, and economic gains and losses are experienced by the issuing company but not recognized on the financial statements. However, under the fair market value option, companies using either U.S. GAAP or IFRS can account for long-term debt at fair market value.

 Operating leases, capital leases, and off-balance-sheet financing.

Operating and capital leases are categories created by generally accepted accounting principles that define the methods used to account for lease contracts. Four criteria that determine whether the lessor or lessee bears the risks and rewards of owning the leased asset are listed, and if any

one of the criteria is met, the lease is considered a capital lease. Under IFRS these four criteria are not used. Rather, capital lease accounting is required if ownership has transferred. Capital leases are treated as installment purchases for financial reporting purposes, requiring that the lessee record both an asset and a liability in the amount of the present value of the future lease payments, discounted at the effective interest rate. The asset is subject to depreciation, and the liability is amortized using the effective interest method. Operating lease payments are simply accounted for as rental expense by the lessee. Companies can practice off-balance-sheet financing by structuring lease contracts so that none of the four criteria are met, which, in turn, allows them to account for leases as operating leases that may in economic substance be capital leases. Such treatment keeps the liability associated with the lease off the balance sheet.

KEY TERMS

Note: Definitions for these terms are provided in the glossary at the end of the text.

Bonds payable (p. 485)
Call provision (p. 497)
Capital leases (p. 507)
Certificates of deposit (p. 513)
Collateral (p. 489)
Covenants (p. 496)
Debentures (p. 497)
Default (p. 489)
Discount on bonds payable (p. 500)
Discount rate (p. 513)
Effective interest method (p. 492)
Effective interest rate (p. 490)
Face, principal, or maturity value (p. 488)
Hedging (p. 516)
Installment obligation (p. 488)
Interest (p. 488)
Interest-bearing obligations (p. 488)
Interest payment (p. 496)
Interest rate swap (p. 516)
Lease (p. 506)

Leasehold obligations (p. 485)
Life (p. 495)
Maturity date (p. 485)
Mortgage (p. 492)
Non-interest-bearing obligations (p. 488)
Notes payable (p. 485)
Operating leases (p. 506)
Prime interest rate (p. 513)
Proceeds (p. 496)
Redeemed (p. 504)
Refinancing (p. 492)
Restrictive covenants (p. 489)
Risk-free (or riskless) return (p. 513)
Risk premium (p. 513)
Secured notes (p. 492)
Stated interest rate (p. 488)
Treasury notes (p. 513)
Unsecured bonds (p. 497)
Unsecured notes (p. 492)

ETHICS in the Real World

A review of the financial statements of Lowe's and Home Depot shows that both companies lease a large portion of their facilities. A closer examination of the lease arrangements reveals that, while the contractual terms of the leases held by the two companies are quite similar, Lowe's considers 10 percent of its leases as capital leases compared to 13 percent for Home Depot.

According to GAAP, "capital" leases must be represented as balance sheet liabilities, while "operating" leases do not. Although the FASB has provided criteria that should be followed when making such a classification, applying these criteria requires much judgment, and many companies structure their lease contracts in ways that give them the flexibility to classify them as "operating." Such a strategy can be construed as a form of "off-balance-sheet financing," enabling a company to raise debt capital without having to include it on the balance sheet as a liability. In this way, the company can avoid violating debt covenants, protect its credit ratings, and generally encourage shareholders and others to believe that the company is carrying less debt than it really is.

ETHICAL ISSUE Is it ethical for a company to structure its leasing contracts in a manner that allows it to avoid reporting debt?

INTERNET RESEARCH EXERCISE

Access Ready Mix's current financial reports at www.readymixinc.com. Briefly explain how the company has managed the somewhat difficult situation introduced at the beginning of the chapter.

BRIEF EXERCISES

REAL DATA

BE11–1

Inferring debt transactions

The following table was taken from the 2009 annual report of RadioShack.

Long-term debt (in millions)

	2009	2008
Notes payable (interest 2.5%)	$375.0	$375.0
Notes payable (interest 7.375%)	306.8	350.0
Other	5.4	7.7
Unamortized discount	(59.4)	(73.2)

a. Briefly explain the transactions entered into by RadioShack during 2009. Which financial statements were affected?
b. Approximately how much interest expense was recognized in 2009 on the 2.5 percent notes?
c. Assume that RadioShack paid $300 million to retire the 7.375 percent notes in 2009. How much gain or loss would RadioShack have recognized on the transaction? Where in the financial statements would it be found?

REAL DATA

BE11–2

Bond issuance

In October 1997, Hewlett-Packard issued zero coupon (stated interest rate = zero) bonds with a face value of $1.8 billion, due in 2017, for proceeds of $968 million.

a. What is the life of these bonds?
b. What is the stated interest rate on these bonds?
c. Estimate the effective rate of interest on these bonds.
d. How many bonds did HP issue?

REAL DATA

BE11–3

Operating and capital leases

During fiscal 2007, the SUPERVALU grocery chain paid approximately $569 million on its lease contracts—$168 million on capital leases and $401 million on operating leases.

a. How did the operating lease payments affect the income statement, balance sheet, and statement of cash flows?
b. How did the capital lease payments affect the income statement, balance sheet, and statement of cash flows?
c. Discuss whether SUPERVALU is practicing off-balance-sheet financing.

EXERCISES

E11–1

Disclosing debt and debt covenants

The balance sheet as of December 31, 2011, for Melrose Enterprises follows:

Assets		Liabilities and Shareholders' Equity	
Current assets	$200,000	Current liabilities	$200,000
Noncurrent assets	700,000	Long-term liabilities	300,000
		Shareholders' equity	400,000
		Total liabilities and	
Total assets	$900,000	shareholders' equity	$900,000

During 2011 Melrose entered into a loan agreement that required the company to maintain a debt/equity ratio of less than 2:1.

a. How much additional debt can Melrose take on before it violates the terms of the loan agreement?

b. Assume that during 2012 Melrose had revenues of $950,000 and expenses of $800,000. Assume that all revenues and expenses were in cash. How much additional debt can Melrose take on before it violates the terms of the loan agreement?

c. Assume again that during 2012 Melrose has cash revenues of $950,000 and cash expenses of $800,000. If Melrose pays a cash dividend of $100,000, how much additional debt can it take on before violating the terms of the loan agreement? If Melrose declares, but does not pay, the dividend during 2012, does it make a difference in the amount of additional debt the company can take on?

E11–2

Annual or semiannual interest payments?

Hathaway Manufacturing issued long-term debt on January 1, 2011. The debt has a face value of $300,000 and an annual stated interest rate of 10 percent. The debt matures on January 1, 2016.

a. Assume that the debt agreement requires Hathaway Manufacturing to make annual interest payments every January 1. Set up a timeline that indicates the timing and magnitude of the future cash outflows of this long-term debt.

b. Assume that the debt agreement requires Hathaway Manufacturing to make semiannual interest payments every July 1 and January 1. Set up a timeline that indicates the timing and magnitude of the future cash outflows for this long-term debt.

c. Under the conditions of (a) and (b), compute the present value of these two debt agreements, assuming that the effective rate of interest is equal to the stated rate of interest.

E11–3

The relationship among the stated rate, effective rate, and issuance price of a liability

The stated and effective interest rates for several notes and bonds follow:

Note/Bond	Stated Interest Rate	Effective Interest Rate
1	10%	10%
2	7	8
3	9	8
4	11.5	9

Indicate whether each note/bond would be issued at a discount, par value, or a premium.

E11–4

Computing the proceeds from various notes

Compute the proceeds from the following notes payable. Interest payments are made annually.

Proceeds	Stated Interest Rate	Effective Interest Rate	Face Value	Life
?	0%	8%	$ 1,000	4 years
?	0	6	5,000	6 years
?	4	12	8,000	6 years
?	8	8	3,000	7 years
?	10	6	10,000	10 years

E11–5

Notes issued at a discount and the movement of interest expense

Tradewell Rentals purchased a piece of equipment with an FMV of $11,348 in exchange for a five-year, non-interest-bearing note with a face value of $20,000.

a. Compute the effective interest rate on the note payable.

b. Prepare the journal entry to record the purchase.

c. How much interest expense should Tradewell recognize on the note payable during the first year?

d. What is the balance sheet value of the note at the end of the first year?

e. Will the interest expense recognized by Tradewell in the second year be greater than, equal to, or less than the interest expense recognized in the first year? Why?

f.   Will the interest expense recognized in the third year be greater than, equal to, or less than the interest expense recognized in the second year?

E11–6

Accounting for notes payable with various stated interest rates

Candleton borrowed cash, signing a two-year, interest-bearing note payable with a face value of $8,000 and an effective interest rate of 8 percent. Interest payments on the note are made annually.

Provide the journal entries that would be recorded over the life of the note, assuming the following stated interest rates:

a.   8 percent
b.   0 percent
c.   6 percent

E11–7

Determining the effective interest rate

On January 1, 2012, Wilmes Floral Supplies borrowed $2,413 from Bower Financial Services. Wilmes Floral Supplies gave Bower a $2,500 note with a maturity date of December 31, 2013. The note specified an annual stated interest rate of 8 percent.

a.   Compute the present value of the note's future cash flows at the following discount rates:
    (1)   8 percent
    (2)   10 percent
    (3)   12 percent
b.   What is the effective interest rate of the note?
c.   Determine the effective interest rate on the note if Wilmes Floral Supplies originally borrowed $2,500.

E11–8

Financing asset purchases with notes payable

Morrow Enterprises purchased a building on January 1, 2012, in exchange for a three-year, non-interest-bearing note with a face value of $693,000. Independent appraisers valued the building at $550,125.

a.   At what amount should this building be capitalized?
b.   Compute the present value of the note's future cash flows, using the following discount rates:
    (1)   6 percent
    (2)   8 percent
    (3)   10 percent
c.   What is the effective interest rate of this note?
d.   Explain how one could more quickly compute the effective interest rate on the note.

E11–9

Inferring an effective interest rate from the financial statements

The following information was extracted from the financial records of Leong Cosmetics:

	2013	2012
Balance Sheet		
Notes payable	$200,000	$200,000
Less: Discount on notes payable	12,000	14,400
Income Statement		
Interest expense	$ 16,400	$ 16,200

a.   What is the effective interest rate on the notes payable?
b.   Prepare the journal entry to record interest expense during 2013.

REAL DATA

E11–10

Bond discounts

At the beginning of 2002 Southwest Airlines issued ten-year notes with a face value of $385 million. The stated interest rate on the notes was 6.5 percent, and proceeds from the issuance approximated $380 million.

a.   Estimate the effective interest rate of the issuance.
b.   Compute the interest expense associated with this note recorded in 2002.
c.   Explain why the market paid less than $385 million for these notes.

E11–11

Computing bond
issuance proceeds and
the movement
of balance sheet value
and interest expense
over the bond's life

Three different bond issuances are listed here with interest payments made semiannually:

Bond Issuance	Face Value	Stated Interest Rate	Effective Interest Rate	Life
A	$100,000	6%	6%	10 years
B	$400,000	8	6	10 years
C	$600,000	6	8	5 years

a. Compute the proceeds of each bond issuance.
b. For each bond issuance, indicate whether the balance sheet value of the bond liability will increase, decrease, or remain constant over the life of the bond.
c. For each bond issuance, indicate whether the interest expense recognized each period will increase, decrease, or remain constant over the life of the bond.

E11–12

Accounting for bonds
issued at face value

On January 1, 2011, Collins Copy Machine Company issued thirty $1,000 face-value bonds with a stated annual rate of 10 percent that mature in ten years. Interest is paid semiannually on June 30 and December 31. The bonds were issued at face value.

a. Prepare the entry to record the issuance of these bonds on January 1, 2011.
b. Prepare all the entries associated with these bonds during 2011 (excluding the entry to record the issuance).
c. Compute the balance sheet value of the bond liability as of December 31, 2011.
d. Compute the present value of the bond's remaining cash flows as of December 31, 2011, using the effective rate at issuance.
e. Repeat (c) and (d) as of December 31, 2012, and explain the relationship between the balance sheet value and the present value.

E11–13

Accounting for bonds
issued at a discount

Tingham Village issued 500 five-year bonds on July 1, 2012. The interest payments are due semiannually (January 1 and July 1) at an annual rate of 6 percent. The effective interest rate on the bonds is 8 percent. The face value of each bond is $1,000.

a. Prepare the journal entry that would be recorded on July 1, 2012, when the bonds are issued.
b. Prepare the journal entry that would be recorded on December 31, 2012.
c. Compute the balance sheet value of the bond liability as of December 31, 2012.
d. Compute the present value of the bond's remaining cash flows as of December 31, 2012, using an effective interest rate of 8 percent. Explain the relationship between the balance sheet value and the present value.

E11–14

Accounting for bonds
issued at a premium

Coral Sands Marina issued 100 ten-year bonds on July 1, 2012. The interest payments are due semiannually (January 1 and July 1) at an annual rate of 8 percent. The effective rate on the bonds is 6 percent. The face value of each bond is $1,000.

a. Prepare the journal entry that would be recorded on July 1, 2012, when the bonds are issued.
b. Prepare the journal entries that would be recorded on December 31, 2012.
c. Compute the balance sheet value of the bond liability as of December 31, 2012.
d. Compute the present value of the bond's remaining cash flows as of December 31, 2012, using the effective rate at the time the bonds were issued. Explain the relationship between the balance sheet value of the liability and the present value of the future cash payments.

E11–15

Changing market
interest rates and
economic gains
and losses

Treadway Company issued bonds with a face value of $20,000 on January 1, 2011. The bonds were due to mature in five years and had a stated annual interest rate of 8 percent. The bonds were issued at face value. Interest is paid semiannually.

a. As of December 31, 2011, market interest rates had decreased by 2 percent, and the market price of Treadway bonds reflected the entire change. Compute the present value of Treadway's bond liability as of that date, using the new effective interest rate (6 percent), and determine the economic gain or loss experienced by the company.

b. Assume instead that as of December 31, 2011, market interest rates had increased by 2 percent, and the market price of Treadway's bonds reflected the entire change. Compute the present value of Treadway's bond liability as of that date, using the new effective interest rate (10 percent), and determine the economic gain or loss experienced by the company.

c. What is the intuition underlying such gains and losses, and why are they not reflected on the financial statements? If you were analyzing the financial statements of Treadway, what could you do to improve the reported numbers?

E11–16

Redeeming bonds not originally issued at par

On September 10, 2009, Mooney Plastic Products issued bonds with a face value of $500,000 for a price of 96. During 2012, Mooney exercised a call provision and redeemed the bonds for 101. At the time of the redemption, the bonds had a balance sheet value of $490,000.

a. Prepare the journal entry to record the redemption.

b. Assume that the bonds were issued in 2009 for 102, and at the time of redemption they had a balance sheet value of $507,000. Prepare the journal entry to record the bond redemption.

REAL DATA

E11–17

Refinancing debt

When Eli Lilly, a major pharmaceutical company, chose to refinance some of its outstanding bonds payable, the company paid off the outstanding debt and replaced it with a new bond issuance. At the time of the refinancing, the balance sheet value of the outstanding debt was approximately $35 million. On the company's income statement a loss of $7.2 million (net of $4.8 million in tax benefits) was reported.

a. Compute the payment made by Eli Lilly to retire the original debt.

b. How did the company benefit from the $4.8 million tax effect?

c. Lilly uses the indirect method of presentation for the statement of cash flows. How was the loss treated on that statement?

d. How was the loss disclosed on the income statement?

REAL DATA

E11–18

Refinancing debt

During 2004, American Greetings Corporation, a large producer of greetings cards, repurchased some of its outstanding long-term debt. Shortly thereafter the company issued new debt. At the time of the refinancing, where old debt was replaced by new debt, the balance sheet value of the repurchased debt was $142.2 million. The company's 2004 income statement contained a $39.0 million loss related to the cost of the debt repurchase.

a. How much cash did American Greetings pay to repurchase the outstanding debt?

b. Explain why a loss was recognized on the transaction.

c. Why would a company repurchase debt if it led to a loss being recognized on the income statement?

E11–19

Updating amortization and retiring a bond issuance

Marker Musical Products issued bonds with a face value of $100,000 and an annual stated interest rate of 8 percent on January 1, 2009. The effective interest rate on the bonds was 10 percent. Interest is paid semiannually on July 1 and January 1. As of December 31, 2011, the company reported the following dollar amounts for these bonds:

Bonds payable	**$100,000**	
Less: Discount on bonds payable	**3,546**	**$96,454**

Marker Musical Products retired the bonds on July 2, 2012, by repurchasing them for $91,700 in cash.

a. Provide the journal entry recorded on July 1, 2012, when the interest payment is made.

b. Prepare the journal entry to record the retirement of the bonds.

E11–20

Analyzing bond
disclosures and
market values

The following information was taken from the balance sheet of Beasley Brothers as of December 31, 2011:

Bond payable	**$100,000**	
Less: Unamortized discount	**5,350**	**$94,650**

The bonds have a stated interest rate of 5 percent paid annually and will mature on December 31, 2013. The market value of the bonds as of December 31, 2011, is $98,167.

a.   Compute the effective interest rate when the bonds were issued.
b.   What effective rate would an investor be earning by purchasing the bonds on December 31, 2011, at the market price and holding the bonds until maturity?
c.   Assume that Beasley reported net income of $27,000 for the period ending December 31, 2011. Adjust net income for the gain or loss experienced by the company on these outstanding bonds due to the change in market interest rates. Ignore income taxes. Do you believe that the gain or loss represents an increase or decrease in the wealth of the company? Why?
d.   Assume that Beasley retired the bonds by purchasing them on the open market. Record the journal entry, and compare the gain or loss recognized on the retirement with the gain or loss computed in (c) above. Discuss.

E11–21

Analyzing bond
disclosures and
market values

The information below was taken from the balance sheet of Cohort Enterprises as of December 31, 2012:

Bond payable	**$200,000**	
Less: Unamortized discount	**6,941**	**$193,059**

The bonds have a stated interest rate of 5 percent and will mature on December 31, 2014. The market value of the bonds as of December 31, 2012, is $186,479.

a.   Compute the effective interest rate when the bonds were issued.
b.   What effective rate would an investor be earning by purchasing the bonds on December 31, 2012, at the market price and holding the bonds until maturity?
c.   Assume that Cohort reported net income of $38,500 for the period ending December 31, 2012. Adjust net income for the gain or loss experienced by the company on these outstanding bonds due to the change in market interest rates. Ignore income taxes. Do you believe that the gain or loss represents an increase or a decrease in the wealth of the company? Why?
d.   Assume that Cohort retired the bonds by purchasing them on the open market. Record the journal entry, and compare the gain or loss recognized on the retirement with the gain or loss computed in (c) above. Discuss.

E11–22

Accounting
for leases

On January 1, 2011, Q-Mart entered into a five-year lease agreement requiring annual payments of $10,000 on December 31 of each year. The fair market value of the facility was estimated by appraisers to be $39,927.

a.   Record the journal entries required over the five-year period, assuming that Q-Mart accounts for this arrangement as an operating lease.
b.   Compute the effective interest rate on the lease, and record the journal entries required over the five-year period if Q-Mart accounts for this arrangement as a capital lease. Assume that the capitalized asset is depreciated over a five-year period, using the straight-line method with no salvage value.
c.   Compare the effects of the two accounting methods on the financial statements. Discuss.

E11–23

Accounting for
leases and the
financial statements

Tradeall, Inc., leases automobiles for its sales force. On January 1, 2011, the company leased 100 automobiles and agreed to make lease payments of $10,000 per automobile each year. The lease agreement expires on December 31, 2015, at which time the automobiles can be purchased by Tradeall for a nominal price. Assume an effective rate of 10 percent.

a.   Compute the annual rental expense if the lease is treated as an operating lease.
b.   Prepare the journal entry on January 1, 2011, if the lease is treated as a capital lease. What dollar amount represents an approximation of the fair market value of the automobiles?

c. Assume that the automobiles are depreciated over a five-year life, using the straight-line method with no salvage value. Compute the total rental expense (interest and depreciation) associated with the lease during the first year if the lease is treated as a capital lease.

d. Which of the two methods of treatment (operating or capital) would give rise to a higher net income in the first year? Which method would give rise to a lower debt/equity ratio?

e. Define off-balance-sheet financing, and explain how leases can be arranged to practice it.

E11–24

Financing asset purchases

Watts Motors plans to acquire a building and can either borrow cash from a bank to finance the purchase or lease the building from the current owner. The sales price of the building is $149,388. If the company wishes to finance the purchase with a bank loan, it must sign a ten-year note with a face value of $149,388 and a stated interest rate of 12 percent. If the company leases the building, it must make an annual lease payment of a constant-dollar amount for ten years, at which time the building can be purchased for a nominal fee.

a. Compute the annual lease payment that would make the two alternatives equivalent. Ignore the nominal purchase fee at the end of Year 10.

b. Describe how the timing of the cash flows would differ between the two alternatives.

c. Provide the journal entries that would be recorded when the building is acquired if the company (1) finances the purchase with a bank loan, (2) leases the building and accounts for it as a capital lease, or (3) leases the building and accounts for it as an operating lease.

d. If the company leases the building and accounts for it as a capital lease, compute the balance sheet value of the lease liability after the second lease payment.

e. Compute the present value of the remaining lease payments as of the end of the second year.

E11–25

Inferring the effective rate of interest

Compute the effective rate of interest on the following long-term debts. Interest payments on the notes are made annually, and interest payments on the bonds are made semiannually.

Debt	Fair Market Value of Receipt	Face Value	Life	Stated Interest Rate
Note	$10,000	$ 10,000	6 years	8%
Note	35,056	100,000	8 years	0
Note	922	1,000	5 years	7
Bond	11,635	10,000	10 years	6
Bond	54,323	50,000	15 years	9

E11–26

Appendix 11A: The decision to purchase a bond

Dylander bonds are selling on the open market at 89.16. The bonds have a stated interest rate of 8 percent and mature in eight years. Interest payments are made semiannually.

a. Assume that your required rate of return is 12 percent. Would you buy the bonds? Why or why not?

b. At what required rate of return would you be indifferent to purchasing the bonds?

E11–27

Appendix 11C: Managing interest rate risk

On March 1, 2011, Bonneville Printers issued long-term debt with a fixed stated annual interest rate of 4 percent and a maturity date of February 28, 2021. The debt was issued at a discount. The company's financial managers are seeking ways to reduce the risk related to the value of the debt fluctuating over its life as market interest rates change.

a. Explain how the value of Bonneville's debt would be affected if market interest rates fell in 2012.

b. Advise Bonneville regarding how it could manage this risk, and explain how it would work.

PROBLEMS

P11–1

Computing the face value of a note payable

On December 31, 2011, East Race Kayak Club decided to borrow $20,000 for two years. The Bend Bank currently is charging a 10 percent effective annual interest rate on similar loans.

REQUIRED:

a. Assume that the club borrows $20,000 and signs a two-year note with a 10 percent stated annual interest rate. What would be the face amount of the note payable?
b. Assume that the club borrows $20,000 and signs a two-year note with a stated annual interest rate of zero. What would be the face amount of the note payable?
c. Prepare the journal entry to record the note payable, assuming that the club signs
    (1) the note in (a).
    (2) the note in (b).
d. Prepare the entries necessary on December 31, 2013, assuming that the club signs
    (1) the note in (a) (interest payable on December 31).
    (2) the note in (b).

P11–2

Accounting for bonds with an effective rate greater than the stated rate

Hartl Enterprises issued ten $1,000 bonds on September 30, 2011, with a stated annual interest rate of 8 percent. These bonds will mature on October 1, 2021, and have an effective rate of 10 percent. Interest is paid semiannually on October 1 and April 1. The first interest payment will be made on April 1, 2012.

REQUIRED:

a. Without computing the present value of the bonds, will they be issued at par value, at a discount, or at a premium? Explain your answer.
b. Prepare the entry to record the issuance of the bonds on September 30, 2011.
c. Prepare any adjusting journal entries necessary on December 31, 2011.
d. Prepare the entry to record the interest payment on April 1, 2012.

P11–3

The balance sheet value of debt and the long-term debt/equity ratio

The balance sheet as of December 31, 2011, for Manheim Corporation follows:

Assets		Liabilities and Shareholders' Equity	
Current assets	**$ 85,000**	**Current liabilities**	**$ 70,000**
Noncurrent assets	**125,000**	**Long-term liabilities**	**40,000**
		Shareholders' equity	**100,000**
		Total liabilities and	
Total assets	**$210,000**	**shareholders' equity**	**$210,000**

REQUIRED:

a. Compute Manheim Corporation's long-term debt/equity ratio.
b. Assume that Manheim Corporation is considering borrowing money and signing a five-year note with the following terms:

Face value	**$40,000**
Stated interest rate	**0%**
Effective interest rate	**11%**

Compute the proceeds of the note, and compute the company's long-term debt/equity ratio if it decides to borrow the money.

c. Assume that Manheim Corporation is considering issuing bonds that mature on December 31, 2031. The bonds have a face value of $40,000, a stated interest rate of 10 percent, and an effective interest rate of 8 percent. Compute the proceeds from the bond issuance, and compute the company's long-term debt/equity ratio if it issues the bonds. The bonds pay interest semiannually.

P11–4

Accounting for notes issued at a discount and at face value

Patnon Plastics needs some cash to finance expansion. Patnon issued the following debt to acquire the cash:

1. A five-year note with a stated interest rate of zero, a face value of $20,000, and an effective interest rate of 10 percent.

2. An eight-year note with an annual stated rate of 8 percent and a face value of $35,000. Interest is paid annually on December 31. The effective interest rate is 10 percent.
3. A ten-year note with an annual stated rate of 8 percent and a face value of $50,000. Interest is paid semiannually on June 30 and December 31. The effective interest rate is 8 percent.

All three notes were issued on January 1, 2012.

REQUIRED:
a. Compute the proceeds from each of the three notes.
b. Prepare the entries to record the issuance of each note.
c. Prepare the entry to record the interest paid on June 30, 2012, on the ten-year note.
d. Prepare the entries to record the interest paid on December 31, 2012, on the eight-year note and the ten-year note.
e. Prepare the adjusting entry required on December 31, 2012, to recognize accrued interest on the five-year note.

P11–5

The effects of various notes payable on the financial statements

The balance sheet as of December 31, 2012, for Boyton Sons follows:

Assets		Liabilities and Shareholders' Equity	
Current assets	$ 40,000	Current liabilities	$ 30,000
Noncurrent assets	80,000	Long-term liabilities	60,000
		Shareholders' equity	30,000
		Total liabilities and	
Total assets	$120,000	shareholders' equity	$120,000

The company needs capital to finance operations and purchase new equipment. Boyton is not certain how much money it will need and is considering one of the following three-year notes payable. Each note would mature on January 1, 2016.

(A) Face value = $50,000	**Stated interest rate = 0%**	**Proceeds = $37,566**
(B) Face value = $50,000	**Stated interest rate = 10%***	**Proceeds = $50,000**
(C) Face value = $50,000	**Stated interest rate = 6%***	**Proceeds = $45,027**

*Interest paid annually.

REQUIRED:
a. Determine the effective interest rate of each note.
b. Compute the amounts that would complete the following table:

	Interest Expense (A)	Interest Expense (B)	Interest Expense (C)
Year 1			
Year 2			
Year 3			

c. Assume that Boyton can earn a 12 percent return on the borrowed money and that it reinvests all interest that it earns. Compute the annual income (return − interest expense) generated from each of the three notes.
d. Compute the amounts that would complete the following chart. (*Hint:* Consider the effect of annual income from (c) on shareholders' equity as well as the new debt.)

	Debt/Equity (A)	Debt/Equity (B)	Debt/Equity (C)
12/31/13			
12/31/14			
12/31/15			

e. Discuss some of the trade-offs involved in choosing among the three notes.

P11–6

The difference
between cash
interest payments
and interest
expense

Earl Rix, president of Rix Driving Range and Health Club, has provided you with the following information:

	2013	2012
Balance Sheet		
Notes payable	$800,000	$800,000
Less: Discount on notes payable	55,000	70,000
Income Statement		
Interest expense	$ 95,000	

The stated annual interest rate on the notes is 10 percent, and interest is paid annually on December 31. The $95,000 in interest expense is due solely on these notes. While reviewing the company's 2013 financial statements, Mr. Rix is having difficulty understanding why the amount charged to interest expense does not equal the amount of cash actually disbursed during 2013 in payment of the interest on these notes.

REQUIRED:

a. Assuming that Rix Driving Range and Health Club makes all of its interest payments on time, how much cash was actually disbursed during 2013 for interest payments on these notes?
b. Explain to Mr. Rix why interest expense does not equal the amount of cash disbursed for interest. What does the difference between the cash disbursed and the amount charged as interest expense represent?
c. What was the effective interest rate at the time the notes were issued?
d. Provide the journal entry to record the payment of interest on December 31, 2013.

P11–7

The effective
interest method,
interest expense,
and present value

Hartney Enterprises issued twenty $1,000 bonds on June 30, 2012, with a stated annual interest rate of 6 percent. The bonds mature in six years. Interest is paid semiannually on December 31 and June 30. The effective interest rate as of June 30, 2012, the date of issuance, was 8 percent.

REQUIRED:

a. Compute the present value of the cash flows associated with these bonds on June 30, 2012, using the following format:

Face value	XX
Present value of cash payments at maturity	XX
Present value of cash interest payments	+XX
Less: Total present value	XX
Discount (premium) on bonds	XX

b. Compute the present value of the remaining cash flows associated with these bonds on December 31, 2012. What does the present value on December 31, 2012, represent?
c. What does the difference between the present value of the remaining cash flows associated with these bonds on June 30, 2012, and December 31, 2012, represent?
d. Prepare the entry to record the interest payment on December 31, 2012, using the effective interest method. Is the amount of discount on bonds payable amortized in this entry the same as the amount found in (c)? Why or why not?

P11–8

The effective
interest method and
the straight-line
method: Effects on
the financial
statements

Ross Running Shoes issued ten $1,000 bonds with a stated annual rate of 10 percent on June 30, 2012. These bonds mature on June 30, 2015. The bonds have an effective interest rate of 8 percent, and interest is paid semiannually on December 31 and June 30.

REQUIRED:

a. How much must Ross Running Shoes invest in a bank on June 30, 2012, at an annual rate of 8 percent, compounded semiannually, to meet all the future cash flow requirements of these bonds and have no money left after repaying the principal on June 30, 2015?

b. Prepare the entry to record the interest payment on December 31, 2012. Assume that the company uses the effective interest method.

c. Prepare the entry to record the interest payment on December 31, 2012. Assume that the company amortizes an equal amount of premium each year (i.e., straight-line method).

d. Which method (effective interest or straight-line) of amortizing the premium will allow Ross Running Shoes to recognize the higher amount of net income in 2012?

e. Which method (effective interest or straight-line) of amortizing the premium will allow Ross Running Shoes to recognize the higher amount of net income in 2015?

P11-9

Why the effective interest method is preferred to the straight-line method

Consider the three notes payable listed here. Each was issued on January 1, 2012, and matures on December 31, 2014. Interest payments are made annually on December 31.

Note	Face Value	Stated Interest Rate	Effective Interest Rate
A	$1,000	10%	6%
B	$1,000	10	10
C	$1,000	6	10

REQUIRED:

a. Compute the present value of the remaining cash outflows for each note at each date:

Note	1/1/12	12/31/12	12/31/13
A			
B			
C			

b. Compute the balance sheet values of each note payable at each of the above dates, using the effective interest method.

c. Compute the balance sheet values of each note payable at each of the above dates, using the straight-line method (i.e., amortize an equal amount of the discount or premium each year).

d. Why is the effective interest method preferred to the straight-line method for financial reporting purposes?

P11-10

Redemption and updating amortization

Ginny & Bill Eateries reported the following account balances in the December 31, 2011, financial report:

Bonds payable	**$500,000**
Premium on bonds payable	12,600

The bonds have a stated annual interest rate of 8 percent and an effective interest rate of 6 percent. Interest is paid on June 30 and December 31.

REQUIRED:

a. Compute the gain or loss recorded on January 1, 2012, if the bonds are called at 104.

b. Compute the gain or loss recorded on January 1, 2012, if the bonds are called at 108.

c. Compute the gain or loss recorded on July 1, 2012, if the bonds are called at 110.

P11-11

Call provisions and bond market prices

Ficus Tree Farm issued five $1,000 bonds with a stated annual interest rate of 12 percent on January 1, 2012. The bonds mature on January 1, 2017. Interest is paid semiannually on June 30 and December 31. The bonds were sold at a price that resulted in an effective interest rate of 14 percent. The bonds can be called for 103.5 beginning June 30, 2014.

REQUIRED:

a. Prepare the entry on January 1, 2012, to record the issuance of these bonds.

b. Prepare the entry on June 30, 2012, to record the interest payment.

c.   Assume that Ficus wishes to retire the bonds on June 30, 2014. If the bonds are selling on the open market on that date at a price that would result in a return of 10 percent, should Ficus exercise the call provision or simply attempt to buy the bonds at the market price?

d.   Is it likely that Ficus would be able to buy back all outstanding bonds on the bond market at market price?

e.   Prepare the entries necessary on June 30, 2014, if Ficus chooses to exercise the call provision.

P11–12

Tax-deductible bond interest and the present value of cash outflows

Taylor Corporation is contemplating issuing bonds to raise cash to finance an expansion. Before issuing the debt, the controller of the company wants to prepare an analysis of the cash flows and the interest expense associated with the issuance. Taylor Corporation is considering issuing one hundred $1,000 bonds on June 30, 2012, that mature on June 30, 2016. The bonds will have a stated annual interest rate of 6 percent, and interest is to be paid semiannually on December 31 and June 30. The bonds will have an effective interest rate of 10 percent.

REQUIRED:

a.   Compute the amounts that would complete the following table with respect to the bond issuance being considered by Taylor:

Date	Interest Expense	Cash Payment	Unamortized Discount	Balance Sheet Value
6/30/12				
12/31/12				
6/30/13				
12/31/13				
6/30/14				
12/31/14				
6/30/15				
12/31/15				
6/30/16				

b.   Find the difference between the total cash inflow from issuing the bonds and the total cash outflows from interest and principal payments.

c.   Recognizing that cash interest payments are tax deductible and assuming a tax rate of 34 percent, recompute the difference you found in (b).

d.   Repeat (c), but now consider the time value of money by using the effective rate of these bonds to compute the present value of the net future cash outflows due to interest and principal payments.

REAL DATA

P11–13

Capital and operating leases

As of January 31, 2009, Wal-Mart reported balance sheet total assets and total liabilities of $163 billion and $98 billion, respectively. In the footnotes the company disclosed future operating lease payments of $12.8 billion. Future capital lease payments of $5.5 billion were discounted to $3.5 billion and disclosed at that amount on the balance sheet.

REQUIRED:

a.   Describe the difference between a capital lease and an operating lease.

b.   Explain why a company might want to treat its leases as operating leases.

c.   Compute the effect on Wal-Mart's total liability/total assets ratio if the company treats all its leases as capital leases. Assume that future operating lease payments are discounted at the same rate as future capital lease payments.

d.   Explain how this kind of analysis may be useful to an analyst trying to compare the financial position and performance of two companies that rely heavily on leasing.

P11–14

Accounting for a capital lease

Mackey Company acquired equipment on January 1, 2011, through a leasing agreement that required an annual payment of $30,000. Assume that the lease has a term of five years and that the life of the equipment is also five years. The lease is treated as a capital lease, and

the FMV of the equipment is $119,781. Mackey uses the straight-line method to depreciate its fixed assets. The effective annual interest rate on the lease is 8 percent.

REQUIRED:
a. Compute the amounts that would complete the table:

Date	Balance Sheet Value of Equipment	Leasehold Obligation	Interest Expense	Depreciation Expense	Total Expense
1/1/11					
12/31/11					
12/31/12					
12/31/13					
12/31/14					
12/31/15					

b. Compute rent expense for 2011–2015 if the lease is treated as an operating lease.
c. Compute total expense over the five-year period under the two methods and comment.

P11-15

Some economic effects of lease accounting

The balance sheet as of December 31, 2011, for Thompkins Laundry follows:

Assets		Liabilities and Shareholders' Equity	
Current assets	$10,000	Current liabilities	$10,000
Noncurrent assets	60,000	Long-term liabilities	20,000
		Shareholders' equity	40,000
		Total liabilities and	
Total assets	$70,000	shareholders' equity	$70,000

The $20,000 of long-term debt on the balance sheet represents a long-term note that requires Thompkins to maintain a debt/equity ratio of less than 1:1. If the covenant is violated, the company will be required to pay the entire principal of the note immediately. On January 1, 2012, Thompkins entered into a lease agreement. The agreement provides the company with laundry equipment for five years for an annual rental fee of $5,000.

REQUIRED:
a. Compute Thompkins's debt/equity ratio as of January 1, 2012, if the company treats the lease as an operating lease.
b. Compute Thompkins's debt/equity ratio as of January 1, 2012, if the company treats the lease as a capital lease. Assume an effective interest rate of 12 percent.
c. Compare the expenses recognized during 2012 if the lease is treated as operating to the expenses recognized during 2012 if the lease is treated as capital. Assume that the leased equipment has a five-year useful life and is depreciated using the straight-line method.
d. Discuss some of the reasons why Thompkins would want to treat the lease as an operating lease. How might the company arrange the terms of the lease so that it will be considered an operating lease?

P11-16

Financing asset purchases with notes and inferring the effective rate of interest

Memminger Corporation purchased equipment on January 1, 2012. The terms of the purchase required that the company pay $1,000 in interest at the end of each year for five years and $20,000 at the end of the fifth year. The FMV of the equipment on January 1, 2012, was $17,604.

REQUIRED:
a. Prepare the journal entry that would be recorded on January 1, 2012.
b. Compute the effective interest rate on the note payable.
c. Prepare the journal entry that would be recorded when the first interest payment is made on December 31, 2012.
d. Compute the net book value of the note payable as of December 31, 2012.

P11–17

Appendix 11A:
Determinants of
bond market prices

Hodge Sports bonds are selling on the open market at par value. The bonds have a stated interest rate of 9 percent and mature in five years. You have determined that the risk-free rate is 7 percent.

REQUIRED:

a. What is the maximum risk premium you could attach to these bonds and still be willing to purchase them?

b. Assume that Standard & Poor's lowers the credit rating of Hodge Sports bonds, and this action causes you to increase your risk premium to 5 percent. The bonds have a face value of $1,000 and pay interest semiannually. What price would you be willing to pay for the bonds?

c. Independent of (b), assume that you read in the *Wall Street Journal* that the prime rate has been cut by 1 percent. All other factors being equal, would this news tend to increase or decrease the market price of Hodge Sports bonds? Why? Assume that reducing the prime rate by 1 percent reflects a reduction in the risk-free rate of 1 percent, and estimate the magnitude of this effect on the price of Hodge Sports bonds.

P11–18

Appendix 11B:
Bond investments

On June 1, 2011, Mayberry Imports purchased bonds on the open market, paying $92,994. The bonds had a face value of $100,000, a stated annual interest rate of 4 percent, and a remaining time to maturity of two years. Interest was paid semiannually on November 30 and May 31, and Mayberry intended to hold the bonds until the maturity date.

REQUIRED:

a. Compute the effective interest rate on the bonds.

b. Record the entries made by Mayberry when it received the interest payments on November 30, 2011, and May 31, 2012.

c. Compare the market value of the bond investment to its book (balance sheet) value on May 31, 2012, assuming that market interest rates as of that date were 6 percent.

ISSUES FOR DISCUSSION

REAL DATA

ID11–1

Repurchasing
outstanding debt

Sun Company, an oil-refining concern, purchased all of its outstanding 8.5 percent (stated rate) debentures as part of a restructuring plan. The balance sheet value of each outstanding debenture at the time of the repurchase was $875, and the company paid $957.50 for each $1,000 face value bond.

REQUIRED:

a. What is a debenture? Would such bonds tend to be issued at higher or lower prices than secured bonds? Why?

b. Briefly discuss why a company would repurchase its outstanding debt.

c. Explain how this repurchase would affect (increase, decrease, or have no effect on) the components of the accounting equation: assets, liabilities, shareholders' equity. Would a gain or loss be recognized on the transaction?

d. Would the gain or loss be recognized if Sun Company had not repurchased the bonds? Why or why not?

REAL DATA

ID11–2

Bonds with a stated
interest rate of zero

Several years ago, JCPenney Company issued bonds for 33.24 (percent of face value), with a face value of $200 million and a stated interest rate of zero, which matured eight years later. That same year, Martin Marietta, Northwest Industries, and Alcoa also issued bonds with stated interest rates of zero.

REQUIRED:

a. Why would an investor purchase a bond with a stated interest rate of zero?

b. Compute the effective interest rate on the bond issuance.

c.   In terms of its cash flows, explain why a company might wish to issue bonds with a stated interest rate of zero.

d.   At what price would the bonds have been issued if the stated interest rate had been 5 percent? 18 percent? Assume that interest payments would be made annually.

REAL DATA

ID11–3

Buy or lease:
Financial
statement effects

Assume that Southwest Airlines is planning to purchase a jet passenger plane with a price of $45,636,480 from The Boeing Company. Southwest is considering structuring the transaction in one of two ways. In Alternative 1, Southwest would borrow the necessary cash from Federal City Bank and sign a note requiring payments of $6 million at the end of each year for fifteen years. The proceeds from the loan would then be used to purchase the airplane. In Alternative 2, Southwest would lease the airplane from Boeing and make annual lease payments of $6 million for fifteen years, at which time it could purchase the airplane from Boeing for a nominal sum. Southwest depreciates its aircraft over a useful life of fifteen years, using the straight-line method.

REQUIRED:

a.   Determine the effective interest rate on the note and the lease arrangement.

b.   Provide the journal entries that would be recorded under Alternative 1 to reflect the borrowing and the purchase of the airplane.

c.   Provide the journal entry that would be recorded under Alternative 2 when the lease agreement is signed if the lease is treated as a capital lease.

d.   Compare the effects on the financial statements caused by (b) and (c).

e.   Provide the journal entry that would be recorded under Alternative 2 when the lease agreement is signed if the lease is treated as an operating lease.

f.   Which of the three alternative treatments (borrowing, capital lease, operating lease) could be considered off-balance-sheet financing? Explain why Southwest might want to structure the transaction in this way.

REAL DATA

ID11–4

Long-term
debt disclosures

The following information was taken from the footnotes to Johnson & Johnson's 2008 financial statements (dollars in millions):

Zero coupon debentures due 2020	**$ 183**	**3.00**
4.95% debentures due 2033	**500**	**4.95**
3.80% debentures due 2013	**500**	**3.82**
6.95% notes due 2029	**294**	**7.14**
6.73% debentures due 2023	**250**	**6.73**
6.625% notes due 2009	**199**	**6.80**
5.55% debentures due 2017	**1,000**	**5.55**
5.95% notes due 2037	**995**	**5.99**
5.50% notes due 2024	**731**	**5.71**
4.75% notes due 2019	**1,390**	**5.35**
5.15% debentures due 2012	**599**	**5.18**
5.86% debentures due 2038	**700**	**5.86**
5.15% debentures due 2018	**898**	**5.15**
Other	**102**	**—**
Total	**$8,341**	
Less current portion	**(221)**	
	$8,120	

REQUIRED:

a.   Which amounts appeared on Johnson & Johnson's balance sheet and where?

b.   What is a zero coupon debenture, and how does the effective interest rate affect the debenture? Explain.

c.   Which of the long-term debts above were issued at face value (i.e., sold at par)?

d.   Is the face value of the 6.95 percent notes due 2029 greater than, less than, or equal to the balance sheet value? Explain.

REAL DATA

ID11–5

Long-term
debt and
the fair market
value option

Johnson & Johnson reported long-term debt of $8.3 billion and $7.1 billion as of the end of 2008 and 2007, respectively. The company reported that "the excess of the fair value over the carrying value of the debt was $1.4 billion in 2008 and $0.3 billion in 2007." The effective interest rate was similar for the long-term debt in both years.

REQUIRED:

a. What must have happened during 2008 to cause the difference between the market value and the book value of the debt to be so much larger at the end of 2008?

b. If Johnson & Johnson exercised the option to account for the long-term debt at fair market value, what entry would have been recorded at the end of 2008?

c. Record the entry Johnson & Johnson would have made if it did not exercise the fair market value option, but chose to retire the debt at the end of 2008.

d. Compare the entries you made in b and c above, and discuss.

As the United States slid deeper into a recession, companies with high amounts of cash relative to their debt were coveted by the stock market, while companies with high levels of debt slashed dividends, payrolls, and capital expenditures to stay afloat. High debt, combined with slower sales and increasing energy and labor costs, proved to be a deadly combination for a number of companies. Standard & Poor's found that both dividend decreases and omissions were up. Defaults on corporate notes and bonds payable rose to a record level as companies missed debt payments. Moody's Investors Service noted that at the time an average of only 41 percent of the face value of defaulted debt was recovered by investors; secured bondholders recovered an average of 67 percent of the face value, while holders of debentures recovered an average of only 23 percent.

REQUIRED:

a. U.S. corporations have dramatically increased their debt levels in recent years. Discuss how high levels of debt may influence the way in which a company is managed. That is, how might management concerns and decisions be different because a company is carrying a large amount of debt?

b. Describe the financial statement effects of this borrowing activity, and explain how these effects could have helped investors and creditors to avoid the losses incurred during the recession. How and why might the reported levels of debt on the balance sheet be less than the actual levels of debt carried by the company?

c. Define a debenture and explain why defaults on debentures would lead to a lower recovery rate for investors than defaults on secured bonds.

Home Depot and Lowe's are the leading home improvement retail chains in the United States. In 2009, Home Depot reported $41 billion in total assets and $23 billion in total liabilities, while Lowe's reported $33 billion in total assets and $15 billion in total liabilities. Both companies, as is the case with most large retailers, lease most of their stores. At the time, Home Depot incurred about $10.1 billion per year in lease payments, treating about 87 percent of its leases as operating leases for financial reporting purposes. Lowe's incurred about $6.8 billion per year in lease payments and treated about 92 percent of its leases as operating leases. The approximate present values of the future cash flows associated with the operating leases of Home Depot and Lowe's were $2.7 billion and $3.6 billion, respectively.

REQUIRED:

a. Compute the liabilities/total assets ratio for both companies.

b. Assume that both companies accounted for all their leases as capital leases, and recompute their liabilities/total assets ratios.

c. By how much did Lowe's adjusted ratio exceed that of Home Depot? Did the adjustment make much of a difference? Why or why not?

d. Explain why an analyst may wish to make the adjustments required above.

REAL DATA

ID11-8

Subprime mortgage problems

Most homeowners purchase their houses by borrowing the funds in what is called a mortgage loan. Banks and other financial institutions that make the mortgage loans often package the loans for resale to investors, pooling many mortgage loans together into a "mortgage-backed bond." Investors purchase the bonds and earn interest to compensate for the risk of default by the homeowner on the mortgage loan. In the years leading up to 2007 a very active segment of the mortgage loan market was made up of "subprime" mortgages, loans made to individuals with less-than-stellar credit histories. The subprime mortgages were also pooled together and sold as bonds to investors.

The subprime bonds were graded by Moody's and Standard & Poor's, along with other ratings agencies. However, many of the subprime mortgage-backed bonds were highly rated by the agencies even as the housing market began to struggle and defaults by homeowners increased. Often, investors purchased the bonds in part based on the ratings provided by the agencies. Those investors began to lose money in 2007 as the underlying home mortgages defaulted when homeowners could not afford the payments.

REQUIRED:
a. What is a ratings agency, and how does it grade debt securities?
b. How does a rating affect the interest rate on a bond issue, and how does that interest rate affect the price of a bond issue?
c. What risks would a ratings agency look for when reviewing a bond issue composed of loans to borrowers with "subprime" credit?

REAL DATA

ID11-9

Long-term debt and covenants

The following excerpt was taken from the 2008 annual report of JCPenney:

The . . . Credit Agreement includes a requirement that the Company maintain, as of the last day of each fiscal quarter, a Leverage Ratio (a ratio of Funded Indebtedness to Consolidated EBITDA) . . . of no more than 3.0 to 1.0.

Assume that Funded Indebtedness approximates long-term debt on the balance sheet. As of year-end 2008, JCPenney had long-term debt of $3,505 million and earnings before interest, taxes, depreciation, and amortization (EBITDA) of $1,604 million.

REQUIRED:
a. How much long-term debt can JCPenney add to its 2008 balance sheet and still remain in compliance with the financial covenant described above?
b. Why would the creditors of JCPenney limit the company's indebtedness relative to the cash flow of the company?
c. Describe some possible actions if the company violates the financial covenant.

REAL DATA

ID11-10

Lease accounting revolution

"It is time for a second overhaul of lease-accounting rules," says Peter Holgate. In 1981, when the current lease rules were developed, there was a reasonably clear distinction between leases that were equivalent to purchasing an asset (capital leases) and others that were in the nature of short-term hire (operating leases). Though unpopular, the new rule was well accepted. Gradually, though, the leasing industry became more sophisticated: The capital/operating distinction became blurred through innovation as financial engineers sought to keep debt off the balance sheet. This was particularly prevalent in the United States. A result of this innovation is that it is now time for another lease-accounting revolution. The basic idea is to abolish the distinction between capital leases and operating leases and require lessees to show all leases on the balance sheet as a liability and an asset.

REQUIRED:
a. What is the difference between a lease that is "equivalent to purchasing an asset" and "others that were in the nature of short-term hire"?
b. Why was the lease-accounting rule passed in 1981 unpopular with industry?
c. How have financial engineers sought to keep debt off the balance sheet?
d. Do you agree with Mr. Holgate's proposal? Why or why not?

REAL DATA

ID11-11

Appendix 11A:
Risk premiums
and bond prices
in a recession

The *Wall Street Journal* reported (8/21/2009) that many companies took advantage of the depressed market values of their own debt, and bought their own bonds at steep discounts to the debt's face value. Companies such as Beazer Homes, Harrah's Entertainment, and Tenet Healthcare saw that the 2008–2009 crisis in the financial markets had depressed the trading value of their own debt and purchased the debt "on the cheap" to save millions of dollars in principal and interest payments.

REQUIRED:

a. Explain how the market values of these companies' long-term debts could decrease in an economic environment where interest rates were also decreasing.
b. What advantages would a company experience by retiring its debt for less than face value?
c. How would the financial statements be affected by such a transaction?

REAL DATA

ID11-12

Appendix 11B:
Interest rate swaps

The following excerpt was taken from the annual report of Bristol-Myers Squibb, a leader in pharmaceutical and health care products.

Derivative financial instruments are used principally in the management of its interest rate . . . exposures. . . . The Company has entered into fixed to floating interest rate swaps for $3.9 billion of its long-term debt . . . in conjunction with the new issuance of $1.25 billion 5.87% Notes . . . the Company executed several fixed to floating interest rate swaps to convert the fixed rate debt . . . to variable rate debt.

REQUIRED:

Explain the meaning of this footnote, and why a company would enter into an interest rate swap.

REAL DATA

ID11-13

The SEC Form
10-K of NIKE

The SEC Form 10-K of NIKE is reproduced in Appendix C.

REQUIRED:

Review the NIKE SEC Form 10-K, and answer the questions below.

a. Compute NIKE's long-term debt (include deferred income taxes and other long-term liabilities) to total asset ratio for 2008 and 2009. Discuss the change.
b. What interest rates are stated in the various long-term obligations of NIKE?
c. What additional risk applies to the long-term debt of the subsidiary NIKE Logistics YK?
d. Review the financing section of the statement of cash flows and comment on the change in the company's reliance on long-term debt over the last three years.
e. Comment on the comparison between the market value of NIKE's long-term debt and its carrying value on NIKE's balance sheet.
f. How does NIKE reduce the risk of interest rate fluctuations?

Shareholders' Equity

KEY POINTS

The following key points are emphasized in this chapter:

- The three forms of financing and their relative importance to major U.S. corporations.

- Distinctions between debt and equity.

- Economic consequences associated with the methods used to account for shareholders' equity.

- Rights associated with preferred and common stock and the methods used to account for stock issuances.

- Distinctions among the market value, book value, and par (stated) value of a share of common stock.

- Treasury stock.

- Cash dividends and dividend strategies followed by corporations.

- Stock dividends and stock splits.

General Electric announced in February of 2009 that it was cutting its cash dividends by 68 percent, reducing the quarterly payout from 31 to 10 cents per share, the first such drop in 71 years. GE estimated that the annual savings would amount to $9 billion. The company was not alone. The *Wall Street Journal* (2/28/2009) reported that stalwart names such as JPMorgan Chase, Dow Chemical, Pfizer, Textron, CBS, and Citigroup announced similar plans to reduce dividends and retain capital. In early 2009 very few companies were immune to the need to maintain their equity bases, as former high fliers, including Blackstone Group, either cut or eliminated their dividends. The shortage of capital became even more apparent when the federal government stepped in to inject equity into such well-known names as General Motors, Chrysler, insurance giant AIG, and most of the nation's top banking companies.

What is equity? What purpose does it serve? In what forms is equity disclosed on the financial statements, and how do companies account for changes in equity? These questions are covered in this chapter.

Companies generate assets from three sources: (1) borrowings, (2) issuing equity securities, and (3) retaining funds generated through profitable operations. Each of these sources is represented on the right side of the basic accounting equation (balance sheet), which is depicted in Figure 12–1.

FIGURE 12–1 The basic accounting equation	**SHAREHOLDERS' EQUITY**
	Assets = (1) Liabilities + (2) Contributed Capital + (3) Earned Capital
	Preferred stock　　　　　Retained earnings
	Common stock　　　　　Accum. comp.
	Additional paid-in　　　　income

Chapters 10 and 11 were devoted to current and long-term liabilities, which represent the first of the three financing sources illustrated in Figure 12–1. This chapter focuses on shareholders' equity, which comprises the other two financing sources: (2) contributed capital and (3) earned capital. **Contributed capital,** which reflects contributions from a company's owners, consists of three components: preferred stock, common stock, and additional paid-in capital. The major component of **earned capital** is retained earnings, a measure of the assets that have been generated through a company's profitable operations and not paid to the owners in the form of dividends. **Accumulated comprehensive income** consists of all nonowner-related changes in shareholders' equity that do not appear on the income statement and are not reflected in the balance of retained earnings.[1] The total dollar amount of shareholders' equity represents the investment made by the shareholders in the company and is also referred to as **net assets, book value, or net worth.**

Under U.S. GAAP, companies must provide a description of the changes in comprehensive income during the year as either a separate statement or part of the statement of changes in shareholders' equity. Under IFRS, companies must also provide a description of the changes in comprehensive income, but as a separate statement or an extension of the income statement. Under IFRS, this statement is normally referred to as the statement of recognized income and expense (SORIE).

---

1. As discussed in Chapter 8 and again in Chapter 13, examples of accumulated comprehensive income include holding gains and losses due to price changes of available-for-sale securities and foreign currency translation gains and losses.

Contributed and earned capital are important financing sources for many major U.S. companies. Funds used to acquire other companies, purchase machinery and equipment, finance plant expansion, pay off debts, and support operations are often generated by issuing preferred stock, issuing common stock, and retaining funds provided by profitable operations. Recent estimates indicate that new stock is issued in the United States at the rate of more than $200 billion per year.

THE RELATIVE IMPORTANCE OF LIABILITIES, CONTRIBUTED CAPITAL, AND EARNED CAPITAL

Figure 12–2 illustrates the relative importance of the three forms of financing (liabilities, contributed capital, and retained earnings) for our selected firms. Overall, liabilities (with a few exceptions) are the primary financing source. Interest costs are tax deductible, reducing the cost of borrowing, and as discussed before, leverage is a popular way to provide returns to shareholders without using their capital. Most Internet firms have not relied heavily on leverage for several reasons: (1) several years ago their stock prices were trading at huge premiums, which encouraged equity financing; (2) the speed of their growth created uncertainty associated with their future increased risks, discouraging debt capital providers; and (3) Internet firms had little collateral that could be used to secure loans. However, recently Cisco Systems has been issuing debt and repurchasing shares of its own stock. Its strong track record has opened up its borrowing ability.

FIGURE 12–2

The relative importance of liabilities, contributed capital, and retained earnings (percentage of total assets)

	Liabilities	Contributed Capital	Retained Earnings
Manufacturing:			
General Electric (Manufacturer)	.87	−.02	.15
Chevron (Oil drilling and refining)	.46	−.09	.63
Retail:			
Kroger (Grocery retail)	.78	−.10	.32
Lowe's (Hardware retail)	.45	.03	.52
Internet:			
Yahoo! (Internet search engine)	.22	.42	.36
Cisco (Internet systems)	.43	.51	.06
General Services:			
AT&T (Telecommunications services)	.64	.22	.14
Wendy's/Arby's (Restaurant services)	.49	−.59	−.08
Financial Services:			
Bank of America (Banking services)	.90	.06	.04
Goldman Sachs (Investment services)	.93	.02	.05

Note also that non-Internet firms rely very little on contributed capital; in fact, for GE, Chevron, and Kroger, the percent under contributed capital is negative. These companies are well-established, successful firms that have repurchased large amounts of their outstanding shares over the years at prices far exceeding the price at which the shares were originally issued. As we discuss later in the chapter, these transactions

reduce the amount of contributed capital. Finally, the companies that rely heavily on retained earnings as a source of financing have had a history of high profitability and/or have chosen not to pay high levels of dividends. The negative retained earnings amount for Wendy's/Arby's was caused by a large loss reported by the company in 2008, the year when Wendy's merged with Arby's.

The 2008 annual report for Amazon.com, the Internet retailer, shows total assets of $8.314 billion and the following financing sources: current liabilities ($4.796 billion), long-term liabilities ($0.896 billion), contributed capital ($3.402 billion), and negative retained earnings ($0.730 billion). Explain what must have happened to create the company's capital structure since its inception in 1995.

DEBT AND EQUITY DISTINGUISHED

Chapters 10 and 11 presented the basic characteristics of the debt contracts between a company and its creditors. This section describes how the nature of this relationship differs from that between a company and its shareholders. As will be discussed later, such a distinction is important to investors, creditors, management, and auditors.

Characteristics of Debt

When a company borrows money, it establishes a relationship with an outside party, a *creditor* or *debtholder,* whose influence on the company's operations is defined by a formal legal contract containing a number of specific provisions. These provisions were discussed in Chapters 10 and 11, and they are summarized in Figure 12–3, along with characteristics of equity.

FIGURE 12–3
Characteristics of debt and equity

Debt	Equity
1. Formal legal contract	1. No legal contract
2. Fixed maturity date	2. No fixed maturity date
3. Fixed periodic interest payments	3. Discretionary dividend payments
4. Security in case of default	4. Residual asset interest
5. No direct voice in management; influence through debt covenants	5. Vote for board of directors
6. Interest is an expense.	6. Dividends are not an expense, but a distribution of retained earnings.

Characteristics of Equity

When a corporation raises capital by issuing stock, it establishes a relationship with an owner, often referred to as an *equity holder,* or *shareholder.* Unlike debt, an equity relationship is not evidenced by a precisely specified contract. There is no maturity date, because a shareholder is an owner of a company until it ceases operations or until the equity interest is transferred to another party. Dividend payments are at the discretion of the board of directors, and shareholders have no legal right to receive dividends until

they are declared. In case of bankruptcy, the rights of the shareholders to the available assets are subordinate (secondary) to the rights of the creditors, who are paid in an order that can usually be determined by examining the terms in the debt contracts. The shareholders receive the assets that remain. That is, a corporation's owners have a **residual interest** in the corporation's assets in case of bankruptcy.

Shareholders, however, can exert significant influence over corporate management. Each ownership share of common stock carries a vote that is cast in the election of the board of directors at the annual shareholders' meeting. The board, whose function is to represent the interests of the shareholders, declares dividends, determines executive compensation, has the power to hire and fire management, and sets the general policies of the corporation. In addition, certain significant transactions, such as the issuance of additional stock, often must be approved by vote of the shareholders.

Finally, distributions by a corporation to the shareholders (dividends) are not considered operating expenses by either generally accepted accounting principles (U.S. or international) or the Internal Revenue Service. They are considered a return on the owners' original investments. Consequently, dividends are neither included as expenses on the income statement nor considered deductible expenses in the computation of taxable income. On the financial statements, dividends serve to reduce retained earnings without passing through the income statement.

> In its 2009 annual report, Fortune Brands, Inc. reported interest expense of $216 million and dividends of $152 million. The interest expense appeared on the income statement, while the dividends appeared on the statement of shareholders' equity. Describe the difference between interest and dividends and explain why they are treated differently on the financial statements.

Why Is It Important to Distinguish Debt from Equity?

It is important to distinguish debt from equity for a number of reasons, depending primarily on the perspective of the interested party: capital provider (investor or creditor), management, and accountant and external auditor.

DEBT VS. EQUITY: THE CAPITAL PROVIDER'S PERSPECTIVE

Capital providers include individuals and entities who hold debt and equity securities. Debt securities primarily include notes receivable and bonds, and equity securities include stocks. Active markets (e.g., the New York Stock Exchange) exist where such securities are purchased and sold.

EQUITY: HIGHER RISK. Owning an equity security is usually riskier than owning a debt security. The interest and principal payments associated with debt investments are backed by legal contracts and, in general, are more predictable and dependable than returns on equity investments. Debt contracts often include security provisions, and in case of bankruptcy, debtholders have higher priority claims to the existing assets than do equity holders, who are often left with nothing. As evidence of the riskier nature of equity securities, stock prices tend to be more volatile than bond prices on the major security exchanges.

EQUITY: HIGHER RETURNS. A characteristic of the additional risk associated with equity investments is that they can produce higher returns than debt investments. When companies perform exceptionally well, equity holders often receive exceedingly large returns, either in the form of dividends or price appreciation of their securities.

Debtholders, on the other hand, are limited only to the interest and principal payments specified by the debt contract. During 2009, for example, Emerson Electric had an exceptional year; the price of its common stock increased by approximately 35 percent. In contrast, during that same year the company paid about a 5 percent return to its debtholders (i.e., interest rate on outstanding loans). Historically, annual equity returns have approximated 10–15 percent.

The Independent, a London newspaper, reported that "bonds have long been regarded as boring. Investors are only meant to buy them when they are too nervous of the excitement in the stock market." Explain the reasoning underlying this statement.

DEBT VS. EQUITY: MANAGEMENT'S PERSPECTIVE

The decision by management to raise capital by issuing debt or equity is complex. Factors such as present and future interest rates, the company's credit rating, the relative amount of debt and equity in the company's capital structure and balance sheet, the condition of the economy, and the nature of the company's operations are usually relevant.

DEBT: CONTRACTUAL RESTRICTIONS. Issuing debt limits a company in a number of important ways. Contractual interest and principal payments must be met in the future, and assets often must be pledged as security (collateral) during the period of the debt. At the end of 2009, for example, Macy's reported that lease obligations were expected to require future cash payments of approximately $2.8 billion. Additional debt may also lower a company's credit rating and reduce its ability to borrow in the future. Routinely, Standard & Poor's and Moody's Investors Service lower credit ratings of major U.S. companies when they incur large amounts of debt. Finally, the debt contract itself may restrict a company's future borrowing power, limit dividends, or require that certain accounting ratios be maintained at or above specified levels.

DEBT: LESS EXPENSIVE. On the other hand, raising capital by issuing debt is attractive because interest payments are *tax deductible*. General Electric, for example, saved over $4.3 billion in federal income taxes during 2008 because it was able to deduct for tax purposes the interest on its outstanding debts. Issuing debt, therefore, is generally considered less expensive than issuing equity, as dividend payments are not tax deductible. In general, if management can use debt capital to earn revenues that exceed the after-tax cost of the debt, it is using a concept called **leverage** to provide a return for the shareholders. As indicated in Figure 12–2, such a practice appears to be common in that many large U.S. corporations tend to rely more heavily on debt than on equity. The tax deductibility of interest, which significantly reduces the cost of issuing debt, is definitely one of the main reasons.

EQUITY: DILUTION OF OWNERSHIP. Another advantage of raising capital by issuing debt instead of equity is that issuing equity can dilute the ownership interests of the existing shareholders. Suppose, for example, that Mr. Jones owns 10 percent of XYZ Corporation, 1,000 of the 10,000 outstanding shares. If XYZ issues an additional 10,000 shares, and Mr. Jones purchases none, his ownership interest decreases from 10 percent to 5 percent (1,000/20,000).[2] Such **dilution,** if not accompanied by higher

---

2. Some stock certificates carry with them a preemptive right, which allows existing shareholders to share proportionately in any new issue of stock. Also, additional stock issuances sometimes require the approval of the existing shareholders.

profits, can reduce both the future dividends paid to Mr. Jones and the market price of his shares. For example, a 450 million euro stock issuance by Rhodia, France's largest chemical maker, surprised some analysts because it did not depress the company's stock. However, whether the issuance produces capital that creates the basis for adequate future returns remains to be seen.

Dilution also reduces the proportionate control of the existing shareholders and, accordingly, can increase the likelihood of a **takeover** by an outsider. In a takeover, another company, an investor, or group of investors (sometimes called a *raider*) purchases enough of the outstanding shares to gain a controlling interest in the purchased company. If the takeover is "hostile," the voting power attached to the acquired shares is often used by the "raider" to elect a new board of directors. Such action can be followed by the replacement of existing management and substantial changes in the nature of the purchased company.

Corporate managers whose jobs are threatened by takeovers are understandably concerned about the dilutive effects of equity issuances. Many companies, such as Merck, PepsiCo, Citigroup, and Home Depot, have entered into programs of buying back their own previously issued shares. Such transactions, called **treasury stock** purchases because the acquired shares are often held in the corporation's treasury for reissuance at a later date, make a company less attractive as a takeover target by reducing its cash balance and increasing the proportionate control of the remaining shareholders. For example, the management of Safeway Stores, Inc. once purchased all of its publicly traded outstanding stock to elude a takeover attempt by Dart Group Corporation. In other words, the company *went private*—the only shares left outstanding were those held by shareholder-managers who withdrew them from the public markets.

Over a 3-year period, the search engine company Google, Inc. made three equity issuances, raising over $7.5 billion, while taking on no additional debt. As of the end of that period, the company had contributed capital of $7.4 billion and no long-term debt. Explain some of the reasons that may have encouraged Google to rely on equity instead of debt financing.

DEBT VS. EQUITY: THE ACCOUNTANT'S AND AUDITOR'S PERSPECTIVE

The substantive differences between debt and equity give rise to different accounting treatments: (1) debt and equity issuances are disclosed in different sections of the balance sheet, and (2) debt transactions affect the income statement, while equity transactions do not.

Debt issuances are disclosed in the liabilities section of the balance sheet, while equity issuances are included in the shareholders' equity section. Proper classification is important because the debt/equity distinction affects a number of financial ratios, which are used by investors and creditors and in debt covenants and executive compensation agreements.

Interest payments on outstanding debts and book gains and losses, recognized when debt is redeemed, appear on the income statement and affect the computation of net income. In contrast, transactions involving equity securities, like dividends and the reissuance of treasury stock, do not enter into the computations of net income. Figure 12–4 summarizes why distinctions between debt and equity are important to investors and creditors, management, and accountants and auditors. These distinctions give rise to economic consequences that are discussed in the following section.

FIGURE 12–4

Distinctions between debt and equity from different perspectives

Interested Party	Debt	Equity
Investors and Creditors	Lower investment risk Fixed cash receipts (contractual interest and principal)	Higher investment risk Variable cash receipts (discretionary dividends and stock appreciation)
Management	Contractual future cash payments Effects on credit rating Interest is tax deductible	Dividends are discretionary Effects of dilution/takeover Dividends are not tax deductible
Accountants and Auditors	Liabilities section of balance sheet Income statement effects from debt transactions	Shareholders' equity section of balance sheet No income statement effects from equity transactions

During 2008, Honeywell International paid $3.48 billion to capital providers—$456 million for interest, $754 million to reduce debt principal, $1.459 billion to repurchase outstanding common stock, and $811 million for dividends. Explain the effect of each payment on the basic accounting equation. Why are they accounted for differently?

THE ECONOMIC CONSEQUENCES ASSOCIATED WITH ACCOUNTING FOR SHAREHOLDERS' EQUITY

The economic consequences associated with accounting for shareholders' equity arise in part from the effects of financial ratios (e.g., return on equity) that include the dollar amount of shareholders' equity or its components. Such ratios affect a company's stock prices, credit rating, and any debt covenants that restrict additional borrowings, the payment of dividends, or the repurchase of outstanding equity shares (i.e., treasury stock purchases). We argued in Appendix 5A that return on equity (net income divided by shareholders' equity) is the most important indicator of whether management is creating value for the shareholders. Indeed, the ROE model is designed to explain why return on equity increases or decreases. Four of Dun & Bradstreet's fourteen key business ratios explicitly use the dollar value of shareholders' equity (net worth) in their calculations: (1) current liabilities/net worth, (2) total liabilities/net worth, (3) fixed assets/net worth, and (4) return on net worth. Dun & Bradstreet uses the values of these ratios to determine a company's credit rating, which in turn can affect the terms (e.g., market price, interest rate, security, restrictive covenants) of the company's debt issuances.

Many companies "manage" their debt/equity ratios to maintain or improve their credit ratings. In general, as a company's debt/equity ratio increases, its credit ratings fall. When American Stores, a supermarket and drugstore chain, acquired Lucky Stores, Inc., it raised additional capital, which it reported as debt on its balance sheet, increasing the company's debt/equity ratio. Moody's Investors Service responded by lowering the credit rating on American Stores' outstanding bonds, which was followed by a decrease in the market price of the company's stock.

As companies reduce their reliance on debt and increase their reliance on equity issuances and especially retained earnings as sources of financing, their credit ratings tend to rise. General Motors claimed to "strengthen its balance sheet" when it announced plans to sell as much as $1 billion in stock. In its annual report, General Electric commented that during the year its debts were "substantially reduced," leading the major debt-rating agencies to evaluate the company's credit rating as being of the highest standing, *AAA*. Such a rating enabled General Electric to get the best possible terms on its debt issuances as well as maintain or increase the value of the company's outstanding debt securities.

Another important economic consequence associated with the shareholder equity section of the balance sheet relates to restrictions on dividend payments and the repurchase of previously issued, outstanding stock imposed by certain debt covenants. Such restrictions can be very significant. Under the terms of covenants with its debtholders, Turner Broadcasting System, Inc. (now part of Time Warner), for example, had been prohibited from paying cash dividends altogether. Similar restrictions may be less binding. A recent annual report of Owens Corning states, "As is typical for bank credit facilities, the agreements . . . contain restrictive covenants, including . . . limitations on . . . the payment of dividends and purchase of company stock."

Such restrictions protect the interest of creditors by keeping a company from paying all of its available cash to the shareholders through excessive dividends or stock repurchases. Note also that the methods used to account for stock issuances, dividends, treasury stock purchases, and retained earnings, which are covered later in the chapter, can determine whether such restrictions have been violated. Finally, recall that the methods used to account for assets and liabilities affect the recognition of expenses and revenues, which in turn affect retained earnings.

> Some believe, as indicated above, that the most direct measure of value creation is return on shareholders' equity (net income/average shareholders' equity). During 2009, Procter & Gamble, the consumer products conglomerate, issued equity, bought back outstanding shares, and paid dividends. Assuming that these transactions all occurred at the end of the year, explain how each affected return on equity. How might these effects influence an analyst who considers return on equity an important metric of corporate performance?

ACCOUNTING FOR SHAREHOLDERS' EQUITY

The shareholders' equity section of a corporate balance sheet consists of two major components: (1) contributed capital, which primarily reflects contributions of capital from shareholders and includes preferred stock, common stock, and additional paid-in capital[3] less treasury stock, and (2) earned capital, which reflects the amount of assets earned and retained by the corporation and consists essentially of retained earnings and accumulated comprehensive income. An example of the shareholders' equity section of a corporate balance sheet appears in Figure 12–5. Spend a moment to review it because it provides an outline of the remaining discussion in this chapter. Note that most companies disclose treasury stock at the bottom of the shareholders' equity section even though it represents a reduction of contributed capital.

---

3. While the title *additional paid-in capital* is the most common, there is some variation across companies. For example, The New York Times Company uses *additional capital*, Goodyear Tire & Rubber uses *capital surplus*, and Chevron Texaco Corporation uses *capital in excess of par value*.

FIGURE 12–5
Shareholders'
equity section of
balance sheet

Contributed capital:		
Preferred stock (authorized, issued, and outstanding shares, asset preference, dividend preference, par value, cumulative, nonparticipating)	$ 3,000	
Common stock (authorized, issued, and outstanding shares, par value/stated value/no par)	15,000	
Additional paid-in capital (preferred stock, common stock, treasury stock, stock dividends)	86,000	
Total contributed capital		$104,000
Earned capital:		
Retained earnings	$120,000	
Accumulated comprehensive income	5,000	
Total earned capital		125,000
Less: Treasury stock (cost method)		(20,000)
Total shareholders' equity		$209,000

Non-U.S. companies, many of which publish IFRS-based financial statements, use different terms to describe the shareholders' equity accounts. Unilever, for example, uses "share capital" and "share premium" to describe the stock and additional paid-in capital sections, "other reserves" to describe accumulated comprehensive income and treasury stock, and "retained profit" instead of retained earnings. In these cases it is often best to refer to the footnotes to ascertain exactly what is included in each account.

Preferred Stock

Preferred stock is so called because preferred shareholders have certain rights that are not shared by common shareholders. These special rights relate to the receipt of dividends and/or to claims on assets in case of liquidation. **Preferred stock as to dividends** confers the right, if dividends are declared by the corporation's board of directors, to receive dividends. **Preferred stock as to assets** carries a claim to the corporation's assets, in case of liquidation, with a higher priority than the claim carried by common stock. The exact characteristics and terms of preferred stock vary from one issue to the next. The following sections describe some of the more important features of preferred stock.

AUTHORIZED, ISSUED, AND OUTSTANDING PREFERRED SHARES

Authorized preferred shares are the number of shares a corporation is entitled to issue by its corporate charter. Additional authorizations must be approved by the board of directors and are often subject to shareholder vote.

Issued preferred shares have been issued previously by a corporation and may or may not be currently outstanding. Some issued shares may have been repurchased by the corporation and held as treasury stock. **Outstanding** preferred shares are the shares presently held by the shareholders. Issued shares less repurchased shares equal outstanding shares. *Accounting Trends and Techniques* (AICPA, 2009) reports that, of the major U.S. corporations surveyed, approximately 7 percent had outstanding preferred issuances.

The number of authorized, issued, and outstanding preferred shares should be disclosed in the annual report. Priceline.com, for example, recently disclosed in its annual report that the shareholders had authorized and issued 80 million shares of preferred stock, of which over 13 million were presently outstanding.

Many major U.S. corporations have authorized preferred stock issuances but have chosen not to issue them. In such cases, the number of authorized shares should still be disclosed in the financial report. As of the end of 2008, for example, Goodyear Tire & Rubber Company (50 million shares), Hewlett-Packard (300 million shares), and Johnson & Johnson (2 million shares) disclosed authorized preferred shares, none of which had been issued.

?

During the 2008–2009 financial crisis, the U.S. government took unprecedented steps to shore up the capital positions of major banks by injecting them with equity capital. Many critics argued that the equity injections were a bad idea, stating that these companies should have been allowed to fail. Outlined below is an excerpt of the 2008 annual report of Citigroup, the holding company for Citibank (dollars in millions):

	2008	2007
Preferred Stock	$70,664	—

Based on the information provided above, discuss the mechanism used by the government to protect the banking system and the implications to Citigroup of having the U.S. government as a shareholder.

PREFERRED DIVIDEND PAYMENTS

The terms of preferred stocks usually include a specific annual dividend that is paid to the preferred shareholders before any payments are made to the common shareholders, assuming that a dividend is declared by the board. The remaining amount of the dividend is then paid to the common shareholders. The amount of the preferred annual dividend payment is normally expressed as either an absolute dollar amount or a percentage of a dollar amount referred to as the par value of the preferred stock.[4]

For example, if dividends are declared in a given year, the holder of one share of $5 preferred stock will receive a $5 dividend. The holder of one share of 4 percent preferred stock with a par value of $100 would receive a $4 (4% × $100) dividend. Agway, an agriculture co-op, had three kinds of preferred shares outstanding, differentiated by, among other characteristics, the per-share amount of the annual dividend payment: 6 percent, 7 percent, and 8 percent, all on a par value of $100.

To illustrate the allocation of a dividend between preferred and common stock, several years ago the board of directors of DuPont declared and paid a total dividend of $802 million. During the year, approximately 1.68 million shares of $4.50 preferred stock, 0.7 million shares of $3.50 preferred stock, and 240 million shares of common stock were outstanding. The dividend allocation to the preferred and common shareholders is shown in Figure 12–6.

---

4. The concept of par value is discussed more completely later in the chapter when we cover common stock. At that time, we point out that par value has little or no economic meaning. In the case of preferred stock, however, par value is meaningful in that it is sometimes used to determine the annual dividend payment to the preferred shareholders.

FIGURE 12–6

Allocation of a
dividend between
preferred and
common stock

Preferred dividend:		
$4.50 preferred stock × 1.68 million shares	$7.55 million	
$3.50 preferred stock × 0.7 million shares	2.45 million	$ 10 million
Common dividend ($3.30 × 240 million shares)		792 million
Total dividend		$802 million

FIGURE 12–6

Allocation of a dividend between preferred and common stock

CUMULATIVE PREFERRED STOCK

With **cumulative preferred stock,** when a corporation misses a dividend, **dividends in arrears** are created in the amount of the missed preferred dividend. In future periods, as dividends are declared, dividends in arrears are first paid to the preferred shareholders, who then receive their normal annual dividend. Finally, the common shareholders are paid from what remains. If the preferred stock is *noncumulative,* no dividends in arrears are created for missed dividends, and the preferred shareholders receive only their normal annual dividend in future periods as dividends are declared.

It is important to realize that dividends in arrears are not liabilities to the corporation and therefore are not listed on the balance sheet. They do not represent legal obligations to the preferred shareholders, because dividends are at the discretion of the board of directors. The liability is created at the time the dividends are declared and only in the amount of the dividends. However, the corporation must keep track of dividends in arrears because they must be clearly disclosed in the financial report. Such information is particularly interesting to creditors as well as potential and existing shareholders because it may signal a shortage of cash in the corporation. The amount of dividends in arrears may also affect the dividends that common shareholders can expect to receive in the future.

The following excerpt was taken from a recent Sears annual report:

In the event that dividends payable on preferred stock are in arrears for six quarterly periods, holders of such stock shall have the right to elect two additional directors of the Company until all cumulative dividends have been paid or set apart for payment. Additionally, dividends cannot be paid on the Company's common shares if dividends on preferred shares are in arrears.

Who would insist on such a policy and why?

Almost all preferred stock issuances are cumulative, and among major U.S. companies, dividends in arrears are relatively rare. Several years ago, however, Stelco (Canada's second-largest steelmaker) omitted dividends on its cumulative preferred stocks as it attempted to turn around its money-losing operations. Accordingly, the company disclosed dividends in arrears in its financial report. The company had not missed a dividend payment in seventy-five years.

PARTICIPATING PREFERRED STOCK

If preferred stock carries a **participating** feature, the preferred shareholders not only have a right to the annual dividend payment, but they also share in the remaining amount of the dividend with the common shareholders. The extent to which the preferred shareholders participate in the remaining dividend is often expressed as a percentage of the par value of the preferred stock. Nonparticipating preferred stock, which is much more common, carries no rights to share in the remaining dividend.

PREFERRED STOCKS: DEBT OR EQUITY?

We have described how most preferred stocks (1) carry higher priority than common stocks in the event of liquidation, (2) specify annual dividend payments of a fixed amount, (3) are cumulative, and (4) do not contain a participation feature. In addition, preferred stocks normally do not carry a right to vote in the election of the board of directors, and many contain a call provision that allows the corporation to redeem the stock for a specified price after a specified date.

Recall the discussion earlier in the chapter on the characteristics of debt and equity (see Figure 12–3), and note how the features listed above closely resemble debt. In some cases the Internal Revenue Service has allowed corporations to deduct from taxable income the dividends paid on securities classified on the balance sheet as preferred stocks because such dividends were construed as interest. Preferred stocks are definitely hybrid securities, which have characteristics of both debt and equity. They are, therefore, difficult to classify on the balance sheet. In most cases, the preferred stock account is disclosed at the top of the shareholders' equity section, where it is located immediately below long-term liabilities. In some cases, however, preferred stocks are disclosed as debt. On its 2008 balance sheet, for example, The Washington Post Company reported $11.8 million in preferred stock in the long-term liabilities section of the balance sheet. Financial statement users interested in computing ratios that involve distinctions between debt and equity (e.g., debt/equity) may find it more useful to treat the preferred stock account as a long-term liability.

Classifying hybrid securities, like preferred stocks, is indeed a difficult area for accountants and auditors, primarily because the distinction between debt and equity is not always clear-cut. Also, the guidelines specified by generally accepted accounting principles are not very specific. In an article in *Forbes,* the national director of accounting and auditing at a major accounting firm noted: "The distinction between debt and equity has become so muddied that the accounting rules seem more arbitrary than ever . . . preferred stocks are clever ways to raise cash . . . simply [a form of] off-balance-sheet financing masquerading as equity."

Consequently, by issuing certain kinds of preferred stock, management can raise what is essentially debt capital without increasing the liabilities reported on the balance sheet. Because preferred stock carries no voting power, such a strategy also avoids the problems of dilution and possible takeover associated with issuing common stock. As noted in *Forbes:*

Companies anxious to protect their credit ratings, and unwilling to issue more [common] stock for fear of diluting earnings per share or inviting takeover bids, have turned to these ingenious instruments [preferred stocks] to lower the cost of raising money. But pity the poor accountant who must categorize these hothouse hybrids.

Energy company PG&E Corporation notes in its 2008 annual report that it is authorized to issue two types of preferred stock: 75 million shares of $25 par value preferred stock and 10 million shares of $100 par value preferred stock. The company specifies that 5.8 million shares of the $25 stock be nonredeemable without mandatory redemption. The remainder of the $25 stock and all of the $100 stock may be issued as either redeemable or nonredeemable. Furthermore, the company recently retired a third series of preferred stock; in 2005 the company redeemed the last of $25 par value preferred stock that was subject to mandatory redemption provisions. Why would a company authorize three different types of preferred stock? Where on the balance sheet should these shares be listed, as debt or as equity?

Common Stock

Unlike preferred stock, common stock is typically not characterized by a wide variety of features that differ from issuance to issuance. Moreover, common stock is not designed to provide a fixed return over a specified period of time. Rather, as a true equity security, common stock is characterized by three fundamental rights: (1) the right to receive dividends if they are declared by the board of directors, (2) a residual right to the corporation's assets in case of liquidation, and (3) the right to exert control over management, which includes the right to vote in the annual election of the board of directors and the right to vote on certain significant transactions proposed by management (e.g., the authorization of additional shares, large purchases of outstanding shares, major acquisitions).

The value of the common stock issued by a corporation can be described in a number of different and often confusing ways. This section clarifies some of this confusion by differentiating among the market value, book value, and par value of a share of common stock.

Market Value

The **market value** of a share of stock, common or preferred, at a particular point in time is the price at which the stock can be exchanged on the open market. This amount varies from day to day, based primarily on changes in investor expectations about the financial performance and condition of the issuing company, interest rates, and other factors. The market prices of the common stocks of publicly traded companies must be disclosed in their financial reports. For example, the market price of JPMorgan Chase's common stock fluctuated from a low of approximately $16 per share to a high of over $47 during the year ending December 31, 2009.

> **?** Google, Inc. first sold shares of its stock to the public on August 19, 2004. The shares in the initial public offering (IPO) opened at $100. As of February 25, 2010, Google shares were trading for $526.43. Who received the $100 on the date of the initial sale? Who has received the trading profit of $426.43 in the six years since the company went public? Do companies benefit from an increase in stock price? Discuss.

Book Value

The *book value* of a share of common stock is determined by the following formula:

$$\text{Book Value of Common Stock} = \frac{\text{Shareholders' Equity} - \text{Preferred Capital}}{\text{Number of Common Shares Held by the Shareholders}}$$

It is simply the book value of the corporation (less preferred capital), as indicated on the balance sheet, divided by the number of common shares presently held by the shareholders. This value rarely approximates the market value of a common share, because the balance sheet, in general, does not represent an accurate measure of the market value of the company. As of December 31, 2009, the book value of JPMorgan Chase common stock was $39.84 per share, while the market value during 2009 ranged from $16 to $47 per share.

Market-to-Book Ratio

Dividing the market value of a company's common stock by its book value (**market-to-book ratio**) provides a ratio that indicates the extent to which the market believes that the balance sheet reflects the company's true value. Ratios equal to 1 indicate that a company's net book value (as measured by the balance sheet) is perceived by the market to be a fair reflection of the company's true value. More commonly, market-to-book ratios are somewhat larger than 1, indicating that the balance sheet is perceived to be a conservative measure of the company's true value. Large ratios can be attributed to a number of reasons: Balance sheet assets are at cost, not fair market value; the financial statements report on past, not future, events; important intangibles are ignored on the balance sheet; and/or accounting methods are conservative.

High market-to-book ratios also indicate that investors expect high growth relative to the invested capital indicated on the balance sheet. Market-to-book ratios vary substantially across and within companies. As of the end of 2009, for example, JPMorgan Chase's market-to-book ratio was approximately 1.2:1, 3M's was 4.4:1, and the ratio for General Electric has ranged from 4:1 to almost 10:1 in recent years.

Par Value

The **par value** (sometimes called stated value) of a share of common stock has no relationship to its market value or book value and, for the most part, has little economic significance. At one time it represented a legal concept, instituted by some states, that was intended to protect creditors, but over time the concept proved to be largely ineffective.[5] It is not uncommon for corporations to issue either no-par common stock or common stock with extremely low par values. For example, the par value of JPMorgan Chase's common stock is only $1.00 per share.

While the par (stated) value of a share of common stock has limited legal or economic significance, these values do have financial accounting significance. As the next section demonstrates, under generally accepted accounting principles, these values are used in the journal entries to record certain common stock transactions. Many believe that attributing any significance, accounting or otherwise, to the par or stated value of common stock is unwarranted.

> **?** As discussed earlier, as of the end of 2009, there were large differences among the market value, book value, and par value of a share of JPMorgan Chase common stock. Discuss why they are so different.

ACCOUNTING FOR COMMON AND PREFERRED STOCK ISSUANCES

As with preferred stock, common stock issuances must be authorized in the corporate charter and approved by the board of directors and sometimes the shareholders. Similarly, the number of shares of common stock outstanding may differ from the number of common shares originally issued. As of December 31, 2008, for example, the corporate charter and shareholders of Johnson & Johnson had authorized over 4 billion

5. In some states the concept of stated value was substituted for par value, but like par value, this concept has limited economic meaning. Note, however, that state laws differ in this area.

shares of common stock, over 3 billion shares had been issued, and over 2.7 billion shares were currently outstanding—approximately 350 million shares had been repurchased by the company and were held in the form of treasury stock.

The methods used to account for common stock issuances are essentially the same as those used for preferred stock. When no-par common or preferred stock is issued for cash, the cash account is debited for the proceeds and the common (or preferred) stock account is credited for the entire dollar amount. For example, when Apple Computer, Inc. issued 4.98 million shares of no-par common stock for an average price of $17.592 per share (total cash proceeds of $87.61 million), the company recorded the following journal entry (dollars in millions):

Cash (+A)	87.61	
Common Stock (+CC)		87.61
Issued no-par common stock		

When common or preferred stock with a par value is issued for cash, the cash account is debited for the total proceeds, the common (or preferred) stock account is credited for the number of shares issued multiplied by the par value per share, and the additional paid-in capital (common or preferred stock) account is credited for the remainder. The dollar amount credited to the additional paid-in capital account represents the difference between the total issuance price of the stock and the par value of the issuance. For example, when Coca-Cola Enterprises issued 71.4 million shares of $1 par value common stock for $15.62 per share, the company recorded the following journal entry (dollars in millions):

Cash (+A)	1,115.27	
Common Stock (+CC)		71.40*
Additional Paid-In Capital, C/S (+CC)		1,043.87*
Issued $1 par value common stock		

*71.4 million sh. × $1

When Weyerhaeuser Company issued 147,000 shares of $1 par value preferred stock for $11 per share, it recorded the following journal entry:

Cash (+A)	1,617,000*	
Preferred Stock (+CC)		147,000**
Additional Paid-In Capital, P/S (+CC)		1,470,000
Issued $1 par value preferred stock		

*147,000 sh. × $11
**147,000 sh. × $1

> The discount airline JetBlue sold 15.2 million shares of common stock in its initial public offering for $12 per share. One year later the company sold an additional 4.5 million shares at $28.33 per share. The common stock has a par value of .01 per share. Explain how the two issuances affected the basic accounting equation.

Treasury Stock

Outstanding common stock is often repurchased and either (1) held *in treasury,* awaiting reissuance at a later date, or (2) retired.[6] Repurchases of this nature normally must

6. Repurchased preferred shares are normally retired and are not held as treasury stock. Most repurchased common shares, on the other hand, are held in treasury. Treasury shares have the status of authorized and unissued shares.

be authorized and approved by the board of directors. On August 30, 2007, Ditech Networks offered to purchase for cash up to 9.1 million shares of common stock from its shareholders at a price not to exceed $5.50/share. At the time the shares were trading for about $5.00/share. Treasury stock carries none of the usual rights of common stock ownership. That is, while common shares are held in treasury, they lose their voting power and their right to receive dividends.

WHY COMPANIES PURCHASE TREASURY STOCK

Corporations purchase outstanding common shares and hold them in treasury for many reasons. Perhaps the most common is to support employee compensation plans. Johnson & Johnson, for example, purchased treasury stock in the amount of over $2.1 billion in 2009. During that time period, treasury stock in the amount of $1.4 billion was reissued as part of an employee compensation plan.

Other companies, such as Walt Disney, Avco, Gillette, and Safeway, have entered into common stock buy-back programs to fend off possible takeover attempts. We mentioned earlier that by purchasing its own outstanding common stock, a company can discourage takeovers by reducing its cash balance and increasing the proportionate control of the remaining shareholders. Gillette, for example, entered into a plan to purchase 11 million of its outstanding common shares. In doing so, the company blocked a takeover attempt by purchasing the 13.9 percent interest held at that time by the Revlon Group, Inc. Columbia Broadcasting System (CBS) once blocked a takeover attempt by Ted Turner (Turner Broadcasting System, Inc.) by repurchasing a substantial portion of its outstanding common stock.

Purchasing treasury stock may also be related to increases in the market price of a company's outstanding stock. Prudential Securities analyst Ed Keon reported in a study in *CFO.com* that companies that made large stock buy-backs outperformed the stock market average over the following year.

Treasury stock purchases are often viewed as a sign of financial strength. When stock prices dip, companies with strong cash positions, such as Merck, PepsiCo, and Home Depot, often take advantage of the reduced prices on the stock market by purchasing large quantities of their own shares. Many of these shares are reissued later at much higher prices.

Companies in a strong financial position often purchase treasury stock to maintain their levels of leverage without having to rely heavily on borrowing. During 2008, for example, Walt Disney purchased $4.5 billion of its own common stock while increasing its debt by only about $400 million. During the year the company's leverage level decreased by only 2 percent. Had the treasury stock not been purchased, its leverage would have decreased by 6 percent. Recall from Chapter 5 that leverage is a direct determinant of return on equity (ROE), an important indicator of shareholder value creation.

A treasury stock purchase can also serve to increase a company's earnings per share (net income/outstanding common shares). IBM's CFO once claimed that a series of large stock buybacks " has been an important contributor toward growing earnings per share."

Finally, treasury stock purchases are often made to return cash to shareholders. In this sense, it is much like a dividend, especially if the treasury stock purchase is proportionate across the shareholders. Consider, for example, a company that has 6,000 common shares outstanding, held in equal amounts of 2,000 shares by three shareholders. Each shareholder owns one-third of the company. If 1,000 common shares are repurchased from each shareholder for $2 per share, each receives $2,000

and still maintains a one-third interest in the company—the exact result that would have occurred had the company paid a $1 per share dividend.

In both 2007 and 2008 the financing section of the statement of cash flows for Unilever Group, which publishes IFRS-based financial statements, showed share repurchases of 1.5 billion euros. Comment on why a company might want to enter into a share repurchasing program.

ACCOUNTING FOR TREASURY STOCK: THE COST METHOD

There are two methods of accounting for treasury stock: (1) the cost method and (2) the par value method. Although either method is acceptable under GAAP, the cost method is covered below because it is simpler and much more widely used.[7]

PURCHASING TREASURY STOCK. Under the cost method, when a company purchases its own outstanding common stock and holds it in treasury, a permanent account, called "treasury stock," is debited for the cost of the purchase.[8] This account is disclosed below retained earnings in the shareholders' equity section of the balance sheet (see Figure 12–5). For example, when Dell purchased treasury stock for a total cost of over $2.8 billion, it recorded the following journal entry (dollars in millions):

Treasury Stock (−CC)	**2,867**	
Cash (−A)		**2,867**

Purchased shares of treasury stock

This transaction brought the total investment in treasury shares held by Dell to $28 billion, and the shareholders' equity section of Dell's fiscal 2008 balance sheet appeared as in Figure 12–7.

FIGURE 12–7 Disclosure of treasury stock	**Dell Computer** **Balance Sheet** **Shareholders' Equity Section** **January 30, 2009** **(in millions of dollars)**

Preferred stock	$ 0
Common stock	11,189
Retained earnings	20,677
Less: Cost of common stock in treasury	(27,904)
Comprehensive income (loss)	309
Total shareholders' equity	$ 4,271

7. *Accounting Trends and Techniques* (2009) indicated that 70 percent of the companies surveyed reported treasury stock, and 94 percent of those used the cost method.

8. If outstanding stock, preferred or common, is repurchased and then retired, the stock account is debited and the cash payment is credited. If the payment exceeds the stock account, which is frequently the case, additional paid-in capital and/or retained earnings is debited to balance the entry.

Although treasury stock represents a reduction of contributed capital, the treasury stock account is disclosed immediately below retained earnings. In many states, dividends cannot legally exceed retained earnings less the cost of all shares held in treasury. Such laws are designed to protect creditors by keeping a corporation from distributing all of its cash to the shareholders in the form of dividends or stock repurchases. By subtracting the dollar amount in the treasury stock account from retained earnings, financial statement readers can determine the maximum amount of cash that legally can be paid to the shareholders as of the balance sheet date.[9]

From 2007 to 2009 Johnson & Johnson purchased $14.3 billion of its own common shares. During that time period its capital structure leverage (total assets/total shareholders' equity) stayed at 1.87. See below (dollars in billions):

	2009	2007
Total assets	$94.6	$80.9
Shareholders' equity	50.5	43.3
Capital structure leverage	1.87	1.87

Compute the change in the company's capital structure leverage had it chosen not to purchase the treasury shares and instead used the cash to increase assets. Briefly discuss how purchasing treasury shares can help to maintain leverage, and why a company might want to do it.

REISSUING TREASURY STOCK FOR MORE THAN ACQUISITION COST. Common stock held in treasury is often reissued at a later date. If it is reissued at a price greater than its acquisition cost, the cash account is debited for the proceeds, the treasury stock account is credited for the cost, and the difference is credited to the additional paid-in capital (treasury stock) account. For example, when PepsiCo, Inc. reissued 139,000 shares of treasury stock, which had an acquisition cost of $2.7 million, for a total of $5.3 million, the company recorded the following journal entry (dollars in millions):

Cash (+A)	5.3	
Treasury Stock (+CC)		2.7
Additional Paid-In Capital, T/S (+CC)		2.6
Reissued treasury stock		

REISSUING TREASURY STOCK FOR LESS THAN ACQUISITION COST. If treasury stock is reissued for less than the acquisition cost, the cash account is debited for the proceeds, the treasury stock account is credited for the acquisition cost, and additional paid-in capital (treasury stock) is debited for the difference, *if there is a sufficient balance in the account to cover this difference.* If the difference between the acquisition cost and the proceeds exceeds the balance in the additional paid-in capital (treasury stock) account, retained earnings is debited.

For example, when Eli Lilly and Company reissued 1.2 million treasury shares, with an acquisition cost of $68.5 million, for $44.5 million, the balance in the additional paid-in capital (treasury stock) account exceeded $24 million, the difference

---

9. Recently, some major companies (e.g., Wal-Mart) reduced retained earnings directly when outstanding stock was purchased and retired. This accounting treatment may be questioned in that it confuses the distinction between earned and contributed capital.

between the cost and the proceeds. Thus, the following journal entry was recorded to reflect the transaction (dollars in millions):

Cash (+A)	44.5	
Additional Paid-In Capital, T/S (−CC)	24.0	
Treasury Stock (+CC)		68.5

Reissued treasury stock

When the Pillsbury Company reissued 300,000 shares of treasury stock, which had an acquisition cost of $12.9 million, for a total of $11.7 million, the balance in the additional paid-in capital (treasury stock) account at the time was zero. Accordingly, the following journal entry was recorded (dollars in millions).

Cash (+A)	11.7	
Retained Earnings (−SE)	1.2	
Treasury Stock (+CC)		12.9

Reissued treasury stock

Note that in all three preceding examples, an income statement gain or loss is not recognized when treasury stock is reissued for an amount more than or less than the acquisition cost. Reissuing treasury stock is a capital transaction and as such should not affect the income statement.

> The 2008 annual report of Boston Scientific, a manufacturer of medical technology, reports a reissuance of treasury stock that decreased the treasury stock account by $142 million and decreased additional paid-in capital by $52 million. How much cash did Boston Scientific receive from the stock issuance, and was the reissuance price above or below the original cost of the treasury stock? How did the transaction affect the basic accounting equation, and was it reflected on the statement of cash flows?

THE MAGNITUDE OF THE TREASURY STOCK ACCOUNT

The dollar value of the treasury stock account on the balance sheets of major U.S. corporations is often quite significant. As indicated in Figure 12–8, it is not unusual for it to exceed the dollar value of the corporation's total contributed capital (preferred stock, common stock, and additional paid-in capital). This phenomenon can occur because treasury stock is often acquired at prices considerably higher than the original issuance prices of the shares.

FIGURE 12–8

The dollar value of treasury stock/total contributed capital (dollars in millions)

Company	Treasury Stock/Contributed Capital
Amazon.com	$\frac{600}{4,002} = 0.15$
Dell	$\frac{27,904}{11,498} = 2.43$
Goodrich	$\frac{793}{2,243} = 0.35$
Eli Lilly	$\frac{99}{820} = 0.12$
Exxon Mobil	$\frac{148,098}{5,314} = 27.87$

Source: 2008 annual reports.

Stock Options

Many corporate executives in the United States are compensated with **stock options.** These arrangements give executives an option to purchase company stock at a given price (e.g., $10/share) for a given period of time (e.g., five years). If the price of the stock increases during that time period (e.g., $15/share), the executive benefits by purchasing the stock at $10/share and then immediately selling it for $15/share, an instant profit of $5/share. If the stock price decreases, the executive simply chooses not to exercise the option. This form of compensation is very popular because it creates a financial incentive for executives to increase stock prices, which is consistent with shareholder goals, and requires no cash payment from the corporation. In addition, the executive enjoys great upside potential and little downside risk, and if structured correctly, stock option compensation can create tax advantages for both the executive and the corporation.

Accounting standard setters argue that options are costly to companies (and to shareholders) because they allow executives to buy stock at discounted prices. In the illustration just given, where the stock price rose from $10 to $15, the company would be issuing stock worth $15/share to executives for a discounted price of $10/share. Consequently, existing shareholders would be giving up some percentage of their ownership in return for a dollar amount less than the market believes it is worth. On this basis, accounting standard setters now require that compensation expense be recognized when stock options are issued.

Below we illustrate the entries associated with the recognition of stock option compensation expense, and the stock issuance when the options are exercised.

STOCK OPTION COMPENSATION EXPENSE

Assume that during 2010 options to purchase 100 shares of stock at the current market price ($10) are granted to executives, and the options can be exercised any time over the next two years. The options are valued, using an acceptable valuation formula, at $5 per share. The following adjusting entry would be made to record the 2010 compensation expense at year end.

Stock option compensation expense (E, −RE)	**500***	
Additional paid-in capital, S/O (+CC)		**500**

*100 shares × $5 per share

When stock option compensation expense is recognized, shareholders' equity is increased (additional paid-in capital − stock options). This treatment recognizes that the cost of the option is in the form of an investment made by the existing shareholders.

In the operating section of Target's 2008 statement of cash flows, share-based compensation expense of $72 million is added back to net earnings. Why?

EXERCISING STOCK OPTIONS

Assume that the stock price increases, and during 2011 the options are exercised to purchase 100 shares of stock for $10 per share; 100 shares of treasury stock (purchased previously at $8 per share) are issued to the executives.

Cash (+A) [100 shares × $10/sh]	**1,000**	
Additional paid-in capital, S/O (−CC)	**500**	
Treasury stock (+CC) [100 shares × $8/sh]		**800**
Additional paid-in capital, T/S (+CC) [plug]		**700**

This entry recognizes the receipt of cash associated with the stock issuance and removes the additional paid-in capital established when the compensation expense was recognized. The issuance of treasury stock to support the options represents, as illustrated in the previous section, treasury stock issued for more than its acquisition cost. If the treasury stock had been purchased previously for more than $15 per share, the "plug" would reduce additional paid-in capital, T/S (i.e., appear on the left side of the entry).

> In the financing section of Target's 2008 statement of cash flows, stock options exercised show a positive $43 million. Explain.

The above entries illustrate only the basics involved in accounting for stock option compensation. In reality, the entire amount of the expense is not recognized all at once, but is allocated instead over the service life of the employee, the period of time between when the options are granted and when the employee becomes eligible to exercise them. However, the dollar amount of the costs associated with issuing stock options can be very significant. While these costs are especially high in high-tech companies, where stock option compensation is a major form of executive compensation, a relatively recent study estimates that recognizing stock option compensation expense leads to large reductions in reported earnings for a number of well-known, traditional U.S. companies, including Lucent (20 percent); Kmart (13 percent); PepsiCo (12 percent); Morgan Stanley (12 percent); DuPont (9 percent); and Motorola (6 percent).

The value of the options is determined by a complicated and controversial formula, and many companies state in the footnotes to the financial statements that this formula is not well suited for valuing the options granted to their executives. These concepts are covered in intermediate financial accounting texts.

> Backdating a stock option means that a corporation has reset the date at which the option was granted to the employee, picking an earlier date when the option price was lower and thus making the option more valuable to the employee. Regulators have accused several companies over the years of backdating options. In 2010 the *New York Times* news Web site listed several companies being investigated by the SEC for options backdating, including Engineered Support Systems, Broadcom, and KB Homes. In each case the government was concerned that the companies changed the date for the option price to a period when the stock was at its low point. If stock options are a form of employee compensation, how does backdating affect the financial statements? How would backdating affect the shareholders?

Retained Earnings

Retained earnings is a measure of previously recognized profits that have not been paid to the shareholders in the form of dividends. As indicated in Figure 12–2, major U.S. corporations rely heavily on internally generated funds as a source of capital. This section discusses two factors that affect the retained earnings balance: (1) dividends and (2) appropriations.

DIVIDENDS

Dividends are distributions of cash, property, or stock to the shareholders of a corporation. They are declared by a formal resolution of the corporation's board of directors (usually quarterly), and the amount is usually announced on a per-share basis. Cash dividends represent distributions of cash to the shareholders. Property dividends (dividends in kind) are distributions of property, usually debt or equity securities in other companies.[10] **Stock dividends** are distributions of a corporation's own shares. Cash dividends are by far the most common. *Accounting Trends and Techniques* (AICPA, 2009) reported that of the major U.S. companies surveyed, 70 percent paid cash dividends during 2008, 1 percent paid property dividends, and zero paid dividends in the form of stock.[11]

As Figure 12–9 shows, three dates are relevant when dividends are declared: (1) the **date of declaration,** when the dividends are declared by the board; (2) the **date of record,** which determines who is to receive the dividend; and (3) the **date of payment,** when the distribution is actually made.

FIGURE 12–9
Important dividend dates

Date of Declaration	Date of Record	Date of Payment
Board of directors declares dividend and liability is established.	**Shareholders holding stock at this date receive the dividend when paid.**	**Dividend is paid to shareholders of record.**

A typical dividend announcement reads as follows:

The Board of Directors of Bennet Corporation, at its regular meeting of March 10, 2009, declared a quarterly dividend of $5 per share, payable on April 20, 2009, to shareholders of record on April 2, 2009.

In this announcement, March 10 is the date of declaration, April 2 the date of record, and April 20 the date of payment.

DIVIDEND STRATEGY. When and how much of a dividend to declare depends on a number of factors, such as the nature, financial condition, and desired image of the company, as well as legal constraints. If dividends are to be paid in cash, the board of directors must first be certain that the corporation has sufficient cash to meet the payment. Such a determination requires a projection of the operating cash flows of the company, including, for example, analyses of the company's current cash position, future sales, receivables, inventory purchases, and fixed-asset replacements, and the company's desired debt/equity ratio. It is usually wise to make sure that the company's operating cash needs and leverage goals can be met before cash dividends are paid.

The goals of a corporation and the nature of its activities may also have a bearing on dividend policy. Many young, fast-growing companies have adopted policies of paying no dividends. Such companies, often called growth companies, reinvest their earnings primarily to support growth without having to rely too heavily on debt and dilutive equity issuances. The shareholders receive their investment returns in the form of stock price appreciation. The following excerpt is from a recent annual report of Toys "R" Us, Inc., a company that pays no dividends:

The Company has followed the policy of reinvesting earnings in the business and, consequently, has not paid any cash dividends. At the present time, no change in this

---

10. Accounting for property dividends is normally covered in intermediate financial accounting.
11. Some companies distributed more than one kind of dividend, and others distributed no dividends of any kind.

policy is under consideration by the Board of Directors. The payment of cash dividends in the future will be determined by the Board of Directors in light of conditions then existing, including the Company's earnings, financial requirements and condition, opportunities for reinvesting earnings, business conditions, and other factors.

More established companies, such as General Electric and Johnson & Johnson, normally pay quarterly dividends in the amount of 30–40 percent of net income and also attempt to consistently increase their dividend payments from year to year. This policy, which provides a consistent dividend while retaining some funds to finance available growth opportunities, tends to reflect an image of stability, strength, and permanence. The following excerpt is from an annual report of General Electric:

Based on past performance and current expectations, in combination with the financial flexibility that comes with a strong balance sheet and the highest credit ratings, we believe that we are in a sound position to grow dividends, continue making selective investments for the long-term growth, and continue to execute for $25 billion share repurchase program.

Dividend payments from 2007 to 2009 for Abbott Laboratories, a successful pharmaceutical company, are listed below (dollars in billions).

	2009	2008	2007
Dividend payment	$2.2	$2.0	$1.8
Percent of net income	46%	55%	105%

Comment on Abbott's dividend payment policy.

Some companies consistently increase dividends from year to year, but the distributions do not represent a consistent percentage of net income. Bristol-Myers Squibb, for example, increased its dividends each year since 1999. However, as a percentage of net income, dividend payments over that time period varied from less than 50 percent to well over 100 percent. Apparently, the boards of such companies believe that dividend payments should show consistent growth regardless of how well the company does from one year to the next.

State laws and debt covenants can also limit the payment of dividends. In most states, the dollar amount of retained earnings less the cost of treasury stock sets a limitation on the payment of dividends. In addition, the terms of debt contracts may further limit dividend payments to an even smaller portion of retained earnings. Several years ago, for example, Sears, Roebuck & Company had a balance of retained earnings of almost $9 billion. Yet, certain indenture agreements existing at the time limited dividend payments to a maximum amount of $8 billion.

Intel pays cash dividends consistently each year; Microsoft, after paying no dividends for many years, recently issued a huge special dividend to its shareholders; and Cisco Systems follows a policy of paying no dividends. Comment on these three dividend policies and what they may indicate about each company.

ACCOUNTING FOR CASH DIVIDENDS. When the board of directors of a corporation declares a cash dividend, a liability in the amount of the fair market value of the dividend is created on the date of declaration. At this time, a cash dividend account is debited, and a current liability account, "dividends payable," is credited for a dollar value equal to the per-share amount multiplied by the number of outstanding shares. Cash dividend is a temporary account that is closed directly to retained earnings at the end of the accounting period. The dividends payable account is removed from the balance sheet when the dividend is paid on the date of payment. No entry is recorded on the date of record. The shareholders as of the date of record are simply the recipients of the dividend.

To illustrate, when the board of directors of Marriott Corporation declared a fourth-quarter cash dividend of $0.20 per share on 118.8 million common shares outstanding, the following journal entry was recorded (dollars in millions):

Cash Dividend (−RE)	**23.76**	
Dividends Payable (+L)		**23.76**

Declared a cash dividend (118.8 million sh. × $0.20/sh.)

Marriott recorded the following entry on the date of payment (dollars in millions):

Dividends Payable (−L)	**23.76**	
Cash (−A)		**23.76**

Paid a cash dividend

Unilever, a Dutch-based consumer-goods company that publishes IFRS-based financial statements, reported dividend payments of 2.09 billion euros on its 2008 statement of cash flows. That same year it reported dividends of 2.05 billion euros on its statement of shareholders' equity. Explain, and discuss whether this difference is due to the fact that Unilever reports under IFRS and not U.S. GAAP.

STOCK SPLITS AND STOCK DIVIDENDS. Corporations can distribute additional shares to existing shareholders by declaring either a stock split or a stock dividend. For practical purposes, there is very little difference between these two actions. In both cases, the existing shareholders receive additional shares, and in neither case are the assets or liabilities of the corporation increased or decreased.

In a **stock split,** the number of outstanding shares is simply "split" into smaller units, which requires the corporation to distribute additional shares. A 2:1 stock split, for example, serves to double the number of outstanding shares, which requires that the company distribute an additional share for each common share outstanding. A 3:1 stock split effectively triples the number of outstanding shares, which the company executes by distributing two additional shares for each one outstanding. In a 3:2 stock split, one additional share is issued for every two outstanding.

In a stock dividend, additional shares, usually expressed as a percentage of the outstanding shares, are issued to the shareholders. Large stock dividends have essentially the same effect as stock splits. Both a 100 percent stock dividend and a 2:1 stock split, for example, double the number of outstanding shares. Similarly, both a 50 percent stock dividend and a 3:2 stock split increase outstanding shares by 50 percent. Professional accounting standards recommend that relatively large stock dividends (over 25 percent) be referred to as **stock splits in the form of dividends.** Stock splits and stock splits in the form of dividends are not very common. *Accounting Trends and*

Techniques (AICPA, 2009) reports that, of the major U.S. companies surveyed, only 2 percent reported a stock split or a large stock dividend during 2008. Relatively small stock dividends (less than 25 percent), which are even less common than either stock splits or stock splits in the form of dividends, are referred to as **ordinary stock dividends.**

The Dow Jones News Service reported after long stock market "bull" runs: "Many companies have stock prices well into triple digits that are daunting to investors, particularly retail customers and individuals. When stock prices are perceived as too high, companies may consider stock splits." How do stock splits work, and why might a company want to lower the average market price of its shares? As of March 10, 2010, Google common shares were selling for $570 each. If it issued a 5:1 stock split, what would have happened to the per-share market price?

ACCOUNTING FOR STOCK DIVIDENDS AND STOCK SPLITS. Stock dividends and splits can be divided into three categories: (1) stock dividends (<25 percent), (2) stock splits in the form of dividends (>25 percent), and (3) stock splits. While each category is accounted for in a slightly different manner, it is important to realize that such actions affect neither the corporation's assets nor its liabilities. Only the accounts within the shareholders' equity section (i.e., common stock, additional paid-in capital, or retained earnings) are adjusted. Below, we cover ordinary stock dividends and stock splits.[12]

ORDINARY STOCK DIVIDENDS. When the board of directors of a corporation declares an ordinary stock dividend, a dividend account is debited for the number of shares to be issued multiplied by the fair market value of the shares, the common stock account is credited for the number of shares issued multiplied by the par value, and additional paid-in capital is credited for the remainder.[13]

To illustrate, assume that ATP International has 100,000 shares of $1 par value common stock outstanding, each with a fair market value of $25. The company would record the following journal entry if the board of directors decided to distribute 5,000 additional shares by declaring a 5 percent stock dividend:

Stock Dividend (−RE)	125,000*	
Common Stock (+CC)		5,000**
Additional Paid-In Capital, Stock Dividend (+CC)		120,000

Declared 5 percent stock dividend

*(100,000 × .05) × $25/sh.
**5,000 sh. × $1/sh.

Note that no assets or liabilities are involved in the transaction; all of the activity takes place in the shareholders' equity section. Retained earnings is reduced after the stock dividend account is closed at the end of the accounting period, and common stock and additional paid-in capital (stock dividend) are both increased. In other words, retained earnings has been *capitalized.* Earned capital has been transferred to contributed capital. Note also that if the issued stock has a par value of zero, the entire amount of the stock dividend is credited to the additional paid-in capital account.

STOCK SPLITS. Under generally accepted accounting principles, no entry is recorded in the books when stock splits are declared. The corporation should simply record the fact that the par value of the issued stock has been reduced in proportion to the size of

---

12. We do not cover stock splits in the form of dividends because we believe, as many others do, that they are effectively stock splits and should be accounted for as such.
13. We assume here that the stock dividend is declared and issued on the same day.

the split. A 3:1 split, for example, triples the number of outstanding shares and reduces the par value of each share to one-third of its original value. If the stock has no par value, the par value need not be adjusted.

To illustrate, when the board of directors of Procter & Gamble approved a 2:1 stock split, the company recorded no journal entry to reflect the action. The 1.35 billion outstanding shares, each with a par value of $2, were simply replaced by 2.7 (1.35 × 2) billion outstanding shares, each with a par value of $1 ($2/2). In other words, one additional share with a par value of $1 was distributed for each share outstanding.

WHY DO COMPANIES DECLARE STOCK DIVIDENDS AND STOCK SPLITS? To understand the reasons behind stock dividends and stock splits, it is important to realize that (1) such actions do not distribute additional assets to the shareholders and (2) their proportionate ownership of the company after the dividend or split is the same as it was before the dividend or split. For example, a shareholder who owns 10 of a company's 100 outstanding shares, each with a market value of $6, owns 10 percent of the company that has a theoretical value of $600 (100 shares × $6). After a 2:1 stock split, the shareholder will own 20 shares of stock, but each share should drop in value to $3 and the 20 shares will still represent only 10 percent of the 200 outstanding shares. Consequently, unlike cash or property dividends, corporations do not declare stock dividends or stock splits to distribute assets to the shareholders.

Perhaps the most popular reason for declaring a stock split or a large stock dividend is to reduce the per-share price of the outstanding shares so that investors can more easily purchase them. When IBM, for example, declared a 4:1 stock split, which quadrupled the number of outstanding shares, the per-share price of IBM stock immediately decreased from $300 to $75 ($300/4). The managements of many corporations believe that such an action encourages better public relations and wider stock ownership. It is also true that a company's stock price often increases after a stock split is announced. *Business Week* once noted: "As the market booms, companies are increasingly splitting their stock to both make it more affordable and boost the price."

While it is unclear why stock prices jump when stock splits are announced, many believe that such announcements signal to investors that company management believes that it can maintain the value of the stock in the future. Perhaps this signal provides investors with positive information about the company's prospects that was unavailable prior to the announcement.

The reasons for stock dividends are even less clear. Such distributions have a relatively small effect on the number of outstanding shares and thus do little to reduce per-share prices and broaden stock ownership. They do not place assets in the hands of shareholders, which is supported by the IRS position of not considering stock dividends received as taxable income. It is possible that cash-poor corporations distribute stock dividends instead of cash dividends so that shareholders are at least receiving something, but this strategy could be interpreted simply as a publicity gesture. It may satisfy shareholders, especially if they believe that they have received additional assets, but more likely, it may signal financial problems. Finally, corporations may issue stock dividends to capitalize a portion of retained earnings. By reducing retained earnings, a stock dividend places a more restrictive limitation on future dividend payments.

? The same year that Hershey Foods declared a 100 percent stock dividend, Urban Outfitters and Knight Transportation declared 2:1 and 3:2 splits, respectively. Briefly explain how each transaction affected the basic accounting equation, and discuss why a company might declare a stock dividend or a stock split.

APPROPRIATIONS OF RETAINED EARNINGS

An **appropriation of retained earnings** is a book entry that serves to restrict a portion of retained earnings from the payment of future dividends. It involves no asset or liability accounts and no shareholders' equity accounts other than retained earnings. Such entries are executed either at the discretion of the board of directors or in conformance with the terms of contracts (e.g., debt covenants).

Suppose, for example, that the board of directors of Rosebud Corporation plans to expand the company's main manufacturing plant. To save cash so that the expansion can be funded internally, the board has decided to place a restriction on the payment of future dividends. Accordingly, a resolution is passed stating that the company cannot pay dividends that reduce retained earnings below $300,000. Assuming that the balance in the company's retained earnings account before the appropriation was $500,000, the shareholders' equity section of Rosebud's balance sheet after the resolution would appear as in Figure 12–10.

FIGURE 12–10

Disclosing an appropriation of retained earnings

Rosebud Corporation
Balance Sheet
December 31, 2012

Shareholders' Equity

Common stock		$1,200,000
Additional paid-in capital		2,500,000
Retained earnings:		
Restricted	$300,000	
Unrestricted	200,000	500,000
Total shareholders' equity		$4,200,000

Appropriations of retained earnings that result from contractual restrictions are disclosed in a similar manner. In practice, most companies simply disclose the existence, nature, and dollar amount of restricted retained earnings. Nordstrom, for example, once disclosed the following information about restricted retained earnings in its annual report and chose not to adjust the balance of retained earnings:

Senior Note Agreements contain restrictive covenants which . . . restrict dividends to shareholders to a formula amount (under the most restrictive formula, approximately $247,342 of retained earnings was not restricted).

NEGATIVE RETAINED EARNINGS: A MIXED SIGNAL

The retained earnings account becomes negative if a company's accumulated net losses plus its dividends from previous years exceeds the accumulation of its past profits. Negative retained earnings can indicate serious company problems in that it reflects previous losses. However, young and ultimately very successful companies often experience losses in the early years as they start up their businesses, and these companies frequently show negative retained earnings on the balance sheet. At no time in recent history has this phenomenon been more common than in this era of high technology and the Internet. Well-known Internet providers, such as Amazon.com and others, consistently showed losses in their earlier years, yet their stock prices remained extremely

strong. Consider, for example, Priceline.com—recognized as a leading provider of online travel services. As of the end of 2009, the company had only recently posted consistent profits and still had an accumulated deficit in retained earnings (of over $450 million). Interestingly, the company's stock jumped from around $70 per share to over $200 by the end of 2009, not so much because the company showed a profit and reduced its retained earnings deficit, but because the market seemed to sense something (e.g., a strong future) not captured on the financial statements. By February 2010, the shares were up to $226 despite the deficit.

> The 2002 balance sheet of Yahoo!, an Internet search engine, indicated an accumulated deficit in retained earnings of $7.5 million, down from a deficit of $50 million the previous year. By the end of 2003, retained earnings was a positive $230 million. How could a well-known company like Yahoo! accumulate a deficit in retained earnings, and what must have happened in 2002 and 2003 to reduce the deficit?

RETAINED EARNINGS AND PRIOR PERIOD ADJUSTMENTS

All items on the income statement are eventually transferred (closed) to retained earnings, so net income (loss) appears as an adjustment to retained earnings on the statement of shareholders' equity. We have noted that the financial effects of other events, such as the declaration of dividends, the appropriation of retained earnings, and the sale of treasury stock for an amount less than its acquisition cost, are also booked directly to the retained earnings account.

In addition to these items, generally accepted accounting principles require that the financial effects of several rather unusual events be booked directly to retained earnings. One is the correction in the current period of an accounting error made in a previous period. When such a correction is made, a journal entry is recorded to correct the misstated asset or liability and the other half of the entry serves to increase or decrease retained earnings directly. Another is the effect of a change in accounting method in cases when it is not practical for the company to determine the effects of the change on prior years' financial statements. These entries are called **prior period adjustments.**

THE STATEMENT OF SHAREHOLDERS' EQUITY

Generally accepted accounting principles require that the changes during the period in the dollar balances of the separate accounts comprising the shareholders' equity section be disclosed in the financial report. A company can disclose such changes either in the footnotes or in a separate financial statement called the **statement of shareholders' equity.** The consolidated statement of shareholders' equity for Emerson Electric Company appears in Figure 12–11.

INTERNATIONAL PERSPECTIVE: THE RISE OF INTERNATIONAL EQUITY MARKETS

We have referred many times in this text to the New York and American Stock Exchanges and the important roles they play in the buying and selling of equity securities in the United States. As the world of business has become internationalized, however, stock

FIGURE 12–11
Consolidated
statements of
shareholders'
equity

Consolidated Statements of Stockholders' Equity
Emerson Electric Co. & Subsidiaries
Years Ended September 30
(Dollars in millions, except per share amounts)

	2007	2008	2009
Common stock			
Beginning balance	$ 238	477	477
Adjustment for stock split	239	—	—
Ending balance	477	477	477
Additional paid-in capital			
Beginning balance	161	31	146
Stock plans and other	31	115	11
Adjustment for stock split	(161)	—	—
Ending balance	31	146	157
Retained earnings			
Beginning balance	11,314	12,536	14,002
Net earnings	2,136	2,412	1,724
Cash dividends (per share:			
2007, $1.05; 2008, $1.20; 2009, $1.32)	(837)	(940)	(998)
Adjustment for stock split	(77)	—	—
Adoption of FIN 48	—	(6)	—
Adoption of FAS 158 measurement date			
provision (net of tax of $7)	—	—	(14)
Ending balance	12,536	14,002	14,714
Accumulated other comprehensive income			
Beginning balance	306	382	141
Foreign currency translation	459	(30)	(104)
Pension and postretirement (net of tax of:			
2007, $(1); 2008, $51; 2009, $334)	2	(144)	(568)
Cash flow hedges and other (net of tax of:			
2007, $29; 2008, $51; 2009, ($29))	(56)	(67)	35
Adoption of FAS 158 liability provisions			
(net of tax of $193)	(329)	—	—
Ending balance	382	141	(496)
Treasury stock			
Beginning balance	(3,865)	(4,654)	(5,653)
Purchases	(849)	(1,128)	(695)
Issued under stock plans and other	60	129	51
Ending balance	(4,654)	(5,653)	(6,297)
Total shareholders' equity	$8,772	9,113	8,555
Comprehensive income			
Net earnings	$2,136	2,412	1,724
Foreign currency translation	459	(30)	(104)
Pension and postretirement	2	(144)	(568)
Cash flow hedges and other	(56)	(67)	35
Total	$2,541	2,171	1,087

See accompanying Notes to Consolidated Financial Statements.

exchanges outside the United States have become increasingly important. The stock of JCPenney, for example, is traded not only on the New York Exchange, but also on exchanges in Antwerp and Brussels; General Electric is traded in New York, London, and Tokyo; Coca-Cola is traded in Frankfurt in addition to five different exchanges in Switzerland; and American Express stock is listed on no less than fifteen stock exchanges, eleven of which are outside the United States. It is also true that many companies outside the United States list their equity securities on U.S. exchanges. Approximately 50 percent of Sony's equity is held in New York, and each year billions of dollars are raised through equity issuances on U.S. stock exchanges by non–U.S. companies. A "world stock exchange" seems to be emerging. In the words of Neil Osborn, author of *The Rise of the International Equity:* "It is quite possible to trade in a Japanese stock with a buyer in Saudi Arabia, a seller in London, and a U.S. broker without the transaction going near Tokyo."

The increasing level of international equity trading has important implications for accountants who must provide the financial reports necessary to support this investment activity. Each stock exchange, for example, establishes its own reporting requirements, and issuing companies must prepare their financial statements and supporting disclosures in a manner that conforms to those requirements. To date, the requirements of the U.S. exchanges have been the most difficult to meet, which, in turn, has discouraged many companies from listing their securities on the U.S. exchanges. The *Wall Street Journal* once noted that "the major roadblock to foreign companies listing their overseas stock on U.S. exchanges has long been the big difference between accounting standards in the United States and abroad."

But as we have noted many times before, IFRS are becoming increasingly important and the U.S. exchanges now accept them. As a result, IFRS-based financial statements are becoming more and more common, and U.S. investors now have to contend with the challenges associated with comparing company financial statements prepared on different sets of reporting standards.

ROE EXERCISE: RETURN ON EQUITY AND VALUE CREATION

The ROE model, introduced and illustrated in Appendix 5A, provides a framework linking the management of a company's operating, investing, and financing activities to its return on the shareholders' investment (return on equity). The balance in the shareholders' equity section of the balance sheet represents the investment made by the shareholders, and it is management's responsibility to provide a return on that investment exceeding the return the shareholders could have generated if they chose to invest their funds in other equally risky investments. If this objective is achieved, management has "created value" for the shareholders. If return on equity (ROE) is 20 percent in a particular year, for example, and in that year other equally risky investment alternatives generate a return, on average, of 15 percent, management has achieved **value creation.**

Transactions that influence the shareholders' equity balance have a direct influence on ROE (net income ÷ average shareholders' equity) because they directly affect the denominator used in its calculation. A stock issuance, for example, increases the shareholders' investment, which immediately reduces ROE, placing pressure on management to manage the cash collected from the issuance in a way that generates a return that more than offsets the drop in ROE. Similarly, reported net income increases shareholders' equity, and if retained in the business, represents an additional investment made by the shareholders, providing management with additional capital through which a return must be generated. Dividend payments and treasury stock

purchases, on the other hand, have the opposite effect. By returning cash to the shareholders, these transactions reduce the shareholders' investment and decrease the capital available to management that can be used to generate shareholder returns.

ROE ANALYSIS

An important part of ROE analysis involves assessing the level and changes in the shareholders' investment (equity) as well as the returns generated by management on the capital provided or used by those changes. Access the Web site http://wiley.com/college/pratt and conduct ROE analyses on Biogen Idec, Inc. versus Baxter and/or International Paper versus Mead Westvaco Corporation, paying special attention to changes in ROE and transactions that affect shareholders' equity.

REVIEW PROBLEM

The following data pertain to the shareholders' equity transactions of Pike Place Corporation over its first three years of operations: 2010, 2011, and 2012. Transactions are described and followed by the appropriate journal entries. The shareholders' equity section of the balance sheet is shown for each of the three years.

2010

(1) The company issued 1,000 shares of $1 par value stock for $70 per share.

Cash (+A)	70,000*	
Common Stock (+CC)		1,000**
Additional Paid-In Capital, C/S (+CC)		69,000
Issued common stock		

*1,000 sh. × $70/sh.
**1,000 sh. × $1 par value/sh.

(2) The company issued 500 shares of no par value, cumulative preferred stock for $50 per share.

Cash (+A)	25,000	
Preferred Stock (+CC)		25,000
Issued preferred stock (500 sh. × $50/sh.)		

(3) Net income during the year = $2,000
Dividends = $0

Pike Place Corporation
Balance Sheet
December 31, 2010

SHAREHOLDERS' EQUITY

Preferred stock (500 sh., no par value)	$25,000
Common stock (1,000 sh. @ $1 par value)	1,000
Additional paid-in capital (C/S)	69,000
Retained earnings	2,000
Total shareholders' equity	$97,000

Note: Dividends in arrears on cumulative preferred stock = $2,500 (500 sh. × $5/sh.)

2011

(1) The company purchased 200 treasury (common) shares for $60 per share.

Treasury Stock (−CC)	**12,000**	
Cash (−A)		**12,000**

Acquired treasury stock (200 sh. × $60/sh.)

(2) Net income for the year = $20,000
Dividends = $6,600: $5,000 for preferred shareholders [$2,500 dividends in arrears and $2,500 (500 sh. × $5/sh.)] for 2011, and $1,600 for the common shareholders (800 outstanding sh. × $2/sh.). The dividends were declared and paid.

Preferred Dividends (−RE)	**5,000**	
Common Dividends (−RE)	**1,600**	
Dividends Payable (+L)		**6,600**

Declared dividends

Dividends Payable (−L)	**6,600**	
Cash (−A)		**6,600**

Paid dividends

Pike Place Corporation
Balance Sheet
December 31, 2011

SHAREHOLDERS' EQUITY

Preferred stock (500 sh., no par value)	**$25,000**
Common stock (1,000 sh. @ $1 par value)	**1,000**
Additional paid-in capital (C/S)	**69,000**
Retained earnings	**15,400***
Less: Treasury stock (200 sh. × $60/sh.)	**(12,000)**
Total shareholders' equity	**$98,400**

$2,000 + $20,000 − $6,600

2012

(1) The company reissued 100 treasury shares for $65 each.

Cash (+A)	**6,500***	
Treasury Stock (+CC)		**6,000****
Additional Paid-In Capital, T/S (+CC)		**500**

Reissued treasury stock

*100 sh. × $65/sh.
**100 sh. × $60/sh.

(2) The company reissued 50 treasury shares for $40 each.

Cash (+A)	**2,000***	
Additional Paid-In Capital, T/S (−CC)	**500**	
Retained Earnings (−CC)	**500**	
Treasury Stock (+CC)		**3,000****

Reissued treasury stock

*50 sh. × $40/sh.
**50 sh. × $60/sh.

(3) The company declared a 10 percent stock dividend. There were 950 common shares outstanding at the time of the split, each with a fair market value of $5.

Stock Dividend (−RE)	475*	
Common Stock (+CC)		**95****
Additional Paid-In Capital (+CC)		380

Declared stock dividend

*Closed to Retained Earnings
**95 sh. × $1 par value/sh.

(4) The company entered into a debt covenant that required a minimum retained earnings balance of $30,000. The board of directors voted to restrict retained earnings of $30,000.
(5) Net income at the end of the year = $35,000
Dividends = $4,590: $2,500 to preferred shareholders and $2,090 to common shareholders (1,045 sh. outstanding × $2/sh.). The dividends were declared but unpaid at year-end.

Preferred Dividends (−RE)	2,500	
Common Dividends (−RE)	2,090	
Dividends Payable (+L)		4,590

Pike Place Corporation
Balance Sheet
December 31, 2012

SHAREHOLDERS' EQUITY

Preferred stock (500 sh., no par value)		$ 25,000
Common stock (1,045 sh. @ $1 par value)		1,045[a]
Additional paid-in capital		69,380[b]
Retained earnings:		
Restricted	$30,000	
Unrestricted	14,835	44,835[c]
Less: Treasury stock		(3,000)[d]
Total shareholders' equity		$137,260

[a]*$1,000 + $45*
[b]*$69,000 + $500 − $500 + $380*
[c]*$15,400 − $500 − $475 + $35,000 − $4,590*
[d]*50 sh. × $60/sh. or $12,000 − $6,000 − $3,000*

SUMMARY OF KEY POINTS

The three forms of financing and their relative importance to major U.S. corporations.

Companies can generate assets from three sources: (1) borrowings, (2) issuing equity securities, and (3) retaining funds generated through profitable operations. Borrowings are represented by liabilities on the balance sheet, equity issuances are represented by contributed capital (preferred stock, common stock, and additional paid-in capital), and retaining funds are represented by earned capital (retained earnings). Major U.S. corporations generally rely more heavily on

liabilities as a form of financing than on the combined total of contributed and earned capital. Earned capital is typically more important than contributed capital. The additions of contributed and earned capital represent the shareholders' investment in the company.

 Distinctions between debt and equity.

Debt involves a contractual relationship with an outsider. The contract usually states a fixed maturity date, interest charges, security in case of default, and additional provisions designed to protect the interests of the debtholders. Interest is an expense on the income statement and is deductible for tax purposes. In case of liquidation, creditors have rights to the company's assets before owners. Creditors do not vote in the annual election of the board of directors.

Equity involves a relationship with an owner. There is no legal contract, fixed maturity date, or periodic interest payment. Dividends are at the discretion of the board of directors. They are not considered an expense on the income statement and are not tax deductible. Equity holders have lower asset priority than debtholders in case of liquidation, but they have a direct voice in the operation of the company, primarily through voting power over the board of directors.

Distinguishing debt from equity is important to investors and creditors because equity investments are generally riskier than debt investments but offer the potential for higher returns. From the company's perspective, issuing debt involves the commitment of future cash outflows, but interest is tax deductible. Issuing equity, while avoiding fixed contractual cash outflows, dilutes the ownership of the existing shareholders and makes it easier for outside investors to gain significant control. From the accountant's perspective, debt and equity are classified in different sections of the balance sheet, and unlike interest payments and debt redemptions, exchanges of equity are never reflected on the income statement.

Economic consequences associated with the methods used to account for shareholders' equity.

The economic consequences associated with accounting for shareholders' equity arise from the effects of financial ratios that include the dollar amount of shareholders' equity or its components on a company's stock prices, credit rating, or any debt covenants that restrict additional borrowings, the payment of dividends, or the repurchase of outstanding equity shares. Such ratios are also commonly used to define restrictions in debt covenants imposed on management. The use of financial ratios in these ways can encourage management, for example, to structure debt financing in a way that resembles equity so that additional debt need not be reported on the balance sheet. Issuing certain forms of preferred stock and other hybrid securities may represent such a strategy.

Rights associated with preferred and common stock and the methods used to account for stock issuances.

Stock that is preferred as to dividends carries the right, if dividends are declared by the board, to receive a certain specified dividend payment before the common shareholders receive a dividend. If the preferred stock is cumulative and the corporation misses a dividend, dividends in arrears are created in the amount of the missed preferred dividend. In future periods, as dividends are declared, dividends in arrears are paid first to the preferred shareholders, the preferred shareholders are then paid their normal, annual dividend, and finally, the common shareholders are paid from what remains. If the preferred stock carries a participating feature, the preferred shareholders not only receive their initial specified amount, but they also share in the remaining dividends with the common shareholders. Stock that is preferred as to assets carries a claim to the corporation's assets, in case of liquidation, that has higher priority than the claim carried by common stock. In many ways preferred stock resembles debt.

Common stock is characterized by three fundamental rights: (1) the right to receive dividends if they are declared by the board, (2) a residual right to the corporation's assets in case of liquidation, and (3) the right to exert control over corporate management, which is exercised primarily by voting in the election of the board at the annual shareholders' meeting.

When preferred or common stock with no par value is issued for cash, the cash account is debited for the proceeds, and the stock account is credited for the entire dollar amount. When stock with a par (or stated) value is issued for cash, the cash account is debited for the total proceeds, the stock account is credited for the number of shares issued multiplied by the par value per share, and the additional paid-in capital account is credited for the remainder.

● *Distinctions among the market value, book value, and par (stated) value of a share of common stock.*

The market value of a share of stock is the price at which the stock can be purchased and sold on the open market. The book value of a share of stock is equal to the book value of the corporation, as indicated on the balance sheet (shareholders' equity or net assets), less preferred capital and divided by the number of common shares outstanding. The par (stated) value of a share of stock has no relationship to its market value or book value and, for the most part, has limited economic significance.

● *Treasury stock.*

Outstanding common stock is often repurchased by companies. Such stocks are either (1) held in treasury, to be reissued at a later date, or (2) retired. Treasury stock purchases normally must be authorized and approved by the company's board of directors and shareholders. While held in treasury, stock shares carry none of the usual rights of ownership.

Companies purchase treasury stock to support employee compensation plans, to fend off possible takeover attempts, to prepare for merger activity, to increase the market price of the company's outstanding stock, to maintain leverage levels, to increase the company's earnings per share (net income/outstanding common shares), and to distribute cash to the shareholders. In general, treasury stock purchases reduce the scale of a company's operations.

When a company purchases its own outstanding common stock under the cost method, a permanent account, called treasury stock, is debited for the cost of the purchase. This account is disclosed below retained earnings in the shareholders' equity section of the balance sheet. If treasury stock is reissued at a price greater than its original cost, the cash account is debited for the proceeds, the treasury stock account is credited for the cost, and the difference is credited to the additional paid-in capital (treasury stock) account. If treasury stock is reissued at an amount less than the original cost, the cash account is debited for the proceeds, the treasury stock account is credited for the original cost, and additional paid-in capital (treasury stock) is debited for the difference, if there is a sufficient balance in the account to cover the difference. If the difference between the cost and the proceeds exceeds the balance in the additional paid-in capital account, retained earnings is debited.

● *Cash dividends and dividend strategies followed by corporations.*

Cash dividends represent distributions of cash to the shareholders. When a cash dividend is declared, a cash dividend account is debited and a current liability account, dividends payable, is credited on the date of declaration. The dollar amount is equal to the cash dividend per share multiplied by the number of outstanding shares. The dividend account is a temporary account that is closed directly to retained earnings at the end of the accounting period. On the date of record, no entry is made in the books of the corporation. The shareholders as of this date are the recipients of the dividends. On the date of payment, the cash dividend is paid, and the dividends payable liability is removed from the balance sheet.

When to declare a dividend and how much to declare depend on the nature, financial condition, and desired image of the company, as well as legal constraints. If dividends are to be paid in cash, the board of directors must first be certain that the corporation has sufficient cash to meet the payment. Some companies have adopted policies of paying no dividends. Such companies reinvest their earnings primarily to support growth without having to rely too heavily on debt and equity financing. Other companies pay quarterly dividends at the rate of a relatively fixed percentage of net income and also attempt to increase their dividend payments consistently from year to year. Some companies consistently increase dividends from year to year, but the distributions do not represent a consistent percentage of net income.

● *Stock dividends and stock splits.*

In a stock split, the number of outstanding shares is simply split into smaller units, which requires the corporation to distribute additional shares. In a stock dividend, additional shares, usually expressed as a percentage of the outstanding shares, are issued to the shareholders. Professional accounting standards recommend that relatively large stock dividends (over 25 percent)

be referred to as stock splits in the form of dividends and that relatively small stock dividends (less than 25 percent) be referred to as ordinary stock dividends.

Stock splits or stock dividends in the form of splits are often declared to reduce the per-share price of the outstanding shares so that investors can more easily purchase them. The reasons for small stock dividends are less clear. Such distributions have a relatively small effect on the number of outstanding shares and do little to reduce per-share prices and broaden stock ownership. Corporations that are short of cash may distribute stock dividends instead of cash dividends so that the shareholders are at least receiving something. Corporations may also issue stock dividends to capitalize a portion of retained earnings, rendering them unavailable for future dividends. In any case, the issuance of a stock split or stock dividend does not involve a distribution of assets to the shareholders.

KEY TERMS

Note: Definitions for these terms are provided in the glossary at the end of the text.

Accumulated comprehensive income (p. 540)
Appropriation of retained earnings (p. 566)
Authorized (shares) (p. 548)
Book value (of company/share) (p. 540)
Contributed capital (p. 540)
Cumulative preferred stock (p. 550)
Date of declaration (p. 561)
Date of payment (p. 561)
Date of record (p. 561)
Dilution (p. 544)
Dividends in arrears (p. 550)
Earned capital (p. 540)
Issued (shares) (p. 548)
Leverage (p. 544)
Market-to-book ratio (p. 553)
Market value (of stock) (p. 552)
Net assets (p. 540)

Net worth (p. 540)
Ordinary stock dividends (p. 564)
Outstanding (shares) (p. 548)
Par value (p. 553)
Participating (preferred stock) (p. 550)
Preferred stock as to assets (p. 548)
Preferred stock as to dividends (p. 548)
Prior period adjustments (p. 567)
Residual interest (p. 543)
Statement of shareholders' equity (p. 567)
Stock dividends (p. 561)
Stock options (p. 559)
Stock split (p. 563)
Stock splits in the form of dividends (p. 563)
Takeover (p. 545)
Treasury stock (p. 545)
Value creation (p. 569)

ETHICS in the Real World

Two years in a row, Hampton Industries, a men's clothing manufacturer that relies heavily on low-cost labor in Third-World countries, declared 10 percent stock dividends. Although no assets were transferred to shareholders, millions of dollars were transferred from retained earnings to the common stock and paid-in capital accounts. More recently, the company faced some very difficult times, violating debt covenants and entering into a plan to liquidate assets. Some have speculated that the board of directors declared the stock dividends to mislead the shareholders into believing that the company was still able to distribute something of value even though profits were down and falling fast, perhaps in an attempt to delay an inevitable stock price collapse.

ETHICAL ISSUE Does a stock dividend represent something of value? Was the board of directors acting ethically if it attempted to delay an inevitable stock price collapse by issuing a stock dividend?

INTERNET RESEARCH EXERCISE

Kellogg Company manufactures products on six continents, and these products are sold in more than 160 countries. Review the company's most recent annual report, specifically the statement of shareholders' equity, which can be found via www.kelloggs.com. Briefly describe the main transactions between the company and its shareholders over the previous three-year period. Has the company issued stock, declared stock splits, purchased its own shares, or declared dividends, and have the company's executives exercised any stock options?

BRIEF EXERCISES

REAL DATA

BE12-1

Inferring shareholders' equity transactions

The following information was taken from the 2008 statement of shareholders' equity of The Home Depot (dollars in millions).

	Common Stock	Additional Paid-In Capital	Retained Earnings	Treasury Stock
Beginning balance	$85	$5,800	$1,388	($314)
Net income			2,260	
Shares issued under				
employee stock plans,		369		
stock options, other		248		
Repurchase of common stock				(58)
Cash dividends			(1,533)	

a. What portion of net income was paid out in dividends during the year?
b. Explain how the issuance of shares affected the basic accounting equation.
c. Explain how the purchase of treasury stock affected the basic accounting equation.
d. How much cash was distributed to the company's shareholders during the year?
e. What was the balance sheet value of the retained earnings account at the end of the year?

REAL DATA

BE12-2

Stock splits and market values

When Tandy (RadioShack) Corporation announced a 2:1 stock split, the company had 97 million shares outstanding, trading at $100 per share.

a. Estimate the number of shares outstanding and market price per share immediately after the split.
b. Estimate the company's overall market value, and explain whether you expect the company's overall market value to change due to the split.

REAL DATA

BE12-3

Treasury stock purchases

The following information was taken from the 2009 annual report of Coca-Cola (dollar and share amounts in millions).

	Treasury Shares	Dollar Amount
2007 Share repurchases	34	$1,756
2008 Share repurchases	18	1,044
2009 Share repurchases	26	1,484

a. At what average price did the company repurchase its shares in 2007?
b. At what average price did the company repurchase its shares in 2008?

c. The December 31, 2009, balance in treasury stock was ($25,398). If Coca-Cola reissues treasury shares in the amount of $1,200 to support 2010 employee compensation plans, what will be the December 31, 2010 balance in the treasury stock account?

EXERCISES

E12–1

The effects of transactions on shareholders' equity

The following are possible transactions that affect shareholders' equity:

1. A company issues common stock above par value for cash.
2. A company declares a 3-for-1 stock split.
3. A company repurchases 10,000 shares of its own common stock in exchange for cash.
4. A company declares and issues a stock dividend. Assume that the fair market value of the stock is greater than the par value.
5. A company reissues 1,000 shares of treasury stock for $75 per share. The stock was acquired for $60 per share.
6. A company pays a cash dividend that had been declared fifteen days earlier.
7. A company generates net income of $250,000.

For each transaction above, indicate the following:

a. The accounts within the shareholders' equity section that would be affected.
b. Whether these accounts would be increased or decreased.
c. The effect (increase, decrease, or no effect) of the transaction on total shareholders' equity.

E12–2

Debt, contributed and earned capital, and the classification of preferred stock

The balance sheet of Lamont Bros. follows:

ASSETS		LIABILITIES AND SHAREHOLDERS' EQUITY	
Current assets	**$ 85,000**	**Current liabilities**	**$ 52,000**
Noncurrent assets	**315,000**	**Long-term note payable**	**35,000**
		Preferred stock	**50,000**
		Common stock	**80,000**
		Additional paid-in capital:	
		Preferred stock	**50,000**
		Common stock	**100,000**
		Retained earnings	**113,000**
		Less: Treasury stock	**(80,000)**
		Total liabilities and	
Total assets	**$400,000**	**shareholders' equity**	**$400,000**

a. What portions of Lamont's assets were provided by debt, contributed capital, and earned capital? Reduce contributed capital by the cost of the treasury stock.
b. Compute the company's debt/equity ratio. Compute the debt/equity ratio if the preferred stock issuance was classified as a long-term debt.
c. In most states, to what dollar amount of dividends would the company be limited?

E12–3

Authorizing and issuing preferred and common stock

Deming Contractors was involved in the following events involving stock during 2012:

1. Authorized to issue: (a) 100,000 shares of $100 par value, 8 percent preferred stock; (b) 150,000 shares of no-par, $5 preferred stock; and (c) 250,000 shares of $5 par value, common stock.
2. Issued 10,000 shares of $5 par value common stock for $30 per share.
3. Issued 25,000 shares of the $100 par value preferred stock for $150 per share.
4. Issued 50,000 shares of no-par preferred stock for $50 each.

Prepare entries, if appropriate, for each event, describe how each event affects the basic accounting equation, and explain the economic significance of par value.

REAL DATA
E12–4

Effects of treasury
stock purchases on
financial ratios

Before the merger of Wendy's and Arby's, Wendy's made a huge purchase of its own shares and in total bought back over 26 million shares for approximately $1 billion. Before the purchase, 125.5 million shares were outstanding, and the financial statements appeared as follows (dollars in millions).

INCOME STATEMENT

Revenue	$2,439
Expenses	2,345
Net income	94

BALANCE SHEET

Assets	$3,060
Liabilities	$1,048
Shareholders' equity	$2,012

a. Provide the journal entry for the treasury stock purchase.
b. Compute the ratio of total liabilities to shareholders' equity before and after the purchase.
c. Compute earnings per share before and after the purchase.
d. Comment on why a company might choose to purchase treasury stock.

E12–5

Reissuing
treasury stock

Twin Lakes incorporated on April 1, 2012, and was authorized to issue 100,000 shares of $5 par value common stock and 10,000 shares of $8, no-par preferred stock. During the remainder of 2012, the company entered into the following transactions.

1. Issued 25,000 shares of common stock in exchange for $500,000 in cash.
2. Issued 5,000 shares of preferred stock in exchange for $60,000 in cash.
3. Purchased 3,000 common shares for $15 per share and held them in the form of treasury stock.
4. Sold 1,000 treasury shares for $18 per share on the open market.
5. Issued 1,000 treasury shares to executives who exercised stock options for a reduced price of $5 per share.

The company entered into no other transactions that affected shareholders' equity during 2012.

a. Prepare entries for each of the transactions.
b. Assume that Twin Lakes generated $500,000 in net income in 2012 and did not declare any dividends during 2012. Prepare the shareholders' equity section of the balance sheet as of December 31, 2012.

E12–6

Reissuing
treasury stock

The shareholders' equity section of Rodman Corporation as of December 31, 2011, follows:

Common stock	$ 80,000
Additional paid-in capital (C/S)	10,000
Retained earnings	60,000
Total shareholders' equity	$150,000

During 2012, the company entered into the following transactions:

1. Purchased 1,000 shares of treasury stock for $60 per share.
2. As part of a compensation package, reissued half of the treasury shares to executives who exercised stock options for $20 per share.
3. Reissued the remainder of the treasury stock on the open market for $66 per share.

a. Provide the journal entries for each transaction, and prepare the shareholders' equity section of the balance sheet as of December 31, 2012. Rodman Corporation generated $20,000 in net income during 2012 and did not declare any dividends.
b. What portion of the additional paid-in capital account is attributed to treasury stock transactions?

E12-7

Treasury stock exceeds contributed capital

In 2002, Stuart Corporation began operations, issuing 100,000 shares of $1 par value common stock for $25 per share. Since that time, the company has been very profitable. The shareholders' equity section as of December 31, 2011, follows:

Common stock	$ 100,000
Additional paid-in capital (C/S)	2,400,000
Retained earnings	4,500,000
Total shareholders' equity	$7,000,000

In 2012, the company entered into a program of buying back some of the outstanding shares. During the year, the company purchased 30,000 outstanding shares at $95 per share.

a. Prepare the journal entry to record the purchase of the treasury shares.
b. Assuming that net income of $350,000 was earned and dividends of $50,000 were declared during the year, prepare the shareholders' equity section of the balance sheet as of the end of 2012.
c. Explain how the dollar value of the treasury stock account can be larger than the dollar amount of contributed capital.

REAL DATA

E12-8

Book value per share, stock issuances, and treasury stock purchases

The condensed 2008 balance sheet of Honeywell International follows (dollars in millions):

Assets	$35,490	Liabilities	$28,303
		Shareholders' equity	7,187
	_____	Total liabilities and	
Total assets	$35,490	shareholders' equity	$35,490

Seven hundred thirty-five million shares of common stock and no preferred stock were outstanding. The following requirements are independent:

a. Compute the book value per common share.
b. Compute the book value per common share if the company issues 50 million shares of common stock at $32 per share.
c. Compute the book value per common share if the company issues 50 million shares of common stock at $20 per share.
d. Compute the book value per outstanding share of common stock if the company purchases 50 million shares of treasury stock at $32 per share.
e. Compute the book value per outstanding share of common stock if the company purchases 50 million shares of treasury stock at $20 per share.
f. What effect does issuing stock have on the book value of the outstanding shares? Upon what does this effect depend?
g. What effect does purchasing treasury stock have on the book value of the outstanding shares? Upon what does this effect depend?

E12-9

Inferring equity transactions from the statement of shareholders' equity

The following information was taken from the statement of shareholders' equity of Chinook Furs:

	2012	2011
Preferred stock (no par)	$ 700	$400
Common stock ($1 par value)	1,000	900
Additional paid-in capital:		
Common stock	40	20
Treasury stock	10	—
Less: Treasury stock	130	150

Provide the journal entries for the following:

a. The issuance of preferred stock during 2012.
b. The issuance of common stock during 2012.
c. The sale of treasury stock during 2012.

E12–10

Inferring equity transactions from the statement of shareholders' equity

The following information was taken from the statement of shareholders' equity of Zielow Siding as of December 31, 2012. The par value of the Zielow stock is $5, and as of the beginning of 2012, the company held 400 shares in treasury.

	Common Stock	Additional Paid-In Capital	Retained Earnings	Treasury Stock
Beginning balances	$10,000	$25,000	$34,000	$ 8,000
Acquisition of Timeco	5,000	23,000		
Treasury share purchases				4,000
Exercised stock options	1,000	800		
Net income			5,600	
Cash dividends			(3,520)	
Ending balances	$16,000	$48,800	$36,080	$12,000

a. Zielow issued common stock at one time prior to 2012. How many shares were issued and at what price per share?
b. Zielow purchased treasury stock at one time prior to 2012. How many shares were purchased and at what price?
c. During 2012, Zielow acquired Timeco and issued its own shares as payment in the transaction. How many shares were issued, and what was the market value of Timeco at the time of the acquisition?
d. At what price were the stock options exercised, and how did that price compare to the market value of Zielow stock at the time?
e. Compute the per-share dividend rate paid by Zielow during 2012. Assume that treasury shares acquired in 2012 were purchased at the same price per share prior to 2012.

E12–11

Inferring equity transactions from the statement of shareholders' equity

The following information was taken from the statement of shareholders' equity of Kidd Sports as of December 31, 2012. The par value of Kidd stock is $1, and as of the beginning of 2012, the company held 1,500 shares in treasury.

	Common Stock	Additional Paid-In Capital	Retained Earnings	Treasury Stock
Beginning balances	$8,000	$32,000	$27,000	$18,000
Exercised stock options			(2,750)	(3,000)
Net income			5,600	
Cash dividends			(3,500)	
Stock dividend	700	9,800	(10,500)	
Ending balances	$8,700	$41,800	$15,850	$15,000

a. Kidd issued common stock at one time prior to 2012. How many shares were issued and at what price per share?
b. Kidd purchased treasury stock at one time prior to 2012. How many shares were purchased and at what price?
c. At what price were the stock options exercised, and how did that price compare to the market value of Kidd stock at the time? Assume that the stock options were exercised immediately prior to the issuance of the stock dividend, which was recorded at market value.
d. Compute the per-share dividend rate paid by Kidd during 2012, assuming that the cash dividends were declared prior to the stock dividend but after the stock options were exercised.

E12–12

Issuing cash dividends on outstanding common stock

The board of directors of Enerson Manufacturing is in the process of declaring a dividend. The company is considering paying a cash dividend of $12 per share. Enerson Manufacturing is authorized to issue 800,000 shares of common stock. The company has issued 375,000 shares to date and has reacquired 50,000 shares. These 50,000 shares are held in treasury.

a. How many shares of common stock are eligible to receive a dividend?
b. Assume that the board declares the dividend. Prepare the appropriate journal entries on the (1) date of declaration, (2) date of record, and (3) date of payment.

E12–13

Cumulative
preferred stock and
dividends in arrears

The shareholders' equity section of Mayberry Corporation, as of the end of 2012, follows. Mayberry began operations in 2008. The 5,000 shares of preferred stock have been outstanding since 2008.

Preferred stock (10,000 sh. authorized, 5,000 issued,	
cumulative, nonparticipating, $5 dividends, $10 par value)	**$ 50,000**
Common stock (500,000 sh. authorized, 200,000 sh. issued,	
50,000 held in treasury, no par value)	**1,600,000**
Additional paid-in capital (P/S)	**140,000**
Retained earnings	**110,000**
Less: Treasury stock	**(80,000)**
Total shareholders' equity	**$1,820,000**

The company has paid the following total cash dividends since 2008:

2008	$ 0
2009	30,000
2010	80,000
2011	15,000
2012	40,000

a.   Compute the dividends paid to the preferred and common shareholders for each of the years since 2008.

b.   Compute the balance of dividends in arrears as of the end of each year.

c.   Should dividends in arrears be considered a liability? Why or why not?

E12–14

Stock dividends and
stock splits

The shareholders' equity section of Pioneer Enterprises as of December 31, 2012, follows:

Common stock (10,000 shares issued @ $6 par)	**$ 60,000**
Additional paid-in capital (C/S)	**100,000**
Retained earnings	**60,000**
Less: Treasury stock (2,000 shares @ $12)	**(24,000)**
Total shareholders' equity	**$196,000**

Prepare journal entries for the following *independent* transactions:

a.   The company declares and distributes a 2 percent stock dividend on the outstanding shares. The market price of the stock is $70 per share.

b.   The company declares a 3:2 stock split on the outstanding shares.

c.   The company declares a 10 percent stock dividend on the outstanding shares. The market price of the stock is $80 per share.

d.   The company declares a 2:1 stock split on the outstanding shares.

e.   Compute the ratio of contributed capital to earned capital after independently considering each of the four actions listed above. Reduce contributed capital by the cost of the treasury stock. Comment on the difference between a stock dividend and a stock split.

E12–15

Why do companies
declare stock
dividends?

The December 31, 2011, balances in retained earnings and additional paid-in capital for Railway Shippers Company are $135,000 and $50,000, respectively. Five thousand $10 par value common shares are outstanding with a market value of $85 each. The company's cash position at year-end is lower than usual, so the board of directors is considering issuing a stock dividend instead of the normal cash dividend. They are considering the following options.

Option 1: A 10 percent stock dividend: 500 new shares would be issued.
Option 2: A 20 percent stock dividend: 1,000 new shares would be issued.
Option 3: A 2:1 stock split: 5,000 new shares would be issued.

a.   Prepare the journal entries for Options 1 and 2, and comment on why these alternatives may not be attractive. Why do companies issue stock dividends?

b.   What effect would Option 3 have on the financial statements?

c.   Why do companies split their stock?

E12–16

Appropriating
retained earnings

Taylor Manufacturing entered into a borrowing arrangement that requires the company to maintain a retained earnings balance of $500,000. The company also wishes to finance internally a major plant addition in the not-too-distant future. Accordingly, the board of directors has decided to appropriate $350,000 of the retained earnings balance. Prior to the board's action, the balance in the retained earnings account was $800,000.

a. Why would the board of directors appropriate retained earnings in the situation described above, and why might an auditor insist that it be done?
b. Show how retained earnings would be disclosed on the balance sheet after the appropriation.
c. Discuss the constraints with respect to dividend payments that have been imposed on the board by the debt covenant and the appropriation.

PROBLEMS

P12–1

Hybrid securities
and debt covenants

Lambert Corporation issued 1,000 shares of $100 par value, 8 percent, cumulative, nonparticipating preferred stock for $100 each. The stock is preferred to assets, redeemable after five years at a prespecified price, and the preferred shareholders do not vote at the annual shareholders' meeting. The condensed balance sheet of Lambert prior to the issuance follows:

Assets	$580,000	Liabilities	$250,000
		Shareholders' equity	330,000
		Total liabilities and	
Total assets	$580,000	shareholders' equity	$580,000

Lambert has entered into a debt agreement that requires the company to maintain a debt/equity ratio of less than 1:1.

REQUIRED:
a. Provide the journal entry to record the preferred stock issuance, and compute the resulting debt/equity ratio, assuming that the preferred stock is considered an equity security.
b. Compute the debt/equity ratio, assuming that the preferred stock is considered a debt security.
c. What incentives might the management of Lambert have to classify the issuance as equity instead of debt? Do you think that the issuance should be classified as debt or equity? What might Lambert's external auditors think?

P12–2

The effects of
treasury stock
transactions
on important
financial ratios

The balance sheet of Alex Bros. follows:

Assets	$840,000	Liabilities	$300,000
		Preferred stock	50,000
		Common stock	300,000
		Additional paid-in capital (C/S)	100,000
		Retained earnings	130,000
		Less: Treasury stock	(40,000)
		Total liabilities and	
Total assets	$840,000	shareholders' equity	$840,000

Of the 200,000 common shares authorized, 50,000 shares were issued for $8 each when the company began operations. There have been no common stock issuances since; 45,000 shares are currently outstanding, and 5,000 shares are held in treasury. Net income for the year just ended was $45,000.

REQUIRED:
a. Compute the par value of the issued common shares.
b. Compute the book value of each common share.

c.   At what average price were the treasury shares purchased?

d.   Alex is considering reissuing the 5,000 treasury shares at the present market price of $10 per share. What effect would this action have on the company's debt/equity ratio, book value per outstanding share, and earnings-per-share ratio?

P12–3

The significance of par value

Several independent transactions are as follows.

1.   10,000 shares of no-par common stock are issued for $50 per share.
2.   10,000 shares of $1 par value common stock are issued for $40 per share.
3.   10,000 shares of $10 par value common stock are issued for $30 per share.
4.   5,000 shares of no-par preferred stock are issued for $80 per share.

REQUIRED:

a.   Prepare journal entries for each transaction.

b.   What is the significance of par value from a financial accounting standpoint? Is par value significant in any economic sense?

P12–4

Cash and stock dividends

Royal Company is currently considering declaring a dividend to its common shareholders, according to one of the following plans:

1.   Declare a cash dividend of $15 per share.
2.   Declare a 10 percent stock dividend. Royal Company would distribute one share of common stock for every 10 shares of common stock currently held. The company's common stock is currently selling for $50 per share.

Royal Company is authorized to issue 100,000 shares of $10 par value common stock. To date, the company has issued 55,000 shares and is currently holding 8,000 shares in treasury stock.

REQUIRED:

a.   How many shares of common stock are eligible to receive a dividend?

b.   Prepare the entries necessary on the date of declaration, date of record, and date of payment for the cash dividend.

c.   Prepare the entry to record the stock dividend, assuming that the dividend is declared and issued on the same date.

d.   Describe how each dividend would affect Royal's debt/equity ratio.

e.   Which of the two dividends would you, as a shareholder, prefer to receive? Why?

P12–5

Dividend payments and preferred stock

The following information was extracted from the financial records of Maverick Corporation:

Preferred stock: 15,000 shares outstanding, 10 percent, $50 par value
Common stock: 50,000 shares outstanding, $15 par value

Maverick began operations on January 1, 2006. The company has paid the following amounts in cash dividends over the past seven years:

2006	$ 65,000
2007	100,000
2008	70,000
2009	50,000
2010	125,000
2011	110,000
2012	99,000

REQUIRED:

Prepare a sheet to contain the following schedule.

Year	Total Dividends Declared	Dividends to Preferred	Dividends to Common	Dividend per Share (Preferred)	Dividend per Share (Common)

a. Complete this schedule for each year from 2006 through 2012, assuming that the preferred stock is noncumulative and nonparticipating.

b. Complete this schedule for each year from 2006 through 2012, assuming that the preferred stock is cumulative and nonparticipating.

P12-6

The maximum
dividend

The following selected financial information was extracted from the December 31, 2011, financial records of Cotter Company:

	Debit	Credit
Cash	25,000	
Short-term investments (2,500 shares of Oreton Corporation)	80,000	
Common stock ($10 par value, 100,000 shares authorized, 50,000 issued)		500,000
Additional paid-in capital (C/S)		100,000
Retained earnings (before closing)		245,000
Net income for 2011		43,000

The company's board of directors is currently contemplating declaring a dividend. The company's common stock is presently selling for $40 per share.

REQUIRED:

a. Given the present financial position of Cotter Company, how large a cash dividend can the board of directors declare?

b. How large a stock dividend can the board legally declare?

c. Assume that the dividends are declared and issued on the same day. Prepare the journal entry to record the maximum dividend in each case above.

d. If the company sold its short-term investments, how large a cash dividend could it declare and pay? The current selling price of Oreton Corporation is $50 per share.

P12-7

Stock splits and
stock dividends

Stevenson Enterprises is considering the following items:

1. The company may declare a 10 percent stock dividend, issuing an additional share of common stock for every ten shares outstanding; the common stock is currently selling for $25 per share.

2. The company may issue a 2:1 stock split.

Prior to these events, Stevenson Enterprises reports the following:

Common stock ($6 par value, 650,000 shares authorized, 70,000 issued, 60,000 outstanding, and 10,000 held as treasury stock)	$ 420,000
Additional paid-in capital (C/S)	525,000
Retained earnings	695,000
Less: Treasury stock	(100,000)
Total shareholders' equity	$1,540,000

REQUIRED:

a. Assume that Stevenson Enterprises declares the stock dividend but not the stock split. Prepare the necessary journal entry. Prepare the shareholders' equity section of the balance sheet to reflect the stock dividend.

b. Assume that Stevenson Enterprises declares the stock split but not the stock dividend. Prepare the shareholders' equity section of the balance sheet to reflect the stock split.

c. Assume that Stevenson Enterprises declares the stock dividend and then the stock split. Prepare the necessary journal entries. Prepare the shareholders' equity section of the balance sheet to reflect both actions.

d. Assume that Stevenson Enterprises declares the stock split and then the stock dividend. Prepare the necessary journal entries. Prepare the shareholders' equity section of the balance sheet to reflect both actions. Assume that the market price of Stevenson's stock drops to $12.50 per share following the stock split.

REAL DATA

P12–8

Stock issuances

The 2008 statement of shareholders' equity of Starbucks, the coffee shop retailer, included the following information concerning common stock (dollars in thousands):

	Shares	Dollar Amount
2007:		
Exercised stock options	6,600	$77,400
Sale of common stock	2,800	41,900
Repurchase of stock	12,200	194,500
2008:		
Exercised common stock	4,900	35,900
Sale of common stock	2,500	26,800

REQUIRED:

a. Compute the average prices at which the shares in 2007 and 2008 were issued and purchased.
b. Were the shares to exercise the stock options issued at a higher or lower price than the shares issued for the sale of common stock? Explain how the two sets of shares could be issued for different purposes. What does the repurchase indicate about the stock price trend?

P12–9

Miscellaneous shareholders' equity transactions

The shareholders' equity section of Rudnicki Corporation contained the following balances as of December 31, 2011:

Preferred stock (10%, $10 par value, cumulative)	**$1,000**
Preferred stock (12%, $10 par value, noncumulative)	**1,500**
Common stock ($1 par value, 5,000 shares	
authorized, 3,500 issued and 400	
held in treasury)	**3,500**
Additional paid-in capital:	
Preferred stock (10%)	**1,050**
Preferred stock (12%)	**1,275**
Common stock	**2,345**
Retained earnings	**4,256**
Less: Treasury stock	**(5,750)**
Total shareholders' equity	**$9,176**

During 2012, Rudnicki Corporation entered into the following transactions affecting shareholders' equity:

1. On May 13, the company repurchased 50 shares of its common stock in the open market at $20 per share.
2. On September 26, the company issued 200 shares of its 10 percent preferred stock at $19 per share.
3. On October 19, the company reissued 30 shares of the stock held in treasury. They sold for $22 per share; all of the shares reissued were purchased prior to May 13 for $12 per share.
4. On December 2, the company declared a cash dividend of $750, which was paid on December 27. The company has not declared a dividend since 2010. (Rudnicki Corporation uses a separate dividend account for each type of stock.)
5. On December 27, the company pays the dividend declared on December 2.
6. On December 29, the company declares a 2:1 stock split on the company's common stock.

REQUIRED:

a.   Prepare the necessary entries for each transaction.
b.   Assume that Rudnicki Corporation earned net income of $899 during 2012. Prepare the shareholders' equity section as of December 31, 2012.

P12–10

Inferring
transactions from
the balance sheet

The shareholders' equity section of Buzytown Industries' balance sheet reports the following:

	2012	2011
Preferred stock (9%, $100 par value)	$ 200,000	$ 110,000
Common stock ($10 par value, 750,000 shares		
authorized, 90,000 issued, and 5,000 held		
in treasury)	900,000	750,000
Additional paid-in capital:		
Preferred stock	150,000	35,000
Common stock	465,000	298,000
Retained earnings	575,000	495,000
Less: Treasury stock	(110,000)	—
Total shareholders' equity	$2,180,000	$1,688,000

REQUIRED:

a.   How many shares of preferred stock were issued during 2012? What was the average issue price?
b.   How many shares of common stock were issued during 2012? What was the average issue price?
c.   Prepare the entry to record the repurchase of the company's own stock during 2012. What was the average repurchase price?
d.   Assume that the treasury shares were purchased on the last day of 2012. Did the purchase increase or decrease the book value of the outstanding shares? By how much?

P12–11

Inferring shareholders'
equity transactions
from information on
the balance sheet

Tracey Corporation reports the following in its December 31, 2011, financial report:

	2011	2010
Cumulative preferred stock (10%, $100 par value)	$ 400,000	$ 400,000
Common stock ($10 par value, 11,000 shares		
authorized, issued, and outstanding)	110,000	70,000
Additional paid-in capital:		
Common stock	625,000	500,000
Treasury stock	124,000	55,000
Retained earnings	975,000	250,000
Less: Treasury stock	(84,000)	(105,000)
Total shareholders' equity	$2,150,000	$1,170,000

The total balance in treasury stock on December 31, 2010, represents the acquisition of 1,500 shares of common stock on March 3, 2009.

REQUIRED:

a.   Compute the number of shares of common stock issued during 2011.
b.   Compute the average market price of the common shares issued during 2011.
c.   Assume that Tracey Corporation earned net income of $2 million during 2011. Compute the amount of dividends that were declared during 2011.
d.   If Tracey Corporation did not declare or pay any dividends during 2010, and again assuming a net income during 2011 of $2 million, compute the amount declared as dividends to common stockholders during 2011.
e.   Prepare the entry that would have been necessary on March 3, 2009, to record the purchase of the treasury stock.

f. Assume that all shares of treasury stock reissued during 2011 were reissued at the same time and at the same price. Prepare the entry to record the reissuance of the treasury stock.

g. At what per-share price was the treasury stock reissued?

P12–12

Shareholders'
equity over a
four-year period

Aspen Industries became a corporation in the state of Colorado on March 23, 2009. The company was authorized to issue 1 million shares of $6 par value common stock. Since the date of incorporation, Aspen Industries has entered into the following transactions that affected contributed and earned capital:

1. On March 23, 2009, the company issued 50,000 shares of common stock in exchange for $15 per share.
2. On December 5, 2009, the company issued a 10 percent stock dividend. The market value of the stock is $18 per share.
3. On May 6, 2010, the company issued 60,000 shares of common stock in exchange for $22 per share.
4. On September 24, 2010, the company repurchased 15,000 shares of its own stock for $25 per share.
5. On December 1, 2010, the company reissued 5,000 shares held in treasury for $27 per share.
6. On February 14, 2011, the company declared a 3:1 stock split and adjusted the par value of the stock. (*Hint:* Consider the effect of the stock split on treasury stock.)
7. On August 19, 2011, the company reissued 8,000 shares held in treasury for $10 per share.
8. On December 27, 2011, the company declared a cash dividend of $50,000.
9. On January 3, 2012, the company paid the dividend declared on December 27, 2011.
10. On October 31, 2012, the company reissued 2,000 shares held in treasury for $15 per share.

REQUIRED:

a. Prepare the necessary journal entries to record these transactions.
b. Prepare the shareholders' equity section of Aspen's balance sheet as of December 31, 2012. Assume that net income for 2009, 2010, 2011, and 2012 was $400,000, $100,000, $100,000, and $20,000, respectively.

P12–13

Blocking takeovers
and treasury stock
purchases

Five shareholders together own 35 percent of the outstanding stock of Edmonds Industries. The remaining 65 percent is divided among several thousand shareholders. There are 400,000 shares of Edmonds stock currently outstanding. A condensed balance sheet follows:

ASSETS		LIABILITIES AND SHAREHOLDERS' EQUITY	
Cash	$ 3,150,000	Liabilities	$ 1,250,000
Other current assets	4,200,000	Common stock	8,000,000
Noncurrent assets	8,220,000	Retained earnings	6,320,000
		Total liabilities and	
Total assets	$15,570,000	shareholders' equity	$15,570,000

It has become known that Vadar, Inc. is planning to take over Edmonds by purchasing a controlling interest of the outstanding stock. Vadar hopes to gain enough control to elect a new board of directors and replace Edmonds's current management. The current board of directors, on which the five major shareholders serve, is considering how to block the apparent takeover attempt.

REQUIRED:

a. Describe how the company might be able to block the takeover attempt through a program of treasury stock purchases. How many shares would the company need to purchase to concentrate ownership enough to keep Vadar from acquiring a controlling interest? Assume that the other members of the board own no stock.

b. The current market price of the outstanding stock is $45, but the board feels that any major buyback would have to be at a premium—approximately $50 per share. How much cash would Edmonds need to purchase enough shares to block the takeover attempt?

c. Assume that Edmonds was able to borrow $4 million and used the cash to buy back the necessary number of shares. Prepare the balance sheet of Edmonds after stock had been purchased.

d. Compute the debt/equity ratio for Edmonds both before and after the treasury stock purchase. Comment on the effect of the purchase on the company's financial position.

P12–14

Bankruptcy and protecting the interests of the creditors

The balance sheet of Natathon International is as follows:

ASSETS		LIABILITIES AND SHAREHOLDERS' EQUITY	
Current assets	**$200,000**	**Liabilities**	**$400,000**
Fixed assets	**500,000**	**Common stock**	**150,000**
		Additional paid-in capital	**50,000**
		Retained earnings	**100,000**
		Total liabilities and	
Total assets	**$700,000**	**shareholders' equity**	**$700,000**

Although the balance sheet appears reasonably healthy, Natathon is on the verge of ceasing operations. Appraisers have estimated that, while current assets are worth $200,000, the fixed assets of the company can be sold for only $450,000. There are 1,000 outstanding shares of common stock owned by ten shareholders, each with a 10 percent interest (i.e., 100 shares). Before ceasing operations, the board of directors, which is composed primarily of the major shareholders, is considering several alternative courses of action.

1. Liquidate the assets, declare a $250-per-share dividend, and distribute the remaining assets to the creditors.
2. Liquidate the assets, declare a $400-per-share dividend, and distribute the remaining assets to the creditors.
3. Liquidate the assets, purchase the outstanding shares for $250 each, and distribute the remaining assets to the creditors.
4. Liquidate the assets, and purchase the outstanding shares for $650 each.

REQUIRED:

a. Prepare the journal entry to reflect the write-down of the fixed assets.
b. Prepare the journal entry to accompany each alternative course of action.
c. Comment on the legality of each of the board's proposals, and explain how the assets should be distributed after liquidation.

ISSUES FOR DISCUSSION

REAL DATA

ID12–1

Do stock dividends represent economic exchanges between a corporation and its shareholders?

When Hershey Foods declared a 100 percent stock dividend, 149.5 million of its shares were outstanding. Assume that the stock dividend was declared and paid on the same day.

REQUIRED:

a. How many shares of stock were outstanding after the dividend?
b. The market price of the stock was approximately $46 per share, and the par value was $1 per share on the day the dividend was declared and paid. Provide the journal entry to record the distribution.
c. Compute the value of Hershey if all outstanding shares, prior to the stock dividend, could have been sold for $46 each. Using this value, compute the per-share value of the company's outstanding shares after the stock dividend.

d. Assume that Mr. Jones owned 1 million shares prior to the stock dividend. How many shares did Mr. Jones own after the stock dividend? What percentage of the company did Mr. Jones own before and after the stock dividend? What was the value of Mr. Jones's total shareholdings before and after the stock dividend based on the amounts from part (c)?

e. Does a stock dividend actually represent an economic exchange between a corporation and its shareholders? Why or why not?

f. Provide several reasons why a company would issue a stock dividend.

REAL DATA

ID12–2

Dividend strategy

When companies cut dividends, it is usually a bad sign for the stock. But apparently not at Monsanto. Several years ago, the company cut its dividend and the stock price went up.

REQUIRED:

Explain how a dividend cut could lead to increasing stock prices.

REAL DATA

ID12–3

Economic consequences of treasury stock purchases and cash dividends

The *Wall Street Journal* once reported, "Philip Morris Cos., in an aggressive move to boost its stock price, announced a $6 billion stock buyback plan and raised its quarterly dividend nearly 20%. . . . The announcement, which came after a regularly scheduled board meeting, raised the company's stock to a 52-week high. . . . Separately, rating agencies Standard & Poor's Rating Group and Moody's Investors Service Inc. confirmed their ratings on Philip Morris's debt. While both agencies said Philip Morris is continuing to generate strong cash flow, Moody's . . . placed Philip Morris at the low end of its current rating level."

REQUIRED:

Explain how this announcement can increase the stock price of Philip Morris (now known as Altria Group) while at the same time reduce its credit rating.

REAL DATA

ID12–4

Treasury stock purchases

In an article entitled "Buybacks or Giveaways," *CFO.com* reported that "large repurchase programs require a whole lot of capital. Critics of buybacks contend that companies can put their cash to better use. They also point out that investors are more likely to reward a company that attempts to grow its business—rather than artificially inflate its stock price." The article goes on to quote an investment banker as saying that "[stock repurchase programs] can be a sign that a company can't find anything better to do with its cash."

REQUIRED:

a. Describe some other uses for a company's cash. How could these uses benefit shareholders more than a stock repurchase?

b. Why might the stock market interpret a company's purchase of its own shares as a way to "artificially inflate" its stock price?

c. If the stock market is trading at very high levels, what risks do companies face with their stock repurchasing plans?

REAL DATA

ID12–5

Debt or equity?

Preferred stock is often seen as a hybrid security as it has characteristics of both debt and equity. The *Wall Street Journal* once reported two new securities used by companies going public: income deposit securities and enhanced income securities, both of which carry characteristics of both debt and equity. The securities are sold to investors, who will receive two payments from the company—one based on the company's equity shares and one based on the company's outstanding debt. The securities are being underwritten and marketed by such investment banking firms as Canadian Imperial Bank of Commerce, Goldman Sachs, and Lehman Brothers.

REQUIRED:

a. What is a hybrid security, and how should it be reflected on the balance sheet, income statement, statement of cash flows, and statement of shareholders' equity?

b. Describe some reasons why an investor might want to purchase a hybrid security and some reasons why a company might want to issue a hybrid security.

c.   What are some characteristics that would make these securities look more like debt? More like equity?

REAL DATA

ID12–6

Contracts based
on net worth

For twenty years, Westinghouse Electric Corp. used PCBs in the manufacture of electrical capacitors at its plant in Bloomington, Indiana. A federal consent decree has ordered the company to be prepared to build an incinerator in the future to destroy the PCB-contaminated materials. The decree, with which Westinghouse agrees, contains a clause stating that if Westinghouse's net worth (balance sheet assets less balance sheet liabilities) drops to $1.9 billion, the company is required to place in escrow (set aside) $325 million to ensure that funds will be available if and when the incinerator is built.

A pronouncement from the FASB required that Westinghouse, as well as other companies, change the way in which they account for certain employee retirement costs. After adopting this mandated change, Westinghouse's net worth plunged to $1.85 billion, which is below the dollar amount indicated in the consent decree. According to the agreement, therefore, Westinghouse should transfer $325 million to an escrow account. Westinghouse has refused to make the payment, however, claiming that the reduction in net worth was due to a new accounting standard not in effect at the time the agreement was signed.

REQUIRED:
Discuss this issue from the perspective of the following:
a.   An executive of Westinghouse
b.   A representative of the federal government
c.   A resident of Bloomington, Indiana

REAL DATA

ID12–7

Shareholder returns,
dividends, and
buy-backs

The *Wall Street Journal* reported (April 13, 2007) that shareholders of Kraft Foods "can afford to give management more time to improve its brands, sales margins, and earnings" because of the dividends paid by the company and the share buy-back program. Kraft Foods has been losing market share in its cheese and processed-meat product categories and has not been keeping up with private-label competition, as well as new food offerings in healthy snacks and foods. However, due to the dividends and buy-backs, share price appreciation is not the only form of return to the investors.

REQUIRED:
a.   How does a shareholder receive a return on his or her investment in a company?
b.   Do companies that pay dividends have creation advantage over companies that do not pay dividends and choose to retain all earnings?
c.   What signs will investors look for to see if Kraft's management is successful in its strategy? Where in the financial statements will this evidence be presented?

REAL DATA

ID12–8

Market value vs.
book value

The stock in Dow Jones & Co., Inc. (the publisher of the *Wall Street Journal*) has a book value (shareholders' equity per share) of approximately $6. Prior to a buyout offer, the stock had been trading (market value) for $36 per share. Rupert Murdoch and his News Corporation made an unsolicited offer of $60 per share during the summer of 2007. As of August 14, 2007, the market value was $58.60 per share.

REQUIRED:
a.   What are the differences between book value and market value? How are these values determined?
b.   Calculate the price-to-book ratio for Dow Jones.
c.   Why would News Corporation offer to pay $60 per share (for a total of $5 billion) to buy a stock trading for $36 per share?
d.   The *Wall Street Journal,* similar to other newspapers, has struggled against competition posed by the Internet and other electronic outlets. Discuss the effect that macroeconomic factors can have on the value of a stock.

REAL DATA

ID12–9

Common stock issuances

The following information was taken from Google, Inc.'s statement of cash flow in the company's 2006 annual report (amounts in millions):

	2004	2005	2006
Net proceeds from public offerings	$1,161	$4,287	$2,064

The following information was taken from Google's statement of shareholders' equity (amounts in millions):

	Class A and B Common Stock Number of Shares
2004	
Issuance of common stock in connection with IPO	17.0
2005	
Issuance of common stock	14.9
2006	
Issuance of common stock	7.7

REQUIRED:
a. What is meant by "net proceeds" on the statement of cash flow? What is the difference between "net" and "gross"?
b. What happened with the share price of Google from 2004 to 2006? Discuss your calculations.
c. List some reasons for the trend in share price.

REAL DATA

ID12–10

Equity issuances

Bloomberg News Service reported that Rhodia, SA, France's largest specialty chemicals company, announced plans to sell 450 million euros in shares, in addition to a 600 million euro bond issue, to raise cash to prevent a liquidity crisis. Rhodia had posted losses for the three previous years and projected losses for the next two. Rhodia's largest shareholder, the French drug firm Aventis, will subscribe to the new offering to maintain its ownership stake at 15.3 percent.

Segway, LLC, the much-publicized manufacturer of the Segway scooter, raised $31 million in new equity to augment $100 million previously raised. The *Wall Street Journal* reported that the original funds have been depleted because "operating expenses were exceeding revenue."

REQUIRED:
a. Both companies had similar reasons for the equity issuance. On which financial statement would the reasons be evident? How would the influx of funds after the issuances be reflected on the financial statements?
b. Why would Aventis want to purchase additional shares in a company in which it already has a significant investment? Would the holders of the $100 million in equity in Segway have similar issues?
c. Imagine you are an investor interested in these two offerings. What evidence would you have to observe before making this investment?

REAL DATA

ID12–11

Stock split and stock prices

When Walt Disney Co. declared a 4:1 split of its common stock, the announcement boosted the entertainment company's shares up by $3.50 per share.

REQUIRED:
a. What is a 4:1 stock split, and how did it affect the financial statements of Walt Disney Co.?
b. Why should the market value of Disney's stock rise?
c. The *Wall Street Journal* once reported that the stock split was "a psychological boost and an indication that management has confidence in their performance and that the stock price can be sustained." Explain how this explanation could account for the stock price increase.

REAL DATA

ID12-12

Share repurchases
during volatile
economic periods

During the 2008–2009 financial crisis, stock prices fluctuated wildly. The S&P 500 Index was 1,549.38 in October 2007, then dropped all the way to 735.09 in February 2009, and then rebounded to 1,104.49 by February 2010. Companies that actively repurchased their own stock shares were buyers in this volatile market. Movie rental company Netflix, for example, repurchased $130 million of its own stock in the third quarter of 2009 and publicly stated that it would borrow additional money to continue the buy-backs. Amazon.com's board of directors authorized a $2 billion stock buy-back, despite the fact that its shares were trading at 45 times the company's projected 2010 earnings. Sears spent $134 million by August 1, 2009, to repurchase 2.7 million shares. Apple, Inc., on the other hand, did not repurchase any of its shares during this time period.

REQUIRED:
a.   What is meant by a stock price selling for "45 times" its earnings?
b.   What does a volatile stock market do to a company with an announced plan to repurchase its own shares?
c.   Explain how repurchases followed by stock issuances affect the financial statements.
d.   Netflix borrowed to finance share repurchases. How would this sequence of events affect its leverage position?
e.   If companies reissue previously purchased treasury stock at prices that differ from the costs of the repurchases, are gains and losses recognized on the income statement? Why or why not?

REAL DATA

ID12-13

Stock option expense

In July 2005 Microsoft adopted SFAS 123 (R), *Share-based Payment,* which required companies to recognize expenses related to stock options. In the company's 2009 annual report, Microsoft reported net income of $14.6 billion, 17.7 billion, and $14.1 billion in 2009, 2008, and 2007, respectively. It also reported "stock-based compensation expense" on the statement of shareholders' equity of $1.7 billion, $1.5 billion, and $1.6 billion for 2009, 2008, and 2007, respectively.

REQUIRED:
a.   Explain the nature of stock-based compensation expense.
b.   Why would it appear on the statement of shareholders' equity, and on what other financial statement would it also appear?
c.   Would you consider stock option expense to be material for Microsoft, and why?
d.   Explain why many companies resisted SFAS 123 (R).

REAL DATA

ID12-14

Statement of
shareholders' equity

Refer to the statement of shareholders' equity reported by Emerson Electronics located at the end of the chapter.

REQUIRED:
Describe Emerson's dividend and treasury stock transactions and policies over the three-year period 2007–2009.

REAL DATA

ID12-15

Different treasury
stock strategies

Hewlett-Packard and Apple, Inc., two very successful technology firms, show no investment in their own shares (treasury stock) on their 2008 balance sheets. Bear Stearns, on the other hand, was reported in a 2004 edition of the *Wall Street Journal* to have launched a $1 billion stock repurchase plan. By 2008 the share price of Bear Stearns had dropped from $133 to $10, the price at which the company was acquired by JPMorgan Chase. From 2006 to early 2010 Apple shares increased from $75 to over $200 per share, while HP increased from $30 to $50 per share.

REQUIRED:
a.   Discuss the implications of the corporate strategy of repurchasing outstanding shares of stock.
b.   Compare and contrast the outcomes of this financial strategy among the three companies above.
c.   Discuss the various methods companies can employ to create wealth for their shareholders.

REAL DATA

ID12–16

Comprehensive
income—U.S. GAAP
vs. IFRS

Unilever Group, a Dutch-based consumer-goods company that publishes IFRS-based financial statements, reported a net profit on its 2008 income statement of 5.3 billion euros. That same year the company reported "total recognized income and expense" of only 1.1 billion euros, and on its 2008 balance sheet it reported accumulated recognized income and expense of 1.8 billion euros.

Johnson & Johnson, a U.S. consumer-goods company that publishes U.S. GAAP-based financial statements, reported net profit on its 2008 income statement of $12.2 billion. It reported 2008 comprehensive income of $14.1 billion, and accumulated comprehensive income in the shareholders' equity section of the 2008 balance sheet of $70.3 billion.

REQUIRED:

a. Explain the difference between net profit and comprehensive income, which is referred to as total recognized income and expense under IFRS.

b. Explain the difference between comprehensive income for a given year and accumulated comprehensive income, which appears on the balance sheet as of the end of that year.

c. On which financial statement could you find a reconciliation of the beginning and ending balances of comprehensive income (or total recognized income and expense) for a given period of time?

REAL DATA

ID12–17

The SEC Form 10K
of NIKE

The SEC Form 10K of NIKE is reproduced in Appendix C.

REQUIRED:

Review the NIKE 10K, and answer the following questions.

a. What percentage of NIKE's total assets were provided by liabilities, contributed capital, and retained earnings?

b. How many shares of common stock had been authorized, issued, and outstanding as of May 31, 2009?

c. How much cash did the company use to purchase its outstanding common stock and pay dividends over the past three years? Are those amounts growing or decreasing? Discuss.

d. Why does NIKE list redeemable preferred stock as a liability?

e. Explain why stock-based compensation appears on the statement of cash flows.

f. Within what ranges did NIKE's market price fall over the last two years, and what amount of dividends per share were paid during that period?

g. At what average prices did the company issue stock in support of exercised stock options over the past three years?

h. What is NIKE's accumulated balance of comprehensive income as of May 31, 2009? What does the balance primarily consist of, and what was the comprehensive income amount for the year? Was it greater than or less than net income?

Income and Cash Flows

Manpower Inc. is a world leader in employment services, providing clients with temporary, contract, and permanent employees. The company is often cited as a bellwether for the health of the job market as well as the overall economy. From 2007 to 2008, annual revenues rose from $20.5 billion to $21.6 billion, a 5.1 percent jump in a difficult economic environment. Yet profits fell 55 percent, from $485 million to $219 million. At the same time, cash flows from operations increased an outstanding 83 percent, from $432 million to $792 million. Three different measures of operating success seemed to be moving in vastly different directions. How can revenues shoot up, while profits lag and operating cash flows jump so dramatically? These kinds of questions are addressed in Chapters 13 and 14, which cover the income statement and statement of cash flows, respectively.

CHAPTER 13
The Complete Income Statement

CHAPTER 14
The Statement of Cash Flows

The Complete Income Statement

KEY POINTS

The following key points are emphasized in this chapter:

- Economic consequences associated with reporting net income.

- Two different concepts of income: matching and fair market value.

- A framework for financing, investing, and operating transactions.

- Categories that constitute a complete income statement and how they provide measures of income that address the objectives of financial reporting.

- Intraperiod tax allocation.

- Earnings per share disclosure on the income statement.

The income statement from pharmaceutical giant Merck's 2009 annual report is provided below (dollars in billions).

	2009	2008	2007
Sales	$27.4	$23.8	$24.2
Costs and expenses:			
Materials and production	(9.0)	(5.6)	(6.1)
Marketing and administrative	(8.5)	(7.4)	(7.6)
Research and development	(5.8)	(4.8)	(4.9)
Restructuring costs	(1.6)	(1.0)	(0.3)
Equity income from affiliates	2.2	2.6	3.0
U.S. Vioxx settlement charge	0	0	(4.9)
Other income	10.7	2.3	0.1
Income before taxes	15.3	9.9	3.5
Taxes on income	2.3	2.0	0.1
Net income	$13.0	$ 7.9	$ 3.4

Net income appears to have increased from $3.4 billion (2007) to $7.9 billion (2008) to $13 billion (2009), a very steep upward slope both in terms of raw numbers and as a percentage of sales. Indeed, Merck's future looks rosy! Yet, what about expense and income items like restructuring costs, equity income, the Vioxx settlement, and "other" income? They have all been included in the net income calculation, but are they part of Merck's core operations, and can they be expected to persist in the future? And taxes—why only $0.1 billion in 2007, but $2.3 billion in 2009? The rules governing income statement disclosure, which are covered in this chapter, are designed to help.

This chapter covers (1) the economic consequences associated with income measurement and disclosure, (2) conceptual issues of income measurement, and (3) the disclosure rules that must be followed when preparing an income statement.

THE ECONOMIC CONSEQUENCES ASSOCIATED WITH INCOME MEASUREMENT AND DISCLOSURE

Income is the most common measure of a company's performance. It has been related to stock prices, suggesting that equity investors use income in their decisions to buy and sell equity securities. An article in the *Journal of Accountancy* stated that "[accounting] research . . . has provided some well-established conclusions. Perhaps the most conclusive finding is the importance of accounting income to investors." Almost daily the *Wall Street Journal* reports how stock prices respond to corporate earnings reports.

Income has also been related to bond prices, which indicates that debt investors use income in their decisions to buy and sell corporate bonds. Credit-rating agencies, such as Standard & Poor's and Dun & Bradstreet, use income numbers to establish credit ratings. In response to "improved financial statements," for example, Standard & Poor's raised the credit rating on bonds issued by two of China's top four banks (Bank of China and China Construction Bank) from BBB− to BB+ which, in turn, increased the market value of their outstanding debt. In addition, three of Dun & Bradstreet's fourteen key business ratios (return on sales, return on assets, and return on net worth) explicitly use a measure of income in the formula, and most of the numbers used in the remaining eleven ratios are indirectly affected by the dollar amount of reported income.

Due to the importance attached to income, periodic public earnings announcements, which appear in newspapers such as the *Wall Street Journal* and in corporate

annual reports, are also considered important news items, having important effects on the economy. For example, an article in *USA Today* titled "Do Profits Matter?" noted:

Profit is the compass of the free enterprise system. When it dries up, the repercussions echo at every level of society. . . . Profits keep a free-market economy humming. They help pay for the development of new plants, products, and jobs. A sizable chunk of profits helps finance government in the form of taxes. Another chunk goes as dividends to shareholders—often the pension funds that pay for your retirement. Says an economist from the University of Chicago: "Economies . . . won't grow without corporate profit."

Various measures of income are also found in contracts written among shareholders, creditors, and managers. Such contracts are normally designed either to protect the interests of creditors or to control managers and encourage them to act in the interests of the shareholders. Loan agreements relating to the outstanding debts of Marriott Corporation, for example, limit the company's annual dividends to a portion of net income. Such covenants serve to protect the investments of corporate creditors by limiting the amount of cash that can be paid to shareholders in the form of dividends. The board of directors of pharmaceutical giant Eli Lilly encourages company employees to act in the shareholders' interests by providing incentive compensation in the form of a profit-sharing plan. As reported in the 2008 annual report, the payment of this compensation is based on changes in the company's annual earnings per share.

The measurement, definition, and disclosure of income are important to investors, creditors, managers, auditors, and the general public in a number of different ways. Students of accounting, therefore, must understand how income is measured and presented.

THE MEASUREMENT OF INCOME: DIFFERENT MEASURES FOR DIFFERENT OBJECTIVES

According to the *Statement of Financial Accounting Concepts No. 1,* the objectives of financial reporting are to provide information that is: (1) useful to those making investment and credit decisions who have a reasonable understanding of business and economic activities; (2) helpful to current and potential investors, creditors, and others in assessing the amounts, timing, and uncertainty of future cash flows; and (3) about economic resources, the claims to those resources, and changes in them.[1] Three important features of this objective relate directly to the income statement and the measure of income. The statement focuses on supplying useful information to those who provide debt and equity capital to the firm; the information should help to predict future cash flows; and the information should reflect changes (increases or decreases) in the company's resources. No single measure of income can achieve this set of broad objectives, and income statements prepared under GAAP are designed to provide a variety of different measures of income. It is important that financial statement users understand how they differ and the situations under which each should be used.

To achieve this understanding, one must be familiar with several important definitions that appear in the *Statement of Financial Accounting Concepts No. 6.*[2] Figure 13–1 contains the definitions of ten key concepts, referred to as the elements of financial statements.

1. "Objectives of Financial Reporting by Business Enterprises," *Statement of Financial Accounting Concepts No. 1* (Stamford, Conn.: FASB, November 1978), pars. 5–8.
2. "Elements of Financial Statements," *Statement of Financial Accounting Concepts No. 6* (Stamford, Conn.: FASB, December 1985), pp. ix and x.

The objectives and elements of income under IFRS are very similar to those discussed under U.S. GAAP.

FIGURE 13–1
Elements of the financial statements

Assets. Probable future economic benefits obtained or controlled by a particular entity as a result of past transactions or events.

Liabilities. Probable future sacrifices of economic benefits arising from present obligations of a particular entity to transfer assets or provide services to other entities in the future as a result of past transactions or events.

Equity. Residual interest in the assets of an entity that remains after deducting its liabilities. In a business enterprise, the equity is the ownership interest.

Investments by Owners. Increases in net assets of a particular enterprise resulting from transfers to it from other entities of something of value to obtain or increase ownership interests (or equity) in it. Assets are most commonly received as investments by owners, but that which is received may also include services or satisfaction or conversion of liabilities of the enterprise.

Distributions to Owners. Decreases in net assets of a particular enterprise resulting from transferring assets, rendering services, or incurring liabilities by the enterprise to owners. Distributions to owners decrease ownership interests (or equity) in an enterprise.

Comprehensive Income. Change in equity (net assets) of an entity during a period from transactions and other events and circumstances from nonowner sources. It includes all changes in equity during a period except those resulting from investments by owners and distributions to owners.

Revenues. Inflows or other enhancements of assets of an entity or settlement of its liabilities (or a combination of both) during a period from delivering or producing goods, rendering services, or other activities that constitute the entity's ongoing major or central operations.

Expenses. Outflows or other using up of assets or incurrences of liabilities (or a combination of both) during a period from delivering or producing goods, rendering services, or carrying out other activities that constitute the entity's ongoing major or central operations.

Gains. Increases in equity (net assets) from peripheral or incidental transactions of an entity and from all other transactions and other events and circumstances affecting the entity during a period except those that result from revenues or investments by owners.

Losses. Decreases in equity (net assets) from peripheral or incidental transactions of an entity and from all other transactions and other events and circumstances affecting the entity during a period except those that result from expenses or distributions to owners.

You may be familiar with many of these definitions already, but several points are of special interest here. Revenues and expenses, which are ongoing and central to the company's operations, for example, are distinguished from gains and losses, which are peripheral or incidental to operations. Revenues and expenses occur frequently and are part of a company's core activities and, therefore, are related to the company's future cash flows. Gains and losses, however, tend to be infrequent and/or tangential

to the company's core activities. Such items would not be expected to reflect future cash flows, yet they would be part of a company's comprehensive income and reflect changes in a company's resources.

To illustrate, consider two transactions entered into by a company: (1) sale of inventory with a cost of $50 million for $75 million, and (2) winning a settlement of $25 million in a one-time lawsuit. Both transactions increased the company's net assets by $25 million, making the company wealthier. Should they be included in income and reflected on the income statement? Transaction (1) involved the sale of inventory, a transaction that occurs frequently and is part of the company's core activities. It is likely to occur again, so it both reflects future cash flows and increases the company's resources. It seems that including this transaction on the income statement helps it to meet the objectives of financial reporting under almost any definition of income. Transaction (2) is a different story. The lawsuit was one-time, so it is not expected to occur again, and winning lawsuits is not part of the company's core activities. Consequently, this transaction would not be a good indicator of future cash flows, but it did increase the company's resources. It could be included, therefore, under a broad definition of income.

> Refer to the Merck income statement introduced at the beginning of this chapter. What is the Vioxx settlement charge, and should it be included on the income statement? How did including the charge in 2007 instead of 2008 affect the apparent growth of Merck's earnings? As an analyst, would you consider this expense in the same way you consider operating expenses? As reported, Merck's earnings more than doubled from 2007 to 2008. Do you agree?

Comprehensive income represents a broad definition of income, including any change in the company's equity due to nonowner transactions. In June 1997, the FASB issued *SFAS No. 130,* "Reporting Comprehensive Income," which established standards for the reporting and display of comprehensive income and its components. This concept of income encompasses items not included in the computation of net income, such as foreign currency translation adjustments and unrealized gains and losses on available-for-sale securities (see Chapter 8). The standard does not change the display or components of net income, but it requires that the components of comprehensive income be displayed with the same prominence as the other financial statements. The following disclosure, which was taken from the 2009 annual report of Campbell Soup, was placed as a part of the statement of shareholders' equity (dollars in millions).

	2009	2008	2007
Net earnings	$ 736	$1,165	$ 854
Foreign currency translation adjustments	(148)	112	43
Cash flow hedges, net of tax	(25)	11	9
Minimum pension liability, net of tax	(409)	(136)	51
Comprehensive income	$(582)	$1,152	$(957)

This discussion demonstrates that there are different ways to measure income, and different measures of income address different objectives of financial reporting. It also shows that the nature of individual transactions must be considered to determine if and how they should be reflected in income. The following section develops a framework for different kinds of transactions and relates them to the different measures of income used in financial statements.

Under IFRS, an entity must present a statement of comprehensive income, often called the statement of recognized income and expenses (SORIE). The SORIE below was taken from the 2008 annual report of Unilever Group, a Dutch-based consumer-goods company that publishes IFRS-based financial statements (in million euros).

	2008	2007	2006
Net profit	5,285	4,136	5,015
Fair value gains (losses) on cash flow hedges	(118)	84	6
Fair value gains (losses) on available-for-sale securities	(46)	2	15
Actuarial gains (losses) on pensions	(2,293)	542	853
Currency retranslation gains (losses)	(1,688)	(413)	(335)
Total recognized income and expense	1,140	4,351	5,554

Which of the numbers—net profit or total recognized income and expense—represents a more accurate metric of Unilever's past performance? Which provides a better indication of future performance? Why?

Two Different Concepts of Income: Matching and Fair Market Value

Through most of the text we have described income as the result of the **matching process**—first, revenues are recognized in a particular time period in line with the principles of revenue recognition, and then the costs necessary to generate the revenues (expenses) are subtracted from them in the computation of net income. This basic procedure, illustrated below, has provided the basis for income measurement for many, many years.

$$\text{Revenues (n)} - \text{Expenses (n)} = \text{Net Income (n)}$$

Recently, there has been an increased emphasis on measuring income in terms of changes in the fair market values of a firm's assets and liabilities. IFRS relies more heavily on fair market value accounting than does U.S. GAAP, and just a few years ago the United States introduced the fair value option for financial instruments, which allows companies to book gains and losses when the values of their financial assets and liabilities change. This notion of income does not rely on a matching process. Rather, it simply computes income for a given period by comparing the fair market value of a firm's net assets (assets – liabilities) at the end of a particular period to the fair market value of the firm's net assets at the beginning of the period, as illustrated below.

$$\text{FMV Net Assets (end)} - \text{FMV Net Assets (beginning)} = \text{Net Income (n)}$$

To illustrate the difference between these two ways of measuring income, assume that you purchased a machine for $1,000. The machine had a five-year useful life, and you rented it to another company, receiving $300 per year for five years. Under the matching principle, you would capitalize the $1,000 cost of the machine, and depreciate it over the five-year life. Net income on the machine each year would be the $300 in revenue less the depreciation taken in each year. If you used straight-line depreciation ($1,000/5 = $200), net income each year would be $100 ($300 − $200). The balance sheet carrying amount (book value) of the machine would be the original cost less the accumulated depreciation.

Under the fair market value approach, net income each year would be the $300 rent collected plus or minus the change in the machine's fair market value during the year. If the fair market value of the machine decreased, the amount of the decrease would be subtracted from the $300. If the fair market value increased, the increase would be added to the $300. The balance sheet carrying value of the machine would be its fair market value.

The current system of measuring income—under both U.S. GAAP and IFRS—is a hybrid of these two approaches. We still rely heavily on the recognition of revenue and the matching of expenses, but in certain cases we now book gains and/or losses when the values of certain assets (e.g., marketable securities) and liabilities change. Depending on the rules, some of these changes are reflected directly on the income statement, while others do not appear on the income statement; instead, they appear as other comprehensive income items, affecting only shareholders' equity. It is important that you understand the basics of these two forms of income measurement, and how income is reported both on the income statement and, more generally, on the statement of comprehensive income.

Financing, Investing, and Operating Transactions: A Framework

Financing and investing transactions basically involve setting up a company so that it can conduct operations, while **operating transactions** entail the actual conduct of the operations. Figure 13–2 represents a continuum for classifying financing, investing, and operating transactions. Note that five categories of transactions are described, and each is placed at a point along the continuum. Category 1 at the extreme left contains purely financing transactions, and Category 5 contains operating transactions. Categories 2, 3, and 4 increasingly resemble operating activities. Later, we point out that operating transactions can also be subdivided into categories, based primarily on how germane they are to a company's normal, everyday operating activities. Review the figure closely because we will be discussing it in detail in the following paragraphs.

FIGURE 13-2   Classifying financing, investing, and operating transactions

Financing and Investing Transactions				Operating Transactions
	Balance Sheet			Income Statement
1	2	3	4	5
Exchanges with shareholders	Exchanges of liabilities and shareholders' equity	Issues and payments of debt	Purchases, sales, and exchanges of assets	Revenues Expenses

1. Exchanges with shareholders: stock issuances, stock redemptions, and dividend payments.
2. Exchanges of liabilities and shareholders' equity: debt refinancing and conversion of convertible bonds and stocks.
3. Issues and payments of debt: cash borrowings evidenced by notes payable, issuing bonds, and payments on debts, including the redemption of debt.
4. Purchases, sales, and exchanges of assets: purchases, sales, and exchanges of all assets.
5. Revenues: inflows of assets (or outflows of liabilities) due to operations.
   Expenses: outflows of assets (or inflows of liabilities) due to the generation of revenues.

(1) EXCHANGES WITH SHAREHOLDERS

Exchanges with owners include (1) issuances of preferred or common stock, (2) purchases, retirements, and reissuances of treasury stock, and (3) cash, property, and stock dividends. This group is located on the far left side of the continuum because these are

purely financing transactions involved exclusively with the formation and dissolution of the company's equity capital and the returns (i.e., dividends) to the company's owners. The most distinctive and important feature of the transactions in this category is that they never affect the income statement. Even when treasury stock is reissued for an amount different from its cost, the dollar amount of the difference is not recognized as a gain or a loss on the income statement.

During 2008, clothing retailer The Gap reissued treasury stock with a cost of $24 million, receiving $23 million. Did the company recognize a $1 million loss on the reissuance? Why or why not?

(2) EXCHANGES OF LIABILITIES AND SHAREHOLDERS' EQUITY

Exchanges of liabilities and shareholders' equity refer to transactions in which liabilities are exchanged for other liabilities (debt refinancing arrangements) or converted into shareholders' equity (conversion of convertible bonds or preferred stocks to common stock). Such exchanges are considered financing transactions because they deal only with a company's capital structure. Accordingly, they generally do not affect the income statement. However, these transactions are located to the right of exchanges with shareholders because in certain limited circumstances they can give rise to gains or losses that appear on the income statement.[3]

(3) ISSUES AND PAYMENTS OF DEBT

Issues and payments of debt include cash borrowings associated with the issuance of notes or bonds payable as well as the cash payments required to service or retire such liabilities. These transactions involve exchanges with a company's creditors and thus are reflected in the liabilities section of the balance sheet. They are considered financing transactions because they involve how a company pays for its operations through debt. However, these transactions are not completely separate from a company's operations. Interest payments on debt are directly reflected on the income statement through interest expense; book gains and losses are recognized when debt is retired; premiums and discounts on notes and bonds are amortized to the income statement (via interest expense) over the life of the debt, and under the fair value option, changes in the fair market value of liabilities can be reflected in income. Consequently, this category of transactions is located to the right of exchanges of liabilities and shareholders' equity.

During 2008, Honeywell International issued long-term debt in the amount of $1.5 billion and paid $884 million to reduce debt and cover interest. How did these transactions influence the basic accounting equation, and how was the income statement affected?

(4) PURCHASES, SALES, AND EXCHANGES OF ASSETS

Category 4 includes the purchase, sale, or exchange of all assets. Such assets include marketable securities, inventories, prepaid expenses, long-term investments, and long-lived

---

3. The methods used to account for refinancing arrangements and the conversion of convertible bonds and stocks are complex and controversial, and we do not discuss them in this textbook. For our purposes, it is sufficient to note that, according to current generally accepted accounting principles, such transactions rarely give rise to income statement gains and losses.

assets. These transactions, all of which are capitalized, represent both investing and operating activities. Activity involving long-term assets is considered investing, while activity involving short-term assets is considered operating. This category is located next to the operating section of the continuum because it is only a matter of time before these capitalized costs appear on the income statement. Prepaid expenses and long-lived assets, for example, are amortized, depleted, or depreciated on the income statement over their useful lives. Capitalized inventory costs, investments, and long-lived assets are matched against revenues when they are sold.[4] Also, under fair value accounting, changes in the values of these assets can be reflected in income.

> **?** During 2008, Southwest Airlines invested approximately \$923 million in property and equipment. How does this transaction affect the income statement in the current year and future years?

(5) REVENUES AND EXPENSES

The right side of the continuum includes exchanges that are considered operating transactions. Revenues represent inflows of assets (or outflows of liabilities) due to a company's operating activities, and in line with the matching principle, expenses represent outflows of assets (or inflows of liabilities) associated with the generation of the revenues.

Classifying Operating Transactions

Income statements include transactions ranging from those that are fundamental and necessary to a company's operations to those that are only marginally related to operations. Figure 13–3 shows three groups of operating transactions, based primarily on how germane the transactions are to the normal operations of a company and how frequently they occur.

FIGURE 13–3
Classifying operating transactions

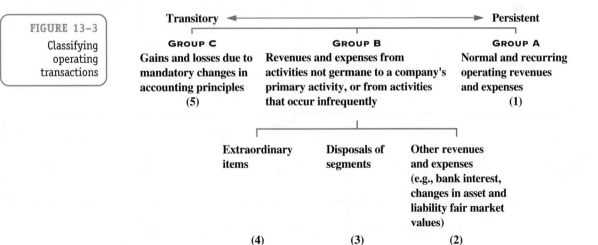

4. Many companies also sell outstanding accounts receivable to financial institutions for immediate cash, and an income statement gain or loss is recognized in the amount of the difference between the book value of the receivable and the cash proceeds. These transfers accelerate cash collections from sales on account as well as pass on the risks and costs associated with uncollectible accounts to the financial institution. Such exchanges are called *factoring* arrangements. Sales made on credit using major credit cards, such as VISA, American Express, and MasterCard, represent factoring arrangements.

Group A contains revenues and expenses that result from transactions that are normal to company operations and occur frequently. Examples include the sale of the company's inventories or services and the payment and recognition of expenses due to such items as wages, utilities, rent, insurance, depreciation, and other administrative and selling activities.

Group B contains items that are much less germane to the normal activities of a company or that may occur infrequently. Examples include interest earned on bank savings accounts held by manufacturing, retail, and service companies; rent earned from temporarily leasing company property planned to be used later for other purposes; gains and losses recognized on sales of long-lived assets and debt retirements; write-downs due to long-lived asset impairments and restructurings; and gains and losses related to such items as litigation, employee strikes, infrequent natural disasters, and changes in the values of certain assets and liabilities.

Group C contains gains and losses recognized from changes in accounting principles mandated by new financial standards, which reflect very little about the operations occurring during the periods in which such changes were made. They are simply bookkeeping entries that do not reflect an economic event.

In the past, there was considerable controversy over the proper classification and disclosure of the transactions contained in Groups B and C. Some accountants argued that transactions from Group C should not enter into the computation of net income. Others took an even more extreme view and suggested that transactions in both Groups B and C were not germane to operations and, accordingly, should not appear on the income statement, which should be limited to operating revenues and expenses in the strictest sense.

The accounting profession has now adopted the position that nonoperating items (Groups B and C) should be included on the income statement, but they must be separately and clearly disclosed in specific categories. Specifically, the income statement should consist of five categories: (1) operating revenues and expenses, (2) other revenues and expenses, (3) disposals of business segments, (4) extraordinary items, and (5) mandated changes in accounting principles. In terms of Figure 13–3, Category 1 corresponds to Group A, Categories 2, 3, and 4 come from Group B, and Category 5 corresponds to Group C.[5]

The different categories on the income statement allow users to assess the significance of the items in each category and to choose to include or exclude them in the computation of net income as the situation dictates. The next section defines and illustrates the five categories of a complete income statement.

From 2006 to 2008, Time Warner, Inc. included the following items on its income statement: cost of revenue, asset impairments, gain (loss) on disposal of assets, and discontinued operations. Classify each of these items in the groups illustrated in Figure 13–3.

A COMPLETE INCOME STATEMENT: DISCLOSURE AND PRESENTATION

Figure 13–4 provides an income statement that contains each of the five categories introduced in the previous section. Review the statement carefully. The following discussion first considers the income statement in general and then covers each category individually.

---

5. A recent financial standard requires that the financial effects of discretionary accounting changes should no longer affect net income.

FIGURE 13-4   A complete income statement[a]

XYZ Company
Income Statement
for the Period Ending December 31, 2012

Gross sales	$325	⎫
Less: Sales discounts and returns	25	⎬ 1. Operating revenues
Net sales	$300	⎭
Less: Cost of goods sold:		⎫
Beginning inventory	$ 75	
+ Gross purchases	150	
− Purchase discounts and returns	(5)	
+ Freight-in	20	
− Ending inventory	(80)	160
Gross profit	$140	
Operating expenses:		⎬ 1. Operating expenses
Wages and salaries	$ 30	
Advertising	10	
Insurance	8	
State and local taxes	7	
Depreciation	25	
Utilities	20	
Miscellaneous	15	115 ⎭
Net operating income	$ 25	
Other revenues	10	⎫
Less: Other expenses	(13)	⎬ 2. Other revenues and expenses
Net income from continuing operations	$ 22	
before tax		
Less: Federal income tax	7	
Net income from continuing operations	$ 15	
Income (loss) on segment up to disposal		
(net of tax)	(3)	⎫
Gain (loss) on disposal of segment (net of tax)	5	⎬ 3. Disposal of business segment
Net income before extraordinary items	$ 17	
Extraordinary gain (loss) (net of tax)	(5)	⎬ 4. Extraordinary item
Net income before change in accounting principle	$ 12	
Income effect due to change in accounting		
principle (net of tax)	7	⎬ 5. Mandated changes
Net income	$ 19	in accounting principles
Earnings per share (100 shares outstanding):		
Net income from continuing operations		
(after tax)	$ .15	
Disposal of business segment	.02	
Extraordinary items	(.05)	
Change in accounting principle	.07	
Total earnings per share	$ .19	

[a]Most real-world income statements are variations of two basic formats: (1) single-step or (2) multistep. This income statement uses the multistep format. Under the single-step format, all revenues and expenses above "net income from continuing operations" are grouped into two separate categories. Below "net income from continuing operations," the two formats are identical.

The computation of net income on the income statement involves five major components, each representing one of the five categories. In general, as one moves from the top to the bottom of the income statement, the events become increasingly less important to the operations of the business. Net operating income (operating revenues less operating expenses) reflects financial performance resulting from transactions that are both fundamental to a company's normal activities and occur frequently. Other revenues and expenses and disposals of business segments reflect the financial effects of events that are either not part of a company's normal operations or do not occur frequently. Extraordinary gains and losses result from events that are both highly unusual and infrequent, and gains and losses due to mandated changes in accounting principles result simply from book entries.

The income statement is divided into these categories to enable users to distinguish transactions that are due to operations from those due to unusual, infrequent, and sometimes uncontrollable events (e.g., extraordinary items) or simply to changes in accounting principles. Presumably, measures of profit disclosed near the top of the income statement (e.g., net operating income) better reflect management's performance and are more indicative of the future than are those disclosed near the bottom of the statement (e.g., net income). The boards of directors of many companies, for example, express their management compensation agreements in terms of net operating income instead of net income. The boards apparently believe that if management acts to increase net operating income, it will increase the long-term earnings of the company and thus further the interests of the shareholders. Consider the following excerpt from a recent annual report of The Pillsbury Company:

Certain employees of the Company participate in compensation programs which include a base salary plus incentive payments based on the level of operating earnings.

(1) Operating Revenues and Expenses: Usual and Frequent

Operating revenues and expenses refer to asset and liability inflows and outflows related to the acquisition and delivery of the goods or services provided by a company. They are considered usual and frequent. The term **usual** refers to the normal operations of the business. If a company is in business to sell furniture, for example, *usual* revenues come from furniture sales. Automobile dealerships, on the other hand, are in business to sell and service automobiles; for them, revenues generated from selling office furniture would not be considered usual.

The term **frequent** refers to how often the revenue is generated or the expense incurred. Revenues and expenses are considered frequent if they are expected to recur in the foreseeable future. They are not "one-shot," unpredictable events. For many companies, the sale of a fixed asset or a long-term investment, for example, which can generate either a gain or a loss, is a transaction that tends to occur infrequently.

Which of the following two companies would likely consider a gain on the sale of investments a usual and frequent transaction—Bank of America or JCPenney? Why?

(2) Other Revenues and Expenses: Unusual or Infrequent

The section of the income statement headed "other revenues and expenses" contains revenues and expenses related to a company's secondary or auxiliary activities. The most common examples are interest income and interest expense, which relate to the

company's investments and debt financing, respectively. While interest is important and recurring, with the exception of financial institutions, it is not directly a part of the acquisition and selling of a company's goods and services. IBM Corporation and Coca-Cola Enterprises, like many other large U.S. companies, include both interest income and interest expense in this category. Another item commonly disclosed in this section is income (or loss) from long-term investments accounted for under the equity method. Both Yahoo and AT&T, for example, disclosed equity earnings from associated companies in this manner on their 2008 income statements.

Other examples include dividend income from investments, gains and losses from price changes in trading securities, gains and losses from sales of investments and long-lived assets, long-term asset and goodwill impairments, receivable and inventory write-downs, gains and losses on foreign currency transactions, losses due to employee strikes, income from the rental of excess warehouse space, and gains and losses due to litigation. Many companies, like Hewlett-Packard, Merck, and Intel, restructured their operations during 2008 and reported the associated costs in this section of the income statement. During 2008, Boston Scientific recorded a $250 million gain on the divestiture of a subsidiary, and Sears reported a gain of $51 million on the sale of assets in the same manner. Over a recent three-year period, Goodyear Tire & Rubber Company recorded gains and losses from asset sales and write-downs, workforce reductions, and lawsuits in this section of the income statement.

The key feature of the items in this section of the income statement is that they are "unusual or infrequent, but not both." Interest and dividend income, for example, are considered unusual because they are not germane to the normal operations of the business. They are secondary to the major activities of most companies. At the same time, interest and dividend revenue may be recognized every year and are therefore considered to occur frequently. Receivables and inventory write-downs and losses from employee layoffs, on the other hand, though part of the normal business risks faced by virtually all companies, occur infrequently. They are, therefore, considered to be infrequent but not unusual.

The nature of a particular business and the environment in which it operates must be considered when deciding what is unusual and/or infrequent. Dividend and interest income, for example, are secondary to the operations of manufacturing, retailing, and service companies, yet they represent the primary revenues for financial institutions. Interest income for Bank of America Corporation, for example, normally represents 80–85 percent of total revenues generated by the company. Consequently, for Bank of America, interest income is an operating item, both usual and frequent.

In April 2008 Limited Brands sold its share of a joint venture, resulting in a gain of $128 million. Net income for Limited Brands in 2008 was $220 million. In what section of the income statement did the gain appear and why?

(3) Disposal of a Business Segment

A **business segment** is defined as a separate line of business, product line, or class of customer involving an operation that is independent from a company's other operations. Highly diversified companies consist of many independent segments. DuPont, for example, consists of nine different segments: agriculture, biomedical products, coal, fibers, industrial and consumer products, petroleum exploration, petroleum refining, marketing and transportation, and polymer products. Each of DuPont's segments generates well over $1 billion in revenue each year. The sale or discontinuance of any

one of these segments would be referred to as a disposal of a business segment, and the related financial effects would be disclosed separately on the income statement. It is not uncommon for companies to sell major business segments. In recent years, for example, Whirlpool Corporation, Goodyear Tire & Rubber, and DuPont all disposed of major business segments. Indeed, several years ago DuPont recognized a $6 billion gain on its sale of DuPont Pharmaceuticals.

The disposal of a business segment is a significant and complex transaction that is subject to a number of detailed rules under generally accepted accounting principles. We do not cover these detailed rules here. For our purposes, it is sufficient to view the disposal of a segment as similar to the sale or retirement of a long-lived asset: more specifically, the sale or retirement of a large piece of equipment that generates revenues and incurs expenses that are independent of the company's other operations.

Note in the complete income statement in Figure 13–4 that two separate disclosures are associated with a disposed business segment. The first reflects the income or loss associated with the segment's operations for the time period extending from the previous balance sheet date to the point when the segment is actually disposed of. Since the segment is an independent entity, the expenses associated with it can be matched against its revenues to provide a net income or loss for that time period. The second disclosure reflects the gain or loss recognized when the segment is actually disposed of. At that time, the assets and liabilities of the segment are written off the books, the proceeds (if the segment is sold) are recorded, and a gain or loss on the disposal is recognized in the dollar amount of the difference between the book value of the segment and the proceeds. This dual disclosure allows users to separately ascertain both the profitability of the segment and the book gain or loss on the disposal.

To illustrate, during 2008 Campbell Soup Company sold the Godiva chocolate business, as management considered the unit not related to the "core" operations of the company. Since the earnings of this unit would no longer be part of Campbell's normal and recurring operations, GAAP requires that these earnings be disclosed separately on the income statement, along with the gain or loss from the actual sale. The disclosures below were taken from Campbell Soup's 2008 income statement (dollars in millions). They show that during 2008 the company recorded operating profits on the Godiva unit of $494 million, and after taxes the gain on sale of the unit (proceeds less costs) was $462 million. Together, these two profit numbers exceeded the profits booked by Campbell Soup associated with its continuing operations ($671 million).

Earnings from continuing operations	**$671**
Gain on sale of business, net of $236 taxes	462
Earnings from discontinued operations	494

(4) Extraordinary Items: Unusual and Infrequent

Extraordinary items are defined as material events of a character significantly different from the typical, customary business activities of an entity, which are not expected to recur frequently in the ordinary operating activities of a business. In other words, extraordinary items are both unusual and infrequent. *Accounting Trends and Techniques* (AICPA, 2009) reports that, of 500 major U.S. companies surveyed, only 2 (<1 percent) disclosed an extraordinary item on the income statement.

The concept of extraordinary items does not exist under IFRS.

Examples of extraordinary items include gains and losses from terminating pension plans; gains and losses from litigation settlements; losses resulting from casualties like floods, earthquakes, tornadoes, hurricanes, droughts, and volcanoes; and gains and losses resulting from expropriations (forced government takeovers or purchases of company property) and prohibitions under new law. Note, however, that losses due to employee layoffs, inventory write-downs due to obsolescence, receivables writedowns, and foreign currency translation gains and losses should never be classified as extraordinary according to generally accepted accounting principles. Such items are considered to arise from normal operating business risks.

> **?**
>
> Dole, a major food company with fruit groves in many warm-weather locations, once reported two special charges—$100 million to reflect crop damage from a hurricane and $20 million to reflect damage to citrus groves caused by freezing temperatures in California. In neither case did the company consider these charges extraordinary. Explain why.

(5) Mandatory Changes in Accounting Principles

Chapter 4 defines the concept of consistency and mentions that once a company chooses an acceptable principle or method of accounting (e.g., straight-line depreciation, FIFO inventory valuation, etc.), it must continue to use that method consistently from one year to the next. Consistency helps to maintain the credibility of accounting reports, enabling investors, creditors, and other interested parties to make more meaningful comparisons and to identify more easily the trends in a company's performance across time.

Companies change their accounting methods either by choice or by mandate. Discretionary accounting changes are allowed if management can convince the independent auditor that the business environment has changed such that a new accounting method better reflects the company's economic position and performance. A recent accounting standard requires that the effects of discretionary accounting changes should not be disclosed on the income statement and therefore not influence the computation of net income. They should be handled retrospectively, which means that prior years' financial statements should be restated as if the new method was always in place. In cases where this treatment is impractical, the standard requires that the cumulative adjustment affect the beginning balance of retained earnings.

Accounting changes mandated by new financial reporting standards are implemented in the manner set forth by the standard. Some may require retrospective application; others may involve adjustments to retained earnings; and still others may be disclosed on the income statement and affect net income. For example, in recent years the FASB issued new standards covering asset impairments, goodwill, and stock option compensation. In each case, a number of companies changed their accounting methods to conform with these new standards, and these changes were accompanied by prominent disclosure in the footnotes, on the income statement, and in the audit opinion. In 2008 pharmaceutical company Eli Lilly booked a $1.9 billion charge due to adopting the new standard on accounting for asset retirements.

Mandated changes in accounting methods must be disclosed in three prominent places in the financial report: (1) The auditor's report to the shareholders must mention the change, (2) the footnotes to the financial statement must clearly describe the change, and, if applicable, (3) the cumulative effects of the change on net income must be disclosed (net of tax) separately on the income statement, immediately below extraordinary items. Figure 13–5 shows how Starbucks disclosed the accounting change in its 2006 annual report.

FIGURE 13–5
Starbucks
excerpts from the
annual report

For the Year Ended October 1, 2006

NOTES TO THE FINANCIAL STATEMENTS

On October 1, 2006 Starbucks adopted FASB Interpretation No. 47
"Accounting for Conditional Asset Retirement Obligations" . . .

AUDITOR'S REPORT TO THE SHAREHOLDERS

As discussed in Note 1 . . . the Company changed its method of accounting for
conditional asset retirement obligations" . . .

2006 INCOME STATEMENT (THOUSANDS OF DOLLARS)

Earnings before cumulative effect of change in accounting principle	$581,473
Cumulative effect of accounting change	(17,214)
Net earnings	$564,259

Mandated changes in accounting principles can make it more difficult to compare a company's financial performance across time because in the annual report the financial statements from periods prior to the change are prepared using the previous accounting methods. However, generally accepted accounting principles require that net income on a **pro forma (as if) basis** be disclosed on the face of the income statement for all periods presented, as if the newly adopted principle had been applied to those periods. This disclosure enables users to make more meaningful comparisons, at least across the periods presented on the face of the income statement.

One final point: It is important to realize that an accounting method differs from an accounting estimate, which is used to implement an accounting method. The allowance method of accounting for bad debts is implemented by estimating the amount of bad debts at the end of each year. This section has discussed how to account for a change in an accounting method. How to account for revisions in accounting estimates was described in Chapter 9.

The following excerpt was taken from information in the 2006 annual report of Avis Budget Group, Inc. (dollars in millions):

	2006	2005	2004
Income (loss) from continuing operations	($451)	($11)	$71
Income from discontinued operations, net of tax	478	1,088	1,822
Gain (loss) on disposal of discontinued operations, net of tax	(1,957)	549	198
Net income (loss) before cumulative effect of accounting change	(1,930)	1,626	2,091
Cumulative effect of accounting change, net of tax	(64)	(8)	—
	$(1,994)	$1,618	$2,091

Comment on the income trend across time before and after considering the effects of discontinued operations and the change in accounting method. Which of the trends would you consider to be more valid?

INTRAPERIOD TAX ALLOCATION

Federal income taxes, which do not include state and local taxes, are disclosed in two different ways on the income statement. The first income tax disclosure immediately follows net income from continuing operations (before tax). It represents the tax expense resulting from all taxable revenues and deductible expenses except for those listed below it on the income statement.[6]

The dollar amounts associated with the remaining items (disposal of business segments, extraordinary items, and changes in accounting principles) are all disclosed *net of tax*. Such presentation means that each of these revenue and expense items is disclosed on the income statement after the related income tax effect has been removed. The practice of including the income tax effect of a particular transaction with the transaction itself on the income statement is known as **intraperiod tax allocation.** It enables users to assess the total financial impact of these special transactions as well as the tax benefit or cost associated with them.

For example, when Ralston Purina Company sold its Van Camp Seafood division for $260 million, the book value of Van Camp was $147.3 million, and a gain of $112.7 million was recognized on the transaction with the following journal entry (dollars in millions):

Cash (+A)	**260**	
Net Assets of Van Camp Seafood (−A)		**147.3**
Gain on Disposal of Segment (Ga, +RE)		**112.7**

Sold business segment

The gain, however, was included in Ralston Purina's taxable income and increased the company's tax liability by $42.5 million. The increase in tax liability was recorded with the following journal entry (dollars in millions), and Ralston Purina disclosed a $70.2 million ($112.7 − $42.5) gain on its income statement. The gain appeared under disposals of business segments.

Gain on Disposal of Segment (−Ga, −RE)	**42.5**	
Income Tax Liability (+L)[7]		**42.5**

Recorded increase in tax liability

The general formula for computing the net-of-tax dollar amount for a revenue or expense item is:

Net-of-Tax Dollar Amount = (Gross Revenue or Expense) × (1 − Tax Rate)

If, for example, an accounting change leads to a book and tax gain or loss of $10,000, and the company's federal income tax rate is 35 percent, the net-of-tax dollar amount disclosed on the income statement would be calculated as follows:

Net-of-Tax Dollar Amount = $10,000 × (1 − 35%)
= $6,500

> ?
>
> When General Electric adopted a new accounting standard concerning goodwill accounting, it booked a one-time $1.2 billion charge, but only $1 billion appeared on the income statement. Explain.

---

6. Appendix 10B, which covers deferred income taxes, provides a more complete description of tax expense listed in the income statement.

7. If the income tax effect of the transaction is not realized in the current year due to timing differences between tax rules and GAAP, the account "deferred income taxes" is debited or credited.

EARNINGS-PER-SHARE DISCLOSURE

Generally accepted accounting principles also require that earnings per share be disclosed on the face of the income statement and that the specific dollar amounts associated with (1) net income from continuing operations (after tax), (2) disposals of business segments, (3) extraordinary items, and (4) changes in accounting principles be disclosed separately. Note the form of this disclosure in Figure 13–4. The earnings-per-share amount for each category is calculated by dividing the dollar amount of the gain or loss associated with that category by the number of common shares outstanding. The income statement in Figure 13–6 was taken from the 2008 annual report of Bristol-Myers Squibb. Note, in particular, the earnings-per-share disclosure near the bottom. These breakdowns allow users to focus on the components of earnings per share.

Generally accepted accounting principles require an additional disclosure, called **diluted earnings per share,** for companies that have the potential for significant dilution. Many companies, for example, have issued and presently have outstanding options to purchase their common stocks or bonds that can be converted to common stocks in the future. If and when these options and conversion privileges are exercised, the number of outstanding common shares will increase, which, in turn, will dilute the ownership interests of the existing common shareholders. The calculation of diluted earnings per share, which is described in intermediate and advanced financial accounting textbooks, reflects these possibilities by essentially increasing the denominator of the earnings-per-share ratio and thereby reducing its dollar value. The extent of potential dilution, as measured by the difference between diluted and unadjusted (basic) earnings per share, can be useful information to existing or potential shareholders who are concerned with maintaining the value of their investments.

?

Review the income statement of Bristol-Myers Squibb in Figure 13–6 and estimate the number of common shares outstanding as of the end of 2008, 2007, and 2006. By how much would the number of shares increase in 2008 if all potentially dilutive securities were converted to common shares?

INCOME STATEMENT CATEGORIES: USEFUL FOR DECISIONS BUT SUBJECTIVE

The income statement classifications discussed in this chapter introduce a very important concept to those who use financial accounting information to predict the future cash flows of an enterprise. The concept is called **earnings persistence,** and it reflects the extent to which a particular earnings dollar amount can be expected to continue in the future and, thus, generate future cash flows. Earnings amounts with high levels of persistence are expected to continue in the future, while those with low levels of persistence are not. The income statement classifications are useful because, for the most part, they are defined in terms of their persistence. Net operating income is the result of usual and frequent activities that can be expected to continue in the future; "other revenues and expenses" are considered to have somewhat less persistence; and disposals of segments, extraordinary items, and accounting changes are all considered to be "one-shot" events that should not be counted on in the future. Financial statement users

FIGURE 13-6 Financial statements and supplementary data

BRISTOL-MYERS SQUIBB COMPANY
CONSOLIDATED STATEMENT OF EARNINGS
Dollars and Shares in Millions, Except Per Share Data

Item 8. **FINANCIAL STATEMENT AND SUPPLEMENTARY DATA.**

	Year Ended December 31		
	2008	2007	2006
EARNINGS			
Net Sales	$20,597	$ 18,193	$16,208
Costs of products sold	6,396	5,868	5,420
Marketing, selling and administrative	4,792	4,516	4,469
Advertising and product promotion	1,550	1,415	1,304
Research and development	3,585	3,227	2,951
Acquired in-process research and development	32	230	—
Provision for restructuring, net	218	183	59
Litigation expense, net	33	14	302
Gain on sale of product lines and businesses	(159)	(273)	(200)
Equity in net income of affiliates	(617)	(524)	(474)
Gain on sale of ImClone shares	(895)	—	—
Other expense, net	191	351	292
Total Expenses, net	15,126	15,007	14,123
Earnings from Continuing Operations Before Income Taxes and Minority Interest	5,471	3,186	2,085
Provision for income taxes	1,320	682	431
Minority interest, net of taxes	996	763	440
Net earnings from Continuing Operations	3,155	1,741	1,214
Discontinued Operations:	113	424	371
Earnings, net of taxes	1,979	—	—
Gain on Disposal, net of taxes	2,092	424	371
Net earnings	$ 5,247	$ 2,165	$ 1,585
Earnings per Common Share			
Basic:			
Net earnings from Continuing Operations	$ 1.60	$ 0.88	$ 0.62
Discontinued Operations:			
Earnings, net of taxes	0.05	0.22	0.19
Gain on Disposal, net of taxes	1.00	—	—
Net Earnings per Common Share	$ 2.65	$ 1.10	$ 0.81
Diluted:			
Net earnings from Continuing Operations	$ 1.59	$ 0.88	$ 0.62
Discontinued Operations:			
Earnings, net of taxes	0.05	0.21	0.19
Gain on Disposal, net of taxes	0.09	—	—
Net Earnings per Common Share	$ 2.63	$ 1.09	$ 0.81
Average Common Shares Outstanding:			
Basic	1,977	1,970	1,960
Diluted	2,001	1,980	1.963
Dividends declared per common share	$ 1.24	$ 1.15	$ 1.12

cannot ignore these classifications since they contain valuable information about a company's future prospects.

In terms of the objectives of financial accounting, earnings numbers with high persistence are considered to reflect future cash flows, while low persistence earnings are not. Both kinds of earnings, however, reflect changes in the company's resources and in that respect are considered useful.

It is also important to realize that income statement classifications can be quite subjective, and management has incentives to use its discretion to disclose the financial results of certain events in categories that serve its interests. For example, management may use its reporting discretion to include certain "gains" in the operating section and certain "losses" in the nonoperating sections of the income statement. By using such a strategy, management might influence users to believe that the "gains" are persistent while the "losses" are not. As noted in *Forbes* magazine: "clever accountants can find all sorts of different meanings in those simple sounding words [usual and frequent]. . . . It all comes down to a judgement."

> Review The Bristol-Myers Squibb statement of earnings on the prior page, and note that it does not include a section called "other gains and losses" and an item called "net income from operations." What items would you consider to fall in the "other" category, and what would you consider net income from operations for 2006, 2007, and 2008?

Consider Western Savings of Phoenix, a savings and loan company that reported $49 million in *operating* income, almost half of which ($24 million) was due to the sale of one large investment. Many accountants agreed that this particular sale was nonrecurring and that similar gains could not be expected in the future. Consequently, the gain on this transaction should not have been included in the operating section of the income statement. *Forbes* pointed out that this and other accounting practices followed by the company suggested that "Western is a classic case of how reported profits can misrepresent economic reality."

The *Wall Street Journal* once noted that many companies use subjective restructuring charges to manage earnings. Often, they prematurely recognize expenses within a charge that is disclosed on the income statement outside of the operating section. This activity reduces future operating expenses and increases net income from operations. The article went on to say: "The most obvious way restructuring charges make companies' earnings look better is if the company can convince investors that operating earnings—before the charges—provide a more meaningful indication of trends."

The subjectivity associated with classifying gains and losses in different sections of the income statement can give rise to other significant economic consequences. We noted earlier in the chapter, for example, that The Pillsbury Company, now part of General Mills, has instituted a compensation plan that rewards management on the basis of operating income. An important question is whether interest expense is considered to be an operating or a nonoperating expense in the measurement of operating income as defined by the plan. Including interest as an operating expense could discourage management from borrowing needed funds; including it as a nonoperating expense, on the other hand, could encourage managers to borrow too much. Classifying interest as operating or nonoperating is a subjective decision, yet it can influence the manner in which a company functions.

Robert A. Olstein, a veteran accounting expert and manager of the Olstein Financial Alert mutual fund, noted in the *New York Times:* "We are always looking around and between the numbers to see what a company's real or repetitive earnings are." What does he mean, and how is the income statement designed to help him?

INTERNATIONAL PERSPECTIVE: INVESTMENTS AND INCOME STATEMENT DISCLOSURE

Many times in this textbook we have commented that U.S. businesses are increasingly investing in foreign markets and operations. Such investments introduce certain risks and opportunities that are different from those characterizing domestic business activities. The following quote from Coca-Cola's annual report provides an illustration:

The Company distributes its products in nearly 170 countries and [transacts in approximately 40 different currencies]. Approximately 80 percent of total operating income is generated outside the United States. International operations are subject to certain risks and opportunities, including currency fluctuation and government actions. The Company closely monitors its methods of operating in each country and adopts strategies responsive to changing economic and political environments.

Such a strong international presence increases the number of transactions that require special disclosure on the income statement. Owens Corning, for example, has significant investments in six different non–U.S.-affiliated companies (two in Saudi Arabia and one each in Canada, Japan, Brazil, and Mexico). A portion of the income reported by these affiliates is disclosed, under the equity method, as a special item on the company's income statement. Merck & Co., Inc., which has investments in foreign assets that total over $2.5 billion, has sold and restructured foreign subsidiaries frequently over the last several years. For example, the company sold subsidiaries in South Africa, Lebanon, and Nigeria and restructured operations in Argentina, Brazil, and Venezuela. These activities led to special disclosures in its income statement.

The unique risks associated with investments in countries with high inflation and volatile economies also often give rise to special income statement disclosures. Johnson & Johnson once disclosed two special charges on the income statement: (1) a $104 million write-off for permanently impaired assets and operations in Latin America, which was disclosed in the operating section of the income statement; and (2) a $36 million loss from the liquidation of Argentine debt. The company's annual report also mentions the risks of foreign currency fluctuations and describes how the company hedges these risks.

In such an international investment environment, financial statement users must be particularly aware of, and carefully interpret, the special gains and losses that are reported on the income statement. They should attempt to completely understand the underlying transaction and appreciate the context in which it occurred. An article in the *Wall Street Journal* cautions investors about gains that arise from foreign currency translations in particular:[8]

Foreign exchange gains resulting from the dollar's [recent] tumble . . . raise questions about the quality of soon-to-be-released earnings reports for those U.S. firms

---

8. An example of foreign currency gains/losses is provided at the end of Chapter 6.

with big foreign operations. For example, American Family Corp., Gillette Co., American Brands Inc., and Colgate-Palmolive Co. all derive more than 60 percent of their sales from foreign operations. . . . Investors should [not overemphasize the importance of] currency-related earnings . . . because they're really a one-time gain that could easily reverse itself.

These issues underline the importance of carefully reading the footnotes in an annual report. Most of the information required to make the assessments discussed in this section is not disclosed on the face of the financial statements but is buried somewhere in the footnotes.

ROE EXERCISE: USING THE RIGHT EARNINGS NUMBER

The ROE model, introduced and illustrated in Appendix 5A, provides a framework linking the management of a company's operating, investing, and financing activities to its return on the shareholders' investment (return on equity). A key question addressed by analysts using the ROE model involves choosing the most appropriate earnings number. Since the ROE model is designed to explain ROE, and earnings represent the numerator of that ratio, the quality of ROE analysis can be no better than the quality of the chosen earnings number. "Bottom-line" net income, as discussed in this chapter, includes components that vary in terms of the extent to which they reflect a change in the company's wealth as well as their persistence, and consequently may not be the best choice in all cases.

While no hard-and-fast rules exist covering how to choose an appropriate earnings number, in most cases it is best to use a number that is both a reasonable measure of the wealth change experienced by the company and expected to persist in the future. Some analysts believe that after-tax operating earnings are best in this regard. Conducting several ROE analyses using several earnings numbers (including and excluding special charges like restructurings, assert impairments, gains and losses on asset sales, etc.) is often a useful practice. It can help to ascertain whether the conclusions are sensitive to the choice of the earnings number and to what extent. Finally, the analysis should be conducted across time and across similar companies, and any comparisons should use earnings numbers measured as similarly as possible.

ROE ANALYSIS

Access the Web site http://www.wiley.com/college/pratt and conduct ROE analyses on Ford Motor Company versus Toyota and/or Abbott versus Bristol-Myers Squibb, paying special attention to earnings numbers used in the analysis.

REVIEW PROBLEM

The operating revenues and expenses of Panawin Enterprises for 2012 follow, along with descriptions of and entries for several additional transactions. Assume that income taxes on income from continuing operations are $7,000, the effective income tax rate on other items is 34 percent, the balance in retained earnings as of December 31, 2011, is $106,000, and dividends declared during 2012 total $16,000.

Operating revenues	$85,000
Operating expenses	62,000
Net operating income	$23,000

1. Machinery with an original cost of $14,000 and a book value of $11,000 was sold for $9,000. The transaction was considered unusual but not infrequent.

Cash (+A)	9,000	
Accumulated Depreciation (+A)	3,000	
Loss on Sale of Machinery (Lo, −RE)	2,000	
Machinery (−A)		14,000
Sold machinery		

2. A separate line of business (segment) was sold on March 14, 2012, for $18,000 cash. The book values of the assets and liabilities of the segment as of the date of the sale were $10,000 and $4,000, respectively. The business segment recognized revenues of $18,500 and expenses of $14,000 from January 1, 2012, to March 14, 2012.

Revenues of the Segment	18,500	
Expenses of the Segment		14,000
Income Summary		4,500
Recognized business segment income		
(closing entry recorded at time of sale)		
Income Summary (E, −RE)	1,530	
Income Tax Liability (+L)		1,530
Recognized income tax liability related to		
2012 operations ($4,500 × 34%)		
Cash (+A)	18,000	
Liabilities (−L)	4,000	
Assets (−A)		10,000
Gain on Sale (Ga, +RE)		12,000
Sold business segment		
Gain on Sale (−Ga, −RE)	4,080	
Income Tax Liability (+L)		4,080
Recognized additional tax liability ($12,000 × 34%).		

3. On September 12, 2012, Panawin retired, before maturity, outstanding bonds with a face value of $120,000, for a cash payment of $130,000. The bonds were originally issued at a premium, and the unamortized premium as of the date of retirement was $3,000. The loss on the retirement is considered extraordinary.

Bonds Payable (−L)	120,000	
Unamortized Premium (−L)	3,000	
Loss on Retirement (Lo, −RE)	7,000	
Cash (−A)		130,000
Retired outstanding bonds		
Income Tax Liability (−L)	2,380	
Loss on Retirement (−Lo, +RE)		2,380
Recognized tax benefit ($7,000 × 34%)		

4. The company changed its method of accounting for inventories in line with a new mandated standard. This change increased the ending inventory balance for 2012 by $8,000.

Inventory (+A)	8,000	
Income from Accounting Change (Ga, +RE)		8,000
Recognized change in accounting method		
Income from Accounting Change (−Ga, −RE)	2,720	
Income Tax Liability (+L)		2,720
Recognized additional tax liability ($8,000 × 34%)		

The income statement is shown in Figure 13–7, and the reconciliation of retained earnings is shown in Figure 13–8.

FIGURE 13–7   Income statement for review problem

Panawin Enterprises
Income Statement
for the Year Ended December 31, 2012

Operating revenues	$85,000	(given)
Operating expenses	62,000	(given)
Net operating income	$23,000	
Loss on sale of machinery	(2,000)	
Net income from continuing operations before tax	$21,000	
Less: Federal income tax	7,000	(given)
Net income from continuing operations	$14,000	
Income from disposed segment (net of tax)	2,970	($4,500 − $1,530)
Gain on sale of segment (net of tax)	7,920	($12,000 − $4,080)
Net income before extraordinary items	$24,890	
Extraordinary loss on retirement of debt (net of tax)	(4,620)	(−$7,000 + $2,380)
Net income before change in accounting principle	$20,270	
Income effect from change in inventory accounting		
(net of tax)	5,280	($8,000 − $2,720)
Net income	$25,550	
Earnings per share (10,000 shares outstanding):		
Net income from continuing operations	$ 1.40	($14,000 ÷ 10,000)
Disposal of business segment	1.09	[($2,970 + $7,920) ÷ 10,000]
Extraordinary item	(.46)	[$(4,620) ÷ 10,000]
Change in accounting principle	.53	($5,280 ÷ 10,000)
Total earnings per share	$ 2.56	($25,550 ÷ 10,000)

FIGURE 13–8
Reconciliation of retained earnings for Review Problem

Panawin Enterprises
Reconciliation of Retained Earnings
for the Year Ended December 31, 2012

Beginning retained earnings balance	$106,000
Plus: Net income	25,550
Less: Dividends	(16,000)
Ending retained earnings balance	$115,550

SUMMARY OF KEY POINTS

 Economic consequences associated with reporting net income.

Income is the most common measure of a company's performance. It has been related to stock prices, suggesting that equity investors use income in their decisions to buy and sell equity securities. It has been related to bond prices, indicating that debt investors use income in their decisions to buy and sell corporate bonds. Income is also used by credit-rating agencies to establish credit ratings. Various income measures are also found in contracts written among shareholders, creditors, and managers. Such contracts are normally designed either to protect the interests of creditors or to encourage managers to act in the interests of the shareholders.

Two different concepts of income: Matching and fair market value

The matching process measures income by first recognizing the revenues of a particular period and then subtracting from them the expenses necessary to generate the revenues. The fair market value concept measures income by comparing the fair market value of the firm's net assets at the end of a period to the fair market value of the net assets at the beginning of the period. For years the matching principle has provided the basis for income measurement, and it still does for both U.S. GAAP and IFRS. However, both systems now rely on a combination of the two concepts. IFRS allows the use of fair market value accounting for a variety of assets and liabilities, and U.S. GAAP, in addition to requiring fair market value accounting for trading securities, has recently adopted a fair market value option for financial instruments in general. Astute readers of financial statements must understand both concepts of income, and how they affect both the income statement and the statement of comprehensive income.

A framework for financing, investing, and operating transactions.

Financing and investing transactions involve setting up a company so that it can conduct operations. Operating transactions entail the actual conduct of the operations. The text identifies five categories of transactions: (1) exchanges with shareholders, (2) exchanges of liabilities and shareholders' equity, (3) issues and payments of debt, (4) purchases, sales, and exchanges of assets, and (5) operating transactions (revenues and expenses). Generally accepted accounting principles consider categories 1–3 as financing transactions, category 4 as investing transactions, and category 5 as operating transactions.

Exchanges with shareholders are involved exclusively with the formation and dissolution of the company's equity capital and the returns to the company's shareholders. Exchanges of liabilities and shareholders' equity deal only with a company's capital structure. Issues and payments of debt involve exchanges with a company's creditors and are reflected in the liabilities section of the balance sheet. Purchases, sales, or exchanges of assets are considered capital transactions because assets represent the capital base on which operations are conducted.

Categories that constitute a complete income statement and how they provide measures of income that address the objectives of financial reporting.

The financial effects of five types of events warrant special disclosure and presentation on the income statement: (1) operating revenues and expenses, (2) other revenues and expenses, (3) disposals of business segments, (4) extraordinary items, and (5) mandated changes in accounting principles.

These classifications highlight income numbers that vary in persistence. In terms of the objectives of financial accounting, earnings numbers with high persistence (e.g., operating earnings) are considered to reflect future cash flows, while low-persistence earnings are not. Both kinds of earnings, however, reflect changes in a company's resources and, in that respect, are considered useful.

Intraperiod tax allocation.

Federal income taxes are disclosed in two different ways on the income statement. The first income tax disclosure immediately follows net income from continuing operations (before tax). It

represents the tax expense recognized by the company due to taxable revenues and deductible expenses not related to the items listed below net income from continuing operations on the income statement.

The dollar amounts associated with the remaining items (disposal of business segments, extraordinary items, and changes in accounting principles) are all disclosed *net of tax.* Such presentation means that each of these revenue and expense items is disclosed on the income statement after the related income tax effect has been removed. The practice of including the income tax effect of a particular transaction with the transaction itself on the income statement is known as *intraperiod tax allocation.*

● *Earnings-per-share disclosure on the income statement.*

Generally accepted accounting principles require that earnings per share be disclosed on the face of the income statement and that the specific amounts associated with (1) net income from continuing operations (after tax), (2) disposals of business segments, (3) extraordinary items, and (4) mandated changes in accounting principles be disclosed separately. The calculation involves dividing the dollar amounts of each of the four items listed by the average number of shares outstanding during the accounting period.

KEY TERMS

Note: Definitions for these terms are provided in the glossary at the end of the text.

Business segment (p. 608)	Frequent (p. 607)
Comprehensive income (p. 600)	Intraperiod tax allocation (p. 612)
Diluted earnings per share (p. 613)	Matching process (p. 601)
Earnings persistence (p. 613)	Operating transactions (p. 602)
Extraordinary items (p. 609)	Pro forma (as if) basis (p. 611)
Financing and investing transactions (p. 602)	Usual (p. 607)

ETHICS in the Real World

The boards of directors of most major U.S. companies have established executive compensation plans that base executive pay on some measure of company performance. While these plans differ widely across companies, a large percentage use some form of reported earnings as the measure of performance. Recognizing that there are many different ways to measure earnings, these compensation contracts must be very specific about which earnings measure is used. Pillsbury, for example, bases its formula on operating earnings, the result of subtracting operating expenses from operating revenues, excluding such items as interest expense, interest income, gains and losses on asset sales, extraordinary gains and losses, and the effects of accounting changes. Other companies, such as DuPont and Ashland Oil, base their formulas on net income after such items—the "bottom line."

Consider a company that has a compensation plan like that of DuPont, where compensation is a function of earnings after interest expense, and assume that management is analyzing how to finance a particular capital investment—that is, should it be financed with debt or equity? Management knows that if debt is chosen, net income and its compensation will be reduced by the interest expense recognized on the debt. On the other hand, if management chooses equity, there will be no interest expense to reduce its compensation amount.

ETHICAL ISSUE Is it ethical for management to consider the impact of the financing decision on its compensation amount, or should such impact be completely ignored when choosing between debt and equity?

INTERNET RESEARCH EXERCISE

Yahoo reports a number of items on its 2007–2009 consolidated statements of earnings that one could consider non-operating. Identify these items and comment on their persistence. Begin your search at the company home page (yahoo.com).

BRIEF EXERCISES

REAL DATA

BE13–1

Nonrecurring items

Revenues for Goodrich Corporation increased from $6.4 billion in 2007 to $7.1 billion in 2008 (a 10.5 percent increase), but earnings increased by over 40% from $483 million to $674 million. In recent years the company has reported losses from debt retirements, accounting changes, and discontinued operations. Explain how these items could influence your conclusions about Goodrich's comparative performance from 2007 to 2008.

REAL DATA

BE13–2

Effects on the basic accounting equation

When Anheuser-Busch Company recognized a $160 million charge on its income statement for the closure of Tampa Breweries, it consisted of a write-down of plant assets of $113.7 million, employee severance costs of $19.4 million, and other disposal costs of $26.9 million. The following year the company disclosed a $54.7 million gain associated with the sale of the St. Louis Cardinals baseball team. The team was sold for $150 million.

For each of the elements of these disclosures, discuss how the basic accounting equation could have been affected.

REAL DATA

BE13–3

Interpreting non-operating items

Refer to the Merck income statement presented at the very beginning of the chapter, and note that the company reported climbing profits of $3.4 billion, $7.9 billion, and $13 billion in 2007, 2008, and 2009, respectively. Restructuring charges rose across the three years; equity income affiliates fell across the three years; and there were two very large non-operating items during the three-year period. In 2007 Merck booked a $4.9 billion charge associated with a litigation settlement, and in 2009 the company booked $10.7 billion in "other income." Discuss how each of these non-operating items influenced the basic accounting equation, and compute Merck's net operating income for the three years. Comment on Merck's earnings trend.

REAL DATA

BE13–4

Understanding comprehensive income and how it is reflected on the financial statements

In the shareholders' equity section of its 2008 and 2009 balance sheets, H&R Block reported accumulated other comprehensive income balances of $2.5 million and negative $11.6 billion, respectively. The 2009 income statement reported net income of $486 million. During 2009 the net holding loss for the available-for-sale securities held by H&R Block was $4 million, and the company incurred an additional $10 million loss on foreign currency translations. Neither item affected earnings, but both reduced shareholders' equity.

a. Compute comprehensive income for 2009.
b. Describe how these activities are reflected on H&R Block's balance sheet, income statement, and statement of shareholders' equity.

EXERCISES

E13–1

Which statement is affected?

Listed below are transactions or items that are frequently reported in financial statements.

1. Income effect due to changing from the double-declining-balance method to the straight-line method of depreciation.
2. Collection of accounts receivable.

3. Purchase of an insurance policy on December 31 that provides coverage for the following year.
4. Accrued wages earned by the employees.
5. Estimated uncollectible accounts receivable using the aging method.
6. Recognized a gain on the sale of plant equipment.
7. Recognized a loss when the government expropriated land for a highway.
8. Declared a dividend valued at $100,000.
9. Under the requirements of a debt covenant, appropriated a portion of retained earnings.
10. Received dividends on stocks held as a short-term investment. The dividends were declared and paid on the same day.
11. Recognized the cost of inventory sold during the year under the periodic method.
12. Paid rent for the current year.

a.   Indicate whether each item would be included on the company's income statement, statement of shareholders' equity, or neither, using the following codes:

IS   Income statement
SE   Statement of shareholders' equity
N   Neither

b.   Indicate whether the items you coded IS would be considered (1) usual and frequent, (2) unusual or infrequent, (3) unusual and infrequent, or (4) other.
c.   Provide a brief explanation of your choice in (b) of (1), (2), (3), or (4).

E13–2

Classifying
transactions

Transactions include the following:

1. Declaration of a stock dividend.
2. Purchase of 50 percent of the outstanding stock of another company.
3. Payment of previously accrued interest payable.
4. Accrual of interest expense.
5. Purchase of machinery.
6. Recognition of depreciation on machinery.
7. Purchase of treasury stock.
8. Sale of treasury stock at a price less than its original cost.
9. Conversion of debt to common stock.
10. Receipt of cash on an outstanding receivable.
11. Sale of inventory on account.
12. Purchase of inventory on account.
13. Declaration of dividends.
14. Receipt of dividends on short-term marketable securities.
15. Early retirement of outstanding long-term debt.

a.   Refer to Figure 13–2 in the text, and classify each transaction in one of the following categories:
    (1) Exchanges with shareholders
    (2) Exchanges of liabilities and shareholders' equity
    (3) Issues and payments of debt
    (4) Purchases, sales, and exchanges of assets
    (5) Operating transactions
b.   Briefly explain why the transactions are considered increasingly operating (or decreasingly financing) as the categories move from (1) to (5).

E13–3

Comprehensive
income

The December 31, 2012, balance sheet of Smedley Company is as follows:

Assets	$70,000	Liabilities	$15,000
		Shareholders' equity	55,000
		Total liabilities and	
Total assets	$70,000	shareholders' equity	$70,000

During 2013 the company entered into the following transactions:

1. Common stock was issued for $35,000 cash.
2. Services were performed for $50,000 cash.
3. Cash expenses of $24,000 were incurred.
4. Long-term liabilities of $15,000 were paid.
5. Dividends of $7,000 were declared and paid.

a. Classify each transaction as operating, investing, or financing and then prepare an income statement.
b. Compute comprehensive income, and compare it to the income amount calculated in (a).
c. Explain why the two dollar amounts are equal.

E13–4

Debt covenants
expressed in terms
of income

Morton Manufacturing maintains a credit line with First Bank that allows the company to borrow up to $1 million. A covenant associated with the loan contract limits the company's dividends in any one year to 20 percent of net income. The 2012 income statement data of Morton Manufacturing is as follows:

Net sales	**$840,000**
Less: Cost of goods sold	570,000
Gross profit	**$270,000**
Selling and administrative expenses	120,000
Net operating income	**$150,000**
Gain on sale of securities	14,000
Interest expense	(4,000)
Net income from continuing operations before tax	**$160,000**
Less: Income tax	51,200
Net income from continuing operations	**$108,800**
Extraordinary gain (net of tax)	22,000
Net income before change in accounting principle	**$130,800**
Income effect due to change in accounting principle	52,000
Net income	**$182,800**

a. Compute the maximum amount of dividends Morton can pay if the debt covenant is expressed as 20 percent of each of the following:
   (1) Net income
   (2) Income before change in accounting principle
   (3) Income before extraordinary items (from continuing operations)
   (4) Net operating income
b. Explain why the bank may wish to state the contractual limitation on dividends in terms of income from operations instead of net income.

REAL DATA

E13–5

Special items

In a three-year period AT&T, the telecommunications provider, reported net income of $1.9 billion (Year Three), a net loss of $13 billion (Year Two), and net income of $7.7 billion (Year One). Included in these numbers were the following special items:

Year One: losses from equity investments ($7.5 billion); net loss from discontinued operations ($4 billion); gain on disposition of discontinued operations ($1.3 billion); and gain from accounting changes ($904 million).

Year Two: losses from equity investments ($400 million); net loss from discontinued operations ($14.5 billion); gain on disposition of discontinued operations ($1.3 billion); and loss from accounting changes ($856 million).

Year Three: losses from equity investments ($12 million); net loss from discontinued operations ($13 million); and gain from accounting changes ($15 million).

a. Describe each special item.
b. Comment on AT&T's performance across the three-year period.

E13-6

Disposal of a
business segment

LTB Enterprises consists of four separate divisions: building products, chemicals, mining, and plastics. On March 15, 2012, LTB sold the chemicals division for $625,000 cash. Financial information related to the chemicals division follows:

(1/1–3/15/12)		(3/15/12)	
Sales	$175,000	Assets	$1,850,000
Operating expenses	160,000	Liabilities	1,400,000
Net operating income (loss)	$ 15,000		

a.   Provide the journal entry (or entries) to record the sale of the chemicals division. Assume an income tax rate of 35 percent.

b.   Prepare the section of LTB's 2012 income statement that relates to the disposal of the business segment.

E13-7

Management choices
and earnings
persistence

It is December 2012, and Sharon Sowers, the CEO of Mallory Services, has decided to sell the clerical division. She has received an offer for $105,000 but is undecided about whether she wishes to complete the sale in 2012 or 2013. She is currently evaluating the effects of the sale on 2012 reported net income. Income from continuing operations for 2012 is estimated to be $950,000 (excluding the activities of the clerical division), and information about the clerical division is provided as follows. The company's tax rate is 35 percent.

Year Ended 2012		December 2012	
Revenues	$35,000	Assets	$93,000
Expenses	23,000	Liabilities	26,000

a.   Prepare the 2012 income statement, beginning with net income from continuing operations, assuming that Sharon accepts the offer, and explain how a user might interpret the items on the income statement in terms of earnings persistence.

b.   Prepare the 2012 income statement, beginning with net income from continuing operations, assuming that Sharon chooses not to sell the division in 2012, and explain how a user might interpret the items on the income statement in terms of earnings persistence.

c.   Describe some of the important trade-offs Sharon faces as she decides whether to complete the sale in 2012 or 2013.

E13-8

Management choices
and earnings
persistence

It is December 2012, and Rob Blandig, the CEO of Carmich Industries, has decided to sell the chemical division. He has received an offer for $350,000, but he is undecided about whether he wishes to complete the sale in 2012 or 2013. He is currently evaluating the effects of the sale on 2012 reported net income. Income from continuing operations for 2012 is estimated to be $1,930,000 (excluding the activities of the chemical division and management's bonus), and the company anticipates a weak year in 2013. Information about the division follows. The company's tax rate is 35 percent, and company management is paid a bonus each year in the amount of 20 percent $\times$ net income from continuing operations. For purposes of the bonus calculation, net income from continuing operations is not reduced by the bonus.

Year Ended 2012		December 2012	
Revenues	$145,000	Assets	$437,000
Expenses	120,000	Liabilities	218,000

a.   Prepare the 2012 income statement, beginning with net income from continuing operations, assuming that Rob accepts the offer, and explain how a user might interpret the items on the income statement in terms of earnings persistence.

b.   Prepare the 2012 income statement, beginning with net income from continuing operations, assuming that Rob chooses not to sell the division in 2012, and explain how a user might interpret the items on the income statement in terms of earnings persistence.

c.   Describe some of the important trade-offs Rob faces as he decides whether to complete the sale in 2012 or 2013.

REAL DATA

E13-9

Interpreting
non-operating items
on IFRS-based income
statements

The 2007 income statement for Group Danone, a French-based food processor that publishes IFRS-based financial statements, is provided below (in million euros).

	2007
Net sales	12,776
Operating expenses	(11,230)
Operating income	1,546
Net cost of debt	(177)
Income before taxes	1,369
Income tax	(410)
Income from consolidated companies	959
Net income of equity-accounted affiliates	87
Net income from continuing operations	1,046
Net income from discontinued operations	3,292
Net income	4,338

a. Briefly explain each of the line items on the income statement.
b. Explain what must have happened at Danone in 2007 that boosted net income by so much, and comment on possible implications for Danone's future.

E13–10

Accounting for
unusual losses

You are currently auditing the financial records of Paxson Corporation, which is located in San Francisco, California. During the current year, inventories with an original cost of $2,325,000 were destroyed by an earthquake. The company was unsure how to record this loss and is seeking your advice. The loss is deductible for tax purposes, and the company's tax rate is 35 percent.

a. Prepare the journal entry (or entries) to record the loss of the inventory if the loss is not considered extraordinary.
b. Prepare the journal entry (or entries) to record the loss of the inventory if the loss is considered extraordinary.
c. Should the loss be classified as an extraordinary loss or as an ordinary loss? Explain.
d. Would your answer to (c) change if the plant had been located in Miami, Florida? Explain.

E13–11

Economic
consequences of an
extraordinary item

The management of Sting Enterprises shares in a bonus that is determined and paid at the end of each year. The amount of the bonus is defined by multiplying net income from continuing operations (after tax) by 12 percent. The bonus is not used in the calculation of income from continuing operations. During 2012, Sting was a defendant in a lawsuit and was required to pay $480,000 over and above the amount covered by insurance. The loss is tax deductible, and the company's tax rate is 35 percent. The company was last involved in a lawsuit five years ago. Net income from continuing operations (before tax) for 2012, excluding the loss from the lawsuit, was $800,000.

a. Compute management's 2012 bonus, assuming that the lawsuit is considered unusual but not infrequent.
b. Compute management's 2012 bonus, assuming that the lawsuit is considered extraordinary.
c. Repeat (a) and (b) above, assuming that Sting was awarded the $480,000 settlement instead of having to pay it.
d. Explain how the decision to include or exclude an item as extraordinary can have significant economic consequences.

E13–12

Earnings-per-share
disclosure

The following income statement was reported by Battery Builders for the year ending December 31, 2012:

Sales	$85,000
Rent revenue	23,000
Interest income	7,000

(Continued)

Total revenues		$115,000
Cost of goods sold	$52,000	
Operating expenses	24,000	
Interest expense	12,000	
Loss on sale of fixed asset	6,000	
Total expenses		94,000
Income from continuing operations (before tax)		$ 21,000
Less: Income tax		10,000
Income from continuing operations		$ 11,000
Income from disposed segment (net of tax)		3,000
Gain on sale of disposed segment (net of tax)		2,000
Income before extraordinary items		$ 16,000
Extraordinary loss (net of tax)		7,000
Income before change in accounting principle		$ 9,000
Income due to change in accounting principle (net of tax)		6,000
Net income		$ 15,000

Show how Battery Builders would report earnings per share on the face of the income statement, assuming the following:

a. An average of 15,000 shares of common stock was outstanding during 2012.
b. An average of 25,000 shares of common stock was outstanding during 2012.
c. An average of 30,000 shares of common stock was outstanding during 2012.

E13–13

Intraperiod tax allocation and the financial statements

The following information was taken from the 2012 financial records of Rothrock Consolidated. All items are pretax.

	Debit	Credit
Operating revenues		87,000
Operating expenses	32,500	
Gain on sale of short-term investments		5,200
Loss on sale of business segment	21,000	
Income earned on disposed business segment		3,000
Extraordinary loss	5,000	
Income due to change in accounting principle		12,500
Retained earnings (beginning balance)		72,000
Dividends declared	18,000	

The company's income tax rate is 35 percent, and the items above are treated identically for financial reporting and tax purposes.
  Prepare the following:

a. An income statement.
b. A reconciliation of retained earnings.

E13–14

Intraperiod tax allocation

The following pretax amounts were obtained from the financial records of Watson Company for 2012:

	Debit	Credit
Retained earnings (1/1/09)		847,000
Sales revenues		1,385,000
Rent revenue		360,000
Cost of goods sold	475,000	
Administrative expenses	100,000	
Depreciation expense	250,000	
Selling expenses	189,000	

(Continued)

Extraordinary loss	202,000
Loss on sale of fixed assets	105,000
Dividends declared	460,000

The company's tax rate is 35 percent.

a.   Prepare an income statement for the year ended December 31, 2012, using the multistep format.
b.   Prepare a reconciliation of retained earnings for the year ended December 31, 2012.
c.   What is the income tax effect associated with each item that is reported net of tax? Assuming that no taxes were owed at the beginning of 2012 and no tax payments were made during 2012, what is the total income tax liability at the end of 2012?

E13–15

Covenant restrictions and income reporting

Kennington Company has outstanding debt that contains restrictive covenants limiting dividends to 15 percent of net income from continuing operations. During 2012, the company reported net income from operations of $235,000 after taxes, excluding the following items—all of which ignore tax effects.

1.   A $25,000 gain was recognized on the sale of an investment.
2.   A $62,000 loss was recognized on a lawsuit.
3.   A $38,000 loss was recognized on the early retirement of debt.

Assume that the gain in (1) is taxable, the losses in (2) and (3) are tax deductible, and the company's tax rate is 35 percent.

a.   Provide the income statement, beginning at net income from operations, and compute the maximum amount of dividends that the company can declare, assuming that (1) the investment in (1) is a business segment that broke even during 2012 and (2) lawsuits are common for Kennington.
b.   Provide the income statement, beginning at net income from operations, and compute the maximum amount of dividends that the company can declare, assuming that (1) the investment in (1) is a short-term equity security and (2) lawsuits are very rare for Kennington.

E13–16

Stock market reactions to income reporting

Madigan International is planning a major stock issuance in early 2013. During 2012, the company reported net income from operations of $865,000 before taxes. The four items below describe major events that occurred during 2012. The company's accountants chose to include items (1) and (4) in the computation of net income from continuing operations and to disclose items (2) and (3) as extraordinary items.

1.   A $42,000 gain was recognized on the sale of a subsidiary.
2.   Inventory was written down by $53,000 due to earthquake damage.
3.   An outstanding account receivable of $38,000 was written off when a major customer declared bankruptcy.
4.   A $25,000 gain was recognized due to the change of an accounting principle.

Assume that items (1) and (4) are taxable, items (2) and (3) are tax deductible, and the company's tax rate is 35 percent.

a.   Present the income statement, beginning with net income from operations.
b.   Critique the accounting treatment chosen by Madigan's accountants, and provide an income statement that is consistent with generally accepted accounting principles.
c.   Discuss how Madigan's accounting treatment could influence the price at which the company's stock is sold in 2013, and provide a rationale for why Madigan may have made such choices.

E13–17

Different ways to measure income

Brinkley Leasing purchases farm machinery and leases it to farms. At the beginning of 2011 the company paid $1,000,000 for a fleet of tractors, and estimated their useful lives at five years. Brinkley immediately leased the vehicles for an annual charge of $250,000. Assume that all lease payments were made, the vehicles were disposed of after five years, and at the end of each year the following fair market values for the fleet were estimated.

December 31, 2011	$790,000
December 31, 2012	$622,000
December 31, 2013	$432,000
December 31, 2014	$227,000
December 31, 2015	0

a. Compute the net income and balance sheet value associated with the fleet for each year using the matching concept and assuming that Brinkley uses straight-line depreciation.
b. Compute the net income and balance sheet value associated with the fleet for each year using the matching concept, assuming that Brinkley uses double-declining-balance depreciation.
c. Compute net income and balance sheet value associated with the fleet for each year using the fair market value concept.
d. Discuss the differences.

PROBLEMS

P13–1

Classifying
transactions

Lundy Manufacturing produces and sells football equipment. The company was involved in the following transactions or events during 2012:

1. The company purchased $250,000 worth of materials to be used during 2013 to manufacture helmets and shoulder pads.
2. The company sold football equipment for $500,000. The inventory associated with the sale cost the company $375,000.
3. One of the company's plants in San Francisco was damaged by a minor earthquake. The total amount of the damage was $100,000.
4. The company issued ten ($1,000 face value) bonds at a discount (.98).
5. The company incurred $143,000 in wage expenses.
6. The company was sued by a high school football player who was injured while using some of the company's equipment. The football player will probably win the suit, and the amount of the settlement has been estimated at $10,000. This is the sixth lawsuit filed against the company in the past three years.
7. The company switched from the double-declining-balance depreciation method to the straight-line depreciation method.
8. The company declared and paid $50,000 in dividends.
9. The company incurred a loss when it sold some securities that it was holding as an investment.

REQUIRED:
a. Classify each of these transactions as financing, investing, or operating.
b. Refer to Figures 13–2 and 13–3 in the text, and identify the category in which each of the items listed should be placed.
c. Which of these items should be included on the company's income statement? Briefly describe how they should be disclosed.

P13–2

Bonus contracts
based on income
can affect management's
business decisions

The managers of Martin House are paid a salary and share in a bonus that is determined at the end of each year. The total bonus is determined by multiplying the company's income from operations by 25 percent. The bonus is not considered an operating expense. Interest on borrowed funds is considered an operating expense when computing the bonus.

During 2012, the company decided to expand its plant facility. The estimated cost of the expansion was $1 million. To raise the necessary funds, the company could either borrow $1 million at an annual interest rate of 8 percent or issue 50,000 shares of common stock at

$20 each. The company raised the funds using one of these two methods, and income from operations (excluding any interest charges) for 2012 was reported as follows:

Operating revenues	**$6,800,000**
Operating expenses (excluding interest)	**5,600,000**
Income from operations	**$1,200,000**

REQUIRED:

a. Assume that on January 1, 2012, Martin House borrowed the $1 million. Compute the total bonus shared by the company's managers.

b. Assume that on January 1, 2012, Martin House issued common stock to raise the $1 million. Compute the total bonus shared by the company's managers.

c. Why might management choose to issue equity instead of borrowing the $1 million? Is such a decision necessarily in the best interest of the company's shareholders?

d. Repeat (a) and (b) above, assuming that the interest expense is not considered an operating expense when computing the bonus.

P13–3

Financing, investing, and operating transactions

Raleigh Corporation began operations on February 10, 2012. During 2012, the company entered into the following transactions:

1. Issued $110,000 of common stock and $25,000 of preferred stock.
2. Performed services for $580,000.
3. Issued $475,000 in long-term debt for cash.
4. Incurred expenses: $125,000 for wages, $35,000 for supplies, $80,000 for depreciation, and $75,000 for miscellaneous expenses.
5. Purchased fixed assets for $250,000 cash.
6. Declared, but did not pay, cash dividends of $10,000.
7. Purchased fixed assets in exchange for a long-term note valued at $85,000.

REQUIRED:

a. Classify each transaction as either operating, investing, or financing.
b. Prepare an income statement.
c. Compute comprehensive income and compare it to the income reported on the income statement. Discuss.

P13–4

Preparing an income statement

Excerpts from Crozier Industries' financial records as of December 31, 2012, follow:

	Debit	Credit
Sales		977,000
Sales returns	9,000	
Costs of goods sold	496,000	
Dividends	50,000	
Rent expense	90,000	
Wages payable		175,000
Loss on sale of food services division	2,000	
Loss incurred by food services division	10,000	
Depreciation expense	100,000	
Cumulative effect on income of change in fixed asset accounting	130,000	
Gain on land appropriated by the government		92,000
Insurance expense	12,000	
Inventory	576,000	
Administrative expenses	109,000	
Prepaid insurance	48,000	
Gain on sale of short-term investments		142,000

The amounts shown do not include any tax effects. Crozier's tax rate is 35 percent. Assume that all items are treated the same for accounting and income tax purposes.

REQUIRED:
a. Indicate which items should be included on the company's income statement. Classify each item to be included on the income statement as one of the following:
   (1) Usual and frequent
   (2) Unusual or infrequent
   (3) Disposal of business segment
   (4) Unusual and infrequent
   (5) Mandated change in accounting method
b. Prepare an income statement using the single-step format, and assess the persistence of each item on the income statement.

P13–5

Disclosing extraordinary items

In its 2012 financial report, Meeks Company reported $850,000 under the line item "extra-ordinary losses" on the income statement. The company's tax rate is 35 percent. The foot-note pertaining to extraordinary losses indicates that the $850,000 loss, before tax, is composed of the following items:

1. A loss of $260,000 incurred on a warehouse in Florida damaged in a hurricane.
2. A loss of $150,000 incurred when Meeks sold the assets of a business segment.
3. A loss of $225,000 incurred when a warehouse in Iowa was blown up by a disgruntled employee.
4. Accounts receivable written off in the amount of $125,000.
5. A loss of $90,000 incurred when one of the company's distribution centers in Arizona was damaged by a flood.

REQUIRED:
a. Discuss how each of these items should be disclosed in the financial statements, includ-ing whether or not they should be disclosed net of tax.
b. Show how the "extraordinary items" section of the income statement should have been reported.

P13–6

Intraperiod tax allocation, income tax expense, and income tax liability

The following information has been obtained from the internal financial records of MTM Company:

Retained earnings, December 31, 2011	**$1,259,000**
Dividends declared and paid during 2012	**100,000**
Dividends declared during 2012 but not paid	**75,000**
Dividends declared during 2011 and paid in 2012	**90,000**
2012 income from continuing operations (before taxes)	**850,000**
Extraordinary losses in 2012 (before tax effect)	**135,000**

The company's tax rate is 35 percent. Assume that financial accounting income equals income for tax purposes.

REQUIRED:
a. What is the company's net income for the year ended December 31, 2012?
b. Compute income tax expense reported in MTM's 2012 income statement.
c. Prepare a reconciliation of retained earnings for the year ended December 31, 2012.
d. Assume that the income tax liability account had a balance of $70,000 on January 1, 2012, and that tax payments of $200,000 were made during 2012. What should be the balance in this account on December 31, 2012?

The lower portion of the 2006 income statement for McDonald's follows (dollars in millions):

Income from continuing operations	**$2,875.0**
Income from discontinued operations net of taxes	671.2
Net income	**$3,544.2**
Basic net earnings per share:	
Continuing operations	**$ 2.33**
Discontinued operations	0.54
	$ 2.87
Diluted net earnings per share:	
Continuing operations	**$ 2.30**
Discontinued operations	0.53
	$ 2.83

REQUIRED:
a.   Why is there a distinction between net earnings from continuing operations and net earn-
     ings from discontinued operations?
b.   Estimate the number of common shares outstanding.
c.   Why is there a distinction between basic net earnings per share and diluted net earnings
     per share?
d.   Estimate the number of common shares that would be outstanding if all potentially dilu-
     tive securities were converted to common shares.

The lower portion of the 2008 income statement for Duke Energy Corporation follows (dollars
in millions, except per-share amounts):

Income from continuing operations	**$1,279**
Income from discontinued operations, net of tax	16
Income before extraordinary items	1,295
Extraordinary items, net of tax	67
Net income	**$1,362**
Earnings per share from continuing operations	
Basic	**$ 1.01**
Diluted	**$ 1.01**
Earnings per share from discontinued operations	
Basic	**$ 0.02**
Diluted	**$ 0.01**
Earnings per share before extraordinary items	
Basic	**$ 1.03**
Diluted	**$ 1.02**
Earnings per share from extraordinary items	
Basic	**$ 0.05**
Diluted	**$ 0.05**
Earnings per share	
Basic	**$ 1.08**
Diluted	**$ 1.07**

REQUIRED:
a.   Why is there a distinction among income from continuing operations, income from dis-
     continued operations, and income from extraordinary items?
b.   Estimate the number of common shares outstanding.
c.   Why is there a distinction between basic earnings per share and diluted earnings per share?
d.   Estimate the number of common shares that would be outstanding if all potentially dilutive
     securities were converted to common shares.

P13–9

Disclosing net of tax, and the earnings-per-share calculation

Woodland Farm Corporation has the following items to include in its financial statements:

	Debit	Credit
Extraordinary loss from a flood	250,000	
Extraordinary gain from bond retirement	55,000	
Sale of inventory		250,000
Loss on disposal of business segment	100,000	
Income effect due to change in accounting method		80,000
Advertising expense	50,000	
Income earned by disposed business segment		150,000

None of the listed amounts includes any income tax effects. The company's tax rate is 35 percent.

REQUIRED:

a. Describe how each item above would be disclosed on the income statement or statement of retained earnings.
b. Compute the tax effect of each of the items that should be disclosed net of tax. What dollar amount would be shown on the financial statements for each of these items?
c. Assume that income from continuing operations (after tax) was $600,000, and 200,000 shares of common stock were outstanding during the year. Provide the earnings-per-share calculation.

P13–10

Preparing an income statement

Tom Brown, controller of Microbiology Labs, informs you that the company has sold a segment of its business. Mr. Brown also provides you with the following information for 2012:

	Continuing Operations	Discontinued Segment
Sales	$10,000,000	$850,000
Cost of goods sold	2,500,000	600,000
Operating expenses	750,000	100,000
Loss on sale of office equipment	60,000	—
Gain on disposal of discontinued segment		250,000

The following information is not reflected in any of the above amounts:

1. Microbiology Labs is subject to a 35 percent tax rate.
2. During 2012, Microbiology Labs retired outstanding bonds that were to mature in 2014. The company incurred a loss of $80,000, prior to taxes, on the retirement of the bonds.
3. Microbiology Labs owns several apple orchards as part of its operations. During 2012, the company's apple crop was destroyed by an infestation of a rare insect. This unusual and infrequent loss, prior to taxes, totaled $800,000.
4. Two million shares of common stock were outstanding throughout 2012.

REQUIRED:

Prepare an income statement for the year ended December 31, 2012, including the recommended earnings-per-share disclosures. In terms of the objectives of financial accounting, comment on the usefulness of each of the different measures of income.

REAL DATA

P13–11

Special items and earnings trends

Over a two-year period Sears reported an 83 percent earnings drop: Net income of $309 million on sales of $10 billion dropped to net income of $53 million on sales of $8.8 billion. It so happened, however, that the $309 million in profits was boosted by a hefty gain on the sale of its credit card division, while the following year was marred by a big restructuring charge, including asset write-downs and an accrual for employee severance packages.

REQUIRED:

a. Where on the income statement would you find the charges related to asset sales and restructuring?
b. Describe how analysts might treat these special items, and comment on Sears's performance across the two years.

REAL DATA
P13–12
Recognized income
and expense
under IFRS

Group Danone, a French-based food processor that publishes IFRS-based financial statements, reported 2008 net income of 1.5 billion euros. Accumulated currency translation adjustments and net holding gains/losses from securities, both of which directly affected shareholders' equity but were not reflected on the income statement, together had balances of 311 million euros and negative 955 million euros at the beginning and end of 2008, respectively.

REQUIRED:

a. Recognized income and expense under IFRS is similar to what concept under U.S. GAAP?
b. Prepare a statement of recognized income and expense (SORIE) for Danone.
c. Which of the financial statements—income statement, balance sheet, statement of cash flows, and/or statement of shareholders' equity—contain information about the currency translation adjustments and the net holding gains/losses referred to above?

P13–13
Comprehensive
problem

Laidig Industries has prepared the following unadjusted trial balance as of December 31, 2012:

	Debit	Credit
Cash	$110,000	
Accounts receivable	340,000	
Allowance for doubtful accounts		$ 50,000
Inventory (balance 1/1/12)	467,000	
Prepaid insurance	60,000	
Fixed assets	850,000	
Accumulated depreciation		287,000
Accounts payable		200,000
Dividends payable		45,000
Bonds payable		500,000
Common stock		100,000
Retained earnings		673,000
Sales		1,256,000
Gain on sale of land		76,000
Extraordinary loss	35,000	
Income effect due to change in accounting principle	60,000	
Purchases	750,000	
Administrative expenses	100,000	
Selling expenses	255,000	
Interest expense	25,000	
Dividends	135,000	

ADDITIONAL INFORMATION:

1. A physical count of inventory on December 31, 2012, indicated that the company had $480,000 of inventory on hand.
2. An aging of accounts receivable indicates that $75,000 is uncollectible.
3. The company uses straight-line depreciation. The assets have a ten-year life and zero salvage value.
4. The company used a third of the remaining insurance policy during 2012.
5. The company pays interest for its bond payable on December 31 of every year. The coupon rate and the effective rate are both 10 percent per year.

(Continued)

6. The company's tax rate is 35 percent. All income tax charges are recorded at the end of the year.
7. 200,000 shares of common stock were outstanding during 2012.

REQUIRED:
Prepare the following:

a. The necessary adjusting and closing entries on December 31, 2012.
b. An income statement including recommended earnings-per-share disclosures.
c. A reconciliation of retained earnings.
d. In terms of the objectives of financial accounting, discuss the usefulness of the various measures of income included on the statement.

ISSUES FOR DISCUSSION

REAL DATA

ID13–1

Comprehensive income

The components of 2008 comprehensive income for CVS Caremark and for Caterpillar, Inc. are outlined below (dollars in millions):

	CVS	Caterpillar
Net income	$3,696	$3,557
Foreign currency translation	——	(488)
Pension/post-retirement benefits	7	(3,272)
Derivative financial instruments	1	69
Available-for-sale securities	——	(97)

REQUIRED:

a. The net incomes for the two firms are very similar. Discuss how the total changes to equity due to nonowner transactions compare for the two firms.
b. CVS is a U.S.-based chain of retail pharmacies, while Caterpillar is a global manufacturer of heavy-duty construction equipment. How are the companies' business models reflected in their respective comprehensive incomes?
c. How would an analyst reading the financial statements of the two companies compare their relative financial changes over the course of a year? What specific areas might concern an analyst looking at Caterpillar that would not affect CVS?

REAL DATA

ID13–2

Ratings agencies and assessing risks

Ratings agencies such as Moody's and Standard & Poor's rate securities to give investors an independent grading of the risks involved in financial transactions. During 2007 both Moody's and S&P reported large increases in profits due to the increased volume of securities being issued and the consequent need for their services. Moody's reported a 20 percent rise in net profits during the first quarter of 2007, while the parent company of S&P (McGraw-Hill) indicated its financial services business (including S&P) recorded a 38 percent increase in operating profits. Both companies cited the growth in issuances as the driver of their profits.

Shortly after these earnings announcements in 2007, financial markets tightened in response to the collapse of the "subprime" mortgage market. Subprime home mortgages were bundled together by issuing lenders and sold to investors in what are called mortgage-backed securities, which are rated by agencies like Moody's and S&P. In fact, both companies have come under fire for not accurately rating the risks associated with the subprime securities.

REQUIRED:

a. What will the tightening of credit markets do to the business volume of the ratings agencies?
b. Where on the financial statements will Moody's and S&P reflect the drop in issuing activity?

c. Assume that the two companies are held responsible for their inaccurate ratings on the mortgage-backed securities. What possible entries might appear on future income statements if the companies' reputation and business are hurt due to the subprime collapse?

Weyerhaeuser Company is engaged principally in the growing and harvesting of timber and the manufacture, distribution, and sale of forest products. When Mount St. Helens, a volcano located in Washington State, erupted, 68,000 acres of the company's standing timber, logs, buildings, and equipment were destroyed. As a result, the company recognized a $36 million (net of tax) extraordinary loss on its income statement.

REQUIRED:

a. What must have been true for Weyerhaeuser to classify this event as extraordinary?
b. If Mount St. Helens continues to erupt periodically, would future related losses necessarily be classified by Weyerhaeuser as extraordinary? Why or why not?
c. At the same time of the eruption, Weyerhaeuser's income tax rate was approximately 48 percent. Compute the entire loss (ignoring the tax effect) incurred by the company, and provide the journal entries prepared by the company's accountants to record the loss and the related income tax effect.

REAL DATA

ID13–4

Disclosing
nonoperating items
on the income
statement

Several years ago, PepsiCo's earnings either rose or fell, depending on the source of the information. Standard & Poor's reported that PepsiCo experienced a 25 percent earnings gain, while Value Line, another investor service, reported that PepsiCo experienced a 7 percent loss. The discrepancy involved a "normal but nonrecurring charge" taken by PepsiCo to write down foreign bottling assets. Standard & Poor's ignored the charge in its earnings calculation, while Value Line included the charge.

REQUIRED:

a. Provide reasonable arguments that Standard & Poor's and Value Line could have used to support the decision either to ignore or include the charge in the calculation of PepsiCo's income.
b. Briefly describe the categories comprising a complete income statement and explain how such categories are usually disclosed.
c. *Forbes* once reported that "most financial analysts [are not concerned about] the geographic location of such items on the income statement." It is only important that they be disclosed. Explain why financial analysts might take such a position. At the same time, provide an argument suggesting that the specific location of an item on the income statement is important in an economic sense. State your argument in terms of earnings persistence and how income numbers are used in contracts.

Many e-tailers (retailers via the Internet) were not profitable in their early years. Analysts who believed in the futures of these firms, therefore, were forced to focus on other positive metrics of performance, such as revenues and gross profit margins (sales less cost of goods sold). The *Dow Jones News Service* (June 2, 2000) reported that the FASB had recently come out with a new rule requiring companies to include shipping and handling costs, significant in the e-tailing industry, in the cost-of-goods-sold category instead of as part of selling and administrative expense. Even though this reporting requirement had no effect on the bottom line, e-tailers like Amazon.com lobbied aggressively against it.

REQUIRED:

a. Why might analysts be interested in companies that were not recording profits?
b. What specific effect did the new FASB rule have on the income statement of companies like Amazon.com, and why would these companies lobby aggressively against the rule?
c. What impact would this new rule have on the reported cash flows of the company?
d. Do you think that the stock market prices of e-tailers would decrease in response to this ruling by the FASB? Why?

REAL DATA

ID13-6

Litigation, reported
income, and
stock prices

In 1990, Eastman Kodak recorded a third-quarter net loss of $206 million, but at the same time, it posted a 22 percent rise in operating earnings to $835 million. Much of the loss was due to a $909.5 million charge taken to cover the costs associated with a patent infringement ruling, at which time Kodak was ordered to pay almost $1 billion to Polaroid for infringing on Polaroid's instant photography patents. The dollar amount awarded Polaroid was far below the company's multibillion-dollar claim. Kodak's shares jumped $1.25 to $29.75 in response to the news.

REQUIRED:

a.   Where on Kodak's income statement should the charge be disclosed, and should the amount be reported net of tax? If so, assume a 34 percent tax rate and compute the net amount.

b.   The patent infringement case between Kodak and Polaroid was well publicized and extended over several years. How do you think this situation was reported in Kodak's 1989 annual report? In Polaroid's 1989 annual report?

c.   Explain why Kodak's stock could have increased in value in response to news that the company reported a $206 million net loss for the quarter.

REAL DATA

ID13-7

Income statement
categories

In its 2008 annual report, which included a statement of comprehensive income, Bristol-Myers Squibb reported the following items (dollars in millions):

Net earnings from discontinued operations	**$ 113**
Research and development	**(3,585)**
Foreign currency translation	**(123)**
Net gain on disposal of business	**1,979**
Provision for restructuring	**(218)**
Gain on sale of assets	**159**
Cost of products sold	**(6,396)**
Litigation charges	**(33)**
Equity in net income of affiliates	**617**

REQUIRED:

a.   Explain the nature of each item, describe where they would be disclosed on the income statement (including comprehensive income), and state whether or not they would be reported net of taxes.

b.   Discuss each item in terms of its persistence.

REAL DATA

ID13-8

Analyzing special
income statement
items

Indicate how the income effects of the following items would be disclosed on the income statement and whether they represent a wealth change and/or can be expected to persist in the future.

a.   Federal Express reported $17 million on operating gains from an insurance settlement for a DC-10 aircraft destroyed by fire.

b.   Over a three-year period Motorola reported net gains of $443 million on asset sales.

c.   Owens Corning reported a $68 million restructuring charge, equity in net income of affiliates of $11 million, and a $15 million cumulative effect of an accounting change.

d.   Owens Corning reported an $875 million charge related to expected litigation claims due to asbestos injuries.

REAL DATA

ID13-9

Recurring vs.
nonrecurring items

When luxury car maker BMW recently released earnings, the *Wall Street Journal* reported that it compared poorly to the prior year for a number of reasons, including:

• rising raw material costs
• strength of the euro
• a large gain booked during the year
• rising costs to introduce new models

These factors contributed to a 38 percent drop in quarterly income despite a 2.9 percent increase in sales.

REQUIRED:
a. Discuss where the above reasons would be represented in the financial statements.
b. Which of the above reasons might be considered permanent and recurring?
c. How is net income different from comprehensive income?
d. On the day of the earnings announcement, BMW's stock price rose 1 percent. What other factors would an analyst review in addition to the earnings?

REAL DATA

ID13–10

Classification differences under both IFRS and U.S. GAAP

The Volkswagen Group, a German auto manufacturer, and Carrefour, a French retailer, both publish financial statements under IFRS, denominated in euros. Sony, the Japanese electronics giant, publishes financial statements under U.S. GAAP, denominated in yen. Excerpts taken directly from their 2008 income statements are provided below. Note that the items are in the order in which they appeared on the income statement.

Volkswagen (million euros):

Operating profit	6,333
Share of profits and losses from equity-accounted investments	910
Finance cost	(1,815)

Carrefour (million euros):

Finance costs	(562)
Net income from operations	1,471
Net income from equity method companies	52

Sony (billion yen):

Equity in net income of affiliates	101
Operating income	475
Interest expense	23

REQUIRED:
a. Identify differences in the definitions of operations used by the three companies.
b. Comment on possible reasons for these differences.
c. How might an analyst handle these differences?

REAL DATA

ID13–11

The SEC Form 10-K of NIKE

Portions of NIKE's SEC form 10-K are reproduced in Appendix C.

REQUIRED:
Review the NIKE SEC Form 10-K, and answer the following questions.

a. Describe how nonoperating items affected NIKE's reported net income over the last three years. Did they increase or decrease net income, and by how much?
b. What was NIKE's net income per share of common stock? Has it been increasing or decreasing over the last three years? How much potential dilution do existing shareholders face?
c. How does NIKE disclose other comprehensive income items, and what was the comprehensive income amount for 2009? Was it above or below net income, and why?

CHAPTER 14   The Statement of Cash Flows

KEY POINTS

The following key points are emphasized in this chapter:

- The structure and format of the statement of cash flows.

- Cash flows from operating, investing, and financing activities.

- How the statement of cash flows complements the other financial statements and how it can be used by those interested in the financial condition of a company.

- Important investing and financing transactions that do not appear on the statement of cash flows and how they are reported.

- Economic consequences associated with the statement of cash flows.

- Preparing a statement of cash flows from the information contained in two balance sheets, an income statement, and a statement of shareholders' equity.

MicroStrategy was a red-hot software company in the business-to-business Internet sector. Unlike many other Internet companies, MicroStrategy reported profits early and often. Then, the bottom fell out when news was released that MicroStrategy had been "cooking the books" by overstating revenues and profits. The stock price plunged and Zack's Research Report noted that, at the time, nine out of ten analysts had recently published "buy" or "strong buy" recommendations. Interestingly, well in advance of the stock price collapse, the company's cash flow from operations told a sobering story—negative $2.5 million instead of a profit of $9 million. Should the analysts have been looking at net cash from operations instead of net income? This chapter, which covers the statement of cash flows, answers that question, and discusses what cash flow is, how it should be used, and how earnings quality can be assessed by comparing net income to cash flow from operations.

Like U.S. GAAP, IFRS requires the presentation of a statement of cash flows, and the format of the statement is largely the same.

The statement of cash flows contains a summary of a company's transactions that involve the cash account over a period of time. It is designed to highlight the cash flows associated with three aspects of the company's economic activities: (1) operations, (2) investments, and (3) financing. The basic structure of the statement of cash flows is provided in Figure 14–1. The reported numbers were taken from the 2008 annual report of Southwest Airlines, currently one of the few companies in the airline industry generating consistent positive cash flows from operations.

FIGURE 14–1

Sample statement of cash flows

Southwest Airlines
Statement of Cash Flows
for the Year Ended December 31, 2008
(in millions)

	2008	2007	2006
Cash provided (used) by operating activities	$(1,521)	$2,845	$ 1,406
Cash provided (used) by investing activities	(978)	(1,529)	(1,495)
Cash provided (used) by financing activities	1,654	(493)	(801)
Increase (decrease) in cash	$ (845)	$ 823	$ (890)
Cash—beginning of year	2,213	1,390	2,280
Cash—end of year	$ 1,368	$2,213	$ 1,390

Recall that the statement of cash flows has already been presented and discussed. Chapter 1 introduced the statement and provided an example. Chapter 2 discussed the basic nature of the statement and related it to the income statement, balance sheet, and statement of shareholders' equity. Chapter 4 explained how a statement of cash flows can be prepared from the cash T-account, and Appendix 4A contained an exercise where a statement of cash flows was prepared from two balance sheets and an income statement. Chapter 5 described how it can be interpreted to assess solvency, and subsequent chapters covered the effects of a variety of transactions on the statement of cash flows. Thus, you have already been exposed to the fundamentals of the statement of cash flows. This chapter provides a more complete discussion of the nature of the statement, how it can be used, and how it is prepared.

The statement of cash flows was established as a standard of financial reporting in 1987 when the Financial Accounting Standards Board decided (in FASB *Statement No. 95, Statement of Cash Flows*) to modify the statement of changes in financial position, which had been required since 1971.

On its 2009 statement of cash flows, Starbucks Corporation reported net cash flows from operating activities of $1.4 billion. The same year, reported net income was only $391 million. Briefly explain how net cash flow from operating activities can be so much higher than net income.

THE DEFINITION OF CASH

Chapter 6 of this text defines cash for purposes of balance sheet disclosure and points out that it consists of coin, currency, and available funds on deposit at the bank. Negotiable instruments such as money orders, certified checks, cashier's checks, personal checks, and bank drafts are also considered cash. The total of these items as of the balance sheet date is the cash amount that appears on the balance sheet.

When preparing the statement of cash flows, companies commonly consider as cash the items already mentioned as well as certain **cash equivalents,** which include commercial paper and other debt investments with maturities of less than three months.[1] They do so because these items can be converted to cash immediately; for all intents and purposes, therefore, they are virtually the same as cash. In the remainder of this chapter, where we illustrate the statement of cash flows, we will also treat cash equivalents as cash.

Bristol-Myers Squibb considers securities with maturities of less than three months to be cash equivalents. Would such securities be included in the cash account and reported on the statement of cash flows or in the marketable securities account on the balance sheet? Why?

A GENERAL DESCRIPTION OF THE STATEMENT OF CASH FLOWS

Take a moment now and refer back to Chapter 2. It describes the statement of cash flows in terms of the other financial statements, explaining the change in the cash balance from one balance sheet date to the next. Figure 14–2 illustrates the statement of cash flows more completely. This statement is divided into three sections (operating activities, investing activities, and financing activities) and shows the cash inflow and outflow categories that normally comprise each section.

---

1. Commercial paper and short-term debt instruments were discussed in Chapter 10. Also, some corporations, like McDonnell Douglas, Eli Lilly, and Walt Disney, also include short-term investments, such as marketable securities, in the definition of cash for purposes of the statement of cash flows. Such a practice is acceptable under generally accepted accounting principles because marketable securities, by definition, are highly liquid.

FIGURE 14–2

Standard
statement of
cash flows

XYZ Corporation
Statement of Cash Flows
for the Year Ended December 31, 2011

Operating activities:		
Cash received from customers	$ 7,000	
Cash paid for operations (to suppliers, employees, and others)	(5,200)	
Cash provided (used) by other operating items	(870)	
Net cash provided (used) by operating activities		$ 930
Investing activities:		
Cash outflows for the purchase of noncurrent assets	$(3,000)	
Cash inflows from sale of noncurrent assets	400	
Net cash provided (used) by investing activities		(2,600)
Financing activities:		
Cash inflows from borrowings	$ 3,000	
Cash inflows from stock issuances	2,000	
Cash outflows for debt retirements	(1,460)	
Cash outflows for treasury stock purchases	(1,550)	
Cash outflows for dividend payments	(200)	
Net cash provided (used) by financing activities		1,790
Net increase (decrease) in cash and cash equivalents		$ 120
Cash and cash equivalents at the beginning of the year		100
Cash and cash equivalents at the end of the year		$ 220

Cash Provided (Used) by Operating Activities

Cash provided (used) by **operating activities** includes those cash inflows and outflows associated directly with the acquisition and sale of the company's inventories and services. This category includes the cash receipts from sales and accounts receivable as well as cash payments for the purchase of inventories, payments on accounts payable, selling and administrative activities, and interest and taxes. Under generally accepted accounting principles (both U.S. GAAP and IFRS), there are two acceptable ways to present the operating section of the statement of cash flows: the direct method and the indirect method.

THE DIRECT METHOD

The statement of cash flows illustrated in Figure 14–2 was prepared using the **direct method.** It is so called because the computation of cash provided (used) by operating activities ($930) consists of cash inflows and outflows that can be traced *directly* to the cash T-account. For example, the $7,000 collected from customers, the $5,200 paid for operations, and the $870 used for other operating items all represent aggregate totals of entries initially recorded in the journal and posted to the cash account in the ledger.

THE INDIRECT METHOD

Another method of computing and disclosing cash provided (used) by operating activities that is acceptable under GAAP is called the **indirect method.** Under this method, cash provided (used) by operating activities is computed *indirectly* by beginning with the net income figure, which appears on the income statement, and adjusting it for the

differences between cash flows and accruals. The indirect method of computing cash from operating activities is illustrated in Figure 14–3. An example of how to prepare the operating section of the statement of cash flows under the indirect method is contained in Appendix 4A.

FIGURE 14–3 Cash from operating activities: Indirect method	**Operating activities:**

Operating activities:	
Net income	$1,085
Noncash charges to noncurrent accounts:	
Depreciation, amortization, and other noncash charges on noncurrent items	$ 400
Book losses	50
Book gains	(450)
Changes in current accounts other than cash:	
Net decreases (increases) in current assets	105
Net increases (decreases) in current liabilities	(260)
Net cash provided (used) by operating activities	$ 930

In general, items added back to net income in the computation of cash provided (used) by operating activities (e.g., depreciation, amortization, book losses, and decreases in current assets) decrease net income on the income statement but involve no cash outflows. Items subtracted from net income in this computation (e.g., book gains, decreases in current liabilities) increase net income on the income statement but involve no cash inflows. Note also that these adjustments are separated into two categories: (1) noncash charges to the noncurrent accounts and (2) changes in current accounts. The first category includes depreciation and amortization charges as well as book gains and losses recognized on the transfer of long-term assets and liabilities. The second category includes the changes during the period in the current asset and current liability accounts other than cash, marketable securities, and dividends payable.[2]

> A depreciation charge of $538 million is included on the 2009 statement of cash flows for Biomet, a medical technology company. Does the company use the direct or indirect method of presenting the statement of cash flows? Why would an income statement expense like depreciation appear on the statement of cash flows?

THE FASB'S POSITION

Both the direct and the indirect methods result in the same dollar amount ($930) for cash provided (used) by operating activities; in that respect, they simply represent two different forms of presentation. In fact, when the FASB made the statement of cash flows a requirement, it allowed either the direct or the indirect method. If the direct method is chosen, however, the FASB requires that it be accompanied by a schedule of the adjustments that reconcile net income to cash provided (used) by operating activities. This schedule can appear either in the footnotes to the financial statements or on the face of the statement itself. Also, generally accepted accounting principles require that under either method cash amounts paid for taxes and interest must be separately disclosed.

---

2. Changes in marketable securities and dividends payable are reflected in the investing and financing sections, respectively.

Since the adjustments on this schedule are the same as those disclosed under the indirect method, the direct method (including the accompanying schedule) discloses more about the changes in the cash account than the indirect method. To encourage increased disclosure and what the FASB believes to be a more straightforward presentation, it has recommended that companies use the direct method. However, the vast majority of major U.S. companies choose not to follow this recommendation; they use the indirect method probably because it requires fewer disclosures.[3]

?

World Sources Online once reported that the principal advantage of the direct method is that it shows operating cash receipts and payments, while the principal advantage of the indirect method is that it focuses on the differences between net income and net cash from operations. Explain how each advantage could be useful to an analyst.

Cash Provided by Investing Activities

Cash provided (used) by **investing activities** includes the cash inflows and outflows associated with the purchase and sale of a company's noncurrent assets.[4] This section includes the cash effects from purchases and sales of long-term investments, long-lived assets, and intangible assets. The statement of cash flows in Figure 14–2, for example, shows that $3,000 was used to purchase such items, and $400 was collected from selling noncurrent assets. These cash inflows and outflows all can be traced to entries in the cash account in the company's ledger.

Cash Provided (Used) by Financing Activities

Cash provided (used) by **financing activities** includes cash inflows and outflows associated with a company's two sources of outside capital: liabilities and contributed capital. This category primarily includes the cash inflows associated with borrowings and equity issuances as well as the cash outflows related to debt repayments, treasury stock purchases, and dividend payments. The statement of cash flows in Figure 14–2 shows that the company borrowed $3,000, raised $2,000 by issuing stock, made principal payments on debt in the amount of $1,460, used $1,550 to purchase treasury stock, and paid cash dividends of $200. These cash flows also can be traced to the cash account in the company's ledger.

Note also that cash interest payments are not included in this section, even though they represent a cost of financing. Instead, such payments are included in the operating section of the statement of cash flows. This practice has been questioned because it confuses the distinction between financing and operating activities. Figure 14–4 provides an example of a recently published statement of cash flows prepared under the indirect form of presentation. It was taken from the April 25, 2009, annual report of La-Z-Boy, a well-known furniture manufacturer.

3. *Accounting Trends and Techniques* (2009) reports that, of the 500 major U.S. companies surveyed, only five used the direct form of presentation. The remaining 495 used the indirect form.
4. Investing activities can include the purchase and/or sale of securities listed as short-term, but sometimes these investments are included as cash equivalents, and in many cases they are not material.

FIGURE 14–4   La-Z-Boy statement of cash flows

La-Z-Boy Incorporated
Consolidated Statement of Cash Flows

	Fiscal Year Ended		
(Amounts in thousands)	4/25/2009	4/26/2008	4/28/2007
Cash flows from operating activities			
Net income (loss)	$(121,347)	$(13,537)	$ 4,139
Adjustments to reconcile net income (loss) to cash provided by operating activities			
(Gain) loss on sale of assets	(2,813)	270	(14,147)
Write-down of investments	5,140	—	—
Write-down of intangibles	47,677	8,426	—
Write-down of long-lived assets	7,503	—	—
Write-down of assets from businesses held for sale (net of tax)	—	2,159	14,936
(Gain) loss on sale of discontinued operations (net of tax)	—	3,696	(935)
Restructuring	12,460	8,135	11,033
Provision for doubtful accounts	25,254	8,550	3,790
Depreciation and amortization	23,479	24,696	27,204
Stock-based compensation expense	3,819	4,527	3,959
Change in receivables	27,223	20,956	5,064
Change in inventories	36,995	23,471	4,486
Change in payables	(14,544)	(10,394)	(11,607)
Change in other assets and liabilities	(37,961)	(25,689)	1,701
Change in deferred taxes	38,803	(6,027)	(16,390)
Total adjustments	173,035	62,776	29,094
Net cash provided by operating activities	51,688	49,239	33,233
Cash flows from investing activities			
Proceeds from disposals of assets	9,060	8,761	46,974
Proceeds from sale of discontinued operations	—	4,169	42,659
Capital expenditures	(15,625)	(27,386)	(25,811)
Purchases of investments	(11,330)	(34,562)	(18,165)
Proceeds from sales of investments	34,675	35,580	17,342
Change in restricted cash	(18,207)	160	(116)
Change in other long-term assets	(581)	(705)	(955)
Net cash provided by (used for) investing activities	(2,008)	(13,983)	61,928
Cash flows from financing activities			
Proceeds from debt	50,794	93,861	91,787
Payments on debt	(92,139)	(144,790)	(128,483)
Stock issued/(canceled) for stock and employee benefit plans	—	(269)	1,340
Repurchases of common stock	—	—	(6,947)
Dividends paid	(5,177)	(20,746)	(24,886)
Net cash used for financing activities	(46,522)	(71,944)	(67,189)
Effect of exchange rate changes on cash and equivalents	(901)	109	(456)
Change in cash and equivalents	2,257	(36,579)	27,516
Cash acquired from consolidation of VIEs	631	—	—
Cash and equivalents at beginning of period	14,476	51,055	23,539
Cash and equivalents at end of period	$ 17,364	$ 14,476	$ 51,055

The accompanying Notes to Consolidated Financial Statements are an integral part of these statements.

Google, Inc. reported the following cash flows over the three-year period 2007–2009 (dollars in millions).

	2009	2008	2007
Operating cash flows	$9,316	$7,853	$5,775
Investing cash flows	(8,019)	(5,319)	(3,682)
Financing cash flows	233	88	403

Discuss Google's cash management over the three-year period.

HOW THE STATEMENT OF CASH FLOWS CAN BE USED

The statement of cash flows is used primarily to assess performance in two basic areas: (1) a company's ability to generate cash and (2) the effectiveness of a company's cash management. The ability to generate cash is determined by the strength of the company's operating activities as well as its **financial flexibility,** which reflects the company's capacity to borrow, issue equity, and sell nonoperating assets (e.g., investments). During 2009, for example, the drugstore chain Walgreens generated $4.1 billion through its operating activities, which was sufficient to finance $2.8 billion of additional investments, repurchase $279 million of its own stock, pay a $446 million dividend, and maintain its cash balance. On the other hand, the national retailer Saks needed to raise over $156 million in financing to fund its investments of $123 million because cash from operations was a negative $1.5 million.

Effective cash management requires that two competing objectives be balanced. On one hand, cash must be available to meet debts as they come due. That is, **solvency** must be maintained. On the other hand, cash must be invested in productive assets that provide returns. Sources of cash include the sale of inventories and services, borrowings, equity issuances, and the selling of long-term assets. Uses of cash include purchasing and manufacturing inventories, covering selling and administrative costs, making debt interest and principal payments, purchasing long-term assets, purchasing treasury stock, and paying dividends. Effective cash management involves managing these cash sources and uses in a way that provides a high return without bearing too great a risk of insolvency.

Review Figure 14–4 and comment on La-Z-Boy's cash management over the three-year period covering fiscal years 2007, 2008, and 2009.

Analyzing the Statement of Cash Flows

Questions like the following can be answered by referring to the statement of cash flows: Is the company's cash balance increasing or decreasing? What portion of the company's cash is generated through operations, the sale of investments, or the issuance of debt and equity securities? What portions of the company's cash payments go toward supporting operations, capital investments, repayments of debt, purchasing treasury stock, and dividends? In Chapter 5, we discussed cash flow analysis. There we distinguished between operating performance, financial flexibility, and liquidity, and

illustrated how the statement of cash flows can be used to identify cash flow profiles of companies. You may wish to review this material now.

The Importance of Cash from Operating Activities

The amount of cash generated through operating activities is especially important to financial statement users because the successful sale of a company's services or inventories is a prerequisite for a successful business. Also, while cash flows from investing and financing activities tend to vary from one year to the next, operating activities, by definition, are normal and expected to recur. Consequently, positive net cash flows from operations, especially across several periods of time, can indicate financial strength.

It is generally desirable to finance asset purchases and debt payments with cash generated from operations. Companies able to follow such a strategy consistently tend to have higher credit ratings and are generally viewed as financially more stable than those unable to do so. DuPont, for example, one of the ten largest companies in the world with an AAA credit rating, commented in an annual report:

Cash provided by operations was sufficient to finance the company's capital expenditures, repurchase 1,968,000 shares of the company's common stock, reduce borrowings, and pay dividends.

The management of AT&T, a leader in the communications industry, stated:

Strong cash flow from operations permitted us to continue efforts toward increased financial flexibility. We redeemed $830 million of preferred stock and retired $147 million of long-term debt. Our external financing was limited to $343 million. Consequently, for the second consecutive year, we have reduced our utilization of external sources of financing.

In 2008, Swiss chocolate company Nestlé, which uses IFRS, reported net income of 19 billion Swiss francs (CHF) and cash from operations of only 10.8 billion CHF. The prior year the company reported net income of 11.4 billion CHF, and a higher cash from operations of 13.4 billion CHF. Provide reasonable explanations for how the relationship between net income and cash from operations could be so different from one year to the next for a single company.

The items that explain the difference between net income and net cash from operating activities also can be used to assess the quality of reported earnings in a given year. Examine the operating section of La-Z-Boy's 2009 statement of cash flows (Figure 14–4), for example, and note that net cash provided by operating activities exceeds net income by over $173 million. One of the major reasons for this difference is the numerous asset write-downs.

A review of La-Z-Boy's income statement would reveal that net income was reduced by the $60.3 million due to asset write-downs (excluding the restructuring charge), and the disclosure on the statement of cash flows (added back to net income) indicates that the write-downs had no cash impact. That is, net income was reduced by the change, but cash flow was unaffected. Consequently, an analyst might discount the effect of the write-down on net income, concluding that the change represented a one-time effect that signaled little about La-Z-Boy's financial performance in 2009.

Business Credit, a trade journal for analysts, states that financial analysis can be plagued by GAP ("games accountants play") in deriving the earnings number—the so-called sins of accrual accounting. The effect of these actions is to either increase current profits or hide them for a later date. It is important for analysts to understand the effects of these games on cash flows. Explain how understanding these cash flows effects can be useful to analysts.

The Importance of Significant Noncash Transactions

The statement of cash flows includes only those transactions that directly affect cash or cash equivalents. Many important transactions, however, neither increase nor decrease cash and, as a result, are excluded from the face of the statement. For example, the purchase of a long-lived asset in exchange for a long-term note payable can be a significant capital transaction, yet as illustrated by the journal entry below, it has no effect on the cash account.

Equipment (+A)	**20,000**	
Notes Payable (+L)		**20,000**

Purchased equipment financed with a long-term note

Similarly, the acquisition of land in exchange for a note payable, the acquisition of a subsidiary by issuing stock, the payment of a debt with common stock, and the declaration of a dividend are capital transactions that are not found on the statement of cash flows.

These kinds of capital transactions can be very important to a company's financial condition, and the FASB requires in its standard on cash flows that they be described clearly in the footnotes to the financial statements. It is important that such information be accessible to readers who are interested in examining the financing and investing activities of a company. For example, when MCI acquired Satellite Business Systems (SBS) and selected other assets from IBM, MCI issued common stock and signed a note payable. No cash was exchanged in the transaction, and accordingly, neither the acquired assets nor the increases in the common stock and notes payable accounts appeared on MCI's statement of cash flows. However, the transaction was important enough to warrant disclosure, and MCI reported it directly below the statement of cash flows in the following manner:

Acquisition of SBS (in millions):	
Common stock issued to acquire SBS	$ 376
Communications systems acquired	(428)
Other assets acquired	(52)
Current obligations assumed	104
Cash outflow to acquire SBS	$ 0

THE STATEMENT OF CASH FLOWS: ECONOMIC CONSEQUENCES

The economic consequences associated with the statement of cash flows result primarily from investors, creditors, and other interested parties using it to assess the investment potential and creditworthiness of companies and the equity and debt securities that they issue. *Forbes* magazine reported: "a number of stock advisers are basing their

work in part on cash flow . . . an investor who ignores cash flow in picking stocks is being deprived of one of the most valuable tools in an arsenal." Furthermore, many writers have claimed that had investors relied more heavily on cash flow numbers, instead of working capital and the current ratio, famous bankruptcies, like W. T. Grant, Penn Central, Sambo's Restaurants, AM International, and Wickes, might have been foreseen earlier. As one survey found: "The evidence could not be clearer. Investors use the statement of cash flows more, and the income statements less, than previously."[5]

The increasing importance of cash flow information to investors and creditors creates incentives for management to **window dress** the statement of cash flows. Such incentives can be troublesome because in the short run it is relatively easy for management to present a favorable cash position. Delaying payments on short-term payables, for example, can significantly boost the amount of cash provided (used) by operating activities. Selling investments, even if it is not in the shareholders' long-term interests, can increase cash inflows from investing activities, while delaying debt payments and dividends can inflate cash from financing activities.

In 2009, Kyocern, a Japanese electronics manufacturer that uses IFRS, reduced its accounts payable balance by over $784 million. Net cash from operations that year was $988 million. What could Kyocern have done to report an even higher net cash from operations?

Those who use the statement of cash flows must be careful not to place too much importance on the cash flows of a particular period, which can be manipulated. However, such manipulation is much less effective when statements are viewed across several periods because payments that are delayed in one period must normally be paid in the next. For this reason, the FASB requires that cash flow statements from at least the previous three years be disclosed.

From management's standpoint, it is also important to realize that decisions designed to manipulate the disclosures on the statement of cash flows can be counterproductive. While such decisions may improve the appearance of a company's cash position in the current period, they can (1) represent poor business decisions, (2) make the cash position of the company look worse in the future, (3) reduce the credibility of the company and its financial reports in the eyes of investors, creditors, and other interested parties, and (4) if fraudulent, can expose management to future lawsuits. In addition, such manipulations may simply be unethical.

A *Wall Street Journal* article titled "Analysts Increasingly Favor Using Cash Flow over Reported Earnings in Stock Valuations" describes how some analysts are losing faith in the earnings number, choosing instead to rely on various measures of cash flows in the assessments of a company's future performance. They claim that cash flow across time is less variable, less subject to manipulation, and easier to predict. Briefly discuss how cash flow from operations might be easier to predict than net income.

5. Marc J. Epstein and Moses L. Paun, "How Useful Is the Statement of Cash Flows?" *Management Accounting,* July 1992, p. 52.

DERIVING CASH FLOW FROM ACCRUAL FINANCIAL STATEMENTS

In Chapter 4 of this text, we prepared a simple statement of cash flows by focusing on the cash effects of the individual transactions of the period. That is, we prepared the statement from the entries to the cash T-account. This section demonstrates how the statement of cash flows can be prepared when the analysis of individual transactions is either impractical or, in some cases, impossible. We show that the statement can be prepared primarily from the information contained in two balance sheets, the intervening income statement, and the statement of shareholders' equity. This method is followed by most companies, and the resulting statement of cash flows is the same as that prepared from analyzing the entries to the cash T-account. In most cases, however, the method we illustrate here is far more practical. Figure 14–5 contains the December 31, 2011 and 2012, balance sheets of ABC Enterprises and the related income statement and statement of shareholders' equity. Additional information is disclosed in the section that appears below the statements.

In the sections that follow, we prepare a statement of cash flows under both the direct and indirect methods from the information contained in Figure 14–5. Cash provided (used) by operating activities is derived first, followed by the cash provided

FIGURE 14–5

The financial statements of ABC Enterprises

ABC Enterprises, Inc.
Balance Sheets
for December 31, 2011 and 2012

	2012	2011
ASSETS		
Cash	$ 5,900	$ 8,000
Accounts receivable	23,200	12,000
Less: Allowance for doubtful accounts	(1,300)	(1,000)
Inventory	4,000	3,000
Prepaid insurance	1,000	2,000
Land	30,000	20,000
Machinery	6,000	8,000
Less: Accumulated depreciation	(2,500)	(2,000)
Building	30,000	—
Less: Accumulated depreciation	(1,500)	—
Patent	6,000	8,000
Total assets	$100,800	$58,000
LIABILITIES AND SHAREHOLDERS' EQUITY		
Accounts payable	$ 9,000	$12,000
Accrued payables	3,000	1,500
Income taxes payable	200	500
Payments in advance	—	3,000
Dividends payable	3,000	1,000
Notes payable	24,000	25,000
Less: Discount on notes payable	(1,800)	(2,000)
Common stock	42,000	10,000
Additional paid-in capital	19,300	2,000
Retained earnings	2,100	6,000
Less: Treasury stock	—	(1,000)
Total liabilities and shareholders' equity	$100,800	$58,000

ABC Enterprises, Inc.
Income statement
for December 31, 2012

Sales		$ 32,000
Fees earned		3,000
Cost of goods sold		(11,000)
Gross profit		$ 24,000
Operating expenses:		
Miscellaneous expenses	$11,000	
Insurance expense	1,000	
Bad debt expense	1,100	
Depreciation expense (machinery)	1,000	
Depreciation expense (building)	1,500	
Amortization of patent	2,000	17,600
Net operating income		$ 6,400
Nonoperating revenues and expenses:		
Loss on sale of machinery	$ 100	
Interest expense	2,000	2,100
Net income from continuing operations		
before taxes		$ 4,300
Less: Income tax expense		1,200
Net income		$ 3,100

ABC Enterprises, Inc.
Statement of Shareholders' Equity
for the Year Ended December 31, 2012

	Common Stock	Additional Paid-In Capital	Retained Earnings	Treasury Stock	Total
Beginning balance	$10,000	$ 2,000	$6,000	$(1,000)	$17,000
Stock issuance for building	20,000	10,000			30,000
Stock issuance for cash	10,000	5,000			15,000
Net income			3,100		3,100
Dividends					
Cash			(3,000)		(3,000)
Stock	2,000	2,000	(4,000)		
Treasury stock reissuance		300		1,000	1,300
Ending balance	$42,000	$19,300	$2,100	0	$63,400

Additional information:
1. Two thousand shares of common stock ($10 par; $15 fair market value) were issued for a building early in 2012.
2. A 5 percent stock dividend on 4,000 outstanding shares was distributed late in 2012 when the fair market value of the $10 par value stock was $20 per share.
3. Treasury stock that was originally purchased for $1,000 was reissued for $1,300.

(used) by investing activities, and cash provided (used) by financing activities. In the figures that appear throughout these sections, italics are used to indicate dollar amounts taken directly from the information in Figure 14–5.

Cash Provided (Used) by Operating Activities

This section analyzes the cash flows associated with each income statement account: sales and bad debt expense, fees earned, cost of goods sold, miscellaneous expenses, insurance expense, depreciation of machinery and of building, amortization of patent, loss on sale of machinery, interest expense, and income tax expense.

SALES AND BAD DEBT EXPENSE

The cash inflow from sales can be determined by analyzing the changes in accounts receivable and allowance for doubtful accounts. Refer to the T-accounts and related journal entries in Figure 14–6.

FIGURE 14–6   Determining cash inflow from sales

Sales	Accounts Receivable	Allowance for Doubtful Accounts	Bad Debt Expense

Effect on Accounts:

Transactions	Accounts	Debit (Net)	Credit (Net)
(1)	Accounts Receivable	32,000	
	Sales		32,000
(2)	Bad Debt Expense	1,100	
	Allowance for Doubtful Accounts		1,100
(3)	Allowance for Doubtful Accounts	800	
	Accounts Receivable		800
(4)	Cash	20,000	
	Accounts Receivable		20,000

Cash collections from sales: $20,000

The beginning and ending balances in accounts receivable and the allowance for doubtful accounts appear on the balance sheets in Figure 14–5. We assume that all sales were made on account, and therefore, $32,000 (see income statement) was debited to accounts receivable during the year.[6] The $1,100 bad debt expense (see income

---

6. In this illustration we assume that all sales were made on account. Similarly, when analyzing future accounts (e.g., fees earned, inventory purchases, miscellaneous expenses), we make similar assumptions. These assumptions simplify the analysis, but they are not necessary. Any of a number of reasonable assumptions could be made, leading to the exact same result.

statement) was credited to allowance for doubtful accounts at year-end, which (when the beginning and ending balances in the allowance account are considered) implies that uncollectibles in the amount of $800 must have been written off and credited to accounts receivable. Therefore, an additional credit of $20,000 to accounts receivable must have been entered during the year. The corresponding debit represents cash receipts on outstanding accounts during the year.

FEES EARNED

The cash inflow related to fees earned can be determined by analyzing the change in the payments in advance account. Refer to Figure 14–7.

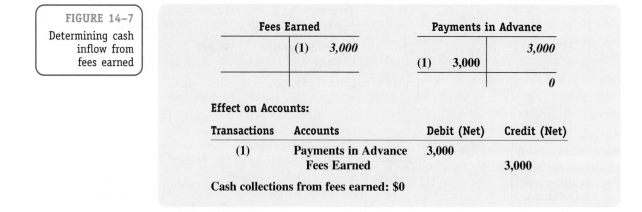

FIGURE 14–7
Determining cash inflow from fees earned

The beginning ($3,000) and ending ($0) balances in the payments in advance account appear on the balance sheets in Figure 14–5. The recognition of $3,000 in fees earned (see income statement) involved a $3,000 debit to payments in advance. This entry accounts for the entire change in the payments in advance account, indicating that no cash inflow was associated with fees earned.

COST OF GOODS SOLD

The cash outflow associated with cost of goods sold can be determined by analyzing the changes in the inventory and accounts payable accounts. Refer to Figure 14–8.

The beginning and ending balances in inventory and accounts payable appear on the balance sheets in Figure 14–5. The $11,000 debit to cost of goods sold (see income statement) was credited to inventory, which (when the beginning and ending balances in the inventory account are considered) implies that inventory purchases of $12,000 must have been made during the year. Assuming that all inventory purchases were made on account, $12,000 must have been credited to accounts payable. Considering the beginning and ending balances in accounts payable, an additional debit of $15,000 must have been recognized during the year. The corresponding credit represents cash payments of $15,000 on accounts payable during the year.

MISCELLANEOUS EXPENSES

The cash outflow related to miscellaneous expenses can be determined by analyzing the change in the accrued payables account. Refer to Figure 14–9.

The beginning ($1,500) and ending ($3,000) balances in accrued payables appear on the balance sheets in Figure 14–5. Assuming that all miscellaneous expenses were

FIGURE 14-8

Determining cash outflow from inventory purchases

Cost of Goods Sold			Inventory			Accounts Payable		
(1)	11,000		3,000					12,000
				(1)	11,000		(2)	12,000
		(2)	12,000			(3) 15,000		
			4,000					9,000

Effect on Accounts:

Transactions	Accounts	Debit (Net)	Credit (Net)
(1)	Cost of Goods Sold	11,000	
	Inventory		11,000
(2)	Inventory	12,000	
	Accounts Payable		12,000
(3)	Accounts Payable	15,000	
	Cash		15,000

Cash paid to suppliers: $15,000

FIGURE 14-9

Determining cash outflow from miscellaneous expenses

Miscellaneous Expenses			Accrued Payables		
(1)	11,000				1,500
				(1)	11,000
			(2) 9,500		
					3,000

Effect on Accounts:

Transactions	Accounts	Debit (Net)	Credit (Net)
(1)	Miscellaneous Expenses	11,000	
	Accrued Payables		11,000
(2)	Accrued Payables	9,500	
	Cash		9,500

Cash paid for miscellaneous expenses: $9,500

accrued, the debit of $11,000 to miscellaneous expenses (see income statement) must have involved an $11,000 credit to accrued payables. Considering the beginning and ending balances in accrued payables, a $9,500 debit must have been entered in the account. The corresponding credit represents cash payments on accrued payables.

INSURANCE EXPENSE

The cash outflow related to insurance expense can be determined by analyzing the change in the prepaid insurance account. Refer to Figure 14–10.

The beginning ($2,000) and ending ($1,000) balances in prepaid insurance appear on the balance sheets in Figure 14–5. The debit of $1,000 to insurance expense (see income statement) involved a $1,000 credit to prepaid insurance. This entry accounts for the entire change in the prepaid insurance account, indicating that no cash was paid for insurance during the year.

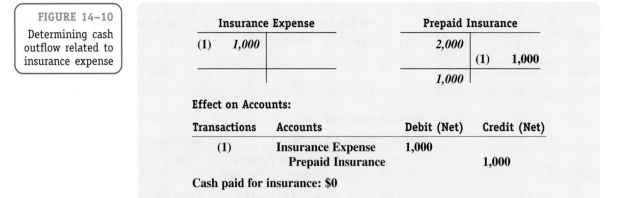

FIGURE 14–10
Determining cash
outflow related to
insurance expense

Insurance Expense		Prepaid Insurance	
(1) *1,000*		*2,000*	
			(1) *1,000*
		1,000	

Effect on Accounts:

Transactions	Accounts	Debit (Net)	Credit (Net)
(1)	Insurance Expense	1,000	
	Prepaid Insurance		1,000

Cash paid for insurance: $0

DEPRECIATION OF MACHINERY, DEPRECIATION OF BUILDING, AMORTIZATION OF PATENT, AND LOSS ON SALE OF MACHINERY

There are no operating cash effects associated with depreciation, amortization, or book gains and losses.

INTEREST EXPENSE

The cash outflow related to interest expense can be determined by analyzing the change in the discount on notes payable account. Refer to Figure 14–11.

FIGURE 14–11
Determining cash
outflow related to
interest expense

Interest Expense		Discount on Notes Payable	
(1) *2,000*		*2,000*	
			(1) *200*
		1,800	

Effect on Accounts:

Transactions	Accounts	Debit (Net)	Credit (Net)
(1)	Interest Expense	2,000	
	Discount on Notes Payable		200
	Cash		1,800

Cash paid for interest: $1,800

The beginning ($2,000) and ending ($1,800) balances in the discount on notes payable account appear on the balance sheets in Figure 14–5. The $200 difference between the beginning and ending balances indicates that the discount was amortized in the amount of $200 during the year. Discounts are amortized into interest expense, as illustrated in Figure 14–11. Thus, $1,800 cash must have been paid for interest during the year.

INCOME TAX EXPENSE

The cash outflow related to income tax expense can be determined by analyzing the changes in the income tax payable account. Refer to Figure 14–12.

The beginning ($500) and ending ($200) balances in the income tax payable account appear on the balance sheets in Figure 14–5. The debit of $1,200 to income tax expense (see income statement), assuming that income taxes were accrued, involved a $1,200 credit to income tax payable. Considering the beginning and ending balances in

Income Tax Expense			Income Tax Payable		
(1)	1,200				500
				(1)	1,200
			(2)	1,500	
					200

Effect on Accounts:

Transactions	Accounts	Debit (Net)	Credit (Net)
(1)	Income Tax Expense	1,200	
	Income Tax Payable		1,200
(2)	Income Tax Payable	1,500	
	Cash		1,500

Cash paid for income taxes: $1,500

income tax payable, $1,500 must have been debited to the account during the year. The corresponding credit represents cash payments for income taxes.

Cash Provided (Used) by Investing Activities

In this section, we determine the cash inflows and outflows associated with investing activities by analyzing changes in the long-lived asset accounts. Specifically, we analyze the $10,000 increase in the land account and the $2,000 decrease in the machinery account. The building was acquired in exchange for stock and involved no cash exchange, while the $2,000 decrease in the patent account reflects amortization, which also involved no cash receipt or payment.

PURCHASE OF LAND

The $10,000 increase in the land account (see Figure 14–5) indicates that land was acquired during the period. Since there is no indication that noncash assets were exchanged for the land or a liability was credited, we assume that the land was purchased for a $10,000 cash payment. Refer to Figure 14–13.

SALE OF MACHINERY

The cash inflow from the sale of machinery can be determined by using the available information to reconstruct the journal entry that recorded the transaction. Refer to Figure 14–14.

Land		
	20,000	
(1)	10,000	
	30,000	

Effect on Accounts:

Transactions	Accounts	Debit (Net)	Credit (Net)
(1)	Land	10,000	
	Cash		10,000

Cash payment for land: $10,000

FIGURE 14-14   Determining cash inflow from sale of machinery

Machinery	Accumulated Depreciation	Loss on Sale of Machinery	Depreciation Expense
8,000		2,000	(2) 100	(1) 1,000
(2) 2,000	(1) 1,000		
	(2) 500		
6,000	2,500		

Effect on Accounts:

Transactions	Accounts	Debit (Net)	Credit (Net)
(1)	Depreciation Expense	1,000	
	Accumulated Depreciation		1,000
(2)	Cash	1,400	
	Accumulated Depreciation	500	
	Loss on Sale of Machinery	100	
	Machinery		2,000

Cash receipt for sale of machinery: $1,400

The beginning and ending balances in the machinery and accumulated depreciation accounts can be found on the balance sheets in Figure 14–5. Depreciation expense of $1,000 on the machinery (see income statement) was recognized during the period; accordingly, $1,000 must have been credited to accumulated depreciation. The accumulated depreciation account, therefore, must have been debited for $500 when the machine was sold. Given the $100 loss on the sale (see income statement), the $2,000 reduction in the machinery account, and the $500 debit to accumulated depreciation, the journal entry to record the sale can be reconstructed and the amount of cash received ($1,400) can be determined.

Cash Provided (Used) by Financing Activities

In this section, we determine the cash inflows and outflows associated with financing activities by analyzing changes in the long-term liability and shareholders' equity accounts. Specifically, we analyze the $1,000 decrease in the notes payable account, the increase in the common stock and additional paid-in capital accounts, the issuance of treasury stock for $1,300, and the declaration of a $3,000 cash dividend.

PRINCIPAL PAYMENT ON NOTES PAYABLE

We have no indication that the $1,000 decrease in the notes payable account (see Figure 14–5) was due to anything other than the payment of cash. Refer to Figure 14–15.

ISSUANCE OF COMMON STOCK AND TREASURY STOCK

The cash inflows from the issuance of common stock and treasury stock can be determined by analyzing the changes in the common stock, additional paid-in capital, and

FIGURE 14–15
Determining cash
outflow from
payments
on notes

Notes Payable

			25,000
(1)	1,000		
			24,000

Effect on Accounts:

Transactions	Accounts	Debit (Net)	Credit (Net)
(1)	Notes Payable	1,000	
	Cash		1,000

Cash payment of notes payable: $1,000

treasury stock accounts. Note that the statement of shareholders' equity and the "additional information" section of Figure 14–5 indicate that a building was acquired for common stock, a stock dividend was distributed, and treasury stock was sold for $1,300. Refer to Figure 14–16.

FIGURE 14–16
Determining cash
inflow from
stock issuances

Building

0	
(1) 30,000	
30,000	

Treasury Stock

1,000			
	(3)	1,000	
0			

Stock Dividend

(2)	*4,000*	

Common Stock

		10,000
(1)	20,000	
(2)	2,000	
(4)	10,000	
		42,000

Additional Paid-In Capital

		2,000
(1)	10,000	
(2)	2,000	
(3)	300	
(4)	5,000	
		19,300

Effect on Accounts:

Transactions	Accounts	Debit (Net)	Credit (Net)
(1)	Building	30,000	
	Common Stock		20,000
	Additional Paid-In Capital		10,000
(2)	Stock Dividend	4,000	
	Common Stock		2,000
	Additional Paid-In Capital		2,000
(3)	Cash	1,300	
	Treasury Stock		1,000
	Additional Paid-In Capital		300
(4)	Cash	15,000	
	Common Stock		10,000
	Additional Paid-In Capital		5,000

Cash receipts from issuance of treasury stock: $1,300
Cash receipts from issuance of common stock: $15,000

The beginning and ending balances in common stock, additional paid-in capital, and treasury stock appear on the balance sheets and the statement of shareholders' equity in Figure 14–5. The purchase of the $30,000 building increased common stock and additional paid-in capital by $20,000 and $10,000, respectively. Common stock and additional paid-in capital each increased by $2,000 when the $4,000 stock dividend was distributed. Additional paid-in capital increased by $300 when the treasury stock was issued for $1,300 cash, which was greater than its $1,000 cost. The additional information that follows the financial statement in Figure 14–5 describes these three transactions. Given the ending balances in common stock and additional paid-in capital, there must have been a stock issuance for cash in the amount of $15,000 during the year.

CASH DIVIDENDS

The cash dividend payment can be determined by analyzing the changes in the dividends payable account. Refer to Figure 14–17.

The beginning ($1,000) and ending ($3,000) balances in the dividends payable account appear on the balance sheets in Figure 14–5. The declaration of the $3,000 cash dividend (see statement of shareholders' equity) created a $3,000 dividend payable liability. Therefore, $1,000 must have been debited to dividends payable during the year, which represents cash payments to the shareholders.

FIGURE 14–17
Determining cash outflow from dividend payments

	Cash Dividends		Dividends Payable		
(1)	*3,000*				*1,000*
			(2)	*1,000*	(1) *3,000*
					3,000

Effect on Accounts:

Transactions	Accounts	Debit (Net)	Credit (Net)
(1)	Cash Dividends	3,000	
	Dividends Payable		3,000
(2)	Dividends Payable	1,000	
	Cash		1,000

Cash payment for dividends: $1,000

THE COMPLETE STATEMENT OF CASH FLOWS

We have now derived the cash flows of the period and can prepare the statement of cash flows. The following sections cover the direct method and the indirect method.

The Direct Method

A statement of cash flows prepared under the direct method is provided in Figure 14–18. Note that the dollar amounts are identical to the cash flows derived in the previous section.

FIGURE 14–18

Statement of cash
flows for
ABC Enterprises:
Direct method

ABC Enterprises, Inc.
Statement of Cash Flows
for the Year Ended December 31, 2012

Operating activities:		
Cash collections from sales and accounts receivable	$ 20,000	
Cash paid to suppliers	(15,000)	
Cash paid on miscellaneous expenses	(9,500)	
Cash paid for interest	(1,800)	
Cash paid for income taxes	(1,500)	
Net cash provided (used) by operating activities		$(7,800)
Investing activities:		
Purchase of land	$(10,000)	
Sale of machinery	1,400	
Net cash provided (used) by investing activities		(8,600)
Financing activities:		
Proceeds from issuing common stock	$ 15,000	
Proceeds from sale of treasury stock	1,300	
Cash dividends	(1,000)	
Principal payment on outstanding note payable	(1,000)	
Net cash provided (used) by financing activities		14,300
Net increase (decrease) in cash balance		$(2,100)
Beginning cash balance		8,000
Ending cash balance		$ 5,900

Note that cash outflows due to interest are disclosed in the operating section under U.S. GAAP. Under IFRS, firms can choose to disclose interest in the operating or financing sections.

The Indirect Method

The statement of cash flows under the indirect method is exactly the same as the direct method, except for the presentation of the operating section and the derivation of net cash provided (used) by operating activities. The operating section presented under the indirect method for ABC Enterprises, Inc. is illustrated in Figure 14–19. Note first that the dollar amount of net cash provided (used) by operating activities is the same (−$7,800) whether the direct or the indirect method is used. The difference is in the way in which the amount is computed. Under the indirect method, net cash provided by operating activities (−$7,800) is computed by adjusting net income ($3,100), which appears on the income statement, for the timing difference between operating accruals and cash flows. As indicated earlier in this chapter, these adjustments are classified into two categories: (1) noncash charges to noncurrent accounts (e.g., depreciation, amortization, and book gains and losses) and (2) changes in the current noncash accounts (e.g., accounts receivable, inventory, accounts payable, income tax and miscellaneous accruals, payments in advance, and prepaid insurance), except for short-term

FIGURE 14–19

Statement of
cash flows:
Indirect method

ABC Enterprises, Inc.
Statement of Cash Flows
for the Year Ended December 31, 2012

Operating activities:		
Net income	$ 3,100	
Noncash charges to noncurrent accounts:		
Depreciation of machinery	1,000	
Depreciation of building	1,500	
Amortization of patent	2,000	
Loss on sale of machinery	100	
Decrease in discount on notes payable	200	
Changes in current noncash accounts:		
Increase in net accounts receivable	(10,900)	
Increase in inventory	(1,000)	
Decrease in accounts payable	(3,000)	
Increase in accrued payables and taxes payable	1,200	
Decrease in payments in advance	(3,000)	
Decrease in prepaid insurance	1,000	
Net cash provided (used) by operating activities		$(7,800)

investments and dividends payable, which are reflected in the investing and financing sections, respectively.

The first category of adjustments, "noncash charges to noncurrent accounts," affected net income but did not affect cash flows. Depreciation and amortization charges, for example, simultaneously reduced the dollar amounts of long-lived assets and created expenses, which reduced net income. The entries to record depreciation and amortization, however, do not reduce cash. Consequently, when deriving cash flows from net income, as is done under the indirect method, depreciation and amortization charges are added back. Similarly, gains and losses on the disposal of long-lived assets do not affect operating cash flows. Note in Figure 14–19 that the loss on sale of machinery is added back in the computation of net cash provided (used) by operating activities. Such transactions often involve cash flows, but these cash flows are reflected in the investing—instead of the operating—section of the statement of cash flows. Other common examples, where changes in non-current assets affect net income—but not cash flow—include long-term investments accounted for under the equity method, deferred income taxes, and the amortization of discounts and premiums on long-term debt.

Kyocern, the Japanese electronics manufacturer which uses IFRS, reports the following four items in the operating section of its 2009 statement of cash flows (dollars in millions):

- Provision for doubtful accounts +$6.8
- Inventory write-downs +$88
- Gains on sales of property −$84
- Equity earnings −$65

Explain why.

FIGURE 14–20

Explaining current adjustments to net income in the calculation of net cash provided (used) by operating activities

	Current Assets	Current Liabilities
Increase	**Subtract from Accrual Numbers**	**Add to Accrual Numbers**
Decrease	**Add to Accrual Numbers**	**Subtract from Accrual Numbers**

One way to better understand the adjustments included in the second category, "changes in current noncash accounts," is to refer to Figure 14–20. Here, four possible combinations are illustrated. Increases (decreases) in current assets and decreases (increases) in current liabilities are subtracted from (added to) net income in the computation of net cash provided (used) by operating activities. The logic is fairly straightforward. Increases in accounts receivable, for example, must mean that revenues are being recognized faster than cash is being collected from customers—that is, net income, not backed by cash receipts, is being recorded. Accordingly, an increase in accounts receivable is subtracted from net income in the calculation of net cash provided (used) by operating activities. Similarly, growing current payables must mean that expenses are being recognized faster than cash is being paid. Net income must be adjusted upward, therefore, in the computation of net cash provided (used) by operating activities. Note how Figure 14–20 explains each of the adjustments under the heading "changes in current noncash accounts."

That same year, Kyocern adds the decrease in accounts receivable, and subtracts the decrease in short-term payables in the operating section. Why?

ANALYZING THE STATEMENT OF CASH FLOWS: AN APPLICATION

Now that the statement of cash flows has been prepared, we can use it to assess ABC Enterprises' cash management policies. ABC's cash position decreased (from $8,000 to $5,900) during 2012. For the most part, this decrease was caused by investing and operating activities, which required $8,600 and $7,800, respectively. Financing activities, which provided $14,300, almost made up for these cash deficits. While the exact sources and uses of cash in each of these three areas should be examined, the $7,800 cash deficit due to operating activities appears to be the most troublesome and definitely deserves special attention.

Summarizing the Cash Effects of Operating Transactions

ABC's income statement shows that net income for 2012 totaled $3,100. At the same time, the operations that produced net income reduced the cash balance by $7,800. Interestingly, these two measures produced significantly different numbers that are used to evaluate the same (operating) activities.

The statement of cash flows under the indirect method (Figure 14–19) explains the difference between net income and cash provided (used) by operations. Four items appear to be the most important: (1) the $10,900 buildup in net accounts receivable, (2) the $3,000 decrease in accounts payable, (3) the $3,000 decrease in payments in advance, and (4) the depreciation and amortization of the long-lived assets.

The net accounts receivable buildup increased net income but not cash. This could indicate aggressive revenue recognition policies. Coupled with the decrease in accounts payable, it indicates that ABC paid its suppliers more quickly than it received payments from its customers. Such a strategy can give rise to cash flow problems. The $3,000 decrease in payments in advance was reflected in revenues (and thus net income) but produced no cash. Presumably, the $3,000 was received some time before December 31, 2011. The depreciation and amortization of long-lived assets reduced net income by a total dollar amount of $4,500 ($1,000 + $1,500 + $2,000) but required no cash.

Keep in mind also that the management of ABC could have manipulated cash provided (used) by operating activities. For example, had management chosen to defer cash payment on accounts payable, cash provided (used) by operating activities would have been considerably higher. This particular decision would have had no effect on net income.

> In the operating section of its 2008 statement of cash flows, McDonald's reported three items: depreciation and amortization (+$1.2 billion), provision for impairment charges (+$6 million), and gains on sales of investments (−$160 million). Explain why these items are added to or subtracted from net income in the computation of net cash provided by operations.

Summarizing the Cash Effect of Investing and Financing Transactions

ABC Enterprises relied heavily on stock issuances for its cash needs during 2012. The statement of cash flows shows that common stock was issued for cash in the amount of $15,000 and that the sale of treasury stock produced $1,300. Both issuances diluted ABC's outstanding stock. The sale of a piece of machinery produced $1,400.

The cash produced by the financing and investing sources was used primarily to cover the cash deficit from operating activities (−$7,800) and to purchase land ($10,000). Dividend and principal payments on outstanding loans amounted to $1,000 each.

Note that ABC Enterprises issued 2,000 shares of common stock, valued at $15 each, for a building (see Figure 14–5). While this transaction does not affect ABC's cash balance and does not appear on the statement of cash flows, it is nonetheless very important and should be reported in the footnotes to the financial statements. Apparently, ABC relied even more heavily on equity issuances and purchased more long-term assets than the statement of cash flows indicates.

> During 2008, Safeguard Scientifics, Inc. reported a loss of $52 million, yet boosted its investments by over $14 million. Explain how the company must have financed these investments and indicate where one could find this information on the financial statements.

Two Additional Observations

Now that we have covered the nature, use, and preparation of the statement of cash flows, two additional observations might be helpful. First, the statement of cash flows provides very little new information over and above that provided by the balance sheet, income statement, and statement of shareholders' equity. After all, we just illustrated how the statement can be derived from these statements. Its significant value comes from the way in which it is organized and its focus on cash. It is the only statement that reports on the operating, investing, and financing activities of a business from a cash perspective, and many believe that cash management is a key to business success. Professor Loyd Heath, whose writings did much to motivate the development of the statement of cash flows, describes it as being "complementary to the income statement and balance sheet," and the project manager for the FASB once said that "cash flow is one of the best measures of corporate liquidity." A well-known article published in the *Wall Street Journal,* titled "Why Cash Is King in the Current Climate," noted that, during economic downturns, "companies with high amounts of cash relative to debt are likely to be coveted by investors as economic growth turns increasingly sluggish. Cash may be a new gauge of value in the stock market."

A second observation is that normally one cannot explain the adjustments in the operating section of the statement of cash flows (indirect method) of a major U.S. company by computing the changes in the current accounts on its balance sheet. For example, the 2008 statement of cash flows of SUPERVALU reported an accounts receivable decrease of about $68 million. The change computed from the 2007 and 2008 balance sheets, however, indicated a decrease of approximately $78 million. The difference can be explained by the consolidation process. When a company such as SUPERVALU acquires another company, the cash decrease is reflected in the investing section—not the operating section—of the statement of cash flows. When the accounts are consolidated at the end of the year, the current assets and liabilities of the acquired company are added to those of the parent. The result is an inconsistency. In the SUPERVALU case, the $78 million decrease in accounts receivable indicated on the balance sheet reflects revenues that are being recognized slower than cash is being collected, but it also reflects receivables that have been purchased in other companies. The inconsistency arises because the cash outflows associated with these purchases are reflected in the investing section, rather than the operating section, of the statement of cash flows.

During 2008, Motorola sold off businesses for $93 million, and purchased businesses for $282 million. Would you expect the change in receivables indicated on the statement of cash flows to be greater than or less than the change in receivables computed from the 2007 and 2008 balance sheets? Why?

INTERNATIONAL PERSPECTIVE: THE STATEMENT OF CASH FLOWS

The importance of debt capital to many foreign companies places a premium on cash flow information, which banks and other lenders use to assess solvency. As indicated earlier, international financial reporting standards (IFRS) require a statement of cash flows in the same format as required by U.S. GAAP.

Interpreting the statement of cash flows for a multinational company can be tricky. Multinational companies, based in the United States and elsewhere, conduct operations in a variety of countries, many of which use different currencies. A U.S. corporation, for

example, may sell goods or services to a customer in France, giving rise to a receivable expressed in euros. When the value of the euro changes relative to that of the U.S. dollar, the value of the receivable on the U.S. company's balance sheet must be restated, which, in turn, gives rise to a gain or loss reported on the income statement.

Foreign currency exchange gains and losses, however, involve no cash flow. Consequently, when the statement of cash flows is prepared under the indirect method, an adjustment must be made to net income. Partly because these adjustments are becoming more and more significant, accounting pronouncements now require that they be disclosed separately at the bottom of the statement, immediately before "net increase (decrease) in cash and cash equivalents."

Refer to Figure 14–4, the statement of cash flows of La-Z-Boy, and find the adjustment for foreign currency exchange rate changes. What are the dollar amounts? Are they negative or positive, and what do they indicate?

REVIEW PROBLEM

Figure 14–21 contains balance sheets (December 31, 2011 and 2012) for XYZ Enterprises and the intervening income statement. Following these statements are several selected pieces of information that more completely describe the activity of XYZ during 2012. The two forms of the statement of cash flows are contained in Figures 14–22 (direct method) and 14–23 (indirect method). We have included relevant calculations on the statements to explain how the numbers were derived. Examine each cash flow statement closely, and trace the calculations back to the original financial statements and information given in Figure 14–21.

FIGURE 14–21

Financial statements for XYZ Enterprises

XYZ Enterprises
Balance Sheets
for December 31, 2011 and 2012

	2012	2011
ASSETS		
Cash	$ 3,000	$ 2,500
Accounts receivable	4,500	4,000
Inventory	10,500	8,000
Prepaid rent	3,000	2,000
Fixed assets	40,000	35,000
Less: Accumulated depreciation	(12,000)	(10,000)
Patent	8,000	9,000
Total assets	$57,000	$ 50,500
LIABILITIES AND SHAREHOLDERS' EQUITY		
Accounts payable	$ 6,500	$ 3,000
Other current payables	7,000	10,000
Bonds payable	19,000	19,000
Plus: Premium on bonds payable	2,500	3,000
Common stock	15,000	10,000
Additional paid-in capital	4,000	3,000
Retained earnings	3,000	2,500
Total liabilities and shareholders' equity	$57,000	$ 50,500

XYZ Enterprises
Income Statement
for the Year Ended Dec. 31, 2012

Sales	$55,000
Less: Cost of goods sold	35,000
Gross profit	$20,000
Rent expense	(2,000)
Interest expense	(2,000)
Miscellaneous expense	(9,000)
Depreciation of fixed assets	(5,000)
Amortization of patent	(1,000)
Gain on sale of machinery	1,000
Net income	$ 2,000

FIGURE 14–22   Statement of cash flows for XYZ Enterprises: Direct method

XYZ Enterprises
Statement of Cash Flows
for the Year Ended December 31, 2012

OPERATING ACTIVITIES:

INCOME STATEMENT		ADJUSTMENT/EXPLANATION	OPERATING CASH FLOWS	
Sales	$55,000	(500) [increase in accounts receivable]	$54,500	
COGS	(35,000)	(2,500) [increase in inventory]		
		+3,500 [increase in accounts payable]	(34,000)	
Rent	(2,000)	(1,000) [increase in prepaid rent]	(3,000)	
Interest	(2,000)	(500) [decrease in premium]	(2,500)	
Misc.	(9,000)	(3,000) [decrease in other current payables]	(12,000)	
Depreciation	(5,000)	[no cash effect]	0	
Amortization	(1,000)	[no cash effect]	0	
Gain	1,000	[no cash effect]	0	
Net income	$ 2,000	Net cash from operations		$3,000
INVESTING ACTIVITIES:				
Sale of machinery		[see note below]	$ 3,000	
Purchase of machinery		[see note below]	(10,000)	
Net cash provided (used) by investing activities				(7,000)
FINANCING ACTIVITIES:				
Issue of common stock		[increase in common stock and APIC]	$ 6,000	
Cash dividends		[see change in retained earnings		
		plus net income]	(1,500)	
Net cash provided (used) by financing activities				4,500
Increase (decrease) in cash balance				$ 500
Beginning cash balance				2,500
Ending cash balance				$3,000

(Continued)

NOTE:

		COST OF FIXED ASSETS	**ACCUMULATED DEPRECIATION**	
Beginning balance		$35,000		$10,000
Plus: Increases	(purchases)	10,000	(depreciation expense)	5,000
Less: Decreases	(sales)	(5,000)	(sold machinery)	(3,000)
Ending balance		$40,000		$12,000

Cash (+A)	3,000	
Accumulated Depreciation (+A)	3,000	
Machinery (−A)		5,000
Gain on Sale of Machinery (Ga, +RE)		1,000

Additional information

1. Purchased $3,000 of prepaid rent.
2. Sold a piece of machinery (cost: $5,000; accumulated depreciation: $3,000) for $3,000 cash. Purchased additional machinery for $10,000 cash.
3. Paid annual interest of $2,500 on note payable.
4. Issued 500 shares of $10 par value common stock for $12 per share.

FIGURE 14–23

Statement of cash flows for XYZ Enterprises: Indirect method

XYZ Enterprises
Statement of Cash Flows
for the Year Ended December 31, 2012

OPERATING ACTIVITIES:		
Net income	$ 2,000	
Noncash charges to noncurrent accounts:		
Depreciation of fixed assets	5,000	
Amortization of patent	1,000	
Gain on sale of machinery	(1,000)	
Decreases in premium	(500)	
Changes in current accounts other than cash:		
Increase in accounts receivable	(500)	
Increase in inventory	(2,500)	
Increase in prepaid rent	(1,000)	
Decrease in other payables	(3,000)	
Increase in accounts payable	3,500	
Cash provided (used) by operating activities		$3,000
INVESTING ACTIVITIES:		
Sale of machinery	$ 3,000	
Purchase of machinery	(10,000)	
Cash provided (used) by investing activities		(7,000)
FINANCING ACTIVITIES:		
Issue of common stock	$ 6,000	
Cash dividends	(1,500)	
Net cash provided (used) by financing activities		4,500
Net increase (decrease) in cash balance		$ 500
Beginning cash balance		2,500
Ending cash balance		$3,000

SUMMARY OF KEY POINTS

 The structure and format of the statement of cash flows.

The statement of cash flows explains the change in a company's cash account from one accounting period to the next. It is divided into three sections: (1) cash provided (used) by operating activities, (2) cash provided (used) by investing activities, and (3) cash provided (used) by financing activities. Each of these sections contains the cash inflows and outflows of the period that were associated with the indicated activity.

Cash flows from operating, investing, and financing activities.

Cash flows from operating activities include those cash inflows and outflows associated directly with the acquisition and sale of a company's inventories and services. Such activities include the cash receipts from sales and accounts receivable, as well as cash payments from the purchase of inventories, payments on accounts payable, selling and administrative expenses, and interest and taxes. The sale or purchase of inventory on account is an operating transaction that does not appear on the statement of cash flows.

Cash flows from investing activities include the cash inflows and outflows associated with the purchase and sale of a company's noncurrent assets. Cash activities include the cash effects from the purchase and sale of long-term investments, long-lived assets, and intangible assets.

Cash flows from financing activities include cash inflows and outflows associated with a company's two sources of outside capital: liabilities and contributed capital. Such activities include the cash inflows associated with borrowings and equity issuances as well as the cash outflows associated with debt repayment, treasury stock purchases, and dividends.

How the statement of cash flows complements the other financial statements and how it can be used by those interested in the financial condition of a company.

While the income statement provides a summary of a company's operating transactions on an accrual basis, and the balance sheet represents the accumulated accruals of the company's operating, investing, and financing transactions as of a particular point in time, neither statement indicates much about the cash effects of the company's operating, investing, and financing activities. The statement of cash flows is designed to fill this void by summarizing the cash effects of the company's operating, investing, and financing transactions.

The statement of cash flows is used primarily to evaluate a company's ability to generate cash (i.e., financial flexibility) as well as the effectiveness of its cash management policies. Financial flexibility reflects a company's ability to generate cash through operations, borrowings, issuing equity, or selling noncurrent assets. Effective cash management involves investing cash to provide a high rate of return while maintaining enough cash to meet debts as they come due (i.e., solvency). The statement of cash flows is helpful to this evaluation in three interrelated ways: (1) it explains the change in the cash balance, (2) it summarizes the cash effects of operating transactions, and (3) it summarizes the cash effects of capital (investing and financing) transactions.

Important investing and financing transactions that do not appear on the statement of cash flows and how they are reported.

The statement of cash flows includes only those transactions that either increase or decrease the cash account. Many important operating and capital transactions do not affect the cash account and are therefore excluded from the statement. For example, the purchase of machinery in exchange for a long-term note payable, the acquisition of land or the payment of a debt with capital stock, and the declaration of a dividend are all capital transactions that have no effect on the cash account and are therefore excluded from the statement.

The FASB requires that capital transactions that do not affect the cash account be described clearly in the footnotes to the financial statements. No special disclosures are required for operating transactions that do not affect the cash account, because the effects of such transactions can be inferred from the reconciliation of net income to net cash provided (used) by operating activities.

Economic consequences associated with the statement of cash flows.

The economic consequences associated with the statement of cash flows occur when investors, creditors, and other interested parties use it to assess the investment potential and creditworthiness of companies and the equity and debt securities they issue. The rising importance of cash flow information to report users creates incentives for managers to "window dress" the statement of cash flows. Such incentives can present problems, because in the short run, it is relatively easy for management to present a favorable cash position. Such manipulation is much less effective, however, when statements are viewed across several periods, because payments delayed in one period must normally be paid in the next. For this reason, the FASB requires that cash flow statements from at least the previous three years be disclosed in the financial report.

● *Preparing a statement of cash flows from the information contained in two balance sheets, an income statement, and a statement of shareholders' equity.*

One can prepare the statement of cash flows, under either the direct or indirect method, by reconstructing the T-account for each balance sheet account, posting the transactions that are reflected on the income statement and statement of shareholders' equity, and deriving the related cash flows.

KEY TERMS

Note: Definitions for these terms are provided in the glossary at the end of this text.

Cash equivalents (p. 641)
Direct method (p. 642)
Financial flexibility (p. 646)
Financing activities (p. 644)
Indirect method (p. 642)

Investing activities (p. 644)
Operating activities (p. 642)
Solvency (p. 646)
Window dress (p. 649)

ETHICS in the Real World

MicroStrategy, a software maker in the business-to-business Internet industry, was introduced at the beginning of the chapter. Since it revised its earnings numbers downward, the company continued to report net losses for some time. Clearly, company management was under considerable pressure from shareholders, bankers, and the investment community to turn things around. While the company's cash flow situation appeared somewhat more promising, a closer look at the numbers indicates that net cash from operations was buoyed by huge increases in the company's accounts payable balance. It is possible, for example, that MicroStrategy intentionally delayed some payments to suppliers in an effort to put as positive a spin as possible on the company's cash flow position.

ETHICAL ISSUE Is it ethical for a company in weak financial condition to manage the timing of its cash receipts and payments to delay signaling that weakness to the public?

INTERNET RESEARCH EXERCISE

General Motors was once the largest and most dominant auto manufacturer in the world. In an unprecedented move, the U.S. government stepped in to salvage the business, funding over $19 billion to the company before it filed bankruptcy, and billions more afterward. At the time the federal government owned a majority of the company. GM statement of cash flows showed cash used by operating activities of $12.1 billion for the year ending 12/31/2008, coupled with

$1.7 billion used for investing activities for that year. Given the tumult in the financial markets in fall 2008 and GM's deteriorating condition, any cash from financing activities was not enough to keep the company afloat. You can view the 12/31/2008 10-K financial statement on www.gm.com/corporate/investor_information/. Review the statement of cash flows and look at the cash generated by the company and the many drains on that cash flow.

BRIEF EXERCISES

REAL DATA

BE14–1

The indirect presentation

The 2008 statement of cash flows for technology company Hewlett-Packard reported net earnings of $8.3 billion and net cash provided by operating activities of $14.6 billion. Depreciation and amortization totaled $3.4 billion. HP used the indirect form of presenting the statement of cash flows.

a. How is depreciation disclosed on the statement of cash flows? Why?
b. Why doesn't net earnings plus depreciation equal net cash provided by operating activities?
c. Provide an estimate of the net change in current assets and current liabilities for HP during 2008.

REAL DATA

BE14–2

Cash vs. accruals

Pier 1 Imports reported retail sales for fiscal 2008 of $1.3 billion. During the year, accounts receivable decreased from $24.2 million to $19.1 million.

Estimate the cash collected by Pier 1 from its customers during 2008.

REAL DATA

BE14–3

Inferring inventory transactions

Pier 1 Imports reported cost of sales of $957 million for fiscal 2008. Inventory decreased during the year from $412 million to $316 million, and accounts payable (related to inventory purchases) decreased from $106 million to $81 million.

a. Estimate the cost of inventories purchased during 2008.
b. Estimate the cash payments made to inventory suppliers during 2008.

REAL DATA

BE14–4

Interpreting the statement of cash flows

The following information was taken from the 2008 statements of cash flow for Agilent Technologies and Advanced Micro Devices (dollars in millions):

Company	Net Income/ (Loss)	Cash from Operating	Cash from Investing	Cash from Financing
Agilent	$ 693	$ 756	$(399)	$(774)
AMD	(3,098)	(692)	(27)	220

a. Compute the change in cash for both companies.
b. Describe the cash management profile for each company—that is, what is the source of each company's cash, and how is each company using it?
c. Discuss why cash from operating for AMD and Agilent is greater than profits. What does the cash from financing figure tell you about the companies' activities?

REAL DATA

BE14–5

Interpreting IFRS-based statements of cash flow across time

The statement of cash flow for Nestlé Group, a Swiss-based food conglomerate that publishes IFRS-based financial statements, contained the following numbers (in million Swiss francs—CHF).

	2008	2007
Profit	19,051	11,382
Operating cash flow	10,763	13,439
Cash flow from investing activities	4,699	(15,753)
Cash flow from financing activities	(16,884)	3,397

a. Explain how profit could be below operating cash flow in one year and above it the next.
b. Analyze Nestlé's cash management activities in 2007 and contrast them with 2008.

EXERCISES

E14–1

Classifying transactions

Classify each of the following transactions as an operating, investing, or financing activity, even those that would not appear explicitly on the statement of cash flows. Some transactions may be classified in more than one category.

1. Purchase of machinery for cash
2. Issuance of common stock for cash
3. Sale of inventory on account
4. Purchase of outstanding stock (treasury stock) for cash
5. Sale of land held as a long-term investment
6. Purchase of a building for cash and a mortgage payable
7. Cash payment for principal and interest on an outstanding debt
8. Cash payment on accounts payable
9. Payment of a cash dividend
10. Payment of wages to employees

E14–2

Operating, investing, or financing activity?

The following are several activities that Wallingford, Inc. engaged in during 2012:

1. Wrote off an open receivable as uncollected.
2. Purchased a piece of plant equipment.
3. Reacquired 5,000 shares of its common stock.
4. Sold a building in exchange for a five-year note.
5. Declared, but did not pay, a cash dividend.
6. Retired bonds payable by issuing common stock.
7. Collected on a long-term note receivable.
8. Issued a stock dividend.
9. Recorded depreciation on fixed assets. (Assume that the direct method is used.)
10. Paid interest on long-term debt.
11. Purchased inventory on account.
12. Collected open accounts receivable.
13. Exchanged a building for land.
14. Issued 75,000 shares of preferred stock.
15. Purchased a two-year fire insurance policy.

Assume that each of these transactions involved cash unless otherwise indicated. Indicate in which section of the statement of cash flows each transaction would be classified. Classify each transaction as one of the following:

a. An operating activity
b. An investing activity
c. A financing activity
d. Not included on the statement of cash flows

E14–3

Cash management policies across companies

Summaries of the 2012 statements of cash flows for five different companies follow. For each company compute the missing dollar amount, and briefly describe the company's cash management policy for 2012.

| Company | Cash Provided (Used) by | | | Net Increase (Decrease) |
	Operations	Investments	Financing	
AAA	$320	?	$(180)	$ (38)
BBB	219	$(450)	190	?
CCC	?	(414)	80	$(137)
DDD	120	(130)	?	420
EEE	?	(120)	(100)	70

E14–4

Cash management
across companies

Excerpts of statements of cash flows reported by Kraft Foods, Kellogg's, and General Mills, three companies in the food industry, are provided below (dollars in millions).

Company	Cash from Operations	Cash from Investments	Cash from Financing	Net Change in Cash
Kraft Foods	$5,084	$?	$(2,988)	$857
Kellogg's	1,643	(370)	(1,194)	?
General Mills	?	(289)	(1,450)	89

For each company compute the missing dollar amount, and briefly describe the company's cash management policy.

E14–5

Journalizing
and classifying
transactions

Presented below is a list of transactions entered into by Kaitland Manufacturing during 2012.

1.   Recorded depreciation expense of $170,000.
2.   Sold 10,000 shares of common stock ($10 par value) for $18 per share.
3.   Purchased 5,000 shares of IBM for $75 per share.
4.   Purchased a three-year insurance policy for $27,000.
5.   Purchased a building with a fair market value of $200,000 in exchange for a twenty-five-year mortgage. The agreement called for a down payment of $40,000.

Assume that each transaction is independent. Indicate how each transaction affects the accounting equation and how the cash effect, if any, would be disclosed on the company's statement of cash flows. That is, provide

a.   the dollar amount of the cash effect,
b.   whether it increases or decreases cash, and
c.   the section of the statement of cash flows in which it would appear.

E14–6

Converting accrual to
cash numbers

The following are several account titles that could appear on an income statement:

1. Cost of Goods Sold
2. Insurance Expense
3. Sales Revenue
4. Rent Expense
5. Dividend Revenue

6. Wage Expense
7. Supplies Expense
8. Interest Expense
9. Rent Revenue
10. Depreciation Expense

Several possible balance sheet accounts follow.

A. Cash
B. Merchandise Inventory
C. Retained Earnings
D. Unearned Sales Revenue
E. Interest Payable
F. Dividends Receivable
G. Fixed Assets
H. Rent Payable
I.   Accounts Payable
J.   Accounts Receivable
K. Premium on Bonds Payable
L. Allowance for Doubtful
     Accounts

M. Deferred
     Income Taxes
N. Prepaid Rent
O. Wages Payable
P. Common Stock
Q. Supplies Inventory
R. Discount on Bonds Payable
S. Unearned Rent
T. Marketable Securities
U. Prepaid Interest
V. Bonds Payable
W. Accumulated Depreciation
X. Prepaid Insurance

a.   Assume that you wish to compute the cash inflow or outflow associated with each income statement account. Match each income statement account with the related balance sheet account (or accounts) that you would analyze in this computation.
b.   For Sales Revenue, Cost of Goods Sold, and Interest Expense indicate whether an increase in the related balance sheet accounts (identified in [a]) would be added to or deducted from the income statement item when computing the cash effect.

E14–7

Depreciation:
A source of cash?

Your boss asks you to examine the following income statements of Hamilton Hardware and Watson Glass:

	Hamilton Hardware	Watson Glass
Sales	$900,000	$900,000
Cost of goods sold	(400,000)	(400,000)
Depreciation expense	(50,000)	(100,000)
Other expenses	(200,000)	(200,000)
Net income	$250,000	$200,000

In the notes to the financial statements, you notice that Hamilton Hardware uses the straight-line method of depreciation and that Watson Glass uses the double-declining-balance method.

a.   Assume that the dollar amounts for sales, cost of goods sold, and other expenses reflect total cash collections from customers, total cash paid for inventory, and total cash paid for other expenses, respectively. Compute cash provided (used) by operating activities for each company, using each of the following:
   1.   The direct method format
   2.   The indirect method format
b.   Why is the cash provided (used) by operations different from net income? Which of the two methods shows this more clearly?
c.   Would you agree or disagree with the following statement? *Depreciation is an important source of cash for most companies.* Explain your answer.

E14–8

Preparing a statement
of cash flows from
original transactions

Tony began a small retailing operation on January 1, 2012. During 2012, the following transactions occurred:

1.   Tony contributed $20,000 of his own money to the business.
2. $60,000 was borrowed from the bank.
3.   Long-lived assets were purchased for $25,000 cash.
4.   Inventory was purchased: $25,000 cash and $15,000 on account.
5.   Inventory with a cost of $25,000 was sold for $80,000: $20,000 cash and $60,000 on account.
6.   Cash payments included $18,000 for operating expenses, $5,000 for loan principal, and a $2,000 dividend.
7. $15,000 in expenses were accrued at the end of the year.

a.   Prepare journal entries for each economic event.
b.   Prepare a balance sheet as of the end of 2012 and an income statement and reconciliation of retained earnings for 2012 for Tony's business.
c.   Prepare a cash T-account and a statement of cash flows using the direct method.
d.   Prepare a statement of cash flows using the indirect method, but this time prepare it from the company's two balance sheets, the income statement, and the reconciliation of retained earnings. Tony's first balance sheet contains all zero balances.

E14–9

Preparing a
statement of cash
flows from the
cash account
in the ledger

Driftwood Shipbuilders entered into the following transactions during 2012:

1. Sold $6,000 of no-par common stock.
2. Purchased $6,000 of inventory on account.
3. Purchased new equipment for $5,000 in cash.
4. Collections on accounts receivable totaled $10,000.
5. Made payments of $5,000 to suppliers.
6. Declared and paid dividends of $2,000.
7. Paid rent of $6,000 for the last six months of 2011 and $6,000 for the first six months of 2012.
8. Made sales totaling $100,000: $35,000 on account and the remainder for cash.
9. Paid $40,000 in cash for miscellaneous expenses.
10. Sold investments with a cost of $20,000 for $25,000.

a. Prepare journal entries for each transaction.
b. Prepare a cash T-account and post all transactions affecting cash to the account. Assume a beginning cash balance of $25,000.
c. Prepare a statement of cash flows (direct method) from the cash T-account.

E14–10

Computing cash outflows from accrual information

The following year-end totals were taken from the records of Landau's Supply House. Compute the cash outflows associated with insurance and wages during 2012.

	2012	2011
Prepaid insurance	$7,000	$4,200
Wages payable	6,000	0
Insurance expense	3,000	4,700
Wage expense	8,500	3,000

E14–11

Reconstructing a transaction and its cash effect

The following information was taken from the records of Dylan's Toys:

	2012	2011
Machinery	$ 45,000	$ 20,000
Accumulated depreciation	$(15,000)	$(10,000)
Depreciation expense	7,000	6,000
Gain on sale of machinery	2,000	500

Machinery with a cost of $8,000 was sold during 2012.

a. How much machinery was purchased during 2012?
b. How much cash was collected on the sale of the machinery during 2012?
c. Provide the journal entry to record the sale of the machinery.

REAL DATA

E14–12

Compute cash flows from accrual numbers

Excerpts from the 2008 financial statements of SUPERVALU supermarkets are as follows (dollars in millions):

	2008	2007
Sales	$44,564	$44,048
Cost of sales	34,451	33,943
Accounts receivable	887	965
Inventory	2,709	2,776
Accounts payable	2,441	2,579

Compute estimates of cash receipts from customers and cash payments to suppliers. Assume that all sales are on account and that accounts payable includes only accounts with suppliers.

E14–13

Computing cash provided by operations from accrual information

Income statement and balance sheet excerpts of Shevlin and Liberty for the period ending December 31, 2012, follow. Compute cash provided (used) by operating activities for the period ending December 31, 2012. Use both the direct and indirect forms of presentation.

INCOME STATEMENT EXCERPTS

Sales		$48,000
Cost of goods sold		30,000
Gross profit		$18,000
Wage expense	$4,000	
Advertising expense	1,000	
Depreciation expense	2,000	7,000
Net income		$11,000

BALANCE SHEET EXCERPTS	2012	2011
Accounts receivable	$4,000	$ 5,000
Deferred revenues	0	3,000
Inventory	9,000	11,000
Accounts payable	3,000	4,000
Wages payable	1,800	900
Prepaid advertising	3,000	1,200
Accumulated depreciation	5,000	3,000

E14-14

Preparing a statement of cash flows from information contained in the other financial statements

The following information was taken from the records of Grimes Pools. Prepare a statement of cash flows (direct method) for the period ending December 31, 2012. Assume that all transactions involve cash.

	2012	2011
Cash	$ 4,000	$ 6,000
Noncash operating assets	15,000	15,000
Nonoperating assets	20,000	28,000
Operating liabilities	2,000	8,000
Nonoperating liabilities	6,000	4,000
Contributed capital	26,000	30,000
Retained earnings	5,000	7,000
Revenues	35,000	
Expenses	34,000	
Dividends	3,000	

E14-15

Preparing a statement of cash flows from information contained in the other financial statements

The following information was taken from the records of Romora Supply House. Prepare a statement of cash flows (direct method) for the period ending December 31, 2012. Assume that all transactions involve cash.

	2012	2011
Cash	$12,000	$ 5,000
Noncash operating assets	18,000	23,000
Nonoperating assets	27,000	23,000
Operating liabilities	7,000	2,000
Nonoperating liabilities	6,000	8,000
Contributed capital	35,000	32,000
Retained earnings	9,000	9,000
Revenues	64,000	
Expenses	61,000	
Dividends	3,000	

E14-16

Computing net income from cash provided by operating activities

The operating cash flows and balance sheet excerpts of Schlee and Associates for the period ending December 31, 2012, follow. Compute net income for the period ending December 31, 2012.

OPERATING ACTIVITIES

Cash inflows from sales	$ 65,000
Cash payments for inventories	$(40,000)
Cash payments for wages	(6,000)
Cash payments for advertising	(1,000)
Cash provided (used) by operating activities	$ 18,000

BALANCE SHEET EXCERPTS	2012	2011
Accounts receivable	$ 3,000	$ 9,000
Deferred revenues	4,000	1,000
Inventory	18,000	10,000
Accounts payable	7,000	3,000
Salaries payable	2,100	1,300
Prepaid advertising	5,000	8,000
Accumulated depreciation	8,000	5,000

E14–17

Preparing the operating section of the statement of cash flows: Direct and indirect methods

The following balance sheet and income statement data were taken from the records of L. L. Beeno for the year ended December 31, 2012:

	2012	2011
BALANCE SHEET		
Cash	$ 3,000	$ 2,800
Accounts receivable	5,600	4,500
Inventory	7,500	7,800
Prepaid insurance	600	900
Total current assets	$16,700	$16,000
Machinery (net)	29,000	26,000
Total	$45,700	$42,000
Accounts payable	$ 5,600	$ 7,300
Wages payable	4,500	3,400
Total current liabilities	$10,100	$10,700
Bonds payable (net)	14,000	14,800
Capital stock	5,000	5,000
Retained earnings	16,600	11,500
Total	$45,700	$42,000

INCOME STATEMENT	
Revenues	$47,000
Cost of goods sold	25,000
Gross profit	$22,000
Wage expense	(6,200)
Insurance expense	(4,200)
Interest expense	(1,600)
Depreciation expense	(3,300)
Net income before taxes	$ 6,700
Tax expense	1,200
Net income	$ 5,500

Prepare the operating section of the statement of cash flows, and present it under both the direct and indirect methods.

E14–18

Preparing the operating section of the statement of cash flows: Direct and indirect methods

The following balance sheet and income statement data were taken from the records of Martland Stores for the year ended December 31, 2012.

	2012	2011
BALANCE SHEET		
Cash	$ 6,000	$ 1,400
Accounts receivable	12,000	13,500
Inventory	4,500	9,800
Prepaid insurance	900	1,200
Total current assets	$23,400	$25,900
Machinery (net)	38,000	37,500
Total	$61,400	$63,400

	2012	2011
Accounts payable	$12,600	$13,100
Wages payable	9,500	7,400
Total current liabilities	$22,100	$20,500
Bonds payable (net)	17,000	17,000
Capital stock	15,000	15,000
Retained earnings	7,300	10,900
Total	$61,400	$63,400

INCOME STATEMENT

Revenues	$96,000
Cost of goods sold	64,000
Gross profit	$32,000
Wage expense	(18,600)
Insurance expense	(9,200)
Interest expense	(2,100)
Depreciation expense	(5,700)
Net loss	$ 3,600

Prepare the operating section of the statement of cash flows, and present it under both the direct and indirect methods.

E14–19

Preparing the operating section of the statement of cash flows: Direct and indirect methods

The following balance sheet and income statement data were taken from the records of Mako Retail Supply for the year ended December 31, 2012.

	2012	2011
BALANCE SHEET		
Cash	$ 6,000	$ 5,400
Accounts receivable	11,200	9,000
Inventory	15,000	15,600
Prepaid rent	1,200	1,800
Total current assets	$ 33,400	$31,800
Equipment (net)	58,000	52,000
Total	$ 91,400	$83,800
Accounts payable	$ 11,200	$14,600
Wages payable	9,000	6,800
Interest payable	1,500	2,200
Unearned revenue	6,500	4,700
Total current liabilities	$ 28,200	$28,300
Bonds payable (net)	28,000	28,400
Capital stock	10,000	10,000
Retained earnings	25,200	17,100
Total	$ 91,400	$83,800

INCOME STATEMENT

Revenues	$109,100
Cost of goods sold	56,000
Gross profit	$ 53,100
Wage expense	(15,200)
Rent expense	(9,000)
Interest expense	(2,900)
Depreciation expense	(6,200)
Loss on sale of equipment	(4,200)
Net income before taxes	$ 15,600
Tax expense	4,400
Net income	$ 11,200

Prepare the operating section of the statement of cash flows, and present it under both the direct and indirect methods.

E14–20

Preparing the operating section of the statement of cash flows: Direct and indirect methods

The following balance sheet and income statement data were taken from the records of Steeler and Jones for the year ended December 31, 2012:

	2012	2011
BALANCE SHEET		
Cash	$ 6,400	$ 7,400
Accounts receivable	11,900	13,000
Inventory	14,100	15,600
Prepaid rent	1,300	900
Total current assets	$ 33,700	$ 36,900
Equipment (net)	52,000	66,000
Total	$ 85,700	$102,900
Accounts payable	$ 9,200	$ 14,600
Wages payable	4,500	6,800
Interest payable	1,500	1,300
Unearned revenue	6,500	8,700
Total current liabilities	$ 21,700	$ 31,400
Bonds payable (net)	16,500	24,300
Capital stock	20,000	25,000
Retained earnings	27,500	22,200
Total	$ 85,700	$102,900
INCOME STATEMENT		
Revenues	$ 87,400	
Cost of goods sold	46,700	
Gross profit	$ 40,700	
Wage expense	$(13,200)	
Rent expense	(11,000)	
Interest expense	(1,900)	
Depreciation expense	(5,700)	
Plus: Gain on sale of equipment	5,200	
Net income before taxes	$ 14,100	
Tax expense	4,800	
Net income	$ 9,300	

Prepare the operating section of the statement of cash flows, and present it under both the direct and indirect methods.

E14–21

Preparing the operating section of the statement of cash flows: Direct and indirect methods

The following balance sheet and income statement data were taken from the records of Harbaugh Auto Supply for the year ended December 31, 2012:

	2012	2011
BALANCE SHEET		
Cash	$ 10,100	$ 8,400
Accounts receivable	14,400	13,900
Inventory	21,600	18,700
Interest receivable	1,200	1,500
Prepaid rent	2,600	1,400
Total current assets	$ 49,900	$ 43,900
Investments	35,400	32,100
Equipment (net)	98,000	91,700
Total	$183,300	$167,700

	2012	2011
Accounts payable	$ 18,700	$ 21,300
Wages payable	9,800	11,200
Interest payable	2,300	1,700
Dividend payable	1,700	1,200
Taxes payable	3,100	4,300
Unearned revenue	12,300	15,100
Total current liabilities	$ 47,900	$ 54,800
Long-term notes payable (net)	68,300	62,800
Capital stock	42,000	42,000
Retained earnings	25,100	8,100
Total	$183,300	$167,700

INCOME STATEMENT

Sales revenues	$ 47,500
Service revenue	35,200
Interest revenue	9,300
Cost of goods sold	(21,200)
Wage expense	(17,600)
Rent expense	(15,300)
Interest expense	(6,200)
Depreciation expense	(11,500)
Add: Gain on sale of investments	13,200
Net income before taxes	$ 33,400
Tax expense	9,100
Net income	$ 24,300

The company sells goods and provides services. All sales are made on account, and cash is received in advance on services with service revenues being recognized after services are performed.

Prepare the operating section of the statement of cash flows, and present it under both the direct and indirect methods.

E14–22

Preparing the operating section of the statement of cash flows: Direct and indirect methods

The following balance sheet and income statement data were taken from the records of Standard Center Manufacturing for the year ended December 31, 2012.

The company sells goods and provides services. All sales are made on account, and cash is received in advance on services with service revenues being recognized after services are performed.

Prepare the operating section of the statement of cash flows, and present it under both the direct and indirect methods.

	2012	2011
BALANCE SHEET		
Cash	$ 20,200	$ 22,800
Accounts receivable	28,800	34,800
Inventory	42,900	43,900
Interest receivable	4,100	6,300
Prepaid rent	3,900	1,200
Total current assets	$ 99,900	$109,000
Investments	18,200	23,500
Equipment (net)	43,900	62,500
Total	$162,000	$195,000

	2012	2011
Accounts payable	$ 12,500	$ 8,600
Wages payable	11,100	11,500
Interest payable	1,800	2,100
Dividend payable	900	1,700
Taxes payable	1,200	3,200
Unearned revenue	7,200	9,600
Total current liabilities	$ 34,700	$ 36,700
Long-term notes payable (net)	75,400	97,300
Capital stock	25,000	25,000
Retained earnings	26,900	36,000
Total	$162,000	$195,000

INCOME STATEMENT

Sales revenues	$67,500
Service revenue	28,200
Interest revenue	7,300
Cost of goods sold	(19,500)
Wage expense	(28,400)
Rent expense	(21,500)
Interest expense	(7,200)
Depreciation expense	(4,300)
Loss on sale of investments	(17,900)
Net income before taxes	$ 4,200
Tax expense	1,400
Net income	$ 2,800

REAL DATA

E14-23

Working with
an IFRS-based
operating section
of the statement
of cash flows

The information below was taken from the IFRS-based 2008 financial statements published by Carrefour, a French retailer (in million euros).

Income before tax	2,214
Tax	624
Provision for amortization	1,946
Net gains on sales of assets	219
Provision for impairment	642
Net increase in working capital	964

From the information above, estimate net cash from operations.

PROBLEMS

P14-1

Placing transactions
on the statement
of cash flows

The following events occurred during 2012 for Frames Unlimited:

1. Purchased inventory for $60,000 in cash.
2. Recorded $40,000 in insurance expense for the portion of an insurance policy acquired in 2011 that expired during 2012.
3. Paid $40,000 for rental space that the company will not use until 2013.
4. Sold land with a cost of $80,000 for $94,000 cash.
5. Paid $90,000 on a long-term note. Included in the $90,000 is $15,000 in interest, $9,000 of which was accrued in 2011.
6. Recorded bad debt expense in the amount of $30,000 (allowance method).

7. Reissued 5,000 shares of treasury stock for $30 per share. The stock was acquired at $18 per share.
8. Declared and issued a stock dividend. Ten thousand shares of common stock ($10 par value) were issued with a fair market value of $25 per share at the time.
9. Issued $500,000 face value bonds for cash at a total discount of $25,000.
10. Purchased a building for $100,000 in cash, $50,000 in common stock, and a note with a present value of $217,000.
11. Recorded $35,000 in sales to customers on account.

Frames Unlimited is in the process of preparing a statement of cash flows under the direct method.

REQUIRED:
Use a chart like the one in this problem to indicate the following:

a. The section of the statement of cash flows in which each transaction should be listed. Use the following terms:
   (1) Operating—for operating activities
   (2) Investing—for investing activities
   (3) Financing—for financing activities
   (4) N/A—for items that would not be included on the statement of cash flows
b. Whether the transaction would involve an inflow or an outflow of cash.
c. The dollar amount, if appropriate, that the company would report on the statement of cash flows.

The first transaction is done for you as an example.

Transaction	Section	Inflow	Outflow	Amount
1.	Operating		X	$60,000

P14-2

Placing transactions on the statement of cash flows

Endnote Enterprises entered into the following transactions during 2012:

1. Sold merchandise for $52,000 in cash.
2. Purchased a parcel of land. The company paid $12,000 in cash and issued a $30,000 note payable for the remainder.
3. Purchased a three-year insurance policy for $30,000.
4. Purchased a building in exchange for a long-term note with a face value and present value of $115,000.
5. Collected $100,000 on a long-term note receivable. Included in the $100,000 is $6,000 in interest earned and accrued in the previous period and $4,000 in interest earned in the current period.
6. Collected from customers $45,000 that will not be earned until 2013.
7. Reacquired 5,000 shares of its common stock for $10 per share.
8. Declared and paid a cash dividend of $40,000.
9. Paid $25,000 for wages accrued in a prior year.
10. Retired $500,000 in bonds payable. The company gave the creditor $300,000 in cash and $200,000 in common stock.
11. Purchased $60,000 of inventory on account.
12. Wrote off an open account ($5,000) as uncollectible (allowance method).
13. Recorded $84,000 in depreciation expense for the year.

Endnote Enterprises is in the process of preparing its statement of cash flows under the direct method.

REQUIRED:

Use the chart format below and on the next page to indicate the following:

a. The section of the statement of cash flows in which each transaction would be listed. Use the following terms:
   (1) Operating—for operating activities
   (2) Investing—for investing activities
   (3) Financing—for financing activities
   (4) N/A—for items that would not be included on the statement of cash flows
b. Whether the transaction would involve an inflow or an outflow of cash.
c. The dollar amount, if appropriate, that the company would report on the statement of cash flows.

The first transaction is done for you as an example.

Transaction	Section	Inflow	Outflow	Amount
1.	Operating	X		$52,000

P14–3

Classifying transactions and their cash effects

MHT Enterprises entered into the following transactions during 2012:

1. Sold a piece of equipment with a book value of $8,000 for $1,200.
2. Purchased a parcel of land for $13,000.
3. Purchased a three-year insurance policy for $9,000.
4. Issued 1,000 shares of common stock at $7 per share.
5. Collected a short-term note, including interest, in the amount of $2,500.
6. Collected $3,000 from customers that will not be earned until 2013.
7. Purchased a building in exchange for a long-term note with a face value of $15,000 (the present value of the note is $12,000).
8. Declared and paid a cash dividend of $7,000.
9. Paid $5,000 in wages.
10. Converted an outstanding receivable into a short-term note receivable that matures in February 2013.
11. Purchased $4,500 of inventory on account.
12. Wrote off an account ($500) as uncollectible (allowance method).
13. Recorded $9,000 in depreciation expense for the year.

REQUIRED:

a. The controller of MHT Enterprises is trying to explain the change in the company's cash balance from January 1, 2012, to December 31, 2012. The controller has asked you to analyze each of the transactions. You are to indicate whether cash was provided, used, or not affected by each transaction. If the cash balance is affected by the transaction, indicate the dollar amount of the increase or decrease. Unless otherwise indicated, assume that all transactions involve cash.
b. Classify each transaction identified in (a) as affecting cash as one of the following:
   (1) An operating activity
   (2) An investing activity
   (3) A financing activity

P14–4

Comparing cash flow policies across companies in the Internet industry

Cash flows from three well-known Internet companies are provided below (dollars in millions):

Priceline:	2009	2008	2007
Operations	$510	$316	$156
Investing	(501)	(152)	(221)
Financing	(169)	(169)	19

Amazon.com:	2009	2008	2007
Operations	$3,293	$1,697	$1,405
Investing	(2,337)	(1,199)	42
Financing	(280)	(198)	50

eBay:	2009	2008	2007
Operations	$2,908	$2,882	$2,641
Investing	(1,149)	(2,057)	(693)
Financing	(946)	(1,674)	(694)

REQUIRED:
Describe the similarities and differences of the cash flow policies across the three companies.

P14–5

Classifying transactions and their cash effects

Several transactions entered into by Travis Retail during 2012 follow:

1. Received $50,000 for wine previously sold on account.
2. Paid $55,000 in wages.
3. Sold a building for $100,000. The building had cost $170,000, and the related accumulated depreciation at the time of sale was $55,000.
4. Declared and paid a cash dividend of $70,000.
5. Repurchased 10,000 shares of outstanding common stock at $50 per share.
6. Purchased a two-year, $100,000 fire and storm insurance policy on June 30.
7. Purchased some equipment in exchange for 1,000 shares of common stock. The stock was currently selling for $75 per share.
8. Purchased $500,000 in equity securities considered to be long-term.
9. Issued $200,000 face value bonds. The bonds were sold at 101.
10. Owed $30,000 in rent as of December 31.

REQUIRED:
Record each transaction on a chart like the following. Classify the sections of the statement of cash flows as a cash flow from operating, investing, or financing activities. Transaction (1) is done as an example.

Transaction	Effect on Cash	Section of Statement	Explanation
1.	+50,000	Operating	Operations is defined in terms of inventory activity.

P14–6

A company's cash management policy across time

Ruttman Enterprises began operations in early 2010. Summaries of the statement of cash flows for the years 2010, 2011, and 2012 follow:

	2012	2011	2010
Cash provided (used) by operating activities	$?	$(202)	$?
Cash provided (used) by investing activities	160	?	(500)
Cash provided (used) by financing activities	(150)	280	900
Increase (decrease) in cash	$?	$ (24)	$ 110
Cash balance at beginning of year	86	?	0
Cash balance at end of year	$ 176	$ 86	$?

REQUIRED:
a. Compute the missing dollar amounts.
b. Briefly comment on the company's cash management policy over the three-year period.

P14-7

Cash management across time

The following information was taken from the 2008 annual report of Hewlett-Packard, a leading technology manufacturer (dollars in millions):

	2008	2007	2006
Cash provided (used) by operating activities	$14,591	$?	$11,353
Cash provided (used) by investing activities	(13,711)	(9,123)	?
Cash provided (used) by financing activities	?	(5,590)	(6,077)
Increase (decrease) in cash	(1,140)	?	2,489
Cash balance at beginning of year	?	16,400	13,911
Cash balance at end of year	$10,153	$11,293	$?

REQUIRED:
a. Compute the missing dollar amounts.
b. Comment on the company's cash management policies across the three-year period.

P14-8

Deriving the cash effects of investing transactions

Webb Industries reported the following information concerning the company's property, plant, and equipment in its 2012 financial report:

	2012	2011
Buildings	$ 750,000	$820,000
Accumulated depreciation	(100,000)	(80,000)
Equipment	500,000	380,000
Accumulated depreciation	(75,000)	(85,000)
Land	250,000	250,000
Depreciation expense—buildings	40,000	25,000
Depreciation expense—equipment	15,000	12,000

Listed here are four independent cases involving buildings, equipment, and land during 2012.

1. The company purchased a building for $60,000.
2. The company sold equipment in December 2012 that was purchased for $50,000. It recorded a gain of $5,000 on the sale.
3. The company sold a piece of land for $300,000 at a gain of $75,000.
4. The company acquired a building in exchange for land. The land had a book value of $150,000 and a market value of $600,000.

REQUIRED:
a. For each case, explain the change from 2011 to 2012 in the affected buildings, equipment, and land accounts. (For example, in case [1] explain the change in the building account, the related accumulated depreciation account, and the balance in the related depreciation expense account.)
b. For each case, compute the effect on the cash balance, and indicate the appropriate disclosure on the statement of cash flows.

P14-9

Deriving the cash generated from a common stock issuance

The shareholders' equity section of Mountvale Associates is as follows:

	2012	2011
Common stock ($1 par value)	$128,000	$100,000
Additional paid-in capital (C/S)	95,000	12,000
Retained earnings	41,000	35,000
Total shareholders' equity	$264,000	$147,000

The following selected transactions occurred during 2012:

1. 1/1/12: A 20 percent stock dividend was issued. The fair market value of the stock at the time was $3 per share.
2. 8/25/12: Land was purchased in exchange for 6,000 shares of common stock. The fair market value of the stock was $3 per share.
3. 12/31/12: Common stock was issued for cash.

REQUIRED:
How many shares of common stock did Mountvale issue on December 31, 2012, and how much cash did the issuance generate? Show all calculations clearly. (*Hint:* Calculate the number of shares of common stock issued for cash.)

P14–10

Converting cash flow numbers to accrual numbers and vice versa

Taylor Brothers began operations in 2011. The following selected information was extracted from its financial records:

	2012	2011
Sales returns	$ 25,000	$ 20,000
Cost of goods sold	375,000	250,000
Inventory	110,000	130,000
Accounts receivable	150,000	95,000
Insurance expense	50,000	35,000
Cash collected on sales	500,000	350,000
Accounts payable	115,000	105,000
Cash paid for insurance	90,000	65,000

REQUIRED:
a. Compute gross sales (accrual basis) for 2011 and 2012.
b. Calculate the amount of cash paid to suppliers during 2012 for inventory.
c. Compute the balance in the prepaid insurance account as of December 31, 2011, and December 31, 2012.

P14–11

Reconciling the income statement, the direct method, and the indirect method

Battery Builders, Inc. prepared statements of cash flows under both the direct and indirect methods. The operating sections of each statement under the two methods follow:

DIRECT METHOD

Collections from customers	$26,000
Payments to suppliers	(13,000)
Payments for operating expenses	(10,000)
Cash provided (used) by operating activities	$ 3,000

INDIRECT METHOD

Net income	$9,000
Depreciation	3,000
Gain on sale of equipment	(2,000)
Increase in inventory	(3,000)
Increase in accounts receivable	(3,000)
Increase in accounts payable	1,000
Decrease in accrued payables	(2,000)
Cash provided (used) by operating activities	$3,000

REQUIRED:
Prepare an income statement from the information provided.

P14–12

Manipulating dollar amounts on the statement of cash flows

Pendleton Enterprises began operations on January 1, 2010. Balance sheet and income statement information for 2010, 2011, and 2012 follow:

	2012	2011	2010
Cash	$ 6,000	$ 9,000	$7,000
Accounts receivable	8,000	5,000	4,000
Accounts payable	5,000	3,000	2,000
Revenues	12,000	14,000	8,000
Expenses	14,000	9,000	6,000

REQUIRED:

a. Prepare the operating sections of the statement of cash flows for 2010, 2011, and 2012 under the direct method.

b. Assume that the $4,000 of outstanding accounts receivable on December 31, 2010, was actually collected before the end of 2010 but that the accounts receivable balances for 2011 and 2012 are unchanged. Prepare the statements of cash flows under the direct method for all three years.

c. Ignore the assumption in (b), and assume alternatively that the company deferred an additional $3,000 on the payment of accounts payable as of December 31, 2010 (i.e., accounts payable equal $5,000, and cash equals $10,000 on December 31, 2010). The accounts receivable balances for 2011 and 2012 are unchanged. Prepare the operating section of the statements of cash flows for all three periods.

d. How can managers manipulate cash provided (used) by operations, and what usually happens in the subsequent period?

P14–13

Preparing the statement of cash flows from two balance sheets and an income statement

The 2011 and 2012 balance sheets and related income statement of Watson and Holmes Detective Agency follow:

	2012	2011
BALANCE SHEET		
ASSETS		
Cash	$10,000	$ 6,000
Accounts receivable	7,000	2,000
Less: Allowance for doubtful accounts	(1,000)	(500)
Inventory	8,000	10,000
Long-lived assets	12,000	11,000
Less: Accumulated depreciation	(4,000)	(2,000)
Total assets	$32,000	$26,500
LIABILITIES AND SHAREHOLDERS' EQUITY		
Accounts payable	$ 5,000	$ 6,000
Deferred revenues	1,000	2,000
Long-term note payable	10,000	10,000
Less: Discount on note payable	(800)	(1,000)
Common stock	12,000	6,000
Retained earnings	4,800	3,500
Total liabilities and shareholders' equity	$32,000	$26,500
INCOME STATEMENT		
Revenues	$42,000	
Cost of goods sold	(24,000)	
Depreciation expense	(2,000)	
Interest expense	(3,000)	
Bad debt expense	(2,000)	
Other expense	(9,000)	
Net income	$ 2,000	

REQUIRED:

Prepare a statement of cash flows under both the direct and indirect methods for 2012.

P14–14

Paying short-term debts: Effects on working capital, the current ratio, and the statement of cash flows

ISS Inc. began operations on January 1, 2012. It engaged in the following economic events during 2012:

1. Issued 6,000 shares of no-par common stock for $10 per share.
2. Purchased on account 20,000 units of inventory for $1 per unit.
3. Paid and capitalized $7,000 for rent covering 2012 and 2013.

4. Purchased furniture for $30,000, paying $20,000 in cash and signing a long-term note for the remaining balance.
5. Sold on account 8,800 units of inventory for $4 per unit.
6. Paid one-half of the outstanding accounts payable.
7. Received $12,000 from customers on open accounts.
8. Paid miscellaneous expenses of $10,000 for the year.
9. Depreciation recorded on the furniture totaled $5,000.
10. Accrued interest on the long-term note payable amounted to $1,000.
11. Declared dividends of $3,000 at year-end to be paid in January 2013.
12. Recorded entry for $3,000 of rent expired during 2012.

REQUIRED:

a. Prepare journal entries for these events.
b. Prepare an income statement, statement of shareholders' equity, balance sheet, and statement of cash flows (indirect method).
c. Compute working capital and the current ratio.
d. Assume that the company pays the outstanding accounts payable on the final day of 2012. Recompute working capital, the current ratio, and cash provided (used) by operating activities.

P14–15

Preparing the statement of cash flows and reconciling the operating section with the income statement

Sunshine Enterprises included the following statements in its 2012 financial report:

INCOME STATEMENT	2012	
Marketing revenue	**$1,000,000**	
Salary expense	**(250,000)**	
Office supplies expense	**(175,000)**	
Depreciation expense	**(100,000)**	
Insurance expense	**(60,000)**	
Rent expense	**(120,000)**	
Net income	**$ 295,000**	

BALANCE SHEET	2012	2011
Cash	**$100,000**	**$ 120,000**
Accounts receivable	**150,000**	**105,000**
Office supply inventory	**75,000**	**85,000**
Prepaid insurance	**50,000**	**10,000**
Office furniture	**500,000**	**465,000**
Less: Accumulated depreciation	**(325,000)**	**$(225,000)**
Total assets	**$550,000**	**$ 560,000**
Rent payable	**$ 20,000**	**$ 8,000**
Common stock ($10 par value)	**100,000**	**100,000**
Additional paid-in capital	**125,000**	**125,000**
Retained earnings	**305,000**	**327,000**
Total liabilities and shareholders' equity	**$550,000**	**$ 560,000**

REQUIRED:

a. Convert each of the accrual-basis income statement accounts to a cash basis. Would you classify this method as directly or indirectly computing cash provided (used) by operating activities?
b. Prepare a proof of results. That is, begin with net income and adjust net income to arrive at cash provided (used) by operating activities. Would you classify this method as directly or indirectly computing cash provided (used) by operating activities?
c. Refer to Figure 14–19, and use the same format to reconcile the income statement with operating cash flows.

P14–16

Preparing the
statement of cash
flows from two
balance sheets
and an income
statement:
Book losses and
amortized discounts

The following information was taken from the financial records of Bower Manufacturing Industries:

INCOME STATEMENT	2012
Sales	$190,000
Cost of goods sold	(80,000)
Depreciation expense	(30,000)
Interest expense	(10,000)
Salary expense	(12,000)
Supplies expense	(7,000)
Loss on sale of marketable sec.	(4,000)
Loss on sale of fixed assets	(10,000)
Net income	$37,000

BALANCE SHEETS	2012	2011
Cash	$ 747,000	$ 593,000
Marketable securities	85,000	140,000
Accounts receivable	450,000	400,000
Supplies inventory	10,000	12,000
Inventory	150,000	175,000
Short-term notes receivable	100,000	50,000
Machinery and equipment	550,000	500,000
Less: Accumulated depreciation	(90,000)	(75,000)
Total assets	$2,002,000	$1,795,000
Accounts payable	$ 60,000	$ 95,000
Salaries payable	10,000	10,000
Bonds payable	500,000	500,000
Discount on bonds payable	(5,000)	(10,000)
Common stock ($10 par value)	200,000	100,000
Additional paid-in capital	900,000	800,000
Retained earnings	337,000	300,000
Total liabilities and shareholders' equity	$2,002,000	$1,795,000

The company purchased machinery in exchange for 10,000 shares of common stock. The stock was selling for $20 per share at that time. The short-term receivable was received from a customer in exchange for the sale of merchandise inventory.

REQUIRED:
Prepare a statement of cash flows for the year ended December 31, 2012, using both the direct and indirect methods.

P14–17

Preparing the
statement of cash
flows from two
balance sheets
and an income
statement:
Book gains and
amortized premiums

The following information was taken from the 2012 financial records of Price Restaurant Supply Company:

INCOME STATEMENT	
Sales	$160,000
Cost of goods sold	(100,000)
Depreciation expense	(12,000)
Insurance expense	(10,000)
Interest expense	(11,000)
Gain on sale of plant equipment	10,000
Net income	$ 37,000

BALANCE SHEETS	2012	2011
Cash	$173,000	$120,000
Accounts receivable	60,000	65,000
Inventory	210,000	110,000
Prepaid insurance	14,000	24,000
Plant equipment	275,000	350,000
Less: Accumulated depreciation	(67,000)	(75,000)
Total assets	$665,000	$594,000
Accounts payable	$ 51,000	$ 50,000
Bonds payable	200,000	200,000
Premium on bonds payable	3,000	5,000
Common stock ($10 par value)	75,000	40,000
Additional paid-in capital	125,000	95,000
Retained earnings	211,000	204,000
Total liabilities and shareholders' equity	$665,000	$594,000

The company sold a piece of plant equipment for cash that had originally cost $100,000. The accumulated depreciation associated with the equipment at the time of sale was $20,000.

REQUIRED:
Prepare a statement of cash flows for the year ended December 31, 2012, using both the direct and indirect methods.

P14–18

Preparing the statement of cash flows and using it to set dividend policy

Lynch Engineering Firm provided the following income statement for 2012 in its annual financial report:

		2012		2011
Sales		$5,967,000		$5,590,000
Salary expense	$2,025,000		$1,794,000	
Advertising expense	755,000		710,000	
Bad debt expense	275,000		260,000	
Administrative expenses	898,000		832,000	
Janitorial expense	132,000		120,000	
Supplies expense	281,000		299,000	
Depreciation expense	963,000	5,329,000	978,000	4,993,000
Net income		$ 638,000		$ 597,000

1. The company declared and paid a dividend of $550,000 in 2011 but did not declare any dividends in 2012.
2. 2011:
   (a) Thirty-five percent of the sales were on account.
   (b) The accounts receivable balance decreased by $2,980,000 from January 1 to December 31.
   (c) As of December 31, the company still owed $145,000 in wages and $67,000 on the supplies used during the year.
3. 2012:
   (a) Seventy-five percent of the sales were on account.
   (b) The accounts receivable balance increased by $1,671,750 from January 1 to December 31.
   (c) As of December 31, the company still owed $25,000 in wages and $50,000 in advertising.
   (d) On January 1, 2011, the company had a balance of $13,245 in cash.
4. The company had no write-offs or recoveries of accounts receivable during 2011 or 2012.

REQUIRED:

a.   Prepare the operating section of the statement of cash flows for 2011 and 2012, using the direct method.

b.   Assume that you are a member of the board of directors of the Lynch Engineering Firm. Several influential shareholders have called you and complained that the company generated more net income in 2012 than in 2011, yet chose not to declare a dividend in 2012. How would you explain the board's position on dividends in 2011 versus 2012?

P14–19

Preparing a complete set of financial statements from a set of original transactions

Mick's Photographic Equipment began operations on January 1, 2011. During 2011, the company entered into the following transactions:

1.   Issued 50,000 shares of $15 par value common stock for $30 per share in exchange for cash. Also issued, for cash, 1,000 shares of 10 percent, $100 par value preferred stock for $102 per share.
2.   Purchased $750,000 of fixed assets in exchange for cash.
3.   Issued twenty bonds, each with a face value of $1,000, at 146 (annual coupon rate = 16 percent and annual yield rate = 10 percent). The bonds pay interest semiannually on December 31 and June 30.
4.   Purchased land in exchange for 1,000 shares of $15 par value common stock. The shares were selling for $40 per share at the time.
5.   Purchased $2,000,000 of inventory on account. $1,075,000 was subsequently paid during 2005.
6.   Sold $2,050,000 of merchandise in exchange for cash. The related inventory had cost $875,000.
7.   Purchased a two-year insurance policy for $80,000.
8.   Purchased short-term marketable securities for $250,000.
9.   Sold $880,000 of merchandise on account. The related inventory had a cost of $490,000. $500,000 of the sales made on account were collected during the year.
10. Paid $500,000 in miscellaneous expenses (rent, utilities, and wages).
11. Declared, but did not pay, a $100,000 dividend.
12. Made the first interest payment on the bonds on December 31.

Adjusting entries include:

a.   The fixed assets were purchased on January 1 and had an estimated useful life and salvage value of five years and $50,000, respectively. The company uses the straight-line depreciation method.
b.   The company used one-fourth of the insurance policy during 2011.
c.   The market value of the marketable securities on December 31 was $225,000.
d.   As of December 31, the company had incurred, but had not yet paid, $75,000 in miscellaneous expenses.
e.   The company estimates that 8 percent of credit sales will prove uncollectible.
f.   The market value of the inventory was $5,000 less than the cost.

REQUIRED:

a.   Prepare journal entries for each of the original and adjusting transactions. Establish T-accounts for each account. Post the entries to the T-accounts.
b.   Prepare the necessary closing entries. Post these entries.
c.   Prepare the income statement and balance sheet for Mick's Photographic Equipment for the year ended December 31, 2011.
d.   Prepare the statement of cash flows for Mick's Photographic Equipment for the year ended December 31, 2011, using both the direct and indirect methods.

ISSUES FOR DISCUSSION

REAL DATA

ID14–1

Using the cash flow
statement to spot
earnings quality
problems

An article in *BusinessWeek* described how Bob Olstein, a successful stock analyst, predicts that the prices of stocks issued by firms that "engage in aggressive accounting practices" will go down, stating that other "investors have unrealistic expectations of the earnings potential." He cites Mattel as an example by noting that big changes in net receivables, inventories, and deferred income taxes, as well as foreign currency translation gains that produced no cash, accounted for most of Mattel's earnings growth. The company's debt also jumped "from $440 million to $630 million in about two years."

REQUIRED:

a. Explain how the statement of cash flows, especially if prepared under the indirect format, can be used to identify "quality of earnings" and "earnings persistence" problems.

b. Specifically describe how the information mentioned above about Mattel was used to indicate these kinds of problems.

c. Do you think that it is possible to identify over- and undervalued stocks by identifying firms that use aggressive accounting practices?

REAL DATA

ID14–2

Equity in
unconsolidated
affiliates

As of January 3, 2010, The Washington Post Company held significant, but not controlling, interest in Bowater Mercy Paper Company and other companies. These investments totaled $54.7 million on the company's 2009 balance sheet. In its 2009 annual report, The Washington Post Company included a statement of cash flows, presented in the indirect form, which covered the three-year period of 2009, 2008, and 2007. A line item was included in the operating section of that statement, titled "equity in losses of affiliates, net of distributions," and the dollar amounts for this item for 2009, 2008, and 2007 were $30.1 million, $9.1 million, and $(3.8) million, respectively.

REQUIRED:

a. Briefly describe the accounting methods used for unconsolidated affiliates, in which a company has a "significant influence." (For a review, see the equity method in Chapter 8.)

b. Explain why the dollar amounts were added to net income on the statement of cash flows.

c. What does the phrase "net of distributions" mean?

d. On the same statement of cash flows, The Washington Post Company reported another line item in the operating section, titled "net loss on sale or write-down of property, plant, and equipment," which included dollar amounts for 2009, 2008, and 2007 of $19.7 million, $4.5 million, and $3.1 million, respectively. Describe the transactions that led to these disclosures and explain why the three-dollar amounts are added to net income in the calculation of net cash flow from operating activities. Would these amounts appear on any of the other financial statements, and if so, which one?

REAL DATA

ID14–3

Accrual and cash
flow accounting

Loan officer Han Blackford once commented that cash flow analysis has risen in importance due to a "trend over the past twenty years toward capitalizing and deferring more and more expenses. Although the practice may match revenues and expenses more closely, a laudable intent, it has also made it harder to find the available cash in a company—and easier for lenders to wind up with a loss." He further noted that recessions draw attention to the need for better warning signals of the sort cash flow analysis could provide.

REQUIRED:

a. Why would the process of capitalizing match revenues and expenses more closely, yet make it harder to find the cash available in a company?

b. Discuss the difference between earning power and solvency, why both are essential for a successful business, and how present-day financial accounting statements provide measures of each.

c. Explain why a wave of bankruptcies would draw attention to cash flow analysis.

REAL DATA

ID14-4

Analyzing the
operating section
of the statement of
cash flows

SUPERVALU is one of the largest grocery chains in the United States. Its February 28, 2009, statement of cash flows included the following (dollars in thousands):

SUPERVALU INC. and Subsidiaries
Consolidated Statements of Cash Flows
(in millions)

	February 28, 2009 (53 weeks)	February 23, 2008 (52 weeks)	February 24, 2007 (52 weeks)
Cash flows from operating activities			
Net earnings (loss)	$(2,855)	$ 593	$ 452
Adjustments to reconcile net earnings (loss) to net cash provided by operating activities:			
Goodwill and intangible asset impairment charges	3,524	—	—
Asset impairment and other charges	169	14	26
Depreciation and amortization	1,057	1,017	879
LIFO charge	78	30	18
Gain on sale of assets	(9)	(23)	(15)
Deferred income taxes, net of effects from acquisition and dispositions of businesses	(118)	(74)	44
Stock-based compensation	44	52	42
Other	(25)	(15)	(6)
Changes in operating assets and liabilities, net of effects from acquisition and dispositions of businesses:			
Receivables	68	103	258
Inventories	(12)	(20)	28
Accounts payable and accrued liabilities	(216)	(278)	(683)
Income taxes and currently payable	(83)	319	(224)
Other	(88)	14	(18)
Net cash provided by operating activities	1,534	1,732	801
Cash flows from investing activities			
Proceeds from sale of assets	117	195	189
Purchases of property, plant and equipment	(1,186)	(1,191)	(837)
Business acquisitions, net of cash acquired	—	—	(2,402)
Release of restricted cash	—	14	238
Other	55	14	52
Net cash used investing activities	(1,014)	(968)	(2,760)
Cash flows from financing activities			
Proceeds from issuance of long-term debt	215	41	3,313
Payment of long-term debt and capital lease obligations	(581)	(692)	(1,490)
Proceeds from settlement of mandatory convertible securities	—	52	—
Dividends paid	(145)	(142)	(113)
Net proceeds from the sale of common stock under option plans and related tax benefits	11	153	252
Payment for purchase of treasury shares	(23)	(218)	(220)
Payment of Albertsons standalone drug business payables	—	—	(299)
Net cash (used in) provided by financing activities	(523)	(806)	1,443
Net decrease in cash and cash equivalents	(3)	(42)	(516)
Cash and cash equivalents at beginning of year	243	285	801
Cash and cash equivalents at end of year	$ 240	$ 243	$ 285

(Continued)

SUPPLEMENTAL CASH FLOW INFORMATION

The Company's non-cash activities were as follows:			
Capital lease asset additions and related obligations	$ 26	$ 36	$ 73
Purchase of property, plant and equipment included in Accounts payable	$ 98	$ 154	$ 105
Interest and income taxes paid:			
Interest paid (net of amount capitalized)	$ 614	$ 743	$ 545
Income taxes paid (net of refunds)	$ 274	$ 107	$ 310

See Notes to Consolidated Financial Statements.

REQUIRED:

a. Depreciation and amortization are added back to net earnings in the computation of net cash provided by operations. Does this mean that depreciation and amortization are sources of cash?

b. What is meant by "impairment charges"? What event would lead to such an expense? Why is it added back to net earnings?

c. Explain why the "gain on the sale" of assets is subtracted from net earnings, while "loss on sale" is added. Describe the entries that led to these disclosures.

d. Comment on the trends across time of the company's current accounts, especially inventory and receivables.

e. Comment on the quality of the company's earnings over the three-year period.

REAL DATA

ID14–5

Misunderstandings in the financial press

The financial press often uses the term *cash flow* to refer to a company's "net income + depreciation." In a well-known article in *Barron's* titled "No Substitutions, Please," Intel was criticized for relying heavily on a number the company called "cash earnings," computed by adding amortization of intangible assets to net earnings.

REQUIRED:

Do you believe that using cash flow measures like the ones described above are superior to using net cash from operations as disclosed in the operating section of the statement of cash flows? Explain.

REAL DATA

ID14–6

Analyzing the statement of cash flows

The operating section of the 2008 consolidated statement of cash flows for Imation Corporation, a global technology company, is excerpted below (dollars in millions):

	2008	2007	2006
Net income (loss)	$(33.3)	$(50.4)	$ 76.4
Adjustments:			
Depreciation	25.9	28.6	29.1
Amortization	23.4	18.3	9.3
Deferred income taxes	0.2	(10.7)	9.7
Asset impairments	39.7	102.5	7.2
Gain on sale of company	—	—	(2.1)
Stock-based compensation	9.5	10.2	11.0
Pension settlement/curtailment	5.7	2.4	1.7
Excess tax benefit—stock options	—	—	(3.3)
Other	4.9	3.5	0.6
Changes in operating accounts			
Accounts receivable	129.0	(33.7)	(37.6)
Inventory	0.2	7.8	(49.3)
Other assets	(2.9)	(9.1)	1.5
Accounts payable	(61.5)	(8.7)	30.5
Other liabilities	(56.1)	26.8	12.8
Net cash provided by operating activities	$ 84.7	$ 87.5	$ 97.5

REQUIRED:

a. Review the trends across time of depreciation. Does the company's growth strategy seem to involve investing in property, plant, and equipment? Explain.

b. Why is stock-based compensation added back to net income?

c. Has the inventory balance increased or decreased during the years shown? Explain.

d. Explain the cash flows associated with the asset impairments and the sale of a subsidiary company.

REAL DATA

ID14-7

Analyzing an IFRS-based statement of cash flows

The IFRS-based 2007 and 2008 statements of cash flows published by the Danone Group, a French food processor, are provided below. Briefly describe each of the line items, and comment on the company's cash management policies.

CONSOLIDATED STATEMENTS OF CASH FLOWS

(In € millions)	Notes	Year Ended December 31 2007	Year Ended December 31 2008
Net income attributable to the Group		4,180	1,313
Net income attributable to minority interests		158	178
Net income from discontinued operations		(3,292)	(269)
Net income of equity-accounts affiliates		(87)	(62)
Depreciation and amortization		420	525
Dividends received from equity-accounted affiliates		30	29
Other flows with impact on cash	26	—	(113)
Other flows with no impact on cash	26	21	98
Cash flows provided by operating activities, excluding changes in net working capital		1,430	1,699
(Increase) decrease in inventories		(51)	3
(Increase) decrease in trade accounts receivable		(39)	(74)
Increase (decrease) in trade accounts payable		244	36
Changes in other working capital items		27	90
Net change in current working capital		181	55
Cash flows provided by (used in) operating activities		1,611	1,754
Capital expenditures		(726)	(706)
Purchase of businesses and other investments net of cash and cash equivalents acquired	26	(12,100)	(259)
Proceeds from the sale of businesses and other investments net of cash and cash equivalents disposed of	26	4,699	329
(Increase) decrease in long-term loans and other long-term assets		(142)	67
Changes in cash and cash equivalents of discontinued operations		171	—
Cash flows provided by (used in) investing activities		(8,098)	(569)
Increase in capital and additional paid-in capital		66	48
Purchases of treasury stock (net of disposals)		(439)	46
Dividends		(622)	(705)
Increase (decrease) in non-current financial liabilities		3,069	1,338
Increase (decrease) in current financial liabilities		2,614	(1,901)
(Increase) decrease in marketable securities		1,708	63
Cash flows provided by (used in) financing activities		6,396	(1,111)
Effect of exchange rate changes on cash and equivalents		(16)	(31)
Increase (decrease) in cash and cash equivalents		(107)	43
Cash and cash equivalents at beginning of period		655	548
Cash and cash equivalents at end of period		548	591
Supplemental disclosures			
Cash paid during the year:			
—net interests[1]		152	433
—income tax		369	221

(1) In 2007, net interests corresponded to interest expense on net debt ("interest") for € 252 million net interest income on net debt for € 100 million.

The following information was taken from the 2008 annual report and statement of cash flows of Eli Lilly, a major pharmaceutical (dollars in millions):*

	2008	2007	2006
Net income (loss)	$(2,072)	$2,953	$2,663
Net cash from operations	7,296	5,155	3,976
Net cash from investing activities	(7,269)	(4,328)	608
Net cash from financing activities	(2,346)	(845)	(4,579)
Change in cash	2,276	111	103

*Change in the cash balance does not always equal the sum of cash from operations, investing, and financing due to adjustments for exchange rate changes.

REQUIRED:
a. Discuss the cash management profile of Lilly across the three-year period. Where did the company get its cash, and what did it do with it?
b. Explain how the cash management profile relates to the company's financial condition and performance over this time period.

Starbucks is a relatively young, fast-growing company that is a pioneer and leader in its industry. Excerpts from its 2009 statement of cash flows are as follows (dollars in millions):

	2009	2008	2007
Net income	$ 391	$ 316	$ 673
Net cash from operations	1,389	1,259	1,331
Net cash from investing activities	(421)	(1,087)	(1,202)
Net cash from financing activities	(642)	(185)	(172)
Change in cash	330	(12)	(3)

*Change in the cash balance does not always equal the sum of cash from operations, investing, and financing due to adjustments for exchange rate changes.

REQUIRED:
a. Discuss the cash management profile of Starbucks across the three-year period. Where did the company get its cash, and what did it do with it?
b. Explain how the cash management profile may be representative of a young, fast-growing company.
c. Comment on how this profile reflects the company's financial condition and performance.
d. What do you think Starbucks' future cash will look like? Will the company maintain the same profile or change to a new profile? Why?

The 10-K of NIKE is reproduced in Appendix C.

REQUIRED:
Review the 10-K, and answer the following questions.

a. What are the major sources of cash for the company, and what is it doing with that cash?
b. Were there any significant transactions in 2007, 2008, or 2009 that did not affect cash but were reported on the statement of cash flows?
c. Why is the gain on divestitures a negative number?
d. Discuss NIKE's handling of its accounts receivable over the three years. How does it compare to sales growth, and what might the differences indicate?
e. Analyze NIKE's cash management policies across the three-year period (2007–2009).

The Time Value of Money

Financial accounting information is useful because it provides investors, creditors, and other interested parties with measures of solvency and earning power. In developing these measures, the valuation of the transactions in which the company participates and ultimately the valuation of a company's assets and liabilities as well as the company itself are very important. It is essential, therefore, that investors, creditors, managers, auditors, and others understand the concepts of valuation. This is especially true as IFRS, which relies extensively on fair market value, plays a larger role, and U.S. GAAP continues to move toward a fair market value framework (e.g., the fair value option for financial instruments).

The economic value of an asset or liability is its present value. In computing present value, the future cash inflows and outflows associated with an asset or liability are predicted and then adjusted in a way that reflects the **time value of money** (i.e., a dollar in the future is worth less than a dollar at present). Financial accounting statements rely extensively on the concept of present value. In theory, providing measures of present value is the ultimate goal of financial accounting.

This appendix covers the time value of money and, specifically, the concept of present value. We first point out that money has a price (interest). The price of money gives it a time value; it ensures that money held today has a greater value than money received tomorrow. We then introduce the notion of compound interest and proceed to work a number of examples that equate future cash flows to present values. We conclude by discussing how present value fits into the financial accounting system.

INTEREST: THE PRICE OF MONEY

Money, like any other scarce resource, has a price. Individuals wishing to borrow money must pay this price, and those who lend it receive this price. The price of money is called *interest* and is usually expressed as a percentage rate over a certain time period (often per year but sometimes per month). The dollar amount of interest is the result of multiplying the percentage rate by the amount of money borrowed or lent (*principal*). For example, a 10 percent interest rate per year on a principal of $100 will produce $10 (10% × $100) of interest after one year.

TIME VALUE

In an environment that charges interest for the use of money, would you rather have one dollar now or receive one dollar one year from now? If you choose to receive the dollar immediately, you could lend it, and it would grow to some amount greater than one dollar after a year has passed. Someone, perhaps a bank, would be willing to pay you interest for the use of that dollar. Therefore, in a world where money has a price, a dollar today is worth more than a dollar at some time in the future. The difference between the value of a dollar today and the value of a dollar in the future is called the time value of money. For example, if the interest rate is 10 percent, $1 placed in a bank today will grow to $1.10 ($1 × 1.10) in one year. In this example, the time value of a dollar is $0.10.

Size of Time Value

Let's go one step further and explore the factors that determine the size of the time value of money. That is, what factors determine whether the time value of money is large or small? The first factor is obviously the price of money, or the interest rate. If there were no interest rate, the time value of money would be zero. Accordingly, as the interest rate gets larger, so does the difference between the value of a dollar today and the value of a dollar in the future. The higher the interest rate, the greater the time value of money. In the example above, a 20 percent interest rate would give rise to a time value of money equal to $0.20.

The second factor determining the magnitude of the time value of money is the length of the time period. Which do you think is larger: the difference in value between a dollar today and a dollar tomorrow or the difference in value between a dollar today and a dollar one year from now? Clearly, a dollar will grow much more in one year than it will in one day. Thus, the longer the time period, the greater the time value of money.

Inflation

One additional important point should also be noted. We have assumed in the discussion so far that interest is simply the price of money. You might view this price as a rental fee for the use of money. Just as you pay rent for the use of someone else's apartment, you must also pay rent for the use of someone else's money.

However, in addition to the rental price of money, there is another reason someone would prefer a dollar today to a dollar in the future. In times of rising prices (inflation), for example, one would definitely prefer a dollar today to a dollar in the future because today's dollar will buy more goods than the future dollar. In inflation, the prices of today's goods are less than the prices for the same goods in the future. Thus, in an inflationary environment, there are actually two reasons one would prefer a dollar today to a dollar in the future: (1) the rental price charged for using the dollar (time value) and (2) the erosion of the purchasing power of the dollar in the future (inflation).

In the real world, interest rates are set so that they reflect both factors. A 10 percent interest rate, for example, might be viewed as a 6 percent rental fee and a 4 percent inflation factor. Unfortunately, when using an interest rate to compute the time value of money, it is quite difficult to clearly separate the rental factor from the inflation factor. As a practical matter, there is little one can do other than to realize that both factors

exist and that they are nearly impossible to separate accurately. As indicated previously in Chapter 3, financial accounting ignores this problem by assuming that inflation does not exist.

TIME VALUE COMPUTATIONS

Computations involving the time value of money can be viewed from either of two perspectives: (1) the future value of a sum of money received today or (2) the present value of a sum of money received in the future. The following sections discuss these two perspectives.

Future Value

In our discussion of the time value of money, we stated that $1 invested at a given interest rate for a period of time will grow to an amount greater than $1. This dollar amount is called the **future value.**

SIMPLE INTEREST

As in the example above, $1 invested at a 10 percent per year interest rate will grow to $1.10 ($1 × 1.10) at the end of one year. This $1.10 is referred to as the future value in one year of $1, given a 10 percent interest rate. In such a situation, an individual would be indifferent as to receiving $1 now or $1.10 in one year. A simple interest calculation for one year is as follows.

Now ————⟶ 1 year
$1 ————⟶ $1.10

COMPOUND INTEREST

If we wish to compute the future value of $1 at the end of more than one period (say, two years), given a 10 percent interest rate, we use the notion of **compound interest.** That is, in the second year, the 10 percent interest rate is applied to both the original $1 principal and the $0.10 interest earned in the first year. Here, the future value of $1 at the end of two years, given a 10 percent interest rate compounded annually, is equal to $1.21. An individual would be indifferent as to whether to receive $1 now, $1.10 in one year, or $1.21 in two years, given a 10 percent interest rate compounded annually. The computation is depicted as follows.

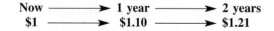

Now ————⟶ 1 year ————⟶ 2 years
$1 ————⟶ $1.10 ————⟶ $1.21

TABLE FACTORS

This same basic procedure could be used to calculate the future value of $1 for any number of periods in the future. After very many periods, though, this computation becomes quite time-consuming. Try, for example, to compute the future value of $1 in 40 years, given an 8 percent interest rate compounded annually. Fortunately, tables have been developed that expedite these calculations considerably. Turn now to the time value of money tables—specifically Table 1, located at the end of this appendix. (The factors in this table and in Tables 2, 3, 4, 5, and 6 are carried out to five digits beyond the decimal point. In our discussions, however, we round the factors to two or three digits beyond the decimal point to simplify calculations.) This is a future value

table. It enables you to quickly compute the future value of any amount for any number of periods in the future. To compute a future value, first find the intersection of the interest rate and the number of periods. This amount is called the **table factor.** Then, simply multiply this table factor by the dollar amount. For example, find the table factor for a 10 percent interest rate and two periods. It equals 1.21. Multiplying this factor by $1 gives you the future value in two years of $1 invested at a 10 percent annual interest rate. Multiplying this factor by $20 gives you the future value in two years of $20 invested at a 10 percent annual interest rate.

Note that the table factor in this example (1.21) is equal to 1.10×1.10, or $(1.10)^2$. In general, the formula for the future value calculation is as follows:

Future Value = A $(1 + i)^n$
where   **A = money amount**
            i = annual interest rate
            n = number of periods

Figure A–1 illustrates the future value calculation of $100 invested at 8 percent, 10 percent, and 12 percent for one, two, and three periods.

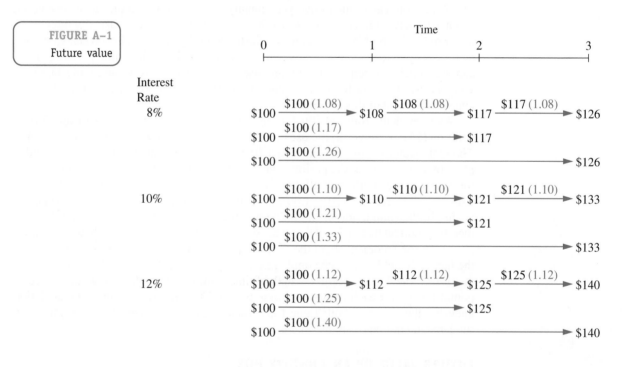

FIGURE A–1
Future value

The chart demonstrates three important points. First, it shows that the factors found on the future value table are nothing more than an individual interest factor $(1 + i)$ multiplied by itself for the number of periods $(1 + i)^n$. For example, the table factor for $n = 3$, $i = 12$ percent is 1.40 ($1.12 \times 1.12 \times 1.12$). Can you find the table factor for three periods and an 8 percent interest rate on the future value table? Can you derive it?

Note also in Figure A–1 that in each of the three time periods, as the interest rate gets higher, the time value of money is larger. In Period 3, for example, the time value of money at an 8 percent interest rate is $26 ($126 − $100). At 10 percent, it is $33 ($133 − $100), and at 12 percent, it is $40 ($140 − $100). And finally, as the time

period becomes longer, the time value of money becomes greater. These last two points illustrate the idea mentioned earlier that the magnitude of the time value of money is determined by two factors: (1) the size of the interest rate and (2) the length of the time period.

FUTURE VALUE OF ORDINARY ANNUITIES

It often happens in business transactions that cash payments of equal amounts are made periodically throughout a period of time. Installment payments on loans, for example, are typically set up in this manner. A flow of cash payments of equal amounts paid at periodic intervals is called an **annuity.** If these payments are made at the end of each period, the flow of payments is called an **ordinary annuity,** or an *annuity in arrears.* An ordinary annuity is illustrated below. This five-year ordinary annuity shows $100 payments made at the end of each year for five years.

Now ⟶ 1 ⟶ 2 ⟶ 3 ⟶ 4 ⟶ 5
       $100 $100 $100 $100 $100

How would one go about computing the future value of this entire ordinary annuity? What would an ordinary five-year annuity of $100 grow to at the end of five years, given a 10 percent interest rate compounded annually? There are basically three ways to approach this problem, and they are illustrated in Figure A–2: (1) you can view each payment separately and compute its growth over each individual time period, (2) you can view each payment separately and use the table for future value (Table 1), or (3) you can use the table for future value of an ordinary annuity (Table 2). Both tables appear at the end of this appendix.

As is evident from the illustration, all three methods bring you to the correct solution ($610). However, the use of Table 2 requires the fewest computations by far. The table factor for five periods and a 10 percent interest rate (6.10) is simply multiplied by the amount of the periodic annuity payment ($100). Note that this table factor is simply the addition of all the individual table factors used in Method 2 (6.10 = 1.46 + 1.33 + 1.21 + 1.10 + 1.00). Thus, the factor in Table 2 for a given time period is simply the summation of the individual time period factors in Table 1. Table 2 is merely a shortcut that makes it easier to compute the future values for ordinary annuities.

Think for a moment about the simple interest factor $(1 + i)$. As we have discussed, the factors in Table 1 are the simple interest factors compounded, or $(1 + i)^n$. A given factor in Table 2 for a specified length of time is the result of adding together the compound factors for each component time period. Thus, the simple interest calculation underlies the factors in both Table 1 and Table 2. In each, we have built upon the very fundamental notion of simple interest.

FUTURE VALUE OF AN ANNUITY DUE

Annuities are often paid at the beginning of each period rather than at the end. Such a series of equal cash payments is referred to as an **annuity due** and is frequently observed when, for example, lease agreements require payments in advance. Calculating the future value of an annuity due follows the same concepts as those for an ordinary annuity. The only difference comes from the obvious fact that annuity due payments come one period earlier and thus earn one period more of interest than ordinary annuities. Table 3 provides table factors for future value of an annuity due calculations.

In the same manner that Figure A–2 illustrated the future value of an ordinary annuity calculation, Figure A–3 illustrates three approaches to computing the future value of a five-year annuity due, given a 10 percent interest rate compounded annually.

FIGURE A–2   Future value of ordinary annuities

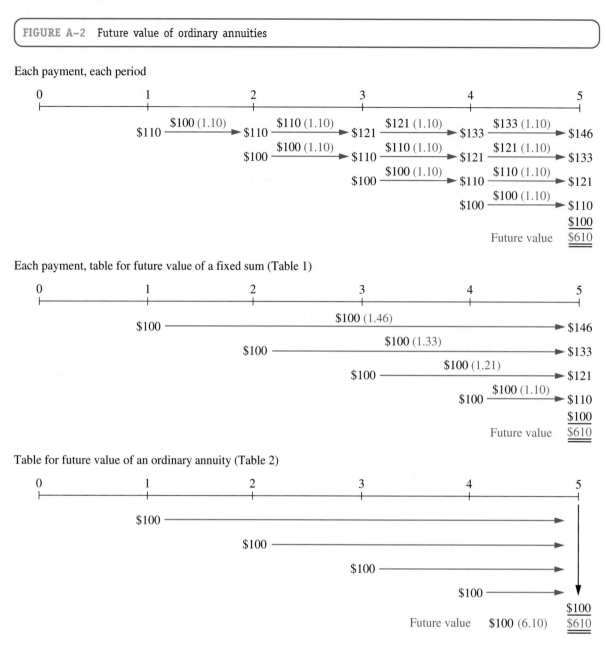

Each payment, each period

Each payment, table for future value of a fixed sum (Table 1)

Table for future value of an ordinary annuity (Table 2)

Again, while all three methods come to the correct solution, Method 3, which uses the factor found on Table 3 (6.71), is by far the easiest.

Compare the computations on this chart to those illustrating the future value of an ordinary annuity on Figure A–2. The future value here is $61 ($671 − $610) greater than the ordinary annuity future value. Why? This difference occurs because each annuity due payment comes one period earlier than each ordinary annuity payment and thus earns more interest over the annuity's life. The fifth $100 payment earns an extra $10 over one period, the fourth payment an extra $11 over two periods, the third an extra $12 over three periods, the second an extra $13 over four periods, and the first an extra $15 over five periods (61 = 10 + 11 + 12 + 13 + 15).

FIGURE A-3   Future value of an annuity due

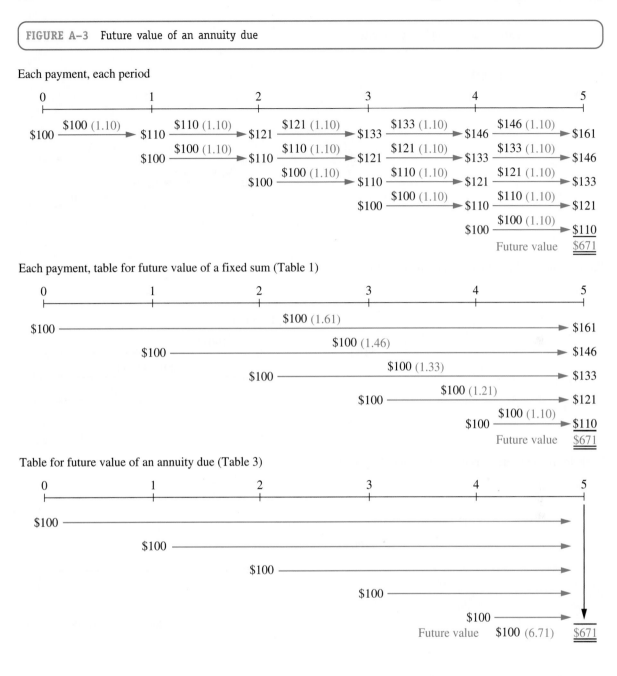

Each payment, each period

Each payment, table for future value of a fixed sum (Table 1)

Table for future value of an annuity due (Table 3)

Present Value

Now that we have covered the concept of future value, it should be relatively easy to look at the other side of the coin. Rather than asking about the future value of a current payment, we now focus on the question, "What is the present value of a future payment?"

In the original example, we stated that $1 would grow to $1.10 after one year, given a 10 percent interest rate. This relationship can just as easily be stated in the opposite way. That is, $1 is the present value of $1.10 received one year in the future,

given a 10 percent interest rate. As investors, we would be indifferent between $1 now (the present value) or $1.10 (future value) one year in the future.

The computation of present value is exactly the reciprocal of the future value computation. Recall that the simple interest factor for the future value in one period at 10 percent interest is $(1 + i)$. The simple interest factor for present value is the reciprocal, $1 \div (1 + i)$. In the future value example presented earlier, $1 \times (1 + 0.10)$ equaled $1.10, the future value. To compute the present value, we simply multiply $1.10 by $1 \div (1 + 0.10)$ to arrive at $1. The present value computation is illustrated as follows.

Now ◄———— 1 year
  $1 ◄———— $1.10

If the present value computation involves more than one period, just as in the future value case, the notion of compounding must be considered. The present value factor, once again, is simply the reciprocal of the future value factor, $1 \div (1 + i)^n$. A two-period, 10 percent interest rate example follows.

Now ◄———— 1 ◄———— 2
  $1 ◄———— $1.10 ◄———— $1.21
  $1 ◄———————————— $1.21

This example demonstrates that the present values of both $1.21 in two years and $1.10 in one year are equal to $1, given a 10 percent interest rate compounded annually. In such a case, an investor would be indifferent among having $1 now, receiving $1.10 in one year, or receiving $1.21 in two years. The example also shows that the present value of a future payment can be calculated in several different ways.

As with future values, there are tables (Tables 4, 5, and 6) designed to expedite the computations required to calculate present values. The factors contained in these tables are the reciprocals of the corresponding factors in the future value tables. Table 4 contains the table factors for the present values of single payments in the future. In the illustration above, one could use the table by multiplying $1.21 by 0.826 (Table 4, $n = 2$, $i = 10\%$) to arrive at the $1 present value. Obviously, as the number of time periods increases, the time savings from using the tables also increases.

Present values for ordinary annuities and annuities due must also be computed from time to time, and Table 5 (ordinary annuity) and Table 6 (annuity due) are designed for that purpose. As with future values, there are basically three ways to compute the present value of ordinary annuity and annuity due payment streams; they are depicted in Figures A–4 (ordinary annuity) and A–5 (annuity due). In both cases, a $100, five-year annuity at a 10 percent interest rate is illustrated.

Again compare the two charts and note that the present value of an annuity due is $38 ($417 − $379) greater than the present value of the ordinary annuity. The fact that each of the five payments in the annuity due is one period earlier than the corresponding ordinary annuity payment accounts for this difference.

An Illustration

You may quickly grasp the general concepts of future and present value, yet still have difficulty making the appropriate computations for a specific situation. We have designed the following example to demonstrate how straightforward future and present value computations can be and also how many different ways one can approach the same problem. We also introduce a concept we call **equivalent value.** It can be useful in understanding the notion of time value.

FIGURE A–4   Present value of an ordinary annuity

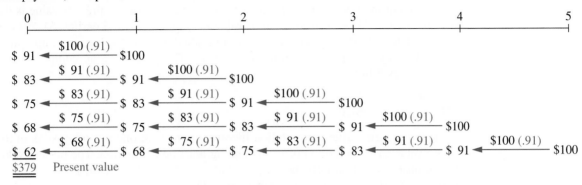

Each payment, each period

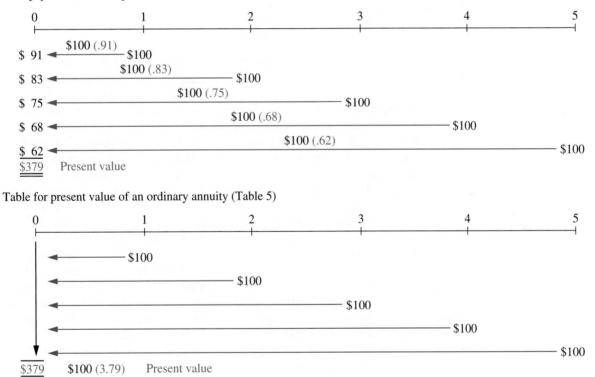

Each payment, table for present value of a fixed sum (Table 4)

Table for present value of an ordinary annuity (Table 5)

Assume a $500, five-year, ordinary annuity at a 12 percent interest rate compounded annually. The cash flows are illustrated below. Let's see how many different ways we can compute the future and present value of this payment stream. Five such examples are shown in Figure A–6.

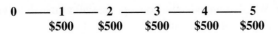

> FIGURE A–5   Present value of an annuity due

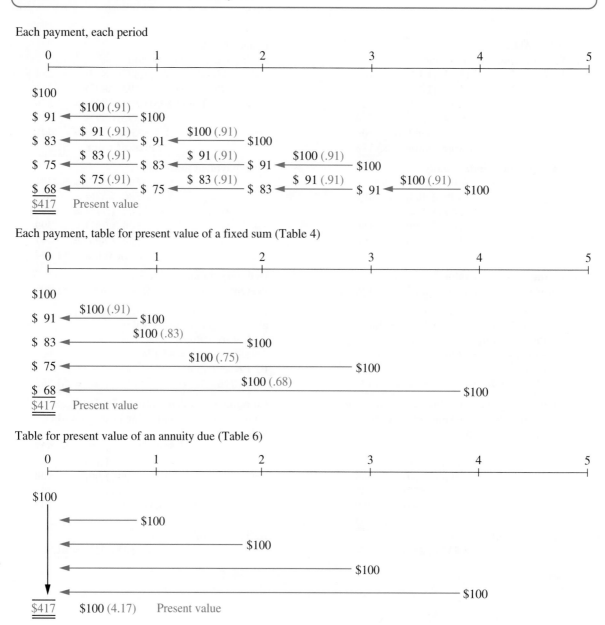

Each payment, each period

Each payment, table for present value of a fixed sum (Table 4)

Table for present value of an annuity due (Table 6)

Can you follow each of the five methods shown? Note that each method brings you to a future value of $3,176 and a present value of $1,804. No matter how many different ways one tackles this problem, the same future and present values emerge.

EQUIVALENT VALUE

To understand the concept of equivalent value, view the $500 annuity payments, the present value, and the future value as being indifference amounts. That is, in this example, an investor would be indifferent as to a five-year, $500 ordinary annuity, or

FIGURE A-6 Example calculations

FUTURE VALUE

1. Each payment, each period

$$\$500\ (1.12)(1.12)(1.12)(1.12) = \$\ \ 787$$
$$\$500\ \ (1.12)(1.12)(1.12) = \ \ \ 702$$
$$\$500\ (1.12)(1.12) = \ \ \ 627$$
$$\$500\ (1.12) = \ \ \ 560$$
$$\$500 = \ \ \ 500$$

Future value $3,176

2. Each payment individually

$$\$500\ (1.574) = \$\ \ 787$$
$$500\ (1.405) = \ \ \ 702$$
$$500\ (1.254) = \ \ \ 627$$
$$500\ (1.120) = \ \ \ 560$$
$$500\ (1.000) = \ \ \ 500$$

Future value $3,176

3. Ordinary annuity table

Future value $500\ (6.353) = \$3,176$

4. Compute present value, and then compute future value of present value

A. Present value
$$\$500\ (3.604) = \$1,802$$
B. Future value
$$\$1,802\ (1.7623) = \$3,176$$

5. Compute equivalent value at Period 3, and then compute future value of that number

A. Value at Period 3
$$\$500\ (1.254) = \$\ \ 627$$
$$500\ (1.120) = \ \ \ 560$$
$$500\ (1.000) = \ \ \ 500$$
$$500\ \ (.893) = \ \ \ 447$$
$$500\ \ (.797) = \ \ \ 399$$
$$\$2,533$$
B. Future value
$$\$2,533\ (1.254) = \$3,176$$

PRESENT VALUE

Each payment, each period

$$\$500\ (.893)(.893)(.893)(.893)(.893) = \$\ \ 284$$
$$\$500\ (.893)(.893)(.893)(.893) = \ \ \ 318$$
$$\$500\ (.893)(.893)(.893) = \ \ \ 356$$
$$\$500\ (.893)(.893) = \ \ \ 399$$
$$\$500\ (.893) = \ \ \ 447$$

Present value $1,804

Each payment individually

$$\$500\ \ (.567) = \$\ \ 284$$
$$500\ \ (.636) = \ \ \ 318$$
$$500\ \ (.712) = \ \ \ 356$$
$$500\ \ (.797) = \ \ \ 399$$
$$500\ \ (.893) = \ \ \ 447$$

Present value $1,804

Ordinary annuity table

Present value $500\ (3.604) = \$1,802^*$

Compute future value, and then compute present value of future value

A. Future value
$$\$500\ (6.353) = \$3,176$$
B. Present value
$$\$3,176\ (.5674) = \$1,802^*$$

Compute equivalent value at Period 3, and then compute present value of that number

Value at Period 3
$$\$500\ (1.12)(1.12) = \$\ \ 627$$
$$\$500\ (1.12) = \ \ \ 560$$
$$500\ (1.00) = \ \ \ 500$$
$$500\ \ (.893) = \ \ \ 447$$
$$500\ (.893)(.893) = \ \ \ 399$$
$$\$2,533$$
B. Present value
$$\$2,533\ (.712) = \$1,804$$

Rounding difference.

$1,804 now, or $3,176 five years from now. These three payments are, in other words, equivalent in value.

    The idea of equivalent value is further illustrated in the fifth computation in Figure A–6. It involves two steps. We first compute the amount that would be equivalent to the five-year ordinary annuity if one lump sum were received at the end of Period 3 ($2,533). This amount is the equivalent value of this particular annuity at the end of Period 3. We then adjust this amount to present or future value by multiplying it by the appropriate table factor. Figure A–7 illustrates the equivalent values of the five-year ordinary annuity if lump-sum payments were made at the end of each of the five periods.

Figure A–7 demonstrates that given a 12 percent interest rate compounded annually, an investor would be indifferent among the following seven payments. Can you derive these amounts?

1. A five-year, $500 ordinary annuity
2. $1,804 now (present value)
3. $2,021 at the end of one year
4. $2,262 at the end of two years
5. $2,533 at the end of three years
6. $2,839 at the end of four years
7. $3,176 at the end of five years (future value)

FIGURE A–7   Equivalent values

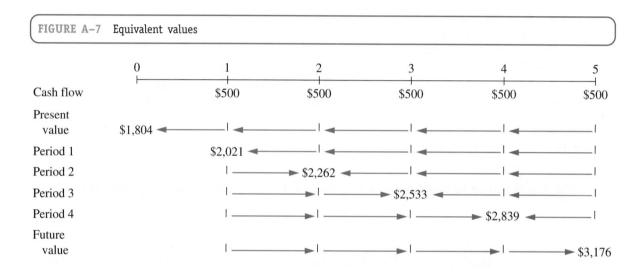

COMPUTING IMPLICIT RATES OF RETURN AND INTEREST RATES

In many business situations it is helpful, or even necessary, to compute the expected or actual rate of return (or interest) generated by an investment (or note). Consider a company, for example, that plans to invest $1,000 in a project expected to generate $300 per year over a five-year period. What rate of return is expected from that project? Similarly, consider a company that finances a piece of property with a fair market value of $100,000 by signing a note that requires annual cash payments of $20,000 for six years. What interest rate is the company paying on the note? These and similar questions can be answered by computing the rate of return (or interest rate) that is implied given the facts of the situation. Such computations are based on the present value computation, which can be viewed in terms of the following equation.

Present value = Future cash flow × (Table factor; _n_ = years, _i_ = interest rate)

So far, we have computed present values after being given a future cash flow, the number of periods (_n_), and an interest rate (_i_). For example, the value of $1,000 to be received in five years at a 10 percent interest rate can be computed as follows.

Present value = $1,000 × (Table 4 "present value of a single sum"; _n_ = 5, _i_ = 10%)
= $1,000 × 0.62092
= $620.92

However, a number of cases arise, similar to those mentioned above, where we wish to compute the interest rate (i) by either knowing—or having to estimate—the present value, the future cash flows, and the time period (n). Consider again the company that plans to invest $1,000 in a project expected to produce cash receipts of $300 per year (assume at the end of each year) for five years. In this case the investment amount ($1,000) can be viewed as the present value, the future cash flow is a $300 ordinary annuity, and the time period (n) is five years. As illustrated in Figure A-8, the implicit rate of return (i) can be computed by first finding the table factor (3.33) and then finding that interest rate on that table where the period of time (five years) matches the table factor. The answer is approximately 15 percent.

FIGURE A–8   Computing an implicit rate of return

Present value	=	future cash flow	×	(Table factor; n = years, i = interest rate)
$1,000	=	$300	×	(Table 5 "present value of an ordinary annuity"; $n = 5, i = $?)

Rearranging,
Table factor   = $1,000/$300
Table factor   =   3.33

On Table 5, a 15 percent interest rate over a five-year period leads to a table factor of approximately 3.33.

In other words, if the company pays $1,000 for an investment that produces $300 at the end of each year for five years, that investment will generate an annual rate of return of approximately 15 percent.

In a similar way, implicit interest rates can be computed on notes payable and receivable. Consider again a company that purchases a piece of property with a fair market value of $100,000, paying for it by signing a note payable requiring cash payments of $20,000 at the beginning of each year for six years. Figure A-9 illustrates the computation of the interest rate (8 percent) implicit in the note payable.

FIGURE A–9   Computing an implicit interest rate

Present value	=	future cash flow	×	(Table factor; n = years, i = interest rate)
$100,000	=	$20,000	×	(Table 6 "present value of an annuity due"; $n = 6, i = $?)

Rearranging,
Table factor   = $100,000/$20,000
Table factor   =   5.00

On Table 6, an 8 percent interest rate over a six-year period leads to a table factor of approximately 5.00.

PRESENT VALUE AND FINANCIAL ACCOUNTING

We stated earlier that present value is the economic form of valuation. Investors, creditors, and managers use it to compare the values of alternative investments. Bankers, lawyers, and other business decision makers use it to derive the terms of contracts like mortgages, leases, pensions, and life insurance. Virtually any transaction that can be broken down into periodic cash flows utilizes the time value of money concept and can be reduced to present value, future value, and other equivalent values. The time value of money is covered in finance, economics, accounting, and other business courses. You may have already studied present value in previous courses, and you will probably see it again in the future. The uses of present value in business decision making are almost limitless.

The study of financial accounting and its reliance on the time value of money concept is no exception. As you already know, financial accounting information is useful because it helps investors, creditors, and other interested parties evaluate and control the business decisions of management. Such evaluation and control requires that financial accounting information be used to assess value: the value of entire companies, the value of individual assets and liabilities, and the value of specific transactions. Since present value is the economic form of valuation, financial accounting information must reflect present value if it is to be useful.

However, a critical problem is associated with using present value on the financial statements. The present value calculation requires that both future cash flows and future interest rates be predicted. In the vast majority of cases, predicting the future cash flows associated with a particular asset or liability with a reasonable degree of confidence is almost impossible. For example, how would one go about predicting the future cash inflows and outflows associated with the purchase of a specific piece of equipment like an automobile? Moreover, accurately predicting interest rates has for years eluded even the best economists. The predictions that management must make to apply present value are simply too subjective for financial statements that are to be used by those outside the company. Auditors are unwilling and unable to verify such subjective judgments. The legal liability faced by both managers and auditors makes such verification potentially very costly.

For these reasons, although present value remains an important goal of financial measurement, most of the valuation bases on the financial statements represent surrogate (substitute) measures of present value. Historical cost, fair market value, replacement cost, and net realizable value can all be viewed as surrogate measures of present value. These valuation bases are used primarily because present value is simply too subjective and unreliable for a system that requires auditors to verify financial statements prepared by management for shareholders and other outside interested parties. Present value calculations, in general, violate the principle of objectivity.

In some cases, however, the future cash flows associated with an asset or a liability are predictable enough to allow for sufficiently objective present value calculations. As discussed in Chapter 3, contractual agreements like notes receivable and payable meet the criterion of objectivity. Mortgages, bonds, leases, and pensions are other examples of contracts that underlie cash flows and thus remove much of the subjectivity associated with cash flow prediction. In these cases, the present value calculation is used in the preparation of the financial statements (see Chapter 11—Long-Term Liabilities: Notes, Bonds, and Leases).

In summary, there are two reasons accounting students must understand present value. First, present value is the economic form of valuation and is therefore an important

goal of accounting measurement. It is the standard against which all financial accounting measurements must be compared and evaluated. Second, in those cases where cash flow prediction is sufficiently objective (e.g., contracts), present value methods are used, and present values are actually incorporated into the financial statements. The balance sheet valuation of the assets and liabilities arising from such contracts results from the present value calculation.

EXERCISES

EA-1

Future value/
single sum

If $150 were invested today, how large a sum could be withdrawn at the end of the following time periods at the following compound interest rates? Complete the following table.

Compound Interest Rates	Time Periods (Years)		
	5	10	15
5%			
10%			
15%			

EA-2

Present value/
single sum

Compute the present value of $10,000 received at the end of the following time periods at the following discount rates. Complete the following table.

Compound Interest Rates	Time Periods (Years)		
	5	10	15
5%			
10%			
15%			

EA-3

Future value/
ordinary annuity

If $150 were invested at the end of each year over the following time periods at the following interest rates, how large a sum could be withdrawn at the end of the final time period? Complete the following table.

Compound Interest Rates	Time Periods (Years)		
	5	10	15
5%			
10%			
15%			

EA-4

Future value/
annuity due

If $150 were invested at the beginning of each year over the following time periods at the following interest rates, how large a sum could be withdrawn at the end of the final time period? Complete the following table.

Compound Interest Rates	Time Periods (Years)		
	5	10	15
5%			
10%			
15%			

EA-5

Present value/
ordinary annuity

Compute the present value of $10,000 received at the end of each year over the following time periods at the following discount rates. Complete the following table.

	Time Periods (Years)		
Compound Interest Rates	5	10	15
5%			
10%			
15%			

EA–6

Present value/
annuity due

Compute the present value of $10,000 received at the beginning of each year over the following time periods at the following discount rates. Complete the following table.

	Time Periods (Years)		
Compound Interest Rates	5	10	15
5%			
10%			
15%			

EA–7

Present value of
different payment
patterns

Compute the present value of the payment patterns provided below, given an 8 percent discount rate.

a. $50 at the end of Year 2; $100 at the end of Year 5; $80 at the end of Year 8.
b. $100 at the end of Years 1, 2, 3, 4; $100 at the end of Year 8.
c. $60 at the end of Years 5, 6, 7, 8; $100 at the end of Year 10.
d. $90 at the end of Years 7, 8, 9.

EA–8

Present value of
different payment
patterns

Compute the present value of the payment patterns provided below, given an 8 percent discount rate.

a. $50 at the end of Year 2; $100 at the end of Year 5; $80 at the beginning of Year 8.
b. $100 at the beginning of Years 1, 2, 3, 4; $100 at the beginning of Year 8.
c. $60 at the beginning of Years 5, 6, 7, 8; $100 at the beginning of Year 10.
d. $90 at the beginning of Years 7, 8, 9.

EA–9

Future and
present values

Ben Watson found $25,000 lying on the sidewalk and decided to invest the money. He believes that he can earn a 10 percent rate (compounded annually) on his investment for the first four years, 12 percent for the following three years, and 15 percent for the following five years.

a. How much money will Ben have at the end of four years, seven years, and twelve years?
b. If someone offered to pay him $36,000 at the end of four years for the $25,000, should he accept? Why or why not?

EA–10

Present value of
future bond
payments—
ordinary annuity
and annuity due

Rudnicki Corporation raises money by issuing bonds. The bond agreement states that Rudnicki must make interest payments in the amount of $40,000 at the end of each year for ten years and make a $500,000 payment at the end of the tenth year. Assume that the discount rate is 10 percent.

a. What amount, as a lump sum, would the company have to invest today to meet the $40,000 annual interest payments and the $500,000 principal payment at the end of the tenth year?
b. What amount would have to be invested if the bond agreement stated that the interest payments were to be made at the beginning of each of the ten years and the $500,000 payment was still at the end of the tenth year?

EA–11

The highest
present value

Congratulations! You have just won the lottery. The lottery board offers you three different options for collecting your winnings:

1. You will receive payments of $500,000 at the end of each year for twenty years.
2. You will receive a lump-sum payment of $4,500,000 today.
3. You will receive a lump-sum payment of $1 million today and payments of $2,100,000 at the end of Years 5, 6, and 7.

Assume that all earnings can be invested at a 10 percent annual rate. Which option should you choose and why?

EA–12

Comparing ordinary annuities and annuities due

Consider a three-year, $700 ordinary annuity (the first payment is due one year from now) and a three-year, $700 annuity due (the first payment is due now). Assume a discount rate of 10 percent. For each of the two annuities, compute the equivalent value as of the following points in time.

a. Now
b. The end of Period 1
c. The end of Period 2
d. The end of Period 3
e. Which of the above is referred to as the present value?
f. Which of the above is referred to as the future value?
g. Which of the two annuities is most valuable and by how much?

EA–13

Different terms of financing

Dunn Drafting Company is considering expanding its business by purchasing new equipment. Because of constraints on how much the company can spend for new equipment, the president wants to make sure that the company enters into the best possible deal. Dunn Drafting has four options for paying for the new equipment.

1. Make a lump-sum payment of $240,000 today.
2. Make a lump-sum payment of $500,000 eight years from now.
3. Make a lump-sum payment of $600,000 ten years from now.
4. Make payments of $50,000 at the beginning of each year for six years. The first payment is due now.

a. Compute the present value of each option. Assume that the relevant interest rate is 12 percent.
b. If you were the president of Dunn Drafting Company, which option would you select?
c. Would your answer to (b) change if the annual interest rate was 8 percent? If so, which option would you now prefer?

EA–14

Saving for a college education— future value

The Croziers have a three-year-old son named Ryan, and they want to provide for Ryan's college education. They estimate that it will cost $40,000 per year for four years when Ryan enters college fifteen years from now. Assume that all investments can earn a 10 percent annual interest rate and that the four annual payments will be made at the beginning of each year.

a. How much would the Croziers have to invest today to meet Ryan's college expenses?
b. How much would the Croziers have to invest at the end of each year for fourteen years to meet Ryan's college expenses?
c. Answer questions (a) and (b) above, assuming an 8 percent annual interest rate.

EA–15

Saving for a college education— future value

The Taylors have a nine-year-old daughter named Emily, and they wish to provide for her college education. They estimate that it will cost $30,000 per year for four years when Emily enters college ten years from now. Assume that all investments can earn an 8 percent annual interest rate and that the four annual payments will be made at the beginning of each year.

a. How much would the Taylors have to invest today to meet Emily's college expenses?
b. How much would the Taylors have to invest at the end of each year for nine years to meet Emily's college expenses?
c. Answer questions (a) and (b) above, assuming a 6 percent annual interest rate.

EA–16

Computing an implicit rate of return

Begley Enterprises is considering investing in a project estimated to produce annual cash flows of approximately $10,000 over the next ten years. The initial cost of the investment is $53,280. Assume that the cash flows will be received at the end of each of the ten years.

a. Compute the implicit interest rate on the investment.
b. If Begley has to borrow the $53,280 from a bank at an annual interest rate of 8 percent, should it pursue this project? Why or why not?

EA–17

Computing an
implicit rate
of return

Barnhiser Goods needs $100,000 to finance a project. It is negotiating a loan, and the bank has offered several different payment schedules. Compute the effective interest rate on each schedule and identify the schedule with the lowest effective interest rate.

a. $14,900 payments at the end of each year for ten years.
b. $10,000 payments at the end of each year for five years, and a $100,000 payment at the end of the fifth year.
c. $10,300 payments at the end of each year for fifteen years.

PROBLEMS

PA–1

The value of
common stock

Christie Bauer is contemplating investing in South Bend Ironworks. She estimates that the company will pay the following dividends per share at the end of the next four years and that the current price of the company's common stock ($100) will remain unchanged.

Year 1	Year 2	Year 3	Year 4
$5	$6	$7	$8

Christie wants to earn 12 percent on her investment.

REQUIRED:

Assume that Christie plans to sell the investment at the end of the fourth year. How much would she be willing to pay for one share of common stock in South Bend Ironworks?

PA–2

Computing future value,
present
value, and
equivalent value

Wharton Company is planning to make the following investments.

1. $1,000 at the end of each year for five years at a 10 percent annual rate. Wharton Company will leave the accumulated principal and earnings in the bank for another five years at a 12 percent annual rate.
2. $3,000 at the end of each year for seven years at a 15 percent annual rate. Wharton will not make the first $3,000 payment until four years from now.

REQUIRED:

a. How much money will Wharton have at the end of ten years?
b. How much would Wharton have to invest in a lump sum today to have an equivalent amount at the end of ten years, given a 12 percent annual rate of return?

PA–3

Computing present
value and
equivalent value of
contract cash flows

The terms of three different contracts follow.

1. $8,000 received at the beginning of each year for ten years, compounded at a 6 percent annual rate.
2. $8,000 received today and $20,000 received ten years from today. The relevant interest rate is 12 percent.
3. $8,000 received at the end of Years 4, 5, and 6. The relevant annual interest rate is 10 percent.

REQUIRED:

a. Compute the present value of each contract.
b. Compute the equivalent value of each contract at the end of Years 5 and 10.

PA–4

The highest
present value?

J. Hartney, president of Doyle Industries, has a choice of three bonus contracts. The first option is to receive an immediate cash payment of $25,000. The second option is a deferred payment of $60,000, to be received in eight years. The final option is to receive an immediate cash payment of $5,000, a deferred payment of $27,000 to be received in three years, and a deferred payment of $20,000 to be received in twenty years. Assume that the relevant interest rate is 9 percent. Which bonus option should Hartney accept and why?

PA–5

Computing
equivalent values

Boulder Wilderness Adventures purchased rafting and kayaking equipment by issuing a note to Recreational Co-op, the seller of the equipment. The note required a down payment of $5,000, annual payments of $10,000 at the end of each year for five years (the first payment to be one year from now), and a final payment of $15,000 at the end of the fifth year (this payment is in addition to the $10,000 annual payments). Assume that 10 percent is the relevant annual interest rate.

REQUIRED:

Recreational Co-op is indifferent between receiving the cash flows described above or any other cash flow that represents an equivalent value. Compute equivalent values as of the following points in time:

a. Today
b. At the end of two years
c. At the end of four years
d. At the end of five years

PA–6

Present and
future values

Assume an annual interest rate of 8 percent for each of the following independent cases. Compute the value at time 0 and the value at the end of the investment period for all the cash flows described.

a. $10,000 is invested and held for four years.
b. $2,000 is invested at the end of each year for eight years.
c. $5,000 is invested at the beginning of each year for three years.
d. $3,000 is invested at the end of each year for five years. The balance is left to accumulate interest for an additional five years.
e. A company will receive $25,000 at the end of seven years.
f. A company will receive $3,000 at the end of each year for two years.
g. A company will receive $4,000 at the beginning of each year for three years.

PA–7

Computing implicit
rates of return

Joy Don Corp. sells a building to Trifle and Life in exchange for a note. The note specifies a lump sum payment of $300,000 ten years in the future and annual payments (beginning today) of $2,000 at the beginning of each year for ten years. Assume an annual interest rate of 10 percent.

REQUIRED:

a. Would Joy Don be wise to accept $110,000 now instead of the note? Why or why not?
b. At what interest rate would Joy Don be wise to accept the $110,000 instead of the note? (*Hint:* Use a trial-and-error approach. The answer is an integer.)

TABLE 1 Future value of $1 (future amount of a single sum)

Periods (n)	2%	3%	4%	5%	6%	7%	8%
1	1.02000	1.03000	1.04000	1.05000	1.06000	1.07000	1.08000
2	1.04040	1.06090	1.08160	1.10250	1.12360	1.14490	1.16640
3	1.06121	1.09273	1.12486	1.15763	1.19102	1.22504	1.25971
4	1.08243	1.12551	1.16986	1.21551	1.26248	1.31080	1.36049
5	1.10408	1.15927	1.21665	1.27628	1.33823	1.40255	1.46933
6	1.12616	1.19405	1.26532	1.34010	1.41852	1.50073	1.58687
7	1.14869	1.22987	1.31593	1.40710	1.50363	1.60578	1.71382
8	1.17166	1.26677	1.36857	1.47746	1.59385	1.71819	1.85093
9	1.19509	1.30477	1.42331	1.55133	1.68948	1.83846	1.99900
10	1.21899	1.34392	1.48024	1.62889	1.79085	1.96715	2.15892
11	1.24337	1.38423	1.53945	1.71034	1.89830	2.10485	2.33164
12	1.26824	1.42576	1.60103	1.79586	2.01220	2.25219	2.51817
15	1.34587	1.55797	1.80094	2.07893	2.39656	2.75903	3.17217
20	1.48595	1.80611	2.19112	2.65330	3.20714	3.86968	4.66096
30	1.81136	2.42726	3.24340	4.32194	5.74349	7.61226	10.06266
40	2.20804	3.26204	4.80102	7.03999	10.28572	14.97446	21.72452

Periods (n)	9%	10%	11%	12%	14%	15%
1	1.09000	1.10000	1.11000	1.12000	1.14000	1.15000
2	1.18810	1.21000	1.23210	1.25440	1.29960	1.32250
3	1.29503	1.33100	1.36763	1.40493	1.48154	1.52088
4	1.41158	1.46410	1.51807	1.57352	1.68896	1.74901
5	1.53862	1.61051	1.68506	1.76234	1.92541	2.01136
6	1.67710	1.77156	1.87041	1.97382	2.19497	2.31306
7	1.82804	1.94872	2.07616	2.21068	2.50227	2.66002
8	1.99256	2.14359	2.30454	2.47596	2.85259	3.05902
9	2.17189	2.35795	2.55804	2.77308	3.25195	3.51788
10	2.36736	2.59374	2.83942	3.10585	3.70722	4.04556
11	2.58043	2.85312	3.15176	3.47855	4.22623	4.65239
12	2.81266	3.13843	3.49845	3.89598	4.81790	5.35025
15	3.64248	4.17725	4.78459	5.47357	7.13794	8.13706
20	5.60441	6.72750	8.06231	9.64629	13.74349	16.36654
30	13.26768	17.44940	22.89230	29.95992	50.95016	66.21177
40	31.40942	45.25926	65.00087	93.05097	188.88351	267.86355

TABLE 2   Future value of an ordinary annuity of $1

Periods (n)	2%	3%	4%	5%	6%	7%	8%
1	1.00000	1.00000	1.00000	1.00000	1.00000	1.00000	1.00000
2	2.02000	2.03000	2.04000	2.05000	2.06000	2.07000	2.08000
3	3.06040	3.09090	3.12160	3.15250	3.18360	3.21490	3.24640
4	4.12161	4.18363	4.24646	4.31013	4.37462	4.43994	4.50611
5	5.20404	5.30914	5.41632	5.52563	5.63709	5.75074	5.86660
6	6.30812	6.46841	6.63298	6.80191	6.97532	7.15329	7.33593
7	7.43428	7.66246	7.89829	8.14201	8.39384	8.65402	8.92280
8	8.58297	8.89234	9.21423	9.54911	9.89747	10.25980	10.63663
9	9.75463	10.15911	10.58280	11.02656	11.49132	11.97799	12.48756
10	10.94972	11.46388	12.00611	12.57789	13.18079	13.81645	14.48656
11	12.16872	12.80780	13.48635	14.20679	14.97164	15.78360	16.64549
12	13.41209	14.19203	15.02581	15.91713	16.86994	17.88845	18.97713
15	17.29342	18.59891	20.02359	21.57856	23.27597	25.12902	27.15211
20	24.29737	26.87037	29.77808	33.06595	36.78559	40.99549	45.76196
30	40.56808	47.57542	56.08494	66.43885	79.05819	94.46079	113.28321
40	60.40198	75.40126	95.02552	120.79977	154.76197	199.63511	259.05652

Periods (n)	9%	10%	11%	12%	14%	15%
1	1.00000	1.00000	1.00000	1.00000	1.00000	1.00000
2	2.09000	2.10000	2.11000	2.12000	2.14000	2.15000
3	3.27810	3.31000	3.34210	3.37440	3.43960	3.47250
4	4.57313	4.64100	4.70973	4.77933	4.92114	4.99338
5	5.98471	6.10510	6.22780	6.35285	6.61010	6.74238
6	7.52333	7.71561	7.91286	8.11519	8.53552	8.75374
7	9.20043	9.48717	9.78327	10.08901	10.73049	11.06680
8	11.02847	11.43589	11.85943	12.29969	13.23276	13.72682
9	13.02104	13.57948	14.16397	14.77566	16.08535	16.78584
10	15.19293	15.93742	16.72201	17.54874	19.33730	20.30372
11	17.56029	18.53117	19.56143	20.65458	23.04452	24.34928
12	20.14072	21.38428	22.71319	24.13313	27.27075	29.00167
15	29.36092	31.77248	34.40536	37.27971	43.84241	47.58041
20	51.16012	57.27500	64.20283	72.05244	91.02493	102.44358
30	136.30754	164.49402	199.02088	241.33268	356.78685	434.74515
40	337.88245	442.59256	581.82607	767.09142	1342.02510	1779.09031

TABLE 3   Future value of an annuity due of $1

Periods (n)	2%	3%	4%	5%	6%	7%	8%
1	1.02000	1.03000	1.04000	1.05000	1.06000	1.07000	1.08000
2	2.06040	2.09090	2.12160	2.15250	2.18360	2.21490	2.24640
3	3.12161	3.18363	3.24646	3.31013	3.37462	3.43994	3.50611
4	4.20404	4.30914	4.41632	4.52563	4.63709	4.75074	4.86660
5	5.30812	5.46841	5.63298	5.80191	5.97532	6.15329	6.33593
6	6.43428	6.66246	6.89829	7.14201	7.39384	7.65402	7.92280
7	7.58297	7.89234	8.21423	8.54911	8.89747	9.25980	9.63663
8	8.75463	9.15911	9.58280	10.02656	10.49132	10.97799	11.48756
9	9.94972	10.46388	11.00611	11.57789	12.18079	12.81645	13.48656
10	11.16872	11.80780	12.48635	13.20679	13.97164	14.78360	15.64549
11	12.41209	13.19203	14.02581	14.91713	15.86994	16.88845	17.97713
12	13.68033	14.61779	15.62684	16.71298	17.88214	19.14064	20.49530
15	17.63929	19.15688	20.82453	22.65749	24.67253	26.88805	29.32428
20	24.78332	27.67649	30.96920	34.71925	38.99273	43.86518	49.42292
30	41.37944	49.00268	58.32834	69.76079	83.80168	101.07304	122.34587
40	61.61002	77.66330	98.82654	126.83976	164.04768	213.60957	279.78104

Periods (n)	9%	10%	11%	12%	14%	15%
1	1.09000	1.10000	1.11000	1.12000	1.14000	1.15000
2	2.27810	2.31000	2.34210	2.37440	2.43960	2.47250
3	3.57313	3.64100	3.70973	3.77933	3.92114	3.99338
4	4.98471	5.10510	5.22780	5.35285	5.61010	5.74238
5	6.52333	6.71561	6.91286	7.11519	7.53552	7.75374
6	8.20043	8.48717	8.78327	9.08901	9.73049	10.06680
7	10.02847	10.43589	10.85943	11.29969	12.23276	12.72682
8	12.02104	12.57948	13.16397	13.77566	15.08535	15.78584
9	14.19293	14.93742	15.72201	16.54874	18.33730	19.30372
10	16.56029	17.53117	18.56143	19.65458	22.04452	23.34928
11	19.14072	20.38428	21.71319	23.13313	26.27075	28.00167
12	21.95338	23.52271	25.21164	27.02911	31.08865	33.35192
15	32.00340	34.94973	38.18995	41.75328	49.98035	54.71747
20	55.76453	63.00250	71.26514	80.69874	103.76842	117.81012
30	148.57522	180.94342	220.91317	270.29261	406.73701	499.95692
40	368.29187	486.85181	645.82693	859.14239	1529.90861	2045.95385

TABLE 4   Present value of $1 (present value of a single sum)

Periods (n)	2%	3%	4%	5%	6%	7%	8%
1	0.98039	0.97087	0.96154	0.95238	0.94340	0.93458	0.92593
2	0.96177	0.94260	0.92456	0.90703	0.89000	0.87344	0.85734
3	0.94232	0.91514	0.88900	0.86384	0.83962	0.81630	0.79383
4	0.92385	0.88849	0.85480	0.82270	0.79209	0.76290	0.73503
5	0.90573	0.86261	0.82193	0.78353	0.74726	0.71299	0.68058
6	0.88797	0.83748	0.79031	0.74622	0.70496	0.66634	0.63017
7	0.87056	0.81309	0.75992	0.71068	0.66506	0.62275	0.58349
8	0.85349	0.78941	0.73069	0.67684	0.62741	0.58201	0.54027
9	0.83676	0.76642	0.70259	0.64461	0.59190	0.54393	0.50025
10	0.82035	0.74409	0.67556	0.61391	0.55839	0.50835	0.46319
11	0.80426	0.72242	0.64958	0.58468	0.52679	0.47509	0.42888
12	0.78849	0.70138	0.62460	0.55684	0.49697	0.44401	0.39711
15	0.74301	0.64186	0.55526	0.48102	0.41727	0.36245	0.31524
20	0.67297	0.55368	0.45639	0.37689	0.31180	0.25842	0.21455
30	0.55207	0.41199	0.30832	0.23138	0.17411	0.13137	0.09938
40	0.45289	0.30656	0.20829	0.14205	0.09722	0.06678	0.04603
50	0.37153	0.22811	0.14071	0.08720	0.05429	0.03395	0.02132
60	0.30478	0.16973	0.09506	0.05354	0.03031	0.01726	0.00988

Periods (n)	9%	10%	11%	12%	14%	15%
1	0.91743	0.90909	0.90090	0.89286	0.87719	0.86957
2	0.84168	0.82645	0.81162	0.79719	0.76947	0.75614
3	0.77218	0.75131	0.73119	0.71178	0.67497	0.65752
4	0.70843	0.68301	0.65873	0.63552	0.59208	0.57175
5	0.64993	0.62092	0.59345	0.56743	0.51937	0.49718
6	0.59627	0.56447	0.53464	0.50663	0.45559	0.43233
7	0.54703	0.51316	0.48166	0.45235	0.39964	0.37594
8	0.50187	0.46651	0.43393	0.40388	0.35056	0.32690
9	0.46043	0.42410	0.39092	0.36061	0.30751	0.28426
10	0.42241	0.38554	0.35218	0.32197	0.26974	0.24718
11	0.38753	0.35049	0.31728	0.28748	0.23662	0.21494
12	0.35553	0.31863	0.28584	0.25668	0.20756	0.18691
15	0.27454	0.23939	0.20900	0.18270	0.14010	0.12289
20	0.17843	0.14864	0.12403	0.10367	0.07276	0.06110
30	0.07537	0.05731	0.04368	0.03338	0.01963	0.01510
40	0.03184	0.02209	0.01538	0.01075	0.00529	0.00373
50	0.01345	0.00852	0.00542	0.00346	0.00143	0.00092
60	0.00568	0.00328	0.00191	0.00111	0.00039	0.00023

> **TABLE 5**   Present value of an ordinary annuity of $1

Periods (n)	2%	3%	4%	5%	6%	7%	8%
1	0.98039	0.97087	0.96154	0.95238	0.94340	0.93458	0.92593
2	1.94156	1.91347	1.88609	1.85941	1.83339	1.80802	1.78326
3	2.88388	2.82861	2.77509	2.72325	2.67301	2.62432	2.57710
4	3.80773	3.71710	3.62990	3.54595	3.46511	3.38721	3.31213
5	4.71346	4.57971	4.45182	4.32948	4.21236	4.10020	3.99271
6	5.60143	5.41719	5.24214	5.07569	4.91732	4.76654	4.62288
7	6.47199	6.23028	6.00205	5.78637	5.58238	5.38929	5.20637
8	7.32548	7.01969	6.73274	6.46321	6.20979	5.97130	5.74664
9	8.16224	7.78611	7.43533	7.10782	6.80169	6.51523	6.24689
10	8.98259	8.53020	8.11090	7.72173	7.36009	7.02358	6.71008
11	9.78685	9.25262	8.76048	8.30641	7.88687	7.49867	7.13896
12	10.57534	9.95400	9.38507	8.86325	8.38384	7.94269	7.53608
15	12.84926	11.93794	11.11839	10.37966	9.71225	9.10791	8.55948
20	16.35143	14.87747	13.59033	12.46221	11.46992	10.59401	9.81815
30	22.39646	19.60044	17.29203	15.37245	13.76483	12.40904	11.25778
40	27.35548	23.11477	19.79277	17.15909	15.04630	13.33171	11.92461
50	31.42361	25.72976	21.48218	18.25593	15.76186	13.80075	12.23348
60	34.76089	27.67556	22.62349	18.92929	16.16143	14.03918	12.37655

Periods (n)	9%	10%	11%	12%	14%	15%
1	0.91743	0.90909	0.90090	0.89286	0.87719	0.86957
2	1.75911	1.73554	1.71252	1.69005	1.64666	1.62571
3	2.53129	2.48685	2.44371	2.40183	2.32163	2.28323
4	3.23972	3.16987	3.10245	3.03735	2.91371	2.85498
5	3.88965	3.79079	3.69590	3.60478	3.43308	3.35216
6	4.48592	4.35526	4.23054	4.11141	3.88867	3.78448
7	5.03295	4.86842	4.71220	4.56376	4.28830	4.16042
8	5.53482	5.33493	5.14612	4.96764	4.63886	4.48732
9	5.99525	5.75902	5.53705	5.32825	4.94637	4.77158
10	6.41766	6.14457	5.88923	5.65022	5.21612	5.01877
11	6.80519	6.49506	6.20652	5.93770	5.45273	5.23371
12	7.16073	6.81369	6.49236	6.19437	5.66029	5.42062
15	8.06069	7.60608	7.19087	6.81086	6.14217	5.84737
20	9.12855	8.51356	7.96333	7.46944	6.62313	6.25933
30	10.27365	9.42691	8.69379	8.05518	7.00266	6.56598
40	10.75736	9.77905	8.95105	8.24378	7.10504	6.64178
50	10.96168	9.91481	9.04165	8.30450	7.13266	6.66051
60	11.04799	9.96716	9.07356	8.32405	7.14011	6.66515

TABLE 6   Present value of an annuity due of $1

Periods (n)	2%	3%	4%	5%	6%	7%	8%
1	1.00000	1.00000	1.00000	1.00000	1.00000	1.00000	1.00000
2	1.98039	1.97087	1.96154	1.95238	1.94340	1.93458	1.92593
3	2.94156	2.91347	2.88609	2.85941	2.83339	2.80802	2.78326
4	3.88388	3.82861	3.77509	3.72325	3.67301	3.62432	3.57710
5	4.80773	4.71710	4.62990	4.54595	4.46511	4.38721	4.31213
6	5.71346	5.57971	5.45182	5.32948	5.21236	5.10020	4.99271
7	6.60143	6.41719	6.24214	6.07569	5.91732	5.76654	5.62288
8	7.47199	7.23028	7.00205	6.78637	6.58238	6.38929	6.20637
9	8.32548	8.01969	7.73274	7.46321	7.20979	6.97130	6.74664
10	9.16224	8.78611	8.43533	8.10782	7.80169	7.51523	7.24689
11	9.98259	9.53020	9.11090	8.72173	8.36009	8.02358	7.71008
12	10.78685	10.25262	9.76048	9.30641	8.88687	8.49867	8.13896
15	13.10625	12.29607	11.56312	10.89864	10.29498	9.74547	9.24424
20	16.67846	15.32380	14.13394	13.08532	12.15812	11.33560	10.60360
30	22.84438	20.18845	17.98371	16.14107	14.59072	13.27767	12.15841
40	27.90259	23.80822	20.58448	18.01704	19.94907	14.26493	12.87858
50	32.05208	26.50166	22.34147	19.16872	16.70757	14.76680	13.21216
60	35.45610	28.50583	23.52843	19.87575	17.13111	15.02192	13.36668

Periods (n)	9%	10%	11%	12%	14%	15%
1	1.00000	1.00000	1.00000	1.00000	1.00000	1.00000
2	1.91743	1.90909	1.90090	1.89286	1.87719	1.86957
3	2.75911	2.73554	2.71252	2.69005	2.64666	2.62571
4	3.53129	3.48685	3.44371	3.40183	3.32163	3.28323
5	4.23972	4.16987	4.10245	4.03735	3.91371	3.85498
6	4.88965	4.79079	4.69590	4.60478	4.43308	4.35216
7	5.48592	5.35526	5.23054	5.11141	4.88867	4.78448
8	6.03295	5.86842	5.71220	5.56376	5.28830	5.16042
9	6.53482	6.33493	6.14612	5.96764	5.63886	5.48732
10	6.99525	6.75902	6.53705	6.32825	5.94637	5.77158
11	7.41766	7.14457	6.88923	6.65022	6.21612	6.01877
12	7.80519	7.49506	7.20652	6.93770	6.45273	6.23371
15	8.78615	8.36669	7.98187	7.62817	7.00207	6.72448
20	9.95011	9.36492	8.83929	8.36578	7.55037	7.19823
30	11.19828	10.36961	9.65011	9.02181	7.98304	7.55088
40	11.72552	10.75696	9.93567	9.23303	8.09975	7.63805
50	11.94823	10.90630	10.03624	0.30104	8.13123	7.65959
60	12.04231	10.96387	10.07165	9.32294	8.13972	7.66492

Quality of Earnings Cases: A Comprehensive Review

CASE 1: LIBERTY MANUFACTURING

You have recently been hired by Capital City Bank as a credit analyst. One of the tasks of your new position is to review the financial statements submitted by loan applicants. You have been instructed to assess the solvency and earning power of the applicants as well as the quality and persistence of the reported earnings number. After completing your analysis, you should report your conclusions to your supervisor, recommending whether the applicant should be further considered for the loan and why.

Company Description

You are now asked to review the file of a loan applicant, Liberty Manufacturing, which has applied for a long-term $500,000 loan. This company is a medium-sized, family-run operation that manufactures a component used in a wide variety of engines. Liberty has been in existence for approximately twenty years and has grown consistently during that time, reporting profits in each of the last ten years. The company has recently begun to move into foreign markets and is seeking the loan to finance investments in property, plant, and equipment and to complete the acquisition of a small foreign supplier, Packer Technical.

The demand for Liberty's product seems stable, and the company has made recent technical advancements in product design that may lead to increased sales in the future. At present, the company appears to hold a solid position in its industry. Prices in the industry, both input and output, have been rising at an above-average rate, and the industrywide inflation rate in 2011 was approximately 5 percent.

Note from Your Supervisor

Contained in the file is a note from your supervisor, Anne Mayor, who has made a cursory review of the financial statements. In addition to your task of assessing Liberty's solvency, earning power, and quality and persistence of the reported earnings number, she raises several other points that you should address in your report.

First, Anne would like you to closely examine the investing activities entered into by Liberty in late 2010 and during 2011. It seems that the company both acquired and sold property, plant, and equipment, land, and short-term investments. It also made a large investment in an affiliate company, Packer, which it intends to increase with the proceeds from the loan under consideration. Is Packer a profitable company, and will this be a prudent investment? Perhaps your analysis can shed some light on why the company entered into these transactions and how they affect the financial statements.

Anne also notes that there were large changes in the accounts receivable, inventory, and accounts payable balances, and suggests that you should pay particular attention to these developments. With respect to receivables, for example, she wonders just how much cash was generated from customers and what was the dollar value of the actual bad debt write-offs during the year. Is the allowance for uncollectibles sufficient?

Finally, Anne is curious about the foreign currency translation gain reported by Liberty. Specifically, she wonders whether it can be considered persistent and what exchange rate between Swiss francs and U.S. dollars as of the balance sheet date gave rise to the $12,500 gain.

Financial Statements

The financial statements and selected additional information are provided below and on the following pages. Based on this information only, prepare a report for your supervisor. The following financial statements have been audited by a major public accounting firm and have received an unqualified opinion. Dollar amounts on the statements are in thousands.

ADDITIONAL INFORMATION

SHORT-TERM INVESTMENTS. Short-term investments are carried at market value and consist solely of an investment in a single firm, Fredericks Ltd., which has 500,000 shares outstanding. As of December 31, 2010, Liberty held 40,000 shares, which cost $4 per share when they were acquired in 2010, and all shares are accounted for as available-for-sale securities. On December 16, 2011, Liberty sold all 40,000 shares for $6 per share. The price remained constant for the next few days, and on December 20, Liberty purchased 46,667 Fredericks shares.

RECEIVABLES. Uncollectibles on accounts receivable are accounted for under the allowance method. On December 1, 2011, Liberty completed a service for Bundes A.G., a manufacturer located in Switzerland. Liberty received a note from Bundes promising a payment of 200,000 Swiss francs within thirty days. On December 1, 2010, two francs exchanged for one U.S. dollar.

INVENTORIES. The last-in, first-out (LIFO) method is used, and inventories are carried at the lower-of-cost-or-market value. Inventories at December 31, 2010, consisted of 10,000 units @ $12 each, 10,000 units @ $6 each, and 30,000 units @ $2 each. Inventory costs have risen consistently in recent years. During 2011, 50,000 units were sold @ $20 each, and 25,000 units were purchased @ $16 each.

INVESTMENTS. On December 20, 2010, Liberty purchased a tract of land for $80,000; it sold the land on December 18, 2011. On January 2, 2011, Liberty purchased 100,000 shares of Packer Technical @ $5.00 per share. Packer has 250,000 shares outstanding (including those held by Liberty). As of December 31, 2011, the share price of Packer shares had fallen to $4 per share.

Liberty Manufacturing
Income Statement
for the Period Ended December 31, 2011

Revenues:		
Sales	$1,000	
Fees earned	100	$1,100
Cost of goods sold		590
Gross profit		$ 510
Miscellaneous operating expenses		(240)
Interest expense		(90)
Depreciation expense		(100)
Bad debt expense		(40)
Gain on sale of plant		10
Realized gain on short-term investments		80
Gain on sale of land		4
Income on equity investment		40
Foreign currency translation gain		25
Net income before taxes		$ 199
Income taxes		40
Net income		$ 159

Liberty Manufacturing
Balance Sheet
December 31, 2011

	2011	2010
ASSETS		
Cash	$ 58	$ 20
Short-term investments	280	168
Accounts receivable	550	300
Less: Allowance for uncollectibles	(10)	(20)
Notes receivable	125	0
Inventory	50	240
Investment in affiliate	530	0
Investment in land	0	80
Property, plant, and equipment	1,100	1,000
Less: Accumulated depreciation	(284)	(200)
Total assets	$2,399	$1,588
LIABILITIES AND SHAREHOLDERS' EQUITY		
Accounts payable	$ 220	$ 100
Other short-term payables	180	180
Long-term liabilities	1,200	600
Common stock	400	400
Unrealized price increase on available-for-sale investments	0	8
Retained earnings	399	300
Total liabilities and shareholders' equity	$2,399	$1,588

Liberty Manufacturing
Statement of Cash Flows
for the Period Ended December 31, 2011

Operating activities:	
Net income	$ 159
Depreciation	100
Realized gain on short-term investments	(80)
Gain on sale of plant	(10)
Gain on sale of land	(4)
Income not received in cash on equity investment	(30)
Increase in net accounts receivable	(260)
Decrease in inventory	190
Increase in notes receivable	(125)
Increase in accounts payable	120
Net cash from operating activities	$ 60
Investing activities:	
Investment in property, plant, and equipment	$(120)
Sale of plant	14
Investment in affiliate	(500)
Sale of land	84
Investment in short-term securities	(280)
Sale of short-term securities	240
Net cash used by investing activities	(562)
Financing activities:	
Issuance of long-term note	$ 600
Payment of dividend	(60)
Net cash from financing activities	540
Increase in cash	$ 38
Beginning cash balance	20
Ending cash balance	$ 58

Liberty Manufacturing
Statement of Shareholders' Equity
for the Period Ended December 31, 2011

	COMMON STOCK	RETAINED EARNINGS	UNREALIZED PRICE CHANGES	TOTAL
12/31/10 balance	$400	$300	$8	$708
Net income		159		159
Sale of securities			(8)	(8)
Dividends		(60)		(60)
12/31/11 balance	$400	$399	$0	$799

PROPERTY, PLANT, AND EQUIPMENT. Property, plant, and equipment is depreciated using the straight-line method.

OUTSTANDING DEBTS. Interest rates on outstanding loans range from 9 percent to 12 percent.

CASE 2: MICROLINE CORPORATION

You work in the finance and investment department of Mega Industries, which recently purchased several small high-tech companies. An additional company, Microline Corporation, is presently under consideration. You have been asked to serve on a project team that is preparing a recommendation to the chief financial officer about whether Mega should attempt to acquire Microline. Your duty on this team is to review the company's financial statements and write a memo to the team leader, Sharon Sonneborn. The memo should analyze Microline's solvency position, earning power potential, and the extent to which the reported financial statements reflect the company's "true" financial position and performance. After a brief review of Microline, Sharon believes that you should also address in your report the following important questions:

1. Is there any evidence that management's bonus caused it to enter into any transactions, especially at year-end, that may not have been in the shareholders' interest?
2. Has the debt covenant imposed any restrictions that may have influenced any of management's reporting choices?
3. What was the acquisition price of Littleton when it was purchased by Microline?
4. Is Microline's bad debt allowance sufficient?
5. How much cash was received by Ellery Inc. during 2011, and what percentage of Ellery's total income was paid out in the form of dividends?
6. How much cash was collected from customers during 2011?

Microline's most recent financial statements are as follows (dollars in thousands).

Microline Corporation
Income Statements
for the Periods Ending December 31, 2011 and 2010

	2011	2010
Sales	$60,000	$52,500
Cost of goods sold	34,000	31,500
Gross profit	$26,000	$21,000
Selling and administrative expenses	(22,750)	(17,500)
Bad debt expense	(250)	(350)
Depreciation expense	(2,500)	(2,100)
Interest expense	(1,000)	(600)
Other gains (losses)	5,250	1,250
Net income before taxes	$ 4,750	$ 1,700
Income tax expense	1,500	800
Net income	$ 3,250	$ 900
Earnings per share	$ 0.26	$ 0.072

FOOTNOTES (DOLLARS IN THOUSANDS)

SHORT-TERM EQUITY INVESTMENTS. Short-term equity investments consist of trading securities and available-for-sale securities. The trading securities were valued

Microline Corporation
Balance Sheets
December 31, 2011 and 2010

	2011	2010
ASSETS		
Cash	$ 1,200	$ 1,100
Short-term investments in equity securities	2,500	1,000
Accounts receivable (net)	5,700	3,650
Inventory	6,750	5,250
Prepaid interest expense	350	750
Total current assets	$16,500	$11,750
Investment in affiliate	6,000	5,000
Land	7,500	6,000
Property, plant, and equipment	20,000	17,500
Less: Accumulated depreciation	(4,000)	(3,000)
Goodwill	5,250	5,250
Total assets	$51,250	$42,500
LIABILITIES AND SHAREHOLDERS' EQUITY		
Accounts payable	$ 4,000	$ 3,000
Dividends payable	1,500	1,000
Miscellaneous payables	1,500	1,500
Unearned rent revenue	6,000	7,000
Total current liabilities	$13,000	$12,500
Long-term notes payable	14,500	7,500
Common stock	12,500	12,500
Accumulated unrealized revaluations on equity inv.	250	0
Retained earnings	11,000	10,000
Total liabilities and shareholders' equity	$51,250	$42,500

at $2,000 and $750 as of December 31, 2011 and 2010, respectively. The available-for-sale securities consists of 50,000 common shares of Acme Inc. that were held throughout 2011. During 2011, equity investments classified as trading securities were actively traded, and related sales generated $1,000 in cash.

ACCOUNTS RECEIVABLE. The allowance for bad debts was $400 and $350 as of December 31, 2011 and 2010, respectively. Microline estimates bad debts as a percentage of credit sales.

INVENTORY. Microline carries inventories using the LIFO cost flow assumption and the lower-of-cost-or-market method. The LIFO reserve was $1,400 and $1,250 as of December 31, 2011 and 2010, respectively.

EQUITY INVESTMENTS. Microline acquired 40 percent of the outstanding voting stock of Ellery Incorporated, a highly leveraged financial institution, at the beginning of 2010. The corporation paid an amount equal to 40 percent of Ellery's book value at the

Microline Corporation
Statement of Cash Flows
for the Period Ending December 31, 2011

Cash flows from operating activities:	
Net income	$ 3,250
Depreciation	2,500
Loss on sale of machinery	900
Unrealized revaluation of equity investments	250
Gain on sale of land	(1,500)
Undistributed affiliate income	(1,000)
Increase in accounts receivable (net)	(2,050)
Increase in inventory	(1,500)
Decrease in prepaid interest expense	400
Increase in accounts payable	1,000
Decrease in unearned rent revenue	(1,000)
Net cash from operating activities	$ 1,250
Cash flows from investing activities:	
Purchases of plant and equipment	$(10,000)
Purchases of land	(4,000)
Proceeds from sale of machinery	5,100
Proceeds from sale of land	4,000
Net cash used by investing activities	(4,900)
Cash flows from financing activities:	
Increases in long-term notes (net)	$ 7,000
Dividend payments	(1,750)
Net cash from financing activities	5,250
Increase in cash and short-term equity investments	$ 1,600
Beginning balance in cash and short-term equity investments	2,100
Ending balance in cash and short-term equity investments	$ 3,700

time of the acquisition and uses the equity method to account for this investment. During 2010, Ellery reported income of $1,000 and declared and paid dividends of $400.

LAND. Microline deals in land as an investment. The land is carried on the balance sheet at cost. As of December 31, 2011, the market value of the land was approximately equal to its cost. As of December 31, 2010, the market value of the land was approximately $1,500 in excess of its cost. Land values remained constant throughout 2011. Near the end of the year, Microline sold one parcel of land and immediately purchased another similar parcel.

PROPERTY, PLANT, AND EQUIPMENT. Microline depreciates its plant and equipment using accelerated rates for both financial reporting and income tax purposes.

GOODWILL. Microline has acquired only one company, Littleton Enterprises, since its inception. Goodwill was recognized on the acquisition in the amount by which the purchase price exceeded the fair market value of the individual assets and liabilities of Littleton. At the time of the acquisition, the net fair market value of the assets and liabilities of Littleton was $7,500.

OTHER GAINS (LOSSES). The following chart provides further details about the other gains (losses) that Microline recognized during 2011 and 2010.

	2011	2010
Rent revenue	$2,400	$1,600
Inventory write-down		(750)
Realized gains on short-term equity securities	400	
Unrealized gains on short-term equity securities	100	
Gain on sale of land	1,500	
Foreign exchange gain	500	
Income from affiliate	1,250	400
Loss on sale of machinery	(900)	
Total	$5,250	$1,250

EXCHANGE GAIN. On December 3, 2011, Microline sold goods to a customer in Canada and agreed to accept 4,000 Canadian dollars in payment. The receivable was still outstanding as of December 31, 2011, at which time the exchange rate of Canadian to U.S. dollars was 1.6/1. No other transactions were conducted outside U.S. borders during 2010 or 2011.

SHORT-AND LONG-TERM DEBT. On November 15, 2011, Microline signed a 90-day note payable in the amount of $4,000. As of December 31, 2011, this note was classified as long term because Microline intends to refinance it indefinitely. Microline also signed a long-term note in the amount of $3,000. This ten-year note includes an interest rate of 8 percent and requires that Microline maintain a current ratio of greater than 1.0 over the ten-year life.

INCOME TAXES. Microline's effective income tax rate is 34 percent.

EXECUTIVE COMPENSATION. At the end of each year, Microline's executives share equally in a bonus, which is equal to 25 percent of the dollar amount by which the corporation's net income exceeds 10 percent of the shareholders' equity dollar amount at the beginning of the year.

REVENUE RECOGNITION. All sales made by Microline are on credit, and Microline recognizes revenue when goods are shipped.

CASE 3: TECHNIC ENTERPRISES AND SONAR-SUN INC.

You are an investment analyst for Timken Brothers, a small brokerage firm. Recent developments in the medical equipment industry have caused a number of Timken's customers to inquire about two particular companies, Technic Enterprises and Sonar-Sun Incorporated. You have been asked to analyze the financial statements of these two companies and—on that basis only—rate them on a scale from 1 (very weak) to 10 (very strong) with respect to (1) solvency position, (2) earning power and persistence, and (3) earnings quality. In addition to the ratings, you have been asked to provide a memo stating why the ratings on these three dimensions do (or do not) differ between the two companies. The ratings and the memo will comprise part of a report that will be used by Timken's brokers to guide their buy/sell recommendations. The financial statements of Technic Enterprises and Sonar-Sun Inc. follow.

Technic Enterprises

The financial statements of Technic Enterprises and selected additional information are provided on the following pages. Dollar amounts are in thousands.

Technic Enterprises
Income Statement
for the Period Ended December 31, 2011

Revenues:		
Sales	$30,000	
Fees earned	3,000	
Less: Bad debt charge	(1,200)	$31,800
Cost of goods sold		(17,700)
Gross profit		$14,100
Miscellaneous operating expenses		(7,200)
Interest expense		(2,700)
Depreciation expense		(3,000)
Income on equity investment		1,200
Miscellaneous gains and losses (net)		4,440
Net income before taxes and accounting change		$ 6,840
Income tax expense		2,100
Net income before accounting change		$ 4,740
Income effect of change in inventory costing method		750
Net income		$ 5,490

Technic Enterprises
Balance Sheets
December 31, 2011 and 2010

	2011	2010
ASSETS		
Cash	$ 750	$ 600
Short-term investments	8,700	4,800
Accounts receivable	16,500	9,000
Less: Allowance for uncollectibles	(300)	(600)
Notes receivable	3,750	0
Inventory	3,300	7,200
Total current assets	$32,700	$21,000
Investment in affiliate	15,900	0
Investment in land	2,100	2,400
Property, plant, and equipment	32,700	30,000
Less: Accumulated depreciation	(8,700)	(6,000)
Total assets	$74,700	$47,400
LIABILITIES AND SHAREHOLDERS' EQUITY		
Accounts payable	$ 8,100	$ 3,000
Other short-term payables	7,200	5,400
Total current liabilities	$15,300	$ 8,400
Long-term liabilities	36,000	18,000
Common stock	12,000	12,000
Unrealized price decrease on short-term investments	(600)	0
Retained earnings	12,000	9,000
Total liabilities and shareholders' equity	$74,700	$47,400

Technic Enterprises
Statement of Cash Flows
for the Period Ended December 31, 2011

Operating activities:	
Net income	$ 5,490
Depreciation	3,000
Gains on short-term investments	(3,300)
Gain on sale of building	(240)
Gain on sale of land	(600)
Equity income in excess of cash received	(900)
Increase in net accounts receivable	(7,800)
Decrease in inventory	3,900
Increase in notes receivable	(3,750)
Increase in accounts payable	5,100
Increase in other short-term payables	1,800
Net cash from operating activities	$ 2,700
Investing activities:	
Investment in property, plant, and equipment	$ (3,120)
Sale of building	360
Investment in affiliate	(15,000)
Investment in land	(2,100)
Sale of land	3,000
Investment in short-term investments	(8,400)
Sale of short-term investments	7,200
Net cash used by investing activities	(18,060)
Financing activities:	
Issuance of long-term note	$18,000
Payment of dividend	(2,490)
Net cash from financing activities	15,510
Increase in cash	$ 150
Beginning cash balance	600
Ending cash balance	$ 750

Technic Enterprises
Reconciliation of Retained Earnings
for the Period Ended December 31, 2011

Beginning balance in retained earnings	$ 9,000
Plus: Net income	5,490
Less: Dividends	(2,490)
Ending balance in retained earnings	$12,000

FOOTNOTES (DOLLARS IN THOUSANDS, EXCEPT PER-SHARE AMOUNTS)

REVENUE RECOGNITION. All sales of inventory are on credit and are recorded in the sales account when goods are shipped. Services are exchanged for short-term notes and recorded in the fees earned account when the service is substantially complete.

UNCOLLECTIBLES. The allowance method is used to account for bad debts, and accounts are written off when payment is not made within one year.

NOTES RECEIVABLE. On November 15, 2011, Technic completed a service for Belton A.G., a manufacturer located in Switzerland. Technic received a note from Belton promising payment of 6,000 Swiss francs within 30 days, and on that date two Swiss francs exchanged for one U.S. dollar. Technic has no other exposure to foreign currency exchange risk.

SHORT-TERM INVESTMENTS. Short-term investments are carried on the balance sheet at market value and consist of equity securities classified as either trading or available-for-sale. As of December 31, 2010, trading securities were valued at $3,900. During 2011, no available-for-sale securities were acquired or sold.

INVENTORY. Technic uses the first-in, first-out (FIFO) cost flow assumption and carries inventories at the lower-of-cost-or-market value. All inventory purchases are made on account and recorded as accounts payable.

In addition, during 2011, Technic adopted a new accounting standard requiring a change in the method used to allocate labor costs to cost of goods manufactured. To achieve a better matching of revenues and expenses, the company now allocates certain of these costs to inventory that previously were charged directly to operating expenses. The change increased 2011 net income by $750, net of applicable income taxes.

INVESTMENT IN AFFILIATE. On January 30, 2010, Technic purchased 40 percent (50,000 shares) of the outstanding equity of Lehmon Financial Services @ $300 per share. No goodwill was recognized on the purchase. The information below refers to Lehmon Financial Services.

	2011	2010
Assets	$29,700	$24,900
Liabilities	24,900	22,500
Shareholders' equity	4,800	2,400
Stock price per share (Dec. 31)	25.50	31.05

LAND INVESTMENTS. During 2010, Technic invested in ten equivalent parcels of land, paying approximately $240 for each parcel. In November of 2011, the company sold these parcels, but chose to repurchase seven of them in December, when it revised its estimate of future real estate appraisal rates.

PROPERTY, PLANT, AND EQUIPMENT. Technic uses the straight-line method of depreciation and depreciates property, plant, and equipment over time periods ranging from five to forty years.

Miscellaneous Gains and Losses. Miscellaneous gains and losses consist of the following items:

Write-down of inventory to market value	$ (450)
Gain on sale of building	240
Realized gain on short-term investments	2,400
Unrealized gain on short-term investments	900
Gain on sale of land	600
Foreign currency translation gain	750
Total	$4,440

ADDITIONAL INFORMATION. Interest rates on outstanding loans range from 6 to 10 percent, and general inflation during 2011 was approximately 5 percent. The company's effective income tax rate is 34 percent.

Sonar-Sun Inc.

The financial statements of Sonar-Sun Inc. and selected additional information are provided on the following pages. Dollar amounts are in thousands.

Sonar-Sun Inc.
Statement of Cash Flows
for the Period Ended December 31, 2011

Operating activities:		
Net income	$20,700	
Depreciation	10,000	
Write-down of equipment	2,000	
Dividends received over income from affiliates	700	
Increase in accounts receivable	(3,500)	
Increase in prepaid insurance	(1,000)	
Increase in inventory	(6,000)	
Increase in accounts payable	11,000	
Increase in unearned revenues	10,000	
Increase in other short-term payables	1,000	
Net cash from operating activities		$44,900
Investing activities:		
Investments in equity securities	$ (2,000)	
Acquisition of Wallingford Atlantic	(24,000)	
Sale of real estate	2,000	
Net cash used by investing activities		(24,000)
Financing activities:		
Issuance of common stock	$ 5,000	
Dividends paid	(20,000)	
Net cash used by financing activities		(15,000)
Increase in cash balance		$ 5,900
Beginning cash balance		2,600
Ending cash balance		$ 8,500

Sonar-Sun Inc.
Income Statement
for the Period Ended December 31, 2011

Sales	$145,000
Revenues from services	35,000
Income from affiliate	4,000
Cost of goods sold	(63,000)
Operating expenses	(65,000)
Depreciation expense	(10,000)
Bad debt expense	(1,000)
Write-downs	(5,000)
Loss on translation of foreign currencies	(1,500)
Interest expense	(5,800)
Net income before taxes	$ 32,700
Income tax expense	(12,000)
Net income	$ 20,700

Sonar-Sun Inc.
Balance Sheet
December 31, 2011 and 2010

	2011	2010
ASSETS		
Cash	$ 8,500	$ 2,600
Accounts receivable (net)	17,200	13,700
Inventory	39,000	33,000
Prepaid insurance	4,000	3,000
Total current assets	$ 68,700	$ 52,300
Equity investments	7,000	4,000
Investments in affiliate	11,300	12,000
Real estate	28,000	25,000
Property, plant, and equipment (net)	44,000	37,000
Goodwill	13,000	8,000
Total assets	$172,000	$138,300
LIABILITIES AND SHAREHOLDERS' EQUITY		
Accounts payable	$ 24,000	$ 13,000
Dividends payable	12,000	13,000
Unearned revenues	15,000	5,000
Other payables	15,000	14,000
Total current liabilities	$ 66,000	$ 45,000
Long-term bank notes	45,000	40,000
Common stock	20,000	15,000
Unrealized price increase on equity investments	1,000	0
Retained earnings	40,000	38,300
Total liabilities and shareholders' equity	$172,000	$138,300

FOOTNOTES (DOLLARS IN THOUSANDS)

REVENUE RECOGNITION. All sales of inventory are made on account. Sonar-Sun recognizes revenue on such sales when goods are shipped. Revenues on services, where cash is received in advance, are estimated at year-end, based on the extent to which the service is completed.

ACCOUNTS RECEIVABLE. Sonar-Sun uses the allowance method to account for uncollectible accounts. The dollar value in the allowance account as of the end of 2011 was $800. Outstanding receivables are written off when they are deemed uncollectible, and during 2011, $500 of such accounts were removed from the books.

INVENTORY. Inventory is carried at the lower-of-cost-or-market rule using the last-in, first-out (LIFO) inventory cost flow assumption. Current costs of the inventory as of the end of 2011 and 2010 were $45,000 and $37,000, respectively.

EQUITY INVESTMENTS. Equity investments listed as noncurrent are considered available-for-sale securities. No sales of such securities were made during 2011.

INVESTMENT IN AFFILIATE. Sonar-Sun owns 25 percent of the outstanding voting stock of EDM Suppliers, and this investment is carried on the financial statements under the equity method.

PROPERTY, PLANT, AND EQUIPMENT. Sonar-Sun uses accelerated methods to depreciate its plant and equipment for both reporting and tax purposes. At the end of 2011 and 2010, accumulated depreciation totaled $12,000 and $8,000, respectively.

WHOLLY OWNED SUBSIDIARIES. Sonar-Sun owns 100 percent of the outstanding voting stock of two companies: Kenworth South and Wallingford Atlantic. The stock of Kenworth South was purchased for cash on January 1, 2008. The stock of Wallingford Atlantic was purchased near the end of 2011. The purchase price consisted of $24,000 in cash and a $5,000 long-term note. Wallingford was composed of machinery and real estate only.

Write-Downs. Sonar-Sun reduced the book value of its inventory by $3,000 to replacement cost in accordance with the lower-of-cost-or-market rule. It also wrote off certain equipment at a book loss of $2,000.

FOREIGN CURRENCY. Sonar-Sun purchases a considerable portion of its inventory from a Mexican supplier, paying its accounts in pesos. Certain accounts payable owed to this supplier were revalued as of year-end to reflect the advance of the peso against the dollar (from 7 pesos per dollar to 8 pesos per dollar).

INCOME TAXES. Sonar-Sun's effective tax rate is 34 percent.

CASE 4: AVERY CORPORATION

Tracy Sellers, a retired musical artist, and his two brothers own a substantial amount of the outstanding common stock of Avery Corporation, a young and fast-growing manufacturer of cartons, containers, and a wide variety of packaging materials. The company's home office is in Cleveland, Ohio, and regional sales offices are operating at several locations across the United States.

Tracy and his brothers, who recently inherited the stock from their aunt, know very little about the business. Just a few days ago, each received the company's 2011 annual report, and Tracy plans to attend the annual shareholders' meeting in Cleveland, scheduled next month. He would also like to take an active part at the meeting—representing both his own and his brothers' interests—especially because doubts about the quality of the company's board of directors and management have recently been raised. However, he knows very little about analyzing annual report information and has hired you to help him prepare for the meeting.

Tracy begins by showing you Avery's 2011 annual report, which includes a letter from Avery's chief executive officer, Arnold Tennenden, a set of consolidated financial statements, and the related footnotes. He cautions you that he wonders whether the CEO's letter accurately characterizes the company's performance and financial position, and he is asking you to ascertain whether this letter reasonably represents Avery's

financial situation. Tracy suspects that many of the comments made by Arnold at the upcoming shareholders' meeting will be similar to those contained in the annual report letter, and he hopes to be able to accurately evaluate and respond to them. The CEO's letter is provided below.

Letter from the Chief Executive Officer

To the Shareholders:

Avery has just completed another successful year, demonstrating strong earning power. Total revenues increased by almost 8 percent, and profits increased by a whopping 30 percent. The profit rise would have been even greater had management chosen not to record a highly unusual $5 million write-off due to the obsolescence of certain inventory items.

The company used the resources generated from these earnings to make an important acquisition, to increase its investment in property, plant, and equipment, and to increase common shareholder dividends. Indeed, Avery has grown substantially in this recent year and the shareholders have prospered. It is particularly impressive that Avery has been able to maintain its rate of growth without relying heavily on debt financing. The company's debt/equity ratio as of the end of 2011 is only 0.65, and profits are more than adequate to cover debt interest payments.

In sum, I am proud to report to you that Avery is an extremely solvent company with great earning power potential. Management plans to keep it that way far into the future.

Arnold Tennenden
Chief Executive Officer

Tracy has also attempted to review the statements himself, and in addition to evaluating the CEO's letter, he would like you to answer the questions listed below.

1. Why did the company's 2011 earnings-per-share number decrease even though net income seems to have increased?
2. How many shares of stock were issued in the 2011 stock dividend, and how did this issuance affect the assets and liabilities of the company?
3. Is it likely that the company will exercise its option to call its outstanding bonds in the near future? Why?
4. The company's debt/equity ratio as of December 31, 2011, is only 0.65. Is that ratio an accurate measure of the company's actual debt position?
5. Is the 2011 sales number disclosed in the footnotes a measure of the cash collected from customers during 2011? If not, how much cash was actually collected from customers in that year? How much cash was paid in 2011 to Avery's suppliers for inventory purchases?
6. Inventory and accounts receivable levels have increased dramatically over the past two years. Is that a positive sign?
7. Are the elements that make up the increase in profits from 2010 to 2011 likely to persist in future years?
8. What was the value of Buckeye's property, plant, and equipment when Buckeye was acquired by Avery in 2011?
9. What was the book value of the equipment that was sold by Avery in December of 2011?
10. How much cash did Avery contribute to its pension fund during 2011?

Avery Corporation
Consolidated Statement of Cash Flows
(in thousands of dollars)
for the Years Ended December 31, 2011 and 2010

	2011	2010
Operating activities:		
Net income	$ 7,333	$ 5,626
Depreciation	5,000	5,000
Inventory write-down	5,000	—
Income in excess of cash from affiliate	(1,050)	(900)
Amortization of bond discount	467	424
Gain from sale of property, plant, and equipment	(6,000)	—
Deferred income taxes	(41)	476
Increase (decrease) in unfunded pension liability	2,000	3,000
(Increase) decrease in net accounts receivable	(9,950)	(9,950)
(Increase) decrease in inventory	(15,000)	(15,000)
Increase (decrease) in accounts payable	7,800	2,200
Increase (decrease) in accrued payables	8,000	(1,700)
Increase (decrease) in unearned revenues	(8,000)	8,000
Net cash used by operating activities	$ (4,441)	$ (2,824)
Investing activities:		
Cash payments for acquisitions	$(50,000)	$ —
Cash payments for equipment purchases	(14,000)	—
Cash from equipment sales	20,000	—
Net cash used by investing activities	$(44,000)	$ 0
Financing activities:		
Cash from preferred stock issuance	$ —	$80,000
Cash from exercise of executive stock options	10,000	—
Cash payments for treasury stock purchases	—	(18,000)
Cash payments for dividends	(6,000)	(4,000)
Net cash from financing activities	$ 4,000	$58,000
Increase (decrease) in cash balance	$(44,441)	$55,176
Beginning plus marketable securities cash balance	58,676	3,500
Ending cash plus marketable securities balance	$ 14,235	$58,676

Footnotes to the Financial Statements

1. REVENUE RECOGNITION. The company recognizes revenue when goods are shipped, and all sales are made on credit. The dollar amounts for operating revenues reported on the consolidated statement of income include the following items (dollars are in thousands):

Item	2011	2010
Sales	$115,000	$120,000
Income from affiliate	1,800	1,500
Gain on sale of equipment	6,000	—
Special services	8,000	—
Total	$130,800	$121,500

Avery Corporation
Consolidated Balance Sheet
(in thousands of dollars)
December 31, 2011, 2010, and 2009

	2011	2010	2009
ASSETS			
Cash plus marketable securities	$ 14,235	$ 58,676	$ 3,500
Accounts receivable	45,000	35,000	25,000
Less: Allowance for uncollectibles	(600)	(550)	(500)
Inventory	55,000	45,000	30,000
Investment in affiliate	11,950	10,900	10,000
Property, plant, and equipment	94,000	50,000	50,000
Less: Accumulated depreciation	(19,000)	(20,000)	(15,000)
Goodwill	15,000	—	—
Total assets	$215,585	$179,026	$103,000
LIABILITIES AND SHAREHOLDERS' EQUITY			
Accounts payable	$ 16,000	$ 8,200	$ 6,000
Accrued payables	14,000	6,000	7,700
Unearned revenues	—	8,000	—
Unfunded pension liability	7,339	5,339	2,339
Bonds payable	50,000	50,000	50,000
Less: Unamortized discount	(4,868)	(5,335)	(5,759)
Deferred income taxes	3,155	3,196	2,720
Preferred stock	50,000	50,000	—
Common stock	5,350	5,000	5,000
Additional paid-in capital	64,900	55,000	25,000
Retained earnings	27,709	31,626	30,000
Less: Treasury stock	(18,000)	(38,000)	(20,000)
Total liabilities and shareholders' equity	$215,585	$179,026	$103,000

Avery Corporation
Consolidated Statement of Shareholders' Equity
(in thousands of dollars)
for the Years Ended December 31, 2011 and 2010

TRANSACTION	PREFERRED STOCK	COMMON STOCK	ADDITIONAL PAID-IN CAPITAL	RETAINED EARNINGS	TREASURY STOCK
Beginning balance (12/31/09)	$ 0	$5,000	$25,000	$30,000	$(20,000)
Net income				5,626	
Cash dividends				(4,000)	
Issue of preferred stock	50,000		30,000		
Purchase of treasury stock					(18,000)
Ending balance (12/31/10)	$50,000	$5,000	$55,000	$31,626	$(38,000)
Net income				7,333	
Preferred stock dividend				(6,000)	
Exercise of stock options					10,000
Issue for acquisition			5,000		10,000
Stock dividend		350	4,900	(5,250)	
Ending balance (12/31/11)	$50,000	$5,350	$64,900	$27,709	$(18,000)

Avery Corporation
Consolidated Income Statement
(in thousands of dollars, except per-share numbers)
for the Years Ended December 31, 2011 and 2010

	2011	2010
Operating revenues	$130,800	$121,500
Less: Cost of goods sold	(60,500)	(60,000)
Selling and administrative expenses	(23,000)	(25,000)
Depreciation expense	(5,000)	(5,000)
Accrued pension expense	(10,000)	(8,000)
Bad debt expense	(500)	(450)
Operating lease expense	(10,000)	(10,000)
Net income from operations	$ 21,800	$ 13,050
Loss due to inventory write-down	(5,000)	—
Interest expense	(4,467)	(4,424)
Pretax income from continuing operations	$ 12,333	$ 8,626
Income tax expense	5,000	3,000
Net income	$ 7,333	$ 5,626
Earnings per share:		
From continuing operations	$ 3.20	$ 3.75
Due to extraordinary loss	(1.30)	—
Total	$ 1.90	$ 3.75

2. INVENTORY. Inventory is carried at lower of cost or market under the first-in, first-out cost flow assumption. Inventory purchase costs have risen consistently over the past several years. The company wrote off certain inventories during 2011 due to obsolescence.

3. PROPERTY, PLANT, AND EQUIPMENT. Property, plant, and equipment are carried at cost less accumulated depreciation. Depreciation is calculated on a straight-line basis, assuming no salvage value and a ten-year useful life. In December of 2011, the company sold equipment with a cost of $20 million and soon thereafter purchased additional equipment for $14 million.

4. ACQUISITIONS. In December of 2009, the company acquired 30 percent of the outstanding common stock of Spartan Savings, a highly leveraged financial institution, for $10 million. The company has held this interest through December of 2011.

In early December of 2011, the company acquired 100 percent of the outstanding common stock of Buckeye Corporation, which consisted primarily of property, plant, and equipment and goodwill. The purchase price included $50 million cash and 1,000,000 shares of the company's common stock, which had been held in treasury. The stock had a market value at the time of the acquisition of $15 per share.

5. EMPLOYEE PENSION. The amount of pension expense accrued each year is based on a number of actuarial assumptions regarding the life expectancy of the current

workforce and other factors. Payments to the pension fund have met all regulatory requirements.

6. BOND ISSUANCE. In January of 2009, the company issued 50,000 bonds, each with a face value of $1,000, a stated interest rate of 8 percent, and a maturity date of January 2014. The bonds sold for $877.10 each, producing an effective interest rate of 10 percent. The terms of the issuance state that beginning in 2012, and thereafter, the company can call the bonds for 2 percent above the face value. Current market interest rates are 8 percent.

7. DEFERRED INCOME TAXES. The deferred income tax account arises solely from the company's choice to use straight-line depreciation for financial reporting purposes and double-declining-balance for income tax reporting purposes. For both purposes property, plant, and equipment are assumed to have a ten-year life and no salvage value. The company's effective tax rate is 0.38.

8. LEASES. The company leases certain facilities in which operations are conducted. Under the lease contract, the company is responsible for maintenance and can acquire the leased properties at the end of the lease term for an amount that is equal to 50 percent of the market value at that time. The current lease was entered into in January of 2008 and will expire in January of 2018. Lease payments are set at $10 million per year over the period of the lease.

9. STOCK TRANSACTIONS. In 2009, the company was authorized to issue 10,000,000 shares of $1 par value common stock, and it chose to issue 5,000,000 shares for a price of $6 per share. Later that year, the company repurchased 2,000,000 of these shares for $10 per share and held them in treasury. Additional treasury shares were purchased in 2010 for $12 per share.

In December of 2009, the company issued 1,000,000 shares of $50 par value preferred stock for $80 per share. Annual dividend payments are set at 12 percent of par value, and the shares are callable at par value by the company in 2015. There are 1,000,000 authorized but unissued shares of preferred stock.

Company executives are paid bonuses in the form of options to purchase common stock. In 2011, 1,000,000 options were exercised. Five million options are outstanding as of December 31, 2011.

10. STOCK DIVIDEND. At the end of 2011, the company declared and issued a 10 percent stock dividend on all outstanding common shares. At the time of the issuance, the common stock had a market value of $15 per share.

CASE 5: ZENITH CREATIONS

It is early in January 2012. You have just been hired by Zenith Creations and assigned to the accounting department. The company specializes in creative sales displays used to market point-of-purchase goods, and it has several large customers that annually hire Zenith to design and manufacture displays for retail outlets. The company has grown quickly and recently has moved from a pure manufacturing firm to one that provides both manufacturing and creative services. In fact, the company's name was just changed from Zenith Manufacturing.

Recently, two giant companies in the industry have shown a serious interest in acquiring Zenith, which has caused Zenith's management to be particularly concerned with how the financial statements are interpreted by outside parties—especially the potential buyers, who will likely base their offers on assessments of Zenith's financial condition and performance. At the same time, management is considering several actions and wants to know in advance how these actions will affect the financial statements, financial ratios, and outsider evaluations of Zenith's financial condition and performance. The actions are listed below.

- Purchase treasury stock at the current market price.
- Write off a relatively large uncollectible accounts receivable.
- Issue a 20 percent stock dividend.
- Redeem the remaining notes payable for $23,200,000.
- Sell the real estate received in the acquisition of Lyon Real Estate for $12,000,000.
- Change the inventory cost flow assumption from LIFO to FIFO.

Your supervisor has asked you to prepare a memo that will be part of a report presented to Zenith's board of directors concerning the possible acquisition. Your memo should consist of two parts: (1) an objective evaluation of Zenith's financial condition and performance and (2) an assessment of how each of the actions listed above will affect that evaluation. Zenith's financial statements and related footnotes are contained on the following pages.

Zenith Creations
Consolidated Income Statement
(in thousands of dollars, except per-share numbers)
for the Years Ended December 31, 2011 and 2010

	2011	2010
Operating revenues	$109,800	$125,800
Less: Cost of goods sold	(47,000)	(52,000)
Selling and administrative expenses	(27,000)	(23,000)
Depreciation expense	(6,000)	(5,000)
Accrued pension expense	(8,000)	(7,500)
Bad debt expense	(1,500)	(1,000)
Operating lease expense	(8,000)	(8,000)
Net income from operations	$ 12,300	$ 29,300
Interest expense	(3,848)	(3,771)
Loss on inventory write-down	(2,000)	—
Restructuring charge	(15,000)	—
Pretax income (loss) from continuing operations	$ (8,548)	$ 25,529
Income tax expense	500	6,000
Net income (loss) from continuing operations	$ (9,048)	$ 19,529
Extraordinary loss due to debt retirement	2,462	—
Net income (loss)	$(11,510)	$ 19,529
Earnings (loss) per share:		
From continuing operations	$ (1.24)	$ 1.86
Due to extraordinary loss	(.23)	—
Total (excludes stock dividend)	$ (1.47)	$ 1.86

Zenith Creations
Consolidated Balance Sheet
(in thousands of dollars)
December 31, 2011, 2010, and 2009

	2011	2010	2009
ASSETS			
Cash plus marketable securities	$ 43,933	$ 30,260	$ 3,500
Accounts receivable	15,900	16,800	28,000
Less: Allowance for uncollectibles	(1,400)	(800)	(1,000)
Inventory	22,500	23,500	30,500
Investment in affiliate	4,900	5,600	6,000
Property, plant, and equipment	82,000	85,000	60,000
Less: Accumulated depreciation	(14,000)	(20,000)	(15,000)
Goodwill	20,000	20,000	—
Total assets	$173,833	$160,360	$112,000
LIABILITIES AND SHAREHOLDERS' EQUITY			
Accounts payable	$ 19,000	$ 6,000	$ 3,000
Accrued payables	14,700	9,700	7,700
Unearned revenues	4,000	8,000	5,000
Restructuring reserve	14,000	—	—
Unfunded pension liability	5,900	3,900	2,400
Notes payable	25,000	50,000	50,000
Less: Unamortized discount	(5,335)	(11,518)	(12,289)
Deferred income taxes	4,920	6,420	5,220
Preferred stock	12,500	—	—
Common stock ($1 par value)	13,555	12,500	10,000
Additional paid-in capital	61,605	47,500	25,000
Retained earnings	23,488	47,658	35,969
Less: Treasury stock	(19,500)	(19,800)	(20,000)
Total liabilities and shareholders' equity	$173,833	$160,360	$112,000

Footnotes to the Financial Statements (Dollar Amounts, Except per Share, in Thousands):

1. REVENUE RECOGNITION. The company recognizes revenue when goods are shipped or services are provided, and all sales are made on credit. The dollar amounts for operating revenues reported on the consolidated statement of income include the following items:

Item	2011	2010
Sales	$110,000	$120,000
Income (loss) from affiliate	(200)	800
Loss on sale of equipment	(4,000)	—
Special services	4,000	5,000
Total	$109,800	$125,800

2. INVENTORY. Inventory is carried at lower of cost or market under the LIFO cost flow assumption. LIFO reserves for 2009, 2010, and 2011 are $1,400, $1,250, and

Zenith Creations
Consolidated Statement of Cash Flows
(in thousands of dollars)
for the Years Ended December 31, 2011 and 2010

	2011	2010
Operating activities:		
Net income (loss)	$(11,510)	$ 19,529
Depreciation	6,000	5,000
Affiliate distributions over earnings	700	400
Amortization of bond discount	848	771
Loss from sale of property, plant, and equipment	4,000	—
Loss on debt retirement	2,462	
Noncash restructuring charge	14,000	
Deferred income taxes	(1,500)	1,200
Increase (decrease) in unfunded pension liability	2,000	1,500
(Increase) decrease in net accounts receivable	1,500	11,000
(Increase) decrease in inventory	1,000	7,000
Increase (decrease) in accounts payable	13,000	3,000
Increase (decrease) in accrued payables	5,000	2,000
Increase (decrease) in unearned revenues	(4,000)	3,000
Net cash from operating activities	$ 33,500	$ 54,400
Investing activities:		
Cash payments for acquisitions	$ —	$(10,000)
Cash payments for equipment purchases	(15,000)	(10,000)
Cash from equipment sales	2,000	—
Net cash used by investing activities	$(13,000)	$(20,000)
Financing activities:		
Cash from preferred stock issuance	$ 15,000	$ —
Cash from exercise of executive stock options	300	160
Cash payment to retire debt	(22,127)	—
Cash payments for dividends	—	(7,800)
Net cash used by financing activities	$ (6,827)	$ (7,640)
Increase (decrease) in cash balance	$ 13,673	$ 26,760
Beginning cash balance	30,260	3,500
Ending cash balance	$ 43,933	$ 30,260

$1,100, respectively. The company has experienced LIFO liquidations in each of the three years, but the effects on income due to the liquidations have been immaterial. The company wrote off certain inventories at the end of 2011 due to obsolescence.

3. PROPERTY, PLANT, AND EQUIPMENT. Property, plant, and equipment are carried at cost less accumulated depreciation. Depreciation is calculated on a straight-line basis, assuming no salvage value and a ten-year useful life. During 2011, the company sold equipment with an original cost of $18,000.

4. ACQUISITIONS. In January of 2009, the company acquired 40 percent of the outstanding common stock of University Services for $5,000. The company has held this equity interest through December of 2011.

In December of 2010, the company acquired 100 percent of the outstanding common stock of Lyon Real Estate, which consisted of land and goodwill. The purchase

Zenith Creations
Consolidated Statement of Shareholders' Equity
(in thousands of dollars)
for the Years Ended December 31, 2011 and 2010

TRANSACTION	PREFERRED STOCK	COMMON STOCK	ADDITIONAL PAID-IN CAPITAL	RETAINED EARNINGS	TREASURY STOCK
Beginning balance (12/31/09)	$ 0	$10,000	$25,000	$35,969	$(20,000)
Net income				19,529	
Cash dividends				(7,800)	
Issue for acquisition		2,500	22,500		
Exercise of stock options				(40)	200
Ending balance (12/31/10)	$ 0	$12,500	$47,500	$47,658	$(19,800)
Net loss				(15,510)	
Exercise of stock options					300
Issue of preferred stock	12,500		2,500		
Stock dividend		1,055	11,605	(12,660)	
Ending balance (12/31/11)	$12,500	$13,555	$61,605	$19,488	$(19,500)

price included $10,000 cash, and the company issued 2,500,000 shares of common stock. The stock had a market value at the time of the acquisition of $10 per share.

5. EMPLOYEE PENSION. The amount of pension expense accrued each year is based on a number of actuarial assumptions regarding the life expectancy of the current workforce and other factors. Payments to the pension fund have met all regulatory requirements.

6. NOTE PAYABLE. In December of 2009, the company signed a note with a face value of $50,000, a stated interest rate of 6 percent, and a maturity date of December 2009. The annual effective interest rate is 10 percent, and the proceeds at issuance were $37,711. Half of the notes were redeemed in December 2011, and a loss of $2,462 was recognized on the redemption.

7. DEFERRED INCOME TAXES. The deferred income taxes are recognized on timing differences between taxable income and reported net income. The company's effective income tax rate is 35 percent.

8. LEASES. The company leases certain facilities in which operations are conducted. Under the lease contract, the company is responsible for maintenance and can acquire the leased properties at the end of the lease term for an amount equal to 90 percent of the market value at that time. The current lease was entered into in January of 2005 and will expire in January of 2025. Lease payments are set at $8 million per year over the period of the lease.

9. STOCK TRANSACTIONS. The company is authorized to issue 25 million, $1 par value, common shares. During 2009, in its only treasury stock purchase, the company acquired 2 million shares at $10 each.

In December of 2010, the company issued 500,000 shares of $25 par value preferred stock for $30 per share. Annual dividend payments are set at 10 percent of par value, and the shares are callable at par value by the company after 2015. There are 500,000 authorized but unissued shares of preferred stock.

10. EXECUTIVE COMPENSATION. Company executives are paid bonuses in the form of options to purchase common stock. The option price is equal to the per-share market price at the time options are issued to the executives. Certain of these options were exercised in 2011 and 2010.

11. STOCK DIVIDEND. At the end of 2011, the company declared and issued a 10 percent stock dividend on all outstanding common shares.

12. RESTRUCTURING. During 2011, the company began a major restructuring and chose to accrue certain future costs associated with employee layoffs, plant closings, and equipment replacement. A $15,000 charge was taken against 2011 income, and a restructuring reserve was established for the future costs. The portion of the reserve due to expected layoffs is considered a current liability.

CASE 6: PIERCE AND SNOWDEN

Pierce and Snowden is an established manufacturer of a wide variety of household items sold through retailers all over the United States. Wellington Mart and Wagner Stores, two retailers, have recently expressed an interest in carrying a number of Pierce and Snowden products. While these two potential customers could generate considerable volume for the company, both retailers would require the extension of a significant amount of credit, and in general, retail sales throughout the United States have been somewhat slow for several years.

You work in the finance department of Pierce and Snowden and have been asked to serve on a team whose task is to make a recommendation to management about whether, or how much, credit should be extended to Wellington Mart and Wagner Stores. The recommendation in part will be based on the solvency position and earning power of these two companies.

Your assignment is to analyze the financial statements of these two companies and—on that basis only—rate them on a scale from 1 to 10 (weak to strong) with respect to solvency position, earning power and persistence, and earnings quality. In addition to the ratings, provide a memo to the team captain stating why the ratings on these three dimensions do (or do not) differ between the two companies. The financial statements of Wellington Mart and Wagner Stores follow.

Wellington Mart
Consolidated Statement of Shareholders' Equity
(in thousands of dollars)
for the Year Ended December 31, 2011

TRANSACTION	PREFERRED STOCK	COMMON STOCK	ADDITIONAL PAID-IN CAPITAL	RETAINED EARNINGS	TREASURY STOCK
Beginning balance (12/31/10)	$50,000	$20,000	$35,860	$44,680	$(36,080)
Net loss				(10,878)	
Stock dividend		2,100	8,400	(10,500)	
Stock issue for options			3,900		7,500
Stock issue for acquisition		6,000	24,000		
Ending balance (12/31/11)	$50,000	$28,100	$72,160	$23,302	$(28,580)

Wellington Mart
Consolidated Balance Sheet
(in thousands of dollars)
December 31, 2011 and 2010

	2011	2010
ASSETS		
Cash	$ 1,870	$ 2,650
Trading securities	2,000	3,500
Net accounts receivable (net)	18,450	12,000
Inventory	4,200	15,800
Investment in affiliate	28,700	34,200
Investment in real estate	45,500	10,500
Buildings, machinery, and equipment	122,500	119,500
Less: Accumulated depreciation	(7,900)	(12,400)
Goodwill	45,000	—
Total assets	$260,320	$185,750
LIABILITIES AND SHAREHOLDERS' EQUITY		
Accounts payable	$ 22,400	$ 8,900
Accrued payables	25,200	11,200
Current maturities of long-term debts	6,100	6,100
Income tax liability	3,050	5,050
Long-term notes payable	26,100	12,200
Bonds payable	16,788	16,540
Retirement liability	6,200	—
Deferred income tax	9,500	11,300
Preferred stock	50,000	50,000
Common stock	28,100	20,000
Additional paid-in capital	72,160	35,860
Retained earnings	23,302	44,680
Less: Treasury stock	(28,580)	(36,080)
Total liabilities and shareholders' equity	$260,320	$185,750

Footnotes to the Financial Statements of Wellington Mart (Dollar Values, Except Per-Share Amounts, Are in Thousands)

1. REVENUE RECOGNITION. The company recognizes revenue when goods are shipped, and all sales are made on credit.

2. OTHER REVENUES AND EXPENSES. Other revenues and expenses consist of the following items (dollars in thousands):

Gain on sale of trading securities	$ 2,000
Unrealized gain on trading securities	500
Translation gain on outstanding accounts payable	1,500
Income from affiliate	2,500
Inventory write-down to market	(1,600)
Restructuring charge	(9,000)
Total	$(4,100)

Wellington Mart
Income Statement
(in thousands of dollars, except per-share numbers)
for the Year Ended December 31, 2011

	2011
Sales	$150,000
Cost of goods sold	(90,000)
Gross profit	$ 60,000
Selling and administrative expenses	(45,000)
Depreciation	(7,500)
Bad debt expense	(1,550)
Interest expense	(2,328)
Net loss from operations	$ (3,622)
Other revenues and expenses	(4,100)
Net loss before taxes	$ (478)
Income tax expense	(4,200)
Net loss before change in accounting method	$ (4,678)
Write-off due to change in accounting method	
(net of tax)	(6,200)
Net loss	$ (10,878)
Loss per outstanding common share:	
Before write-off due to change in accounting method	$ (5.49)
Write-off due to change in accounting method	(2.68)
Total	$ (8.17)

3. TRADING SECURITIES. In the only transaction involving trading securities during 2011, 50 common stock shares of Mammoth Corporation were sold in April.

4. ACCOUNTS RECEIVABLE. A further breakdown of the net accounts receivable balances is provided below.

	Gross Accounts Receivable	Allowance	Net
12/31/10	$12,300	$300	$12,000
12/31/11	19,400	950	18,450

5. INVENTORY. Inventory is carried at lower of cost or market under the LIFO cost flow assumption. Inventory purchase costs have remained relatively constant over the past several years. The LIFO reserve was $730 and $750 as of December 31, 2011 and 2010, respectively. The company wrote off certain inventories during 2011 due to obsolescence.

6. AFFILIATE. The company owns 49 percent of the outstanding voting stock of Ellery, Inc. A condensed balance sheet for Ellery as of December 31, 2011, is provided below (dollar amounts are in thousands).

Current assets	$24,000	Current liabilities	$21,000
Noncurrent assets	46,000	Long-term liabilities	45,000
		Shareholders' equity	4,000
Total assets	$70,000	Total liabilities and shareholders' equity	$70,000

Wellington Mart
Consolidated Statement of Cash Flows
for the Year Ended December 31, 2011

	2011	
Operating activities:		
Net loss	$(10,878)	
Depreciation	7,500	
Noncash restructuring charge	8,000	
Write-off due to change in accounting method	6,200	
Amortization of discount on bonds payable	248	
Dividends from affiliate (net of income recognized)	5,500	
Decrease in deferred income taxes	(1,800)	
Increase in net accounts receivable	(6,450)	
Decrease in inventory	11,600	
Increase in accounts payable	13,500	
Increase in accrued payables	14,000	
Decrease in income tax liability	(2,000)	
Net cash flow from operating activities		$45,420
Investing activities:		
Investment in buildings	$ (8,000)	
Investment in machinery and equipment	(15,000)	
Acquisition of Marilyn Real Estate	(50,000)	
Net cash flow used by investing activities		(73,000)
Financing activities:		
Increase in long-term notes payable	$13,900	
Stock issuances for exercised options	11,400	
Net cash flow from financing activities		25,300
Decrease in cash and trading securities		$ (2,280)
Beginning balance in cash and trading securities		6,150
Ending balance in cash and trading securities		$ 3,870

7. BUILDINGS, MACHINERY, AND EQUIPMENT. Buildings, machinery, and equipment are carried at cost less accumulated depreciation. Depreciation is calculated on a straight-line basis over estimated useful lives ranging from five years for machinery and equipment to twenty years for buildings. The cost and related accumulated depreciation for buildings and for machinery and equipment are as follows.

	12/31/10	Increases	Decreases	12/31/11
Buildings:				
Cost	$65,000	$ 8,000	$20,000	$53,000
Accumulated depreciation	10,400	3,000	12,000	1,400
Machinery and equipment:				
Cost	54,500	15,000	—	69,500
Accumulated depreciation	2,000	4,500	—	6,500

In December of 2011, the company closed a plant with an original cost of $20,000. A loss, which included cash payments required to complete the closure, was recognized in 2011 as a restructuring charge.

8. ACQUISITIONS. In January of 2011, the company acquired 100 percent of the outstanding common stock of Marilyn Real Estate. The company paid cash and issued 600,000 common shares to the shareholders of Marilyn in the acquisition, and the $80 million purchase price was allocated between real estate and goodwill.

9. LONG-TERM DEBT. Long-term notes outstanding as of December 31, 2010, are being paid off in equal installments of $6,100, of which the current portion is listed as a current liability. The interest rate on these notes is approximately 5.5 percent, and the book value of the notes is approximately equal to the market value. An additional note payable was issued during 2011.

The outstanding bond liabilities listed on the balance sheet were issued on January 1, 2008. The bond issuance has a face value of $18,000, an annual stated interest rate (payable semiannually) of 6 percent, and a maturity date of December 31, 2012. The bonds were issued to yield an annual effective rate of return of 8 percent. As of December 31, 2011, the annual market rate of interest on similar bond issuances was 10 percent, and the company has the right to call the bonds any time after December 31, 2011, at face value. A covenant in the bond indenture requires that the company's ratio of total liabilities to total assets cannot exceed 0.60 during the term of the bonds.

10. ACCOUNTING CHANGES. The company adopted a new accounting standard requiring the recognition of a large accrual for retirement costs at the end of 2011. The present value of the future liability associated with these costs was estimated, and the entire dollar amount of the liability was charged against income.

11. DEFERRED INCOME TAXES. Deferred income taxes are recognized on timing differences between income recognized for tax purposes and income for financial reporting purposes. Increases to the deferred tax liability arise primarily because the company uses straight-line depreciation for financial reporting purposes and accelerated depreciation for income tax reporting purposes. Decreases to the deferred income tax liability arose from charges to reported income for restructuring, retirement costs, inventory write-downs, and certain bad debt expenses. The company's effective tax rate for 2011 was 34 percent.

12. SHAREHOLDERS' EQUITY TRANSACTIONS. In December of 2008, the company issued 500,000 shares of 8 percent preferred stock, each with a par value of $100. The shares are callable, cumulative, and nonparticipating. As of December 31, 2011, dividends in arrears on these shares totaled $4,000.

As of December 31, 2011, the company was authorized to issue 3,000,000 shares of $10 par value common stock; 2,810,000 have been issued; 2,310,000 were outstanding; and 500,000 were held in treasury. During 2011, the company issued 600,000 common shares in the acquisition of Marilyn Real Estate, issued 300,000 treasury shares to executives who exercised stock options, and on December 20, 2011, declared a 10 percent common stock dividend.

13. EMPLOYEE PENSION. The company has a defined contribution pension plan that covers all employees, and the payments associated with this plan are expensed as incurred.

14. LEASES. The company leases certain facilities in which operations are conducted. Under the lease contract, the company is responsible for maintenance, and at the end of the lease term, it can either acquire the leased properties for an amount equal to 25 percent of the market value or renew the contract. The current lease was entered into in January of 2007 and will expire in January of 2017. Required lease payments,

included in selling and administrative expenses, are equal to $12 million per year over the period of the lease and are paid at the beginning of each period.

15. CONTINGENCIES. The company is currently under investigation by the Environmental Protection Agency for toxic waste management violations. In several cases, the company has been identified by the agency as a "potentially responsible party," and it is likely that the company will be required to clean up certain waste sites in the future. It is also possible that the company will be subject to certain fines and punitive damages. At this time, there is no way to reliably estimate these possible costs, which management believes to be somewhere between $1 million and $25 million.

Wagner Stores
Income Statement
(in thousands of dollars, except per-share numbers)
for the Year Ended December 31, 2011

	2011
Sales	$72,000
Cost of goods sold	(28,000)
General operating expenses	(14,000)
Operating leases	(6,200)
Insurance expense	(2,800)
Depreciation	(1,200)
Bad debt expense	(150)
Income tax expense	(6,300)
Operating income	$13,350
Other income (losses)	(5,267)
Net income	$ 8,083
Earnings per share*	$16

Net income divided by the weighted average of the common shares outstanding during 2010.

Wagner Stores
Statement of Shareholders' Equity
(in thousands of dollars)
for the Year Ended December 31, 2011

TRANSACTION	PREFERRED STOCK	COMMON STOCK	ADDITIONAL PAID-IN CAPITAL	RETAINED EARNINGS	TREASURY STOCK
Beginning balance (12/31/10)	$5,000	$ 6,400	$4,200	$ 9,850	$(3,200)
Net income				8,083	
Cash dividends				(3,000)	
Stock dividend issued		500	100	(600)	
Common stock issuance		5,000	800		
Exercise of stock options			(1,000)		1,800
Treasury stock purchases					(2,500)
Ending balance (12/31/11)	$5,000	$11,900	$4,100	$14,333	$(3,900)

Wagner Stores
Consolidated Balance Sheet
(in thousands of dollars)
December 31, 2011 and 2010

	2011	2010
ASSETS		
Cash	$ 4,920	$ 6,200
Trading securities	1,050	800
Accounts receivable (net)	7,250	9,400
Inventory	16,700	12,300
Prepaid insurance	1,800	2,500
Notes receivable	2,586	3,320
Investment in affiliate	10,600	8,000
Property, plant, and equipment (net)	42,200	12,400
Goodwill	900	900
Total assets	$88,006	$55,820
LIABILITIES AND SHAREHOLDERS' EQUITY		
Accounts payable	$ 9,700	$ 4,700
Accrued payables	4,000	3,300
Income tax payable	1,700	600
Dividend payable	700	500
Bonds payable (net)	28,502	13,242
Capital lease obligations	4,771	5,228
Deferred income taxes	7,200	6,000
Preferred stock	5,000	5,000
Common stock	11,900	6,400
Additional paid-in capital	4,100	4,200
Retained earnings	14,333	9,850
Less: Treasury stock	(3,900)	(3,200)
Total liabilities and shareholders' equity	$88,006	$55,820

Footnotes to the Financial Statements of Wagner Stores

1. TRADING SECURITIES. Trading securities are carried at fair market value as of the balance sheet date. During 2011, trading securities with a total book value of $250 were sold.

2. REVENUE RECOGNITION AND ACCOUNTS RECEIVABLE. Sales are recorded when goods are shipped, and all sales to customers are on account. Accounts receivable are carried at net realizable value with an allowance for uncollectibles. The dollar amounts in the allowance account were $100 and $120 at the end of 2011 and 2010, respectively.

3. INVENTORY. Inventory is carried at lower-of-cost-or-market value under the first-in, first-out assumption. All inventory purchases are made on account.

4. NOTE RECEIVABLE. On January 1, 2010, the company received an installment note in exchange for services. The note is accounted for under the effective interest

Wagner Stores
Statement of Cash Flows
(in thousands of dollars)
for the Year Ended December 31, 2011

	2011	
Operating activities:		
Net income	$ 8,083	
Noncurrent adjustments:		
Depreciation	1,200	
Loss on write-down of equipment lines	3,200	
Increase in deferred income taxes	1,200	
Amortization of discount on long-term debt	260	
Equity income not received in cash	(300)	
Realized and unrealized gains on trading securities	(150)	
Gain on sale of vehicles	(200)	
Current adjustments:		
Decrease in net accounts receivable	2,150	
Increase in inventory	(4,400)	
Decrease in prepaid insurance	700	
Increase in accounts payable	5,000	
Increase in accrued payables	700	
Increase in income tax payable	1,100	
Net cash from operating activities		$18,543
Investing activities:		
Investments in trading securities	$ (400)	
Proceeds from sales of trading securities	300	
Investment in affiliate	(2,300)	
Receipts of principal on notes receivable	734	
Investments in property, plant, and equipment	(34,500)	
Proceeds from sales of vehicles	500	
Net cash used by investing activities		(35,666)
Financing activities:		
Proceeds from bond issuance	$15,000	
Principal payments on capital leases	(457)	
Proceeds from common stock issuance	5,800	
Treasury stock purchases	(2,500)	
Proceeds from treasury stock issuances	800	
Dividend payments	(2,800)	
Net cash from financing activities		15,843
Decrease in cash balance		$ (1,280)
Beginning cash balance (12/31/10)		6,200
Ending cash balance (12/31/11)		$ 4,920

method and specifies that the company receive a fixed amount of cash at the end of 2010, 2011, 2012, 2013, and 2014.

5. INVESTMENT IN AFFILIATE. For several years, the company has held a 45 percent interest in Truax Incorporated, a financial holding company, which in turn holds interests in a wide variety of financial institutions. At the end of 2011, the company acquired a 25 percent interest in Billingsly Financial. The company uses the equity method to account for these investments.

6. PROPERTY, PLANT, AND EQUIPMENT. This category includes all properties used in the operations of the business, including assets acquired through capitalized leases. Straight-line methods are used to depreciate the assets in this category. Accumulated depreciation totaled $2,700 and $3,000 as of the end of 2011 and 2010, respectively. During 2011, one of the company's lines of equipment was discontinued, and the book value of this line was written off the books. In addition, the company sold a small fleet of vehicles with an original cost of $800.

7. GOODWILL. The company acquired 100 percent of the outstanding stock of Machen Suppliers at the beginning of 2010, accounting for the acquisition as a purchase and recognizing goodwill.

8. ACCOUNTS PAYABLE. Accounts payable includes only outstanding account balances with the company's inventory suppliers.

9. ACCRUED PAYABLES. Accrued payables refer to the company's general operating expenses.

10. BONDS PAYABLE. On January 1, 2009, the company issued ten-year bonds with a face value of $16,000 and a stated interest rate of 5 percent. Interest payments are made at the end of each year, and the bonds were issued at a discount to yield an 8 percent effective interest rate. The company has the option to call these bonds at a premium of 2 percent above the face value. The market value of these bonds as of December 31, 2011, is $14,350. At the end of 2011, the company issued additional ten-year bonds at face value. These bonds have a stated interest rate of 9 percent.

11. LEASE OBLIGATIONS. The company leases most of its facilities and machinery. Lease payments during 2011 totaled $7,180. Projected future lease payments under capitalized leases are $980 per year until December 31, 2017. Projected future lease payments under operating leases are $6,200 at the end of each year for the next twenty years. Both projections exclude executory costs.

12. DEFERRED INCOME TAXES. Deferred income taxes arise due to timing differences between financial reporting and tax reporting. In general, the company attempts to minimize its income tax liability by accelerating expense recognition and deferring revenue recognition within the rules of the Internal Revenue Service. For example, the company uses straight-line depreciation for financial reporting purposes and accelerated methods for income tax reporting purposes. Such practices have accumulated a deferred income tax obligation, which is reported on the balance sheet. The company's effective income tax rate is 35 percent, which is expected to be constant in the foreseeable future.

13. PENSION OBLIGATION. The company carries a defined contribution pension plan on all its employees. During 2011, the company contributed $1,500 to the plan, which is reflected in the general operating section of the income statement.

14. STOCK OPTION PLAN. The company maintains a stock option plan, which compensates certain executives with ten-year options to purchase the company's stock at a price that equals the stock's market value as of the date of the issuance. Certain options were exercised during 2011.

15. SHAREHOLDERS' EQUITY. At December 31, 2010, the company had issued 640 shares of $10 par value stock, 400 of which were held in treasury. During 2011, the company issued 500 shares of $10 par value common stock; 150 shares were issued when executive stock options were exercised; and 224 additional treasury shares were

acquired. At the end of 2011, the company issued a 7.5 percent stock dividend on all outstanding shares.

In addition, the company has 500 shares of preferred stock outstanding, which pays annual dividends at a rate of 10 percent of the par value. The nonvoting preferred shares are cumulative and nonparticipating, and the preferred shareholders have an option to require redemption at par value beginning in 2013.

16. OTHER INCOME (LOSSES). The other income (losses) account consists of the following items:

Interest revenue earned on note receivable	$ 266
Realized and unrealized gains on trading securities	150
Equity income	1,500
Gain on sale of vehicles	200
Interest expense	(1,583)
Loss on write-down of inventory to market	(2,600)
Loss on discontinued equipment	(3,200)
Net loss	$(5,267)

SECURITIES AND EXCHANGE COMMISSION
Washington, D.C. 20549

Form 10-K

(Mark One)

☑ **ANNUAL REPORT PURSUANT TO SECTION 13 OR 15(d) OF THE SECURITIES EXCHANGE ACT OF 1934**
For the fiscal year ended May 31, 2009

or

☐ **TRANSITION REPORT PURSUANT TO SECTION 13 OR 15(d) OF THE SECURITIES EXCHANGE ACT OF 1934**
For the transition period from   to   .

Commission File No. 1-10635

NIKE, Inc.
(Exact name of Registrant as specified in its charter)

Oregon	**93-0584541**
(State or other jurisdiction of incorporation)	*(IRS Employer Identification No.)*
One Bowerman Drive	**(503) 671-6453**
Beaverton, Oregon 97005-6453	*(Registrant's Telephone Number, Including Area Code)*
(Address of principal executive offices) (Zip Code)	

Securities registered pursuant to Section 12(b) of the Act:

Class B Common Stock	New York Stock Exchange
(Title of Each Class)	*(Name of Each Exchange on Which Registered)*

Securities registered pursuant to Section 12(g) of the Act:

None

Indicate by check mark if the registrant is a well-known seasoned issuer, as defined in Rule 405 of the Securities Act. Yes ☑   No ☐

Indicate by check mark if the registrant is not required to file reports pursuant to Section 13 or Section 15(d) of the Act. Yes ☐   No ☑

Indicate by check mark whether the Registrant (1) has filed all reports required to be filed by Section 13 or 15(d) of the Securities Exchange Act of 1934 during the preceding 12 months (or for such shorter period that the Registrant was required to file such reports), and (2) has been subject to such filing requirements for the past 90 days. Yes ☑   No ☐

Indicate by check mark whether the registrant has submitted electronically and posted on its corporate Website, if any, every Interactive Data File required to be submitted and posted pursuant to Rule 405 of Regulation S-T (§229.405 of this chapter) during the preceding 12 months (or for such shorter period that the registrant was required to submit and post such files). Yes ☐   No ☐

Indicate by check mark if disclosure of delinquent filers pursuant to Item 405 of Regulation S-K (§229.405 of this chapter) is not contained herein, and will not be contained, to the best of Registrant's knowledge, in definitive proxy or information statements incorporated by reference in Part III of this Form 10-K or any amendment to this Form 10-K.   ☑

Indicate by check mark whether the Registrant is a large accelerated filer, an accelerated filer, a non-accelerated filer, or a smaller reporting company. See definitions of "large accelerated filer," "accelerated filer" "non-accelerated filer" and "smaller reporting company" in Rule 12b-2 of the Exchange Act.

Large accelerated filer ☑	Accelerated filer ☐
Non-accelerated filer ☐	Smaller Reporting Company ☐

Indicate by check mark whether the registrant is a shell company (as defined in Rule 12b-2 of the Act). Yes ☐   No ☑

As of November 30, 2008, the aggregate market value of the Registrant's Class A Common Stock held by nonaffiliates of the Registrant was $221,932,688 and the aggregate market value of the Registrant's Class B Common Stock held by nonaffiliates of the Registrant was $20,688,140,567.

As of July 24, 2009, the number of shares of the Registrant's Class A Common Stock outstanding was 95,299,318 and the number of shares of the Registrant's Class B Common Stock outstanding was 390,631,331.

DOCUMENTS INCORPORATED BY REFERENCE:

Parts of Registrant's Proxy Statement for the annual meeting of shareholders to be held on September 21, 2009 are incorporated by reference into Part III of this Report.

NIKE, INC.

ANNUAL REPORT ON FORM 10-K

TABLE OF CONTENTS

NIKE, INC.

CONSOLIDATED STATEMENTS OF INCOME

	Year Ended May 31,		
	2009	**2008**	**2007**
	(In millions, except per share data)		
Revenues	$19,176.1	$18,627.0	$16,325.9
Cost of sales	10,571.7	10,239.6	9,165.4
Gross margin	8,604.4	8,387.4	7,160.5
Selling and administrative expense	6,149.6	5,953.7	5,028.7
Restructuring charges (Note 16)	195.0	—	—
Goodwill impairment (Note 4)	199.3	—	—
Intangible and other asset impairment (Note 4)	202.0	—	—
Interest income, net (Notes 1, 7 and 8)	(9.5)	(77.1)	(67.2)
Other (income) expense, net (Notes 17 and 18)	(88.5)	7.9	(0.9)
Income before income taxes	1,956.5	2,502.9	2,199.9
Income taxes (Note 9)	469.8	619.5	708.4
Net income	1,486.7	1,883.4	1,491.5
Basic earnings per common share (Note 12)	$ 3.07	$ 3.80	$ 2.96
Diluted earnings per common share (Note 12)	$ 3.03	$ 3.74	$ 2.93
Dividends declared per common share	$ 0.98	$ 0.875	$ 0.71

The accompanying notes to consolidated financial statements are an integral part of this statement.

NIKE, INC.

CONSOLIDATED BALANCE SHEETS

	May 31,	
	2009	**2008**
	(In millions)	

ASSETS

Current assets:

Cash and equivalents	$ 2,291.1	$ 2,133.9
Short-term investments	1,164.0	642.2
Accounts receivable, net (Note 1)	2,883.9	2,795.3
Inventories (Notes 1 and 2)	2,357.0	2,438.4
Deferred income taxes (Note 9)	272.4	227.2
Prepaid expenses and other current assets	765.6	602.3
Total current assets	9,734.0	8,839.3
Property, plant and equipment, net (Note 3)	1,957.7	1,891.1
Identifiable intangible assets, net (Note 4)	467.4	743.1
Goodwill (Note 4)	193.5	448.8
Deferred income taxes and other assets (Notes 9 and 18)	897.0	520.4
Total assets	$13,249.6	$12,442.7

LIABILITIES AND SHAREHOLDERS' EQUITY

Current liabilities:

Current portion of long-term debt (Note 8)	$ 32.0	$ 6.3
Notes payable (Note 7)	342.9	177.7
Accounts payable (Note 7)	1,031.9	1,287.6
Accrued liabilities (Notes 5 and 18)	1,783.9	1,761.9
Income taxes payable (Note 9)	86.3	88.0
Total current liabilities	3,277.0	3,321.5
Long-term debt (Note 8)	437.2	441.1
Deferred income taxes and other liabilities (Note 9)	842.0	854.5
Commitments and contingencies (Notes 15 and 18)	—	—
Redeemable Preferred Stock (Note 10)	0.3	0.3

Shareholders' equity:

Common stock at stated value (Note 11):

Class A convertible — 95.3 and 96.8 shares outstanding	0.1	0.1
Class B — 390.2 and 394.3 shares outstanding	2.7	2.7
Capital in excess of stated value	2,871.4	2,497.8
Accumulated other comprehensive income (Note 14)	367.5	251.4
Retained earnings	5,451.4	5,073.3
Total shareholders' equity	8,693.1	7,825.3
Total liabilities and shareholders' equity	$13,249.6	$12,442.7

The accompanying notes to consolidated financial statements are an integral part of this statement.

NIKE, INC.

CONSOLIDATED STATEMENTS OF CASH FLOWS

	Year Ended May 31,		
	2009	2008	2007
	(In millions)		
Cash provided by operations:			
Net income	$ 1,486.7	$ 1,883.4	$ 1,491.5
Income charges (credits) not affecting cash:			
Depreciation	335.0	303.6	269.7
Deferred income taxes	(294.1)	(300.6)	34.1
Stock-based compensation (Note 11)	170.6	141.0	147.7
Impairment of goodwill, intangibles and other assets (Note 4)	401.3	—	—
Gain on divestitures (Note 17)	—	(60.6)	—
Amortization and other	48.3	17.9	0.5
Changes in certain working capital components and other assets and liabilities excluding the impact of acquisition and divestitures:			
Increase in accounts receivable	(238.0)	(118.3)	(39.6)
Decrease (increase) in inventories	32.2	(249.8)	(49.5)
Decrease (increase) in prepaid expenses and other current assets	14.1	(11.2)	(60.8)
(Decrease) increase in accounts payable, accrued liabilities and income taxes payable	(220.0)	330.9	85.1
Cash provided by operations	1,736.1	1,936.3	1,878.7
Cash (used) provided by investing activities:			
Purchases of short-term investments	(2,908.7)	(1,865.6)	(2,133.8)
Maturities of short-term investments	2,390.0	2,246.0	2,516.2
Additions to property, plant and equipment	(455.7)	(449.2)	(313.5)
Disposals of property, plant and equipment	32.0	1.9	28.3
Increase in other assets, net of other liabilities	(47.0)	(21.8)	(4.3)
Settlement of net investment hedges	191.3	(76.0)	—
Acquisition of subsidiary, net of cash acquired (Note 4)	—	(571.1)	—
Proceeds from divestitures (Note 17)	—	246.0	—
Cash (used) provided by investing activities	(798.1)	(489.8)	92.9
Cash used by financing activities:			
Proceeds from issuance of long-term debt	—	—	41.8
Reductions in long-term debt, including current portion	(6.8)	(35.2)	(255.7)
Increase in notes payable	177.1	63.7	52.6
Proceeds from exercise of stock options and other stock issuances	186.6	343.3	322.9
Excess tax benefits from share-based payment arrangements	25.1	63.0	55.8
Repurchase of common stock	(649.2)	(1,248.0)	(985.2)
Dividends — common and preferred	(466.7)	(412.9)	(343.7)
Cash used by financing activities	(733.9)	(1,226.1)	(1,111.5)
Effect of exchange rate changes	(46.9)	56.8	42.4
Net increase in cash and equivalents	157.2	277.2	902.5
Cash and equivalents, beginning of year	2,133.9	1,856.7	954.2
Cash and equivalents, end of year	$ 2,291.1	$ 2,133.9	$ 1,856.7
Supplemental disclosure of cash flow information:			
Cash paid during the year for:			
Interest, net of capitalized interest	$ 46.7	$ 44.1	$ 60.0
Income taxes	765.2	717.5	601.1
Dividends declared and not paid	121.4	112.9	92.9

The accompanying notes to consolidated financial statements are an integral part of this statement.

NIKE, INC.

CONSOLIDATED STATEMENTS OF SHAREHOLDERS' EQUITY

	Common Stock				Capital in Excess of Stated Value	Accumulated Other Comprehensive Income	Retained Earnings	Total
	Class A		Class B					
	Shares	Amount	Shares	Amount				
				(In millions, except per share data)				
Balance at May 31, 2006	127.8	$0.1	384.2	$2.7	$1,447.3	$ 121.7	$4,713.4	$6,285.2
Stock options exercised			10.7		349.7			349.7
Conversion to Class B Common Stock	(10.2)		10.2					—
Repurchase of Class B Common Stock			(22.1)		(13.2)		(962.0)	(975.2)
Dividends on Common stock ($0.71 per share)							(357.2)	(357.2)
Issuance of shares to employees			1.2		30.1			30.1
Stock-based compensation (Note 11):					147.7			147.7
Forfeiture of shares from employees			(0.1)		(1.6)		(0.5)	(2.1)
Comprehensive income (Note 14):								
Net income							1,491.5	1,491.5
Other comprehensive income:								—
Foreign currency translation and other (net of tax expense of $5.4)						84.6		84.6
Net loss on cash flow hedges (net of tax benefit of $9.5)						(38.1)		(38.1)
Reclassification to net income of previously deferred losses related to hedge derivatives (net of tax benefit of $3.6)						21.4		21.4
Comprehensive income						67.9	1,491.5	1,559.4
Adoption of FAS 158 (net of tax benefit of $5.4) (Note 13):						(12.2)		(12.2)
Balance at May 31, 2007	117.6	$0.1	384.1	$2.7	$1,960.0	$ 177.4	$4,885.2	$7,025.4
Stock options exercised			9.1		372.2			372.2
Conversion to Class B Common Stock	(20.8)		20.8					—
Repurchase of Class B Common Stock			(20.6)		(12.3)		(1,235.7)	(1,248.0)
Dividends on Common stock ($0.875 per share)							(432.8)	(432.8)
Issuance of shares to employees			1.0		39.2			39.2
Stock-based compensation (Note 11):					141.0			141.0
Forfeiture of shares from employees			(0.1)		(2.3)		(1.1)	(3.4)
Comprehensive income (Note 14):								
Net income							1,883.4	1,883.4
Other comprehensive income:								
Foreign currency translation and other (net of tax expense of $101.6)						211.9		211.9
Realized foreign currency translation gain due to divestiture (Note 17):						(46.3)		(46.3)
Net loss on cash flow hedges (net of tax benefit of $67.7)						(175.8)		(175.8)
Net loss on net investment hedges (net of tax benefit of $25.1)						(43.5)		(43.5)
Reclassification to net income of previously deferred losses related to hedge derivatives (net of tax benefit of $49.6)						127.7		127.7
Comprehensive income						74.0	1,883.4	1,957.4
Adoption of FIN 48 (Note 9)							(15.6)	(15.6)
Adoption of EITF 06-2 Sabbaticals (net of tax benefit of $6.2)							(10.1)	(10.1)
Balance at May 31, 2008	96.8	$0.1	394.3	$2.7	$2,497.8	$ 251.4	$5,073.3	$7,825.3
Stock options exercised			4.0		167.2			167.2
Conversion to Class B Common Stock	(1.5)		1.5					—
Repurchase of Class B Common Stock			(10.6)		(6.3)		(632.7)	(639.0)
Dividends on Common stock ($0.98 per share)							(475.2)	(475.2)
Issuance of shares to employees			1.1		45.4			45.4
Stock-based compensation (Note 11):					170.6			170.6
Forfeiture of shares from employees			(0.1)		(3.3)		(0.7)	(4.0)
Comprehensive income (Note 14):								
Net income							1,486.7	1,486.7
Other comprehensive income:								
Foreign currency translation and other (net of tax benefit of $177.5)						(335.3)		(335.3)
Net gain on cash flow hedges (net of tax expense of $167.5)						453.6		453.6
Net gain on net investment hedges (net of tax expense of $55.4)						106.0		106.0
Reclassification to net income of previously deferred net gains related to hedge derivatives (net of tax expense of $39.6)						(108.2)		(108.2)
Comprehensive income						116.1	1,486.7	1,602.8
Balance at May 31, 2009	95.3	$0.1	390.2	$2.7	$2,871.4	$ 367.5	$5,451.4	$8,693.1

The accompanying notes to consolidated financial statements are an integral part of this statement.

NIKE, INC.

NOTES TO CONSOLIDATED FINANCIAL STATEMENTS

Note 1 — Summary of Significant Accounting Policies

Description of Business

NIKE, Inc. is a worldwide leader in the design, marketing and distribution of athletic and sports-inspired footwear, apparel, equipment and accessories. Wholly-owned Nike subsidiaries include Cole Haan, which designs, markets and distributes dress and casual shoes, handbags, accessories and coats; Converse Inc., which designs, markets and distributes athletic and causal footwear, apparel and accessories; Hurley International LLC, which designs, markets and distributes action sports and youth lifestyle footwear, apparel and accessories; and Umbro Ltd., which designs, distributes and licenses athletic and casual footwear, apparel and equipment, primarily for the sport of soccer.

Basis of Consolidation

The consolidated financial statements include the accounts of NIKE, Inc. and its subsidiaries (the "Company"). All significant intercompany transactions and balances have been eliminated.

Recognition of Revenues

Wholesale revenues are recognized when the risks and rewards of ownership have passed to the customer, based on the terms of sale. This occurs upon shipment or upon receipt by the customer depending on the country of the sale and the agreement with the customer. Retail store revenues are recorded at the time of sale. Provisions for sales discounts, returns and miscellaneous claims from customers are made at the time of sale.

Shipping and Handling Costs

Shipping and handling costs are expensed as incurred and included in cost of sales.

Advertising and Promotion

Advertising production costs are expensed the first time the advertisement is run. Media (TV and print) placement costs are expensed in the month the advertising appears.

A significant amount of the Company's promotional expenses result from payments under endorsement contracts. Accounting for endorsement payments is based upon specific contract provisions. Generally, endorsement payments are expensed on a straight-line basis over the term of the contract after giving recognition to periodic performance compliance provisions of the contracts. Prepayments made under contracts are included in prepaid expenses or other assets depending on the period to which the prepayment applies.

Through cooperative advertising programs, the Company reimburses retail customers for certain costs of advertising the Company's products. The Company records these costs in selling and administrative expense at the point in time when it is obligated to its customers for the costs, which is when the related revenues are recognized. This obligation may arise prior to the related advertisement being run.

Total advertising and promotion expenses were $2,351.3 million, $2,308.3 million, and $1,912.4 million for the years ended May 31, 2009, 2008 and 2007, respectively. Prepaid advertising and promotion expenses recorded in prepaid expenses and other assets totaled $280.0 million and $266.7 million at May 31, 2009 and 2008, respectively.

NIKE, INC.

NOTES TO CONSOLIDATED FINANCIAL STATEMENTS — (Continued)

Cash and Equivalents

Cash and equivalents represent cash and short-term, highly liquid investments with maturities of three months or less at date of purchase. The carrying amounts reflected in the consolidated balance sheet for cash and equivalents approximate fair value.

Short-term Investments

Short-term investments consist of highly liquid investments, primarily commercial paper, U.S. Treasury, U.S. agency, and corporate debt securities, with maturities over three months from the date of purchase. Debt securities which the Company has the ability and positive intent to hold to maturity are carried at amortized cost, which approximates fair value. At May 31, 2009, the Company did not hold any short-term investments that were classified as held-to-maturity. Short-term investments of $124.9 million as of May 31, 2008 were classified as held-to-maturity and were primarily comprised of U.S. Treasury and U.S. agency securities.

Available-for-sale debt securities are recorded at fair value with net unrealized gains and losses reported, net of tax, in other comprehensive income, unless unrealized losses are determined to be other than temporary. The Company considers all available-for-sale securities, including those with maturity dates beyond 12 months, as available to support current operational liquidity needs and therefore classifies these securities as short-term investments within current assets on the consolidated balance sheet. As of May 31, 2009, the Company held $1,005.0 million of available-for-sale securities with maturity dates within one year and $159.0 million with maturity dates over one year and less than five years.

Investments classified as available-for-sale consist of the following at fair value:

	As of May 31,	
	2009	2008
	(In millions)	
Available-for-sale investments:		
U.S. treasury and agencies	$ 772.8	$194.1
Corporate commercial paper and bonds	391.2	323.2
Total available-for-sale investments	$1,164.0	$517.3

Included in interest income, net for the years ended May 31, 2009, 2008, and 2007, was interest income of $49.7 million, $115.8 million and $116.9 million, respectively, related to short-term investments and cash and equivalents.

Allowance for Uncollectible Accounts Receivable

Accounts receivable consists principally of amounts receivable from customers. We make ongoing estimates relating to the collectibility of our accounts receivable and maintain an allowance for estimated losses resulting from the inability of our customers to make required payments. In determining the amount of the allowance, we consider our historical level of credit losses and make judgments about the creditworthiness of significant customers based on ongoing credit evaluations. Accounts receivable with anticipated collection dates greater than twelve months from the balance sheet date and related allowances are considered non-current and recorded in other assets. The allowance for uncollectible accounts receivable was $110.8 million and $78.4 million at May 31, 2009 and 2008, respectively, of which $36.9 million and $36.7 million was recorded in other assets.

NIKE, INC.

NOTES TO CONSOLIDATED FINANCIAL STATEMENTS — (Continued)

Inventory Valuation

Inventories related to our wholesale operations are stated at lower of cost or market and valued on a first-in, first-out ("FIFO") or moving average cost basis. Inventories related to our retail operations are stated at the lower of average cost or market using the retail inventory method. Under the retail inventory method, the valuation of inventories at cost is calculated by applying a cost-to-retail ratio to the retail value inventories. Permanent and point of sale markdowns, when recorded, reduce both the retail and cost components of inventory on hand so as to maintain the already established cost-to-retail relationship.

Property, Plant and Equipment and Depreciation

Property, plant and equipment are recorded at cost. Depreciation for financial reporting purposes is determined on a straight-line basis for buildings and leasehold improvements over 2 to 40 years and for machinery and equipment over 2 to 15 years. Computer software (including, in some cases, the cost of internal labor) is depreciated on a straight-line basis over 3 to 10 years.

Impairment of Long-Lived Assets

The Company reviews the carrying value of long-lived assets or asset groups to be used in operations whenever events or changes in circumstances indicate that the carrying amount of the assets might not be recoverable. Factors that would necessitate an impairment assessment include a significant adverse change in the extent or manner in which an asset is used, a significant adverse change in legal factors or the business climate that could affect the value of the asset, or a significant decline in the observable market value of an asset, among others. If such facts indicate a potential impairment, the Company would assess the recoverability of an asset group by determining if the carrying value of the asset group exceeds the sum of the projected undiscounted cash flows expected to result from the use and eventual disposition of the assets over the remaining economic life of the primary asset in the asset group. If the recoverability test indicates that the carrying value of the asset group is not recoverable, the Company will estimate the fair value of the asset group using appropriate valuation methodologies which would typically include an estimate of discounted cash flows. Any impairment would be measured as the difference between the asset groups carrying amount and its estimated fair value.

Identifiable Intangible Assets and Goodwill

In accordance with SFAS No. 142 "Goodwill and Other Intangible Assets" ("FAS 142"), the Company performs annual impairment tests on goodwill and intangible assets with indefinite lives in the fourth quarter of each fiscal year, or when events occur or circumstances change that would, more likely than not, reduce the fair value of a reporting unit or an intangible asset with an indefinite life below its carrying value. Events or changes in circumstances that may trigger interim impairment reviews include significant changes in business climate, operating results, planned investments in the reporting unit, or an expectation that the carrying amount may not be recoverable, among other factors. The impairment test requires the Company to estimate the fair value of its reporting units. If the carrying value of a reporting unit exceeds its fair value, the goodwill of that reporting unit is potentially impaired and the Company proceeds to step two of the impairment analysis. In step two of the analysis, the Company measures and records an impairment loss equal to the excess of the carrying value of the reporting unit's goodwill over its implied fair value should such a circumstance arise.

The Company generally bases its measurement of fair value of a reporting unit on a blended analysis of the present value of future discounted cash flows and the market valuation approach. The discounted cash flows model indicates the fair value of the reporting unit based on the present value of the cash flows that the Company expects the reporting unit to generate in the future. The Company's significant estimates in the discounted cash flows model include: its weighted average cost of capital; long-term rate of growth and profitability of the

NIKE, INC.

NOTES TO CONSOLIDATED FINANCIAL STATEMENTS — (Continued)

reporting unit's business; and working capital effects. The market valuation approach indicates the fair value of the business based on a comparison of the reporting unit to comparable publicly traded companies in similar lines of business. Significant estimates in the market valuation approach model include identifying similar companies with comparable business factors such as size, growth, profitability, risk and return on investment and assessing comparable revenue and operating income multiples in estimating the fair value of the reporting unit.

The Company believes the weighted use of discounted cash flows and the market valuation approach is the best method for determining the fair value of its reporting units because these are the most common valuation methodologies used within its industry; and the blended use of both models compensates for the inherent risks associated with either model if used on a stand-alone basis.

Indefinite-lived intangible assets primarily consist of acquired trade names and trademarks. In measuring the fair value for these intangible assets, the Company utilizes the relief-from-royalty method. This method assumes that trade names and trademarks have value to the extent that their owner is relieved of the obligation to pay royalties for the benefits received from them. This method requires the Company to estimate the future revenue for the related brands, the appropriate royalty rate and the weighted average cost of capital.

Foreign Currency Translation and Foreign Currency Transactions

Adjustments resulting from translating foreign functional currency financial statements into U.S. dollars are included in the foreign currency translation adjustment, a component of accumulated other comprehensive income in shareholders' equity.

The Company's global subsidiaries have various assets and liabilities, primarily receivables and payables, that are denominated in currencies other than their functional currency. These balance sheet items are subject to remeasurement under SFAS No. 52, "Foreign Currency Translation," ("FAS 52"), the impact of which is recorded in other (income) expense, net, within our consolidated statements of income.

Accounting for Derivatives and Hedging Activities

The Company uses derivative financial instruments to limit exposure to changes in foreign currency exchange rates and interest rates. The Company accounts for derivatives pursuant to SFAS No. 133, "Accounting for Derivative Instruments and Hedging Activities," as amended and interpreted ("FAS 133"). FAS 133 establishes accounting and reporting standards for derivative instruments and requires all derivatives be recorded at fair value on the balance sheet. Changes in the fair value of derivative financial instruments are either recognized in other comprehensive income (a component of shareholders' equity), debt or net income depending on the underlying exposure being hedged and the extent to which the derivative is effective.

See Note 18 — Risk Management and Derivatives for more information on the Company's risk management program and derivatives.

Stock-Based Compensation

On June 1, 2006, the Company adopted SFAS No. 123R "Share-Based Payment" ("FAS 123R"), which requires the Company to record expense for stock-based compensation to employees using a fair value method. Under FAS 123R, the Company estimates the fair value of options granted under the NIKE, Inc. 1990 Stock Incentive Plan (the "1990 Plan") and employees' purchase rights under the Employee Stock Purchase Plans ("ESPPs") using the Black-Scholes option pricing model. The Company recognizes this fair value, net of estimated forfeitures, as selling and administrative expense in the consolidated statements of income over the vesting period using the straight-line method.

NIKE, INC.

NOTES TO CONSOLIDATED FINANCIAL STATEMENTS — (Continued)

The Company adopted the modified prospective transition method prescribed by FAS 123R, which does not require the restatement of financial results for previous periods. In accordance with this transition method, the Company's consolidated statements of income for the years ended May 31, 2009, 2008 and 2007 includes (i) amortization of outstanding stock-based compensation granted prior to, but not vested, as of June 1, 2006, based on the fair value estimated in accordance with the original provisions of SFAS No. 123, "Accounting for Stock-Based Compensation" ("FAS 123") and (ii) amortization of all stock-based awards granted subsequent to June 1, 2006, based on the fair value estimated in accordance with the provisions of FAS 123R.

To calculate the excess tax benefits available for use in offsetting future tax shortfalls as of the date of implementation, the Company is following the alternative transition method discussed in FASB Staff Position No. 123R-3, "Transition Election Relating to Accounting for the Tax Effects of Share-Based Payment Awards."

See Note 11 — Common Stock and Stock-Based Compensation for more information on the Company's stock programs.

Income Taxes

The Company accounts for income taxes using the asset and liability method. This approach requires the recognition of deferred tax assets and liabilities for the expected future tax consequences of temporary differences between the carrying amounts and the tax basis of assets and liabilities. United States income taxes are provided currently on financial statement earnings of non-U.S. subsidiaries that are expected to be repatriated. The Company determines annually the amount of undistributed non-U.S. earnings to invest indefinitely in its non-U.S. operations. The Company recognizes interest and penalties related to income tax matters in income tax expense. See Note 9 — Income Taxes for further discussion.

Earnings Per Share

Basic earnings per common share is calculated by dividing net income by the weighted average number of common shares outstanding during the year. Diluted earnings per common share is calculated by adjusting weighted average outstanding shares, assuming conversion of all potentially dilutive stock options and awards. See Note 12 — Earnings Per Share for further discussion.

Management Estimates

The preparation of financial statements in conformity with generally accepted accounting principles requires management to make estimates, including estimates relating to assumptions that affect the reported amounts of assets and liabilities and disclosure of contingent assets and liabilities at the date of financial statements and the reported amounts of revenues and expenses during the reporting period. Actual results could differ from these estimates.

Reclassifications

Certain prior year amounts have been reclassified to conform to fiscal year 2009 presentation, including a reclassification to investing activities for the settlement of net investment hedges in the consolidated statement of cash flows. These reclassifications had no impact on previously reported results of operations or shareholders' equity and do not affect previously reported cash flows from operations, financing activities or net change in cash and equivalents.

NIKE, INC.

NOTES TO CONSOLIDATED FINANCIAL STATEMENTS — (Continued)

Recently Adopted Accounting Standards

On December 1, 2008, the Company adopted Statement of SFAS No. 161, "Disclosures about Derivative Instruments and Hedging Activities — an amendment of FASB Statement No.133" ("FAS 161"), which provides revised guidance for enhanced disclosures about how and why an entity uses derivative instruments, how derivative instruments and the related hedged items are accounted for under FAS 133, and how derivative instruments and the related hedged items affect an entity's financial position, financial performance and cash flows. The adoption of FAS 161 did not have an impact on the Company's consolidated financial position or results of operations. For additional information, see Note 18 — Risk Management and Derivatives.

On June 1, 2008, the Company adopted SFAS No. 157, "Fair Value Measurements" ("FAS 157") for financial assets and liabilities, which clarifies the meaning of fair value, establishes a framework for measuring fair value and expands disclosures about fair value measurements. Fair value is defined under FAS 157 as the exchange price that would be received for an asset or paid to transfer a liability in the principal or most advantageous market for the assets or liabilities in an orderly transaction between market participants on the measurement date. Subsequent changes in fair value of these financial assets and liabilities are recognized in earnings or other comprehensive income when they occur. The effective date of the provisions of FAS 157 for non-financial assets and liabilities, except for items recognized at fair value on a recurring basis, was deferred by Financial Accounting Standards Board ("FASB") Staff Position FAS 157-2 ("FSP FAS 157-2") and are effective for the fiscal year beginning June 1, 2009. The adoption of FAS 157 for financial assets and liabilities did not have an impact on the Company's consolidated financial position or results of operations. The adoption of FAS 157 for non-financial assets and liabilities is not expected to have an impact on the Company's consolidated financial position or results of operations. For additional information on the fair value of financial assets and liabilities, see Note 6 — Fair Value Measurements.

Also effective June 1, 2008, the Company adopted SFAS No. 159, "The Fair Value Option for Financial Assets and Financial Liabilities" ("FAS 159"), which allows an entity the irrevocable option to elect fair value for the initial and subsequent measurement for certain financial assets and liabilities on a contract-by-contract basis. As of May 31, 2009, the Company has not elected the fair value option for any additional financial assets and liabilities beyond those already prescribed by accounting principles generally accepted in the United States.

In October 2008, the FASB issued Staff Position No. FAS 157-3, "Determining the Fair Value of a Financial Asset in a Market That Is Not Active" ("FSP FAS 157-3"). FSP FAS 157-3 clarifies the application of FAS 157 in a market that is not active and defines additional key criteria in determining the fair value of a financial asset when the market for that financial asset is not active. FSP FAS 157-3 applies to financial assets within the scope of accounting pronouncements that require or permit fair value measurements in accordance with FAS 157. FSP FAS 157-3 was effective upon issuance and the application of FSP FAS 157-3 did not have a material impact on the Company's consolidated financial statements.

Recently Issued Accounting Standards

In May 2009, the FASB issued SFAS No. 165, "Subsequent Events" ("FAS 165"), which establishes general standards of accounting and disclosure for events that occur after the balance sheet date but before financial statements are issued. The provisions of FAS 165 are effective for the quarter ending August 31, 2009. The Company does not expect the adoption will have a material impact on its consolidated financial position or results of operations.

In April 2009, the FASB issued Staff Position No. FAS 107-1 and APB 28-1, "Interim Disclosures about Fair Value of Financial Instruments" ("FSP FAS 107-1 and APB 28-1"), which amends SFAS No. 107, "Disclosures about Fair Value of Financial Instruments", and APB Opinion No. 28, "Interim Financial

NIKE, INC.

NOTES TO CONSOLIDATED FINANCIAL STATEMENTS — (Continued)

Reporting", to require disclosures about fair value of financial instruments in interim and annual reporting periods. The provisions of FSP FAS 107-1 and APB 28-1 are effective for the quarter ending August 31, 2009. The Company does not expect the adoption will have an impact on its consolidated financial position or results of operations.

In December 2007, the FASB issued SFAS No. 141 (revised 2007), "Business Combinations" ("FAS 141(R)") and SFAS No. 160, "Noncontrolling Interests in Consolidated Financial Statements" ("FAS 160"). These standards aim to improve, simplify, and converge international standards of accounting for business combinations and the reporting of noncontrolling interests in consolidated financial statements. FAS 141(R) is effective for business combinations for which the acquisition date is on or after June 1, 2009. Generally, the effects of FAS 141(R) will depend on future acquisitions. FAS 160 is effective for the Company beginning June 1, 2009. The Company does not expect the adoption of FAS 160 will have a material impact on its consolidated financial position or results of operations.

In April 2008, the FASB issued Staff Position No. FAS 142-3, "Determination of the Useful Life of Intangible Assets" ("FSP FAS 142-3"). FSP FAS 142-3 amends the factors that should be considered in developing renewal or extension assumptions used to determine the useful life of a recognized intangible asset under FAS 142. The intent of the position is to improve the consistency between the useful life of a recognized intangible asset under FAS 142 and the period of expected cash flows used to measure the fair value of the asset under FAS 141(R), and other U.S. generally accepted accounting principles. The provisions of FSP FAS 142-3 are effective for the fiscal year beginning June 1, 2009. The Company does not expect the adoption of FSP FAS 142-3 will have a material impact on its consolidated financial position or results of operations.

Note 2 — Inventories

Inventory balances of $2,357.0 million and $2,438.4 million at May 31, 2009 and 2008, respectively, were substantially all finished goods.

Note 3 — Property, Plant and Equipment

Property, plant and equipment includes the following:

	As of May 31,	
	2009	2008
	(In millions)	
Land	$ 221.6	$ 209.4
Buildings	974.0	934.6
Machinery and equipment	2,094.3	2,005.0
Leasehold improvements	802.0	757.3
Construction in process	163.8	196.7
	4,255.7	4,103.0
Less accumulated depreciation	2,298.0	2,211.9
	$1,957.7	$1,891.1

Capitalized interest was not material for the years ended May 31, 2009, 2008 and 2007.

NIKE, INC.

NOTES TO CONSOLIDATED FINANCIAL STATEMENTS — (Continued)

Note 4 — Acquisition, Identifiable Intangible Assets, Goodwill and Umbro Impairment

Acquisition

On March 3, 2008, the Company completed its acquisition of 100% of the outstanding shares of Umbro, a leading United Kingdom-based global soccer brand, for a purchase price of 290.5 million British pounds sterling in cash (approximately $576.4 million), inclusive of direct transaction costs. This acquisition is intended to strengthen the Company's market position in the United Kingdom and expand NIKE's global leadership in soccer, a key area of growth for the Company. This acquisition also provides positions in emerging soccer markets such as China, Russia and Brazil. The results of Umbro's operations have been included in the Company's consolidated financial statements since the date of acquisition as part of the Company's "Other" operating segment.

The acquisition of Umbro was accounted for as a purchase business combination in accordance with SFAS No. 141 "Business Combinations." The purchase price was allocated to tangible and identifiable intangible assets acquired and liabilities assumed based on their respective estimated fair values on the date of acquisition, with the remaining purchase price recorded as goodwill.

Based on our preliminary purchase price allocation at May 31, 2008, identifiable intangible assets and goodwill relating to the purchase approximated $419.5 million and $319.2 million, respectively. Goodwill recognized in this transaction is deductible for tax purposes. Identifiable intangible assets include $378.4 million for trademarks that have an indefinite life, and $41.1 million for other intangible assets consisting of Umbro's sourcing network, established customer relationships, and the United Soccer League Franchise. These intangible assets will be amortized on a straight line basis over estimated lives of 12 to 20 years.

During the quarter ended February 28, 2009, the Company finalized the purchase-price accounting for Umbro and made revisions to preliminary estimates, including valuations of tangible and intangible assets and certain contingencies, as further evaluations were completed and information was received from third parties subsequent to the acquisition date. These revisions to preliminary estimates resulted in a $12.4 million decrease in the value of identified intangible assets, primarily Umbro's sourcing network, and an $11.2 million increase in non-current liabilities, primarily related to liabilities assumed for certain contingencies and adjustments made to deferred taxes related to the fair value of assets acquired. These changes in assets acquired and liabilities assumed affect the amount of goodwill recorded.

The following table summarizes the allocation of the purchase price, including transaction costs of the acquisition, to the assets acquired and liabilities assumed at the date of acquisition based on their estimated fair values, including final purchase accounting adjustments (in millions):

	May 31, 2008 Preliminary	Adjustments	May 31, 2009 Final
Current assets	$ 87.2	—	$ 87.2
Non-current assets	90.2	—	90.2
Identified intangible assets	419.5	(12.4)	407.1
Goodwill	319.2	23.6	342.8
Current liabilities	(60.3)	—	(60.3)
Non-current liabilities	(279.4)	(11.2)	(290.6)
Net assets acquired	$ 576.4	$ —	$ 576.4

The pro forma effect of the acquisition on the combined results of operations for fiscal 2008 was not material.

NOTES TO CONSOLIDATED FINANCIAL STATEMENTS — (Continued)

Umbro Impairment

In accordance with FAS 142 "Goodwill and Other Intangible Assets," the Company performs annual impairment tests on goodwill and intangible assets with indefinite lives in the fourth quarter of each fiscal year, or when events occur or circumstances change that would, more likely than not, reduce the fair value of a reporting unit or intangible assets with an indefinite life below its carrying value. As a result of a significant decline in global consumer demand and continued weakness in the macroeconomic environment, as well as decisions by Company management to adjust planned investment in the Umbro brand, the Company concluded that sufficient indicators of impairment existed to require the performance of an interim assessment of Umbro's goodwill and indefinite lived intangible assets as of February 1, 2009. Accordingly, the Company performed the first step of the goodwill impairment assessment for Umbro by comparing the estimated fair value of Umbro to its carrying amount, and determined there was a potential impairment of goodwill as the carrying amount exceeded the estimated fair value. Therefore, the Company performed the second step of the assessment which compared the implied fair value of Umbro's goodwill to the book value of goodwill. The implied fair value of goodwill is determined by allocating the estimated fair value of Umbro to all of its assets and liabilities, including both recognized and unrecognized intangibles, in the same manner as goodwill was determined in the original business combination.

The Company measured the fair value of Umbro by using an equal weighting of the fair value implied by a discounted cash flow analysis and by comparisons with the market values of similar publicly traded companies. The Company believes the blended use of both models compensates for the inherent risk associated with either model if used on a stand-alone basis, and this combination is indicative of the factors a market participant would consider when performing a similar valuation. The fair value of Umbro's indefinite-lived trademark was estimated using the relief from royalty method, which assumes that the trademark has value to the extent that Umbro is relieved of the obligation to pay royalties for the benefits received from the trademark. The assessments of the Company resulted in the recognition of impairment charges of $199.3 million and $181.3 million related to Umbro's goodwill and trademark, respectively, during the third quarter ended February 28, 2009. A deferred tax benefit of $54.5 million was recognized as a result of the trademark impairment charge. In addition to the above impairment analysis, the Company determined an equity investment held by Umbro was impaired, and recognized a charge of $20.7 million related to the impairment of this investment. These charges are included in the Company's "Other" category for segment reporting purposes.

The discounted cash flow analysis calculated the fair value of Umbro using management's business plans and projections as the basis for expected cash flows for the next twelve years and a 3% residual growth rate thereafter. The Company used a weighted average discount rate of 14% in its analysis, which was derived primarily from published sources as well as our adjustment for increased market risk given current market conditions. Other significant estimates used in the discounted cash flow analysis include the rates of projected growth and profitability of Umbro's business and working capital effects. The market valuation approach indicates the fair value of Umbro based on a comparison of Umbro to publicly traded companies in similar lines of business. Significant estimates in the market valuation approach include identifying similar companies with comparable business factors such as size, growth, profitability, mix of revenue generated from licensed and direct distribution and risk of return on investment.

Holding all other assumptions constant at the test date, a 100 basis point increase in the discount rate would reduce the adjusted carrying value of Umbro's net assets by 12%.

NIKE, INC.

NOTES TO CONSOLIDATED FINANCIAL STATEMENTS — (Continued)

Identified Intangible Assets and Goodwill

All goodwill balances are included in the Company's "Other" category for segment reporting purposes. The following table summarizes the Company's goodwill balance as of May 31, 2009 and 2008 (in millions):

Goodwill, May 31, 2007	$ 130.8
Acquisition of Umbro Plc	319.2
Other[1]	(1.2)
Goodwill, May 31, 2008	448.8
Purchase price adjustments	23.6
Impairment charge	(199.3)
Other[1]	(79.6)
Goodwill, May 31, 2009	$ 193.5

[1] Other consists of foreign currency translation adjustments on Umbro goodwill.

The following table summarizes the Company's identifiable intangible asset balances as of May 31, 2009 and 2008.

	May 31, 2009			May 31, 2008		
	Gross Carrying Amount	Accumulated Amortization	Net Carrying Amount	Gross Carrying Amount	Accumulated Amortization	Net Carrying Amount
			(In millions)			
Amortized intangible assets:						
Patents	$ 56.6	$(17.2)	$ 39.4	$ 47.5	$(14.4)	$ 33.1
Trademarks	37.5	(10.9)	26.6	13.2	(7.8)	5.4
Other	40.0	(19.6)	20.4	65.2	(19.7)	45.5
Total	$134.1	$(47.7)	$ 86.4	$125.9	$(41.9)	$ 84.0
Unamortized intangible assets —						
Trademarks			$381.0			$659.1
Identifiable intangible assets, net			$467.4			$743.1

The effect of foreign exchange fluctuations for the year ended May 31, 2009 reduced unamortized intangible assets by approximately $98.2 million, resulting from the strengthening of the U.S. dollar in relation to the British pound sterling.

Amortization expense, which is included in selling and administrative expense, was $11.9 million, $9.2 million and $9.9 million for the years ended May 31, 2009, 2008, and 2007, respectively. The estimated amortization expense for intangible assets subject to amortization for each of the years ending May 31, 2010 through May 31, 2014 are as follows: 2010: $12.6 million; 2011: $12.2 million; 2012: $11.5 million; 2013: $9.6 million; 2014: $7.6 million.

During the year ended May 31, 2008, the gross carrying amount of unamortized and amortized trademarks were reduced by $59.6 million and $37.5 million, respectively, as a result of the Company's divestitures of the Starter brand business and NIKE Bauer Hockey during the year ended May 31, 2008. See Note 17 — Divestitures for more information the Company's divestitures.

NIKE, INC.

NOTES TO CONSOLIDATED FINANCIAL STATEMENTS — (Continued)

Note 5 — Accrued Liabilities

Accrued liabilities include the following:

	May 31,	
	2009	2008
	(In millions)	
Compensation and benefits, excluding taxes	$ 491.9	$ 538.0
Endorser compensation	237.1	203.5
Taxes other than income taxes	161.9	147.6
Restructuring charges[1]	149.6	—
Dividends payable	121.4	112.9
Advertising and marketing	97.6	121.4
Fair value of derivatives	68.9	173.3
Import and logistics costs	59.4	78.8
Other[2]	396.1	386.4
	$1,783.9	$1,761.9

[1] Accrued restructuring charges primarily consist of severance costs relating to the Company's restructuring activities that took place during the fourth quarter of fiscal 2009. See Note 16 — Restructuring Charges for more information.

[2] Other consists of various accrued expenses and no individual item accounted for more than 5% of the balance at May 31, 2009 or 2008.

Note 6 — Fair Value Measurements

Effective June 1, 2008, the Company adopted FAS 157, "Fair Value Measurements" for financial assets and liabilities. FAS 157 establishes a hierarchy that prioritizes fair value measurements based on the types of inputs used for the various valuation techniques (market approach, income approach, and cost approach). FAS 157 is applied under existing accounting pronouncements that require or permit fair value measurements and, accordingly, does not require any new fair value measurements.

The levels of hierarchy are described below:

- Level 1: Observable inputs such as quoted prices in active markets for identical assets or liabilities.

- Level 2: Inputs other than quoted prices that are observable for the asset or liability, either directly or indirectly; these include quoted prices for similar assets or liabilities in active markets and quoted prices for identical or similar assets or liabilities in markets that are not active.

- Level 3: Unobservable inputs in which there is little or no market data available, which require the reporting entity to develop its own assumptions.

The Company's assessment of the significance of a particular input to the fair value measurement in its entirety requires judgment and considers factors specific to the asset or liability. Financial assets and liabilities are classified in their entirety based on the most stringent level of input that is significant to the fair value measurement.

The following table presents information about the Company's financial assets and liabilities measured at fair value on a recurring basis as of May 31, 2009 and indicates the fair value hierarchy of the valuation techniques utilized by the Company to determine such fair value.

NIKE, INC.

NOTES TO CONSOLIDATED FINANCIAL STATEMENTS — (Continued)

	Fair Value Measurements Using			Assets /Liabilities at Fair Value	Balance Sheet Classification
	Level 1	Level 2	Level 3		
		(In millions)			
Assets					
Derivatives	$ —	$ 378.7	$ —	$ 378.7	Other current assets and other long-term assets
Available-for-sale securities	240.0	1,314.8	—	1,554.8	Cash equivalents
Available-for-sale securities	467.9	696.1	—	1,164.0	Short-term investments
Total assets	$707.9	$2,389.6	$ —	$ 3,097.5	
Liabilities					
Derivatives	$ —	$ 68.9	$ —	$ 68.9	Accrued liabilities and other long-term liabilities
Total Liabilities . .	$ —	$ 68.9	$ —	$ 68.9	

Derivative financial instruments include foreign currency forwards, option contracts and interest rate swaps. The fair value of these derivatives contracts is determined using observable market inputs such as the forward pricing curve, currency volatilities, currency correlations, and interest rates, and considers nonperformance risk of the Company and that of its counterparties. Adjustments relating to these risks were not material for the year ended May 31, 2009.

Available-for-sale securities are primarily comprised of investments in U.S. Treasury and agency securities, corporate commercial paper and bonds. These securities are valued using market prices on both active markets (level 1) and less active markets (level 2). Level 1 instrument valuations are obtained from real-time quotes for transactions in active exchange markets involving identical assets. Level 2 instrument valuations are obtained from readily-available pricing sources for comparable instruments.

The Company had no material Level 3 measurements as of May 31, 2009.

In accordance with the requirements of SFAS No. 107, "Disclosures about Fair Value of Financial Instruments", the Company annually discloses the fair value of its debt, which is recorded on the consolidated balance sheets at adjusted cost. Refer to Note 8 — Long-Term Debt for additional detail.

NIKE, INC.

NOTES TO CONSOLIDATED FINANCIAL STATEMENTS — (Continued)

Note 7 — Short-Term Borrowings and Credit Lines

Notes payable to banks and interest-bearing accounts payable to Sojitz Corporation of America ("Sojitz America") as of May 31, 2009 and 2008, are summarized below:

	May 31,			
	2009		2008	
	Borrowings	Interest Rate	Borrowings	Interest Rate
		(In millions)		
Notes payable:				
Commercial Paper	$100.0	0.40%	$ —	—
U.S. operations	31.2	1.81%[1]	18.6	0.00%[1]
Non-U.S. operations	211.7	4.15%[1]	159.1	6.80%[1]
	$342.9		$177.7	
Sojitz America	$ 78.5	1.57%	$ 65.9	3.51%

---

[1]   Weighted average interest rate includes non-interest bearing overdrafts.

The carrying amounts reflected in the consolidated balance sheet for notes payable approximate fair value.

The Company purchases through Sojitz America certain athletic footwear, apparel and equipment it acquires from non-U.S. suppliers. These purchases are for the Company's operations outside of the United States, the Europe, Middle East, and Africa Region and Japan. Accounts payable to Sojitz America are generally due up to 60 days after shipment of goods from the foreign port. The interest rate on such accounts payable is the 60-day London Interbank Offered Rate ("LIBOR") as of the beginning of the month of the invoice date, plus 0.75%.

As of May 31, 2009, the Company had $100.0 million outstanding under its commercial paper program at a weighted average interest rate of 0.40%. No borrowings were outstanding at May 31, 2008.

In December 2006, the Company entered into a $1 billion revolving credit facility with a group of banks. The facility matures in December 2012. Based on the Company's current long-term senior unsecured debt ratings of A+ and A1 from Standard and Poor's Corporation and Moody's Investor Services, respectively, the interest rate charged on any outstanding borrowings would be the prevailing LIBOR plus 0.15%. The facility fee is 0.05% of the total commitment. Under this agreement, the Company must maintain, among other things, certain minimum specified financial ratios with which the Company was in compliance at May 31, 2009. No amounts were outstanding under this facility as of May 31, 2009 or 2008.

NIKE, INC.

NOTES TO CONSOLIDATED FINANCIAL STATEMENTS — (Continued)

Note 8 — Long-Term Debt

Long-term debt, net of unamortized premiums and discounts and swap fair value adjustments, is comprised of the following:

	May 31,	
	2009	2008
	(In millions)	
5.375% Corporate Bond, payable July 8, 2009	$ 25.1	$ 25.5
5.66% Corporate Bond, payable July 23, 2012	27.4	26.1
5.4% Corporate Bond, payable August 7, 2012	16.2	15.4
4.7% Corporate Bond, payable October 1, 2013	50.0	50.0
5.15% Corporate Bonds, payable October 15, 2015	111.1	104.5
4.3% Japanese yen note, payable June 26, 2011	108.5	99.6
1.5% Japanese yen note, payable February 14, 2012	51.7	47.4
2.6% Japanese yen note, maturing August 20, 2001 through November 20, 2020	54.7	54.5
2.0% Japanese yen note, maturing August 20, 2001 through November 20, 2020	24.5	24.4
Total	469.2	447.4
Less current maturities	32.0	6.3
	$437.2	$441.1

The scheduled maturity of long-term debt in each of the years ending May 31, 2010 through 2014 are $32.0 million, $6.9 million, $167.1 million, $46.9 million and $56.9 million, at face value, respectively.

The fair value of long-term debt is estimated based upon quoted prices for similar instruments. The fair value of the Company's long-term debt, including the current portion, was approximately $456.4 million at May 31, 2009 and $450.8 million at May 31, 2008.

In fiscal years 2003 and 2004, the Company issued a total of $240 million in medium-term notes of which $215 million, at face value, were outstanding at May 31, 2009 and 2008. The outstanding notes have coupon rates that range from 4.70% to 5.66% and maturity dates ranging from July 2009 to October 2015. For each of these notes, except the $50 million note maturing in October 2013, the Company has entered into interest rate swap agreements whereby the Company receives fixed interest payments at the same rate as the notes and pays variable interest payments based on the three-month or six-month LIBOR plus a spread. Each swap has the same notional amount and maturity date as the corresponding note. At May 31, 2009, the interest rates payable on these swap agreements ranged from approximately 1.5% to 3.2%.

In June 1996, one of the Company's Japanese subsidiaries, NIKE Logistics YK, borrowed ¥10.5 billion (approximately $108.5 million as of May 31, 2009) in a private placement with a maturity of June 26, 2011. Interest is paid semi-annually. The agreement provides for early retirement of the borrowing.

In July 1999, NIKE Logistics YK assumed a total of ¥13.0 billion in loans as part of its agreement to purchase a distribution center in Japan, which serves as collateral for the loans. These loans mature in equal quarterly installments during the period August 20, 2001 through November 20, 2020. Interest is also paid quarterly. As of May 31, 2009, ¥7.7 billion (approximately $79.2 million) in loans remain outstanding.

In February 2007, NIKE Logistics YK entered into a ¥5.0 billion (approximately $51.7 million as of May 31, 2009) term loan that replaced certain intercompany borrowings and matures on February 14, 2012. The interest rate on the loan is approximately 1.5% and interest is paid semi-annually.

NIKE, INC.

NOTES TO CONSOLIDATED FINANCIAL STATEMENTS — (Continued)

Note 9 — Income Taxes

Income before income taxes is as follows:

	Year Ended May 31,		
	2009	**2008**	**2007**
	(In millions)		
Income before income taxes:			
United States	$ 845.7	$ 713.0	$ 805.1
Foreign	1,110.8	1,789.9	1,394.8
	$1,956.5	$2,502.9	$2,199.9

The provision for income taxes is as follows:

	Year Ended May 31,		
	2009	**2008**	**2007**
	(In millions)		
Current:			
United States			
Federal	$ 410.1	$ 469.9	$352.6
State	46.1	58.4	59.6
Foreign	307.7	391.8	261.9
	763.9	920.1	674.1
Deferred:			
United States			
Federal	(251.4)	(273.0)	38.7
State	(7.9)	(5.0)	(4.8)
Foreign	(34.8)	(22.6)	0.4
	(294.1)	(300.6)	34.3
	$ 469.8	$ 619.5	$708.4

NIKE, INC.

NOTES TO CONSOLIDATED FINANCIAL STATEMENTS — (Continued)

Deferred tax assets and (liabilities) are comprised of the following:

	May 31,	
	2009	2008
	(In millions)	
Deferred tax assets:		
Allowance for doubtful accounts	$ 17.9	$ 13.1
Inventories	52.8	49.2
Sales return reserves	52.8	49.2
Deferred compensation	160.9	158.4
Stock-based compensation	93.7	55.2
Reserves and accrued liabilities	66.7	57.0
Property, plant, and equipment	—	7.9
Foreign loss carry-forwards	31.9	40.1
Foreign tax credit carry-forwards	32.7	91.9
Hedges	1.1	42.9
Undistributed earnings of foreign subsidiaries	272.9	—
Other	46.2	40.5
Total deferred tax assets	829.6	605.4
Valuation allowance	(26.0)	(40.7)
Total deferred tax assets after valuation allowance	803.6	564.7
Deferred tax liabilities:		
Undistributed earnings of foreign subsidiaries	—	(113.2)
Property, plant and equipment	(92.2)	(67.4)
Intangibles	(100.7)	(214.2)
Hedges	(86.6)	(1.3)
Other	(4.2)	(0.7)
Total deferred tax liability	(283.7)	(396.8)
Net deferred tax asset	$ 519.9	$ 167.9

At the end of fiscal 2009, the Company reported a net deferred tax asset of $272.9 million associated with its investment in certain non-U.S. subsidiaries. Prior to fiscal 2009, the Company reported a net deferred tax liability for book to tax differences in its investment in non-U.S. subsidiaries. The change to a deferred tax asset position at the end of fiscal 2009 is due primarily to the impact of the impairment of Umbro's goodwill, intangible and other assets as described in Note 4 — Acquisition, Identifiable Intangible Assets, Goodwill and Umbro Impairment.

A reconciliation from the U.S. statutory federal income tax rate to the effective income tax rate follows:

	Year Ended May 31,		
	2009	2008	2007
Federal income tax rate	35.0%	35.0%	35.0%
State taxes, net of federal benefit	1.2%	1.4%	1.6%
Foreign earnings	-14.9%	-12.9%	-4.1%
Other, net	2.7%	1.3%	-0.3%
Effective income tax rate	24.0%	24.8%	32.2%

NIKE, INC.

NOTES TO CONSOLIDATED FINANCIAL STATEMENTS — (Continued)

The effective tax rate for the year ended May 31, 2009 of 24.0% decreased from the fiscal 2008 effective tax rate of 24.8%. The effective tax rate for the year ended May 31, 2009 was favorably impacted by a benefit associated with the impairment of goodwill, intangible, and other assets of Umbro (see Note 4 — Acquisition, Identifiable Intangible Assets, Goodwill and Umbro Impairment), the impact of the resolution of audit items and the retroactive reinstatement of the research and development tax credit. The Tax Extenders and Alternative Minimum Tax Relief Act of 2008, which was signed into law during the second quarter of fiscal 2009, reinstated the U.S. federal research and development tax credit retroactive to January 1, 2008. The effective tax rate for the year ended May 31, 2008 of 24.8% decreased from the fiscal 2007 effective tax rate of 32.2%. Over the few years preceding fiscal 2008, a number of international entities generated losses for which the Company did not recognize offsetting tax benefits because the realization of those benefits was uncertain. The necessary steps to realize these benefits were taken in the first quarter of fiscal 2008, resulting in a one-time reduction of the effective tax rate for the year ended May 31, 2008. Also reflected in the effective tax rate for the years ended May 31, 2009 and May 31, 2008 is a reduction in our on-going effective tax rate resulting from our operations outside of the United States, as our tax rates on those operations are generally lower than the U.S. statutory rate.

The Company adopted FASB Interpretation No. 48, "Accounting for Uncertainty in Income Taxes" ("FIN 48") effective June 1, 2007. Upon adoption, the Company recognized an additional long-term liability of $89.4 million for unrecognized tax benefits, $15.6 million of which was recorded as a reduction to the Company's beginning retained earnings, and the remaining $73.8 million was recorded as a reduction to the Company's noncurrent deferred tax liability. In addition, the Company reclassified $12.2 million of unrecognized tax benefits from income taxes payable to other long term liabilities in conjunction with the adoption of FIN 48.

At the adoption date of June 1, 2007, the Company had $122.5 million of gross unrecognized tax benefits, excluding related interest and penalties, $30.7 million of which would affect the Company's effective tax rate if recognized in future periods. Including related interest and penalties and net of federal benefit of interest and unrecognized state tax benefits, at June 1, 2007, the Company had $135.0 million of total unrecognized tax benefits, $52.0 million of which would affect the Company's effective tax rate if recognized in future periods. As of May 31, 2009, the total gross unrecognized tax benefits, excluding related interest and penalties, were $273.9 million, $110.6 million of which would affect the Company's effective tax rate if recognized in future periods. Total gross unrecognized tax benefits, excluding interest and penalties, as of May 31, 2008 was $251.1 million, $60.6 million of which would affect the Company's effective tax rate if recognized in future periods. The Company does not anticipate total unrecognized tax benefits will change significantly within the next 12 months.

The following is a reconciliation of the changes in the gross balance of unrecognized tax benefits:

	May 31,	
	2009	2008
	(In millions)	
Unrecognized tax benefits, as of the beginning of the period	$251.1	$122.5
Gross increases related to prior period tax positions	53.2	71.6
Gross decreases related to prior period tax positions	(61.7)	(23.1)
Gross increases related to current period tax positions	71.5	87.7
Settlements	(29.3)	(13.4)
Lapse of statute of limitations	(4.1)	(0.7)
Changes due to currency translation	(6.8)	6.5
Unrecognized tax benefits, as of the end of the period	$273.9	$251.1

NIKE, INC.

NOTES TO CONSOLIDATED FINANCIAL STATEMENTS — (Continued)

The Company recognizes interest and penalties related to income tax matters in income tax expense. Upon adoption of FIN 48 at June 1, 2007, the Company had $32.0 million (excluding federal benefit) accrued for interest and penalties related to uncertain tax positions. The liability for payment of interest and penalties increased $2.2 million and $41.2 million during the years ended May 31, 2009 and 2008, respectively. As of May 31, 2009 and 2008, accrued interest and penalties related to uncertain tax positions was $75.4 million and $73.2 million, respectively (excluding federal benefit).

The Company is subject to taxation primarily in the United States, China and the Netherlands as well as various state and other foreign jurisdictions. The Company has concluded substantially all U.S. federal income tax matters through fiscal year 2006. The Company is currently subject to examination by the Internal Revenue Service for the 2007, 2008 and 2009 tax years. The Company's major foreign jurisdictions, China and the Netherlands, have concluded substantially all income tax matters through calendar year 1998 and fiscal year 2002, respectively.

The Company has indefinitely reinvested approximately $2.6 billion of the cumulative undistributed earnings of certain foreign subsidiaries. Such earnings would be subject to U.S. taxation if repatriated to the U.S. Determination of the amount of unrecognized deferred tax liability associated with the permanently reinvested cumulative undistributed earnings is not practicable.

Deferred tax assets at May 31, 2009 and 2008, respectively, were reduced by a valuation allowance relating to tax benefits of certain foreign subsidiaries with operating losses where it is more likely than not that the deferred tax assets will not be realized. The net change in the valuation allowance was a decrease of $14.7 million during fiscal 2009 and a decrease of $1.6 million during fiscal 2008.

The Company does not anticipate any foreign tax credit carry-forwards will expire. A benefit was recognized for foreign loss carry-forwards of $13.1 million at May 31, 2009. Such losses will expire as follows:

	Year Ending May 31, 2014	Indefinite
	(In millions)	
Net Operating Losses	$2.2	$10.9

During the years ended May 31, 2009, 2008, and 2007, income tax benefits attributable to employee stock-based compensation transactions of $25.4 million, $68.9 million, and $56.6 million, respectively, were allocated to shareholders' equity.

Note 10 — Redeemable Preferred Stock

Sojitz America is the sole owner of the Company's authorized Redeemable Preferred Stock, $1 par value, which is redeemable at the option of Sojitz America or the Company at par value aggregating $0.3 million. A cumulative dividend of $0.10 per share is payable annually on May 31 and no dividends may be declared or paid on the common stock of the Company unless dividends on the Redeemable Preferred Stock have been declared and paid in full. There have been no changes in the Redeemable Preferred Stock in the three years ended May 31, 2009, 2008 and 2007. As the holder of the Redeemable Preferred Stock, Sojitz America does not have general voting rights but does have the right to vote as a separate class on the sale of all or substantially all of the assets of the Company and its subsidiaries, on merger, consolidation, liquidation or dissolution of the Company or on the sale or assignment of the NIKE trademark for athletic footwear sold in the United States.

NIKE, INC.

NOTES TO CONSOLIDATED FINANCIAL STATEMENTS — (Continued)

Note 11 — Common Stock and Stock-Based Compensation

The authorized number of shares of Class A Common Stock, no par value, and Class B Common Stock, no par value, are 175 million and 750 million, respectively. Each share of Class A Common Stock is convertible into one share of Class B Common Stock. Voting rights of Class B Common Stock are limited in certain circumstances with respect to the election of directors.

In 1990, the Board of Directors adopted, and the shareholders approved, the NIKE, Inc. 1990 Stock Incentive Plan (the "1990 Plan"). The 1990 Plan provides for the issuance of up to 132 million previously unissued shares of Class B Common Stock in connection with stock options and other awards granted under the plan. The 1990 Plan authorizes the grant of non-statutory stock options, incentive stock options, stock appreciation rights, stock bonuses and the issuance and sale of restricted stock. The exercise price for non-statutory stock options, stock appreciation rights and the grant price of restricted stock may not be less than 75% of the fair market value of the underlying shares on the date of grant. The exercise price for incentive stock options may not be less than the fair market value of the underlying shares on the date of grant. A committee of the Board of Directors administers the 1990 Plan. The committee has the authority to determine the employees to whom awards will be made, the amount of the awards, and the other terms and conditions of the awards. The committee has granted substantially all stock options at 100% of the market price on the date of grant. Substantially all stock option grants outstanding under the 1990 plan were granted in the first quarter of each fiscal year, vest ratably over four years, and expire 10 years from the date of grant.

The following table summarizes the Company's total stock-based compensation expense recognized in selling and administrative expense:

	Year Ended May 31,		
	2009	2008	2007
	(In millions)		
Stock options[1]	$128.8	$127.0	$134.9
ESPPs	14.4	7.2	7.0
Restricted stock	7.9	6.8	5.8
Subtotal	151.1	141.0	147.7
Stock options and restricted stock expense — restructuring[2]	19.5	—	—
Total stock-based compensation expense	$170.6	$141.0	$147.7

[1] In accordance with FAS 123R, stock-based compensation expense reported during the years ended May 31, 2009, 2008 and 2007 includes $56.3 million, $40.7 million and $36.3 million, respectively, of accelerated stock-based compensation expense recorded for employees eligible for stock option vesting upon retirement.

[2] In connection with the restructuring activities that took place during the fourth quarter of fiscal 2009, the Company recognized stock-based compensation expense relating to the modification of stock option agreements, allowing for an extended post-termination exercise period, and accelerated vesting of restricted stock as part of severance packages. See Note 16 — Restructuring Charges for further details.

As of May 31, 2009, the Company had $82.3 million of unrecognized compensation costs from stock options, net of estimated forfeitures, to be recognized as selling and administrative expense over a weighted average period of 2.0 years.

NIKE, INC.

NOTES TO CONSOLIDATED FINANCIAL STATEMENTS — (Continued)

The weighted average fair value per share of the options granted during the years ended May 31, 2009, 2008 and 2007, as computed using the Black-Scholes pricing model, was $17.13, $13.87 and $8.80, respectively. The weighted average assumptions used to estimate these fair values are as follows:

	Year Ended May 31,		
	2009	2008	2007
Dividend yield	1.5%	1.4%	1.6%
Expected volatility	32.5%	20.0%	19.0%
Weighted average expected life (in years)	5.0	5.0	5.0
Risk-free interest rate	3.4%	4.8%	5.0%

The Company estimates the expected volatility based on the implied volatility in market traded options on the Company's common stock with a term greater than one year, along with other factors. The weighted average expected life of options is based on an analysis of historical and expected future exercise patterns. The interest rate is based on the U.S. Treasury (constant maturity) risk-free rate in effect at the date of grant for periods corresponding with the expected term of the options.

The following summarizes the stock option transactions under the plan discussed above:

	Shares (In millions)	Weighted Average Option Price
Options outstanding May 31, 2006	40.4	$32.31
Exercised	(10.7)	27.55
Forfeited	(1.6)	37.17
Granted	11.6	39.54
Options outstanding May 31, 2007	39.7	$35.50
Exercised	(9.1)	33.45
Forfeited	(0.9)	44.44
Granted	6.9	58.50
Options outstanding May 31, 2008	36.6	$40.14
Exercised	(4.0)	35.70
Forfeited	(1.3)	51.19
Granted	7.5	58.17
Options outstanding May 31, 2009	38.8	$43.69
Options exercisable at May 31,		
2007	15.3	$29.52
2008	16.2	32.35
2009	21.4	36.91

The weighted average contractual life remaining for options outstanding and options exercisable at May 31, 2009 was 6.3 years and 5.0 years, respectively. The aggregate intrinsic value for options outstanding and exercisable at May 31, 2009 was $535.6 million and $433.5 million, respectively. The aggregate intrinsic value was the amount by which the market value of the underlying stock exceeded the exercise price of the options. The total intrinsic value of the options exercised during the years ended May 31, 2009, 2008 and 2007 was $108.4 million, $259.4 million and $204.9 million, respectively.

NIKE, INC.

NOTES TO CONSOLIDATED FINANCIAL STATEMENTS — (Continued)

In addition to the 1990 Plan, the Company gives employees the right to purchase shares at a discount to the market price under employee stock purchase plans ("ESPPs"). Employees are eligible to participate through payroll deductions up to 10% of their compensation. At the end of each six-month offering period, shares are purchased by the participants at 85% of the lower of the fair market value at the beginning or the ending of the offering period. Employees purchased 1.0 million shares, 0.8 million shares, and 0.8 million shares during the years ended May 31, 2009, 2008 and 2007, respectively.

From time to time, the Company grants restricted stock and unrestricted stock to key employees under the 1990 Plan. The number of shares granted to employees during the years ended May 31, 2009, 2008 and 2007 were 75,000, 110,000 and 345,000 with weighted average values per share of $56.97, $59.50 and $39.38, respectively. Recipients of restricted shares are entitled to cash dividends and to vote their respective shares throughout the period of restriction. The value of all of the granted shares was established by the market price on the date of grant. During the years ended May 31, 2009, 2008 and 2007, the fair value of restricted shares vested was $9.9 million, $9.0 million and $5.5 million, respectively, determined as of the date of vesting.

During the year ended May 31, 2007, the Company also granted shares of stock under the Long-Term Incentive Plan ("LTIP"), adopted by the Board of Directors and approved by shareholders in September 1997. During the year ended May 31, 2007, LTIP participants agreed to amend their grant agreements to eliminate the ability to receive payments in shares of stock; shares of stock are no longer awarded. Prior to the amendment, the LTIP provided for the issuance of cash or up to 2.0 million shares of Class B Common Stock to certain executives based on performance targets established over three-year time periods. Once performance targets are achieved, cash or shares of stock are issued. The shares are immediately vested upon grant. The value of the shares is established by the market price on the date of issuance. Under the LTIP, 3,000 shares with a price of $38.84 were issued during the year ended May 31, 2007 for the plan year ended May 31, 2006. Compensation expense recognized relating to shares issued during the year ended May 31, 2007 was not material. The Company recognized $17.6 million, $35.9 million and $30.0 million of selling and administrative expense related to the cash awards during the years ended May 31, 2009, 2008 and 2007, respectively.

Note 12 — Earnings Per Share

The following represents a reconciliation from basic earnings per common share to diluted earnings per common share. Options to purchase an additional 13.2 million, 6.6 million and 9.5 million shares of common stock were outstanding at May 31, 2009, 2008 and 2007, respectively, but were not included in the computation of diluted earnings per share because the options were antidilutive.

	Year Ended May 31,		
	2009	2008	2007
	(In millions, except per share data)		
Determination of shares:			
Weighted average common shares outstanding	484.9	495.6	503.8
Assumed conversion of dilutive stock options and awards . . .	5.8	8.5	6.1
Diluted weighted average common shares outstanding	490.7	504.1	509.9
Basic earnings per common share	$ 3.07	$ 3.80	$ 2.96
Diluted earnings per common share	$ 3.03	$ 3.74	$ 2.93

NIKE, INC.

NOTES TO CONSOLIDATED FINANCIAL STATEMENTS — (Continued)

Note 13 — Benefit Plans

The Company has a profit sharing plan available to most U.S.-based employees. The terms of the plan call for annual contributions by the Company as determined by the Board of Directors. A subsidiary of the Company also has a profit sharing plan available to its U.S.-based employees. The terms of the plan call for annual contributions as determined by the subsidiary's executive management. Contributions of $27.6 million, $37.3 million, and $31.8 million were made to the plans and are included in selling and administrative expense for the years ended May 31, 2009, 2008 and 2007, respectively. The Company has various 401(k) employee savings plans available to U.S.-based employees. The Company matches a portion of employee contributions with common stock or cash. Company contributions to the savings plans were $37.6 million, $33.9 million, and $24.9 million for the years ended May 31, 2009, 2008 and 2007, respectively, and are included in selling and administrative expense.

The Company has pension plans in various countries worldwide. The pension plans are only available to local employees and are generally government mandated. The liability related to the unfunded pension liabilities of the plans was $82.8 million and $90.6 million at May 31, 2009 and 2008, respectively. Upon adoption of SFAS No. 158, "Employers' Accounting for Defined Benefit Pension and Other Postretirement Plans" ("FAS 158") on May 31, 2007, the Company recorded a liability of $17.6 million related to the unfunded pension liabilities of the plans.

Note 14 — Accumulated Other Comprehensive Income

The components of accumulated other comprehensive income, net of tax, are as follows:

	May 31,	
	2009	2008
	(In millions)	
Cumulative translation adjustment and other	$ 64.6	$ 399.9
Net deferred gain (loss) on net investment hedge derivatives	62.5	(43.5)
Net deferred gain (loss) on cash flow hedge derivatives	240.4	(105.0)
	$367.5	$ 251.4

Note 15 — Commitments and Contingencies

The Company leases space for certain of its offices, warehouses and retail stores under leases expiring from one to twenty-five years after May 31, 2009. Rent expense was $397.0 million, $344.2 million and $285.2 million for the years ended May 31, 2009, 2008 and 2007, respectively. Amounts of minimum future annual rental commitments under non-cancelable operating leases in each of the five years ending May 31, 2010 through 2014 are $330.2 million, $281.3 million, $233.6 million, $195.6 million, $168.6 million, respectively, and $588.5 million in later years.

As of May 31, 2009 and 2008, the Company had letters of credit outstanding totaling $154.8 million and $193.4 million, respectively. These letters of credit were generally issued for the purchase of inventory.

In connection with various contracts and agreements, the Company provides routine indemnifications relating to the enforceability of intellectual property rights, coverage for legal issues that arise and other items that fall under the scope of FASB Interpretation No. 45, "Guarantor's Accounting and Disclosure Requirements for Guarantees, Including Indirect Guarantees of Indebtedness of Others." Currently, the Company has several

NOTES TO CONSOLIDATED FINANCIAL STATEMENTS — (Continued)

such agreements in place. However, based on the Company's historical experience and the estimated probability of future loss, the Company has determined that the fair value of such indemnifications is not material to the Company's financial position or results of operations.

In the ordinary course of its business, the Company is involved in various legal proceedings involving contractual and employment relationships, product liability claims, trademark rights, and a variety of other matters. The Company does not believe there are any pending legal proceedings that will have a material impact on the Company's financial position or results of operations.

Note 16 — Restructuring Charges

During the fourth quarter of fiscal 2009, the Company took necessary steps to streamline its management structure, enhance consumer focus, drive innovation more quickly to market and establish a more scalable, long-term cost structure. As a result, the Company reduced its global workforce by approximately 5% and incurred pre-tax restructuring charges of $195 million, primarily consisting of severance costs related to the workforce reduction. As nearly all of the restructuring activities were completed in the fourth quarter of fiscal 2009, the Company does not expect to recognize additional costs in future periods relating to these actions. The restructuring charge is reflected in the corporate expense line in the segment presentation of pre-tax income in Note 19 — Operating Segments and Related Information.

The activity in the restructuring accrual for the year ended May 31, 2009 is as follows (in millions):

Restructuring accrual — June 1, 2008	$ —
Severance and related costs	195.0
Cash payments	(29.4)
Non-cash stock option and restricted stock expense	(19.5)
Foreign currency translation and other	3.5
Restructuring accrual — May 31, 2009	$149.6

The accrual balance as of May 31, 2009 will be relieved throughout fiscal year 2010 and early 2011, as severance payments are completed. The restructuring accrual is included in Accrued liabilities in the Consolidated Balance Sheet.

As part of its restructuring activities, the Company reorganized its NIKE brand operations geographic structure. In fiscal 2009, 2008 and 2007, NIKE brand operations were organized into the following four geographic regions: U.S., Europe, Middle East and Africa (collectively, "EMEA"), Asia Pacific, and Americas. In the fourth quarter of 2009, the Company initiated a reorganization of the NIKE Brand business into a new operating model. As a result of this reorganization, beginning in the first quarter of fiscal 2010, the NIKE brand operations will consist of the following six geographies: North America, Western Europe, Central/Eastern Europe, Greater China, Japan, and Emerging Markets.

Note 17 — Divestitures

On December 17, 2007, the Company completed the sale of the Starter brand business to Iconix Brand Group, Inc. for $60.0 million in cash. This transaction resulted in a gain of $28.6 million during the year ended May 31, 2008.

NIKE, INC.

NOTES TO CONSOLIDATED FINANCIAL STATEMENTS — (Continued)

On April 17, 2008, the Company completed the sale of NIKE Bauer Hockey for $189.2 million in cash to a group of private investors ("the Buyer"). The sale resulted in a net gain of $32.0 million recorded in the fourth quarter of the year ended May 31, 2008. This gain included the recognition of a $46.3 million cumulative foreign currency translation adjustment previously included in accumulated other comprehensive income. As part of the terms of the sale agreement, the Company granted the Buyer a royalty free limited license for the use of certain NIKE trademarks for a transitional period of approximately two years. The Company deferred $41.0 million of the sale proceeds related to this license agreement, to be recognized over the license period.

The gains resulting from these divestitures are reflected in other (income) expense, net and in the corporate expense line in the segment presentation of pre-tax income in Note 19 — Operating Segments and Related Information.

Note 18 — Risk Management and Derivatives

The Company is exposed to global market risks, including the effect of changes in foreign currency exchange rates and interest rates, and uses derivatives to manage financial exposures that occur in the normal course of business. The Company does not hold or issue derivatives for trading purposes.

The Company formally documents all relationships between hedging instruments and hedged items, as well as its risk management objective and strategy for undertaking hedge transactions. This process includes linking all derivatives to either specific firm commitments, forecasted transactions or net investments. The Company also enters into foreign exchange forwards to mitigate the change in fair value of specific assets and liabilities on the balance sheet; these are not designated as hedging instruments under FAS 133. Accordingly, changes in the fair value of hedges of recorded balance sheet positions are recognized immediately in other (income) expense, net, on the income statement together with the transaction gain or loss from the hedged balance sheet position.

Substantially all derivatives outstanding as of May 31, 2009 are designated as either cash flow, fair value or net investment hedges. All derivatives are recognized on the balance sheet at their fair value and classified based on the instrument's maturity date. The total notional amount of outstanding derivatives as of May 31, 2009 was $7.1 billion, which is primarily comprised of cash flow hedges denominated in Euro, Japanese yen and British pound.

Glossary

A

accelerated methods of depreciation Accelerated methods of depreciation are used to depreciate fixed assets. Under these methods, more costs are allocated to earlier periods than are allocated to later periods. Examples include double-declining-balance and sum-of-the-years'-digits. These methods are considered conservative since they recognize large amounts of depreciation in the early years of an asset's life.

accounting equation The accounting equation is the basis for the four financial statements. It is a mathematical equation stating that the dollar value of a company's assets equals the dollar value of its liabilities plus the dollar value of its shareholders' equity. The balance sheet is a statement of this equation; transactions are recorded on the financial statements in a way that maintains the equality of this equation.

accounting period An accounting period is the period of time between the preparation of the financial statements. Statements are often prepared monthly, quarterly, semiannually, or annually. Most companies report on a calendar-year basis, but for various reasons, some companies report on other 365-day cycles, called fiscal years.

accounts payable Accounts payable are dollar amounts owed to others for goods, supplies, and services purchased on open account. They arise from frequent transactions between a company and its suppliers that are normally not subject to specific, formal contracts. These extensions of credit are the practical result of a time lag between the receipt of a good, supply, or service and the corresponding payment. Accounts payable are normally included on the balance sheet under current liabilities.

accounts payable turnover *Cost of sales/Average accounts payable.* Accounts payable turnover measures how quickly, on average, accounts payable are paid to a company's suppliers. It reflects the number of times, during a given period, that these supplier accounts are turned over. Dividing this activity ratio by 365 changes it into an expression indicating how many days, on average, are required to pay off an account.

accounts receivable Accounts receivable is a balance sheet account indicating the dollar amount due from customers from sales made on open account. It arises when revenues are recognized before receipt of the associated cash payment. Accounts receivable is normally included as a current asset and for some companies can be quite large.

accounts receivable turnover *Net credit sales/Average accounts receivable.* Accounts receivable turnover reflects the number of times a company's accounts receivables are recorded and collected during a given period. This ratio is often divided into 365 days, which indicates how many days, on average, receivables are outstanding—often referred to as the collection period.

accrual accounting The accrual basis is a system of accounting that recognizes revenues and expenses when assets and liabilities are created or discharged because of operating activities. Accrual accounting differs from cash flow accounting, which reflects only cash inflows and outflows, and is the basis upon which the statement of cash flows is prepared. Statements prepared under accrual accounting, like the income statement, are designed to measure earning power.

accruals Accruals are accounting entries designed to ensure that the assets and liabilities created or discharged due to the operating activities of the current period are recognized as revenues or expenses on the income statement of that period. The recognition on the income statement occurs at a time different from the related cash flow, so

a receivable or payable must be recorded on the balance sheet. Common examples include accrued payables, bad debts, warranties, and deferred revenues.

accrued payables Accrued payables are obligations on the balance sheet that must be recognized at the end of each period because they build up over time. Accrued payables are normally included as current liabilities because they are expected to be paid with the use of assets presently listed as current on the balance sheet. Accrued payables normally include obligations associated with salaries, wages, interest, warranties, and taxes.

accumulated comprehensive income Accumulated comprehensive income is an account in the shareholders' equity section of the balance sheet that contains the accumulated balances of items that affect the wealth of the firm but are not reflected on the income statement. Examples include unrealized gains and losses on securities accounted for as available-for-sale, unrealized gains and losses on certain derivative securities, pension adjustments, and foreign currency translation adjustments.

accumulated depreciation Accumulated depreciation is a contra asset account on the balance sheet that reflects the dollar value of the total depreciation that has been previously recognized on the fixed assets up to the date of the balance sheet.

activity method The activity method is a method of depreciating fixed assets or depleting natural resource costs that allocates the cost of the long-lived asset to future periods on the basis of its activity. This method is used primarily in the mining, oil, and gas industries to deplete the costs associated with acquiring the rights to and extracting natural resources. The estimated life under the activity method is expressed in terms of units of activity (e.g., miles driven, units produced, barrels extracted) instead of years, as is done under the other common methods of depreciation (e.g., straight-line, double-declining-balance, sum-of-the-years'-digits).

activity ratios Activity ratios measure the speed with which assets or accounts payable move through operations. They involve the calculation of a number called turnover, which indicates the number of times during a given period that assets (or payables) are acquired, disposed of, and replaced. Dividing 365 by the turnover number produces the average number of days during the year that the assets (or payables) were carried on the balance sheet. Turnover is commonly calculated for accounts receivable, inventory, fixed assets, total assets, and accounts payable.

actuary An actuary is a statistician who estimates risks for a wide variety of purposes, including the determination of insurance premiums, the funding of pension and health plans, and other purposes that involve assessing future demographic trends.

additional paid-in capital Additional paid-in capital is included in the shareholders' equity section of the balance sheet and reflects capital contributions to the firm over and above the par value of issued common stock or preferred stock. It can also appear as the result of issuing stock dividends, stock options, and treasury stock, and is part of contributed capital.

aging schedule Aging is a method of estimating and analyzing uncollectible accounts receivable that categorizes individual accounts on the basis of the amount of time each has been outstanding. Each category is then multiplied by a different uncollectible percentage, under the assumption that older accounts are more likely than new accounts to be uncollectible. This method is used primarily by management to identify and maintain control over uncollectible accounts receivables.

allowance method The allowance method, under generally accepted accounting principles (GAAP), is the preferred method to account for uncollectibles and sales returns, both of which have a direct effect on the reported value of accounts receivable. The allowance method involves estimating the dollar amount of the uncollectibles or sales returns at the end of each accounting period and, based on that estimate, records an entry that reduces both net income and the balance in accounts receivable with a contra account called "allowance for uncollectibles."

amortization Amortization is the systematic allocation of deferred charge (e.g., prepaid expense, fixed asset, bond discount or premium, deferred revenue, intangible asset) over its life. Amortization is often used to describe the allocation of the cost of intangible assets to earnings, but prepaid expenses and discounts and premiums on long-term receivables and payables are also amortized to earnings. Depreciation is the amortization of fixed assets, and depletion is the amortization of natural resource costs.

analytic review Analytic review is an important part of financial statement analysis that focuses on whether balances in financial statement accounts deviate from expected levels and seeks to explain why such deviations occur. It includes analyzing common-size financial statements to identify relative changes in the sizes of financial accounts across periods as well as comparing these changes in an effort to infer management actions.

annual report An annual report is a document that a company publishes each year, containing the financial statements, a description of the company and its operations, an audit report, a management letter, footnotes to the financial statements containing supporting schedules, and other financial and nonfinancial information.

annuity An annuity is a periodic cash flow of an equal amount over time. Bond interest payments, lease and rental payments, and insurance payments are examples.

appropriation of retained earnings An appropriation refers to the act of making a portion of the retained

earnings account unavailable for the payment of dividends. Such restrictions can be imposed contractually or voluntarily and are designed to ensure that cash is available in the future for some specific purpose.

asset An asset is an item listed on the left side of the balance sheet that has been acquired by the company in an objectively measurable transaction and has future economic benefit—additional purchasing power, cash, or the ability to generate revenues.

asset depreciation range (ADR) The Asset Depreciation Range (ADR) System contains guidelines published by the Internal Revenue Service that define the minimum allowable useful lives and maximum depreciation rates for various kinds of long-lived assets. These lives are used when depreciating long-lived assets in the computation of taxable income.

asset impairment An asset impairment occurs when the value of an asset is judged to be permanently reduced. See **asset retirement** and **restructuring charges.**

asset mix Asset mix is the combination of assets listed on the balance sheet as of a given date. For example, the percent of current assets, long-term investments, fixed assets, and intangibles to total assets can represent a company's asset mix. Common-size analysis across time can identify changes in a company's asset mix.

asset retirement An asset retirement refers to the discontinuation of the use of a fixed asset.

asset turnover *Sales/Average total assets.* Asset turnover measures how efficiently a company is using its assets to produce sales. A high ratio indicates that a company is producing a large amount of sales with relatively few assets. Asset turnover times profit margin equals return on assets, which is a direct determinant of return on equity.

audit An audit is an examination conducted by an individual or entity, having no financial interest in the company (i.e., independent), to determine whether the financial statements of the company fairly reflect its financial condition, whether the statements have been prepared in conformance with generally accepted accounting principles, and whether the company's internal control system is effective. The outcome of the audit is an audit report, or opinion letter, signed by the auditor, which states the extent of the auditor's activities and the conclusions.

audit committee The audit committee is a subcommittee of the board of directors, made up entirely of non-management directors, that works with management to choose the external auditor and monitor the audit so that it is conducted in a thorough, objective, and independent manner.

audit opinion See **audit report.**

audit report The audit report, which is written and signed by the external auditor, states whether, and to what extent, the information in the financial statements fairly reflects the financial performance and condition of the company. See **audit.**

authorized shares Authorized shares refers to the number of shares of stock a corporation is entitled to issue by its corporate charter, which is normally granted by the state in which the company is incorporated. Additional authorizations must be approved by the board of directors and are often subject to shareholder vote. Both preferred and common shares must be authorized before they can be issued.

available-for-sale securities Available-for-sale securities refer to relatively small investments (less than 20 percent of the outstanding voting stock) in marketable equity or debt securities that are not considered trading securities. Available-for-sale securities are readily marketable but are not intended to be sold in the near future—they can be listed as either current or noncurrent depending upon management's intention, and they are carried on the balance sheet at fair market value.

averaging assumption In addition to first-in, first-out (FIFO) and last-in, first-out (LIFO), averaging is one of the three most common inventory cost flow assumptions. Under the average method, cost of goods sold and ending inventory are determined by computing a weighted average cost of the items sold and the items remaining, respectively.

B

bad debts See **uncollectibles.**

balance sheet The balance sheet is a financial statement that indicates the financial condition of a business as of a given point in time. It includes assets, liabilities, and stockholders' equity, and it represents a statement of the basic accounting equation. The assets and liabilities are divided into current and noncurrent classifications on the basis of liquidity, and comparisons of assets and liabilities often provide an indication about the company's ability to meet obligations as they come due (i.e., solvency).

bank reconciliation A bank reconciliation is a document that lists items explaining the difference between the cash balance indicated in the company's ledger and the cash balance indicated in the company's bank statement. Differences between the two balances arise from outstanding checks, unrecorded deposits, and bank charges. Maintaining up-to-date bank reconciliations is one component of a good internal control system.

basic earnings per share See **earnings per share.**

betterment A betterment is a material expenditure made after the acquisition of a long-lived asset that improves the asset by increasing its life, increasing the quality or quantity of its output, or decreasing the cost of operating it.

"Big 4" The four public accounting firms that audit most of the large companies in the United States are known as

the Big 4. They are Deloitte & Touche, Ernst & Young, KPMG Peat Marwick, and PricewaterhouseCoopers.

board of directors The board of directors is a group of individuals, elected annually by the stockholders of a corporation to represent the interests of those stockholders. In addition to setting overall corporate policies, the board has the power to declare dividends, set executive compensation, and hire and fire management. The board also appoints and monitors the compensation committee and audit committee.

bond Bonds are debt securities issued by an entity to a large number of investors to raise cash. The issuing company, in return, normally agrees to make cash interest payments to the bondholders until a specific future date (called maturity), usually five to thirty years in the future, at which time a large principal payment is made and the obligation is terminated. Companies issue bonds to raise large amounts of cash, and they are normally issued (sold) to the public through a third party (called an underwriter), such as an investment banker or financial institution. After bonds are initially issued, they are generally freely negotiable; that is, they can be purchased and sold in the open market.

bonds payable Bonds payable represents a balance sheet liability reflecting the book value of bonds that have been previously issued and are presently outstanding. This liability is normally considered to be long-term, except for the portion that is due within the time period of current liabilities. Bonds payable are carried on the balance sheet at the present value of the future cash (interest and principal) payments specified by the terms of the bonds, discounted at the effective interest rate at the time of issuance.

book gain/loss A book gain (or loss) is the difference between the value received (or given up) and the book value of the asset (or liability) disposed of. If, for example, an asset with a book value of $10,000 is sold for $12,000, a $2,000 book gain is recognized. Selling the same asset for $7,000 would create a book loss of $3,000.

book value Book value is the value of an account, a company, or a share of stock as indicated by the balance sheet. It is often referred to as balance sheet value.

borrowing capacity Borrowing capacity is the ability of a company to raise capital by issuing debt securities or other borrowings. Borrowing capacity is critical for successful businesses because debt financing is a method of raising much-needed capital to support operations, invest in assets, or pay off outstanding debts.

business acquisition In a business acquisition, a company (investor) acquires a controlling interest (51 percent or more of the voting stock) in another (investee) company. The investor company is called the parent, and the investee company is called the subsidiary; both companies normally continue to operate. The financial statements of the parent are prepared on a consolidated basis, where the assets, liabilities, income, and cash flows of the combined entity are included together. The financial statements of the subsidiary are unaffected.

business combination See **merger.**

business environment A business environment is the economic setting in which a company's operating, investing, and financing activities are conducted. The business environment consists of many items, most of which are not within management's control—including interest rates, market values of certain assets, competitive forces, the general state of the economy, changes in customer tastes and preferences, characteristics of the workforce, and government regulation.

business segment A business segment is a separate line of business, production line, or class of customer representing an operation that is independent of a company's other operations. Many large companies have multiple lines of business, and if material, the assets, liabilities, revenues, and profits associated with these separate lines are disclosed in the footnotes to the financial statements.

C

call provision A provision in a debt contract that allows the issuing company to repurchase outstanding debt (e.g., bonds) after a specified date for a specified price is a call provision. Call provisions protect issuing companies from situations where market interest rates drop significantly. In such cases, issuing companies can exercise their call provisions (repurchase the debt) and reissue debt at lower interest rates.

capital Capital refers to funds (usually cash) generated by a company to support its operations. In a general sense, capital can refer to funds produced through issuing either debt or equity securities, but the capital section of the balance sheet normally refers to owners' or stockholders' (shareholders') equity—sources of equity capital.

capital asset pricing model The cost of equity can be estimated using the capital asset pricing model, which expresses the return an investor can reasonably expect on an equity investment (cost of equity) as a function of two factors: (1) the expected risk-free rate of return and (2) the expected risk premium associated with an investment in the firm itself.

capital employed Capital employed is an expression used to describe funds invested. See **capital.**

capital lease A capital lease is a lease treated as a purchase for purposes of financial accounting. If, at the date of the lease agreement, a lease meets certain criteria, it is classified and accounted for as a capital lease by the lessee. Under a capital lease, the lessee is considered to have the economic ownership of the leased asset,

which is financed through the periodic lease payments. The resulting accounting treatment recognizes both a balance sheet asset and a liability, which are initially placed on the books at the present value of the future cash payments, discounted at the effective rate of interest. The asset is then depreciated, and the effective interest method is used to amortize the liability as the lease payments are made.

capital market Transactions involving the buying and selling of debt and equity investments are conducted in the capital market. This market includes the global stock and bond markets and the banking system.

capital structure Capital structure refers to a company's financing sources: (1) borrowings or liabilities, (2) contributed capital, and (3) earned capital (primarily retained earnings). It is represented by the right side of the balance sheet—liabilities and shareholders' equity.

capital structure leverage *Average total assets/Average stockholders' equity.* Capital structure leverage or financial leverage indicates the extent to which a company relies on debt financing. As the ratio increases (decreases), the amount of debt financing is greater (less). A ratio of "1" indicates that there is no debt in the company's capital structure. Capital structure leverage is a direct determinant of return on equity.

capitalization ratios Capitalization ratios help analysts evaluate the capital structure of a company or, in general, the composition of the liability and shareholders' equity side of the balance sheet. They include: (1) debt/equity, (2) debt ratio, (3) capital structure leverage, and (4) common equity leverage.

capitalize To capitalize an expenditure means to place the cost of an expenditure on the balance sheet as an asset. Expenditures can be either expensed or capitalized.

cash conversion cycle *Accounts receivable turnover (days) + Inventory turnover (days) − Accounts payable turnover (days).* This metric combines three turnover measures in a way that indicates the time period over which a company's major working capital requirements must be financed. As this measure increases, it indicates a longer time period, a greater working capital investment, and higher financing requirements. See **operating cycle.**

cash discount When a good or service is sold on credit, the selling company wishes to collect the cash as soon as possible. To encourage prompt payment, many companies offer cash discounts on the gross sales price. Cash discounts specify that an amount of cash less than the gross sales price is sufficient to satisfy the obligation.

cash equivalent Cash equivalents are securities that can be converted into cash in a very short time. Examples include commercial paper and other debt instruments with maturity dates less than three months in the future. Such items are often included in the definition of cash for purposes of the balance sheet and the statement of cash flows.

cash flow Cash flow is the movement of cash associated with a company's operating, investing, and financing activities. Cash flow involves inflows and outflows of cash, and a company's cash flow is considered to be strong if it can generate large amounts of cash relatively quickly. Cash flow is an important part of solvency, and a historical description of cash flow is provided by the statement of cash flows.

cash flow accounting Cash flow accounting is a system that keeps a balance of cash and a record of cash inflows and outflows. The statement of cash flows is based on cash flow accounting.

cash flow from financing Cash flow from financing activities represents cash generated during a particular period through a company's financing activities. These cash flows are disclosed in the financing section of the statement of cash flows and reflect cash flows associated with additional long-term borrowings and repayments, equity issuances and treasury stock purchases, and dividend payments.

cash flow from investing Cash flow from investing activities includes cash inflows and outflows during a particular period from a company's investing activities. These flows are disclosed in the investing section of the statement of cash flows and reflect cash inflows and outflows associated with the acquisition and sale of a company's investments and long-lived assets.

cash flow from operations Cash flows from operating activities include cash receipts and payments during a particular period associated with a company's operating activities. Also called net cash flow from operations, these flows are disclosed in the operating section of the statement of cash flows and can be computed and presented in either of two ways: (1) a direct method, which lists the cash flow effects of each income statement item, or (2) the more common indirect method, which arrives at cash from operations by adjusting net income for differences between accruals and operating cash flows.

cash flow projection Cash flow projection is the process of predicting the amount and timing of future cash inflows and outflows and plays an important role in financial statement analysis.

cash management Cash management is the manner in which a company plans and executes the inflows and outflows of cash.

certificate of deposit A certificate of deposit is a short-term bank obligation that pays a given rate of interest for a specified period of time, ending on the maturity date. Often interest penalties are assessed when cash is withdrawn prior to the maturity date.

certified public accountant A certified public accountant (CPA) is an individual who has met a set of educational

requirements to sit for the national CPA exam, passed the exam, and met the experience requirements of the states in which he or she practices. Certified public accountants must also pass an ethics exam, periodically participate in continuing education courses, and maintain their membership with the American Institute of Certified Public Accountants (AICPA). CPAs are empowered to sign audit reports.

classified balance sheet A classified balance sheet is a balance sheet that is divided into classifications—including current assets, long-term investments, fixed assets, intangible assets, current liabilities, long-term liabilities, and shareholders' equity.

clean audit opinion See **standard audit report.**

collateral Collateral represents assets designated to be paid to a creditor in case of default on a loan by a debtor—often referred to as security on the loan. The balance sheet, which contains a listing of a company's assets, and the footnotes to the financial statements may help to identify various sources of collateral. Lenders often require that loans be backed by collateral, as a way of reducing the cost associated with default.

collection period See **accounts receivable turnover.**

commercial paper Commercial paper is a fast-growing means of providing short-term financing; it represents short-term notes (30 to 270 days) issued for cash by companies with good credit ratings to other companies.

common equity leverage (*Net income − Preferred stock dividends*)/(*Net income − Interest expense* [*1 − Tax rate*]). Common equity leverage measures the portion of the return to the stockholders relative to the return to all capital providers (stockholders and creditors). Higher levels of this ratio indicate that greater amounts of the return generated by the company are available to the stockholders, an indication of the effectiveness of the company's leverage.

common stock Common stock is a certificate that represents an ownership (equity) interest in a corporation, carrying with it the right to receive dividends if they are declared and the right to vote for the corporation's board of directors at the annual shareholders' meeting. It also carries with it the right to the assets of the corporation, but this right is subordinate to that of the corporate creditors. Issuing common stock is a popular way used by corporations to raise capital.

common-size financial statements Common-size financial statements express dollar values as percentages of other dollar values on the same statement. On a common-size income statement, for example, expense items and the various measures of income (e.g., operating income, net income) are expressed as percentages of sales. On a common-size balance sheet, assets and liabilities are expressed as percentages of total assets (or liabilities plus shareholders' equity).

compensating balance Compensating balances are minimum cash balances that must be maintained in savings or checking accounts until certain loan obligations are satisfied. Compensating balances help financial institutions reduce the risks of default on outstanding loans by ensuring that at least some cash is available for scheduled loan payments.

compensation committee The compensation committee is a subcommittee of the board of directors charged with establishing the compensation packages of the company's officers. It is made up entirely of outside directors (not part of company management).

compensation contracts Compensation contracts specify the form and amount of compensation paid to the executives, managers, or employees of a company.

comprehensive income A measure of income that includes not only net income, but also other increases in a company's wealth not reflected on the income statement. Examples include unrealized price changes on available-for-sale securities and translation gains and losses related to the consolidation of foreign subsidiaries. A statement of comprehensive income, detailing the change in comprehensive income over a period of time, must be included in the financial statements.

conservatism Conservatism is an exception to the principles of accounting measurement stating that when in doubt, financial statements should understate assets, overstate liabilities, accelerate the recognition of losses, and delay the recognition of gains.

consignment A consignment is an agreement by which a consignor (owner) transfers inventory to a consignee (receiver) who takes physical possession and places the items up for sale. When the inventory is sold, the consignee collects the sales proceeds, keeps a percentage, and returns the remainder to the consignor.

consistency Consistency is a principle of accounting measurement stating that, although there is considerable choice among accounting methods, companies should choose a set of methods and use them from one period to the next. Consistency helps financial statement users to make useful comparisons across time.

consolidated financial statements Consolidated financial statements include a company's assets and liabilities as well as the assets and liabilities of its majority-owned subsidiaries. See **business acquisition and merger.**

contingency A contingency represents an existing condition, situation, or set of circumstances involving uncertainty concerning a possible gain or loss to a company. The uncertainty will ultimately be resolved when one or more future events occurs or fails to occur.

contingent liability See **contingency** and **loss contingency.**

contra account A contra account is a balance sheet account that offsets another balance sheet account.

contributed capital Contributed capital represents that portion of the shareholders' equity section of the

balance sheet of a corporation, reflecting contributions from stockholders. It represents the amount of a company's assets that have been generated through issuances of stock (common and preferred), including the dollar amounts of both the stock and additional paid-in capital accounts. Treasury stock purchases reduce contributed capital because they represent returns of capital to the shareholders.

controlling interest Technically, a controlling interest is ownership of 51 percent or more of the outstanding voting stock of a company. In such cases, consolidated financial statements must be prepared. Control may be possible, however, with less than 51 percent of the stock. A significant influence on either the board of directors or operations of the company, especially in cases where the remaining ownership is spread across many entities, may also represent control.

convertible bonds Convertible bonds are bonds that can be converted to other corporate securities (usually common stock) during some specified period of time. Convertible bonds combine the benefits of a bond (guaranteed interest) with the privilege of exchanging it for stock (potential appreciation and dividends) at the holder's option. They are considered hybrid securities because they possess features of both debt and equity.

copyright Copyrights are exclusive rights granted by law to control literary, musical, or artistic works. They are granted for fifty years beyond the life of the creator. The cost of acquiring a copyright is capitalized on the balance sheet as an intangible asset and normally amortized over its legal life, not to exceed forty years.

corporate governance Mechanisms that encourage management to report in good faith to—and act in the interest of—the stockholders. Effective corporate governance is critical for an effective financial reporting system. Components of corporate governance include financial information users and capital markets, contracts between management and debt and equity investors, financial reporting regulations and standards, independent auditors, boards of directors and audit committees, internal controls ensuring that the company is in compliance with financial reporting regulations, legal liability, professional reputation, and ethics.

corporation A corporation is a legal entity, separate and distinct from its owners (stockholders), who annually elect a board of directors, which in turn represents the stockholders' interests in the management of the business. A corporation has an indefinite life, which continues regardless of changes in ownership. Stockholders of a corporation are usually free to transfer their ownership interests. In a corporation, the liability of the stockholders is limited to the dollar amount of their investments, and in this way, the corporate structure provides a shield that protects the personal assets of the shareholders from corporate creditors.

Companies in need of large amounts of capital therefore normally take the corporate form.

cost See **historical cost.**

cost expiration Cost expiration is the process of converting a capitalized cost to an expense. Accounting entries recorded at the end of the period are often used to expire previously capitalized costs, which appear as assets on the balance sheet.

cost method Under the cost method of accounting, assets are carried on the balance sheet at their original (historical) costs, and when an asset is sold, a gain or loss is recognized on the difference between the balance sheet value of the asset and the proceeds from the sale.

cost of capital If a company has available cash, cost of capital is the expected return forgone by investing the cash in a project rather than in comparable financial securities. If a company does not have available cash, it is the cost of acquiring the cash—i.e., the cost of raising debt (effective interest) capital or the cost of raising equity capital (dilution). Value is created for the shareholders when the management of operations and investments creates a return that exceeds the cost of capital.

cost of debt Because interest is tax deductible, the explicit cost of debt is equal to the annual debt-related interest expense times 1 minus the income tax rate (interest expense $\times$ [1 – tax rate]). Debt may have implicit costs as well, including covenant-imposed restrictions and security (collateral) requirements.

cost of equity The return an investor can reasonably expect on an equity investment in a firm, or the return (expressed as a percentage) forgone by a firm's shareholders, who have chosen to invest their funds in the firm instead of other equally risky investments. It can be estimated by the capital asset pricing model. Value creation, the key metric of management's success, is defined as the extent to which return on equity exceeds the cost of equity.

cost of goods sold Cost of goods sold appears on the income statement, indicating the cost of inventory sold during the period. In retail companies, cost of goods sold consists primarily of the cost of acquiring the inventory; in manufacturing companies, cost of goods sold consists of material, labor, and overhead costs.

covenant See **debt covenant.**

CPA See **certified public accountant.**

credit quality Credit quality refers to the likelihood that an individual or entity will pay an outstanding account in a timely manner. Customers or clients with high credit quality have a history of paying their obligations on time.

credit rating A credit rating is an assessment by an independent agency of the risk associated with a company and especially its outstanding debts. Credit ratings are usually expressed in alphabetic and/or numerical grades (e.g., AA1), and credit-rating agencies include

Standard & Poor's, Dun & Bradstreet, and Moody's Investors Service.

credit terms Credit terms are the contractual terms associated with outstanding credit (accounts receivable and accounts payable) accounts.

creditor A creditor is an individual or entity to which a company owes money or services or to which the company has an outstanding debt.

cumulative preferred stock Cumulative preferred stock is a type of preferred stock with a cumulative feature, which means that when a company misses a dividend on cumulative preferred stock, the missed dividend becomes a dividend in arrears. Most preferred stock is cumulative.

current assets Current assets are assets on the balance sheet expected to be converted to cash or expired in one year or the operating cycle, whichever is longer.

current cost See **replacement cost.**

current liabilities Current liabilities refers to obligations listed on the balance sheet expected to be paid with the use of current assets listed on the balance sheet.

current maturity of long-term debts Current maturity of long-term debts is a balance sheet current liability representing that portion of a long-term liability due in the current period. This liability is expected to require the use of current assets.

current ratio *Current assets/Current liabilities.* The current ratio is often used to assess a company's current asset management and its solvency position. It is normally an important part of financial statement analysis.

D

debenture A debenture is an unsecured bond.

debt Debt is a form of financing a borrowing that involves an obligation, stated in a formal contract, which indicates the time period of the obligation in addition to the amount and timing of the required cash payments. Often, the contract also identifies security (collateral) in the case of default and other provisions (debt covenants) normally designed to protect the interests of the lender.

debt covenant A debt covenant is an agreement between a company's debtholders and its managers that often restricts the managers' behavior. These restrictions are usually designed to protect the debtholder's investment (i.e., increase the likelihood of receiving the contractual debt payments on a timely basis), and they are often written in terms of numbers and ratios taken from the financial statements. Violating a debt covenant puts the issuing company (debtor) into technical default.

debt investment A debt investment involves the purchase of a debt security or a loan of goods or services to another entity, with the expectation that some payment (principal and interest) will be received in return. Debt investments are usually backed by contracts that specify the terms of the arrangement—maturity date interest and principal payments, security, and collateral as well as other features that transfer risk from one party to the other (e.g., debt covenants, call provisions).

debt ratio *Total liabilities/Total assets.* Assets are generated from three sources: borrowings, contributions from owners, and profitable operations not paid out in the form of dividends. The debt ratio reflects that portion provided by borrowings.

debt redemptions See **redemption.**

debt/equity ratio *Total liabilities (both current and non-current)/Shareholders' equity. (Note: Sometimes contractual debt only is used in the numerator.)* The debt/equity ratio indicates the extent to which a company can sustain losses without jeopardizing the interests of its creditors. Creditors have priority claims over stockholders, and in case of liquidation, the creditors have first right to a company's assets. From an individual creditor's standpoint, therefore, the amount of equity in the company's capital structure can be viewed as a buffer, helping to ensure that there are sufficient assets to cover individual claims. It also represents a measure of the extent to which a company is relying on leverage as a source of financing.

default A default occurs when an individual or entity fails to make a contractual payment on a debt. See **technical default.**

deferred cost A deferred cost is a miscellaneous category of assets listed on the balance sheet that often includes prepaid expenses extending beyond the current accounting period and intangible assets such as organizational costs, capitalized legal fees, and other startup costs.

deferred income See **deferred revenue.**

deferred income taxes Deferred income taxes can appear in either the liability or asset section of the balance sheet—arising when companies recognize revenues and expenses for financial reporting and income tax purposes in different time periods. Deferred income tax liabilities (assets) arise in periods when temporary timing differences between tax and financial reporting cause taxable income to be different from net income on the income statement. Deferred tax liabilities (assets) represent expected increases (decreases) in taxes payable in future periods when these temporary timing differences reverse—at which time the deferred income tax liabilities (assets) are written off the books.

deferred revenue Deferred revenue is a balance sheet liability reflecting services yet to be performed by a company for which cash payments have already been collected. Deferred revenues are also referred to as payments in advance, deferred income, and unearned revenues.

defined benefit pension plan In a defined benefit pension plan, an employer promises to provide each employee

with a specified benefit at retirement. This promise is difficult to plan for because the benefits are received by the employees in the future. The benefits must be predicted, and the employer must contribute enough cash to a pension fund so that the contributions plus the earnings on the fund assets will be sufficient to provide the promised benefits. See **defined contribution pension plan.**

defined contribution pension plan In a defined contribution pension plan, an employer agrees only to make a series of contributions of a specified amount to a pension fund. These periodic cash payments are often based on employee wages or salaries, and each employee's percentage interest in the total fund is determined by the proportionate share contributed by the employer on the employee's behalf. Under this type of plan, the employer makes no promises regarding how much the employees will receive upon retirement.

depletion Depletion is the amortization of the costs incurred to acquire rights to mine natural resources. For mining and oil and gas companies, such costs can be substantial, and these costs are normally depleted as the natural resource is extracted, using the activity method.

depreciation Depreciation is the periodic allocation of the cost of a fixed asset to the income statement over the asset's useful life. Such allocation is necessary if the costs are to be matched against the benefits produced by the asset. For financial reporting purposes, management has much discretion over how depreciation is computed. For income tax purposes, there is much less leeway.

depreciation base The depreciation (amortization) base is the portion of the cost of a long-lived asset subject to depreciation or amortization—capitalized cost less estimated salvage value.

depreciation expense A depreciation expense is an item on the income statement, reducing net income, that reflects the depreciation recognized on a company's fixed assets during the period of time covered by the income statement. Depreciation is a cost expiration; it does not represent a cash outflow.

diluted earnings per share Diluted earnings per share is a disclosure required by generally accepted accounting principles (GAAP) for companies that have the potential for significant dilution. This ratio, which must be disclosed on the face of the income statement, is computed by adjusting the earnings per share ratio for an estimate of the equity securities likely to be issued in the near future. Diluted earnings per share is less than earnings per share because the potential for additional equity issuances increases the denominator of the earnings per share ratio.

dilution Dilution is the reduction in a stockholder's relative ownership interest due to the issuance of additional equity securities to others.

dilutive securities Dilutive securities are outstanding securities that can lead to future equity issuances. Shareholders and potential shareholders should be aware of dilutive securities because when the options on dilutive securities are exercised, the equity positions of the existing shareholders are diluted. Examples include stock options and convertible bonds. Fully diluted earnings per share, which is a required disclosure under generally accepted accounting principles (GAAP), reflects the dilutive effects of these kinds of securities.

direct method Under the direct method of presentation in the operating section of the statement of cash flows, the cash effects of the operating expenses are subtracted from the cash effects of the operating revenues in the computation of net cash from operating activities. This form of presentation is called the direct method because the cash inflows and outflows are taken directly from the cash account in the ledger— that is, they represent real cash flows.

direct write-off method The direct write-off method of accounting for bad debts records bad debt expense and removes the outstanding receivable from the balance sheet at the point in time when a specific account is deemed uncollectible. This method of accounting for bad debts is normally considered unacceptable under generally accepted accounting principles (GAAP) because it does not attempt to record all expected bad debts in the same period in which the sales revenue is recorded, thereby violating the matching principle.

discount on bond payable Discount on bond payable is a contra liability account representing the amount by which the face (maturity) value of a bond exceeds the present value of the bond's future cash payments, discounted at the effective rate of interest as of the date when the bonds were issued. Such discounts are amortized over the remaining life of the bond issuance under the effective interest method, increasing periodic interest expense to reflect the fact that the bonds were issued at a discount (i.e., the proceeds at the initial bond issuance were less than the face value of the bond).

discount rate Discount rate is used to describe the rate used in present value computations. To compute the present value of a future cash flow, for example, the cash flows are discounted at the discount rate, which reflects both the timing of the cash flows and the risk associated with receiving them. In this sense, the discount rate reflects the company's cost of capital—the cost of its debt and/or its equity.

dissimilar asset Dissimilar asset is a classification of long-lived assets used in determining the proper method of accounting for long-lived asset exchanges. The methods used to account for exchanges of dissimilar assets are different from those used to account for exchanges of similar assets. When dissimilar

assets are exchanged, book gains or losses are recognized on the transactions—in the amount of the difference between the market value of that received and the market value of that given up. When similar assets are exchanged, book gains or losses are not recognized. Instead, the difference between the market value of that received and the market value of that given up serves to adjust (increase or decrease) the cost of the asset received in the exchange. See **trade-in.**

divestiture A divestiture is the sale of an asset or investment and normally refers to the sale of a major equity interest in another company.

dividend yield *Dividends per share/Market price per share.* Dividend yield indicates the cash return on the stockholders' investment. Recall that a return on an investment in common stock can come in two forms: dividends and market price appreciation. This financial ratio measures the size of the first. Dividend yields tend to be relatively small, especially for fast-growing companies that choose to pay little or no dividends.

dividends Dividends are payments made to the stockholders of a corporation that provide a return on their equity investments. Dividends are declared by the board of directors and are normally paid in the form of cash, although dividends in the form of other assets and shares of stock in the company are not unusual.

dividends in arrears Dividends in arrears are missed dividends on preferred stock with a cumulative feature. Dividends in arrears are not listed on the balance sheet as liabilities, but they must be disclosed in the footnotes to the financial statements, and they must be paid if and when the company declares a dividend.

double taxation Double taxation is a phenomenon that occurs when corporate profits and dividends received by the shareholders are both subject to federal income taxes. Double taxation occurs because the Internal Revenue Service treats corporations and their shareholders as separate taxable entities. It is a major disadvantage of the corporate form of business.

double-declining-balance method Double-declining-balance is the most extreme form of accelerated depreciation. Each period, depreciation expense is computed by multiplying the book value of the depreciable asset (cost − accumulated depreciation) by two times the straight-line rate (1/estimated useful life). This conservative method recognizes large amounts of depreciation expense in the early periods of the asset's life and small amounts in the later periods. It is very popular for tax purposes.

DuPont (ROE) Model Using the DuPont (ROE) Model to analyze financial ratios provides an important starting point for financial statement analysis. While there are a number of different forms of this model, all are designed to explain the changes in return on equity by breaking it down into the following components: profit margin, asset turnover, and leverage.

E

earned capital Earned capital is a measure of the amount of a company's assets that has been generated through profitable operations and not paid out in the form of dividends. On the balance sheet, earned capital is part of the shareholders' equity section and is composed of retained earnings and other accumulated comprehensive income.

earning power Earning power is the ability of a company to generate profits and increase net assets in the future. Net income, especially the persistent components of net income, is considered an indication of earning power.

earnings See **net income.**

earnings management The expression "earnings management" refers to cases when management uses its discretion to produce financial statements that place management's performance in a particular light, often reducing the ability of the financial statements to fairly represent the financial performance and condition of the company. Earnings management can involve reporting discretion or the structuring of transactions to achieve certain reporting goals (called real earnings management).

earnings per share *Net income/Average number of common shares outstanding.* Earnings per share or basic earnings per share is perhaps the best known of all financial ratios, largely because it is often treated by the financial press as the primary measure of a company's performance. According to generally accepted accounting principles (GAAP), earnings per share must appear on the face of the income statement and be calculated in accordance with an elaborate set of complex rules. See **diluted earnings per share.**

earnings persistence Earnings persistence is the extent to which a particular earnings dollar amount can be expected to continue in the future and thus generate future cash flows. Earnings amounts with high levels of persistence are expected to continue in the future, while those with low levels of persistence are not.

earnings quality Earnings quality refers to the extent to which net income reported on the income statement differs from true earnings. This difference is the result of two factors: (1) financial reports based on an objective application of generally accepted accounting principles (GAAP) are inherently limited and (2) management uses its subjective discretion to apply GAAP when preparing the statements (earnings management). Low earnings quality means that GAAP financial statements do not accurately reflect the company's true financial situation and/or management has used much of its discretion in preparing the financial statements.

economic entity assumption The economic entity assumption states that the financial statements refer to entities that are distinct from both their owners and all other economic entities. This assumption is important in determining the methods to account for consolidated financial statements, investments in equity securities, and business segments.

economic value added Economic value added (EVA) represents the extent to which a return generated by management exceeds the cost of the capital (debt and equity) invested to generate that return. See value creation.

effective interest method The effective interest method is used to value long-term liabilities (e.g., bonds) and long-term notes receivable and the related interest charges, so that the book value of the note represents an estimate of the present value of the note's future cash flows. The future cash flows are discounted using the effective rate of interest as of the date the note was issued. The effective interest method is required under generally accepted accounting principles (GAAP).

effective interest rate The effective rate of interest is the actual rate of interest on an obligation or receivable, and it often differs from the stated interest rate. It is that rate which, when used to discount the future cash payments associated with the obligation or receivable, results in a present value equal to the fair market value of that which was initially exchanged for the obligation or receivable. Generally accepted accounting principles (GAAP) require that the effective interest rate be used to compute the periodic interest expense and revenue that appears on the income statement.

equity Equity is an ownership interest. Equity holders in a company own common stocks that have been issued by that company. Two rights are associated with owning a common stock: (1) the right to vote for the board of directors at the annual shareholders' meeting and (2) the right to receive dividends if they are declared by the board. The shareholders' equity section of the balance sheet represents the investment made by the equity holders in the company and is a measure of the assets that would remain for the equity holders after all liabilities have been paid.

equity investment An equity investment is the purchase of an ownership interest (e.g., common stock) in a company.

equity issuance An equity issuance is the sale of common shares (stock). Equity issuances raise funds—often large amounts—for a variety of reasons, including business acquisitions, investments in long-lived assets, payments on outstanding debt, or simply to support operations.

equity method The equity method is used to account for equity investments in the amount of 20 to 50 percent of the investee company's outstanding common (voting) stock. Such a significant influence on the investee company indicates a substantive economic relationship between the two companies and may also be evidenced, for example, by representation on the board of directors, the interchange of management personnel between companies, frequent or significant transactions between companies, or the technical dependency of one company on the other.

equity security See **equity investment.**

ERISA The Employment Retirement Income Securities Act passed by Congress in 1974 requires employers to fund their pension plans at specified minimum levels and provide other safeguards designed to protect employees. See **defined benefit pension plan.**

escrow Escrow is the state of an item (e.g., cash) that has been put into the custody of a third party until certain conditions are fulfilled. Damage deposits on rental agreements, for example, are often held in escrow until the end of the rental period.

exchange rate The exchange rate is the value of one currency expressed in terms of another currency. Like the prices of all goods and services, the exchange rates among currencies vary from one day to the next. Companies that transact in more than one currency face the risks associated with fluctuating exchange rates, which can give rise to gains and losses—some of which are reflected on the financial statements. Hedging is a strategy that can be used to reduce such risks.

expense An expense is the outflow of assets or the creation of liabilities in an effort to generate revenues for a company. Examples include cost of goods sold, salaries, interest, advertising, taxes, utilities, depreciation, and others. Revenues less expenses is equal to net income—the income statement. While some expenses involve cash outflows, many do not; expenses can also be accrued (e.g., salaries, wages, interest) or the result of cost expirations (e.g., depreciation, amortization).

expensed Expensed means to treat an expenditure as an expense by running the account through the income statement and closing it to retained earnings. Expense items appearing on the income statement have been expensed.

external financing External financing refers to the generation of funds to support operations and growth through the issuance of debt and/or equity, instead of retained earnings. Externally financed companies normally have capital structures with relatively large balances in debt and/or contributed capital.

extraordinary item Extraordinary items appear on the income statement and represent the financial effects of events that are significantly different from the typical, customary business activities of an entity. Such events are not expected to recur frequently in the ordinary activities of the business. Extraordinary items are neither usual nor frequent.

F

face value See **maturity value.**

fair market value Fair market value is the dollar amount at which an item can be sold—exchanged for cash.

fair market value accounting Fair market value accounting is a method of accounting for an asset or liability that carries the asset or liability on the balance sheet at its fair market value, and changes in price from one period to the next either directly affect shareholders' equity (other comprehensive income) or are reported on the income statement and ultimately are reflected in retained earnings.

fair value option Fair value option is a relatively recent U.S. reporting standard that allows companies to use fair market value accounting for their financial instruments.

fees earned See **service revenue.**

financial accounting Financial accounting is a process through which managers report financial information about an economic entity to a variety of individuals who use this information for various decision-making purposes. The financial accounting process produces the financial statements and the associated footnotes.

financial accounting standards In the U.S., financial accounting standards represent the official statements of the Financial Accounting Standards Board (FASB) and its predecessor bodies as well as the official statements from the Securities and Exchange Commission (SEC). The complete set of financial accounting standards currently in force comprises U.S. generally accepted accounting principles (GAAP). Many non-U.S. countries have their own financial accounting standards, and International Financial Accounting Standards (IFRS) are also used by many non-U.S. firms. IFRS are established by the International Accounting Standards Board (IASB), successor to the International Accounting Standards Committee (IASC), which was formed in 1973 to develop worldwide accounting practices. The IASC's pronouncements are known as International Accounting Standards (IAS).

Financial Accounting Standards Board The Financial Accounting Standards Board (FASB) is the professional body currently responsible for establishing financial accounting standards. The FASB consists of seven well-compensated, full-time individuals who have severed all ties with previous employers and represent many business backgrounds. Since 1973, this private-sector body has issued well over 100 statements of financial accounting standards, covering a wide variety of topics.

financial condition Financial condition refers to the economic strength of a company as of a specific point in time. The balance is designed to measure financial condition.

financial flexibility Financial flexibility refers to a company's capacity to raise cash through methods other than operations. Examples include short- and long-term borrowings, issuing equity, or selling assets. Financially flexible companies can readily borrow, issue equity, and/or sell liquid assets that are not essential to their operations.

financial performance Financial performance refers to the economic success of a company over a specified time period. The income statement is designed to measure financial performance.

financial ratio analysis Financial ratio analysis is one of several techniques used to analyze financial statements in an effort to assess earning power, solvency, and earnings persistence. Financial ratio analysis involves computing and analyzing ratios that use two or more financial statement numbers. These ratios are often divided into five categories: (1) profitability, (2) solvency, (3) activity, (4) capitalization, and (5) market ratios. The DuPont (ROE) Model is used by many analysts to asses the determinants of return on equity (ROE), which is directly related to shareholder value creation (ROE – cost of equity).

financial statement analysis Financial statement analysis is the process of reading, studying, and analyzing the information contained in the annual report and other relevant documents to predict the future financial performance and condition of a company. Financial statement analysis involves assessing (1) earning power, (2) solvency, (3) earnings persistence, and (4) earnings quality.

financial statements Financial statements are a summary of the financial condition and performance of a company, prepared by its management and in some cases reviewed by independent auditors. The financial statements consist of the income statement, balance sheet, statement of cash flows, statement of shareholders' equity, and related footnotes. The ability to read, understand, and interpret the financial statements is a key element of financial statement analysis.

financing activities Financing activities are the activities of a company that affect its capital structure. They involve the collection of capital through equity or debt issuances and any related payments such as dividends, debt payments, and treasury stock purchases.

financing cost Financing cost is an expression used to describe the cost of financing an activity. It includes the cost of debt and the cost of equity. See **cost of capital, cost of debt**, and **cost of equity.**

first-in, first-out First-in, first-out (FIFO) is a cost flow assumption used to value inventory and cost of goods sold. It assumes that the first items purchased are the first items sold. FIFO is one of three commonly used cost flow assumptions; last-in, first-out (LIFO) and averaging are the other two.

fiscal period assumption The fiscal period assumption states that the life of an economic entity can be divided into fiscal periods and that performance can be measured over those periods. This assumption allows the measurement of income for a given period of time (quarterly or annually) and raises questions about how the benefits and costs of a company should be allocated across periods for financial accounting purposes.

fiscal year Fiscal years end on dates other than December 31. Most companies report on a calendar-year (December 31) basis (e.g. seasonality), but for various reasons, some companies report on other 365-day cycles, called fiscal years.

fixed asset turnover *Net sales/Average fixed assets.* Fixed asset turnover is a measure of how efficiently a company is using its fixed assets. For many companies, this activity ratio is an important component of asset turnover and, in general, financial ratio analysis. Asset turnover times profit margin equals return on assets, a direct determinant of return on equity.

fixed assets Fixed assets, sometimes called property, plant, and equipment, is a category of long-lived assets including buildings, machinery, and equipment.

FOB destination FOB (free on board) destination represents freight terms indicating that the seller is responsible for the sold merchandise until it is received by the buyer. Goods shipped FOB destination are considered owned by the seller until they reach their destination. See **FOB shipping point.**

FOB shipping point FOB (free on board) shipping point describes freight terms indicating that the seller is responsible for the sold merchandise only to the point from where it is shipped. Goods shipped FOB shipping point are considered owned by the seller until they reach the designated shipper, at which time they become the responsibility of the buyer. See **FOB destination.**

footnotes Footnotes are descriptions and schedules included in the annual report that further explain the numbers on the financial statements. The footnotes are audited by the independent auditor, and they are considered part of the financial statements.

forward contract A forward contract enables the holder to buy or sell an asset or liability at a future date at a prespecified price. Forward contracts are also written to enable the holder to buy or sell currencies at a pre-specified exchange rate. Companies enter into forward contracts often to hedge the risks of holding assets and/or liabilities denominated in foreign currencies.

freight-in Freight-in, also called transportation-in, is the freight cost associated with purchased inventory.

frequent transactions A frequent transaction is an operating transaction that affects the income statement and is expected to recur repeatedly in the foreseeable future. See **extraordinary item.**

G

gain contingency A gain contingency refers to an event that leads to a possible future outcome involving an increase in assets or a decrease in liabilities. See **loss contingency.**

generally accepted accounting principles Generally accepted accounting principles (GAAP) are the standards that guide the preparation of financial accounting statements. See **financial accounting standards, U.S. GAAP,** and **international financial reporting standards (IFRS).**

going concern A going concern is an entity that is expected to exist into the foreseeable future. No financial problems indicating financial failure over the planning horizon are apparent. Going concern is an assumption that underlies the financial statements, and auditors are expected to qualify their audit reports if there is doubt about the ability of the audited company to continue as a going concern.

goods in transit Goods in transit are between the buyer and the seller as of the end of an accounting period. See **freight-in, FOB destination,** and **FOB shipping point.**

goodwill In general, goodwill often refers to items of value to a company that are not listed on the balance sheet. However, a goodwill account is often recognized on the balance sheet when a company purchases another company in a business acquisition for a dollar amount greater than the fair market value of the purchased company's net assets (assets – liabilities). This purchased goodwill is the difference between the purchase price and the fair market value of the purchased company's net assets; it represents the purchaser's assessment that the purchased company is worth more as a working unit than is indicated by the value of its individual assets and liabilities.

government accounting See **nonprofit entity** and **not-for-profit accounting.**

gross margin *Gross profit/Sales.* Gross margin measures the extent to which the selling price of sold inventory exceeds its cost.

gross profit Gross profit is equal to sales revenues minus cost of good sold. See **gross margin.**

H

hedging Hedging is a strategy used by management to reduce the risk associated with fluctuations in the values of assets and liabilities.

hidden reserves Hidden reserves refer to subjectively understated assets or overstated liabilities. Building hidden reserves is a reporting strategy used by management that allows it to "smooth" reported earnings from one period to the next. It is accomplished by subjectively recognizing accounting losses, normally in periods of high income, which reduces earnings in the

current period and ensures that these losses are not recognized in future periods when reported earnings may be lower.

historical cost Historical cost is the dollar amount incurred to acquire an asset (investment) or bring it to sellable (inventory) or serviceable (long-lived asset) condition. Historical cost is also referred to as original cost or cost.

human capital Human capital refers to a company's human resources, including its workforce and management.

human resources See **human capital.**

hurdle rate See **cost of capital.**

hybrid security Hybrid securities have characteristics of both debt and equity. Issuing these securities is becoming an increasingly popular means of corporate financing.

I

income See **net income.**

income smoothing Income smoothing is an expression used to describe a management practice where accounting discretion is used to maintain a smooth earnings stream across time. See **earnings management** and **hidden reserves.**

income statement The income statement is a financial statement, prepared on an accrual basis, indicating the performance of a company during a particular period (usually a quarter or a year). It consists of revenues minus expenses, leading to net income, an important indication of a company's earnings power.

independent auditor Independent auditors have no personal or financial interest in their clients. To ensure objective audits, the audit profession requires that auditors maintain complete independence from their clients when conducting audits.

indirect method Under the indirect method, the operating section of the statement of cash flows contains a series of adjustments that reconcile net income with net cash from operations. This form of presentation is called the indirect method because net cash from operating activities is computed indirectly—starting with net income and then adjusting it for the differences between accrual and cash flow accounting.

industry An industry is a classification of a group of companies based on the similarity of their operations, product lines, and/or customers. Three basic categories are manufacturing, retailing, and services (general and financial).

inflation Inflation refers to the eroding of the purchasing power of a monetary unit over time. In an inflationary environment, a dollar at the beginning of a period of time will buy fewer goods and services than at the end of the period.

input market The input market is where an entity purchases the inputs for its operations. Historical cost, which is used extensively on the balance sheet, represents the cost of a company's inputs (e.g., inventory and long-lived assets) when they were acquired previously. Replacement cost, which is used selectively on the balance sheet (e.g., lower of cost or market applied to inventory), represents the current cost of a company's inputs.

installment obligation An installment obligation requires periodic payments covering both interest and principal. Installment obligations are normally represented in the long-term liability section of the balance sheet, but the current installment is often carried as a current liability.

intangible asset Intangible assets are characterized by the rights, privileges, and benefits of possession rather than by physical existence. Also, they are normally considered to have a higher degree of uncertainty than tangible assets.

intention to convert Intention to convert is a phrase that describes one of the criteria by which an investment in a security is classified in the current assets section of the balance sheet. For an asset to be listed as current, management must intend and be able to convert the investment into cash within the time period that defines current assets.

interest Interest is the price, usually expressed as an annual percentage rate, associated with transferring (borrowing or lending) money for a period of time. See **stated interest rate, effective interest rate,** and **cost of debt.**

interest coverage ratio See **times interest earned.**

interest-bearing obligation Interest-bearing obligations are notes requiring periodic interest payments determined as a percentage of face value; notes with stated annual rates of interest greater than zero. Interest-bearing obligations differ from non–interest-bearing obligations, where no interest payments are made until the maturity date. Both interest- and non–interest-bearing notes (receivables and payables) are accounted for under the effective interest method.

interest rate swaps An interest rate swap is a contract that serves to exchange a fixed-interest obligation for interest payments at market rates. Such contracts are used to hedge the risk of holding fixed-interest debt. See **hedging.**

internal control system The internal control system consists of procedures and records designed and followed by company personnel to ensure that (1) the company's assets are adequately protected from loss or misappropriation and (2) all relevant and measurable economic events are accurately reflected in the company's financial statements.

internal financing Internal financing refers to the generation of funds to support operations and growth through profits instead of debt or equity capital. Internally financed companies normally have capital structures

with relatively large balances in retained earnings, usually a sign of financial strength.

Internal Revenue Code The Internal Revenue Code contains the official federal income tax laws. The Internal Revenue Service monitors and enforces adherence to these laws.

Internal Revenue Service The Internal Revenue Service is the government agency charged with monitoring and enforcing the payment of federal income taxes. See **Internal Revenue Code.**

International Accounting Standards Board (IASB) The IASB is a private-sector body, based in Britain and successor to the International Accounting Standards Committee, formed in 1973. The IASB, which represents over one hundred countries, has issued a number of international financial reporting standards (IFRS) recognized as acceptable financial reporting by many of the major stock exchanges in the world, and may soon be accepted by the U.S. Securities and Exchange Commission.

international financial reporting standards (IFRS) IFRS are the financial reporting standards issued by the International Accounting Standards Board. These standards are considered as acceptable reporting in most of the stock exchanges throughout the world, and may soon be accepted by the U.S. Securities and Exchange Commission.

inter-period tax allocation Inter-period tax allocation refers to the methods used to account for the timing differences that arise between tax and financial reporting across periods. It involves accounting for deferred income taxes.

intra-period tax allocation Intra-period tax allocation is the practice of disclosing the income tax effect of certain non-operating items on the income statement or statement of retained earnings with the item itself. The income taxes associated with operating income are disclosed on the income statement in a single line item immediately below operating income. The effects on income of non-operating items—such as disposals of segments, extraordinary items, changes in accounting principles, and prior-period adjustments—are disclosed on the financial statements net of their income tax effects.

inventory Inventory refers to items or products that are either available for sale in the normal course of business or support the operations of the business. See **merchandise inventory** and **supplies inventory.**

inventory recovery Inventory recovery is an expression used to describe an increase in the value of an inventory item that has previously been written down. The recovery can be no larger than the amount of the write-down. Inventory recoveries are recognized under IFRS, but not under U.S. GAAP.

inventory turnover *Cost of goods sold/Average inventory.* Inventory turnover measures the speed with which inventories move through operations. This activity ratio compares the amount of inventory carried by a company to the volume of goods sold during the period, reflecting how quickly, in general, inventories are sold. By dividing this ratio into 365 days, it can be converted to an expression indicating how many days it takes, on average, to turn over the inventory. For retail and manufacturing companies this ratio is an important component of asset turnover, which, when multiplied times profit margin, equals return on assets, a direct determinant of return on equity.

investing activities Investing activities involve the management of a company's long-term assets. The investment activities of a given period are summarized in the investing section of the statement of cash flows, involving primarily purchases and sales of fixed assets and investments in equity securities.

L

land Land refers to real estate held for investment purposes, usually appearing in the long-term investments section of the balance sheet. Land used in the operations of a business is considered a long-lived asset and is normally referred to as property. Land is carried at historical cost on the balance sheet, not fair market value, and is normally not subject to depreciation.

last-in, first-out Last-in, first-out (LIFO) is a cost flow assumption used to value inventory and cost of goods sold. It assumes that the last items purchased are the first items sold. LIFO is one of three commonly used cost flow assumptions; FIFO (first-in, first-out) and averaging are the other two. See **LIFO conformity rule, LIFO liquidation,** and **LIFO reserve.**

lease A lease is a contract granting use or occupation of property during a specified period of time in exchange for some form of payment, usually cash. Leases are a popular way to finance business activities. Companies often lease, rather than purchase, land, buildings, machinery, equipment, and other holdings, primarily to avoid the risks and associated costs of ownership. For purposes of financial accounting, leases are divided into two categories: operating leases and capital leases.

leasehold obligation Leasehold obligations are the balance sheet liabilities associated with capital leases reported by the lessee. This liability is equal to the present value of the future payments associated with a capital lease, discounted at the effective interest rate existing at the original date of the lease. Leasehold obligations are listed on the balance sheet as long-term and are accounted for under the effective interest method.

Level 1, 2, or 3 measurements Because fair market values can be very subjective, an important disclosure that is required when a company uses market values on its balance sheet relates to the basis for the market

value estimate. Market values based on quoted prices in active markets for identical securities are called **Level 1 measurements;** market values based on less reliable, less observable, indirect inputs are called **Level 2 measurements;** and market values based on much less reliable, unobservable inputs are called **Level 3 measurements.** These disclosures help the reader to better assess the uncertainties inherent in the market value estimates.

leverage Leverage involves borrowing funds and investing them in assets that produce returns exceeding the after-tax cost of the borrowing. In such cases, a company is managing its debt effectively and creating benefits for the stockholders, which should manifest themselves as increases in return on equity. Leverage, however, involves the commitment of future cash outflows, which increases the risk associated with the leverage company.

liability A liability is a probable future sacrifice of economic benefits arising from present obligations of a particular entity to transfer assets or provide services to other entities in the future as a result of past transactions or events.

life of a bond The life of a bond is the period of time from the issuance of the bond to the maturity date, at which time the face value is paid to the bondholders. See **bond.**

LIFO conformity rule The LIFO conformity rule is a federal income tax requirement stating that if a company uses the LIFO cost flow assumption to value inventory for tax purposes, it must also use the LIFO assumption when preparing its financial statements. Consequently, those companies that use LIFO to save taxes must report the LIFO cost of goods sold amount on the income statement—normally leading to lower reported net income values.

LIFO liquidation A LIFO liquidation occurs when companies that use the LIFO cost flow assumption have sales that exceed production. LIFO users must pay close attention to inventory levels because when inventory liquidations occur, abnormally high profits can be reported. This is due to matching inventory having old (often lower) costs against current revenues.

LIFO reserve The LIFO reserve is the difference between inventory reported under LIFO and inventory reported under FIFO. Under U.S. GAAP, companies that use LIFO are required to report what inventory would have been had they used FIFO. The difference between these two amounts (the LIFO reserve) represents the accumulated amount by which net income reported by the LIFO user has been understated, relative to FIFO, since the adoption of LIFO. The increase (decrease) in the LIFO reserve over the current period, when added to (subtracted from) LIFO net income for that period, is equal to FIFO net income (before taxes) for that period.

line of credit A line of credit is a borrowing arrangement granted to a company by a bank or group of banks, allowing it to borrow up to a certain maximum dollar amount, with interest being charged only on the outstanding balance.

liquidation Liquidation is the process of selling assets for cash. When companies go through liquidation, they normally sell their existing assets for cash, which is used to pay off creditors in order of priority. Any remaining cash is distributed to the stockholders. Liquidation is also used to describe an inventory reduction, where sales in a given period exceed inventory production or acquisition. See, for example, **LIFO liquidation.**

liquidity Liquidity is the speed with which an asset can be converted into cash. Assets on the balance sheet are listed roughly in order of liquidity. For example, current assets are considered to be more liquid than intangible assets. Of the current assets, cash is considered to be more liquid than accounts receivable, which is more liquid than inventory, which is more liquid than prepaid expenses.

listed company A listed company has its equity shares listed on a public stock exchange. See **stock market** and **stock price.**

loan contract A loan contract is a written agreement describing the terms of a borrowing arrangement, including the timing of cash payments (interest and principal), the maturity date, collateral (security) in case of default, and restrictions on the actions of management (called covenants).

loan covenant See **debt covenant.**

long-lived assets Long-lived assets are used in the operations of a business, providing benefits that extend beyond the current operating period. Examples include property, plant, and equipment and intangible assets.

long-term debt Long-term debt refers to obligations listed on the balance sheet, backed by formal contract, expected to be paid with the use of assets listed as noncurrent on the balance sheet. See **debt and liability.**

long-term debt ratio *Total long-term liabilities/Total assets.* The long-term debt ratio reflects that portion of assets provided by long-term borrowings.

long-term investments Long-term investments refer to assets on the balance sheet that are not intended to be sold in the near term, and are expected to generate benefits over a time period extending beyond that which defines current assets.

loss A loss occurs when the expenses of a given period exceed the revenues. Loss also refers to a situation where an item on the balance sheet is exchanged for something with a value lower than the item's book value.

loss contingency A loss contingency (or contingent loss) is an existing condition, situation, or set of circumstances

involving uncertainty concerning a possible loss to a company that will ultimately be resolved when one or more future events occurs or fails to occur. See **contingency** and **gain contingency.**

lower-of-cost-or-market rule Lower-of-cost-or-market is a rule applied to accounting for inventories, which states that the balance sheet value of inventory will be its historical cost or its market value, whichever is lower.

M

MACRS The Modified Accelerated Cost Recovery System is the set of rules defining the maximum amount of depreciation that can be recognized on a fixed asset for the purpose of determining taxable income in a given year. To determine this amount, a fixed asset is placed into one of eight categories, based on its estimated useful life as specified in the Asset Depreciation Range (ADR) system. Each of the eight categories is then linked with an allowable depreciation method.

maintenance expenditure A maintenance expenditure is a post-acquisition expenditure that serves to repair or maintain a fixed asset in its present operating condition.

management accounting Management accounting systems produce information used for decisions within a company. Such systems produce reports that cover such areas as performance evaluation, production output, product costs, and capital budgeting. This information is not available to individuals outside the company.

management discretion Management discretion refers to the latitude exercised by management when applying accounting methods. Management can choose from a variety of accounting methods, estimates, and assumptions when preparing the financial statements and still be within the guidelines defined by GAAP. The financial statements are also influenced by the timing and execution of transactions planned in advance by management. By using its discretion in these ways, management can make choices that serve its own interest—choices that may or may not be in the best interest of the company's owners. This discretion also makes it difficult for analysts to ascertain a company's true financial condition and performance from the financial reports.

management letter The management letter appears in the annual report and normally states that management is responsible for the preparation and integrity of the financial statements. While management letters differ from one company to the next, most contain references to GAAP, ethical and social responsibilities, the quality and reliability of the company's internal control system, the independent audit, and the audit committee of the board of directors.

manufacturing company Manufacturing companies acquire raw materials and, through a process, combine labor and overhead to manufacture inventory. Manufacturing companies are normally characterized by large investments in property, plant, and equipment and inventory.

margin See **profit margin** and **gross margin.**

mark-to-market accounting Under mark-to-market accounting, investments are carried on the balance sheet at their market values. Realized gains and losses are recognized on the income statement, and unrealized gains and losses are either reflected on the income statement or in the shareholders' equity section of the balance sheet, depending on the classification of the investment. See **marketable securities.**

markdown A markdown is a reduction in sales price normally due to decreased demand for an item. Markdowns are very common in the retail industry, especially at the close of the seasons. These discounts are designed to accelerate sales of old items (boosting inventory turnover), making room for new inventories.

market price The market price is the price at which an asset can be exchanged in the open (output) market as of a particular point in time. See **fair market value** and **stock price.**

market ratios The market ratios are the financial ratios that measure returns to common stockholders due to changes in the market price of the common stock and the receipt of dividends.

market share Market share is the proportion of the total market for a particular good or service held by a company. For example, if the total market for boys' tennis shoes is $50 million per year and Company A sells boys' tennis shoes valued at $5 million in a given year, Company A has a 10 percent market share. Market share and changes in market share measure how well a company is competing with other firms in a given market.

market value See **market price** or **fair market value.**

market-to-book ratio (*Number of outstanding common shares $\times$ Market price per share)/Net assets.* The market-to-book ratio indicates the extent to which the market believes that shareholders' equity on the balance sheet reflects the company's true market value.

marketable securities Marketable securities are investments that are readily marketable and intended to be sold within the time period of current assets. They are carried on the balance sheet at current market prices. See **short-term investments.**

matching principle The matching principle is a measurement principle of financial accounting stating that performance is measured by matching efforts against benefits in the time period in which the benefits are realized. Net income on the income statement is the result of matching expenses against revenues in the time period when the revenues are realized. The matching principle

is applied by first recognizing revenues and then matching against those revenues the expenses required to generate them.

materiality Materiality is an exception to the principles of financial accounting stating that only those transactions dealing with dollar amounts large enough to make a difference to financial statement users need be accounted for in a manner consistent with GAAP. The dollar amounts of some transactions are so small that the method of accounting has virtually no impact on the decisions based upon information in the financial statements. Such transactions are referred to as immaterial, and management is allowed to account for them as expediently as possible.

maturity date The maturity date is the date when a loan agreement ends. As of the maturity date, if all payments (interest and principal) have been made on the loan, the associated debt is satisfied. For most bonds, the face value of the bond is paid to the holder on the maturity date.

maturity value The maturity value is the dollar amount written on the face of the note or bond certificate that is paid to the holder at the maturity date. Face value and par value are terms often used interchangeably with maturity value.

measurement theory Underlying the measurement of assets, liabilities, revenues, and expenses—the key components of the financial statements—is a theoretical framework consisting of assumptions, principles, and exceptions. The assumptions include economic entity, stable dollar, fiscal period, and going concern; the principles include objectivity, matching, revenue recognition, and consistency; and the exceptions include materiality and conservatism.

merchandise inventory Merchandise inventory represents items held for sale in the ordinary course of business. It is especially important to retail and manufacturing enterprises, whose performance depends significantly on their ability to market their inventory. Indeed, the demand for such companies' products is often the most important determinant of their success.

merger A merger is a business combination whereby two or more companies combine to form a single legal entity. In most cases, the assets and liabilities of the smaller company are merged into those of the larger company, and the stock of the smaller, merged company is retired.

misclassification Misclassification involves including a financial statement account in an inappropriate section of the financial statements.

mortgage A mortgage is a cash loan exchanged for an installment note that is secured by real estate. The mortgage gives the holder the right to take possession of the real estate in case of default.

mortgage payable A mortgage payable is a balance sheet account that indicates the outstanding obligation associated with a mortgage. Mortgage payables are included in the long-term liability section of the balance sheet, except for that portion expected to use assets presently listed as current. This portion is included as a current liability.

multinational corporation Multinational corporations have their home in one country but operate and have subsidiaries operating within and under the laws of other countries.

multistep format Under a multistep format, the income statement is designed in a way that separates cost of goods sold from operating expenses, highlighting gross profit. This format also separates usual and frequent operating items from those that are unusual and/or infrequent, often referred to as other revenues and expenses or extraordinary items.

N

natural resource cost Natural resource costs are the costs of acquiring the rights to extract natural resources. Natural resource costs, which appear in the long-lived asset section of the balance sheet, are quite large in the extractive (e.g., oil, gas, mining) industries, and they are normally depleted under the activity (units-of-production) method.

net assets Net assets equals total assets minus total liabilities, or shareholders' equity. A company's net assets are also referred to as the company's book value, balance sheet value, and net worth.

net book value Net book value is the dollar value assigned to an item on the balance sheet. When used in reference to an entire company, net book value is equal to net assets or shareholders' equity. The net book value of a company is also referred to as simply the company's book value, balance sheet value, shareholders' equity, and net worth.

net credit sales Net credit sales is equal to gross sales on account less an estimate of sales returns and allowances.

net earnings See **net income.**

net income Net income is the difference between the revenues generated by a company in a particular time period and the expenses required to generate those revenues. Net income is the "bottom line" of the income statement.

net of tax To disclose an item net of tax on the income statement means to reduce its dollar value by the income tax effect associated with the item.

net operating income Net operating income is equal to the operating revenues minus operating expenses. It is also referred to as operating income.

net profit See **net income.**

net realizable value Net realizable value is the net cash amount expected from the sale of an item, usually equal to the selling price of the item less the cost to complete and sell it.

net sales Net sales is equal to gross sales less an estimate of sales returns and allowances.

net worth See **net assets** and **net book value.**

non–interest-bearing notes Non–interest-bearing notes are debt instruments that do not require periodic interest payments determined as a percentage of the face value; the entire interest amount is paid at maturity. Non–interest-bearing notes have stated annual rates of interest equal to zero, but the effective (actual) rate of interest is greater than zero.

nonoperating items Nonoperating items appear on the income statement below net operating income and are considered unusual and/or infrequent. Nonoperating items are considered less persistent than operating items.

nonparticipating preferred stock Nonparticipating preferred stock, a common form, carries the right—if dividends are declared—only to an amount designated by the dividend percentage expressed in the terms of the preferred stock. Unlike participating preferred stock, there is no right to an additional dividend.

nonprofit entity A nonprofit entity is an organization where the operations are not designed to make a profit. Rather, most nonprofit entities generate funds through contributions, user fees, or taxes and use these funds to achieve some organizational or social purpose. Nonprofit entities are also referred to as not-for-profit and/or government entities.

nonsufficient funds penalty A nonsufficient funds penalty is an assessment charged by banks against their customers for writing checks that are not backed by adequate funds.

not-for-profit accounting See **nonprofit entity.**

notes payable Notes payables are obligations evidenced by formal notes. They involve direct borrowings from financial institutions or other companies, and often are established to finance the purchase of long-lived assets. Notes payable appear on the balance sheet in either the current or long-term debt section.

notes receivable Notes receivable are assets backed by formal loan contracts. They normally arise from issuing loans, the sale of inventory, or the provision of a service and are often listed in the long-term assets section of the balance sheet.

O

objectivity Objectivity is a principle of financial accounting measurement stating that the values of transactions and the assets and liabilities created by them must be verifiable, i.e., backed by documents and prepared in a systematic and reasonable manner.

obsolescence Obsolescence, often referred to as physical obsolescence, is the state of an asset when repairs are no longer economically feasible.

off-balance-sheet financing Off-balance-sheet financing is a reporting strategy designed to depict a company as less reliant on debt than it actually is. For example, managers have been known to structure financing transactions and choose certain accounting methods so that liabilities need not be reported in the liability section of the balance sheet.

open account An open account is an informal credit trade agreement used in cases where frequent credit transactions are conducted and a running balance of the obligation or receivable is maintained. If payments are made regularly within reasonable time periods, interest charges are not usually assessed. Open account is normally used to describe the trade terms underlying accounts receivable and accounts payable.

operating activities Operating activities are the activities of a company associated with the acquisition and sale of a company's products and services.

operating cycle Operating cycle is the time it takes, in general, for a company to begin with cash, convert the cash to inventory (or a service), sell the inventory (or service), and receive cash payment.

operating expenses Operating expenses are the costs incurred to generate operating revenues associated with the normal activities of a company. They are disclosed in the operating section of the income statement, leading to net operating income.

operating income See **net operating income.**

operating lease An operating lease is treated as a simple rental for financial reporting purposes, where the periodic lease payments are treated as an expense, and no asset or liability is recognized on the balance sheet. See **capital lease** and **off-balance-sheet financing.**

operating margin Operating margin equals net operating income divided by sales. It indicates the number of cents of operating income earned from every dollar of sales.

operating performance An operating performance represents a company's ability to increase its net assets through operating activities.

operating revenues Operating revenues are revenues generated through the usual and frequent transactions of a company. They are disclosed in the operating section of the income statement, leading to net operating income.

operating transactions Operating transactions are usual and frequent transactions involving the acquisition and sale of a company's inventories or services.

opinion letter See **audit report.**

ordinary stock dividend An ordinary stock dividend is a relatively small dividend paid in the form of a company's own equity shares. It is normally expressed as a percent of a company's outstanding shares. For example, a 5 percent stock dividend declared by a company with 100,000 shares outstanding would involve the issuance of 5,000 (100,000 × 0.05) new shares to the stockholders. Under an ordinary stock dividend, the number of shares issued represents less than 25 percent of the

number of shares outstanding before the issuance. Ordinary stock dividends are also just called stock dividends.

organizational forms The most common forms of business organization are sole proprietorship, partnership, subchapter S corporation, and corporation.

original cost See **historical cost.**

other comprehensive income Other comprehensive income is a concept that refers to items that affect the firm's wealth but are not reflected on the income statement. See **comprehensive income, accumulated comprehensive income, statement of comprehensive income,** and **statement of recognized income and expense.**

other gains and losses Other gains and losses appear in the nonoperating section of the income statement and refer to transactions that are either unusual or infrequent, but not both. This section of the income statement is also called other revenues and expenses.

other revenues and expenses See **other gains and losses.**

output market The output market is the market where an entity sells the outputs from its operations. Fair market value, market price, and net realizable value are all output market values.

outstanding shares Outstanding shares are shares of stock that have been issued and are presently held by stockholders. They have not been repurchased (as treasury stock) by the company.

overhead Overhead refers to manufacturing costs that cannot be directly linked to particular products.

overstating financial performance and condition Overstating financial performance and condition, sometimes called providing a favorable financial picture, is a reporting strategy in which management attempts to depict a more favorable picture of the financial statements by overstating the company's financial performance and condition.

owners' equity Owners' equity refers to the section of the balance sheet that measures the results of the activities (contributions and withdrawals) of the owners of a partnership or sole proprietorship. See **stockholders' equity,** the term used to describe these activities for the owners (stockholders) of a corporation.

P

paper profits Paper profits is an expression used to describe profits that appear on the income statement but do not reflect increases in a company's economic wealth. Paper profits can be created by cosmetic changes in accounting estimates, judgments, and methods. Quality of earnings assessment is designed to identify and remove paper profits from the financial statements.

par value In the context of preferred stock, par value is often used in the determination of the amount of the annual preferred dividend payment. It also determines the dollar amount disclosed in the preferred stock account on the balance sheet. In the context of common stock, par value has little economic significance, but it is used to determine the dollar amount disclosed in the common stock account on the balance sheet.

parent company Parent companies own controlling interests in other companies, called subsidiaries. The consolidated financial statements of the parent company include the financial statements of all subsidiaries under its control. See **business acquisition** and **merger.**

participating preferred stock Participating preferred stock carries the right, if dividends are declared, not only to an annual dividend amount (determined by the dividend percentage expressed in the terms of the preferred stock) but also to a portion of the remaining dividend paid to the common stockholders. Most preferred stock is nonparticipating.

partnership A partnership is an organizational form where two or more people agree, by means of a contract, on how the business is to be conducted and how the profits and losses will be shared. A partnership is not a legal entity; the partners are legally liable for each other's business activities and the partnership itself is not subject to federal income taxes. The partners themselves are taxed on their share of the partnership profit.

patent Patents are granted by the U.S. Patent Office and give the holders exclusive rights to use, manufacture, or sell a product or process for a period of ten years. See **intangible asset.**

payments in advance See **deferred revenue.**

pension A pension is a sum of money paid to a retired or disabled employee, the amount of which is usually determined by the employee's years of service. For most large companies, pensions are an important part of the employees' compensation packages, and they are part of almost all negotiated wage settlements. There are two primary types of pension plans: a defined-contribution plan and a defined-benefit plan.

percentage-of-credit-sales approach The percentage-of-credit-sales approach is a method of estimating bad debts that multiplies a given percentage by the credit sales of a given accounting period. Percentage-of-credit-sales is a common method of estimating uncollectibles, used in conjunction with the allowance method, when accounting for accounts receivable.

periodic inventory method The periodic inventory method is a method of accounting for inventory that does not record the outflow of inventory at each sale, but relies on an inventory count at the end of the accounting period to compute ending inventory and cost of goods sold. It does not maintain a perpetual record of the inventory balance.

perpetual method The perpetual method is a method designed to keep track of, and close control over,

inventories. It maintains an up-to-date record, recording each purchase as it occurs and recording an inventory outflow at each sale. The perpetual method is becoming increasingly popular, especially with retailers, because it helps to maintain close control over inventories. Also, computer systems have dramatically reduced the cost of using this method. Bar code sensor systems, for example, are used to implement the perpetual method.

physical obsolescence See **obsolescence.**

portfolio A portfolio is a group of securities, investments, or assets held by an individual or company.

postacquisition expenditures Postacquisition expenditures refer to costs incurred subsequent to the acquisition or manufacture of a long-lived asset. They serve either to improve the existing asset (betterment) or merely to maintain it (maintenance expenditure).

postretirement costs Postretirement costs refer to health care and insurance costs incurred by employees after retirement. Most large companies cover a portion of such costs, and similar to pensions, such coverage is part of employee compensation and is earned over an employee's years of service.

preemptive right A preemptive right, which is attached to some equity shares, allows the holder to purchase a proportionate interest in any new equity issuance. It enables shareholders to maintain their relative equity interests, reducing the dilutive effect associated with a new issuance.

preferred stock Preferred stock is issued by companies to raise capital. It has special rights that make it a hybrid between debt and equity. These rights relate either to the receipt of dividends or to claims on assets in case of liquidation.

premium on bonds payable Bond premium is a financial statement account, included in the liability section of the balance sheet and added to the bond liability, representing the fact that the proceeds of a bond issuance exceeded the face value (i.e., the bonds were issued at an effective rate of interest greater than the stated rate of interest). Bond premiums are amortized over the life of the bonds, reducing interest expense. See **effective interest method.**

prepaid expenses Prepaid expense is an asset account that reflects payments for certain items (e.g., insurance and rent) before the corresponding service or right is actually used. Prepaid expenses are considered assets because they represent benefits to be enjoyed by the company in the future. For most companies, prepaid expenses are a relatively small, often insignificant, part of total assets.

present value Present value is a technique used to place a value, as of the present day, on a set of future cash flows. It is computed by discounting future cash flows at an interest rate that reflects a company's cost of capital.

price/earnings ratio *Market price per share/Earnings per share.* The price/earnings (P/E) ratio is a measure of the extent to which the stock market believes that a company's current reported earnings signals future cash inflows.

prime interest rate The prime interest rate is the rate charged by a bank to its best (lowest-risk) customers.

principal Principal is the sum of money owed as a debt, upon which interest is calculated. In the case of a bond, the principal can be referred to as the face value, par value, or maturity value.

prior period adjustment Prior period adjustment refers to the financial effects of certain events that result in direct adjustments to the retained earnings account. They are relatively unusual and are disclosed on the statement of shareholders' equity, normally representing corrections of errors made in prior periods.

private company Private companies have equity shares that are not listed and traded on the public stock exchanges.

proceeds Proceeds refers to the amount of cash collected on a sale, a borrowing, a bond issuance, or a stock issuance.

production capacity Production capacity refers to the number of goods or services a company can produce over a specified period of time given its resources. Production capacity tends to increase when (1) companies expand through business acquisitions and investments in long-lived assets and/or (2) companies increase the efficiency of their available resources. Companies act to increase production capacity when present capacity is insufficient to meet the existing and/or future demand for the company's products and services.

production efficiency Production efficiency refers to the number of items produced (of a given quality) divided by the cost of producing those items. Companies are continually attempting to improve production efficiency by producing more high-quality output at lower costs.

pro forma financial statements Pro forma financial statements are financial statements projected into the future.

pro forma reporting Pro forma reporting is a controversial management disclosure where management recalculates reported net income in a manner it considers to be more meaningful. For example, by highlighting truly one-time items and removing them from the income statement in arriving at pro forma earnings, management may be helping users to more clearly interpret the results of current operations and better predict future results. Pro forma reporting could also be presented by management to undo the distortions generated by accounting rules that may not fit the situation.

profit See **net income.**

profit and loss statement See **income statement.**

profit margin See **return on sales.**

profitability See **earning power.**

profitability ratios Profitability ratios assess performance, normally measured in terms of some measure of earnings as a percent of some level of activity or investment. Profitability ratios are designed to measure earning power and include return on equity, return on assets, earnings per share, return on sales (profit margin), and the times interest earned ratio.

property Property is a long-lived asset account representing the real estate upon which a company's operations are conducted. It is not subject to depreciation and normally not held for sale in the normal course of business. It is carried on the balance sheet at historical cost.

property, plant, and equipment See **fixed assets.**

prospectus A prospectus is a document containing a set of pro forma financial statements and other relevant information (e.g., contractual terms of debt agreements) that is filed with the SEC when a company issues equity or debt to the public.

provision Provision is an accounting expression used often by non-U.S. companies, many of which use IFRS, to describe a contingency write-down. Provisions normally appear as liabilities on the balance sheet, and usually result from relatively subjective accruals made by management. The expression is sometimes used by U.S. firms to describe accruals and contingent liabilities.

proxy statement A proxy statement is mailed to the stockholders of the company, inviting them to attend and vote for the board of directors at the annual shareholders' meeting. It also contains extensive information about the company and the compensation packages of the board of directors and management.

public accounting firms Public accounting firms are concerned primarily with providing independent audits of financial statements prepared by companies. The result of the audit is an opinion letter, signed by a certified public accountant, that provides a brief description of the auditor's procedures and responsibilities and states whether the statements present fairly the financial condition and performance of the company and are in conformance with GAAP, and whether the internal control system is considered effective. In addition to auditing, public accounting firms also perform tax and business advisory services for their clients.

purchase method Under the purchase method of accounting for business acquisitions, the assets and liabilities of the acquired company (subsidiary) are added to those of the parent at their fair market values as of the time of the acquisition. The difference between the purchase price and the fair market value of the subsidiary's assets is recorded as goodwill.

purchasing power Purchasing power is the amount of goods and services a monetary amount can buy at a given point in time. See **inflation.**

Q

qualified audit report A qualified audit report departs from the language in the standard audit report. The departure can be due to any of a wide variety of reasons—some of which are serious, others not. See **audit report.**

quick ratio (*Cash + Marketable securities accounts receivable*)/*Current liabilities.* The quick ratio compares a company's highly liquid assets to its current liabilities, providing a measure of the portion of the current liabilities that could be paid off in the near future.

quality of earnings See **earnings quality.**

R

rate of return See **return on investment.**

readily marketable Readily marketable refers to how quickly an asset can be converted to cash. It is normally used in the context of short-term investments (marketable securities) and describes securities that can be sold and converted into cash on demand. Securities traded on the public stock exchanges are considered readily marketable.

realized gain or loss A realized gain or loss occurs when an asset (liability) is exchanged for another asset (liability) with a market value that differs from the book value of the asset (liability) given up.

recognized gain or loss A recognized gain or loss occurs when a gain or loss is recorded on the financial statements. All gains and losses disclosed on the income statement are recognized.

recovery Recovery refers to an increase in the value of an asset that has previously been written down. The amount of the recovery is limited to the amount of the previous write-down. Recoveries tend to be recognized under IFRS, but not under U.S. GAAP.

redemption Redemption normally refers to the repurchase of outstanding debt (e.g., bonds) either before or at the maturity date. Depending on the terms of the debt, such repurchases can be at the option of either the issuing company or the debtholders, and the price of the repurchase can be prespecified or at the market price existing at the time of the transaction.

refinancing A refinancing occurs when a company satisfies an outstanding debt by issuing another outstanding debt. A company may also refinance by first redeeming debt and then issuing new debt.

related party transaction A related party transaction occurs when a company executes a transaction with an owner, an officer, or someone with a special interest in the welfare of the company. These transactions should be viewed cautiously by analysts because they may be

designed to benefit the related party, often at the expense of the other stakeholders in the company.

replacement cost Replacement cost is the current price a company would have to pay in the input market to replace an existing asset while maintaining operations at the present level.

reporting strategies Reporting strategies are policies used by management when choosing accounting methods, normally designed to achieve specific reporting objectives. There are four common strategies: (1) overstating financial performance and condition, (2) building hidden reserves, (3) taking a bath, and (4) off-balance-sheet financing.

residual interest Residual interest represents the right of the common stockholders to receive corporate assets in case of liquidation, after the creditors and preferred stockholders, in that order, have received their shares. The shareholders' equity section of the balance sheet represents one rough measure of the value of the stockholders' residual interest.

restrictive covenant See **debt covenant.**

restructuring charges A restructuring charge is an expense or loss that appears on the income statement in a given year, reflecting anticipated future costs. Many companies restructure their operations, planning to close plants, lay off employees, and incur other related expenses, choosing to record a charge to income in a period prior to the time they actually close the plants, lay off the employees, etc.

retail company A retail company purchases inventory and attempts to sell it for a price greater than its cost. Retailers purchase inventory from manufacturers or wholesalers and sell it to customers—providing primarily a distribution service, doing little to change or improve the inventory product.

retained earnings Retained earnings is an account listed in the shareholders' equity section of the balance sheet, representing the dollar amount of the company's assets generated through prior profits and not paid out in the form of dividends.

retirement In the context of business activities, retirement normally refers to either discontinuing the use of a fixed asset or purchasing outstanding debt.

return on assets (*Net income + Interest expense* $[1 - Tax\ rate])/Average\ total\ assets$. Return on assets measures the returns to both the stockholders (net income) and the creditors (interest expense) on their total investment in the firm (average total assets). The cost of interest is reduced by $(1 - Tax\ rate)$ because interest is tax deductible. Changes in this ratio can be explained by changes in return on sales and asset turnover. Return on assets is a direct determinant of return on equity. See **DuPont Model, financial statement analysis,** and **profitability ratios.**

return on equity (*Net income − Preferred stock dividends)/Average stockholders' equity*. Return on equity

compares the profits generated by a company to the investment made by the company's stockholders. Net income, which appears in the numerator, is viewed as the return to the company's owners, while the balance sheet value of stockholders' equity, which appears in the denominator, represents the amount of resources invested by the stockholders. Changes in this ratio can be explained by changes in return on assets, common equity leverage, and capital structure leverage. Value is created for the shareholders when return on equity exceeds the cost of equity.

return on equity from financial leverage *Return on equity − Return on assets*. The difference between the two ratios measures the extent to which the return to the stockholders exceeds the return to all capital providers, including creditors. When return on equity is greater (less) than return on assets, it is a measure of the economic benefit (loss) to stockholders from financial leverage. When a company has no liabilities, then the return on equity will equal return on assets.

return on equity (ROE) model See **DuPont Model.**

return on investment (*Market price*$[n − 1]$ − *Market price*$[n]$ + *Dividends*$[n−1])/Market\ price[n]$. Return on investment provides a measure of the pretax performance of an investment in a share of common stock. The numerator reflects the pretax return to the stockholder (market price appreciation and dividends), and the denominator reflects the amount of the stockholders' investment.

return on sales (*Net income + Interest expense* $[1 − Tax\ rate])/Net\ sales$. Return on sales provides an indicator of operating efficiency—increasing if operating expenses increase (decrease) at a slower (faster) rate than net sales. An efficient company, for example, will generate increased net sales with a constant level of operating expenses. Changes in this ratio can be analyzed by examining how the items on the income statement changed as a percentage of sales (i.e., common-size income statement). Return on sales times asset turnover equals return on assets, a direct determinant of return on equity. See **profit margin.**

revaluation adjustment Revaluation adjustments are designed to bring the dollar amount of certain accounts on the financial statements in line with the existing facts.

revenue Revenue refers to inflows or other enhancements of assets of an entity or settlement of its liabilities (or a combination of both) during a period from delivering or producing goods, rendering services, or performing other activities that constitute the entity's ongoing major or central operations.

revenue recognition Revenue recognition is a principle of accounting measurement that determines when revenue from the sale of a good or the provision of a service is entered into the financial statements. Revenue recognition is a critical question in the matching process because

the expenses incurred to generate revenues should not be reflected on the income statement until the revenues are recognized. The sale of a good or provision of a service normally involves a series of steps—including ordering the good or service, producing it, transferring it to the customer, and receiving payment. The principle of revenue recognition helps to determine at which of these steps the revenue should be recorded in the books.

reverse account analysis Reverse account analysis (also called T-account analysis) is a mechanical process that involves examining the activity in a given balance sheet account to acquire information not directly disclosed in the financial statements or footnotes.

risk Risk refers to variation in the returns of a given investment. Risky investments are characterized by large fluctuations in their returns across time—providing large returns in some periods while providing small, zero, or even negative returns in other periods. Risk, when applied to a potential borrower, refers to the probability of receiving timely interest and principal loan payments, sometimes called the risk of default. Equity and debt investors normally require larger expected returns to compensate for bearing additional risk.

risk premium Risk premium refers to the percentage return on investment over and above the risk-free rate that reflects the level of risk associated with an uncertain investment. The risk-free rate plus the risk premium equals the expected rate of return that must be met before an investment will be accepted. In short, larger expected returns are necessary for higher-risk investments.

risk-free return The risk-free return is the return provided by riskless securities (e.g., treasury notes, certificates of deposit). It varies across time due to macroeconomic factors such as economic activity, inflation, exchange rates, and monetary policy, but recently has been relatively low (4–5 percent).

S

sales Sales is a revenue associated with the sale of a good or product. Sales for a given period is computed by multiplying the number of items sold by the sales price, and it is typically the major revenue for manufacturers and retail companies.

sales growth Sales growth is an important indicator of a company's performance over a period of time. It can be determined by comparing sales dollar amounts on the income statement across reporting periods. It normally reflects changes in customer demand for a company's goods or services—due to changing prices and/or quantities sold.

sales returns Sales returns refer to recorded sales that are subsequently returned to the seller. The returns may be due to faulty merchandise and customer dissatisfaction; in a large number of cases, relatively open returns are part of normal business practices.

salvage value Salvage value refers to the dollar value of a long-lived asset at the completion of its useful life. Salvage values must be estimated before long-lived assets are placed into service so that the depreciable base can be depreciated, or amortized, over the estimated useful life. Estimating salvage values is extremely subjective, so many companies assume them to be zero.

Sarbanes–Oxley Act In an attempt to bolster corporate governance and restore confidence in the U.S. financial reporting system, this Act was passed by Congress in 2002. It enacted sweeping changes in the responsibilities of management, financial disclosures, independence and effectiveness of auditors and audit committees, and oversight of public companies and auditors. The Act requires the principal executive and financial officers to certify that the financial reports have been reviewed, do not contain untrue statements or omit important information, and fairly present the company's financial condition and performance. It also places additional responsibilities on management and the auditor to ensure that adequate internal controls are in place to provide reasonable assurance that the financial records are complete and accurate. Management must also file an annual report on internal control over financial reporting, and the external auditor must attest to and report on management's assessment of internal controls.

secured note Secured notes are formal promissory notes backed by assets (collateral) that are distributed to creditors in the event of default.

Securities and Exchange Commission In 1934, the U.S. Congress created the Securities and Exchange Commission, a federal agency with powers to implement and enforce the Securities Act of 1933 and the Securities Exchange Act of 1934. The Securities Act of 1933 requires that companies issuing securities on the public security markets file a registration statement (Form S-1) with the SEC prior to the issuance. The Securities Exchange Act of 1934 states that companies with securities listed on the public security markets must (1) annually file audited financial reports with the SEC (Form 10-K), (2) file quarterly financial statements with the SEC (Form 10-Q), and (3) provide audited financial reports annually to the stockholders. The SEC is also currently active in establishing financial accounting standards.

security See **collateral.**

service company A service company provides a service, as opposed to a good, for its clients or customers. Service companies carry no inventories and do not recognize cost of goods sold on the income statement. Service revenue or fees earned represent its main revenues. The service industry is normally divided into two groups: general services and financial services.

service revenue Service revenue (also called fees earned) represents revenues from the provision of services.

This account is normally found in the operating section of the income statement.

SG&A SG&A refers to selling, general, and administrative expenses—often one of the most important expense categories on the income statement.

shareholders See **stockholders.**

shareholders' equity Shareholders' equity consists of contributed capital and earned capital. Contributed capital represents the original investment in the company made by the shareholders, and earned capital primarily represents funds earned by the entity that the shareholders (normally through the board of directors) have chosen to reinvest in the entity, called retained earnings. Earned capital can also include accumulated comprehensive income, a measure of changes in the wealth of the entity not reflected on the income statement. In total, shareholders' equity represents the total investment made by the owners in the entity.

short-term debt Short-term debt refers to obligations on the balance sheet, backed by formal contract, expected to be paid with the use of assets presently listed as current on the balance sheet. Short-term debt is normally listed in current liabilities.

short-term investments Short-term investments consist of investments in equity securities, bonds, and similar financial instruments that are both readily marketable and intended by management to be sold within the time period that defines current assets. Companies often purchase these kinds of securities to earn income with cash that would otherwise be idle for a short time. These investments are carried on the balance sheet at fair market value and, according to GAAP, must be classified as either trading securities or available-for-sale securities.

similar asset Similar assets are those that perform essentially the same function. See **trade-in.**

sole proprietorship A sole proprietorship is considered to be a partnership with a single partner. It is not a legal entity and therefore not subject to federal income taxes. The sole proprietor is taxed and is personally liable for the activities of the business.

solvency Solvency refers to a company's ability to meet debts as they come due. Assessing solvency is a very important part of financial statement analysis.

solvency ratios Solvency ratios refer to financial ratios designed to measure a company's ability to meet its debts as they come due. The current and quick ratios are the two solvency ratios.

special-purpose entities (SPE) Special-purpose entities are created by a company solely to carry out an activity or series of transactions directly related to a specific purpose. The most common purposes include raising funds and transferring risk. The main accounting issue with SPEs concerns whether to consolidate the SPE into the financial statements of the creating company.

specific identification Specific identification is a procedure used to value cost of goods sold and inventory. It is used when companies can specifically identify the inventory items acquired and sold during the period, as well as those that remain at the end of the period. In such cases, the actual costs of the items sold and retained can be allocated to cost of goods sold and inventory, respectively.

stable dollar assumption The stable dollar assumption states that the value of the monetary unit used to measure a company's performance and financial condition is stable across time. That is, the inflation rate is assumed to be zero. This assumption allows mathematical operations (addition, subtraction, multiplication, and division) to be performed on account values that are established at different points in time.

standard audit report A standard audit report, often referred to as an unqualified report, states that the auditor was able to conduct an appropriate audit and render an opinion that the financial statements were prepared in accordance with GAAP and fairly reflect the financial performance and condition of the company, and the internal control system is effective. See **qualified audit report.**

stated interest rate The stated interest rate is the annual rate of interest stated on the face of a formal promissory note or bond certificate. The stated interest rate times the face value determines the periodic interest payments.

statement of cash flows The statement of cash flows is a financial statement that provides a summary of the activity in a company's cash account over a period of time. This statement divides cash activity into three categories: (1) operating, (2) investing, and (3) financing activities.

statement of cash flows (direct method) The direct method is evident when the operating section of the statement of cash flows contains the actual cash inflows and outflows associated with the operating activities of the company.

statement of cash flows (indirect method) The indirect method is evident when the operating section of the statement of cash flows begins with net income, which is followed by accrual adjustments in the computation of net cash from operations.

statement of comprehensive income The statement of comprehensive income contains net income for the period as well as other objectively measurable items that affect the firm's wealth but are not reflected on the income statement. This statement is not required under U.S. GAAP, but a reconciliation between net income and comprehensive income is required. This statement is very similar to the statement of recognized income and expense, which is required under IFRS. See **comprehensive income** and **other comprehensive income.**

statement of recognized income and expense (SORIE) The statement of recognized income and expense is required under IFRS and contains net income for the period as well as other objectively measurable items that affect the firm's wealth but are not reflected on the income statement. This statement is very similar to the statement of comprehensive income, which is required under U.S. GAAP.

statement of retained earnings The statement of retained earnings represents the portion of the statement of shareholders' equity that reconciles the balance in the retained earnings account at the beginning of an accounting period with the balance at the end of the period. It normally takes the following form: beginning retained earnings plus (minus) net income (loss) less dividends equals ending retained earnings. See **internal financing.**

statement of shareholders' equity The statement of shareholders' equity is a financial statement included in the annual reports of major U.S. companies. It explains the changes in the accounts of the shareholders' equity section of the balance sheet during an accounting period. GAAP requires that these changes be described somewhere in the annual report, and many companies include them in the footnotes.

stock In the United States, the term stock normally refers to common or preferred stock. On occasion, especially outside the United States (e.g., Britain), the term stock refers to inventory.

stock dividend See **ordinary stock dividend.**

stock market The stock market consists of a number of stock exchanges where equity securities are traded in a public forum. The New York Stock Exchange, the American Stock Exchange, and the Over-the-Counter (OTC) market are located in the United States and are the most active in the world. However, there are a number of other exchanges located in virtually all major cities outside the United States.

stock options A stock option is an option to purchase common stock at a prespecified price during a specific time period.

stock price Stock price is the market price of an equity security that has been previously issued and is presently listed on one of the public stock markets. Stock prices increase and decrease as investor expectations about a company change.

stock split Stock splits are used by corporations to increase the number of shares outstanding and simultaneously reduce the market price. Stock splits are expressed in terms of a ratio that describes how the existing shares are to be divided. In a 2:1 split, for example, the existing shareholders each receive an additional share for every share owned. Consequently, the number of outstanding shares are doubled, and the market price per share is approximately cut in half.

A 3:1 stock split effectively triples the number of outstanding shares, which the company executes by distributing two additional shares for each one outstanding. In a 3:2 stock split, one additional share is issued for every two outstanding.

stock split in the form of a dividend Stock splits in the form of dividends are relatively large stock dividends where 25 percent or more of the outstanding stock is issued, as a dividend, to the existing shareholders. They are treated as stock splits.

stockholders Stockholders (also called shareholders) are individuals or entities that hold ownership interests in a corporation. These interests include (1) the right to vote in the elections of the board of directors, (2) the right to receive dividends if they are declared by the board of directors, (3) a residual interest to the corporation's assets in the event of liquidation, and, in some cases, (4) a preemptive right. *Stockholder* and *shareholder* are used interchangeably.

stockholders' equity Stockholders' equity is the section of a corporate balance sheet that represents the stockholders' interests (or investment) in the corporation. It consists primarily of contributed capital and earned capital (retained earnings + other accumulated comprehensive income). The total dollar value of stockholders' equity also represents the company's net book value and its net worth.

straight-line method The straight-line method is a procedure for depreciating or amortizing long-lived assets that recognizes equal amounts of depreciation or amortization in each year of the asset's useful life. To compute straight-line depreciation for a given period, divide the depreciation base by the estimated useful life. Straight-line is the most common method for depreciating fixed assets and amortizing intangible assets.

subchapter S corporation A subchapter S corporation is primarily the same as a corporation, with one important difference: It is taxed like a partnership. It is popular with many small businesses because it has the advantages of a corporation (e.g., stockholders are liable only up to the amount of their investment) without one of the major disadvantages (double taxation).

subsidiary A subsidiary is a company with the majority of its common stock owned by another company, called the parent. Normally, the subsidiary prepares its own financial statements separately from the parent, but these statements are usually not available to the public because the shares of the subsidiary owned by the parent are no longer publicly listed. Under GAAP, the parent must prepare consolidated financial statements.

sum-of-the-years'-digits method Sum-of-the-years'-digits is a method of accelerated depreciation that is less extreme than the double-declining-balance method. To compute depreciation for a given period, the depreciation base is multiplied by a ratio—the

Glossary

remaining estimated life serves as the numerator and the sum of the estimated life's digits serves as the denominator. This method recognizes relatively large amounts of depreciation in the early periods of an asset's life and smaller amounts in later periods.

supplies inventory Supplies inventory refers to items available to support the operations of a business, such as office supplies and spare parts. Supplies inventory can be listed on the balance sheet under either current assets (e.g., office supplies) or long-lived assets (e.g., spare parts used to maintain long-lived assets). Supplies inventory is normally a relatively small asset on the balance sheet.

T

T-account analysis See **reverse account analysis.**

takeover In a takeover, an investor, group of investors, or another company purchases enough of the outstanding voting stock to gain a controlling interest (51 percent or more) in the acquired company. Takeovers are often classified as "unfriendly" (the existing board of directors and management are removed) or "friendly" (the existing board of directors and management are maintained). The threat of a takeover creates an important incentive for the board of directors and management to act responsibly and in the interest of the shareholders. Takeovers are accounted for under either the purchase or pooling-of-interests method.

taking a bath Taking a bath is a reporting strategy that recognizes excessive losses or expenses in a single period. This strategy helps to ensure that future periods will show improved performance because losses and expenses recognized in the current period will not have to be recognized in the future.

tax accounting Tax accounting systems produce information that is reported to the Internal Revenue Service and is used in the computation of the company's tax liability.

tax deductible An expense is tax deductible if—according to tax law—it is an allowable reduction of taxable income, the dollar amount upon which the tax liability is based. Many transactions are structured so that the related costs and expenses can be deducted for tax purposes.

taxable income Taxable income is the number used to determine income tax liability. It is computed by subtracting tax-deductible expenses from revenues that must be included for tax purposes. Deductible expenses and includible revenues are determined primarily by the Internal Revenue Code. Taxable income normally differs from net income reported on the income statement, which is based on GAAP.

technical default In a technical default, a company violates the terms of a debt covenant. For example, a debt covenant may require that the company maintain a current ratio of at least 1.0. If the company allows the ratio to fall below 1.0, it is in technical default. Technical default normally leads to renegotiation of the debt terms and is normally a negative signal for the company.

technical obsolescence Technical obsolescence is the state of an asset when technical advances have rendered its services no longer useful.

term loan Term loans are paid in installments over a period longer than one year from the operating cash flow of a business.

times interest earned *Net income before interest and taxes/Interest expense.* Times interest earned, also referred to as interest coverage, is a financial ratio that measures the extent to which a company's annual profits cover its annual interest expense. The profit number in the numerator should reflect the primary, recurring business operations of the company and should be calculated before income taxes because interest is deductible for tax purposes. The denominator, interest expense, can usually be found on the income statement.

trade-in In a trade-in, an old asset (and usually cash) is exchanged for a new asset. The methods used to account for trade-ins depend upon whether the assets in the exchange are similar or dissimilar.

trademark or trade name Granted by the U.S. Patent Office, a trademark or trade name is a word, phrase, or symbol that distinguishes or identifies a particular enterprise or product. Trademarks last for a fixed period of time but can be renewed indefinitely. See **intangible asset.**

trading securities Trading securities are relatively small investments (less than 20 percent of the outstanding voting stock) in marketable equity (or debt) securities that are purchased and held principally for the purpose of selling them in the very near future with the objective of generating a profit on short-term price changes. Trading securities are always listed as current assets on the balance sheet and are carried at market value. Changes in the market prices of trading securities are reflected as income or loss on the income statement, normally in the nonoperating section.

transportation-in See **freight-in.**

treasury notes Treasury notes are obligations of the federal government that pay interest at a specified rate for a specific period of time, usually less than six months. These notes are very low risk, and companies often purchase treasury notes to temporarily earn interest with excess cash. Such investments are classified as short-term on the balance sheet. The rate paid by treasury notes can also be used as a measure of the riskless rate of return. See **short-term investments.**

treasury stock Treasury stock is previously issued stock that has been repurchased by the issuing company and

held in the corporate treasury. It is often reissued at a later date.

turnover Turnover is an expression used to describe how quickly certain assets (receivables, inventories, noncurrent assets, and total assets) and liabilities are used in the operations of a company. See **inventory turnover, accounts receivable turnover, fixed asset turnover, asset turnover,** and **accounts payable turnover.** Turnover is also used by many non-U.S. companies to describe sales.

U

uncollectibles Uncollectibles, sometimes called bad debts, refer to outstanding accounts or notes receivable that will never be received. Under GAAP, management is required to estimate the value of uncollectibles periodically and recognize an expense on the income statement as well as reduce receivables on the balance sheet.

unearned revenue See **deferred revenue.**

uniformity Uniformity would be achieved if all businesses used the same accounting methods.

unqualified audit report See **standard audit report.**

unrealized gain or loss An unrealized gain or loss occurs when the market value of an asset (liability) on the balance sheet changes and no exchange has taken place. When the market value of an asset increases, for example, an unrealized gain occurs.

unsecured notes Unsecured notes are formal promissory notes (contracts) that are not backed by any form of security—collateral. For this reason, they tend to be high risk but normally can only be successfully issued by strong companies. The presence of unsecured debt on the balance sheet of a company, therefore, is often a signal of financial strength; that company's creditors apparently have not required that the debt be secured by the company's assets. Unsecured bonds are called debentures.

useful life The useful life of an asset is the estimated time period, or activity, over which a long-lived asset is expected to provide revenue-producing services. The estimated lives of intangible assets can be as long as forty years, while fixed asset lives normally range from three to thirty years. The estimated useful life of an automobile may be more appropriately expressed in terms of miles driven (e.g., 150,000 miles), instead of years.

U.S. GAAP U.S. GAAP refers to generally accepted accounting principles used in the United States.

usual transactions Usual transactions are part of the normal operating activities of a company. They involve the sale of a company's merchandise inventory or the provision of services expected in the normal course of business. If these transactions occur frequently, they are considered operating transactions and are disclosed as part of net operating income. If they occur infrequently, they are considered nonoperating items and classified as such on the income statement.

V

valuation base Valuation base refers to the values (e.g., historical cost, replacement cost, fair market value, net realizable value, present value) used to determine the dollar amount of an entity's assets and liabilities on the balance sheet.

value creation Value creation is a key metric of management's success, defined as the extent to which return on equity exceeds the cost of equity. It can be computed as a percentage (return on equity – cost of equity) or as a dollar value (net income – [cost of equity × average shareholders' equity]), and the market value of the firm can be expressed in terms of the book value of the firm plus the discounted future value creation.

W

warranty A warranty is an agreement by which a seller promises to remove deficiencies in the quantity, quality, or performance of a product sold to a buyer.

window dressing Window dressing is a phrase used to describe the activity of managers who use accounting methods, judgments, and estimates or make operating decisions purely to make the financial statements appear more attractive to financial statement users.

working capital *Current assets − Current liabilities.* Working capital measures the extent to which a company's current assets cover its current liabilities. It is viewed as a measure of solvency and is often used in debt covenants to ensure that the borrower maintains a sufficient buffer of current assets to current liabilities. Like the current and quick ratio, however, working capital is a relatively weak measure of a company's solvency position.

Subject Index

An index of company names can be found following the subject index.

Company Index